Lecture Notes in Computer Science 2453

Edited by G. Goos, J. Hartmanis, and J. van Leeuwen

Springer
Berlin
Heidelberg
New York
Barcelona
Hong Kong
London
Milan
Paris
Tokyo

Abdelkader Hameurlain Rosine Cicchetti
Roland Traunmüller (Eds.)

Database and Expert Systems Applications

13th International Conference, DEXA 2002
Aix-en-Provence, France, September 2-6, 2002
Proceedings

Volume Editors

Abdelkader Hameurlain
Université Paul Sabatier, IRIT
118 route de Narbonne, 31062 Toulouse Cedex, France
E-mail: hameur@irit.fr

Rosine Cicchetti
Université Aix-Marseille II, IUT, Département Informatique
413 Avenue Gaston Berger, 13625 Aix-en-Provence Cedex 1, France
E-mail: cicchetti@lim.univ-mrs.fr

Roland Traunmüller
University of Linz, Institute of Applied Computer Science
Altenbergerstr. 69, 4040 Linz, Austria
E-mail: traunm@ifs.uni-linz.ac.at

Cataloging-in-Publication Data applied for

Die Deutsche Bibliothek - CIP-Einheitsaufnahme

Database and expert systems applications : 13th international conference ;
proceedings / DEXA 2002, Aix-en-Provence, France, September 2 - 6, 2002.
Abdelkader Hameurlain ... (ed.). - Berlin ; Heidelberg ; New York ;
Barcelona ; Hong Kong ; London ; Milan ; Paris ; Tokyo : Springer, 2002
(Lecture notes in computer science ; Vol. 2453)
ISBN 3-540-44126-3

CR Subject Classification (1998): H.2, H.3, I.2.1, H.4, H.5, J.1

ISSN 0302-9743
ISBN 3-540-44126-3 Springer-Verlag Berlin Heidelberg New York

Springer-Verlag Berlin Heidelberg New York
a member of BertelsmannSpringer Science+Business Media GmbH

http://www.springer.de

Typesetting: Camera-ready by author, data conversion by Steingräber Satztechnik GmbH, Heidelberg
Printed on acid-free paper SPIN: 10871136 06/3142 5 4 3 2 1 0

Preface

2002 DEXA, the 13th International Conference on Database and Expert Systems Applications was held on September 2–6, 2002, at the Université Aix–Marseille II, France. The quickly growing field of information systems required the establishment of more specialized discussion platforms (the DaWaK conference, EC-Web conference, eGOV conference and DEXA workshops), and there were held in parallel with DEXA, also in Aix-en-Provence.

The resulting book was prepared with great effort. Starting with the preparation of submitted papers, the papers went through the reviewing process. The accepted papers were revised to final versions by their authors and arranged to the conference program. This year 241 papers were submitted and our thanks go to all who have contributed. The program committee and the supporting reviewers produced altogether about 730 referee reports, on average three reports per paper, and selected 89 papers for presentation. The papers presented here encompass the extensive domain of databases; together with the other conferences and workshops of the DEXA event cluster a vast part of applied computer science was covered. In this way DEXA has blazed the trail.

At this point we would like to acknowledge to all institutions which actively supported this conference and made it possible. These are:

- IUT (Université Aix – Marseille II),
- FAW,
- DEXA Association,
- the Austrian Computer Society,
- and Microsoft Research

A conference like DEXA would not be possible without the dedicated work of several people in the background. So we want to thank the whole program committee for the thorough refereeing process. We specially appreciated the essential commitment of Gabriela Wagner (FAW, University of Linz).

September 2002

Rosine Cicchetti (IUT, Université Aix–Marseille II)
Abdelkader Hameurlain (IRIT, Université Paul Sabatier, France)
Roland Traunmüller (University of Linz)

Program Committee

General Chairperson
Abdelkader Hameurlain, IRIT, Université Paul Sabatier, France

Conference Program Chairpersons
Lotfi Lakhal, University of Marseille, France
Roland Traunmüller, University of Linz, Austria

Workshop Chairpersons
A Min Tjoa, Technical University of Vienna, Austria
Roland R. Wagner, FAW, University of Linz, Austria

Publication Chairperson
Vladimir Marik, Czech Technical University, Czech Republic

Program Committee Members
Michel Adiba, IMAG - Laboratoire LSR, France
Hamideh Afsarmanesh, University of Amsterdam, The Netherlands
Jens Albrecht, Oracle GmbH, Germany
Ala Al-Zobaidie, University of Greenwich, UK
Bernd Amann, CNAM, France
Frederic Andres, NII, Japan
Kurt Bauknecht, University of Zurich, Switzerland
Trevor Bench-Capon, University of Liverpool, United Kingdom
Alfs Berztiss, University of Pittsburgh, USA
Sourav S Bhowmick, Nanyang Technological Univ., Singapore
Jon Bing, University of Oslo, Norway
Omran Bukhres, Purdue University, USA
Luis Camarinah-Matos, New University of Lisbon, Portugal
Antonio Cammelli, IDG-CNR, Italy
Wojciech Cellary, University of Economics at Poznan, Poland
Stavros Christodoulakis, Technical University of Crete, Greece
Panos Chrysanthis, Univ. of Pittsburgh & Carnegie Mellon Univ., USA
Paolo Ciaccia, University of Bologna, Italy
Rosine Cicchetti, University of Marseille, France
Christine Collet, LSR-IMAG, France
Carlo Combi, University of Verona, Italy
William Bruce Croft, University of Massachusetts, USA
John Debenham, University of Technology, Sydney, Australia
Misbah Deen, University of Keele, United Kingdom
Nina Edelweiss, University of Rio Grande do Sul, Brazil
Johann Eder, University of Klagenfurt, Austria
Thomas Eiter, Technical University of Vienna, Austria
Gregor Engels, University of Paderborn, Germany

Peter Fankhauser, GMD-IPSI, Germany
Eduardo Fernandez, Florida Atlantic University, USA
Simon Field, IBM Research Division, Switzerland
Burkhard Freitag, University of Passau, Germany
Peter Funk, Mälardalen University, Sweden
Antonio L. Furtado, University of Rio de Janeiro, Brazil
Georges Gardarin, University of Versailles, France
Parke Godfrey, The College of William and Mary, Canada
Paul Grefen, University of Twente, The Netherlands
William Grosky, University of Michigan, USA
Igor T. Hawryszkiewycz, University of Technology, Sydney, Australia
Mohamed Ibrahim, University of Greenwich, UK
Yahiko Kambayashi, Kyoto University, Japan
Magdi N. Kamel, Naval Postgraduate School, USA
Nabil Kamel, American University in Cairo, Egypt
Gerti Kappel, University of Linz, Austria
Kamalar Karlapalem, University of Science and Technology, Hong Kong
Randi Karlsen, University of Tromsö, Norway
Rudolf Keller, Zühlke Engineering AG, Switzerland
Myoung Ho Kim, KAIST, Korea
Masaru Kitsuregawa, Tokyo University, Japan
Gary J. Koehler, University of Florida, USA
Donald Kossmann, Technical University of Munich, Germany
Jaques Kouloumdjian, INSA, France
Petr Kroha, Technical University Chemnitz-Zwickau, Germany
Josef Küng, University of Linz, Austria
Jiri Lazansky, Czech Technical University, Czech Republic
Michel Leonard, University of Geneve, Switzerland
Tok Wang Ling, National University of Singapore, Singapore
Mengchi Liu, University of Regina, Canada
Fred Lochovsky, Hong Kong Univ. of Science & Technology, Hong Kong
Peri Loucopoulos, UMIST, United Kingdom
Sanjai Kumar Madria, University of Missouri-Rolla, USA
Akifumi Makinouchi, Kyushu University, Japan
Heinrich C. Mayr, University of Klagenfurt, Austria
Vladimir Marik, Czech Technical University, Czech Republic
Simone Marinai, University of Florence, Italy
Subhasish Mazumdar, New Mexico Tech, USA
Robert Meersman, Free University Brussels, Belgium
Elisabeth Metais, CEDRIC/CNAM of Paris, France
Mukesh Mohania, IBM-IRL, India
Tadeusz Morzy, Poznan University of Technology, Poland
Noureddine Mouaddib, University of Nantes, France
Günter Müller, University of Freiburg, Germany
Erich J. Neuhold, Fraunhofer-IPSI, Germany
Gultekin Ozsoyoglu, University Case Western Research, USA
Georgios Pangalos, University of Thessaloniki, Greece

Stott Parker, University of Los Angeles (UCLA), USA
Oscar Pastor, Technical University of Valencia, Spain
Marco Patella, University of Bologna, Italy
Barbara Pernici, Politecnico di Milano, Italy
Günter Pernul, University of Essen, Germany
Gerald Quirchmayr, University of Vienna, Austria
Fausto Rabitti, CNUCE-CNR, Italy
Isidro Ramos, Technical University of Valencia, Spain
Harald Reiterer, University of Konstanz, Germany
Norman Revell, Middlesex University, UK
Sally Rice, Unversity of South Australia, Australia
John Roddick, Flinders University of South Australia, Australia
Colette Rolland, University Paris I, Sorbonne, France
Elke Rundensteiner, Worcester Polytechnic Institute, USA
Domenico Sacca, University of Calabria, Italy
Marinette Savonnet, University of Bourgogne, France
Erich Schweighofer, University of Vienna, Austria
Michael H. Smith, University of California, USA
Giovanni Soda, University of Florence, Italy
Harald Sonnberger, EUROSTAT, Luxembourg
Günther Specht, University of Ulm, Germany
Uma Srinivasan, CSIRO, Australia
Bala Srinivasan, Monash University, Australia
Olga Stepankova, Czech Technical University, Czech Republic
Zbigniew Struzik, CWI, Amsterdam, The Netherlands
Makoto Takizawa, Tokyo Denki University, Japan
Katsumi Tanaka, Kyoto University, Japan
Zahir Tari, University of Melbourne, Australia
Stephanie Teufel, University of Fribourg, Germany
Jukka Teuhola, University of Turku, Finland
Bernd Thalheim, Technical University of Cottbus, Germany
Jean Marc Thevenin, University of Toulouse, France
Helmut Thoma, IBM Global Services Basel, Switzerland
A Min Tjoa, Technical University of Vienna, Austria
Aphrodite Tsalgatidou, University of Athens, Greece
Susan Urban, Arizona State University, USA
Krishnamurthy Vidyasankar, Memorial Univ. of Newfoundland, Canada
Pavel Vogel, Technical University of Munich, Germany
Roland R. Wagner, University of Linz, Austria
Michael Wing, Middlesex University, UK
Werner Winiwarter, EC3, Austria
Vilas Wuwongse, Asian Institute of Technology, Thailand
Gian Piero Zarri, CNRS, France
Arkady Zaslavsky, Monash University, Australia
Aidong Zhang, State Univ. of New York at Buffalo, USA

External Reviewers

Vassilios Stoumpos
Dimitrios Theotokis
Mara Nikolaidou
Thomi Pilioura
Olli Nevalainen
Stéphane Grandcolas
Mohand-Said Hacid
Noel Novelli
Werner Retschitzegger
Wieland Schwinger
Morad Benyoucef
Angela Bonifati
Michael Hanus
Carlo Meghini
Pasquale Savino
Giuseppe Amato
Claudio Gennaro
Gillian Dobbie
Eng Koon Sze
Maria Indrawan
Campbell Wilson
Manish Bhide
Upendra Sharma
Andreas Goerdt
Marco Guenther
Kaiyang Liu
Jie Mei
Joshua Pun
Jiying Wang
Jose Martinez
Mohammed Quafafou
Masato Oguchi
Masatoshi Arikawa
Tadashi Ohmori
Haruo Yokota
Miyuki Nakano
Krishina Reddy
Xiaofang Zhou
Harald Kosch
Christian Koncilia
Wolfgang Gruber
Elisabetta Grazzini
Andrea Passerini
Alessandro Vullo
Cesar Garita
Ammar Benabdelkader
Ersin Kaletas
Anne Frenkel
Y.D. Chung
J.H. Son
J.H. Kim
Maciej Zakrzewicz
Marek Wojciechowski
Zbyszko Krolikowski
Matilde Celma
José Ramón Mendivil
Pedro Sánchez Palma
Fredj Dridi
Holger Grabow
Markus Hütten
Torsten Priebe
Torsten Schlichting
Andreas Gruenhagen
Steffen Rost
Genoveva Vargas Solar
J. L. Zechinelli-Martini
Tuyet-Trinh Vu
Cyril Labbe
Jérome Gensel
Khalid Belhajjame
Yimin Wu
Yong Shi
Vicente Pelechano
Emilio Insfran
Juan Sanchez
Beatrice Finance
Fabio Porto
Sean W. Siqueira
S. Chatvichienchai
Akira Okada
Predrag Knezevic
Rodolfo Stecher
Thomas Risse
Wendy Wu
Tony Stockman
Wojciech Wiza
Krzysztof Walczak
Franck Morvan
Carina Dorneles
Fábio Zschornack
Mirella Moura Moro
R. De Matos Galante
Sandro Da Silva
Camargo
Andreas Erat
Thomas Schlienger
Martin Steinert
Thomas Christoffel
Wijnand Derks
Rik Eshuis
Djoerd Hiemstra

Table of Contents

Invited Talk

Web I

Workflow

Web II

Data Warehouses and Datamining I

Applications I

Data Warehouses and Datamining II

Applications II

XML

Applications III

Distributed Systems I

Applications IV

Distributed Systems II

Knowledge Engineering I

Knowledge Engineering II

Advanced Databases I

Invited Talk

Advanced Databases II

Query I

Advanced Databases III

Query II

Advanced Databases IV

Query III

Invited Talk

Information Retrieval I

Query IV

Information Retrieval II

Indexing I

Information Retrieval III

Indexing II

Issues in Monitoring Web Data

Serge Abiteboul

INRIA and Xyleme

Abstract. The web is turning from a collection of static documents to a global source of dynamic knowledge. First, HTML is increasingly complemented by the more structured XML format augmented with mechanisms for providing semantics such as RDF. Also, we believe that the very passive vision of web sites promoted by the current HTTP will soon turn into a much more active one based on pub/sub and web services. Thus, the monitoring of the web is likely to raise new challenges for many years. We consider here some applications involving web monitoring and some issues they raise.

1 Introduction

The web constitutes the largest body of universally accessible information throughout the history of humanity and keeps growing at a healthy pace. This new frontier that was first developed and used by a small number of experts is now turning into a huge distributed information base available to the public at large. However, besides its size, distribution and heterogeneity, the web is difficult to use because in some respect, it is also a huge, evolving junk yard:

- A lot of the information cannot be trusted, e.g., spamming, rumors, etc.
- a lot of the information on the web is stale, e.g., dead web sites or pages no longer maintained.
- even when a site or a page is alive, our vision of it may be out-to-date, e.g., full-text indexes on the web are often not aware of recent changes of pages.

To overcome this difficulty, we need to "monitor" the web. More precisely, web robots need to permanently look for new information on the web, typically by crawling it or by querying databases published on the web. Robots then need to analyze this information, e.g., to evaluate the quality of data that has been found and classify it. Finally, they need to monitor (in the sense of performing some surveillance) the data in order to detect changes.

We first consider the nature of the data one may wish to monitor on the web. We then look at typical applications involving web monitoring. While doing so, we consider technical issues raised by web monitoring. The present paper is motivated by recent works of the author. In particular, it has been motivated by works on the creation of a warehouse of XML data found on the web [11] that lead to the creation of a start-up named Xyleme [20]. The present paper presents a biased vision of a very diverse and active field and is not in any sense a comprehensive survey.

R. Cicchetti et al. (Eds.): DEXA 2002, LNCS 2453, pp. 1–8, 2002.

2 The Nature of Data to Monitor

The web was first developed very homogeneously around HTML. In other words, the bulk of the web consisted of hypertext documents. While maturing, the web became increasingly complex. Nowadays, the following information may be found:

- HTML still forms the backbone of the web, but popular document formats such as DOC, PDF, PS are massively present.
- A new web exchange format, namely XML [19], promoted by the w3c [21] and the industry, is radically changing the web. XML marries, in some sense, the document world with the database world [1]. XML can be used to represent documents, but also structured or semistructured data [1].
- A lot of web data is typically retrieved as a result of queries, in particular queries to database systems. Typically, this means that data (query parameters) has to be fed to obtain more data. The term deep web or hidden web [10] are used for such accesses typically via forms, scripts or using a new standard for web services, SOAP [15].
- Finally, multimedia formats for images, sound, video are crucial components of the web that we will not discuss here.

Note that web robots mostly reach the HTML portion of the web although some may index other formats (e.g., PDF for Google [13]) or crawl XML as well (e.g. Xyleme [20]). Databases are typically seen as stop points by crawlers. So, the deep web (larger than the surface web) is still out of the reach of crawlers. However, most people would probably agree that they use more regularly the deep web (e.g., for ordering tickets, or when querying yellow pages) than the surface web. With the web maturing, we believe that this will be increasingly the case.

When considering the nature of data to monitor, one should also mention:

- Public vs. private web: the private web is typically accessible on an Intranet or on the Internet protected by passwords. The main issue here is the control of access rights. From a technical perspective, there is no real difference between private and public data.
- Static vs. dynamic. One can imagine a static page that is kept very fresh by 24-hour operators and similarly a dynamic page that for years will return the same value. The main issues are those already mentioned: the format of the data and whether or not there is a need to provide query parameters.

3 Difference with Traditional Databases

Although XML is often presented as a new model for data storage with its query language (Xquery [18]), we prefer to view XML here essentially as an exchange format ignoring the nature of the storage (relational, native or other) or the way the data has been produced. Indeed, in this spirit, there is more and more interest in "stream" queries for XML data, see, e.g., [3]. By this we mean that the query refers to data that is being received vs. data that is stored in a database. Note that the problem is intrinsically different. The core of database technology consists in secondary storage management and in taking advantage of indexes. Stream queries are typically applied to main memory data and indexes are not available a-priori. Data management in a web context presents other particularities that we mention next.

First, web data is by nature distributed and heterogeneous. This is in the spirit of distributed databases or more precisely in the spirit of federated databases that stress the independence of data sources that are components of such systems. A main new aspect when considering, for instance, data integration on the web, is the number of sources (tens, hundreds, thousands). Moreover, federated databases typically consider environments where the semantics of data in sources of interest is well understood. This assumption does not scale to the web. We have to be able to discover new sources dynamically and analyze them to understand their semantics on the fly. This clearly complicates monitoring that now has to include a significant artificial intelligence component.

Last but not least, another difference (say, to federated databases) is that the web does not provide for change control on data we are interested in. For HTML pages, it is possible to register with services providing notifications when pages of interest change. This is clearly a very primitive form of change control compared to the sophisticate triggering mechanisms supported by traditional database systems. One can measure the limitations of such approaches when one knows that this is typically implemented by regularly (once a day, a week, a month, more?) reading the page to check whether it has changed and inspecting some hash value of the text of the page.

In the remainder of the paper, we consider applications that deal with web monitoring and mention some technical issues they raise.

4 Electronic Commerce

One of the most popular applications concerns comparative shopping. Some system already provide unique entry points to collections of catalogues. The issue here is the integration of information from the various catalogues. One main difficulty is to "wrap" the various sources to extract their information (nature of the product, price, terms of delivery, etc.) Monitoring is another major issue. Information changes at the sources. In some cases, changes may be so rapid (e.g. prices for air travel) that one prefers to use a "mediator" approach. So, instead of extracting the information and monitoring changes, one asks queries each time a user is looking for information. In many cases still, a warehouse approach with data extracted, stored and monitored is used.

Automatic site wrapping and monitoring. The wrapping of data sources is mostly performed today semi-automatically from HTML pages. An engineer examines a collection of pages with similar structure and tailors a program to extract information from it. The weakness of this approach is that it has to remain limited to a reasonably small number of sites and page styles. Also, when the pages layout is modified in a site, the wrapper has to be modified. With XML, the situation is somewhat easier and it is possible to use the information contained in tags to automatically understand the semantics of pages and thus wrap them automatically. When one moves to forms or web services, the situation becomes more intricate since one needs to find which data to input in order to obtain information. Intuitively, an automatic system would have to apply a heavy dose of artificial intelligence to understand the semantics of a web site and automatically extract information from it. Now let us assume that the owner of a site is willing to let others use the information. Then the site owner may "publish" the semantics of the site (e.g., in RDF [14]) and the means to obtain information from it using standards such as WSDL [17] and UDDI [16]. Indeed, one may even expect that entire domains will standardize the way data is published on the web, e.g., NewsML for the news industry. This is raising the issue of the semantic web and is mentioned here primarily to stress that an intelligent monitoring of the web should rely on semantics published by web sites, which seems to take us a bit far into the future.

5 Web Archiving

The content of the web is an increasingly valuable source of information that is worth being archived. Indeed, there are attempts to archive the entire web (Internet web archive [12]) or portions of it. For instance, we are studying with the Bibliothèque Nationale de France [9] the archiving of the French web [6]. This would be a service to future generations of historians, somewhat like libraries for today's historians. Even the viewpoint that the web is a huge junk yard suggests the need for archiving it when considering the importance of prehistoric junk yards for today's archaeologists. Companies may also want to archive their web (private or public) although the motivation is different here: the "memory" of the enterprise is an important asset. Finally, one may want to archive a web site on some specific topics as part of the service provided by the site (e.g., newspaper websites).

Better web crawlers. Because of the lack of change control on the web, one issue in constructing web archives is to decide when to version a particular page. The crawlers have to visit the web and detect changes. They must do so by taking advantage of their network bandwidth. Crawling is in principle a trivial process: start from some page in the "core" of the web and follow links to discover new pages. There are subtleties such as avoiding rapid firing, i.e., requesting too rapidly too many pages from the same web server, an action considered unfriendly. There is also the technical challenge of managing billions of URLs. But most importantly the real problems come from the limitations of network-bandwidth compared to the size of the web.

> Suppose 4 million pages are read per day with a single PC (the rate of Xyleme crawlers for instance); with 25 crawlers, 100 million pages can

be read per day, which already requires a very large network bandwidth. Still, it takes a month to read 3 billion pages. By that time a lot of the pages that have been read are already stale and reaction to changes is too slow. By accessing once every month the pages of, say the New York Time, a lot of important information is missed.

To overcome this problem, one should use the network bandwidth more intelligently. In particular, one should not access all pages with the same frequency. A solution should distinguish between important pages (e.g., pages with high page rank in Google terminology [13] that are read regularly) and less or unimportant pages. A solution should also take into account some estimate of the change frequency of the page (it is not interesting to keep reading an archive) and, last but not least, it should be tailored to the specific goal of the archive.

There are many other issues in web archiving. For instance, web archives have motivated a new research on versioning mechanisms [8]. The data we archive is a rapidly changing graph and this raises complex issues. To illustrate, suppose that we take some first-generation crawler to create the archive. Say the crawler uses some breadth-first traversal of the graph of the web. Then a large time interval may occur between the visit of a page and the visit of the pages it points to. These pages are very likely to have changed or may even have disappeared by the time we access them. This is a very important cause of inconsistencies in the archive. Finally, perhaps the most critical technical challenge for such applications is to be able to also archive data from the deep web.

6 Web Surveillance

Web surveillance can be applied in a variety of fields ranging from anti-criminal or anti-terrorist intelligence (e.g., detecting suspicious acquisition of technology) to business intelligence (e.g., discovering potential customers, partners or competitors). Such applications combine web monitoring with data mining and text (or sound or image) understanding. The two main issues from a monitoring viewpoint are (i) to obtain the data (using better web crawlers that were already discussed) and (ii) to filter it (using new query processing technology).

Stream and continuous queries. One can distinguish two main approaches:

1. Continuous queries: the same query is evaluated regularly by a query engine and the difference between the answers is analyzed. In other words, we separate data acquisition (crawling and indexing) and query processing; see for instance [5].
2. Stream queries: streams of data are brought from the web (typically from web robots) and these streams of data are filtered; see, e.g., [7].

Typically, stream queries are more appropriate for fast detection of simple patterns on rapidly changing data (e.g., data that is brought in by sensors) whereas continuous queries are more feasible when considering the detection of complex patterns, e.g., patterns involving joins of data from several sources. In this context, we need to develop new optimization techniques for continuous and stream queries. Also, there is a need for a query language to specify such queries since SQL simply misses the points: It does not provide the necessary constructs for querying streams or specifying continuous queries. The query language should allow to specify a number of aspects such as the pattern that one would like to detect, on what data should the query be performed, how often, what should be done with results (should they be posted on the web, sent by email, how often, etc.) A classical query is in some sense very simple: it is a function that returns a result. A continuous or a stream query is more complex in the sense that it creates in some way a contract between the client and the server, it takes time into account in an essential manner, and also some notion of state of the client (e.g., when we compare the last result of a continuous query to the current one).

7 Mobile Devices

Mobile devices are certainly becoming more and more popular, e.g. laptops, PDA's, cellular phones, embedded devices, etc. This leads to a vision of lots of data changing rapidly (position of PDA's) and rather volatile (plugging and unplugging laptops). Perhaps a most critical aspect is geography. For instance, a query such as "where is this particular movie showing" should get a different answer depending on the location of the person asking the query. Indeed, the location and the nature of device used are key components of the user's profile that should be taken into account in answering queries.

These mobile devices should be considered, as participating to the web, e.g., by publishing information on it. The rapidly evolving and massive nature of the web is thus amplified. Furthermore, monitoring is particularly critical in a mobile context, e.g., if I want to be alerted when some cultural events happen nearby or whether a friend happens to be in the neighborhood.

To conclude this quick tour of the topic, we consider active web sites.

8 Active Web Sites

In the previous discussion, we somewhat assumed that web sites were "passive" and that some servers were in charge of the surveillance. This is mostly the situation today. However, one should expect the future web sites to include more and more active features (in the style of active databases) that will facilitate friendly web surveillance. In particular, mobile devices should be viewed as peers willing to share data resources with other peers.

Bringing active database features to the web. The most important concept in active databases is that of triggers. One would like web sites to be friendly enough to let us install triggers in, say XML documents they manage; see [4]. Suppose I am interested in the price of a particular camera in the Amazone catalogue. I would like to introduce the trigger (specified in an ad-hoc syntax):

When the price of the Cannon CAN344 changes do email-me

More generally, one would like to have web peers that are willing to cooperate using (continuous) methods and offering services such as change notification. Research in that direction is certainly needed; see Active XML [2] for a proposal in this spirit.

We are still a long way from truely active web sites. However, web services already provide the technology for enabling more active web sites. To illustrate, consider a bibliography database. It is straightforward to implement a web interface for it using, for instance, SOAP services. A service for notifying the addition of new bibliography references can be easily proposed by combining a database trigger with a call to a SOAP service. Similarly, a service for sending (say once a week) the incremental changes to the database may be easily implemented. What is perhaps more critically missing is a global view of the distributed information system this is leading to. In particular, there are challenging semantics and optimization issues.

9 Conclusion

Let us try to abstract a few main ideas from the applications we considered. The high-level vision we sketched is that the web is moving from a collection of static documents to a world of dynamic knowledge. The knowledge may range from implicit (buried in text or other unstructured media), to somewhat explicit via semantic annotations in the form of XML tags attached to data, to very explicit using future standards such as RDF. One should expect to see more and more semantics specified explicitly on the web, because this is the only feasible path if we are to make effective use of this massive amount of data. In this vision of the web as a world-wide knowledge base, an essential aspect is that the knowledge changes in time. Web knowledge has to be monitored to make available a timely version of information.

Acknowledgment

We would like to thank all the people involved in the Xyleme project [11] and the Xyleme company (www.xyleme.com). We would also like to thank those who work on Active XML and in particular, Omar Benjelloun, Angela Bonifati, Ioana Manolescu, Tova Milo, and those who discussed with me the French web archive, Gregory Cobena and Julien Massanes. Finally, we thank Victor Vianu for his comments on a first draft of this paper.

References

1. S. Abiteboul, P. Buneman, and D. Suciu. Data on the Web. Morgan Kauffman, 1999.
2. Serge Abiteboul, Omar Benjelloun, Tova Milo. Towards a Flexible Model for Data and Web Services Integration, proc. Internat. Workshop on Foundations of Models and Languages for Data and Objects, 2001.
3. Brian Babcock; Shivnath Babu; Mayur Datar; Rajeev Motwani; Jennifer Widom. Models and Issues in Data Stream Systems, PODS, 2002.
4. Angela Bonifati, Daniele Braga, Alessandro Campi, Stefano Ceri: Active XQuery. ICDE 2002
5. Jianjun Chen, David J. DeWitt, Feng Tian, Yuan Wang: NiagaraCQ: A Scalable Continuous Query System for Internet Databases. SIGMOD Conference 2000: 379-390
6. S. Abiteboul, G. Cobéna, J. Masanes, G. Sedrati, A First Experience in Archiving the French Web, to appear in ECDL, 2002.
7. Benjamin Nguyen, Serge Abiteboul, Grégory Cobena, Mihai Preda, Monitoring XML data on the Web, SIGMOD, 2001.
8. Amelie Marian, Serge Abiteboul, Grégory Cobena, Laurent Mignet, Change-Centric Management of Versions in an XML Warehouse, VLDB, 2001.
9. Julien Masanès, The BnF project for Web archiving, Preserving online content for future generation, ECDL Workshop, 2001.
10. Raghavan, S. and H. Garcia-Molina. Crawling the Hidden Web. in 27th International Conference on Very Large Data Bases. 2001. Rome, Italy.
11. Lucie Xyleme (a nickname for the people who worked on the Xyleme project). A dynamic warehouse for XML Data of the Web. IEEE Data Engineering Bulletin 24(2): 40-47 (2001)
12. The Internet Archive, www.archive.org
13. Google, www.google.com
14. Resource Description Framework, www.w3.org/RDF
15. Simple Object Access Protocol (SOAP) 1.1, http://www.w3.org/TR/SOAP/
16. Universal Description, Discovery and Integration of Businesses for the Web, www.uddi.org
17. Web Service Definition Language, www.w3.org/TR/wsdl
18. XQuery 1.0: An XML Query Language, http://www.w3.org/TR/xquery
19. Extensible Markup Language (XML), www.w3.org/XML
20. Xyleme SA, www.xyleme.com
21. The World Wide Web Consortium, www.w3.org

Controlled Caching of Dynamic WWW Pages

Costas Vassilakis and Giorgos Lepouras

University of Athens, Department of Informatics and Telecommunications
Panepistimiopolis, TYPA Buildings, Athens 157 71 Greece
{C.Vassilakis, G.Lepouras}@di.uoa.gr

Abstract. In order to increase flexibility and provide up-to-date information, more and more web sites use dynamic content. This practice, however, increases server load dramatically, since each request results to code execution, which may involve processing and/or access to information repositories. In this paper we present a scheme for maintaining a server-side cache of dynamically generated pages, allowing for cache consistency maintenance, without placing heavy burdens on application programmers. We also present insights to architecture scalability and some results obtained from conducted experiments.

Introduction

Content offered by WWW servers can be classified in two categories, *static* and *dynamic*. Static content comprises of HTML pages and images stored in files; dynamic content is created by the WWW servers upon receipt of a relevant request, through the execution of server-side program/script (CGI, ASP, JSP etc). Usually, these programs accept some parameters, included in the request and extract data from an information repository (e.g. a database) to formulate the HTML page that will be sent back to the requestor. While in the early days of WWW dynamical content was rare, its share is constantly increasing due to the need for increased flexibility in HTML page formulation and the desire to provide up-to-date information.

Dynamic content, however, increases server workload, since it necessitates the execution of a (possibly costly) code fragment, while additional overheads (environment setup, housekeeping etc.) are inherent in such an approach. This workload may prove overwhelming for heavily accessed servers, and techniques used for static HTML pages (e.g. client-side caching, proxy servers) may not be employed for reducing it. This is due to the fact that such techniques do not take into account the particularities of dynamic content, such as the existence of parameters and the possibility that either data, or even the program that were used to formulate the page may have changed in the meantime. This paper presents a scheme for maintaining a *server-side cache* for dynamic content, which may reduce drastically server workload, without compromising the advantages offered by the usage of dynamic content.

In the rest of this paper, section 2 covers related work and outlines open issues. System architecture is presented in section 3, and cache consistency maintenance is discussed in section 4. Section 5 focuses on scalability and resource utilization and section 6 presents experimental results. Section 7 concludes and outlines future work.

R. Cicchetti et al. (Eds.): DEXA 2002, LNCS 2453, pp. 9–18, 2002.

Related Work

In [11] a cost model for the materialization of web views, i.e. subsets of a server's dynamically computed information content, is presented. In [12] pre-generation of Web pages is discussed and changes in the information repository are addressed, but no algorithm for selecting the most appropriate pages for caching is presented. Caching of dynamic content is also discussed in [3], [13] and [6] and [9] presents techniques for reducing a web server's workload, regarding dynamic content creation.

In [15], two categories of dynamic content caching are described, *active cache* and *server accelerators*. In *active cache* [4] servers supply cache applets that are attached to documents and are executed when a user "hits" a cached object. Although this scheme reduces network load, it has a significant CPU cost. On the other hand, *web server accelerators* reside in front of web servers. Such techniques were used to improve performance at the Web Site for the 1996 Olympics [10] and for the 1998 Winter Games [6]. In the 1998 Games the Data Update Algorithm was used to maintain data dependence information between cached objects and the underlying data, enabling cache hit rates close to 100% compared to 80% of an earlier version. However, this approach suffers when it comes to web sites that offer a large number of dynamic pages [19], because it depends on keeping up to date a fine-grain graph that describes dependencies among each web page and the underlying data. In [19] a different approach is proposed, where the caching mechanism resides behind the web server and the fine grain method described in [6, 10] is supplemented with coarse grain dependencies between data and groups of dynamic pages. The caching algorithm uses a URL class based invalidation method and selective precomputing.

Commercial products implementing caching of dynamic content exist as well. Cold Fusion [1] offers the capability to designate programs that produce non-changing dynamic pages, and Cold Fusion engine arranges so that outputs from this program are cached and reused, while XCache [18] can be integrated into the IIS Web server to maintain a cache of dynamically generated Pages, providing an additional API for update applications so as to inform the cache engine for outdated pages.

All techniques presented insofar, however, require from application programmers an amount of additional development and maintenance for adapting programs to the caching scheme, for reasons of update propagations and consistency management. Moreover, invalidated pages are designated using proprietary specifications or APIs, increasing thus overall system complexity. Finally, most implementations are coupled to specific web servers, reducing interoperability and portability.

Maintaining a Cache of Dynamically Generated Pages

A server-side cache of dynamic content may be maintained in a controlled fashion using the architecture depicted in Figure 1. The proposed scheme complements the existing web site installation with two additional software modules, the *cache manager* and the *update manager*, which are responsible for maintaining the cache and ensuring that the cache is consistently updated or invalidated, when data is modified. The proposed scheme places the new modules as a *front end* to the existing installation, without any need to affect the latter; some additions may only be needed for update programs, as explained later. This characteristic was one of the design goals, since site administrators would be reluctant to employ a scheme that would require major changes to their site.

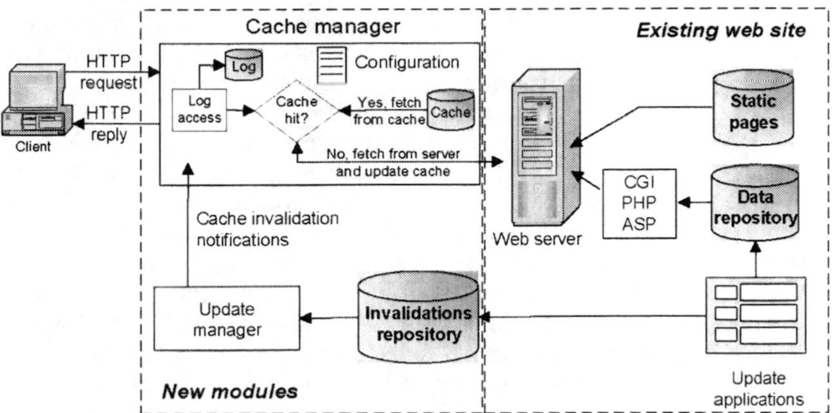

Fig. 1. Architecture for maintaining a cache of dynamic content

Upon start-up, the Cache Manager reads its configuration, which is derived from the class-based cache management for dynamic web content, described in [23]. Under this scheme, web pages are grouped into classes, based on page URLs and client information. The URL information used for classifying pages includes network paths, program names and parameters. Client information may complement the specification of a class and include cookies, client domain names or IPs, browser information (e.g. HTTP_ACCEPT_ENCODING, HTTP_USER_AGENT), or any other piece of information designated in the HTTP protocol for the server-side program environment. Figure 2 presents example cache specifications for three classes. We note that our approach does not use the *Dependence* specification described in [23], since a different mechanism (see section 4) is used for change tracking and page invalidations.

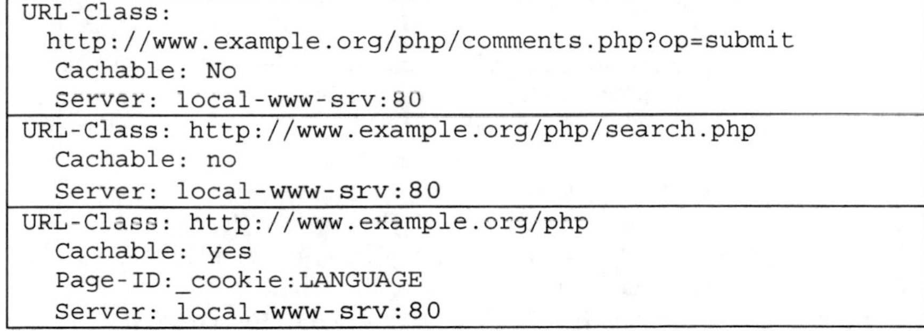

```
URL-Class:
  http://www.example.org/php/comments.php?op=submit
   Cachable: No
   Server: local-www-srv:80
```

```
URL-Class: http://www.example.org/php/search.php
   Cachable: no
   Server: local-www-srv:80
```

```
URL-Class: http://www.example.org/php
   Cachable: yes
   Page-ID:_cookie:LANGUAGE
   Server: local-www-srv:80
```

Fig. 2. Cache specification for two document classes

The first class designates that pages generated by server-side program (SSP) *comments.php* with the parameter *op* set to the value *submit* are not eligible for caching (due to side effects of execution); the second class denotes that search results are not cacheable either (due to the small probability that two users will use the same search text). The third class defines that pages generated by SSPs within the *php* catalogue are cacheable, but additionally states that the page contents depend on the value of the *LANGUAGE* cookie. In all three cases, the *Server* lines (an addition to the specifications presented in [23]) designate that the web server producing these pages is named *local-www-srv* and may be contacted at port *80*. The name *local-www-srv* need not be known to the clients, since only the Cache Manager uses it.

After initialisation, the Cache Manager awaits for web requests. For each request, it checks whether the requested page has been cached or not. A *page*, in the context of dynamic content, is identified by the URL, the parameters passed to the SSP and any cookies and HTTP variables pertaining to the class in which the request falls. If the page is found in the cache, it is returned to the client immediately. If not, the Cache Manager requests the page from the web server and forwards the results to the client. In order to rapidly determine if the target page exists in the cache, the Cache Manager employs the algorithm described in [16], which computes an MD5 checksum of the requested URL and matches it against the checksums of the cached pages.

Subsequently, the Cache Manager inspects its configuration to determine whether the page just served is eligible for caching. In this case, the page is placed in the cache, so that it becomes available for later requests. If the page is not eligible for caching, the results returned to the client are simply dropped. In the case that the cache is full and a page needs to be inserted to it, the Cache Manager removes some previously cached pages from the cache to make space available for the new page. The page(s) that will be removed are determined using the Greedy Dual-Size [5] algorithm, and more specifically the variation aiming to maximize the hit ratio, since it has been found to achieve superior performance, compared to other algorithms within the context of web caching [2].

The Cache Manager cooperates with the *Update Manager* module, described in section 4, to guarantee that the pages sent to the clients are not outdated, due to changes in the data or the server-side programs that generate the pages.

Handling Data and Program Changes

Pages generated by SSPs and stored within the cache may become obsolete, since the underlying data, or even the server-side programs themselves may be modified. In these cases, the affected pages in the cache must be located and either be removed, or re-generated. The responsibility for update tracking is assigned to the *Update Manager*, which is a distinct software module that may be run on the same machine as the cache manager or on a different one. The *Update Manager* monitors the *invalidations repository*, to locate *patterns* describing the pages that have become obsolete. Each such pattern contains the following information:

1. A designation of the program(s) that have generated the affected pages.
2. The parameters and the respective values that must match the server-side program's invocation data, so as to consider the page invalid.

Figure 3 presents some examples of invalidation patterns.

Each invalidation pattern is complemented with a *criticality designation*, which draws values from the domain *{hard, soft}*. A value of *soft* indicates that the outdated version of the page *may* be used as a reply to the requesting client, in the event of high server load, whereas a *hard* criticality designation states that sending outdated pages is unacceptable, and the respective cached pages should be invalidated immediately. Updates having a *soft* criticality designation are assigned to a low-priority thread of the Cache Manager, which uses idle CPU cycles to refresh outdated pages.

(Path, Parameters)	Remarks
("http://www.example.org/categories.php", "catid=2")	All pages generated by *categories.php* with the parameter *catid* equal to 2, regardless of the values of other parameters or cookies.
("http://www.example.org/admin/*", "")	All pages generated by any program in the *admin* directory, regardless of parameters.
("http://www.example.org/index.php", "__cookie:LANGUAGE=en")	All pages generated by *index.php* with the cookie *LANGUAGE* set to the value *en*.

Fig. 3. Examples of patterns within the invalidations repository

Once the Update Manager detects a new invalidation entry within the invalidations repository, it reads the respective data and propagates them to the Cache Manager, so that the respective page invalidations or regenerations may be performed. The Cache Manager communicates with the Update Manager using a private protocol, which is not needed to be known to the applications that modify the data repository, contrary to the practice employed in [23] and [10]. These applications need only insert the corresponding invalidation entries to the invalidations repository (which may be a database table, an operating system file etc.), using familiar programming techniques.

Using an additional repository for registration of invalidation patterns and the introduction of the update manager were design decisions, aiming to relieve the update application programmers from using proprietary APIs, the need to know details about the number of Cache Managers and their addresses, or handling communication errors. Furthermore, using a standard information repository for invalidations, such as a database, facilitates interventions from the Web administrators that could not be foreseen at the time of update application development. For instance, in order to force the invalidation of all pages generated by the */categories.php* script (e.g. due to changes in the script), the Web administrator may append the respective entry to the invalidations repository by using e.g. SQL:

```
insert into cache_invalidations(script_path, params, criticality)
values('http://www.example.org/categories.php', '', 'hard');
```

If invalidation information were communicated to the cache manager through an API, it would be necessary to write compile and execute a –simple– program that would arrange for sending the respective information. Moreover, invalidation records use a format very familiar to web programmers and administrators; therefore it is expected that web site maintenance will run more smoothly, compared to cases that employ proprietary protocols or specifications.

Finally, if the data repository supports active features, application programmers may be totally relieved from the burden of registering the invalidation patterns within the invalidations repository. This approach is outlined in section 4.2.

Locating Affected Pages within the Cache

When the Cache Manager receives an invalidation notification, it must locate all pages matching the patterns for the script path and the parameters and either remove them from the cache or refresh them (in immediate or deferred mode, as specified by the *criticality* designation). Since the model presented in this paper allows for specifying *parameter subsets* or *wildcards* within the script paths, the MD5 checksum of the URL, stored for the purpose of serving client requests, cannot be used to locate the affected pages, since hash functions can only be used for full key search [8]. To avoid scanning the full table of cached pages, which would be expensive, the following techniques are used, together with the primary MD5 checksum hashing:

1. An additional MD5 checksum is computed on the program path portion of the URL for each page within the cache, and a hash structure is maintained based on this checksum. This hash structure is used to locate the pages generated by a specific server-side program, when the *script path* field of an invalidation entry does not contain wildcards. For each of these pages, standard substring searching is used to further filter pages matching the specified parameters, if necessary.
2. A secondary B-tree index is built on the *script path* field of the cached pages. This index is used to locate the affected pages when the invalidation entry's *script path* field *does* contain wildcards. Since the maintenance of this index is more costly than the maintenance of MD5 hash tables, an administrative option is provided to disable it; in this case, however, wildcard matching in script paths is not supported.
3. An *optimisation hint* may be attached to an invalidation entry, specifying that the page designation is *complete*, i.e. it includes *all* parameters to the SSP. In this case, the primary MD5-checksum hashing algorithm may be used to locate the *single* page that has become obsolete, minimizing thus housekeeping overheads.

Separating Invalidations from Update Applications

In the approaches presented in the literature insofar, application programs that modify the data repository need to notify in some way the Cache Managers regarding the pages that have become obsolete. This is a burden for programmers and introduces another source of application maintenance activities, when the mapping between data items and dependent web pages changes. In these cases, all programs modifying the respective data need to be tracked and updated.

The approach presented in this paper allows for exploitation of active features offered by the data repository to relieve programmers from the extra coding and maintenance. Such active features may be found in many DBMSs, e.g. *triggers* in Oracle, *rules* in INGRES etc. These active features may be used to implement automatic entry addition to the invalidation repository when the underlying data changes. For instance, the PL/SQL code

```
create trigger category_invalidations
after insert or delete on stories for each row begin
insert into cache_invalidations (script_path, params, criticality)
values('http://www.example.org/categories.php', 'catid=' || catid,
      'hard');
end;
```

arranges for automatically inserting into the cache invalidations repository the appropriate record for invalidating the pages generated by the script *categories.php*, when its *catid* (category id) parameter matches the category id of an inserted or deleted item in the *stories* table.

Similar results may be obtained by using *stored procedures* within the information repository, in order to modify the data, instead of direct SQL (or other information repository-dependent) statements. For instance, the addition of a story may be performed using the statement

```
exec procedure insert_story(800, 3, 'New story', 'Very interesting');
```

where *insert_story* may be defined as

```
create procedure insert_story(sid number, cid number, title varchar2,
body varchar2) as begin
insert into stories values(sid, cid, title, body);
insert into cache_invalidations(script_path, params, criticality)
values(' http://www.example.org/categories.php', 'catid=' || cid,
    'hard');
end;
```

Both the trigger-based and the stored procedure-based techniques are feasible because invalidations are stored within a data repository, instead of being communicated to the Cache Manager via a custom interface, which –in general- cannot be directly used from within a database. Moreover, both cases present the additional advantage of *centralising* the mapping between updated data and affected pages; thus when this mapping changes, only a single modification is required (within the database schema), rather than one update for each affected application.

Architecture Scalability and Resource Utilisation

When the number of requests to the web site increases, the cache manager may become the performance bottleneck of the installation. This may be tackled by using an *array of cache managers* rather than a single one, as depicted in Figure 4. Client requests may be distributed amongst the servers within the array using any appropriate technique (e.g. clustering, round-robin DNS, or specialised hardware [7]).

In this configuration, cache managers maintain independent caches, serving client requests using the algorithm described in section 3. Although in some cases it would be preferable for a Cache Manager to fetch a pre-generated page from a *sibling cache*, rather than from the web server, the current implementation does not support ICP [19], cache digests [14], or any protocol for communication between cache servers.

When updates to underlying data take place, the invalidations repository is populated with the appropriate entries, as presented in section 4. The Update Manager monitors new additions and arranges for communicating the relevant data to the Cache Managers, whose addresses are registered within the Update Manager's configuration file. Each Cache Manager proceeds then to the invalidation of the affected pages, following the algorithm described in section 4.1. The Update Manager is the sole responsible for handling communication errors, retransmissions to failed nodes etc.

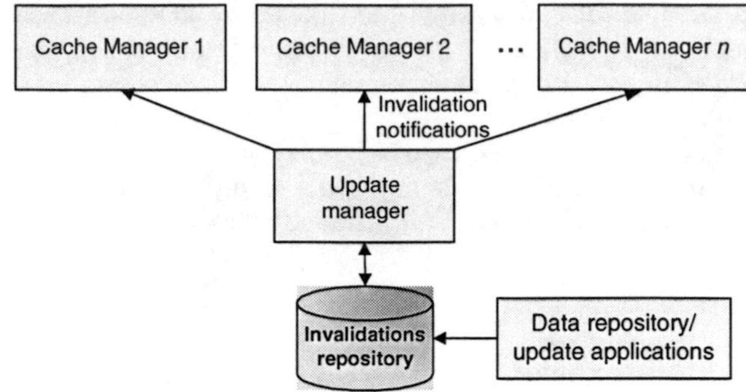

Fig. 4. Load balancing through introduction of multiple caching servers

We would like to note that although the web server, the Cache Manager and the Update Manager appear as distinct modules in Figure 4, it is possible that two of these modules (or even all of them) run on the same machine, in order to save resources. In medium configurations it is expected that only one Cache Manager will be used and the Update Manager will be hosted in the same machine as the cache manager. In large installations, the Cache Manager might be placed in a separate machine. Finally, a single Cache Manager may be used to cache multiple web sites, if this is desirable.

Experiment Results

In order to assess the various aspects of our approach, a number of experiments were conducted. The experiments were selected so as to vary in different aspects, such as update frequency, average page size, update propagation criticality and the existence of personalised pages. For each experiment, stress tests were performed under different loads, so as to quantify the benefits derived from using the caching scheme.

The first experiment was conducted on a web portal implemented using the PHP-Nuke system. In this experiment, a number of stories were added daily; when a story was added, the main page (*/index.php*) should be refreshed instantly, whereas pages hosting news falling in specific categories (*/categories.php*) were updated with softer time constraints. Personalised pages (implemented via cookies) were not cached, as log analysis showed that each such page was used only 1.2 times in average.

The second experiment was conducted for a sports site, offering "live" information about the scores of soccer and basketball games. Pages served from this site were classified in three categories: (a) a summary page for all soccer games (b) a summary page for all basketball games (c) one detail page for each match (basketball or soccer). In this experiment, the soccer summary page was updated once every two minutes, in average, whereas the basketball summary page was updated constantly as game scores evolved. Out of these two summary pages, only the first one was cached. Regarding detail pages, the average update rate for soccer pages was once every 3':30", while the corresponding rate for basketball match pages was once every 28". Refresh information sent to clients dictated page refreshing every 30" for both soccer and basketball pages. "Impatient" users, however, often requested page refreshes every 3"-5", especially during the last few minutes of games.

Both experiments were conducted using two site configurations. In the first configuration, a single machine hosted all software modules, i.e. the web server, the Cache Manager and the Update Manager. In the second configuration, two machines were used, with the first one running the Cache Manager, and the second one hosting the Update Manager and the web server. The results from these experiments are summarised in Figure 5.

Single-server	*Cache hit ratio*			*Avg. response time reduction*		
# clients	*50*	*250*	*500*	*50*	*250*	*500*
Web portal	62%	73%	78%	61%	72%	67%
Sports site	43%	60%	65%	51%	62%	59%
Dual-server	*Cache hit ratio*			*Avg. response time reduction*		
# clients	*50*	*250*	*500*	*50*	*250*	*500*
Web portal	62%	73%	78%	59%	70%	76%
Sports site	43%	60%	65%	49%	59%	66%

Fig. 5. Experiment results using a dual-machine configuration

In these results, it is worth noting that in the single-machine configuration, although the cache hit rate increases when the number of users grows from 250 to 500, the average response time reduction drops. This is due to *server saturation*, since the server cannot handle all three tasks under this heavy load. The situation is remedied when the cache manager is separated from the web server, in the second configuration, where the load is balanced between the two servers.

Conclusions – Future Work

This paper proposes a caching scheme for dynamic web pages, which isolates the caching mechanism from the web server. Although this separation duplicates the parsing of URLs and headers, it presents a number of advantages:

- the caching server can interoperate with any web server, thus no web-server specific implementations are required
- the two servers (web and caching) may reside on different systems
- any upgrade/modification to any of the servers does not affect the others.

The architecture presented minimises the additional workload for dynamic page developers, by allowing separation of the rules describing the dependencies between underlying data and derived pages from the application programs that perform the data updates. These dependencies can be stored within the database schema, in a centralised fashion, leaving update applications intact. This requirement can be easily met when the database offers triggering mechanisms, or stored procedures.

The caching scheme was tested in several cases, proving quite efficient and well behaved in cases of information repository or server-side program updates. The results showed that the proposed caching mechanism offers improved network performance with minimum CPU overhead. It should, however, be noted that the results are dependent on the nature of the dynamic pages. If the underlying data change too often (e.g. stock exchange), the caching scheme will probably not improve the web site performance. Further research is underway to form a set of guidelines and tools to aid developers in assessing the suitability of dynamic content for caching.

Future work will focus on supporting cache population using anticipatory rules, to cater for expected access patterns over time periods, and extending cache techniques to the client side, so as to limit the required network traffic. Cooperation between sibling caches, and its effect on performance is another area that will be investigated.

References

1. Allaire Corporation: Cold Fusion White Paper. Version 4.0. (1999). http://www.allaire.com
2. Arlitt M., Friedrich R., Jin T.: Performance Evaluation of Web Proxy Cache Replacement Policies. Proceedings of the 10th International Conference, Tools '98, Palma de Mallorca, Spain, (1998) 193-206
3. Atzeni P., Mecca G., Merialdo P.: Design and Maintenance of Data Intensive Web Sites. Proceedings of the Conference of Extending Database Technology, Valencia, Spain (1998)
4. Cao P., Zhang J., Beach K. Active Cache: Caching Dynamic Contents on the Web. Proceedings of IFIP International Conference on Distributed Systems Platforms and Open Distributed Processing (Middleware '98). (1998) 373-388.
5. Cao P., Irani S.: Cost-Aware WWW Proxy Caching Algorithms. Proceedings of USENIX Symposium on Internet Technologies and Systems. Monterey, California (1997) 193-206
6. Challenger J., Iyengar A., Dantzig P. A Scalable System for Consistently Caching Dynamic Web Data. Proceedings of the IEEE Infocom 99 Conference. New York, (1999)
7. Coyote Point Systems Inc. The Equalizer Network Appliance. Available through http://www.coyotepoint.com/equalizer.shtml
8. Elmarsi R., Navathe S. Fundamentals of Database Systems. Benjamin/Cummings Publishing Company Inc. (1994)
9. D. Florescu et al. Run-Time Management of Data Intensive Web-sites. Proceedings of the Workshop of Web and Databases (WebDB 99), Philadelphia, Pensylvania. (1999)
10. Iyengar A., Challenger J. Improving Web Server Performance by Caching Dynamic Data. Proceedings of the USENIX Symposium on Internet Technologies and Systems, Monterey, California (1997).
11. Labrinidis A., Roussopoulos N. On the Materialization of Web Views. Proceedings of the Workshop of Web and Databases (WebDB 99), Philadelphia, Pensylvania (1999)
12. Pröll B. et al. Ready for Prime-Time – Pre-Generation of WEB Pages in TIScover. Proceedings of the Workshop of Web and Databases, Philadelphia, Pensylvania (1999)
13. Sindoni G. Incremental Maintenance of Hypertext Views. Proceedings of the Workshop of Web and Databases (1998)
14. Hamilton M., Rousskov A., Wessels D. Cache Digest specification - version 5. Available through http://www.squid-cache.org/CacheDigest/cache-digest-v5.txt
15. Wang J. A Survey of Web Caching Schemes for the Internet. ACM Computer Communication Review, (29) (1999) 36--46
16. Wessels D. Squid Internet Object Cache. http://www.squid-cache.org
17. Wessels D., Claffy K. Internet Cache Protocol (ICP), version 2 – RFC 2186. Available through http://www.cis.ohio-state.edu/cgi-bin/rfc/rfc2186.html
18. XCache Technologies, XCache Product Information. http://www.xbuilder.net/home/
19. Zhu H., Yang T. Class-based Cache Management for Dynamic Web Content. IEEE INFOCOM, 2001.

Deriving and Verifying Statistical Distribution of a Hyperlink-Based Web Page Quality Metric

Devanshu Dhyani, Sourav S. Bhowmick, and Wee Keong Ng

School of Computer Engineering, Nanyang Technological University, Singapore 639798
{assourav, awkng}@ntu.edu.sg

Abstract. In this paper, we discuss issues related to metrics for *Web page quality*. These metrics are used for ranking the quality and relevance of Web pages in response to user needs. We focus on the problem of ascertaining the statistical distribution of some well-known hyperlink based Webpage quality metrics. Based on empirical distributions of Webpage degrees, we derived analytically the probability distribution for the Pagerank metric. We found out that it follows the familiar inverse polynomial law reported for Webpage degrees. We verified the theoretical exercise with experimental results that suggest a highly concentrated distribution of the metric.

1 Introduction

The significance of a Web page can be viewed from two perspectives—its *relevance* to a specific information need such as a user query, and its absolute *quality* irrespective of particular user requirements. Relevance metrics relate to the similarity of Web pages with driving queries using a variety of models for performing the comparison. Quality metrics typically use link information to distinguish frequently referred pages from less visible ones. Specifically, a well-known set of metrics for measuring the quality of Web pages is based on hyperlink citations, for example Pagerank [2] and Authorities/Hubs [4]. As these measures depend upon Web page in and out-degrees, knowledge of degree distribution can lead to their probability density functions. In this paper, we study the measurement of hyperlink information at a microscopic level in assessing the quality or relevance of page. We demonstrate an approach for deriving the distribution of Pagerank from the empirical distributions of topological primitives. We also experimentally verify the probability distribution of Pagerank. There are several reasons why this exercise is instructive. Firstly, it illustrates a generic methodology that can be extended to other hyperlink metrics. Secondly, a distribution derived theoretically from observations of more primitive determinants is likely to be more reliable than an empirically obtained one that is inextricably linked to the experimental setup. This conforms with the conventional wisdom of making measurements as fundamental as possible before deriving more comprehensive metrics. Additionally, in the case of Web hyperlink metrics such as Pagerank, we

R. Cicchetti et al. (Eds.): DEXA 2002, LNCS 2453, pp. 19–28, 2002.

avoid running computationally expensive algorithms. Finally, a theoretical distribution serves as a model that can help us predict precisely and consistently the effect of changes in certain parameters without incurring the cost of carrying out complex measurements again.

2 Distribution of Quality Metrics

Quality measures depend upon Web page in and out-degrees, knowledge of degree distribution can lead to their probability density functions. Knowing, say the cumulative distribution of Pagerank for the Web F_R, one can determine the number of high-quality pages according to some threshold say r, given the size of the Web N. That is, the number of pages with Pagerank greater than r can be estimated as $N' = N \cdot \Pr(R > r) = N(1 - F_R(r))$. The value of N' can be useful for crawlers looking for high quality Web pages in deciding optimum size versus quality configurations for search engine indexes. The distribution can also help Web crawlers give greater priority to visiting more important, high quality pages first.

In this section, we demonstrate an approach for deriving the distribution of Pagerank from the empirical distributions of topological primitives. We first revisit the formulation of Pagerank and explain its key determinants. The Pagerank R_i of a page i having in-degree n can be defined in terms of the Pagerank of each of the n neighboring pages and their out-degrees. Let us denote by j $(1 \leqslant j \leqslant n)$, the index of neighboring pages that point to i and by X_j the out-degree of page j. Then for a fixed parameter d in [0,1] the Pagerank R_i of i is given as $R_i = (1-d) + d\sum_{j=1}^{n} \frac{R_j}{X_j}$. We refer to d $(0 \leqslant d \leqslant 1)$ as the damping factor for the calculation of Pagerank.

We derive the distribution of a simplified version of Pagerank, ignoring the recurrent relationship of R_i with the Pagerank of other pages R_j and assuming the formulation to be

$$R_i = (1-d) + d\sum_{j=1}^{N_i} \frac{1}{X_j} \tag{1}$$

Computationally, the determination of Pagerank for a graph of k pages can be seen as equivalent to the steady state solution $(n \to \infty)$ of following matrix product relationship:

$$\begin{pmatrix} R_1^{n+1} \\ R_2^{n+1} \\ \vdots \\ R_k^{n+1} \end{pmatrix} = \begin{pmatrix} 1-d \\ 1-d \\ \vdots \\ 1-d \end{pmatrix} + d \begin{pmatrix} \frac{1}{x_{11}} \cdots \frac{1}{x_{i1}} \cdots \frac{1}{x_{k1}} \\ \frac{1}{x_{12}} \cdots \frac{1}{x_{i2}} \cdots \frac{1}{x_{k2}} \\ \vdots \quad\quad \vdots \quad\quad \vdots \\ \frac{1}{x_{1k}} \cdots \frac{1}{x_{ik}} \cdots \frac{1}{x_{kk}} \end{pmatrix} \cdot \begin{pmatrix} R_1^n \\ R_2^n \\ \vdots \\ R_k^n \end{pmatrix}$$

where R_i^n denotes the Pagerank of page i at the nth iteration and x_{ij} the number of links from page i to j. If there are no outgoing links from page i to j, i.e., $x_{ij} = 0$, then the corresponding entry in the matrix $(1/x_{ij})$ is set to zero. Repeated multiplication of inverse out-degree matrix with the Pagerank vector yields the dominant eigenvector of the latter. Pagerank can thus be seen as the stationary probability distribution over pages induced by a random walk on the Web, that is, it represents the proportion of time a "random surfer" can be expected to spend visiting a page. It is clear that the steady state distribution of the Pagerank vector (R_i^n) depends entirely on the value of d and the right hand vector of inverse out-degrees. Our simplification of Equation 1 aims at finding the distribution of this vector at $n = 0$. The distribution of (R_i^1) gives us an idea of the steady state distribution at $n \to \infty$ which can itself be obtained by applying the above computation on the initial distribution. We further assume that initially Pagerank is uniformally distributed, that is, $R_i^0 = 1/k$ for all i $(1 \leqslant i \leqslant k)$.

We interpret R_i, X_j and N_i in Equation 1 as random variables denoting Pagerank of i, the out-degree of j and the in degree of i respectively. Although both X_j and N_i are known to have the same distribution, X_j is continuous while N_i is discrete. It is clear that R_i for all values of i are identically distributed. The same holds for the in- and out-degrees denoted by X_j and N_i. We therefore represent the common probability densities of these sets of random variables as $f_R(r)$, $f_X(x)$ and $f_N(n)$ respectively. The problem now is to find the density $f_R(r)$ given the relationship of R_i with X_j and N_i as represented by Equation 1.

2.1 The Lotka Density

The derivation of the distribution of Pagerank is based on observations of distribution of Web page degrees. These measurements carried out on Webgraphs by Broder *et al* [1] and Kleinberg *et al* [5] have been reported to follow the well-known *Lotka distribution*. The Lotka density is given as

$$f_X(x) = \begin{cases} \dfrac{C}{x^\alpha} & \text{if } x \geqslant 1, \\ 0 & \text{otherwise.} \end{cases}$$

where $\alpha \approx 2$ and C is a constant. In our derivation, we invoke both the continuous and discrete versions of this law. Here we distinguish between the two and examine the implications of each. If we interpret X as a continuous random variable, the constant C is found using the fact that the area under a probability density curve sums to unity. That is, $\int_{-\infty}^{\infty} f_X(x)dx = 1$. Applying this to the continuous Lotka density above, we have

$$\int_1^\infty \frac{C}{x^2} dx = 1 \tag{2}$$

Solving this we obtain $C = 1$. The continuous version of Lotka's law can then simply be stated as follows:

$$f_X(x) = \begin{cases} \dfrac{1}{x^2} & \text{if } x \geqslant 1, \\ 0 & \text{otherwise.} \end{cases}$$

In the case of the discrete version, the integral of Equation 2 changes to a discrete summation, hence, $\sum_{x=1}^{\infty} \frac{C}{x^2} = 1$. If we factor the constant C from the summation on the left, we are left with the sum $\sum_{x=1}^{\infty} x^{-2}$ which is the well-known *Riemann zeta function* $\zeta(2)$. Several analytical methods exist for computing the zeta function. Here we use the following general definition for even arguments, i.e., $n \equiv 2k$, $\zeta(n) = \frac{2^{n-1}|B_n|\pi^n}{n!}$ where $|B_n|$ is a Bernoulli number. Given $B_2 = 1/6$, we have for $n = 2$, $\zeta(2) = \frac{\pi^2}{6}$. Substituting this we obtain the expression for C as $C = \frac{1}{\zeta(2)} = \frac{6}{\pi^2} \approx 0.608$.

Although the in- and out-degree distributions on the WWW have been discovered principally as discrete distributions, we apply the continuous approach in examining the relationship between degree and Pagerank distributions because the apparatus of infinitesimal calculus makes the mathematical formulation easier. Indeed, as the number of pages being considered increases, the differences between the continuous and discrete approaches become insignificant.

To approximate the Lotka distribution function $F_X(x) = \Pr(X \leqslant x)$, we integrate the density function $f_X(\cdot)$ within the continuous range $(1, \infty)$: $F_X(x) = \int_1^x f_X(z)dz = \int_1^x \frac{1}{z^2}dz = 1 - \frac{1}{x}$.

2.2 The Pagerank Distribution

The non-recurrent definition of Pagerank in Equation 1 may be viewed as a composition of three primitive functions of random variables enumerated below.

The inverse of individual out-degrees of pages: The individual out-degrees are independent identically distributed random variables, X_j with the index j ranging from 1 to the in-degree of the page being considered. If we represent the inverse of the out-degree of the jth neighboring page as a random variable Y_j then, $Y_j = \frac{1}{X_j}$. It is known that the density of out-degrees, $f_X(x)$ is the Lotka function introduced earlier. We denote the density function of Y_j as $f_Y(y)$, since Y_j is identically distributed for all j.

The sum of out-degree inverses: We denote by a random variable Z_i, the sum of out-degree inverses Y_j. That is, $Z_i = \sum_{j=1}^{N_i} Y_j$. The upper limit to the sum is itself a random variable denoting the out-degree of the page in question. Fortunately, this random variable N_i, the out-degree of page i, is Lotka distributed. We must note however, that N_i is necessarily a discrete random variable as must any index to a discrete summation. Thus, N_i has the probability density obtained earlier for the Lotka distribution

$$f_N(n) = \begin{cases} \dfrac{6}{\pi^2}\dfrac{1}{n^2} & \text{if } n \geqslant 1, \\ 0 & \text{otherwise.} \end{cases}$$

Finally, the Pagerank function of Equation 1 can be expressed as a linear function of the random sum Z_i above as

$$R_i = (1 - d) + dZ_i \tag{3}$$

We now determine the densities of the random variables Y_i, Z_i and R_i introduced above. Consider Y_i, the inverse of X_i that represents the out-degree of page i. We first note that Y_i is a strictly decreasing function in the range of X_i (with the latter defined on positive values only). The probability distribution of Y_j can be expressed in terms of the distribution of X_j as follows $F_Y(y) = \Pr(Y_j \leqslant y) = \Pr\left(\frac{1}{X_j} \leqslant y\right) = \Pr\left(X_j \geqslant \frac{1}{y}\right)$ since $\frac{1}{\mathrm{X_j}}$ is strictly decreasing $= 1 - \Pr\left(X_j < \frac{1}{y}\right) = 1 - F_X\left(\frac{1}{y}\right)$. Differentiating this to convert to probability densities, we have: $f_Y(y) = \frac{d}{dy}F_Y(y) = -f_X\left(\frac{1}{y}\right)\frac{d}{dy}\left(\frac{1}{y}\right) = \frac{1}{y^2}f_X\left(\frac{1}{y}\right)$. Substituting the Lotka continuous density function for $f_X(\cdot)$ to the above result and applying the range $[1, \infty]$ to the argument $1/y$, we obtain the uniform density for Y_j over the converted range $(0, 1]$.

$$f_Y(y) = \begin{cases} 1 \text{ if } 0 < y \leqslant 1, \\ \\ 0 \text{ otherwise.} \end{cases}$$

The above result, that the inverse of a Lotka distributed random variable has a uniform distribution is an interesting coincident. Intuitively it implies that even though the probability that the out-degree of a page is in a given range follows an inverse square law, the probability of out-degree inverse is uniformally distributed, i.e., independent of the value of Y_j.

The sum of out-degree inverses Z_i given by $\sum_{j=1}^{n} Y_j$ has a variable number of terms equal to n, the number of pages that point to i or the out-degree of i. We model the limit of the summation itself as a discrete random variable N_i. Such a sum is commonly referred to as a *random sum*. As noted earlier, N_i is Lotka distributed and similar to X_i except that the distribution here is the discrete version of the Lotka function. Note that Z_i for all values of i are identically distributed so the common density can be denoted $f_Z(z)$ as done earlier for the random variables X_i and Y_i. We first find the density of Z_i conditioned on the summation limit N_i, that is $f_{Z|N}(z|n)$.

A sum of random variables has a density which is the convolution of the densities of individual random variables. For n identically distributed summands, this specializes to the n-fold convolution of their common density, in this case $f_Y(y)$. This n-fold convolution $f_Y^{(n)}(y)$ is defined recursively as follows: $f_Y^{(1)}(y) = f_Y(y)$ and $f_Y^{(n)}(y) = \int_{-\infty}^{\infty} f_Y^{(n-1)}(y-u) f_Y(u) du$ for $n > 1$. The above definition can be applied to $f_Y(y)$ derived earlier to obtain the following formula for the density of the random sum Z_i conditioned upon the out-degree of page i. Figure 1 shows the n-fold convolutions of the uniform density for several values of n. Observe that for higher values of n, the curve flattens out resembling a normal distribution. This is predicted by the central limit theorem which states that the sum of n independent random variables tends to a uniform distribution as $n \to \infty$, $f_{Z|N}(z|n) = f_Y^{(n)}(y)$ where

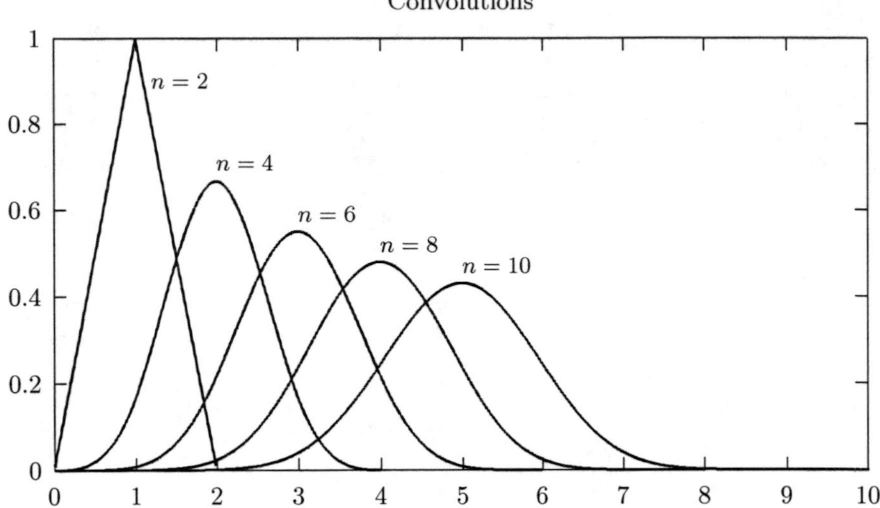

Fig. 1. Convolutions of n uniform densities.

$$f_Y^{(n)}(y) = \begin{cases} \dfrac{1}{(n-1)!} \displaystyle\sum_{j=0}^{x} (-1)^j \binom{n}{j} (x-j)^{n-1} & \text{if } 0 < x < n, \\ 0 & \text{otherwise.} \end{cases}$$

By the law of total probability, the continuous marginal density of the sum Z_i can be found as $f_Z(z) = \sum_{n=1}^{\infty} f_{Z|N}^{(n)}(z|n) \cdot f_N(n)$. Substituting for the above expression for $f_{Z|N}(z|n)$ and the discrete Lotka density for $f_N(n)$ we have

$$f_Z(z) = \begin{cases} \dfrac{6}{\pi^2} \displaystyle\sum_{n=1}^{\infty} \dfrac{1}{n^2(n-1)!} \displaystyle\sum_{j=0}^{x} (-1)^j \binom{n}{j} (x-j)^{n-1} & \text{if } 0 < x < n, \\ 0 & \text{otherwise.} \end{cases}$$

It is difficult to simplify the above summation since the inner sum does not have a closed form. Figure 2 shows the approximate curve for the density $f_Z(z)$. The parameter n_0 represents the *minimum in-degree* considered for computing the random sum. Notice that the sharp peak for the curve $n_0 = 2$ occurs due to the influence of the 2-fold convolution of Figure 1. For higher starting values of n, signifying more densely connected pages the curve becomes more even.

Finally, to derive the density $f_R(r)$ of a linear function of Z_i, we adopt a similar approach as before for finding the density of out-degree inverse, except that the function $\phi(Z_i) = 1 - d + dZ_i$ is strictly increasing. We have from Equation 3 $F_R(r) = \Pr(R_i \leqslant r) = \Pr(1 - d + dZ_i \leqslant r) = \Pr\left(Z_i \leqslant \frac{r-1}{d} + 1\right)$ since ϕ is strictly increasing. Therefore,

$$= F_Z\left(\frac{r-1}{d} + 1\right) \tag{4}$$

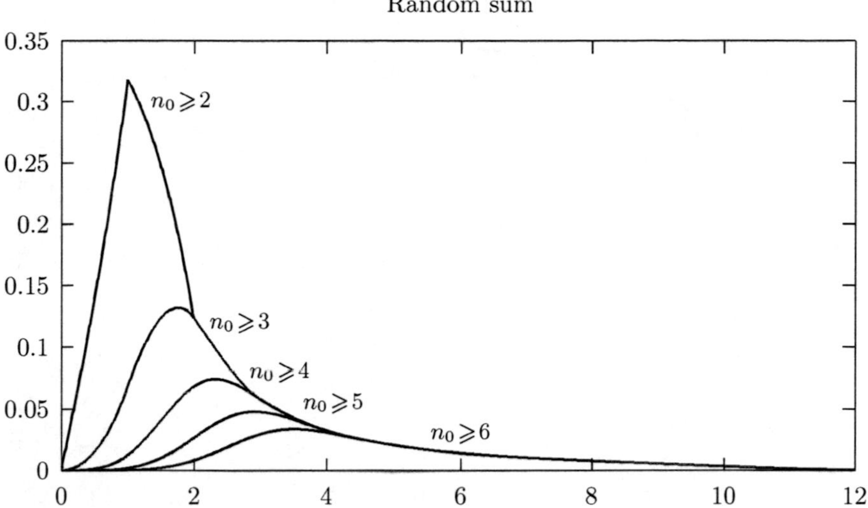

Fig. 2. Density of a sum of uniformally distributed random variables. Each curve represents the density function given by $\sum_{n=n_0}^{\infty} f_{Z|N}(z|n)f_N(n)$. For computation purposes we approximated the upper limit to be $n = 20$.

and differentiating to obtain probability density,

$$\begin{aligned} f_R(r) &= \frac{d}{dr}F_R(r) = f_Z(\phi^{-1}(r))\frac{d}{dr}(\phi^{-1}(r)) \\ &= \frac{1}{d}f_Z\left(\frac{r-1}{d}+1\right) \end{aligned} \tag{5}$$

Figure 3 shows the unnormalized Pagerank distribution $F_R(r)$ denoting the probability $\Pr(R < r)$. For $n_0 = 2$, nearly two-thirds pages have a Pagerank within 10% of its total range which means that Pagerank follows a highly concentrated distribution as do Web page in- and out-degrees. This confirms our earlier conjecture that Pagerank distribution is affected by the degree distributions.

3 Experimental Verification

We have conducted experiments to verify the theoretical exercise of the previous section. We summarize our results here. Detailed discussion on the experiments is given in [3]. We do so in two parts—first we verify that Web page out-degrees follow a Lotka distribution and then compare the derived theoretical distribution for Pagerank with the observed distribution of the metric, computed over a given sample of pages. Our experiments required large crawls of the WWW and were undoubtedly limited by the scale of available computing resources, primarily memory and network bandwidth. Our crawls were different from those performed by a typical search engine in that they did not download pages for storage, but merely obtained the URL and hyperlink connectivity of visited pages. Web crawls

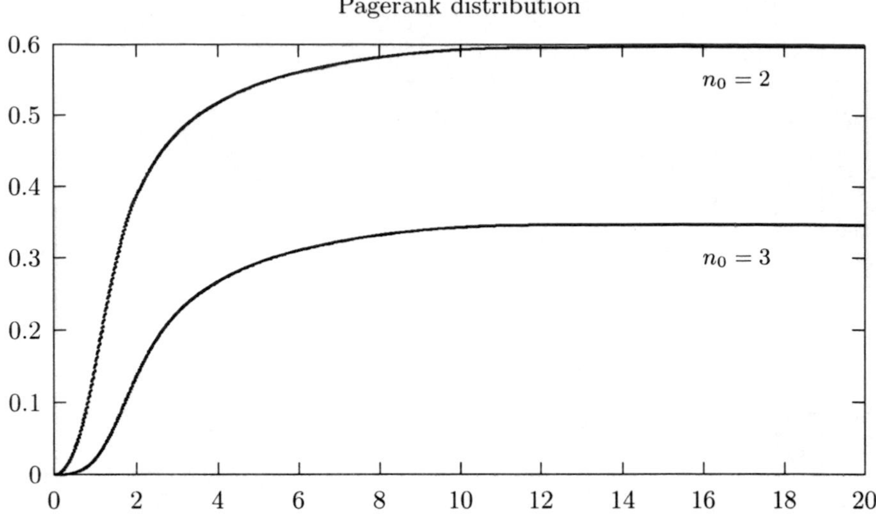

Fig. 3. Derived Pagerank probability distribution $F_R(r)$ with parameter $d = 0.5$ for two values of minimum in-degree n_0.

for our experiments were performed using a Java-based toolkit for developing customized crawlers, known as SPHINX (for Site-oriented Processors for HTML Information) [6]. To test the power law phenomenon which serves as our own starting hypothesis in the theoretical determination of Pagerank distribution, we conducted experiments on a crawl of over 2000 pages. A log-log plot of out-degree distributions is shown in Figure 4. This plot appears linear as expected for a power law distribution. We computed the Pagerank of over 2000 pages ($\beta = 40$) with the objective of confirming the theoretically derived distributions of the previous section. Following graph completion, the computation converged with residual error below a threshold of 10^{-4}. We used a damping factor of 0.5. A log-log frequency plot of Pagerank values suggests that Pageranks also follow a power law distribution. We confirmed this intuition by fitting the observed Pagerank distribution with a power law function shown in Figure 5.

Finally, we present in Figure 6 the comparison of the *cumulative* Pagerank distribution with its theoretically derived counterpart $F_R(r)$ from the previous section (see Equation 4). As mentioned earlier, the theoretical expression for Pagerank distribution employs infinite convolutions of uniform densities. For computation purposes, we approximated this with a limit of 20-fold convolution. The derived cumulative distribution was obtained by integrating the area under the density curve of Equation 5 using the *trapeziod rule*. We see that the observed distribution of Pagerank compares reasonably with the distribution of Equation 4, derived from out-degree distributions.

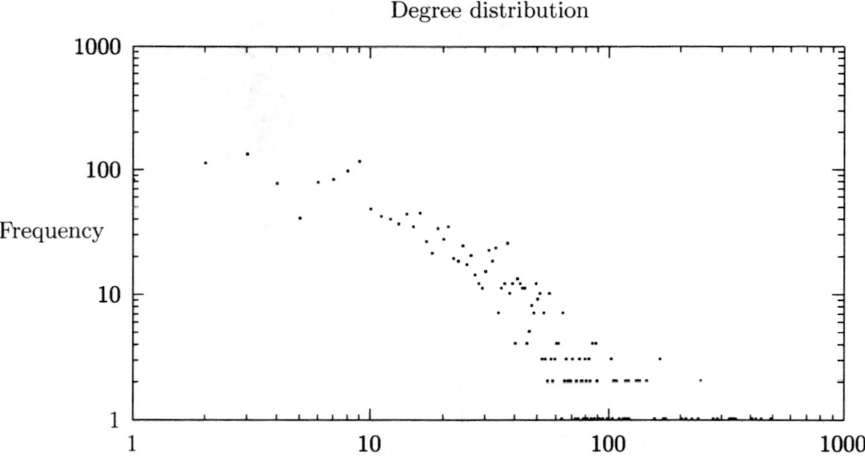

Fig. 4. Log-log plot of out-degree distribution of 2024 Web pages in the NTU domain.

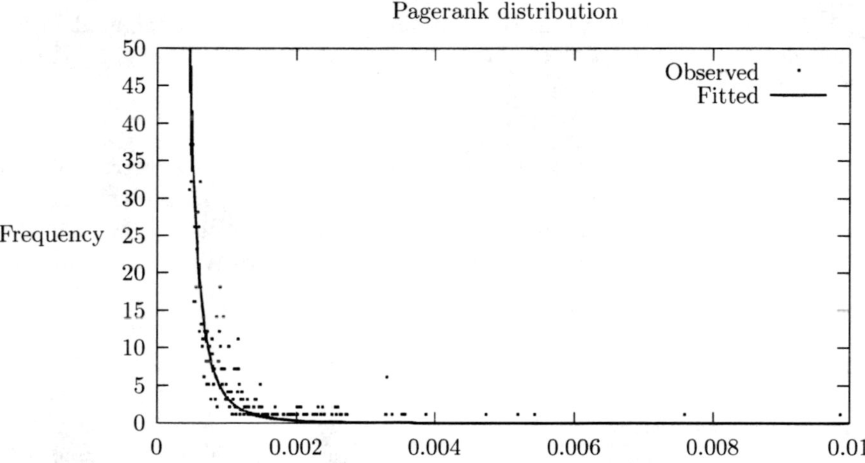

Fig. 5. Pagerank distribution for 1889 pages in the NTU domain fitted to the analytical curve $y = \alpha x^{-\beta}$ where $\alpha = 1.7 \times 10^{-10}$, $\beta = 3.43$. Goodness of fit parameters: $\chi^2 = 47.78$, asymptotic standard errors for α and β were 180.9%, 6.84% respectively.

4 Conclusions

In this paper we treated the problem of ascertaining the statistical distribution of some well-known hyperlink based Webpage quality metrics. Based on empirical distributions of Webpage degrees, we derived analytically the probability distribution for the Pagerank metric and found it to follow the familiar inverse polynomial law reported for Webpage degrees. We verified the theoretical exercise with experimental results that suggest a highly concentrated distribution of the metric. Our work on distributions of hyperlink metrics can be extended

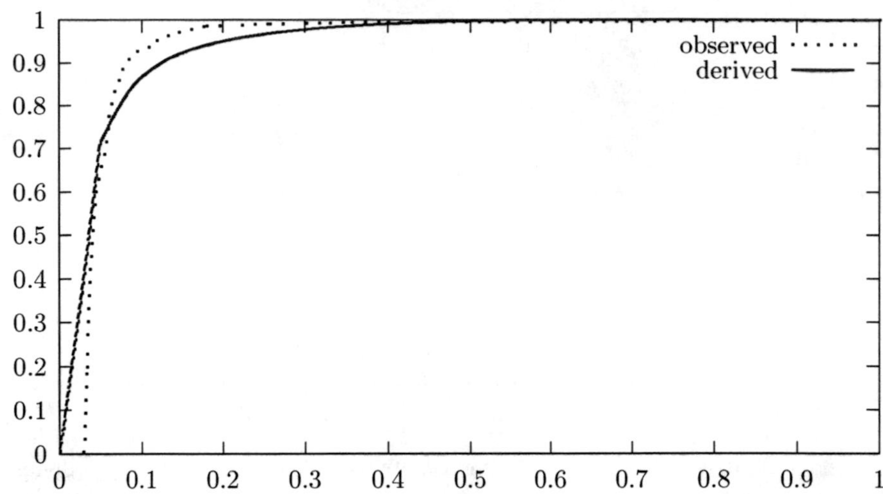

Fig. 6. Theoretical probability distribution function of Pagerank (computed with 20-fold convolution) and the observed normalized cumulative distribution of NTU Pagerank for a crawl of 2026 pages.

by conducting similar exercises for other types of significance metrics for both quality and relevance. It is not clear whether the high concentration depicted by hyperlink metrics is a special consequence of the power law behavior of Webpage degrees or the manifestation of a general regularity in Webpage significance, irrespective of the metric in particular.

References

1. A. Broder, R. Kumar, F. Maghoul, P. Raghavan, S. Rajagopalan, R. Stata, A. Tomkins, J. Wiener. Graph Structure of the Web. *Proceedings of the Ninth World Wide Web Conference*, Amsterdam, Netherlands, May 2000.
2. S. Brin, L. Page. The Anatomy of a Large-Scale Hypertextual Web Search Engine. *Proceedings of the Seventh World Wide Web Conference,* Brisbane, Australia, April 1998.
3. D. Dhyani. Measuring the Web: Metrics, Models and Methods. *Master's Dissertation,* School of Computer Engineering, Nanyang Technological University, Singapore, 2001.
4. J. Kleinberg. Authoritative Sources in a Hyperlinked Environment. *Proceedings of the ACM-SIAM Symposium on Discrete Algorithms,* 1998.
5. J. Kleinberg, R. Kumar, P. Raghavan, S. Rajagopalan, A. Tomkins. The Web as a graph: measurements, models, and methods. *Proceedings of the Fifth International Conference on Computing and Combinatorics, COCOON*, Tokyo, Japan, July 1999.
6. R. Miller, K. Bharat. SPHINX: A framework for Creating Personal, Site-specific Web Crawlers. *Proceedings of the Seventh International World Wide Web Conference,* Brisbane, Australia, April 1998.

MWM: Retrieval and Automatic Presentation of Manual Data for Mobile Terminals *

Masaki Shikata[1], Akiyo Nadamoto[2], Kazutoshi Sumiya[3], and Katsumi Tanaka[3]

[1] Graduate School of Science & Technology, Kobe University,
Rokkodai, Nada, Kobe 657-8501, Japan
shikata@db.cs.kobe-u.ac.jp

[2] Communication Research Labolatory, Seikatyouhikaridai, Sagara, Kyoto 619-0289, Japan
nadamoto@crl.go.jp

[3] Graduate School of Informatics, Kyoto University, Yoshida Honmachi, Sakyo, Kyoto
606-8501, Japan
{sumiya, ktanaka}@i.kyoto-u.ac.jp

Abstract. In this paper, we propose a new way of retrieving and presenting manual data from the Web, based on a state transition diagram and data conversion into synchronized multi-modal contents. The manual data of a target device is assumed to consist of three parts: (1) manual documents in XML, (2) state transition diagrams in XML, and (3) three-dimensional computer graphics (3D CG) of the target device, which are also in XML. The prototype under development is called a Mobile Web Manual (MWM). The major features of MWM are as follows: (a) acquisition of the present state of a target device by wireless communication, (b) retrieval of manual data by finding a path between the present state and a given goal state, (c) automatic generation of 3D animation from the retrieved manual data, and (d) presentation by 3D animation synchronized with synthesized speech.

1 Introduction

Recently, due to the rapid progress of mobile communications technologies, it is possible to use not only the Internet but also a short-distance wireless network, such as Bluetooth[1] and 802.11b. With these mobile communications technologies, mobile terminals can communicate with other types of equipment, acquire the present state of devices, and perform real-time operations. However, not only do most mobile terminals have small displays, but they also do not have full keyboards. This makes it difficult for mobile terminals to display the ordinary, text-based manual data that can be displayed with conventional Web browsers. In other words, mobile terminals impose many restrictions on content presentation and user interactions. We have proposed [2][3] a way of viewing information together with 3D CG (three-dimensional computer graphics) in a

* This research is partly supported by the joint research project with NTT DoCoMo, and the research is also partly supported by the Japanese Ministry of Education, Culture, Sports, Science and Technology under Grant-in-Aid for Scientific Research on "New Web Retrieval Services Based on Discovery of Web Semantic Structures", No. 14019048, and "Multimodal Information Retrieval, Presentation, and Generation of Broadcast Contents for Mobile Environments", No. 14208036.

R. Cicchetti et al. (Eds.): DEXA 2002, LNCS 2453, pp. 29–39, 2002.

more automatic, passive style. With our approach, several attributes or description data concerned with a 3D CG object can be viewed passively in mobile terminals, because our approach automatically transforms the attribute data or description data of a 3D CG object into multi-modal synchronized contents. That is, our approach automatically generates 3D CG animation, which is synchronized with speech synthesized from its attribute or description data.

A number of research groups are working on controlling smart appliances from a single handheld device based on those mobile terminals, which will be able to communicate with smart appliances using a short-range wireless network. Philips Pronto[4] is the universal remote controls that are available today for controlling many different consumer electronic products. The interface, which is displayed on mobile terminals to control appliance, must be hand-programmed in Pronto's system. Correspondingly, Jeffrey et al.[5], Abrams et al.[6],the IBM project[7] are working on automatically generating interface, which is displayed on mobile terminals to control appliance. These works are using XML-based language to describe user interface.

Many research groups are working on automatic generation of a help or a manual of software. For example, Roberto et al.[8] presented the system that generates hypertext-based help about data presented in application displays, commands to manipulate data, and interaction techniques to invoke commands. Fiorella et al.[9] proposed that explanation by Animated Agent is generated automatically. Our research is in agreement with these researches in respect of automatically generating and representing explanation.

Harold Thimbleby et al.[10][11][12] proposed a way of generating user manuals in terms of design integration, so that all aspects of usability (e.g., user interface, help systems, training, documentation) evolve concurrently. He implemented a prototype system called HyperDoc, which animates models of interactive devices, generates user manuals, and supports device analysis. However, few system designers and manual writers use a manual-generating system such as HyperDoc. The feature common to HyperDoc and our proposed approach are the introduction of a finite state machine (FSM) model to describe the behaviors of the target device. HyperDoc does not use XML. In our proposed system, the behavior of the target device is described in XML as a hierarchical state transition diagram (i.e., a state chart) as well as XML-based manual documents. Also, HyperDoc does not take mobile terminals into consideration, but our system does.

In this paper, we propose a mechanism of presenting the manual data of device operation using 3D animation and synthesized speech manual text with mobile terminals. We call this mechanism the Mobile Web Manual (MWM). The MWM can relate the state transition, the manual document, and the 3D CG, each of which is written in XML. Usually, a computer operation manual may use text, images, 3D CG, and movies. MWM targets the text and the 3D CG.

The left side of Fig.1 shows a system image of the MWM. Users input into the mobile terminals the target operations (goal state) that they want to perform. The mobile terminal can acquire the present state of a device by short-distance wireless communication. The system computes the shortest path of the state transition between the target operations and the present state in the state chart. The shortest path of the state transition can be the action scenario of the 3D animation. The system retrieves the manual from the state

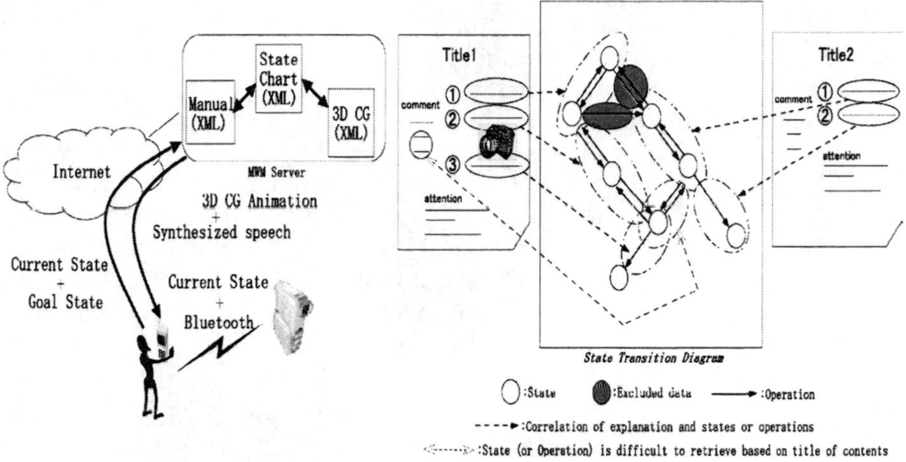

Fig. 1. Mobile Web Manual(MWM) and Correspondence manual and state transition diagram

chart and generates the speech scenario of the 3D animation from the manual. Then, the system creates the 3D animation automatically, based on the action and speech scenarios. The functions of the MWM are as follows:

- Get the present state of a smart device by short-distance wireless communication.
- Create 3D CG animation automatically by using the state chart, the text manual, and 3D CG, each in XML.
- Present the 3D CG animation manual based on the 3D CG animation and synthesized speech.

The remainder of this paper is divided as follows: Section 2 discusses the retrieval of the manual data based on the FSM model. Section 3 discusses the presentation of the operation manual on mobile terminals. Section 4 presents a prototype system. Section 5 summarizes our work.

2 Retrieval of Manual Data by FSM Model

In this section, we describe a mechanism to retrieve the necessary portions of the operation manual data using the FSM (finite state machine) model. As stated previously, in our system, the manual data for devices consists of the following three components:

- A manual document, written in XML
- A state transition diagram, written in XML
- 3D CG data of target devices, written in XML

In order to retrieve the manual data for user requests, the system uses the current state and the desired state of the target device to construct the scenario of the 3D CG manual. The desired state is computed by the path to the goal state. It is possible for the system to acquire the current state of the target device with using the short-distance wireless communications network. We will describe the procedure of specifying state transitions. The system retrieves the desired states by user-specified keywords. This is important because some users may not understand the meaning of operation (i.e.,sequence) names. For a set of user-specified keywords and an acquired current state, we need to retrieve all the reachable states whose corresponding text segment contains the user-specified keywords. In the following, we show an algorithm to retrieve all the reachable states. The input to the algorithm includes (1) an XML-based operation manual document, M, (2) a user-specified keyword, key. The output of the algorithm is a list of reachable state names. Let T_{key} denotes a text segment that contains the user-specified keyword key. Here, we assume that the manual document has a tree structure that represents the logical structure defined in XML. That is, the manual document forms a tree structure whose vertices are tags, text segments or images (See the upper left portion of Fig.2). Text nodes and image nodes are all leaves of the tree.

Step 1 Search the manual document tree for all the text segment nodes each of which contains the user-specified keyword key.

Step 2 For each text segment node T_{key} containing the keyword key, find the minimal tagged areas (corresponding to a subtree of the manual document tree) that contain both the text segment node T_{key} and a non-leaf node with the attribute which is the state or transition. The reason for having applied the minimal tag region is that the neighborhood tags of the sentence that contains user specified keyword are assumed matched with the target state. Here, a tagged area denotes a continuous portion of the manual document, M, which starts at an arbitrary tag X and ends at the corresponding tag X.

Step 3 For each minimal tagged area which is found in Step 2, retrieve the corresponding state name in the state chart.

Fig.2 shows an illustrative example of the algorithm. The right portion of the figure shows an XML manual document. The upper left portion of the figure shows the XML logical structure of the manual document represented as a tree. The lower portion of the figure shows the correlation between XML tags with the attribute and the state/transition in the state chart. Here, t_i denotes a text segment node or an image node. $< X* >$ denotes a tag with an attribute which corresponds to a state or a transition in the state chart. $< X >$ denotes a tag that does not correspond to a state or a transition. S_j is an attribute data of $< X* >$, and it denotes a state and j is the state number. T_{kl} is also an attribute data of $< X* >$, and denotes a transition edge in the state chart. (k is the start state number of the transition, and l is the end state number.) The state or the end state of the transition has the potential to be an item in the output candidate list.

The following is an example of the above algorithm for the Fig.2. $t_i (i = 1, 2, ..., 11)$ are leaf nodes. In this case, the text node, which includes user specified keyword, is assumed only t_{10}. Each broken line surrounds the minimal tagged regions of t_{10}. Each region's non-leaf node with the attribute, which is the state/transition, becomes $< P* >$ or $< Q* >$. $< P* >$'s attribute's value is S_3, and $< Q* >$'s attribute's is T_{34}. Then S_3 and S_4 become the item of the candidate list.

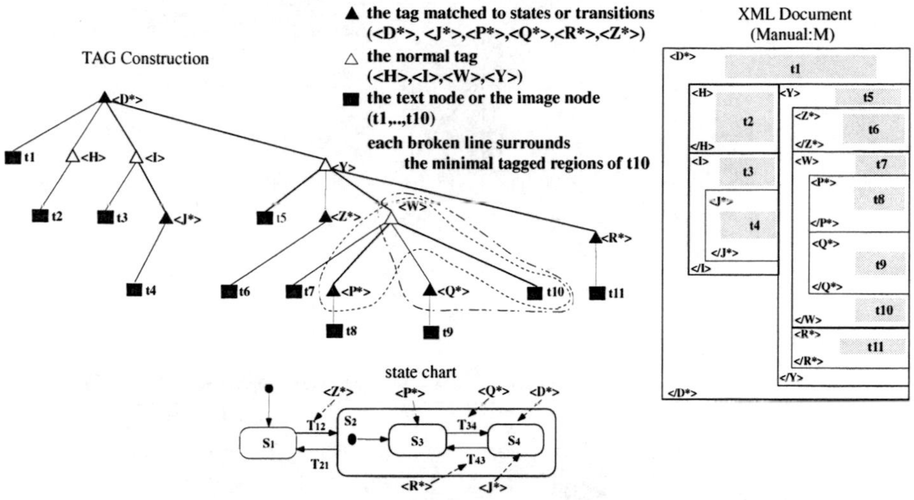

Fig. 2. Correlation between titles and states/transitions

3 Presentation of Operation Manual on Mobile Terminals

Users select the goal state from the obtained candidate list of states, and send it to the MWM server. Then, the shortest path from the current state to the goal state is calculated. The MWM server retrieves the necessary portions of manual data that correspond to the shortest path. This shortest path should be the scenario for constructing the 3D CG manual. Each state or transition attaches surfaces to the 3D CG, plus images and text data as materials. The presentation data is automatically generated and organized based on the scenario and materials (See Fig.3). Generated and organized manual data is presented in a multi-modal manner. That is, our system generates a 3D CG animation synchronized with speech guidance. Using 3D CG enables users to recognize spatial positions and operation directions intuitively. However, it may be easier for some users to understand an operation by using still images or movies. Consequently, the movement from one operation to another operation is presented by a rotating 3D CG model of the devices. The explanation of an operation is presented by a still image that is synchronized with the synthesized speech. Fig.3 shows the flow of the presentation. The presentation data in this paper is as follows:

- Speech data: explanations, attentions and annotations, which are transformed from the retrieved text data in an operation manual
- 2-D visual data: still images
- 3-D visual data: 3D CG model

In order to determine the correlation between portions of a manual document and the states/transitions in a state chart, we designed the XML tags and attributes, which are shown in Table 1. These tags are identified with an `mwm` namespace. These tags and attributes are used in a state chart. We defined the tags and attributes in order to

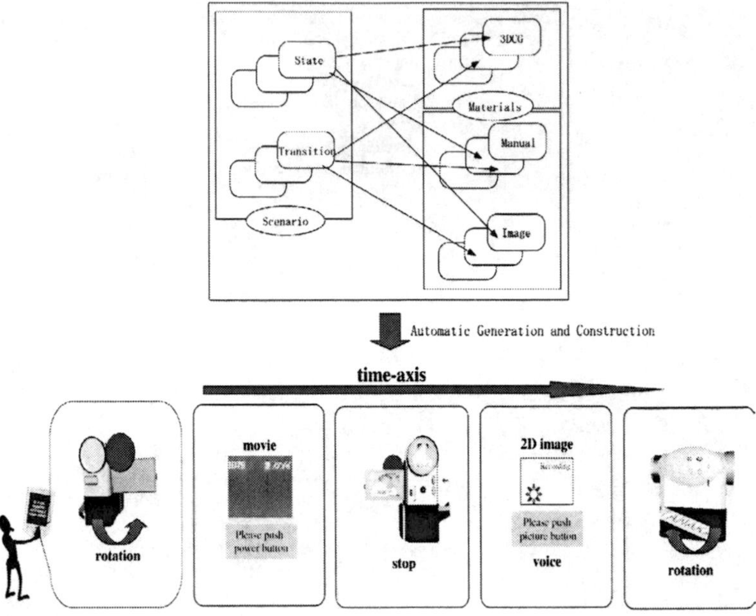

Fig. 3. Presentation Data Generated and Organized based on Scenario and Materials

Table 1. MWM's tags and attributes in a state transition diagram

Element	Attribute	Specification
manual		Root element to describe manual data in state chart.
sequence		As is the case with < *seq* > in SMIL, data on and after it is in sequential order
parallel		As is the case with < *par* > in SMIL, data on and after it is in parallel order
explanation		explanation text in speech
	file	manual filename
	id	explanation ID
annotation		annotation or attention text in speech out.
	file	annotation or attention in speech
	id	annotation ID
image		an image file represented in explanation
	file	a still-image file name
operationface		This tag matches state (or transition) to the surface of 3D CG
	file	3D CG file name
	face	the surface which is used to generate rotation of 3D CG animation

specify the data that should be synchronized with speech guidance. For this purpose, the `id` attribute is used. The `id` attribute is added to a tagged area that includes text in the manual document. The text should be transformed into voice speech. However, sometimes only a certain portion of a text segment is transformed into synthesized speech. Therefore, it is difficult to specify a text portion only by these tags. For this purpose, we introduce the following tags to specify the necessary text portion:

- `explanation`: the region surrounded by this tag denotes the data needed for the voice explanation of operations (transitions) with the attribute `explanation ID`.
- `annotation`: the region surrounded by this tag denotes the data needed for voice annotation or voice attention of states or operations (transitions) with attribute `annotation ID`.

If tags are used in a still image that has a text caption as its attribute value, then the text caption is transformed into speech data. The goal is to represent an operation manual on a mobile terminal in a multi-modal manner. However, most mobile terminals have a physically narrow display, and they do not have full keyboards. Therefore, mobile terminals impose many restrictions are on content presentation and user interactions. We generate a 3D CG animations based on the state charts. Fortunately, most Web3D[13] representations of 3D CG models are based on XML, and therefore, it is easy to make a correlation between the state chart and the 3D CG model description. MWM makes a correlation between the surfaces of the 3D CG model and the states/transitions of the state chart. In X3D[14], the `IndexedFaceSet` tag denotes a surface tag. We define the `facename` attribute for the `IndexedFaceSet` tag. The `facename` attribute value provides a unique name for a surface. In a state chart, `operationface` tag is used to denote the corresponding data of the 3D CG model, and the `face` attribute is defined for the `operationface` tag (See Table 1). The `face` attribute is the `facename` attribute for the `IndexedFaceSet` tag. In this way, MWM matches the `IndexedFaceSet` tag of X3D and the `operationface` tag of a state chart.

Fig.4 is a simple example that illustrates the correlation between a state chart and presentation data. The upper left portion of Fig.4 shows the XML description of a state transition in a state chart. XMI(XML Metadata Interchange)[17], UXF(UML eXchange Format)[18],etc. exist as a format which describes the state chart. In our work, we use UXF to describe a state chart. However our work is independent of specific format, because our purpose is using the ease of the extendibility of XML and applying our system to any XML formats. We describe a state transition from `Recording` state to `Ready` state. The lower left portion of this figure shows the presentation flow by the state chart. The upper right portion of the figure shows a description of the 3D CG model in X3D, and the lower right portion shows a fragment of a manual document described in XML. The presentation flow is as follows:

1. First, the 3D CG model is presented. It rotates from its display screen area to the area having a stop button.
2. After the rotation, the text, which is specified for explanation, is transformed into voice speech and is played. After the speech is finished, the stop button turns to the users.
3. After the voice speech is over, the 3D CG model rotates from the stop button to the display area.
4. After the rotation, the device's still image is presented. At the same time, in a synchronized manner, the text, which is specified as annotation text, is read as voice speech.

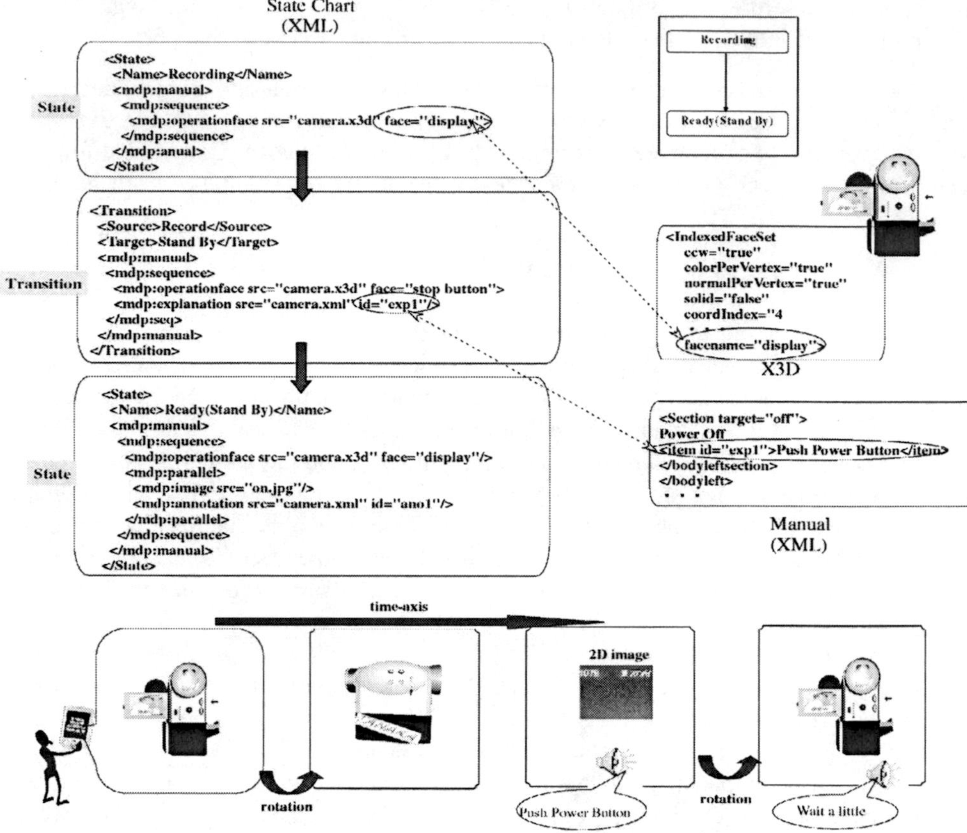

Fig. 4. Presentation control by a state chart and manual data

4 Prototype System

In this section, we describe a prototype system based on our MWM. The prototype system was developed by Java and transported into a celluler phone, which is used for FOMA[15] service. (FOMA service is the 3rd-generation cellular-phone service currently offered in Japan by NTT DoCoMo.) Since it is difficult for us to develop a device that supports a FSM and a wireless communications network, we created a 3D CG model as a virtual device on a desktop PC. Also, since a viewer to represent the 3D CG model described in XML on FOMA Platform dose not exist, we utilized i-motion[16] that is service to reproduce specified format video data on a FOMA terminal. That is, 3D CG animation synchronized with synthesized speech guidance, which is changed into the video format for FOMA in advance, and it performed communicating the video of suitable explanation to FOMA. On the MWM server side, we used X3D to represent 3D CG, by which the final CG animation is generated in the form of a VRML file. In order to describe the state charts in XML, we utilized UXF, which is an XML format, to represent UML(Unified Modeling Language). Fig.5 shows the information flow of our

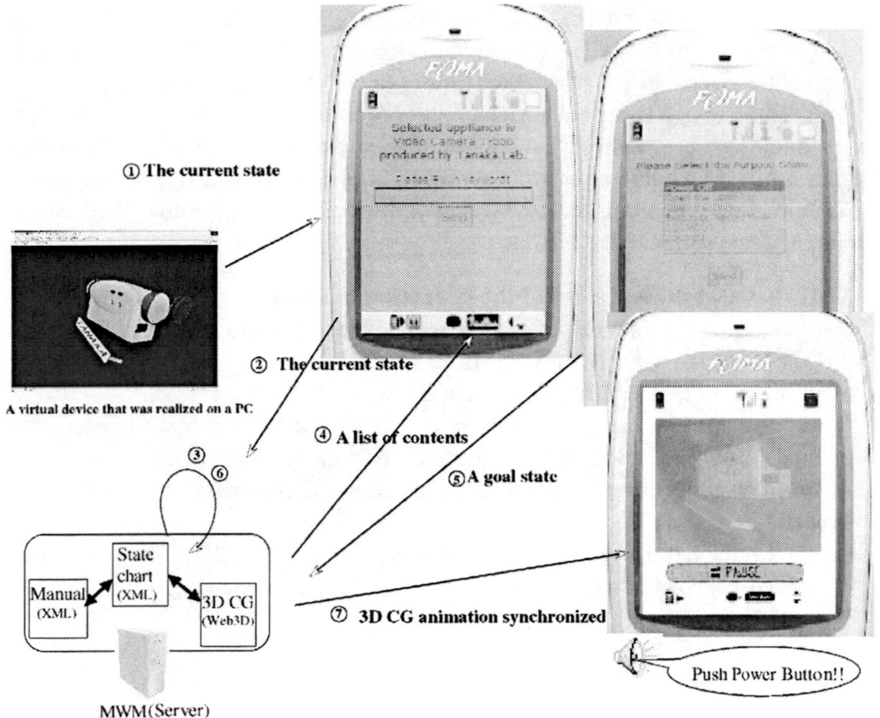

Fig. 5. Information Flow of Our MWM Prototype System

prototype system. The following is one example of possible uses of our MWM prototype system:

1. A user wants to change the state of a device (e.g., video camera), and obtain its current state by using a FOMA terminal.
2. The obtained current state, the product data (e.g., product ID, etc.) and related keywords are transported from the FOMA terminal to the MWM server.
3. The system retrieves manual data based on the current state and the state chart.
4. The user receives a list of the candidates, selects a goal state from this list, and sends the selected goal state to the MWM server.
5. The MWM server automatically generates the 3D CG animation of the retrieved manual data, which is an operation sequence from the current state to a goal state.
6. 3D CG animation, synchronized with synthesized speech guidance, is displayed on the FOMA terminal.(This prototype system represents movie data which is translated from 3D CG animation.)

5 Concluding Remarks

In this paper, we proposed both of a new way of retrieving manual data by a sta te transition diagram and a way of presenting retrieved data in a multi-modal manner by mobile terminals. The manual data of a target device is assumed to consist of three parts: (1) manual documents in XML, (2) state transition diagrams described in XML, and (3) a 3D CG of the target device. The major features of MWM are as follows: (a) acquisition of the present state of a target device by wireless communication, (b) retrieval of manual data by finding a path between the present state and a given goal state, (c) automatic generation of 3D CG animation from retrieved manual data, and (d) presentation (by 3D CG animation synchronized with synthesized speech). The main contributions of the present paper are summarized as follows:

- **XML-based representation of the operation manual**
  Operation manual data of devices consist of manual documents, state charts, and the 3D CG of the devices, all in XML.
- **Manual data retrieval by FSM (state chart)**
  Based on a current state acquired from the devices and a goal state, portions of the manual data are retrieved by finding a shortest path in a state chart.
- **Automatic generation of 3D CG animation synchronized with synthesized speech**
  Retrieved manual data is automatically transformed into a 3D CG animation synchronized with synthesized speech for the user's passive viewing.

References

1. Bluetooth Available at http://www.bluetooth.com/
2. N.Nadamoto, M.Shikata, T.Yabe, K.Tanaka:Autonomous Presentation of 3Dimensional CG Contents and Their Attribute Information, submitted to journal.
3. M.Shikata, A.Nadamoto, K.Tanaka:Retrieval and Reorganization of Operation Manual and Obtain Machine State Information by Mobile Terminals, (in Japanease), Technical Report of IPSJ, Vol.2001, No.70 01-DBS-125(1), pp.343-350, 2001.
4. Philips.Pronto Available at http://www.pronto.philips.com/
5. J.Nichols, B.A.Myers, M.Higgins, J.Hughes, T.K.Harris K.Harris, R.Rosenfeld, M.Pignol: Generating Remote Control Interfaces for Complex Appliances, Submitted for Publication.
6. M.Abrams, C.Phanouriou, A.L.Batongbacal, S.M.Williams: UIML:An Appliance-Independent XML User Interface Language, Computer Networks, Vol. 31, 1999, pp. 1695-1708.
7. K.Eustice, T.Lehman, A.Morales, M.C.Muson, S.Edlund, M.GuillenF: A Universal Information Appliance, IBM Systems Journal, 1999, 38(4),pp.575-601. http://www.research.ibm.com/journal/sj/384/eustice.html
8. B.De Carolis, F.de Rosis, S.Pizzutilo: Automated generation of agent behavior from formal models of interaction, in Proceedings of AVI2000, Palermo (Italy), 24-26 May 2000, pp.193-199, ACM Press.
9. R.Moriyon, P.Szekely, R.Neches: Automatic generation of help from interface design models. Proceedings of CHI94, Boston, 1994.
10. H.Thimbleby, M.Addison: Intelligent adaptive assistance and its automatic generation, Interacting with Computers, 8(1), pp51-68, 1996.
11. H.Thimbleby: Combining systems and manuals, HCI'93, pp479-488, 1993.
12. H.Thimbleby: Creating User Manuals for Use in Collaborative Design, ACM Conference on Computer-Human Interaction, CHI'96, pp279-280, 1996.

13. Web3D Available at http://www.web3d.org/
14. X3D Available at http://www.x3d.org/
15. FOMA Available at http://foma.nttdocomo.co.jp/english/
16. i-motion Available at http://www.nttdocomo.co.jp/english/p_s/i/imotion/
17. XMI Available at http://www.omg.org/technology/documents/formal/xmi.htm
18. UXF Available at http://www.yy.cs.keio.ac.jp/%7Esuzuki/project/uxf/uxf.html

Ensuring Recovery for SACReD Web Transactions in the E-commerce Applications

Muhammad Younas[1] and Barry Eaglestone[2]

[1]School of Mathematical and Information Sciences, Coventry University, UK
M.Younas@coventry.ac.uk
[2]Department of Information Studies, University of Sheffield, UK
B.Eaglestone@sheffield.ac.uk

Abstract. This paper presents an extension to a novel Web transaction management protocol, previously defined for a failure-free environment, such that it provides reliable recovery from failure in e-commerce applications. This protocol manages complex Web transactions upon multiple distributed Web services, and overcome limitations of two-phase commit protocols by applying correctness criteria based upon semantic atomicity. Further, it supports enhanced transaction resilience through the use of compensating and alternative transactions. The protocol has been prototyped in a CORBA environment. An evaluation carried out on this prototype shows that the new recovery mechanism minimises the logging cost, increases fault tolerance, and permits independent recovery of autonomous systems.

1. Introduction

Limitations of Web-transaction management (W-TM) currently restrict the scope of e-commerce [14]. Specifically, W-TM does not effectively manage complex transactions that aggregate sub-transactions on distributed Web services and data sets. Our contribution is a reliability procedure for managing transactions of this type. Our protocol, which enforces correctness criteria based upon semantic atomicity and transaction resilience (SACReD criteria) [16], has been formally defined and analysed for a failure free environment [17]. Here we extend this work by formally considering the protocol in the presence of failures. Specifications are given in CCS (Calculus of Communicating Systems) notations [8].

Section 2 reviews related work and identifies limitations of current approaches to Web transaction recovery. Section 3, presents a protocol that enforces SACReD criteria for Web transactions in the absence of failures [16, 17], and then extends it by formally specifying a new recovery mechanism which will enforce the SACReD criteria in the presence of failures. Section 4 describes a CORBA-compliant prototype tool that implements the recovery mechanism and the results of an evaluation using it.

R. Cicchetti et al. (Eds.): DEXA 2002, LNCS 2453, pp. 40–49, 2002.

2. Related Work

Communications and component system failures on the Web are frequent. However, most W-TM approaches either do not address recovery within the Web environment [11,12,19,20], or rely on two-phase commit (2PC) based protocols to enforce ACID criteria for transaction correctness [1, 5, 10, 3, 7, 6, 2].

Usefulness of 2PC-based solutions is limited by their failure recovery strategy, i.e., aborting the transaction and all subtransactions. This severely affects systems throughput and fault tolerance. Also, performance is impeded by the overhead of logging state changes of Web transactions, and excessive consumption of systems resources. The latter occurs particularly where participating systems cannot communicate with each other to terminate a transaction [17, 13]. A more serious limitation is that, for 2PC to operate, underlying information systems must support either access to prepare-to-commit state or undergo modification to provide this support. The former limits heterogeneity, while the later violates autonomy. Also, in e-commerce application component systems may belong to autonomous businesses, and system modifications for participation in 2PC protocols may not be feasible.

Alternatives to 2PC-based W-TM are conversational transactions [11, 12] and Jpernlite [19]. The former comprise autonomous independent transactions, related only in the context of a specific conversation. Jpernlite incorporates extended transactions for Web-enabled software engineering applications (using plug-in codes). Both approaches mainly concern concurrency control mechanisms. The issue of execution guarantees for e-services is raised in [15, 9], but this work has limited scope, since it concerns specific applications, e.g. payment protocols. Also, none of these approaches cover recovery aspects of applications; they do not address system-wide failures of the Web transactions. A concurrency control mechanism for flexible transactions in heterogeneous database environments is proposed in [20], such that alternative subtransaction sets can be specified to execute to compensate or as alternatives to subtransaction within the context of a global transaction. However, simultaneous execution of alternative sets of subtransactions can result in performance degradation [18].

The above limitations motivate our research in which we have defined transaction correctness criteria, which we argue are more appropriate to the Web environment, and protocols to enforce those criteria. Our correctness criteria are based upon semantic atomicity, which requires transactions to commit either all subtransactions, or if any is aborted to reverse, using compensating transactions, the effects of committed subtransactions. This allows subtransactions to unilateral commit and therefore intermediate states of local databases become accessible. This means that consistency is enforced only at component database level, and transactions are not isolated from the effects of others. However, in practice isolation may be undesirable when transactions involve co-operation and negotiation between users. We add resilience as a desirable, but not mandatory property. Web-transactions are vulnerable to failure due to unreliability of the Internet, autonomy of local systems and consequentially increased likelihood of subtransaction failure through system failure or unavailability of requested services, i.e., semantic failure. The resiliency property concerns the capability of transactions to cope with semantic failures, and is therefore an *a priori* property of a transaction, rather than an *a posteriori* measure of correctness of its execution. Resilience is increased by associating alternative transactions with subtransactions, to create alternative subtransaction sequences that result in successful completion. Thus, our new criteria (called SACReD criteria [16]) comprise **S**emantic **A**tomicity, **C**onsistency, and **Re**silience, while **D**urability remains a requirement, as in ACID criteria.

A protocol to enforce SACReD criteria in the absence of failure is formally specified and implemented [17, 18]. Performance evaluation shows improvements over 2PC-based W-TM, in that it is less costly in terms of information logging, while providing relief from system resource blocking. In addition, it increases resilience to systems and semantic failures, while preserving autonomy of participating Web and database servers. In the remainder of this paper we extend the formal definition of the Web Transaction Protocol to recover from failures.

3. Web Transaction Protocol

The protocol, P1, defined in this section enforces SACReD criteria in the presence of failures. After establishing basic definitions and assumptions (3.1), the basic protocol procedure, P1, is presented (3.2). P1 is informally specified, (see [17] for its formal specification). The extension to P1 for recovery from failures, is formally defined in 3.3 and 3.4. Section 3.3 covers the failure detection and restart procedures of P1, while 3.4 describes the failure and recovery of P1.

3.1. Basic Definitions and Assumptions

A Web transactions, T_{web}, is defined as the execution of a Web application which can be divided into well defined units that provide semantically correct transitions between consistent states (with possibly temporarily invalid intermediate states) of shared database systems [17]. T_{web} is therefore decomposable into subtransactions, ST_i which are compensatable if the effects on a database can be semantically undone by a compensating transaction, and replaceable if there is an associated alternative transaction, i.e., a subtransaction can be compensatable-only (CO), replaceable-only (RO), replaceable and compensatable (R-C), or non-compensatable and non-replaceable (NC-RC).

Two types of failure can occur: (i) Component system failures (F2) occur if participating systems experience hardware or software failures. These may halt component systems, thus causing lose of information stored in volatile memory. (ii) Internet failures (F3) give rise to communication failures resulting in lost of messages or delivery failure. As in [13, 18, 1], other types of failures, e.g., improperly ordered messages, failures of CPUs, main memory, and disks, are not considered.

The protocol recovers from failure using information relating to previous states of the transaction, written to log files. Logged information includes transaction and subtransaction identifiers, types and status, recorded in the log files at different stages of the protocol. For example, identity of a Web transaction is recorded when it is created. Logging is performed using simple-write or forced-write operations. A simple-write does not suspend the protocol. A forced-write suspends the protocol until information is recorded in the log file. Thus forced-writes significantly affect the performance of the Web transactions.

3.2 The Basic Protocol Procedures

Protocol procedures are defined as a multi-process program; WTC (Web transaction coordinator) and each WTA (Web transaction agent) are processes (see 4.). Here we provide informal narrative of their operation.

1. A new transaction, T_{web}, is assigned to a WTC, which records the start of T_{web} in a log file using a simple write and initiates the subtransaction, ST_i. WTC then enters into a *wait* state, awaiting messages from WTAs concerning completion of subtransactions. (Note, WTC does not send a prepare messages to WTAs, as is necessary in the IYV protocol [4]. Also, WTAs can votes after processing STs, since WTC starts the protocol as soon as it starts the execution of T_{web}).
2. When a new ST_i is assigned to a WTA, it records the beginning of ST_i in the log file using a simple write. After processing ST_i, WTA sends a commit or abort vote to WTC. If the latter, WTA forcibly records the abort of ST_i, sends an abort vote to WTC, and declares ST_i to be local-aborted. Otherwise, WTA forcibly writes a commit decision, sends a commit vote to WTC and awaits WTC's decision.
3. WTC receives WTAs' votes, ignoring any duplicates. If all votes register a commit decision, WTC globally commits, by forcibly writing the commit decision and sending global commit messages to all WTAs. It then terminates T_{web} and starts the processing of a new Web transaction.
4. If any aborted subtransaction, ST_i, is replaceable, WTC initiates the alternative subtransaction and awaits the WTA's decision regarding commit or abort of the alternative subtransaction. If ST_i is not replaceable WTC globally aborts, by forcibly writing the abort decision, sending global abort messages to all WTAs, and terminating the transaction.
5. After receiving a global commit decision, WTA simply writes the global commit of ST_i and changes ST_i's status from *local-committed* to *global-committed*. If ST_i is *locally-committed* and WTA receives an abort message, WTA must execute the compensating transaction for ST_i. This is logged by WTA by simply writing the compensation decision and then marking the end of ST_i.

3.3. Recovery Mechanism for SACReD Web Transactions

We now consider type F2 and F3 failures. Timeout [13,1,17] is used by WTC and WTAs to detect these. It is assumed that an appropriate timeout value is pre-determined using the relation: Time-out > $Decision_T$ + $Message_T$; where $Decision_T$ is the worst case time WTC and WTAs take to reach a commit/abort decision, and $Message_T$ is the worst case time needed to receive a decision.

3.3.1 WTC Restart Process

The WTC restart process ensures recovery on the coordinator side, and is designed to respond to the following three situations in which failures of type F2 can occur:

Case-1: WTC log file is searched for the commit record of T_{web} to establish whether T_{web} has committed at the time of failure. This activity is modeled as follow:

$$\text{WTC-Restart}\ (T_{web}) \stackrel{def}{=} \text{read-log (decision)} \,.\, \text{WTC-Restart}'\ (\text{decision}, T_{web})$$

$$\text{WTC-Restart}'\ (\text{decision}, T_{web}) \stackrel{def}{=} \textbf{If}\ \text{decision} = \text{commit-decision}$$

$$\textbf{then}\ \text{send-commit}'\ (0, \text{no-of-ST})\ \textbf{else}\ \text{WTC-Restart}''\ (\text{decision}, T_{web})$$

$$\text{send-commit}'\ (n, \text{no-of-ST}) \stackrel{def}{=} \textbf{if}\ n = \text{no-of-ST}\ \textbf{then}\ \text{Global-commit}\ \textbf{else}$$

$$\sum_{k=1}^{\text{no-of-ST}} [\overline{\text{g} - \text{commit}}_k \,.\, \text{send-commit (n+1, no-of-ST)} + \text{timeout} \,.\, \text{send-commit}'\ (\text{n+1, no-of-ST})]$$

$$\text{Global-commit} \stackrel{def}{=} \overline{\text{Terminate}}\ (T_{web})$$

In the above, no-of-ST represents the number of subtransactions ($\in T_{web}$). If a commit record is found in WTC log file, then each ST_i has committed. Thus WTC must inform all WTAs of the global commit decision. WTC then terminates T_{web}.

Case-2: WTC log file is searched for the abort record of T_{web} so as to determine whether T_{web} aborted at the time of failure, as follow.

$$\text{WTC-Restart}''(\text{decision}, T_{web}) \stackrel{def}{=} \textbf{If}\ \text{decision} = \text{abort-decision}$$

$$\textbf{then}\ \text{send-abort}'\ (0, \text{no-of-ST})\ \ \textbf{else}\ \text{WTC-Restart}'''\ (0, T_{web})$$

$$\text{send-abort}'\ (n, \text{no-of-ST}) \stackrel{def}{=} \textbf{if}\ n = \text{no-of-ST}\ \textbf{then}\ \text{Global-abort}\ \textbf{else}$$

$$\sum_{k=1}^{\text{no-of-ST}} [\overline{\text{g} - \text{abort}}_k \,.\, \text{send-abort}'\ (n+1, \text{no-of-ST}) + \text{timeout} \,.\, \text{send-abort}'\ (n+1, \text{no-of-ST})]$$

$$\text{Global-abort} \stackrel{def}{=} \overline{\text{Terminate}}\ (T_{web})$$

If an abort decision is found in WTC log file, then T_{web} was already aborted when failure occurred. WTC must send abort decision to all WTAs, and then terminate T_{web}.

Case-3: If no global decision is found in the log file then T_{web} was active, and therefore there exist one or more outstanding ST_i ($\in T_{web}$) at WTA sites. Consequently, WTC must communicate with the WTAs to correctly terminate pending ST_i. To do this, WTC must retrieve each outstanding ST_i's status from respective WTAs to determine if they are active, committed, or aborted, and take action accordingly.

$$\text{WTC-Restart}'''\ (n, T_{web}) \stackrel{def}{=} \textbf{if}\ n = \text{no-of-ST}\ \textbf{then}\ \text{WTC-commit}\ (T_{web})$$

$$\textbf{else}\ (\text{get}_n\ (\text{status}) \,.\, \text{check}(n, \text{status}, T_{web})) + (\text{timeout} \,.\, \text{WTC-abort}\ (n, ST_i, T_{web}))$$

In the above, n is the number of outstanding subtransactions. If WTC can retrieve the status of ST_i from WTA then WTC proceeds according to check(n, status, T_{web}) and takes appropriate action. If WTC cannot retrieve the ST_i status, then WTA has failed. Thus WTC will timeout for that WTA and will proceed with WTC-abort (n, ST_i, T_{web}) since it will assume ST_i has aborted.

$$\text{check}(n,\text{status},T_{web}) \overset{def}{=} \textbf{if } ST_i\text{-status= local-committed } \textbf{then } (\text{local-committed}_i)) \,.\, \text{WTC-Restart}''' (n+1, T_{web})$$

$$\textbf{else if } ST_i\text{-status = local-aborted } \textbf{then } \overline{s - write}\,(\text{local-aborted}_i)) \,.\, \text{WTC-abort}\,(n, ST_i, T_{web})$$

$$\textbf{else if } ST_i\text{-status = active } \textbf{then } \text{vote}_i(\text{vote}) \,.\, \text{check}(n, \text{status}, T_{web})$$

If ST_i has committed, WTC records its commit in the log file and proceeds to the next subtransaction by following WTC-Restart''' (n+1, T_{web}). WTC executes WTC-commit (T_{web}) provided all ST_i ($\in T_{web}$) are committed. If any ST_i is aborted then WTC logs its abort and proceeds according to WTC-abort (n, ST_i, T_{web}). If ST_i is active WTC must receive the vote from the WTA and check if it is committed or aborted.

$$\text{WTC-commit}\,(T_{web}) \overset{def}{=} \overline{f - write}\,(\text{commit-decision}) \,.\, \text{send-commit}'\,(0, \text{no-of-ST})$$

$$\text{send-commit}'\,(n, \text{no-of-ST}) \overset{def}{=} \textbf{if } n = \text{no-of-ST } \textbf{then } \text{Global-commit } \textbf{else}$$

$$\sum_{k=1}^{\text{no-of-ST}} [\,\overline{g - \text{commit}}_k \,.\, \text{send-commit}'\,(n + 1, \text{no-of-ST}) + (\text{timeout} \,.\, \text{send-commit}'\,(n, \text{no-of-ST}))]$$

$$\text{Global-commit} \overset{def}{=} \overline{\text{Terminate}\,(T_{web})}$$

WTC forcibly writes the commit decision to the log file and sends global commit messages to all WTAs. It then terminates the transaction according to Global-commit.

$$\text{WTC-abort}\,(n, ST_i, T_{web}) = \textbf{if } \text{replaceable}\,(ST_i) \textbf{ then } \text{WTC-Restart}'''\,(n, T_{web})$$

$$\textbf{else } \overline{f - write}\,(\text{abort-decision}) \,.\, \text{send-abort}\,(0, \text{no-of-ST})$$

If ST_i is replaceable, it is replaced by an alternative subtransaction. Otherwise, WTC forcibly writes the abort decision and proceeds according to send-abort(n, no-of-ST):

$$\text{send-abort}\,(n, \text{no-of-ST}) \overset{def}{=} \textbf{if } n = \text{no-of-ST } \textbf{then } \text{Global-abort } \textbf{else}$$

$$\sum_{k=1}^{\text{no-of-ST}} [\,\overline{g - \text{abort}}_k \,.\, \text{send-abort}\,(n+1, \text{no-of-ST}) + (\text{timeout} \,.\, \text{send-abort}\,(n+1, \text{no-of-ST}))]$$

$$\text{Global-abort} \overset{def}{=} \overline{\text{Terminate}\,(T_{web})}$$

WTC must then send global-abort messages to all the WTAs, and terminate the transaction.

From the above, the following definition of a reliable WTC is deduced.

$$\text{Reliable-WTC} \overset{def}{=} \text{WTC} \mid (\text{restart}(T_{web}) + \text{WTC-Restart}(T_{web}))$$

3.3.2 WTA Restart Process

The WTA restart process is designed to respond to four situations that can occur when an F2 failure occurs.

Case-1: When WTA restarts its execution, it must determine the status of ST_i from the log file in the following manner.

$$\text{WTA-Restart}(ST_i) \stackrel{def}{=} \text{read-log (status)} \,.\, \text{check}(ST_i\text{-status})$$

$$\text{check }(ST_i\text{-status}) \stackrel{def}{=} \textbf{if } ST_i\text{-status} = \text{committed } \textbf{then} \text{ local-committed }(ST_i)$$

$$\textbf{else if } ST_i\text{-status} = \text{aborted } \textbf{then} \text{ local-aborted }(ST_i) \textbf{ else if } ST_i\text{-status=active } \textbf{then } WTA^{/}(ST_i)$$

$$\textbf{else if } ST_i\text{-status} = \text{compensated } \textbf{then } \overline{\text{Terminate}}\,(ST_i)$$

If ST_i is committed, then WTA proceeds according to local-committed (ST_i), otherwise it follows local-aborted (ST_i). If ST_i is active, WTA follows $WTA^{/}(ST_i)$. If ST_i is compensated then WTA needs not to take any action and will terminate ST_i, as it has already compensated the effects of the locally committed ST_i.

Case-2: In this case, the status of the active subtransactions is determined, whether they are committed or aborted.

$$WTA^{/}(ST_i) \stackrel{def}{=} \textbf{if } \text{g-abort } \textbf{then} \text{ abort }(ST_i) \textbf{ else if } ST_i\text{-commit } \textbf{then} \text{ local-committed }(ST_i)$$

$$\textbf{else} \text{ local-aborted }(ST_i)$$

$$\text{abort }(ST_i) \stackrel{def}{=} \text{abort-}ST_i \,.\, \overline{\text{Terminate}}\,(ST_i)$$

If WTA receives a global-abort message from WTC amid the processing of ST_i then it will abort and terminate ST_i. This arises when WTC receives an abort vote for a non-replaceable subtransaction. It must then send global abort messages to all WTAs. Consequently WTAs abort all active subtransactions. If ST_i is committed then WTA must follow local-committed(ST_i), otherwise WTA will follow local-aborted (ST_i).

Case-3: This case concerns the situation when ST_i is locally aborted.

$$\text{local-aborted }(ST_i) \stackrel{def}{=} \overline{\text{f - write}}\text{ (abort-decision)} \,.\, \overline{\text{vote}}_i\text{(abort)} \,.\, \overline{\text{Terminate}}\,(ST_i)$$

WTA forcibly writes the abort of ST_i in a log file, sends abort vote to WTC, and declares ST_i as local-aborted. It then terminates ST_i.

Case-4: This case concerns the situation when a subtransaction, ST_i, is locally committed.

$$\text{local-committed }(ST_i) \stackrel{def}{=} \overline{\text{f - write}}\text{ (commit-decision)} \,.\, \overline{\text{vote}}_i\text{ (commit)} \,.\, \text{Wait (WTC-decision))}$$

WTA sends commit vote to WTC (if it has not sent before), and then waits for WTC's decision. But before sending the commit decision, WTA forcibly writes commit decision in the log file.

$$\text{Wait (WTC-decision)} \overset{def}{=} \text{get(WTC-decision)} . (\text{global-commit} . \text{global-commit } (ST_i)) + (\text{global-abort}. \text{global-abort } (ST_i))$$

In a wait state, WTA contacts WTC to query the global commit or abort decision. If WTA receives a global-commit message from WTC, it acts according to global-commit (ST_i), otherwise it proceeds with global-abort (ST_i).

$$\text{global-commit } (ST_i) \overset{def}{=} \overline{\text{s - write}} . (ST_i\text{-global-commit}) . \overline{\text{Terminate}} (ST_i)$$

WTA simply writes the global commit for ST_i and changes the status of ST_i from local-committed to global-committed in the log file. WTA then terminates ST_i.

$$\text{global-abort}(ST_i) \overset{def}{=} \text{compensate}(ST_i) . \overline{\text{s - write}} (ST_i\text{-compensated}) . \overline{\text{Terminate}} (ST_i)$$

WTA first executes the compensating transaction for the committed ST_i. WTA then simply writes the compensation decision in the log file, and marks the end of ST_i.

The following definition of a reliable WTA is deduced from the above algorithm.

$$\text{Reliable-WTA} = \text{WTA} \mid (\text{restart}(ST_i) + \text{WTA-Restart } (ST_i))$$

3.4. Failures and Recovery

We now describe P1 (section 3.2) in the presence of failures of types F2 and F3.

WTC passes through the states: *initial*, *wait*, and *decision*. When WTC recovers from failures in the *initial* state, it must restart T_{web} from the beginning, as no information is logged about the beginning of T_{web}. If there is no failure then WTC changes to a *wait* state.

1. In *wait* state, WTC waits for the WTA votes. If any vote fails to arrive due to F3, WTC timeouts and assume ST_i has aborted. WTC will interpret this as a WTA site failure. WTC aborts ST_i if it receives an abort vote or if it times out due to lack of a response from WTA.
2. After recovery in the *wait* state, WTC executes the restart process, WTC-Restart process (see 3.3.1), and waits for votes from pending WTAs. If no failure occurs, it will commit or abort T_{web}, as appropriate.
3. If WTC fails after having written the global commit or abort decision, it re-sends the decision messages to all WTAs, using WTC-Restart process (see 3.3.1) as some messages may have been received by the WTAs, whereas others may not.

WTA passes through the following states: *initial*, *processing*, *voting*, *wait*. The behaviour of WTA in these states when errors of type F2 and F3 occur, is as follow:

1. If WTA fails in the *initial* state, it must re-execute ST_i after recovering from failure. Since ST_i has not yet started, no information is available in the log file. In the case of no failure, WTA records the beginning of ST_i and starts processing.

2. If WTA fails during the *processing* of ST_i, it has to follow the WTA-Restart process (see 3.3.2), which checks the status of ST_i from the log file. If failure does not occur, WTA changes to the *voting* state.
3. If WTA fails after writing the local commit or abort decision in the log file, but has not sent its vote to WTC, the following must happen. After recovery, WTA will follow the WTA-Restart process, in which case, either WTA sends an abort vote to the WTC and terminate ST_i, or it sends a commit vote to WTC and waits for WTC's decision concerning global commit or abort.
4. If WTA fails while waiting for the WTC decision, the following must occur. After recovery, WTA will query WTC to determine that global decision. This is done by following the WTA-Restart process, because it is possible that WTC might have sent the decision while WTA was unable to operate due to failure.

Note that the correctness of the recovery procedure (presented in 3.3 and 3.4) is formally verified in [18], but we are unable to present that due to page limit.

4. Summary and Discussion

We have defined a W-TM protocol [17] for reliable recovery of complex transaction from system and communication failures. Novel features are the application of the SACReD correctness criteria which we argue are more suited to the Web environment than the conventional ACID criteria [16], and recovery from failures.

This protocol has been validated and evaluated through the development of a CORBA-compliant prototype. This comprises two parts: Web transaction coordinator (WTC), and Web transaction agent (WTA). Both are implemented as CORBA objects, which may be located at different nodes of the Internet. The commit/abort of the Web transaction and its subtransactions, and occurrence of the site failures, are simulated using probability approach.

Evaluation of the protocol using the prototype demonstrates performance improvements. Logging costs were reduced by requiring fewer forced writes to the log file. These affects performance, since execution of the protocol must pause while information is logged. Our protocol uses n + 1 forced-write operations to process a Web transaction; where 'n' is the number of the subtransactions, compared to 2n + 1 required by 2PC-based protocols. Resilience of a W-TM system is increased by use of alternative transactions. Our evaluation shows that if there exist 0.3 (30%) alternative transactions per Web transaction, the commit probability of a Web transaction increases from (i) 0.9 to 0.927 (ii) 0.8 to 0.848, and so on (see [18] for details). The recovery mechanism does not cause cascading restarts of component systems. Instead, restart processes are executed independently, though they must exchange messages after independently recovering from failures. Ensuring independent recovery is important in e-commerce applications, because component systems providing cross-organizational e-commerce services are largely autonomous [11, 14]. Finally, W-TM systems independently recover from failures of participating systems, and do not require modification to participate in the protocol. Thus autonomy of component systems is maintained.

References

1. D. Billard: Transactional Services for the Internet. Proc. of Int. Workshop on Web and Database (WebDB'98), Valencia, Spain, March 27-28, 1998.
2. Sylvanus A. Ehikioya, K. Barker: A Formal Specification Strategy for Electronic Commerce. IDEAS, Montreal, Canada, August, 1997.
3. K. Evans, J. Klein, J. Lyon: Transaction Internet Protocol: Requirements and Supplemental Information. Internet-Draft, October 1997.
4. Yousef J. Al-Houmaily, P.K. Chrysanthis: Two-Phase Commit in Gigabit-Networked Distributed Databases. 8th Int. Conf. on Parallel & Dist. Comp. Sys. Sept., 1995.
5. J. Lyon, K. Evans, J. Klein: Transaction Internet Protocol: Version 3.0. Internet-Draft, April 1998 (http://www.ietf.org/ids.by.wg/tip.html)
6. M.C. Little, S.K. Shrivastava, S.J. Caughey, D.B. Ingham: Constructing Reliable Web Applications using Atomic Actions. 6th Int. WWW Conf., USA, April, 1997.
7. M.C. Little, S.K. Shrivastava: Java Transactions for the Internet. Proc. of 4th USENIX Conference on O-O Technologies and Systems, April 1998.
8. Rubin Milner: Communication and Concurrency. C.A.R. Hoare Series Editor, Prentice Hall, International Series in Computer Science, 1989.
9. C. P. Martin, K. Ramamritham: Guaranteeing Recoverability in Electronic Commerce. 3rd International Workshop on Advanced Issues of E-Commerce and Web-based Information Systems, 21-22 June, 2001, San Jose, California.
10. OMG: CORBAservices: Common Object Service Specification. November 1997 (http://www.omg.org/corba/csindx.htm)
11. J.Ouyang, A.Sahai, V. Machiraju: An Optimistic Commit Protocol for Conversational Transactions. Technical Report HPL-2001-02, Hewlett-Packard Labs, 2001
12. J. Ouyang, A. Sahai, V. Machiraju: An approach to Optimistic Commit and Transparent Compensation for E-Service Transactions. 14th International Conf. on Parallel and Distributed Computing Systems (PDCS 2001), Dallas TX
13. T.Ozsu, P. Valduriez: Principles of Distributed Database Systems. Prentice-Hall, 1991
14. H. Schuldt, A. Popovici: Transactions and Electronic Commerce. 8th Int. Workshop on Foundations of Models and Languages for Data and Objects: Transactions and Database Dynamics, Schloss Dagstuhl, Germany , 1999, Springer LNCS No.1773.
15. J.D. Tygar: Atomicity versus Anonymity: Distributed Transactions for Electronic Commerce. Proceeding of 24th International Conference on Very Large Databases (VLDB), August 24-27, 1998, New York City
16. M. Younas, B. Eagelstone, R. Holton: A Review of Multidatabase Transactions on the Web: From the ACID to the SACReD. British National Conf. on Databases (BNCOD), Exeter, UK, July 3-5, Springer LNCS, 2000.
17. M. Younas, B. Eagelstone, R. Holton: A Formal Treatment of a SACReD Protocol for Multidatabase Web Transactions. 11th International Conf., DEXA2000, Greenwich, London, 5-8 September, 2000, Springer LNCS, 2000
18. M. Younas: Web Transaction Management for Multidatabase Applications. Ph.D. Thesis, University of Sheffield, UK, 2001.
19. J.Yang, G.E.Kaiser: JPernLite: An Extensible Transaction Server for the World Wide Web. IEEE TKDE, 1999.
20. A. Zhang, M. Nodine, B. Bhargava: Global Scheduling for Flexible Transactions in Heterogeneous Distributed Database Systems. IEEE TKDE 13(3), 2001, 439-450

Workflow Simulation across Multiple Workflow Domains

Xiaohui Zhao

Department of Computer Science
Harbin Institute of Technology, P.R. China
wallace@dip1.hit.edu.cn

Abstract. In the scenario of multiple homogenous intra enterprise workflow domains, several partial processes cooperate according to certain interoperability models. In this case, workflow simulation requires more flexible and powerful mathematical models. In this paper, BCMP queuing network is imported to workflow based business process simulation filed for the first time. With its special multi-class and multi-chain characteristics, we can provide a workflow simulation across multiple domains using three basic interoperability models. This simulation approach accords well with the dynamic and randomness of workflow. Thus, we can report some performance indexes and analysis before deploying.

1 Introduction

1.1 Introduction

Workflow is the computerized facilitation or automation of a business process, in whole or part. Workflow management system (WfMS) uses one or more functional components to perform business activities, to interact with workflow participants (persons or applications), to manipulate workflow process instances' implementation and supervise the runtime state of process instance [1-3].

Traditional workflow system requires each workflow model to be instantiated first to analyze before applied in practice. However, with workflow simulation, we can predict its performance before deploying. In this paper, a simulation method, based on BCMP queuing network, is proposed, which supports the chained, nested and parallel synchronized interoperability models across multiple workflow domains.

1.2 Related Works

There are many researches about integrating workflow representation and simulation/performance analysis together, such as the following:
ARIS (Architecture of Integrated Information System), a process-oriented model architecture proposed by Dr. Scheer of University Saarland, which defines four

R. Cicchetti et al. (Eds.): DEXA 2002, LNCS 2453, pp. 50–59, 2002.

views, i.e. function/process view, organization view, data view and control view [4,5]; GRAI (Graphical Results and Activities Interrelated), a method to describe and analyze production management system, proposed by GRAI lab of University Bordeaux [6]; QSGM (Qualitative Simulation Graph Methodology), developed by Ingalls, et al, a general purposes qualitative discrete-event simulation (QDES) framework that can be well suited to address the PERT (Performance Evaluation Review Technology) scheduling with resource problem [7,8]; A performance analysis approach to very large workflow systems, proposed by Dr. Kwang-Hoon Kim, based on MOL (Method of Layers) in order to evaluate performance of possible spectrum of workflow architectures proposed in the framework [9,10].

1.3 Compare with Petri Net

Aiming at model's organizational structure and dynamic behavior, Petri net is easy to represent the change condition and post change state, especially when timed and Stochastic Petri nets come forth. Anyway, it is widely accepted that Petri net is good at distributed, parallel, synchronized system analysis [11-13]. However, Petri net is unfit to represent the change of data value or attributes. In the course of large, complex system modeling, Petri net always encounters the problem of too large state space, which blocks its application area very much. Compared to Petri net, queuing network is specific at having product form solutions. This point can simplify the solution computing a lot, which is much valuable in practice. In addition, the hybrid queuing network may represent the characteristics of both transaction handling and batch workload [14,15].

2 Multiple Domain Design Based on Workflow Interoperability

2.1 Design of Multiple Workflow Domains

During the process of intra enterprise information revolution, such as a workflow based ERP (Enterprise Resource Planning) project to a manufacturing enterprise, the functional parts of the ERP system can be separated into several workflow domains according to the business logic relationship and business contact frequency. Such workflow domain is relatively independent and autonomous, each domain only manage the business that contacts with functional parts in the domain. This new design approach is apt to the changing environment, and is more flexible and reliable than the original long life cycle management.

Each workflow domain can be represented as a tri-tuple

Domain•(Eng, PD, FC)

PD={Process Definition1, … , Process Definition n}

'PD' is a set of process definitions in this workflow domain.

Process Definition = (BA, BR)

Each Process Definition contains two sets – 'BA' and 'BR', which denote the set of business activities involved in a business process and the set of the business rules among these activities respectively.

FC={Functional Component1, … , Functional Component n}

'FC' in is the set of functional components, charged by the engine of the domain, which can deal with certain business activities.

The concept of functional component is extended to denote the executor of one or more activities defined in set 'BA'. Moreover, it can be not only a software system, but also a person or a combination of both. Functional components belonged to the same workflow domain can interpret the same workflow process definition, and share workflow control data and process instance.

'Eng', representing the special workflow engine in the domain, is up to interpret the process definitions in set 'PD', and deal the corresponding business process by invoking functional components in set 'FC'.

Because various business processes may involve some certain activities, the executors – the functional components may appear in the intersection of proper domains.

Fig. 1 shows a typical domain design to ERP system. The detailed dividing algorithm can be found in reference [16].

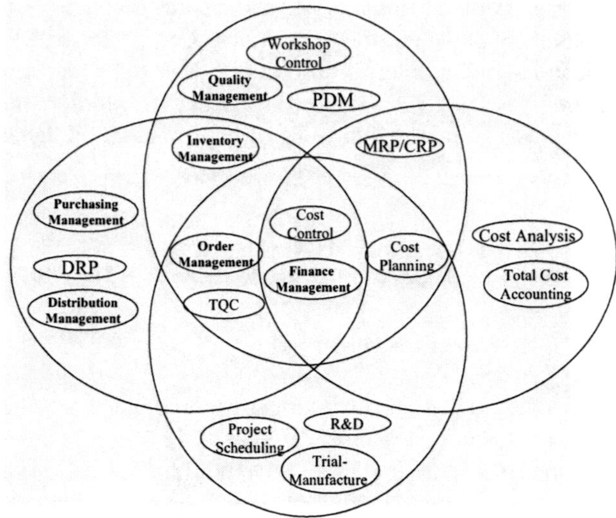

Fig. 1. Petal-like multiple domain design

The workflow engines of these domains have the same structure and running mechanism. They may use the same modeling language, and all the functional components can be built on the same development platform, such as CORBA or J2EE. However, one domain can only deal with a specific set of processes.

2.2 Interoperability Models

There are three kinds of classical interoperability models that support the interoperability across workflow domains, i.e. chained service, nested sub process, chained service and parallel-synchronized model [17,18].

Chained Service Model allows one process instance to be joined to another. The two joint nodes can be not only the start and end nodes, but also any two nodes of the process instance. Fig.2a shows such a simple example. This model supports one workflow engine to transfer a process instance to another engine of other domain, then the receiver can deal the process instance itself, and the two engines need no longer to be synchronized.

In Nested Sub Processes Model, as Fig.2b shows, a process instance running in a workflow domain just acts as a sub process of one process of another workflow domain.

Parallel Synchronized Model (as Fig.2c shows) allows two processes to operate essentially independently, possibly across separate domains, but require that synchronization points exist between the two processes. Synchronization requires that once the processes each reach a predefined point within their respective execution sequences, a common event be generated. However, we do not encounter such cases frequently, because such cases are always tight-coupled ones, most of which have already been gathered into one proper domain.

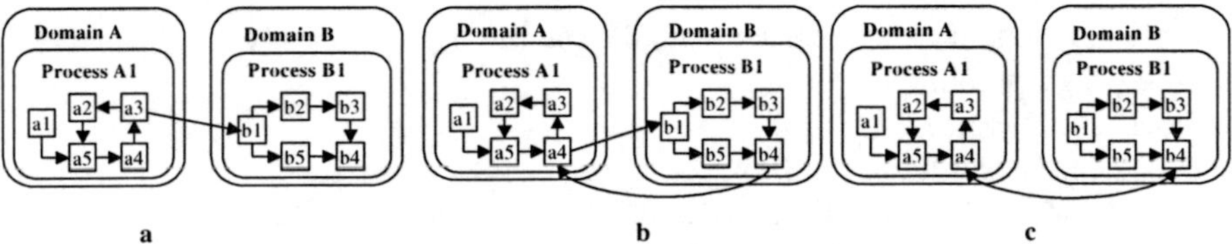

Fig. 2. Interoperability models

3 BCMP Queuing Network

3.1 Introduction to BCMP Queuing Network

Queuing networks are widely used to analyze the performance of multi-programmed computer systems. The theory dates back to the 1950s, when Jackson first published an analysis of a multiple device system [19]. In 1967, Gordon and Newell simplified the notational structure of these results [20]. Baskett, et al. extended the results to include different queuing disciplines and multiple classes of jobs [21], and they also named it with the capitals of their names, i.e. BCMP network. In this paper, BCMP network is imported to workflow based business process simulation field for the first time. Moreover, Table 1. shows the similarities between the BCMP and workflow.

Table 1. Similarities between BCMP network and workflow

BCMP	Workflow
Task class may change during marching period.	A process instance may be transferred to be an instance of another process under the scenario of interoperability.
Task direction may change during marching period.	Process definition maybe modified dynamically during implementation period.
Tasks of multi classes may be in one network.	Processes of multi definitions are always implementing simultaneously.
Each node has stochastic service time.	Activity service time may change with different process.
Tasks get to each node stochastically.	Dynamic workflow may add or delete some activities temporally.
Each node has a task queue.	Each functional component has a work item queue.

Anyway, all of the above use the theory of stochastic process, which begins with the following Stochastic Hypothesis:

The behavior of the real system during a given period of time is characterized by the probability distributions of a stochastic process.

However, it should be mentioned that Stochastic Hypothesis is an assertion about the causes underlying the behavior of a real system. It can never be established beyond doubt through any measurement.

3.2 Mapping to Workflow

First of all, it should be announced that all to be discussed in this section depends on the following assumptions:

Stochastic Hypothesis;

Each queue has infinite capacity;

Each component follows the service rule of First Come First Served (FCFS);

Each functional component can only deal one transaction at one time;

Task arrivals as a Poisson process;

As Fig.3 shows, the processes across workflow domains can be mapped to a BCMP network as a directed graph, which consists of a set of service centers and transitions. Each service center comprises a task queue and a functional component, which is to perform some business activities.

A process instance coming to this network will go through it along a certain route. Different from single class queuing network, BCMP network supports multiple classes of tasks, such as instances of engineering process and instances of PDM process. Furthermore, a certain task may change its original route, e.g. an Engineering process instance may go back to do shape design or contrail design again instead of the next activity, when it finishes the performance analysis. Thus, it is called a multi-chain network, as each task may own more than one route.

An instance of a certain process r (r=1,2, ... , R), goes through a network with M functional components, which are marked as 1,2, ... , M. The transition probability of each component is defined in set $\{q_{ir;js}\}$. $q_{ir;js}$ denotes that the probability that an instance goes from component i to j with its process definition changing from r to s.

Two processes of r and s are interchangeable if an instance of process r can change into another process s, while one of process s can also do this adversely. According to this point, such process definitions are collected into one same subset, if they are interchangeable. As to these subsets, we define the term of routing chain as the following:

{*(i,r)*| component *i* can be accessed by instances of process *r*, *r• P*}

P is a subset derived from the mentioned method.

Thus, a routing chain contains the information about all components that can be accessed by a certain process. In Fig.3, there are two routing chains, which are connected by solid and hollow arrows respectively.

Let e_{ir} denotes the times that functional component i is accessed by the instances of process r in routing chain c. As to component i and process r, $(i,r)\in c$, we have,

$$\sum_{(j,s)\in c} e_{js}q_{js;ir} + q_{0;ir} = e_{ir} \tag{1}$$

$q_{0;ir}$ is the probability that an instance comes from external to component i and changes to process r.

As to component i, we define μ_{ir} denotes component i's service speed to process r. for each FCFS component, it has the same μ_{ir} to every process r;

There is another representation form to describe the communication traffic in the network –using the "visit ratio". Define visit ratio, v_{ir}, means the average visit times of an instance of process r during its staying period, and there are γ_r instances come to the network from external. Then we have,

$$v_{ir} = \frac{e_{ir}}{\gamma_r} \tag{2}$$

The detailed mathematical justification can be found in reference [21].

Divide ① by ②, we get

$$v_{ir} = q_{0;ir} + \sum_{(j,s)\in c} v_{js}q_{js;ir} \tag{3}$$

Define D_{ir} means the total service time of component i to one instance of process r, then we get $D_{ir} = \sum_{(j,s)\in c} \frac{e_{js}}{\mu_{js}}$. In addition, D_{ir} can also be represented as, $D_{ir} = \frac{v_{ir}}{\mu_{ir}} = \frac{\rho_{ir}}{\gamma_r}$, which is equivalent to $\rho_{ir} = \gamma_r D_{ir}$. At last, we get

$$\rho_{ir} = \gamma_r \sum_{(j,s)\in c} \frac{e_{js}}{\mu_{js}} \tag{4}$$

and then, we can get some important performance parameters, such as

$$\rho_i = \sum_c \rho_{ir} \tag{5}$$

$$l_i = \frac{\rho_i}{1-\rho_i} \tag{6}$$

$$L = \sum_{i=1}^{M} \frac{\rho_i}{1-\rho_i} \tag{7}$$

ρ_i denotes the time utilization of component i.

l_i denotes the average queue length of component i.

L denotes the total queue length of the network.

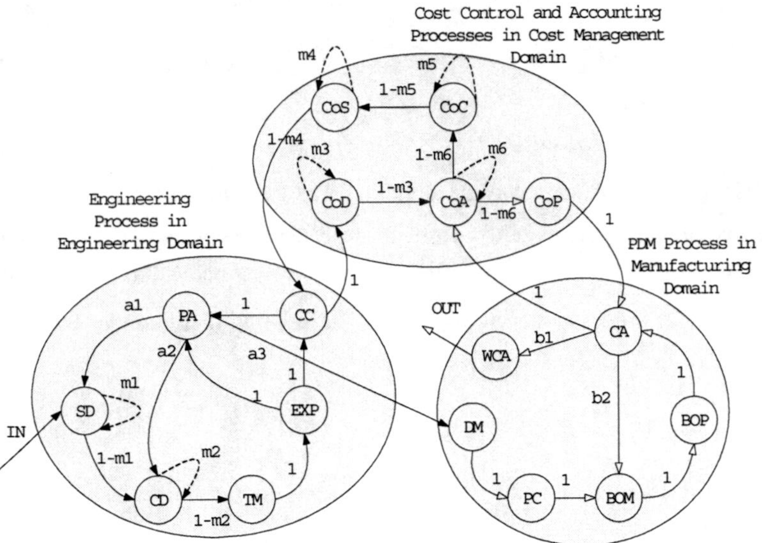

Fig. 3. Workflow BCMP network.

Table 2. Acronyms and Activities in Fig.3.

•	Abbr	Activity	•	Abbr	Activity	•	Abbr	Activity
1	SD	Shape Design	7	DM	Drawingsheet Management	13	CoD	Cost Decomposition
2	CD	Contrail Design	8	PC	Part Coding	14	CoA	Cost Analysis
3	TM	Trial Manufacturing	9	BOM	Bill of Material	15	CoP	Cost Planning
4	EXP	Experiment	10	BOP	Bill of Process	16	CoC	Cost Computation
5	CC	Cost Control	11	CA	Cost Accounting	17	CoS	Cost Solution
6	PA	Performance Analysis	12	WCA	Work Center Design			

4 Simulation

4.1 Simulation

In Fig.3, the numbers, above the arcs, denote the route probability. The cost control process acts as a sub process of the engineering process, and so does the cost accounting and PDM (Production Data Management) processes. In addition, the engineering and PDM processes follow the chained service mechanism.

Anyway, the service time of some activities vary with the complexity of practical process instances, which doesn't permit the Stochastic Hypothesis. In this case, we apply an alternative method, which is to add some self-pointing arcs (represented in the dashed) to convert time chanciness into route chanciness.

The simulation consists of two steps:

Firstly, determine the basic parameters, i.e. $\{q_{ir;js}\}$, $\{\gamma_r\}$ and $\{\mu_{ir}\}$;

$\{\mu_{ir}\}$ can be gotten from past experience, $\{\gamma_r\}$ depends on the input speed and $\{q_{ir;js}\}$. As to $\{q_{ir;js}\}$, besides experience, we need to generate some dummy process instances, which are initiated only with the transition information and corresponding parameters. These dummy instances are driven through the network under the workflow transition rules. Thus we can determine the routing probabilities.

Secondly, compute the performance parameters using the mentioned formulas;

4.2 Result Analysis

Ten random generated transactions are started every time, and we assume the transaction interval defers to hypo dispersion of [5,15] days, based on the experience from ETO (Engineer to Order) type enterprise.

The gray bars in Fig.4a show time utilization of activities in the three processes. The numbers under the horizon axis represent these activities, and the mapping relationship is listed in table 2. From Fig.4a, we can see that cost analysis activity's utilization is relatively higher than other cost activities. The same conclusion can be got in Fig.4b, which shows task queue length of each activity. The cost control activity's task queue is relatively longer, which means it may defer the whole business process's implementation time. Then an estimated conclusion can be drawn that cost analysis activity may be the bottleneck of the whole flow.

After a careful study, we can see that typical cost analysis contains five steps, i.e. create activity model, collect cost data, classify cost data, trace to activity and cost analysis. A redesign scheme is to removing the first two steps to the activities of cost decomposition and cost accounting.

The black bars in Fig.4ab show the utilization and task queue length after modification respectively. From these two figures, we can see that cost analysis activity's burden has been reduced to some extent, and so do the activities of cost control process.

Most of the other activities' utilizations increase, which may be caused by the shortened life cycle of the whole business process. And the task queue length of each activity tends to be balanced. What's surprising is the mean task sum (as Table.3 shows) still falls when the life cycle has been shortened after the modification.

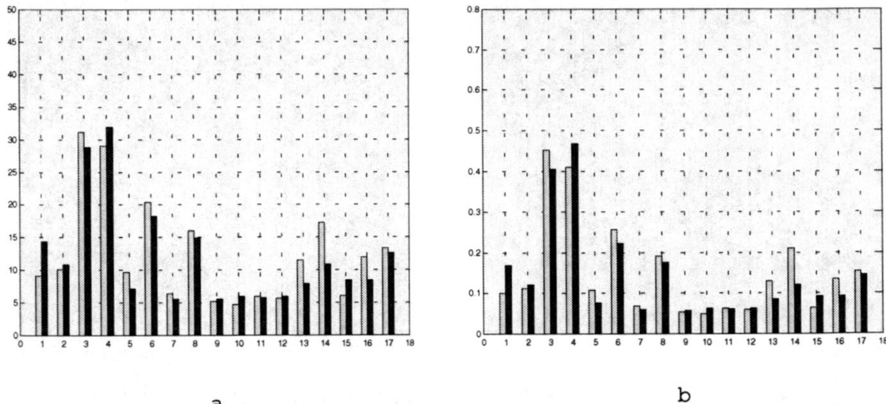

Fig. 4. Simulation results

Table 3. Mean task sum

	Before modification	After modification
Mean task sum	2.6180	2.4778

5 Conclusion

By mapping workflow functional components to BCMP network nodes, business process flow acts as a series of activities upon this network. Thus, some valuable performance indexes can be computed from this simulation, such as resource utilization, task queue length and etc. Then we can find out the bottleneck factors of original business process, and to test various modified schemes to refine the best solution. Therefore, a closed loop, from process design, evaluation to redesign, has been built up. Likewise, this does contribution to system design and business process reengineering.

The short point is that it mainly concentrates on the route selections, while other important aspects, e.g. human factors, are not considered very much.

References

1. G.Alonso, D.Agrawal, A.El Abbadi and C.mohan: Functionality and Limitations of Current Workflow Management systems, IEEE Expert, Vol. 12 (1997), pp: 0-29.
2. WfMC. Workflow Management Coalition Terminology and Glossary (WfMC-TC-1011). Technical Report, Workflow Management Coalition.
3. WfMC. Workflow Management Coalition The Workflow Reference Model (WfMC-TC-1003). Technical Report, Workflow Management Coalition.
4. Scheer, A.W.: Architecture of Integrated Information Systems - Foundations of Enterprise Modeling, Springer-Verlag Berlin, Heidelberg, (1992).
5. Scheer, A.W.: ARIS Business Process Frameworks, 2nd Edition, Springer, Berlin.
6. Doumemeingts G.: GRAI approach to designing and controlling advanced manufacturing systems in CIM environment. In Advanced Information Technologies for Industrial Material Flow Systems, New York; Springer, (1989).
7. Ingalls, R.G.; Morrice, D.J.: PERT scheduling with resources using qualitative simulation graphs Simulation Conference, 2000. Proceedings. Winter , Volume: 1 (2000). pp:362-370.
8. Ingalls, R. G., D. J. Morrice, A. B. Whinston: Implementation of Temporal Intervals in Qualitative Simulation Graphs. ACM Tracnsactions on Modeling and computer Simulation (2000).
9. Kwang-Hoon Kim; Dong-Soo Han: Performance and scalability analysis on client-server workflow architecture. ICPADS 2001. Proceedings. Eighth International Conference on Parallel and Distributed Systems (2001) pp: 179 –186.
10. Kwang-Hoon Kim, Clarence A.Ellis: Workflow performance and scalability analysis using the layered queuing modeling methodology" in Proceedings of the 2001 International ACM SIGGROUP Conference on Supporting Group Work - Volume 2001 September (2001).
11. Petri C A.: Communication with Automata, New York: Griffiss Air Force Base. Tech. Rep. RADC-TR-65-377, 1(1), (1996).
12. Feldbrugge F, Jensen K.: Petri net tool overview (1986). In: LNCS, 1987, 255: 20-61
13. Best and Fernandez C.: Notations and terminology on Petri net theory. Petri Net Newsletters 23, (1986), pp: 21-46.
14. P.J. Denning and J.P.Buzen: The Operational Analysis of Queuing Network Models, ACM Computing Survey, Vol. 10, No.3, Sep. (1978), pp:225-261.
15. E.D.Lazowska, et al.: Quantitative System Performance, Computing System Analysis Using Queuing Network Models, (http://www.cs.washington. edu/homes/lazowska/qsp/).
16. Xiaohui Zhao: Process Integration based on Interoperability across Multiple workflow Domains (submitted to publish).
17. C. Bussler: Enterprise-Wide Workflow Management. IEEE Concurrency Journal, July, (1999), pp: 94-100.
18. WfMC. Workflow Management Coalition Reference Model Interface 4 Workflow Interoperability The Key to E-Commerce and to process, Workflow Management Coalition.
19. Jackson, J. R.: Networks of Waiting Lines. Oper. Res. 5 (1957), pp: 518-521.
20. Gordon, W. J.; Newell, G. F.: Closed Queuing Systems with Exponential Queuing Network Familiy. Acta Inf. 7.2 (1976) pp: 123-136.
21. F.Baskett, K.M.Chandy, R.R.Muntz, F.Palacios-Gomez: Open, Closed and Mixed Networks of Queues with Different Classes of Customers, J.ACM, vol.22, No.2, (1975), pp: 248-260.

Transactional Workflows or Workflow Transactions?

Paul Grefen

Computer Science Department, University of Twente
P.O. Box 217, 7500 AE Enschede, Netherlands
http://www.cs.utwente.nl/~grefen

Abstract. Workflows have generally been accepted as a means to model and support processes in complex organizations. The fact that these processes require robustness and clear semantics has generally been observed and has lead to the combination of workflow and transaction concepts. Many variations on this combination exist, leading to many approaches to transactional workflow support. No clear classification of these approaches has been developed, however, resulting in a badly understood field. To deal with this problem, we describe a clear taxonomy of transactional workflow models, based on the relation between workflow and transaction concepts. We show that the classes in the taxonomy can directly be related to specification language and architecture types for workflow and transaction management systems. We compare the classes with respect to their characteristics and place existing approaches in the taxonomy – thus offering a basis for analysis of transactional workflow support.

1 Introduction

Workflows have generally been accepted as a paradigm for modeling and supporting processes in complex organizations. Often workflow processes have a business character, but workflow concepts have also been used for other processes types, e.g., scientific processes or software production processes. The use of workflows for core processes of organizations has lead to the requirements of clear process semantics and robustness in process execution, both in regular process execution and under exception or error conditions. The notions of transaction management, already used for several decades in the database world, have been combined with workflow notions to satisfy these requirements. Resulting from this, the notion of transactional workflow or workflow transaction has emerged. Many variations on the notion of transactional workflow or workflow transaction have been developed, however, by merging the worlds of workflow and transaction management in different ways – the two more or less synonymous terms are an omen of this. No clear classification has been developed yet that provides a framework for the analysis of transactional workflow models and systems supporting these models. Matching models and systems with application requirements and comparing approaches is therefore not easy.

In this paper, we present a classification framework that provides two main classes for the combination of workflows and transactions, based on the relation between workflow and transaction concepts. The main classes are further refined into subclasses with specific properties, resulting in six basic classes. We show that the conceptual classes can directly be mapped to specification language and architecture classes for workflow and transaction management support. We analyze the classes with respect to their goal, means to achieve this goal, and advantages and disadvantages. The

R. Cicchetti et al. (Eds.): DEXA 2002, LNCS 2453, pp. 60–69, 2002.

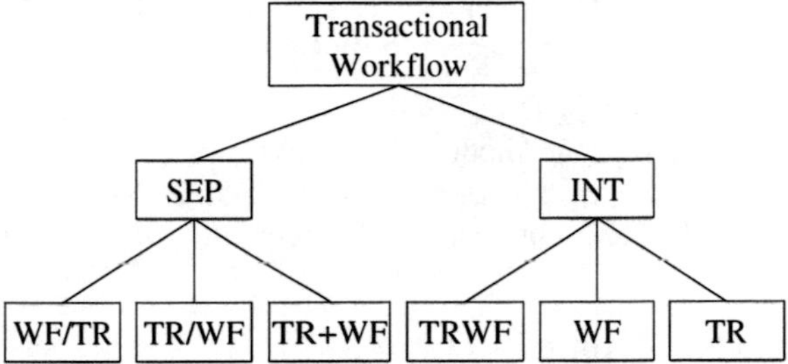

Figure 1. Transactional workflow taxonomy

framework and analysis together provide a clear basis for comparing approaches and selecting specific approaches for specific application classes.

The structure of this paper is as follows. In Section 2, we describe our basic taxonomy that underlies the classification presented in this paper. In Section 3, we present the conceptual point of view of our classification, focused around language aspects. Section 4 presents the system point of view, centered on architecture aspects. In Section 5, we apply the framework by comparing the various classes and classifying existing approaches to transactional workflows. Section 6 contains conclusions.

2 The Taxonomy

To support transactional workflows, there are two basic approaches: either transactional aspects and workflow aspects are treated as separate issues, or they are seen as one integrated issue. In the former case, separate transaction and workflow models exist that are combined to obtain transactional workflows. In the latter case, one single transactional workflow model is used. These two main classes are refined below.

In the situation where we have separate workflow and transaction models, we need to relate these two models. We have three possible basic relations, based on the abstraction relation between the models:

Workflows over transactions (WF/TR): workflows are more abstract than transactions – transaction models are used to provide semantics to workflow models.

Transactions over workflows (TR/WF): transactions are more abstract than workflows – workflow models are used to provide process structure to transaction models.

Transactions and workflows as peers (TR+WF): workflow and transaction models exist at the same abstraction level – workflow and transaction models can be seen as two submodels of an implicit, loosely coupled process model.

In the case of one single model for both workflow and transaction aspects, obviously there is no relation between models. There are, however, three main variants with respect to the nature of the single model:

Hybrid transactional workflow model (TRWF): a single hybrid model is used that contains both transaction and workflow concepts.

Transactions in workflows (WF): a single workflow model is used, in which transactional aspects are mapped to workflow primitives.

Workflows in transactions (TR): a single transaction model is used, in which workflow aspects are mapped to transaction primitives.

The resulting taxonomy is depicted in Figure 1, in which the 'SEP' main class contains basic classes with separate models for workflows and transactions, the 'INT' main class contains basic classes with a single integrated model. We use this taxonomy to discuss conceptual and architectural characteristics of each of the classes.

3 The Conceptual Point of View

In this section, we discuss the conceptual point of view of our framework. To do so, we will take the specification language perspective, which we explain below. Then, the various classes of our taxonomy are discussed from this language perspective.

In the conceptual point of view, we are interested in the conceptual specification of transactional workflows formulated in one or more specification languages. Given the two main classes in the taxonomy of Figure 1, we can have two situations. In the first situation, there is a separate language for specifying workflow aspects, the workflow definition language (WFDL), and a separate language for specifying transaction aspects, the transaction definition language (TRDL). In the second situation, there is an integrated language for specifying both workflow and transaction aspects, the transactional workflow definition language (TRWFDL).

If we have two languages, the languages can have two relations: either one language is a refinement of the other, or the two languages are orthogonal with respect to each other. If the two languages have a refinement relation, we have the following. A language offers primitives to specify transitions in a state space. A language L_2 is a refinement of a language L_1 if there is a notion of correspondence (a relation in the mathematical sense) between its state space and that of L_1, and between its primitives and those of L_1, such that the transitions specified by the primitives maintain the correspondence between states (see [11] for a further explanation). If the TRDL is a refinement of the WFDL, the WFDL level contains workflow attributes and the intermediate states at the TRDL level are related to transaction states. If the WFDL is a refinement of the TRDL, the TRDL level contains transactional attributes and the intermediate states at the WFDL level are related to control flow states.

In the integrated approach, all aspects are merged into a single language, covering a state space that is the cross product of the two state spaces discussed above.

3.1 Separate Languages

The main reason for using two separate languages is separation of concerns in dealing with control flow and transaction aspects in complex applications. Below, we discuss the three basic classes of the separate models approach.

In the WF/TR case, the control flow aspect is leading in the specification of transactional workflows. Low-level workflow semantics are based on transactional semantics of individual workflow tasks or groups of workflow tasks. Hence, the TRDL is a refinement of the WFDL. Primitives of the WFDL are mapped to primitives of the TRDL. Transaction semantics are often imported from the data management level – the TRDL is a sublanguage of a data manipulation language (DML) in this case. The WF/TR approach is taken in most commercial workflow management systems that support (usually limited) transactional behavior of workflows. Below, we show a simple example in which individual workflow tasks can be parameterized to behave as business transactions (atomic and isolated units of execution). On the left, we see the specification of a workflow task. The second and third lines of this specification are expanded on a lower abstraction level to the transaction specification shown on the right. When executed, the TRDL specification will induce intermediate states with respect to the WFDL specification.

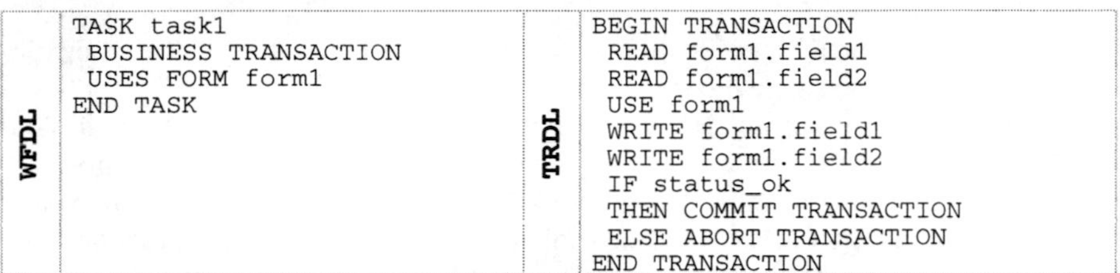

WFDL

```
TASK task1
 BUSINESS TRANSACTION
 USES FORM form1
END TASK
```

TRDL

```
BEGIN TRANSACTION
 READ form1.field1
 READ form1.field2
 USE form1
 WRITE form1.field1
 WRITE form1.field2
 IF status_ok
 THEN COMMIT TRANSACTION
 ELSE ABORT TRANSACTION
END TRANSACTION
```

In the TR/WF class, transactional behavior is the leading aspect in the specification of transactional workflows. High-level transactional semantics are specified with a workflow as elaboration of the underlying process structure. Hence, the WFDL is a refinement of the TRDL. The TR/WF approach is applied for example in workflow management for e-commerce applications. Here, the transaction between two business partners is the starting point and the elaboration of the control flow a refinement of the transaction. We show a simplified example below. On the left, we see a TRDL specification of a transaction that states transactional properties. The control flow is seen as an implementation detail to be specified at a lower level of abstraction. This is elaborated in the WFDL specification on the right. Note that the WFDL specification concerns a non-linear process, which is not easy to specify in traditional TRDLs. The execution of the WFDL specification will introduce intermediate states with respect to the execution of the TRDL specification.

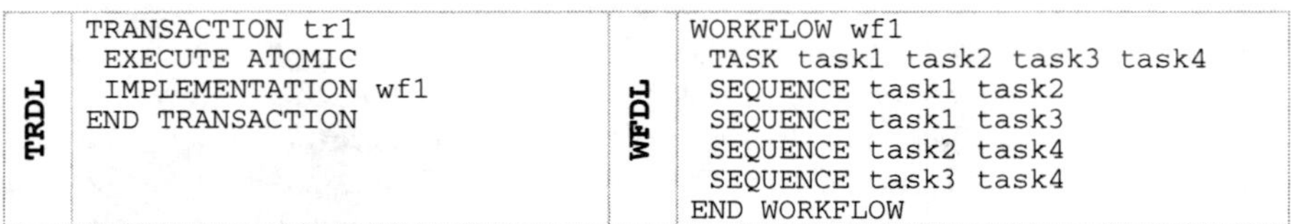

TRDL

```
TRANSACTION tr1
 EXECUTE ATOMIC
 IMPLEMENTATION wf1
END TRANSACTION
```

WFDL

```
WORKFLOW wf1
 TASK task1 task2 task3 task4
 SEQUENCE task1 task2
 SEQUENCE task1 task3
 SEQUENCE task2 task4
 SEQUENCE task3 task4
END WORKFLOW
```

In the TR+WF approach, there is a balance between control flow and transactional behavior. High-level transactional semantics are defined on the same conceptual level as workflow processes. Hence, workflow and transaction specifications refer to each other on the same level of abstraction. Below, we show a stylized example. On the left, we see a WFDL specification that specifies a control flow and refers to the TRDL specification for the transactional properties. The TRDL specification shown on the right imports the task list from the WFDL specification and specifies transactional properties over this. The TRDL specification specifies compensating tasks [5] and a safepoint [10] to allow flexible rollback by compensation. Control flow and compensation functionality can be changed independently of each other, thus creating a separation of concerns between workflow and transaction specification.

WFDL		TRDL	
	WORKFLOW wf1 REFERS TRANSACTION tr1 TASK task1 task2 task3 SEQUENCE task1 task2 SEQUENCE task2 task3 END WORKFLOW		BEGIN TRANSACTION tr1 REFERS WORKFLOW wf1 COMP ctask1 task1 COMP ctask2 task2 SAFEPOINT task1 END TRANSACTION

3.2 Integrated Models

In the integrated model class of the taxonomy, workflow and transaction semantics are combined into one single model.

In the TRWF class of our taxonomy, we find hybrid workflow and transaction models. These models are reflected in hybrid transactional workflow specification languages. These languages contain typical workflow-related primitives – e.g., to express control flows – and transaction-related primitives – e.g., to express atomicity or isolation requirements. An obvious way to create a TRWF language is to 'merge' a pair or languages of the TR+WF class. Following this approach, we can obtain the example below from the TR+WF example shown above. Clearly, the TRWF and TR+WF approaches are exchangeable to some extent.

TRWFDL

```
WORKFLOW wf1
 TASK task1 COMP ctask1 SAFEPOINT
 TASK task2 COMP ctask2
 TASK Task3 COMP none
 SEQUENCE task1 task2
 SEQUENCE task2 task3
END WORKFLOW
```

In the WF class, transactional semantics are expressed in workflow processes. Specific process patterns are used to express transaction behavior of workflow processes. An example is the specification of compensation patterns in workflow definitions to achieve relaxed atomicity characteristics for a workflow. We show an example below. In the WF specification, we see the definition of regular tasks and a regular control flow (three consecutive tasks) and the definition of compensating tasks and compensating control flow (two consecutive tasks). The compensating control flow is linked to the regular control flow through or-splits (alternative paths). At an or-split, a condition is evaluated to check whether rollback of the workflow is required – if not, the regular control flow is followed – if so, the compensating control flow is followed. Note that the example is in fact a static specification of all possible cases of the dynamic compensation behavior of the TRWF example above.

WFDL

```
WORKFLOW wf1
 TASK task1 task2 task3  # regular tasks
 TASK ctask1 ctask2      # compensating tasks
 SPLIT or1 or2
 SEQUENCE task1 or1      # start regular control flow
 SEQUENCE or1 task2
 SEQUENCE task2 or2
 SEQUENCE or2 task3
 SEQUENCE or1 ctask1     # start compensation control flow
 SEQUENCE or2 ctask2
 SEQUENCE ctask2 ctask1
END WORKFLOW
```

In the TR class of the taxonomy, workflow semantics are expressed in transaction specifications. In this approach, transactions have structured processes as their action specification. An example is shown below. Here we see a transaction consisting of two subtransactions that can be executed in parallel – thus constituting a rudimentary form of control flow.

TRDL

```
TRANSACTION tr1
 SUBTRANSACTION s1
  action1; action2
 END SUBTRANSACTION
 SUBTRANSACTION s2
  action3; action4
 END SUBTRANSACTION
 PARALLEL s1 s2
END TRANSACTION
```

4 The System Point of View

After having discussed the conceptual point of view in the previous section, we turn to the system point of view in this section. Where the conceptual point of view explains the 'what', the system point of view explains the 'how' – i.e., the support of workflow and transaction models.

We base the system point of view on the architecture aspect, focusing on the high-level structure of transactional workflow support systems. We use abstract architectures to identify the elementary system characteristics of the classes of the taxonomy. We relate these abstract architectures to concrete architectures in Section 5. In the description of the architectures, we place workflow management and transaction management modules on top of a function and data support (FDS) layer. The details of this layer are not relevant in the context of this paper.

Below, we turn to the various classes of transactional workflows, again organized as depicted in Figure 1.

4.1 Separate Models

In the separate models category of our taxonomy, we have separate workflow and transaction management modules in the architecture (WFM respectively TRM). These modules can have three architectural relations (as depicted in Figure 2): WFM as client of a TRM server, TRM as client of a WFM server, and WFM and TRM as peer-to-peer modules. These three architectures coincide with the three classes WFM/TRM, TRM/WFM and TRM+WFM. In discussing the characteristics of the three classes, the focus is on the WFM-TRM interface, as indicated by triangles in Figure 2. This interface is used in all three architectures to synchronize the control flow state in the WFM and transaction state in the TRM.

The WFM/TRM architecture is depicted in the left hand side of Figure 2. The interface between WFM and TRM is both a control and a data channel. The WFM uses the TRM interface to open a transaction context and perform data manipulation operations in this context. In this class, TRM and FDS are often integrated into one database application environment based on a DBMS with built-in transaction management functionality. The WFM/TRM architecture is 'standard' for commercial systems.

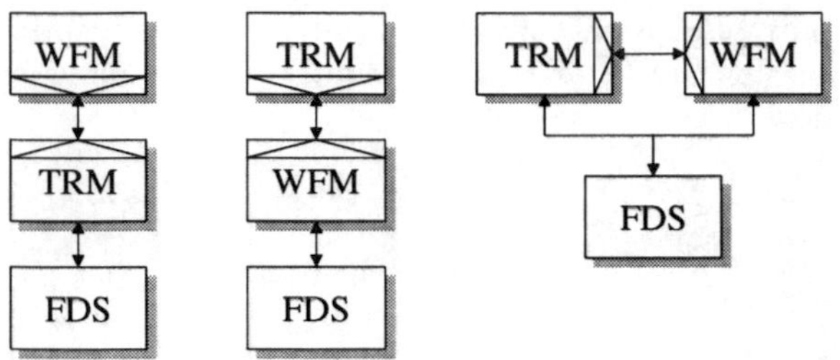

Figure 2. WFM/TRM, TRM/WFM and TRM+WFM architectures

The TRM/WFM architecture is depicted in the center of Figure 2. The interface between TRM and WFM is both a control and a data channel. The TRM uses the WFM interface to open a workflow context and next to invoke control flow primitives. We observe this architecture class in e-commerce environments where a high-level transaction engine invokes processes supported by workflow management technology.
The TRM+WFM architecture is depicted in the right hand side of Figure 2. In this architecture, we have a TRM as transaction server and a WFM as process server in a peer-to-peer relation. The interface between WFM and TRM is strictly a control channel: the WFM communicates process states to the TRM, the TRM communicates transaction contexts and workflow commands to effectuate transactional effects on process states to the WFM. Note that this interface is not a standard interface as defined by the WfMC – its Interface 4 standard describes communication between two workflow servers [17]. The TRM+WFM architecture is – trivially – fit for TR+WF language support. TRWF language support is possible by filtering a TRWF specification into the right parts for TRM and WFM.

4.2 Integrated Models

In the integrated models class of our taxonomy, we have a single transactional workflow management module in the architecture. This can either be a transactional workflow manager (TRWFM), a traditional workflow manager (WFM), or an advanced transaction manager (TRM). The three cases are shown in Figure 3.
The TRWFM offers integrated support for transaction management and workflow management. A hybrid transaction and workflow state is maintained within the TRWFM. It supports languages in the TRWF and TR+WF classes. To handle TR+WF specifications, the two subspecifications are merged into one specification by a preprocessor.
In the WFM architecture class, the state of a transactional workflow is completely maintained by WFM. Transactional attributes of this state are mapped to workflow attributes. The WFM can only interpret specifications in the WF class. Specifications in other classes (typically TRWF) have to be translated to WF format. This architecture class is fit for support by commercial workflow management systems.
In the TRM class, the state of a transactional workflow is completely maintained by the TRM. Control flow attributes of this state are implemented by transaction attributes. The TRM can only interpret specifications in the TR class. Specifications in other classes (typically TRWF) have to be translated to TR format. Nested process

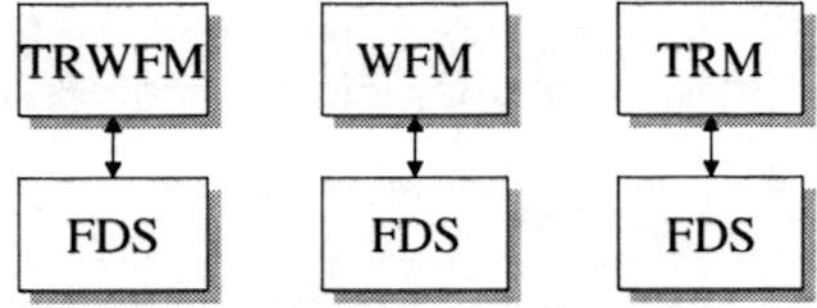

Figure 3. TRWFM, WFM and TRM architectures

structures can be supported by standard transaction management technology. More advanced structures are typically only supported by research prototypes.

5 Application of the Framework

In this section, we apply the taxonomy we have developed in two ways: we present a comparison of the various classes with respect to their characteristics and we place existing work in our taxonomy.

5.1 Comparing the Classes

In Table 1, we show a comparison of the classes in our taxonomy. For each class, we list the main goal, the means used to achieve this goal, and a brief list of advantages and disadvantages – which we explain in the sequel.

Flexibility in coupling models and separation of concerns between workflow and transaction aspects are main advantages of the classes with separate models. Problems with integration of models (and support based on these models) form the downside of this aspect. Consistency of specifications is a main advantage of the single-model approach: there are no separate models to be kept consistent. Consistency can certainly be a problem in the TR+WF class, as two specifications of a transactional workflow exist without a 'leading' specification. Limited expressiveness is a clear disadvantage of the WF and TR classes, as possible semantics of transaction aspects are limited by available workflow primitives and vice versa. The TRWF class does generally not have this problem, but a complex formalism with equally complex semantics usually is the basis for models in this class. Finally, system support is (cur-

Table 1. Comparison of classes

class	goal	means	advantages	disadvantages
WF/TR	WF with robust character	data management in WFs	sep. of concerns, flexibility, support	integration
TR/WF	TR with complex control flow	process management in TRs	separation of concerns, flexibility	integration
TR+WF	integrated WF and TR	coupled process and data mngmnt	separation of concerns, flexibility	integration, consistency
TRWF	integrated WF and TR	hybrid process and data management	integration, consistency	complex formalism, inflexibility
WF	WF with robust character	advanced process management	simple formalism, consist., support	limited expressiveness
TR	TR with complex control flow	advanced TR management	simple formalism, consistency	limited expressiveness

rently) best for the WF/TR class (supported by combinations of existing WFM and TRM systems) and the WF class (implementable on commercial WFM systems).

5.2 Positioning Existing Approaches

In this subsection, we place a selection of existing approaches in our taxonomy. For reasons of brevity, the overview is far from complete. We first discuss approaches in the separate models category, then turn to the integrated model category, and finally pay attention to an approach that combines aspects of both categories. A more elaborate analysis is presented in [11].

In the Mercurius initiative [8], a WF/TR architecture has been proposed: workflow management functionality is placed on top of transaction management functionality. The CrossFlow approach [9, 16] is an example of the TR/WF class. In the CrossFlow language perspective, cross-organizational transactions are specified in an electronic contract that is mapped to workflow definitions. In the CrossFlow architecture perspective, inter-organizational transaction management functionality is placed on top of workflow management systems. In [4], an approach to a language in TR+WF class is proposed in which independence between specification of control flow on the one hand and transactional characteristics on the other hand is a starting point.

In the context of the FlowMark WFMS, an approach for the support of business transactions has been developed [14]. It uses specification of transactional spheres in a workflow process that is interpreted by extended workflow technology – the approach can hence be placed in the TRWF class. ObjectFlow [12] can also be placed in the TRWF class. In the Exotica approach [1], a language is proposed in TRWF class. This language is preprocessed to be interpretable by an architecture in the WF class. In the FlowBack project [13], a similar approach has been developed. In the WF language class, we find work in which transactional characteristics are coded into Petri Nets [3]. The ConTracts model [15] is an approach in the TR class providing an environment for reliable execution of long-lived computations. The control flow primitives of the ConTracts language have been used for the realization of transactional workflows. TSME [6] is an approach in the TR class with comparable goals.

In the WIDE project, an approach has been developed that combines aspects of both main classes of our taxonomy. The WIDE workflow specification language belongs in the TRWF class, as it is a 'classical' workflow definition language extended with (among other things) transactional primitives. The WIDE architecture contains three levels [7]. The two high-level transaction management levels GTS [10] and LTS [2] belong in the TR+WF class, the low-level LTI level [2] belongs in the WF/TR class.

6 Conclusions and Outlook

In this paper, we have described a taxonomy for transactional workflow support, paying attention to both the conceptual and system point of view. Characteristics of the conceptual point of view have been described in terms of specification language classes. System characteristics have been discussed in terms of architecture topologies and interfaces. The result is a taxonomy that provides a background for selecting or analyzing transactional workflow support. Choosing appropriate classes from our taxonomy for the conceptual and system points of view is a basis for the configuration

of transactional workflow support in complex applications, where functional requirements and architectural context both play an important role. The choice can be different in both points of view to some extent, but a mapping must be possible.
Completing the analysis of existing approaches to obtain an overview of the state of the art is an obvious follow-up of the presented work. Extending the framework to better cover multi-level transaction support is an important research direction.

Acknowledgments. Maarten Fokkinga is acknowledged for his assistance with respect to language concepts and his feedback on the draft version of this paper.

References

1. G. Alonso et al.; *Advanced Transaction Models in Workflow Contexts;* Procs. Int. Conf. on Data Engineering, 1996; pp. 574-581.
2. E. Boertjes et al.; *An Architecture for Nested Transaction Support on Standard Database Systems*; Procs. 9th Int. Conf. on Database and Expert System Appls., 1998; pp. 448-459.
3. J. Dehnert; *Four Systematic Steps towards Sound Business Process Models*; Procs. 2nd Int. Colloq. on Petri Net Techn. for Modeling Comm. Based Systems, 2001; pp. 55-63.
4. W. Derks et al.; *Customized Atomicity Specification for Transactional Workflows*; Procs. 3rd Int. Symp. on Cooperative Database Systems for Adv. Appls., 2001; pp.155-164.
5. H. Garcia-Molina, K. Salem; *Sagas*; Procs. 1987 ACM SIGMOD Int. Conf. on Management of Data, 1987; pp. 249-259.
6. D. Georgakopoulos, M. Hornick, F. Manola; *Customizing Transaction Models and Mechanisms in a Programmable Environment Supporting Reliable Workflow Automation*; IEEE Trans. on Knowledge and Data Engineering, (8)4, 1996; pp. 630-649.
7. P. Grefen et al.; *Two-Layer Transaction Management for Workflow Management Applications*; Procs. 8th Int. Conf. on Database and Expert System Appls., 1997; pp. 430-439.
8. P. Grefen, R. Remmerts de Vries; *A Reference Architecture for Workflow Management Systems*; Journ. of Data & Knowledge Engineering, (27)1, 1998; pp. 31-57.
9. P. Grefen et al.; *CrossFlow: Cross-Organizational Workflow Management in Dynamic Virtual Enterprises*; Int. Journ. of Computer Systems Science & Engineering, (15)5, 2000; pp. 277-290.
10. P. Grefen, J. Vonk, P. Apers; *Global Transaction Support for Workflow Management Systems: from Formal Spec.to Practical Impl.*; VLDB Journal, (10)4, 2001; pp. 316-333.
11. P. Grefen; *A Taxonomy for Transactional Workflows*; CTIT Technical Report 02-11; University of Twente, 2002.
12. M. Hsu, C. Kleissner; *ObjectFlow and Recovery in Workflow Systems*; in: V. Kumar, M. Hsu; *Recovery Mechanisms in Database Systems*; Prentice Hall, 1998; pp. 505-527.
13. B. Kiepuszewski, R. Muhlberger, M. Orlowska; *FlowBack: Providing Backward Recovery for WFMs*; Procs. ACM SIGMOD Int. Conf. on Management of Data, 1998; pp. 555-557.
14. F. Leymann; *Supporting Business Transactions via Partial Backward Recovery in WFMs*; Procs. Datenbanksysteme in Büro, Technik und Wissenschaft, 1995; pp. 51-70.
15. A. Reuter, K. Schneider, F. Schwenkreis; *Contracts Revisited*; in: S. Jajodia, L. Kerschberg; *Adv.Transaction Models and Architectures*; Kluwer Academic, 1997; pp. 127-151.
16. J. Vonk et al.; *Cross-Organizational Transaction Support for Virtual Enterprises*; Procs. 5th Int. Conf. on Cooperative Information Systems, 2000; pp. 323-334.
17. *Workflow Management Coalition Workflow Standard – Interoperability Abstract Specification*; Doc. No. WfMC TC-1012; Workflow Management Coalition, 1996.

Collaboration Flow Management: A New Paradigm for Virtual Team Support

Jacques Lonchamp

LORIA, BP 239, 54506 Vandœuvre lès Nancy Cedex, France
jloncham@loria.fr

Abstract. Collaboration flow management is a new paradigm for virtual team support which departs from the classical 'workflow management' and 'collaborative computing' paradigms. The aim is to support the opportunistic flow of collaboration within a distributed project, considered as a living and self-organizing system. Such a flow includes informal and formal, synchronous and asynchronous, task-oriented and project-oriented collaborative sessions. Some of them are elements of model-driven session-based process fragments. The paper defines the paradigm and describes our Java prototype of collaboration flow management system through a realistic scenario.

1 Introduction

A virtual team (VT) is a *team distributed across space, time, and organization boundaries*, and *linked by webs of interactive technology*. As every team, a VT is a group of people who work interdependently with a shared goal. Teams exist for some *task-oriented purpose*, and differ from social groups (virtual communities, electronic groups) and decision groups (virtual government, direct participation). The growing importance of the VT concept is related to several well known reasons: the diversification of organizational structures towards more distributed, decentralized, and flexible organizations, the globalization of the economy, with the development of worldwide organizations and projects, the rapid growth of telecommunications and Internet in particular. Cross-organizational VTs, such as virtual enterprises, or networked projects, are the most in need of new ways to work and technology-support infrastructures. VTs can improve work performance by reducing costs (cutting travel costs and time), shortening cycle time (moving from serial to parallel processes), increasing innovation (permitting more diverse participation, and stimulating creativity), and leveraging learning (capturing knowledge in the natural course of doing the work, gaining wider access to expertise, and sharing best practices).

Communication tools, especially those aiming at geographical distribution transparency, such as video/audio conferencing systems, are obviously useful for VTs but not sufficient. The success of a VT depends on a set of psychological, organizational, and cognitive factors [11]. A computerized support for VTs should take into account these factors and include them in its basic requirements. First, a sense of identity and

R. Cicchetti et al. (Eds.): DEXA 2002, LNCS 2453, pp. 70–80, 2002.

membership is necessary for VTs. Periodically performing informal virtual meetings is not sufficient for developing a collaborative attitude. Participants must feel that the supporting environment helps them to *do important and constructive things together, in synergy* (R1). Secondly, traditional authority is minimized in VTs, which develop an inner authority based on competencies. In VTs, power comes from information, expertise, and knowledge, not from position. The important things done together through the supporting environment should include *expression of competencies, externalization of knowledge and mental models* related to the task in hand (R2). Third, trust is the key to VTs. People work together because they trust one another. People make deals, set goals, and lend one another resources. Without face-to-face cues, and the nuances of person-to-person interaction, trust is harder to attain. But trust can be built with *the recognition of the contribution that everyone makes, the clarity of positions and commitments* (R3). Finally, project and process management is a critical ingredient for successful distributed work. Co-located teams can quickly clarify goals, correct misunderstandings, and work through problems. VTs need to be *more explicit in their planning and their processes* (R4). When considering these requirements, we claim that no existing paradigm for cooperative systems, neither the 'workflow management paradigm' nor the 'workgroup computing paradigm', is satisfying. A *new paradigm* is required for VT support. The second section of this paper elaborates this idea and defines such a paradigm, called the *collaboration flow management paradigm*. The third section describes our current Java prototype of *collaboration flow management system* through a realistic scenario. Finally, the last section compare our proposal with related work and draw some conclusions.

2 The Collaboration Flow Management Paradigm

The fourth requirement (R4) stresses the importance of supporting the VT life cycle process. VT projects usually follow a life cycle with an alternation of divergence phases, during which people work individually, and collaborative convergence phases, during which people *build some shared understanding*, discuss for *discovering and solving the divergences accumulated during individual work*, and *drive the project*. Cognitive ergonomists draw a similar distinction for collective design tasks between individual design steps, requiring operative synchronization mechanisms, and collaborative co-design steps, requiring *cognitive synchronization mechanisms* [4].

A classical Workflow Management System (WfMS) provides support for coordinating individual activities, as those occurring during divergence phases. Generally, a WfMS provides no support for collaborative activities, as those constituting convergence phases. The three first requirements (R1 to R3) imply that a VT environment should mainly support convergence phases. The 'workgroup computing paradigm' is not a satisfying solution because it considers collaborative tasks in isolation and does not support the life cycle process as a whole. A computerized environment for VTs should support more or less structured processes *whose steps are collaborative sessions* either synchronous or asynchronous, informal or formal. On the basis of requirements (R1 to R3), we analyze these sessions as working sessions, during which participants express their views, competencies, positions, and commitments about the task in hand. Cognitive ergonomists distinguish between 'production activities', for the collaborative production of artifacts (idea lists, concept graphs, ontologies, design sketches,...), and 'evaluation activities', for the collaborative evaluation and integration of individually produced artifacts. We consider also collaborative sessions for project orientation and project organization (objectives, to do lists, plans,...). At a very abstract level, we feel that *issue resolution* is the basic building block which can be used for describing all these activities. Participants discuss and solve various issues about the artifacts, the shared context, and the collaboration process itself. The computerized environment should support *the definition and management of more or less structured processes whose steps are issue-based synchronous or asynchronous, informal or formal, collaborative sessions.*

Otherwise, a VT is a *living and self-organizing system.* For Peter and Trudy Johnson-Lenz [7], post-mechanistic groupware, like all living systems, are 'rhythmic' and made of 'containers' with flexible and permeable 'boundaries'. The VT computerized environment should support in particular a range of session (containers) types providing different collaboration rhythms, in accordance with the task urgency and the required depth of issue analysis, and different group boundaries, through the evolving definition of a 'core team' and an 'extended team'. Core team members are strongly involved in the project and use directly the computerized environment. Extended team members should only be involved through standard communication technologies, such as annotating Web pages or participating to Usenet-like forums. Procedures (process models), context, and timing are the three other primitives of post-mechanistic groupware [7]. The choice between these forms (containers, rhythms, boundaries, procedures) should be made *dynamically and collectively during the course of the project.*

From above, the following four basic functionalities can be identified. (F1) *Support different types of short/rapid, more or less formal, synchronous sessions for the core team,* such as artifact-centered informal sessions (around a shared document or a free hand drawing) or formal argumentation sessions (with different rhythms and styles of interaction: free, turn talking, circle, moderated). Composite synchronous sessions can mix formal and informal times. (F2) *Support longer/slower/deeper, formal, asynchronous sessions for the core team, controlled through the enactment of issue-based and session-based collaborative process model fragments.* Such model fragments can specify for instance different structured brainstorming processes, document inspection processes, knowledge elicitation processes, solution evaluation processes (comparative, analytical, analogical). When needed, an asynchronous issue-based session within a process fragment can be *transformed* into a synchronous session for continuing with a faster rhythm the resolution of conflicting issues. (F3) *Support the overall collaboration flow:* some asynchronous *Project Management (PM) process* enables project initiators to launch synchronous sessions and asynchronous process fragments (see Fig.1). This PM process is the spring of the *opportunistic flow of collaboration that the VT generates,* which can include in particular other PM processes better suited to the circumstances and which *replace* the initial one (see section 3.3). (F4) *Play the role of a project memory*, storing all project related information: artifacts, debates, free hand drawings, messages, process trace, etc. These elements should be *externalized* as HTML/XML documents, for easier access and feedback from the extended team during *asynchronous informal sessions* on the Web (see Fig.2).

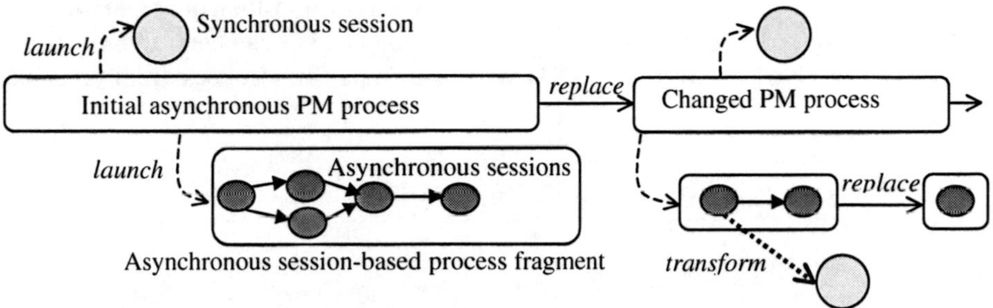

Fig. 1. Main elements of a collaboration flow

Session types	*Typical examples*
synchronous informal	artifact-centered informal session
synchronous formal	formal argumentation session
asynchronous formal	instance of a session type within an issue-based and session-based collaborative process model fragment
asynchronous informal	informal annotation of 'externalized' artifacts using the Web

Fig. 2. Summary table of the four basic session types with typical examples

3 A Prototype of Collaboration Flow Management System

In this section, we describe a scenario supported by our current prototype of *Collaboration flow Management System* (CfMS). Our lab plans an extension of its building. A VT has been created for discussing different aspects of this project with the point of view of the future residents. The team includes representatives of lab members and participants coming from the university, the town, and the firm of architects. A kick-off informal 'orientation meeting' has first planned a set of virtual meetings about several specific questions. These synchronous sessions are organized by the project manager through the asynchronous PM process (see section 3.3).

3.1. Synchronous Session Support

The session described here is about car parking near the lab. Such a synchronous session does not follow any predefined execution path: the session moderator can describe the problem and organize the work by using the audio channel. In our scenario, the problem is first informally discussed through textual or graphical annotations on the overall building plan (see Fig.3). Social protocols, such as author identification with colors, can be negotiated. Written clarifications may be obtained through the chat tool. In a second time, emerging controversial issues can be formally discussed with pro and con arguments, for instance by using a 'turn talking' policy ('free' and 'moderated' policies are also available). On the basis of the resulting argumentation trees (described in more details in section 3.2.2), the session moderator can select some solutions and measure the consensus within the core team with the voting tool. All produced documents (drawings, annotated documents, argumentation trees, vote results) can be saved as HTML documents for feedback from other lab members.

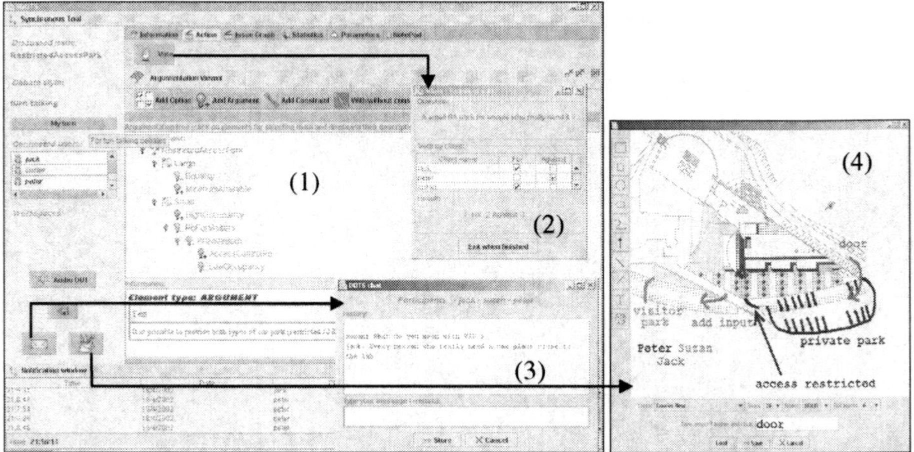

Fig. 3. The synchronous session support, with a formal argumentation (1), a vote result (2), an informal discussion (3) about the freely annotated architectural plan of the lab (4).

3.2. Model-Driven Collaborative Process Fragment Support

Later in the course of the project, the VT has planned an asynchronous model-driven process fragment for a systematic study of the existing cafeteria dysfunctions and for proposing a consensual list of possible causes and solutions for the new cafeteria.

3.2.1. The Meta Model

The process modeling language is defined by a *meta model*, which extends the classical *process view* and *organizational view* of WfMSs with a *decision view* and a *knowledge view* (see Fig.4). The *process view* mainly includes ProcessFragment and Session types. Each process fragment instance is structured into a network of session instances (also called 'phases'), with precedence relationships, and special phase instances corresponding to the classical workflow operators (AND split, OR split, AND join, OR join phase types). The *knowledge view* mainly includes Artifact, Component, and ApplicationTool types. Artifact types specialize generic types such as Text, List, Table, Graph (concept map), or Image. Component types specialize generic types such as ListElement, GraphNode, or GraphVertex. ApplicationTool types mirror the specialization of artifact types, with specializations of generic types such as TextViewer, ListViewer, TableViewer, or GraphViewer. Each Session type grants access to some ApplicationTool types. The *organizational view* mainly includes Role and Actor types. The *decision view* describes collaborative work at a fine grain level. Each Session type is defined internally by a set of Issue types, which must be solved either individually or collectively. Each Issue type is characterized by a set of Option types, which describe the possible solutions. At run time, one option is chosen trough an argumentation process. Each Option type can trigger, when it is chosen, some Operation type, which can change some Artifact or Component, or change the process state (e.g. termination of a Session), or change the process definition itself.

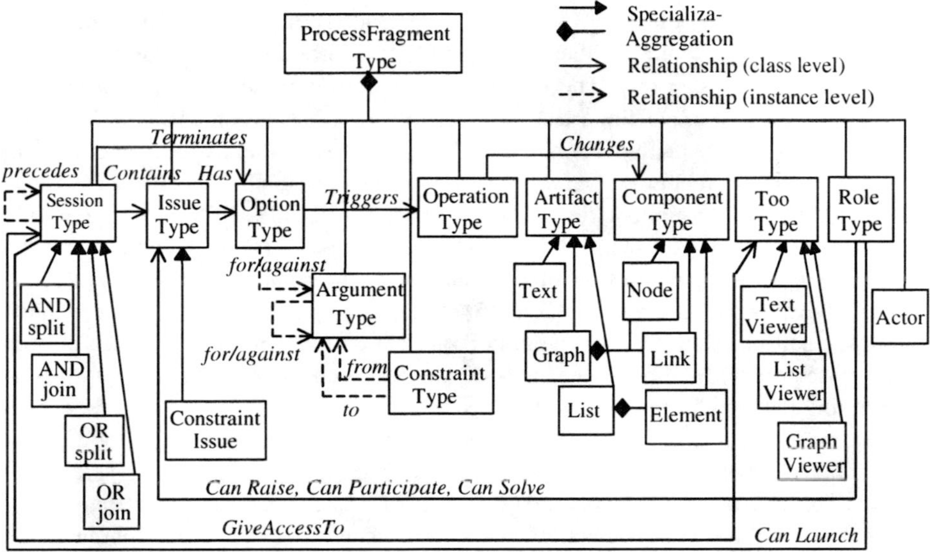

Fig. 4. The basic concepts of the meta model

3.2.2. The Scenario

A process model fragment is selected and instantiated (see section 3.3). The fragment implements the DIPA approach [10] which formalizes collaborative problem solving for synthesis situations (design of solutions), and for analysis situations (diagnosis). A typical DIPA-based analysis process includes three steps: first, the problem is described and *data* ('symptoms') are collected; secondly, data are used to find *interpretations*, i.e. possible causes; lastly, interpretations are used to devise *solutions* that serve as reparations suppressing the causes of the symptoms. The process model fragment includes three session types. The ProblemDefinition session type contains issues types for defining the problem (individual), proposing a symptom (individual), and terminating the phase (collective). The ProblemAnalysis session type contains issue types for proposing a cause (individual), linking a cause to a symptom (individual), challenging -keeping or discarding- a cause (collective), adding new symptoms (individual), and terminating the phase (collective). The ProblemResolution session type contains issue types for proposing a solution (individual), linking a solution to a cause (individual), challenging a solution (collective), and terminating the phase (collective). The instantiated process is a sequence of one phase of each type.

When a user, say Jack, logs in a process fragment where he plays a role, he can use the What can I do? guidance query and the Whats'new? awareness query (for knowing elements that have changed since his last logout). He can also browse various textual and graphical representations of the model types and the process instances. All participants only act by solving typed issue instances. If Jack wants to propose a new cause, he raises an individual ProposeCauseIssue. Then he has to explain his intention as an argument. This individual issue is automatically solved and triggers an operation which creates a new Cause component. If Jack wants to challenge a cause given by Peter, he raises a collective ChallengeCauseIssue. Then, he gives an argument in favor of the Discard option. Other participants can react (support the Keep option or challenge Jack's argument). The debate takes the form of an argumentation tree, possibly with qualitative importance constraints between arguments. Such a constraint ('more/ less/equally important than') opens a sub issue, called a 'constraint issue', for debating about the value of the constraint. Participants can access various representations of argumentations, like a threaded discussion form (Fig.3) or a graphical form with a 'playback' facility (Fig.5). At each argumentation move, the system computes a preferred option by using an *argumentative reasoning technique* close to the approach proposed in Zeno [5]. The system provides also statistical charts about the participation, the favorite option of each participant, and the 'level of conflict', based on the number of changes of the preferred option. Suzan, who plays a role giving the capability to solve this type of issue, terminates the debate by choosing one option. The issue resolution triggers an operation that either keeps or discards the challenged cause. Different tools, like table or graph viewers, are available to the session participants for accessing the process artifacts, such as the symptom/cause/solution concept graph of Fig.5. The process guidance, the argumentation and decision-making support, the awareness facilities, and the way to transform an asynchronous debate into a synchronous one are described in more details in [12], which also gives some information about the current Java implementation.

A model fragment can include '*open points*' for refining the model at run time. In our model an open point is an instance of a model refinement phase type including a *model refinement issue type*, with one option type for each possible refinement. At run time, one of these options is chosen, either individually by an actor playing the role of project manager, or collectively by the core team. The resulting operation deploys the refinement by instantiating new phase instances and new phase precedence relationships. By this way, artifact production and process refinement are performed similarly.

3.3 The Project Management Process

In our scenario, the initial PM process follows a very simple model with a PM phase followed by a refinement phase. During the PM phase a participant playing the role of

ProjectManager can plan synchronous sessions and asynchronous process fragments by solving CreateSessionOrProcess individual issue instances. Each resolution adds a new description (name, date, objective, participants, status,…) to a ProjectPlan artifact and calls people for participation through email generation. This planning activity can also result from synchronous 'orientation meetings' with the core team. The ProjectManager can also publish in a ProjectRepository artifact, HTML documents produced by the terminated processes/sessions (PublishResult issue type). A dedicated tool for accessing each document is generated and appears in the tool list of the PM session (see Fig.6). The refinement phase enables the project manager (possibly after a debate with the core team) to change the PM policy by instantiating a new PM fragment. For instance, a richer model can include an issue type for publicizing individual tasks by publishing them in the ProjectPlan artifact. Participants can commit themselves to do a given task, and their commitments are published in the ProjectPlan. Model-driven process fragments can also be used within a PM session for defining and installing dynamically ('on line') and consensually new model fragments as it is proposed in [6]. It is perhaps not a realistic approach because participants should be aware of all the details of the modeling approach and language. Another way is to use informal sessions for debating the general characteristics of the process model fragment, possibly around high level graphical descriptions. The model programming and installation is then performed 'off line' by model developers using the specialized model development environment (editor, compiler, static analyzer, and instantiation tool [12]).

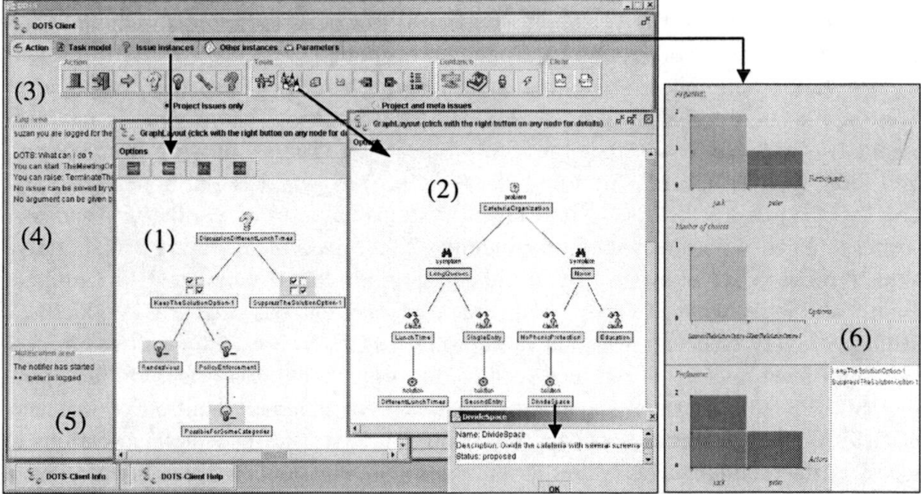

Fig. 5. The asynchronous process-centered session support, with a graphical view of an issue (1), the DISA concept graph built during the session (2), the action panel (3) with a 'What Can I do?' guidance query (4), the notification panel (5), and the statistical analysis of the debate.

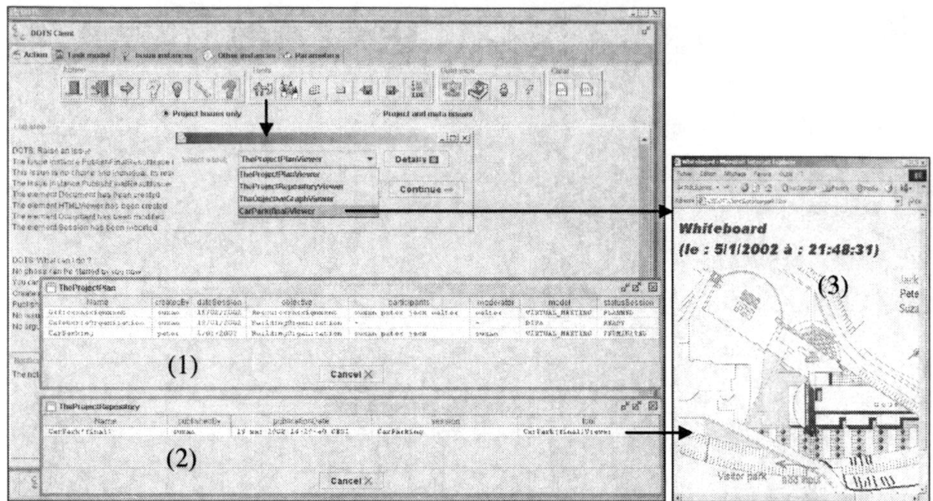

Fig. 6. The asynchronous project session support with the project plan (1) and the project repository (2). A dedicated tool is generated for each published result (3).

4 Conclusions and Future Work

Our approach is rooted in a wealth of research projects. Among the most important precursors, we can cite Conversation Builder [8] (for genericity, process model fragments, asynchronous collaboration), Cognoter/Argnoter [17] and gIBIS/rIBIS [3] (for argumentation and concept mapping). Our approach reflects also the evolution, in many application domains, from hard-coded tools to model-based generic environments. It is the case for instance for review/inspection systems, moving from specialized tools such as ICICLE, Scrutiny, etc. (see [15]) to generic environments such as CSRSv3 [18] or ASSIST [16]. Two recent systems have strong similarities with our proposal. First, we share with Compendium [2] the idea of modeling collaborative work through a set of typed issues, called 'question-based templates' in Compendium. We share with SCOPE [6] the idea of 'session based process modeling'. SCOPE roughly coincides with our definition of a CfMS. But SCOPE does not provide high level interaction services such as our argumentation service. On the opposite, SCOPE aims at satisfying a larger set of system requirements. For instance, SCOPE provides a specific concurrency control mechanism for enabling sessions to access artifacts simultaneously and for preventing inconsistent changes. In our view, a CfMS only provides the core services for collaboration, such as the management of collaboration-oriented artifacts local to the different sessions. A document sharing system for distributed teams such as BSCW [1] or our Java Motu prototype (available at http://motu.sourceforge.net) should complement the CfMS for managing (sharing, versioning) application artifacts, such as the architectural plans in our scenario. By this way, *collaboration is not tied to some particular document management policy.*

Similarly, no support is provided for coordinating individual tasks. *A cooperative WfMS* could complement our CfMS for this aspect.

The 'collaboration flow management paradigm' aims at satisfying the basic requirements of VT support, in particular *fluidity*. As many researchers we have first focused on technical solutions such as structural reflection and meta object protocols (in a early Smalltalk prototype [14]). In the current Java prototype, structural reflection ('linguistic reflection' [9]) is not a very practical solution in complex cases which require dynamic coding in the process modeling language followed by a long transformation process (starting with our specific compiler producing Java code followed by the persistency pre processor, the regular Java compiler, and the instantiation process). More realistically, PM process fragments include *predefined reflective issue types* for simple cases such as modifying the class level relationships of Fig.4 (e.g. adding/suppressing existing issue types or tool types accessibility from a given phase type) or creating new types when the code can be generated from a set of user-provided parameters (e.g. creating new role types). Today, we think that fluidity is a larger problem, with *multiform technical and organizational aspects* such as fluidity of group boundaries (core team vs extended team), fluidity of roles (in the context of each session), fluidity of containers (sessions) definition and organization (capability to start a formal debate asynchronously and to terminate it synchronously), fluidity in rhythms (between different styles of synchronous interaction), fluidity in formalization (from informal debates to formal argumentation, from to do list to model-driven processes), etc. Our approach deals with a large range of such technical and organizational aspects. Concerning the core services of CfMSs, future work will be directed towards a better support *for the VT project memory* by using XML technologies. Such a memory should store and restore *both in human-readable and machine-readable forms* all kinds of information, such as the collaboration artifacts, the process history, the argumentation trees, and even the process model fragments themselves. Another important objective is to provide a larger *library of reusable process model fragments*, either task-oriented or PM-oriented, and to evaluate them through scenarios and experiments, such as those already performed with our previous prototype [13].

References

1. Bentley, R., Appelt, W., Busbash, U., Hinrichs, E., Kerr, D., Sikkel, K., Trevor, J., and Woetzel, G.: Basic support for cooperative work on the World Wide Web. International Journal of Human-Computer Studies, 46 (1997) 827-846
2. Conklin, J., Selvin, A., Buckingham Shum, S., Sierhuis M.: Facilitated Hypertext for Collective Sense making: 15 Years on from gIBIS. Tech. Report KMI-TR-112, KMI (2001)
3. Conklin, J., Begeman, M.: gIBIS: A hypertext tool for exploratory policy discussion. ACM Transaction on Office Information System, 6, 4 (1988) 303-331
4. Falzon, P., Darses, F., Béguin, P.: Collective Design Processes. Proc. COOP'96, Juan Les Pins, France, INRIA (1996) 141-149
5. Gordon, T.F., Karacapidilis, N.: The Zeno argumentation framework. Proc. 6th Int. Conf. on AI and Law (ICAIL'97), Melbourne, Australia, ACM Press (1997) 10-18

6. Haake, J.M., Wang, W: Flexible support for business processes: extending cooperative hypermedia with process support. Information and Software Technology, 41, 6 (1999)
7. Johnson-Lenz, P., Johnson-Lenz, T.: Post mechanistic groupware primitives: rhythms, boundaries and containers. Int. Journal Man-Machine Studies, 34 (1991) 395-417
8. Kaplan, S., Caroll, A.: Supporting collaborative processes with Conversation Builder. Computer communications, 15, 8 (1992)
9 Kirby, G.N.C., Morrison, R., Stemple, D.W.: Linguistic reflection in Java. Software Practice & Experience, 28, 10 (1998) 1045-1077
10. Lewkowicz, M., Zacklad, M.: MEMO-net, un collecticiel utilisant la méthode de résolution de problème DIPA. Proc. IC'99, Palaiseau, France (1999) 119-128
11. Lipnack, J., Stamps, J.: Virtual teams. John Wiley & Sons, New York (2000)
12. Lonchamp, J., Muller: Computer-Supported Deliberations for Distributed Teams. Proc. I2CS 2001, Ilmenau, Germany, LNCS, Springer-Verlag (2001) 167-174
13. Lonchamp, J., Denis, B.: Fine-grained process modeling for collaborative work support: experiences with CPCE. Journal of Decision Systems, 7 (1998) 263-282
14. Lonchamp, J.: Object-oriented collaborative process modeling. Technology of Object-Oriented Languages and Systems (TOOLS 16). Prentice Hall (1995) 17-27
15. Macdonald, F., Miller, J.: Automatic generic support for software inspection. Proc. 10th International Quality Week, San Francisco (1997)
16. Macdonald, F., Miller, J., Brooks, A., Roper, M., Wood, M.: A review of tool support for software inspection. Proc. 7th Int. Workshop on CASE (1995)
17. Stefik, M., Foster, G., Bobrow, D., Kahn, K., Lanning, S., Suchman, L.: Beyond the chalkboard: computer support for collaboration and problem solving in meetings. CACM, 1, (1987) 32-47
18. Tjahjono, D.: Building software review systems using CSRS. Tech. Report ICS-TR-95-06, University of Hawaii, Honolulu (1995)

Domain Knowledge-Based Automatic Workflow Generation*

Soon Ae Chun, Vijayalakshmi Atluri, and Nabil R. Adam

CIMIC and MS/IS Department
Rutgers University
Newark, New Jersey, USA
{soon,atluri,adam}@cimic.rutgers.edu

Abstract. The traditional workflow design paradigm relies heavily on humans who statically specify business processes. However, such a manual design approach is not suitable for many cases: (a) *Inter-agency workflows* that cross autonomous organizational boundaries require experts who possess knowledge required for defining workflows composed of services from the constituent organizations; (b) *Customized workflows* that require many variations make it infeasible and error-prone to predefine the complex workflow in advance. This paper presents an alternative design paradigm that allows automatic on-the-fly generation of a workflow schema. This *dynamically integrated workflow composition approach* utilizes conceptual ontologies of domain services (tasks) and domain integration knowledge that serves as a model for workflow integration (composition) rules. It also uses user profiles (preferences) as part of (transient) compositional rule base. We present a prototype system for "registering a new business" in the State of New Jersey that implements this automatic workflow design methodology.

1 Introduction

Workflow management systems (WFMS) have made it possible to automate the coordinated execution of different business processing activities. WFMS take over the responsibility of controlling the coordinated execution of tasks from human coordinators. This automation is possible with well-formed workflow specifications. Currently, tasks and interdependency conditions among tasks need to be fully specified by humans, before the workflow is executed. Various modeling techniques have been proposed [5,7], but the modeling process remains manual. Graphical tools [14] can be helpful, however, the graphical objects still need to be put together manually. The workflow design process typically requires to specify all the possible use cases and different execution environments. Once the workflow has been designed, modification of the workflow definition is costly and time consuming. Manual workflow specification needs automation, given the fact that workflow technology is widely being adopted for web-based B2B and

* This work is partially supported by the National Science Foundation under grant EIA-9983468 and by MERI (the Meadowlands Environmental Research Institute).

R. Cicchetti et al. (Eds.): DEXA 2002, LNCS 2453, pp. 81–93, 2002.

B2C e-commerce transactions as well as eGovernment services in G2G, G2B and G2C.

Often, government services span agency boundaries e.g., for new business registrations [1], welfare and social services [4], etc. The workflow for these services is referred to as *inter-agency workflow*. An inter-agency workflow is composed of component services provided by autonomous government agencies. The decentralized execution model proposed in [3] allows automatic execution with the collaborative coordination of participating agencies' services and information systems, while maintaining autonomy of each agency. In this paper, we emphasize that inter-agency workflow design needs to be dynamic and automatic rather than static and manual.

Our approach is based on a knowledge-based workflow design method. An ontology of services serves as a domain model for component services (tasks) and their relationships. An ontology of government regulations serves as a domain model for compositional rules. We present a *dynamic workflow model* that makes use of the tasks and rules in the ontology hierarchies, and of user profiles. Compositional rules consist of selection rules that select obligatory and preference tasks, and coordination rules that glue tasks together in order. Each rule is represented as Condition-Action pair. The composition algorithm evaluates compositional rules against a user profile, automatically generating the customized inter-agency workflow. This knowledge-based approach allows automating the complex inter-agency workflow design as well as provides a customized workflow that requires fewer evaluations at run time.

Problem: In the following, we provide two example scenarios to illustrate the need for a dynamic and automatic workflow design method.

Example 1. *A developer, Bill, wishes to build a warehouse complex on his property on the bank of the Hackensack River in Little Ferry, NJ. His property of 15 acres (block 108.04, lot 2.04) is currently vacant and designated as "Light Industrial and Distribution B" zone. His property is only two feet below the maximum tide level. He will need to fill it with some material to secure a sound foundation.*

A workflow designer needs to know that (1) Bill needs to acquire a zoning certificate from the NJMC; (2) if the parcel falls into the so-called environmentally sensitive area, such as wetlands, riparian land, and flood plains, etc., Bill may need permits from local, state and federal agencies, including NJ Department of Environmental Protection (NJDEP) Waterfront Development Permit, Stream Encroachment Permit, Water Quality Certificate, Army Corps of Engineers Section 10 or Section 404 permit, Riparian Grant, etc.

The designer needs knowledge on local, state, and federal regulations in order to properly design a workflow for Bill. In addition, the designer needs to consider not only Bill's case, but many others with different geo-spatial characteristics. Specifying all the possible variations for every user in one workflow is not feasible. The next example illustrates the need for variant workflows for "busines registration process."

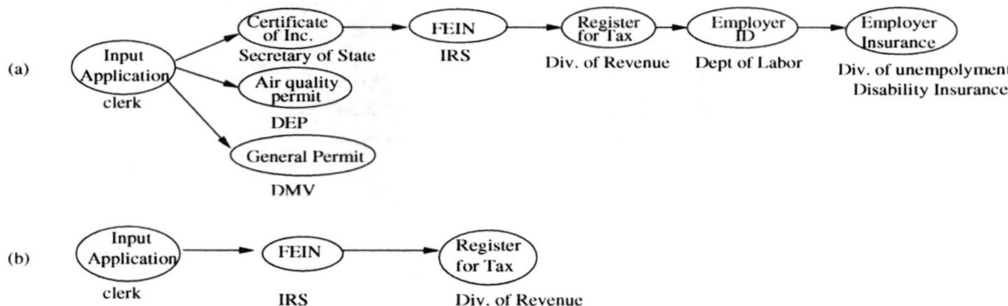

Fig. 1. Customized business registration process

Example 2. *John Smith would like to start a new auto body repair shop in New Jersey. Jane Carlson would like to open a convenience store. John Smith wants to locate his business in downtown Newark, Essex county. Jane Carlson wants to have her shop near her home in Mercer county. John wants to have the business incorporated with several employees, while Jane wants to have it in sole proprietorship without any employees.*

According to these requirements, two different inter-agency service specifications are needed as shown in figures (1a) and (1b) for John and Jane, respectively. While both entrepreneurs need to file the tax-related business registration application at the Division of Taxation, their required steps and tasks differ. John will also need a certificate of incorporation and employee related insurance as well as an air quality permit. Our automatic workflow design methodology benefits the designer, and also citizens who without the automated design system need to find which regulations by which agency apply for their particular situations. This is time-consuming and complex process, as different regulations are enforced by different autonomous agencies. Moreover, there are few people with comprehensive knowledge of the regulations and services of different agencies.

In Section 2, we present the domain knowledge-based workflow generation model Section 3 presents an algorithm to generate the workflow definition and describes our prototype system. Section 4 discuss related work, followed by conclusions and future research in Section 5.

2 Automatic Workflow Composition Model

2.1 Task and Service Ontology

For service discovery and composition, services are described as service interfaces for external use and internal implementations. We argue that descriptions of individual services do not capture the inter-relationships among services. The linear set of individual services without any structures can result in inefficiency in service discovery and identification. For this reason, we use an ontology of services. An ontology is defined as a description of concepts and relationships that

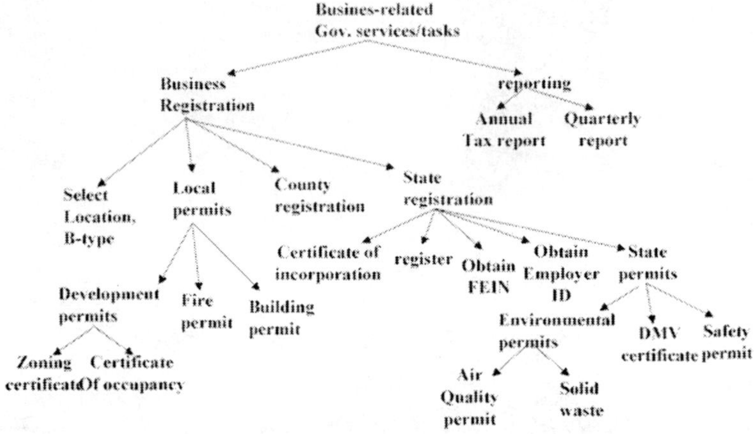

Fig. 2. Component Hierarchy for a Service of opening a new business

exist among them [8]. For example, the knowledge of a composite service *Open a New Business* is represented as a *component hierarchy* (Figure 2). Each node represents a service, and each down link (up link) represents a *has-component* (*component-of*) relationship. The *has-component* relationship emanating at a service, s, defines all the component services of s. The knowledge of tasks and their relationships explicitly considered in our workflow generation model facilitates the search for appropriate component tasks via *component-of* relationships and provides necessary interface and connection information needed for composing integrated services.

Definition 1. **[Domain Services/Tasks Ontology]** *A domain service ontology SO is defined as a set of services* $S = \{s_1, s_2, ...\}$ *where each* $s_i \in S$ *is defined as a triple* $\langle id, SA, SR \rangle$*, where id is a service identifier, SA is a set of service attributes and SR a set of relationships that are associated with* s_i*. The service attribute SA is represented as a 5-tuple* $s_i = \langle a, Pre, A, Input, Output \rangle$*, where a denotes the execution agent, or service provider of* s_i*, Pre denotes the precondition set for* s_i*, A the set of activities (or operations) within* s_i*, Input the set of input parameters to* s_i*, and Output the set of output parameters of* s_i*. SR is a set of relationships* $\{rel_1, rel_2, ...\}$ *where each* rel_i *is a triple* $\langle name, N, mode \rangle$ *with name for relationship name, N for a set of services that bear* rel_i *relationship with* s_i *and mode to denote whether relationship* rel_i *is obligatory or optional with tasks linked in the service ontology.*

We use the notation $rel_i(s_i)$ to retrieve all the services that bear the relationship rel_i to s_i, i.e. N. A relationship $SR = \{$*has-component component-of, implement* $\}$ for s_i defines a set of all component services for s_i, a set of services that s_i is a component of, and a set of regulatory rules that s_i enforces, respectively.

2.2 Ontology of Government Regulations

Government services implement federal, state and local regulations [12,9]. Obvious examples include: "a drivers license is required for vehicle operation," "low income households are entitled to social benefits," etc. However, some regulations are not so obvious. Moreover, as seen in examples in 1, regulatory knowledge required for designing an inter-agency workflow crosses the boundaries of local, state, and federal agencies. Regulatory rules may include different types:

1. Semantic Rules: These are the rules that affect the activities involved in a workflow. For example, an environmental protection regulation states that any business type, such as an autobody shop, that releases a certain level of spray paint into the air is required to obtain an air quality permit.
2. Spatial Rules: These rules are concerned with the geographic features of a business [10], e.g. (1) If a development project includes construction of a structure along, in, or across the stream channel, or 100 year flood plain of any stream, then a stream encroachment permit is required. (2) If a business is located in municipalities under a certain agency jurisdiction, then a development application needs to be filed and approved by that agency.
3. Temporal Rules: Temporal rules may state the absolute and relative deadlines for a task. For instance, if a public records filing for a new business entity is submitted, then tax registration forms must be submitted within 60 days.
4. Sequencing Rules: These rules specify the obligatory sequences among tasks. For example, obtaining a certificate of incorporation is required before business registration.

The comprehensive knowledge about regulations is conceptually modeled as regulatory topic ontology (Figure 3). This topic-subtopic hierarchy allows the identi-

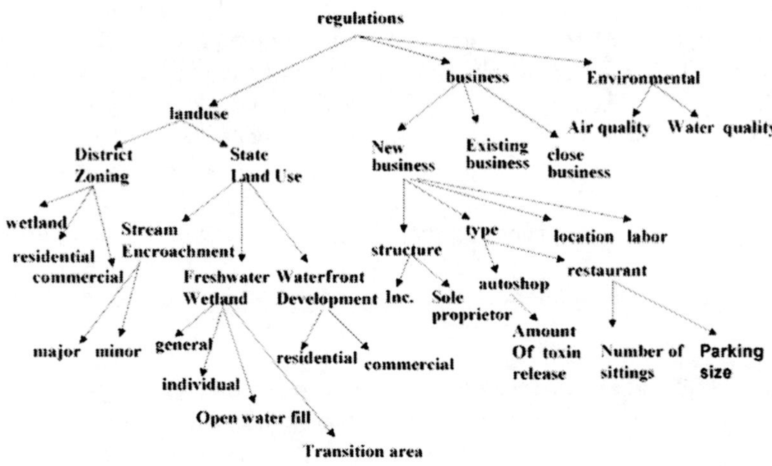

Fig. 3. Government Regulations Ontology

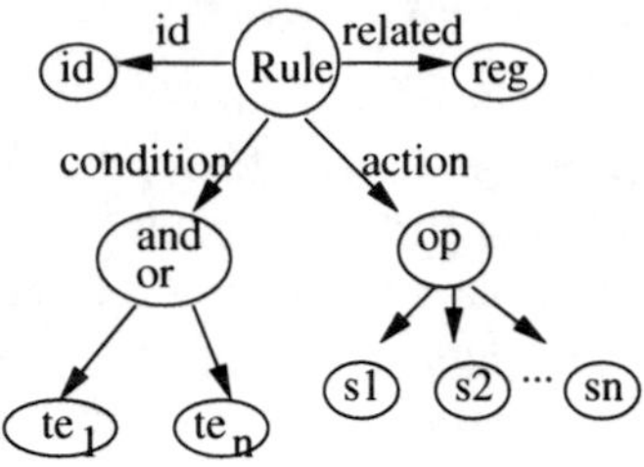

Fig. 4. Model of a compositional rule

fication of necessary information (e.g. type, location and kind of a new business) and regulation information. Each leaf node is associated with a regulatory rule. The rule nodes are modeled as Condition-Action relations (Figure 4), where Condition is a logical expression and Action is an operation on services (e.g. insert, parallel, order). This rule node has a link to the text document containing the regulation. The rule node also has a link to actual services that implement it (i.e. an *implemented-by* relationship). For example, the leaf node on the subtopic of *incorporated* has a relationship *is-subject-to* pointing to a regulatory rule *reg*. The rule *reg* is associated with the text document containing regulations such as "If the business structure is incorporation, then it is required to obtain a certificate of incorporation." It also has a relationship of *implemented-by* to a service "Obtain a certificate of incorporation" in the service hierarchy described above.

The following definitions formalize the regulations ontology and composition rules.

Definition 2. [**Domain Rules Ontology**] *Domain rules ontology RO is defined as a set of rule topics* $O = \{o_1, o_2, ...\}$. *Each* $o \in O$ *is defined as a 4 tuple* $< id, RA, Rel, R >$, *where id denotes an rule topic identifier, RA denotes a set of attributes, Rel a set of relationships that c bears, and R is a set of domain rules,* $\{r_1, r_2, \ ...\}$ *where each* $r_i \in R$ *is defined as a triple of* $(id, body, reg)$ *where id denotes the rule identifier and body is denoted as Condition-Action pair* $\langle c, a \rangle$ *where c and a are expressions for the antecedent and consequent of the rule, respectively. The regulation that is related to the rule is denoted by reg, which has a set of attributes* $\{rat_1, rat_2, ...\}$ *and a set of rule relationships* $\{rrel_1, rrel_2, ...\}$.

The condition c is defined as a logical expression, called trigger expression, as follows:

Definition 3. [**Trigger Expression**] *Given an alphanumeric string variable* $v \in \mathcal{S}$, *a function* $f \in \mathcal{F}$ *which is a set of predefined functions, a relational operation* $op \in OP = \{<, \ , =, \neq, \not<, \not\geq, \leq, \not\geq, \not\leq, \in, \subset, \subseteq, \notin, \not\subset, \not\subseteq, \supset, \supseteq, \not\supset, \not\supseteq\}$ *and a literal* $l \in \{\mathcal{S}, \mathcal{N}\}$ *for strings* $\mathcal{S}$ *and numbers* $\mathcal{N}$, *the* trigger expression *te is defined as follows:*

1. $(v\ op\ l)$ *is a trigger expression*
2. $(f(\boldsymbol{x})\ op\ l)$ *is a trigger expression*
3. If te_1 *and* te_2 *are trigger expressions, then* $\neg te_1$, $te_1 \vee te_2$, *and* $te_1 \wedge te_2$, *are also trigger expressions.*

The function f represents predefined semantic, spatial and temporal functions such as *amount(x), distance(x, y), after(x, y), etc.* An example trigger expression is $(number(employee) \geq 1)$. The action $a \in r_i$ is an operation $o \in \{insert, order, parallelize, ...\}$, that can be applied to tasks T in a workflow. Following shows semantics of actions: $insert(t_1)$ is an action to insert task t_1; $order(t_1, t_2)$ imposes an order: t_1 before t_2; $parallelize(t_1, t_2)$ allows t_1 and t_2 to be executed in parallel. The following is an example of a rule defined above:

(R1, ⟨ *amount(spray-paint)* $\geq$ *1/2 gallon per hour, insert(obtain air-quality-permit)* ⟩, REG_1)

$R1$ states that if the amount of spray paint used is more than half a gallon per hour, then insert task *obtain air quality permit* into the workflow and add the trigger expression *amount(spray-paint)* $\geq$ *1/2 gallon per hour* as the precondition for the task. This rule is related to regulation REG_1.

2.3 User Profile Model

While the service ontology and regulatory ontology are static most of the time, the *user profile* varies from case to case. Our approach contains a user profile for customization as an important part of the model. The individual user profile is modeled as a goal and a set of preference attributes and their values. The user goal in the model identifies a domain (i.e., a set of services) for a composite service, and user preferences are used for composition rule evaluation to select component services. User preferences include functional preferences (e.g. the type of business), geographic preferences (e.g. business location), or temporal preferences (e.g. business opening date), and others.

The preference attributes required for composing a workflow are also derived from the regulatory topic hierarchy. For example, the business registration related user profile attributes include business type, location, kind and labor information.

Definition 4. [**User Profile**] *A user profile* P *is defined as a pair of* $\langle g, PR \rangle$ *where* g *is a user's goal service* $g \in S$ *that a user intends to initiate, and* PR *is a set of service preferences* $\{p_1, p_2 ..., p_n\}$. *Each* p_i *is represented as a pair of an attribute and its value,* $\langle at, v \rangle$.

The following is a profile for John Smith:

– P_{John} =⟨ *open new business,* { ⟨ *type, in corporated* ⟩ , ⟨ *name, Car Care* ⟩ , ⟨ em kind, Autobody shop ⟩, ⟨ *location, 80 Mercer Street, Newark, NJ 07052* ⟩, ⟨ *employee_number,* $\geq$ *3* ⟩ } ⟩

2.4 Workflow Composition Function

Definition 5. **[Workflow Composition Functions]** *Given S, a set of services in service ontology SO, R a set of rules in rule ontology RO and P a set of user preferences, A rule selection function σ is defined as $\sigma : (S \times R \times P) \rightarrow CR$, where $CR = \{r_1, r_2, ..\} \subseteq R$ where each r_i is a pair $\langle c, a \rangle$ for condition c and action. Given CR from σ, workflow composition functions h and k denote task selection function and task coordination function, respectively, and are defined as follows:*
1. $h : CR \rightarrow T$, h is a function that selects a set of tasks $T \in a(CR)$ where $a(CR)$ is an action a of each rule $r \in CR$. for each $t \in T$, and $Pre(t) = te$ is precondition value is set to a trigger expression $te \in c(CR)$
2. $k : CR \rightarrow D$, k maps all tasks $T \in CR$ into dependency set $D = T \times T$ according to the coordination action $a \in CR$.

Definition 6. **[Workflow]** *A workflow W is defined as a directed graph $G = (T, D)$ where $T \subseteq S$ is a node set representing a set of tasks selected by composition function h and $D \subseteq (T \times T)$ is an edge set for coordination dependencies among T, generated by composition function k.*

Intertask dependencies D support a variety of workflow coordination requirements. Basic types of task dependencies include *control-flow dependencies* which specify the flow of control based on the outcome state of a task (e.g. begin-on-success), *value-dependencies* which specify the control flow based on the output value of a task (e.g. number of employee ≥ 2), and *external dependencies* which specify the control flow based on certain conditions satisfied by parameters external to the workflow (e.g. task t starts at 9:00am) [2,13,3].

3 Dynamic Workflow Composition

This section presents components and an algorithm to dynamically generating a customized workflow.

3.1 Profile Gathering

User profile attributes are derived from the rule ontology and hierarchically organized. The profile attribute data required for registering a new business shown in Figure 5 consist of attributes like structure, location, name, type and employee, and so on. A leaf node represents an attribute that assumes a value. For instance, the attribute *structure*, can take a value from the set {*incorporated, sole proprietorship, limited partnership, ...*}.

This hierarchical profile organization is represented as a set of profile rewrite rules (Table 1). These rules are used to gather profile information by dynamically expanding the LHS of a rule with RHS nodes and collapsing RHS nodes when all the attributes are filled with values. Figure 6 illustrates the expansion and shrinkage of the tree structure as the profile information is gathered.

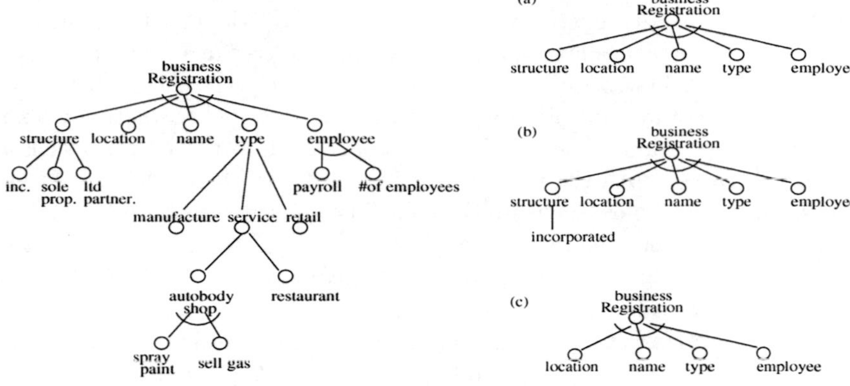

Fig. 5. Profile Attribute Hierarchy

Fig. 6. Tree Structure for Profile Evaluation

Table 1. Profile Rewrite Rules

P1: *business registration* $\rightarrow$ *structure* $\wedge$ *location* $\wedge$ *name* $\wedge$ *type* $\wedge$ *employee*
P2: *structure* $\rightarrow$ *incorporated*
P3: *structure* $\rightarrow$ *sole proprietorship*
P4: *location* $\rightarrow$ *street* $\wedge$ *county* $\wedge$ *state* $\wedge$ *zip*
P5: *type* $\rightarrow$ *manufacture*
P6: *type* $\rightarrow$ *service*
P7: *service* $\rightarrow$ *autobody repair*
P8: *autobody repair* $\rightarrow$ *amount(spray paint)* $\geq 1/2$ *gallonhr* $\wedge$ *sell gas*
P9: *employee* $\rightarrow$ *payroll* $\geq$ \$1000 $\wedge$ *number(employee)* ≥ 1

Table 2. Service Selection and Coordination Rules

R1: $\langle$*struct = incorporated, insert(t1)* $\wedge$ *insert(t2)*$\rangle$
R2: $\langle$*struct = limited liabilitycompany, insert(t1)* $\wedge$ *insert(t2)*$\rangle$
R3: $\langle$*struct = limited partnership, insert(t1)* $\wedge$ *insert(t2)*$\rangle$
R5: $\langle$*struct = sole proprietorship, insert(t3)*$\rangle$
R7: $\langle$*register business, register business for tax*$\rangle$
R8: $\langle$*register business, obtain federal employer id*$\rangle$
R9: $\langle$*register business, certificate of incorporation* $\prec$ *register business for tax*$\rangle$
R10: $\langle$*register business, fein* $\prec$ *register business for tax*$\rangle$

3.2 Automatic Integration of Customized Workflows

Given a set of customization rules and a user profile, the customization process generates an individualized workflow, selecting only relevant component services (i.e. tasks) and obeying other constraints such as sequence ordering rules. Given the customization rule base in Tables 2, and user profile, the customization process automatically selects tasks and arranges these tasks according to the coordination rules. For instance, when a user enters *incorporated* as his business structure, the system finds rule R1 in Table 2, and inserts t_1 and t_2 into the workflow. Here, we assume t_1= *register business name with the State of NJ*, t_2 = *file original business certificate*, and t_3 = *register business's name with the County Clerk*. If the user prefers to establish a business of *sole proprietorship*, then R5 fires. As a result, t_3 is inserted into the workflow. As soon as a rule fires, the profile evaluation tree shrinks, and the next profile attribute evaluation starts (Figure 6). This process repeats until all the attributes of the profile tree acquire values and are used to fire appropriate rules. The end result of this process is a workflow. In addition to the tasks selected based on preferences, there exist obligatory tasks required for all users. For instance, *register-business-for-tax* is required for all applicants. These obligatory tasks are inserted by rules such as R7 and R8 in Table 2. All the tasks in the workflow are then subjected to the inter-task sequencing rules to ensure the coordination requirements, such as R9 and R10 in Table 2. For instance, rule R9 states that if the process is *register business*, then the task *obtain a certificate of incorporation* should be finished before *register business for tax.*

The following algorithm generates an inter-agency workflow given a user's request for a service g. It uses the ontologies defined in 2.1 and 2.2.

```
Algorithm 1.[Generate Customized workflow]
Input: g: user's desired service
Output: W=(T, D) W=workflow with set of tasks T and dependency D
BEGIN
T = ∅, D = ∅
S =has-component(g) /* identify all component services for G */
R = ∅ /* set of rules applicable to services in S */
For each s_i ∈ S { /* identify regulations and rules related to S */
    reg = implement(s_i)
    r = related-to(reg)
    R = R ∪ r }
For each r = (c, a) ∈ S { /* add obligatory service in workflow tasks T */
    if (c(r) = ∅ {
       T = T ∪ t ∈ a(r) }
For each t_i ∈ T and r = (c, a) ∈ R { /* add dependencies among tasks */
    if a(r) = order(t_i, t_j) {
       D = D ∪ (t_i, t_j)
       Pre(t_j) = bs
       R = R − r }
S = S -T
PR = gather-profile*(g) /* gather relevant user profile */
While(PR ≠ empty ) Do { /* while preference list is not empty */
      Given p ∈ PR
      For each r = (c, a) ∈ R { /* evaluate preference rules */
          if (eval(c, p) = true) {
             if a = insert(t_i) { /* add a task into workflow */
                T = T ∪ t_i
                Pre(t_i) = te ∈ c } /* add trigger expression as precondition for t_i */
                For each t_i ∈ T { /* add dependency */
                    if a = order(t_i, t_j) {
                       D = D ∪ (t_i, t_j)
                       Pre(t_j) = Pre(t_j) ∧ bs
                       R = R − r }}}}
      PR = PR − p
      S = S − t_i }
W = (T, D) }
END
```

*We assume the function *gather-profile* returns a set of attribute and value sets required for a service g.

The algorithm first identifies all the candidate component tasks based on the user requested service, g, as specified in the component service ontology. Second, it identifies applicable regulatory rules that are used to select obligatory and other tasks and determine dependencies among tasks. Selected tasks are composed according to the order related rules. The output of this algorithm is the customized composite workflow $W = (T, D)$ for the requested service g.

3.3 Prototype System

We have developed a prototype system[1] of generating customized workflows for the NJ State government [1]. Specifically, we have built an inter-agency service, called "a new business registration" process that requires information and coordination of various State agencies including Department of Revenue, Division of Commercial Recording, Division of Community Affairs, Department of Environmental Protection, Department of Public Health and Safety and others. The prototype system gathers the user profile information through an interview session, which is guided by interview rules which are based on case analysts' expert knowledge, i.e. ontology, such that only questions relevant to a specific business of the user are asked. The user profile gathered at the interview session and the business related regulations database are matched to generate a customized workflow. Web-based client applications for entrepreneurs include (1) a GIS-based business location service; (2) an interview interface; and (3) a workflow interface.

4 Related Work

Industry standards and research efforts such as WSDL, UDDI, ebXML, DAML-S, describing the semantics and metadata of web services, facilitate discovery and access of services, but they go only half way toward automating integration of services. The automation of service integration requires the selection and control knowledge that specifies what services are needed in certain circumstances. This knowledge of service composition and selection is left to domain experts to define manually, or for program developers to combine with the application code. Our approach of utilizing a domain model provides the capability to automate the integration and customization of workflow design.

Platforms for developing composite e-services proposed in eFlow [6], E-speak [11], and CMI (Collaboration Management Infrastructure) [15] are compositional models, similar to our approach. However, their design of e-services (compositional process) is still manual, while our approach uses a workflow definition model where the workflow task selection and ordering knowledge is explicitly modeled for automating the generation of the workflow definition.

5 Conclusions and Future Work

We have presented a formal model for *automatic workflow generation* that uses *domain knowledge* represented as service ontology, regulatory ontology and a user profile. We have presented the composition algorithm and data structures used for automatic generation of the workflow. This framework can be easily adopted to process definitions in other application domains where process design needs to obey company policies and other constraints. Our future work includes semi-automatically constructing the ontology of regulations and extracting business rules from documents. We also plan to address the workflow analysis and verification which provide validation of the automatically generated workflow. The

[1] http://cimic.rutgers.edu/dgov/demos1.html

dynamic modifications of workflow definitions to run-time changes in regulations, user profiles, or services are also under investigation.

References

1. N. Adam, F. Artigas, V. Atluri, S. Chun, S. Colbert, M. Degeratu, A. Ebeid, V. Hatzivassiloglou, R. Holowczak, O. Marcopolus, P. Mazzoleni, and W. Rayner. E-government: Human centered systems for business services. In *The First National Conference on Digital Government*, pages 48–55, May 2001.
2. Nabil R. Adam, Vijayalakshmi Atluri, and Wei-Kuang Huang. Modeling and Analysis of Workflows using Petri nets. *Journal of Intelligent Information Systems, Special Issue on Workflow and Process Management,*, 10(2), March 1998.
3. V. Alturi, S. Chun, and Pietro Mazzoleni. A Chinese Wall Secuity Model for Decentralized Workflow Systems. In *Eighth ACM Conference on Computer and Communications Security (CCS-8)*, Philadelphia, Pennsylvania, USA, November 2001.
4. A. Bouguettaya, A. Elmagarmid, B. Madjahed, and M. Quzzani. A web-based architecture for government databases and services. In *The First National Conference on Digital Government*, pages 56–59, May 2001.
5. F. Casati, S. Ceri, B. Pernici, and G. Pozzi. Conceptual Modeling of Workflows. In *Proceedings of the 1995 OOER Conference*, December 1995.
6. Fabio Casati, Ski Ilnicki, and Li-Jie Jin. eflow: a platform for developing and managing composite eservices. Technical report, HP Laboratories Palo Alto, March 2000.
7. Dimitrios Georgakopoulos, Mark Hornick, and Amit Sheth. An Overview of Workflow Management: From Process Modeling to Workflow Automation Infrastructure. *Distributed and Parallel Databases*, pages 119–153, 1995.
8. T.R. Gruber. Toward principles for the design of ontologies used for knowledge sharing. In N. Guarino and R. Poli, editors, *Proceedings of International Workshop on Formal Ontology*, Padova, Italy, 1993.
9. C. S. Han. *Computer Models and Methods for a Disabled Access Analysis Design Enviroment.* PhD thesis, Department of Civil and Environmental Engineering, Stanford University, June 2000.
10. R. Holowczak, S. Chun, F. Artigas, and V. Atluri. Customized geospatial workflows for e-government services. In *ACM-GIS 2001, The Ninth ACM International Symposium on Advances in Geographic Information Systems*, Atlanta, GA, USA, November 2001.
11. Alan Karp. E-speak e-xplained. Technical report, HP Laboratories Palo Alto, July 2000.
12. Shawn Kerrigan, Gloria Lau, Liang Zhou, Gio Wiederhold, and Kincho H. Law. Information infrastructure for regulation management and compliance checking. In *The First National Conference on Digital Government*, pages 167–170, May 2001.
13. Marek Rusinkiewicz and Amit Sheth. Specification and Execution of Transactional Workflows. In W. Kim, editor, *Modern Database Systems: The Object Model, Interoperability, and Beyond.* Addison-Wesley, 1994.
14. Asim Sadiq and Mria Orlowska. Applying a generic conceptual workflow modeling technique to document workflows. In *The second Australian Document Computing Symposium*, Melbourne, Australia, April 1997.
15. H. Schuster, D. Georgakopoulos, A. Cichocki, and D. Baker. Modeling and composing service-based and reference process-based multi-enterprise processes. In *Proceedings of the Inernational Conference on Advanced Information Systems Engineering (CAiSE)*, Stockholem, Sweden, June 2000.

A Comparison of Alternative Encoding Mechanisms for Web Services[1]

Min Cai, Shahram Ghandeharizadeh, Rolfe Schmidt, Saihong Song

Computer Science Department
University of Southern California
Los Angeles, California 90089-0781
{mincai,shahram,rrs,saihong}@usc.edu

Abstract. A web service is a modular application that is published, advertised, discovered, and invoked across a network, i.e., an intranet or the Internet. It is based on a "software-as-services" model and may participate as a component of other web services and applications. Binary and XML are two popular encoding/decoding mechanisms for network messages. Binary encoding is used when performance is critical and XML encoding is employed when interoperability with other web services and applications is essential. With each, one may employ compression to reduce message size prior to its transmission across the network. These decisions have a significant impact on response time and throughput. This paper reports on our experiences with a decision support benchmark, TPC-H, using these alternatives on different hardware platforms. We focus on queries and make the following observations. First, compression reduces the message size and enhances the throughput of a shared network. With XML, we present numbers from XMill, a compression technique that employs XML semantics. For queries that produce more than one megabyte of XML data, XMill compressed XML messages are almost always smaller than the Zip compressed Binary messages. While this improves the throughput of a networked environment with a fixed bandwidth, the response time of XMill compressed messages are at times twice slower than Zip compressed Binary messages. The processor speed has a significant impact on the observed response times.

1 Introduction

Many organizations envision web services as an enabling component of Internet-scale computing. A web service is either a computation or an information service with a published interface. Its essence is a remote procedure call (RPC) that consumes and processes some input data in order to produce output data. It is a concept that renders web applications extensible: By identifying each component of a web application as a web service, an organization can combine these web services with others to rapidly develop new web applications. The new web application may consist of web services that span the boundaries of several (if not many) organizations.

---

[1] This research is supported using an un-restricted cash gift from Microsoft research.

R. Cicchetti et al. (Eds.): DEXA 2002, LNCS 2453, pp. 93–102, 2002.

Serialization is an integral component of both web services and network-centric database applications. It is the process of converting objects and their state information into a form appropriate for transmission across the network (and storage in a flat file). With a network connection, the receiving process consumes arriving messages, re-assembles the transmitted objects, and processes them. This process is termed de-serialization. Two common encoding mechanisms are XML and Binary. XML produces human readable text and is employed when interoperability with other web services and applications is essential. Binary produces streams that are compact and fast to parse, but not human-readable.

The focus of this study is to quantify the performance tradeoff associated with these two alternatives for a decision support benchmark. We do not report on the query execution times and have eliminated it from the presented response times. In addition, we analyze the role of compression in reducing the number of transmitted bytes with each encoding mechanism. With XML, we analyze two compression schemes: Zip/GZip library and XMill [Liefke & Suciu]. Both employ techniques based on Lempel-Ziv algorithm [Ziv & Lempel]. Our results demonstrate that without compression, the XML encoder results in message sizes that are at times five times larger than their Binary representation. With Zip, compressed XML messages are at most twice the size of their compressed Binary representation. With XMill, compressed XML messages are at times smaller than their Zip compressed Binary representation. This trend holds true for large messages (more than one megabyte). Otherwise, Zip compressed Binary messages are smaller.

We also investigated two alternative protocols, namely, TCP/IP [Postel] and HTTP [Fielding et. al.]. Our experiments reveal that these two protocols provide comparable performance. This is because the Hypertext Transfer Protocol (HTTP) is an application-level protocol that employs a reliable transport protocol. In our experimental configuration, it employs TCP/IP connections. HTTP does transmit more bytes based on its request-response paradigm [Fielding et. al.]. However, this is negligible when compared with the message size. We do not investigate the role of HTTP intermediary, i.e., proxy, gateway, and tunnel. To simplify discussion, we eliminate HTTP from further consideration.

We use the obtained results to develop analytical models that compute the throughput of the system when the network is a shared resource. An analysis of these models reveals compression can significantly enhance system throughput when the network bandwidth is limited. The rest of this paper is organized as follows. Section 2 provides an overview of our experimental environment and the obtained results. Section 3 describes analytical models that compute system throughput using network as a bottleneck. We offer brief conclusions and future research directions in Section 4.

2 Performance Evaluation

We quantified the performance of alternative transmission protocols using TPC-H benchmark [Poess & Floyd] because it is a standard that provides documented queries and data sets. This enables others to re-create our experiments. TPC-H includes both retrieval and refresh queries. The refresh commands generate large requests and small responses. The retrieval queries offer a mix of commands that generate either (a) large requests and small responses, and (b) large requests and large responses. This motivated us to focus on retrieval queries and ignore refresh queries from further consideration. We report on 21 out of 22 queries because we could not implement query 15 in a timely manner.

Our hardware platform consists of two PCs. One is a server and the other is a client. (We analyze results with PCs configured with three different processor speeds: 450 MHz, 1 GHz, and 2 GHz.) The client and server were connected using a LINKSYS Ethernet (10/100 megabit per second, mbps) switch. Each machine is configured with a 20-gigabyte internal disk, 512 megabytes of memory (unless specified otherwise), and a 100 mbps network interface card. The server is configured with Microsoft Windows 2000 Server, SQL Server 2000, and Visual Studio .NET Beta 2 release. The client is configured with Microsoft Windows 2000 Professional and Visual Studio .NET Beta 2 release. The server implements a web service that accepts one TPC-H retrieval query, processes the query using ADO.NET, and returns the obtained results back to the client. The client employs a TPC-H provided component that generates SQL retrieval query strings, invokes the server's web service, and receives the obtained results.

The communication between the client and server uses the .NET remoting framework. For transmission, we use the TCP and HTTP channels provided with the .NET framework. For message formatting we use the SOAP [Box et. al.] and Binary formatters provided with the .NET framework. We extended this framework with two new formatters: a) compression using Zip/GZip library written entirely in C#, and b) XMill compression scheme [Liefke & Suciu]. XMill employs zlib, the library function for gzip. We modified XMill to consume its input from buffers (instead of a file). This framework configures channels and encoders without requiring modification of the application code. When performing our experiments, our system reconfigures at runtime to repeat a query workload while communicating over different channels with different encoders. All of our experiments were conducted in a single user mode with no background load on the underlying hardware. The client was configured to invoke the web service in an asynchronous manner.

2.1 Obtained Results

We used a 1 Gigabyte TPC-H database for evaluation purposes. The presented results ignore the query execution time. They pertain to only the encoding, transmission, and decoding times for processing a query. Different TPC-H queries produce a different amount of data. With the binary formatter, the message sizes vary from a few hundred bytes to a few megabytes. With the XML formatter, the message varies from a few hundred bytes to tens of megabytes. The server produces the largest volume of data for Query 10, approximately 25 megabytes of data with XML.

A compression scheme such as Zip can be applied to both the Binary and XML formatters. XMill compresses XML data using its semantics. Figure 1 shows a comparison of these alternatives using Zip compressed Binary (Zip-Binary) messages as a yardstick. The y-axis of this figure shows the ratio in size between a technique such as XMill-XML and Zip-Binary. For example, with Query 1, Zip-XML messages are 1.5 times larger than their Zip-Binary counterparts. A y-axis value less than 1.0 implies a smaller message size relative to Zip-Binary. XMill compressed XML (XMill-XML) produce smaller messages than Zip-Binary, i.e., 0.84 times the size with Query 2. In our experiments, in the worst-case scenario, Zip compressed XML (Zip-XML) messages are twice the size of Zip-Binary messages, see Figure 1. In the best case, they are approximately the same size. This is because a loss-less compression technique can effectively compress the repeated XML tags. To illustrate, Figure 2 shows the compression factor for Zip-XML, and XMill-XML. In general, compression factor is higher with XML. With Binary, compression factor ranges from 1.4 to 5.5. With XML, the Zip compression factor ranges from 2.1 to 19.6. With XMill, the compression factor is as high as 26 with query 16.

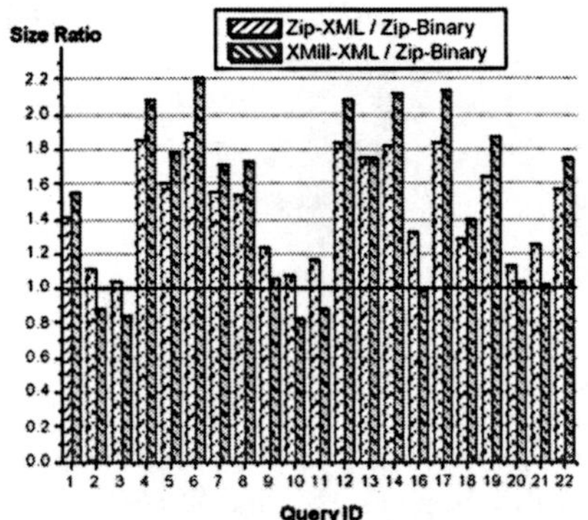

Fig. 1. Comparison of XML and Binary message sizes with and without compression

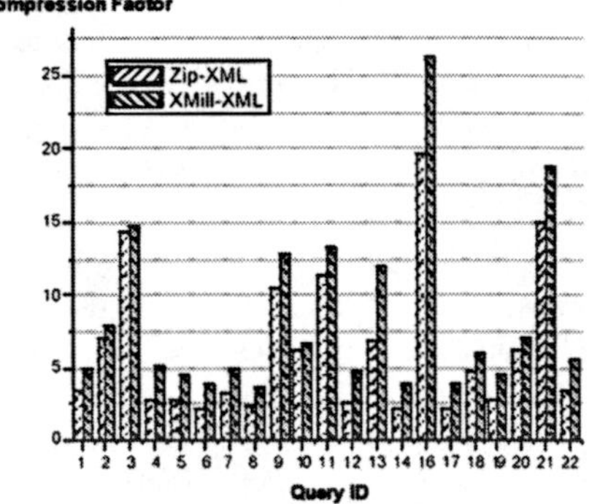

Fig. 2. Impact of compression on each encoding scheme

Figure 1 shows that XMill-XML messages are at times smaller than Zip-Binary messages, e.g., see query 2. This is because XMill groups data items with related meaning into containers and compresses each independently [Liefke & Suciu]. This column-wise compression is generally better than row-wise compression [Iyer and Wilhite]. At the same time, Figures 1 and 2 show that XMill is not always superior to Zip compression technique for XML messages, e.g., queries 1, 4, 5, 6, 7, 8, 12, 13, 14, 17, 18, 19 and 22. Generally speaking, when compared with Zip, XMill is more effective with large messages. The aforementioned queries transmit fewer than 9000 bytes. With the remaining queries that produce XML messages that are tens of thousands of bytes in size, XMill outperforms Zip.

Table 1 shows the response time of TPC-H Query 10 with the alternative formatters with three different processor configurations: a) 450 MHz, b) 1 GHz, and c) 2 GHz. In each case, we used two identical PCs with the same processor speed, one as the client and the other as the server. Each machine was configured with 512 megabytes of memory. The network configuration was identical in each case; see the beginning of Section 2. In these experiments, Binary provides the fastest response times. While Zip-Binary transmits fewer bytes, it is slightly slower because it includes the overhead of compressing the message at the transmitter and uncompressing it at the receiver. This observation applies to a comparison of Zip-XML with XML. These trends change when the network characteristics are less than ideal, e.g., either network latency or loss rate is high, see [Ghandeharizadeh et. al.].

In Table 1, XMill-XML provides the worst response time which is an inaccurate characterization of XMill. It is inaccurate because of how our experimental environment manages memory in conjunction with Microsoft SQL server, increasing XMill compression time dramatically. We invoked our modified XMill-XML on the result of query 10 (without running SQL server) and observed average total compression and decompression time of 4.6 seconds. The average total time with Zip-XML is 3.1 seconds. The resulting compressed file is smaller with XMill-XML. Hence, XMill-XML should provide a response time comparable to Zip-XML. We intend to investigate this memory limitation and resolve it in the near future.

Table 1. Response time(millisecond) of alternative formatters for TPC-H Query 10

	450 MHz	1 GHz	2 GHz
Binary	100,148	74,849	35,655
Zip-Binary	113,187	75,645	37,694
XML	183,902	112,200	64,365
Zip-XML	184,062	113,930	64,276
XMill-XML	296,311	176,278	91,547

Figure 3 shows the speedup observed for each formatter as a function of the processor speed. In each case, the speedup is sub-linear. This is because the memory's clock speed is the same for all configurations. This is important because query 10 requires the system to read and write a large amount of data for encoding, compression, transmission, decompression and decoding.

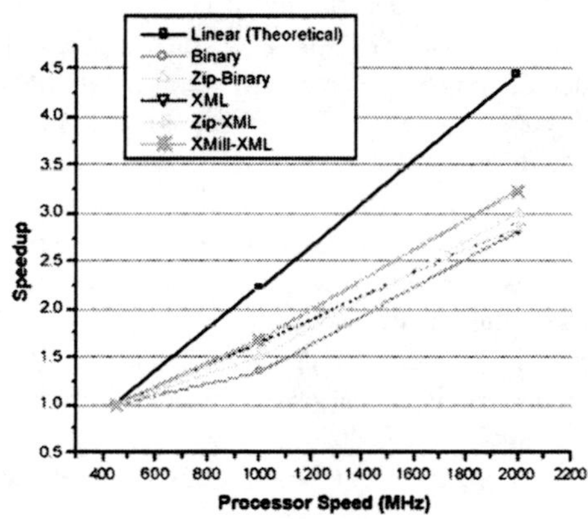

Fig. 3. Speedup of each technique as a function of processor (clock) speed

3 Analytical Models of Transmission to Estimate Throughput

The results of Section 2 demonstrate the impact of alternative formatters on the number of transmitted bytes per TPC-H query. This can quickly dominate and determine the throughput of the environment in realistic Internet deployments when network bandwidth is limited. Here we present an analytical model to compute upper bounds on the throughput of a system as a function of fixed bandwidth between a server and multiple clients. Using these models and the experimental results of Section 2, we quantify the throughput of each formatter with different network characteristics. We start with a simple model of throughput. Next, we use a Markov process to model transmission failures. Finally, we apply these models with different system parameters to compare the alternative encoders.

3.1 A Simple Model

In the following discussion, assume a fixed application and communication channel. Moreover, lets assume the average request message size is Q megabits (Mb) and the average response message size is A Mb. The server component resides on a machine that is linked to the network with a bandwidth of B Mb/sec. We use T to denote the system throughput. Its upper bound is defined as:

$$T \leq B \div (Q + A) \tag{1}$$

No matter what improvements are made to the server or the transmission protocol, this theoretical upper bound cannot be surpassed.

3.2 Transmission Failures

Our techniques employ TCP transmission protocol. This reliable protocol may retransmit packets in order to compensate for packet loss, resulting in increased traffic on the underlying shared network. We use a Markov process to model TCP packet transmission. This model computes the expected number of bits to transmit a message based on failure rates, packet sizes, and available bandwidth. Using this expectation, we derive upper bounds on throughput.

We start by explaining our model for environments that transmit a single packet of size P. Next, we extend this model to a message that consists of N packets. There are three basic states for transmitting a single packet:

1. The packet is sent, but not received. This state is termed t, or "transmitted".
2. The packet is sent and received, but the ACK has not been received. This state is termed r, or "received".
3. The packet is sent and received, and the ACK has also been received. This is the terminal state.

The following state transition diagram (Figure 4) shows these different states assuming: a) every packet has a failure probability λ that is independent of its size, and b) the ACK message has size ε bits.

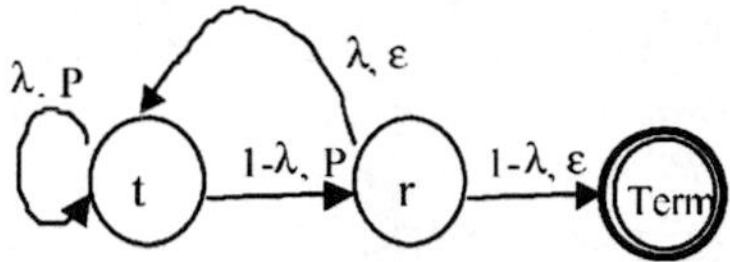

Fig. 4. The state transition diagram for three basic states

Where each transition is labeled with the probability of the transition and the number of bits transmitted during the transmission. Given this diagram we can compute P*, the expected number of bits transmitted over the network before successfully completing the transmission. If no failures occur (with probability of $(1-\lambda)^2$) then a total of P + ε bits are transmitted. When there is a failure, the system restarts with state t. This is described as:

$$P^* = (1-\lambda)^2 (P+\varepsilon) + \lambda(P+P^*) + \lambda(1-\lambda)(P+\varepsilon+P^*) \quad \mathbf{(2)}$$

Which can be reduced to:

$$P^* = P \div (1-\lambda)^2 + \varepsilon \div (1-\lambda) \quad \mathbf{(3)}$$

The extension of this to a message that consists of N packets is trivial. We represent this as N "transmitted" states $t_0, t_1, t_2, \ldots, t_N$, and "received" states $r_0, r_1, r_2, \ldots, r_N$. After successfully receiving ACK for the ith packet, the system moves to state $t_{(i+1)}$: transmitted the $(i+1)^{th}$ packet. The new diagram is shown in Figure 5.

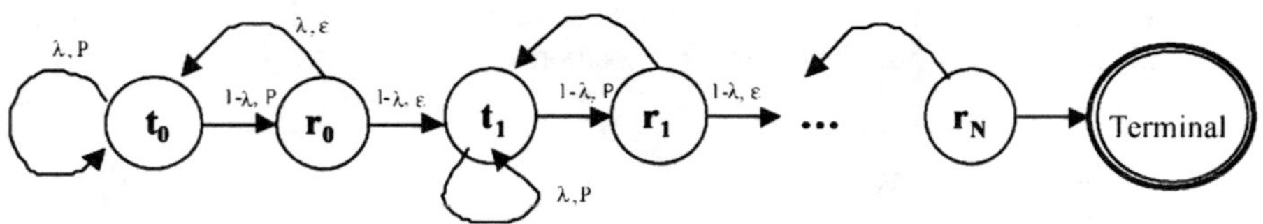

Fig. 5. The state transition diagram for the message transmission Markov chain

Note that once we reach state t_i, we will never visit state t_j for any $j < i$, motivating the following two propositions:

Proposition 1: The expected number of bits sent over the network to transmit a message of size M with failure rate λ and packet size P is:

$$M^* = M[1 \div (1-\lambda)^2 + \varepsilon \div (P-P\lambda)] \quad \mathbf{(4)}$$

With this analysis, we employ our simple model to estimate the expected throughput as a function of the failure rate, packet size, and bandwidth:

$$T(\lambda, P, B) = (1-\lambda) B \div [(Q+A)[1 \div (1-\lambda) + \varepsilon \div P]] \quad \mathbf{(5)}$$

In fact we can say more about this estimation, see Proposition 2.

Proposition 2: For a workload of W queries, T(λ, P, B) is a good estimate for the expected throughput when average total message size is M, where M = Q + A. In particular:

$$T(\lambda, P, B) \leq \text{Expected Throughput} \leq T(\lambda, P, B) + O(1 \div (WM^2)) \quad \mathbf{(6)}$$

Proof: First define μ to be the random variable representing the total number of bytes transmitted to finish the workload. Using Proposition 1, $E[\mu] = WM^*$. Now note that we always have $\mu > 0$, and the function $F(\mu) = 1/\mu$ is convex in this range. This allows us to use Jensen's inequality [Folland] to state:

$$\text{Expected Throughput} = E[B \div \mu] = B\,E[\Phi(\mu)] \geq B\,\Phi(E[\mu]) = T(\lambda, P, B) \quad \textbf{(7)}$$

Proving that T is a lower bound. To prove the upper bound, we use the Taylor expansion of Φ around the point WM^*. Denoting the minimum number of bytes that must be transmitted to complete the workload by μ_{min} we can find a function $\alpha(\lambda, P)$ so that the following holds when $x > \mu_{min}$

$$\Phi(x) \leq 1 \div WM^* - (x - WM^*) \div (WM^*)^2 + \alpha(\lambda, P)\,(x - WM^*)^2 \div (WM^*)^3 \quad \textbf{(8)}$$

Now write

$$\text{Expected Throughput} = B\,E[\Phi(\mu)] = B \sum \Phi(i)\Pr[\mu = i] \quad \textbf{(9)}$$

$$\begin{aligned} &\leq B \div (WM^*) - \sum (i - WM^*) \div (WM^{*2})\Pr[\mu = i] \\ &\quad + \alpha(\lambda, P)\,\Sigma\,(I - WM^*)^2 \div (WM^*)^3 \Pr[\mu = i] \\ &\leq T(\lambda, P, B) + \alpha(\lambda, P)\,BW\,\mathrm{Var}[\mu] \div (WM^*)^3 \\ &= T(\lambda, P, B) + \alpha(\lambda, P)\,BW^2M\,\mathrm{Var}[p] \div (WM^*)^3 \\ &= T(\lambda, P, B) + O(1 \div (WM^2)) \end{aligned}$$

Where p is a random variable denoting the number of bytes needed to transmit a single packet. This completes the proof of proposition 2.

3.3 Implications of the Model

This formula has several intuitive implications, and can be used to quantify our basic thesis that when bandwidth is limited, an encoding mechanism that transmits fewer bytes results in a higher throughput. Inspection of the formula for $T(\lambda, P, B)$ leads to the following basic observation: The throughput bound increases as a function of bandwidth, larger packet size, and reduced packet loss rate.

We now use these throughput estimates to study the data reported in Section 2. Figures 6-8 plot throughput estimates on the TPC-H query workload using XML, Binary, ZIP-Binary, Zip-XML, XMill-XML. For these figures, we used the average message sizes (request plus esponse) for the 21 TPC-H queries. These are as follows: for the XML formatter is 1.65 MB, for the Binary formatter is 0.54 MB, for the Zip-XML formatter is 0.22 MB, for the Zip-Binary is 0.21 MB, and for the XMill-XML is 0.17 MB. These plots serve two purposes: First, they show how the throughput bound varies over realistic choices of parameter values. Second, they quantify the benefit of XMill-XML format in a variety of realistic settings.

Figure 6 shows the theoretical upper bounds on throughput for a workload of random TPC-H queries as a function of bandwidth to the server. The bandwidth varies from 56Kbps to 1Gbps, and both x-axes and y-axes use a log scale. Because the average message size is the same for TCP and HTTP channels, only the TCP data are displayed. This figure assumes each packet is eight kilobytes, P = 8K, and each acknowledgement packet is one kilobyte, ε = 1K. In Figure 6, XMill-XML encoder provides substantial performance improvement: its throughput is 270 times higher than that of the binary channel (and 800 times higher than the XML encoder).

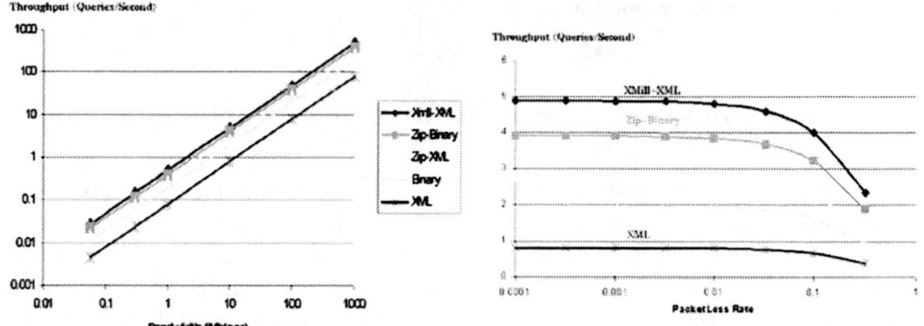

Fig. 6. Throughput estimates as a function of server bandwidth for a packet loss rate of 0.01%

Fig. 7. Throughput estimates as a function of packet loss rate for 10 Mbps link

Figure 7 shows the throughput as a function of the packet loss rate when the server's network bandwidth is limited to 10 Mbps. Once again, XMill-XML provides a higher throughput because it tansmits fewer bytes, i.e., packets. This figure also shows that while performance improves with increased reliability, the improvement is marginal with loss rates less than 10%. For example, as we reduce the packet loss rate from 10% to 0.01%, the through put improves 21%.

Finally we studied the impact of packet size on throughput. This study assumes the packet loss rate is independent of the packet size. (The models can be extended to remove this assumption.) Figure 8 shows the throughput of the alternative communication formatters assuming a 10 Mbps connection to the server and a 0.01 packet loss rate. The obtained results demonstrate a higher throughput with a larger packet size. This is because the number of acknowledgements and retransmissions are reduced with larger packet sizes.

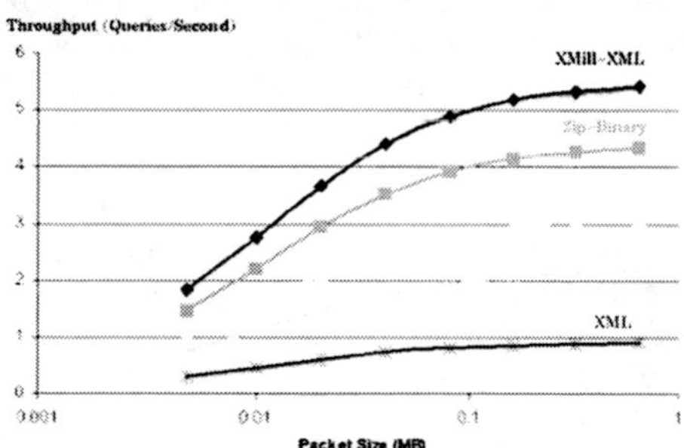

Fig. 8. Throughput as a function of packet size for a 10 Mbps link and a 0.01% retransmission rate

Collectively, these figures make the following observation: when a fixed amount of bandwidth is available to a server, one may increase system throughput by either increasing bandwidth, decreasing message size, or a combination of these two options. For the query workload given by the TPC-H queries, compressing XML messages improves throughput significantly. Furthermore, these savings can be exploited by reconfiguring existing applications to use a new compressed XML formatter with the communication channel.

4 Conclusion and Future Research Directions

This paper presents a performance study of XML and Binary formatters supported by Microsoft .NET (Beta 2) and the role of compression to reduce the number of transmitted bytes. The obtained results demonstrate a tradeoff between response time and throughput. XMill compressed XML messages might be smaller than compressed Binary messages, resulting in a higher throughput for a shared network with a fixed bandwidth. However, this might result in a higher response time depending on the overhead of compression and network characteristics, see [Ghandeharizadeh et. al.].

As a future research direction, we intend to investigate a dynamic framework that decides between XML and compressed XML at run-time. The objective would be to develop a framework that adjusts itself to the evolving characteristics of an environment and the target application, maximizing system performance when XML is essential. It would choose between the alternative compression schemes, namely, Zip versus XMill, when bandwidth is scarce. To render intelligent decisions, it considers the performance requirements of a target application, the amount of physical memory, the network characteristics, and the message size. If the network bandwidth is scarce then it must employ a compression scheme. If the message size is large (larger than 1 megabyte) then it should employ XMill.

References

1. Box, D., Ehnebuske, D., Kakivaya, G. Layman, A., Mendelsohn, N., Nielsen, H. F., Thatte, S., and Winer, D. Simple Object Access Protocol (SOAP) 1.1 *W3C Note 08,* May 2000.
2. Fielding R. T., J. Gettys, J. Mogul, H. Nielsen, L. Masinter, P. Leach, T. Berners-Lee. Hypertext Transfer Protocol – HTTP/1.1. *W3C RFC 2616,* June 1999.
3. Folland, G. B. *Real Analysis: Modern Techniques and Their Applications* Wiley-Interscience, 1999.
4. Ghandeharizadeh S., C. Papadopoulos, M. Cai and K. Chintalapudi. Performance of Networked XML-Driven Cooperative Applications. Submitted for publication.
5. Iyer B., and D. Wilhite. Data Compression Support in Databases. In Proceedings of the 20th International Conference on Very Large Data Bases, 1994.
6. Liefke H., and D. Suciu. XMill: An Efficient Compressor for XML Data. University of Pennsylvania Technical Report MSCIS -99-26. M.
7. Poess, M., and C. Floyd. New TPC Benchmarks for Decision Support and Web Commerce. In ACM SIGMOD Record, Volume 29, Number 4, December 2000.
8. Postel, J. Transmission Control Protocol. *Request for Comments 793*, September 1981.
9. Ziv, J., and A. Lempel. A Universal Algorithm for Sequential Data Compression. *IEEE Trans. Inform. Theory 23*, 3 (May), 337-343, 1977.

Capturing Semantics in HTML Documents

Mengchi Liu

School of Computer Science, Carleton University
Ottawa, Ontario K1S 5B6, Canada
mengchi@scs.carleton.ca

Abstract. Most documents available over the web confirm to the HTML specification. They are intended to be human readable through a web browser and thus are constructed following some common conventions. Based on such common conventions, the Conceptual Model for HTML was proposed recently to automatically capture the hierarchical structure within web documents. However, certain key semantic information about the contents in the documents, which are obvious to human, are often omitted. As a result, web data processing, manipulation and integration are still quite difficult. In this paper, we discuss how to extend the Conceptual Model for HTML to capture the intended semantics of the HTML documents. We show that with the new constructs introduced, using an Intelligent Wrapper, and limited human interaction, semantics can be transferred from human into the Extended Conceptual Model so that further meaningful processing, manipulation and integration of web documents become possible.

1 Introduction

With the ever-growing popularity of the World Wide Web, the Internet has become a major source for various kinds of information. How to make meaningful processing, manipulation and integration and provide semantically correct answers has become a major research issue.

Several different approaches have been exploited to retrieve information from the web: using information retrieval techniques to identify predefined concepts, extracting structure in documents based on formatting information [1,9,11,12,16], or focusing on reconstructing the web documents using wrappers, and developing powerful query languages [1,2,3,6,13]. Other proposals use database techniques and tools to manage web data, as found in [2,7,10], which discuss approaches based on ER models, SQL, relational algebra and other database techniques. For a survey see [8].

These various approaches reveal the same fact: the need for capturing the structure and semantics about the information over the web. Most web documents are human-oriented. They don't support explicit structure and semantics within the documents. However, they normally follow some common conventions and often exhibit some hierarchical structure. Based on such common conventions, the Conceptual Model for HTML was proposed to automatically capture

R. Cicchetti et al. (Eds.): DEXA 2002, LNCS 2453, pp. 103–112, 2002.

the hierarchical structure within the web document with a few simple constructs in [13]. It provides a simple way to describe web documents at a high level close to human visualization. However it is still not sufficient as a basis for further semantics-based processing as certain key semantic information about the contents, which are obvious to human, are often omitted in the documents. The constructs provided in the Conceptual Model are too simple and the semantic information if any cannot be expressed naturally. In particular, tuple-like information and lists are all represented as lists, which causes some ambiguity in both object notion and relationships between objects. Furthermore, table is the most used construct in HTML documents for presenting complicated information in a simply way. However, in the Conceptual Model, tables are converted into nested lists, which can be quite complicated, but neither natural nor informative.

In this paper, we discuss how to extend the Conceptual Model for HTML to capture both structural and semantic information in HTML documents. We show that with the new constructs introduced, using an Intelligent Wrapper, and limited human interaction, semantics can be transferred from human into the Extended Conceptual Model so that further meaningful processing, manipulation and integration of web documents become possible.

The rest of the paper is organized as follows. In section 2, we discuss how to extend the Conceptual Model. In section 3, we discuss how the Extended Conceptual Model is used in our Web Query and Inference System. Finally, we summarize and point out further research issues.

2 Extending the Conceptual Model for HTML

The purpose of models is not to fit the data but to sharpen the questions [15]. In databases we distinguish attributes from values and we simply use attributes to query the database even though they are deeply nested. For web documents, if we can identify attributes, then we can query web documents in the same way. This is the idea behind the Conceptual Model for HTML in [13], which provides a simple way to represent the complex hierarchical structure within web documents using attribute and value pairs, lists, etc.

However, the objects in the Conceptual Model may still not be meaningful. Consider a simplified web document shown in Figure 1. It is about the people in the Department of Computer Science and is quite meaningful to human. It is represented in the Conceptual Model as follows:

$$\begin{aligned} People \Rightarrow \{ & \{Anne, Lecturer, B200, 520\text{-}2500, Anne@cs.abc.ca\} \\ & \{Gary, Professor, B210, 520\text{-}2600, gary@cs.abc.ca\}, \\ & \{John, Professor, B190, 520\text{-}2400, john@cs.abc.ca\}, \\ & \{Mark, Student, B170, 520\text{-}2300, mark@cs.abc.ca\}, \\ & \{Mary, Staff, B130, 520\text{-}2100, mary@cs.abc.ca\}, \\ & \{Tony, Professor, B150, 520\text{-}2200, tony@cs.abc.ca\}\} \end{aligned}$$

where *People* is an attribute and the list after ⇒ is its value. The list consists of four nested lists as well.

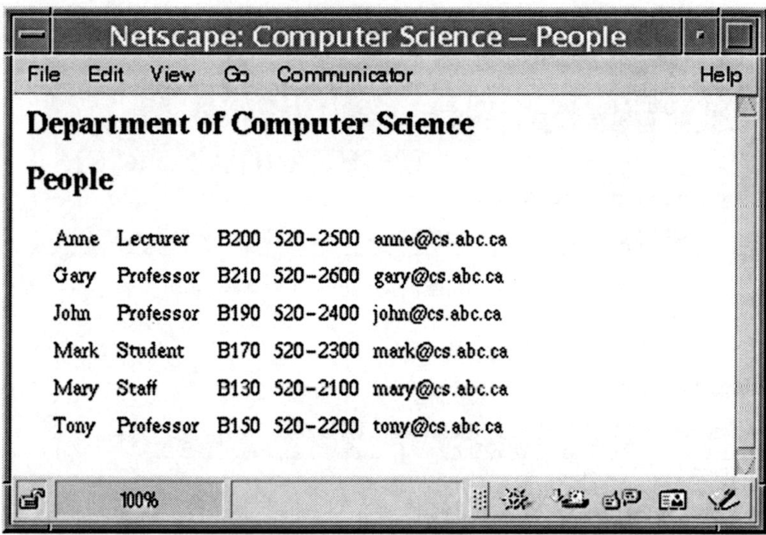

Fig. 1. Sample Document

In databases, lists are normally used to represent sequences of similar objects, while tuples are normally used to represent different aspects of similar objects. Using lists for tuples loses some semantic information and is an obvious deficiency of the model. The above object is better represented as follows:

$$
\begin{aligned}
People \Rightarrow \{ & [Anne, Lecturer, B200, 520\text{-}2500, Anne@cs.abc.ca], \\
& [Gary, Professor, B210, 520\text{-}2600, gary@cs.abc.ca], \\
& [John, Professor, B190, 520\text{-}2400, john@cs.abc.ca], \\
& [Mark, Student, B170, 520\text{-}2300, mark@cs.abc.ca], \\
& [Mary, Staff, B130, 520\text{-}2100, mary@cs.abc.ca], \\
& [Tony, Professor, B150, 520\text{-}2200, tony@cs.abc.ca]\}
\end{aligned}
$$

In this way, we know at least that the data items in a tuple represent some aspect of a person and there are six people altogether and this view is close to what we see in Figure 1. Thus, our first extension is to add tuple construct to the Conceptual Model.

For another example, consider part of the latest DBLP bibliography server of Michael Ley at *www.informatik.uni-trier.de/~ley/db* shown in Figure 2. Its representation with the new tuple construct is shown in Figure 3 where a_1, b_1, etc. are simplified URLs to fit in the paper.

Consider again the sample document in Figure 1. If we want to find all people using a query, then we can use the attribute *People* to get what we want. In other words, *People* is the semantic information that describes the contents in the document and can be used to interpret or query the document. However, if we want information about individual person such as office, phone number, or email address, we do not have any semantic information to use in our queries.

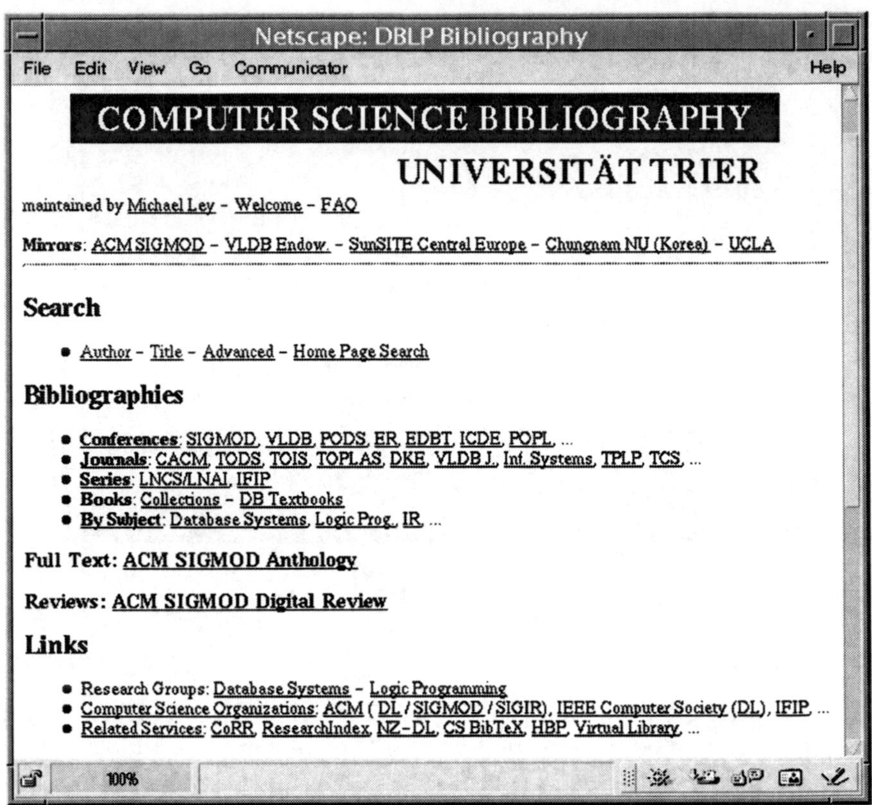

Fig. 2. DBLP Bibliography Web Page

What we can do is to transfer human knowledge to the Conceptual Model. However, the Conceptual Model does not have proper constructs that can be used to represent such semantic information.

In databases, a list of tuples is a table and the schema of the table is the most important part for table queries and is normally separated from the table. What we are lacking in the above example is just the schema. Unlike in databases, if we want to add schema for a table, the schema should not be separated from the table. Instead, the schema should be kept together with the table so that the system can use it to interpret data, just like the element tags and attribute names in XML [4].

Thus, our second extension to the Conceptual Model is the notion of table. We use $\{...\}^T$ to represent a table of tuples and the first tuple is the schema of the table and we use $[...]^S$ to represent this tuple so that it can be distinguished from ordinary tuples.

With these new constructs and knowledge transfer from human, the above object can be represented meaningfully as follows:

[
...
Title ⇒*DBLP Bibliography*,
Search ⇒ {*Author*$\langle a_1 \rangle$, *Title*$\langle a_2 \rangle$, *Advanced*$\langle a_3 \rangle$, *Home Page Search*$\langle a_4 \rangle$},
Bibliographies ⇒ [
    Conferences$\langle b_1 \rangle$ ⇒{*SIGMOD*$\langle b_{11} \rangle$, *VLDB*$\langle b_{12} \rangle$, *PODS*$\langle b_{13} \rangle$, ...},
    Journals$\langle b_2 \rangle$ ⇒{*CACM*$\langle b_{21} \rangle$, *TODS*$\langle b_{22} \rangle$, *TOIS*$\langle b_{23} \rangle$, ... },
    Series$\langle b_3 \rangle$ ⇒{*LNCS/LNAI*$\langle b_{41} \rangle$, *DISDBIS*$\langle b_{42} \rangle$},
    Books ⇒{*Collections*$\langle b_{51} \rangle$, *DB Textbook*$\langle b_{52} \rangle$},
    By Subjects$\langle b_4 \rangle$ ⇒{*Database Systems*$\langle b_{61} \rangle$, *Logic Prog*$\langle b_{62} \rangle$, *IR*$\langle b_{63} \rangle$},
  ]
Full Text ⇒*ACM SIGMOD Anthology*$\langle c_1 \rangle$,
Reviews ⇒*ACM SIGMOD Digital Review*$\langle c_2 \rangle$,
Links ⇒ [
    Research Groups ⇒{*Database Systems*$\langle d1 \rangle$, *Logic Programming*$\langle d2 \rangle$},
    Computer Science Organization$\langle e_1 \rangle$ ⇒{
        ACM$\langle e_{11} \rangle$ (*DL*$\langle e_{12} \rangle$, *SIGMOD*$\langle e_{13} \rangle$, *SIGIR* $\langle e_{14} \rangle$),
        IEEE Computer Society$\langle e_{15} \rangle$(*DL*$\langle e_{16} \rangle$)}
    Related Services $\langle f_1 \rangle$ ⇒{
        CoRR$\langle f_{11} \rangle$, *Research Index*$\langle f_{12} \rangle$, *NZ-DL*$\langle f_{13} \rangle$,
        CS BibTex$\langle f_{14} \rangle$, *HBP*$\langle f_{15} \rangle$, *Virtual Library* $\langle f_{16} \rangle$}
  ]
  ...
]

Fig. 3. DBLP Web Object with Simplified URLs

People ⇒{[**Name**, **Position**, **Office** , **Phone**, **Email**]^S
[*Anne*, *Lecturer*, *B200*, *520-2500*, *Anne@cs.abc.ca*],
[*John*, *Professor*, *B190*, *520-2400*, *john@cs.abc.ca*],
[*Gary*, *Professor*, *B210*, *520-2600*, *gary@cs.abc.ca*],
[*Mark*, *Student*, *B170*, *520-2300*, *mark@cs.abc.ca*],
[*Mary*, *Staff*, *B130*, *520-2100*, *mary@cs.abc.ca*],
[*Tony*, *Professor*, *B150*, *520-2200*, *tony@cs.abc.ca*]}^{T}

Sometimes, the semantic information may be present in the table already. Consider another web document shown in Figure 4. This document has complete semantic information about the data and its representation is the same as the table shown above.

Often, we may find web documents that contain partial semantic information. Consider the web document shown in Figure 5. This document is similar to the previous one but some semantic information is missing. With our table construct, we can capture partial information as follows so that rooms are made for knowledge transfer:

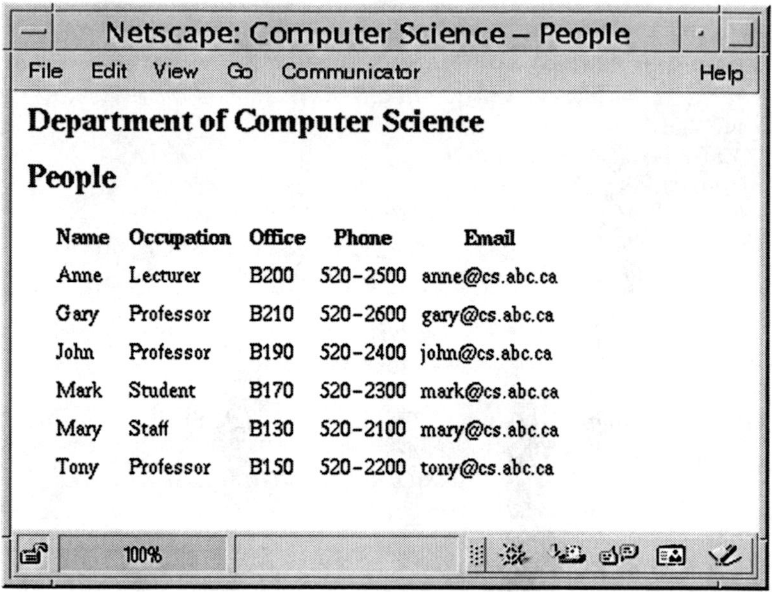

Fig. 4. Sample Document 2

$$
\begin{array}{lllllll}
\textit{People} \Rightarrow \{ & [\quad , & \quad , & \textbf{Office}, & \textbf{Phone}, & \textbf{Email} &]^S \\
 & [\textit{Anne}, & \textit{Lecturer}, & \textit{B200}, & \textit{520-2500}, & \textit{Anne@cs.abc.ca} &] \\
 & [\textit{Gary}, & \textit{Professor}, & \textit{B210}, & \textit{520-2600}, & \textit{gary@cs.abc.ca} &], \\
 & [\textit{John}, & \textit{Professor}, & \textit{B190}, & \textit{520-2400}, & \textit{john@cs.abc.ca} &], \\
 & [\textit{Mark}, & \textit{Student}, & \textit{B170}, & \textit{520-2300}, & \textit{mark@cs.abc.ca} &], \\
 & [\textit{Mary}, & \textit{Staff}, & \textit{B130}, & \textit{520-2100}, & \textit{mary@cs.abc.ca} &], \\
 & [\textit{Tony}, & \textit{Professor}, & \textit{B150}, & \textit{520-2200}, & \textit{tony@cs.abc.ca} &]\}^T
\end{array}
$$

With the semantic information available, we can query web documents as in databases. For example, if we want to get the complete information of Professor Tony, we can use the following XPath [5] like expression:

$$/People/\$Prof[Name \Rightarrow Tony,\ Occupation \Rightarrow Professor]$$

where *$Prof* is a variable that matches one tuple at a time that satisfies the selection condition in the tuple [*Name* ⇒ *Tony*, *Occupation* ⇒ *Professor*]. Similarly, if we want to get people who are not professor, we can use the following two expressions:

$$/People/\$Prof[Occupation \Rightarrow \$P],\ \$P \neq Professor$$

where *$Prof* still matches a tuple at a time and *$P* matches the occupation value of the tuple. Only the tuples that satisfies the second expression will be selected in the result.

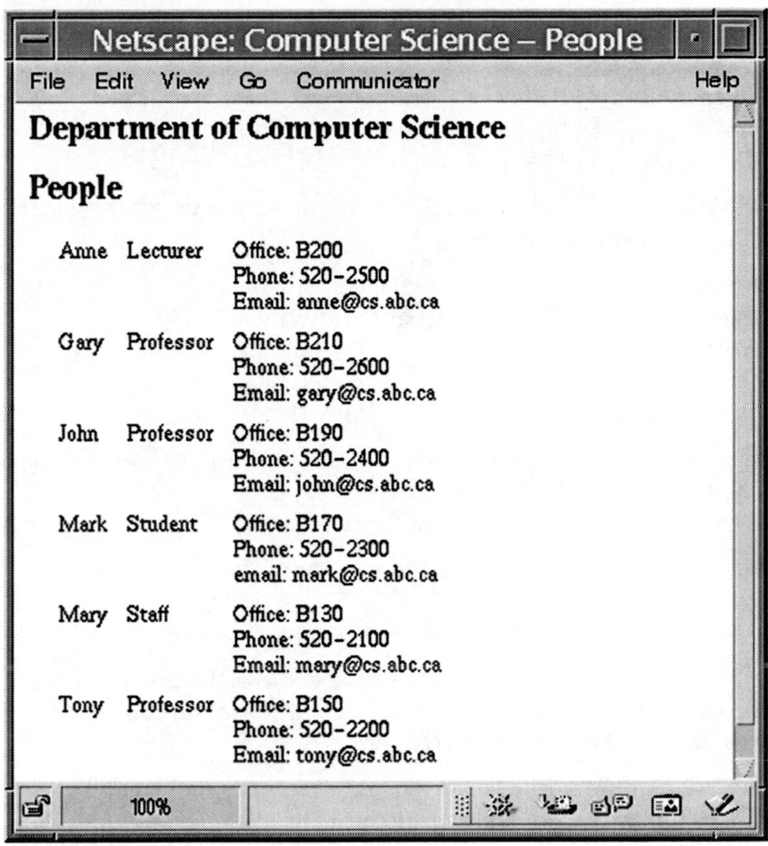

Fig. 5. Sample Document 3

For another example, if we simply want the email address of Professor Tony, then we can use the following expression:

$$/People/[Name \Rightarrow Tony,\ Occupation \Rightarrow Professor,\ Email \Rightarrow \$Email]$$

In fact, table is the most used construct of HTML. It is used for presenting complicated information in a simply way. With the introduction of tuple and table constructs, it is quite simple now to convert HTML documents into our Extended Conceptual Model. Consider the following table in HTML:

```
<table>
<caption align = top>Bear Sightings</caption>
<tr>
<td><br><th>Babies<th>Adults<th>Total
<tr><th>Northampton<td>2<td>4<td>6
<tr><th>Becket<td>5<td>22<td>27
<tr><th>Worthington<td>7<td>5<td>12
</table>
```

It is represented in the original Conceptual Model as follows:

Bear Sightings ⇒{
  Northampton⇒{*Babies* ⇒*2*, *Adults* ⇒*4*, *Total* ⇒*6* },
  Becket ⇒{*Babies* ⇒*5*, *Adults* ⇒*22*,*Total* ⇒*27*},
  Worthington ⇒{*Babies* ⇒*7*, *Adults* ⇒*5*, *Total* ⇒*12*}}

Its representation in the Extended Conceptual Model with semantic information *Place* added is shown below:

Bear Sightings ⇒{
  [**Place**, **Babies**, **Adults**, **Total**]^S,
  [*Northampton*, *2*, *4*, *6*],
  [*Becket*, *5*, *22*, *27*],
  [*Worthington*, *7*, *5*, *12*]}^{T}

With this new representation, we can ask for various questions about the table. The following are several examples:

Find the total number of bears at Northamption:

Bear Sightings/[Total ⇒$Total, Place ⇒Northampton]

Find how many more babies that Worthington has than Northampton:

Bear Sightings/[Babies ⇒$WBabies, Place ⇒Worthington]
Bear Sightings/[Babies ⇒$NBabies, Place ⇒Northampton]
$MoreBabies = $WBabies - $NBabies

In fact, we can use a rule-based language to query and construct the result. Due to space limitation, we omit the detail here.

3 Implementation

Based on the Extended Conceptual Model described above, we have implemented an HTML document query and inference system using Java. The system supports normal HTML document browsing like Internet Explorer and Netscape but not as powerful. However, it allows the user to view HTML documents in the Extended Conceptual Model, capture the semantic information in HTML documents, transfer knowledge into the Extended Conceptual Model representation, and perform query and inference based on such representation. The architecture of the system is shown in Figure 6.

The system is composed of three major components: Extended Conceptual Modeler, Intelligent Wrapper, and Query Processor.

The Extended Conceptual Modeler includes a syntactic Enforcement Interface. When the user accesses the web, it checks syntactical structures and automatically generates the Extended Conceptual Model representation of the HTML document, and send the output to the Intelligent Wrapper.

The user can then interact with the Intelligent Wrapper, and fill in the missing semantic information, if any. The result is stored in Local Data Repository for the Query Processor to use.

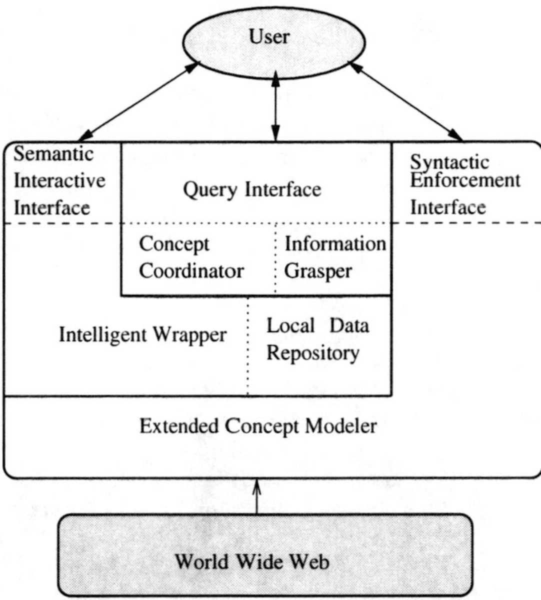

Fig. 6. System Architecture

The Query Processor consists of the Query Interface, Information Grasper, and Concept Coordinator. Information Grasper is responsible for retrieving objects from the Local Data Repository. Concept Coordinator manages concept categories and equivalent terms under each category. It initially stores some simple concept categories and terms and, allows the user to adjust them according to the application. When the user issues a query, the Query Interface contacts the Concept Coordinator for correct terms used in Local Data Repository and then load the objects from the Local Data Repository for query and inference processing. The result is returned to the user through the Query Interface.

4 Conclusion

In this paper, we have discussed our extension to the Conceptual Model for HTML with two important constructs that are common to advanced data models: tuple and table, in order to capture semantic information. We have also described our HTML document web query and Inference system that is based on the Extended Conceptual Model. We have showed that through the introduction of an Intelligent Wrapper, and with limited human interaction, the semantics that is missing in the web documents can be transferred from human into our Extended Conceptual Model and then used in queries and inferences. Thus we not only build a model which can express the semantics in web documents in a natural way, but also create a basis for further data manipulation and integration [14], where data are meaningful and can be interpreted by the system.

Currently, we are building an intelligent web search engine so that the user can obtain precise information in a meaningful way. The Extended Conceptual Model and the system implemented are used to gather data from the web for the project.

References

1. N. Ashish and C. Knoblock. Modeling Web Sources for Information Integration. In *Proc. Workshop on Management of Semistructured Data*, 1997.
2. P. Atzeni, G. Mecca, and P. Merialdo. Semistructured and structured data in the web: Going back and forth. In *Workshop on Management of Semistructured Data*, 1997.
3. C. Bornhvd. Semantic Metadata for the Integration of Web-Based Data for Electronic Commerce. In *International Workshop on Advance Issues of E-Commerce and Web-Based Information Systems*, 1999.
4. T. Bray, J. Paoli, and C. M. Sperberg-McQueen. Extensible Markup Language (XML) 1.0. *http://www.w3.org/TR/1998/REC-xml-19980210*, February 1998.
5. J. Clark and S. DeRose. XML Path Language (XPath) Version 1.0. *http://www.w3.org/TR/1999/REC-xpath-19991116*, November 2001.
6. M. Fernandez, D. Florescu, and A. Levy. A Query Language for a Web-Site Management System. *SIGMOD Record*, 26(3):4–11, 1997.
7. T. Fiebig, J. Weiss, and G. Moerkotte. Raw: A relational algebra for the web. *http://www.research.att.com/ suciu/workshop-paper/paper05.ps*, 1997.
8. D. Florescu, A. Levy, and A. Mendelzon. Database Techniques for the World-Wide Web: A Survey. *SIGMOD Record*, 27(3):59–74, 1998.
9. Hamme, Garcia-Molina, Cho, Aranha, and Crespo. Extracting Semistructured Information from the Web. In *Proceedings of Workshop on Management of Semistructured Data*, 1997.
10. V. Kashyap and M. Rusinkiewicz. Modeling and querying textual data using e-r model and sql. *http://citeseer.nj.nec.com/kashyap97modeling.html*, 1997.
11. C. A. Knoblock, S. Minton, J. L. Ambite, N. Ashish, P. J. Modi, I. Muslea, A. G. Philpot, and S. Tejada. Modeling Web Sources for Information Integration. In *Proceedings of the 15th National Conference on AI*, 1998.
12. M. Liu and T. W. Ling. A Data Model for Semistructured Data with Partial and Inconsistent Information. In *Proceedings of the International Conference on Advances in Database Technology (EDBT 2000)*, pages 317–331, Konstanz, Germany, March 27-31 2000. Springer-Verlag LNCS 1777.
13. M. Liu and T. W. Ling. A Conceptual Model and Rule-based Query Language for HTML. *World Wide Web Journal*, 4:49–77, 2001.
14. M. Liu and T. W. Ling. Towards semistructured data integration. In A. Dahanayake and W. Gerhard, editors, *Web-Enabled Systems Integration: Practice and Challenges*, chapter 2, pages 19–39. Idea Group Publishing, 2003.
15. P. O'neil and E. O'Neil. *Database Principles: Programming, and Performance.* Morga Kaufmann Publishers, 2 edition, 2000.
16. D. Smith and M. Lopez. Information extraction for semi-structured documents. In *Proceedings of Workshop on Management of Semistructured Data*, pages 225–238, 1997.

Assessment of Spatial Data Mining Tools for Integration into an Object-Oriented GIS (GIDB)

Roy Ladner and Fredrick E. Petry

Naval Research Laboratory
Digital Mapping Charting and Geodesy Analysis Program
Stennis Space Center, MS 39529 USA
(rladner,fpetry)@nrlssc.navy.mil

Abstract. A variety of data mining techniques are under evaluation on the spatial data of concern in our setting. We are planning to integrate a number of these techniques into our geospatial system (GIDB). Three approaches are under special consideration and are described in the paper. A COTS data mining system has been successfully used to develop predictive models of near-shore conditions such as wave height for naval amphibious operations. Attribute generalization was applied to seafloor data to obtain statements about conditions relevant to mine warfare. Finally an extension of association rule discovery applied to fuzzy spatial data that is under development is discussed.

1 Introduction

Data mining or knowledge discovery generally refers to a variety of techniques that have developed in the fields of databases, machine learning and pattern recognition. The intent is to uncover useful patterns and associations from large databases. We are concerned with applications of data mining to spatial and temporal data.

In this paper we describe the geospatial system that will be the source of the data we are attempting to enhance with data mining for a number of Naval planning applications. Then we describe our experiences with three diverse data mining techniques that we have found applicable to the spatial data of interest in our setting and summarize their potential for integration into an overall enhanced system.

2 Background

We are developing approaches for spatial data mining in an environment in which there is considerable concern about the development of ways for processing large amounts of spatio-temporal data especially of oceanographic and littoral regions and including meteorological information. Our plan is to integrate the data mining techniques into the geospatial system described below. The ultimate goal is to provide

R. Cicchetti et al. (Eds.): DEXA 2002, LNCS 2453, pp. 113–122, 2002.

knowledge-enhanced information to decision tools that will be used by US Navy and Marine planners.

The Digital Mapping, Charting and Geodesy Analysis Program (DMAP) at the Naval Research Laboratory has been actively involved in the development of a digital geospatial mapping and analysis system since 1994. This work started with the Geospatial Information Database (GIDB™), an object-oriented, CORBA-compliant spatial database capable of storing multiple data types from multiple sources. Data is accessible over the Internet via a Java Applet [3].

The GIDB includes an object-oriented data model, an object-oriented database management system (OODBMS) and various analysis tools. While the model provides the design of classes and hierarchies, the OODBMS provides an effective means of control and management of objects on disk such as locking, transaction control, etc. The OODBMS in use is Ozone, an open-source database management system. This has been beneficial in several aspects. Among these, access to the source code allows customization and there are no costly commercial database licensing fees on deployment. Spatial and temporal analysis tools include query interaction, multimedia support and map symbology support. Users can query the database by area-of-interest, time-of-interest, distance and attribute. For example, statistics and data plots can be generated to reflect wave height for a given span of time at an ocean sensor. Interfaces are implemented to afford compatibility with Arc/Info, Oracle 8i, Matlab, and others.

The object-oriented approach has been beneficial in dealing with complex spatial data, and it has also permitted integration of a variety of raster and vector data products in a common database. Some of the raster data include satellite and motion imagery, Compressed ARC Digitized Raster Graphics (CADRG), Controlled Image Base (CIB), jpeg and video. Vector data includes Vector Product Format (VPF) products from the National Imagery and Mapping Agency (NIMA), Shape, real-time and in-situ sensor data and Digital Terrain Elevation Data (DTED). The VPF data includes such NIMA products as Digital Nautical Chart (DNC), Vector Map (VMAP), Urban Vector Map (UVMAP), Digital Topographic Data Mission Specific Data Sets (DTOP MSDS), and Tactical Oceanographic Data (TOD).

Over the years, the system has been expanded to include a communications gateway that enables users to obtain data from a variety of data providers distributed over the Internet in addition to the GIDB. These providers include Fleet Numerical Meteorology and Oceanography Center (FNMOC), USGS, Digital Earth/NASA, and the Geography Network/ESRI. A significant FNMOC product is the Coupled Ocean/Atmosphere Mesoscale Prediction System (COAMPS) data. The atmospheric components of COAMPS are used operationally by the U.S. Navy for short-term numerical weather prediction for various regions around the world. Our communications gateway provides a convenient means for users to obtain COAMPS data and incorporate it with other vector and raster data in map form. The gateway establishes a well-defined interface that brings together such heterogeneous data for a common geo-referenced presentation to the user. An illustration of the interface for a typical data request is shown in Figure 1.

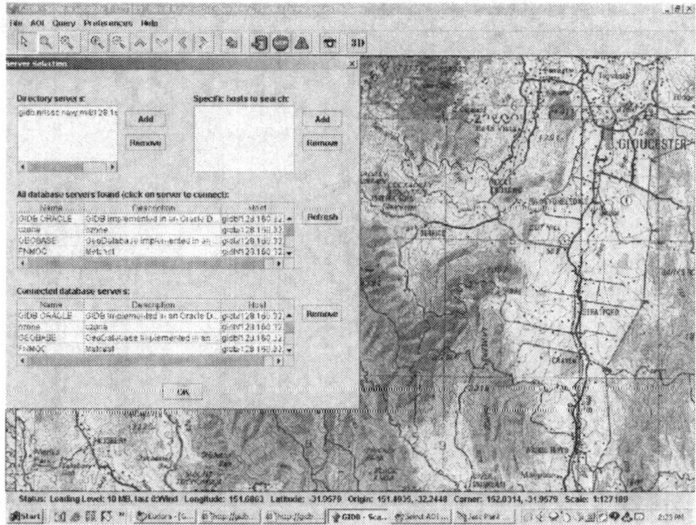

Fig. 1. The GIDB Interface.

3 Spatial Data Mining Techniques

3.1 Predictive Modeling

For this technique we used a COTS data mining system (the KXEN Knowledge Extraction Engines) based on the Support Vector (SV) approach. It is based on the VC (Vapnik-Chervonenkis) learning theory, which does not depend on dimensionality and can be applied to any function estimation problem [7].

The particular component we utilized is a regression algorithm, which builds predictive models. The support vector machine approach is an extension of the linear hyperplane classification of perceptrons to more complex surfaces. This is done by extending the measurement space so that it includes transformations of the raw variables. The distinct aspect of this approach is the score function called the margin. This is used to optimize the decision boundary between the classes such that it is likely to lead to the best possible generalization performance [5].

We have approximately 20 years of data observations of sea conditions at the Field Research Facility in Duck, North Carolina USA. Sensors record changing waves, winds, tides and currents on approximately an hourly basis. These are stored in the GIDB and were selectively used for the data mining experiments.

The application for which we wish to utilize this type of data is that of providing advisory information to tactical Naval planners for amphibious operations. One critical factor is the wave conditions near the beach for mine removal, landing craft operation, etc. In particular we considered wave height and wave periodicity. In doing this we were concerned with the ability to predict conditions that would jeopardize the mission. Thus we focus on prediction of the wave heights in the upper quartile of the recorded data. We needed to provide a qualified prediction as to

the recorded data. We needed to provide a qualified prediction as to whether the wave height would exceed a given operational capability for the equipment being planned for the mission as input by a user. For example based on prescribed operational requirements, the mission would have to be cancelled if the wave heights exceeded 1-½ meters.

For predicted wave heights we must consider two situations. The first is where we have overestimated wave heights. If a prediction is an overestimate that exceeds the specified limits, the operation might be erroneously scrubbed, thus missing an opportunity but not jeopardizing equipment or personnel.

On the other hand an underestimate might cause a planner to decide on continuing a mission in an unacceptable and potentially dangerous sea condition. This is clearly the more important error and the one presented in the table.

Training was done based on years 1999-2000 with a total of 13,591 observations. This model was then used to predict the wave heights for years 1993-1995 and 1997-1998. Data was not available for the entire year 1996. Consider the 1993 data in which there were 7773 observations (1943 in the upper quartile). In the upper quartile 1004 of these were underestimates (since very few are exact predictions in general we either have under or over estimates). The range of wave heights in the upper quartile was .60 - 2.0 meters. For the upper quartile, the average error for the underestimates was 24.7% and the average wave height of the underestimates was 0.95 meters. So the typical error in the underestimate was 0.27 meters in this critical range. This error was deemed to be generally acceptable although this is of course situation dependent.

Table 1. Duck, NC Wave Height Predictions

Year	Number of Observations	#Upper Quartile Under Estimate	Avg. Wave Height Under Estimate	Average % Under Estimate	Std. Dev
1993	7773	1004	0.95	24.75	0.19
1994	7735	625	0.92	24.86	0.16
1995	7767	876	0.94	29.79	0.20
1997	6162	1282	1.02	31.85	0.22
1998	6729	1461	1.06	32.10	0.22

3.2 Attribute Generalization

Both this technique of attribute-oriented induction and association rule generation are intended to provide a generalization or summarization of some potentially relevant aspects of the data being considered.

The attribute-oriented induction approach produces a generalized representation by either attribute removal or attribute generalization. After this step the processed data is aggregated by merging identical tuples in the database and counting the number of tuples merged to indicate significance [4]. Attributes are removed if there is no hierarchy for the attribute or if it can be expressed in terms of higher-level concepts of other attributes. Attribute generalization examines an attribute to ascertain if there are too large a number of distinct values (exceeding a given threshold). Then if a generalization hierarchy is available for this attribute, it is generalized and the common tuples merged.

We applied this technique to sea bottom data from 10 locations (such as areas in the Philippines, Mediterranean, Persian Gulf, etc.). Here the intended application was to characterize various sea bottom areas for the planning of a mine deployment/hunting mission. The spatial data was queried to formulate the files from which the attribute generalization was done. The basic query was on bottom sediment classification as this was the major characteristic of interest to experts. The data consisted of polygons of the bottom types as classified. Depth was an estimate, and depth and area were binned into three categories

Shown below in Table 2 is generalization of data from the Onslow Bay area. The value of "any" is the root of the concept hierarchy to which the corresponding tuples have been generalized.

Table 2. Generalization of Bottom Data from the Onslow Bay Area.

Area	Type	Depth	Count
any	pure sand	shallow	46
any	pure sand	deep	44
any	sandy mix	deep	26
small	sandy mix	shallow	15
mid	sandy mix	shallow	9
mid	pure sand	mid	1
mid	sandy mix	mid	1
small	sandy mix	mid	1

3.3 Association Rules for Fuzzy Spatial Data

Association rules capture the idea of certain data items commonly occurring together. For example an analysis of the soils and vegetation in a certain region might reveal that 30% of the total area has co-occurring sandy soil and scrub cover and for any sandy soil area, 75% of these area had scrub cover. Thus we can obtain the rule

$$Sandy\ soil \rightarrow Scrub\ cover \quad (1)$$

that could be used for planning and environmental decision makers. This rule is said to have a 75% degree of confidence and a 30% degree of support.

The process of generating rules requires the determination of the values of support and confidence and if a potential rule has values for these that exceed the user the user provided minimums it is called a strong rule [1]. Let R = { T_1, T_2, ...} be the results of a query that obtains the data of interest. To determine if there is a strong relation between values (possibly sets) A and B, the tuples in R must be examined and a count made of the number containing A and B where T_i contains A (B) if A (B) $\subseteq T_i$. Two measures are used to determine rules. First, the percentage of tuples that contain both A and B is called the <u>support</u> *s*. Second, if T_i contains A then it also contains B - called the <u>confidence</u> *c*. The Apriori algorithm [1] proceeds by first obtaining the sets of values (called itemsets) that satisfy the minimum support. It uses an iterative level-wise search where sets of k items are used to consider the set at the next level of k + 1 items. The final result is called the frequent itemsets. Then using the confidence value the strong association rules are extracted from the frequent itemsets

Now if the data we are interested in, as is typical of much spatial data [2], has uncertainty associated, we can model this using fuzzy sets [3]. So in general we will have fuzzy membership values associated to the tuples of R. The count to determine the support for finding frequent itemsets in the case of fuzzy data is developed by using the idea of the Σ count, which extends the ordinary concept of set cardinality to fuzzy sets [8]. Using this the fuzzy support count for the set A becomes:

$$FSC_R\,(A) = \Sigma\,\text{Count}\,(A) = \sum_j \mu_{ti}\,. \tag{2}$$

Finally to produce the association rules from the set of relevant data R retrieved from the spatial database we can now extend the ideas of fuzzy support and confidence as

$$FS = FSC_R(\,A \cup B\,)\,/\,|\,R\,|\,, \tag{3}$$

$$FC = FSC_R\,(\,A \cup B\,)\,/\;FSC_R\,(\,A\,)\,. \tag{4}$$

3.3.1 Example of Spatial Association Rules

We will consider an example that requires data mining on a spatial database to provide assistance in the logistical planning for a military operation. Assume that an area of operational interest has been divided into several zones (1, 2, etc.) and we would like to know some of the important relationships of relevant attributes in each zone to provide guidance in planning and selection of a zone for the particular mission. From this point of view small cities are of interest as they would have sufficient infrastructure but would not pose difficulties in which to operate, as would large cities. The major logistical concern is with transportation (railroads, highways, airfields) and terrain (soils, ground cover) within about 5 kilometers of the city.

The first step we must take to discovering rules that may be of interest in a given zone is to formulate a SQL query using the fuzzy function NEAR (Figure 2) to represent those objects within about 5 kilometers of the cities. Additionally we use the fuzzy function of Figure 3 to select the cities with a SMALL population.

Sample SQL.

```
SELECT City C, Road R, Railroad RR, Airstrip A,
Terrain T
```

```
FROM Area of Interest Zone 1

WHERE {NEAR (C.loc, R.loc), NEAR (C.loc, RR.loc),

     NEAR (C.loc, A.loc), NEAR (C.loc, T.loc)}

and C.pop = SMALL

AT Threshold Levels = .80, .75, .70
```

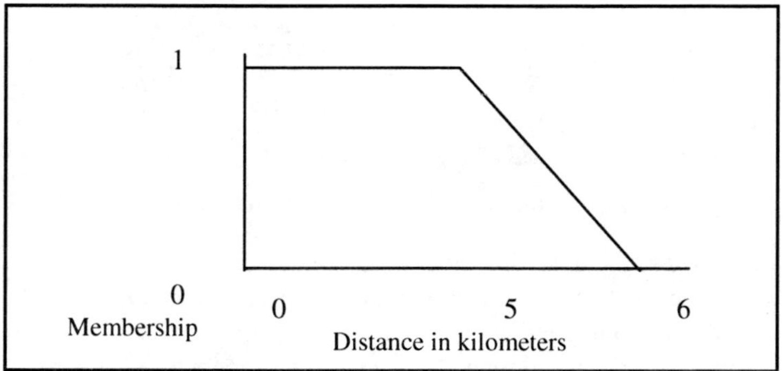

Fig. 2. Fuzzy Membership Function for Distance.

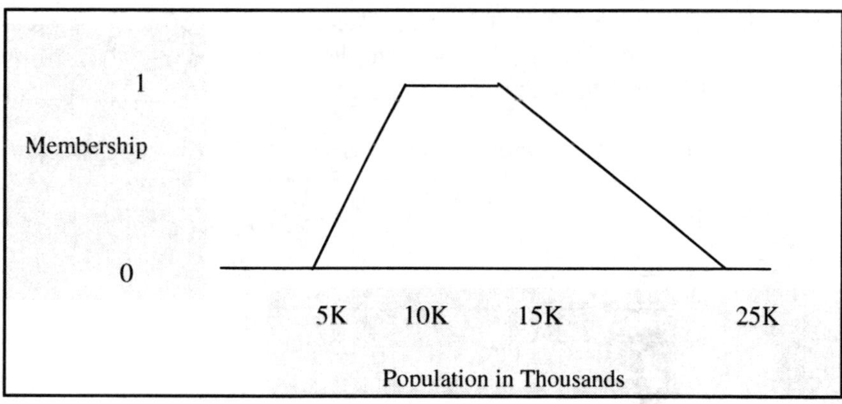

Fig. 3. Fuzzy Membership Function for Small City.

We evaluate for each city in a selected zone the locations of roads, railroads and airstrips using the NEAR fuzzy function. The terrain attribute value is produced by evaluation of various factors such as average soil conditions (e.g. firm, marshy), relief (e.g. flat, hilly), coverage (fields, woods), etc. These subjective evaluations are then combined into one membership value, which is used to provide a linguistic label based on fuzzy functions for these. Note that the evaluation for terms such as "good" can be context dependent. For logistical purposes an open and flat terrain is suitable whereas for an infiltration operation a woody and hilly situation would be desirable.

Each attribute value in the intermediate relation then has a degree of membership. The three threshold levels in the query are specified for the NEAR, SMALL and the terrain memberships. The final relation R is formulated based on the thresholds and the tuple membership computed as a minimum of the individual memberships from the intermediate relation.

Table 3. The Final Result of the Example Query – R.

City	Roads	Railroads	Airstrips	Terrain	μ_t
A	Rte.10	RRx	None	Good	0.89
B	{Rte.5,Rte.10}	None	A2	Fair	0.79
F	Rte.6	RRx	None	Good	0.92
...	...	...	...	...	...

In R the value 'None' indicates for the attribute that no value was found NEAR – within the five kilometers. For such values no membership value is assigned and so μ_t is just based on the non-null attribute values in the particular tuple.

Now in the next step of data mining we generate the frequent itemsets from R using the fuzzy support count. At the first level for itemsets of size 1 (k=1), airstrips are not found since they do not occur often enough in R to yield a fuzzy support count above the minimum support count that was pre-specified. The level k=2 itemsets are generated from the frequent level 1 itemsets. Here only two of these possibilities exceed the minimum support and none above this level, i.e. k=3 or higher. This gives us the following table of frequent itemsets:

Table 4. The Frequent Itemsets Found for the Example.

k	Frequent Itemsets	Fuzzy Support-Count
1	{Road Near}	11.3
1	{Good Terrain}	10.5
1	{Railroad Near}	8.7
2	{Road Near, Good Terrain}	9.5
2	{Good Terrain, Railroad Near}	7.2

From this table of frequent itemsets we can extract various rules and their confidence. Rules will not be output unless they are strong – satisfy both minimum support and confidence. A rule produced from a frequent itemset satisfies minimum support by the manner in which frequent itemsets are generated, so it only necessary to use the fuzzy support counts from the table to compute the confidence. The small city clause that will appear in all extracted rules arises because this was the general condition that selected all of the tuples that appeared in query result R from which the frequent itemsets were generated.

Let us assume for this case that the minimum confidence specified was 85%. So, for example, one possible rule that can be extracted from the frequent itemsets in Table 4 is:

> If C is a small <u>city</u> and has good <u>terrain</u> nearby then there is a <u>road</u> nearby with 90% confidence.

Since the fuzzy support count for {Good Terrain} is 10.5 and the level 2 itemset {Road Near, Good Terrain} has a fuzzy support count of 9.5, the confidence for the rule is 9.5 / 10.5 or 90%. This is above the minimum confidence of 85%, so the rule is strong and will be an output of the data mining process.

If we had specified a lower minimum confidence such as 80% we could extract (among others) the rule:

> If C is a small <u>city</u> and has a <u>railroad</u> nearby then there is good <u>terrain</u> nearby with 83% confidence.

Since the fuzzy support count for {Railroad Near} and {Railroad Near, Good Terrain} are 8.7 and 7.2, the confidence is 7.2 / 8.7 or 83% and so this rule is also output.

4 Conclusions

We have found the data mining approaches we have described to be basically satisfactory in our preliminary evaluations. We are continuing with more extensive testing and evaluation with various sets of spatio-temporal data that are available to us.

There are three aspects of integrating these and similar data mining tools within our GIDB system. The first is the specification of the query to obtain the relevant data for the particular data mining tool(s) to be applied. As seen in some of our examples, for user query specification we should provide an interface that allows the query to be generated from selection of the data as it is displayed. Also as in the case of association rules, but applicable to other approaches as well, we must be able to deal with fuzzy function specification for the query. Considerable work has appeared that we can utilize for this in fuzzy set research [8]. Next for most techniques the user must provide some parameters and values for the techniques such as hierarchies in attribute generalization or support and confidence thresholds for association rule generation. Finally and related to the parameters specification is the issue of appropriate display of results to the user. This is more complex for the domain of spatial data. This is of concern not only for the final results but also based on the common assumption that the data mining will be an iterative process in which a user may be changing the input parameters and specifications as they obtain various preliminary results.

Acknowledgements

We would like to thank the Naval Research Laboratory's Base Program, Program Element No. 0602435N for sponsoring this research.

References

1. Agrawal R, Imielinski T, and Swami A, 1993, Mining Association Rules between sets of items in large databases. In *Proceedings of the 1993 ACM-SIGMOD International Conference on Management of Data.* New York, NY, ACM Press:207-216.
2. Burrough P, and Frank A (eds.), 1996 *Geographic Objects with Indeterminate Boundaries,* GISDATA Series Vol. 2, London, UK , Taylor and Francis.
3. Chung M, Wilson R, Ladner R, Lovitt T, Cobb M, Abdelguerfi M, and Shaw K, 2001 TheGeospatial Information Distribution System (GIDS). In Chaudhri A and Zicari R (eds) *Succeeding with Object Databases.* New York, NY, Wiley and Sons:357-378.
3. M. Cobb, F. Petry and V. Robinson (2000), Special Issue: Uncertainty in Geographic Information Systems and Spatial Data, *Fuzzy Sets and Systems*, 113, #1.
4. Han J, and Kamber M 2000 *Data Mining: Concepts and Techniques.* San Diego, CA Academic Press.
5. Hand D, Mannila H, and Smyth P, 2001, *Principles of Data Mining.* Cambridge, MA, MIT Press.
6. Lu W, Han J, and Ooi B, 1993, Discovery of general knowledge in large spatial databases. In *Proceedings of Far East Workshop Geographic Information Systems.* Singapore, World Scientific Press: 275-289.
7. Vapnik V, 1995, *The Nature of Statistical Learning Theory.* Berlin, GDR, Springer-Verlag.
8. Yen J, and Langari R, 1999, *Fuzzy Logic: Intelligence, Control and Information.* Upper Saddle River, NJ, Prentice Hall.

A Model and a Toolkit for Supporting Incremental Data Warehouse Construction

Paolo Naggar[1], Luigi Pontieri[2], Mariella Pupo[3], Giorgio Terracina[4], and Emanuela Virardi[1]

[1] CM Sistemi - Via Nazario Sauro 1, 00100 Roma, Italy
[2] ISI-CNR - Via P. Bucci, 87036 Arcavacata di Rende (CS) Italy
[3] CM Sistemi Sud - Via Galluppi 87100 Cosenza, Italy
[4] DIMET - Università degli Studi "Mediterranea" di Reggio Calabria Via Graziella, Località Feo di Vito, 89100 Reggio Calabria, Italy
{paolo.naggar, mariella.pupo, emanuela.virardi}@gruppocm.it, pontieri@isi.cs.cnr.it, terracina@ing.unirc.it

Abstract. The design of data warehouse is a very relevant issue in supporting the management decisional processes and data analysis. While the design and maintenance of data warehouses are difficult tasks, enterprise managements are increasingly asking for tools capable to support designers in all the activities involving data warehouse construction. In this context it is mandatory to provide designers with the capability to incrementally define data warehouse components. In this paper we propose a conceptual model, called Multidimensional Fact Network (MFN), allowing to incrementally define data marts and a toolkit, called AURORA, based on MFN and providing a comprehensive set of data warehouse design tools.

1 Introduction

In the last years data warehouses have been recognized by a large number of organizations as a solution for exploiting the large quantity of information stored in their operational systems and for improving their decisional processes. A data warehouse collects data coming from various sources, integrated and restructured, in order to support On Line Analytical Processes (OLAP), typically based on the multidimensional paradigm.

The design and maintenance of data warehouses is a difficult task involving challenging issues in the database research. However, since the availability of a data warehouse has been demonstrated to be a key issue for improving both the management decisional processes and data analysis, enterprise managements are increasingly asking for tools capable to support designers in all the activities involving the data warehouse construction.

The most important activities in this context are: *(i)* the integration of the information stored in the enterprise databases, *(ii)* the definition of the data marts and *(iii)* the application of knowledge discovery techniques and workflow tools on constructed data marts. While *(i)* and *(iii)* may be obtained by applying quite standardized techniques, the definition of the data marts is strictly

R. Cicchetti et al. (Eds.): DEXA 2002, LNCS 2453, pp. 123–132, 2002.

related to both the enterprise decisional processes and the kind of analysis to be performed on available data. Moreover, the analysis targets may change quite frequently over time.

These considerations make it clear the necessity to provide designers with tools allowing to incrementally define data warehouse components. Indeed, this seems to be the only way to face frequent changings in the enterprise data warehouse desiderata.

In this paper we propose a conceptual model, called Multidimensional Fact Network (MFN), allowing to both incrementally define data marts and produce networks of multidimensional data marts. Data marts in a network might be obtained either from enterprise data or they can be the result of (possibly complex) transformations on other, previously defined, data marts. MFN is the core of a toolkit, called AURORA [1,2], intended to support designers in all the activities related to the construction and exploitation of a data warehouse, i.e. enterprise data integration, data mart construction and knowledge discovery.

Decision support analysis processes in a data warehouse are typically carried out by exploiting the OLAP paradigm [4], where data are represented in a multidimensional perspective and are queried by means of easy-to-use interactive operations. Since the structure of the multidimensional space imposes strict limitations to the set of queries that may be expressed, the conceptual design of a multidimensional database is a critical task. Several proposals for handling multidimensional data have been presented in the literature. In particular, some of them [3,8,13] define suitable logical data models and query languages which are able to support various OLAP operations. On the contrary, we are mainly interested in the conceptual modelling task, looking at it as a central aspect within the design process. In connection with this aspect, in [5,11] the Entity/Relationship is extended, whereas [6] introduces a new model, called Dimensional Fact Model (DFM), which is capable of representing several aspects of multidimensional data. This latter work defines also a methodology for designing a data warehouse, by deriving a DFM scheme from E/R (or relational) models of the data sources. An object-oriented approach is adopted by [12], which presents a specialization of UML capable of expressing both static and dynamic features of multidimensional data.

Our approach, on the contrary, is devoted to supporting the incremental construction of a data warehouse by introducing a framework for designing new data marts either from enterprise data or from other, previously defined, ones. In particular, the model exploited in our paper is novel with respect to those described so far, mainly because it explicitly represents, at a conceptual level, (possibly complex) transformations among multidimensional data.

The plan of the paper is as follows. In Section 2 the Multidimensional Fact Network model is presented. The AURORA toolkit is described in Section 3. In the Appendix, the exploitation of the MFN model to a real example case is shown.

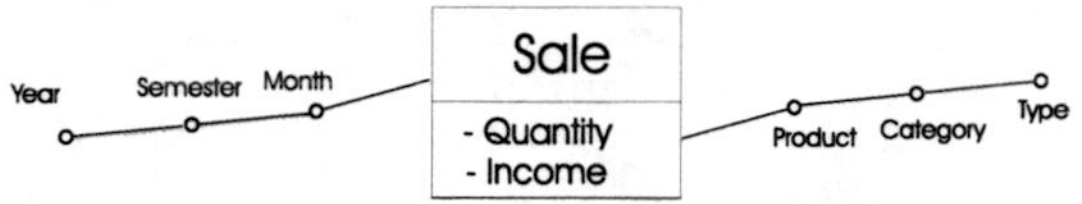

Fig. 1. Example of a DFM scheme

2 The Multidimensional Fact Network

In [6] the DFM conceptual model has been proposed for representing multidimensional facts. DFM is a graphical model conceived for supporting the data mart design. It can be considered as a specialization of the multidimensional model for warehousing applications. One of the main features of the DFM is the graphical representation of *fact schemes*. Basic elements of the fact schemes are *(i)* the *facts*, representing concepts of interest in the decisional process, *(ii)* the *measures*, which are attributes quantitatively describing the fact from different points of view, and *(iii)* the *dimensions*, i.e. discrete valued attributes determining the minimal granularity of the fact representation. An example of DFM scheme is shown in Figure 1.

While the DFM model is a powerful and user-friendly model for representing fact schemes, it is not able to support the designer in the incremental definition of multidimensional data marts. As we have pointed out in the Introduction, the incremental definition of multidimensional data marts allows the designer to reuse previously defined facts for deriving more complex ones. The result of this activity is a network of facts related each other by some mapping functions. In this network, single elements are obtained by transforming, with various kinds of mappings, pre-existing facts possibly integrated with information available in the Business Data Warehouse (BDW) or in master tables external to the data warehouse. This capability of supporting the definition of networks of multidimensional facts is particularly important when we have to deal with complex Business Information Warehouse (BIW) design.

In this section we propose a model, called Multidimensional Fact Network (MFN for short) allowing to define complex networks of multidimensional facts. This model is well suited to be promptly integrated with complex toolkits for data warehouse design such as that developed in the AURORA project.

A Multidimensional Fact Network can be represented as an acyclic graph in which each node is associated with a multidimensional fact, whereas each arc of the form $\langle F_1, F_2 \rangle$ indicates that the fact F_1 participates in the definition of the derived fact F_2. A fact F is said to be *derived* if it is the result of (possibly complex) transformations on other facts, *basic* otherwise. Each fact is associated with a level representing the maximum number of fact transformations necessary to obtain that fact from basic ones.

Derived facts are obtained by transforming and composing dimensions and measures of one or more source facts. These last can be either basic or derived facts themselves. Given a fact F, the bag of facts $[F_i]$ such that an arc $\langle F_i, F \rangle$ exists in the network constitutes the *bag of source facts* of F. A fact can partic-

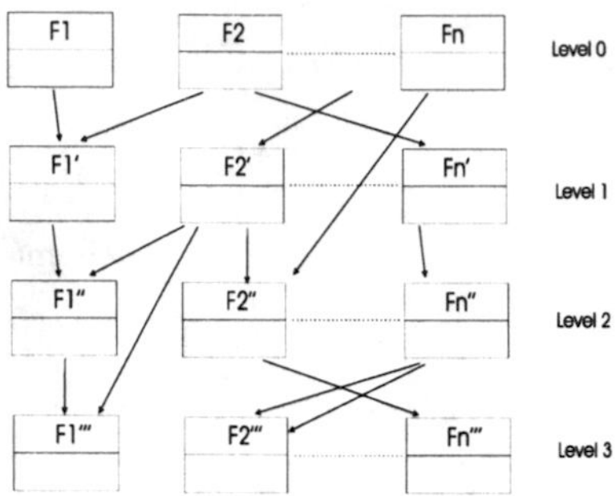

Fig. 2. Example of a generic Multidimensional Fact Network

ipate more than once in the definition of a derived fact and, therefore, we refer to bags of facts instead of sets thereof.

A graphical representation of a generic Multidimensional Fact Network is illustrated in Figure 2 where facts $F_1, \ldots, F_n$ at level 0 are basic facts, whereas the other ones are derived facts. Note that a fact at level $i > 0$ in the network can be obtained from facts of any level $j < i$.

Obviously, the definition of a derived fact requires the formal definition of the transformations involving both the dimensions and the measures of its source facts. In the following section we formalize the representation of basic and derived multidimensional facts in the MFN model.

2.1 Definition of Multidimensional Facts in MFN

As explained in the previous section, facts in MFN can be either basic or derived. Derived facts at level i are obtained from a bag of either basic or derived facts of any level $j < i$ in the network. Moreover, the same fact can participate more than once in the definition of a derived fact. Dimensions and measures of the derived fact are obtained by both applying suitable transformations to the dimensions and measures of the source facts and linking the fact with external master tables and the BDW.

The set of transformations to be applied on source dimensions and measures to obtain derived dimensions and measures can be defined in terms of suitable algebras on the bag of source facts. Each multidimensional fact f in MFN can be represented as a tuple:

$$f = \langle S, FB, AD, AM, lev \rangle, \text{ where}$$

- S is the scheme definition of the fact f;
- FB is the bag of facts f is derived from (this bag is empty if f is basic);
- AD is the algebra for the transformation of the dimensions;
- AM is the algebra for the transformation of the measures;
- lev is the level of f in the network.

Obviously, for basic facts, only S is meaningful. In the following, we will often use the notation $f.x$ to indicate the generic component x of the tuple representing f; as an example, $f.S$ indicates the fact scheme associated to f. In what follows we formalize each of those components, one per subsection.

Scheme Definition of the Fact. The scheme definition of the fact follows the formalization proposed in [6]. The scheme S of a multidimensional fact f is defined as a tuple $\langle M, D, N, R\rangle$, where:

- M is the set of measures of f, each defined by a boolean or numerical expression;
- D is the set of dimensional attributes of f, each characterized by a discrete domain;
- N is a set of non dimensional attributes;
- R is a set of functional dependencies used to represent various aggregation levels along dimensional hierarchies.

As described above, we use the dot notation for indicating the various components of the facts. This also extends to sub-components. As an example $f.S.M$ indicates the set of measures of the fact scheme associated the multidimensional fact f.

Dimension Transformation Algebras. Given a fact f derived from a bag of facts FB, each derived dimension of f is obtained from the dimensions of the facts in FB (we will also call these dimensions *source* dimensions). Generally, the source dimensions are transformed and composed to obtain the derived dimensions. Such manipulations can be described by suitable transformation operators which formally define the way the derived dimensions are obtained from the source ones. Each derived dimension has an associated transformation operator. The set of these operators constitutes the Dimension Transformation Algebra for the fact f into consideration and describes the relationship existing between each dimension of f and the dimensions of the facts in FB. Formally:

Definition 1. Given a multidimensional fact $f = \langle S, FB, AD, AM, lev\rangle$, the Dimension Transformation Algebra AD of f on the bag of source facts $FB = [f_1, \ldots, f_n]$ is defined as:

$$AD = \{\langle op_k, d_k^{'}, \overline{D}_k\rangle \mid op_k \text{ is a well typed computable function,} \\ d_k^{'} \in f.S.D, \emptyset \subset \overline{D}_k \subseteq \bigcup_{f_i \in f.FB} f_i.D, (\forall f_i \in f.FB)(|f_i.S.D \cap \overline{D}_k| \leq 1)\}$$

i.e. the set of transformation operators to be applied on the source dimensions for obtaining the derived dimensions of f. AD contains one tuple for each dimension in $f.D$. □

In the definition above, op_k indicates a generic transformation operator, $d_k^{'}$ is the derived dimension generated by op_k and $\overline{D}_k$ is the (non empty) set of dimensions of the facts in FB generating $d_k^{'}$.

Note that, for each tuple $\langle op_k, d_k^{'}, \overline{D}_k\rangle$, the following conditions must hold:

– op_k must be a well typed computable function defined on the domains of the dimensions in $\overline{D}_k$;
– each element in $\overline{D}_k$ is one of the dimensions of the facts in FB;
– for each fact $f_i \in f.FB$, $\overline{D}_k$ contains at most one of its dimensions.

Definition 1 allows that some of the dimensions of the facts in FB do not generate any derived dimension. This situation might happen either if some source dimensions are not interesting for the definition of the derived ones, or if some source dimensions are heterogeneous so that it can be not meaningful to consider these dimensions in the derived facts. These dimensions can be ignored.

Measure Transformation Algebras. A reasoning analogous to that drawn for obtaining derived dimensions can be exploited for derived measures; indeed, given a fact f derived from a bag of facts FB, each measure of f is obtained from suitable transformations applied on information stored in the facts of FB. However, in this case, the derivation of new measures is a more complex task than the derivation of new dimensions. Derived dimensions, indeed, might be obtained from transformations performed only on other dimensions, whereas derived measures can be obtained from transformations on both measures and either dimensional or non dimensional attributes of the facts in FB; moreover, their derivation can exploit information available in external master tables.

This produces the necessity of defining more complex transformation operators but, conversely, allows to have a powerful tool for the analysis of the data stored in the data warehouse. Obviously, for each derived measure, there must be a transformation operator; the set of such operators constitutes the Measure Transformation Algebra. Formalizing:

Definition 2. Given a multidimensional fact $f = \langle S, FB, AD, AM, lev \rangle$, the Measure Transformation Algebra AM of f on the bag of source facts FB is defined as:

$$\begin{aligned} AM = \{\langle op_k^m, m'_k, \overline{M}_k, \overline{A}_k, \overline{T}_k \rangle \mid\ & op_k^m \text{ is a well typed computable function}, \\ & m'_k \in f.S.M,\ \emptyset \subset \overline{M}_k \subseteq \textstyle\bigcup_{f_i \in f.FB} f_i.S.M, \\ & \emptyset \subseteq \overline{A}_k \subseteq \textstyle\bigcup_{f_i \in f.FB} (f_i.S.D \cup f_i.S.N)\} \end{aligned}$$

i.e. the transformation operators to be applied on *(i)* the source measures, *(ii)* the source dimensional and non dimensional attributes and, possibly, *(iii)* the set of data taken from external master tables $\overline{T}_k$ for obtaining the derived measures of f □

Each transformation operator op_k^m must be defined on at least one measure of the facts in FB, but can involve also dimensional and non dimensional attributes of the facts in FB and data taken from external tables $\overline{T}_k$. The generic transformation operator for a measure must be a well typed and computable function defined as:

$$op_k^m : \overline{M}_k \times \overline{A}_k \times \overline{T}_k \rightarrow \langle \Delta(f) \rightarrow m'_k \rangle$$

where $\Delta(f)$ denotes the space of the derived dimensions of f, i.e. $\Delta(f) = \times_{d' \in f.S.D} Dom(d') = Dom(d'_1) \times \ldots \times Dom(d'_{|f.S.D|})$.

The definition above of op_k^m indicates that each transformation operator produces, starting from $\overline{M}_k$, $\overline{A}_k$ and $\overline{T}_k$, a suitable function defined on the values of the set of derived dimensions. Note that there always exists a relationship between dimensions and measures; transformations on the dimensions are made in order to obtain the new measures of interest. Therefore, it is clear that values of derived measures are obtained from values of derived attributes suitably composed with the values of the elements in $\overline{M}_k$, $\overline{A}_k$ and $\overline{T}_k$.

Note that, in the definition of the Measure Transformation Algebra, no constraint is set for the number and kind of either measures or attributes from which m'_k can be derived. This allows to define complex relationships between the source facts and the derived ones.

The exploitation of the MFN model to a real application case is presented in the Appendix.

3 Tool Description

In this section we illustrate the AURORA toolkit [1,2] developed at CM-Sistemi Sud in collaboration with Università di Reggio Calabria, Università della Calabria, Università di Bologna and ISI-CNR. As pointed out in the Introduction, AURORA aims at providing a comprehensive set of data warehouse design tools for supporting designers in all the activities related to the construction of a data warehouse, i.e. *(i)* the integration of the information stored in the enterprise databases, *(ii)* the definition of the data marts and *(iii)* the application of knowledge discovery techniques and workflow tools on constructed data marts. As for the data warehouse implementation, AURORA exploits a three level architecture allowing to maintain the information source integration and the derivation of multidimensional data for OLAP application two independent tasks. The architecture of AURORA is depicted in Figure 3.

The information owned by the enterprise is integrated by the *Integration Module* which receives in input the schemes relative to the enterprise databases and performs the integration task in order to obtain the set of reconciled data from the operational ones. If necessary, the designer can edit existing or new E/R diagrams by exploiting a graphical interface provided by the *E/R Diagram Designer* module.

The construction of data marts is performed by the *Data Mart Builder* module, which is the core of AURORA architecture. As pointed out in the Introduction, AURORA is based on the Multidimensional Fact Network model, defined in the previous section, to support data mart design. In particular, the *Data Mart Builder* first derives the attribute trees from the source schemes into consideration. On the basis of these attribute trees, the *First Level Multidimensional Facts Builder* module allows the user to build basic multidimensional facts (i.e., first level multidimensional facts in the MFN network). This module is part of a more general one, namely the *Multidimensional Fact Network Builder*. Once first level

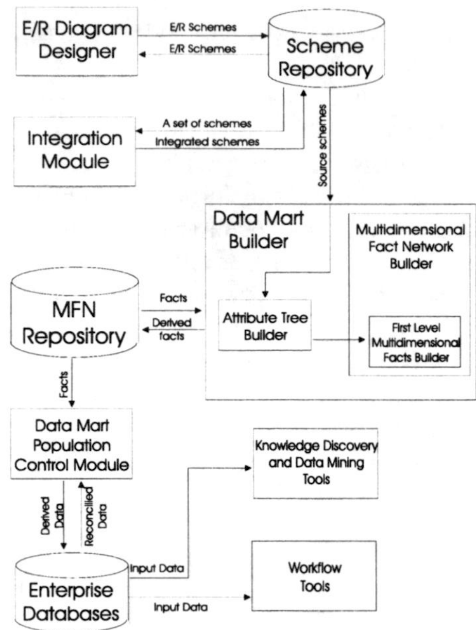

Fig. 3. AURORA architecture

multidimensional facts are derived, the *Multidimensional Fact Network Builder* allows to define more complex multidimensional facts as the result of (possibly complex) transformations on other, previously defined, multidimensional facts. All the produced multidimensional facts, as well as the overall Multidimensional Fact Network, are stored in the *Multidimensional Fact Network Repository*.

The *Data Mart Population Control Module* allows to populate data marts stored in the repository with the enterprise data. These are stored in the *Enterprise Databases*. Finally, *Knowledge Discovery and Data Mining Tools* as well as *Workflow Tools* can be applied on derived data.

A schematic representation of AURORA implementation is shown in Figure 4. AURORA user interface is implemented in standard HTML with java scripts and adopts a client-server architecture so that it can be exploited in Web-based environments such as enterprise Intranets.

The various modules of AURORA architecture described above interact by means of an extended metadata component. This allows AURORA to be easily upgraded if new, more advanced, techniques would become available for some of the phases comprised in the data warehouse construction and exploitation.

In Figure 4, the item named *Methodology* represents a module allowing to trace all the steps of the construction of the data warehouse for an automatic generation of the necessary documentation. The *QDE E/R Design* tool provides the E/R diagram design facilities, whereas *DIKE* [9,10] implements the source integration module. The *MFN* provides the tools for the construction of Data Marts as Multidimensional Fact Networks. *jMINING* [7] is responsible of the

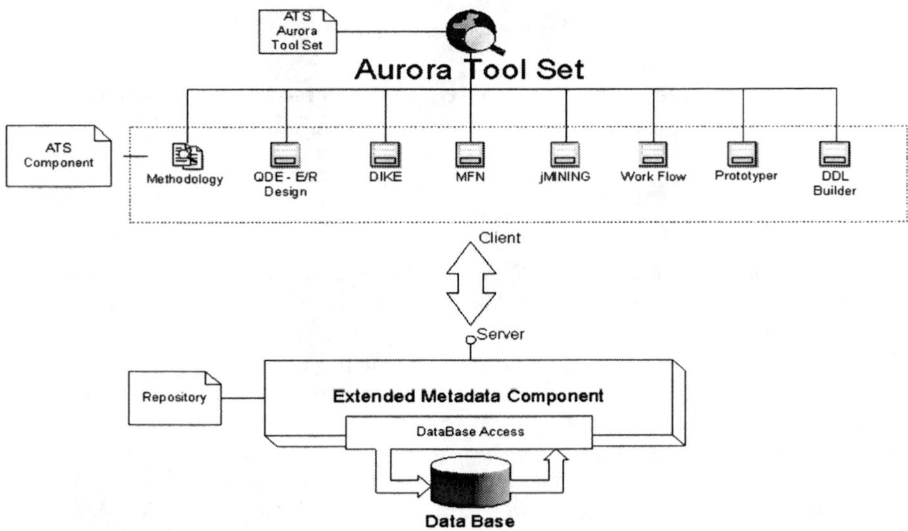

Fig. 4. Schematic representation of AURORA implementation

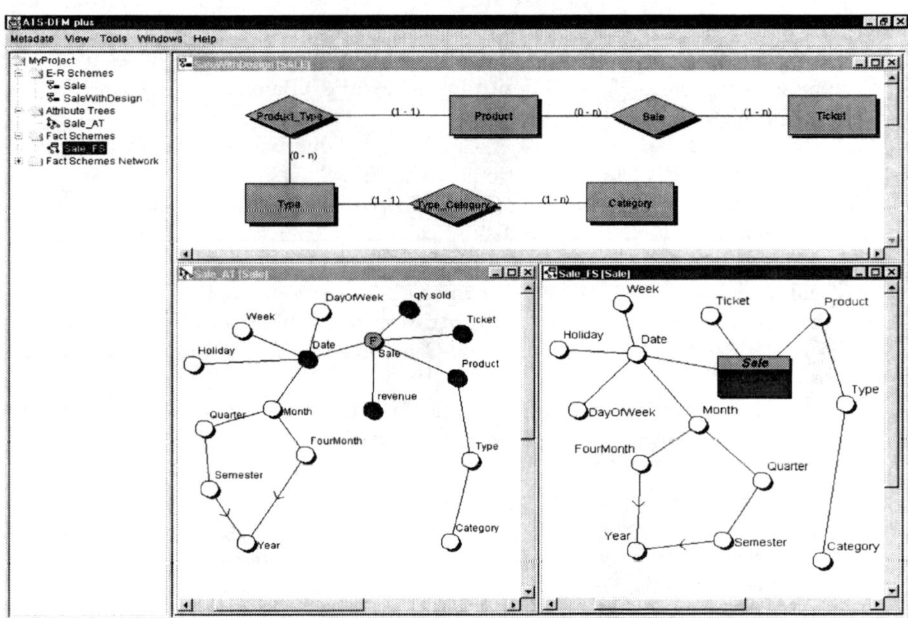

Fig. 5. AURORA screen-shot

front-end to mining techniques. The item named *Workflow* represents the set of workflow tools allowing to overlap workflow based interpretative schemes to derived data marts. The *Prototyper* implements the Data Mart Population Control

Module and, finally, the *DDL* builder is responsible of the automatic generation of DDL scripts for a generic database.

In Figure 5 a screen-shot of AURORA is presented; in particular the figure shows how multidimensional data marts can be defined in a graphical way.

References

1. *Extended metadata component - Specifiche*, Document project number 1704-STEC-01-00-10 in IMI-MURST project "Aurora: un ambiente unitario di realizzazione de sistemi informativi direzionali".
2. *ATS Aurora Toolset - ATS progetto*, Document project number 1704-STECH-01-04-02 in IMI-MURST project "Aurora: un ambiente unitario di realizzazione de sistemi informativi direzionali".
3. L. Cabibbo, R. Torlone. A Logical Approach to Multidimensional Databases. in Proceedings of International Conference on Extending Data Base Technology (EDBT'98), Springer-Verlag, 1998. ACM SIGMOD Record 26(1): 65–74, 1997.
4. S. Chaudhuri, U. Dayal. An Overview of Data Warehousing and OLAP Technology. ACM SIGMOD Record 26(1): 65–74, 1997.
5. E. Franconi, U. Sattler. A Data Warehouse Conceptual Data Model for Multidimensional Aggregation. In Proc. Int. Workshop on Design and Management of Data Warehouses, 1999.
6. M. Golfarelli, D. Maio, S. Rizzi, Conceptual Design of Data Warehouses from E/R Schemes, Proceedings of the Hawaii International Conference on System Sciences, Kona (Hawaii), USA, 1998.
7. S. Greco, E. Masciari, L. Pontieri, "Combining inductive and deductive tools for data analysis", in AI Communications, 14(2), pp. 69–82, 2001.
8. W. Lehner. Modeling Large Scale OLAP Scenarios. In Proc. of Int. Conf. on Extending Database Technology (EDBT), Valencia, Spain, 1998: 153–167.
9. L. Palopoli, G. Terracina and D. Ursino, The System DIKE: Towards the Semi-Automatic Synthesis of Cooperative Information Systems and Data Warehouses, Proc. of Challenges of Symposium on Advances in Databases and Information Systems (ADBIS-DASFAA 2000), Prague, Czech Republic, pp. 108–117, 2000, Matfyzpress
10. L. Palopoli, L. Pontieri, G. Terracina and D. Ursino, Intensional and extensional integration and abstraction of heterogeneous databases, Data & Knowledge Engineering, 35(3), pp. 201–237, 2000
11. C. Sapia, M. Blaschka, G. Höfling, B. Dinter. Extending the E/R Model for the Multidimensional Paradigm. In Proc. of ER Workshops, Singapore, 1998: 105–116.
12. J. C. Trujillo, M. Palomar, J. Gómez. Applying Object-Oriented Conceptual Modeling Techniques to the Design of Multidimensional Databases and OLAP Applications. In Proc. First Int. Conf. Web-Age Information Management (2000): 83–94.
13. P. Vassiliadis. Modeling multidimensional databases, cubes and cube operations. In Proc. of 10th Int. Conf. on Scientific and Statistical Database Management (SSDB), Capri, 1998.

Efficient Automated Mining of Fuzzy Association Rules

Mehmet Kaya[1,*], Reda Alhajj[1,**], Faruk Polat[2], and Ahmet Arslan[3]

[1] Dept of Computer Science, University of Calgary, Calgary, Alberta, Canada
[2] Dept of Computer Engineering, Middle East Technical University, 06531, Ankara, Turkey
[3] Dept of Computer Engineering, Fırat University, 23119, Elazığ, Turkey

Abstract. Mining association rules is one of the important research problems in data mining. So, many algorithms have been proposed to find association rules in databases with either binary or quantitative attributes. One of these approaches is fuzzy association rules mining. However, most of the earlier algorithms proposed for mining fuzzy association rules assume that fuzzy sets are given. In this paper, we propose an automated method for autonomous mining of both fuzzy sets and fuzzy association rules. For this purpose, we first find fuzzy sets by using an efficient clustering algorithm, namely CURE, and then determine their membership functions. Finally, we decide on interesting fuzzy association rules. Experimental results show the efficiency of the presented approach for synthetic transactions.

Keywords: association rules, CURE clustering algorithm, fuzzy sets, data mining, quantitative attributes.

1. Introduction

Data mining is the process of extracting previously unknown and potentially useful hidden predictive information from large amounts of data. Discovering association rules is one of the several data mining techniques described in the literature. Associations allow capturing all possible rules that explain the presence of some attributes according to the presence of other attributes in the same transaction.

An association rule is defined as an implication $X \Rightarrow Y$, where both X and Y are defined as sets of attributes or items. An association rule is a statement of the form "for a specified fraction of the existing transactions, a particular value of an attribute set X determines the value of attribute set Y as another particular value under a certain confidence". For instance, an association rule in a supermarket basket data may be stated as, "in 15% of the transactions, 80% of the people buying milk also buy biscuit in the same transaction"; 15% is called the support and 80% is the confidence. Simply, support is the percentage of transactions that contain both X and Y, while confidence is the ratio of the support of $X \cup Y$ and the support of X. The significance of an association rule is measured by its support and confidence. So, the problem is to find all association rules that satisfy user-specified minimum support and confidence.

---

* on leave from Fırat University, Elazığ, Turkey

** contact author, Email: alhajj@cpsc.ucalgary.ca, Tel: (403) 210 9453. The research of this author is partially supported by NSERC grant and UofC grant.

R. Cicchetti et al. (Eds.): DEXA 2002, LNCS 2453, pp. 133-142, 2002.

Early research in the field concentrated on boolean association rules, which are concerned only with whether an item is present in a transaction or not, without considering its quantity. However, quantity is a very useful piece of information. Realizing the importance of quantity, people started to concentrate on quantitative attributes. The main reason for quantitative association rule mining is that numerical attributes typically contain many distinct values. The support for any particular value is likely to be low, while the support for intervals is much higher.

Although current quantitative association rules mining algorithms can solve some of the problems introduced by quantitative attributes, they introduce some other problems. The major problem is caused by the sharp boundary between intervals. In other words, existing quantitative mining algorithms either ignore or over-emphasize elements near the boundary of an interval. The use of sharp boundary interval is also not intuitive with respect to human perception as illustrated next.

Consider three intervals for the income of a person, namely [0, 30K],]30K, 70K[, and [70K, 120K] to represent poor, moderate and rich, respectively. It is not easy to distinguish the degree of membership for the interval method. For instance, the interval method may classify a person as poor if annual income is less than or equal to $30K and moderate if annual income is greater than $30K. Further, using the interval method, incomes of $70K and $120K may both be classified into the rich category. However, it has intuitively been known that the income of $120K is much richer than the income of $70K. This problem can be handled smoothly by introducing fuzziness into the model as described in this paper.

Unlike classical set theory where membership is binary, the fuzzy set theory introduced by Zadeh [14] provides excellent means to model the "fuzzy" boundaries of linguistic terms by introducing gradual membership. Some example linguistic terms include "poor", "young", "rich", "excellent", etc.

In this paper, we present an automated method to derive fuzzy sets from a set of given transactions by employing an efficient clustering algorithm, namely CURE clustering algorithm [5]. First, we automatically determine fuzzy sets based on the given transactions. Then, membership functions for the determined sets are defined and adjusted accordingly. Finally, we conduct some experiments to test our approach and the obtained results support the efficiency of the proposed method.

The rest of this paper is organized as follows. Related work is discussed in Section 2. The automated process to autonomously find fuzzy sets and their membership functions is presented in Section 3. The definition of fuzzy association rules and an algorithm for mining these rules are described in Section 4. Experimental results for synthetic transactions are given in Section 5. Conclusions are included in Section 6.

2. Related Work

The problem of discovering association rules was first explored in [1] on supermarket basket data, which is the set of transactions that include items purchased by customers. In this pioneering work, the data was considered to be binary, i.e., concerned with whether an item exists in a transaction or not, and the quantity of the item in the transactions was ignored. There are many known algorithms for mining boolean association rules, including Agrawal and Srikant's Appriori, AppriorITID and AppriorIHybrid algorithms [1, 2], and Mannila et al [11].

The problem of mining quantitative association rules was first introduced in [13]. The basic idea of this algorithm is to first map the values of categorical attributes into a set of consecutive integers. Then, each quantitative attribute domain is partitioned into small intervals and adjacent intervals are combined into larger ones such that the combined intervals will have enough support. Finally, the obtained intervals are mapped into consecutive integers. By replacing the original attribute by its attribute-intervals pair, the quantitative problem can be transformed into a boolean one leading to a uniform representation.

Recently, the use of fuzziness in data mining has been considered as one of the key components of data mining systems because of its close similarity with human knowledge representation [10]. Ishibuchi et al. [8] illustrated fuzzy versions of confidence and support that can be used for evaluating each association rule. The authors employed these measures of fuzzy rules for function approximation and pattern classification problems. Hong et al. [7] proposed an algorithm that integrates fuzzy set concepts and Apriori mining algorithm to find interesting fuzzy association rules from given transaction data. Gyenesei [6] presented two different methods for mining fuzzy quantitative association rules, namely *without normalization* and *with normalization*. The experiments of Gyenesei showed that the numbers of large itemsets and interesting rules found by the fuzzy method are larger than the discrete method defined by Srikant and Agrawal [13], our findings described in this paper are in the same direction. Chan and Au [3] utilized adjacent difference analysis and fuzziness in finding the minimum support and confidence instead of having them supplied by a user. They determine both positive and negative associations. Finally, the approach developed by Zhang [15] extends the equi-depth partitioning with fuzzy terms. However, it assumes fuzzy terms as predefined.

All of the above mentioned approaches assume that fuzzy sets and their corresponding membership functions are given beforehand. In other words, they rely on an expert to manually specify the fuzzy sets. On the other hand, Fu et al. [4] proposed an automated method to find fuzzy sets for the mining of fuzzy association rules. The method is based on the CLARANS clustering algorithm [12]. After obtaining the k medoids for each quantitative attribute, these medoids are used to classify each quantitative attribute into k fuzzy sets.

The approach proposed in this paper, uses less centroids than the other approaches described in the literature, and the membership functions of the determined sets are adjusted accordingly.

3. Fuzzy Sets and Membership Functions

One of the most important steps in mining fuzzy association rules is to decide on the fuzzy sets according to which the values of each quantitative attribute are to be classified. In other words, the quality of the results produced relies quite crucially on the appropriateness of the fuzzy sets to the given data. So, fuzzy sets must be consistent with the values of the corresponding attribute. Fuzzy sets can be either provided by an expert or automatically derived from the contents of the existing transactions. However, fuzzy sets provided by experts may not be suitable for mining fuzzy association rules in databases. Also, it is extremely difficult for experts to estimate the most appropriate fuzzy sets.

In order to cope with these problems, we first concentrate on how fuzzy sets are determined automatically from the values of the given attributes. For this purpose, we have used the CURE clustering algorithm. The input parameters to this clustering algorithm are:

The input data set D containing $|D|$-values in n-dimensional space, where $|D|$ is the number of values in the database and n is the number of attributes.

1. The desired number of clusters k
2. Starting with individual values as individual clusters, at each step the closest pair of clusters are merged to form a new cluster. The process is repeated until only k clusters are left. This way, the values of each attribute in the databases are distributed into k cluster. The centroids of the k clusters are the set of midpoints of the fuzzy sets for the corresponding attribute.

To illustrate the process, suppose we want to find fuzzy sets for the i-th attribute, which is quantitative with a range from min(i) to max(i). Let $\{f_{i1}, f_{i2},...f_{ik}\}$ be the set of mid-points of the fuzzy sets for the i-th attribute. Actually, the i-th attribute has also two additional fuzzy sets, which are at intervals of $[\min(i), f_{i1}]$ and $[f_{ik}, \max(i)]$. Then, the total k+2 fuzzy sets will have the following ranges: $[\min(i), f_{i1}]$, $[\min(i), f_{i2}], \ldots, [f_{i(k-1)}, \max(i)]$, and $[f_{ik}, \max(i)]$.

After the fuzzy sets of each quantitative attribute are obtained, for each fuzzy set a corresponding membership function can be generated. In general, a membership function over a numerical universe is convex and normal. The process is illustrated next.

Suppose we want to find membership functions of the fuzzy sets for the i-th attribute, which is quantitative with ranges from min(i) to max(i), and as indicated above, $\{f_{i1}, f_{i2},...f_{ik}\}$ is the set of mid-points of the fuzzy sets for the i-th attribute. We use the following method to find the required membership functions.

For the fuzzy set with a range from min(i) to f_{i1}, the membership function is given by

$$F_0(x) = \begin{cases} \dfrac{x - f_{i1}}{\min(i) - f_{i1}} & \text{if } x \leq f_{i1} \\ 0 & \text{if } x > f_{i1} \end{cases}$$

For each fuzzy set with mid-point f_{ij}, where $1 \leq j \leq k$, the membership function is given by

$$F_{ij}(x) = \begin{cases} \dfrac{x - f_{i(j-1)}}{f_{ij} - f_{i(j-1)}} & \text{if } f_{i(j-1)} \leq x \leq f_{ij} \\ \dfrac{x - f_{i(j+1)}}{f_{ij} - f_{i(j+1)}} & \text{if } f_{ij} \leq x \leq f_{i(j+1)} \end{cases}$$

For the fuzzy set with a range from f_{ik} to max(i), the membership function is given by

$$F_{k+1}(x) = \begin{cases} 0 & \text{if } x \le f_{ik} \\ \dfrac{x - f_{ik}}{\max(i) - f_{ik}} & \text{if } f_{ik} < x \le \max(i) \end{cases}$$

The following example illustrates the whole process. Given a database with a quantitative attribute, say *income* with five different ranges, as shown in Table 1. The values of *income* range from \$10K to \$120K, and can be classified into four fuzzy sets, i.e., two clusters, as shown in Figure 1.

Table 1. The ranges of fuzzy sets found according to CURE clustering algorithm

Income	Range	Centroid
Quite poor	10-30	-
Poor	10-70	30
Moderate	30-120	70
Rich	70-120	-

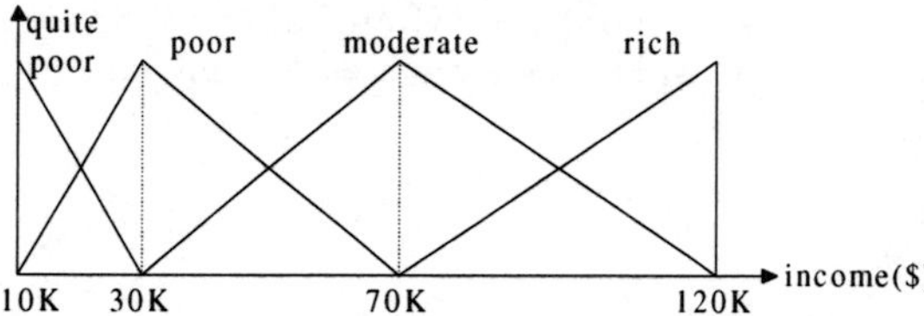

Fig. 1. The membership functions found according to the centroids

4. Fuzzy Association Rules

Given a transaction database $D=\{t_1, t_2, \ldots t_n\}$, its set of attributes I, and the fuzzy sets associated with quantitative attributes in I. Notice that each transaction t_i contains values of some attributes from I. We want to find out some interesting, potentially useful regularities, i.e., rules with enough support and high confidence. We use the following form for fuzzy association rule [8]:

If $X=\{x_1, x_2, \ldots x_p\}$ is $A=\{f_1, f_2, \ldots f_p\}$ then $Y=\{y_1, y_2, \ldots y_q\}$ is $B=\{g_1, g_2, \ldots g_q\}$, Where X, Y are itemsets, i.e., sets of attributes, which are disjoint subsets of I, and A and B contain the fuzzy sets associated with corresponding attributes in X and Y, respectively. In other words, f_i is the set of fuzzy sets related to attribute x_i and g_j is the set of fuzzy sets related to attribute y_j.

As it is the case with binary association rules, "X is A" is called the antecedent of the rule while "Y is B" is called the consequent of the rule. If a rule is interesting, it should have enough support and high confidence value, which are described next within the fuzziness framework.

4.1 Fuzzy Support

To generate fuzzy association rules, we first find all sets of items that have transaction support above a user specified threshold. Itemsets with at least a minimum support are called large itemsets. Fuzzy support is calculated by first summing all votes of each record with respect to the specified itemset, then dividing it by the total number of records. This way, each record contributes to the overall result a vote that falls in [0,1]. Therefore, a fuzzy support value reflects not only the number of records supporting the itemset, but also their degree of support. We use the following formula to calculate the fuzzy support value of a given itemset, say *Z* with corresponding fuzzy sets *C*, denoted <*Z, C*> [8]:

$$S_{<Z,C>} = \frac{\sum_{t_i \in T} \prod_{z_j \in Z} m_{z_j}(c_j \in C, t_i[Z_j])}{|D|}$$

In the above equation, *Z* is a set of attributes z_j and *C* is the corresponding set of fuzzy sets c_j. Here, W is the union of the itemsets on both sides of an association rules and *C* is the union of their corresponding two sets of fuzzy sets. We use $t_i[z_j]$ to obtain the value of w_j in the *i*-th record, then transform the value into membership grade by applying $m_{z_j}(c_j \in C, t_i[z_j])$, which is the membership function of z_j.

4.2 Fuzzy Confidence

The discovered large itemsets are used to generate all possible association rules. Given a large itemset, we know its support and by definition all of its subsets are also large. So, for each large itemset we want to generate fuzzy association rules of the form, "If *X* is *A* then *Y* is *B*". Such a rule will be considered interesting if the union of its antecedent and consequent has enough support and the rule itself has high confidence.

To determine fuzzy confidence, let *Z=X U Y* and *C=A U B*, such that *X* and *Y* are disjoint and *A* and *B* are also disjoint. So, we can calculate fuzzy confidence value by dividing the fuzzy support of <*Z, C*> by the fuzzy support of <*X, A*> as follows [8]:

$$C_{<X,A><Y,B>} = \frac{S_{<Z,C>}}{S_{<X,A>}} = \frac{\dfrac{\sum_{t_i \in T} \prod_{z_j \in X} m_{z_j}(c_j \in C, t_i[z_j])}{|D|}}{\dfrac{\sum_{t_i \in T} \prod_{x_j \in X} m_{x_j}(a_j \in A, t_i[x_j])}{|D|}} = \frac{\sum_{t_i \in T} \prod_{z_j \in X} m_{z_j}(c_j \in C, t_i[z_j])}{\sum_{t_i \in T} \prod_{x_j \in X} m_{x_j}(a_j \in A, t_i[x_j])}$$

We use confidence to help us estimate the interestingness of the generated fuzzy association rules because confidence measures the degree of support given by transactions.

To illustrate this, consider the values in Table 2, which shows a part of a database with two quantitative attributes, *annual income* and *saving*. In spite of having each attribute consists of three fuzzy sets, the table contains only membership scores of the attributes, *medium* and *low*.

Table 2. The membership grades of attributes, annual income and saving according to medium and low

<Annual income, medium>	**<Saving, low>**
0.4	0.5
0.8	0.3
0.6	0.4
0.5	0.4
0.9	0.2

According to Table 2, the fuzzy support and fuzzy confidence of the rule, "if *annual income* is *medium*, then *saving* is *low*" can be calculated as follows:

$$S = \frac{0.20 + 0.24 + 0.24 + 0.20 + 0.18}{5} = 0.212$$

$$C = \frac{0.20 + 0.24 + 0.24 + 0.20 + 0.18}{0.4 + 0.8 + 0.6 + 0.5 + 0.9} = 0.331$$

Finally, the problem of discovering all fuzzy quantitative association rules can be decomposed into two sub-problems:

Find all itemsets that have fuzzy support above the user specified minimum support. These itemsets are called large itemsets.

Use the obtained large itemsets to generate the desired rules. The general idea is that if, say X and Y are large itemsets, then it can be determined whether the rule $X \Rightarrow Y$ holds by computing the ratio described above. If the determined value is larger than the user specified minimum confidence value, then the rule will be considered interesting.

5. Experimental Results

In this section, we present some experiments that have been carried out to test the efficiency of the proposed approach. The database used in the experiments consists of 10000 records with 4 quantitative attributes, namely age of person, savings, annual income and number of persons in family. Each quantitative attribute has three intervals/fuzzy sets.

First, to support our position in using CURE clustering algorithm, we compare two of the well-known clustering algorithms described in the literature, CLARANS and CURE. We have run both clustering algorithms with database size ranging from 100 to 10000 transactions. The number of fuzzy sets is set to 3 for both algorithms, i.e., the number of medoids to be found for CLARANS clustering algorithm is three while it is one for CURE. Figure 2 shows the execution time required by each of the two algorithms to find the required three fuzzy sets per quantitative attribute.

After illustrating the superiority of CURE over CLARANS, we run another experiment to compare discrete and fuzzy methods (both based on CURE) in the association rules construction process. Shown in Table 3 are the ranges of the attributes found by the CURE clustering algorithm with respect to both discrete intervals and fuzzy sets methods.

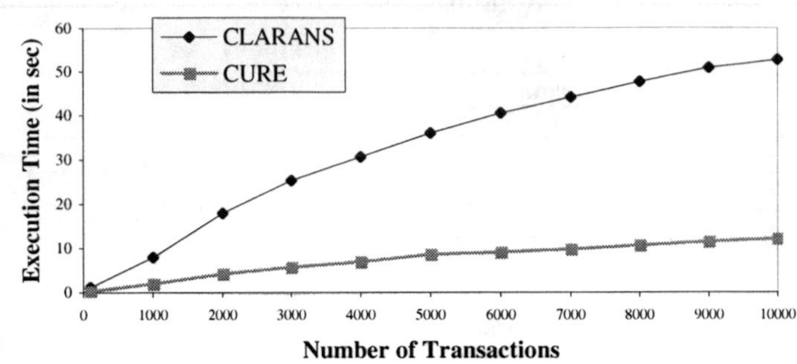

Fig. 2. The execution time required for CURE and CLARANS clustering algorithms to find 3 fuzzy sets

Table 3. The ranges of attributes according to discrete interval and fuzzy set methods

	Label	**Young**	**Medium**	**Old**	Centroids
Age of Person	**Fuzzy Sets**	15-43	15-90	43-90	43
	Discrete Intervals	15-32	32-50	50-90	32, 50
Saving	Label	**Little**	**Medium**	**Large**	-
	Fuzzy Sets	0-100K	0-500K	100K-500K	100
	Discrete Intervals	0-100K	100K-250K	250K-500K	100, 250
Annual Income	Label	**Low**	**Medium**	**High**	-
	Fuzzy Sets	10K-55K	10K-120K	55K-120K	55
	Discrete Intervals	10K-40K	40K-70K	70K-120K	40, 70
Number of Person	Label	**Small**	**Medium**	**Big**	-
	Fuzzy Sets	1-4	1-10	4-10	4
	Discrete Intervals	1-3	3-6	6-10	3, 6

Figure 3 shows the number of large itemsets found according to three different methods for different values of minimum support. As expected, the number of large itemsets decreases as the minimum support value increases from 10% to 50%. The number of large itemsets found by our proposed method is almost the same as that of Fu et al's.

Finally, the number of interesting rules for different values of minimum confidence is given in Figure 4. For this experiment, the minimum support was set to 25%. The results are quite similar to those of Figure 3.

As both Figure 3 and Figure 4 demonstrate, using fuzzy sets results in more large itemsets and more rules than the discrete method. On the other hand, using the CURE algorithm does improve the performance with the outcome unaffected. Some of the determined interesting fuzzy association rules are enumerated next:

IF age of a person is medium AND annual income is high THEN saving is medium.

IF saving is large AND annual income is medium THEN number of persons in family is small.

IF age of person is young AND annual income is high AND number of persons in family is small THEN saving is medium.

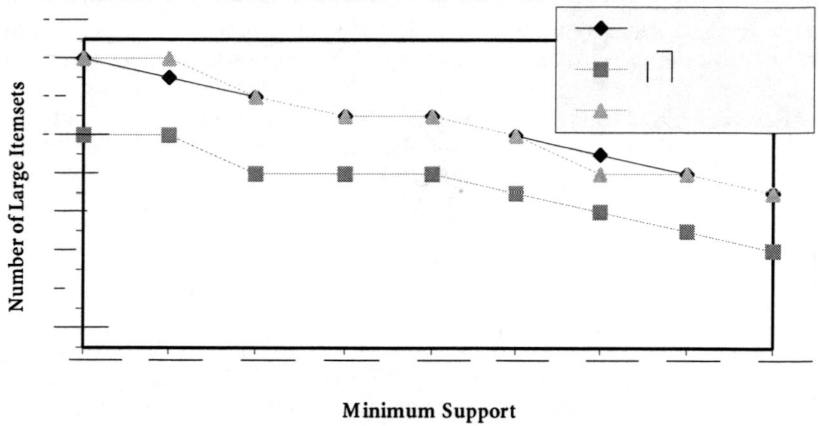

Fig. 3. Number of Large Itemsets for example database

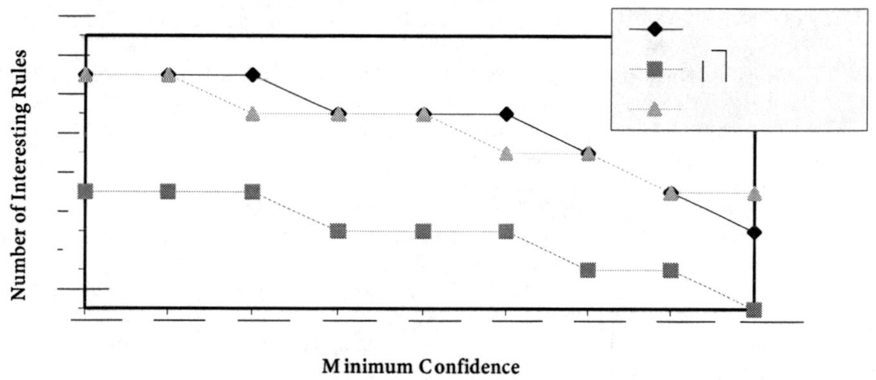

Fig. 4. Number of Interesting Rules for example database

At the end, another advantage of the presented CURE based approach is that the function F_0 decreases between *min*(i) and f_{i1} while this same interval is equal to 1 in CLARANS based Fu et al.'s work. Similarly, the function F_{k+1} increases between f_{ik} and *max*(i) in the former approach while it is again fixed at 1 in the latter approach. Thus, the degree of membership of each attribute value differs in the two approaches.

6. Conclusions

In this paper, we have presented our approach of using CURE clustering algorithm to automate the process of finding fuzzy sets to be used in mining interesting association rules. By using fuzzy sets, we describe association rules in concise manner. It is true that expert users can participate in the process by changing the number and position of the fuzzy sets, which lead to the discovered rules. However, it is unrealistic that users always have the capacity to intervene in the mining process. The approach proposed in this paper is a solution to these deficiencies. The position of the fuzzy sets has been adjusted by using CURE, which is an efficient clustering algorithm. As illustrated by the experiments conducted on the proposed method, three fuzzy sets were determined by finding only one centroid. The experiments done on the synthetics databases showed that the proposed approach produces meaningful results and has reasonable efficiency. Currently, we are investigating the possibility of applying the same fuzzy approach to OLAP.

References

[1] R. Agrawal, T. Imielinski and A. Swami. "Mining association rules between sets of items in large databases", *Proceedings of ACM SIGMOD,* pp.207-216, USA, May 1993.

[2] R. Agrawal and R. Srikant. "Fast algorithms for mining association rules", *Proceedings of VLDB,* pp.487-499, Chile, Sept. 1994.

[3] K.C.C. Chan and W.H. Au, "Mining Fuzzy Association Rules," *Proceedings of ACM CIKM,* Las Vegas, pp.209-215, Nov. 1997.

[4] A. W. C. Fu, M. H. Wong, S. C. Sze, W. C. Wong, W. L. Wong and W. K. Yu. "Finding Fuzzy Sets for the Mining of Association Rules for Numerical Attributes", *Proceedings of IDEL,* pp.263-268, Oct. 1998.

[5] S. Guha, R. Rastogi and K. Shim. "CURE: An Efficient Clustering Algorithm for Large Databases", *Proceedings of ACM SIGMOD,* 1998.

[6] A. Gyenesei. "A Fuzzy Approach for Mining Quantitative Association Rules", *TUCS Technical Report No:336*, Mar. 2000.

[7] T.P. Hong, C. S. Kuo and S. C. Chi. "A fuzzy data mining algorithm for quantitative values", *Proceedings of KBIIES*, pp.480-483, Australia, 1999.

[8] H. Ishibuchi, T. Nakashima and T. Yamamoto. "Fuzzy Association Rules for Handling Continuous Attributes", *Proceedings of IEEE ISIE*, pp.118-121, 2001.

[9] C. M. Kuok, A. W. Fu and M. H. Wong. Mining fuzzy association rules in databases. *SIGMOD Record*, 17(1), pp.41-46, 1998.

[10] A Maeda, et al, "Data Mining System using Fuzzy Rule Induction," Proceedings of IEEE ICFS, Japan, pp.45-46, 1995.

[11] H. Mannila, H. Toivonen and A.I. Verkamo. "Efficient Algorithms for discovering association rules", *Proceedings of AAAI Workshop on KKD*, pp.181-192, 1994.

[12] R. Ng and J. Han. "Efficient and effective clustering methods for spatial data mining", *Proceedings of VLDB,* 1994.

[13] R. Srikant and R. Agrawal. Mining quantitative association rules in large relational tables. *Proceedings of ACM SIGMOD,* pp.1-12, 1996.

[14] L.A. Zadeh, "Fuzzy Sets," Information and Control, Vol.8, pp.338-353, 1965.

[15] W. Zhang, "Mining Fuzzy Quantitative Association Rules," *Proceedings of IEEE ICTAI,* Illinois, pp.99-102, Nov. 1999.

A Two-Phase Stock Trading System Using Distributional Differences

Sung-Dong Kim[1], Jae Won Lee[2], Jongwoo Lee[3], and Jinseok Chae[4]

[1] Dept. of Computer System Engineering, Hansung University,
Seoul 136-792, Korea
sdkim@hansung.ac.kr

[2] School of Computer Science and Engineering, Sungshin Women's University,
Seoul 136-742, Korea
jwlee@cs.sungshin.ac.kr

[3] Division of Information and Communication Engineering, Hallym University,
Chunchon-si, Kangwon-do 200-702, Korea
jwlee44@hallym.ac.kr

[4] Dept. of Computer Science and Engineering, University of Incheon,
Incheon 402-749, Korea
jschae@incheon.ac.kr

Abstract. In the context of a dynamic trading environment, the ultimate goal of the financial forecasting system is to optimize a specific trading objective. This paper presents a two-phase (extraction and filtering) stock trading system that aims at maximizing the rates of returns. Extraction of stocks is performed by searching specific time-series patterns described by a combination of values of technical indicators. In the filtering phase, several rules are applied to the extracted sets of stocks to select stocks to be actually traded. The filtering rules are induced from past data using distributional differences. From a large database of daily stock prices, the values of technical indicators are calculated. They are used to make the extraction patterns, and the distributions of the discretization intervals of the values are calculated for both positive and negative data sets. The values in the intervals of distinctive distribution may contribute to the prediction of future trend of stocks, so the rules for filtering stocks are induced using those intervals. We show the rates of returns by the proposed trading system, with the usefulness of the rule induction method using distributional differences.

1 Introduction

The investor's ultimate goal is to optimize some relevant measures of trading objective, such as profit, economic utility or risk-adjusted return. Considerable research efforts have been devoted to the development of financial forecasting models that try to optimize the goal. This paper addresses the problem of financial forecasting to optimize the rates of returns in stock investment.

Most researches in the financial forecasting community have focused on building predictive models. The prediction models incorporate various types of explanatory variables: so-called technical variables (depending on the past price

R. Cicchetti et al. (Eds.): DEXA 2002, LNCS 2453, pp. 143–152, 2002.

sequence), micro-economic stock-specific variables (such as measures of company profitability), and macro-economic variables (which give information about the business cycle) [1]. There are two types of analysis for predicting the stock market: technical and fundamental analyses. Technical analysis is based on the daily price data and it is difficult to create a valid model for a longer period of time. Fundamental analysis considers information concerning the activities and financial situation of each company. Neural networks are considered to provide state-of-the-art solutions to noisy time series prediction problems such as financial prediction [2]. Rule inference for financial prediction through noisy time series analysis is also performed using neural networks [3]. Most studies focus on the prediction of a stock index, not on the prediction of multiple stocks. The use of the prediction system in trading would typically involve the utilization of other financial indicators and domain knowledge. A general approach to decision making in dynamic stock trading environment is to build a trading system that consists of a predictive model and the decision rules converting the prediction into an action [4].

In this paper we propose a two-phase stock trading system that considers multiple stocks in KOSPI and KOSDAQ, two Korean stock markets. The system is composed of an extraction and a filtering phases and its ultimate goal is to maximize the rates of returns. It is also parameterized by a trading policy, which specifies a target profit ratio, a stop loss ratio, and a maximum holding period. Only technical data is used for technical analysis, so the system is adopted to short-term stock trading. Extraction of stocks is performed through pattern matching and filtering is done based on the decision rules. The pattern is a combination of the values of technical indicators. The decision rules, filtering rules, are induced from past data using distributional differences. They are the rules that classify the states of the extracted stocks by which the investment action takes place. In the stock trading system, buy is based on the extraction and the filtering, and sell is directed by a trading policy.

From a database of daily stock prices, the values of technical indicators are calculated. We make the extraction patterns using the values and collect the pattern-matched stocks that serve as the training data. In order to induce the decision rules, the training data is classified into positive and negative and the values are discretized into intervals. The distributions of the value intervals are calculated for positive and negative data sets respectively. Some intervals show a distinctive distribution and the values in those intervals may contribute to the classification of the stocks. The decision rules are induced using the distinguished intervals.

Section 2 explains the environment for building a stock trading system. Overall structure of the proposed stock trading system is given in Section 3. Extraction patterns, the induction process of decision rules, and the trading policy are also described. The results of hypothetical investments are shown in Section 4. Section 5 draws a conclusion and presents further works.

2 Setup Description

2.1 Stock Database

We construct a database of daily stock prices. It contains data for all stocks in KOSPI and KOSDAQ, now about 1,700 stocks. The data is daily and spans 12 years, from January 1990 to December 2001. Raw data (RD) consists of seven fields and can be represented as follows:

$$RD = (name, date, p_o, p_c, p_h, p_l, v) ,$$

where p_o is a daily open price, p_c is a daily close price, p_h is the daily highest price, p_l is the daily lowest price, and v is a daily trading volume.

From the raw data, technical indicators are calculated such as price moving average and RSI (Relative Strength Index) [5]. Using the values of the indicators, we construct time-series patterns.

2.2 Time-Series Patterns

In the literature about financial prediction, self-organizing maps [6] and neural networks [7] are used to discover time-series patterns. Recently there have been efforts to identify "change point" with data mining techniques [8].

In this paper we construct patterns using stock expert's knowledge, so the patterns are intuitive and empirical ones rather than automatically acquired patterns from time-series data. Three kinds of pattern sets are established: R, $S1$, $S2$. They are based on the support and resistance levels [5]. First set (R) is for patterns that break the resistance level upward and the others ($S1$, $S2$) are for patterns that relate to the support level. The representative patterns of each pattern set are exemplified in Figure 1. Figure 1-(a) is an example of R, 1-(b) is for $S1$, and 1-(c) is a pattern of $S2$.

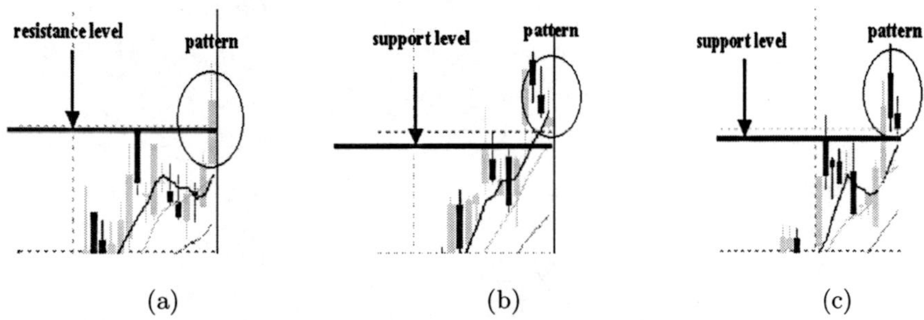

Fig. 1. The examples of patterns in each pattern set

A pattern ($pattern_i$) is represented by a set of questions for the values of the technical indicators:

$$pattern_i = (ques_1(ti_1), ques_2(ti_2), \ldots, ques_n(ti_n)) .$$

The following is a concrete example of a pattern[1]:

$pattern_1 = (Grad5_0 \geq 1.23, RC_0 \geq 0.04, VL_1 < VL_0, Disp5-10_1 < Disp5-10_0)$.

These patterns will be used in extraction phase of the proposed trading system.

2.3 Training Data

The training data is used to build decision rules for filtering phase in our trading system. From the stock database described in Section 2.1, we extract data of the stocks that are matched with patterns in Section 2.2. From January 1998 to June 2000 (30 months), we extract stocks by pattern matching and collect data for the stocks. The collected data ($D(s)$) consists of the values of technical indicators and several trigram values reflecting 3 days trend of technical indicators:

$$D(s) = (ti_1, \ldots, ti_n, tri_1, \ldots, tri_m) , \tag{1}$$

where ti stands for a value of a technical indicator, tri represents a trigram value, and s is an extracted stock. All elements of $D(s)$ are considered in filtering phase, and some of them participate in describing patterns, The trigram consists of 3 ternary symbols ($b_1, b_2, b_3 \in \{-1, 0, 1\}$) obtained by discretizing the original, real value (v) using the "signum" function:

$$b_i = sign(v) = \begin{cases} -1, & \text{if } v < 0 \\ 0, & \text{if } v = 0 \\ 1, & \text{if } v > 0 \end{cases} .$$

Because different technical indicators participate in describing each pattern, the elements of each $D(s)$ are different with each other depending on the matched pattern.

Each of the collected data is tagged as *positive* or *negative*, based on the one-day return $R_1(s)$:

$$R_1(s) = \frac{\text{close price - open price}}{\text{open price}} , \tag{2}$$

where the prices are the next day prices of the extraction day. The class of each training data ($C(s)$) is determined as follows:

$$C(s) = \begin{cases} positive, & \text{if } R_1(s) \geq 0 \\ negative, & \text{if } R_1(s) < 0 \end{cases} .$$

Table 1 shows the number of extracted stocks in each pattern set and statistics of the training data.

---

[1] In the example, subscript 0 means the today and 1 is yesterday. *Grad*5 is the gradient value of 5-day price moving average, RC is the value of rate of change, VL is a trading volume, and $Disp5-10$ is a disparity value between 5-day and 10-day price moving averages.

Table 1. The statistics of the training data

Pattern Set	Total	Positive	Negative
R	12658	5324	7334
$S1$	5572	2628	2944
$S2$	6624	3000	3624

2.4 Discretization

It has been shown in the past that discretizing real-valued financial time-series into symbolic streams and subsequent use of predictive models on such sequences can be of great benefit in many financial tasks [9][10]. However, the question of the number and position of discretization intervals has been largely dealt with in an *ad hoc* manner. For example, [10] quantized daily returns of exchange rates of five currencies into nine intervals and up to seven quantization intervals for the returns were considered in [9]. A data-driven parametric scheme for quantizing real-valued time-series is introduced in [11].

We determine the number of intervals such that standard deviation of the distribution of intervals would be maximized. The distribution of intervals of a technical indicator ($p_{ti}(int_i)$) is calculated by the formula:

$$p_{ti}(int_i) = \frac{\#\text{ of values in } int_i}{\text{total }\#\text{ of values}} , \quad (3)$$

where int_i is the ith interval. We try the number of intervals from 3 to 10. Therefore, the determination of the number of intervals (n_{ti}) is represented as:

$$n_{ti} = \arg\max_k \sigma(p_{ti}^k) ,$$

where $\sigma(p_{ti}^k)$ means the standard deviation of the distribution when the number of intervals is k. The position of the intervals is determined to keep the size of the interval same. For that purpose, the values (v) are sorted in decreasing order and the ith position (pos_i) is determined as follows:

$$pos_i = \max(v) - (\max(v) - \min(v)) \times i .$$

3 Trading System

We present a stock trading system that consists of an extraction and a filtering phases with a parameterized trading policy. Figure 2 shows the structure of the trading system.

3.1 Extraction Phase

In this phase, a stock is described by a set of values of technical indicators calculated using data from a stock database in Section 2.1. The questions of the

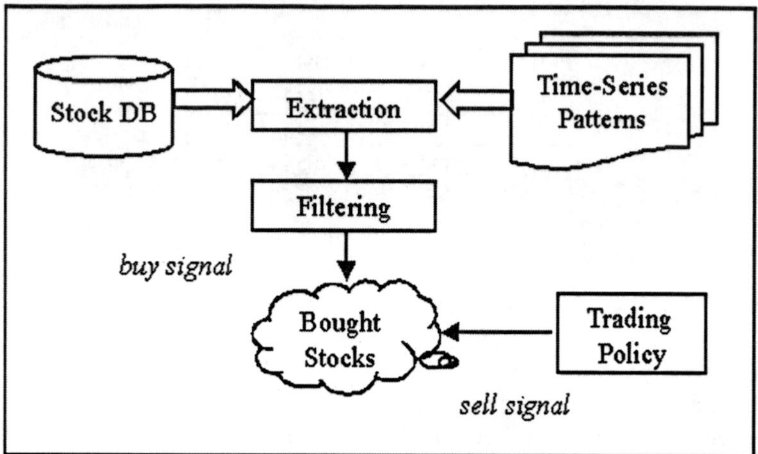

Fig. 2. The structure of the stock trading system

constructed patterns in Section 2.2 are checked with the stock description shown in equation (1). We perform pattern-based extraction rather than the prediction of a single stock because there are multiple stocks in real stock market. The patterns are applied to multiple time-series data and the stocks are matched of which values of indicators satisfy all the questions of a pattern. The set of buying candidates based on the pattern sets ($\mathcal{C}_\mathcal{P}$) is expressed as:

$$\mathcal{C}_\mathcal{P} = \{cs \mid \forall\, ti_i \text{ of } cs,\ cs(v_{ti_i}) \vdash ques_i(ti_i) \in pattern_j(\in \mathcal{P})\}\ , \tag{4}$$

where the subscript $\mathcal{P}$ means a pattern set, *cs* is a candidate stock, $cs(v_{ti_i})$ is the value of technical indicator ti_i of *cs*, and '$\vdash$' means the satisfaction of a question.

3.2 Filtering Phase

In order to take action using the candidates extracted in Section 3.1, we have to select stocks that are most likely to result in high profit. Even if the stocks are extracted using the same pattern, the values of their technical indicators may be different. Therefore, we need to construct classification rules to help the decision making to take a buy action.

Using the training data in Section 2.3, we induce rules that classify the extracted stocks into two categories: *profit-expected, loss-expected.* Only *profit-expected* stocks would be filtered. The overall process of rule induction is illustrated in Figure 3.

The distributions of discretization intervals of technical indicators are calculated respectively for both positive and negative data sets using the equation (3). That is, discretization intervals are considered as random variables and their probability distributions are constructed. For all technical indicators participating in describing a stock, we compare the distributions of intervals. Using

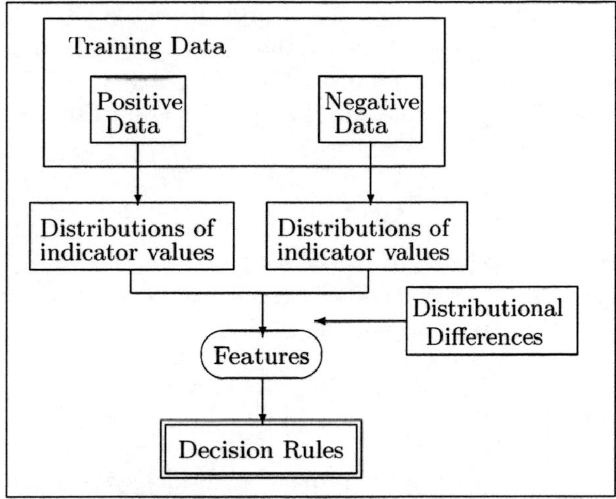

Fig. 3. The overall process of rule induction

distributional differences, we select some intervals as features for building classification rules. A set of selected features (FS_P) is represented as:

$$FS_P = \{f_{ti_i}, f_{tri_j} \mid p_{pos}(f_{ti_i}) > p_{neg}(f_{ti_i}) + \epsilon \text{ or } p_{pos}(f_{tri_j}) > p_{neg}(f_{tri_j}) + \epsilon\} ,$$

where f_{ti_i} is a discretization interval of ti_i, f_{tri_j} is a trigram value, $p_{pos}(f_{ti_i})$ is a probability of f_{ti_i} in positive data set, and $p_{neg}(f_{ti_i})$ is one in negative data set. The constant ϵ is introduced to determine conspicuous features.

For each element in the set, the following rule (r_i) is generated:

$$\text{if } v_{ti_i} \in f_{ti_i}, \quad \text{then } RS(r_i) = p_{pos}(f_{ti_i}) - p_{neg}(f_{ti_i}) \text{ else } RS(r_i) = 0 .$$

A rule score ($RS(r_i)$) is associated with each rule, which can be regarded as a certainty factor.

A buy signal (bs) is generated using the score of the stock and the buy signal function (f_{bs}) is expressed as:

$$f_{bs}(cs) = \begin{cases} 1, & \text{if } \sum_{i=1}^{n} RS(r_i) > \lambda \\ 0, & \text{otherwise} \end{cases} ,$$

where cs is an element of $\mathcal{C}_\mathcal{P}$ in the equation (4) and λ is a threshold value. The filtered set of stocks ($\mathcal{BS}_\mathcal{P}$) is defined as follows and a buy action is to be performed for stocks in the set:

$$\mathcal{BS}_\mathcal{P} = \{s \mid f_{bs}(s) = 1 \text{ and } s \in \mathcal{C}_\mathcal{P}.\} .$$

3.3 Stock Trading Policy

Stock trading policy (STP) specifies a target profit ratio (tpr) and a stop loss ratio (slr) and a maximum holding period (mhp), which directs the sell action:

$$STP = (tpr, slr, mhp) .$$

A buy signal from the filtering phase can be generated after the stock market is closed, so buy is actually performed on the next day. We assume the buy must be done with an open price. Given a stock trading policy, $STP = (\alpha, \beta, \gamma)$, the target profit price (TPP) and the stop loss price (SLP) can be obtained as:

$$TPP = bp \times (1 + \alpha) , \qquad SLP = bp \times (1 - \beta) ,$$

where bp is the buy price. The sell is performed when the target profit price or the stop loss price is reached within the specified maximum holding period. If neither price appears within γ days, the stock would be sold at the close price on the last day of the maximum holding period.

4 Experiments

We simulate stock trading using the proposed trading system on data from July to December 2001 (6 months). Table 2 shows the number of extracted and filtered stocks using three pattern sets in Section 2.2.

Table 2. The statistics of trading stocks

Pattern Set ($\mathcal{P}$)	# of $\mathcal{C}_\mathcal{P}$	# of $\mathcal{BS}_\mathcal{P}$
R	1829	668
$S1$	1116	604
$S2$	1288	895

Using two trading policies, we calculate the rates of returns for each pattern set respectively: $STP_1 = (0.05, 0.05, 1)$, $STP_2 = (0.1, 0.05, 5)$. That is, we evaluate the predictability of daily and weekly returns. Buy is performed on the stocks in $\mathcal{BS}_\mathcal{P}$ and sell is done as a way described in Section 3.3. The rate of return, $R(s)$, is defined somewhat differently from the equation (2):

$$R(s) = \frac{\text{sell price} \; - \; \text{buy price}}{\text{buy price}} \times 100 \, .$$

And, we introduce *profit per trade* (PPT) as an evaluation measure for trading system:

$$PPT = \frac{\sum_{i=0}^{n} R(s)}{n} \; (\%) \, , \quad s \in \mathcal{BS}_\mathcal{P} \text{ and } n = |\mathcal{BS}_\mathcal{P}| \, .$$

Table 3 shows the results of the evaluation. The average holding period in STP_2 is 2.78, 2.88, 2.78 days for pattern sets R, $S1$, and $S2$ respectively. PPT is calculated without the consideration of transaction costs. For performance comparison, the results using decision tree and neural network in filtering phase are also given in Table 3. C4.5 [12] is used to construct decision tree. And, the network is a two-layered feedforward neural network and is trained using the same training data in Section 2.3. As we can see in this table, our method of

Table 3. The results of the evaluation (*PPT*)

Pattern Set		Extraction	Filtering	Decision Tree	Neural Network
R	STP_1	-0.322	0.107	-0.17	-0.01
	STP_2	-0.58	-0.275	-0.35	0.03
S1	STP_1	0.365	0.782	0.757	0.505
	STP_2	0.937	1.683	1.65	1.165
S2	STP_1	-0.03	0.318	0.04	0.145
	STP_2	0.085	0.265	0.344	0.273

rule induction using distributional differences shows better performance. Moreover, we can see that the transaction costs (0.5% per trade) can be overcome in some cases. During the simulation period, KOSPI increased about 16.8% and KOSDAQ rose about -6.4%. The simple cumulative profits of trading for $S1$ pattern sets are 170.328%[2] and 714.532%[3]. Though the results may be different from those of real trading, we can expect more profit than market average with the consideration of the transaction costs.

5 Arguments and Conclusion

We propose a two-phase stock trading system parameterized by the trading policy, which consists of an extraction and a filtering phases. We aim to construct a prediction model for trading multiple stocks. In our trading system, multiple stocks are extracted at the same time and traded. Our trading system is based on the technical analysis, and technical indicators are used in building patterns and inducing classification rules for filtering stocks.

In acquiring decision rules, we adopt a relatively simple method using distributional differences for selecting features on which rules are constructed. Our method uses features that are both independently and jointly predictive, and it would probably miss feature interactions. But we try to capture somewhat manifest features excluding noisy features, which shows a competitive performance. The feature selection method using distributional differences may help fast induction of rules and the reduction of parameters for neural networks training.

The patterns are modeled by expert's knowledge. This trading system plays a role to verify and enhance the knowledge using past data. The proposed framework can be useful in building trading systems based on expert's knowledge.

The results also suggest that the trading policy can affect the expected rate of return. Therefore, the study of finding optimal parameters of a stock trading policy can be considered as future work. Also, more technical indicators can be considered to enhance the performance of the trading system.

[2] $(0.782 - 0.5) \times 604 = 170.328$.
[3] $(1.683 - 0.5) \times 604 = 714.532$.

Acknowledgment

This work was supported by the Korea Science and Engineering Foundation (KOSEF) through the Northeast Asian e-Logistics Research Center at University of Incheon.

References

1. Joumana Ghosn, Yoshua Bengio: Multi-Task Learning for Stock Selection, Advances in Neural Information Processing Systems, volume 9, (1997), 946-952, Michael C. Mozer and Micheal I. Jordan and Thomas Petsche editor, The MIT Press.
2. A. Refenes: Neural Networks in the Capital Markets, (1995), John Wiley and Sons.
3. C. Lee Giles, Steve Lawrence, Ah Chung Tsoi: Rule Inference for Financial Prediction using Recurrent Neural Networks, in Proceedings of IEEE/IAFE Conference on Computational Intelligence for Financial Engineering, (1997), 253-259.
4. N. Towers, A. N. Burgess: Optimisation of Trading Strategies using Parameterised Decision Rules, in Proceedings of IDEAL 98, Perspectives on Financial Engineering and Data Mining, (1998), L. Xu et al editor, Springer-Verlag.
5. Optima Investment Research: Interpreting Technical Indicators, Fourth Edition, (1998), http://www.oir.com.
6. Tak-chung Fu, Fu-lai Chung, Vincent Ng, Robert Luk: Pattern Discovery from Stock Time Series Using Self-Organizing Maps, Workshop Notes of KDD 2001 Workshop on Temporal Data Mining, 26-29 Aug., San Francisco, (2001), 27-37.
7. Jinwoo Baek and Sungzoon Cho: Left Shoulder Detection in Korea Composite Stock Price Index Using an Auto-Associative Neural Network, in Intelligent Data Engineering and Automated Learning - IDEAL 2000, Data Mining, Financial Engineering, and Intelligent Agents, Second International Conference, Springer, (2000), Shatin, N.T. Hong Kong, China.
8. V. Guralnik and J. Srivastava: Event Detection from Time Series Data, in Proceedings of the fifth ACM SIGKDD International Conference on Knowledge Discovery and Data Mining, (1999), 33-42.
9. C. Lee Giles, Steve Lawrence, Ah Chung Tsoi: Noisy time series prediction using a recurrent neural network and grammatical inference, Machine Learning, volume 44, (2000), 161-183.
10. C. P. Papageorgiou: High frequency time series analysis and prediction using Markov models, in Proceedings of IEEE/IAFE Conference on Computational Intelligence Financial Engineering, (1997), 182-185.
11. P. Tino, C. Schittenkopf, G. Dorffner: Volatility trading via temporal pattern recognition in quantized financial time series, Pattern Analysis and Applications, (2001).
12. R. Quinlan: C4.5: Programs for Machine Learning, Morgan Kaufmann, (1992).

A Multi-agent Q-learning Framework for Optimizing Stock Trading Systems

Jae Won Lee[1] and Jangmin O[2]

[1] School of Computer Science and Engineering, Sungshin Women's University, Seoul, Korea 136-742
jwlee@cs.sungshin.ac.kr
[2] School of Computer Engineering, Seoul National University, Seoul, Korea 151-742
jmoh@bi.snu.ac.kr

Abstract. This paper presents a reinforcement learning framework for stock trading systems. Trading system parameters are optimized by Q-learning algorithm and neural networks are adopted for value approximation. In this framework, cooperative multiple agents are used to efficiently integrate global trend prediction and local trading strategy for obtaining better trading performance. Agents communicate with others sharing training episodes and learned policies, while keeping the overall scheme of conventional Q-learning. Experimental results on KOSPI 200 show that a trading system based on the proposed framework outperforms the market average and makes appreciable profits. Furthermore, in view of risk management, the system is superior to a system trained by supervised learning.

1 Introduction

The number of investors in stock market is increasing everyday in this century and intelligent decision support systems aiding them to trade are keenly needed. Many of technical indicators such as moving averages have been developed by researchers in economic area [1]. Also statistical and other computer aided machine learning approaches are prevalent. But many of them, based on supervised learning, have a limitation that they are optimized to prediction criteria without considering trading policies in a unified framework. Recently, as an alternative, reinforcement learning is adopted to optimize trading systems [2][3]. The objective of reinforcement learning is not the minimization of the *sum-of-squares* error which is actually the objective of conventional supervised learning but the acquisition of an optimal policy under which the learning agent achieves the maximal average reward from the environment.

This paper proposes a reinforcement learning framework with multiple cooperative agents to integrate prediction criteria with trading policies more effectively. The agents for buy and sell signals use a matrix named *turning-point structure* in order to model the long-term dependencies of stock prices. To utilize intraday price swings, the agents for ordering executions optimize the short-term policies. Q-learning with neural networks is adopted for training the agents

R. Cicchetti et al. (Eds.): DEXA 2002, LNCS 2453, pp. 153–162, 2002.

to get optimal policies. In addition, the value approximator is trained using a regularizing technique for the prevention of divergence of the parameters. We demonstrate a stock trading system implemented using the proposed framework can significantly outperform the market average and the one implemented by conventional supervised learning algorithm.

The paper is organized as follows. In section 2, we briefly summarize the concept of reinforcement learning and some previous researches on stock market analysis. In section 3, we introduce the overall structure of the framework and explain how the cooperative agents communicate with others. Also, the detailed learning algorithm is presented. In section 4, we describe the experimental setup and results. Finally, in section 5 we conclude with a few future directions.

2 Backgrounds

Reinforcement learning is a computational approach for understanding and automating goal directed learning and decision making. We introduce reinforcement learning following the notations of Sutton [4]. In the reinforcement learning framework, especially in Markov decision process (MDP), there are an agent and an environment interacting with each other at discrete time steps $t = 0, 1, 2, \ldots, T$. The agent selects an action $a_t \in \mathcal{A}$ from its policy π based on the state $s_t \in \mathcal{S}$ of the environment. If certain action is taken by the agent, the environment changes its state to s_{t+1} responding to action a_t and also gives rise to a reward $r_{t+1} \in R$.

If one-step state transition probabilities and one-step expected reward models were available, the environment could be completely described as:

$$p^a_{ss'} = \Pr\{s_{t+1} = s' | s_t = s, a_t = a\} \tag{1}$$

$$r^a_s = \Pr\{r_{t+1} | s_t = s, a_t = a\}, \tag{2}$$

for all $s, s' \in \mathcal{S}$ and $a \in \mathcal{A}$. The objective of the agent is to learn an optimal policy, a mapping from states to actions, that maximizes the expected discounted future reward from state-action pair (s, a), called action-value function $Q^\pi(s, a)$. Given an episodic task which is defined as the history of interactions from the starting state s_0 to the terminal state s_T , $Q^\pi(s, a)$ is defined as:

$$Q^\pi(s, a) = E_\pi\{r_t + \gamma r_{t+1} + \cdots + \gamma^{T-t-1} r_T | s_t = s, a_t = a\}, \tag{3}$$

where $0 \leq \gamma \leq 1$ is a discount-rate. Then optimal policy, denoted Q^*, can be defined as:

$$Q^*(s, a) = \max_\pi Q^\pi(s, a), \tag{4}$$

for all s and a. Though there are many kinds of algorithms for learning optimal policy, they could be grouped into 3 categories according to how their backups are made up. First, dynamic programming uses full backup and can always converge but requires an exact model of the environment. Second, Monte Carlo technique uses only sample backups of the entire episode. It doesn't require any model but needs tremendous episodes for its convergence. Last, the temporal difference (TD) method is a compromise form of both algorithms, It uses both n-step samples and bootstrapping, namely currently learned value model [4], [7]. In practice, TD method is widely used for its easiness of handling but much caution is needed for its convergence [5].

Researches on applying reinforcement learning to stock market analysis have a short history. Neuneier formulated financial market as MDP under some assumptions and simplifications about the market's characteristics [2]. He also modified Q-learning by adding preference to the risk avoiding tendency in [11]. He focused on the asset allocation, that is, how to change one's position to either DAX or DM. Moody et al. formulated a reinforcement learning framework similar to recurrent neural networks [9][10]. Within their framework the policy is directly updated by back propagation through time which is the famous learning technique of recurrent neural networks. He showed that the trained asset allocator could make a profit by changing successfully its position to either S&P 500 or T-Bill market. Xiu et al. also proposed a portfolio management system using Q-learning [8]. Since they used two performance functions, absolute profit and relative risk-adjusted profit, two networks were used in the training process.

Our main interest is not the asset allocation between two markets, but trading stocks in a single stock market. While most reinforcement learning formulations of stock market have one agent, we formulate reinforcement learning with multiple agents.

3 Proposed Framework and Algorithm

In this section, we describe the overall structure of the proposed framework and the details of the Q-learning algorithm for this framework.

3.1 Overall Structure

We propose a multi-agent framework as shown in Fig. 1. This framework aims to maximize the profits of investments by considering not only global trends of stock prices but also intraday price movements of stocks. Each agent has its own goal to achieve and interacts with others to share episodes in the learning process:

- *Buy signal agent* performs prediction by estimating the long-term and short-term information of the states of stocks to produce buy signals.
- *Buy order agent* determines prices for *bids* by estimating the short-term information of the states of stocks. A bid is an order to buy at a given price.
- *Sell signal agent* performs prediction by estimating the long-term and short-term information of the states of stocks and the current profits, to produce sell signals.
- *Sell order agent* determines the prices for *offers* by estimating the short-term information of the states of stocks. An offer is an order to sell at a given price.

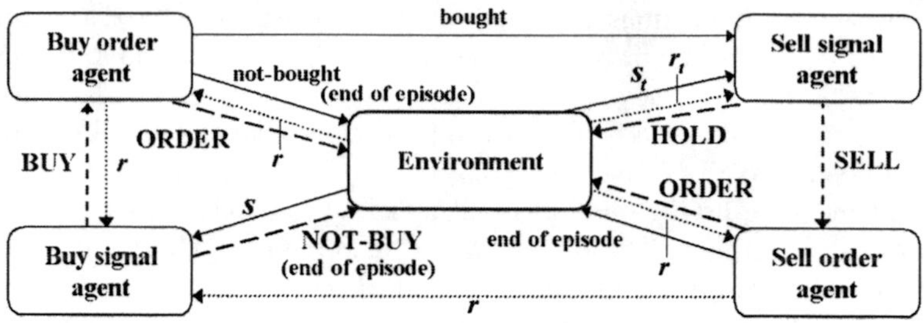

Fig. 1. Structure of the framework

The sell signal agent differs from the buy signal agent in that it also concerns in the policy as well as the prediction for selling. The buy/sell order agents do not perform prediction because their only goal is to provide a policy for optimal order executions in order to increase the success rate of trades.

3.2 States, Actions, and Rewards

One of the most important keys to achieve reasonable performance in machine learning is the representation of the input space. Specially reinforcement learning is an art of the design of state, action and reward. Those in the proposed framework are as follows.

We adopt a binary matrix, the turning-point structure, summarizing the long-term dependencies based on both upper and lower turning points of 5-day moving averages. Fig. 2 shows an example of this matrix. The columns represent the displacement of the day of a turning point from the reference day, and the rows represent the displacement of the price of a turning point from the reference day. The value 'N' means that this slot can not be hit since the price of stocks in KOSPI never reaches that entry[1]. The total number of bits required to represent both matrices for the turning points is 305 with 'N' entries eliminated. In addition to these temporal structures, the buy signal agent shares the short-term technical indicators shown in Table 2, with the ordering agents. After all, the state of the buy signal agent consists of 353 binary bits. The sell signal agent has a few bits more, which represent the current profit rate during a holding period of a stock as shown in Table 1. We confine arbitrarily the profit range as $+30\% \sim -20\%$. So while holding the stock, if its profit rises above $+30\%$ or falls down below -20%, the sell signal agent is compelled to sell the stock forcedly.

The signal agents can take only two kinds of actions. The buy signal agent takes NOT-BUY or BUY and the sell signal agent takes HOLD or SELL. The calculation of reward is as follows. The buy signal agent is given zero reward while it takes NOT-BUY. If it takes BUY the calculation of its reward is postponed until the sell order agent sells the stock. The rate of daily changes of stock prices are given while the sell signal agent takes HOLD. But when it takes SELL, zero

[1] In KOSPI, the restriction of price range for one day is $(+15\%, -15\%)$.

	2	3	5	8	13	21	34	55	89
-89	N	N	N	N	0	0	0	0	0
-55	N	N	0	0	0	0	0	0	0
-34	N	0	0	0	0	0	1	1	1
-21	0	0	0	0	0	1	0	1	1
-13	0	0	0	0	0	0	0	0	1
-8	0	0	0	0	1	0	0	0	1
-5	0	0	0	0	0	0	0	0	0
-3	0	0	0	0	0	0	0	0	0
-2	0	0	0	0	0	0	0	0	0
+2	0	0	0	0	0	0	0	0	0
+3	0	0	0	0	0	0	0	0	0
+5	0	0	0	0	0	0	0	0	0
+8	0	0	0	0	0	0	0	0	0
+13	0	0	0	0	0	0	0	0	0
+21	0	0	0	0	0	0	0	0	0
+34	0	0	0	0	0	0	0	0	0
+55	0	0	0	0	0	0	0	0	0
+89	N	N	N	0	0	0	0	0	0

Upper turning point

	2	3	5	8	13	21	34	55	89
-89	N	N	0	0	0	0	0	0	0
-55	N	0	0	0	0	0	1	1	1
-34	0	0	0	0	0	0	1	1	1
-21	0	0	0	0	0	1	0	0	1
-13	0	0	0	1	1	0	0	0	1
-8	0	0	0	0	0	0	0	0	0
-5	0	0	0	0	0	0	0	0	0
-3	0	0	0	0	0	0	0	0	0
-2	0	0	0	0	0	0	0	0	0
+2	0	0	0	0	0	0	0	0	0
+3	0	0	0	0	0	0	0	0	0
+5	0	0	0	0	0	0	0	0	0
+8	0	0	0	0	0	0	0	0	0
+13	0	0	0	0	0	0	0	0	0
+21	0	0	0	0	0	0	0	0	0
+34	N	0	0	0	0	0	0	0	0
+55	N	0	0	0	0	0	0	0	0
+89	N	N	N	N	0	0	0	0	0

Lower turning point

Fig. 2. An example of turning-point sturucture. 'N' means *not available*

Table 1. Additional bits for the sell signal agent to represent the current profit, which is, 100×(closing price of the current day - buy price)/buy price

Profit	Coding	Profit	Coding
$+(0 \sim 5)$	00000001	$-(0 \sim 3)$	00010000
$+(5 \sim 12)$	00000010	$-(3 \sim 7)$	00100000
$+(12 \sim 20)$	00000100	$-(7 \sim 12)$	01000000
$+(20 \sim 30)$	00001000	$-(12 \sim 20)$	10000000

reward is given because the signal means that it exits the market. When the sell price is determined by the sell order agent, the buy signal agent receives the profit rate, considering the transaction cost, as the reward.

Ordering agents share the state and possible actions shown in Table 2. For a given state, the buy order agent tries to make an optimal bid, that is, the bid at lowest price in the range of stock price changes of the next day. When trading stocks with very high volatility, the buy price may significantly affect to the final profit of the trade. Fig. 3 shows an example of this. Here the bid at 'Low' can decrease the risk of stop-loss selling. The reward of the buy order agent is defined as:

$$r = \begin{cases} e^{-100*d/Low} & \text{bid price} \geq Low, \\ 0 & \text{otherwise}, \end{cases} \tag{5}$$

where d = bid price − Low[2]. If d is 0, the agent receives the maximal reward. Similarly the reward of the sell order agent is defined using $High$[3]:

$$r = \begin{cases} e^{100*d/High} & \text{offer price} \leq High, \\ 0 & \text{otherwise}, \end{cases} \tag{6}$$

where d = offer price − $High$.

[2] The lowest price of the next day.

[3] The highest price of the next day.

Table 2. Coding of state and actions for ordering agents

State	Bits	Action	Coding
Disparity(5)	8	−12%	0000001
Disparity(10)	6	−7%	0000010
Disparity(20)	6	−3%	0000100
MA-Grad(5)	8	0%	0001000
MA-Grad(10)	6	+3%	0010000
MA-Grad(20)	6	+7%	0100000
Body	8	+12%	1000000

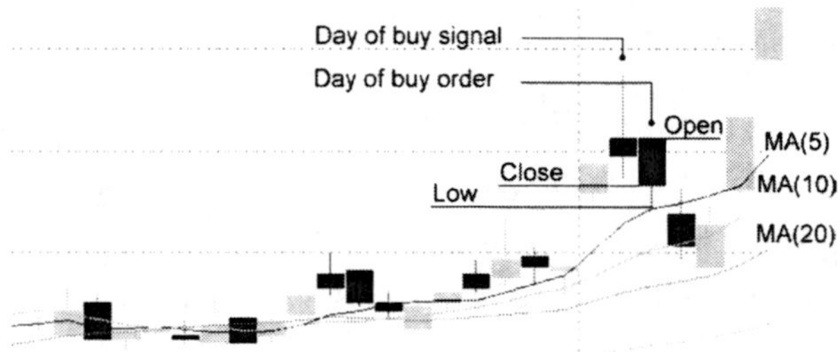

Fig. 3. An example of daily price changes

3.3 Learning Algorithm

An episode starts with a stock at a certain day randomly chosen by the environment. If the buy signal agent takes NOT-BUY as a response to the state of the given stock, the episode ends and a new episode starts. But if the buy signal agent takes BUY, it invokes the buy order agent. The buy order agent refers the state of the stock at the same day and determines the bid price. If the stock can not be purchased, the episode ends and invokes the buy signal agent with 0 as the reward. The whole algorithm including the selling side is shown in Fig. 4. Each agent has equations for reward, delta and Q-value, but all of them are expressed in the same notation for the brevity. Time index is also abbreviated for the same reason. If the sell order agent fails to sell the stock with its offer price, it sells the stock at close, the last traded price of the day. The update rules and function approximation are based on the ordinary Q-learning.

Since the search space of state-action pairs is too large, i.e. 2^{353} for the buy signal agent, to maintain the Q-values in a table, we use neural networks as Q-value approximators. Theoretically there are the situations where simple linear approximators of Q-table can diverge. Baird discussed some theoretical directions to prohibit the divergence of approximators [5]. In this paper, to make the problem simple, we introduce the regularized gradient descent as:

$$\nabla_{\theta_i} \widetilde{Q}(s,a) = \begin{cases} \nabla_{\theta_i} Q(s,a) & \text{if } \theta_i = \text{bias}, \\ \nabla_{\theta_i} Q(s,a) + \nu * \theta_i & \text{otherwise}, \end{cases} \tag{7}$$

Buy signal agent :

1. Environment produces s.

$$a \leftarrow \begin{cases} \arg\max_a Q(s,a) & \text{with prob. } 1-\epsilon, \\ \text{random selection} & \text{with prob. } \epsilon. \end{cases}$$

If a = NOT-BUY Episode ends and goto 1.
Else Invoke the buy order agent and wait for invocations from other agents.
If the invocation is from the buy order agent
 $r \leftarrow 0$
Else
 $r \leftarrow ((1-TC)*SP-BP)/BP$
$\delta \leftarrow r - Q(s,a);\quad \theta \leftarrow \theta + \eta * \delta * \nabla_\theta Q(s,a)$
Episode ends and goto 1.

Buy order agent :

2. Environment produces s.

$$a \leftarrow \begin{cases} \arg\max_a Q(s,a) & \text{with prob. } 1-\epsilon, \\ \text{random selection} & \text{with prob. } \epsilon. \end{cases}$$

$d = MA(5) + \frac{a}{100} * MA(5) - Low$
If $d \geq 0$
 $r \leftarrow e^{-100*d/Low};\quad \delta \leftarrow r - Q(s,a);\quad \theta \leftarrow \theta + \eta * \delta * \nabla_\theta Q(s,a)$
 Invoke the sell signal agent with BP, where $BP = MA(5) + \frac{a}{100} * MA(5)$.
Else
 $r \leftarrow 0;\quad \delta \leftarrow r - Q(s,a);\quad \theta \leftarrow \theta + \eta * \delta * \nabla_\theta Q(s,a)$
 Invoke the buy order agent.

Sell signal agent :

3. Environment produces s.

$$a \leftarrow \begin{cases} \arg\max_a Q(s,a) & \text{with prob. } 1-\epsilon, \\ \text{random selection} & \text{with prob. } \epsilon. \end{cases}$$

If a = HOLD
 $s' \leftarrow Action(s,a);\ r \leftarrow RC;$
 $\delta \leftarrow r + \gamma * \max_{a'} Q(s',a') - Q(s,a);\ \theta \leftarrow \theta + \eta * \delta * \nabla_\theta Q(s,a)$
 Goto 3.
Else Invoke the sell order agent.

Sell order agent :

4. Environment produces s.

$$a \leftarrow \begin{cases} \arg\max_a Q(s,a) & \text{with prob. } 1-\epsilon, \\ \text{random selection} & \text{with prob. } \epsilon. \end{cases}$$

$d = MA(5) + \frac{a}{100} * MA(5) - High$
If $d \leq 0$
 $r \leftarrow e^{100*d/High};\quad \delta \leftarrow r - Q(s,a);\quad \theta \leftarrow \theta + \eta * \delta * \nabla_\theta Q(s,a)$
 Invoke the buy signal agent with BP and $SP(MA(5) + \frac{a}{100} * MA(5))$.
Else
 $r \leftarrow 0;\quad \delta \leftarrow r - Q(s,a);\quad \theta \leftarrow \theta + \eta * \delta * \nabla_\theta Q(s,a)$
 Invoke the buy signal agent with BP and $SP(Close)$.

Fig. 4. Q-learning algorithm for the proposed framework. TC is the transaction cost, SP is the sell price, BP is the buy price, and RC is the rate of change of the closing price

where ν is the constant that controls the degree of weight decay. The regularized gradient descent is a popular technique in the neural network society, and can discourage a component of parameters from increasing indefinitely.

4 Experiment

We compare a stock trading system built according to the proposed framework with another trading system trained by supervised learning using a neural network with the same input space described in section 3. For convenience, the former system is called MAQ and the latter SNN in this section.

Table 3 shows the data set. The network structure of MAQ arbitrarily chosen as two hidden layers with 40×20 neurons. The strategy of shrinkage of the learning rate is not adopted, but the learning rate is fixed $\eta = 0.005$ for all the agents. The weight decay constant is fixed as $\nu = 0.2$ after some preliminary trials. The discount factor γ is set to 0.95 and the exploration factor ϵ is set to 0.1. After each of 20,000 episodes is experienced, the system is verified on the validation set.

Table 3. Partitions and specification of the data set

Partition	Period	Size
Training set	Jan-1999 ~ Dec-2000	32,019
Validation set	Jan-2001 ~ May-2001	6,102
Test set	Jun-2001 ~ Oct-2001	6,213

Fig. 5 shows the tendency of the training performance of MAQ. Before 2,800,000 episodes are experienced, the trades are conducted about 50 times from 20,000 episodes in the training set and never in the validation set. This means that the system is trying to buy and sell through only random exploration of ϵ-policy. In this first period, trades lead to losses, about -1.2% ~ -0.1%[4]. After 2,800,000 episodes, the number of trades and the profit begin to increase in both data set. This means that the system begins to buy and sell stocks by its greedy policy and make profits from those trades. But after 5,900,000 episodes there is, though less significant, degradation of the average profit in the validation set. So the system is stopped to train at that point and is applied to the test set.

Both trading systems, MAQ and SNN, have five subtraders which individually trade their assets according to the strategy of the system they belong to. The trading system evaluates stocks and gathers the upper ranked candidates. From the candidates pool, the target stock is randomly distributed to each subtrader. After some steps of trading, the invest moneys of subtraders are merged and redistributed equally and trades are continued. SNN buys and sells stocks at opening prices while MAQ follows the decision of the ordering agents.

[4] The transaction cost is 0.5% in Korean stock market.

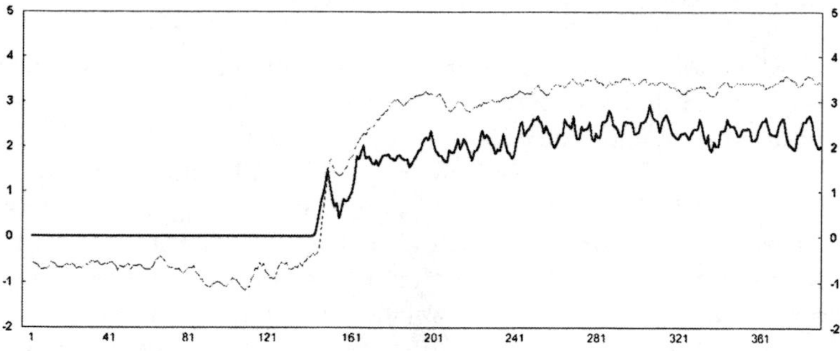

Fig. 5. Average profit rate induced during every 20,000 episodes

Fig. 6 shows the performance of both SNN and MAQ on the test set. KOSPI is 612 point on the starting day of the test period. On the whole, it can be said that MAQ outperforms both the market index and SNN. At the end of the test period, the asset of MAQ increases 28.26% to 785 while that of SNN increases 8.49% to 664.

In view of risk management, MAQ is also superior to SNN. There are two shocks in KOSPI during the test period. One is the internal shock between June to July, that is, the market is in a normal bear trend. The profit of SNN is severely degraded from this shock but MAQ endures the shock with a relatively small loss. The other is an external shock, the tragedy of September 11, 2001. For a week after the tragedy, The Korean stock market suffered from panic selling. Both systems lead to severe losses for this short period. But after the end of September, the market changes to a bull market. In this period, the profit of MAQ is increased steadily while that of SNN somewhat fluctuates.

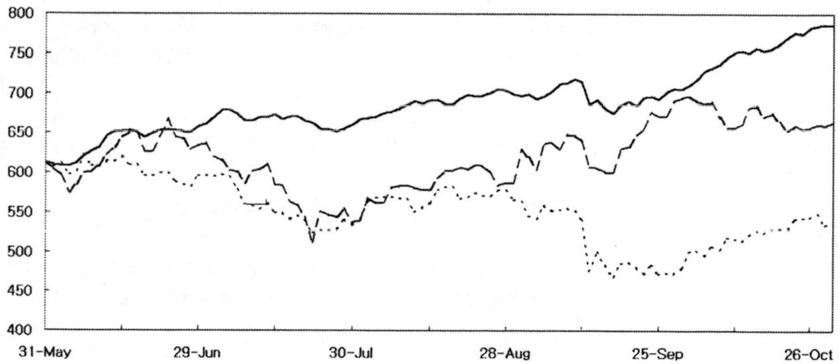

Fig. 6. Profit ratio of SNN (dashed) and MAQ (solid). Each system starts to trade with the asset 612 equivalent to the starting value of KOSPI (dotted) for comparison

5 Conclusion

We proposed a framework for building stock trading systems with multiple cooperative agents formulated under reinforcement learning. Also we designed a data structure for summarizing the historic information of price changes for a long period. The system achieves a higher profit and reasonable risk management compared with the one trained by supervised learning in the Korean stock market. However, there are several additional realistic considerations to be incorporated in a stock trading system. These include the number of portfolios, the distribution of the asset to each portfolio, and adaptation of the trend of the stock market. Reinforcement learning is promising but incorporation of these considerations makes the problem more complex. So making formulations of reinforcement learning with those considerations tractable is the future work.

References

1. Kendall, S. M., Ord, K.: Time Series. Oxford, New York. (1997)
2. Neuneier, R.: Enhancing Q-Learning for Optimal Asset Allocation. Advances in Neural Information Processing Systems 10. MIT Press, Cambridge. (1998) 936–942
3. Lee, J.: Stock Price Prediction using Reinforcement Learning. In Proceedings of the 6th IEEE International Symposium on Industrial Electronics. (2001)
4. Sutton, R. S., Barto, A. G.: Reinforcement Learning : An Introduction. MIT Press, Cambridge. (1998)
5. Baird, L. C.: Residual Algorithms: Reinforcement learning with Function Approximation. In Proceedings of Twelfth International Conference on Machine Learning. Morgan Kaufmann, San Fransisco. (1995) 30–37
6. Bengio, Y., Simard, P., Frasconi, P.: Learning Long-Term Dependencies with Gradient is Difficult. IEEE Transactions on Neural Networks 5(2). (1994) 157–166
7. Jaakkola, M., Jordan, M., Singh, S.: On the Convergence of Stochastic Iterative Dynamic Programming Algorithms. Neural Computation, 6(6). (1994) 1185–2201
8. Xiu, G., Laiwan, C.: Algorithm for Trading and Portfolio Management Using Q-learning and Sharpe Ratio Maximization. In Proceedings of ICONIP 2000, Korea. (2000) 832–837
9. Moody, J., Wu, Y., Liao, Y., Saffell, M.: Performance Functions and Reinforcement Learning for Trading Systems and Portfolios. Journal of Forecasting, 17(5-6). (1998) 441–470
10. Moody, J., Saffell, M.: Learning to Trade via Direct Reinforcement. IEEE Transactions on Neural Networks, 12(4). (2001) 875–889
11. Neuneier, R., Mihatsch., O.: Risk Sensitive Reinforcement Learning. Advances in Neural Information Processing Systems 11. MIT Press, Cambridge. (1999) 1031–1037

Using Adaptive Programming in Legal Advisory Systems

P. Kroha and S. Bürgel

TU Chemnitz,
Department of Computer Science, 09107 Chemnitz, Germany

Abstract. A legal advisory system is in principle an information system that does not collect and store data but regulations. In our system ADONIS regulations are stored in form of an object-oriented model that can be investigated by queries. Since regulations are frequently a subject to changes, the system has been implemented using adaptive programming to achieve a simple, cheap, and reliable maintenance. In this contribution, we present our experience with applying the adaptive programming technology for the purpose described above.

1 Introduction

In this paper, we focus on the problem of maintenance and evolution of systems that extract information from regulations and laws. To simplify, we focus on evolution of the static model especially on evolution of the class structure. The problem is how to minimize impact of these changes, i.e. how to minimize costs of adaptive maintenance.

We describe our experience with the application of adaptive programming technology for this purpose. Problems of modelling of legal advisory systems will be discussed in another paper [12]. The implemented legal advisory system ADONIS, this paper is dealing with, shall support students of our department with respect to the agenda of academic regulations and laws.

The rest of the paper is organized as follows. In Section 2 we discuss the related work. In Section 3 we briefly explain some basics of adaptive programming [14] that are necessary for understanding our paper. Our original solution of the object initialization problem of common object graphs will be presented in Section 4. In Section 5 we present our system ADONIS. In Section 6 our experience with adaptive programming and its tools will be described. In the last section we resume and draw our conclusions.

2 Related Work

Since 1988 [13], the idea of adaptive programming is being used and improved in many ways and supported by many tools. There are very many papers describing all possible theoretical aspects of adaptive programming concerning design and compiling, but only a few projects describing an application experience.

R. Cicchetti et al. (Eds.): DEXA 2002, LNCS 2453, pp. 163–171, 2002.

We have found a compiler project using Demeter/Java [1]. The Secure Internet Gateway System (SIGS) project at GTE Laboratories has a component whose purpose is to perform validation of incoming requests from customers. This component has been used for processing Verizon's agenda and has sustained six iterations of changing requirements. The other compiler would have taken three weeks to build and the DemeterJ version was done in two days.

Another projects uses adaptive programming in compiling too. The goal of project described in [16] is to devise two languages that may be used to automatically convert existing C++ classes into COM objects and interfaces (for use with Microsoft Visual C++). In Motorola Design Pattern Code Generator [17], a code generation tool has been written that was originally developed as a Perl script.

In [7], an application is described that has been used by both internal and external customers to troubleshoot schema problems. A schema is the heart of any hierarchical database such as Novell Directory Services (NDS).

Advantages of adaptive programming for maintenance are supposed since [15], but we have not found any case study that would describe a project using adaptive technology in information systems or advisory systems.

3 On Adaptive Programming

Adaptive programming [14] is a higher-level abstraction of object-oriented programming aiming at the production of better maintainable code. It generally respects the following guidelines: The Law of Demeter,Traversal strategies, Visitor-style programming.

The Law of Demeter [14] restricts targets of message sending in conventional object-oriented programming using the following rules. Suppose we have an object-oriented schema (a class graph representing class relations association and aggregation) and a query Q has to be implemented. This query (called also an operation) will be sent as a message to an object O of a class C, it initiates a chain of messages that will be finished by an answer-message. Methods of the class C are only allowed to send messages to objects of the following classes: classes of the immediate attributes of the current object O, classes of the argument objects of Q (including C itself), and classes of objects created by Q.

This implies that operations have only a limited knowledge about the whole class structure of the model and objects communicate only with closely related objects.

Traversal strategies describe the using of a subset of model's static structures that will be concerned by processing of the given operation. In a typical object-oriented program a high percentage of code fragments is only concerned with passing messages or transporting objects along a chain of collaborating objects. All these trivial operations share common behavior, which can be abstracted out. Traversal strategies exactly accomplish this task. They describe the traversal of all collaborating objects of an operation in a succinct manner. When speaking about a program, we mention traversal of collaborating objects (run-time). In a more abstract sense, when speaking about a traversal graph (a subgraph of the class graph), we use to speak about collaborating classes (compile-time). Sometimes, these two levels of abstraction will not be distinguished very strictly.

A visitor is a class containing a subset of the dynamical model that concern the given operation. It specifies methods to be executed when performing an operation on a set of collaborating objects on the traversal graph. Although traversal strategies generate the whole traversal code for us, they cannot free us from writing non-trivial operation code, i.e. from description of the behavior in nodes. We suppose that any node of the traversal graph, i.e. any collaborating class, can contribute to the semantics of the operation. This task is performed in adaptive programming by so called Adaptive visitors [14] whose idea is an extension of that rooted in Gamma's Visitor design pattern [5].

The main idea of the adaptive programming can be explained on the following cases. Leaf-classes contain data to be processed and usually have a method that contains some nontrivial semantics of the processing. Non-leaf classes propagate the message to their successors in the class graph. For such non-leaf classes that only propagate messages and do not contribute to the semantics of the query, a corresponding program representing only the propagation to the next collaborating object can automatically be generated. For such non-leaf classes that contribute to the semantics of the query processing, their contribution must explicitly be described (using so called wrappers in the language DemeterJ) and assigned to the corresponding class.

This means, that a propagation pattern (traversal strategy + adaptive visitor) must contain at least the semantics of the leaf method, but it can additionally contain some semantic contribution of traversed non-leaf classes. In this way, a propagation pattern can be seen as a novel query notation in OODBMSs.

Summarized, an adaptive program is a sequence of propagation patterns that encapsulate the behavior which will be spread across in methods of classes along the paths of propagation. Each propagation pattern is a navigation specification (including some constraints concerning paths in the class structures) that describes how objects have to be traversed in the corresponding program.

Propagation patterns of the adaptive program are used by the translator for producing an object-oriented program. An adaptive program represents a generic template which is parameterized by the class structure. To obtain a concrete object-oriented program the adaptive program must be instantiated by a concrete class structure.

Using propagating patterns, adaptive operations become flexible against changes in the class structure. We agree that it can bring a benefit in programming legal advisory systems and information systems that are closely related to regulations and law.

4 Initialization of Object Graphs

Similarly to other information systems, we also have to keep objects permanently. Our persistent objects correspond to the concepts stated in the modelled regulations, i.e. objects used in regulations have to be created and stored during the initialization phase. This implies the problem of how to create objects graphs in a simple manner.

Application-specific languages (ASL) used in DemeterJ can solve that problem only partially. The Demeter project utilizes ASLs for the adaptive specification of object structures. In their approach, the class dictionary, which actually describes class structures, is enriched with syntactical elements forming a grammar for an ASL. That ASL is then employed to initialize objects according to their class structure.

This approach has one drawback. The ASLs specified by Demeter are only applicable to the description of object trees. Most real-world domains can not be mapped onto tree-like object structures, though. Hence, we needed a method suitable for – possibly cyclic – object graphs.

We have developed and implemented a solution of our own that is able to describe complete object graphs flexible with respect to class structure evolution using our own object graph description language (OGDL).

The OGDL interpreter is written in DemeterJ itself and comes as a separate component. An object graph described in OGDL can be used with any Java 2 application although it shows particular strength in conjunction with DemeterJ-enabled applications. The main features of OGDL include

- instantiation of tree-like object subgraphs by parsing ASLs,
- instantiation of remaining objects using OGDL (default constructors and value assignments),
- linking objects by 1:1 and 1:n associations.

OGDL takes advantage of the fact that each object graph can be clustered into subgraphs that are completely tree-like. Such subgraphs can be initialized using DemeterJ's built-in ASLs. Moreover, OGDL allows each object within the object graph to be labeled by an unique identifier. Identified objects can be linked together by associations. As a consequence, we are able to successively instantiate and link objects. A welcomed side-effect of this solution is that at least the object subgraphs keep their adaptivity properties.

OGDL is kept very simple. There are no control structures built in. So, the only flow of control is sequential. The connection between the OGDL interpreter and the resulting object graph relies completely on the reflection capabilities of the Java programming language.

5 Legal Advisory System ADONIS

Representing regulations and laws in models for automated processing is an open problem. There are some artificial intelligence approaches using a rule system as a basic modelling unit for legal advisory systems because of the inference possibility. We have found that meaning of many words used in regulations are too much complex, vague, and ambiguous to let a computer derive possible impacts. Therefore, we decided to handle these information without inferencing but in a natural and intuitive way.

In our approach, an analyst transforms the text of regulations into an object-oriented model and the message-flow in the model substitutes the inferencing. This means that some complex semantic transformations run in a human brain during modelling. Because of frequent changes in regulations, we restricted the used object-oriented technology according to adaptive programming principles.

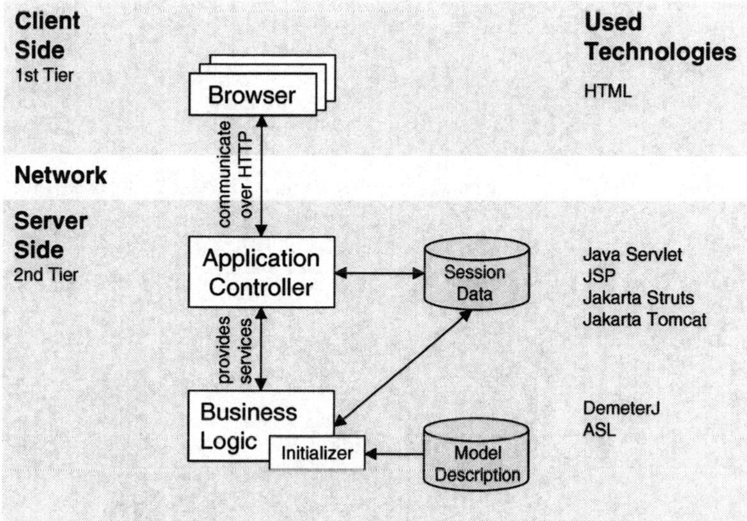

Fig. 1. Architecture of ADONIS prototype

The system ADONIS deals with the agenda of academic regulations and laws of the Department of Computer Science at the Chemnitz University of Technology. Its intended purpose is to assist students with the interpretation and application of regulations and laws that concern their education process.

In case of ADONIS the domain is described in natural language inside the stated regulations and laws. In order to formalize these contents in a more object-oriented way, we have utilized a special analysis tool that is being developed at the TU Chemnitz. The Textual Assistant (TESSI) [8], [11] supports us in turning a natural specification text into the UML model supported further by Rational Rose using an XML interace between both tools.

For ADONIS we have found a two-tier application architecture using the model-view-controller design pattern as best suitable. In our case, we can denote it as a thin client-server Web application. An experimental prototype of ADONIS has been implemented in DemeterJ [3] and Java 2. The system architecture is web-based on top of the Jakarta Struts framework [6] which is further based on Java Servlet and JSP technology.

6 Evaluation of Adaptive Programming

This evaluation is based on our experience from implementing ADONIS. Most of the findings presented in this chapter have been won from our work with DemeterJ 0.8.3, a recent AP implementation. Nonetheless, the majority of our findings addresses the theoretical concepts behind AP and is not only related to that specific implementation. In the following paragraphs we analyze and compare the advantages and disadvantages of AP as we see them from the perspective of our project.

6.1 Advantages

- The separation of class structure and behavior eases the readability and clarity of code.
  Class dictionaries provide a fast overview of the contained classes and their relationships. AP's functionality is grouped by behavior files in a fine-grained manner. Methods and traversal specifications can be arranged into the same behavior file according to their intended purpose. So, each behavior file represents a certain functional category (aspect) which further eases the clarity of complex applications.
- Visitor-style programming allows an intuitive way to implement complex operations.
  Traversal strategies in conjunction with adaptive visitors help to keep the administrative overhead of this programming style low. So, AP users may fully concentrate on the participating classes and their role in an operation.
- AP's higher abstraction level leads to small code.
  Large parts of the underlying object-oriented code are automatically generated. This feature saves a lot of written work. In addition, traversal code is automatically derived from traversal strategies. As a result, a high percentage of AP code is only concerned with the actual problem and not with tedious, frequently repeating tasks.
- AP does not restrict the usage of third party libraries.
  Class dictionaries may have references to external packages or classes. In that case those entities are seen as terminals, i.e. they cannot be included in traversals.

6.2 Disadvantages

- Traversal strategies may become complex especially with recursive class structures.

These class structures regularly introduce alternative traversal paths that must not be included in a traversal. Negative path constraints are able to exclude certain paths from a traversal. It may be hard to specify a traversal strategy in a clean, adaptive manner.

– Traversals may not be broken after modifications of the class structure, but they may deliver wrong results without any warning notifications.
The traversal should be specific enough to visit all necessary classes and relations in right order, but it should also be general enough to evolve with the class structure. If a strategy is too specific, a corresponding traversal may not be found and it will be reported to the developer. Otherwise, if a strategy is too general, a traversal may still work after changing the class structure but may also fail to deliver correct results. We call this behavior "over-adaptivity". Unluckily, the recognition of those misbehaving traversals is not always trivial.
– There exists no support for generating documentation.
Especially traversals and the corresponding visitors could need some form of documentary help. The current state of the art in AP documentation are generated traversal graphs in textual form as well as comments on source code level.
– Exception handling facilities are underdeveloped.
Exceptions may be declared for ordinary methods but not for adaptive visitors or generated getter/setter methods. In case of DemeterJ the only form of exception that can be thrown without being declared is the `RuntimeException` or one of its subclasses. This means that exceptional conditions that occur during a traversal or within setter/getter methods can not be declared by ordinary exceptions. Instead we have to revert to Java's RuntimeException.
– Error tracing is relatively complicated.
As in all preprocessors, the source code is first transformed to some form of intermediate code, which is finally compiled into machine-executable code. If now an error occurs during execution, it can only be traced back to the intermediate code by conventional means.

7 Concluding Remarks

We have found that adaptive programming is also applicable on smaller projects. In ADONIS, for example, we use the generative features of DemeterJ to an extent that allows us to describe loads of small, dumb information classes in a very compact manner. In the current version, there are about 50 classes identified from the regulations (not including GUI and other packages), the adaptive DemeterJ-source code has only about 1000 lines and the corresponding generated Java-code has 18.000 lines. This relation improves the understandability of the program immensely.

The intention behind adaptive programming lies in the field of evolutionary software development. It is sure not the remedy for any problem associated with the evolution of software but it clearly addresses the problem of changing class structures. However, it does not provide any support with respect to functional evolution.

Adaptive programming shall ease the maintainability of software. Here we can give only some presumable answers, because the ADONIS project has not entered the maintenance phase yet.

Currently, we would not recommend to employ adaptive programming in commercially critical projects unless the class hierarchy will change very often. Adaptive programming is still a subject of further research, and the currently available development tools have not left alpha or beta status yet.

On the other hand, adaptive programming is sure a suitable technology for implementing systems whose object-oriented model represents some imaginations of human beings and changes often because of some administrative decisions having a political background. Here, the advantages in maintenance will bring more benefit as the costs of non-maturity in development.

References

1. Blando, L.:The EEL Compiler Using Adaptive Object Oriented Programming and Demeter/Java http://www.ccs.neu.edu/research/demeter/evaluation/gte-labs/aosd2002/after-four.txt
2. Bürgel, S.: ADONIS – A Case Study of a Legal Advisory System Using Adaptive Programming. M.Sc. Thesis, Faculty of Informatics, TU Chemnitz, 2002.
3. Demeter Research Group: Demeter/Java: Adaptive and Aspect-Oriented Programming in Java. Project homepage at http://www.ccs.neu.edu/research/demeter/DemeterJava
4. Demeter Research Group: Project homepage at http://www.ccs.neu.edu/home/lieber/demeter.html
5. Gamma, E., Helm, R., Johnson, R., Vlissides, J.: Design Patterns: Elements of Reusable Object-Oriented Software. Addison-Wesley, 1995
6. http://jakarta.apache.org/struts
7. Jensen, N., Wagstaff, D., Danielson, S.: Can Demeter be used for Real Life Applications? Yes. NTU 737 Final Project http://support.novell.com/misc/patlst.htm.
8. Kroha, P., Strauss, M.: Requirements Specification Iteratively Combined with Reverse Engineering. In: Plasil, F., Jeffery, K. (Eds.): Proceedings of SOFSEM'97, LNCS 1338, Springer Verlag, 1997.
9. Kroha,P.: Advanced Concepts on Top of Object-Oriented Programming. Proceedings of System Integration Conference, 1999.
10. Kroha, P.: Adaptive Programming for Evolutionary Software Systems. Proceedings of the 45 International Scientific Colloquium, Ilmenau Technical University, 2000.
11. Kroha, P.: Preprocessing od Requirements Specification. In: Ibrahim, M., Kung, J., Revell, N. (Eds.): Proceedings of DEXA'2000, LNCS 1873, Springer Verlag, 2000.
12. Kroha, P., Bürgel, S.: Modelling in Legal Advisory Systems. To appear.
13. Lieberherr, K., Riel, A.: Demeter: A CASE Study of Software Growth Through Parameterized Classes. In: Proceedings of the 10th International Conference on Software Engineering (ICSE'88), Singapore, pp. 254-264, IEEE Press, 1988.
14. Lieberherr, K.: Adaptive Object-Oriented Software: The Demeter Method with Propagation Patterns, PWS Publishing Company, 1996.

15. Lieberherr, K., Orleans, D.: Preventive program maintenance in Demeter/Java (research demonstration). In: International Conference on Software Engineering (ICSE '97), Boston, 1997.
16. Miller, A.: C++ COMponent Magic Project - A COM Aspect for C++ Xerox ScanSoft, Inc. http://www.ccs.neu.edu/research/demeter/evaluation/ScanSoft/source/
17. Motorola Design Pattern Code Generator. http://www.ccs.neu.edu/research/demeter/course/f97/projects/motorola/html/project.html

Web Information Retrieval Based on the Localness Degree

Chiyako Matsumoto[1], Qiang Ma[2], and Katsumi Tanaka[2]

[1] Department of Computer and Systems Engineering,
Graduate School of Science and Technology,
Kobe University.
Rokkodai, Nada, Kobe, 657-8501, Japan
chiyako@db.cs.scitec.kobe-u.ac.jp
http://www.db.cs.scitec.kobe-u.ac.jp/

[2] Department of Social Informatics,
Graduate School of Informatics,
Kyoto University.
Yoshida Honmachi, Sakyo, Kyoto, 606-8501, Japan
{qiang,tanaka}@dl.kuis.kyoto-u.ac.jp
http://www.dl.kuis.kyoto-u.ac.jp/

Abstract. A vast amount of information is available on the WWW. There are a lot of Web pages whose content is 'local' and interesting for people in a very narrow regional area. Usually, users search for information with search engines, even though finding or excluding local information may still be difficult. In this paper, we propose a new information retrieval method that is based on the localness degree for discovering or excluding local information from the WWW. Localness degree is a new notion for estimating the local dependence and ubiquitous nature of Web pages. The localness degree is computed by 1) a content analysis of the Web page itself, to determine the frequency of occurrence of geographical words, and the geographical area (i.e., latitude and longitude) covered by the location information given on the page, and 2) a comparison of the Web page with other pages with respect to daily (ubiquitous) content. We also show some results of our preliminary experiments of the retrieval method based on the localness degree.

1 Introduction

The World Wide Web (WWW) is rapidly progressing and spreading. In the year 2000, about 2.1 billion pages were available on the Web, and about 7 million new pages appeared every day [1].

Everyone-both novice and expert- can access the vast amount of information available on the WWW and find what they are looking for. Conventionally, users input keywords or keyword-based user profiles to search for the information of interest. Unfortunately, it's not always easy to specify the keywords of user interest information, especially, for recently posted information, such as new pages and news articles. Ma [2,3] and Miyazaki [4] focused on the time-series feature of information and proposed some meaningful measures, called freshness and popularity, to fetch new valuable information.

R. Cicchetti et al. (Eds.): DEXA 2002, LNCS 2453, pp. 172–181, 2002.

However, while there are many occurrences of local adhesion information on the Web, it is not always easy to find and eliminate local information via conventional methods. Some portal Web sites [5,6] provide the regional information, which is clustered by keywords. In such portal Web sites, users are required to clearly specify their interest by keywords. Moreover, since the regional information is entered by users, the search information may be limited, and some valuable local information may be missed.

In this paper, we propose a non-traditional information retrieval method that is based on the *localness degree*. Localness degree is a new notion for discovering or excluding local information from the WWW.

In this paper, we assume that local information includes:

- information that is only interested by users in some special region or organization (we called regional interest information), and
- information that describe something (event, etc.) about some special region or organization (we called regional content).

From these aspects, regional interest and regional content, we propose two types of localness degree of a Web page: 1) localness of content, and 2) localness of community.

Localness of Content. Localness of Content means that how much the content is concerned with specifical region, according to the aspect of regional content.

We analyze the content of Web page to estimate its region dependence. If a page has high region dependence, it should be regional content. Therefore, its probability of being local information may be high. We call this type of localness as localness of content.

First, we compute the frequency and the level of detail of geographical words appearing on a Web page. In this paper, we assume that geographical words are words of region name, oraganization name, and so on. If geographical words appear frequently and in detail, the localness degree is high. Therefore, it could be regional content and its localness degree of content may be high.

We also compute the coverage of these geographical words with respect to location information (that is, latitude and longitude). If the geographical coverage is small and there are many detailed geographical words (e.g., regional names), the localness degree of the Web page is considered high. In other words, we compute the proportion of the density of geographical words to the geographical coverage to estimate the localness degree. If the density is high, localness degree of content of that page could be high.

Localness of Community. Localness of Community[1] means the localness of the interests, that is, to what extent the interests are bound to a special region, where, the interests is a group of people interested in a special topic (content).

Some events occur anywhere and some events occur only in some special region. Information about the latter is a scoop and may be interested by all users (of all regions). In other words, it may be global interest information more than regional interest information. Therefore, if a page describes such scoop event (the latter), it may not be local information. On the other hand, if a page describes ubiquitous event (the former type.

[1] In this paper, the term 'localness' means physical localness, not logical. For this, we do not consider the logical (virtual) community in this paper.

High similarity between these events excluding the location or time), it may be interested only by users of some special region. For instance, a summer festival is held everywhere in Japan. These events (summer festivals) are similar although the location and time may be different. People may be only interested in the summer festival of his/her town. In other words, a summer festival may be interested by its residents only. We call this kind of information local information of community.

We compare the estimating page with other Web pages, to determine if it represents a ubiquitous topic or event. If a page represents a ubiquitous topic or event, its localness degree of community may be high.

The first step is to exclude geographical words and proper nouns from the Web page. Then, if this page contains many words that often appear in other pages, then it is regarded as ubiquitous information. Ubiquitous information means information that can be found anywhere and anytime. This information could be an event, or information given daily. The localness degree of such a page is considered to be high.

We also note that there may be many pages covering a same event. Such pages should not be local but global or *popular* [2,3,4]. To distinguish from this case, we just need to check the location information of the events, which are reported by the estimating page and the comparison pages. If the locations are different, so we can say that these pages represent different daily events. The localness degree of these pages may be high.

The remainder of this paper is organized as follows: in chapter 2, we give an overview of related work. In chapter 3, we present a mathematical definition of localness degree of Web pages. We show some preliminary evaluation results in chapter 4. Finally, we conclude this paper with some discussion and a summary in chapter 5.

2 Related Work

Mobile Info Search (MIS) [7] is a project that proposes a mobile-computing methodology and services for utilizing local information from the Internet. The goal of MIS is to collect, structure, and integrate distributed and diverse local information from the Internet into a practical form, and make it available through a simple interface to mobile users in various situations or contexts. The researchers in this project do this in a location-oriented way, and have produced a MIS prototype system [8]. The prototype system exchanges information bi-directionally between the virtual Web world and the real world. Our research differs in that we define a new concept, the localness degree of a Web page, for discovering 'local' information from the Web.

Buyukkokten et al. [9] discussed how to map a Web site to a geographical location, and studied the use of several geographical keys for the purpose of assigning site-level geographical context. By analyzing "whois" records, they built a database that correlates IP addresses and hostnames to approximate physical locations. By combining this information with the hyperlink structure of the Web, they were able to make inferences about the geography of the Web at the granularity of a site. They also presented a tool to visualize geographical Web data. Digital City [10] propose an augmented Web space and its query language to support geographical querying and sequential plan creation utilizing a digital city that is a city-based information space on the Internet. The augmented Web space consists of home pages, hyperlinks, and generic links that represent geographical relations between home pages. They have applied the proposed augmented Web space to Digital City Kyoto, a city information service system that is accessed through a 3D walk-through implementation and a map-based interface. In contrast, our work focuses on how to discover local information from Web contextually: content and correlation with others. Geographic Search [11] adds the ability to search for web pages within a particular geographic locale to traditional keyword searching. To accomplish this, Daniel converted street addresses found within a large corpus of documents to latitude-longitude-based coordinates using the freely available TIGER and FIPS data sources, and built a two-dimensional index of these coordinates. Daniel's system provides an interface that allows the user to augment a keyword search with the ability to restrict matches to within a certain radius of a specified address. In consideration of how much a page has stuck to the area, this point differs from our research.

The Clever (Client-side Eigenvector-Enhanced Retrieval) [12,13] system uses algorithmic methods to examine the sites linking to and from a Web site. Clever attempts to ensure that the information it retrieves is useful by pointing users toward one of two classes of sites, called authorities and hubs. Because Clever concentrates on hyperlinks, it can discover communities interested in the same topics. Regional interest information, which is kind of local information in our work, can also be considered as the interested information of a 'physical' regional community.

3 Localness Degree

In this section, we show the approaches to discover local information from aspect of regional content and aspect of regional interest, respectively. As we mentioned, the former is called as localness of content, the latter is called as localness of community.

3.1 Localness of Content

Regional content that describe something (event, etc.) about some special region or organization may have high region dependence: many geographical words, many organization name, and so on. For the localness degree, the frequency of geographical words in the Web page content should be estimated. Usually, if a Web page has many detailed geographical words, its localness degree considered to be high. More specifically, if the frequency of geographical words is high, and if these words represent very detailed location (i.e., place) information, we say that its localness degree might be high. Moreover, with the location data (i.e., latitude and longitude), we can estimate the geographical coverage of the Web page, based on the MBR (Minimum Bounding Rectangle) [14,15]. When the density of geographical words over the covered area is high, we say that the localness degree of the page is considered to be high.

Density of Geographical Words Over Web page's MBR. Usually, if a page covers a narrow geographical area, it may be a type of regional content and its localness degree is considered to be high. In other words, if the content coverage of a page is high, its localness degree should be lower.

We use latitude and longitude to estimate page coverage. First, we transform all of the location information of a geographical word into two-dimensional points (latitude, longitude). We plot all of these points on a map, on which the x-axis and y-axis are latitude and longitude, respectively. So, page coverage corresponds to the MBR (Minimum Bounding Rectangle) [14,15]. When page coverage is narrow, its localness degree should be high.

The number of points plotted on the MBR is also considered well for estimating the localness degree in our approach. In other words, not only the area of MBR, but also the number of plotted points affects the localness degree.

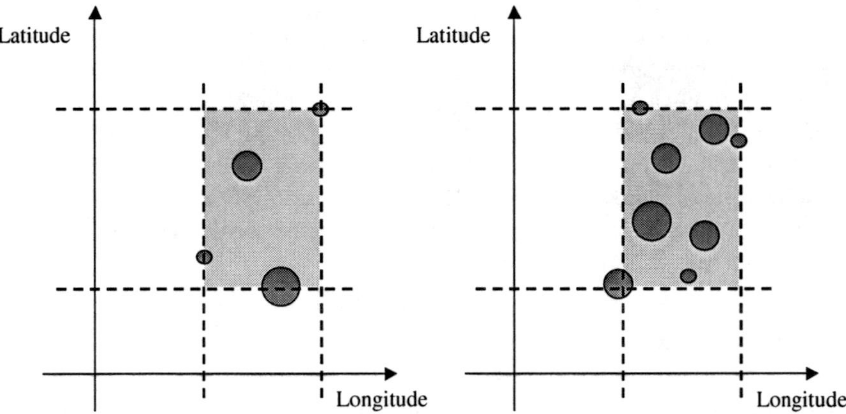

Fig. 1. Example for Influence of Density on Localness

For example, in *Figure 1*, four points are plotted in the left MBR, and eight points in the right MBR. The point size indicates the level of detail of geographical words and organization names. The bigger the point size is, the higher the level of detail of geographical word is. Even if the area of the two MBRs are equal, their localness degree should be different. Fuller discussion about the level of detail and the frequency of geographical words will be described later.

We can compute the density of geographical words over the MBR to estimate localness degree. The higher the density is, the higher the localness degree is considered to be. The formula is defined as follows.

$$\mathrm{Lcl_d}(page_x) = \frac{\sum_{i=1}^{n} \mathrm{weight}(geoword_i)}{MBR_{page_x}} \tag{1}$$

where $\mathrm{Lcl_d}$ is the localness degree, this time with respect to density; $\mathrm{weight}(geoword_i)$ is the function i that we use to estimate the level of detail of geographical words or organization names in $page_x$; MBR_{page_x} is the area of the MBR for $page_x$, which is calculated with Formula (2) and will be described later.

Frequency and Detail of Geographical Words. Generally, a Web page with a high dependence on an area includes a lot of geographical information, such as the names of the country, state (prefecture), city, and so on. Because many organizations are related to a specific location, we can also use the frequency of organization names to estimate the localness degree. In short, if the frequency of geographical words and organization names is high, the page's localness degree is considered to be high.

The level of detail of geographical words and organization names is also considered when we compute the localness degree of a Web page. The level of detail for geographical words depends on their administrative level. For example, a city is at a lower administrative level than a state, so we say that a site is more detailed than a state. Therefore, when computing the frequency, we assign weight values to geographical words [2] and organization names according to their level of detail. The simplest rule is to set up weight values in the following order: country name $<$ organization name $<$ state (prefecture) $<$ city $<$ town.

Location Information Based on Geographical Words. In our current working phase, we use a Japanese location information database [16], which includes latitudinal and longitudinal data for the 3,252 cities, towns, and villages in Japan. We match geographical words with this location data.

We noticed that some detailed place names have no match in the database. In this case, we downgrade the detail level of the place name to find an approximate location. For example, if the location data of "S street, B city, A state" is not found, we could use the location data of "B city, A state" to approximate a match.

Different places may share the same name. To avoid a mismatch, we could analyze the page's context to clearly specify its location. For example, to match up "Futyu city" to its correct location data, we can examine the page content for either "Hiroshima prefecture" or "Tokyo metropolitan" . If "Hiroshima prefecture" appears, we could use the location data of "Futyu city, Hiroshima prefecture" for the "Futyu city" on this page. Another example is "Paris", which maybe mean the Paris city of the USA or the capital city of France.

Therefore, we can compute the area of the MBR, which is based on the geographical words in $page_x$, to estimate the localness degree of $page_x$. If the area is large, the localness degree of $page_x$ is small.

$$\mathrm{MBR}_{page_x} = (lat_{max} - lat_{min})(long_{max} - long_{min}) \tag{2}$$

where MBR_{page_x} is the area of the MBR for $page_x$. The maximum latitude and longitude are lat_{max} and $long_{max}$, respectively. The minimum latitude and longitude are lat_{min} and $long_{min}$, respectively. When only one point exists in a page and MBR_{page_x} is set to 0, it treats as an exception and is referred to as $\mathrm{MBR}_{page_x} = 1$.

---

[2] In our current work, we just consider the level of detail of geographical words based on administrative level. We also observe that the population ratio is also important. We will discuss this issue in our future work

3.2 Localness of Community

Some events occur anywhere and some events occur only in some special region. Information about the latter is a scoop and may be interested by all users (of all regions), who are independent of their region or organization. In other words, it may be global interest information more than regional interest information. Oppositely, a ubiquitous occurrence may have a high localness degree regardless of location. For example, a summer festival, an athletic meet, and so on, are ubiquitous events that happen wherever people are. A ubiquitous occurrence may be a normal part of daily life. Therefore, if a page describes such scoop event (the latter), it may not be local information. On the other hand, if a page describes ubiquitous event (the former), it may be local information.

We define the localness degree by investigating the degree of similarity between pages, and the location where an event happens. If the pages show a high degree of similarity, but a difference in event locations, the localness degree would be considered high, as long as the event locations are irrelevant-meaning the events could be held anywhere.

Excluding the geographical words, the degree of similarity is calculated. The formula for calculating the degree of similarity $sim(A, B)$ between page A and page B is as follows.

$$sim(A, B) = \frac{v(A)v(B)}{|v(A)||v(B)|} \tag{3}$$

where, $v(A)$ and $v(B)$ are keyword vectors of page A and B.

The formula for the localness degree Lcl_r of page $page_x$, with respect to the comparison of other pages, is as follows.

$$\mathrm{Lcl_r}(page_x) = \begin{cases} \frac{m}{N} & (different\ location) \\ 1 - \frac{m}{N} & (same\ \ \ \ \ \ \ location) \end{cases} \tag{4}$$

where m is the number of similar pages, excluding geographical words, organization names, and proper nouns, and N is the number of pages compared.

4 Preliminary Experiments

In this section, we show the results of two preliminary experiments, which are estimating localness of content and localness of community, respectively. In preliminary experiments, we excluded all of the structural information (e.g., HTML tags) and the Ad. content from the HTML source pages. For our preliminary experiments, we used 400 Web pages (written in Japanese) from the Web site ASAHI.COM (`http://www.asahi.com/`), which is a well-known, news Web site in Japan.

4.1 Preliminary Experiment 1: Localness of Content

In preliminary experiment 1, we compute localness degree of content of Web page with Formula (1), which is from the regional content aspect and compute the localness based on the density of geographical words over Web page's MBR. In contrast to all estimated Web pages (400 pages) are organized as regional information by editors of ASAHI.COM. There are 224 pages whose localness degree is greater than threshold 10 and these 224 pages are considered as local page based on our regional content aspect. The recall ratio is 0.624. As our evaluation is a limited one, there are more improving works needed to do. Nevertheless, these results can confirm that localness of community is fit to organize the local information.

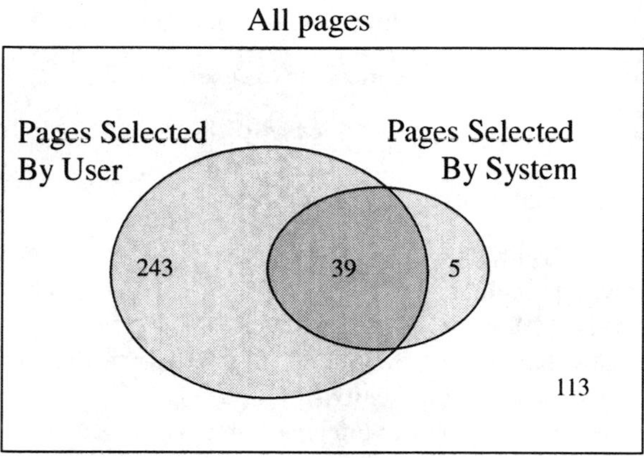

Fig. 2. Results of Preliminary Experiments 2: Localness of Community

4.2 Preliminary Experiment 2: Localness of Community

In preliminary experiment 2, we estimated the localness of community with Formula (4), which is from the aspect of regional interest. As shown in *Figure 2*, 44 pages have greater value of community localness than threshold 0.0875. Such 44 pages are selected as local pages. On the other hand, the number of human-selected local pages is 282. The recall ratio and precision ratios are 0.138 and 0.886, respectively.

The recall ratio is very poor. One of the considerable reasons is: we used the news articles as our example pages for the preliminary experiments. Because news articles are more formal and unique than other Web pages, we maybe fail to compute the similarity between pages for discovering ubiquitous information. The other kind of Web pages is needed to be evaluated. The number of estimated pages is another considerable reason.

5 Conclusion

There are a lot of Web pages whose content is 'local' and only interested by people in a very narrow region. Usually, users search for information with search engines. However, since it's not easy to specify the query for acquiring interest information via the conventional keyword based technologies, the efficiency and ability to acquire or exclude local information are limited. In this paper, we propose a new notion, localness degree, for discovering or excluding local information from the WWW.

We consider the following two kinds of information may be local: 1) regional content, and 2) regional interest information. According to this assumption, we defined two types of localness for Web pages:

1. localness of content, which is based on its content analysis (according to aspect of regional content).
2. localness of community, which is based on comparison with related pages for estimating its ubiquitousness (according to aspect of regional interest).

Our local information discovering mechanism is useful to

- acquire local information, which is not easy to clearly specify in keywords;
- exclude the local information;
- discover local information over plural regions.

The definition of localness degree will be improved and estimated in our future works. For example, for localness of community, we also could analyze the user access history of Web pages. If a Web page is often accessed by users who are from same region, and there is few access from other regions, we could say that this page is regional interest one and its localness of community should be high. The hub/authority style link analysis approach for discovering local information will be discussed in near future. We also plan to develop some applications for local information dissemination based on localness degree of information.

Acknowledgement

This research is partly supported by the Japanese Ministry of Education, Culture, Sports, Science and Technology under Grant-in-Aid for Scientific Research on "New Web Retrieval Services Based on Discovery of Web Semantic Structures", No. 14019048, and "Multimodal Information Retrieval, Presentation, and Generation of Broadcast Contents for Mobile Environments", No. 14208036.

References

1. Cyveillance. http://www.cyveillance.com/web/us/newsroom/releases/2000/2000-07-10.htm.
2. Qiang Ma, Kazutoshi Sumiya, and Katsumi Tanaka. Information filtering based on timeseries features for data dissemination systems. *TOD7*, 41(SIG6):46–57, 8 2000.
3. Qiang Ma, Shinya Miyazaki, and Katsumi Tanaka. Webscan: Discovering and notifying important changes of web sites. In *DEXA*, volume 2113 of *Lecture Notes in Computer Science*, pages 587–598. Springer, 9 2001.
4. Shinya Miyazaki, Qiang Ma, and Katsumi Tanaka. Webscan: Content-based change discovery and broadcast-notification of web sites. *TOD10*, 42(SIG8):96–107, 7 2001.
5. Yahoo!regional. http://local.yahoo.co.jp.
6. MACHIgoo. http://machi.goo.ne.jp. 10 Chiyako Matsumoto, Qiang Ma and Katsumi Tanaka
7. Nobuyuki Miura, Katsumi Takahashi, Seiji Yokoji, andKenichi Shima. Location oriented information integration m̃obile info search 2 experiment ˀ *The 57th National Convention of IPSJ*, 3:637–638, 10 1998.

8. MIS2. http://www.kokono.net/.
9. Orkut Buyukkokten, Junghoo Cho, Hector Garcia-Molina, Luis Gravano, and Narayanan Shivakumar. Exploiting geographical location information of web pages. In *WebDB (Informal Proceedings)*, pages 91–96, 1999.
10. Kaoru Hiramatsu and Toru Ishida. An augmented web space for digital cities. In *SAINT*, pages 105–112, 2001.
11. Daniel Egnor. Geographic search. Technical report, Google Programming Contest, 2002.
12. Soumen Chakurabarti, Btron Dom, David Gibson, Jon M. Kleinberg, S. Ravi Kumar, Prabhakar Raghavan, Sridhar Rajagopalan, and Andrew Tomkins. Hypersearching the web. scientific american, 1999.
13. Jon M. Kleinberg. Authoritative sources in a hyperlinked environment. *Journal of the ACM*, 46(5):604–632, 1999.
14. Antonin Guttman. R-trees: A dynamic index structure for spatial searching. *Proc. ACM SIGMOD Conference on Management of Data*, 14(2):47–57, 1984.
15. Carlo Zaniolo, Stefano Ceri, Christos Faloutsos, Richard T. Snodgrass, V. S. Subrahmanian, and Roberto Zicari. *Advanced Database Systems*. The Morgan Kaufmann, 1997.
16. T. Takeda. The latitude / longitude position database of all-prefectures cities, towns and villages in japan, 2000.

Run-Time Load Balancing System on SAN-connected PC Cluster for Dynamic Injection of CPU and Disk Resource — A Case Study of Data Mining Application —

Kazuo Goda[1], Takayuki Tamura[2], Masato Oguchi[3], and Masaru Kitsuregawa[1]

[1] Institute of Industrial Science, The University of Tokyo
[2] Mitsubishi Electric Corporation
[3] Research and Development Initiative, Chuo University

Abstract. PC cluster system is an attractive platform for data-intensive applications. But the conventional shared-nothing system has a limit on load balancing performance and it is difficult to change the number of nodes and disks dynamically during execution. In this paper, we develop dynamic resource injection, where the system can inject CPU power and expand I/O bandwidth by adding nodes and disks dynamically in the SAN(Storage Area Network)-connected PC cluster. Our experiments with data mining application confirm its effectiveness. We show the advantages of combining PC cluster with SAN.

1 Introduction

PC cluster system is regarded as one of the most promising platforms for the data-intensive applications such as data mining, data warehouse, etc. because of its cost performance.

However, the conventional shared-nothing system, where each node manages its own disk exclusively, has a limit on load balancing performance. In particular it cannot handle the large skew which often occurs e.g. when the system changes the number of nodes. User has to configure the number of nodes, and data placements *before* the execution. The available CPU power and I/O bandwidth are statically bounded by that initial configuration, thus limit the user convenience.

We propose the SAN(Storage Area Network)-connected PC cluster to handle such problems. In this configuration, the whole storage space are virtually shared by all the nodes, so we can achieve much higher load balancing performance. It is also possible to allocate resources, namely CPU power and I/O bandwidth, dynamically during execution. We can inject resource only when it is necessary. It can also free the user from configuration tasks before the execution.

In this paper, we pick up association rule mining as an example of data-intensive applications and we design, implement and evaluate *dynamic resource injection*. In the next section, association rule mining is explained. As the underlying mechanism to access shared disks on SAN-connected PC cluster, we implement *Storage Virtualizer*. The detail is given in Section 3 and its load balancing performance is evaluated in Section 4. Dynamic resource injection is explained and evaluated in Section 5 and Section 6 concludes the paper.

R. Cicchetti et al. (Eds.): DEXA 2002, LNCS 2453, pp. 182–192, 2002.

2 Parallel Data Mining

In this paper, we pick up association rule mining as an example of data-intensive applications. The problem of association rule mining is to find all the rules that satisfy a user-specified minimum support and minimum confidence from a given transaction database, which can be decomposed into two subproblems: 1) To find all *large itemsets*, or combinations of itemsets, which satisfy a given minimum support, 2) To generate the rules which satisfy a given minimum confidence from the large itemsets derived.

Compared with the second subproblem, the first one requires much more processing time, since it has to scan the whole transaction database several times and calculate support values. Then most researchers to date have focused on improvement of the first subproblem.

In this paper, we use *HPA(Hash Partitioned Apriori)*[3], a parallelized algorithm based on *Apriori* proposed by Agrawal[1]. Apriori is one of the most well-known algorithms for association rule mining. Here k-itemset is defined as a set of k items and L_k as a set of large itemsets whose length is k. C_k is a set of candidate itemsets whose length is k. The HPA algorithm is composed of two processes, *SEND* and *RECV*, in each node of the cluster system and runs the following iteration until L_k becomes empty.

1. The SEND process generates a set of candidate itemsets C_k using the set of large itemsets L_{k-1} which is determined by the previous pass, $k-1$.
2. While reading the transaction database, the SEND process generates k-itemsets, applies a hash function to derive the destination node ID and sends the k-itemset to it. The RECV process receives the k-itemsets sent by the SEND process and counts the support value by probing a hash table.
3. After scanning the entire transaction database, the RECV process determines a set of large itemsets L_k and broadcasts it to all the SEND processes.
4. Increments k.

In the above procedure, generation of k-itemsets by the SEND process and support counting using the hash table by the RECV process in the step 2. can produce heavy workloads. Especially the pass 2, where the most candidate itemsets are generated, requires a lot of CPU power and dominates the most part of the execution time. The execution of pass 3 or later requires less CPU power and needs more I/O bandwidth. The pass 2 is CPU-bound while other passes are rather I/O bound instead. So the challenge to improve the performance means that we have to care about both CPU-bound situation and I/O-bound situation.

3 Storage Virtualization and Load Balancing

3.1 Overview of Load Balancing

We have developed *Storage Virtualizer* which consists of a *LVM(Logical Volume Manager)* and a *Meta Server* on our SAN-connected PC cluster system. Fig. 1(a) shows a control model of parallel data mining using Storage Virtualizer.

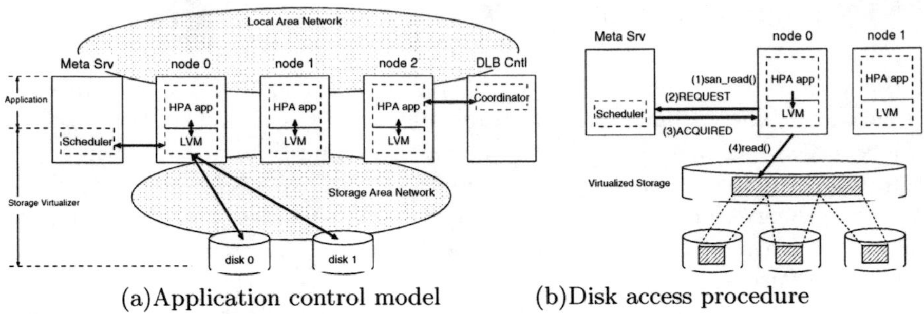

(a)Application control model (b)Disk access procedure

Fig. 1. Parallel data mining over Storage Virtualizer

The LVM is a layer that provides a virtualization service of storage, which corresponds to the file system of operating systems. In our system, it is implemented as API(Application Programming Interface) functions, which replace ordinary system calls(`read()` etc.). Application can access the virtualized storage space by calling functions such as `san_read()`. We also employ a *Dynamic Load Balancing Controller(DLB Cntl)* that takes care of balancing the workload among the nodes. DLB Cntl utilizes hints collected by the application.

3.2 Storage Virtualizer

Since multiple storage devices are shared by multiple host computers in the SAN environment, meta information such as block address, seek pointer, etc. must be consistent across the host computers. The Meta Server of Storage Virtualizer manages all the meta information to keep the consistency and to handle the I/O access of each host computer in the SAN.

Fig. 1(b) shows a disk read procedure as an example of storage access. The LVM sends a request to the Meta Server in response to a first `san_read()` call by the application. The Meta Server builds a plan from the meta information it manages, locks a area of storage devices on the SAN for the requesting node and sends back a notice(ACQUIRED notice) including the meta information such as a device ID, a block address, etc. of the locked area to the LVM. Receiving the notice, the LVM calls `read()` to retrieve data from the SAN devices and passes the retrieved data to the application. In response to the next `san_read()` call, the LVM calls `read()` directly if there are any remaining locked areas that are not yet read. It sends a request again to the Meta Server if no locked area remains.

This mechanism makes it possible for the multiple host computers to virtually share a file distributed across multiple storage devices over the SAN. It potentially resolves the problem on the skew of the amount of data distributed among the disks, known as TPS(Table Placement Skew) on the relational database system. As we will show in Section 4.2, Storage Virtualizer can resolve the soft and medium level of skew. But if the load is extremely skewed, we need introduce more explicit load balancing mechanism, which we will discuss in the next section.

3.3 Dynamic Load Balancer

Usually load balancing of the parallel distributed application is realized by migration of data structure on the memory or threads. This kind of method often becomes very complex especially in data-intensive applications. In order to reduce the difference among the execution times of all the nodes, it is necessary to predict how much data or threads should be migrated from the amount of each node's *unread* data. In addition, as mentioned in Section 4.2, this method cannot handle huge skew that often appears in case of changing the number of nodes dynamically.

When we have the Storage Virtualizer, the data mining application does not have to prepare such complex mechanism. All it has to do is just to prevent the RECV process of each node from monopolizing CPU power. If the CPU utilization of the RECV process became 100%, the receiver queue would be flooded and its node would be the bottleneck of the whole system.

The control method of the dynamic load balancing controller on Storage Virtualizer can be formulated as follows. Let L_{RECVi} and L_{SENDi} be the CPU utilization ratio of the RECV and SEND processes of node i respectively. We can define L_{RECVi} is in proportion to the flow rate(V_{Ri} [itemset/second]) which the RECV process receives, while L_{SENDi} is proportional to the flow rate(V_{Si} [item/second]) which the SEND process sends. Thus we have :

$$L_{RECVi} = \alpha\gamma_i V_{Ri} \sim \alpha\gamma_i C_i \sum_j V_{Sj}$$

$$L_{SENDi} = \beta\gamma_i V_{Si}$$

Here the suffix i means the node ID. α and β are defined as workload coefficients of the RECV and SEND processes. γ_i is a CPU coefficient which is approximately in inverse relation to the clock speed of each node's CPU. C_i is a coefficient which means a weighted size of the hash table. Each node has one CPU so that the condition $L_{RECVi} + L_{SENDi} \leq 1$ must be satisfied.

Here the controller controls the system as follows so that the condition $L_{RECVi} < 1 - \epsilon$ can be satisfied in each node[1] to prevent the RECV process from being a bottleneck.

1. The controller collects statistics from each mining node.
2. The controller calculates the $\alpha\gamma_i$ value of each node from the statistics (L_{RECVi}). If there is any node where the condition $L_{RECVi} < 1 - \epsilon$ is not satisfied, it determines reorganization of the hash tables, called *Data Migration*, and makes a migration plan which balances the L_{RECVi} value of each node.
3. The controller broadcasts the migration plan to all the nodes and each node exchanges its hash lines to each other according to the plan.

This type of control method is subject to how exactly the system can observe parameters, α, β, γ_i and C_i. But we found that our Storage Virtualizer can absorb such perturbation.

[1] In our experiment, ϵ is approximately 5% to 10%.

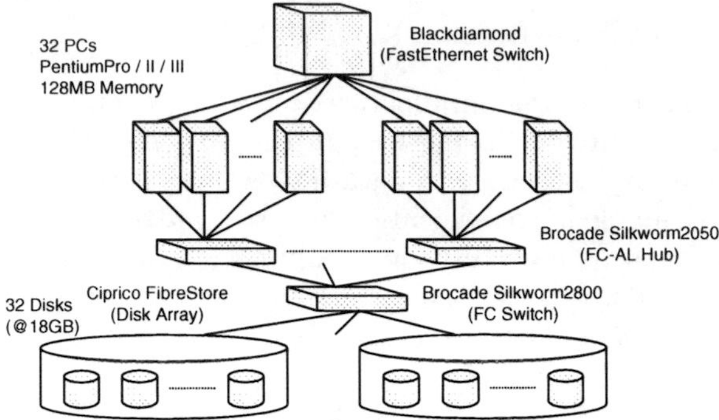

Fig. 2. Overview of the SAN-connected PC cluster system

Table 1. Skew setup for CPU power and Data volume

Node placement

Case	Node 0	Node 1	Node 2	Node 3
c0	P-III 800MHz	P-III 800MHz	P-III 800MHz	P-III 800MHz
c1	P-III 800MHz	P-II 450M	P-II 450MHz	P-II 450MHz
c2	P-III 800MHz	P-III 800MHz	P-III 800MHz	P-II 450MHz
c3	P-III 800MHz	P-III 800MHz	P-III 800MHz	P-Pro 200MHz

Data placement

Case	Disk 0	Disk 1	Disk 2	Disk 3
d0	1,000,000 (84MB)	1,000,000 (84MB)	1,000,000 (84MB)	1,000,000 (84MB)
d1	500,000 (42MB)	500,000 (42MB)	500,000 (42MB)	2,500,000 (210MB)
d2	200,000 (16.8MB)	200,000 (16.8MB)	200,000 (16.8MB)	3,400,000 (285.6MB)

Number of transactions / Size of data volume
P-III: Pentium III, P-II: Pentium II
P-Pro: Pentium Pro

4 Performance Evaluation

4.1 Experimental System

The SAN-connected PC cluster consists of 32 PCs and 32 disks connected through SAN. Each PC node runs the Solaris 8 operating system on Pentium III(800MHz), Pentium II(450MHz) or Pentium Pro(200MHz) with 128 MB of main memory. Each node has two NICs, Intel Pro/100+ for the 100Base-TX Ethernet and Emulex LP8000 for the Fibre Channel. Fig. 2 depicts the organization of the experimental system.

4.2 Performance Evaluation

To evaluate the system as described in Section 3, we prepared various configurations of PCs and transaction databases showed in Table 1. The skew becomes larger from c0 to c3 (CPU skew) and from d0 to d2 (data skew). Notice that the most skewed case is quite extreme. Here the transaction data that mimics retail sales data is generated using the procedure described in [1] with parameters, number of items: 5000 and average size of transactions: 20. The minimum support value is 0.7%. We set the size of read buffer at 64KB and the lock size of the Meta Server at 512KB.

Table 2 shows the execution time of pass 2 measured with respect to each combination of CPU skew and data skew over Storage Virtualizer. We compared

Table 2. Normalized execution time of Pass 2

Storage System	DLB Control	Skew(CPU/data)											
		c0			c1			c2			c3		
		d0	d1	d2	d0	d1	d2	d0	d1	d2	d0	d1	d2
SN	-	100	133	170	100	143	173	129	171	223	220	302	395
	Mig.	100†	120	136	94	104	126	104	120	155	113	192	259
SAN	-	98	102	102	93	95	95	108	112	112	175	176	176
	Mig.	98†	102†	102†	93†	94†	95†	97	100	100	98	99	99

SN: Shared Nothing, Mig.: Data Migration

cases without any application-dependent load balancing mechanism and cases with Data Migration introduced in section 3.3. Table 2 also shows the results in case of dynamic load balancing method for the conventional shared-nothing environment without SAN, described in [4]. This conventional method is denoted by "SN", while "SAN" means the evaluation over Storage Virtualizer. Notice that the meaning of Data Migration in the table differs between the SAN and the SN environment. In the conventional Data Migration for SN environment, the controller considers the data amount remaining in each node to calculate the migration plan, then migrates transaction data from each disk directly through LAN(Local Area Network) in order to reduce the data skew among the disks. † means that Data Migration is not triggered because the controller decides that it is not necessary.

Each value is normalized by the total CPU clock speed. For example, in c1d0 case, the total execution time is normalized by multiplying $\frac{800+3*450}{4*800}$. Since pass 2 is completely CPU-bound, the normalization by CPU clock speed is reasonable. The execution time of c0d0 case, where there is no skew in neither CPUs nor data, in non-SAN is normalized as 100.

Storage Virtualizer. We evaluate the load balancing performance of Storage Virtualizer. With respect to data skew, the execution time in the shared-nothing(SN) case, even with Data Migration, becomes worse, 100, 120 and 136, from d0 to d2, while the execution time in the SAN case without application-dependent control is reasonably stable, 98, 102 and 102, only 4% worse. This result shows the fact that any data skew can be well absorbed by Storage Virtualizer.

As for CPU skew, the result shows that only Storage Virtualizer can balance such a *soft* skew as c1 case without Data Migration. The execution trace graph of c1d0 case without Data Migration is depicted by Fig. 3(a). The heavy, dotted and solid lines mean respectively a disk read throughput, a CPU utilization of the SEND process L_{SENDi} and a CPU utilization of the SEND and RECV processes $L_{SENDi}+L_{RECVi}$. The pass 2 runs between 10 sec. and 300 sec. Since each node has approximately the same size of hash table, L_{RECV0} of the fastest Node0 becomes less than L_{RECVi} of the other node. So the surplus CPU power can be used more for the SEND process. In Node [1-3], whose CPUs are slower, the RECV process uses most of CPU power. But it is still not so dominant such as monopolizing the CPU power. Thus the CPU power of all the nodes are

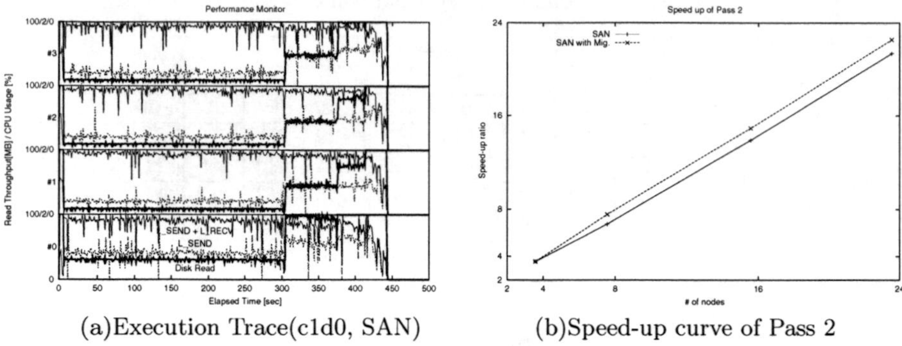

(a)Execution Trace(c1d0, SAN) (b)Speed-up curve of Pass 2

Fig. 3. Experimental result

effectively utilized. This shows that Storage Virtualizer can resolve the soft skew without application-dependent load balancer.

In case of much *harder* case, c2 and c3, where one slower node becomes a bottleneck of the whole system, Storage Virtualizer is not enough to balance the system. The execution time increases 78% from c0 to c3 in d0 case.

It is interesting when there is data skew in addition to CPU skew. The execution times are 192 in c3d1 case and 270 in c3d2 in the shared-nothing case, while in the SAN case the execution times is the same 176 in c3d1 and in the more data-skewed c3d2. These results show that the execution time of data mining in the shared-nothing system is strongly subject to data skew, while SAN can absorb it.

Storage Virtualizer with Load Balancer. In the hard CPU skew case, where Storage Virtualizer alone cannot balance the skew, there is at least one RECV process which becomes a bottleneck ($L_{RECVi} \geq 1 - \epsilon$.) Data Migration over Storage Virtualizer as described in Section 3.3 removes the bottleneck and balances the skew, so that the aggravation of the execution times of various skew cases can be within 2% compared with the basis value of c0d0. The experiment results show that the proposed mechanism works fine no matter how hard the skew is.

Speed Up with More Nodes. We prepare a set of PCs, "Pentium III(800MHz) * $N - 1$ + Pentium II(450MHz) * 1", with transaction database as desribed in case d0. Then we measure the execution time of Pass 2 to evaluate the scalability of the system. Fig. 3(b) shows a scale-up curve, where the X-axis is normalized number of nodes. The result shows almost linear speed-up.

5 Dynamic Resource Injection

Using the load balancing method evaluated in the previous section, we implement and examine *dynamic resource injection*, where CPU power is added and I/O bandwidth is expanded dynamically while data mining application is running.

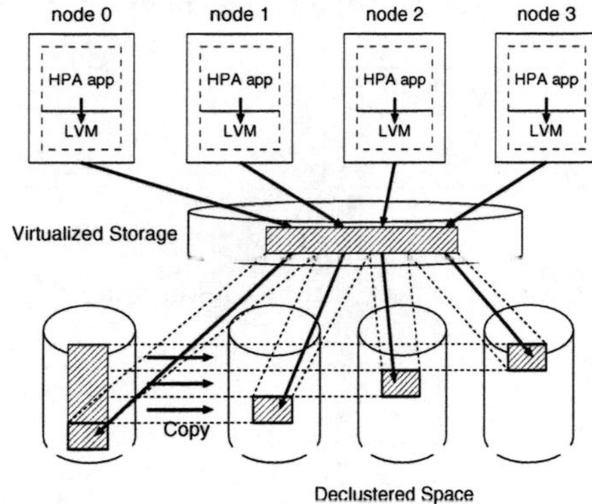

Fig. 4. Overview of dynamic declustering

5.1 Dynamic Injection of CPU Power

We implement a run-time mechanism to inject CPU power of unused nodes as a function of the dynamic load balancing controller. When the controller finds that the system is CPU-bound from the statistics and determines to inject additional CPU power, it invokes the SEND and RECV processes in the injected nodes. The SEND process begins immediately to access the disk through the LVM. And then if required, hash lines are migrated to the new nodes by Data Migration mechanism, however the controller cannot determine how many hash lines should be migrated because the controller has no statistics about the newly injected nodes. If the controller distributed too many hash lines, the injected nodes would be a bottleneck. So the system migrates only a few hash lines at the first-time migration. After enough statistics is acquired, the controller can execute a more aggressive migration.

5.2 I/O Bandwidth Expansion: Dynamic Declustering

Expansion of I/O bandwidth in the SAN environment can be realized by *dynamic declustering*[2]. The data such as transaction database in the storage device can be declustered and copied to the unused device speculatively at the first-time scan, and I/O access becomes parallelized at the next-time scan. This method is efficient for applications that access the large file repeatedly such as data mining. Fig. 4 shows the concept of dynamic declustering.

We implement dynamic declustering as a function of Storage Virtualizer. When dynamic declustering is enabled, the ACQUIRED notice from the Meta Server to the LVM includes meta information of the copy destination at pass 1. Receiving this notice, the LVM reads blocks of the copy source device and copies them to the destination device. After the later passes, the LVM determines *bounding factor*(whether the system is CPU-bound or I/O-bound) and notices it to the Meta Server. When the Meta Server determines that the whole system is I/O-bound, it changes its meta information so that the storage access to the

Table 3. Experimental setup of CPU power and data volume

Node placement

Node 0	Node [1-3]	Node 4	Node [5-23]
P III 800MHz	P II 450MHz	P Pro 200MHz	P III 800MHz

Data placement

Disk 0	Disk [1-3]
20,000K (1.63GB)	Unused Storage

declustered copies can be activated and consequently I/O bandwidth can be expanded.

5.3 Experiment

When the system performance is bounded by resources such as CPU power or I/O bandwith, the cluster system can inject idle resource using dynamic CPU power injection and I/O bandwidth expansion. Basically the system injects new CPU power if it is CPU-bound and it expands I/O bandwidth if it is I/O-bound.

We evaluate dynamic resource injection through real experiments. We use the experimental setup depicted in Table 3. "Unused Storage" in the figure means that the specified device are used as destination devices of declustering copy. Minimum support value is 1.5% and lock size is 1024KB. At the start time of data mining, only Node 0 is active and the other are idle.

Fig. 5 shows a execution trace. At pass 1, transaction database is speculatively declustered and copied. Immediately after pass 2 starts, the dynamic load balancing controller finds that the system is CPU-bound and determines to add new idle nodes, Node [1-7]. The SEND process of the newly injected node starts processing immediately and hash lines are migrated to them so that the skew can be balanced. But the system is still CPU-bound and the controller injected another CPU power of Node [8-15]. After that, the total disk read throughput becomes up to approximately 25 MB/s and the system changes into I/O-bound. Then the Meta Server activates storage access to the declustered copies and the I/O bandwidth is expanded. Once the I/O bandwidth is expanded, the system changed back into CPU-bound and yet another 8 nodes are injected by the controller and finally the number of active nodes becomes 24. In addition, the read throughput of pass 3 and later improves up to approximately 360%.

Finally, we prepare four times as large transaction database as Table 3 and measures the execution time of each pass. The result is showed in Fig. 6. When injecting only CPU power, the execution time of pass 2 improves a lot but its expansion stops at 16 nodes because the system becomes I/O-bound after 16 CPUs are activated. On the other hand, when we inject both CPUs and disks, the number of nodes at pass 2 can be expanded up to 24 and its execution time improves up to about 1800 %. The overhead time that occurred on CPU invocation and on disk I/O expansion are included in the execution time. Improvement of execution time at pass 3 and later is approximately 330 %, which is less than the theoretical upper bound. This is because synchronization overhead between passes is not negligible. Improvement of the overall execution time including pass 1 amounts to about 580 %.

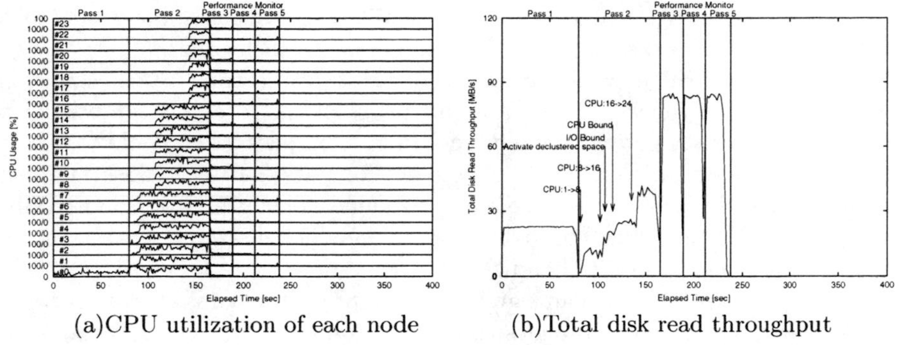

(a)CPU utilization of each node (b)Total disk read throughput

Fig. 5. Execution trace (Dynamic resource injection up to 24 nodes/4 disks, minimum support 1.5%)

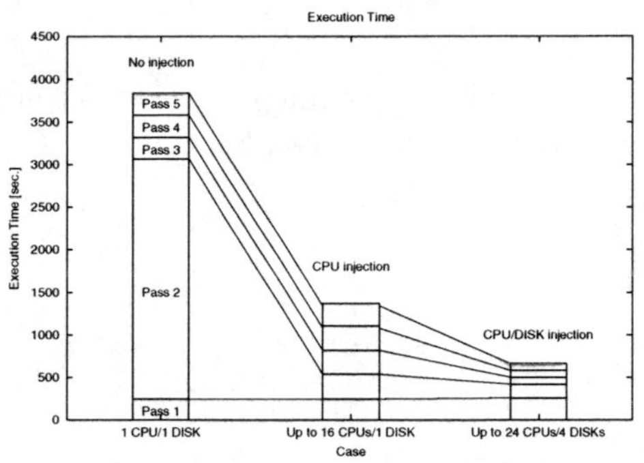

Fig. 6. Comparison of execution time (minimum support 1.5%)

6 Conclusion

First we developed storage virtualization mechanism over SAN-connected PC cluster system. This virtualization can resolve the workload imbalance when the system has soft and medium skew. Skew might happen when the CPU clock speed of each node is different. It would also happen when the amount of data allocated to its storage is different. We configured various skewed PC cluster configuration and evaluated the effectiveness of Storage Virtualizer using the data mining application. We found that it really works effectively. But if the system is highly skewed, Storage Virtualizer is not enough. We have to introduce load balancing methodology which utilizes application knowledge. For the data mining application, load balancer migrates the hash lines between nodes, which we call Data Migration. In principle this works fine if we can collect precise statistics. But it is not necessarily easy and sometimes there incur some errors. Perfect Data Migration is very difficult. But if it is employed with Storage Virtualizer, these two together work synergistically and can improve the performance a lot. That is, Storage Virtualizer can distribute the workload on demand fashion. So it can allocate the workload almost optimally if the skew is not so heavy. On the other hand, Data Migration balances the workload imprecisely but can resolve the large skew. Thus these two are complimentary to each other.

Second we did the experiment on CPU and disk injection. By checking the bounding factor of the system, we are able to inject the resources adaptively at runtime. For the association rule mining application, pass 2 is completely CPU-bound. CPU injection works very effectively for pass 2. But it does not help for pass 3, 4 and so on, since those are I/O-bound. Thus we also proposed disk injection mechanism. Once I/O-bound situation is detected, our system injects disks in order to expand I/O bandwidth. It was shown that by employing both CPU and disk injection, we can significantly improve the total execution time.

We plan to apply our strategies to different types of data intensive applications. Also we are trying to utilize the unused memory space of PCs which runs different tasks.

Acknowledgements

This work is partly supported by the Grant-in-Aid for Scientific Research (S) by the Ministry of Education, Culture, Sports, Science and Technology of Japan.

References

1. R. Agrawal and R. Srikant. Fast Algorithms for Mining Association Rules. In *Proceedings of the Twentieth International Conference on Very Large Data Bases*, 1994.
2. M. Oguchi and M. Kitsuregawa. Dynamic Data Declustering on SAN-Connected PC Cluster for Parallel Data Mining. In *Proc. of the IPSJ Workshop on Database System*, 2001.
3. T. Shintani and M. Kitsuregawa. Hash Based Pararellel Algorithm for Mining Assocication Rules. In *Proceedings of Parallel and Distributed Information Systems*, 1996.
4. M. Tamura and M. Kitsuregawa. Dynamic Load Balancing for Parallel Association Rule Mining on Heterogeneous PC Cluster Systems. In *Proceedings of the Twenty-fifth International Conference on Very Large Data Bases*, 1999.

Variable Sized Partitions for Range Query Algorithms

Tok Wang Ling, Wai Chong Low, Zhong Wei Luo, Sin Yeung Lee, and Hua Gang Li

School of Computing, National University of Singapore
{lingtw, lowwaicl, luozhong, jlee, lihuagan}@comp.nus.edu.sg

Abstract. A range query applies an aggregation operation over all selected cells of an OLAP data cube where selection is specified by the range of contiguous values for each dimension. Many works have focused on efficiently computing range sum or range max queries. Most of these algorithms use a uniformly partitioning scheme for the data cube. In this paper, we improve on query costs of some of these existing algorithms by noting two key areas. First, end-user range queries usually involve repetitive query patterns, which provide a variable sized partitioning scheme that can be used to partition the data cubes. Query costs are reduced because pre-computation is retrieved for entire partitions, rather than computed for a partial region in many partitions, which requires large amounts of cell accesses to the data cube. Second, data in the data cube can be arranged such that each partition is stored in as few physical storage blocks as possible, thus reducing the I/O costs for answering range queries.

1 Introduction

Aggregation is a common and computation-intensive operation in OLAP systems, where data is usually modeled as a multidimensional data cube [5]. Queries typically involve aggregations across various cube dimensions. A range query [4] applies an aggregation operation over selected cells the data cube. Selection is specified by providing a range of values over selected dimensions. Many works have focused on efficiently computing range sum or max queries. These algorithms [1, 2, 3, 4, 6, 7, 8] use a uniformly partitioning scheme for the data cube. Here, we improve on query costs of these existing algorithms by noting two key areas. First, range queries usually involve repeated queries that can be taken advantage of. The ranges of these queries provide a variable sized partitioning scheme that is used to partition data cubes. Query costs are reduced because pre-computation is retrieved for entire partitions, whereas computing for a partial region requires many cell accesses. Next, data in the data cube can be arranged so each partition is stored in a few storage blocks. Since a physical block is read for each I/O, query costs are reduced when data is read sequentially from each logical partition, retrieving very little physical blocks. The combination of these two techniques optimizes existing algorithms for better performance.

R. Cicchetti et al. (Eds.): DEXA 2002, LNCS 2453, pp. 193–202, 2002.

2 Related Works

To improve the range query for the aggregate function sum and max, considerable research has been done in the database community. The foundation stone is to pre-compute a set of results which is used to speed up the processing of a range query. One of the commonly found ideas is the Prefix Sum Method [4]. A prefix cube *PC*, of the same size as the data cube *DC*, stores various pre-computed prefix aggregation. In particular, *PC*[$x_1,\ldots,x_d$] stores the sum of all data in *DC* ranging from [0,…,0] to [$x_1,\ldots,x_d$]. With the use of *PC*, any range-sum query on d dimensions can be answered with a constant (2^d) cell accesses. To illustrate, the sum of all data in *DC* ranging from [2,4] to [6,9] can be computed with four cell accesses of the *PC* by using the formula: sum([2,4],[6,9])=*PC*[6,9]–*PC*[6,3]–*PC*[1,9]+*PC*[1,3].

Although the Prefix Sum Method has a good constant time query cost, it is very expensive to update the prefix sum cube. A single update to data at *DC*[0,…,0] requires an update to every cell in the *PC*. Other methods try to correct this weakness. The Blocked Prefix Sum method [4] uniformly partitions the data cube and pre-computes the prefix sum in each partition, thus constraining updates to one partition. The Hierarchical Cubes [1] improves further to allow a dynamic fine-tuning between the query cost and update cost. To process range max queries efficiently, the Block Range Max Algorithm [7] uniformly partitions the data cube and pre-computes the prefix max in each partition, whereas [6] proposed the Hierarchical Compact Cube, which is a hierarchical structure storing the maximum value and its location of all children sub-cubes. Both approaches use pre-computed maximum values and their locations to prune unnecessary searches, speeding up range max queries.

A typical range query over a partitioned 2-dimensional data cube is illustrated by Fig. 1. Only the partitions and the query regions are shown.

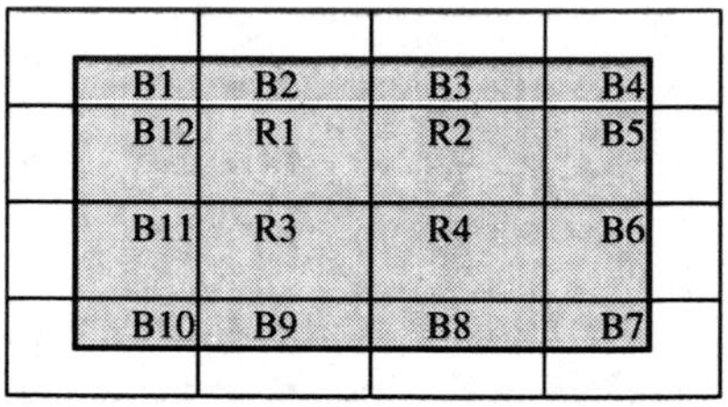

B1	B2	B3	B4
B12	R1	R2	B5
B11	R3	R4	B6
B10	B9	B8	B7

Fig. 1. Typical range query over a partitioned data cube

In the above diagram, the shaded region represents the query region. Sub-regions B1 to B12 do not fully cover a partition each, while regions R1 to R4 each cover an entire partition. We shall refer to regions of type B1 to B12 as *boundary regions* and regions of type R1 to R4 as *internal regions* henceforth.

When answering range queries, the max or sum of internal regions can be directly obtained from pre-computed data. However, to obtain the max or sum of boundary regions, we need to investigate partitions of the original data cube which contain boundary regions. Thus, query performance of partition-based range query algorithms heavily depends on the number of boundary regions which need to be accessed. Our proposed approach reduces the number of boundary regions for these range query algorithms and reduces the number of I/Os for accessing each partition.

3 Variable Sized Partitions

It can be observed that for many database applications, users would likely be interested in a few fixed ranges of values for one or more attributes in the data cube. This results in highly visible patterns in the queries that will be asked of the database. Take for example the following chart taken from the Singapore Statistics web site [9]:

PREVALENCE OF SELECTED DISEASES AND RISK FACTORS AMONG SINGAPOREANS AGED 18 TO 69 YEARS, 1998							
Risk Factor / Disease	Diabetes Mellitus	Hypertension $\geq$ *140/90 mmHg*	Daily Cigarette Smoking *Smoked$\geq$1 cigarette / day*	Regular Physical Activity *Exercised $\geq$ 20 minutes for $\geq$3 days per week*	Obesity *Body Mass Index $\geq$30 kg/m^2*	High Cholesterol *Total blood cholesterol $\geq$ 6.2 mmol/l*	Regular Alcohol Consumption *Consumed Alcohol >4 Days per week*
Overall	9.0	27.3	15.0	16.8	6.0	25.4	2.6
Age Group (years)							
18-29	0.8	-	15.7	18.2	4.4	9.0	1.3
30-39	3.3	9.9	13.8	11.9	5.8	19.7	1.8
40-49	9.6	22.7	16.7	15.8	6.9	31.6	3.4
50-59	21.8	49.5	13.8	19.7	8.2	43.0	4.1
60-69	32.4	64.3	13.8	28.1	5.6	50.1	4.2

Fig. 2. Example chart from Singapore Statistics

Note that the age attribute has been divided into categories. It can be anticipated that queries to this data cube would be made mostly with the age ranges specified in the chart. The domain size of the age attribute is 52. Using the Block Range Max Algorithm [7], the optimal partition size would be $\sqrt{52} \approx 7$. The figure below shows how the age attribute dimension would be partitioned.

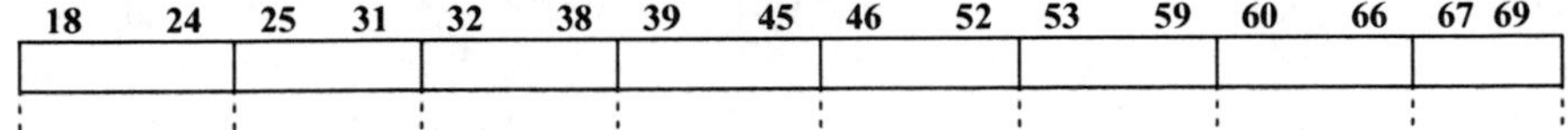

Fig. 3. Fixed Sized Partitions for Age attribute

Since queries made to the data cube would largely consist of ranges specified according to the age categories, most of the queries would produce query regions which would result in many boundary regions. The idea behind the use of variable sized partitions is to take advantage of the patterns of the queries known beforehand, in this case the categories of the ages, to produce non-uniformly sized partitions so as to reduce the number of boundary regions. A better way to partition the age categories might be as follows:

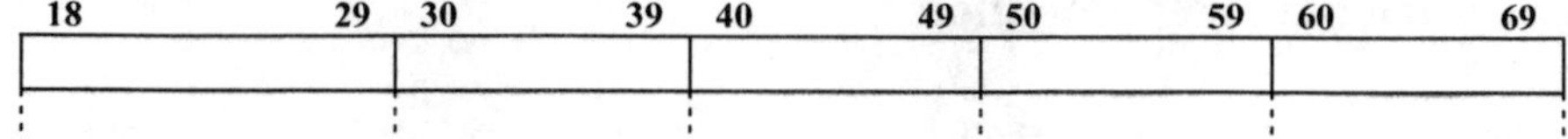

Fig. 4. Variable Sized Partitions for Age attribute

It is clear that if queries were made according to the age categories, there would not be any boundary regions along the age attribute dimension. The query could only cover internal regions, thus the query can be answered using only the pre-computed values stored by the various algorithms. The values in the data cube need not be accessed at all. This reduces the query cost tremendously. If non-uniformly sized partitions were to be used along the other dimension as well, there would be no boundary regions at all.

Observation: Given a range query Q, where the values from l_i to h_i defines the range of each dimension i, and a n-dimensional data cube logically partitioned such for all dimensions i, $i \in \{0, 1, \ldots, n - 1\}$, there exists partitions start at l_i and at h_i+1, the entire range query will be composed of internal regions only.

This is illustrated in the below 2-dimensional data cube example:

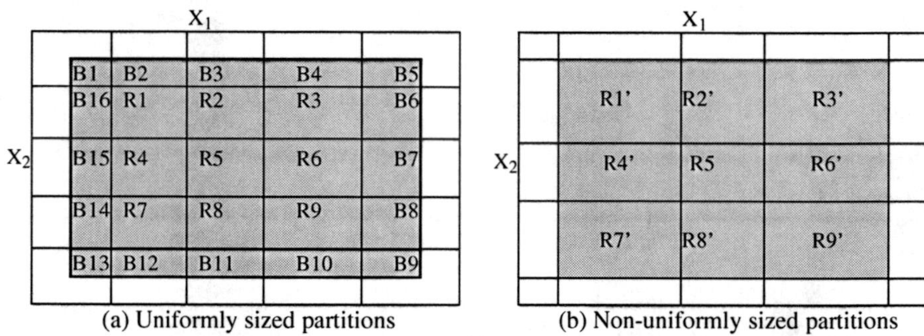

(a) Uniformly sized partitions (b) Non-uniformly sized partitions

Fig. 5. Effect of using non-uniformly sized partitions along both dimensions

In the above figure, it can be observed that there are boundary regions B1 to B16 in the uniformly partitioned data cube. Using the non-uniformly partitioned data cube, they all are replaced by internal regions R1', R2', R3', R4', R6', R7', R8' and R9'. It can also be observed that the total number of queried partitions, created by variable sized partitioning, is reduced. In practice, the query patterns may not be known before partitioning the data cube. In that case, the data cube should be first partitioned using the optimal partition size indicated in [7], $\sqrt{N}$, where N is the size of the attribute along the dimension to partition. And, range-value pairs are stored for analyzing the query patterns. Then the data cube can be re-partitioned according to the query patterns.

Issues with variable sized partitions. However, there are some issues with choosing the ranges that appear most often in the queries, namely a) there is the danger that there are too many range-value pairs; and b) there are too few range-value pairs.

(a) The first issue may result in too many partitions that are too small. The worst case is that each partition may only be 1 cell large. In general, the greater the number of partitions, the larger the number of pre-computed values stored.

This problem can be solved by choosing the most important queries to partition the data cube. A method for choosing these queries is to make use of weights derived from some factors: frequency of the query, hierarchy in dimension attributes, importance of that query, time when the query is run, e.g. during peak hours where other queries are being run, or during off-peak hours. These factors can be multiplied together to give an overall weight for a query, and the queries with the highest weights can be chosen. The user may also define an algorithm or method in which the most important query ranges are identified as well.

In order to constrain the storage overhead for storing range-value pairs, the range-value pairs should be stored and updated periodically. The user can also monitor query pattern changes. If user query behaviors have major changes, then the data cube should be re-partitioned and pre-computed cubes re-constructed.

(b) The second issue may result in exactly the opposite situation. Partitions become too large in size, and queries that do not follow the range-value pairs that make up the partitions would create boundary regions of large areas. In general, if the partitions are too large in size, then the number of pre-computed values stored will be too small. This means that ad-hoc queries are likely to have large boundary regions, which require accessing cells in the data cube, and in turn incur more query cost.

To solve this, partitions that are too large may be divided by the optimal partition size $\sqrt{N}$. However, there may be cases where dividing the partition exactly by $\sqrt{N}$ makes the remaining partition too small in size. For example, if $N = 100$, then the optimal partition size would be 10. However, if a partition is of size 45, then division by $\sqrt{N}$ would result in a remaining partition of size 5 as shown in Fig. 6(a). The remaining last partition would be too far from the optimal partition size.

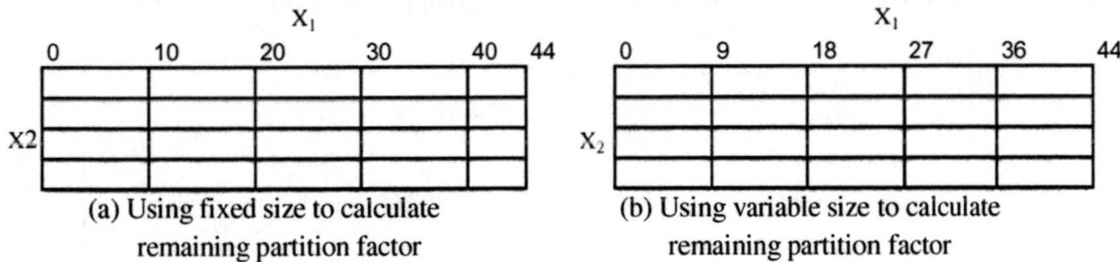

(a) Using fixed size to calculate remaining partition factor

(b) Using variable size to calculate remaining partition factor

Fig. 6. Effects of using variable size to calculate remaining partition size

Partitioning as in Fig. 6(b) would produce partition sizes that are larger and closer to the optimal size [7] and thus produce better results for ad-hoc queries. This is done by dividing the partition size *Z* by $\sqrt{N}$ first and rounding off the result, *p*, to obtain the number of partitions. The next partition is then given the size of $Z_l = Z/p$ rounded off. Then the second partition is given the size of $(Z\text{-}Z_l)/(p\text{-}1)$, and so on. Thus, in Fig. 6(b), where 45 is the partition size suggested by the range query, we divide this by 10, which when rounded off gives a value of 5. Thus each of the smaller partitions introduced will each be of size 9. The following formulation can be used:

Given a partition size *Z*, and a dimension of size *N*, such that the optimal partition size is $\sqrt{N}$, and $Z > \sqrt{N}$, divide *Z* into $p = rnd(Z/\sqrt{N}\ )$ partitions, where *rnd*(*x*) rounds *x* off to the nearest integer. Each partition would have a partition size as follows:

$$Z_i = rnd\left(\frac{Z - \sum_{j=0}^{i-1} Z_j}{p - i}\right), i = 0, \ldots, p\text{-}1;$$

Variable Partitioning Algorithms

Description: Provides partition sizes according to existing range-value pairs

Input: n, the number of dimensions of the data cube
$Q_L[n]$, an array of lists of the most important query ranges for each dimension identified using a separate user defined algorithm A
k, user defined variable to choose the most important queries
$N[n]$, size of domain for each dimension

Output: set of partition sizes for each dimension

Step 1: Separate the lower and upper bound values
For each dimension i, each lower bound value is stored in $\mathrm{Pt}_{\mathrm{start}}[i]$, and each upper bound value in $\mathrm{Pt}_{\mathrm{end}}[i]$ from the query ranges in $Q_L[i]$

Step 2: Output partition sizes for all dimensions of the data cube
Repeat steps 3 to 6 for all dimensions i = 1 to n of the data cube.

Step 3: Incrementing $\mathrm{Pt}_{\mathrm{end}}[i]$ values
For each value in $\mathrm{Pt}_{\mathrm{end}}[i]$, increment that value by 1;

Step 4: Merging $\mathrm{Pt}_{\mathrm{start}}[i]$ and $\mathrm{Pt}_{\mathrm{end}}[i]$
Merge-sort $\mathrm{Pt}_{\mathrm{start}}[i]$ and $\mathrm{Pt}_{\mathrm{end}}[i]$ into an ordered list $\mathrm{Pt}_{\mathrm{all}}$ in ascending order, discarding all duplicates;
Put $n[i]+1$ into $\mathrm{Pt}_{\mathrm{all}}$ as the last entry.

Step 5: Output partition sizes for points in merged list $\mathrm{Pt}_{\mathrm{all}}$
$\mathrm{part}_{\mathrm{var}} = \mathrm{part}_{\mathrm{cur}} = 0$;
while ($\mathrm{Pt}_{\mathrm{all}}$ is not empty) {
remove first entry from $\mathrm{Pt}_{\mathrm{all}}$ and place it in $\mathrm{part}_{\mathrm{var}}$;
$Z = \mathrm{part}_{\mathrm{var}} - \mathrm{part}_{\mathrm{cur}}$;
if ($Z \leq \sqrt{N[i]}$) {
output partition size as Z; }
else {

$$p = rnd\left(\frac{Z}{\sqrt{N[i]}}\right);$$

$$Z_i = rnd\left(\frac{Z - \sum_{j=0}^{i-1} Z_j}{p - i}\right), i = 0, \ldots, p\text{-}1;$$

Output the p partition sizes as $Z_0, Z_1, \ldots, Z_{p-1}$; }
$\mathrm{part}_{\mathrm{cur}} = \mathrm{part}_{\mathrm{var}}$;
}

The age group categories would then divide the data cube in the following manner.

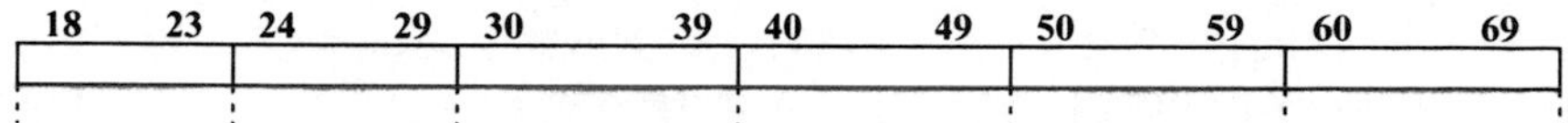

Fig. 7. Using the algorithm to partition according to the age categories

Experiment Results. The experiments were conducted on a PC running Windows 98 using the Block Range Max algorithm. Query ranges and data in the data cube were randomly generated using a uniform distribution. A total of 1000 queries were generated. The following results were obtained from fixing the query range along 1 dimension and 2 dimensions of the data cube to simulate patterns in user queries, but with the query range along the other dimensions randomly generated using a uniform distribution. The two ends of the query ranges were fixed to be in the middle of uniformly sized partitions. This provides an average case for input to the experiments. The query range for each dimension was generated to span about half the number of fixed sized partitions. The partition size is set to $\sqrt{N}$, where N is the dimension size.

Type of Data Cube	**Average Time Taken (millisec)**		**Improvement over [7] (%)**
	[7]	**Variable Partitioning**	
2D 100 x 100	2.97	2.69	9.43
3D 100 x 100 x 100	8.13	5.76	29.15
3D 200 x 200 x 200	13.62	10.60	22.17

Fig. 8. Results using variable sized partitions with queries fixed along 1dimension

Type of Data Cube	**Average Time Taken (millisec)**		**Improvement over [7] (%)**
	[7]	**Variable Partitioning**	
2D 100 x 100	2.92	1.92	34.32
3D 100 x 100 x 100	5.77	3.79	34.32
3D 200 x 200 x 200	10.16	8.13	19.98

Fig. 9. Results using variable sized partitions with queries fixed along 2 dimensions

Similar experiments were conducted for the Blocked Prefix Sum algorithm [4].

Type of Data Cube	**Average Time Taken (millisec)**		**Improvement over [4] (%)**
	[4]	**Variable Partitioning**	
2D 100 x 100	5.93	4.01	32.38
3D 100 x 100 x 100	292.70	202.07	30.96
3D 200 x 200 x 200	1244.60	941.50	24.35

Fig. 10. Results using variable sized partitions using Blocked Prefix Sum along 1 dimension

Type of Data Cube	**Average Time Taken (millisec)**		**Improvement over [4] (%)**
	[4]	**Variable Partitioning**	
2D 100 x 100	5.50	2.20	60.00
3D 100 x 100 x 100	199.40	106.50	46.59
3D 200 x 200 x 200	938.70	525.60	44.01

Fig. 11. Results using variable sized partitions using Blocked Prefix Sum along 2 dimension

Query performance for Block Range Max algorithm is better than Blocked Prefix Sum algorithm, since Block Range Max algorithm prunes many partitions when answering range max queries. That is also why the improvement for Blocked Prefix Sum algorithm outperforms the Block Range Max algorithm, since every boundary region has to be investigated for Blocked Prefix Sum algorithm. Detailed information could be found in [4, 7]. The best improvement is when all dimensions of the data cube are logically partitioned. Queries with query ranges that fall exactly at partition edges along all dimensions can be processed using pre-computed values only.

4 Reducing Physical Blocks Spanned by Logical Partitions

Costs for algorithms dealing with data cubes can be measured in the following three ways: a) number of cell accesses, b) number of disk I/Os, and c) response time. [4, 6, 7] are examples in which cell accesses are equated with the cost of the algorithm. However, this is usually not true in the practice. The number of cells accessed provides a worst case cost in which every cell accessed generates an I/O. This is only true if each cell is read separately from storage media. The method described in this section aims to reduce the number of actual disk I/Os and thus the response time. In practice, to improve I/O efficiency, blocks of data are transferred from disk to memory. Each logical block, the size of which is determined by the operating system, may consist of one or more physical sectors on the disk. This block of memory is usually cached in anticipation of future reads from the same block on the disk. Thus, the way in which data is arranged on the physical drive would make a difference to I/O performance. In Fig. 12(a), data is stored along one dimension of the data cube, with each logical block spanning 2 partitions. In each partition, data is spread over 6 logical blocks. In Fig. 12(b), data is stored according to the partition. The data in each partition is stored in only 3 logical blocks. The number of I/Os to the physical drive is reduced for each partition. Hence, the original data cube should be re-organized using the storage method as shown in Fig. 12(b) to speed up query processing.

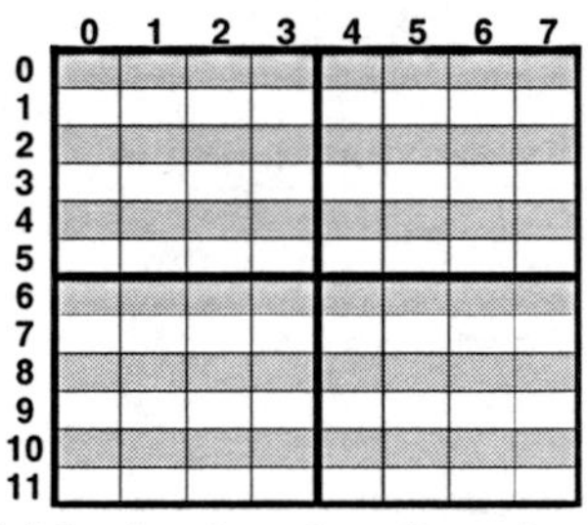

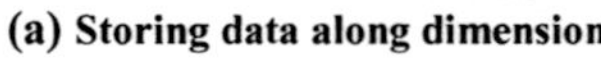
(a) Storing data along dimension

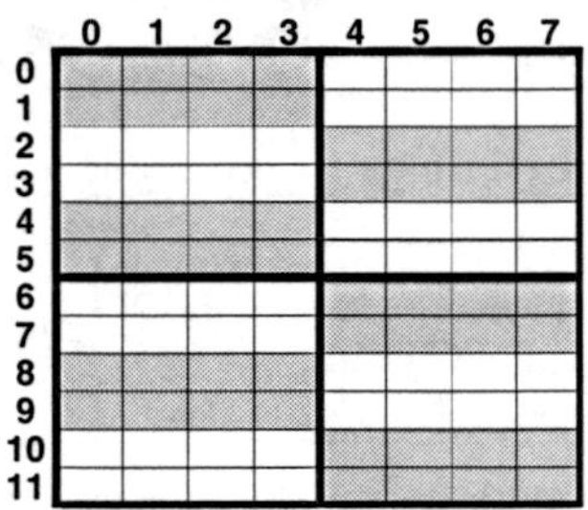

(b) Storing data by minimizing blocks spanned in each partition

Fig. 12. Different ways of physically storing data

Let n be the size of the domain for each dimension of a d-dimensional data cube, assuming the data cube has attributes of the same domain size. And, b is the partition size for each dimension. Let h be the size (in data entries) of a logical block on the physical drive. If the data cube is stored as in Figure 12(b), a partition in the data cube is stored in at most $\lceil b^d/h \rceil$ physical blocks. If the data cube is stored as in Fig. 12 (a), the calculation is more complicated. To simplify the calculation, we assume $(c\text{-}1)n < h \leq cn$, where $1 \leq c \leq n$, i.e. $0 < h \leq n^2$. This assumption is reasonable, when n is large. c is the number of rows in a partition, which are stored in one physical block. Then, the data in each partition of the data cube would span at least $b^{d-2} \times \lceil b/c \rceil$ physical blocks, where $d \geq 2$. For example, when $n = 100$, $d = 3$, $b = 10$, $h = 1024$, c is obtained to be 11. Thus, if the data cube is stored as in Fig. 12 (a), the number of blocks spanned by one partition would be $10^{3-2} \times \lceil 10/11 \rceil$, i.e. 10 blocks. However, if the data cube is stored as in Fig. 12 (b), the number of blocks spanned by one partition would be 1 block. This works out to a savings of 10 times, for the number of I/Os made to one partition. In addition, this method of storage may be applied to non-uniformly sized partitions as well. The real improvements for range max and range sum queries in the following experiments are not as much as we analyzed above, since when answering range queries many partitions are investigated using pre-computed values instead of accessing these partitions in the original data cube.

Experiment Results. The experiments were conducted on a PC running Windows 98 using a FAT32 file system. The cluster size is 4kB large. Each data entry in the data cube took up 4 bytes, so a cluster could store 1024 data entries. The partition size is set to $\sqrt{N}$, where N is the dimension size. Query ranges and data in the data cube were randomly generated using a uniform distribution. A total of 1000 queries were generated. The following table shows results obtained by comparing response times of a data cube stored according to the partitioning structure against that in [7].

Type of Data Cube	Avg Access Time [7] (millisec)	Avg Access Time-Reorganized (millisec)	Improvement in Response Time(%)
2D 1000 x 1000	5.39	4.56	15.40
3D 100 x 100 x 100	7.58	5.33	29.68
3D 200 x 200 x 200	17.08	8.51	50.18

Fig. 13. Results for linearizing storage according to partition using Block Range Max

Similar experiments were conducted for the Blocked Prefix Sum algorithm [4].

Type of Data Cube	Avg Access Time [4] (millisec)	Avg Access Time-Reorganized (millisec)	Improvement in Response Time(%)
2D 1000 x 1000	30.10	17.79	40.90
3D 100 x 100 x 100	45.05	18.84	58.17
3D 200 x 200 x 200	335.10	140.10	58.15

Fig. 14. Results for linearizing storage according to partition using Blocked Prefix Sum

The larger the data cube, the better the improvement, because as the data cube gets larger in size, each partition increases in size, and the number of cells accessed increases. As the partition gets larger, data in each partition is spread over more blocks if stored as in Fig. 12(a). However, if the data cube is stored as in Fig. 12(b), the increase in number of blocks is not as much.

5 Improving Response Time for Existing Algorithms

The techniques in section 3 and 4 can be easily combined to improve overall response times of existing range query algorithms on OLAP data cubes. A few criteria must be met before the techniques can be applied. Firstly, the range query algorithm should involve a partitioning scheme. We would not be able to apply variable sized partitions to Prefix Cube because no logical partitions exist. Secondly, the OLAP application should have a fairly predictable range of queries. This would allow the algorithm in section 3 to partition the dimensions according to the most important queries. If the first two criteria can be met, the use of non-uniform sized partitions can be applied, such as the algorithms in [1, 2, 3, 4, 6, 7, 8]. The third criterion is that the algorithm would access cells in the data cube sequentially in partitions. This means that spanning data in each partition in as few physical blocks as possible would improve performance. For algorithms that access cells far away from each other, as in Prefix Cube, there would be no noticeable improvement since each cell access would likely be in different physical blocks. If this criterion is met, the use of the method in section 4 can be applied, such as the algorithms in [4, 6, 7].

If the range query algorithms meet these three criteria, such as algorithms in [4, 6, 7], then the combination of the methods discussed in this paper would be applicable. Since it is not reasonable for OLAP applications to accept only queries that are based on the variable sized partitioning scheme, arranging the data physically as discussed in section 4 would reduce query response time needed for the other queries.

6 Conclusion

In this paper, we have presented a combination of techniques, involving the use of variable sized partitions as well as packing the data in each partition into as few physical blocks as possible, which if applied to existing range query algorithms which meet the criteria discussed in the previous section, will greatly improve the query cost and response time of these algorithms. We have also shown that these techniques can be applied to range sum and range max query algorithms. These methods can also be applied separately or in conjunction with each other. Since the methods are applied directly to existing algorithms, the benefits of the original algorithm are not affected.

References

[1] Y. Chan and Y.E. Ioannidis, "Hierarchical cubes for range-sum queries", *in Proc. of the Intl. Conf. On Very Large Databases (VLDB), 1999*, pp. 675-686.
[2] S. Geffner, D. Agrawal, A. El Abbadi, "The dynamic data cube", *in Proc. of EDBT, 2000.*
[3] S. Geffner, D. Agrawal, A.E. Abbadi, T. Smith. "Relative Prefix Sum: An Efficient Approach for Querying Dynamic OLAP Data Cubes". In Proc. of the 15th ICDE, 1999.
[4] C. T. Ho, R. Agrawal, R. Megiddo, R. Srikant, "Range Queries in OLAP Data Cubes", *in Proc. of the Intl. ACM SIGMOD Conference, Tucson, Arizona, May 1997,* pp. 73-88.
[5] J. Gray, A. Bosworth, A. Layman, H. Pirahesh. "Data cube: A relational aggregation operator generating group-by, cross-tabs and sub-totals". In Proc. of the 12th ICDE, 1996.
[6] S. Y. Lee, T. W. Ling, H. G. Li, "Hierarchical Compact Cube for Range-Max", *in Proc. of the 26th VLDB Conference Cairo, Egypt, September 2000.*
[7] H. G. Li, T. W. Ling, S. Y. Lee, "Range-Max/Min Query in OLAP Data Cube", *in Proc. of the 11th DEXA Conference, Greenwich, 2000.*
[8] H. G. Li, T. W. Ling, S. Y. Lee, Z. X. Loh, "Range Sum Queries in Dynamic OLAP Data Cubes", *CODAS'2001.*
[9] "Highlights of the 1998 National Health Survey", *http://www.singstat.gov.sg/PUBN/SSN/1Q2000/pg3-8.pdf.*

A Comparison of Data Warehouse Development Methodologies Case Study of the Process Warehouse

Beate List[1], Robert M. Bruckner[1], Karl Machaczek[1], Josef Schiefer[2],

[1] Institute of Software Technology and Interactive Systems
Vienna University of Technology
1040 Wien, Austria
{list, bruckner, machaczek}@ifs.tuwien.ac.at

[2] IBM Research Division, Thomas J. Watson Research Center
Yorktown Heights, NY 10598, United States
josef.schiefer@us.ibm.com

Abstract. Building a data warehouse is a very challenging issue because compared to software engineering it is quite a young discipline and does not yet offer well-established strategies and techniques for the development process. Current data warehouse development methods can fall within three basic groups: data-driven, goal-driven and user-driven. All three development approaches have been applied to the Process Warehouse that is used as the foundation of a process-oriented decision support system, which aims to analyse and improve business processes continuously. In this paper we evaluate all three development methodologies by various assessment criteria. The aim is to establish a link between the methodology and the requirement domain.

1 Introduction

During the last decade data warehouse systems have become an essential component of modern decision support systems in large organisations. Data warehouse systems offer efficient access to integrated and historic data from heterogeneous sources to support managers in their planning and decision-making. A data warehouse by itself does not create value; value comes from the use of the data in the warehouse. Hence, improved decision-making results from the better information available in the data warehouse. According to Watson and Haley, the greatest potential benefits of the data warehouse occur when it is used to redesign business processes and to support strategic business objectives. (see [12]). These are also the most difficult benefits to achieve, because of the amount of top management support, commitment, and involvement and the amount of organisational change required.

R. Cicchetti et al. (Eds.): DEXA 2002, LNCS 2453, pp. 203–215, 2002.

Building a data warehouse is a very challenging issue because compared to software engineering it is quite a young discipline and does not yet offer well-established strategies and techniques for the development process. A lot of projects fail due to the complexity of the development process. As yet there is no common strategy for the development of data warehouses. Current data warehouse development methods can fall within three basic groups: data-driven, goal-driven and user-driven.

In this paper all three development approaches have been applied to the Process Warehouse that is used as the foundation of a process-oriented decision support system, which aims to analyse and improve business processes continuously (see [10]). We evaluate these development methodologies by the means of application areas, supported management method, targeting organisational level, extent of end user involvement, duration of development and completion, skill level of data warehouse designer, complexity of data model, amount of source systems and longevity of data model. The aim is to establish a link between the methodology and the requirement domain.

The following section presents the related work of data warehouse development methodologies. A brief overview of the Process Warehouse is given in section 3. The data-driven development methodology is applied, analysed to the Process Warehouse in section 4, the user-driven development methodology in section 5 and the goal-driven development methodology in section 6. The paper ends with a conclusion and an assessment of the final results.

2 Related Work

Data-Driven Methodologies: Bill Inmon, the founder of data warehousing argues that data warehouse environments are data driven, in comparison to classical systems, which have a requirement driven development life cycle (see [6]). He states that requirements are the last thing to be considered in the decision support development life cycle, they are understood after the data warehouse has been populated with data and results of queries have been analysed by users. The data warehouse development strategy is based on the analysis of the corporate data model and relevant transactions. The approach ignores the needs of data warehouse users a priori. Company goals and user requirements are not reflected at all. User needs are integrated in the second cycle.

Golfarelli, Maio and Rizzi propose a semi-automated methodology to build a dimensional data warehouse model from the pre-existing E/R schemes that represent operational databases (see [5]).

Goal-Driven Methodologies: Böhnlein and Ulbrich-vom Ende present an approach that is based on the SOM (Semantic Object Model) process modelling technique in order to derive the initial data warehouse structure (see [1]). The first stage of the derivation process determines goals and services the company provides to its customers. Then the business process is analysed by applying the SOM interaction schema that highlights the customers and their transactions with the process under study. In a third step sequences of transactions are transformed into sequences of existing dependencies that refer to information systems. The last step identifies measures and dimensions: One has to find enforcing (information request) transactions for measures and get dimensions from existing dependencies. In our opinion this highly complex approach works only well when business processes are designed throughout the company and are combined with business goals.

Kimball proposes a four-step approach where he starts to choose a business process, takes the grain of the process, and chooses dimensions and facts (see [7]). He defines a business process as a major operational process in the organisation that is supported by some kind of legacy system (or systems).

User-Driven Methodologies: Westerman describes an approach that was developed at Wal-Mart and has its main focus on implementing business strategy (see [13]). The methodology assumes that the company goal is the same for everyone and the entire company will therefore be pursuing the same direction. It is proposed to set up a first prototype based on the needs of the business. Business people define goals and gather, prioritise as well as define business questions supporting these goals. Afterwards the business questions are prioritised and the most important business questions are defined in terms of data elements, including the definition of hierarchies. Although the Wal-Mart approach focuses on business needs, business goals that are defined by the organis ation are not taken into consideration at all.

Poe proposes a catalogue for conducting user interviews in order to collect end user requirements (see [11]). She recommends interviewing different user groups in order to get a complete understanding of the business. The questions cover a very board field and include also topics like job responsibilities.

3 The Process Warehouse

Business process reengineering has turned functional organisations into process organisations (see [3], [4]). In order to gain long-term advantages, it is not sufficient merely to reengineer business processes. It is essential that the newly designed business processes are continuously measured and improved. In order to gauge the performance of business processes, a Performance Measurement System is required According to Kueng it should meet the following requirements: the system must be capable of tracking both financial and non-financial performance indicators, include company-internal and external indicators, store collected data on a non-volatile media so that the data can be analysed over a long period of time, provide a user-friendly interface, which will support, for example, an easy data selection mechanism, consider target values for each performance indicator and disseminate results (see [8]). We address these needs by applying a data warehouse approach, called the *Process Warehouse*, which is defined as follows:

The Process Warehouse (PWH) is a separate read-only analytical database that is used as the foundation of a process-oriented decision support system, which aims to analyse and improve business processes continuously [10].

In the Process Warehouse, basic business process theories are reflected in five perspectives in order to represent fundamental process concepts in an explicit way. The *Business Process Perspective* focuses on the process as a complete entity. The *Organisational Perspective* focuses on the organisational structure of a business process and addresses the fact that business processes, which cross organisational boundaries tend to be inefficient because of changing responsibilities [9]. This perspective supports the detection of delay causing organisational units. The *Product / Service Perspective* focuses on the relationship between product or service and the business process. Its target is to identify the complexity drivers that request a change in the process design, e.g. the segmentation of a process or the special treatment of certain cases.

The *Improvement Support Perspective* is based on the histories of several instances together. The aggregation of instances aims at identifying major performance gaps and deviations, which show that there is need for improvement. As single instances do not have an impact on the aggregated performance, gaps reflect a fundamental performance problem. The *Information Detail Perspective* aims at process information on instance level. It enables the analysis of certain instances and their development over time and helps to determine the cause of performance gaps and deviations.

4 Data-Driven Development Methodology

4.1 Motivation and Application Setting

Current Workflow Management Systems (WfMS) lack comprehensive analysis capabilities. The presented case study can be seen as an extension to a WfMS in order to overcome those limitations. We have applied a data-driven methodology to this case study because commercial Workflow Management Systems have hard coded audit trails in the sense that history data cannot be adjusted to the specific needs of an organisation as well as limited audit trails. Consequently, as much information as possible must be retrieved. Basic components of the WfMS, the meta-model and the audit trail, provide the foundation for identifying information requirements.

The meta-model represents the modelling capabilities of the WfMS. It consists of a process model and an organisation model. The utilised WfMS is IBM MQSeries Workflow™. The organisation model of IBM MQSeries Workflow™ is composed of organisational units, roles and individuals. These entities are assigned as process performers to entities of the process model. The process model of IBM MQSeries Workflow™ is composed of processes, process activities (sub process), block activities (loop) and program activities (execute an application). A process type is defined in the build-time environment.

A process instance is executed in the runtime environment according to its process definition. WfMSs can be seen as state event machines; process and activity instances get through events into certain predefined states. All events in the life cycle of a process or an activity instance are recorded in the audit trail that is either a relational database or a file. Each record in the audit trail contains a number of information including, but not limited to following items: date and time when the event takes place, type of event, process identifier, parent process identifier, activity type, activity state, activity identifier, started program name, role or id associated with the event, etc.

4.2 Data Model

In order to get a data model for this Process Warehouse prototype we analysed the data model of the underlying operational sources and identified the relevant transactions. The process and the organisation meta-model represent the underlying operational sources. The state transition machines for activity and process represent the relevant transactions, which are at runtime tracked in the audit trail. Having business process theory in mind, the entities of the meta-model match perfect with dimensions. We used the audit trail for potential measures.

The audit trail tracks any event change with a timestamp. A process instance may have the following states: *running, suspended, terminated, finished* and *deleted*. The initial process instance state is *created*. The process instance state is *running*, when activities are carried out. A process instance goes into the *suspended* state when a user requests this state explicitly. In this state navigation has stopped and no more activities are carried out. A process instances that has *finished* will be *deleted* later on.

An activity instance is in the state *ready* when a work item is assigned to a role. The state *running* indicates that the item is being processed and the state *terminate* indicates an early termination by an authorised user. In certain situations, the activity implementation cannot be carried out correctly. In this case, the activity is put into the *in error* state. The user can carry out the activity outside of the control of the WfMS, through the support of the checkout facility. The user checks out the activity instance, which is put into the *checked out* state. A user can also *suspend* an activity instance. Activity instances may have further states: *disabled, expired, finished, deleted* and *executed*. These states may not resume the activity instance. We decided for process and activity instances to measure the duration of each state.

The conceptual model represents the ADAPT (Application Design for Analytical Processing Technologies, see [2]) notation. The basic elements of ADAPT are *cubes*, *dimensions*, and *formulas*. Measures represent a particular kind of dimension – a measure dimension. Figure 1 shows the Process Warehouse data model with the cubes *Process* and *Activity*. As process and activity instances have different life cycles, we have separated the cubes for process and activity duration. Each cube has its own measure dimension. The measure dimension for the *Process* cube consists of four single measures: *Ready, Running, Suspended* and *Cycle Time* – this fourth measure is calculated by means of a formula. We have not considered the remaining states, as the instance has already finished and may not resume. The *Process* cube has the dimensions *Organisation*, *Process* and *Time*. The *Process* dimension represents the *Business Process Perspective* and consists of the levels process type and process instance. The *Organisation* dimension represents the *Organisational Perspective* and consists of the levels organisation, role and user. The *Organisation* dimension enables the analysis of the process performance of certain organisations, roles or units. The measure dimension for the *Activity* cube consists of six single measures: *Ready, Running, Suspended, Checked Out, In Error* and *Cycle Time* – this measure is calculated by means of a formula. We have not considered the remaining states, as the instance has already finished and may not resume. The *Process* cube has the dimensions *Organisation*, *Process, Activity* and *Time*.

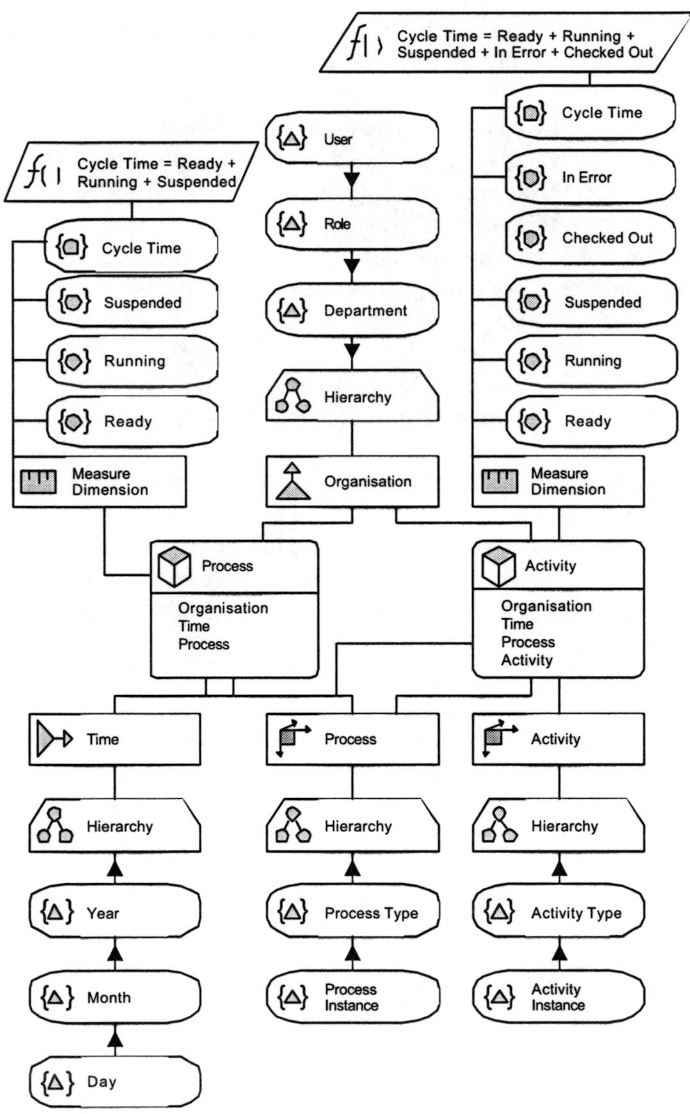

Figure 1: Conceptual design of the Process Warehouse in ADAPT notation

4.3 Evaluation

The data model consists of a few dimensions and a lot of measures. The dimensions represent the basic structure of the WfMS. Measures are time-based and have a very low level of granularity as well as a short-term focus. Basically, measures can be characterised as quantitative, non-financial and unbalanced. Very tight task supervision of individuals can be observed at activity level. In addition to the overall performance of departments, roles and individuals, the development of knowledge can be traced. This approach represents the era of scientific management methods. It supports tayloristic fundamentals of measurement e.g. finding out the best way of doing a job.

Time is not a sufficient key figure to assure long-term process quality. A balance of financial, non-financial, qualitative and quantitative measures, from external and internal sources with the aim of assuring long-term goals is an elementary shortcoming. As the data-driven development methodology allows no scope for long-term strategic visions it is unsuitable for the strategic level of organisation. The tactical level of the organisation or the process owner is only partly supported by the data-driven development methodology. Main shortcomings are the lack of objectives connected to the process definition. Consequently, there is no link to strategic targets. However, the approach is appropriate for managing the process at micro level e.g. management of resources etc. and targets mainly the operational level of the organisational hierarchy.

As the objective of this prototype is to build an extension for a WfMS and the development methodology is based exclusively on the fundamental structure of the system, the integration of end users has not been required. The success of the project fully depends on the skill and experience of the data warehouse designer. No other roles were involved in the project. Due to the lean project structure, the development process was fast and straightforward.

Overall, a data-driven development methodology can generate performance information targeting a non-specified user group at operational level. The information created is suited for tight and narrow monitoring as well as for mining purposes. This approach is especially suited for production workflows, because they generate a high business value, have a high degree of repetition, are customer focused and often time critical. The longevity of the prototype is directly related to the durability of the structure of the WfMS. An integration of external data sources would balance the analysis capabilities of the prototype.

5 User-Driven Development Methodology

5.1 Motivation, Organisational Setting

The goal of the case study that is presented in this chapter was to establish the Process Warehouse in a business environment and to incorporate process performance measurement into the corporate data warehouse. In addition to the advantage of reusing the corporate data warehouse management facilities, it is a first step towards an enterprise-wide performance measurement system. This case study can be also seen as a proof of the Process Warehouse concept in a commercial environment in terms of usability and acceptance. The project was set up as a feasibility study with a strong focus on the production environment. We selected a user-driven development methodology in order to raise the acceptance of the system by constantly interacting with potential users and decision makers. Additionally, it was my concern to convince the company of the merits of this unusual approach for process analysis and to integrate the prototype into the production environment.

The organisation where this case study has been realised is a large insurance company, which is primarily operating in central Europe. The business process is part of the broker business and responsible for proposal processing. IBM MQSeries Workflow™ is utilised to automate the proposal processing business process. In November 2001 a first pilot system went into operation. Today, the workflow engine handles ten users and about 3000 workflow instances per month. The use of this system is limited to two regional offices and a few insurance products. They are planning to launch the system all over Austria and enlarge it on the complete range of product. Up to 150 users will be involved in the processing of some 100.000 instances per year.

5.2 Data Model

We applied the Wal-Mart Model methodology (see [13]), developed by Westerman to this prototype. The insurance company has the significant business need to reduce the process cycle time of the proposal process by more than 50 %. This is the main process goal. Additional goals concerning e.g. quality or cost were not available.

Two data models have been developed. When we finished the first data model, a new person with management experience joined our group and criticised the model as not focusing on top-level management and their decision support requirements. We started again with phase two and developed a second data model.

The second model has had a broader perspective. The focus is on comprehensive business questions e.g. Is the broker responsible for the waiting time?, What insurance product was processed?, etc. and integrated more external data sources. Insurance companies traditionally have a very powerful labour union; therefore we did not analyse the performance of individuals. Compared to the data model in Figure 1, it has got additional dimensions (broker, product, region) that integrate to a larger extent the external environment and fewer measures (working time and waiting time). The *Broker* dimension analyses processes that belong to certain broker and targets the relationship between dealer and cycle time. In this case there was the concern that some brokers deliver incomplete data and increase the cycle time. The *Product* dimension questions whether there is a difference in terms of cycle time between products. Some might be more demanding than others. The *Region* dimension targets different ways of processing the proposal in certain region, e.g. a different skill level. Beside the audit trail, we accessed the proposal database for product, region and broker data. The product, broker and region dimension were reused from the corporate data warehouse.

5.3 Evaluation

The data model contains more dimensions than the model created with data-driven methodology, but has fewer measures, which are time-based and have a low level of granularity as well as a historic and short-term focus. Measures do not represent the state structure of MQ Series Workflow™. Financial measures would have been possible, but were not an issue in the business question definition session. Dimensions represent either the structure of MQ Series Workflow™ or external data sources. The dimension *Product* represents the Product / Service Perspective of the Process Warehouse. The dimension *Broker* partly represents the customer aspect. Basically, measures can be characterised as quantitative, non-financial and unbalanced.

The user-driven development methodology generates performance information that is targeting the organisational level of the people who have been involved in the project. Every person who dominated the data model created a different one. The granularity and the analysis requirements of the models were also different and represented the hierarchical level, the profession, the educational background, the experience and perceptions of the people involved. When the players changed, the requirements changed as well and the complete model might become obsolete. Consequently, the longevity of these models is very short-dated. Overall, the models also represent the company culture, for example the culture of powerful labour union (e.g. very close supervision of individuals has not been a concern).

The fundamental pitfall of the Wal-Mart model is that it is based on the existence of transparent business goals throughout an organisation. At the insurance company, the corporate goals are not communicated to its employees; therefore they are not in a position to support their firm's business strategy. Selected measures, dimensions, the level of granularity and the targeting level of the organisational hierarchy depend on the people involved. The user-driven development methodology requires a project manager with very strong moderation and leadership skills as well as a skilled data warehouse designer. If the business goals are fuzzy, the project manager must act with even more determination. While a user-driven development methodology supports user acceptance, it does not guarantee decision support. It is useful for prototypes and user-sensitive domains, but a monopolisation of this approach is risky and must be avoided.

6 Goal-Driven Development Methodology

6.1 Motivation, Organisational Setting and Data Model

The project (for details see [8]) was in cooperation between one of the authors and the performance measurement group (http://www.measure.ch/) at the University of Fribourg, Switzerland. The motivation for the project was to create a holistic Process Performance Measurement System. Two business processes have been analysed.

The development methodology utilised is a stakeholder driven approach that has been developed by Kueng (see [8]). He suggests starting with identifying stakeholders (e.g. customer, employee, innovation, investor, etc.) for each process. For each stakeholder, process-relevant goals are identified. From the company goals, business process-specific goals are selected. Each goal is measured by at least one indicator. The indicators aim at achieving long-term goals. This leads to a mix of financial, non-financial, qualitative and quantitative measures, from external and internal sources which take various perspectives into consideration.

Five aspects that represent stakeholders were identified for the service process: finance, customer, employee, environment and development. The customer aspect's goal is high service quality and low product price. Customer satisfaction (as revealed in customer surveys), customer complaints and problem solving time are the performance indicators that measure the goal *high service quality*. The goal of a low product price is measured with the ratio to competitors. The finance (investor) aspect has the goal *high profitability* and measures the performance indicators service process margin and operating assets. The employee's goal *good working conditions* and this aspect is measured by the employee satisfaction rate in a survey. The development aspect has the goal *investment in professional training* and measures training days per employee. The environment aspect has the goal *optimise travels* and measures kilometres per visit.

The indicator Customer satisfaction is represented with the *Customer Satisfaction Cube*. The measure dimension for *Customer Satisfaction* consists of three single measures: *Expectation, Perception* and *Performance Gap*. The *Customer Satisfaction Cube* has the dimensions Questionnaire, Process and Time. Any question of a certain questionnaire can be measured for a process type. The indicator problem solving time is represented with the *Duration Cube*, which measures the cycle time of a process. The *Duration Cube* has the dimensions Organisation, Customer, Process and Time.

6.2 Evaluation

The data model contains a few measures, which are balanced and represent a mix of financial, non-financial, qualitative and quantitative measures with a strategic focus. Facts have a moderate level of granularity and do not support a tayloristic monitoring approach. Cubes have few dimensions that support the corporate goals. The prototype integrates a lot of external source systems, in order to achieve a balanced system.

The data model supports users at all organisational levels. The success of the project depends greatly on the support of top management, as the entire organisation is affected. In order to quantify the strategy of the company and to transfer the strategy into key performance indicators, top management, moderators, economists and data warehouse designers are required. End user involvement is exceptional, although this would increase the acceptance of the system. A goal-driven development methodology supports an organisation in turning strategy into action and guides that organisation towards the future desired. This top-down approach provides assistance for modern management methods. On the whole decision support is based upon it.

7 Summary and Conclusion

In this paper we have evaluated data warehouse development methodologies. The empirical background of this work is based on three case studies of the Process Warehouse. This section compares all methodologies and ends up establishing a link between methodology and requirement domain. Results are compared in Table 1.

Basically, a monopolisation of this user-driven development methodology is risky and must be avoided, as it generates performance information that reflects the organisational level of the people involved. Therefore, selected measures, dimensions, the level of granularity and the targeting level of the organisational hierarchy are very unstable. The methodology has a bottom-up tendency, because most employees do not see the organisation from a broad angle, theirs is a narrow-minded, egocentric point of view. The project duration may be long-winded and very costly, as project participants request long discussions on a lot of unnecessary measures and dimensions. Hence, analysing the criteria of the user-driven methodology does not make sense, because results change with the people involved. This development methodology may well raise acceptance of a system, but must be combined with the data-driven or goal-driven development methodology in order to improve the longevity of the system. The more a system suffers rejection, the more user involvement is required beside a focus on organisational strategies or the corporate data model.

The goal-driven development methodology supports modern management methods and is a foundation for decision support at all organisational levels. The level of granularity is much higher compared to that of the data-driven approach. While the Process Warehouse based on the goal-driven development methodology measures only the cycle time for business processes and has only one cube, the Process Warehouse based on the data-driven development methodology measures the duration of all process and activity states as well as the workload of departments and roles. The development duration of the project tends to be very extensive and costly, as a lot of highly qualified professionals and managers take part in numerous workshops and derive performance indicators from strategy. End-users are rarely involved. They are only required when operational detail matters. As the model is aligned with the corporate strategy, it is very stable. Measures and dimensions are balanced: financial, non-financial, qualitative and quantitative aspects are considered. A lot of data sources are integrated, because a holistic approach is based on all aspects of an organisation.

The data-driven development methodology is recommended for data mining and data exploration purposes. The bottom-up approach exploits the database and is suited for tayloristic measurement. The data-driven development methodology is particularly suited for production workflows. These workflows generate a high business value, have a high degree of repetition, are customer focused, often time critical and therefore require tight and close monitoring. All development methodologies have been applied to IBM MQSeries Workflow™ and measure the process cycle time. The goal-driven development methodology measures exclusively the process cycle time. The user-driven development methodology differentiates between working time and waiting time, while the data-driven development methodology measures three states: ready, suspended and running. The working time is equal to the running state.

Methodology Criteria	Data-Driven	User-Driven	Goal-Driven
Basic Approach	Bottom-up	Bottom-up	Top-Down
Supported Management Method	Taylorism Classical School of Management	None Company is culture reflected	Management by Objectives
Project Support	None	Department	Top Management
Application Area / Requirement Domain	Data Exploration and Data Mining	Raise the Acceptance of a System	Foundation for Decision Support
Targeting Organisational Level	Operational Partly Tactical	Depends on the Group of Interview Partners	Strategic Tactical Operational
Focus	Short-Term Focus	Short-Term Focus	Long-Term Focus
Extent of End User Involvement	None	High	Moderate
Project Duration	Low	Very High	High
Skills of Project Members	Data Warehouse Designer	Moderator Data Warehouse Designer	Moderator Economist Data Warehouse Designer
Number of Measures	Many	Many	Few
Type of Measures	Non-Financial and Quantitative Time-Based and Frequency-Based	Non-Financial and Quantitative Time-Based and Frequency-Based	Balanced: Financial and Non-Financial as well as Qualitative and Quantitative
Level of Granularity	Low	Low	High
Number of Dimensions	Few	Many	Few
Type of Dimensions	Represents the Basic Structure of the Application	Represents the Basic Structure of the Application and external Sources	Represents the Strategic Building Blocks of the Organisation
Number of Source Systems	Low	Moderate	High
Longevity / Stability of Data Model	Long	Short	Long
Cost	Low	High	High

Table 1: Comparison of Data Warehouse Development Methodologies

The ready and the suspended states describe the waiting time in more detail. The ready state represents the duration a work item is assigned to a user and has not been accessed before. The suspended state represents the duration a work item is moved off the work list because it cannot be processed because information required is not available. The breakdown of the waiting time into different states enables the detection of work overload, missing resources or lazy employees. Therefore, the insurance company is going to re-engineer the first prototype and apply the data-driven development methodology. The longevity of the data model is directly related to the durability of the structure of the underlying system. Compared to the goal-driven approach, the project duration was very short, as no end users and no other source systems were involved. Due to the limitation of the audit trail, measures and dimensions are time-based. Their main target is the operational level of the organisation.

The data-driven and the goal-driven development methodology do not stress mutual exclusion. As they pursue different purposes they may exist in parallel. The data-driven development methodology can even be seen as a lower level of detail, as the drill-down path of the goal-driven development methodology. These methodologies are complementary and when used in parallel, the benefit is even higher.

8 References

1. Boehnlein, M., Ulbrich vom Ende, A.: Business Process Oriented Development of Data Warehouse Structures. In: Proceedings of Data Warehousing 2000, Physica Verlag (2000)
2. Bulos, D.: OLAP Database Design: A New Dimension, Database Programming & Design, Vol. 9, No. 6, (1996)
3. Davenport, T. H.: Process Innovation – Reengineering Work through Information Technology, Harvard Business School Press, Boston (1993)
4. Hammer, M.: Beyond Reengineering, Harper Collins Publishers (1996)
5. Golfarelli, M., Maio, D., Rizzi, S.: Conceptual Design of Data Warehouses from E/R Schemes. In: Proceedings of the 31st HICSS, IEEE Press (1998)
6. Inmon, W. H.: Building the Data Warehouse. Wiley & Sons (1996)
7. Kimball, R.: The Data Warehouse Toolkit: Practical Techniques For Building Dimensional Data Warehouse. John Wiley & Sons (1996)
8. Kueng, P., Wettstein, Th., List, B.: A Holistic Process Performance Analysis through a Process Data Warehouse. In: Proceedings of the American Conference on Information Systems (2001)
9. Leymann, F., Roller, D.: Production Workflow. Prentice Hall (2000)
10. List, B., Schiefer, J., Tjoa A M., Quirchmayr, G.: Multidimensional Business Process Analysis with the Process Warehouse. In: W. Abramowicz and J. Zurada (eds.): Knowledge Discovery for Business Information Systems, Kluwer Academic Publishers (2000)
11. Poe, V.: Building a Data Warehouse for Decision Support. Prentice Hall (1996)
12. Watson, H., Haley, B.: Managerial Considerations. In Communications of the ACM, Vol. 41, No. 9 (1998)
13. Westerman, P.: Data Warehousing using the Wal-Mart Model, Morgan Kaufmann (2001)

Self-maintainable Data Warehouse Views Using Differential Files[1]

Lee Wookey[1], Yonghun Hwang[2], Suk-Ho Kang[2], Sanggeun Kim[1], Changmin Kim[1], and Yunsun Lee[1]

[1] Computer Science & Management, Sungkyul Univ., Anyang, Korea, 430-742
{wook | sgkim | kimcm | lcy}@sungkyul.edu
[1] Industrial Engineering, Seoul National Univ., Seoul, Korea, 151-742
{yhwang | shkang}@ara.snu.ac.kr

Abstract. Data warehouses materialize views in order to provide fast access to information, but the correctness also should be maintained. The notion of self-maintenance can be a goal that defined as maintaining views by materializing supplementary data. Incremental update mechanisms can now be prospective way to the goal. A discussion with extensive literature is generated on several issues with maintaining data warehouse views. There are issues related to the data warehouse view maintenance: algebraic approaches, the concurrency control problem, database rule related problems. Motivating example derived from TPC-D database is suggested in terms of incremental base relation method, auxiliary view method, and differential method respectively. After quantitative dealings and qualitative measures are reviewed, it is concluded that the differential method is superior to the others in that it is a true self-maintenance method and it does not burden the current base relations.

Index Terms -- data warehouse, materialized view, differential file, self-maintenance

1 Introduction

Data warehouses materialize views in order to provide fast access to information that is integrated from several data sources. The data sources may be heterogeneous or distributed from the data warehouse views. Though the source data is homogeneous, accessing or updating it is usually time consuming due to the sheer volume (+Terabyte), or sometimes its unavailability. One of the critical weaknesses of materialized views in data warehouses is that the views are liable to become outdated or out of synchronization with the source data, as changes are made to the source data upon which the views are defined. In order to guarantee the correctness of the data warehouse, the changes of source data have to be applied to the views. That makes the maintenance of materialized views in a data warehouse different from the maintenance in conventional views [23]. Maintaining materialized views under source

[1] This work was supported by the Korea Science and Engineering Foundation (KOSEF) through the Advanced Information Technology Research Center (AITrc), and the first author was supported by postdoctoral fellowship program from KOSEF.

R. Cicchetti et al. (Eds.): DEXA 2002, LNCS 2453, pp. 216–225, 2002.

updates in a data warehouse is one of the important issues of data warehousing [9, 14, 16, 27].

Data warehouse view maintenance is a complicated as well as a practical problem in real world computing society. Thus in this paper, we have a focus on that what is a practical self-maintenance method. It is kept in mind that in maintaining data warehouse view the current DBMS should not be interfered, which is practically significant. In addition the size of the data and the number of transactions should be minimized. A motivating example modified from TPC-D would be generated and discussed the data warehouse view maintenance.

A discussion on several issues in data warehouse view maintenance with extensive literature will be suggested in more detail. The notion of self-maintenance defined as maintaining views by materializing supplementary data and the incremental update mechanisms are discussed. Then issues on several algebraic approaches for maintaining data warehouse views will be considered. On the issues of concurrency control problem that consistently updating distributed replica in a situation to which several local source data cannot be accessed, a series of approaches have been introduced. On the other hand, rule generation point of view related to the view maintenance will be discussed; recently it is extended up to data warehouse views, among the database rules the referential integrity in DBMS is worth while to consider in depth.

2 The Data Warehouse View

We start with an example showing how a data warehouse view can be maintained without accessing base relations. The views are called data warehouse views and are not considered arbitrary database relations; rather, they are a data warehouse setup that normally has relationships enforced a referential integrity condition among them. The example is obtained from TPC-D [25] that consists of 8 tables in Fig. 1 (a) as follows: A customer (in Customer table) who may optionally be categorized to a Region and may place orders. An order (in Order table) generates items (in LineItems table) placing one of the supplied parts (PartSupp) from a Supplier and a Product. A supplier should be categorized one of the regions.

The TPC-D database can be integrated as data warehouse schema that is suggested in the right hand side as Fig. 1 (b). The schema used in this example would be considered a star schema architecture having four dimensions such as a *RegionCustomerOrder*, *RegionSupplier*, *Part*, and *Time* with a fact table *LineItem* (or called *SUPPART*). The dimensional tables are the joins of the relevant tables: the *RegionSupplier* is a join by *Supplier* with *Region*; the *RegionCustomerOrder* is by the join by three tables *Region*, *Customer*, and *Order*. It is assumed that they are logically connected with primary key and foreign key conditions. The arrows in the Fig. 1 represent referential integrity conditions. We assume that a frequently accessed query is placed on materialized views as three tables as a part (*PART*), a supplier (*SUPPLIER*), and a supplied part table (*SUPPART*), which is suggested in Fig. 2.

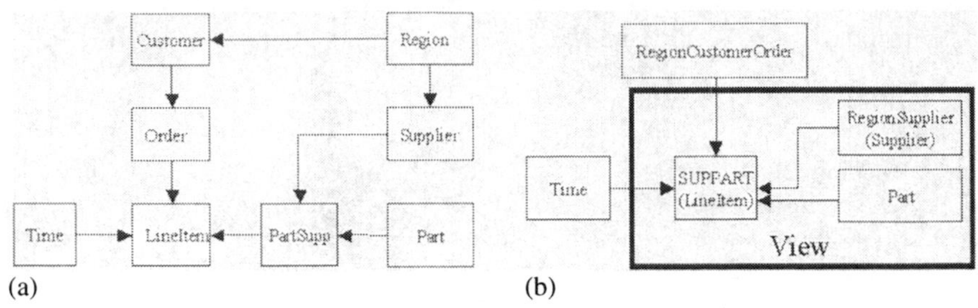

Fig. 1. (a)TPC-D database and (b) Data warehouse view

The table layouts are defined as follow:
PART (P_KEY, P_NAME, P_MFGR, P_PRICE)
/*Primary Key: P_KEY, SF*200,000 are populated */
SUPPLIER (S_KEY, S_NAME, S_ADDRESS)
/* Primary Key: S_KEY, SF*10,000 are populated */
SUPPART (SP_PKEY, SP_SKEY, SP_QTY, SP_SUPPLYPRICE, SP_SUPPLYDATE)
/* Compound Primary Key: SP_PKEY, SP_SKEY */
/* Foreign key SP_SKEY references to P_KEY */
/* Foreign key SP_SKEY references to S_KEY */
/* The SF in the above three tables represents the selectivity factor */
The PART relation contains the part's identifier (P_KEY) as a primary key, a part name (P_NAME), a manufacturer name (P_MFGR), and a price of the part (P_PRICE). The SUPPLIER relation contains the supplier's identifier (S_KEY) as a primary key, a supplier name (S_NAME), and the address of the supplier location (S_ADDRESS). The SUPPART relation contains a concatenated primary key (SP_PKEY, SP_SKEY) that is from the PART relation and the SUPPLIER relation respectively, and a supplied quantity (SP_QTY), the supplied price (SP_SUPPLYPRICE), and the supplied date (SP_SUPPLYDATE). The SP_PKEY references the primary key P_KEY of the PART relation and the SP_SKEY references the primary key S_KEY of SUPPLIER relation as foreign keys respectively. In other words, the following referential integrity constraints hold: (1) from *SUPPART*.SP_PKEY to PART.P_KEY, and (2) from *SUPPART*.SP_SKEY to *SUPPLIER*.S_KEY.

Suppose that each of the three base relations contain a number of tuples listed in the first column of Table 1. Assuming that the selectivity of PART.P_NAME = 'COMPUTER' is .20, *SUPPART*.SP_SUPPLYDATE >= '01/07/2001' is .3, SUPPLIER.S_ADDRESS = 'CA' is .10, *SUPPART*.SUPPLYPRICE > P.PRICE*1.1 is .50, and the join selectivity would be .20 of the transaction with uniform distributions. The three approaches (Base table method, *Auxiliary view* method, and *Differential file* method) are given and each column is divided into two columns of which cardinalities and deltas are suggested respectively in Table 1. It is assumed for the TPC-D that the base relation *SUPPART* has 800,000 transactions, and the base relation PART and SUPPLIER have 200,000 and 10,000 tuples respectively. We illustrate the various maintenance methods for the case when 10,000 tuples are inserted into the base relation *SUPPART*. Table 1 shows the number of tuple accesses incurred by different maintenance methods to update the materialized views.

We use three views as discussed below. Suppose that the manager responsible for computer sales in the state of California is interested in maintaining a view of this year's profitable product supplies (View: *profit_COMP_CA*): all profitable computers supplied in California after July of 2001, where the company calls a sale 'profitable' when the supplied price is 10% greater than the part price. We also define a view called *profit_COMP_** which is the same view as V1 but with area (S.S_ADDRESS), and a view called *profit_*_CA* which is the same view as V1 but with each product (i.e., P.P_NAME).

In keeping the views self-maintainable, in this paper, we do not use auxiliary views, but *differential files*. In the auxiliary view approaches, the view query would be parsed into sub-queries relevant to each relation along with the local selection conditions. In the above example the view would need several auxiliary views having selection conditions such as S_address = 'CA' or P_name = 'computer', etc.

```
CREATE MATERIALIZED VIEW profit_COMP_CA AS SELECT P.P_KEY,
S.S_key, S.S_NAME, (SP.SP_SUPPLYPRICE – P.P_PRICE)*SP.QTY PROFIT
FROM SUPPLIER S, PART P, SUPPART SP
WHERE S.S_KEY = SP.SP_SKEY AND P.P_KEY = SP.SP_PKEY
AND SP.SUPPLYPRICE > P.PRICE*1.1
AND S.S_ADDRESS = 'CA'
AND P.P_NAME = 'COMPUTER'
AND SP.SUPPLYDATE >= '07/01/2001';

CREATE MATERIALIZED VIEW profit_COMP_* AS SELECT P.P_KEY,
S.S_key, S.S_NAME, S.S_address, (SP.SP_SUPPLYPRICE - P.P_PRICE)*SP.QTY
PROFIT
FROM SUPPLIER S, PART P, SUPPART SP
WHERE S.S_KEY = SP.SP_SKEY AND P.P_KEY = SP.SP_PKEY
AND SP.SUPPLYPRICE > P.PRICE*1.1
AND P.P_NAME = 'COMPUTER'
AND SP.SUPPLYDATE >= '07/01/2001';

CREATE MATERIALIZED VIEW profit_*_CA AS
SELECT P.P_KEY, S.S_key, P.P_NAME, SUM((SP.SP_SUPPLYPRICE -
P.P_PRICE)*SP.QTY) SUMofPROFIT
FROM SUPPLIER S, PART P, SUPPART SP
WHERE S.S_KEY = SP.SP_SKEY AND P.P_KEY = SP.SP_PKEY
AND SP.SUPPLYPRICE > P.PRICE*1.1
AND S.S_ADDRESS = 'CA'
AND SP.SUPPLYDATE >= '07/01/2001'
GROUP BY (P.PKEY, S.SKEY);
```

Fig. 2. Example Views

In our approach, we keep the *differential files*, which are relevant to each base relation, and *join differential files* [28]. The *differential file* would be derived from the active log of the relevant base relation. If a transaction would commit, then the record is left in the *differential file*. Thus the file can be said to denote the delta of a relation. The *join differential file* is a file (not a view) generated by a transaction to a *referencing relation*, if a referential integrity rule locates between *referenced relations* and *referencing relation*. The tuple of *join differential file* is consisted of that of the *referenced relation* and placed in the same location. It is appended only when there is an insertion in the *referencing relation* to refer a referential integrity constraint. (See details in [28].)

First of all, the approach managing differential files [22] is extended to improve distributed and data warehouse environment by taking key and referential integrity constraints. In the example, we don't need to materialize any tuples from view, because the key and referential integrity constraints guarantee that existing tuples in SUPPART cannot join with insertions into the other relations. Our approach can dramatically reduce the number of tuples to update the materialized views. Our approach also does not use the auxiliary views, which are deeply dependent upon selections of the relevant base relations. The number of tuples required by our approach to handle base relation insertions in our example appears in the fourth column of Table 1.

Consider the sizes of the database in Table 1. We illustrate the various maintenance methods for the case when 10,000 tuples are updated (inserted, deleted, and modified) into the base relation SUPPART, 1,000 tuples are updated into the base relation PART, and the base relation SUPPLIER is not changed at all. The base relation method represents the same cardinality for the three views, because the method simply uses the three base relations as a bottom line. Our method uses a *differential file* and a *join differential file* that are represented in the last two columns of Table 1.

Table 1. Benefits of *differential file* approach (where $|S|$=cardinality of relation (view) S, dR=delta of relation R, AV= auxiliary view, dAV= delta of auxiliary view, jR=*join differential file* of R)

Relation/ View Name	Base table method		Auxiliary view method		*Differential file* method (Our approach)	
	$\|R\|$	Changes	$\|AV\|$	$\|dAV\|$	$\|dR\|$	$\|jR\|$
SUPPART	800,000	10,000	60,000	1,500	10,000	0
PRODUCT	200,000	1,000	40,000	200	1,000	5,000
SUPPLIER	10,000	0	1,000	0	0	5,000
profit_COMP_CA	19,342,518		637,300		269,620	
*profit_COMP_**	19,342,518		760,212		269,620	
Profit_*_CA	19,342,518		3,547,720		267,620	

It also shows uniform results for the three views, for our method need not require any other additional views or files to update the views. In the auxiliary view approaches, the view query would be parsed into sub-queries relevant to each relation along with the local selection conditions. In the above example the view would need several auxiliary views having selection conditions such as S_address = 'CA' or P_name = 'computer', etc. Thus in the auxiliary view method, people have to invent each auxiliary view(s) in terms of the query condition. (The view designer or a user may have selected a procedure to take an appropriate materialized view among existing ones before inventing an auxiliary view, for this method is strongly dependent on the view condition.) The hardest cases for the auxiliary view method are the situations that cannot use the selection conditions such as in the view *profit_COMP_** and *profit_* _CA* in Table 1. The view *profit_COMP_** suggests not to use the selection condition for the SUPPLIER relation and the view *profit_* _CA* for the PART relation respectively. In other words, the auxiliary view method is dependent upon the combination of the selection conditions, but the differential method is not.

3 Discussions

Self-maintenance is a notion that can be defined as maintaining views by materializing supplementary data so that the warehouse view can be maintained without (or at least minimally) accessing base relations. The notion was originally introduced in Blakeley et al. [2] and enhanced by others [6, 22, 24, 32]. The main ideas are based on a Boolean expression with sufficient and necessary conditions on the view definition for autonomously computable updates that can be called self-maintenance of views. Blakeley's algorithm is a special case of the counting algorithm applied to select project join expressions (no negation, aggregation, or recursion). Segev and Park [22] suggested the view maintenance problem based on net changes as differential files in a distributed environment, but deals with views with no join or aggregation. They also have a focus on the conventional database views, not on the data warehouse view. Several notable articles that deal with self-maintenance aim to develop algorithms related to the integration and the maintenance of information extracted from heterogeneous and autonomous sources [12, 17, 34], recently [14] and [32] extended this concept to temporal views.

On the issues of consistently updating distributed replica in which several local source data cannot be accessed, some approaches have been introduced in [1, 13, 18, 34, 35]. Zhuge et al. [33] introduced ECA algorithms ensuring strong consistency for the cases that considers only a single data source and requires a period of quiescence for the materialized view. The Strobe algorithm [34] considers multiple data sources, requiring the materialized view to contain a key for each of the base relations and also requiring quiescence before installing any changes in the materialized view. The Sweep algorithms are introduced by compensating each Probe separately, and they do not require quiescence [1]. The PSWEEP algorithm extends the SWEEP by introducing the parallel evaluation of updates [35]. The Posse [18] presents an optimal Probe plan algorithm for the DW view with multiple data sources that can minimize the messages between the DW and data sources. The algorithm, however, may cause a latency to update the changes. The TxnWrap [4] presents a multi-version concurrency control strategy that removes the maintenance anomaly problem. Currency control issue is not directly related to our approach. To the best of our knowledge, there is no paper based on the differential file to update the DW views. It is one of our research issues that related the sequence of the updates with concurrency control problem, and we also presented another paper [13].

There exist algebraic approaches in maintaining data warehouse views [10, 12, 20, 21]. Excluding conventional database approaches [2], Quian and Widerhold [21] presented an algorithm for incremental view maintenance based on finite differencing techniques (later corrected in [8]). The algorithm derives the minimal incremental changes in arbitrary relational expression for a view modification by replacing the original relational algebraic expression by an efficient and incremental re-computation, and they considered two types of operations: insertions and deletions. However, the algorithm is liable to include source relations; it requires access to entire base relations for maintaining views. Griffin et al. [8] extends the techniques in [21]. N. Hyun [12] proposes to include functional dependencies and there are integrations on outerjoins [10]. They did not consider the concepts of primary key and foreign key with referential integrity for the maintenance of data warehouse views. Quass [20] addresses the bag algebra to include aggregates and introduced the referential integrity in the view maintenance. But it has serious restrictions that it works only on the tree schema and represents vague descriptions in generating update operation.

Database rules, including the referential integrity, are utilized in maintaining materialized views in several articles such as [15, 16, 20, 29, 30, 31]. Quass [20] and Mohania et al. [16, 26] use the referential integrity constraint partially to update data warehouse views, and [20] extend the works of [21] to transform change propagation equations into more efficient ones. They use auxiliary views (in [16, 20] 'auxiliary relations') in order to maintain a select project join (SPJ) view without accessing base relations at the sources. On relating rules to data warehouse, our motivation starts from the point that database relations are designed to have relationships with each other. If a relation exists alone (without a relationship), it is usually due to a design flaw or the consequence of some semantic miss. Moreover, data warehouses are represented by a specific architecture called a star schema or a snowflake schema, which is a structure having a referential integrity constraint via the primary key and the foreign key relationships among the fact table and dimension tables. In this paper, we take advantage of the fact that the process to check the referential integrity among base relations may generate a clue to maintaining the data warehouse views. Widom et al. [3] is a comprehensive survey on the roles play in data warehouse views. In that paper, the rule is classified as a constraint and a trigger such that the constraint is descriptive and the trigger is procedural. When a referential integrity rule invokes cascade with other rules among database rules in the DBMS, [15] investigates the view maintenance problem having inclusion dependency, not with the referential integrity rules.

Even though they reduce the possibility of accessing base tables in their entirety, they could not eliminate it completely. If a view is defined as the join of several tables, and it does not have any selection condition (e.g., Group-by condition), then it still has to access the base relations. In that case, the auxiliary view would be the base relation per se. Therefore, the method is not truly a self-maintainable view maintenance approach, as long as they do inevitably access base relations.

Another inherent drawback of the auxiliary view method is that the number of auxiliary views is unavoidably increasing along with the number of data warehouse views. Hence, the view selection problem [7, 11] may be pragmatically critical from which a node (indicated by a view) of the cube structure should be materialized.

In applying referential integrity rule to the view maintenance, the auxiliary view method by [16, 20] is the closed related to our approach. It can be said that the auxiliary view method uses the rule in a macroscopic way but we use it in a microscopic way. The auxiliary view method uses the referential integrity rule just to determine which relation is relevant to the view. Because data warehouse views are materialized for frequently accessed queries, the definitions are given in advance. It may practically be a trivial problem in that we can know the table schema and structure in issuing a data warehouse query. Thus what is important is that not to know which relation participates in a data warehouse view, but how to do it with these relations.

The differential method uses the referential integrity rule in such a different way that it determines which tuple is relevant to update the view. It is practically significant for our method is on how to do it. This is one of the innovative features of our approach. For any case of updating *SPJ* views of a data warehouse, the relevant base tables are never accessed. Thus, it can be said to be a true self-maintenance method.

4 Conclusion

Data warehouses materialize views in order to provide fast access to information, but the correctness also should be maintained. The notion of self-maintenance can be a goal that defined as maintaining views by materializing supplementary data. An incremental update mechanism now shows prospective method to the goal. A discussion on several issues in data warehouse view maintenance with extensive literature and a motivating example was suggested.

There are several issues related to the data warehouse view maintenance: algebraic approaches, the concurrency control problem, database rule related problems. There are several theoretic approaches to view maintenance, but an aggregation with referential integrity based on the bag algebra should be devised. Though the concurrency control problem is not directly related to the self-maintainability of data warehouse view, but it is important to deal with the issues of updating distributed replica consistent. Up to now there is no effort to consider the concurrency control issues based on the *differential file* approach in which several local source data cannot be accessed.

Auxiliary view method is a view oriented in that the auxiliary views are generated in terms of updating a view, and thus the auxiliary views can be made from another views. In applying referential integrity rule to the view maintenance, the *auxiliary view* method by [16, 20] is the closed related to our approach. It can be said that the *auxiliary view* method uses the rule in a macroscopic way but we use it in a microscopic way. The *auxiliary view* method uses the referential integrity rule just to determine which relation is relevant to the view. It also means that the number as well as the size of auxiliary views may be increased unendingly. But the differential method is transaction oriented and only one *differential file* (including the *join differential file*) for one base table and referential integrity constraints, thus the size and additional transactions for view maintenance can be minimized. In the differential method the number of supplementary files is required no more, even though the number of data warehouse view is increased. Thus we can conclude that the differential method can be superior to others in that and it does not lock the current database relations at all and it is a true self-maintenance method.

References

1. Agrawal, D., Abbadi, A.E., Singh, A.K. and Yurek, T.: Efficient View Maintenance in Data Warehouses, ACM SIGMOD, (1997) 417-427
2. Blakeley, J., Larson, P. and Tompa, F.: Efficiently Updating Materialized Views, ACM SIGMOD, Washington D.C., (1986) 61-71
3. Ceri, S., Cochrane, R.J. and Widom, J.: Practical Application of Triggers and Constraints: Successes and Lingering Issues, Proc. of the 26th VLDB conference, Egypt, (2000) 254-262
4. Chen, J and Rundensteiner, E.A.: TxnWrap: A Transactional Approach to Data Warehouse Maintenance, CS Technical Report WPI-CS-TR-00-26 (2000)
5. Ceri, S. and Widom, J.: Deriving production rules for incremental view maintenance, In Proc. the 7th Int'l Conf. on VLDB, Spain, September (1991) 577-589
6. Gupta, A. and Blakeley, J.: Using partial information to update a materialized view, Information Systems, Vol. 20, No. 8 (1995) 641-662
7. Gray, J., Chaudhuri, S., Bosworth, A., Layman, A., Reichart, D., Venkatrao, M., Pellow, R. and Pirahesh, H.: Data Cube: A Relational Aggregation Operator Generalizing Group-by, Cross-Tab, and Sub-Totals, Data Mining and Knowledge Discovery, Vol. 1 (1997) 29-53
8. Griffin, T., Libkin, L. and Trickey, H.: An Improved Algorithm for the Incremental Recomputation of Active Relational Expressions, IEEE TKDE, Vol. 9, No. 3 May-June (1997) 508-511
9. Gupta, A. and Mumick I. S.: Maintenance of Materialized Views: Problems, Techniques, and Applications. IEEE Data Engineering Bulletin, 18(2), June (1995)
10. Gupta, H. and Mumick, I.S.: Incremental Maintenance of Aggregate and Outer-join Expressions, Technical report, Stanford University (1999)
11. Harinarayan, V., Rajaraman, A. and Ullman, J.: Implementing data cubes efficiently, In SIGMOD, Montreal, Canada, June (1996) 205-216
12. Huyn, N.: Maintaining Data Warehouse Under Limited Source Access, Ph.D. thesis, Stanford University, August (1997)
13. Kim, Y., Wookey, L., Kim, J. and Kim, S.: Efficient View Maintenance with Consistency at Data Warehouse Environment, Proc. INFORMS, Seoul, Korea (2000) 1935-1941
14. Kotidis, Y. and Roussopoulos, N.: A Case for Dynamic View Management, ACM TODS, Vol. 26, No. 4 (2001) 388-423
15. Laurent, D., Lechtenborger, J., Spyratos, N. and Vossen, G.: Complements for Data Warehouses, Proc. the 15th ICDE (1999)
16. Mohania, M. and Kambayashi, Y.: Making Aggregate Views Self-Maintainable, Data and Knowledge Engineering, Vol. 32, No. 1 (2000) 7-109
17. Mumick, I., Quass, D. and Mumick, B.: Maintenance of Data Cubes and Summary Tables in a Warehouse, ACM SIGMOD, Tuscon, Arizona, May (1997)
18. O'Gorman, K., Agrawal, D. and Abbadi, A.E.: Posse: A Framework for Optimizing Incremental View Maintenance at Data Warehouses, In DaWaK99 (1999) 106-115
19. Quass, D., Gupta, A., Mumick, I. and Widom, J.: Making Views Self-Maintainable for Data Warehousing, Proc. Parallel and Distributed Information Systems, Miami, FL (1996)
20. Quass, D.: Materialized Views in Data Warehouses, Ph.D. thesis, Stanford Univ., Department of Computer Science (1997)
21. Quian, X. and Wiederhold, G.: Incremental Recomputation of Active Relational Expressions," IEEE TKDE, Vol. 3, No. 3 (1991) 337-341
22. Segev, A. and Park, J.: Updating Distributed Materialized Views, IEEE TKDE, Vol. 1, No. 2, June (1989) 173-184
23. Theodoratos, D. and Bouzeghoub, M.: A General Framework for the View Selection Problem for Data Warehouse Design and Evolution, Proc. the ACM workshop on Data Warehousing and OLAP (2000) 1-8
24. Tompa, F. W. and Blakeley, J. A.: Maintaining Materialized Views Without Accessing Base Data, Information Systems, Vol. 13, No. 4 (1988) 393-406

25. http://www.tpc.org/
26. Vincent, M., Mohania, M. and Kambayashi, Y.: A Self Maintainable View Maintenance Technique for Data Warehouses, ACM SIGMOD (1997) 7-22
27. Widom, J.: Research Problems in Data Warehousing," Fourth Intl. Conf. on Information and Knowledge Management (1995) 25-30
28. Wookey, L.: On the Independence of Data Warehouse from Databases in Maintaining Join Views, In DaWak99, LNCS, Springer Verlag Vol. 1676 (1999)
29. Wookey, L., Park, J. and Kang, S.: Replication Server Scheme in Distributed Database Systems, Proc. of `96APDSI conference, Vol. 3 (1996) 1275-1282
30. Wookey, L., Park, J. and Kang, S.: A Distributed Join Data Replicator, Journal of Computer Information Systems, Vol. 38, No. 4 (1998) 108-116
31. Wookey, L., Park, J. and Kang, S.: An Asynchronous Differential Join in Distributed Data Replications, Journal of Database Management, Vol. 10, No. 3 Idea-Group Pub. (1999) 3-12
32. Yang, J. and Widom, J.: Temporal View Self-Maintenance in a Warehousing Environment, Proc. 8th Int. Conf. EDBT2000, LNCS 1777, (2000) 395-412
33. Zhuge, Y., Garcia-Molina, H., Hammer, J. and Widom, J.: View Maintenance in a Warehousing Environment, ACM SIGMOD, (1995) 316-327
34. Zhuge, Y., Garcia-Molina, H. and Wiener, J.L.: The Strobe Algorithms for Multi-Source Warehouse Consistency, Conf. on Parallel and Distributed Information Systems (1996) 146-157
35. Zhang, x. and Rundensteiner, E.A.: Psweep: Parallel view maintenance under concurrent data updates of distributed sources," Technical Report WPI-CS-TR-99-14, Worcester Polytechnic Institute, Computer Science Department, Worcester, MA (1999)

Using ECA Rules in Database Systems to Support Clinical Protocols

Kudakwashe Dube[1], Bing Wu[1], and Jane B. Grimson[2]

[1] Computer Science, School of Computing, Dublin Institute of Technology, Ireland
{kudakwashe.dube, bing.wu}@dit.ie
[2] Computer Science, Trinity College Dublin, Ireland
jane.grimson@cs.tcd.ie

Abstract. Computer-based support for clinical protocols or guidelines is currently a subject of a lot of interest within the Healthcare Informatics community. The Event-Condition-Action (ECA) rule paradigm, as supported in active databases and originating from production rules in expert systems, promises to be of great potential in supporting clinical protocols or guidelines. The problem being addressed in the authors' work is that of managing complex information encountered in the management (i.e., the specification, execution and manipulation as well as querying) of clinical protocols whose specification and execution models are based on the ECA rule paradigm. This paper presents a generic framework and a mechanism for the management of ECA rule-based protocols using modern database technology.

1. Introduction

Computer-based support for clinical guidelines and protocols[1] is currently a subject of active research within the Healthcare Informatics community. Current approaches to computer-based support for clinical guidelines focus mainly on providing expressive specification languages and execution mechanisms that provide enough flexibility and ease-of-use for them to be acceptable by clinicians in daily routine patient care. An important aspect that is lacking in these approaches is the support for easy integration of the guideline support mechanisms with the electronic patient record systems. The *Event-Condition-Action (ECA) rule*[2] paradigm, as found in *active databases* and originating from *production rules* in some expert systems, promises to be an effective means of representing, sharing, enforcing and managing medical knowledge and expertise in the form of clinical protocols. Researchers have highlighted several advantages of ECA rules within database systems [3][4][5][6][7]. The use of the ECA

---

[1] A *clinical guideline* is "a set of schematic plans, at varying levels of detail, for the management of patients who have a particular clinical condition (e.g. insulin-dependent diabetes)" [1]. *Clinical protocols* are highly detailed clinical guidelines and are usually mandatory [2]. In this paper, the terms *clinical guideline* and *clinical protocol* refer to the same concept and are interchangeable.

[2] An ECA rule monitors and reacts to a *situation* by performing a relevant *action* or task. Situation monitoring involves detecting an *event* of interest and evaluating a *condition* associated with the event. The action is performed only if the condition holds [3].

R. Cicchetti et al. (Eds.): DEXA 2002, LNCS 2453, pp. 226–235, 2002.

rule paradigm with database technology also promises to provide an excellent framework for integrating guideline and patient record systems. The rest of this paper is organised as follows: Section 2 covers related work in computer-based support for clinical guidelines/protocols. Section 3 presents our framework for supporting the management of ECA rule-based clinical protocols. Section 4 briefly outlines our ECA rule-based model and language, called PLAN (**P**rotocol **LAN**guage), for specifying clinical protocols and briefs on the database for storing protocol specifications. Section 5 presents the architecture that would support the framework, presented in Section 3, for specifying, storing, executing and manipulating clinical protocols. Section 6 briefly presents a summary and discussion of the framework and architecture, the current and future work. Section 7 concludes this paper.

2. Related Work

This section gives a brief survey of the computer-based support for clinical guidelines with focus on those that use the rule-based formalism. Of special interest to the authors are the guideline support approaches that make use of the ECA rule paradigm in database systems. Several guideline modeling frameworks, architectures and representation languages have been developed for computer-based support of guideline-based care [2][8][9][10][11][12][13][14][15]. More recent approaches make use of Internet Technology such as HTML and XML [16][17][18]. One of the main reasons for the general lack of widespread use of these guideline systems is the difficulty associated with integrating these systems with the medical record so that the systems use the patient's data and present guideline knowledge at the point of care while the clinician is accessing the patient's data [1][19]. To the best of the authors' knowledge, only two previous efforts have been encountered that apply the ECA rule paradigm in supporting clinical guidelines/protocols. These efforts are: the Arden Syntax and Medical Logic Modules (MLMs) [20]; and HyperCare [21].

The Arden Syntax is a language for encoding medical knowledge bases that consists of independent modules, the MLMs. MLMs are ECA rules stored as separate *text files*. An MLM is a set of *slots* categorised into *maintenance* information, *library* information, and the actual medical *knowledg*e [22]. The knowledge slot is expressed in the ECA rule format and is the core of a MLM. The MLMs have been applied to generating alerts, patient management suggestions, management critiques and diagnostic scores[3]. Attempts have also been made to build complex care plans and clinical guidelines/protocols by chaining MLMs in such a way that the action of one MLM evokes the next MLMs [25][26][27]. Since MLMs specifications are stored as individual text files, they cannot be queried and manipulated easily[4]. As a result, a limitation of the Arden Syntax, which is important to this work, is the lack of support

---

[3] The Arden Syntax is currently the only standard for sharing and encoding medical knowledge among systems in various medical institutions[23][24], which is an indication of the promise the ECA Rule paradigm has as a viable technology.

[4] In a study to quantify changes that occur as an MLM knowledge base evolves, 156 MLMs developed over 78 months were studied and 2020 distinct versions of these MLMs were observed. It was also found out that 38.7% of changes occur primarily in the logic slot while 17.8% and 12.4% of the changes occur in the action and data slots respectively [28]. For instance, changes in laboratory testing can cause disruptions in MLM execution unless the code of these MLMs is revised and modified [29].

for the manipulation, querying and the resultant difficulty in maintenance of the MLMs specifications.

HyperCare [21] is a prototype system that employs the ECA rule paradigm in the active object-oriented database, Chimera, to support clinical guideline compliance in the domain of essential hypertension. The limitations of HyperCare are: 1) the difficulty in managing the rules making up the protocol; 2) lack of support for dynamic manipulation, querying, versioning and customisation of clinical protocol specifications and instances; and 3) it is an implementation of a specific guideline and does not attempt to provide a generic formalism to support similar protocols.

In summary, the Arden Syntax and HyperCare make use of the ECA rule paradigm to support clinical protocols. Both the Arden Syntax and HyperCare do not create patient-specific instances; instead rules operate at a global level. The approach presented in this paper differs from the above works in that it permits generic clinical protocols not only to be declaratively specified, stored, and executed but also to be dynamically manipulated (i.e. operated on and queried) at the individual patient level, with both the specification and its instances being manageable on a full-scale.

3. Framework for the ECA Rule-Based Support for Clinical Protocols

This section describes the framework for the computer-based support for the management of clinical protocols. The managed protocols guide the care of patients within clinical categories, which may be disease-based, such as diabetes mellitus and/or its sub-types: type I and type II. The challenge is to provide each patient with an executable care plan that is appropriate for the management of the patient's clinical condition based on the patient's recent pathology.

The framework, illustrated in Figure 1, consists of the three *planes*: specification, execution and management of the protocol specifications and their instances, the individual patient care plans (Figure 1(a)). Protocol specifications are created in the *specification plane*. A declarative specification language, PLAN, is used to describe the protocol [30]. In the *execution plane*, the customisation of protocols produces plans that take into consideration the individual patient's condition and recent pathology.

Also in the execution plane, the patient's care plan is executed. Execution state data is generated and made available for querying and decision-making. The protocol specifications and their instances are managed in the *manipulation plane*. The interaction between the specification and the execution aspects of the problem is illustrated in Figure 1(b). It involves: 1) the *customisation* of a generic specification to suit a specific situation (patient condition); 2) the *instantiation* of a customised specification; and 3) the propagation of *dynamic changes* between the specification and the executing instance. Interaction between the manipulation and the specification aspects involves: 1) the *querying* of specification's components; 2) the *manipulation* of specifications such as adding, deleting and modifying components; and 3) the maintenance of *versions* of the specifications. The interactions between the manipulation and execution planes involve the dynamic querying and manipulation of the execution process. Central to the three planes, are the ECA rule mechanism and the database that form the core technologies employed in this approach.

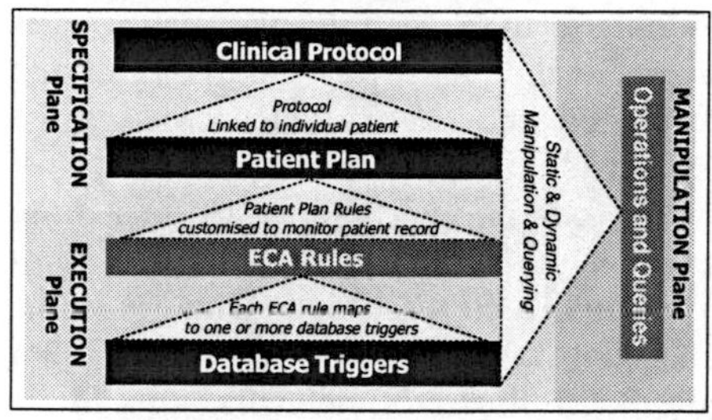

(a) *Planes for supporting the management of clinical protocols*

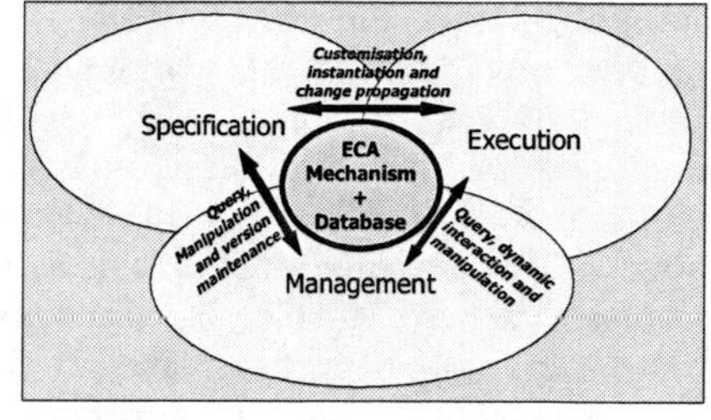

(b) *Interactions between the specification, execution and manipulation planes*

Fig. 1. Framework for supporting the management of clinical protocols using event-condition-action (ECA) rules in a database system

In summary the framework presented here aims at allowing static and dynamic aspects of clinical protocols to be easily manageable on a full-scale. The next sections outline how this is achieved.

4. ECA Rule-Based Clinical Protocol Specification

This section briefly outlines the PLAN model and language. For more details on PLAN, the reader is referred elsewhere [30].

Figure 2 illustrate the entity-relationship model for a clinical protocol specification. Patients are put into clinical categories and sub-categories. Each category has a clinical protocol defined for it. A *Clinical Protocol* is a generic care plan consisting of ECA rule-controlled clinical tasks for the management of patients. The clinical protocol is made up of a collection of a set of *schedules* and one *protocol rule set* for managing a patient in a clinical category. Each patient is associated with a care plan, which consists of one schedule and one set of dynamic rules. The plan is derived from customising the generic protocol to suit the patient. A *schedule* is a set of *static*[5] *rules,* which is a time-driven rule that schedules clinical tasks.

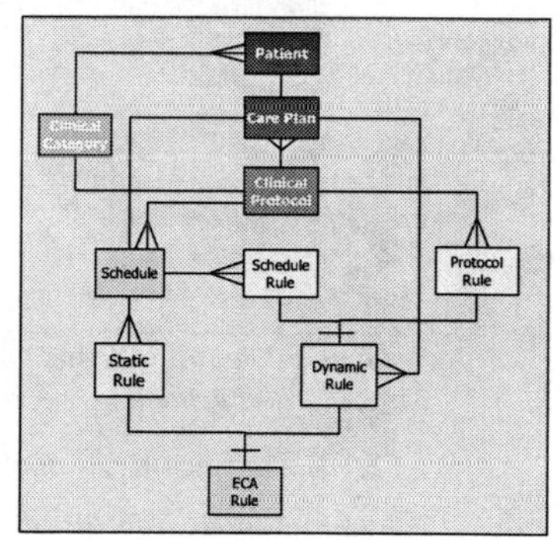

Fig. 2. Entity-Relationship Diagram for the clinical protocol specification using the ECA rule paradigm

The schedule also contains as a set of *schedule rules.* The Schedule, when contained in a patient plan, is a collection of static rules only. Only one schedule is required for a plan. Each schedule in a protocol is associated with entry criteria to be satisfied by a patient before the schedule is selected to be part of the patient's plan.

[5] The concept *static* for describing a rule refers to the idea that the firing time of the rule is predetermined and definite on creation of the rule. Static rules usually react to time events.

The Schedule and the Protocol Rule sets modularise the rules into two distinct sets with elements of one set interacting with elements of the other set. Schedule rules and protocol rules are *dynamic*[6] *rules*, which are placed into one set when creating the patient plan. A Dynamic Rule is an ECA rule that monitors: 1) the state or effects of actions of a static rule or set of static rules and conditionally performs an action; and/or 2) the condition of a patient as reflected in in-coming test results and takes appropriate action. The plan has the ability to monitor and react to: 1) changes in the patient condition over time; and 2) feedback in form of test results and other measurements of the patient's attributes. Figure 3 (a) illustrates the syntax of a Static Rule. Figure 3 (b) illustrates a Dynamic Rule. Figure 3(c) and 3(d) illustrates examples of static and dynamic ECA rules taken from a protocol for diabetes management.

```
<TOPS Static Rule> := ON STARTING <start date>
        EVERY <interval>
        ENDING <end date>
        [IF <condition>]
        DO <action list>
<start date> := <date>,<time>
<interval> := period in milliseconds
<end date> := <date>, <time>
<action list> := list of actions relevant to this rule
```

(a) The syntax for the time-driven static ECA rule in BNF

```
<TOPS Dynamicl Rule>::=ON <protocol event>
    IF <condition> DO { <action list> }
<protocol event>::=patient-entry | lab-result-arrival
        | new-test-order | execution-state-change
<condition>::=<test range check> | <other patient condition>
<action list>::= <action> | <action>, <action list>
<action>::=store-message | send-alert | return-value
        | perform-management-operation
```

(b) The syntax of the dynamic ECA rule in BNF

```
When the patient's HbA1c result has been obtained,
if the result is greater than or equal to the previous
HbA1c result and the patient is in the type 2 diabetes
mellitus category, then give the patient advice on diet
and exercise.

Rule:
ON resultArrival(HbA1c)
IF result("HbA1c") >= previousResult("HbA1c") ) AND
        subtype = "diabetes type 2"
DO advice(diet_and_exercise)
```

(c) An example dynamic rule for diabetes management

```
Every two weeks before the date of the next
consultation, perform HbA1c test.

Rule:
ON STARTING TODAY
EVERY consultation_date – 14 days
ENDING indefinite
DO order("HbA1c")
```

(d) An example temporal/static ECA rule for diabetes management

Fig. 3. The Specification of clinical protocol rules in the PLAN language

A clinical protocol specification is initially created and saved as a text file in PLAN language. After being parsed, the protocol specification and the attributes of the protocol are stored in relational tables of the protocol specification database. Storing the protocol specifications in a database allows queries and manipulation operations to be performed on components of the specification. Individual specifications of ECA rules and other components such as entry criteria can be added, deleted, modified, and queried. This would be difficult if text files only were to be used, as is the case for MLMs [28]. While XML documents can be queried, manipulation operations such as deletions and insertions of components of the XML

[6] The concept *dynamic* refers to the fact that whether or not the rule will fire and/or execute is determined dynamically depending on the situation at any point as the execution process proceeds.

documents are not yet as easy as manipulating structured data in relational tables. The next section presents the architecture for executing and manipulating the clinical protocols that have been specified and stored as described in this and the previous sections.

5. The Architecture for Supporting the Management of Clinical Protocols

This section presents the architecture for supporting the management of clinical protocols using of ECA rules. As illustrated Figure 4, the architecture has three layers. *External* to the system are users and external systems. The *top* layer is the clinical protocol management functionality that allows users to specify, store, execute manipulate and query clinical protocols and external systems to supply and receive information from the system. The *middle* layer provides services that 1) extend the ECA rule execution mechanism of the underlying database system and 2) handle connections to the database. The *bottom* layer is the ECA rule execution mechanism, which is the *ECA rule mechanism* in a modern database system. *Users* of the system may be either clinicians or patients. Typically, users should be subject to security checks and authorization. Currently, basic security is provided through user-names and passwords. Besides users, the system interacts with *external systems* such as the Synapses Server [32] for access to the distributed patient's record and the Laboratory Information System (LIS) for test orders and results. Other systems may want to access information relating to protocol specifications and their execution process.

The Protocol Management Layer generally provides users with the functionality for i) managing patients and patient categories, ii) creation of protocol specifications for patient categories, iii) creating, executing and manipulating patient plans, and iv) querying the system's static and dynamic information.

The ECA Rule Mechanism Extension's main purpose is to provide the functionality that is not adequately supported by the ECA rule execution mechanism in the underlying database system and to perform actions that need to be performed outside the database system. Due to space limitations, the technical aspects, especially for the external actions and the management of the temporal events, will not be presented here. The *Time Events Generator* extends the database trigger mechanism by providing a time event detector. It generates time events of interest to specific rules within each patient plan. The mechanism for supporting time triggers is illustrated in Figure 6. The Java-based subscription and time trigger mechanism is used to give signals for the occurrence of only those time events that are of interest to rules in the patient plans. The Time Events Generator was necessitated by the absence of the support for temporal triggers in most modern database systems.

The *Rule Activity Listener* listens and receives messages from rules executing within the database. Modern database systems do not provide support for rules to communicate externally with applications outside the database. For instance, current *database connectivity* (e.g., JDBC and ODBC) do not support active behaviour or *push* functionality (only *pull* functionality is supported). Hence, there is a need for a separate mechanism to allow rules to communicate externally. With the Rule Activity Listener, rules inside the database can communicate with other modules of the system that are outside the database.

Lastly, the *Dynamic SQL Statement Generator* and the *Database Access Manager* are the two components that are dedicated to handling standard communication through database connectivity between the database system and external components. The Dynamic SQL Statement Generator generates the required SQL statements to allow dynamic manipulation of both rules and data in the database.

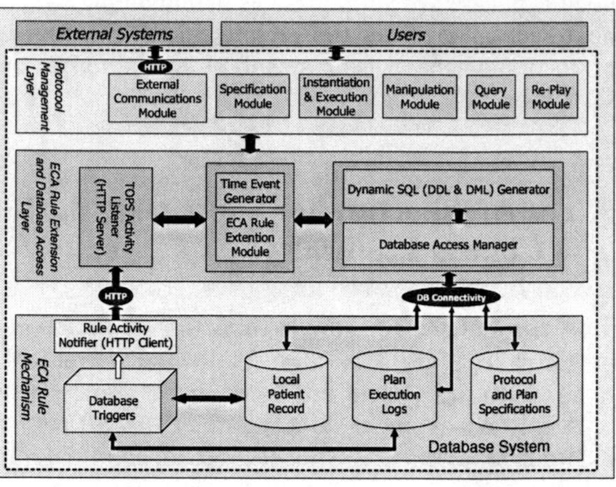

Fig. 4. System architecture for supporting the management of ECA rule-based clinical protocols

The trigger mechanism of a database system is used as the engine for executing the ECA rule-based clinical protocols. One ECA rule in a patient plan is mapped to one or more database triggers. The mapping is predefined for each of the two main types of rules, i.e., the static rules and dynamic rules. A static (time-driven) rule is mapped to one Java-based *time event generator trigger* that signals the occurrence of a time event and one *database trigger* that reacts to this signal. Dynamic rules are mapped to only one database trigger. Each ECA rule in a plan monitors either the patient's record or the plan's execution logs such as the time event log.

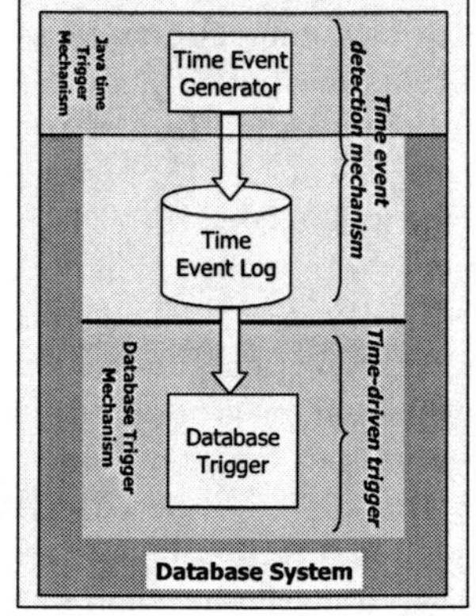

Fig. 5. Mechanism for supporting time-driven ECA rules using the Java-based time event generator

The implementation of the framework and architecture presented in the previous sections is ongoing. Preliminary tests performed using an early limited version of the prototype system conducted ran 100 protocol instances at the same time and proved to be promising. The prototype system is now being prepared for undergoing tests using clinical protocols for the diabetes domain at a Dublin hospital's diabetes clinic within the framework of the MediLink Project[7].

In summary, the architecture presented in Figure 4 attempts to fully utilise the trigger mechanism within the database system in executing the ECA rule-based patient plans. The architecture allows the management of ECA rule-based clinical protocols by providing, within a layered framework, management functionality that allow operations to be performed and queries to be issued dynamically at any time during the execution of patient plans. The architecture provides support for the three planes in the framework presented in Section 4 of this paper. Every ECA rule is mapped to at least one trigger in the database. Issues of concurrency and efficiency in

[7] http://www.cs.tcd.ie/medilink/, June 2002.

rule execution are not of concern as these are handled by the trigger mechanism within the database system with the exception of time driven triggers, which rely on an external time event generator (Figure 5).

6. Summary and Discussion

In our framework clinical protocols are supported through the specification, execution and manipulation planes. A declarative language called PLAN is used to specify clinical protocols. More work still needs to be done to make PLAN more expressive by incorporating advanced research results on ECA rule event specification and event algebra. The protocols are mapped to ECA rules (or triggers) and other schema objects in the database on instantiation in the execution plane. Clinical protocol specifications are stored in the database together with the relevant patient's data. This allows the specifications to be manageable on a full scale using the DML of the underlying database. The protocol specifications are customized using patient data to create individual patient care plans. The ECA rules in a modern database system are used to execute the care plans and to interface the model of the patient, as stored in the database, and the clinical guidelines/protocols from which the plan derives. The manipulation plane imposes modularisation on the underlying ECA rules by viewing them as bundled into sets and subsets making up the patient care plans. The manipulation plane also provides the functionality to manipulate and query both the static specifications and dynamic aspects of the ECA rules that make up the patient care plans. The ECA rule paradigm has the advantage that it can be easily integrated with the electronic medical record if combined with database technology and a way is found to represent guideline tasks using ECA rules. This paper has presented a framework and architecture for the use of ECA rules in database systems to support clinical protocols. An important requirement in supporting clinical protocols is that these protocols must be dynamically manageable on a full-scale in order to be acceptable for routine use in daily practice.

7. Conclusion

It is the authors' strong belief that a method and mechanism to support dynamic management (specification, execution and manipulation as well as querying) of ECA rules or sets of ECA rules in a database system can provide the flexible support for the management of ECA rule-based clinical protocols. Supporting the management of ECA rules and their composites in a modern database system can be used as a basis for providing the flexible management of clinical protocols whose specification and execution models are based on the ECA rule paradigm. The management of the collection of ECA rules in a database system is also an important and challenging requirement that can be of beneficial use in many applications within the healthcare and other domains.

References

1. Shahar Y, (2001) Automated Support to Clinical Guidelines and Care Plans: the Intention-Oriented View, Ben Gurion University, Israel, http://www.openclinical.org/resources/reference/briefingpapers/shahar.pdf, 03/2002.
2. Miksch S (1999). Plan Management in the Medical Domain. AI Communications, 12(4), pp.209-235.
3. Dittrich KR, Gatziu S and Geppert A (1995). The Active Database Management System Manifesto: A Rulebase for ADBMS Features. In: Sellis T (ed): Proc 2nd Workshop on Rules in Database (RIDS), Athens, Greece, September 1995. Lecture Notes in Computer Science, Springer, 1995.
4. Paton NW (1999). Active Rules in Database Systems. Springer, New York.
5. Simon E and Kotz-Dittrich A (1995). Promises and realities of active database systems. In Proceedings 21st VLDB Conference, Zurich, Switzerland, pp.642-653.
6. Appelrath H-J, Behrends H, Jasper H and Zukunft O (1995). Case studies on active database applications: Lessons learned. TR-AIS-9601, Tech. Report, University of Oldenburg, http://citeseer.nj.nec.com/appelrath95case.html, ResearchIndex, 03/2002.
7. Widom J and Ceri S (1996). Active Database Systems: Triggers and Rules for Advanced Database Processing. Morgan Kaufmann, San Francisco, California, 1996.
8. Shortliffe, E. H., Scott, C. A., and Bischoff, M. B. (1981). ONCOCIN: An expert system for oncology protocol management. In Proc. Seventh International Joint Conference on Artificial Intelligence, pages 876--881.
9. Musen MA, Carlson RW, Fagan LM and Deresinski SC (1992). T-HELPER: Automated support for community-based clinical research. Proceedings of the 16th Annual Symposium on Computer Application in Medical Care, Washington, D.C., pp.719-723.
10. Shahar Y, Miksch S, and Johnson P (1998). The Asgaard Project: A Task-Specific Framework for the Application and Critiquing of Time-Oriented Clinical Guidelines. Artificial Intelligence in Medicine 14:29-51, 1998.
11. Fox J, Johns N and Rahmanzadeh A (1998). Disseminating medical knowledge: the PROforma Approach. Artificial Intelligence in Medicine, 14:pp.157-181.
12. Ohno-Machado L, Gennari JH, Murphy S, Jain NL, Tu SW, Oliver DE, et al. The GuideLine Interchange Format: A Model for Representing Guidelines. Journal of the American Medical Informatics Association 1998;5(4):357-372.
13. Peleg M, Boxwala AA, Omolala O, Zeng Q, Tu SW, Lucson R, Bernstam E, Ash N, Mork P, Ohno-Machado L, Shortliffe EH and Greenes RA (2000). GLIF3: The evolution of a guideline representation format. In Overhage MJ, ed, Proceedings 2000 AMIA Annual Symposium, LA, CA, Hanley and Belfus, Philadelphia.
14. C Gordon and M Veloso (1996). The PRESTIGE Project: Implementing Guidelines in Healthcare MIE 96
15. Johnson PD, Tu SW, Booth N, Sugden B and Purves IN (2000). Using scenarios in chronic disease management guidelines for primary care. In: Overhage MJ, ed, Proceedings of the of the 2000 AMIA Annual Symposium (LA, CA, USA), Hanley and Belfus, Philadelphia.
16. Tang TC and Young CY (2001). ActiveGuidelines: Integrating web-based guidelines with computer-based patient records. 2001 AMIA Annual Symposium, http://www.amia.org/pubs/symposia/D200173.PDF, 3/2002.
17. Karras BT, Nath SD, and Shiffman RN 2000). A Preliminary Evaluation of Guideline Content Markup Using GEM—An XML Guideline Elements Model. In Overhage M.J.,, Ed., Proceedings of the 2000 AMIA Annual Symposium (Los Angeles, CA, 2000), 942, Hanley & Belfus, Philadelphia.
18. Shiffman RN, Karras BT, Agrawal A, Chen RC, Marenco L and Nath S (2000). GEM: A proposal for a more comprehensive guideline document model using XML. J. Am. Med. Inform. Assoc., 7:pp.488-498.
19. Tu SW and Musen MA (2001) Representation Formalisms and Computational Methods for Modeling Guideline-Based Patient Care, In: Heller B, Loffler M, Musen M and Stefanelli M (2001). Computer-Based Support for Clinical Guidelines and Protocols, Proceedings of the First European Workshop on Computer-based Support for Clinical Guidelines and Protocols, 2000, Leipzig, p.115-132, IOS Press, Amsterdam.
20. Hripscak G, Luderman P, Pryor TA, Wigertz OB and Clayton PD (1994). Rationale for the Arden Syntax. Computers and Biomedical Research, 27:pp.291-324.
21. Caironni PVC, Portoni L, Combi C, Pinciroli F and Ceri S (1997). HyperCare: a Prototype of an Active Database for Compliance with Essential Hypertension Therapy Guidelines. In: Proc 1997 AMIA Ann Fall Symposium, Philadelphia, PA, Hanley and Belfus, 1997:pp.288-292

22. Clayton PD, Pryor TA, Wgertz OB and Hripcsak G (1989). Issues and Structures for Sharing Medical Knowledge Among Decision-making Systems: The 1989 Arden Homestead Retreat. Proc Annu Symp Comput Appl Med Care, 1989:pp.116-121.
23. ASTM (1992). E-1460: Standard Specification for Defining and Sharing Modular Health Knowledge Bases (Arden Syntax for Medical Logic Modules). In 1992 Annual Book of ASTM Standards, Vol.14.01, pp.539-587. American Society for Testing and Materials, Philadelphia, 1992.
24. HL7 (1999). Arden Syntax for Medical Logic Modules. Standard of the Health Level 7, 1999, http://www.cpmc.columbia.edu/arden/arden-2.1-proposed-120300.doc, March 2002.
25. Starren JB, Hripcsak G, Jordan D, Allen B, Weissman C and Clyaton PD (1994). Encoding a post-operatice coronary artery bypass surgery care plan in Edern Syntax. Comput Biol Med 1994 Sep; 24(5): pp.411-7
26. Sherman EH, Hripcsak G, Starren J, Jenders RA and Clayton P (1995). Using intermediate states to improve the ability of the Arden Syntax to implement care plans and reuse knowledge. Proc Annu Symp Comput Appl Med Care 1995: pp.238-42
27. Sailors RM, Bradshaw RL and East TD (1998). Moving the Arden Syntax Outside of the (Alert) Box: A Paradigm for Supporting Multi-Step Clinical protocols. JAMIA, 5 (Symposium Supplement): pp.1071.
28. Jenders RA, Huang H, Hripcsak G and Clayton PD (1998). Evolution of a knowledge base for a clinical decision support system encoded in the Arden Syntax. In: Proc AMIA Symp, 1998:pp.558-62
29. Jenders RA, Hripcsak G, Sideli RV, DuMouchel W, Zhang H, Cimino JJ, Johnson SB, Sherman EH and Clayton PD (1995). Medical decision support: experience with implementing the Arden Syntax at the Columbia-Presbyterian Medical Center. In: Proc Annu Symb Comput Appl Med care, 1995:pp169-73
30. Wu B and Dube K (2001b) PLAN: a Framework and Specification Language with an Event-Condition-Action (ECA) Mechanism for Clinical Test Request Protocols. In Proceedings of the 34th Hawaii International Conference on System Sciences (HICSS-34): the Mini-Track in Information Technology in Healthcare, Abstracts and CD-ROM of Full Papers, IEEE Computer Society, Los Alamitos, California, p.140.
31. Elmasri R and Navathe SB (2000). Fundamentals of Database Systems, 3rd Edition, Addison-Wesley, Massachusetts, Chap.3-4.
32. W Grimson, D Berry, J Grimson, G Stephens, E. Felton, P Given and R O'Moore. Federated healthcare record server - the Synapses paradigm. International Journal of Medical Informatics, Vol.52, 1998, pp3-27.

Establishment of Virtual Enterprise Contracts

Gerald Quirchmayr[1,3], Zoran Milosevic[2], Roger Tagg[1], James Cole[2], and Sachin Kulkarni[2]

[1] University of South Australia, School of Computer and Information Science
Mawson Lakes, SA-5095, Australia
{Gerald.Quirchmayr |Roger.Tagg}@unisa.edu.au
[2] Enterprise Distributed Systems Technology Centre (DSTC)
Level 7, GP South, University of Queensland,
Brisbane, Q4072, Australia
{zoran |colej |sachink}@dstc.edu.au
[3] University of Vienna, Institute for Computer Science and Business Informatics
Liebiggasse 4, A-1010 Vienna, Austria
Gerald.Quirchmayr@univie.ac.at

Abstract. In this paper we describe an approach to the modelling of virtual enterprise agreements. An important and ever-present issue in the set-up phase of such a virtual enterprise is the virtual enterprise contract. As one of the goals of virtual enterprises is to become operational quickly, the time consumed by the set-up phase must be reduced to a minimum. At the same time it has to be guaranteed that the outcome of this phase leads to a formally correct and executable agreement. Our approach aims at showing how to achieve a formal model of virtual enterprise contracts, which can later be executed and monitored in a particular automated contract management environment.

1 Introduction

Today's business world is characterised by an increasing need for flexible, dynamic, often short-term and task-specific alliances and partnerships. This is a result of growing customer pressures for improved, personalised, more versatile, and yet cost-effective services. Virtual Enterprises (VEs) are a form of enterprise structure through which these demands can be met.

In spite of substantial advantages of VEs, there are also a number of problems associated with them, such as having to set up legally binding contracts under enormous time pressure and with incomplete information. This incompleteness arises from parties not having sufficient background information about the other partners or about the environment in which the VE has to operate.

With appropriate IT systems in place, it is possible to considerably reduce the effort in setting up such alliances. IT systems can provide more information about the partners involved, e.g. their historic behaviour, their reputation, credit rating and so on. IT systems can also enable better compliance with the legal requirements when setting up contracts, helping to ensure their validity and enforceability. They can also provide support for better monitoring of the adherence of parties to the contract and more timely notifications of possible non-fulfilment of contractual obligations.

R. Cicchetti et al. (Eds.): DEXA 2002, LNCS 2453, pp. 236–248, 2002.

As amply documented in the literature [Susskind 1987], [de Korvin et al. 1995], electronic support for contract specification is difficult. One major reason is the highly complex task of transforming natural language representation of contract documents into a representation suitable for automated interpretation, reasoning and execution.

The first stage in setting up a VE is the establishment phase. This phase encompasses all the necessary processes needed for building business relationships between the constituents of a VE [Tagg and Quirchmayr 2001], ultimately leading to the formation of a legally binding contract. The contract specification can be compared to the design specification for some software system and in that sense is similar in its importance for the further stages in the VE life cycle.

In this paper we address the key issue of the VE establishment stage, the use of a contract-based approach to set up legally binding relationships in a VE structure and describe a formal approach that leads to an executable representation.

2 Virtual Enterprises

A Virtual Enterprise (VE) has been described [Davaclu et al 1999] as "a temporary consortium of autonomous, diverse and possibly geographically dispersed organizations that pool their resources to meet short-term objectives and exploit fast-changing market trends". It is implicit that a VE can disband when the objectives have been achieved. A VE is thus somewhat more mobile than a "strategic alliance". In the view of some authors, e.g. [Riempp 1998], a VE also differs from supply chain partnerships in which there is a dominant partner.

2.1 The Virtual Enterprise Lifecycle

Tagg [Tagg 2001] proposed 3 stages in the lifecycle of a Virtual Enterprise, namely *VE Establishment, Business Development and Business Execution.* These stages are not necessarily distinct, but can be interleaved.

The *VE Establishment stage* is primarily concerned with forming the VE in the first place. This will involve the negotiation of contracts between the partners, the terms of which will include the processes to be followed and the information to be passed.

Unless membership of the VE is going to be fixed, processes will be needed for adding (and removing) members, and for guiding the way in which contracts are negotiated with new partners. These activities will be interleaved with the later lifecycle stages discussed below.

Business Development covers the activities through which a VE goes about getting business with outside markets or major customers. The processes for doing this will have been established in the Establishment stage. Activities will include cooperative market research, responding to invitations to tender, joint promotions and the negotiation of contracts with external organizations.

Business Execution refers to the time when the VE is actually fulfilling its business of supplying goods or services to customers. The routine business processes that are followed will have been agreed at the VE Establishment stage - they will involve actors working on different sides of organizational boundaries.

To complete the analogy with lifecycles in the natural world, there should also be a final stage called *Dissolving the VE*. However a more likely scenario is that the VE Establishment and Business Development stages, rather than ending when Business Execution starts, will continue in the background to monitor the activities of the VE and the state of the markets it was formed to address. When Business Development reports that the market has moved on, or when VE Establishment reports that partners are leaving the VE, then it may be time to terminate the VE.

2.2 Establishing Virtual Enterprises

Although the performance of VE contracts is an element of the Business Development and Execution stages, establishment of virtual enterprise contracts belongs primarily to the VE Establishment stage. We can best see the nature of this stage by considering how each of the processes within the VE Establishment stage might apply to an example, in this case the "Helen Club" of textile SMEs (Small to Medium Enterprises) quoted by [Ktendis and Paraskevopoulos 1999]. The list of processes is taken from [Tagg 2001].

Identifying broad areas of market opportunity
An original founding committee of representatives from the most highly motivated SMEs would create a proposal after working on a joint discussion document.

Creating and maintaining a constitution
The committee would create set of rules for the governance of the VE. These would be typically based on a precedent from a similar body. Company secretarial or legal advice might be sought. The rules for altering the constitution would be included. A process for winding up the VE should also be worked out at this stage.

Forming and recruiting an executive and committee members
This would be done following the constitution.

Identification and recruitment of partners
A target list of possible additional partners for the VE would be set up, and a recruitment process initiated. The committee of the Helen Club might give priority to companies providing complementary services, e.g. dyers and finishers to complement spinners and weavers.

Partner applications to join, and credit and reference checking of partners
The Helen Club was intended to be extensible from the beginning, so repeatable and consistent processes are needed to evaluate applicants.

Partner renewal, lapsing and severance processes
Processes are required to monitor the partners in the VE, so that unsatisfactory behaviour can be weeded out. Partners may lapse because of lack of involvement in joint development efforts, or they may proactively resign.

Proposal and approval of agreed processes and protocols between partners
The mainstay of any VE has to be the rules for developing and executing business. Such rules may cover joint marketing effort, main contractor/subcontractor relation-

ships, sales commissions, transport between factories, cross-organization consultancy, respect of commercially sensitive information etc. Well-defined workflows, together with stipulated data flows, may be necessary.

Negotiating contracts between the partners
Each partner company may be required to sign a legally binding contract agreeing to the above processes and protocols and respecting the constitution of the VE.

Such a contract between the partner and the VE would be complemented by contracts that cover the specific needs of the Business Development or Business Execution stages. In Business Development a group of Helen Club manufacturers may agree to participate in a joint marketing activity. In Business Execution, they will deal as an entity with suppliers, customers and each other; contracts will cover how this is to be done and how the outcomes of the operation will be accounted for and settled.

As with most contracts, what happens in the exceptional cases will form a major part of the rule base.

The focus of this paper is the writing and implementation of contracts that support the establishment and operation of Virtual Enterprises, and this is addressed below.

3 A Closer Look at the Process of Constructing and Maintaining a Virtual Enterprise Constitution

The establishment phase of a virtual enterprise is, like that of any other form of enterprise, characterized by setting up agreements on key aspects of the business to be operated through this form of operation and ultimately by the legally binding contracts which are considered as one of the major outputs of this process.

3.1 Structuring Contracts

The primary goal of the establishment phase of a virtual enterprise is to see it becoming operational, governed by a series of agreements and contracts. Agreements represent some mutually accepted rules of engagement between parties, that, when governed by the legalisation of a jurisdiction, lead to contracts, i.e. agreements that have legally binding weight.

The first of these agreements is usually a framework setting the general guidelines and principles for enabling parties to cooperate as a VE, regulating internal and external relationships that come within the scope of a VE. This framework must include key elements such as the common goals of the virtual enterprise, the cooperation structure, and activities to be carried out jointly, and details of how they will be carried out. They will be defined in the form of framework clauses, with each clause specifying one or more of the following: a common goal, a cooperation structure or pattern, activities to be carried out jointly, etc. As shown in figure 1, the class concept representing the generic model of VE contracts can be expressed in a standardized diagram convention such as the UML class diagram.

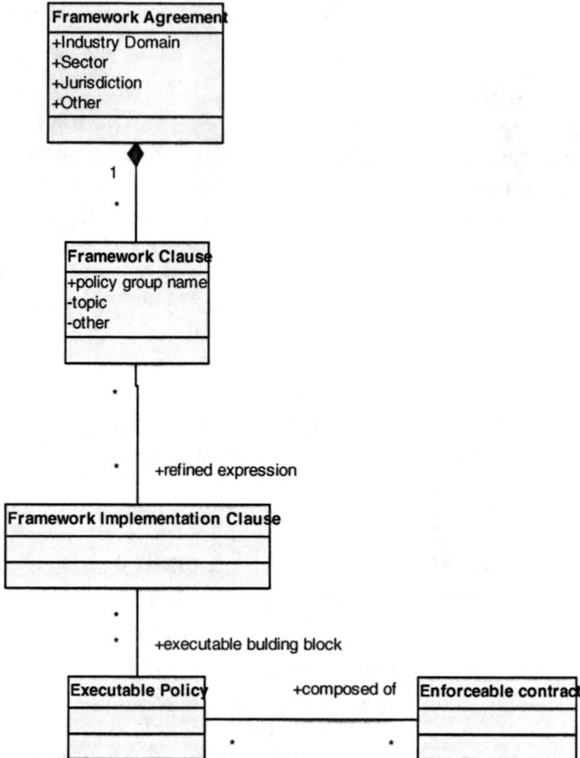

Fig. 1. Model of the Agreement Struture for VE

The structuring of agreements into framework clauses reflects standard legal and commercial practices (cf. framework agreements between suppliers and purchaser and the widespread use of international commercial terms [INCOTERMS]), whereby a clause is typically a logical self-contained unit of rules related to an identifiable topic. Examples of framework clauses in an airline virtual enterprise agreement (usually called an airline alliance) are frequent flyer program conditions, joint purchasing and training policies between partners, joint aircraft maintenance policies and so on (see figure 2). The policies expressed in framework clauses are of a general nature. They provide goals and guidelines for composing legally binding agreements, but they are not sufficiently specific to be legally enforceable.

Each of the framework clauses is further refined in terms of the framework implementation clauses. A framework implementation clause is expressed in terms of policies that are specific and unambiguous enough to form a legally enforceable contract. For example, a frequent flyer program has policies related to the calculation, the accreditation and validity of frequent flyer points.

The enforceability means that it is possible to determine whether the actions of parties to the contract are in accordance with the VE agreement stated in the contract. This determination is traditionally done by human experts and can to a certain extent be supported by automated systems, depending on the degree of ambiguity and incompleteness of the language used.

The issue of transforming clauses/expressions stated in a natural language into a formal representation has been the subject of substantial research, with many problems still remaining unsolved (for an overview see some of the classic literature of Artificial Intelligence, such as [Harmon and King 1985], [Winston 1992] and [Abelson and Sussman 1996]).

3.2 Towards a Formal Representation of Framework and Implementation Clauses

A proven approach for transforming framework implementation clauses into an executable form and for monitoring their execution is to represent them in First Order Predicate Logic (FOL) (for recent work on the representation of legal argumentation see [Kowalski 1994] and [Kowalski 1996]). For example, an airline alliance might include the following framework implementation clause in its frequent flyer program policy:

All participating airlines must have a clause in place in their frequent flyer programs that allows for the accreditation of points earned in flights that are code shared (e.g. QF1/BA7311) with other partners in addition to points earned through its own flights.

This might translate into a formal representation of the form

$$\begin{aligned}&\forall x \in \{Alliance\}\\&R(x) = [Earn(Program(x), Miles * factor) \Leftarrow Flown(Miles, Airline(x));\\&Earn(Program(x), Miles * factor)\\&\Leftarrow Flown(Miles, Airline(y)) \wedge (CodeShare(Airline(x), Airline(y)),\\&y \in \{Alliance\}]\end{aligned} \tag{1}$$

, where *R(x)* stands for rule applicable to x.

In situations where ambiguity and incompleteness prevail, terms will have to be expanded by introducing concepts from Fuzzy Logic [de Korvin et al. 1994], and ultimately by human judgment. The simple equivalence of rules, such as $[A(x) \Leftarrow (B(x) \wedge C(x)) \vee D(x)]$ being equal to $[A(x) \Leftarrow B(x) \wedge C(x); A(x) \Leftarrow D(x)]$ can be checked automatically, but more complicated identities of rules or their combinations might be difficult to prove. Therefore it is highly advisable to also require the partner airlines in our example to follow the same logical structure.

As shown, advanced logic concepts, such as permissions, prohibitions and obligations [Ciampi and Martino 1982], can be expressed in FOL with Obligation (x), being represented as $\forall x A(x)$ Permission (x) as $\exists x A(x)$ Prohibition (x) as $\neg\exists x A(x)$, where *A(x)* represents the action which a role x is obliged to, permitted or prohibited. This approach works if a resolution system similar to the one used in Prolog is provided. (For an excellent guide to Prolog see [Clocksin and Mellish]). As most of the commonly agreed rules in a VE will consist of permissions, prohibitions and obligations, this deontic extension should be sufficient.

3.3 The Role of Meta-rules

Framework clauses, which can in this context be interpreted as a sort of meta-rules, build the shell for executable rules, in our approach called framework implementation clauses. They determine the existence and the content of framework implementation clauses. They can be viewed as meta-rules, which regulate the WHAT and leave the HOW to a lower level. In cases where the aim is to integrate existing implementation clauses, they serve as constraints for checking the overall compliance. In cases where a new partner joins or where the business operation has not existed before, they can also serve as rule generators. A good example of both aims being served is the European Union data protection directive [EU Directive 95/46].

A typical framework clause for airline alliances would have to include an implementation clause stating an obligation for an existence of a rule for the reciprocal accreditation of services delivered by the partners. The implementation clause of this clause (in other words a meta-rule) can then be evaluated against the relevant rules of the frequent flyer programs of participating airlines – to check compliance between individual frequent flyer program rules and this Alliance's rules.

Theoretically it is possible to use the VE policies as generator or even as templates for creating the rules of individual member policies (e.g. frequent flyer programs). In practice, these rules often already exist and thus, the VE policies will be used mostly as a basis for checking the compliance of individual frequent flyer programs with VE principles, i.e. making sure that none of the established constraints is compromised. This has parallels in a number of areas, such as static semantic checking of programs and the testing of correctness of implementation of software design patterns, e.g. [Neal and Linington 2001].

4 Application Example: Modelling Airline Alliance Agreements

There are already several examples of successful VEs, which give the customer the impression of being serviced by just one organisation while in reality a number of enterprises is contributing to the product or service. Some of these examples occur in the automotive, aviation and service industry, while some of the best known examples are frequent flyer programs, airline alliances and telecommunication providers. In some cases, such as the tourism industry, branding for the virtual enterprise has been very successful - leading examples are One World, Star Alliance, and the Qualiflyer Group. Even in situations where some of the partners cannot deliver for some reason (e.g. an airline does not offer a flight to a certain destination), the other members of the VE can cover the services, a highly desirable effect for the customer.

The frequent flyer programs of the larger airline networks have attempted to deliver more and more of their services online, as on-line delivery is suited to the non-tangible nature of frequent flyer points. From a legal and organisational point of view, the most interesting part is the set-up of agreements between participating enterprises, in this case airlines, hotels, and rental car companies. The goal of the VE is to make the sum of the member companies more attractive to customers by delivering value-added services. The cooperation structure is based around the collection, exchange and redemption of points. The strategic task in an airline alliance is to set up a contract harmonizing the frequent flyer programs of all participating airlines and regulating the cross-accreditation of points for services delivered by the partners.

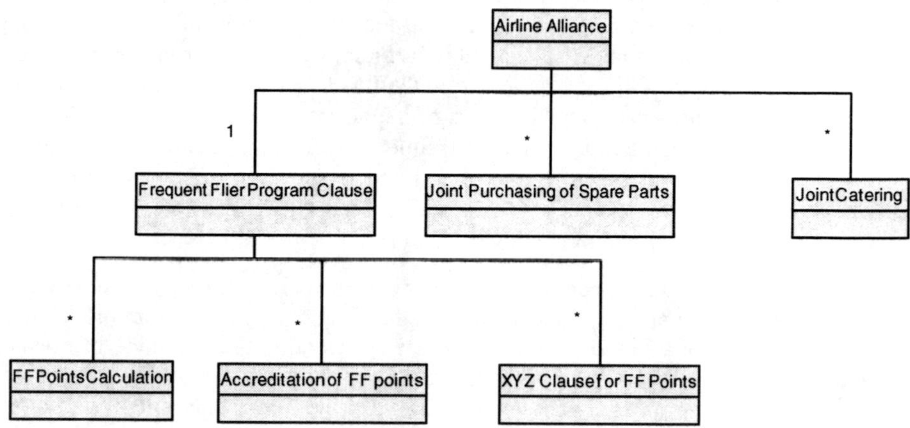

Fig. 2. Agreement Structure for an Airline Alliance VE and its member Airlines

Figure 2: Agreement Structure for an Airline Alliance VE and its member Airlines

The actual monitoring will be the evaluation of the execution of the individual FF program rules by the participating airlines. For this we will apply the BCA monitoring approach as described in section 5 below.

By applying this model to Airline Alliances, we get the following hierarchical structure for the frequent flyer clauses:

- The Frequent Flyer Program Clause.
- The Frequent Flyer Program Implementation Clause, consisting of a set of rules regulating issues such as the calculation of frequent flyer points and their accreditation.
- The actual Frequent Flyer Programs of Participating Airlines.

There will be a similar structure for other areas of cooperation such as Joint Purchasing of Spare Parts, Fuel, Catering and so on.

A realistic scenario might look as follows:

- Airlines A, B, C, D, and E agree to form a strategic alliance called Best Airlines of the World. One of the aims of the alliance is to set up an accreditation scheme for frequent flyer programs.
- All participating airlines should implement rules compliant to the following principles in their frequent flyer programs:
    - Calculation of frequent flyer points: one point is equal to 1 mile flown multiplied by a previously agreed factor. Miles are calculated on a basis of the official distances between the airport of departure and the airport of arrival.

- Accreditation of points: frequent flyer points can be earned on all code share flights, but can be accredited to only one frequent flyer program.

- The frequent flyer program of airline A contains the following rules:
  - Frequent flyer points are earned on the basis of one point being equal to miles multiplied by a factor agreed by airlines participating in the alliance. Miles are calculated on a basis of the official distances between the airport of departure and the airport of arrival.
  - Accreditation of points: frequent flyer points can be earned on all flights of airline A and on all code share flights operated with a *Best Airlines of the World* (BAW) partner airline, but can be accredited to only one frequent flyer program.

For checking the compliance of an airline with the VE agreement, two levels of monitoring have to be applied. Firstly, rules in the frequent flyer program of airline X have to be compliant with the alliance agreement. Secondly, the execution of rules of the individual frequent flyer programs has to be checked by the airline. Altogether therefore, we have a three-tier hierarchy with meta-rules, rules, and the execution of rules.

Assuming that rules can be represented in FOL (for representation of legal rules in First Order Predicate Logic see classics such as [Susskind 1987]). we can then specify them in the form of:

$$A(x) \Leftarrow B(x) \wedge C(x) \wedge D(x) \ . \tag{2}$$

The meta-rules can be represented as

$$\forall x \in X \ \Big| \ R(x) = \big[A(x) \Leftarrow B(x) \wedge C(x) \wedge D(x)\big] \, . \tag{3}$$

If both sets of rules are written in disjunctive form and are not partitioned, the compliance of rules of a frequent flyer program with meta-rules can then be checked by seeing whether or not such a rule $R(x)$ exists. For the monitoring of the actual execution of a rule $R(x)$ we use the BCA monitoring approach, as indicated earlier.

In our example the meta-rules would be

$$\begin{aligned} &\forall x \in \{BAW\} \\ &R(x) = [Earn(Program(x), Miles * factor) \\ &\qquad\qquad \Leftarrow Flown(Miles, Airline(x)); \\ &\qquad Earn(Program(x), Miles * factor) \\ &\qquad\qquad \Leftarrow Flown(Miles, Airline(y)) \wedge \\ &\qquad (CodeShare(Airline(x), Airline(y))), \quad y \in BAW]. \end{aligned} \tag{4}$$

So we need to check with each frequent flyer program of the participating airlines whether they contain such set of rules, i.e. whether the frequent flyer program of airline A contains the rules

$$Earn(Program(A), Miles * factor) \Leftarrow Flown(Miles, Airline(A));$$
$$Earn(Program(A), Miles * factor) \Leftarrow Flown(Miles, Airline(y)) \wedge$$
$$(CodeShare(Airline(A), Airline(y))),\ y \in BAW. \quad (5)$$

Other interesting VE scenarios that could be modelled in this way are joint purchasing strategies, virtual competence centres and alliances between travel enterprises such as hotel chains and rental car companies.

In the following section we will discuss how the rules might be adopted in an automated contract management system.

5 Implementation of the Rule Base

The formalism introduced in the previous section can be used as a starting point for providing an increasing level of automation of those stages in the VE life-cycle that involve contract management activities. These activities cover the creation of contracts and also the management of contracts during the periods of business development and business execution stages, as discussed in 2.1.

In addition, this formalism can be built into the various components of an IT system that can support management of contracts. In this section we demonstrate this with an example of Business Contract Architecture (BCA) – which is one of the early proposals for supporting various levels of automated contract management, as described in [Milosevic and Bond 1995, Goodchild et al. 2000].

First, the BCA allows storing of *standard contract forms* and this component is called as Contract Forms Repository. These predefined forms (i.e. templates) can be used by businesses when agreeing on the specifics terms of a contract and instantiating contracts. Examples are contract forms that govern real-estate transactions, banking and insurance forms, purchase and sale of goods and services and so on. Such repositories can also contain forms for standard *contract clauses* that can be reused when deriving *new* contracts that govern specific business interactions. Availability of standard contract clauses also enables flexible changing/updating of existing contracts by simply providing references to the new contract clause from the existing contract. These changes are quite frequent in cases of long-term contracts and are known as *contract variations* and *contract escalation* clauses. These features of the BCA can thus be used as an effective mechanism for storing specific framework agreements, framework clauses and also framework implementation clauses that are valuable as a collection of pre-defined templates of use in establishing VEs. The contract forms repository can be used as facility for faster setting up and reuse of existing structures that are commonly used when structuring various VE agreements.

Second, BCA supports *digital signing* of contracts, once specific contract terms have been agreed. This can bring significant savings, in particular in cases where contracts involve multiple, geographically distributed trading partners, such as those related to international contracts, and which can involve significant time and transaction costs associated with handling the contract signing process. This is also a useful way of speeding up contract negotiation process. Once a negotiated contract is signed, it can be stored in a separate repository, termed Notary. This negotiated contract specifies a particular set of policies that parties must comply to in order to satisfy a contract. One possible format for expressing these policies can be in the form introduced in 3.2. The Notary for the Frequent Flyer example would store the full agreement structure specific to the BAW partner airlines.

Third, in cases where parties are interested in being notified about some contract non-compliance, BCA supports *Monitoring* of the business interactions governed by a contract. This can be done either by logging of business interactions and their audits at a later stage, or by a more pro-active monitoring which can be particularly applicable in cases of electronic services delivery. Essentially, this monitoring consists of evaluating policies as agreed in the contracts and stored in a Notary and comparing these with the actual execution of contracts – in particular the action of parties that are specified as part of contractual obligations.

In the Frequent Flyer example, monitoring at the Business Development stage would involve testing, against actual data, whether each participating airline had observed agreed rules when advertising their frequent flyer schemes. Likewise at the Execution stage, one could check that operations under the VE had been done properly, e.g. cross-crediting of frequent flyer points.

A special kind of monitoring particularly suitable for longer term and timed contracts *is tracking* of contracts. This allows timely reaction to some important deadlines such as contract termination, thus making it possible to re-negotiate a subsequent contract and put it in place, before or immediately after the existing contract terminates. Such tracking of contracts can be also seen as a mechanism that prevents situations in which businesses continue their interactions after the contract has expired – thus avoiding undesirable circumstances such as penalties and fines.

Finally, in cases when contract terms and conditions were breached it may be useful to provide certain *enforcement* contract terms. Although some of the enforcements can be done electronically, such as in cases of services provision and billing, the ultimate enforcements are to be executed by human decision makers.

We note that there can be several business processes identified in our business contracts model, but our architecture is essentially role-based - to enable support for many types of underlying contracting scenarios (i.e. business processes implementing them).

6 Conclusion and Further Work

In this paper we have shown how providing a formal representation of virtual enterprise contracts can support the establishment of a virtual enterprise. This formal representation serves as basis for consistency and compliance checks as well as for the development of implementation rules. Once these implementation rules have been formulated, they can be plugged into execution and monitoring mechanisms, such as those provided by the BCA facilities. We have therefore been able to point towards a way of effectively supporting the setting up of virtual enterprise contracts and consequently reducing the virtual enterprise's time to operation.

Future plans include a detailed proposal of how the implementation of the rules in BCA would be achieved. This will include generation of rules in a standard format and the checking of sets of rules at one level of the hierarchy against those at the next higher level. There is also a need to access a range of real-world case studies, in order to collect standard contract patterns and their relationship to common B2B situations in supply chains. We will then be in a position to test the concepts in a suitable pilot environment.

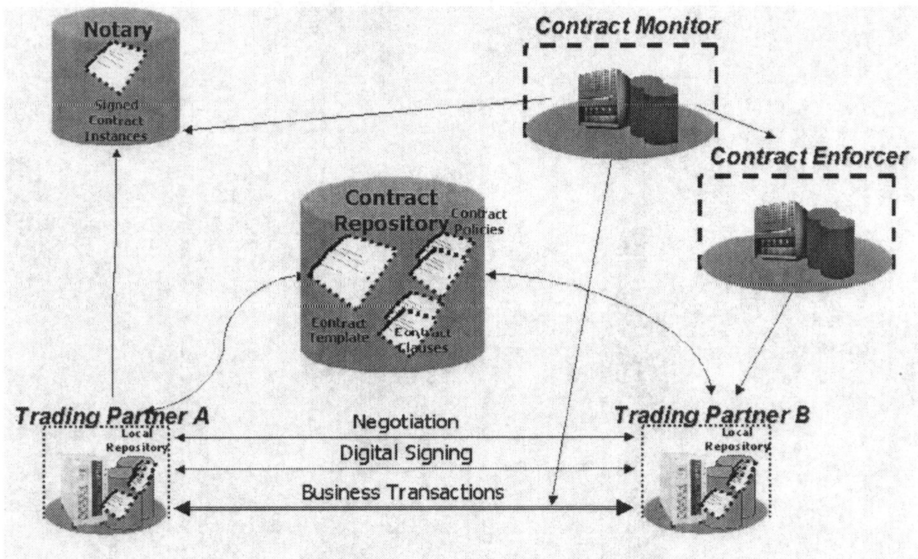

Fig. 3. BCA Architecture

Acknowledgements

The work reported in this paper has been funded in part by the Cooperative Research Centres Program through the Department of the Prime Minister and Cabinet of the Commonwealth Government of Australia.

References

[Abelson and Sussman 1996]). H. Abelson, G. and J. Sussman. Structure and Interpretation of Computer Programs, 1996.

[Ciampi and Martino 1982] C.Ciampi and A.A. Martino (Ed). Artificial Intelligence and Legal Information Systems: Deontic Logic, Computational Linguistics and Legal Information Systems, Elsevier Science Ltd; ISBN: 0444864156.

[Clocksin and Mellish] W. F. Clocksin, C. S. Mellish. Programming in Prolog, Springer, ISBN 3-540-58350-5.

[Davaclu et al 1999] H. Davaclu, M. Kifer, L.R. Pokorny, C.R. Ramakrishnan, I.V. Ramakrishnan, S. Dawson. Modeling and Analysis of Interactions in Virtual Enterprises, in Proceedings of the Workshop on Research Issues in Data Engineering - Information Technology for Virtual Enterprises (RIDE-VE'99), Sydney, Australia, March 1999.

[EU Directive 95/46] Directive 95/46/EC of the European Parliament and of the Council of 24 October 1995, on the protection of individuals with regard to the processing of personal data and on the free movement of such data.

[Goodchild et al. 2000] A.Goodchild, Z. Milosevic and C. Herring. Business Contracts for B2B, CAiSE'00 Workshop on Infrastructures for Dynamic Business-to-Business Service Outsourcing.

[Harmon and King 1985]. P. Harmon and D. King. Expert Systems: Artificial Intelligence in Business, John Wiley & Sons. ISBN 0471808245.

[INCOTERMS] International Chamber of Commerce, Incoterms 2000: ICC Official Rules for the Interpretation of Trade Terms. ICC Publishing New York 2000. ISBN 92-842-1199-9.

[Kowalski 1994] R. Kowalski, F. Toni. Argument and Reconciliation, in: International Symposium on Fifth Generation Computer Systems '94, Workshop on Legal Reasoning, Tokyo (1994).

[Kowalski 1996] R. Kowalski, F. Toni. Abstract Argumentation, In: Artificial Intelligence and Law Journal 4(3-4), Special Issue on Logical Models of Argumentation, H. Prakken and G. Sartor, eds., Kluwer Academic Publishers (1996).

[de Korvin et al. 1994] A. de Korvin, G. Quirchmayr, S. Hashemi. Dealing with Uncertainty in Insurance Contracts. Proc. of the 6th Conference on Expert Systems Applications and Artifical Intelligence, EXPERSYS-94, Houston, Texas, December 1994.

[de Korvin et al. 1995] A. de Korvin, G. Quirchmayr, S. Hashemi. Managing Uncertainty in Contract Law. Proc. of the 7th Conference on Expert Systems Applications and Artifical Intelligence, EXPERSYS-95, p. 191 ff., December 1995.

[Ktendis and Paraskevopoulos 1999] P.D. Ktendis and A.T. Paraskevopoulos. Information and Communication Technology (ICT) Infrastructure fro Small and Medium Enterprises (SMEs) Networks: Achievements and Work-in-Progress from Three European Projects, in Proceedings of the Workshop on Research Issues in Data Engineering - Information Technology for Virtual Enterprises (RIDE-VE'99), Sydney, Australia, March 1999.

[Milosevic and Bond 1995] Z. Milosevic and A. Bond. Electronic Commerce on the Internet: What is Still Missing? The 5th Annual Conference of the Internet Society, INET'95, Honolulu, Hawaii, USA, June 1995.

[Neal and Linnington 2001] S.Neal and P.F.Linington. Tool support for development using patterns. In E.Lupu and A.Wegmann, editors, Proceedings of the fifth International Enterprise Distributed Object Computng Conference, pages 237-248, Seattle, WA, USA, IEEE Computer Society.

[Riempp 1998] G. Riempp. Wide Area Workflow Management, Springer, London 1998.

[Tagg 2001] R. Tagg. Workflow in Different Styles of Virtual Enterprise, in Proceedings of Workshop on Information Technology for Virtual Enterprises (ITVE 2001), Gold Coast, Australia, January 2001.

[Tagg and Quirchmayr 2001] R. Tagg, G. Quirchmayr. Towards an Interconnection Model for Evolution of Shared Workflows in a Virtual Enterprise, in Proceedings of Third Int. Conference on Information Integration and Web-Based Applications and Services, Linz, Austria, September 2001.

[Susskind 1987]. R. E. Susskind. Expert Systems in Law: A Jurisprudential Inquiry. ASIN: 0198252730.

[Winston 1992] P. H. Winston. Artificial Intelligence. 1992. Addison-Wesley Pub Co; ISBN: 0201533774.

Multiple Regression Analysis in Crime Pattern Warehouse for Decision Support

Dale Dzemydiene[1,2] and Vitalija Rudzkiene[1]

[1] Law University of Lithuania,
Ateities 20, LT-2057 Vilnius, Lithuania
vital@ltu.lt

[2] Institute of Mathematics and Informatics
Akademijos 4, LT-2600 Vilnius, Lithuania
daledz@ktl.mii.lt

Abstract. The application domain of crime investigation and prevention deals with incomplete information from a broad variety of data sources and a complex structure of interdependencies of rapidly changing situations. The paper describes an approach of integration of multiple statistical analyses for recognition of crime information patterns in data warehouse. With multiple statistical methods we develop a decision support system based on real data of warehouses of social-economic and crime indicators. The proposed multiple regression models allows gaining new insights into the structure of problem and developing strategies for crime prevention measures.

1 Introduction

Our consideration is concentrated on the intelligence based on conceptual knowledge and analytical logics of different types of statistical models related with the evaluation of a huge quantity of data that reflect criminal events and their relationships. It is of importance, that the integration of different statistics, such as Pearson's sample coefficient correlation, a coefficient of multiple correlation, and a partial correlation coefficient, enhances competitive advantages in the analysis of complicated situations and decision support. These multiple statistical methods jointly with knowledge representation techniques allow extracting more valuable patterns from the information leading to the recognition of important tendencies of crime situation. In some cases, the technique of data mining helps in the analysis of very large databases. Data mining is, in some ways, an extension of statistics, with a few artificial intelligence and machine-learning methods introduced.

The decision support system under construction ensures ease of use and clarity of interpretation in the presentation of analysis results from the data warehouse of crime and social investigations [2]. Statistical techniques and visual representation of characteristics analysed are crucial in supporting decision making and gaining new insights into the structure of problems by generating different views of the decision situation. It is important to recognize meaningful alternatives and strategies for crime prevention measures during the problem-solving process by means of statistical analysis [1].

R. Cicchetti et al. (Eds.): DEXA 2002, LNCS 2453, pp. 249–258, 2002.

The specificity of the judicial system and criminological fields most frequently involves the problem of structuring and describing the phenomena formalised [7]. The development of ontological intelligent systems in this particular field requires the application of additional methods, their task being the description of intricate decision situations [8], informal ways of coming to a decision, possible subjective factors that affect making a particular decision, etc.

The paper proposes the approach of adaptation of multiple statistical analysis for recognition of crime situation and revelation of informative patterns in criminal and social data warehouse. Introduced multiple statistical methods allow us to exercise statistical control, forecast the main crime tendencies and support decisions for crime prevention means. The results obtained are based on the Lithuanian social-economic data and crime statistics.

2 Architectural View of the Decision Support System

The knowledge that helps us to understand how to apply the methods of decision preparation and development of advising systems is of special importance. Intellectual information systems have additional properties that enable structural analysis and storing data in the system, modelling situations, making and explaining decisions [3]. In addition, the knowledge system must be able to abstract information and data about the current situation and to have the possibilities of retrospective analysis and prognoses [4].

Regional bureaus of crime statistics and research collect a great volume of data from different sources that reflect criminal events and their relations. The data is stored in warehouses with multiplex and temporal dimensions. Such data in warehouse sometimes become too extensive and unmanageable for detailed decision making. More often the organizations want the discover knowledge, trends and patterns within the data. Summarization and generalization may be used to reduce data sizes. But summarization can cause problems too [9]. Summarization of the same data set with two sampling or summarization methods may result in the same result, and summarization of the same data set with two methods may produce two different results.

The patterns become more popular in resent software engineering developments. There exist some differences of the terms "design pattern" in the realm of object-oriented software development [10], "data pattern" in data warehouses [5] and "pattern-tables" within relational databases. A pattern warehouse is defined by [9] as an information repository that stores relationships between data items and holds historical patterns rather than historical data. In the context of this research patterns are characterized as generic structures won by experience of modelling in the past, they can be abstract (describing the structure of a model) or concrete (describing one special model).

For the purposes of revealing crime patterns our system can provide the statistics based on local government areas, which break down the reported incidents into categories.

Data access operations such as query and reporting deals with data space of warehouse, statistical analysis uses the multidimensional space and data mining takes place on inference of alternative decisions. Such spaces form a basis of architectural view of the decision support system (Fig. 1).

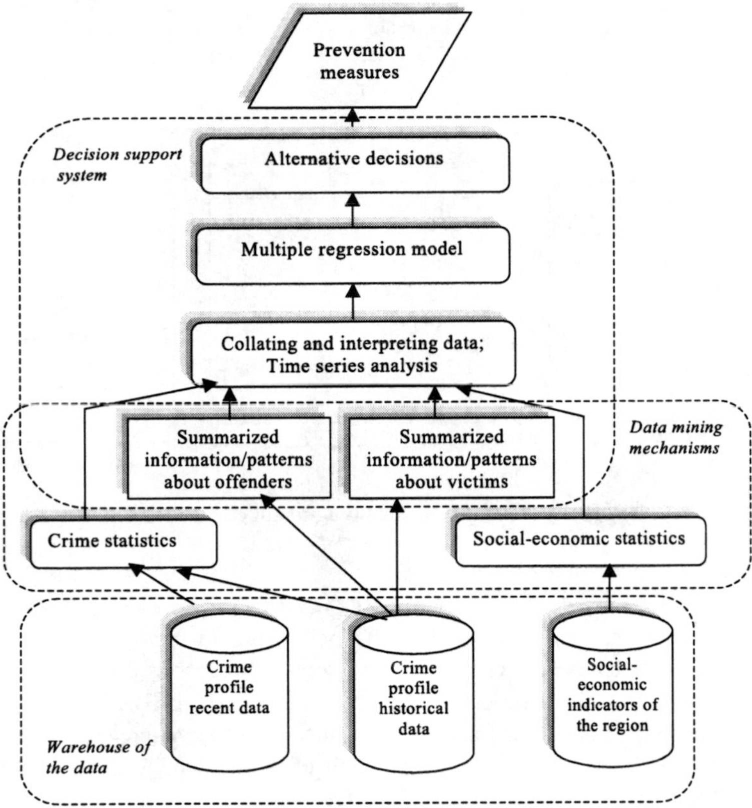

Fig. 1. The architectural view of data integration processes for data mining and decision support

A broad variety of analysis forms could be defined. For instance, crime pattern's analysis, profile analysis, case analysis (course of events immediately before, during and after a serious offence), comparative crime analysis, etc.

2.1 The Topology of Criminal Information

The problems of data conflict are closely related to the data quality as a multidimensional concept with subjective acquisition and temporal variance of data. The data quality control at the staging area of the data warehouse system is an important issue [6]. For these purposes the topology of a warehouse is constructed and stored in the repository of data warehouse. The ontological view based on object-oriented UML semantic model helps us to reveal the knowledge and examine the causal structure of the objects in the domain. It allows the expression of the main principles and substantiation of the "game" rules.

To find out the crime profile structure it is important to reveal information on the type of crime, offenders and victims (Fig. 2).

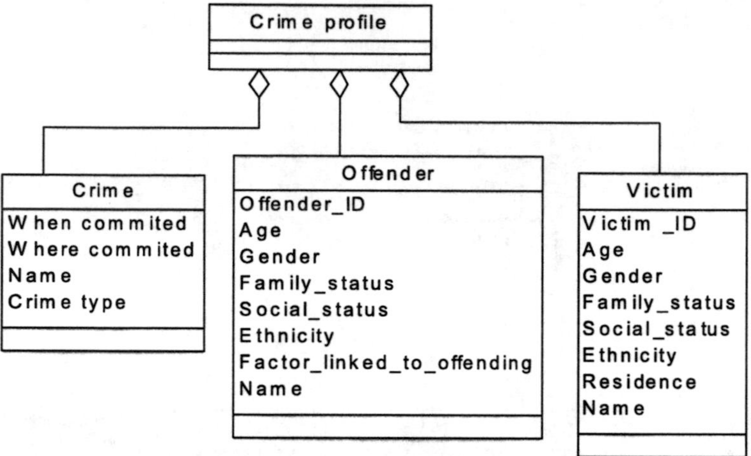

Fig. 2. The example of class diagram of crime profile

Crime statistics and research collect vast quantity of data from different sources reflect criminal events and their relations. They can provide statistics based on local government areas that break down reported incidents in categories, like offences against the person, offences against property and specific offences (Fig. 3).

Crime is a complex phenomenon of social, political and economical impacts. A crime rate is defined as the number of crimes per unit of population. A crime is considered registered if it is included into the centralised Register.

2.2 The Main Social-Economic Indicators

A lot of governments take a census on a regular basis. Governmental offices of statistics usually take a census of population, survey business and economy. Databases are also being created across interstate line on crime, weather, welfare, solid waste disposal, electric power use, and so on. Which part of this information is most important in a specific policy area – social statistics? Relative severity of crime problems compared to other areas is social–economic indicators of state and other similar areas:

- Crime rate;
- Structure of population;
- GDP per capita;
- Unemployment;
- Average disposable income;
- Poverty rate and number of population living under poverty rate, etc.

Economic stratum of population is also very important indicator. The social justice level of society has always had a great influence on criminality. Numerous investigations of this indicator were performed in the 18–20th centuries. The number of crimes does not have a tendency to directly depend and decrease when the economical situation

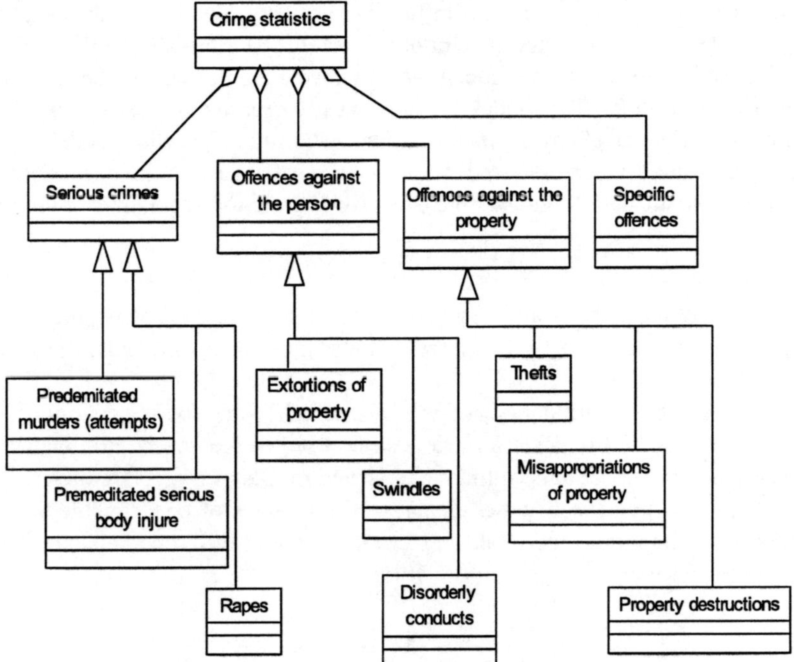

Fig. 3. The components of crime statistics

changes for the better. Therefore we can investigate the ratio between the consumption expenditure of 10 percent of the richest families and 10 percent of the poorest families as a second of the main indicators (further this indicator will be called an *expenditure ratio – ER*). This indicator is calculated by the household budget survey and complies with the main requirements of Eurostat.

A third indicator is the unemployment. A large number of the unemployed, especially young people have always been a reason for anxiety of the society. Data on the unemployed population are registered in two ways: by Labour Exchange Offices and by the public survey of population.

3 The Correlation and Multiple Regression Analysis of Data Warehouse

Most social and economic data take the form of time series – e.g., the Gross National Product by year, indices of consumer and wholesale price, number of offences, to name just a few. Usually the analysis of time-series data focuses on two types of problems:

- Attempting to estimate the factors which produce the pattern of the series;
- Using this estimate in forecasting the future behavior of series.

In reality, the social world is a complicated network of interdependencies, which is rarely captured well by models involving two variables (one of which is time) only.

Typically, the value of any variable is influenced not only by one another variable, but also by two, three, or even a multitude of other variables. Criminality in the region may indeed depend on the civil rights, social security level, unemployment, consumption of alcohol drinks and so on. The model that allows us to exercise statistical control and to determine the influence of any X on Y is called a multiple regression model.

Suppose that there are m independent variables and that the population model relating these variables to the dependent variable y, is given by the following linear relationship:

$$Y = \alpha + \beta_1 X_1 + \beta_2 X_2 + \cdots + \beta_n X_m + \varepsilon. \tag{1}$$

The subscript on each variable represents one of the values in the population. Also, α equals a y-intercept, $\beta_1, \beta_2, \ldots, \beta_m$ are partial regression coefficients, ε represents a disturbance term.

Suppose that Y is criminality and $X_1, X_2, \ldots, X_m$ are social-economic factors, influencing the criminality. Such a model can be used to predict the criminality when social-economic factors do fall within the observed ranges of these variables.

In solving the question whether changes in the values of one variable tend to be associated with changes in the others, we can use several different statistics. The first one is *Pearson's sample coefficient of correlation*

$$p = \frac{\sum XY - m\bar{X}\bar{Y}}{\sqrt{\left(\sum X^2 - m\bar{X}^2\right)\left(\sum Y^2 - m\bar{Y}^2\right)}}, \tag{2}$$

where $\bar{X}, \bar{Y}$ are the means of the variable X and Y, respectively.

The *sample coefficient of multiple determination* is denoted by R^2 and represents the relationship between more than two variables. It equals the proportion of the total variation in the values of the dependent variable Y, which is explained by the multiple regression of Y on $X_1, X_2, \ldots, X_n$, and possibly additional independent variables $X_{n+1}, X_{n+2}, \ldots$.

$$R^2 = \frac{\sum\left(\widehat{Y} - \bar{Y}\right)^2}{\sum\left(Y - \bar{Y}\right)^2}, \tag{3}$$

where $\widehat{Y}$ are estimated values of Y and $\bar{Y}$ is the mean.

The coefficient of multiple correlation indicates a fraction of the total variation in Y accounted for the regression equation and is denoted as a square root of the multiple coefficient of determination $R = \sqrt{R^2}$.

A partial coefficient of determination is a measure of the strength of the relationship between the dependent variable and independent variable, when the linear effect of the rest of the variables is being eliminated. The general formula for this coefficient is presented as:

$$r^2_{i(jk\cdots n)*tu\cdots w} = \frac{R^2_{i*jk\cdots w} - R^2_{i*tu\cdots w}}{1 - R^2_{i*tu\cdots w}} \tag{4}$$

where R^2 are coefficients of multiple determination.

The square root of the partial coefficient of determination $r_{i(jk\cdots n)*tu\cdots w}$ is called *a partial correlation coefficient.*

4 Time-Series of Social-Economic Indicators

Criminal processes in East European countries depend on a similar economic situation and have similar development tendency. Therefore general tendencies of criminality in Lithuania reveal a broad spectrum of problems, which is characteristic of the whole East European region. It is reasonable to investigate data on the criminality in Lithuania not earlier than from 1989, because 1989 was the beginning of the period when changes in the Lithuanian economic and politics state system entailed changes in criminality.

The restitution of independence in Lithuania caused illegal accumulation of capital. This process influenced others social, economic and political relations. In this period consumption expenditure ratio of the poorest and richest families started increasing intensively. The department of Statistics to the Government of the Republic of Lithuania has started the survey of household budget since 1994. By this survey from 1994 to 1996 the ratio between consumption expenditure of 10 percent of the richest families and 10 percent of the poorest families increased about two times, and in 1999 it was 8.1. The main social-economic indicators of Lithuania since 1989 are presented in Fig. 4.

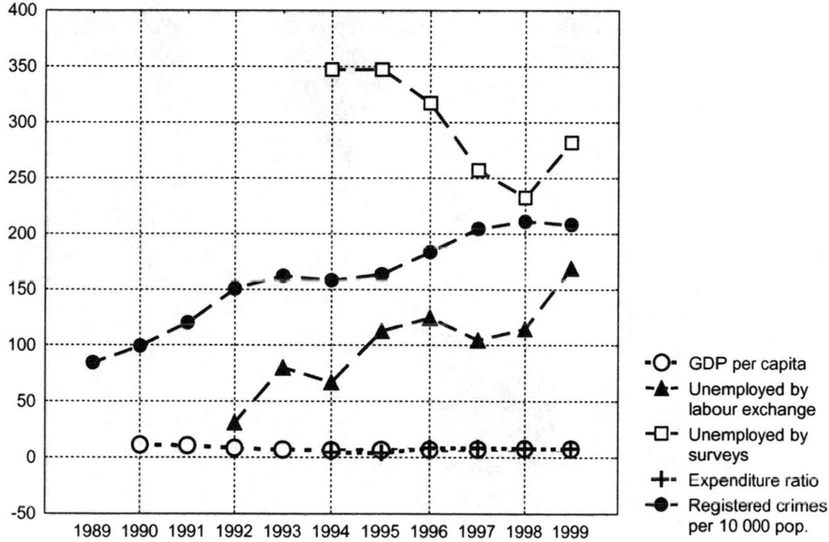

Fig. 4. Dynamics of the main social-economic indicators of Lithuania. GDP per capita is presented in real prices (in thousands of Lt), the number of the unemployed in thousands

Two different series describe data on the unemployed. The Labour Exchange present the first series and the Lithuanian Department of Statistics according to the survey present the second one. The data are dissimilar and the relationship between these series is very weak – Pearson's coefficient of correlation is $p = 0.37$. We may explore common tendencies of data series and in thus evaluate the reliability of data. For example, it is well known that an increase in GDP decreases unemployment. But the estimate of

Pearson's coefficient of correlation between the unemployment registered by survey and GDP per capita is -0.97. The value of the same coefficient between the unemployed registered by the Labour Exchange Offices and GDP per capita is 0.58. It is common knowledge that a large number of the unemployed increases criminality. The estimate of Pearson's coefficient of correlation between the unemployment registered by the Labour Exchange Offices and criminality is 0.64 and between the unemployed by survey and criminality is -0.944.

We see that the data on the unemployed registered by survey do not increase and have a close relationship only with the economic situation. Most likely this indicator reflects the apprehension of losing a job, but not the real situation. Therefore following the data on the unemployed we will use the data presented by the Labour Exchange Offices.

5 The Multiple Regression Model of Criminality

The data series are presented in different scales. Therefore we transform the data series by the formula

$$w_j = \frac{x_j}{x_1} \cdot 100\%, \tag{5}$$

where x_1 is the first year indicator, x_j is the indicator of the jth year. After this transformation we attach the first year indicator to 100%, i.e. $w_1 = 100\%$ (Fig. 5).

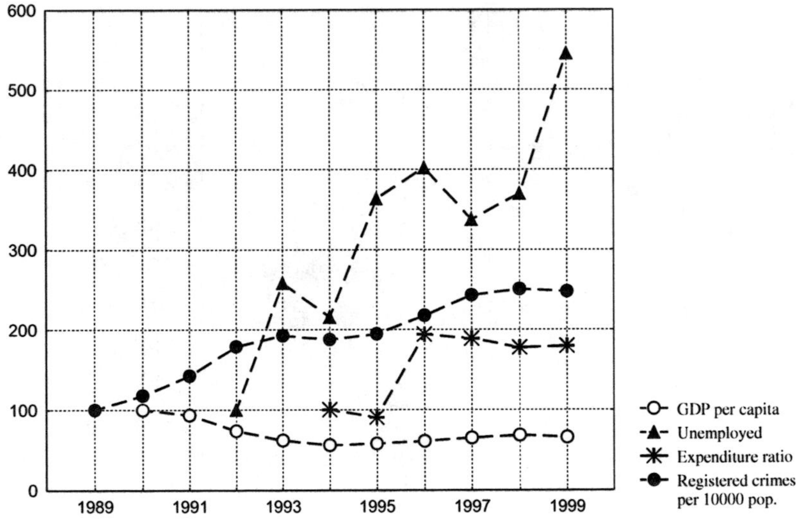

Fig. 5. Data series of social-economic indicators transformed by formula (5)

To assess the relationship between variables (indicators) we calculate the coefficients of multiple correlation R and partial correlation r.

The results show that GDP per capita has a great influence on criminality ($R = 0.984$, $r = 0.975$). The relationship between the criminality and the expenditure ratio

($R = 0.84$, $r = 0.75$) takes the second place. The unemployed registered by the Labour Exchange Offices have a weaker influence ($R = 0.64$, $r = 0.45$).

Since the time period under investigation is rather short the hypothesis that the last coefficient is not significant was tested. As a test statistic we use Fisher's statistic

$$z(r) = \frac{1}{2} \ln \frac{1+r}{1-r}. \tag{6}$$

The significance level $\alpha = 0.05$ implies the critical value $z_{cr} = 0.754$. Hypothesis should be accepted, as the calculated value is lower than the critical value. We can maintain that other indicators replace the influence of this indicator.

Now we can calculate the multiple regression equation between GDP per capita, the expenditure ratio (*ER*) and the criminality (*Cr*)

$$Cr = 70.72 + 34.77 * GDP + 2.28 * ER. \tag{7}$$

But we should remember that data series are short and the estimates of coefficients can be inexact. However this equation presents the common influence of some social-economic indicators on the evolution of criminality.

6 Conclusions

A general conceptual framework has been proposed for the integration multiple statistical methods in decision support system for recognition of crime patterns. The ontological view of data warehouse enable us define the significant concepts and associations used in crime prevention system as well as the level of concord between concepts and their equal comprehensibility. The proposed approach of data mining for joint criminality, social and economic databases is based on multiple regression and correlation analysis. The integration of multiple statistical methods, such as Pearson's sample coefficient correlation, a coefficient of multiple correlation, a partial correlation coefficient, and multiple regression analysis, enhances competitive advantage in the analysis of complicates situations. This method allows us to reveal actual relationships, to investigate time patterns as well as to construct a process management strategy.

The contribution of the paper, we believe, is that it identifies some important problems and issues associated with the inter-relationships of different social-economic parameters that suggested the influence into the criminality.

References

1. Duncan, J.W., Gross, A.C.: Statistics for the 21st century. Irwin. USA (1995)
2. Dzemydiene, D.: Consultative Information Systems in Law Domain. Information Technologies and Management **4**(21) (2001) 38–42
3. Dzemydiene, D.: An Approach of Modelling Expertise in Environmental Pollution Evaluation System. In: Barsdinš, J., Caplinskas, A. (eds.): Databases and Information Systems. Kluwer Academic Publishers (2001) 209–220

4. Dzemydiene, D.: Temporal Information Management and Decision Support for Predictive Control of Environment Contamination Processes. In: Eder, J., Caplinskas, A. (eds.): Advances in Databases and Information Systems. Proc. of Fifth East-European Conference. Vilnius (2001) 158–172
5. Herden, O.: Parameterised Patterns for Conceptual Modelling of Data Warehouses. In: Proc. of the 4th IEEE International Baltic Workshop on Databases and Information systems. Technika. Vilnius (2000) 152–163
6. Hinrichs, H.: Statistical quality control of Warehouse Data. In: Barsdins, J., Caplinskas, A. (eds.): Databases and Information Systems. Kluwer Academic Publishers (2001) 69–84
7. Kovacich, G.L., Boni, W.: High-Technology-Crime Investigator's Handbook: Working in the Global Information Environment. Butterworth-Heinemann (2000)
8. Maskeliunas, S.: Ontological Engineering: Common Approaches and Visualisation Capabilities. Informatica **1**(11) (2000) 41–48
9. Parsaye, K.: Rotational Schemas: Multi-Focus Data Structures for data Mining. Information Discovery Inc. (1996)
10. Pree, W.: Design Patterns for Object-Oriented Software Development. Addison Wesley (1995)
11. Rudzkiene, V.: Mathematical Modelling of Criminality in Lithuania in a Context of the East European Countries. Liet. Matem. Rink., Vol.41, Spec.No. Vilnius (2001) 548–551

A Practical Walkthrough of the Ontology Derivation Rules

Carlo Wouters[1], Tharam Dillon[1], Wenny Rahayu[1], and Elizabeth Chang[2]

[1] Department of Computer Science and Computer Engineering
La Trobe University
Bundoora, Victoria 3086, Australia
{cewouter, wenny, tharam} @cs.latrobe.edu.au
[2] Department of Computer Science and Software Engineering
University of Newcastle
Callaghan, NSW 2308, Australia
chang@cs.newcastle.edu.au

Abstract. To ensure the success of the semantic web, structures that are implemented, usually ontologies, should maintain their validity well into the future. These ontologies can be very extensive, introducing the problem that only parts (sub-ontologies) of them are needed by applications. A number of rules were established to get from such a base ontology to a derived sub-ontology. This paper explores these rules in a practical way, by giving a real-world scenario, and following it through from initial state to target ontology design. Each step and rule is applied to the scenario, and so the more practical side of the theoretical rules and steps is shown.

1 Motivation

To ensure the success of the semantic web, structures that are implemented, usually ontologies, should maintain their validity well into the future. Since it is impossible to model a dynamic, ever-changing domain in a static ontology, methods to dynamically update and modify these ontologies are being developed. The used ontologies also tend to grow larger, to a point where ideally the entire world is modeled in one supra-ontology [1], providing great compatibility and consistency across all sub-domains, but practically it introduces the new problem of being too vast to be used in its entirety by any application. For the first problem; versioning [2] and maintenance of ontologies [3] provide a solution. To address the second problem we need distribution of ontologies [4], but even more so derivation of independent sub-ontologies. In this paper the derivation rules for extracting such a sub-ontology from a given base ontology are demonstrated using a more practical approach. An actual example design in UML (Unified Modeling Language) is used as base ontology. Certain requirements for the derived sub-ontology are set up, representing a possible real world problem. The final goal is to arrive at a design of a smaller ontology (sub-ontology) that caters for all the needs specified in the requirements, while maintaining consistency, cohesiveness, coherency and, most importantly, independency. A full practical workout from start to finish is provided, with references to the theoretical

R. Cicchetti et al. (Eds.): DEXA 2002, LNCS 2453, pp. 259–268, 2002.

research previously carried out [5], [6]. The extraction process presented is divided into two sub-processes; Extraction of core elements, and optimization schemes. Although the focus here is on the first sub-process, the second sub-process is included to arrive at a full, optimized solution. The optimization schemes provide a means of quality assurance, so that developers can be confident they arrive at a design of a sub-ontology that is one of the most appropriate solutions for their specific requirements.

2 Background

This section provides a summary of our earlier work [5], [6], and only provides the rules and theorems actually used in this paper. Whilst the following rules provide a basis of the practical walkthrough for ontology derivation rules in the next sections, the main aim of this paper is to demonstrate the applicability of the rules in a real world domain and how the resulting design can be further optimized.

1) *'No Island' criterium*: In a single ontology no islands may occur, where an island is defined as a group of 1 or more ontological concepts that cannot reach every other ontological concept in the total group. These ontological concepts are said to belong to different ontologies.

2) *Construction of Core Elements*

a) *Step 1: selection of concepts*: All the ontological concepts from the base-ontology that are still needed in the sub-ontology are taken and put as permanent elements of the sub-ontology.

b) *Step 2: selection of attributes*: In this step a selection is made out of all available attributes to obtain a list of the wanted attributes.

i) Detailed rule for step 2 (*Attributes Distribution Rule of Thumb*): If the cardinality from a temporary concept to any permanent concept solely consists of Inheritance Downwards (ID) and One cardinalities (ON), the temporary concept can be removed, and the attributes can be placed in the permanent concept this strong path made a connection to.

c) *Step 3: Definition hybrid relationships*: A hybrid relationship is the relationship that is formed by concatenating the relationship descriptions along a path from a source concept to a target in a certain way.

i) Restriction (*Invalid Path Rule*): Paths cannot contain an adjacent generalization and specialization relationship.

ii) *Shorthand Notation for Sequential Cardinality*:

Table 1. Cardinality Shorthand Notation

Definition	short	0	1	Many
Inheritance upwards	IU		*	
Exactly one (1)	ON		*	
Inheritance downwards	ID	*	*	
Multiple (1 .. m)	MU		*	*
Single (0 .. 1)	SI	*	*	
Many (0 .. m)	MA	*		*

iii) *Definition for Sequential Cardinality*: The Sequential Cardinality of a hybrid relationship consists of two list, one in each direction, containing the shorthand notation of the cardinalities of the individual relationships.

iv) *Definition for Combined Cardinality*: The Combined Cardinality of a hybrid relationship is the cardinality that arises from taking the lowest minimum of the individual cardinalities in the Sequential Cardinality as a minimum, and the highest maximum of the individual cardinalities in the Sequential Cardinality as a maximum.

v) *Definition for Extended Combined Cardinality*: The Extended Combined Cardinality is based on the Combined Cardinality, but providing additional information about the minima and maxima.

vi) *Definition for Lexical Description*: A lexical description of a hybrid relationship is the meaningful description of the relation between the two concepts the relationship connects, derived from a concatenation of the intermediate concepts and the lexical descriptions of the connecting relationships in sequence.

3) *Definition of Optimization Sub-Process*: Optimization is the pruning process of the sub-ontology with all the hybrid relationships still present. This optimization is done according to a prioritized list of optimization schemes.

a) *Definition of Conceptual optimization*: Conceptual optimization is the optimization where the ontology engineer prioritizes the list of hybrid relationships, according to the meaning derived from the lexical descriptions, and their satisfaction level towards the sub-ontology requirements.

b) *Definition of Optimization for Simplicity*: Optimization for simplicity is the optimization scheme where a minimal number of hybrid relationships is chosen to come to a single sub-ontology. All other hybrid relationships are lost. Unless a further detailed optimization scheme is specified, the order in which is chosen is according to the strength of the hybrid relationships.

3 A Walkthrough of a Practical Example

The theoretical rules set out in 2.1 will be used here to demonstrate the solution to a very basic, specific problem, consisting of a base ontology, a scenario (what do we want to achieve), and some requirements (the breakdown of what we want into core elements). Both the initial base ontology and the derived sub-ontology will be given in UML.

3.1 Base Ontology

A rather small and simple ontology has been modeled in Fig. 2. This ontology structures a small part of the publishing world, with a number of simplifications and assumptions to keep the example within an appropriate size frame.

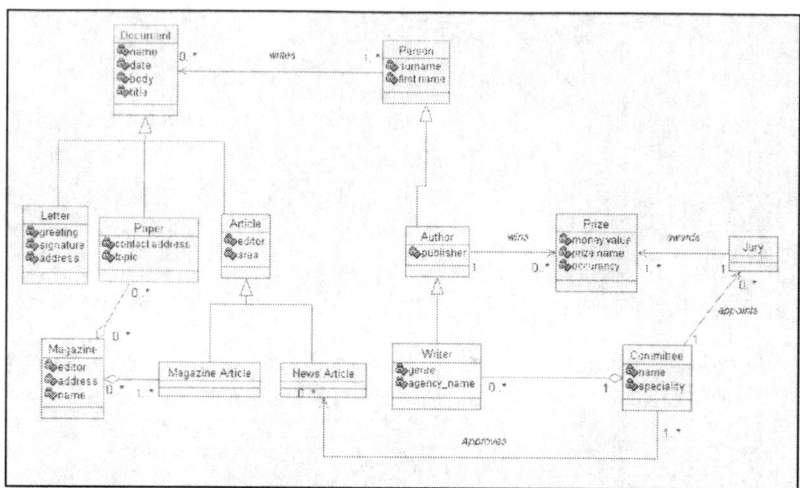

Fig. 1. original base ontology for example

3.2 Example Scenario

In the example scenario presented the base ontology is implemented in a central office, which has a number of magazine daughter companies, amongst others. One of the remote departments has to analyze what magazines won what prizes, when they were won, the consistency throughout time, and so forth. They do not want nor need all the information set out in the big ontology, and because the department is located in a remote office, a local copy of the ontology and data is needed. Here we will go through the process the ontology engineer of the particular department has to go through to derive a consistent sub-ontology from the base ontology.

3.3 Requirements for Solution

For this example, it will be assumed that the ontology engineer has sufficient background knowledge to manually make the conversion from the worded scenario to a low breakdown of the specific requirements. The actual steps to get to these low level core elements has not been given here, as it bears no significance towards proving the practical validity of the derivation rules.

Using this process, as requirements for the low level elements that should be present in the derived sub-ontology, two concepts and attributes out of four concepts are found to be needed. The concepts are **Magazine** and **Prize**, and the attributes are **Address** (attribute of concept Magazine), **Name** (Magazine), **Money Value** (Prize), **Prize Name** (Prize), **Occurrence** (Prize), **Surname** (Person), **First Name** (Person), **Date** (Document), and **Title** (Document).

To get to the solution for the problem that was proposed, four major steps are used in the first sub-process – construction of core elements – and then very briefly the second sub-process – optimization schemes – is demonstrated. For the optimization schemes, we would like to see our solution to display certain conceptual correlations , and also be as quick/simple as possible, so as optimization schemes we have (in order of priority) **conceptual optimization** and **optimization for speed** (here taken equal to **optimization for simplicity**).

3.4 Construction of Core Elements

While constructing these core elements, references to the specific step or rule applied will be given. The list containing the simplified explanation of these references can be found in section 2.

3.4.1 Step 1: Selection of Concepts (2.a)

There are only two concepts that were identified as being important to the sub-ontology. Note that however there were attributes of more concepts than just the two that are proposed now, we do not include these concepts at this stage. Only permanent concepts are identified in this first step.

3.4.2 Step 2: Selection of Attributes (2.b)

Since a list of all the required attributes has already been iterated in section 0, so here the obtained diagram after step 2 is immediately presented.

Fig. 2. Concepts and attributes for sub-ontology

Magazine and **Prize** are considered to be the permanent concepts, while **Document** and **Person** are temporary ones. However, the attributes are necessary in both cases. This means that eventually a solution will need to be sought for the placement of the different attributes. There are three options; either the attributes remain in the temporary concept where they are now, and then the concept becomes permanent as well, or the attributes are moved to one of the permanent concepts (if possible), or finally, the attributes are moved to other, hybrid concepts and these concepts become permanent as well.

The algorithms and rules needed for this decision are also beyond the scope of this paper, but as a simple working rule the following can be used: Attributes can travel along hybrid paths with very strong links, as presented in the theory of hybrid relationships and optimization (see 2.b.i).

The resulting diagram will transform the temporary concept **Document** into a permanent one, and the concept **Person** will be lost completely. The 'floating' attributes of **Person** will be placed as attributes of **Prize**.

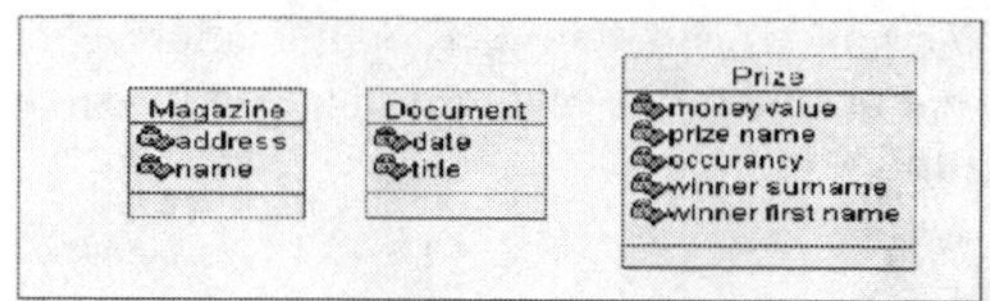

Fig. 3. Permanent attributes and concepts result

3.4.3 Step 3: Characteristics of Hybrid Relationships

In this section all the hybrid relationships will be determined, by following the hybrid paths between the core concepts, and then a number of characteristics have to be worked out for each hybrid relationship. Because of the limited space available here, the characteristics for only one hybrid path are established in this section. The other paths follow a analogue process, and in the appendix (section 6), a full diagram containing the characteristics for all the hybrid relationships, is given.

Step 3.1: Hybrid Relationships (2.c)

The third step in the first sub-process is the most important, and tedious one of all. Not only do we have to establish all the hybrid relationships, but also all the characteristics as defined previously have to be calculated. First all the possible paths between the different concepts will be established.

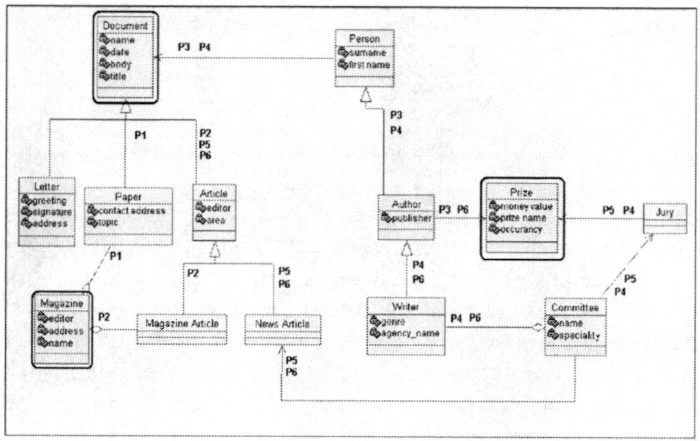

Fig. 4. Base ontology with all the hybrid paths labeled next to the relationships

Path 4

The fourth path is a path between **Document** and **Prize**. Note that we only look in one direction every time. This direction can initially be chosen randomly, but from there on has to be consistent throughout the establishing of the paths, so in this case always from **Document** to **Prize**, and not from **Prize** to **Document**. This means that the same path is not considered into two directions. The path remains always a single one, and is never regarded as a second path (one in the opposite direction).

Path 4 proves to be a longer path if the number of traversed relationships is counted, but, as stated before, this does not necessarily mean it will be a bad option to choose.

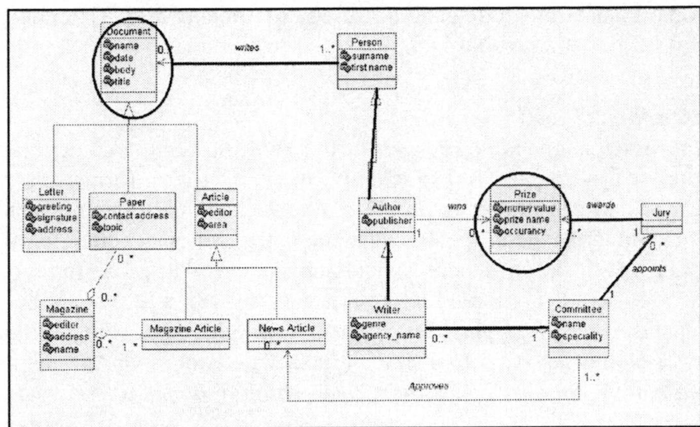

Fig. 5. Hybrid Path 4

<u>*Step 3.2: Characteristics of Hybrid Relationships*</u>

In the previous section, a total of 6 valid hybrid relationships were calculated. Arbitrary numbers were assigned to them, so they can be identified uniquely when specifying the characteristics. The names used in this section will refer to the numbering used in the previous section. As stated in that section already, there is no qualitative significance given to any of the numbers, they are only to identify the paths.

Following the rule for *Sequential Cardinality* (2.c.iii) is fairly straight forward, especially with Fig. 5 as a reference next to it. For Path 4 the following sequential cardinality if found: MU/ID/ID/ON/MA/MU in one direction, and MA/IU/IU/MA/ON/ON in the opposite direction. Note that for the first relation (in this case between **Document** and **Person** the cardinalities for both direction appear as the first ones in their respective lists, i.e. to follow the second one, it has to be read from right to left, going from **Person** to **Document**).

The easiest way of getting to the *Extended Combined Cardinality* (2.c.v) is by putting the individual cardinalities in a table, and defining the minimum and maximum cardinalities for that type of connection.

As with all the other characteristics, the direction in which they are taken does not matter, but as soon as a choice has been made, it needs to be consistent throughout the hybrid relationships between those two concepts.

Table 2. Extended Combined Cardinality for Path 4

	Min	Max		Min	Max
MU	-	M	MA	0	M
ID	0	-	IU	-	-
ID	0	-	IU	-	-
ON	-	-	MA	0	M
MA	0	M	ON	-	-
MU	-	M	ON	-	-

This results in the following ECC for Path 4: **MA(3,3) & MA(2,2)**.

Again, the same method can be used to obtain the Extended Combined Cardinalities for the other paths.

Lexical description (3.c.vi)
The lexical description is very useful to give the ontology engineer a good understanding of what the links actually mean. The information provided by extended combined cardinality is purely mathematical, and does not lend itself very well to human understandability. Because the optimization scheme that was chosen – the conceptual optimization – these lexical descriptions will prove to be of the highest importance. The rather simple grammatical rules [4] will be applied to the six identified paths we have, and for path 4 this will result in following lexical description: *A Document is written by a Person, who can be an Author, who can be a Writer, who can be member of a Committee, which appoints a Jury, which awards a Prize.*

Since the choice of our optimization was conceptual optimization, the ontology engineer just looks at the meaning of these paths, not even considering to what previous grouping they belong. Using the extended combined cardinalities and selected secondary optimization schemes, an optimized solution can then be found.

3.4.4 Step 4: Selection of Hybrid Relationships

In the example requirements that were given, it was said that the views that needed to be made would provide information on the prizes that were won by magazines. The ontology engineer can gain extra information from the managers as to what they consider prizes connected to a magazine, since there are two possible paths from documents to magazine, and both types of documents can possibly win prizes. The managers explain that when an article of any kind wins a prize, that prize is considered to be connected to the magazine, because the name of the magazine will appear in the prize credentials. However, this is not the case for published papers in a magazine, because they usually win a prize first (independently), and only then are published, and potentially by multiple magazines.

This clarification makes the ontology engineer decide that path 1 is not a hybrid relationship that is wanted in the sub-ontology, because prizes connected to a magazine in that fashion should be disregarded anyway. However, path 2 is essential for the working of the sub-ontology. The result is that path 2 is marked as permanent, and path 1 as a definite deletion (even if that would mean the end result would be 2 sub-ontologies instead of one), since it has no connection in the sense of the sub-ontology.

Similarly, it can be concluded by the ontology engineer that all connections going through an actual committee are not what is wanted, thus excluding path 4, 5 and 6. This leaves path 3, which seems what is wanted, but let us assume that the ontology engineer is not sure of this anymore, and thus marks that hybrid relationship as a 'maybe'.

3.4.5 Final Solution Stage

After considering all these steps, and mostly the selection of the hybrid relationships, a single, consistent sub-ontology is built. In the first attempt, only the permanent hybrid relationships are used, since secondary optimization is optimization for simplicity, thus the less relationships, the better. However, it is found that there is no remaining connection between the island containing the concepts **Document** and **Magazine**, and the island containing the concept **Prize**. In this case, this can be concluded easily by just looking at the diagram, but for very complex diagrams, where the visual connectivity might not be as rudimentary, algorithms can be worked out that calculate this automatically, without human interference (very similar again to some networking algorithms).

After including the temporary (marked as 'maybe') hybrid relationships it is found that with inclusion of path 3 a consistent sub-ontology is obtained. Since the secondary optimization was simplicity, no further is looked for more hybrid relationships to add (in this case, there was only 1 temporary path anyway).

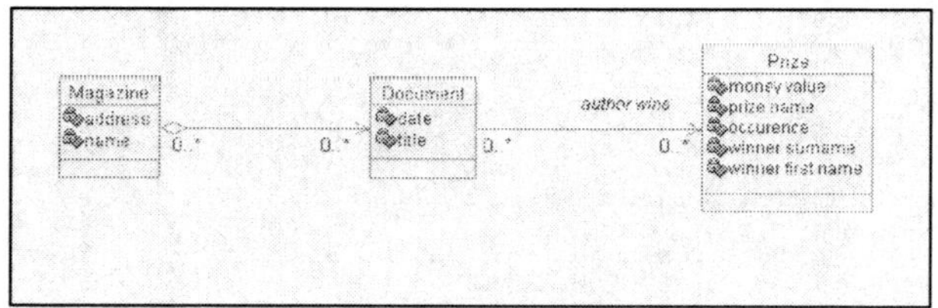

Fig. 6. Final solution

The UML design presented in Fig. 9 is the final solution after optimization. By using such a simplistic example with simple solution it can be easily followed how the steps logically direct engineers towards a good solution, in a well-defined, scalable manner, which would also work for very large ontologies and sub-ontologies.

4 Conclusion

This paper established a more practical approach to the theoretical rules for ontology derivation presented in earlier research [5], [6] and [7]. By showing how all the small rules are broken down into segments that can manually be worked out, the theory will become easier to understand. This paper also provided some information about the possibilities for automation of most of these steps, through indicating similar algorithms already used in different areas of research (such as network routing algorithms).

Using UML designs as a starting point, but also as an end result, it is both shown that the derived sub-ontology is an independent design, as well as the versatility for implementation, as the UML designs can be ported to many platforms and languages.

References

1. Meersman R.: Ontology for Database Semantics. Vrije Universiteit Brussels, seminar at La Trobe University (April 6, 2001)
2. Klein M., Fensel D: Ontology Versioning on the Semantic Web. Proceedings of the Semantic Web Working Symposium (2001)

3. Heflin J., Hendler J.: Dynamic Ontologies on the Web. In Proceedings of American Association for Artificial Intelligence Conference (AAAI-2000)
4. Heflin J., Hendler J., Luke S.: Coping with Changing Ontologies in a Distributed Environment. . Ontology Management. Papers from the AAAI Workshop. WS-99-13. AAAI Press. pp. 74-79 (1999)
5. Wouters C., Dillon T., Rahayu W., Chang E.: Transformational Processes for Sub-Ontology Extraction. (submitted for publication, 2002)
6. Wouters C., Dillon T., Rahayu W., Chang E.: Stepwise Construction of Core Elements for Ontology Derivation Rules. (submitted for publication, 2002)
7. Wouters C., Dillon T., Rahayu W., Chang E.: A Comparison of Versioning and Extraction of Ontologies, using the General Sequential Derivation Diagram. (submitted for publication, 2002)

Appendix: Characteristics Model

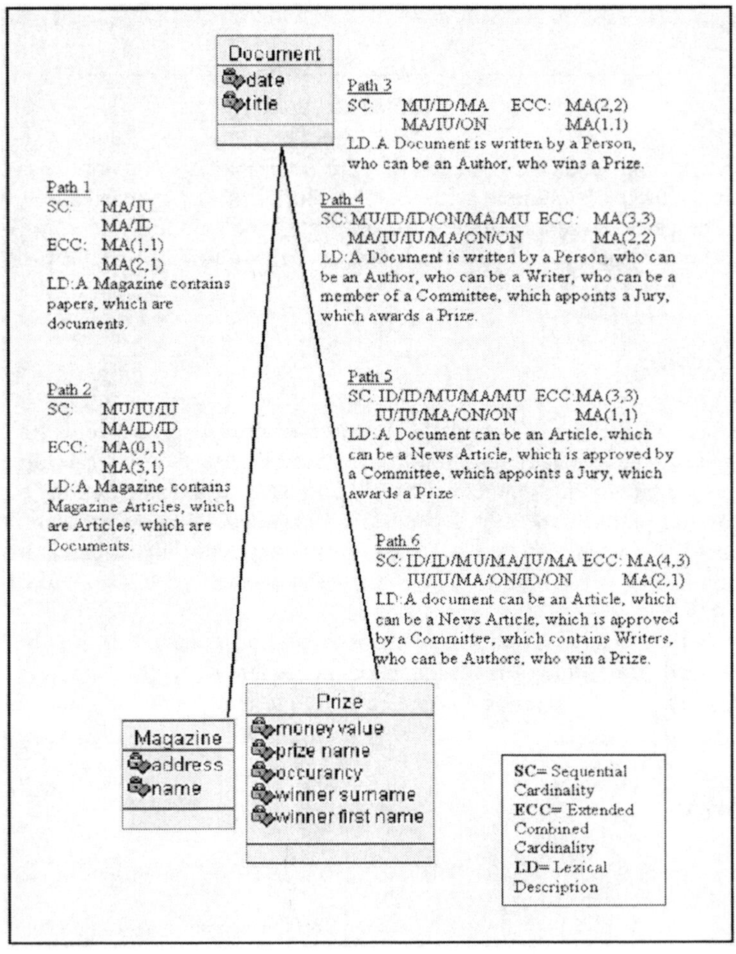

What's Hard about XML Schema Constraints?

Marcelo Arenas[1], Wenfei Fan[2], and Leonid Libkin[1]

[1] Department of Computer Science, University of Toronto.
{marenas,libkin}@cs.toronto.edu
[2] Bell Laboratories
wenfei@research.bell-labs.com

Abstract. Data description for XML usually comes in the form of a type specification (e.g., a DTD) together with integrity constraints. XML Schema allows one to mix DTD features with semantic information, such as keys and foreign keys. It was shown recently [2,7] that the interaction of DTDs with constraints may be rather nontrivial. In particular, testing if a general specification is consistent is undecidable, but for the most common case of single-attribute constraints it is NP-complete, and linear time if no foreign keys are present.
However, XML Schema design did not adopt the form of constraints prevalent in the database literature, and slightly changed the semantics of keys, foreign keys, and unique constraints. In this paper we demonstrate the very costly effect of this slight change on the feasibility of consistency checking. In particular, all the known hardness results extend to the XML Schema case, but tractability results do not. We show that even without foreign keys, and with very simple DTD features, checking consistency of XML-Schema specifications is intractable.

1 Introduction

Any data-central system must provide a data definition language as well as a data manipulation language. For commercial relational DBMSs, these languages are well-understood. As a lot of data is becoming available in XML [11], and much of database research focus is shifting from the traditional relational model to semistructured data and XML [1,6,5,9,10], it is important to understand new issues that arise in the context of describing and querying XML.

One such issue is the semantics of XML data specifications. Traditionally, XML data was described by DTDs [11][1]. But just as in the relational context, where simple SQL's `create table` must be supplemented with various constraints to provide semantic information, constraints must be added to XML specifications as well. Most of the proposals deal with constraints similar to those found in relational databases: keys and foreign keys [3,4,12]. However, unlike traditional relational constraints, XML keys and foreign keys interact in a nontrivial way with DTDs, allowing one to write seemingly perfect specifications that nevertheless are *inconsistent*: no document can satisfy them.

[1] Throughout the paper, by a DTD we mean its type specification; we ignore its ID/IDREF constraints since their limitations have been well recognized [3].

R. Cicchetti et al. (Eds.): DEXA 2002, LNCS 2453, pp. 269–278, 2002.

In [2,7], we studied this problem, and demonstrated the following. First, if arbitrary keys and foreign keys are added to DTDs, the consistency problem is undecidable. Second, with the restriction to one-attribute constraints (*unary* constraints, by far the most common in practice), the problem is intractable: depending on the exact flavor of constraints, it is anywhere from NP-complete (simple element-type absolute constraints [7]) to PSPACE-hard (regular-expression-based constraints [2]) to undecidable (relative constraints [2]). However, without foreign keys, the problem is tractable: it is solvable in *linear* time.

Those results were shown for DTDs and (foreign) keys. These days, the prime standard for specifying XML data is *XML Schema* [14]. It is a rather rich language that supports specifications of both types and integrity constraints. Its types subsume DTDs [11], and its constraints – even keys and foreign keys – have a slightly different semantics from what has been primarily studied in the database literature. In this paper we investigate specifications that consist of a DTD and a set of constraints with the semantics proposed by XML Schema. We show that this little change of semantics complicates things considerably, as far as consistency checking is concerned.

We say that an XML document satisfies a specification if and only if it conforms to the DTD and satisfies the constraints, and that a specification is *consistent* if there is a document that conforms to it. A specification may be inconsistent due to the interaction between the type and the constraint parts.

As an example, consider a specification in XML Schema $S_1 = (D_1, \Sigma_1)$, where D_1 is a simple DTD describing insurance policies for a transportation vehicle and Σ_1 is a set of keys and foreign keys:

D_1:
```
<!ELEMENT  vehicle  ((registr | plate), policy, policy)>
<!ATTLIST  registr  num  CDATA  #REQUIRED>
<!ATTLIST  plate    num  CDATA  #REQUIRED>
<!ATTLIST  policy   ref  CDATA  #REQUIRED>
```

Σ_1: $(vehicle/registr \cup vehicle/plate,\ \{@num\})$,
$(vehicle/policy,\ \{@ref\})$,
$(vehicle/policy,\ \{@ref\}) \subseteq_{FK} (vehicle/registr \cup vehicle/plate,\ \{@num\})$

Here we omit the definition of elements whose type is string. The DTD says that each vehicle must present either a registration number or a plate number, and must purchase two insurance policies. The first constraint in Σ_1 is a key asserting that each vehicle can be uniquely identified by either its registration number or its plate number[2]. The second constraint, another key, says that the policies should use different references. The third constraint in Σ_1 is a foreign key. It says that a policy reference must be either the registration number or the plate number. This schema is inconsistent: on one hand, as indicated in Figs. 1 (a) and (b), for any XML document conforming to the DTD D_1, the `vehicle` element must have either a `registr` or a `plate` subelement, but it cannot have both; on the other hand, the constraints enforce the presence of both a `registr` subelement and a `plate` subelement, since otherwise two `policy` references cannot be distinct. As a result, there is no XML document that both

[2] We define the syntax and semantics of keys and foreign keys in Sec. 2.2.

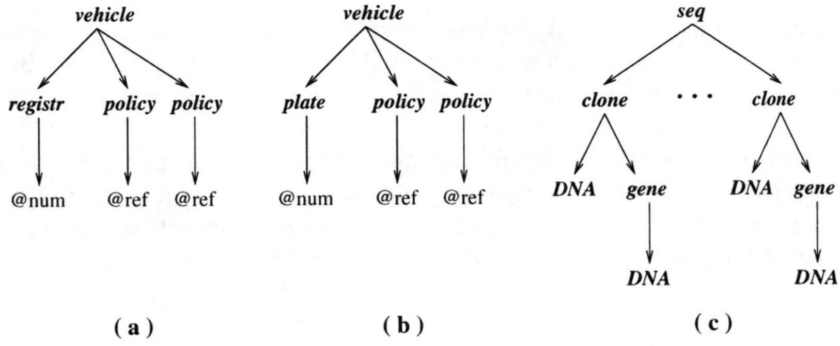

Fig. 1. XML documents (represented as trees) conforming to DTDs D_1 and D_2

conforms to D_1 and satisfies Σ_1. This example demonstrates that the DTD and constraints in an XML-Schema specification may interact with each other, and the interaction leads to the inconsistency of the specification.

Worse still, a specification in XML Schema may not be consistent even in the absence of foreign keys. As another example, consider the following specification $S_2 = (D_2, \Sigma_2)$ for biomedical data:

D_2:
```
<!ELEMENT  seq   (clone+)>
<!ELEMENT  clone (DNA, gene)>
<!ELEMENT  gene  (DNA)>
```
Σ_2: $(seq/clone, \{//DNA\})$

The DTD describes a nonempty sequence of `clone` elements: each `clone` has a `DNA` subelement and a `gene` subelement, and `gene` in turn has a `DNA` subelement, while `DNA` carries text data (PCDATA). The key in Σ_2 attempts to enforce the following semantic information: there exist no two `clone` elements that have the same `DNA` no matter where the `DNA` appears as their descendant. Again this specification is inconsistent. To see this, recall that XML Schema requires that for any XML document satisfying a key, the "fields" (that is, `//DNA` in our example) must *exist* and be *unique*. However, as depicted in Fig. 1 (c), in any XML document that conforms to the DTD D_2, a `clone` element must have two `DNA` descendants. Thus, it violates the uniqueness requirement of the key in Σ_2.

Is it possible to test consistency of an XML-Schema specification at compile time? That is, given a specification (D, Σ), whether or not there exists an XML document that both conforms to the DTD D and satisfies the constraints Σ. We refer to this problem as the *consistency problem* for XML Schema. The question is important as one wants to know whether or not a specification makes sense before attempting to create or validate an XML document w.r.t. it.

The central technical problem investigated in this paper is the consistency problem for XML Schema. Our *main conclusion* is that the semantics of keys and foreign keys in XML-Schema makes the consistency analysis rather intricate and intractable. Indeed, all the hardness and undecidability results of [2,7] carry over to specifications of XML Schema. However, using a new technique, we show that the most important tractable cases under the standard key semantics, become intractable under the semantics of XML Schema. We also identify several restrictions, commonly used in practice, that still allow relatively-efficient consistency checking.

Organization. Sec. 2 introduces a formalism for XML-Schema specifications. We show in Sec. 3 that the consistency problem is highly intricate in general. In Sec. 4 we identify restricted cases that allow relatively efficient consistency checking. We summarize our results in Sec. 5. Proofs can be found in [15].

2 XML Schema

XML Schema [14] defines both a type system and a class of integrity constraints. Its type system subsumes DTDs. It supports a variety of atomic types (e.g., string, integer, float, double, byte), complex type constructs (e.g., sequence, choice) and inheritance mechanisms (e.g., extension, restriction). Its integrity constraints include keys, foreign keys and unique constraints. In XML Schema, a specification for XML data consists of a type and a set of integrity constraints.

The goal of this paper is to understand how types interact with integrity constraints under the XML-Schema semantics. To focus on the nature of the interaction and to simplify the discussion, we consider XML-Schema specifications in which the type is a DTD and the constraints are simple keys and foreign keys[3]. We show that even in this simple setting, the interaction is already highly intricate such that the consistency check of XML-Schema specifications is infeasible. Note that in practice, an XML-Schema specification typically consists of a mild extension of a DTD as its type, as well as simple keys and foreign keys.

In this section, we first provide a formalism of DTDs, and then define keys and foreign keys under the XML-Schema semantics.

2.1 DTDs and XML Trees

Following [5,7], we formalize the definition of DTDs as follows. A *DTD* (Document Type Definition) is a tuple $D = (E, A, P, R, r)$, where:

- E is a finite set of *element types*;
- A is a finite set of *attributes*, disjoint from E.
- For each $\tau \in E$, $P(\tau)$ is a regular expression α, called the *element type definition* of τ: $\alpha \;::=\; \mathtt{S} \mid \tau' \mid \epsilon \mid \alpha|\alpha \mid \alpha, \alpha \mid \alpha^*$, where S denotes the *string* type, $\tau' \in E$, ϵ is the empty word, and "|", "," and "*" denote union, concatenation, and the Kleene closure;
- For each $\tau \in E$, $R(\tau)$ is a set of attributes in A;
- $r \in E$ and is called *the element type of the root*.

We normally denote element types by τ and attributes by $@l$, and assume that r does not appear in $P(\tau)$ for any $\tau \in E$. We also assume that each τ in $E \setminus \{r\}$

[3] We do not consider *relative* keys and foreign keys [2,3] here as the simple constraints suffice to demonstrate the complications caused by their interaction with types.

is *connected to* r, i.e., either τ appears in $P(r)$, or it appears in $P(\tau')$ for some τ' that is connected to r.

For example, recall the two DTDs D_1, D_2 given in the previous section. These DTDs can be naturally expressed in the formalism given above.

Given a DTD $D = (E, A, P, R, r)$, a *path* in D is a string $w_1 \cdots w_m$ over the alphabet $E \cup A \cup \{\mathtt{S}\}$ such that w_{i+1} is a symbol in the alphabet of $P(w_i)$ for each $i \in [1, m-2]$, and $w_m \in R(w_{m-1})$ or w_m is a symbol in the alphabet of $P(w_{m-1})$. Let $Paths(D) = \{p \mid p \text{ is a path in } D\}$. We say that a DTD is *non-recursive* if $Paths(D)$ is finite, and recursive otherwise. We also say that D is a *no-star* DTD if the Kleene star does not occur in any regular expression $P(\tau)$.

An XML document is typically modeled as a node-labeled tree. Below we describe valid XML documents of a DTD along the same lines as XML Schema [14].

Let $D = (E, A, P, R, r)$ be a DTD. An *XML tree* T *conforming to* D, written $T \models D$, is defined to be $(V, lab, ele, att, val, root)$, where

- V is a finite set of *nodes*;
- lab is a function that maps each node in V to a label in $E \cup A \cup \{\mathtt{S}\}$; a node $v \in V$ is called an *element of type* τ if $lab(v) = \tau$ and $\tau \in E$, an *attribute* if $lab(v) \in A$, and a *text node* if $lab(v) = \mathtt{S}$;
- ele is a function that for any $\tau \in E$, maps each element v of type τ to a (possibly empty) list $[v_1, ..., v_n]$ of elements and text nodes in V such that $lab(v_1) \ldots lab(v_n)$ is in the regular language defined by $P(\tau)$;
- att is a partial function from $V \times A$ to V such that for any $v \in V$ and $@l \in A$, $att(v, @l)$ is defined iff $lab(v) = \tau$, $\tau \in E$ and $@l \in R(\tau)$;
- val is a partial function from V to string values such that for any node $v \in V$, $val(v)$ is defined iff $lab(v) = \mathtt{S}$ or $lab(v) \in A$;
- $root$ is the root of T, $root \in V$ and $lab(root) = r$.

For any node $v \in V$, if $ele(v)$ is defined, then the nodes v' in $ele(v)$ are called the *subelements* of v. For any $@l \in A$, if $att(v, @l) = v'$, then v' is called *an attribute* of v. In either case we say that there is a *parent-child edge* from v to v'. The subelements and attributes of v are called its *children*. The graph defined by the parent-child relation is required to be a rooted tree.

For example, Figs. 1 (a) and (b) depict two XML trees that conform to the DTD D_1, and Fig. 1 (c) shows an XML tree that conforms to D_2.

In an XML tree T, the root is a unique node labeled with r. The subelements of an element of τ are ordered and their labels observe the regular expression $P(\tau)$. In contrast, its attributes are unordered and are identified by their labels. The function val assigns string values to attributes and to nodes labeled $\mathtt{S}$.

2.2 Keys and Foreign Keys

Given a DTD $D = (E, A, P, R, r)$, a *key over* D is a constraint of the form

$$(P, \{Q_1, \ldots, Q_n\}), \tag{1}$$

where $n \geq 1$ and P, Q_1, ..., Q_n are regular expressions over the alphabet $E \cup A \cup \{\mathtt{S}\}$. Expression P is called the *selector* of the key and is a regular expression conforming to the following BNF grammar [14].

$$\begin{array}{lll} \textit{selector} & ::= \textit{path} \mid \textit{path} \cup \textit{selector} \\ \textit{path} & ::= r//\textit{sequence} \mid \textit{sequence} \\ \textit{sequence} & ::= \tau \mid \_ \mid \textit{sequence}/\textit{sequence} \end{array}$$

Here _ is a wildcard that matches any element type, $\tau \in E$ and // represents the Kleene closure of _, that is, any possible finite sequence of node labels. The expressions $Q_1, \ldots, Q_n$ are called the *fields* of the key and are defined by [14]:

$$\begin{array}{lll} \textit{field} & ::= \textit{path} \mid \textit{path} \cup \textit{field} \\ \textit{path} & ::= //\textit{sequence}/\textit{last} \mid /\textit{sequence}/\textit{last} \\ \textit{sequence} & ::= \epsilon \mid \tau \mid \_ \mid \textit{sequence}/\textit{sequence} \\ \textit{last} & ::= \mathtt{S} \mid @l \mid @\_ \end{array}$$

Here @_ is a wildcard that matches any attribute and $@l \in A$. This grammar differs from the one above in restricting the final step to match a text node or an attribute. A key containing exactly one field is called *unary*.

It should be mentioned that XML Schema expresses selectors and fields with *restricted* fragments of XPath [13], which are precisely the regular expressions defined above. In XPath, '_' represents *child* and '//' denotes *descendant*[4].

A *foreign key* over a DTD D is an expression of the form

$$(P, \{Q_1, \ldots, Q_n\}) \subseteq_{FK} (U, \{S_1, \ldots, S_n\}), \tag{2}$$

where P and U are the selectors of the foreign key, $n \geq 1$ and $Q_1, \ldots, Q_n, S_1, \ldots, S_n$ are its fields. A foreign key containing one field in its left hand side and one field in its right hand side is called *unary*.

To define the notion of satisfaction of keys and foreign keys, we need to introduce some additional notation. Any pair of nodes x, y in an XML tree T with y a descendant of x uniquely determines the path, $\rho(x, y)$, from x to y. We say that y is *reachable* from x by following a regular expression β over D, denoted by $T \models \beta(x, y)$, iff $\rho(x, y) \in \beta$. For any fixed T, let $\textit{nodes}_\beta(x)$ stand for the set of nodes reachable from a node x by following the regular expression β: $\textit{nodes}_\beta(x) = \{y \mid T \models \beta(x, y)\}$. If there is only one node y such that $T \models \beta(x, y)$, then we define $x.\beta = y$.

Definition 1. *Given an XML tree $T = (V, \textit{lab}, \textit{ele}, \textit{att}, \textit{val}, \textit{root})$, T satisfies a key $(P, \{Q_1, \ldots, Q_n\})$, denoted by $T \models (P, \{Q_1, \ldots, Q_n\})$, if*

1. *For each $x \in \textit{nodes}_P(\textit{root})$ and $i \in [1, n]$, there is exactly one node y_i such that $T \models Q_i(x, y_i)$. Furthermore, $\textit{lab}(y_i) \in A$ or $\textit{lab}(y_i) = \mathtt{S}$.*
2. *For each $x_1, x_2 \in \textit{nodes}_P(\textit{root})$, if $\textit{val}(x_1.Q_i) = \textit{val}(x_2.Q_i)$ for all $i \in [1, n]$, then $x_1 = x_2$.*

That is, the values of $Q_1, \ldots, Q_n$ uniquely identify the nodes reachable from the root by following path P. It further asserts that starting from each one of these nodes there is a single path conforming to the regular expression Q_i ($i \in [1, n]$).

[4] XPath [13] uses '*' to denote wildcard. Here we use '_' instead to avoid overloading the symbol '*' with the Kleene star found in DTDs.

Definition 2. *An XML tree* $T = (V, lab, ele, att, val, root)$ *satisfies a foreign key* $(P, \{Q_1, \ldots, Q_n\}) \subseteq_{FK} (U, \{S_1, \ldots, S_n\})$*, denoted by* $T \models (P, \{Q_1, \ldots, Q_n\}) \subseteq_{FK} (U, \{S_1, \ldots, S_n\})$*, if* $T \models (U, \{S_1, \ldots, S_n\})$ *and*

1. *For each* $x \in nodes_P(root)$ *and* $i \in [1, n]$*, there is exactly one node* y_i *such that* $T \models Q_i(x, y_i)$*. Furthermore,* $lab(y_i) \in A$ *or* $lab(y_i) = \mathtt{S}$*.*
2. *For each* $x \in nodes_P(root)$ *there exists a node* $x' \in nodes_U(root)$ *such that* $val(x.Q_i) = val(x'.S_i)$ *for each* $i \in [1, n]$*.*

The foreign key asserts that $(U, \{S_1, \ldots, S_n\})$ is a key and that for every node x reachable from the root by following path P, there is a node x' reachable from the root by following path U such that the $Q_1, \ldots, Q_n$-values of x are equal to the $S_1, \ldots, S_n$-values of x'.

Observe that condition 1 of Defs. 1 and 2 requires the *uniqueness* and *existence* of the fields involved. For example, the XML tree depicted in Fig. 1 (c) does not satisfy the key $(seq/clone, \{//DNA\})$ because the uniqueness condition imposed by the key is violated. Uniqueness conditions are required by the XML Schema semantics, but they are not present in various earlier proposals for XML keys coming from the database community [3,4,7,2].

Given an XML tree T and a set of keys and foreign keys Σ, we say that T satisfies Σ, denoted by $T \models \Sigma$, if $T \models \varphi$ for each $\varphi \in \Sigma$.

3 Consistency Problem: The General Case

We are interested in the consistency, or satisfiability, problem for XML-Schema specifications; that is, whether a given set of constraints and a DTD are satisfiable by an XML tree. Formally, for a class $\mathcal{C}$ of integrity constraints and a class $\mathcal{D}$ of DTDs, the input of the *consistency problem* $\mathsf{SAT}(\mathcal{D}, \mathcal{C})$ is a DTD $D \in \mathcal{D}$ and a set of constraints $\Sigma \subseteq \mathcal{C}$ and the problem is to determine whether there is an XML tree T such that $T \models D$ and $T \models \Sigma$.

The same problem was considered in [7]. The constraint language introduced there is properly contained in the language defined in the previous section. Given a DTD D, element types τ, τ' and attributes $@l_1, \ldots, @l_n$, $@l'_1, \ldots, @l'_n$, keys and foreign keys in [7] are of the form

$$(r//\tau, \{@l_1, \ldots, @l_n\}), \tag{3}$$

$$(r//\tau, \{@l_1, \ldots, @l_n\}) \subseteq_{FK} (r//\tau', \{@l'_1, \ldots, @l'_n\}), \tag{4}$$

respectively. Then, from [7] we immediately derive:

Corollary 1. *The consistency problem for XML-Schema specifications, i.e., arbitrary DTDs and keys, foreign keys of the form (1) and (2), is undecidable.*

Observe that given an XML tree T conforming to a DTD D, for every node x reachable from the root by following a path $r//\tau$, there exists exactly one node reachable from x by following a path $@l_i$, which correspond to the attribute $@l_i$ of x. In this case, to check the consistency of an XML-Schema specification one does not need to consider the first condition of Defs. 1 and 2. Also from results of [7], for keys of such a form alone, and for arbitrary DTDs, there exists a *linear time* algorithm for the consistency problem.

However, none of the previous results give us any hint as to what happens when the first condition of Defs. 1 is imposed on arbitrary XML-Schema keys. Somewhat surprisingly, this extra condition makes the problem intractable, even for unary keys and very simple DTDs. By using a reduction from SAT-CNF [8], we can show the following:

Theorem 1. *The consistency problem is NP-hard for unary keys of form (1) and for non-recursive and no-star DTDs.* □

From these one can see that the consistency analysis is impossible for general XML-Schema specifications, and it is still not practical even if only unary keys are considered. In light of these we consider restricted cases of specifications in the next section, by imposing restrictions on the fields of keys and foreign keys.

4 Consistency Problem: A Restricted Case

In this section we study a class of XML-Schema constraints that are commonly found in practice, and investigate their consistency analysis. More specifically, we consider keys and foreign keys of the form

$$(P, \{@l_1, \ldots, @l_n\}), \tag{5}$$

$$(P, \{@l_1, \ldots, @l_n\}) \subseteq_{FK} (U, \{@l'_1, \ldots, @l'_n\}), \tag{6}$$

where P and U are regular expressions defined by the BNF grammar for *selector* expressions given in the previous section. Furthermore, if these constrains are defined over a DTD $D = (E, A, P, R, r)$, then they must satisfy the following *existence condition*: for each $\tau \in \mathit{last}(P)$, $\{@l_1, \ldots, @l_n\} \subseteq R(\tau)$, and for each $\tau' \in \mathit{last}(U)$, $\{@l'_1, \ldots, @l'_n\} \subseteq R(\tau')$, where $\mathit{last}(P)$ is the set of element types that are the last symbol of some string in the regular language defined by P. Note that these conditions can be checked in polynomial time.

Observe that the keys and foreign keys satisfying these conditions trivially satisfy requirement 1 of Defs. 1 and 2. For this kind of constraints, one can show the following by reduction to the emptiness problem of finite state automata.

Proposition 1. *For keys of the form (5) satisfying the existence condition and for arbitrary DTDs, the consistency problem is decidable in linear time.*

In practice, *unary* constraints are most commonly used, with the form:

$$(P, \{@l\}), \tag{7}$$

$$(P, \{@l\}) \subseteq_{FK} (U, \{@l'\}). \tag{8}$$

The next result tells us that when constraints are restricted to be unary and defined with attributes, the consistency problem is decidable even in the presence of foreign keys. This follows from results of [2]. However, the complexity is very high.

Proposition 2. *For constraints of the form (7), (8) satisfying the existence condition and for arbitrary DTDs, the consistency problem is PSPACE-hard and decidable.*

Obviously it is completely impractical to solve a PSPACE-hard problem. Thus one may want to consider further restrictions to get lower complexity. One approach is to further restrict constraints. Observe that constraints of the form (3) and (4) are a restriction of (7) and (8): P and U are required to be of the form $(r//\tau)$ for some element type τ. This helps, but not much: from [7] we get:

Proposition 3. *The consistency problem for unary constraints of form (3) and (4) is NP-complete for arbitrary DTDs, and is in PTIME for a fixed DTD.*

Note that Proposition 3 does not require the existence condition as it can be checked in linear time for constraints of form (3) and (4). The motivation for considering a fixed DTD is because in practice, one often defines the DTD of a specification at one time, but writes constraints in stages: constraints are added incrementally when new requirements are discovered.

Alternatively, one may want to further restrict the DTDs involved. However, this again does not help much: even under some rather severe restriction on DTDs, the consistency problem remains intractable. More precisely, we show that even if DTDs contain a fixed number of elements and attributes, the consistency problem for unary keys and foreign keys is NP-hard.

Let $k > 0$ be a fixed constant and let $\mathcal{D}_k$ be the class of DTDs $D = (E, A, P, R, r)$ such that $|E \cup A| \leq k$.

Theorem 2. *If $\mathcal{C}$ is the class of unary keys and foreign of the form (7), (8) satisfying the existence condition, then for each $k \geq 11$, $\mathsf{SAT}(\mathcal{D}_k, \mathcal{C})$ is NP-hard.*

This again is a new result that does not follow from previously published results on the consistency checking for XML.

5 Conclusion

We have shown that the semantics of XML-Schema constraints makes the consistency analysis of specifications rather intricate. The main results of the paper are summarized in Fig. 2, which indicate that static consistency checking for XML-Schema specifications is very hard: in general it is beyond reach (undecidable); for extremely restricted DTDs and constraints, it is still rather expensive

	DTD [7]	XML Schema
Keys and foreign keys	undecidable	undecidable
Unary keys and foreign keys	NP-complete	PSPACE-hard
Keys only	linear time	NP-hard
No constraints	linear time	linear time

Fig. 2. Complexity of the consistency problem

(NP-hard and PSPACE-hard). In particular, with only unary keys, the consistency problem is NP-hard under the XML-Schema semantics, in contrast to its linear-time decidability under the standard key semantics [2,7].

These negative results tell us that under the current semantics of XML-Schema constraints, there is no hope to efficiently check whether or not an XML-Schema specification makes sense. One may find that a seemingly perfect specification turns out to be inconsistent, after repeated failures to validate documents. The designers of XML Schema might want to take these results into account when revising the W3C recommendation.

Acknowledgments

Marcelo Arenas and Leonid Libkin are supported in part by grants from the Natural Sciences and Engineering Research Council of Canada and from Bell University Laboratories. Wenfei Fan is currently on leave from Temple University, and is supported in part by NSF Career Award IIS-0093168.

References

1. S. Abiteboul, P. Buneman and D. Suciu *Data on the Web: From Relations to Semistructured Data and XML.* Morgan Kaufman, 2000.
2. M. Arenas, W. Fan and L. Libkin. On verifying consistency of XML specifications. In *PODS'02*, pages 259–270.
3. P. Buneman, S. Davidson, W. Fan, C. Hara and W. Tan. Keys for XML. In *WWW'10*, 2001, pages 201–210.
4. P. Buneman, S. Davidson, W. Fan, C. Hara and W. Tan. Reasoning about Keys for XML. In *DBPL*, 2001.
5. D. Calvanese, G. De Giacomo, and M. Lenzerini. Representing and reasoning on XML documents: A description logic approach. *J. Logic and Computation* 9(3):295–318, 1999.
6. S. Ceri, P. Fraternali, S. Paraboschi. XML: Current developments and future challenges for the database community. In *EDBT 2000*, pages 3–17.
7. W. Fan and L. Libkin. On XML integrity constraints in the presence of DTDs. In *PODS'01*, pages 114–125.
8. M. Garey and D. Johnson. *Computers and Intractability: A Guide to the Theory of NP-Completeness.* W. H. Freeman and Company, 1979.
9. D. Lee and W. W. Chu. Constraints-preserving transformation from XML document type definition to relational schema. In *ER'2000*, pages 323–338.
10. V. Vianu. A Web odyssey: From Codd to XML. In *PODS'01*, pages 1–15.
11. W3C. Extensible Markup Language (XML) 1.0. W3C Recommendation, Feb. 1998.
12. W3C. XML-Data, W3C Working Draft, Jan. 1998.
13. W3C. XML Path Language (XPath). W3C Working Draft, Nov. 1999.
14. W3C. XML Schema. W3C Recommendation, May 2001.
15. Full version: `http://www.cs.toronto.edu/~marenas/publications/xsc.pdf`.

Application of rUID in Processing XML Queries on Structure and Keyword

Dao Dinh Kha[1], Masatoshi Yoshikawa[1,2], and Shunsuke Uemura[1]

[1] Graduate School of Information Science, Nara Institute of Science and Technology
8916-5 Takayama, Ikoma, Nara 630-0101, Japan
[2] Information Technology Center, Nagoya University
Furo-cho, Chikusa-ku, Nagoya 464-8601, Japan

Abstract. Applying numbering schemes to simulate the structure of XML data is a promising technique for XML query processing. In this paper, we describe SKEYRUS, a system, which enables the integrated structure-keyword searches on XML data using the rUID numbering scheme. rUID has been designed to be robust in structural update and applicable to arbitrarily large XML documents. SKEYRUS accepts XPath expressions containing word-containment predicates as the input, therefore the query expressiveness is significantly extended. The structural feature and the ability to generate XPath axes of rUID are exploited in query processing. Preliminary performance results of SKEYRUS were also reported.

1 Introduction

Presently, Extensive Markup Language (XML) [13] has become a framework for structural information exchange over the Internet. Processing XML data requires new techniques different from the techniques applied in relational databases. XML elements must be assigned unique identifiers in order to be distinguished from each other. In addition, the structure of XML documents may change when elements are inserted or removed. Therefore, an effective mechanism, which can not only generate robust element identifiers but also maintain the information about the structure of XML documents, is essential for processing XML queries. Using a numbering scheme, which generates the identifiers of XML elements in such manner that the hierarchical order within XML documents can be re-established based on the element identifiers, can meet the requirement.

Several numbering schemes for XML data have been proposed in [2,?,?,?]. Among these schemes, the *Unique Identifier* (UID) technique that uses a k-ary tree to enumerate nodes in an XML tree has an interesting property whereby the identifier of a parent node can be determined based on the identifiers of its child nodes. This property is promising in evaluating XML queries because it enables an effective re-establishment of hierarchical order within a tree.

However, the UID technique is not robust in structural update. Furthermore, the value of UID easily exceeds the maximal manageable integer value. In [3], the *recursive UID* numbering scheme has been proposed so as to remove the

R. Cicchetti et al. (Eds.): DEXA 2002, LNCS 2453, pp. 279–289, 2002.

above-mentioned drawbacks. Besides the property that the identifier of a parent node can be determined based on the identifiers of its child nodes, rUID is robust for structural update and applicable to arbitrarily large XML documents.

In this study, we describe SKEYRUS (*S*tructure and *KEY*word search based on *R*ecursive *U*id *S*ystem), that integrates structure and keyword searches on XML data using rUID. SKEYRUS is comprised of the modules for raw data processing and managing, query plan generation, content query processing, and integration. The input of SKEYRUS is a simplified XPath expression with word-containment predicates. Taking into account the feature of query processing using numbering schemes, we have discussed the following issues:

- *A join mechanism.* How to exploit rUID to perform joins effectively?
- *Query plan selection.* Which is the appropriate plan to execute a query?
- *Physical data organization.* How to partition the data into files appropriate to the query processing using rUID?
- *Dealing with the common subqueries.* How to keep the result of the frequent subqueries to save the repeatedly processing cost?

The rest of paper is organized as follows. Section 2 briefly reviews related works. Section 3 presents an overview of the 2-level recursive UID that is the core data structure in SKEYRUS. Section 4 describes the design of SKEYRUS. Section 5 discusses a number of preliminary performance results of SKEYRUS. Section 6 concludes this paper with future work suggestion.

2 Related Works

Numbering scheme proposals. A method to determine the ancestor and descendant relationship using *preorder* and *postorder traversals* has been introduced in [2]. Extensions of the method using the *preorder* and *range* have been presented in [12,?]. Another approach uses the *position* and *depth* of a tree node to process containment queries [17]. The application of XID-map in change management of versions of XML documents have been discussed in [6].

The UID technique has been introduced in [11]. Applications of the technique have been described in [7,?]. In these studies, the problems of structural update and the overflow of identifier have not been discussed.

XML data management approaches. Respecting the role of RDBMS, there are several approaches to implement a system to manage XML data, as follows:

- *All-In*: The system is implemented exclusively based on an RDBMS.
- *All-Out*: The system is implemented without using any RDBMS.
- *Half-In-Half-Out*: An RDBMS is used to store the pre-processed data. The query processing is performed by other modules, which are built originally.

There is a number of works applying the *All-In* approach, [5,?,?]. The transformation of queries from XPath to SQL statements has been described in XRel, [16]. Integration of keyword search to XML query processing has been discussed in [5]. The maturity of the relational database technology and the plenty of RDBMS products are the advantage of the *All-In* approach. The disadvantage is that RDBMS have been designed primarily for the relational data model, not for XML, which also includes the structural information of data.

The recent examples of the *All-Out* approach have been described in [7,?]. The advantage of the *All-Out* approach is the fast performance. On the other hand, the *All-In* approach usually requires an implementation workload heavier than the first approach does.

In the implementation of SKEYRUS, we have adopted the *Half-In-Half-Out* approach. An RDBMS is used to perform the task of managing the pre-processed data. Other modules in SKEYRUS have been implemented originally.

3 Overview of 2-Level rUID

As mentioned above, the rUID numbering scheme is crucial for SKEYRUS. In this section, we describe the main features of 2-level rUID in order to make the paper self-contained. The technical details of rUID has been presented in [3].

3.1 Description

The 2-level rUID numbering scheme manages the identifiers of nodes in XML trees by the *global* and *local* levels.

Definition 1. *(A frame) Given an XML tree $\mathcal{T}$ rooted at $\boldsymbol{r}$, a frame $\mathcal{F}$ is a tree: (1) rooted at $\boldsymbol{r}$, (2) the node set of which is a subset of the node set of $\mathcal{T}$ and (3) for any two nodes $\boldsymbol{u}$ and $\boldsymbol{v}$ in the frame, an edge exists connecting the nodes if and only if one of the nodes is an ancestor of the other in $\mathcal{T}$ and there is no other node $\boldsymbol{x}$ that lies between $\boldsymbol{u}$ and $\boldsymbol{v}$ in $\mathcal{T}$ and $\boldsymbol{x}$ belongs to the frame.*

Definition 2. *(UID-local area) Given an XML tree $\mathcal{T}$ rooted at $\boldsymbol{r}$, a frame $\mathcal{F}$ of $\mathcal{T}$, and a node $\boldsymbol{n}$ of $\mathcal{F}$, a UID-local area of $\boldsymbol{n}$ is an induced subtree of $\mathcal{T}$ rooted at $\boldsymbol{n}$ such that each of the subtree's node paths is terminated either by a child node of $\boldsymbol{n}$ in $\mathcal{F}$ or a leaf node of $\mathcal{T}$, if between the leaf node and $\boldsymbol{n}$ in $\mathcal{T}$ there exists no other node that belongs to $\mathcal{F}$.*

A frame divides an XML tree into local areas, each of these areas is rooted at a frame node. Hereafter, let us refer to the full identifier of a node as its *identifier* and the number assigned to a node locally inside an UID-local area as its *index*. Let κ denote the maximal fan-out of nodes in $\mathcal{F}$. We use a κ-ary tree to enumerate the nodes of $\mathcal{F}$ and let the number assigned to each node in $\mathcal{F}$ be the index of the UID-local area rooted at the node.

Definition 3. *(2-level rUID) The full 2-level rUID of a node $\boldsymbol{n}$ is a triple ($\boldsymbol{g}$, $\boldsymbol{l}$, $\boldsymbol{r}$), where $\boldsymbol{g}$, $\boldsymbol{l}$, and $\boldsymbol{r}$ are called the global index, local index, and root indicator, respectively. If $\boldsymbol{n}$ is a non-root node, then $\boldsymbol{g}$ is the index of the UID-local area containing $\boldsymbol{n}$, $\boldsymbol{l}$ is the index of $\boldsymbol{n}$ inside the area, and $\boldsymbol{r}$ is $\boldsymbol{false}$. If $\boldsymbol{n}$ is the root node of an UID-local area then $\boldsymbol{g}$ is the index of the area, $\boldsymbol{l}$ is the index of $\boldsymbol{n}$ as a leaf node in the upper UID-local area, and $\boldsymbol{r}$ is $\mathbf{true}$. The identifier of the root of the main XML tree is (1, 1, $\mathbf{true}$).*

We construct a table $\mathcal{K}$ having three columns *global index*, *local index*, and *fan-out*. Each row of $\mathcal{K}$ corresponds to an UID-local area and contains the global index of the area, the index of the area's root in the upper area, and the maximal fan-out of nodes in the corresponding area, respectively. The value κ and the table $\mathcal{K}$ are the *global parameters*.

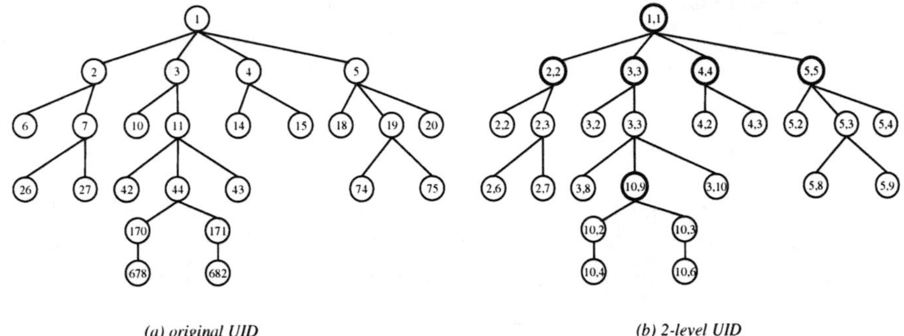

Fig. 1. An original UID and its corresponding 2-level rUID version

Global index	Local index	Local fan-out
1	1	4
2	2	2
3	3	3
4	4	2
5	5	3
10	9	2

Fig. 2. Global parameter table for the 2-level rUID shown in Figure 1(b)

Example 1. Figure 1 depicts examples of the original UID and the new 2-level rUID. The table $\mathcal{K}$ of 2-level rUID is shown in Figure 2.

3.2 Properties of rUID.

The rUID preserves the ability to compute the parent-child relationship. Besides that, rUID has the following properties:

Scalability. rUID is applicable for arbitrarily large trees. In SKEYRUS, 2-level rUID is sufficient for generating the element identifiers of large XML data sets.

Robustness in structural update. Using rUID, the scope of identifier update due to a node insertion or deletion is reduced. For example, if a node is inserted, only the nodes in the UID-local area where the update occurs need to be considered. *Hierarchical summary in the frame.* The global index of rUID can be used to determine the relative position, such as preceding or following, of two nodes in the entire data tree, if these indices are distinguished.

XPath axes expressiveness. Generating the XPath axes is essential in evaluation of location steps in XPath expressions. XPath axes can be constructed using rUID, (see [3] for details).

4 SKEYRUS - An Application of the 2-Level rUID

In this section, we describe an implementation of rUID in a prototype system named SKEYRUS. The system integrates two functions together: querying on structure of XML documents and searching by keywords. More technical details of SKEYRUS can be found in [4].

4.1 Approach

In SKEYRUS, we valuate XML queries by selecting the tested nodes that satisfy conditions on content, and then joining these qualified nodes by axes. The input queries are expressed by XPath expressions having word-containment predicates. The XPath axis construction ability of rUID is useful in processing the structural part of the queries. For the content part, we focus on keyword search, which is a popular request to the Web applications.

4.2 System Design

The system design of SKEYRUS and the components are depicted in Figure 3. **Pre-processing, storing, and indexing.** The input XML documents are parsed by the pre-processing module, and then the resulted XML tree's nodes are numbered using rUID. The global parameters κ and $\mathcal{K}$ are generated and stored in the table *globalParameters*.

In order to generate the structural information, for each XML element and attribute, a tuple `<rUID, EleAttrName, descr>` is generated. The `rUID` is the identifier of the element or attribute `EleAttrName`, and `descr` contains the type

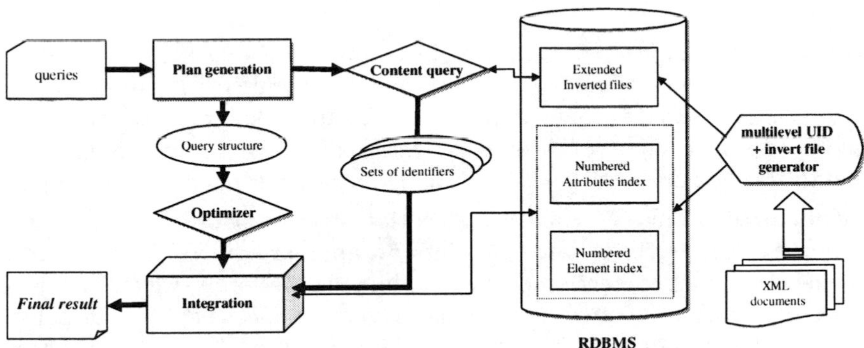

Fig. 3. System design of SKEYRUS

of EleAttrName and its position, which is the address where data resides, in XML documents. The structural information is saved to the table *codeName*.

For each leaf node, an inverted structure of the node content is created. In [5], a structure has been proposed to record the occurrence of a *word* at a *depth* in a *location* of an *element* or *attribute* in XML documents. In SKEYRUS, since the hierarchical level can be computed using rUID, we can discard the *depth* parameter. Therefore, the structure of the rUID-keyword inverted file is <rUID, word, descr>. The content information is saved to the table *codeWord*.

Plan generation in SKEYRUS. An input query is expressed by an XPath location path. An initial *query plan* is generated by parsing the input location path into location steps.

A query plan is stored in a table having the attributes stepID, nodeType1, axisType, nodeType2, Operation, and Output. Each row of the table is a *plan step*. The stepID indicates the order to perform plan steps. The nodeType1 and nodeType2 show candidate node sets joined by the axis axisType. The Operation is the function executed on the candidate node sets to get the qualified nodes. The Output indicates whether the location step produces the output.

Table 1. A query plan for Example 2

stepID	nodeType1	axisType	nodeType2	Operation	Output
1	root	child	doc		
2	doc	child	chapter	position()= 5	
3	chapter	descendant	figure		yes
4	figure	child	title	contains 'genetic'	

Example 2. A query plan of the XPath expression "/child::doc/child::chapter [position()=5]/descendant::figure[contain(child::title,'genetic')]", which selects the figure, the title of which contains the keyword 'genetic', of the fifth chapter of a document, is shown in Table 1.

Shortcut for common subqueries. Common subqueries are extracted from the input. The intermediate result of common subqueries is stored in a table named scomsubqTab having three attributes comquery, startnode, and endnode, where comquery stores the expression of the subquery, startnode and endnode are the nodes, the relationship of which corresponds to the subquery.

Content processing. We evaluate a location step by choosing the candidates, and then projecting these candidates into an appropriate axis. The candidates are generated by the content processing module that performs two tasks: Loading the list of elements or attributes having a given name, and filtering a list of elements or attributes by given keywords. The output of the content processing module is stored in buffer tables in main memory. SKEYRUS manages the buffers using flags and frees a buffer after the buffer become not necessary.

Structure processing. This module joins, using rUID as the key, the tables in main memory according to given axes.

Notation. Let A, $\mathcal{C}$(A), $\mathcal{X}$(A), and $\mathcal{X}$(A, B) denote a list of elements of the type a, the list of items in A satisfying the condition $\mathcal{C}$, the computation of the axis $\mathcal{X}$ from A, and the join of the sorted tables A and B by the axis $\mathcal{X}$, respectively.

Join mechanism. To establish $\mathcal{X}$(A, B), rather than checking all possible pairs from tables A and B, we first generate $\mathcal{X}$(A) and store the finding in an buffer table E. The ability of rUID to compute XPath axes is crucial for this step. The axis mapping is performed in main memory without any disk I/O. The cost of this step is denoted by *cost*($\mathcal{X}$(A)). Next, we sort E by rUID and store in a table E'. The cost of this step is $O(|E| * log|E|)$. Finally, we merge E' with B. Because E' and B are sorted, the cost of this step is $(|E'| + |B|)$ or $(|E| + |B|)$. The total cost of the join equals *cost*($\mathcal{X}$(A)) + $O(|E| * log|E|)$ + $(|E| + |B|)$. The join process is depicted in Figure 4.

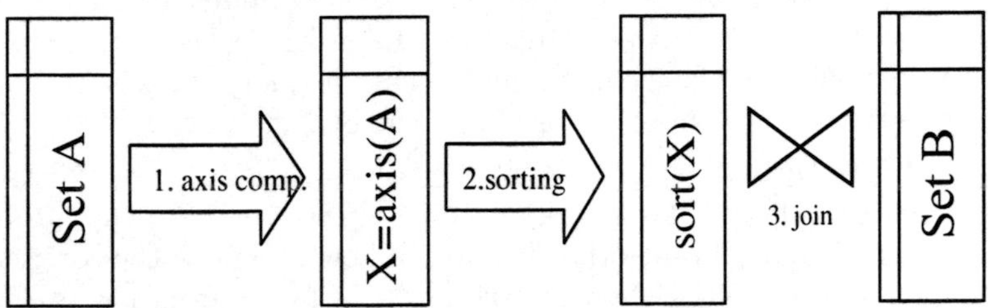

Fig. 4. Join process in SKEYRUS

This join mechanism can be applied for different axis types. For sorting, the hierarchical order is used to decide whether two nodes are swapped.

Rules for query plan selection in SKEYRUS. The general query optimization for XML data has been discussed in [9]. In this part, we discuss several improvement measures specific to query processing on numbering schemes.

Given a query plan, the query steps can be performed in different orders. The different process orders require the different query processing time and main memory for buffering. Regarding the *input/output* and *processing time consumption*, we consider the following illustration example.

Example 3. Consider a simple query "`a/`$\mathcal{X}$`::b[satisfies `$\mathcal{C}$`]`" where $\mathcal{X}$ is an axis, $\mathcal{C}$ is a condition on `b`. The process order is either generating the set of nodes `b` satisfying $\mathcal{C}$ and checking which nodes belong to the axis $\mathcal{X}$ of `a`, or joining `a` and `b` by the axis $\mathcal{X}$ first, and then checking which nodes satisfy $\mathcal{C}$. Let P_1 and P_2 denote these plans, which are shown in Table 2.

The cost difference between P_1 and P_2 is $d =$ *cost*(P_1) - *cost*(P_2), or *cost*($\mathcal{C}$(B)) - *cost*(B) - *cost*($\mathcal{C}$(C)) + *cost*($\mathcal{X}$(A, $\mathcal{C}$(B))) - *cost*($\mathcal{X}$(A, B)). From the cost of the join mechanism, d is found equal to *cost*($\mathcal{C}$(B)) - *cost*(B) - *cost*($\mathcal{C}$(C)) + $|\mathcal{C}(B)|$ - $|B|$. The value depends on the cost of evaluating $\mathcal{C}$ and the size of C.

Table 2. Two query plans for Example 3

stepID	Plan P_1	Plan P_2
1	find $\mathcal{C}$(B)	find A
2	find A	find B
3	find $\mathcal{X}$(A, $\mathcal{C}$(B))	find C = $\mathcal{X}$(A, B)
4		find $\mathcal{C}$(C)

We adopted the following approximate measures to select the query plans:

- *Number of connections between processing modules in main memory and RDBMS*: We must cluster the query steps performed by RDBMS in batches.
- *Cost of the evaluation of* $\mathcal{C}$: If the cost is *cheap* then P_1 is better than P_2. If the cost to verify $\mathcal{C}$ is *expensive* then P_2 is better than P_1. For simplicity, we consider the number of input keywords in $\mathcal{C}$ the cost of $\mathcal{C}$.

Regarding *memory consumption*, we choose the number of buffers used to store the intermediated data as a measure. In order to keeps the number of main memory buffers small, the order to process the query steps is from top and bottom steps toward the step that produces the output.

Database table tuning. When the number of tuples is too large, distributing the tuples into smaller tables is necessary to speed up the query processing. However, the distribution raises the question of how to choose the correct tables to make the I/O operations. Creating the name of tables from the two parts is our solution to the problem. For the tables of *codeName* type, the first part of the name of a table is a common prefix of element names stored in the table. For the tables of *codeWord* type, the first part of the name of a table is the common prefix of words stored in the table. The second part, in both of these cases, is the common global index of rUID.

5 Experiment

In this section, we describe several experiments on SKEYRUS. The details of the experiment platform used in these experiments is presented in [4]

Data sets. We used the Shakespeare's plays formatted by XML available at http://sunsite.unc.edu/pub/sun-info/xml/eg/shakespeare.1.10.xml.zip. In addition, we generated two synthetic data sets that supposedly describe the personnel organization, denoted by `personnel`, of a company. The specification of the synthetic data sets is shown in Table 3.

Comparison of the capacities of UID and rUID. The UID technique failed to numerate entirely the data set I, which has an unbalanced structure and a high degree of recursion. The UID technique can deal with Shakespeare's plays because the documents have a relatively balanced and low tree shape. However, when the plays are grouped in a *collection*, for example by adding a DTD declaration `<!ELEMENT collection (play+)>`, then the UID technique was overflowed, even when only a single play "Love's Labor's Los" was added. Meanwhile, the 2-level UID is successful enumerated both of these data sets.

rUID and XML query processing. We compared the query processing of SKEYRUS with Xalan [15] on the data set *II*. We conducted the experiments using the query input in the following categories:

- Q1: simple XPath expressions having parent and ancestor axes, such as "`//child::person`" and "`//child::person/child::email`".
- Q2: XPath expressions having parent and ancestor axes that require the hierarchical level information, such as "`//child::person/child::*/child::person`" and "`//child::person/child::*/child::*/child::person`".
- Q3: complex XPath expressions having keyword search, such as "`/descendant::person/child::note[contains(self,'academic')]`".
- Q4: XPath expressions having preceding axes, such as "`/descendant::person/preceding::person`".

Let x_p and x_q, s_p and s_q denote the times for data preparing and querying of Xalan and SKEYRUS, respectively. The times for processing these queries are shown in Table 4.

Table 3. Specification of the data sets

Data set	Size	# of ele./attr.	tree height	description
Synthetic set I	7.6Kb	201	11	20 main entities
Love's Labor's Lost	210Kb	5057	7	plays grouped in `collection`
Synthetic set II	3172Kb	50052	11	7104 main entities

Table 4. Times of query processing (*ms*)

Categories	x_p	x_q	x_p+x_q	s_p	s_q	s_p+s_q
Q1.1	860	1312	2172	1344	–	1344
Q1.2	875	1562	2437	2500	865	3365
Q2.1	875	1750	2625	2453	991	3444
Q2.2	875	1875	2750	2500	1084	3584
Q3.	891	1328	2219	2844	20	3044
Q4.	875	X	–	2650	2050	4700

Analysis. From the Table 4, we have made the following observations:

- Accessing RDBMS to retrieve the pre-processed data in SKEYRUS requires more time than parsing a text file in Xalan. This can be best explained that SKEYRUS has to communicate with the RDBMS via ODBC-JDBC.
- When data is loaded into main memory, SKEYRUS is better than Xalan in query processing. In average, the processing time required by SKEYRUS is 50-60% of the time required by Xalan.

– If one of element participants in an axis is unknown, as in Q2.1 and Q2.2, considering all of possibilities of the component is necessary. SKEYRUS deals with the cases using the ability of rUID for hierarchical level determination, so the required time for processing was not increased sharply.
– We tested two query plans for Q3. The result accords with our rule in Section 4.2 for query plan selection based on the number of connections between processing modules and RDBMS.
– For the queries including the axes *preceding* or *following*, such as Q4, the evaluation cost was high. The runs for the query were cancelled in Xalan.

6 Conclusion

Queries on keywords are common user requests whereas XML makes the queries on document structure available. Therefore, it is natural to integrate these tasks to enrich the selectivity of users. In this study, we described SKEYRUS, a system which enables the searches on both keywords and structure of XML documents. The core technique of SKEYRUS is the rUID numbering scheme, which has been designed to be scalable and robust in structural update. The ability of rUID in XPath axes construction has been exploited in query processing. The preliminary experiments have shown the efficiency of rUID and SKEYRUS.

Extensions of this study are underway, including the implementation of an indexing engine based on the B^+-tree structure to index the data tables in SKEYRUS in order to avoid the limitations in using an underlying RDBMS. We also plan to conduct more performance tests in different configurations.

References

1. S.Chien, et al. Storing and Querying Multiversion XML Documents using Durable Node Numbers. Proc. of the Inter. Conf. on WISE, Japan, 270–279, 2001.
2. P.F.Dietz. Maintaining order in a link list. Proceeding of the Fourteenth ACM Symposium on Theory of Computing, California, 122–127, 1982.
3. D.D.Kha, M.Yoshikawa, S.Uemura: A Structural Numbering Scheme for XML Data. EDBT workshop on XML Data Management (XMLDM), Prague, March 2002.
4. D.D.Kha, M.Yoshikawa, S.Uemura: Processing XML Queries on Structure and Keyword in SKEYRUS. Technical report, NAIST, June 2002.
5. D.Florescu, I. Manolescu, D.Kossmann. Intergrating Keyword Search into XML Query Processing. Proc. of the Inter. WWW Conf., Elsevier ,Amsterdam, 2000.
6. A.Marian, S.Abiteboul, G.Cobena, L.Mignet. Change-Centric Management of Versions in an XML Warehouse. Proc. of the Inter. Conf. on VLDB, Italy, 2001.
7. H.Jang, Y.Kim, D.Shin. An Effective Mechanism for Index Update in Structured Documents. Proc. of CIKM, USA, 383–390, 1999.
8. D.Shin. XML Indexing and Retrieval with a Hybrid Storage Model. J. of Knowledge and Information Systems, 3:252–261, 2001.
9. J.McHugh, J.Widom. Query Optimization for XML. Proc. of the Inter. Conf. on VLDB, Edinburgh, Scotland, pages 315–326, 1999.

10. J.Shanmugasundaram, et al. Relational Databases for Querying XML Documents: Limitations and Opportunities. Proc. of the Inter Conf. on VLDB, Scotland, 1999.
11. Y.K.Lee, S-J.Yoo, K.Yoon, P.B.Berra. Index Structures for structured documents. ACM First Inter. Conf. on Digital Libraries, Maryland, 91–99, 1996.
12. Q.Li, B.Moon. Indexing and Querying XML Data for Regular Path Expressions. Proc. of the Inter. Conf. on VLDB, Italy, 2001.
13. World Wide Web Consortium. Extensible Markup Language (XML) 1.0. http://www.w3.org/TR/REC-xml, 2000.
14. World Wide Web Consortium. XML Path Language (XPath) Version 1.0. http://www.w3.org/TR/xpath, 2000.
15. Apache Software Foundation. Apache XML Project. http://xml.apache.org/, 2001.
16. M.Yoshikawa, T.Amagasa, T.Shimura, S.Uemura. XRel: A Path-Based Approach to Storage and Retrieval of XML Documents Using Relational Databases. ACM Transation on Internet Technologies, 1(1), 2001.
17. C.Zhang, et al. On Supporting Containment Queries in Relational Database Management Systems. Proc. of the ACM SIGMOD, USA, 2001.

Translating Access Authorizations for Transformed XML Documents

Somchai Chatvichienchai, Mizuho Iwaihara, and Yahiko Kambayashi

Department of Social Informatics, Kyoto University
Yoshida Sakyo Kyoto 606-8501 Japan
somchai@db.soc.i.kyoto-u.ac.jp,
{iwaihara, yahiko}@i.kyoto-u.ac.jp

Abstract. XML access control models proposed in the literature enforce access restrictions directly on the structure and content of an XML document. Therefore, the authorization must be revised whenever the structure of an XML document is changed. In this paper we present an approach that translates the authorizations for the transformed XML document. We focus on the case where schemas of the source and transformed documents represent the same concept. This approach is strongly based on schema mapping information between the source and transformed XML schemas.

1. Introduction

As XML [3] emerges as an increasingly popular format for representation and exchange of data, it will lead to web data sharing and data integration. Therefore, it becomes critical to define and enforce access restrictions on XML documents to ensure that only authorized users can access to the information. In recent years, contributions [2, 6, 8] have been made to XML access control models. These models enforce access restrictions directly on the structure and content of XML documents. In this way, information in XML format can be protected at a finer level of granularity (e.g., the element level) than the whole document. Each XML document is associated with a set of authorizations specifying access rights of users on information within the document. An object in the authorization is described by path expression identifying an element or attribute within the document. However, the structure of XML documents tend to change over time for a multitude of reasons, for example to correct design errors in the schema, to allow expansion of the application scope over time, or to account for the merging of several businesses into one. When an XML document is transformed to conform to a new schema, the associated authorizations must be translated for the transformed document. However, the translation of authorizations is a complicated task since its scope covers XML data model, schema matching, XML access control model, and application requirements. In general, the schema matching is a laborious manual work. Fortunately, recent contributions have been made in the area of schema matching and document transformation. Xtra [10] provides a set of

R. Cicchetti et al. (Eds.): DEXA 2002, LNCS 2453, pp. 290–299, 2002.

schema transformation operations that establish semantic relationships between two XML document schemas. Xtra also offers an algorithm that discovers XSLT [5] script to transform the source XML document into the target XML document. TranScm [9] examines and finds similarities/differences between the source and target schemas. This is done using a rule-based method that defines a possible common matching between two schema components, and provides means for translating an instance of the first to an instance of the second. These works can provide some schema mapping information needed for authorization translation.

The objective of this paper is to present an approach that translates authorizations of the XML document. To the best of our knowledge, no previous study has addressed authorization translation for XML documents. Our work focuses on the case where schemas of the source and transformed documents represent the same concept. For an XML document that is not associated with a DTD, we may obtain its DTD by applying DTD generating functions of existing XML document processing tools [1, 7]. The goal of authorization translation is that authorizations of the transformed XML document must enforce the same access restrictions as provided by the authorizations of the source XML document. This paper also indicates the limitation of authorization translation.

The rest of the paper is organized as follows. In Section 2 we give basic concepts of XML and an XML access control model. Section 3 discusses the impact of document structure transformation on authorization translation. In Section 4 we present a technique of translating authorizations for the target document. Section 5 introduces an algorithm for translating a path expression of an object to the corresponding path expression of the target schema. Finally, Section 6 concludes our work.

2. Basic Concepts

XML Documents, DTDs and XPath

An XML document is composed of a sequence of nested elements, each delimited by a pair of start and end tags or by an empty tag. An element can have attributes attached to it. These attributes represent properties of the element. Both elements and attributes are allowed to contain values. The structure of an XML document is described by a DTD. A DTD can be modeled as a labeled tree containing a node for each attribute and element in the DTD. An example of XML document and its DTD are depicted in Fig.1(a) and (b), respectively. XPath [4] is a language for locating textual data, elements, and attributes in an XML document. In addition to its use for addressing, XPath can add conditions in the navigation.

An XML Access Control Model

In this paper, we adopt the XML access control model of Damiani [6]. Our approach can be easily adapted to other XML access control models. This model regulates the access of users to elements and attributes within an XML document on the basis of the user's identity and rules, called *authorizations*, which specify for each user the types of accesses that the user can/cannot exercise on each object. Authorizations can be positive or negative to an XML element or attribute. Authorizations specified on an element can be defined as applicable to its attributes only (local authorizations) or, in a recursive approach to its subelements and attributes (recursive authorizations). This model provides document-level and schema-level authorizations. Schema-level authorizations are applicable to all XML documents that are instances of the DTD. Document-level authorizations allows user to tailor security requirements for each document. Document-level authorizations usually take precedence over the schema-level ones. To address the situations where the precedence criteria should not be applied, the model allows users to specify the authorization (either local or recursive) as weak type.

```
<division>
 <dname>Computers</dname>
 <client>
  <cname>Ichiro</cname>
  <class>special</class>
  <po>
   <number>S0210</number>
   <date>20020214</date>
   <items>
    <item>
     <product>Desktop PC</product>
     <price>1200</price>
     <disc_rate>20</disc_rate>
     <qty>1</qty>
    </item>
   </items>
  </po>
 </client>
</division>
```

(a) order.xml

```
<!ELEMENT division (dname, client*)>
<!ELEMENT dname (#PCDATA) >
<!ELEMENT client (cname,class,po*)>
<!ELEMENT cname (#PCDATA) >
<!ELEMENT class (#PCDATA)>
<!ELEMENT po (number,date,items+)>
<!ELEMENT number (#PCDATA)>
<!ELEMENT date (#PCDATA)>
<!ELEMENT items (item+)>
<!ELEMENT item (product,price,disc_rate?,qty)>
<!ELEMENT product (#PCDATA) >
<!ELEMENT price (#PCDATA)>
<!ELEMENT disc_rate (#PCDATA)>
<!ELEMENT qty (#PCDATA)>
```

(b) order.dtd

```
a1: <<manager,*,*>, /division, read, +, R>
a2: <<staff,*,*>, /division/client, read, +, R>
a3: <<staff,*,*>, /division/client[class="special"]//disc_rate, read, -, R>
```

(c) order.xacl

Fig. 1. A sample of XML document (a), DTD (b), and access control list (c).

Definition 1 (Authorization): An authorization is a 5-tuple of the form:
<subject, object, action, sign, type>, where

- *subject* is a user to whom the authorization is granted. *subject* is described by a triple (user-id, IP-address, symbolic-address),
- *object* described by a path expression identifying an element and attribute,
- *action* is the read operation,
- *sign* ∈ {'+', '-'},
- *type* ∈ {*L,R,LW,RW*} is an authorization propagation type (*L*ocal, *R*ecursive, *L*ocal *W*eak, and *R*ecursive *W*eak, respectively).

•

We call an authorization whose object definition is based on values of elements or attributes a *value-dependent* authorization. We call an authorization whose object definition is not based on values of elements or attributes a *value-independent* authorization. An example of access control list for order.xml is shown in Fig.1(c). Authorization a_1 and a_2 are value-independent authorizations. a_2 states that Staff is allowed to read information of the clients. a_3 is a value-dependent authorization. It states that Staff is not allowed to read discount rates of the order items of special class customers. For simplicity, we consider *L* and *LW* as a local type. We consider *R* and *RW* as a recursive type.

3. Impact of XML Document Structure Transformation

We first analyze the impact of XML document transformation on authorization translation. We classify the impact as follows:

Total Mapping / Partial Mapping

Total mapping indicates that every schema element in a schema has relationship with the schema element(s) in another schema. Partial mapping occurs when some schema elements in either schema have no relationship with those in another schema. Note that a schema element is an XML element or attribute. We call a source schema element that has no relationship with any target schema elements an *unmapped source schema element* (USE). We call a target schema element that has no relationship with any source schema elements an *unmapped target schema element* (UTE). In case source and target schemas represent the same concept, USE and UTE are internal elements. We define an authorization for UTEs by three optional policies: Open policy, Authorization-inheritance policy, and User-defined policy. Open policy allows all subjects to access UTEs. Authorization-inheritance policy allows UTEs to inherit authorizations from their parents. User-defined policy allows a security administrator to predefine authorizations for UTEs before translating authorizations.

Semantic Relationship between Source and Target Schema Elements

Semantic relationship between source and target schema elements is classified into one-to-one, one-to-many, many-to-one, and many-to-many relationships. The authorization of a target schema element *e* is computed by combining the authorizations of all source schema elements that have semantic relationships with *e*. In case object of authorization is based on values of schema elements that have one-to-many, many-to-one, or many-to-many relationships with the target elements, the authorization translation needs guidance from the security administrator who knows the value mapping between source and target schema elements.

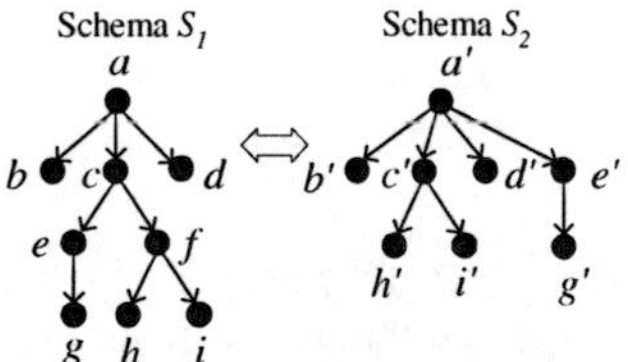

Fig. 2. A sample of change of element-subelement relationship.

Element-subelement Relationship

As an element-subelement relationship is changed, the descendant elements inheriting security policies from a given recursive authorizations may become different. For example, schema S_1 and S_2 that are depicted in Fig.2 represent the same concept. Element *f* of schema S_1 is an USE. Suppose that there exists an authorization *auth*: <<*staff*, *, *>, */a/c*, *read*, +, *R*> for XML document D_1 conforming to schema S_1. Descendant elements of element *c* of schema S_1 are different from those of element *c'* of schema S_2. Therefore, we cannot directly translate this authorization to <<*staff*, *, *>, */a'/c'*, *read*, +, *R*> for the document D_2 that is transformed from D_1 to conform to schema S_2. To solve this problem, we first convert *auth* into a set of authorizations that have the same authorization policies of *auth*. Therefore *auth* is converted to (1) a local authorization for element *c* and (2) recursive authorizations for elements *e*, *h* and *i* that are *c*'s the closest descendant elements, which are not USEs. We next translate path expressions of these authorizations to the corresponding path expressions of schema S_2.

Element and Attribute Values

Due to document transformation, values of some elements and attributes of XML target document may be different from the values of the corresponding elements and attributes of the source document. The security administrator uses value mappings between these source and target elements / attributes for translating value-dependent authorizations.

4. Translating Authorizations

We observe that in many occasions the semantic relationship between source and target schema element is a one-to-one mapping. In these cases, we offer a simple approach for translating authorizations. We first give definitions of a *DTD* graph and partial mapping.

Definition 2 (DTD Graph): A DTD graph is a 3-tuple $DG = (V, E, l)$, where *V* is the set of nodes in the graph, *E* is the set of edges, and *l* is the labeling function representing the properties of a node. We categorize a node based on its label:

(a) Element node: each element node *n* represents an element type. $l(n) = < N(n), A(n) >$ where $N(n)$ is *n*'s name.

(b) Attribute node: each attribute node *a* represents an attribute. $l(a) =< N(a), A(a) >$ where $N(a)$ is *a*'s name.

We assign a symbol in {*, +, ?} on edge e: $n_i \rightarrow n_j$ to indicate how many times n_j occurs in n_i's content model.

•

Definition 3 (Map Function): Let graphs $DG = (V, E, l)$ and $DG' = (V', E', l')$ be DTD graphs of source and target schemas, respectively. *map:* $V \rightarrow V'$ is a partial mapping from the nodes in *V* into the nodes in *V'*. *map* $(v) = v'$, where $v' \in V'$, $v \in V$, and node *v'* has semantic relationship with node *v*.

•

The partial mapping *map* can be derived from the schema matching, which is performed by manual work and a schema-matching tool. We represent *v* and *v'* as absolute path expressions. For example, *map(/client/class)* = */customer/@category*. We now give a formal definition of authorization preservation in translating an authorization.

Let D_1 be a document of schema S_1, D_2 be the document transformed from D_1 to conform to schema S_2, $AUTH = \{auth_1, auth_2, .., auth_m\}$ be a set of authorizations for D_1, and $AUTH' = \{auth'_1, auth'_2, .., auth'_n\}$ be a set of authorizations for D_2.

Definition 4 (Authorization Preservation): Let $V = \{v_1, v_2, .., v_p\}$ be a set of schema elements of S_1, $V' = \{v'_1, v'_2, .., v'_q\}$ be a set of schema element of S_2, $req_i = (subject_r, object_i, action_r)$ be an access request for an instance x of v_i ($1 \leq i \leq p$) of D_1, and $req_j' = (subject_r, object'_j, action_r)$ be an access request for an instance x' of v'_j ($1 \leq j \leq q$) of D_2. *AUTH' preserves* authorization policies of *AUTH* if and only if the following conditions are satisfied:
(for each instance x in v_i) (for each instance x' in v_j) ($v'_j = map(v_i)$) (x' corresponds to x): req_i and req_j' have the same permission decision (either granted or denied) by *AUTH* and *AUTH'*, respectively for ($1 \leq i \leq p$) and ($1 \leq j \leq q$).

•

It is worth to note that $object_i$ does not indicate USEs of schema S_1 while $object'_j$ does not indicate UTEs of schema S_2. We now describe how access control model decides whether to grant permission to a given access request.

Definition 5 (Grant Decision): Let $x \preccurlyeq y$ denote the fact that y is a descendant-or-self of node x, $subject \Rightarrow subject'$ denote the fact that *subject* is satisfied by definition of *subject'*. An access request $req = (subject_r, object_r, action_r)$ is granted by *AUTH* if and only if the following conditions are satisfied:
$(\exists auth_i)$ $(\neg\exists auth_j)$ $(subject_r \Rightarrow subject_i) \wedge (action_r = action_i) \wedge (sign_i = \text{'+'}) \wedge (subject_r \Rightarrow subject_j) \wedge (action_r = action_j) \wedge (sign_j = \text{'-'}) \wedge (((type_i = recursive) \wedge (type_j = recursive) \wedge (object_i \preccurlyeq object_j \preccurlyeq object_r)) \vee (object_j = object_r)))$, where $auth_i = \langle subject_i, object_i, action_i, sign_i, type_i \rangle$ and $auth_j = \langle subject_j, object_j, action_j, sign_j, type_j \rangle$.

•

An access request is denied by *AUTH* if the conditions of definition 5 are not satisfied. For an access request to an instance x of a schema element v, the grant/deny decision is based on the definitions of the authorizations whose path expressions indicate v. Therefore we can derive *AUTH'* that preserves policies of *AUTH* by creating the corresponding authorization $auth'_i$ of each $auth_i$ as an authorization of *AUTH'*. The *subject*, *action* and *sign* of $auth'_i$ are obtained from those of $auth_i$. The *object* of $auth'_i$ is derived by the result of translating the path expression of *object* of $auth_i$ to the corresponding path expression of the target schema. As we discussed in the previous section, there are some cases where we cannot directly translate an authorization of *AUTH*. We now give a formal definition for the authorization that can be directly translated to the corresponding authorization.

Definition 6 (Translatable Form): Let $auth_i = \langle subject_i, object_i, action_i, sign_i, type_i \rangle$ be an authorization of *AUTH* of D_1, $auth_j' = \langle subject_j', object_j', action_j', sign_j', type_j' \rangle$ be an authorization of *AUTH'* of D_2, v and v' be element nodes indicated by $object_i$

and $object_j$', respectively. Let *desc*(*v*) be a set of *v*'s descendant elements that are not USEs, and *desc*(*v*') be a set of *v*' 's descendant elements that are not UTEs. *auth*' *corresponds* to *auth* if and only if: (1) ($subject_i$ = $subject_j$') and ($action_i$ = $action_j$') and ($sign_i$ = $sign_j$'), (2) *v*' = *map*(*v*), (3) *object* corresponds to *object*', and one of the following conditions are satisfied:

- ($type_i$ and $type_j$' are recursive types) and (each schema element in *desc*(*v*) has one-to-one mapping with a schema element in *desc*(*v*')).
- $type_i$ and $type_j$' are local types.

In this case, we say that $auth_i$ is in *translatable* form.

•

We give a formal definition of condition (3) in the next section. For a recursive authorization $auth_i$ whose *object* indicates *v*, if $auth_i$ is not in translatable form, we generate $auth"_1$, $auth"_2$, .. , $auth"_q$ for *v*'s closest descendant elements v_1, v_2, .. , v_q, respectively. Note that v_1, v_2, .. , v_q are not USEs. The *subject, action,* and *sign* of $auth"_j$ ($1 \le j \le q$) are obtained from those of $auth_i$. If v_i is an internal element, the *type* of $auth"_j$ is defined as a recursive type. Otherwise, *type* of $auth"_j$ is defined as a local type. The path expression of $object"_j$ of $auth"_j$ is defined as concatenation value of path expression of *object* of $auth_i$ and $/v_j$. If *v* is not an USE, we change *type* of $auth_i$ to *local.* Otherwise, we remove $auth_i$ from *AUTH*. If $auth"_j$ ($1 \le j \le q$) is not in translatable form, we recursively apply the same approach in generating a set of authorizations for $auth"_j$ until all authorizations are in translatable form. We next translate path expression of *object* of each authorization in *AUTH* to the corresponding path expression of the target schema.

Proposition 1: Given *AUTH* for D_1, we can derive *AUTH"*={$auth"_1$, $auth"_2$, .. , $auth"_n$} from *AUTH* for D_1 where each $auth"_i \in AUTH"$ is in translatable form.

•

Proposition 2: Let *AUTH"* = {$auth"_1$, $auth"_2$, .. , $auth"_n$} be a set of translatable authorizations for D_1, *AUTH'* = {$auth'_1$, $auth'_2$, .. , $auth'_p$} be a set of authorization of D_2. *AUTH'* preserves the authorization policies of *AUTH"* if:
$\forall auth"_i \exists auth'_j$ such that $auth"_i$ corresponds to $auth'_j$, where ($1 \le i \le n$) and ($1 \le j \le p$).

•

5. Translating a Path Expression

This section presents how to translate path expression of object of each authorization to the corresponding path expression of the target schema. We give a definition of the path expression used for defining the objects in the authorizations. We focus on the core part of XPath since it can sufficiently express location of authorized objects. We name the core part *XPathAuth.* We assume that path expression used for defining the objects are given in the form of *PathExpr* of Fig.3(a). From the syntax rule, we observe that the XPathAuth can be represented by the following sequence: $A_1\{P_1\}+$ $A_2\{P_2\}+$ . . . $A_{n-1}\{P_{n-1}\}+ A_n\{P_n\}*$,where $n \ge 1$. A_1 represents a language of nonterminal symbols: *SimpleRegularExpr* or *SimpleAbsoluteRegularExpr,* A_i ($2 \le i \le n$) and P_j ($1 \le j \le n$) represent a language of nonterminal symbols: *SimpleAbsoluteRegularExpr* and *Predicate*, respectively. '{}+' and '{}*' are meta symbols, which represent 'one or many occurrences' and 'zero or many occurrences' respectively. For example, the path expression */division/client[class='special']//disc_rate* can be viewed as a concatenation of A_1, P_1, and A_2 where A_1 is */division/client*, P_1 is *[class='special']*, and A_2 is *//disc_rate*. To clarify the relationship among *SimpleRegularExpr*, *SimpleAbsoluteRegularExpr*, and *predicate* in the path expression of an object, we introduce XPathAuth graph adapted from [11].

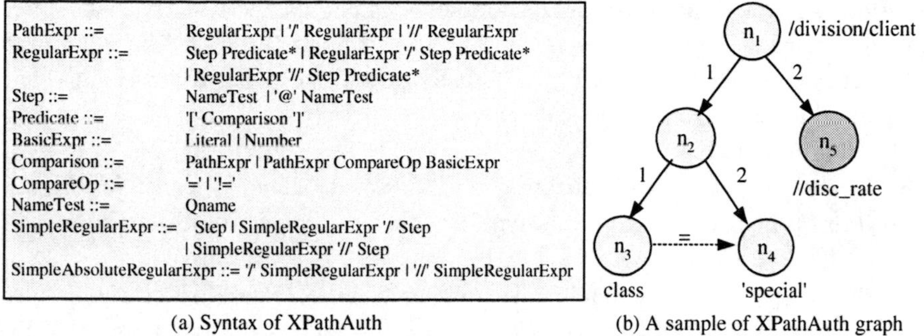

PathExpr ::= RegularExpr | '/' RegularExpr | '//' RegularExpr
RegularExpr ::= Step Predicate* | RegularExpr '/' Step Predicate*
| RegularExpr '//' Step Predicate*
Step ::= NameTest | '@' NameTest
Predicate ::= '[' Comparison ']'
BasicExpr ::= Literal | Number
Comparison ::= PathExpr | PathExpr CompareOp BasicExpr
CompareOp ::= '=' | '!='
NameTest ::= Qname
SimpleRegularExpr ::= Step | SimpleRegularExpr '/' Step
| SimpleRegularExpr '//' Step
SimpleAbsoluteRegularExpr ::= '/' SimpleRegularExpr | '//' SimpleRegularExpr
(a) Syntax of XPathAuth
n1
/division/client
1
2
n2
n5
1
2
//disc_rate
n3
=
n4
class
'special'
(b) A sample of XPathAuth graph

Fig. 3. (a) Syntax of XPathAuth and (b) a sample of XPathAuth graph.

Definition 7 (XPathAuth Graph): The XPathAuth graph is a directed graph *G*(*N*, *E*) satisfying the following constraints:

- Every node has a node type that is one of the following five nonterminal symbols: *SimpleRegularExpr, SimpleAbsoluteRegularExpr, Literal, Number, and Boolean.* Every node that is not *Boolean* type has a value. For a node of type *T*, the value of the node is a language of *T*. There is exactly one node in *N* called the *output node* of *G*. A shaded circle depicts the output node.
- *E* is the union of two mutually disjoint sets of edges: E_t (*tree edges*) and E_c (*comparison edges*). A tree edge is depicted by a solid line. A comparison edge is depicted by a dashed line.
- The graph (N, E_t) is a tree with a root. In (N, E_t), children of a node are ordered. A tree edge from a parent *n* to its *i*-th child *m* is denoted by (*n, i, m*). A comparison edge has a *CompareOp* as a label. A comparison edge from *n* to *m* with a label θ is denoted by (n, θ, m).

•

The XPathAuth graph of the path expression */division/client[class='special'] //disc_rate* is shown in Fig.3(b). Node n_2 is a Boolean node. Intuitively, this path expression has three component paths: */division/client*, */division/client/class*, and */division/client//disc_rate*. These component paths are concatenated values of nodes in XPathAuth graph. The concatenated value is defined as follows.

Definition 8 (Concatenated-value of a Node in XPathAuth Graph) Let *n* be a node of *SimpleRegularExpr* or *SimpleAbsoluteRegularExpr* type in an XPathAuth graph *G*, *value* (*n*) be the value of *n*, and *concat*(*n*) be concatenated-value of *n* (in *G*). *concat*(*n*) is defined recursively as follows:

(1) If n has no ancestor node of *SimpleRegularExpr* or *SimpleAbsoluteRegularExpr* type, *concat*(n) = *value*(n).
(2) Otherwise, let n_a be the closest ancestor node of *SimpleRegularExpr* or *SimpleAbsoluteRegularExpr* type. *concat*(n) is computed as follows:
 - if n is of *SimpleRegularExpr* type, *concat*(n) = *concat*(n_a) & '/' & *value*(n),
 - if n is of the *SimpleAbsoluteRegularExpr* type, *concat*(n) = *concat*(n_a) & *value*(n), where & denotes the concatenation operator.

•

Definition 9 (Path Expression Correspondence): Let *path* and *path'* be path expressions of schema S_1 and S_2, respectively. Let $G(N, E)$ and $G'(N', E')$ be XPathAuth graphs representing *path* and *path'*, respectively. *path* corresponds to *path'* if and only if all the following conditions are satisfied:

(1) $|N| = |N'|$ and $|E| = |E'|$,
(2) $\forall i\ (\exists e_i \in E)\ (\exists e'_i \in E')$ (label of e_i is as same as label *of* e'_i) for $1 \le i \le |E|$,
(3) (For each $n_i \in N$ where n_i's type is either *Literal* or *Number*) $(\exists n'_i \in N')$ $(value(n_i) = value(n'_i))$ for $1 \le i \le |N|$, and
(4) (For each $n_i \in N$ where n_i's type is either *SimpleRegularExpr* or *SimpleAbsoluteRegularExpr*) $(\exists n'_i \in N')$ $(map(v_i) = v'_i)$ for $1 \le i \le |N|$, where v_i and v'_i are full path style of $concat(n_i)$ and $concat(n'_i)$, respectively.

•

We present the algorithm *TranslatePath* (shown in Fig.4) that translates path expression of the object. Given an XPathAuth graph, we first parse the values of nodes of the XPathAuth graph in preorder to obtain the component paths in the XPathAuth graph. We expand the component path from wildcard form into full path. For example, */division/client//disc_rate* is expanded into */division/client/po/items/item/*

TranslatePath (*G, DG, DG', p*)
Input: (1) An XPathAuth graph *G*,
(2) a source DTD graph *DG* = (*V, E, l*), and
(3) a target DTD graph *DG'* = (*V', E', l'*).
Output: A path expression *p*.
Algorithm:
Traversing the nodes in the XPathAuth *G* in preorder.
For each node *m* that is not *Boolean* type, do the following steps:
Let $v_i \in V$ be the schema element indicated by *concat*(*m*), $v_k \in V$ be the schema element indicated by the concatenated-value of the closest ancestor node of *m*, and *val* be the location path from $map(v_k)$ to $map(v_i)$ of the target DTD graph.
If v_i is an USE **then** report translation error on v_i and terminate algorithm.
If node *m* is not connected with comparison edge **then**
p:= *p* & *val*. (where & denotes the concatenation operator)
Otherwise
Let θ be the label on the comparison edge connected to node *m*.
If comparison edge connected to node *m* is an out-edge
Then *p*:= *p* & '[' & *val* & θ. **Otherwise** *p*:= *p* & *val* & ']'.
return *p*.

Fig. 4. The algorithm TranslatePath.

disc_rate. We apply *map* function and the target DTD graph to translate each component path into the corresponding component path of the target DTD. If we can't find the corresponding path for a component path, the algorithm produces translation error report and terminates the translation. We next merge the translated component paths with values of nodes of *Literal* and *Number* types to obtain the corresponding path expression of the target schema.

6. Conclusion

In this paper, we present an approach that translates the authorizations for the XML document that is transformed from an XML source document. We focus on the case where schemas of the source and transformed documents represent the same concept. This approach is strongly based on schema mapping information between the source and transformed schemas. We conclude that XML document structure transformation has strong impact on definitions of authorizations of the transformed document. We have addressed problems and limitations of authorization translation.

References

1. AlphaWorks. Data Descriptors by Example, January 8, 2001. http://www.alphaworks.ibm.com/tech/DDbE.
2. E. Bertino et al., "Specifying and Enforcing Access Control Policies for XML Document Sources," World Wide Web, Baltzer Science Publishers, Netherlands, vol. 3, no. 3, 2000.
3. T. Bray et al. "Extensible Markup Language (XML) 1.0 (Second Edition)". World Wide Web Consortium (W3C). http://www.w3c.org/TR/REC-xml (October 2000).
4. J. Clark et al. "XML Path Language (XPath) Version 1.0". World Wide Web Consortium (W3C). http://www.w3c.org/TR/xpath (November 1999).
5. J. Clark. "XSL Transformations (XSLT) Version 1.0". World Wide Web Consortium (W3C). http://www.w3c.org/TR/xslt (November 1999).
6. E. Damiani, et al., Securing XML documents. In Proceedings of the 2000 International Conference on Extending Database Technology (EDBT'2000), Germany, March 2000.
7. M. H. Kay. SAXON DTDGenerator, http://users.iclway.co.uk/mhkay/saxon/saxon5-5-1/dtdgen.html, 13 April 1999.
8. M. Kudo and S. Hada. "XML Document Security based on Provisional Authorization". Proceedings of the 7th ACM conference on Computer and Communications Security. November 2000, Athens Greece.
9. T. Milo and S. Zohar. Using schema matching to simplify heterogeneous data translation. In VLDB, pages 122-133, 1998.
10. H. Su, H. Kuno, E.A. Rundensteiner, "Automating the Transformation of XML Documents" Advances in Web-Age Information Management, 2nd International Conference WIDM 2001: 68-75, July 9-11, 2001.
11. M. Yoshikawa, et al., XRel: "A Path-Based Approach to Storage and Retrieval of XML Documents Using Relational Databases". ACM Transactions on Internet Technology, Vol.1, No.1, pp.110-141, 2001.

XRL: A XML-based Query Language for Advanced Services in Digital Libraries

Juan Manuel Pérez, María José Aramburu, and Rafael Berlanga

Universitat Jaume I, Castellón, Spain
{martinej, aramburu, berlanga }@uji.es

Abstract. In this paper we present a new XML-based query language for XML documents denoted XRL. This language expresses database conditions concerning the attributes and the structure of documents, as well as Information Retrieval conditions over their contents and their relevance. XRL queries can be stored into a XML repository and manipulated as any other XML document. In order to illustrate the usefulness of this language, we also describe some general guidelines of its current implementation, and present an example application. This application consists in a subscription/notification service of news articles, which are periodically retrieved from a digital library of newspapers according to the preferences of each user.

1 Introduction

New applications of digital libraries store and manipulate large amounts of semi-structured data, mainly multimedia documents with textual data, and provide their access by means of an extensive range of different tools. From our point of view, the main purpose of these applications is to provide users with new Web-based services whose development presents a set of common requirements that could be summarized as follows:

1. When storing and retrieving documents, these services must integrate the usual functions of databases and Information Retrieval (IR) systems, with new techniques for the efficient evaluation of trajectories over document structures.
2. They must have a middleware architecture designed to free the servers from executing the specific tasks required by the user services, and that are too complex to be processed at Web clients.
3. These systems must facilitate query reusing in a uniform way, so that user queries can be stored, retrieved, redefined, interchanged, and executed by applying the same techniques than for documents.

The XML language is the most immediate response to these requirements, as it is designed to represent and manipulate semi-structured documents. At the same time, it allows the transmission of data between software components distributed along heterogeneous architectures. The storage and retrieval of large amounts of XML documents is supported by current technology (e.g.: [1][2]). However, concerning the first and third requirements, we still have some issues without a proper solution. In

R. Cicchetti et al. (Eds.): DEXA 2002, LNCS 2453, pp. 300–309, 2002.

order to solve them we propose a new query language for XML documents with a XML-based syntax in the way explained in [3]. Furthermore, this language should be able to express database conditions over the attributes and the structure of documents, as well as IR conditions over their contents and relevance. Finally, queries should be stored into a XML repository to be manipulated as any other XML document.

In previous works, we have developed new applications of digital libraries for storing documents with a temporal component. The main novelty of the resulting languages and tools is that they allow both the retrieval of documents by their temporal properties, and the historical analysis of past events [4]. Following with this features, and considering the requirements previously explained, in this paper we present a new temporal document retrieval language with a XML-based syntax. This language expresses conditions on the attributes and structure, as well as on the temporal components of the documents. Furthermore, it supports a variety of IR operators [11], the ranking of results by combining different relevance criteria (keywords and document structure), and several ways for presenting the query results.

In order to illustrate the usefulness of this language, in this paper we also describe some general guidelines of its implementation, and present an example application. This application consists on a subscription/notification service of news articles, which are periodically retrieved from a digital library of newspapers according to the preferences of each user. The rest of the paper is organized as follows. Section 2 presents XRL (XML Retrieval Language). In Section 3 we give the implementation guidelines. Section 4 is dedicated to present the subscription/notification service. In Section 5 some related work is analyzed, and, finally in Section 6 we outline some conclusions and future work.

2. The XML Retrieval Language (XRL)

In this section we present the syntax of the XML Retrieval Language (XRL). Briefly, a XRL query is a XML document that specifies a set of advanced IR conditions over XML documents. A XRL document consists of two main parts: the definition of the query variables, and the specification of the queries. The following sections describe in detail these two parts by means of examples.

2.1 Variable definition

The variables of a XRL query are defined by means of *define_var* tags. In XRL a variable represents a relevance ordered list of document components (i.e. XML document sub-trees), which satisfy the given retrieval conditions. These retrieval conditions are specified by means of the *define_var*'s attributes, which are described in turn.

The *id* attribute identifies the variable so that it can be referenced either from queries or from other variables. The *contains* attribute specifies a *boolean* Information Retrieval Expression (IRE) over the textual contents of the document components represented by the variable. For example, the variable *v1* in Figure 1 establishes the following condition: *text must contain the word 'PSG' or the words 'Paris Saint Germain'*. Besides the *contains* attribute, the text marked by the *define_var* tag is also treated as an IRE, which retrieves the document components with the most similar contents to the specified text (see variable *v5* in Figure 1).

```
<xrl id="d1">
   <xrl:definitions>
      <xrl:define_var id="v1" contains="PSG or (Paris Saint Germain)"
          path="/NewsPaper//Sports/Article/*" level="Article" d_ini="1/1/2001" d_end="31/12/2001"/>
      <xrl:define_var id="v2" contains="Champions League" d_ini="1/1/2001" d_end="31/12/2001"
          path="/NewsPaper//Sports/Article/title | /NewsPaper//Sports/Article/subtitle" level="Article" />
      <xrl:define_var id="v3" redefines="v1" contains="Real Madrid" min_rel="10"/>
      <xrl:define_var id="v4" redefines="http://www.my.server.com/xrlqueries.xml#v1" contains="FC Barcelona"
          path="/NewsPaper//Sports/Article/paragraph[1-2]">
      <xrl:define_var id="v5" path="/NewsPaper//Sports//*" level="Article" max="20" d_ini="$v1.d_end">
          Paris Saint-Germain FC beat Olympique de Marseille 7-6 on penalties in the last 16 of the French
          Cup on Sunday, depriving the 1993 UEFA Champions League winners of their last chance to play in
          Europe next season.
      </xrl:define_var>
      <xrl:define_var id="v6" contains="$v1.contains and Final"
          path="/NewsPaper//Sports/Article[@author='Harry']/*" >
   </xrl:definitions>
   <xrl:queries> <! –Query specification elements -- > </xrl:queries>
</xrl>
```

Fig. 1: Example of variable definition in XRL.

The *path* attribute specifies by means of a path expression the document components that must satisfy the retrieval condition. If this attribute is omitted, retrieval conditions will be evaluated over all the components of the documents. The *path* attribute can contain alternative path expressions, like those specified at the definition of the variable *v2*. Moreover, it is possible to specify conditions on the order of the document components (see variable *v4*), and the tag attribute values (see variable *v6*). The *level* attribute establishes the components of the documents that will be retrieved by the variable. If omitted, the variable will represent the last non-wildcard component specified in the *path* attribute. Additionally, the attributes *d_ini* and *d_end* define a time window over the document publication dates.

There are two query attributes that restrict the size of the query variables: the *max* attribute, which indicates the maximum number of document components to be retrieved, and the *min_rel* attribute, which states the minimum relevance for the retrieved document components.

One of the most interesting properties of XRL is the redefinition of variables. The *redefines* attribute allows the definition of a new variable from a previously defined one. For example, in Figure 1 the variable *v3* redefines the variable *v1*. To reference a variable defined in a separate XRL document, we can indicate the URI of that document along with the variable to reuse (see variable *v4*). When defining a variable using the *redefines* attribute, the new variable inherits all the values for its attributes from the referenced variable, except those redefined in the new variable.

Finally, the XRL language includes the *value_of* operator (*$*), whose aim is to reference attribute values of previously defined variables. For example, *v5* takes the value of its *d_ini* attribute from the one defined for the attribute *d_end* of *v1*, and *v6* defines the *contains* attribute starting from that of *v1*.

2.2 Query Specification

In XRL, a query can be seen as a combination of variables. Queries are specified by means of *query* tags (see Figure 2), which indicate the involved variables as well as how to combine their document components for constructing the result. As in the *define_var* tag, the *id* attribute of a *query* tag states an identifier for the query.

When specifying a query, user can select the *relevance* function for ranking the query results. Specifically, the *relevance* attribute can take the values *contents, structural* or *none*. The first one indicates that query results will be ordered according to the relevance given by the keyword frequencies [11]. The second one indicates that query results will be ordered by a combination of the term relevance and the structural relevance [5]. In the third case, query results are not ordered at all.

```
<xrl id="d2">
   <xrl:definitions>  <! –Variable definition elements -- > </xrl:definitions>
   <xrl:queries>
      <xrl:query id="q1" relevance="structural" min_rel="10" max="12" min="5" type="x_doc">
          <union>
               <var id="v1" weight="10"/>
               <intersects>
                    <var id="http://www.my.server.com/xrlqueries.xml#v2"/>
                    <var id="http://www.my.server.com/xrlqueries.xml#q2"/>
               </intersects>
          </union>
      </xrl.query>
      <xrl:query id="q2" min_rel="15" type="x_ref"
          redefines="http://www.myserver.com/xrlqueries.xml#q3(v2=q2_v1, v4=q2_v3)" >
      </xrl:query>
   </xrl:queries>
</xrl>
```

Fig. 2: An example of query specification in XRL.

The attribute *type* specifies how query results are returned to the user. This attribute can take the following values: *x_doc* to obtain the whole document components, *x_ref* to obtain the references to the document components, or *x_count* to obtain the size of the query result. The size of the returned results can be limited by using the *min_rel* attribute. We can also specify a range within the document components of the result by using the *min* and *max* attributes. For example, in Figure 2 query *q1* returns the retrieved document components from 5th to 12th in order of relevance.

The variables involved in a query are specified inside a *query* tag by means of *var* tags. The *id* attribute of a *var* tag is used to reference a previously defined variable. It is also possible to reference the result of another query (see third variable of query *q1* in Figure 2). In order to combine the results of several query variables, XRL introduces the set operators *union*, *intersects* and *difference*, which are expressed as nested tags inside the *query* tag. The semantics of these operators is as usual. However, these operators can change the relevance order of the resulting documents, as shown in Table 1. Finally, the relevance of the results of a variable can be also adjusted by using the *weight* attribute.

Set operator	Relevance recalculation
union(S1,S2)	The resulting relevance of a document appearing at set S1 or at S2 is the maximum of the relevance of this document in the two sets.
intersects(S1,S2)	The resulting relevance of a document appearing at set S1 and at S2 is the minimum of the relevance of this document in the two sets.
difference(S1, S2)	No recalculation is needed.

Table 1. Relevance recalculation implied by the set operators.

The *redefines* attribute of a *query* tag can be applied to reuse the definition of a previously defined query. The example of Figure 2 shows how this attribute is used in the specification of query *q2*. The parameters introduced between parenthesis indicate the correspondence between the original query's variables and the new ones.

3. Implementation Guidelines

In this section we briefly describe the main issues of the current implementation of the XRL query processor. This implementation mainly relies on three indexes, namely:

- *Scodes* [2], which are unique codes, implemented as strings, that represent the trajectories through the XML trees that lead to the terminal elements and attributes. XRL path expressions are efficiently evaluated over *scodes* by using string-matching operations [2].
- *Inverted file*, which records for each term a list with the *scodes* of the XML elements containing it. XRL's *contains* expressions are evaluated over this index.
- *Time index*, which is used to project the document database on a time window.

The current implementation of the XRL query processor uses a relational database with IR capabilities to store the XML documents according to the previous indexes. Specifically, we have defined the following tables:

- repository(id, scode, text), which stores the *text* of each terminal element identified by the corresponding *scode*. The inverted file index is defined on this table.
- repository_att(id, scode, type, value), which stores the *value* of each tag attribute identified by the corresponding *scode*. The type of the value can be either *string*, *number* or *date*, and it is inferred at insertion time.
- type(element, code), which associates a unique code to each XML element or attribute. This code is used to build the *scode* of the document elements.

- insertion_time(scode, time), which stores the insertion time of each document component, identified by its *scode*. Since the insertion of a whole document is usually considered as a transaction, this table only contains the root elements of the XML documents.

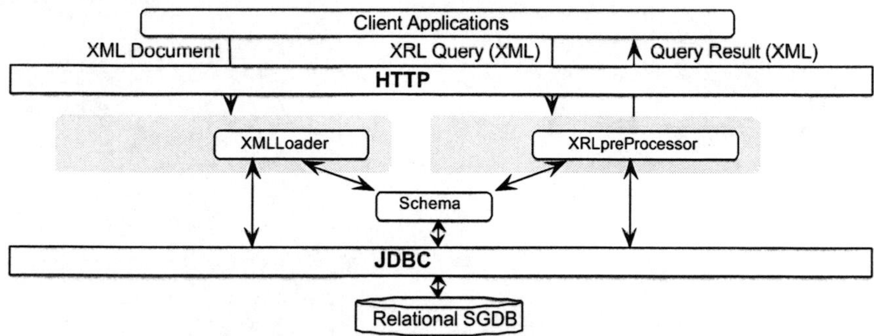

Figure 3. XRL query processor architecture

To store and query XML documents in this database a middleware arquitecture were designed (see Figure 3). The two components that are visible from the client applications are *XMLLoader* and *XRLpreProcessor*, both are implemented as Java Servlets. These two components constitute the wrapper of the relational database. They contain a XML parser to translate the XML documents and XRL queries into the database representation.

The *XRLpreProcessor* is in charge of translating XRL queries into a set of simple SQL queries, usually one for each variable involved in the query. These SQL queries can be efficiently evaluated in parallel by using the presented indexing schema. At this first stage, the *XRLpreProcessor* uses the *Schema* component for translating the path expressions into string-matching expressions over *scodes*. Afterwards, the results of each variable query are combined by union, intersection or difference operations for constructing the final XRL query result.

4. An Example Application

The first application we have developed with the XRL query language is a subscription/notification system for news articles. The users of this system can specify their preferences by means of the interface of Figure 4. Firstly, users can describe the topics of interest by means of an Information Retrieval expression. Additionally, they can specify the newspaper section (e.g. sports, economy, etc.) and the article's component where the retrieval conditions must be evaluated (e.g. title, summary, whole contents, etc.). Afterwards, users can also indicate which parts of the articles must be returned (e.g. title, summary, etc.).

To define the frequency of the subscription evaluation, users specify patterns by selecting a weekly (res. monthly) frequency, and the exact days of the week (res. month) at which they want to be notified.

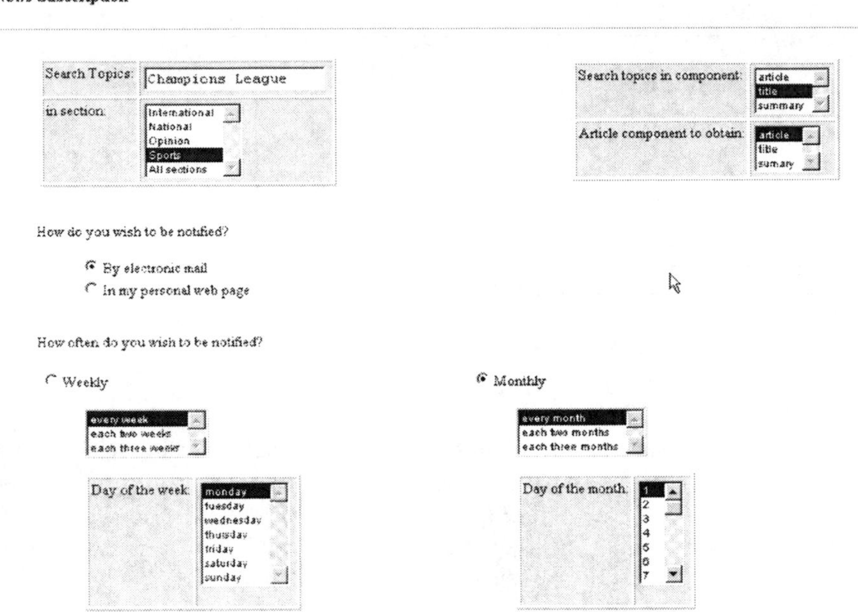

Fig. 4: Interface for the News Subscription System.

Daily the whole contents of the published news articles are inserted into the database in XML format, being indexed by their structure, topics and the temporal attributes. Thus, each user subscription is interpreted by the system as a temporal query over the news database, which must be executed with the specified frequency to retrieve the last novelties related to the user preferences.

Figure 5 schematizes the architecture proposed to implement this system. Firstly, user requirements are processed by a module that updates the users and queries data files. At the same time, a planning module schedules the execution of each query according to the subscription frequency. The planner sends daily to the query processor the queries that must be executed. Once queries are evaluated, their results are passed to the reports generator, so they can be properly presented to the users.

An important feature of this system is that both queries and query results are represented as XML documents. In this way, queries can be easily stored, retrieved, redefined and executed as many times as needed. Additionally, the format of the documents returned by the query processor is flexible, so they can be processed to generate different presentations adapted to the preferences of the users.

4.1 Operation of the System

The subscriber module of Figure 5 is in charge of executing the processes that visualize the user interfaces at the client. Furthermore, this module generates the initial XRL query that retrieves the documents relevant to the user subscription, and inserts it into the queries file. Finally, this module creates an object for each subscription that contains its frequency, its XRL query and the last date it was evaluated. This object is sent to the planner module, which is in charge of determining the next dates at which each subscription must be evaluated.

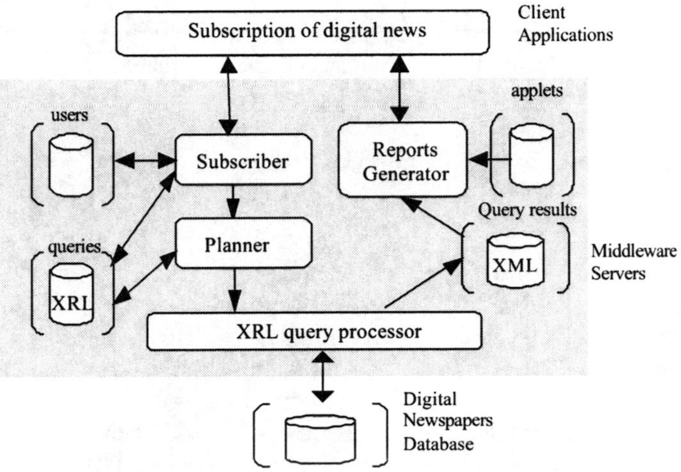

Figure 5. Architecture of the News Subscription System.

Thus, every day the planner retrieves the scheduled XRL queries, and sends them to the query processor, updating accordingly the subscription objects.

As an example consider the XRL query at the left side of Figure 6. This basic XRL query could be initially associated to a subscription that notifies monthly of articles about the "Champions League". As the user wishes to be notified the first day of each month, before being executed, this query must be redefined in order to adjust its temporal projection. The query at the right side of Figure 6 retrieves all the relevant articles published during April, so it must be executed the first day of May. In this way, we make use of the facilities for query reusing and redefinition ensured by XRL as explained in Section 2.

Finally, the reports generator receives the XML file with the query results and produces another XML/HTML document ready to be visualized. Depending on their preferences, users are automatically notified by means of an e-mail, or a new link to this document in their personal Web-pages.

```
<xrl id="example_subscription">
  <xrl: definitions>
       <xrl: define var id="v_basic"
       contains="Champions League"
       path="/NewsPaper//Sports/Article"
       level="Article" >
  </xrl: definitions>
  <xrl:queries>
    <xrl:query id="q_basic" type="x_doc">
       <var id="v_basic/>
    </xrl:query>
  </xrl:queries>
 </xrl>
```

```
<xrl id="example_subscription_april">
  <xrl:definitions>
    <xrl:define_var id="v_april" redefines=
    http://subscrition.server/example.xml#v_basic
    d_ini="01/04/2002" d_end="30/4/2002"/>
  </xrl:definitions>
  <xrl:queries>
    <xrl:query id="q_april" redefines=
    "http://subscrition.server/example.xml#q_basic
    (v_basic=v_april)"/>
   </xrl:query>
  </xrl:queries>
</xrl>
```

Fig. 6: XRL Query for an example subscription.

5. Related Work

In this section we summarise other models and query languages for storing and retrieving XML documents, and we compare these approaches with our work. As presented in Section 2, our language provides mechanisms for specifying document structure conditions by including a subset of Xpath [9]. Other languages like XQuery [10] are based on this proposal. However, they do not provide any Information Retrieval operator nor relevance ranking mechanisms.

In [1], as in our approach, indexing is only performed at the lower/text level of structure of the documents. Their indexing scheme assigns a GID (General element IDentifier) to each element of the document. GIDs can be used for obtaining the ancestors of each element and for accumulating the weights of the terms for relevance ranking. However, it is not clear how the mapping between the query evaluation method and a path expression is performed, specifically when path expressions include wildcards, or the searched elements are at different levels. Under this approach query response time depends on the retrieval level specified by the user, increasing when it is near the root element of the document. They disregard the attributes of tags (present in many XML/SGML documents), the temporal properties of documents, and a structural relevance mechanism.

The work in [6] proposes an expressive model for efficiently indexing and retrieving structured documents. This work consider different structural hierarchies over the same document, with a special hierarchy for the textual contents of the document. As in our approach they use two indexes, one for the document structures and another for the textual contents. Similarly, [7] proposes an index that combines an inverted file with two approaches to codifying the document structure. However, they do not take into account any relevance ranking mechanism for the results.

Finally, YAXQL [8] is a very powerful and expressive XML language for querying XML documents. As in our approach, it provides query reuse and separates the variable definitions from the results specification. Nevertheless, it does not provide any IR operator nor relevance ranking.

6. Conclusions

In this paper we have presented a XML query language for retrieving XML documents. The main goals of this language are to combine structured documents and IR queries, enabling relevance ranking , as well as query reuse. We have described the guidelines of its implementation, and we have shown how this language can be used in a news subscription system. The XRL query processor is currently implemented with Java Servlets and a commercial database. In the future we want to migrate this database into a native XML database with a more appropriate indexing scheme. Over this native database we plan to implement the entire Xpath recommendation [9] for XRL, and to develop optimization techniques for complex XRL queries that combine a large number of variables. Additionally, we plan to introduce advanced presentations for query results, like the histograms and chronicles presented in [5].

Acknowledgements. This work has been funded by the Bancaixa project with contract number PI.1B2000-14, and the CYCIT project with contract number TIC2000-1568-C03-02.

References

1. D. Shin, H. Jang and H. Jin. "BUS: An Effective Indexing and Retrieval Scheme in Structured Documents". Digital Libraries '98, pp. 235-243, 1998.
2. R. Berlanga, M. J. Aramburu and S. Garcia "Efficient Retrieval of Structured Documents from Object-Relational Databases". DEXA'1999, LNCS 1677, Springer-Verlag, 1999.
3. Deutsch, M. F. Fernandez, D. Florescu, A. Y. Levy, D. Maier, D. Suciu "Querying XML Data". IEEE Data Engineering Bulletin 22(3), pp. 10-18, 1999.
4. M. J. Aramburu and R. Berlanga "A Temporal Object-Oriented Model for Digital Librares of Documents" Concurrency: Practice and Experience 13 (11), John Wiley, 2001.
5. R. Berlanga, J.M.Pérez, M.J.Aramburu, and D.Llidó. "Techniques and Tools for the Temporal Analysis of Retrieved Information". DEXA'2001, LNCS 2113, Springer-Verlag, 2001.
6. G. Navarro and R. Baeza-Yates. "Proximal Nodes: A Model to Query Document Databases by Contents and Structure". ACM Trans. on Information Systems 15 (4), 1997.
7. V. Aguilera, S. Cluet, P. Veltri, D. Vodislav and F. Wattez. "Querying XML Documents in Xyleme". VLDB Conference, Roma, 2001.
8. G. Moerkotte. "YAXQL: A powerful and web-aware query language supporting query reuse". Technical Report, University of Mannheim, January 2000.
9. J. Clark and S. DeRose. "XML path language (XPath)". W3C Working Draft 9, July 999.
10. "XQuery 1.0: An XML Query Language". W3C Working Draft, April 2002.
11. R. Baeza-Yates and B.Ribeiro-Neto. "Modern Information Retrieval", Addison-Wesley, 1999.

Norma-System: A Legal Document System for Managing Consolidated Acts

Monica Palmirani and Raffaella Brighi

C.I.R.S.F.I.D, University of Bologna, via Galliera 3,
40100 Bologna, Italy
http://palmiran@cirfid.unibo.it
http://brighi@cirfid.unibo.it

Abstract. The time element inherent in normative systems has become a central topic of the cultural and political debate and is of fundamental concern to legal computer science. The law is under increasing pressure to keep pace with social change: normative texts and amendments follow one another in time and get overlapped. Given this background the Norma-System project, presented in this paper, seeks to use the theoretical, legistic, and legimatic models for facilitating the task of identifying and determining what is the law in force in order to face the multiple problems from which the Italian legal system is currently suffering[1].

1 Introduction

Normative overproduction, a lack of reliable methods for drafting normative texts, the subsequent, overlapping amendments made to such texts, and the ambiguous language used by those who frame our norms—all these factors work against our ability to know and ascertain what the law is. A clearer, better-structured body of norms limits the range of interpretations the same norms are open to, and so makes it possible their correct application. The time element inherent in normative systems has become a central topic of the cultural and political debate and is of fundamental concern to legal computer science. The law is under increasing pressure to keep pace with social change: normative texts and amendments follow one another in time and get overlapped. The citizen, the economic planner, and even the specialist in the law are faced with mounting difficulties in working through the incessant flow of normative innovation and finding the law applicable to the time frames covered by the events subject to regulation.

Considering these scenario, the research project Norma-System got underway in 1993 at the initiative of E. Pattaro, who coordinates a group a researchers[2] engaged in

---

[1] The contributions of this paper are assigned to the co-authors as following: M.Palmirani par. 1, 2, 3.3, 3.4, 3.7, 4; B.Brighi 3.1, 3.2, 3.5, 3.6.

[2] Originally making up the group were E. Pattaro, G. Sartor, A. Capelli, M. Palmirani, and F. Vitali, in collaboration with S. Speranza, J.P. Ballerini, and P. Baldini. Others joined subsequently: among them S. Sola, M. Coppari, R. Brighi, R. Guerra, G. Pasetti, and L. Baroncini.

R. Cicchetti et al. (Eds.): DEXA 2002, LNCS 2453, pp. 310–320, 2002.

working out innovative legistic and legimatic solutions designed to simplify administrative norms process production. Phase one of the project was closed in 1996 and brought out a stand-alone computer system for drafting, managing, and consolidating the norms issued by the City of Bologna. After this, legal document management systems based on Norma-System software were put together for the Italian Treasury Department for a Euro-regulations project (1998 – about 300 acts), the Ministry of Research for funded projects concerning a legal database about IT regulations domain (1999 – about 1000 acts) and a copyright regulations domain (2001 – about 800 acts) and recently the Bologna University for all the local regulations (2002 – about 400 acts).

To meet the aims set for the projects, we integrated into them the technologies used for Web-distributed databases, and this made it necessary to overhaul the entire system. Norma-System now based on seven Web software modules that make it possible to: (i) support practitioners of the law in drafting normative acts, such that from the outset we can prevent unsound lawmaking from undermining the principles of simplification, readability, and certainty; (ii) help program users create consolidated texts; (iii) provide tools with which to create well-framed unified texts (whether to renew or reorder existing norms); (iv) trace the history of a document by searching the temporal axes of its force, and efficacy; (v) apply XML tags to existing documents and make it possible to manage and reuse them; (vi) file old, modificatory, and consolidated documents in XML format so as to facilitate their integration into existing databases; and (vii) publish Internet databases of past and consolidated norms and jurisprudence with advanced search systems that can display data along the temporal lines of the force, and efficacy of norms.

2 System Architecture

The need the Norma project is designed to answer is the current Italian and European lawmaking crisis which invests the entire Italian system of multiple sources of law. On the base of this objective Norma-System is now composed of six base modules and two accessory modules [3]. The base modules are:

1. a Handbook for Drafting Normative Texts[3];
2. a software module for drafting acts;
3. a software module for consolidating acts (producing coordinated texts);
4. a module for filing documents in a database server;
5. a module for publishing and viewing the documents on the Internet;
6. a module for making searching the documents[4].

The accessory modules are:

1. a system-manager module that serves to activate functions for reordering the system and providing DB maintenance;

---

[3] This Handbook is published as appendix in the M. Palmirani, Norma-System, Clueb, Bologna, 2000 and it was created by E. Pattaro, G. Sartor, A. Capelli.

[4] Consultation and research is made possible by a standard Web browser, while drafting and consolidation are effected using a specialized word processor connected with the document management system.

2. a module for defining the structure of normative documents by the creation of the DTD.

This last module is more recent and is designed to enable assigning different structures to the documents and link to these structures differentiated drafting rules, such that the editor and database module can acquire these parameters. This function is based on XML technology, since the module is designed to produce DTD schemes fit to represent all the structural, functional, and semantic elements the drafter/user deems essential to searching and handling the text.

In greater detail, the system is structured as follows:

1. *Norma-Handbook*: a paper handbook for drafting normative texts[5];
2. *Norma-Editor*: an editor for drafting normative texts;
3. *Norma-Consolidation*: a module for creating and managing consolidated texts;
4. *Norma-Database*: a database for filing and retrieving documents using complex search strings;
5. *Norma-Internet*: for generating documents fit for publication on the Internet;
6. *Norma-Query*: for making full-text and structured searches on the Internet;
7. *Norma-DTD*: for creating, modifying, and viewing the structures of DTD documents;
8. *Norma-Admin*: for managing the database from a remote location and for the system manager to reorder versioning operations.

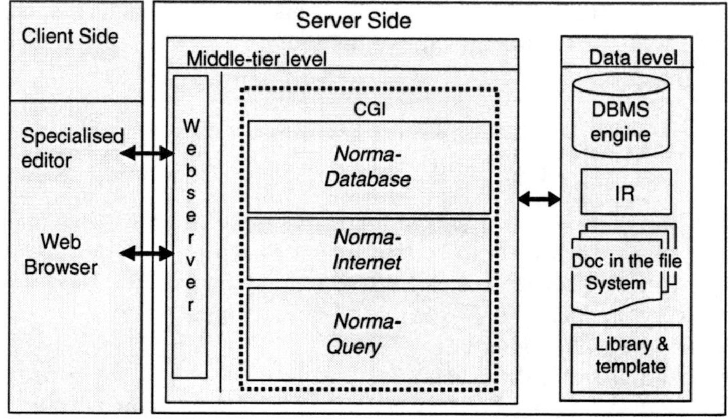

Fig. 1. System Architecture overview

The system's basic architecture is illustrated in the figure 1, where you can see how end users can access a body of norms via a shared browser, and how the expert users can update the database through an editing station Microsoft Word 97.

In what follows we illustrate the chief functions built into each module.

[5] The handbook is not presented here, for its scope is not within the research aims of legistic technique and is rather intended to provide guidelines which the norm-making organs might use in the course of drafting.

3 Modules Presentation

3.1 Norma-Editor

The editor makes it possible to generate new normative acts using the most well-established Italian drafting rules[6] and to mark the information found in the already approved documents. The editor enables you to mark all the information in the course of drafting so that you can later use the same information while reading and consolidating documents. In fact the drafting phase is when you structure the document, link it to other documents, specify the references that make these linkups, put in keywords and subjects for classification, and identify the functional parts of sentences. The aim here is to mark the document with tags (using the XML standard) for each piece of information deemed meaningful and then use all such information to check the text for coherence and make it possible a flexible use of the same text. The editor helps drafters draw up normative texts, whose structure and parameters depend on the user's choice of any of a number of previously set document types. These document types (DTD) provide important information to the editor, which is thereby enabled to help drafters draft and validate documents. The marked document will prove autonomous and equipped with all the data needed for re-processing the document using either Norma-System database or an external, non-proprietary database (after the initial DTD is provided).

Norma-Editor makes it possible to:

1. create new documents using a contextual guide to compilation on the basis of the rules set out in the handbook;
2. customize the constrictive and optional rules depending on the type of document loaded;
3. generate files using as guides the preset modules that load when a document is opened;
4. generate and control document structure;
5. mark all internal, external, abbreviated, and frequent citations;
6. classify citations using different colors keyed to the function served by a reference to another normative text (an added feature that makes the editor an especially powerful tool for all further consolidation operations);
7. manage informative, modifying, and temporal citations [5];
8. manage abbreviations, units of measurements, and acronyms;
9. check the completed text for coherence;
10. mark the documents external to the system using a semi-automated function and manage preexisting norms; this structure marking is fully automated down to article level and semi-automated for references;
11. view the marked document parts by color coding;
12. view and compare the structures automatically recognized by the system through text mapping;
13. access the database to consult filed documents online as well as check for new document markers and references to other acts;
14. connect to the database to upload new documents inside the DB and the file system online;

---

[6] See Annex A of the M. Palmirani, Norma-System, Clueb, Bologna, 2000.

15. manage attached acts, integrative acts, and informative acts;
16. set up a hierarchy connecting the primary documents with its attachments;
17. manage offline references;
18. save document locally in the course of its production phases: draft, preexisting documents, consolidation.

3.2 Norma-Consolidation

The consolidation software helps users provide maintenance for the normative acts by means of a simplified, though restrictive, interface and of computing tools designed as a complement to the user's legal knowledge. This module is essential in helping lawmakers keep up a coherent body of laws, a task defined as "support which the lawmaking techniques provide for policy making" [4]. The Norma-System editor and the module for connecting to the web are a consolidation tool that starts up a sequence of processes in the database. The database becomes a repository for all the versions to each document, thereby making possible the versioning of normative acts. By this means, one can proceed from a document in force to retrieve the norms corpus in force at any date supplied to the system and track the sequence of antecedent documents. The document in question is pegged to a date and contained all and only those normative references pertaining to the time specified. Hence, a user looking to create a coordinated act can call up the modifying document and effect in semi-automated mode all previously marked and classified changed. This procedure is automated when the change affects atomic and well-defined text parts. The system asks for authorisation before effecting the step-by-step automated procedure, since the user is ultimately responsible for legal interpretation. The editing module guides the consolidation operations by effecting (temporal, semantic, and structural) coherence checkups on that the user is doing, and it generates automatically a new document version equipped with explanatory and consolidation notes and with references to the modifying norms. This way the end user can retrieve from any document the documents responsible for bringing about the changes leading to it.

The consolidation software makes it possible to:

1. consolidate documents manually;
2. manage interactive consolidation operations by means of specifically designed keys;
3. manage in fully automated mode the consolidation operations on atomic documents partitions all the while recognizing the partitions on which to operate;
4. consolidate documents proceeding from a list of modified documents;
5. connect to the server via a Web browser controlled by the editor to download documents to be consolidated;
6. activate the locking and security devices in the downloaded documents to maintain a coherent database;
7. activate the temporal-check devices for the consolidation actions, such that disallowed operations are rejected;
8. run coherence checks for the operations effected using the type of normative linkup treated;
9. manage pathological cases (e.g., the modification of a modification);
10. manage the entire creation of consolidation notations;

11.submit the consolidated document to the database;
12.manage versioning when submitting the consolidated document.

3.3 Norma-Database

An SQL-compatible database (a non-proprietary database easily integrated with existing RDBMS engines) makes up the information structure where all the documents are stored and on which all searching and consulting is done, and importantly it is the basis on which all the online publication and consolidation modules rest. The rules for forming documents, the document levels and granularity, the structure of the acts, the tags, and the document-access priorities and relative security levels are all managed by meta-charts linked up with the data charts. Two document types are essential to representing a database document: the original Word document and its HTML (now also in XML) translation with meta-tags used to classify all the information types found in the text. In this structure, the smallest filing unit is the document, while no granularity limits apply to consolidation and consultation. Lastly, the database's multimedia features make it possible to file attachments as charts, graphics, images, visuals, video, and audios: a key function, since normative acts are more and more often accompanied with nontextual material integral to them (e.g. maps, technical plans, handcraft graphics, etc.).

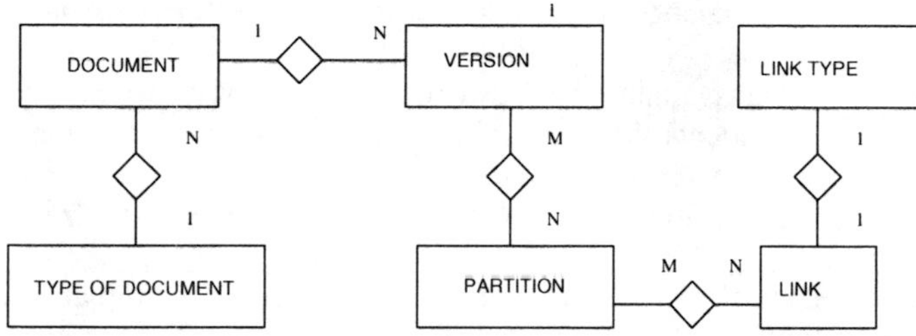

Fig. 2. E-R schema of the Norma-Database

The database makes it possible to:

1. manage documents separately from the database server. The documents are stored only in the file system, or else, when necessary, in the document management system. It is possible to enter documents in different formats. The database now manages files in Word, HTML, PDF, and XML format;
2. the smallest entity is the document, which is treated in its entirety and is the smallest reference unit, even if the marked elements make it possible to handle single part or partitions thereof;
3. build a range of levels and structures into a document and apply to it different kinds of tags. The database (DB) is built keeping separate all the meta-data that define document types and the names of the fields in the DB;
4. manage the multimedia attachments (charts, images, etc.);
5. publish on the Internet the templates foreign to the DBMS logical scheme;
6. index texts using an Information Retrieval (IR) tool;
7. manage each text's dates of issuance, publication, and binding force;
8. query the database by date interval;

9. refine your queries;
10. take a snapshot of a set of documents in force on a given date, framing as well the inbound and outbound links;
11. manage passive and active links;
12. manage statistical data on Web access;
13. version primary documents and attachments;
14. do versioning starting from the date a document comes into force and the date it becomes effective.

3.4 Norma-Internet

Internet consultation forms the basis of Norma-System's new client/server setup, which makes it possible to view on the fly the database documents and the hyperlinks previously marked while editing. Each item of information previously processed, classified, and modified while editing is a tool useful in viewing not only single documents, but also the hypertext network underlying an entire body of coordinated norms. The metadata and tags set into the documents enable users to view in detail a document's the logical map as well as pin down to sub-paragraph level the references to other normative documents. The publication mechanism is based on the use of HTML templates which are external to the database and which lay out page makeups according to user specifications. This way layout design is kept separate from the way the information in the database is managed, a feature which makes the design easy to customise.

The modules makes available the following modes of navigation:

1. searching the documents through a rigid hierarchical structure (list of documents and/or table of contents inside each document);
2. searching through references to other normative documents (references which change as two-way hypertext links are added to the documents);
3. drawing up personalised lists of documents according to dynamically specified criteria (groupings by document type, family, geographic area, area of expertise, etc.);
4. searching via the explicit active (from the current document) and passive (to the current document) references found in a normative text;
5. searching the document's history, with notices appearing along the way;
6. moving from a document to its attachments;
7. select the document and data "frozen" on a given date;
8. looking at the informational notes to the document;
9. viewing and printing the coordinated and text integrated with explanatory notes;
10. viewing lists ordered according to different ordering criteria (as by date, ID number, and enactment authority);
11. viewing the document by enriched logical maps (list of passive references, list of document versions, special information about the document, etc.).

3.5 Norma-Query

The search module for a database collecting normative texts must enable quick document retrieval through the traditional search fields; that is, document ID, enacting authority, date published, and act title. But often these will not suffice, for two reason:

1. the person familiar with such information is typically a legal practitioner, which is to say that accurate searching is possible only given knowledge of preexisting norms. This leaves out of the picture all users not in possession of a document's ID number (ordinary users);
2. anyone looking to do more complex searches will not be able to enter advanced search strings that can yield search results limited to actually meaningful documents (advanced users).

A search tool able to answer the needs of both ordinary users and advanced users will have to provide a number of additional search fields, like act type and enactment date, or more search functions, for example, searching by intervals of values (dates) or by full text using AND, OR, NEAR operators. The indeed indexing are not embedded into the system, but are connected by modules to products out on the market, so that the Norma-Search component stands independent of the information-retrieval tool used.

A feature of the research module enables users to couple searches by structured fields and full text with time parameters: a search can be limited to the date a document comes into force or the date it becomes effective, or to given dates specified by the user, or to date intervals, and these options enable users to take "snapshots" of the body of norms by time periods.

This modules makes possible the following functions:

1. accessing search tools on the fields built into the documents (data identifying the normative acts);
2. doing full-text searches. (the document collection is indexed by an external Information Retrieval tool);
3. viewing the list of active and passive links relative to a text partition;
4. searching by date of enactment, publication, validity, efficacy;
5. searching by time intervals;
6. taking a "snapshot" of a body of documents in force on a given date;
7. viewing search results by documents and document partitions alike.

3.6 Norma-DTD

Norma-System is based on marking the document's structure and features. A principle of polymorphism makes it possible to adapt the entire system to the different structures which normative acts can take on, and on this principle document types customize the editor interface for all uses, from consulting the document to getting search displays.

Even so, the document's structure, and especially the granularity with which users seek to describe a normative domain, is a choice not restricted by the software and is rather entrusted to the persons in charge of the database. Indeed the system makes it possible to specify, according to the desiderata set by the agency using the database, the degree to which the documents are structured and the amount of document types. If the domain to be processed is vast and heterogeneous, as to the norms' provenance and the areas regulated, it will prove useful to define precise typologies for each group of normative documents, so that these can then differentiated by their distinguishing features while editing and while searching. If instead the domain is limited, as to size and range of normative sources, it is advisable not to limit the schemes, this in order not to overburden data entry and access operations, for if a detailed methodology were used, fragmented search results would obtain, and this would work against the quality of the overall view. In other words, ample, complex, and heterogeneous databases are best built using finepoint structure models, such as make it possible to handle the complexity involved, aid users while editing, and supply an interface appropriate to the type of document treated. By contrast, with limited and homogeneous domains it is best to use a single text model, which will prevent fragmenting the database to no avail. The first model (the detailed one) has been used for the legal database about the IT regulations built in 1999 and co-funded by the Ministry of the Research. The database collects 1000-odd documents consisting in Italian and European government-issued legislation and jurisprudence, both primary and secondary. Forty documents types were devised, making possible greater accuracy in data entry and greater control in consolidating and organizing the documents. On the other hand the document type model used for the City of Bologna can be defined with four groups, namely, *city-hall deliberations*, *city-council deliberations*, *city regulations*, and *mayor's ordinances*—no fragmenting into types was needed to build the database. Hence, granularity and differentiation needs to be flexible and easy to handle by the functionaries charged by each agency using a database, whose usage criteria are made to fit the purpose at hand. It is therefore inconceivable that such parameters be built and fixed into the software (by code embedding): they will rather have to be external to it, so that the metadata in each type of document can be accessed when needed.

To manage the specification of these parameters from outside the software code, a tool is needed that makes for easy handling and consultation while enabling users to gather all the technical software-support information.

To this end, a specific software module called Norma-DTD was designed that makes possible two operations by which the structures for the different document types can be defined through the Web.

The first such operation consists in defining the *superclass* to which a given document belongs, meaning by *superclass* a group of documents sharing structural as well as semantic properties: for example, "recommendation" can be made into a class since all recommendations can be described through the same structure: dame ID (regulation number), same number of levels, same kind of normative document (regulation in attachment).

The second operation consists in defining, for each type of regulation, a specific class with specific values, like the authority calling for a norm, the authority issuing the norm, the place of issuance, the document drawn up for official publication (on a gazette or bulletin) as a normative text, the issuance or promulgation formula, the closing formula, the number of signatures, and the names of the persons and institutions underwriting the document. In the case of recommendations we might distinguish the following typologies as pertaining to the same superclass:

1. Recommendation by the European Council
2. Recommendation by the European Central Bank
3. Recommendation by the Commission of European Communities

Each of these entries is a sub-class of the abstract superclass (recommendations) within which it falls. The Norma-DTD software module creates a DTD file for each class of documents and joins to this class a scheme made of markers that by coding differentiate the text's structural and semantic parts.

In the research co-funded by the Ministry of the Research, 40 document superclasses were singled out that bring together 90 calsses. They have been generated automatically by the Norma-DTD module following the DTD standard language and using the data entered online with the software just described.

Increasingly researchers are turning to the problem of defining Italian shared standards for correlating the norms distributed on the Internet, in an effort to create a wide network linking up different sources of normative production and diffusion. To this end, a structured DTD scheme applicable to many types of normative document provides a stepping stone for all subsequent study in the discipline.

3.7 Norma-Admin

The system-administration module, Norma-Admin, is intended for the system administrator and makes possible the following operations:

1. indexing the collection of documents to enable full-text searching. Every now and then it proves necessary to redo the index to make sure that all texts have been processed;
2. regenerating the database in case of some corruption of the files (regeneration proceeds from the collection of marked documents);
3. regenerating the *versioning chains* starting from a document's the date of efficacy. These kind of documents are indeed virtual document generated by the system;
4. removing mistakenly entered documents and synchronize the normative chains of all the DB;
5. assigning access priorities for each user authorising or barring them from performing certain functions (like consolidation);
6. generating the DTD and the dots, meaning the Word models defining each document type entered using Norma-DTD.

4 Conclusion

What emerges from the foregoing considerations is that technology has reached a stage now where it can not only support the entire norm-production cycle, but also deliver the desired certainty in the publication of such consolidated acts as have processed by text marking.

Further, the level of awareness and understanding of legistic and legimatic issues in administrations has grown markedly. In recent years, in a society where information technology is becoming ever more entrenched, the basis has been forming on which to proceed in an effort to bring the advancements made in legimatics to bear on the administrations' experiences in processing legal knowledge by computer. It will be noted here how a number of projects promoted by the public administrations have been weaving progressively the fabric to a new reality. Worthy of mention among in this connection is the *Norme in Rete* [1] project, promoted by

AIPA and the Ministry of Justice and framed to supply the missing link between information technology and the public administrations (both local and central) in the field of legimatics. Specifically, the project has had a major role in an effort to overcome the fragmentation affecting online availability of norms. In the next couple of years we can expect to see increased trust in these legimatic tools, setting the stage for new advancements in streamlining administration and furthering the ends normative production.

For the Norma-System project a new version of the XML editor and database is being developed that will integrate the guidelines set forth by the *Norme in Rete* committees and make it easier to manage XML standards and solve links to norms outside the database. The aim, in other words, it to enable Norma-System to connect to other legislative databases on the Internet so that Norma-Editor documents may be accessed was well by non-proprietary databases, or any database other than Norma-System. This is to increase the availability of legal-drafting tools, whose applications go far beyond text processing, since the wider aim is to develop a solid legistic and legimatic culture.

References

1. multiauthor, "Studio di fattibilità per la realizzazione del progetto «Accesso alle norme in rete»", in Informatica e Diritto, n.1, 2000.
2. M. Palmirani, S. Sola, M. Coppari, P. Baldini, "Norma SQL: un sistema informatico per la gestione del ciclo di produzione normativa", in AA.VV., Atti (su CD-ROM) del Convegno Il diritto nella società dell'informazione, a cura dell'Istituto per la Documentazione Giuridica del CNR, Firenze, 2-5 dicembre 1998.
3. M. Palmirani, Norma-System, Clueb, Bologna, 2000.
4. A. Pizzorusso, La manutenzione del libro delle leggi ed altri studi sulla legislazione, Torino, Giappichelli, 1999.
5. G. Sartor, R. Hernandez Marin, "Time in Legislation", In Time and Law. Is the Nature of Law to Last, Ed. F. Ost & M. Van Hoecke, pp. 425-450, Bruxelles, Bruylant, 1998.

Electricity Market Price Forecasting: Neural Networks versus Weighted-Distance k Nearest Neighbours

Alicia Troncoso Lora[1], José Riquelme Santos[2], Jesús Riquelme Santos[1], José Luís Martínez Ramos[1] and Antonio Gómez Expósito[1]

[1] Department of Electrical Engineering, University of Sevilla, Sevilla, Spain
[2] Department of Languages and Systems, University of Sevilla, Sevilla, Spain
ali@esi.us.es riquelme@lsi.us.es {jesus, camel, age}@us.es

Abstract. In today's deregulated markets, forecasting energy prices is becoming more and more important. In the short term, expected price profiles help market participants to determine their bidding strategies. Consequently, accuracy in forecasting hourly prices is crucial for generation companies (GENCOs) to reduce the risk of over/underestimating the revenue obtained by selling energy. This paper presents and compares two techniques to deal with energy price forecasting time series: an Artificial Neural Network (ANN) and a combined k Nearest Neighbours (kNN) and Genetic algorithm (GA). First, a customized recurrent Multi-layer Perceptron is developed and applied to the 24-hour energy price forecasting problem, and the expected errors are quantified. Second, a k nearest neighbours algorithm is proposed using a Weighted-Euclidean distance. The weights are estimated by using a genetic algorithm. The performance of both methods on electricity market energy price forecasting is compared.

1 Introduction

The new competitive Spanish Electricity Market has been in operation since 1998, and it is mainly based on two separated day-ahead markets [5]:

- The energy market, managed by the Market Operator (MO), where producers and consumers submit production and consumption bids (blocks of hourly energy and the corresponding price in Euros/MWh for each of the 24 hours of the following day). The MO produces a market-clearing price and sets of accepted production and consumption bids for every hour. Additional markets for minor adjustments are also performed on an hourly basis.
- The market for regulation reserves. Once the energy market is cleared, the System Operator establishes the requirements for operating reserves (an hourly margin in MW up and down), that are needed for frequency control, for each of the 24 hours of the following day. The reserve market allocates the margin among the generators that are capable of providing secondary frequency control by using generators' up and down bids which include the offered band (MW) and the price (Euros/MW). A market for additional energy reserves (power that can be provided within 15 minutes for a period of two hours) is also performed.

R. Cicchetti et al. (Eds.): DEXA 2002, LNCS 2453, pp. 321–330, 2002.

In this context, forecasting energy prices is extremely important. In the short term, expected price profiles, both in terms of energy and reserve prices, help market participants to determine their bidding strategies. Consequently, accuracy in forecasting hourly energy & reserve prices is crucial for generation companies (GENCOs) to reduce the risk of over/underestimating the revenue obtained by selling energy.

The motivation of this paper is to present and compare two techniques to deal with energy price forecasting time series: an Artificial Neural Network (ANN) and a combined k Nearest Neighbours (kNN) and Genetic algorithm (GA). First, a customized recurrent Multi-layer Perceptron is developed and applied to the 24-hour energy price forecasting problem, and the expected errors are quantified. Second, a k nearest neighbours algorithm is proposed using a Weighted-Euclidean distance. The weights are estimated by using a genetic algorithm.

2 ANN-Based Market Price Forecasting

The ANN approach has been chosen because of its successful performance in the load forecasting problem [1, 2]. Larger errors are expected in this case, however, as the influence of the load level on market clearing prices is only moderate, and other unpredictable factors play an important role in non-perfect oligopolistic markets.

The study reported in this paper is based on the hourly Spanish spot market prices recorded from January 2001 to August 2001. As weekends and holidays constitute separate cases, only data corresponding to working days have been retained and analyzed.

Figure 1a shows the hourly averages and standard deviations of prices for the working days of March 2001, in cents of Euro per kWh.

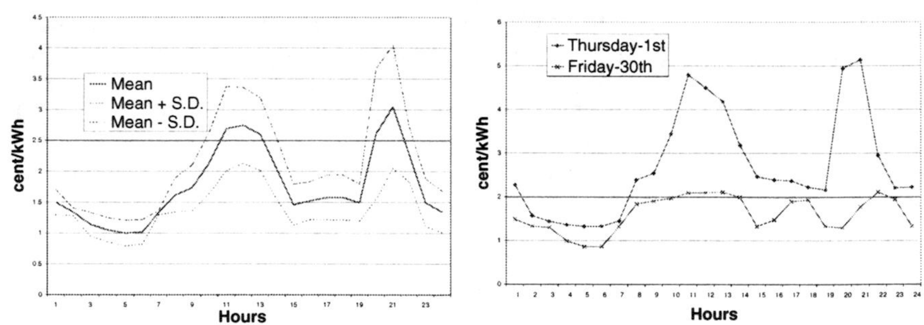

Fig. 1. a) Hourly average of spot market prices for March 2001. **b)** Evolution of energy prices for two days of March 2001.

Average spot prices larger than 2 cent/kWh take place during the morning and evening peak hours (10am-2pm and 8-10pm respectively). Except for a few valley hours, the s.d. of this price exceeds 20% of the mean value, reaching even 40% at 8pm and 9pm.

Figure 1b represents the energy prices for two selected days of March 2001. The significant differences in the prices of the peak hours can not be explained by a change in the demand profile, probably revealing market power mechanisms.

2.1 Structure of the ANN

A brief description of the ANN adopted in this work is provided in this section (the reader interested in ANN background is referred to [3] and [4]).

An ANN is composed of a certain number of perceptrons organized by layers. Each perceptron has several inputs and a single output, whose value is a non-linear function of the inputs. Each perceptron's input is affected by a weighting factor, which must be determined during the training phase. Usually, an ANN is composed of three layers (input, hidden and output), where the outputs of a layer feed the inputs of the next layer.

The two main steps involved in the use of an ANN are:

- Determining its topology, which basically consists of defining the number of perceptrons in the intermediate hidden layer.
- Obtaining the input weighting factors for a given non-linear function (training process).

According to the authors' previous experience, it is decided to feed the ANN with a shifting window of prices comprising 24 hours. This means that the input layer is composed of 24 perceptrons. As far as the number of output perceptrons is concerned, two possibilities have been evaluated.

a) A single output whose value is dictated by the previous 24 hours. Under this scheme, very popular in load forecasting, the window is shifted one hour each time.
b) Twenty four outputs corresponding to the prices of a whole day, whose values are determined by those of the previous day. This implies that the window is shifted 24 hours each time.

Test results have shown better accuracy for scheme b), which is the only one considered in the sequel.

In order to fully define the ANN, it is necessary to determine the number of perceptrons in the intermediate layer and the number of days required for the training process.

Figure 2 shows, for 12, 24 and 36 neurons in the hidden layer, the average forecasting error in the energy price corresponding to the working days of February 2001, versus the number of days used to train the ANN. As can be noted, 20 days are sufficient to train the ANN, the number of neurons not being so important. For the results presented below, 24 neurons in the hidden layer have been used to forecast the spot market energy prices.

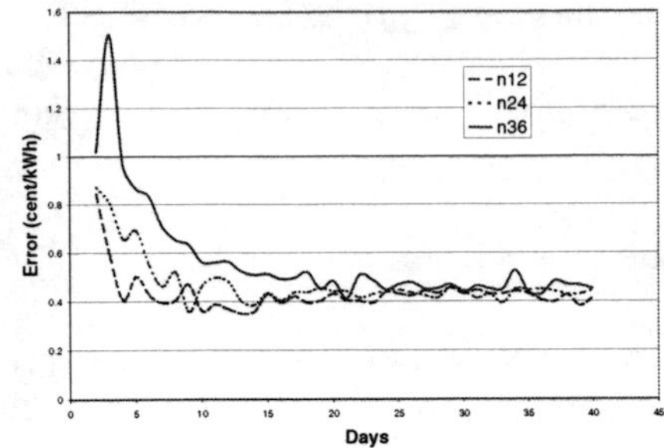

Fig. 2. Average forecasting error in the energy price.

2.2 Results

About two months of the available period (January - February 2001) are used in several experiments to find out and tune the best ANN topology, while the remaining material (March-August 2001) is devoted to check the forecasting errors.

Figure 3a presents the absolute value of the error of the forecasted spot market prices for the two days of March 2001 leading to the largest and smallest average errors.

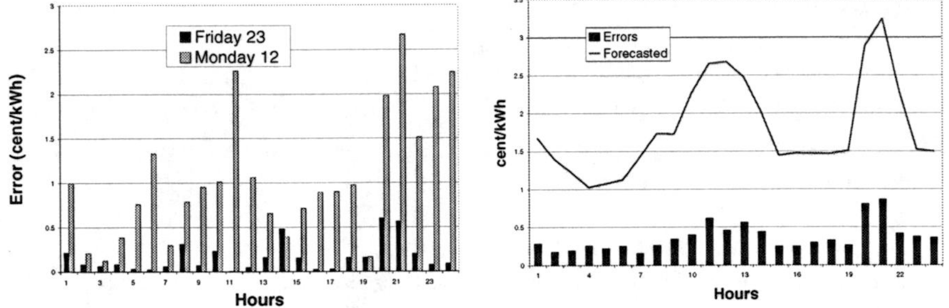

Fig. 3. a) Absolute value of the error of the forecasted energy prices (best and worst prediction). **b)** Hourly average of the forecasted energy prices (March 2001).

	Daily Prices (cent/kWh)			
	Average real price	s. d.	Average absolute error	Maximum error
March-May	2.2588	0.7801	0.3464	2.671
June-August	3.5482	1.0597	0.428	2.0736

Table 1. Forecasting errors for the energy prices.

Figure 3b shows the hourly average of the forecasted energy prices corresponding to March 2001, as well as the resulting prediction errors (obtained by difference with the actual prices of figure 1). Note that the forecasting errors are larger during peak hours.

Finally, table 1 presents the average and s.d. of actual prices, the average absolute value of forecasting errors and the maximum errors for Spring and

Summer seasons. The average error ranges from 12% (Summer) to 15% (Spring) of the hourly average price. As expected, the larger the s.d. of prices the higher the average forecasting error.

3 Nearest Neighbour Based Market Price Forecasting

In this section, a combined kNN [11, 13] and GA [14] for hourly market energy prices forecasting is described. The Genetic Algorithm is used to compute the optimal weights to outweight the most significant hours. The kNN finds the daily market energy prices that are "similar to" the prices of previous days.

The prediction aims at estimating the prices for a certain day from a linear combination of the energy prices of the days that follow the nearest neighbours days.

3.1 K Nearest Neighbours

The prediction of a time series requires the knowledge of some parameters: the time delay, the embedding dimension and the number of nearest neighbours. The optimal determination of these parameters has been studied in the last years [7, 8].

Energy prices are collected every hour and, in consequence, the time delay is an hour.

For short-term forecasting, it has been decided to organize the temporal data with a shifting window of prices comprising 24 hours and consequently the embedding dimension is 24.

As far as the number of steps to predict is concerned, only one possibility has been evaluated: twenty four hours corresponding to the prices of a whole day, whose values are determined by those of the previous day. This possibility implies that the window is shifted 24 hours each time.

Choosing a metric: A time series Y can be considered as a point in a n-dimensional space. Given a sequence query, q, a sequence of Y with the same length as q is searched, z, such that the distance between the sequences is minimum. The choice of the metric to measure similarity between two time series depends mainly on the specific features of the considered series. The most common metric is the square of the Euclidean distance, although other metrics can be used [9]. In this case, the time serie is the electricity market energy prices, and the Weighted-Euclidean distance is preferred because not all the hours of a day have the same influence on the prices of the following day. This distance is defined by

$$d_w^2(q, z) = \sum_{i=1}^{r} w_i \cdot (q_i - z_i)^2 \tag{1}$$

where $r = \text{length}(q)$ and $w_i \in [0, 1]$.

3.2 Prediction

The prediction of stock energy prices for one day $d+1$ is computed through two steps taking into account the weights of all the hours of a day:

1. Calculate the distances between the prices of the day d, P_d, and the preceding points $\{P_{d-1}, P_{d-2}, ...\}$ using (1). Let be v_1,...,v_k the k nearest days to the day d, sorted by closeness.
2. The prediction is:

$$\widehat{P}_{d+1} = \frac{1}{\alpha_1 + ... + \alpha_k} \sum_{l=1}^{l=k} \alpha_l \cdot P_{v_l+1} \tag{2}$$

where

$$\alpha_l = \frac{d_w(P_d, P_{v_k}) - d_w(P_d, P_{v_l})}{d_w(P_d, P_{v_k}) - d_w(P_d, P_{v_1})} \tag{3}$$

The two former steps are repeated during the days of the forecasting horizon.

Notice that $0 \leq \alpha_l \leq 1$, i.e., the weight is equal to zero when the considered day is the most distant and one when the considered day is the nearest.

Also, notice that if the k nearest neighbours for a vector P_d are $[P_{v_1}, ..., P_{v_k}]$, where v_i is the ith nearest neighbour, the set of points $[P_{v_1+1}, ..., P_{v_k+1}]$ will usually be the nearest to P_{d+1}.

3.3 Genetic Algorithm

Genetic Algorithms (GA) are computational techniques based on the mechanics of natural selection in which solutions to a problem are coded in a similar way to the genetic structure of biological organisms. Each individual in the population represents a possible solution to the problem, and a fitness factor is assigned to each member of the population, with the best individuals receiving higher fitness factors. A particular GA is characterized by issues such as population size, mutation rates, and selection and new population creation mechanisms.

In the GA used in this paper, each individual is defined by the weight of each hour throughout the whole day, and the fitness function is the inverse of the average square error (ASE) that results from the aforesaid predicting mechanism.

The basic algorithm can be written as follows [12]:

1. An initial population is randomly selected.
2. The fitness factor of each individual is computed.
3. Parents are randomly selected using a tournament selection technique.
4. Parents are crossbred to create new individuals.
5. Several new individuals are mutated.
6. Members with a low fitness factor are replaced with new individuals.
7. If the maximum number of generations has not been reached, go to step 2.

Notice that, in order to compute the fitness factor of each individual, a Nearest Neighbour Algorithm is needed. In consequence, execution times are mainly determined by the kNN module.

Individuals are represented by real row vectors, with columns corresponding to the 24 hours of a day.

The number of days used for the estimation of the parameters $\{w_i\}_{i=1}^{r}$, and the number of parameters are closely related. If the number of days is too small, the estimated parameters will not be optimal, and if it is too large the estimation of these parameters is computationally very expensive. In consequence, the correct selection of the number of days is quite important to correctly tune the algorithm.

Other implementation issues of the GA are the following:

Initial Population: The initial population is strictly randomly selected.

Fitness function: The fitness function must be able to provide a good measure of the quality of each individual/solution. The kNN+PREDICTION module provides the estimated energy prices according to (2). The fitness function is defined by the inverse of

$$ASE = \frac{1}{n}\sum_{d=1}^{n}(\widehat{P}_d - P_d)^2 \tag{4}$$

where n is the number of days used to calculate the weights. Therefore, in order to calculate the ASE, the k nearest neighbours of the daily prices must be known.

Parent selection and crossover: To produce a new generation, parents are randomly selected using a tournament selection technique that selects the best individuals for reproduction. The probability of a particular individual being selected is in direct proportion to its fitness function, taking into account that the ASE is being minimized.

Regarding the crossover process, the crossover probability has been set to one, i.e., two individuals that have been selected to be parents are always combined to obtain a new individual. Children are obtained by adding the strings that results from random partitions of the row.

Children mutation: Following the crossover process, children are mutated to introduce some new genetic material according to a pre-defined mutation probability. The gene to be mutated is represented by a randomly selected hour, randomly selected individual. The mutation implies adding a random number proportional to the initial value with some previously defined probability.

3.4 Test Results

The kNN+GA has been applied in several experiments to obtain the forecast of Spanish electricity market energy prices. February 2001 has been used to determine the weight of every hour of the day, using the GA described in the former section, and whose main parameters are shown in table 2. The available period of March-August 2001 has been chosen as a test set to check the forecasting errors. The number of neighbours have been considered equal to one in all experiments due to the low influence on the forecasted errors [10].

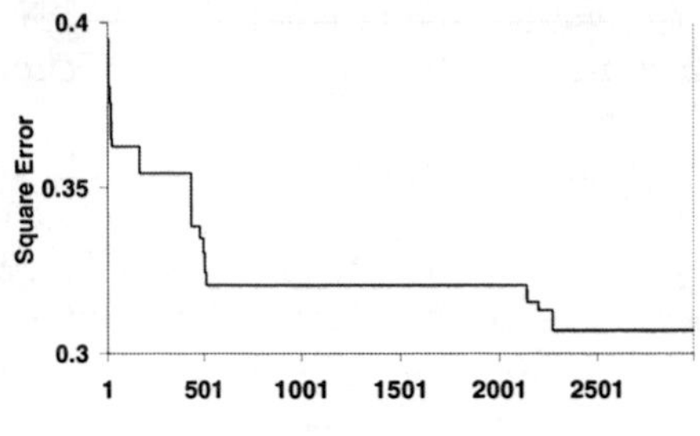

Fig. 4. Evolution of the best individual.

The forecasting errors obtained by the proposed algorithm are compared with the results of an ANN on the same test set described in the first part of this paper.

Figure 4 shows the evolution of the square error of the fittest individual throughout the evolutive process.

Population size	100
Probability of crossover	1
Probability of mutation	0.1
Maximum number of generations	5000

Table 2. GA's main parameters.

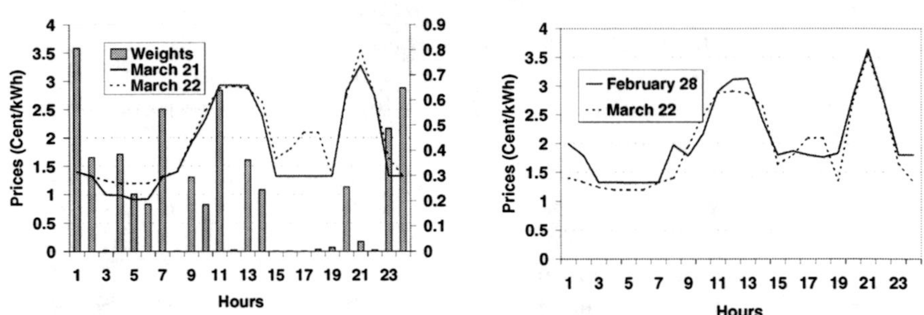

Fig. 5. Nearest neighbour using: **a)** the Weighted-Euclidean, **b)** the Euclidean distance.

Figure 5a represents the relative weights for every hour, along with the energy prices for a selected day, March 22, and its nearest neighbour calculated using the Weighted-Euclidean distance (1). The nearest neighbour corresponds to March 21.

It can be noticed that the hours with larger weights (1am, 7am, 11am, 11pm and 12pm), have almost the same energy prices. However, at 3pm, 4pm, 5pm, 6pm and 7pm, when the differences in prices are greater, the weights are approximately equal to zero.

Figure 5b represents the energy prices of March 22, along with its nearest neighbour calculated using the Euclidean distance. In this case, the nearest neighbour corresponds to February 28. Notice the influence of the chosen distance in the calculation of the nearest neighbour.

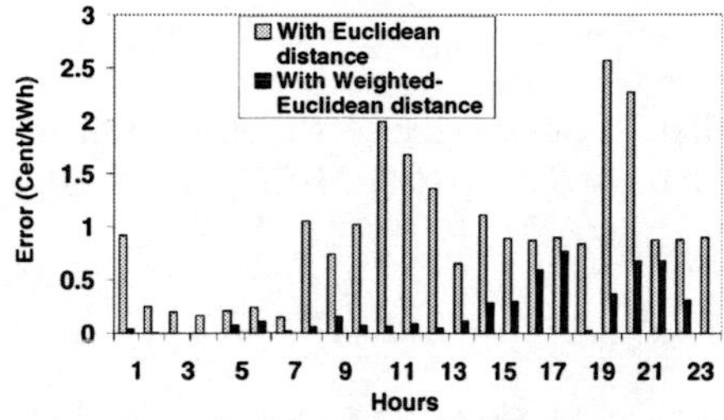

Fig. 6. Absolute value of the error of the forecasted energy prices (March, 23rd).

	Daily Prices (cent/kWh)			
	Average real price	s. d.	Average absolute error	Maximum error
March-May	2.2588	0.2186	0.256	2.13
June-August	3.5482	0.26	0.33	2.36

Table 3. Forecasting errors of energy prices.

Figure 6 presents the absolute value of the error of the forecasted spot market prices for March 23, using the Euclidean distance and the Weighted-Euclidean distance. As expected, the forecasting errors resulting for the selected day are strongly influenced by the calculation of the nearest neighbour.

Finally, table 3 presents the average and s.d. of actual prices, the average absolute value of forecasting errors and the maximum errors for Spring and Summer seasons. Note that, the average error, using an ANN, ranges from 12% (Summer) to 15% (Spring) of the hourly average price, while the average error obtained, by means of a kNN combined with a GA, ranges from 9% (Summer) to 11% (Spring).

Table 4 summarizes the results obtained using both techniques.

4 Conclusions

Optimal bidding strategies are relevant in a competitive market, the computation of a good forecasted price profiles being crucial for the generation companies. In this sense, this paper presents two techniques to deal with forecasting time series: an Artificial Neuronal Network and a combined k Nearest Neighbours and Genetic Algorithm. Both algorithms have been applied to the 24-hour energy price forecasting problems, using real data of the Spanish energy markets, and their performance have been compared. The proposed Weighted-distance kNN reveals much lower forecasting errors for the energy prices that the ANN proposed.

	March-May		June-August	
	kNN+GA	ANN	kNN+GA	ANN
s.d.	0.2186	0.7801	0.26	1.0597
Average absolute error	0.256	0.3464	0.33	0.428
Maximum error	2.13	2.671	2.36	2.0736
Average Relative error (%)	11	15	9	12

Table 4. Comparison of predicted daily prices (Cent/kWh).

Acknowledgments

The authors would like to acknowledge the financial support of the Spanish CICYT under grants PB97-0719, DPI2001-2612 and TIC2001-1143-C03-02.

References

1. R. Lamedia, A. Prudenzi, M. Sforna, M. Caciotta, V. Orsolini Cencellli: A Neural Network Based Technique for Short-Term Forecasting of Anomalous Load Periods. IEEE Trans. on Power System, Vol. 11, pp. 1749-1755. 1996.
2. A. S. Alfuhaid and M. A. El-Sayed: Cascaded Artificial Neural Network for Short-Term Load Forecasting. IEEE Trans. on Power System, Vol. 12, pp. 1524-1529. 1997.
3. M. El-Sharkawi and D. Niebur: Tutorial course on Artificial Neural Networks with Applications to Power Systems. IEEE Catalog Number 96, Tp 112-0, 1996.
4. J. Riquelme, J.L. Martínez, A. Gómez and D. Cros Goma: Possibilities of Artificial Neural Networks in Short-Term Load Forecasting. Proceedings of the IASTED International Conference Power and Energy Systems. pp. 165-170, Marbella, Spain. September 2000.
5. A. Canoyra, C. Illán, A. Landa, J.M. Moreno, J.I. Pérez Arriaga, C. Sallé and C. Solé: The Hierarchical Market Approach to the Economic and Secure Operation of the Spanish Power System. Bulk Power System Dynamic and Control IV, August 24-28, Santorini, Greece.
6. A. J. Conejo, J. Contreras, J.M. Arroyo and S. de la Torre: Optimal Response of an Oligopolistic Generating Company to a Competitive Pool-Based Electric Power Market. To appear in IEEE Trans. on Power System.
7. A. W. Jayawardena, W. K. Li and P. Xu: Neighbourhood selection for local modelling and prediction of hydrological time series. Journal of Hydrology 258, 40-57.
8. James McNames: Local modelling optimization for time serie prediction. Submitted to Physical Review E.
9. D. Berndt and J. Clifford: Using dynamic time warping to find patterns in time series. AAAI-94 Workshop on Knowledge in Databases (KDD-94), Seattle, Washington.
10. R.C. Holte: Very simple classification rules perform well on most commonly used datasets. Machine learning, 11:63-91, 1993.
11. B.V. Dasarathy (Ed): Nearest neighbour (NN) Norms: NN pattern classification techniques. IEEE Computer Society Press, 1991.
12. Z. Michalewicz: Genetic Algorithms + Data Structures = Evolution Programs. Second Edition, Springer-Verlag, 1994.
13. D.W. Aha, D. Kibler and M.K. Albert: Instance-based learning algorithms. Machine Learning 6:37-66, 1991.
14. D. E. Goldberg: Genetic Algorithms in Search, Optimization and Machine Learning. Addison-Wesley, 1989.

Temporal Pattern Mining of Moving Objects for Location-Based Service[1]

Jae Du Chung[1], Ok Hyun Paek[2], Jun Wook Lee[1], and Keun Ho Ryu[1]

[1] Department of Computer Science, Chungbuk National University,
San 48, Gaesin-dong,Cheongju, Chungbuk, Republic of Korea
{chungjaedu,junux,khryu}@dblab.chungbuk.ac.kr
[2] Agency for Defense Development, Republic of Korea
ohpaek@add.re.kr

Abstract. LBS(Location-Based Service) is generally described as an information service that provides location-based information to its mobile users. Since the conventional studies on data mining do not consider spatial and temporal aspects of data simultaneously, these techniques have limited application in studying the moving objects of LBS with respect to the spatial attributes that is changing over time. In this paper, we propose a new data mining technique and algorithms for identifying temporal patterns from series of locations of moving objects that have temporal and spatial dimensions. For this purpose, we use the spatial operation to generalize a location of moving point, applying time constraints between locations of moving objects to make valid moving sequences. Finally, we show that our technique generates temporal patterns found in frequent moving sequences.

1 Introduction

LBS aims to accurately identify individuals' locations and, by applying this information to various marketing and services, provide more personalized and satisfying mobile service to its users. The service can particularly be applicable to the sectors with changeable locations over time, such as PDA, mobile telephone, automobile, airplane, etc. Such changeable entities, in terms of location and pattern over time, are defined as "moving objects"[6,11]. The temporal changes of moving objects tend to possess a unique, regular pattern. This pattern can be traced by using the temporal data mining technique [14]. The pattern of moving objects which is discovered by data mining can be quite useful to location-based information service in identifying users' moving paths [14].

Prior studies, however, have paid little attention to the location data of moving objects. The study of temporal pattern mining for location-based moving objects is similar to the analysis of transaction database [2,10,15] and study of consumer behavior on the web [3,8,9]. It should be pointed out, nonetheless, that since the prior research does not take spatial attributes into account, it is not sufficient to discover

[1] This work was supported in part by KOSEF RRC(Cheongju Univ. ICRC) and KISTI Bioinformatics Research Center.

R. Cicchetti et al. (Eds.): DEXA 2002, LNCS 2453, pp. 331–340.

spatial patterns of moving objects and thus has a limitation when applying the pattern theory to the specific sectors, such as LBS.

In this paper, we adopt a methodological approach that features several distinct stages. First, location information is generalized by applying spatial operation to moving objects in two-dimensional coordinate system, and then transformed into knowledge that conveys the location information of moving objects. Second, a time constraint between locations of moving pattern is imposed in order to transform, in search of moving patterns, uncertain moving sequence into effective transaction. This approach can be attributable to the unclear components of a sequence in moving objects mining. By imposing the maximum time constraint between two areas that constitute a sequence, a sequence is generated only when the time span between two locations satisfies the maximum time constraint. Finally, an algorithm that discovers a significant pattern from the moving sequence of moving object is presented. This algorithm is an appropriate extension and application of Apriori [1] for addressing the issues concerning moving pattern mining.

The paper proceeds as follows. Section 2 explores the definition of moving objects. Section 3 discusses the discovery of moving pattern. Section 4 investigates a new method of moving pattern mining. The proposed method is tested and evaluated through experiments in Section 5. In conclusion, we summarize and provide concluding remarks. Some suggestions for future research design are also provided.

2 Description of Moving Objects

The existing models of data mining are too static to properly identify the location of moving objects, which continues to change over time. Many diverse researches followed to trace moving objects in temporal and spatial dimensions [5,7,8,12,13]. A location change of moving objects may occur in a discrete or continuous pattern, and thus, it can be described as a point in time or time periods. Each description has its merit as well as deficiency and thus far, there is no consistent and well-developed definition of the moving object. Here, we abstract essential definitional components of the term with respect to moving pattern mining. As seen in Fig. 1, the topological attributes of moving objects continue to change sequentially on the two-dimensional coordinate of x- and y-axis.

Since we cannot properly describe the continuous changes of moving objects in the real world setting, we draw the moving locations of objects using discrete points. Each point represents the starting and ending points of the time span. The moving object description adopted in this paper, therefore, embraces only the basic components for generality, implying that the location is sampled at specific points. The spatial attributes of moving objects will be described using a plane coordinate system with x- and y-axis. Mpoint, an abstracted type of moving objects, is defined as follows:

Definition 1. $Mpo\text{int} = oid, \{(VT_1, L_1), (VT_2, L_2), \cdots, (VT_n, L_n)\}$,

where
oid = a discriminator for the object that possesses unique components,
vt = effective time, and
L = location of the sampled object denoted by x, y.

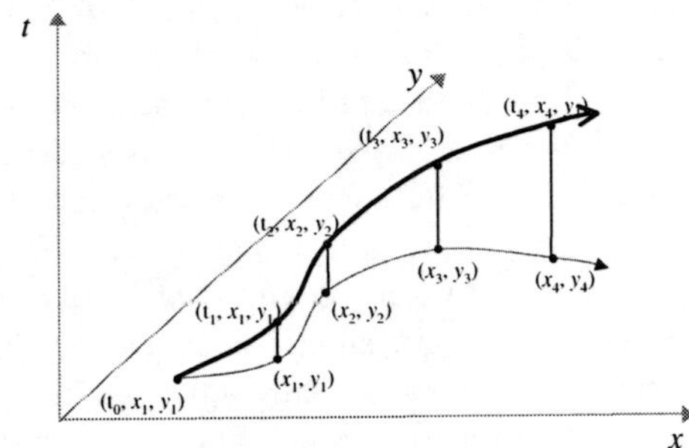

Fig. 1. Location change of the moving objects

Table 1 shows descriptive examples of such moving objects in a form of a relational database table.

Table 1. Example of the moving objects

oid	vt	x	y
100	2001/10/10/13/10	3321000	-233100
100	2001/10/10/13/20	3397000	-463600
100	2001/10/10/13/25	3385000	-523600

3 Problem Definition of Moving Pattern Mining

Let $L = \{l_1, l_2, \cdots, l_m\}$ denote a finite set of coordinates that represent spatial location attributes of moving objects, where $l_i = (x_i, y_i)$ and each x_i, y_i represents the coordinate value of moving object on a two-dimensional coordinate system. Also, let $A = \{a_1, a_2, \cdots, a_n\}$ denote a set of areas that represent the value of spatial location attributes of moving objects, where for $1 \leq j \leq n$, $a_j = (l_1, l_2, ..., l_k)$ and $l_k = (x_k, y_k)$. This allows for the use of representative coordinate values to describe an area, and the spatial attributes of moving objects being described, using coordinate values, can be transformed into an area through spatial operation. This transformation of coordinate values, representing spatial information of moving objects, into an area including those coordinates is called "*generalization of the location*".

A sequence, $S = \{s_1 s_2 \cdots s_k\}$ is an ordered list of the areas, where k denotes the length of a sequence, $s_j = (t_j, a_j)$, t_j denotes the specific time the moving objects were sampled, and $a_i \in A$. Time constraints restrict the time gap between two areas that constitute a sequence. The occurrence times of consecutive movements are denoted by t_j, t_{j-1}. The maximal time gap, *max_gap*, is defined as follows

$$t_j - t_{j-1} \leq max\_gap,\ 2 \leq j \leq k \tag{1}$$

A sequence with k number of lengths, i.e., a sequence composed of k number of areas, is denoted as k-sequence. An area may appear several times in a given sequence. For a given moving object, sequentially arranged areas over time are referred to as the "*moving sequence*". If $a_1 = b_{i_1}, a_2 = b_{i_2}, \cdots, a_n = b_{i_n}$ exist for fixed $i_1 < i_2 < \cdots < i_n$, then the sequence $\langle a_1 a_2 \cdots a_n \rangle$ is a partial sequence of $\langle b_1 b_2 \cdots b_m \rangle$. For example, $\langle 2\ 5\ 9\ 8 \rangle$ is a partial sequence of $\langle 6\ 2\ 1\ 5\ 9\ 3\ 8 \rangle$.

Let $S = \{s_1, s_2, \cdots, s_m\}$ denote a set of moving sequences. Each s_i represents a moving sequence, where $1 \le i \le m$. If sequence s is a partial sequence of s', then it is said that s' contains s. The support of sequence s can be defined as a proportion of entire (including s) moving sequence, i.e., $\sup(s) = |\{s_i \mid s \subseteq s_i\}|/m$. The user-specified minimum support threshold is the lowest value that each frequent sequence satisfies. It is denoted as min_sup. If a sequence s has $\sup(s) \ge$ min_sup, then it is defined as a *frequent sequence*. Although a multiple appearance of an area in a sequence is possible, it is counted no more than once in a given sequence.

Definition 2. Given moving objects database (D), user-assigned minimum support (min_sup), and user-assigned time constraint between areas (max_gap), the moving pattern mining involves searching for all frequent moving sequences that satisfy the minimum support.

4 Temporal Pattern Mining of Moving Objects

In this section, based upon the definitions suggested in section 3, we present a technique used to investigate moving patterns. The algorithm used for moving patterns mining consists of four stages: database arrangement, location generalization, moving sequence extraction, and frequent moving pattern mining.

4.1 Database Arrangement Stage

The database for mining should be orderly arranged by object discriminator as the primary key and by effective time as the assistant key. This provides a well-organized process of transformation when arranging discriminators of the moving objects and bounded time for moving patterns mining. Table 2 shows an example of the database, arranged according to discriminator and time. The unit of the spent time is in minutes.

4.2 Location Generalization Stage

We transform location value of the moving objects into an area with fixed boundary values using a spatial operation. In this process, a spatial operation method is used to test whether an object's x, y point lies within a specified area. A spatial area is represented by a polygon. *Contains* spatial operation algorithm[14] is used to test whether the area includes coordinate points when two random coordinate points and specified areas are entered. 'True' is returned if the point is inside the area, and 'false,' otherwise.

Table 3 demonstrates the application of Contains operation on spatial attribute value of each moving object (from the ordered database in Table 2), transforming it into a generalized area.

Table 2. Example of an arranged database

oid	vt	x	y
1	2001/10/30/13/10	15	10
	2001/10/30/13/15	38	15
	2001/10/30/13/25	55	8
	2001/10/30/13/38	65	19
2	2001/11/01/12/30	5	17
	2001/11/01/12/38	7	35
	2001/11/01/12/45	35	16
	2001/11/01/12/56	51	18
3	2001/10/30/14/11	23	15
	2001/10/30/14/17	59	19
	2001/10/30/14/23	77	12
	2001/10/30/14/58	78	35

Table 3. Location after Contains operation

oid	vt	Location
1	2001/10/30/13/10	A
	2001/10/30/13/15	B
	2001/10/30/13/25	C
	2001/10/30/13/38	D
2	2001/11/01/12/30	A
	2001/11/01/12/38	E
	2001/11/01/12/45	B
	2001/11/01/12/56	C
3	2001/10/30/14/11	B
	2001/10/30/14/17	C
	2001/10/30/14/23	D
	2001/10/30/14/58	H

4.3 Moving Sequence Extraction Stage

In this stage, a moving sequence of each moving object is extracted. That is, a transaction for moving pattern mining is created in this stage.

While a sequence as an object of pattern mining is clearly defined in the transaction database, a sequence as an object of moving pattern mining is not so clearly defined. In order to generate a significant moving sequence, we put a maximum time constraint between areas that constitute a sequence. Only when the time between two locations stay within the maximum time constraint can a sequence be produced.

In addition, during this process, the effective time related to spatial attributes of the objects is examined. If the duration of an object's stay over a specified location exceeds max_gap, the sequences are categorized into either moving sequences before exceeding or after exceeding. Table 4 shows an example of moving sequence of each object, which is extracted from the database in Table 3. In this example, we assume that max_gap is 30 minutes.

Table 4. Moving sequences

Oid	Moving Sequences
1	<A B C D>
2	<A E B C>
3	<B C D>, <H>

4.4 Frequent Moving Pattern Mining Stage

This stage involves mining, from moving sequences, the frequent moving pattern that exceeds the critical value assigned by the user. For this purpose, we use a modified version of Apriori [1] algorithm, the representative association rules algorithm that effectively reduces candidate sets.

F_k represents frequent k -sequence, and C_k represents candidate k -sequence. C_k is the self-join of F_{k-1}, i.e., $F_{k-1} * F_{k-1}$. When the individual moving sequence, $s_1,\ldots,s_{k-1}$ and $s'_1,\ldots,s'_{k-1}$ that exist in F_{k-1}, exists and if the sequence $s'_1,\ldots,s'_{k-1}$ includes $s_1,\ldots,s_{k-2}$, or $s_1,\ldots,s_{k-1}$ includes $s'_1,\ldots,s'_{k-2}$, a join is established. Next, any sequence that includes sequence in C_k but not included in F_{k-1} is eliminated. This procedure is executed based on the observations that super sets (i.e., infrequent sets) do not occur often.

Also, we use hash tree to efficiently scan whether appropriate candidate sets for moving sequence exist and are stored. Assuming that min_sup represent two sequences, the frequent moving pattern extracted from moving sequence in Table 4 is {<A>, <B>, <C>, <D>, <A B>, <A C>, <B C>, <C D>, <A B C>}. Fig. 2 shows this procedure. Thus far, we have categorized the process of moving pattern mining into four stages. The entire process of MP (Moving Pattern mining) algorithm is given in [14].

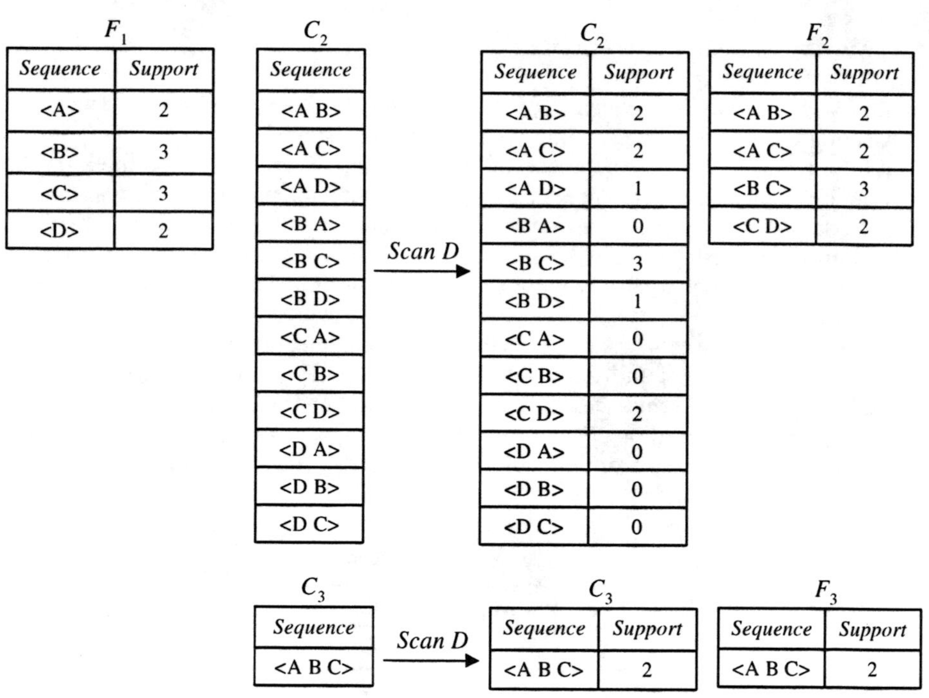

F_1

Sequence	Support
<A>	2
<B>	3
<C>	3
<D>	2

C_2

Sequence
<A B>
<A C>
<A D>
<B A>
<B C>
<B D>
<C A>
<C B>
<C D>
<D A>
<D B>
<D C>

Scan D →

C_2

Sequence	Support
<A B>	2
<A C>	2
<A D>	1
<B A>	0
<B C>	3
<B D>	1
<C A>	0
<C B>	0
<C D>	2
<D A>	0
<D B>	0
<D C>	0

F_2

Sequence	Support
<A B>	2
<A C>	2
<B C>	3
<C D>	2

C_3

Sequence
<A B C>

Scan D →

C_3

Sequence	Support
<A B C>	2

F_3

Sequence	Support
<A B C>	2

Fig. 2. Example of candidate sequence generation

5 Experimental Results

In this section, we analyze the performance of the proposed algorithm using the experimental data.

5.1 Experimental Design and Data Generation

The experiment was conducted using the random data generated via modified version of the data generator used in [1]. A modification is made such that, when moving objects' location properties as represented by coordinates are mapped into the domain of coordinates, |*E*| represents the average number of main lines that form the domain of interest. The data generation parameters are defined in Table 5 and their values are presented in Table 6.

Table 5. Data generating parameters

Input Variables	Description
|D|	The number of total moving sequences to be inputed into database.
|C|	The average number of areas per moving sequence.
|E|	The average number of lines constituting an area.
|S|	The average length of potential frequent sequence.
N_s	The number of potential frequent sequences.
N	The number of areas.

Table 6. Parameter values for data generation

Generated Data	$\|C\|$	$\|E\|$	$\|S\|$
C5.E4.S4	5	4	4
C5.E6.S4	5	6	4
C10.E4.S4	10	4	4
C10.E4.S8	10	4	8

The data generating process for the experiment was designed to generate data by varying the number of regions that constitute a sequence, the number of main lines that constitute domain, and the average length of resulting patterns.

5.2 Performance Evaluation

Using the generated data, performance of the algorithm is evaluated based on the changes in minimum support, the number of total moving sequences, and the average number of domains per moving sequence. Fig. 3 shows the execution time results as the minimum support of each generated dataset decreases from 1% to 0.35%.

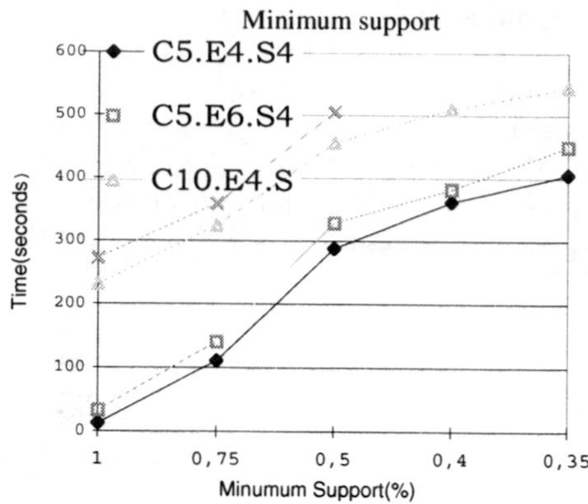

Fig. 3. Execution time in response to changes in minimum support level

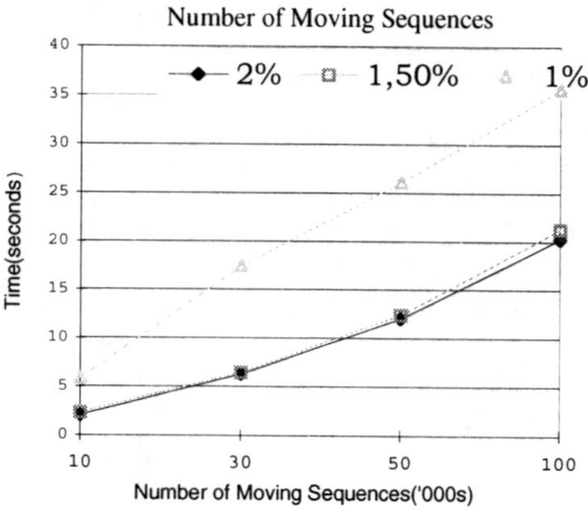

Fig. 4. Execution time in response to changes in number of total moving sequences

Fig. 5 shows the execution time results as the number of areas per moving sequence is increased from 5 to20. We let $|D|$=20000, N_s= 4000, and N= 2000.

In summary, several conclusions can be drawn from the performance evaluation. First, during the entire course of the algorithm, the two steps, location generalization for moving objects and frequent moving pattern mining, do not influence each other's performance. Second, the support level entered by the user greatly influences the performance of the algorithm. As decreased support levels generate increased number of candidate sets, fees associated with scanning the database rise. Third, as the length of the moving sequence grows, especially when the length exceeds 10, the execution time rises, thus alerting the need for efficient algorithm development and improved storage capacity. Finally, with the increase in the size of input database, the execution time for the algorithm gradually escalated.

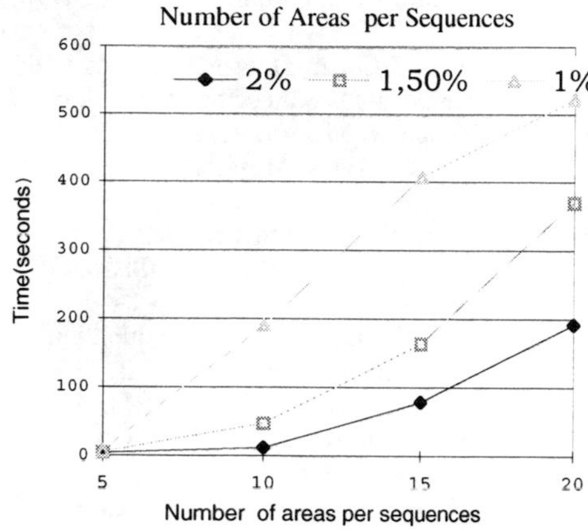

Fig. 5. Execution time in response to changes in number of areas per moving sequence

6 Conclusion and Future Works

In this research, we define individual users as the moving objects, and present an innovative mining technique useful for LSB in discovering significant patterns from users' location information that also change over time. The algorithm used for moving patterns mining consisted of four stages. First, the database is arranged into object discriminator and transaction discriminator, and spatial operators are used on the location information of moving objects to generalize locations. Second, with the location generalization, moving objects' location information is transformed in order to discover significant information. Third, time constraint is imposed to extract effective moving sequence. Finally, the frequent moving patterns are extracted from the generated moving sequences. The results of the experiment show that algorithm efficiency has a negative relation with its support level but positive relations with the length of moving sequences and the size of the database. This mining technique for spatial locations of moving objects is different from the existing techniques that have been used in the analysis of web-log and the transaction analysis. By adopting a simultaneous spatio-temporal approach, there is no doubt that this technique provides useful knowledge for LBS.

Future research in this area should consider not only the moving objects' location information but also incorporate information such as speed and direction, as well as the duration of moving objects' stay in a given area when designing a research in pattern mining.

References

1. Agrawal, R., Srikant, R.: Fast Algorithms for Mining Association Rules. In: Proc. of Int. Conf. on VLDB, Santiago, Chile(1994)

2. Agrawal, R., Srikant, R.: Mining Sequential Patters. In: Proc. of Int. Conf. on Data Engineering, (1995)
3. Chen, M.S., Park, J., Yu, P.S.: Efficient Data Mining for Path Traversal Patterns. IEEE Transactions on Knowledge and Data Engineering, Vol. 10. No.2(1998)
4. Erwig, M., Guting, R.H., Schneider, M., Vazirgiannis, M.: Spatio-Temporal Data Types : An Approach to Modeling and Querying Moving Objects in Databases, GeoInformation, Vol. 3. No. 3.(1999)
5. Forlizzi, L., Guting, R. H., Nardelli, E., Schneider, M.: A Data Model and Data Structures for Moving Objects Databases. In: Proc. of the ACM-SIGMOD Int. Conf. on Management of Data, (2000)
6. Garofalakis, M. N., Rastogi, R., Shim, K.: SPIRIT:Sequential Pattern Mining with Regular Expression Constraints. In: Proc. of Int. Conf. on VLDB,(1999)
7. R. H. Guting, M. H. Bohlen, M. Erwig, C. S. Jensen, N. A. Lorentzos, M. Schneider, M. Vazirgiannis: A Foundation for Representing and Querying Moving Objects, ACM Transactions on Database Systems, (2000).
8. Borges, J., Levene, M.: A Fine Grained Heuristic to Capture Web Navigation Patterns. SIGKDD Explorations, Vol. 2. No. 1 (2000)
9. Pei, J., Han, J., Mortazavi-Asl, B., Zhu, H.: Mining Access Patterns Efficiently from Web Logs. In: Proc. of PAKDD,(2000).
10. Srikant, R., Agrawal, R.: Mining Sequential Patterns : Generalizations and Performance Improvements. In: Proc. of Int. Conf. on Extending Database Technology, Springer-Verlag(1996)
11. Wolfson, O., Sistla, A. P., Xu, B., Zhou, J., Chamberlain, S.: DOMINO: Databases fOr MovINg Objects tracking. In: Proc. of the ACM-SIGMOD Int. Conf. on Management of Data, (1999)
12. Ryu, K., Ahn, Y.: Application of Moving Objects and Spatiotemporal Reasoning. A TimeCenter Technical Report TR-58(2001).
13. Park, S., Ahn, Y., Ryu, K.: Moving Objects Spatiotemporal Reasoning Model for Battlefield Analysis. In: Proceedings of Military, Government and Aerospace Simulation part of ASTC2001, (2001).
14. Paek, O.: A Temporal Pattern Mining of Moving Objects for Location Based Service. Master thesis, Dept. of Computer Science, Chungbuk National University, (2002)
15. Yun, H., Ha, D., Hwang, B., Ryu, K.: Mining Association Rules on Significant Rare Data using Relative Support. Journal of Systems and Software, 2002 (accepted).

MEDWRAP: Consistent View Maintenance over Distributed Multi-relation Sources*

Aparna S. Varde and Elke A. Rundensteiner

Department of Computer Science, Worcester Polytechnic Institute,
Worcester, MA 01609
{aparna|rundenst}@cs.wpi.edu

Abstract. Warehouses today extract information from several sources, each with multiple relations. Incremental View Maintenance (VM) of warehouses in such environments faces the problem of concurrency conflicts due to simultaneous relational updates occurring within and across these (semi-autonomous) sources. Existing VM algorithms only partially solve this issue. Some like ECA and CCA assume a single-source warehouse, while others like Strobe and SWEEP assume a multi-source environment with only one relation per source. However, in practice data sources have multiple relations in one schema. In this paper, we propose a solution called MEDWRAP that applies two-layered compensation. It resolves concurrency conflicts by using single-source compensation at each source wrapper and multi-source compensation at the mediator. We show that this achieves correct and consistent view maintenance. Not requiring intermediate views to be stored at the wrapper, MEDWRAP is space-efficient, a highly desirable feature, given the ever increasing size of modern warehouses.

1 Introduction

Data Warehouse Maintenance. A data warehouse is a materialized repository of integrated information based on the user's needs [CD97]. The system that builds and maintains the warehouse is the Data Warehouse Management System (or DWMS) [Moh96]. *Henceforth, we refer to the DWMS as the mediator.* Due to the ever growing size of data warehouses, it is popular to maintain them *incrementally* [LSK01] when updates occur. Several incremental View Maintenance (VM) algorithms like [ZGMHW95, AESY97] have been proposed. They compute the impact of an update from one source on the warehouse content by sending *maintenance queries* [DZR99] to the other sources. Due to autonomy of sources, other updates may occur concurrently during the processing of a maintenance query, affecting its result. This problem is called a *concurrency conflict.*

State-of-the-Art Solutions. Some VM algorithms like ECA [ZGMHW95] and CCA [Zhu99] solve this problem in a single data source. They utilize remote compensation queries to find out what joins with the conflicting tuple in

* This work was supported in part by the NSF NYI grant #IRI 97–96264, the NSF CISE Instrumentation grant #IRIS 97–29878, and the NSF grant #IIS 9988776.

R. Cicchetti et al. (Eds.): DEXA 2002, LNCS 2453, pp. 341–350, 2002.

each relation of that source. Other VM algorithms like Strobe [ZGMW96] and SWEEP [AESY97] allow relations to spread over multiple sources, restricting each data source to contain a single relation. [ZGMW96] handles data updates from different sources using remote compensation. [AESY97] adopts a local compensation technique that uses data contained in the update notifications received by the mediator to perform correction of maintenance errors. However the assumption that each data source contains only one relation is unrealistic since real-world data warehouses have sources with schemata composed of numerous relations. We need a solution to deal with concurrency conflicts in such environments.

Proposed Approach. In this paper, we propose the MEDWRAP solution that employs two compensation layers, one at the MEDiator of the system and another at the WRAPper of each data source. The wrapper effectively makes each source appear as if it were composed of one virtual relation without storing intermediate *materialized views* [GM96]. It compensates for concurrency conflicts within relations of that source. Thus a VM algorithm that works across multiple sources, assuming one relation per source, can now be used at the mediator. This compensates for concurrency conflicts occurring across sources. With this two-layered compensation however the same concurrent relational update in one source may cause a conflict in processing queries from both the wrapper and the mediator, posing an additional issue. This and other issues encountered in the design of MEDWRAP are discussed in the paper.

Outline. Motivating examples are outlined in Section 2. Section 3 presents the MEDWRAP approach and its architecture. Its design and algorithm appear in Section 4. Section 5 evaluates MEDWRAP and compares it with alternative solutions. Section 6 gives conclusions.

2 Motivating Examples

Concurrency Conflict Problem. Assume two data sources IS_1 with relation R_{11} and IS_2 with relations R_{21} and R_{22}. The view at the mediator is $V = R_{11} \bowtie (R_{21} \bowtie R_{22})$. If update ΔR_{11} occurs at IS_1, then an algorithm like [AESY97] would send the maintenance query $\Delta R_{11} \bowtie (R_{21} \bowtie R_{22})$ to source IS_2. If meanwhile ΔR_{21} had occurred concurrently causing a concurrency conflict, then the incorrect maintenance query result $\Delta R_{11} \bowtie ((R_{21} + \Delta R_{21}) \bowtie R_{22})$ would be returned. To compensate for the conflicting update ΔR_{21}, the mediator would need to subtract the value $\Delta R_{11} \bowtie (\Delta R_{21} \bowtie R_{22})$ from the incorrect query result. But the mediator cannot locally calculate this value since it does not have information about the extent of R_{22} in its update notifications. Hence a local compensation VM algorithm like [AESY97] would fail in this scenario.

First Potential Solution. For the above scenario, consider a wrapper at the source ΔIS_2 that could calculate the effect of any of its update first on its own relations, i.e. $(\Delta R_{21} \bowtie R_{22})$ and send this computed update to the mediator, instead of just sending the pure one-relation update ΔR_{21}. However while the wrapper is doing the above computation, yet another concurrent update ΔR_{22}

may occur, causing a new conflict that cannot be corrected by the mediator. Thus this is not a feasible solution strategy to explore.

Simplistic Approach. Alternatively we propose a simple solution to our problem, henceforth called *the simplistic approach.* The mediator could treat every relation of a source as a separate data source. For our example above, we would have the sources $IS_1.R_{11}$, $IS_2.R21$ and $IS_2.R_{22}$. An algorithm like [AESY97] would then function as before, sending a separate maintenance query down to each and every now single-relation source, receiving its result, and compensating for concurrency conflicts at the mediator. However this is likely to pose tremendous overhead on the system. We would not take advantage of the query processing power of the DBMS engine of the data source in answering a multi-relation join query efficiently. In this paper we develop a practical solution that exploits the power of each data source for compensation to a maximal extent, achieving improved maintenance performance, without storage overhead.

3 The MEDWRAP Approach

MEDWRAP uses **two-layered compensation**. One VM algorithm is used by the mediator that maintains the materialized view at the data warehouse. The other VM algorithm is used at the wrapper dedicated to each source. The wrapper computes a *source update* for every *relational update.*

Definition 1: *A* ***source update*** ΔIS *corresponding to a relational update* ΔR *in that source is the effective change of state in the source based on the view definition V at the data warehouse. The calculation of* ΔIS *is done by using V at the IS to find out the effect of* ΔR *on the portion of V relevant to this IS.*

For example, consider IS_1 with $R_{11}[W, X]$ and IS_2 with $R_{21}[A, B]$, $R_{22}[B, C]$; the view at the warehouse being $V = \pi_W(R_{11}[W, X] \bowtie_{X=A} (R_{21}[A, B] \bowtie R_{22}[B, C]))$. Rewriting this view definition in terms of sources rather than relations, we have $V = \pi_W(IS_1 \bowtie_{X=A} IS_2)$. If in the single-relation source IS_1, ΔR_{11} occurs, then $\Delta IS_1 = \pi_{W,X}(\Delta R_{11})$, since attributes W and X are required in V. In the multi-relation source IS_2, if ΔR_{21} occurs, then $\Delta IS_2 = \pi_A(\Delta R_{21} \bowtie R_{22})$, since attribute A is required in V. Following the same logic as in [ZGMHW95] and related literature, duplicates are retained in the materialized view, by keeping a count of tuples. This enables deletions to be performed incrementally.

Note that the wrapper now effectively makes the source appear as one virtual relation, though without requiring any intermediate storage. Thus, we can employ maintenance strategies like [AESY97] that work across multiple sources, assuming a single relation per source, at the mediator. This is the core idea underlying MEDWRAP. The assumptions regarding tuple representations and message paths in MEDWRAP are similar to those in [DZR99, AESY97].

In MEDWRAP, if we use an algorithm like [AESY97] at the mediator, then a **Global Maintenance Query or GMQ** is a query generated by the mediator in response to a source update, to find out what joins with this update in each of the other sources, based on the view definition at the data warehouse. This is essential to refresh the view based on the source update.

For example, in a system having IS_1 with $R_{11}[W, X]$, and IS_2 with $R_{21}[A, B]$ and $R_{22}[B, C]$, if the materialized view is $V = \pi_W(IS_1 \bowtie_{X=A} IS_2)$, then in response to source update ΔIS_1, the mediator would send the global maintenance query $GMQ = \pi_W(\Delta IS_1 \bowtie_{X=A} IS_2)$ to source IS_2.

Definition 2: *We define a* ***source concurrency conflict*** *as a source update that occurs during the processing of a global maintenance query, affecting the query result returned to the mediator.*

In the above case, if ΔIS_2 occurs during the processing of this GMQ, then it is a source concurrency conflict.

If an algorithm like [Zhu99] is used at the wrapper, then a **Local Maintenance Query or LMQ** is a query generated by the wrapper in response to a relational update in the source, to find out what joins with this update in the other relations of that source, based on the projection of the view definition of the mediator at this source. This is essential to generate a source update from a relational update.

In the example of the GMQ above, if IS_2 has $R_{21}[\phi, \phi]$ and $R_{22}[\phi, \phi]$, [1] and $\Delta R_{21} = +[4, 2]$ occurs, then IS_2 wrapper sends $LMQ = \pi_A(\Delta R_{21} \bowtie R_{22})$ to IS_2. It projects only relevant attribute A, since this is needed in computing $IS_1 \bowtie IS_2$ at the mediator.

Definition 3: *We define a* ***relational concurrency conflict*** *as a relational update that occurs within a particular source, while a local or global maintenance query is being processed in that source, affecting the query result returned to the wrapper or mediator.*

For example, if $\Delta R_{22} = +[2, 5]$, occurs while the above LMQ is being processed, IS_2 returns an incorrect LMQR =+[4]. ΔR_{22} is therefore a relational concurrency conflict. Note that this same ΔR_{22} can also affect the global maintenance query result or GMQR of a GMQ that is being answered by IS_2.

3.1 The Wrapper of MEDWRAP

We employ ideas from existing single-source VM algorithms for the MEDWRAP wrapper. VM algorithms were initially designed to maintain a view. Hence if we were to use an algorithm like [Zhu99] at the wrapper W_i, then it would generate its own local maintenance queries directed towards IS_i in response to relational updates. However, it is not designed to answer global maintenance queries coming from outside the wrapper, in this case from the mediator. Hence we need additional query processing functionality in the wrapper. The simple method of accepting a global maintenance query from the mediator, directing it to the source, and sending results back to the mediator faces the same problem of *relational concurrency conflicts* that cannot be solved by the mediator.

We saw in the example of Definition 3 that the same relational update of a given data source could cause a conflict in both local update processing and

[1] ϕ denotes null or empty

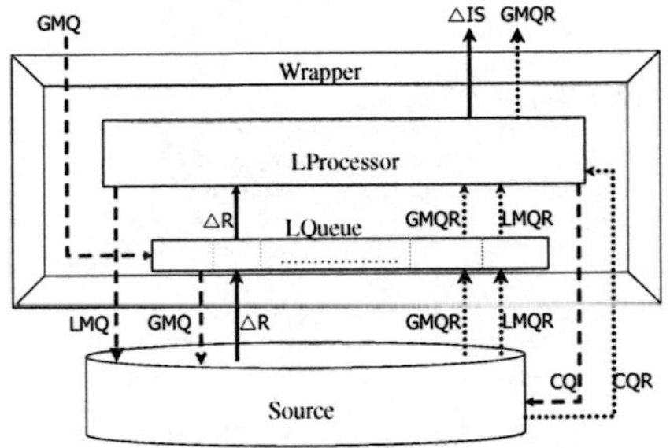

Fig. 1. The MEDWRAP wrapper

Terminology	Meaning
GMQ	Global Maintenance Query
GMQR	Global Maintenance Query Result
LMQ	Local Maintenance Query
LMQR	Local Maintenance Query Result
CQ	Compensating Query
CQR	Compensating Query Result
ΔR	Relational Update
ΔIS	Source Update
LQueue	Queue in the Wrapper
LProcessor	Processor in the Wrapper

Fig. 2. Terminology in wrapper

global query processing in that respective wrapper. Hence, we now propose to employ one common processor for both query and update processing at each data source. This is the **LProcessor** (Fig.1). More importantly, one common queue called **LQueue** is used for both global queries from the mediator and local update handling requests from the IS_i. If relational updates enter **LQueue** after a query and before its result, then we know that they could cause an incorrect query result. Hence they are identified as *relational concurrency conflicts.* Fig.1 has the architecture of the MEDWRAP wrapper. Fig.2 has its terminology.

Following the example from Section 3, we demonstrate the working of the wrapper. The relational update $\Delta R_{21} = +[4,2]$ is sent from the source to the wrapper and collected in **LQueue**. The **LProcessor** picks up the first message from the queue and starts processing. For example, if this is ΔR_{21}, it sends $LMQ = \pi_A(\Delta R_{21} \bowtie R_{22})$ to IS_2. The source computes LMQR and returns it to **LQueue**. If concurrent update ΔR_{22} enters **LQueue** before the LMQR, it is identified as a *relational concurrency conflict.* **LProcessor** sends a *compensating query* in response to each conflict. A **Compensating Query or CQ** is a query generated by the wrapper in response to a relational concurrency conflict during local or global query processing, to find out what joins with the conflicting update in the other relations of that source, based on the projected view definition.

For example, here **LProcessor** would send $CQ_{22} = -\pi_A(\Delta R_{21} \bowtie \Delta R_{22})$ to IS_2. This returns a compensating query result $CQR_{22} = -\pi_A([4,2] \bowtie [2,5]) = -[4]$. **LProcessor** then uses all query results to build a ΔIS corresponding to the ΔR. Thus, $\Delta IS_2 = LMQR + CQR_{22} = +[4] - [4] = \phi$. This is the correct ΔIS_2 in response to $\Delta R_{21} = +[4,2]$, given that R_{22} was empty when ΔR_{21} occurred. Note that since ΔR_{22} occurred after ΔR_{21}, the LMQ for ΔR_{22} would now be answered using the new value of R_{21} i.e. [4,2]. Thus, the later updates incorporate the effect of those previously reported to the mediator.

Similarly, in global maintenance query processing, if there are relational concurrency conflicts while a GMQ is being answered by the source to give GMQR, this compensating query strategy can be used to get the correct GMQR. For details, refer to the additional example in Figure 6. The **LProcessor** sends either the ΔIS or the GMQR to the mediator.

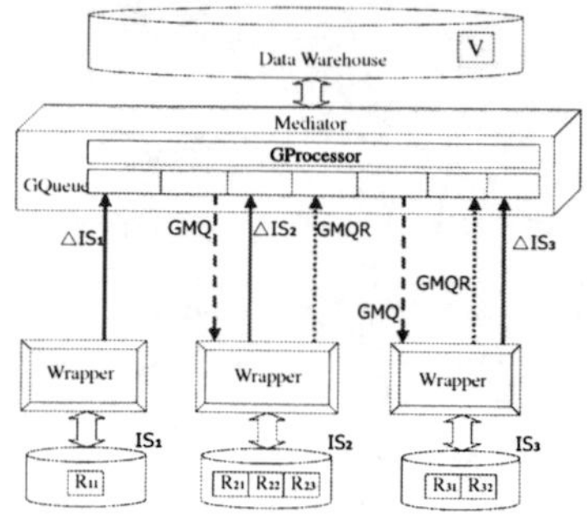

Fig. 3. The MEDWRAP System

Notation	**Meaning**
IS_x	Information Source x
ΔIS_x	Source Update in IS_x
R_{xy}	Relation y of Source x
GMQ	Global Maintenance Query
GMQR	Global Maintenance Query Result
V	Materialized View
GQueue	Queue in the Mediator
GProcessor	Processor in the Mediator

Fig. 4. Notations in MEDWRAP

Theorem 1: *If the wrapper calculates ΔIS for each ΔR, and GMQR for each GMQ using a compensation technique to remove the effect of concurrent ΔRs, then it propagates a consistent state of all the relations in that source at all times.* (For proof refer to [VR02]).

Theorem 2: *If the wrapper propagates a consistent state of all its relations, then each ΔIS and GMQR arriving from the source will have the effect of all the ΔRs previously reported to the mediator from that source.* (Proof in [VR02]).

3.2 The MEDWRAP System

The MEDWRAP system is shown in Fig.3 with its notations in Fig.4. The mediator maintains a materialized view V at the data warehouse. A global processor **GProcessor** performs the computations described below, and a global queue **GQueue** stores messages coming from source wrappers.

On receiving a ΔIS from a source, the mediator sends a GMQ to each source to find out what joins with this update in the other sources. The GMQR arriving from each source is stored in **GQueue.** If any other source update arrives in **GQueue** after a particular GMQ and before its GMQR, then the mediator identifies this as a *source concurrency conflict*. MEDWRAP uses the content of the update notifications in **GQueue** to find out how this conflicting source update joins with the other sources, and performs compensation locally, using an algorithm like [AESY97]. Note that this now works, since we have overcome the problem of *relational concurrency conflicts* due to the compensation-based wrapper at each source. The GMQR for that source generated after compensation is consistent with respect to the current source state. Likewise, the mediator uses the values of GMQRs from each source to build a final view refresh ΔV. It uses this ΔV to update the materialized view. (Detailed example in Figure 6.)

Theorem 3: *If the wrapper sends each ΔIS and GMQR to the mediator in the order that the later ones incorporate the effects of all the previously reported ΔRs, then the mediator can correctly maintain the data warehouse.* (For proof refer to [VR02]).

Theorem 4: *ΔV computed by the mediator from ΔIS in MEDWRAP is identical to ΔV calculated directly from ΔR in the simplistic approach explained in Section 2.* (Proof in [VR02]).

Lemma 1: *The materialized view at the data warehouse will be maintained* ***completely consistent*** *[ZGMW97] with each source state, if the VM algorithms used at the wrapper and the mediator in MEDWRAP individually achieve complete consistency [ZGMW97]. If either algorithm achieves only strong consistency [ZGMW97], then MEDWRAP does VM with* ***strong consistency.***

4 Design of MEDWRAP

Fig.5 gives the MEDWRAP algorithm, with a detailed example in Fig.6. MEDWRAP is designed using techniques similar to [AESY97, Zhu99]. Process **S-up** in the source appends a ΔR from the source to **LQueue** in the wrapper. **LProcessor** gets the first message from the **LQueue**. The **Wrap-up** function in **LProcessor** generates an LMQ if the message is a ΔR, and sends it to **S-qu** in the source. **S-qu** can process LMQs and GMQs. It computes the query result and appends it to **LQueue. LProcessor** gets the LMQR. Its function **Wrap-ans** collects the LMQRs in case of local update processing and GMQRs in case of global query processing. In each case, it sends CQs if there are *relational concurrency conflicts.* It uses all query results to build the ΔIS or the GMQR, and appends it to **GQueue** in the mediator. **GProcessor** gets the first message from the **GQueue**. If the message is a ΔIS, then it sends a GMQ to **S-qu** in each source, one at a time. If the message is a GMQR, it locally compensates for source conflicts, if any. It finally computes the view change ΔV corresponding to ΔIS using all GMQRs after compensation. It then uses this ΔV to update the materialized view V at the warehouse.

LQueue and **GQueue** do implicit time-stamping because these queues store messages in their order of arrival, thus order of maintenance handling, and detect concurrency conflicts by the method outlined above. Thus MEDWRAP does not require explicit clocks as in [DZR99], or versions of transactions/tuples as in [CCR, KM99].

5 Comparative Evaluation

We compare MEDWRAP with two other approaches. One, the materialized Multi Relation Encapsulation Wrapper (MRE) [DZR99] that stores a source view (ISV) at each wrapper, analogous to a materialized view (MV) at the mediator. Two, the simplistic approach of Section 2 that treats every relation as a separate source if there are multiple relations per source. MEDWRAP, MRE and the simplistic approach can all make use of an algorithm like [AESY97] at the mediator. MEDWRAP is inspired by [DZR99], earlier work at WPI.

Space Cost Model. MEDWRAP and the simplistic approach store no views at wrappers. MRE stores one view (ISV) at each wrapper.

```
AT SOURCE:

1. PROCESS S-up:
LOOP
EXECUTE (ΔR_xy);
/* R_xy is relation y of IS_x */
APPEND (ΔR_xy) to LQueue;
FOREVER

2. PROCESS S-qu(Q_i):
LET ss_i := current source state;
/* Q_i is LMQ, GMQ or CQ */
LET QR_i := Q_i[ss_i];
/* query result as per current source state */
IF (Q_i is a CQ) THEN Wrap-ans(CQR_j);
ELSE APPEND (QR_i) TO LQueue;

AT WRAPPER:

1. LQueue:
LET head := φ; /* queue initially empty */
LET msg := message∈LQueue; /* message in LQueue */
/* ΔR_j is a relational update */
LET detectConflict(ΔR_j) := false; /* no conflict assumed */
IF (ΔR_j∈LQueue AFTER Q_i AND BEFORE QR_i)
THEN detectConflict(ΔR_j) := true; /* conflict occurs */

2. PROCESS LProcessor:
LOOP
GET (msg) FROM LQueue.head;
IF (msg == LMQR_y) THEN Wrap-ans(LMQR_y);
ELSE IF (msg == GMQR_x) THEN Wrap-ans(GMQR_x);
ELSE IF (msg == GMQ_x) THEN S-qu(GMQ_x);
ELSE DO /* message is ΔR_xy */
Wrap-up(ΔR_xy);
ENDDO;
FOREVER

2a. FUNCTION Wrap-up(ΔR_xy):
LET LMQ_y := π_attr(V < R_x1 ⋈ ··· ⋈ ΔR_xy ⋈ ··· R_xn >);
/* build LMQ, using info from V */
S-qu (LMQ_y);

2b. FUNCTION Wrap-ans(QR_i):
LET COLLECT[i] := QR_i; /* set to collect query results */
IF (detectConflict(ΔR_j) := true) THEN
/* LQueue acts as implicit time-stamp */
FOR EACH (ΔR_j) DO
/* CQs for relational concurrency conflicts */
LET CQ_j := −π_attr(V < R_x1 ⋈ ··· ⋈ ΔR_xi ⋈ R_xj ⋈ ··· R_xn >
) + CQ_{j−1};
S-qu (CQ_j); /* indirect recursion through S-qu * /
ENDDO; /* for each conflict */
LET output := COLLECT[i];
/* when all CQs answered by recursion */
APPEND (output) TO GQueue;

AT MEDIATOR:

V = IS_1 ⋈ IS_2 ⋈ ··· IS_n; /* initialize the view */
ΔV = φ; /* initial view change is null */

1. GQueue:
LET head := φ; /* queue initially empty */
LET msg := message∈GQueue; /* message in GQueue */
LET detectConflict(ΔIS_a) := false; /* no conflict assumed */
IF (ΔIS_a∈GQueue BEFORE GMQR) /* conflict occurs */
THEN detectConflict(ΔIS_a) := true;

2. PROCESS GProcessor:
LOOP
GET (msg) FROM GQueue.head;
IF (msg == ΔIS_x) THEN DO
TempView := ΔIS_x;
FOR EACH (IS_a <> IS_x) DO
/* poll every IS_a in DW system */
GMQ_a := TempView ⋈ ΔIS_a;
S-qu(GMQ_a); /* send GMQ to S-qu of IS */
ENDDO; /* for each IS */
ENDDO; /* if message is ΔIS */
ELSE DO /* message is a GMQR */
IF (detectConflict(ΔIS_a := true) THEN DO
/*resolve source concurrency conflicts by local compensation */
(GMQR_a := GMQR_a − ΔIS_a ⋈ TempView);
TempView := GMQR_a;
ENDDO; /* for compensation */
ΔV := TempView;
ENDDO; /* if message is GMQR */
V := V + ΔV;
FOREVER
```

Fig. 5. The MEDWRAP algorithm

Space Cost:

Approach	Total Space
MEDWRAP	$MV + 0 = MV$
MRE	$MV + N * ISV$
Simplistic	$MV + 0 = MV$

Time Cost Analysis. When a relational update occurs, the time taken by MEDWRAP to generate a corresponding view update is the sum of the following times: wrapper of one source generating ΔIS for ΔR (compensating for relational concurrency conflicts if any), wrapper sending ΔIS to mediator, mediator in response sending a GMQ each to the other (N-1) wrappers, wrappers processing to give (N-1) GMQRs (compensating for relational concurrency conflicts if any), wrappers sending (N -1) GMQRs to mediator, and mediator processing after each GMQR with or without source conflicts.

On similar lines, we analyze MRE and the simplistic approach. The delays in processing are wrapper delay T_w, mediator delay T_m, I/O delay T_i and CPU delay T_c. Ignoring T_c, since it is negligible compared to the other delays, we tabulate results.

Time Cost:

Approach	Time per Relational Update
MEDWRAP	$(2N + 6X - 1) * T_w + (2N - 1) * T_m + (N + 2X) * T_i$
MRE	$(2N + 3X + 1) * T_w + (2N - 1) * T_m + (X + 1) * T_i$
Simplistic	$(2Z - 1) * T_w + (2Z - 1) * T_m + 2Z * T_i$

Source IS_1	$R_{11} = [A, B]$		
	$Initial = [5, 4]$		
	$\Delta R_{11} = -[5, 4]$		
Source IS_2	$R_{21} = [W, X]$	$R_{22} = [X, Y]$	$R_{23} = [Y, Z]$
	$Initial = [1, 2]$	Initial=$[\phi,\phi]$	Initial=$[\phi,\phi]$
	$\Delta R_{21} = +[4, 2]$	$\Delta R_{22} = +[2, 5]$	$\Delta R_{23} = +[5, 3]$
Source IS_3	$R_{31} = [P, Q]$	$R_{32} = [Q, R]$	
	$Initial = [3, 8]$	$Initial = [8, 5]$	
		$\Delta R_{32} = -[8, 5]$	

Assume IS_1, IS_2, IS_3 as tabulated, and the materialized view (MV) at the mediator: $V = \pi_W(IS_1 \bowtie_{B=W} IS_2 \bowtie_{Z=P} IS_3)$. Thus $IS_1 = \pi_B(R_{11})$, $IS_2 = \pi_W(R_{21} \bowtie R_{22} \bowtie R_{23})$, $IS_3 = \pi_P(R_{31} \bowtie R_{32})$. Initially $V = \phi$, $\Delta V = \phi$. Given a ΔR the following steps calculate ΔV.

1. $\Delta R_{11} = -[5, 4]$ occurs in IS_1. IS_1 has only one relation, so $\Delta IS_1 = \pi_B(\Delta R_{11}) = -[4]$.
2. IS_1 wrapper sends $\Delta IS_1 = -[4]$ to GQueue.
3. GProcessor initializes $TempView := \Delta IS_1 := -[4]$ and sends $GMQ_2 = \pi_W(TempView \bowtie IS_2)$ to S-qu of IS_2.
4. Assume LQueue of IS_2 has messages in the order: ΔR_{21}, GMQ_2, ΔR_{22}, ΔR_{23}, $GMQR_2$
i. At IS_2: S-qu calculates $GMQR_2 = [1], [4]$, based on current source state.
ii. S-qu appends $GMQR_2 = [1], [4]$ to LQueue and LProcessor gets it.
iii. Wrap-ans in LProcessor detects relational concurrency conflicts $\Delta R_{22}, \Delta R_{23}$ since they are in LQueue after GMQ_2 and before $GMQR_2$. Wrap-ans sends $CQ_{22} = -\pi_W(\Delta R_{21} \bowtie [2, 5] \bowtie R_{23})$ and $CQ_{23} = -\pi_W(\Delta R_{21} \bowtie R_{22} \bowtie [5, 3]) + \pi_W(\Delta R_{21} \bowtie [2, 5] \bowtie [5, 3])$ to S-qu.
iv. S-qu sends $CQR_{22} = -([1], [4])$ and $CQR_{23} = \phi$ to Wrap-ans.
v. Wrap-ans calculates $GMQR_2 = GMQR_2 +$ all $CQRs = ([1], [4]) - ([1], [4]) + \phi$. So, $GMQR_2 = \phi$. Wrap-ans sends $GMQR_2 = \phi$ to GQueue.
5. Similarly, IS_2 wrapper independently calculates $\Delta IS_2 = \pi_W(\Delta R_{21} \bowtie R_{22} \bowtie R_{23}) = \pi_W([4, 2] \bowtie \phi \bowtie \phi) = \phi$ and sends it to GQueue. This is ΔIS_2 due to ΔR_{21}.
6. Assume GQueue of mediator has messages in the order: ΔIS_1, GMQ_2, ΔIS_2, $GMQR_2$. The GProcessor detects concurrency conflict ΔIS_2 since it is in the queue before $GMQR_2$. GProcessor applies compensation to get $GMQR_2 = GMQR_2 - \Delta IS_2 \bowtie TempView = \phi$.
7. GProcessor updates $TempView := GMQR_2 = \phi$
8. Likewise GProcessor also sends $GMQ_3 := TempView \bowtie \Delta IS_3$ to IS_3. GQueue receives $GMQR_3 := \phi$ based on the current state of IS_3. GQueue also receives $\Delta IS_3 = \phi$ corresponding to $\Delta R_{32} = -[8, 5]$. Assume ΔIS_3 arrives after $GMQR_3$. GProcessor calculates $TempView := GMQR_3 = \phi$.
9. ΔV due to $\Delta R_{11} = TempView = \phi$.
10. ΔV is used to update the materialized view at the mediator as: $V = V + \Delta V = V + \phi = V$.

Fig. 6. Example for the working of MEDWRAP

In MEDWRAP and MRE, T_i is proportional to the size of each IS. In the simplistic approach, T_i is proportional to the cardinality of each relation. N is the number of information sources, X is the number of relational concurrency conflicts per source, and Z is the total number of relations in the whole system i.e. all sources. For detailed space and time analysis refer to [VR02].

Discussion. MEDWRAP needs substantially less storage space than MRE. Mediator delays T_m in MEDWRAP and MRE are identical. Delays required to overcome *source concurrency conflicts* in MEDWRAP and MRE are identical and negligible in both cases since only CPU operations are involved. MEDWRAP has (3X-1) more wrapper delays and (N+X-1) more I/O delays than MRE. Thus, if the *relational concurrency conflict* rate is very high, MRE is faster, but at the cost of huge storage at all wrappers. Thus, MRE is highly space-consuming. In the simplistic approach, all delays get multiplied by approximately twice the total number of relations in the system, irrespective of concurrency conflicts. Thus, the simplistic approach is very time-consuming. In short, the MEDWRAP approach provides a good space/time trade-off.

6 Conclusions

MEDWRAP provides a consistent solution to incremental view maintenance in distributed multi-source data warehousing environments with multiple relations per source. MEDWRAP offers the flexibility of *semi-autonomous sources* since sources do not participate in view maintenance beyond reporting updates and processing queries, the benefit of *software re-use* by adopting techniques from existing algorithms, and the advantage of *storage efficiency* since no intermediate materialized views are needed at wrappers. Implementation of MEDWRAP and its integration with the existing data warehousing system DyDa at WPI [CZC+O1, LNR01] are ongoing to allow for experimentation.

References

AESY97. D. Agrawal, A. El Abbadi, A. Singh, T. Yurek. Efficient View Maintenance at Data Warehouses. In *SIGMOD-97,* p. 417–427.

CCR. J. Chen, S. Chen, E. Rundensteiner. TxnWrap: A Transactional Approach to Data Warehouse Maintenance. To Appear *ER-02.*

CD97. S. Chaudhuri, U. Dayal. An Overview of Data Warehousing and OLAP Technology. *SIGMOD-97 Record,* 26(1):65-74.

CZC+O1. J. Chen, X. Zhang, S. Chen et. al. DyDa: Data Warehouse Maintenance in Fully Concurrent Environments. In *SIGMOD-01 Demo,* p.619.

DZR99. L. Ding, X. Zhang, E. Rundensteiner. The MRE Wrapper Approach. In *DOLAP-99,* p. 30–35.

GM96. A. Gupta, I. Mumick. What is the data warehousing problem? (Are materialized views the answer?). In *VLDB-96,* p.602.

KM99. S. Kulkarni, M. Mohania. Concurrent Maintenance of Views Using Multiple Versions. In *Intl. Database Eng. and Appl. Symposium- 99,* p. 254–258.

LNR01. A. Lee, A. Nica, E. Rundensteiner. The *E VE* Approach: View Synchronization In Dynamic Distributed Environments. To Appear *IEEE TKDE-01.*

LSK01. K. Lee, J. Son, M. Kim. Efficient Incremental View Maintenance in Data Warehouses. In *SIGMOD-01,* p. 349–356.

Moh96. N. Mohan. DWMS: Data Warehouse Management System. In *VLDB-96,* p. 588–590.

VR02. A. Varde, E. Rundensteiner. The MEDWRAP Strategy. Technical Report, Worcester Polytechnic Institute, Worcester-MA, 2002.

ZGMHW95. Y. Zhuge, J. Widom et. al. View Maintenance in a Warehousing Environment. In *SIGMOD-95,* p. 316–327.

ZGMW96. Y. Zhuge, H. García-Molina et. al. The Strobe Algorithms for Multi-Source Warehouse Consistency. In *Intl. Conf. an Parallel and Distributed Info. Systems-96,* p. 146–157.

ZGMW97. Y. Zhuge, J.Wiener et. al. Multiple View Consistency for Data Warehousing. In *IEEE Intl. Conf. an Data Eng-97,* p. 289–300.

Zhu99. Y. Zhuge. *Incremental Maintenance of* Consistent *Data Warehouses.* Ph.D. Thesis, Stanford University, Stanford-CA, 1999.

Estimating Costs of Path Expression Evaluation in Distributed Object Databases

Gabriela Ruberg, Fernanda Baião, and Marta Mattoso

Department of Computer Science – COPPE/UFRJ
P.O.Box 68511, Rio de Janeiro, RJ, 21945-970 – Brazil
{gruberg, baiao, marta}@cos.ufrj.br

Abstract. Efficient evaluation of path expressions in distributed object databases involves choosing among several query processing strategies, due to the rich semantics involved in object-based data models and to the complexity added by the distribution. This work presents a new cost model for object-based query processors and addresses relevant issues, which are ignored or relaxed in other works in the literature, such as the selectivity of the path expression, the sharing degree of the referenced objects, the partial participation of the collections in the relationships, and the distribution of the database objects across the nodes of a network. These issues allowed us to present more realistic estimates for the query optimizer. Our cost model has been validated against experimental results obtained with an object DBMS prototype running in a distributed architecture, using the OO7 benchmark application.

1 Introduction

The development of realistic and efficient query optimizers is extremely important in enhancing the performance of database systems. In current query languages, path expression processing optimization is a central and difficult issue. Reference attributes in path expressions provide direct (pointer) access through object navigation, such as in object databases, or element navigation in XML [6]. The choice of the best execution plan to process a query with reference attributes is not simple for the query optimizer to make, due to the large number of execution strategies and algorithms to evaluate a path expression. Relevant issues must be considered for this problem, including choosing from binary or n-ary operators, pointer- or value-based algorithms, forward or reverse evaluation directions. These issues are not fully addressed in current cost models for object-based query optimizers, compromising the accuracy of estimate models.

In a distributed environment, the query execution search space is even larger because of fragmented data. Distributed data processing is becoming popular due to performance gains obtained from PC clusters, grid computing, and the Web, among others [11]. However, current path expression optimizers lack practical cost functions for ad-hoc queries in fragmented collections of objects. These functions may not be directly obtained from centralized cost models because some fragmented data may be previously disregarded during the query execution, modifying substantially the query

R. Cicchetti et al. (Eds.): DEXA 2002, LNCS 2453, pp. 351–360, 2002.

costs. Even in a centralized context, a realistic cost model can not be obtained with a simple combination of relevant issues into a single model, because these issues are strongly related to each other and have to be remodeled. Table 1 identifies the presence of important issues in current object database cost models. Next, we discuss the impact of the issues of Table 1 in the cost estimates.

Estimating selectivity factor is essential to the performance analysis of query processing. The selectivity of path expressions can vary significantly according to partial or total participation of a class in a relationship. Partial participation means that only a subset of objects in a class are related to the objects of another class. However, most cost models [1, 2, 7, 8, 9, 10, 13] disregard partial participation. Cho et al.[6] present a realistic method for the estimation of selectivity factors, but only in centralized object databases.

A path expression can be evaluated in a forward direction (from the first to the last collection) or in a reverse direction (in the opposite way). Many cost models [1, 2, 7, 8, 9] are limited to the forward direction. The reverse direction is not obtained by simply changing the index variation, rather other parameters have to be added. The two basic algebra operators for path expression evaluation are the n-ary operator and the binary operator. The execution costs of a path expression may significantly vary for each pair (*evaluation direction*, *algebra operator*), according to the selectivity of the nested predicates and to the partial participation of the collections in the relationships of the path expression. A cost model restricted to a specific direction or execution strategy may prevent the query optimizer from choosing the best execution plan.

The amount of IO operations, estimated in terms of data pages, is often presented as the basic cost in the query processing [1, 2, 5, 8, 9, 10, 13], specially in a centralized execution. The object data model allows complex strategies due to the rich variety of constructors provided, and can drastically affect cost estimates of IO operations if techniques of object clustering are applied. This aspect has been disregarded by most cost models [1, 2, 5, 7, 8, 10, 13]. Very few works analyze CPU costs [9, 10]. Communication costs of distributed evaluation of path expressions in vertically and/or horizontally fragmented classes is not addressed in the literature. Almost all processing cost factors are very influenced by the size of available main memory, although this factor is usually not taken into account. In the small memory hypothesis, the IO reload overhead of a path expression evaluation is traditionally estimated using the collection fan-out parameter [8, 9, 10]. However, we have noticed that practically no additional IO operations are necessary if there is no object sharing in the relationships of the path expression, even if the fan-out is greater than one.

Works on distributed object-based cost functions are dedicated to algorithms for class partitioning in object databases. They are focused on the analysis of primary horizontal (P.H.F.) [1, 2, 7], derived horizontal (D.H.F.) [2], and vertical (V.F) [8] fragmentation methodologies. Their application in a real query optimizer is somewhat restricted, since they disregard important issues in the path expression evaluation, such as the object clustering policy, the evaluation direction, the binary operator and algorithms, and CPU costs. These issues are not trivially included in the cost model of the algorithms.

Table 1. Important issues in path expression processing and related cost models

	Issues / Cost Models	[1]	[2]	[3]	[5]	[7]	[8]	[9]	[10]	[13]	**[14]**
CENTRALIZ.	Partial participation			X	X						**X**
	Physical object clustering							X			**X**
	Evaluation direction			X	X				X	X	**X**
	N-ary operator	X	X			X	X	X	X	X	**X**
	Binary operator				X				X	X	**X**
	IO overhead due to obj. sharing										**X**
	IO costs	X	X		X		X	X	X	X	**X**
	CPU costs							X	X		**X**
DIST.	P.H.F.	X	X			X					**X**
	D.H.F.		X								**X**
	V.F.						X				**X**
	Communication costs										**X**

We present a new cost model that covers the most representative algorithms for binary and n-ary operators, as well as forward and reverse directions for general path expression evaluation, in both centralized and distributed environments. An extended version of this work with detailed cost formulas may be found in [14]. In addition, our cost model has been validated against experimental results obtained in our previous work [15].

The remaining of this paper is organized as follows. Section 2 describes our cost model with emphasis in estimation of selectivity factors. Section 3 shows the validation of our cost model against experimental results, obtained with an object DBMS prototype using the OO7 benchmark. Finally, Section 4 draws some considerations and future work.

2 Cost Model

Invariably, the complexity of optimization problems requires some simplifications in the cost model. We assume that: (i) the query optimizer is able to break the encapsulation property; (ii) objects have a size less than a database page; (iii) the attribute values are uniformly distributed among instances of a class; and (iv) each object collection has just one class as its domain. These assumptions are present in other cost models [1, 2, 3, 5, 8, 9, 10, 13] since they occur in most object-based DBMS, as well as in their typical applications. Thus, they do not limit the expressive power of our cost model.

In our approach for estimating the cost of query execution plans, we consider that queries are issued against collections, thus some statistics are maintained for collections rather than for classes. The parameters of the fragments F_j^i are represented similarly to the parameters of the collections, adding the index j, $1 \le j \le f_i$. Therefore,

SEL'^{i}_{j} represents the selectivity of the path expression over the fragment F^{i}_{j} while $D^{i+1}_{i,j}$ is the total number of distinct pointers from C_i objects to F^{i+1}_{j} objects.

Table 2. Cost Model Parameters

Param	Description
SEL_i	Selectivity of nested predicate p_i over C_i
SEL'_i	Selectivity of the path expression over C_i
$\lVert C_i \rVert$	Cardinality of C_i
$\lvert C_i \rvert$	# pages of C_i
S_{C_i}	Average size of one object of C_i
f_i	# fragments of C_i
$Z_{i-1,i}$	Average # distinct pointers to C_{i+1} objects from C_i objects that have at least one non null reference

$D_{i,i+1}$	Total # distinct pointers from C_i objects to C_{i+1} objects
$X_{i,i+1}$	# C_i objects having all pointers to C_{i+1} objects as null references
sel^{i}_{j}	Selectivity factor over the C_i cardinality according to the F^{i}_{j} cardinality
REF_i	# distinct accessed objects from C_i in the path evaluation.
ref^{i}_{j}	Analogous to REF_i, in F^{i}_{j}
ℓ	Length of the path expression

2.1 Selectivity Factor of Path Expressions

The basis for evaluating query optimization strategies is the estimation of the selectivity factor of selection predicates and joins [5]. The selectivity factor of a path expression is the selectivity factor resultant from the nested predicates and the participation of each class collection in path relationships. Partial participation of a class collection influences the prediction of the path expression selectivity due not only to the estimation of the selectivity of implicit joins, but also due to the estimation of selectivity of nested predicates. Therefore, only the referenced objects in the path expression must be taken into account to estimate the selectivity factors over the collections.

When pointer-based algorithms are used, the path expression selectivity over a collection C_i represents the portion of the C_i objects that will be accessed during the path evaluation. Moreover, the path expression selectivity determines the cardinality of the intermediate results generated by join algorithms (pointer and value-based). Its computation over each collection C_i, $1 \le i \le \ell$, also depends on the direction used to evaluate the path expression. Thus, given a path expression, we may express the number of distinct accessed objects in collection C_i during the path navigation as:

$$REF_i = \lceil SEL'_i \times \lVert C_i \rVert \rceil . \qquad (1)$$

The term SEL'_i, $1 \le i \le \ell$, is obtained according to the evaluation direction:

- In forward, $SEL'_1 = 1$ and $SEL'_i = \dfrac{SEL'_{i-1} \times SEL_{i-1} \times D_{i-1,i}}{\lVert C_i \rVert}$; **(2)**

- In reverse, $SEL'_\ell = 1$ and $SEL'_i = \frac{SEL'_{i+1} \times SEL_{i+1} \times (\|C_i\| - X_{i,i+1})}{\|C_i\|}$. **(3)**

Note that all objects in the starting collection (C_1 or C_ℓ, according to the evaluation direction) are accessed because there is no filter from a previous relationship in the path expression.

In path expressions involving large collections with low selectivity factors, the traditional probabilistic method for selectivity estimation [1, 2, 3, 5, 8, 10] results in an expressive deviation from real values, as shown in section 3. This difference, which is avoided in our method, may be propagated to the estimation of page hits and to all costs that are based on the selectivity factor (IO, CPU and communication costs). Additionally, our method presents low computational complexity, thus improving processing costs in the optimization task.

Fragmentation Effects. Horizontal fragmentation distributes class instances among fragments (object collections) with the same structure, according to a given fragmentation criteria. Analogously, vertical fragmentation splits the logical structure of a class and distributes its attributes (and methods) among fragments with the same cardinality. Let C_i, $1 \le i \le \ell$, be a collection of a path expression with primary horizontal or vertical fragmentation. During the evaluation of this path expression, the query processor can previously identify:

i) a horizontal fragment F_j^i, $1 \le j \le f_i$, where the selectivity of the associated nested predicate p_i is zero; or

ii) a vertical fragment F_j^i, $1 \le j \le f_i$, which attributes are not used in the query.

In both cases, we assume $SEL_j^i = 0$, thus causing the elimination of F_j^i during the query processing. If C_i is fragmented, only the set of fragments of C_i in which $SEL'_j \neq 0$ will be scanned during the query evaluation process. We may define the $Elim_i$ subset containing all C_i fragments eliminated by SEL_j^i as:

$$Elim_i = \{F_j^i, 1 \le j \le f_i \mid SEL_j^i = 0\}. \quad \textbf{(4)}$$

In addition, we may define the subset $Elim'_i$ that refers to the derived horizontal fragments from C_i which were indirectly eliminated by the path expression selectivity (if their primary fragments were eliminated too), as follows:

$$Elim'_i = \{F_j^i, 1 \le j \le f_i \mid (F_j^{i-1} \mapsto F_j^i) \wedge (F_j^{i-1} \in E_{i-1})\}. \quad \textbf{(5)}$$

The term $F_j^{i-1} \mapsto F_j^i$ denotes that the primary fragment F_j^{i-1} determines the derived fragment F_j^i, in the forward evaluation. The reverse evaluation formula is obtained analogously to (5). We may define the set E_i, $1 \le i \le \ell$, with cardinality $\#E_i$, of all C_i fragments that will not be scanned during the path expression evaluation as:

$$E_i = Elim_i \cup Elim'_i. \quad \textbf{(6)}$$

We estimate the selectivity factor of C_i objects that belong to E_i as:

$$selE_i = \sum_{F_j^i \in E_i} sel_j^i \ . \quad \textbf{(7)}$$

The formal definition of set E_i and of its subsets, representing the fragmented data that is disregarded during the query evaluation, allows us to properly estimate the selectivity factors and execution costs of a distributed path expression evaluation.

Path Expression Selectivity in Horizontal Fragmentation. The number of distinct objects retrieved from a horizontally fragmented collection C_i, $1 \le i \le \ell$, during the evaluation of a path expression is given by:

$$REF_i = \sum_{j=1}^{f_i} ref_j^i \ , \quad \textbf{(8)}$$

$$\text{where} \quad ref_j^i = \left| SEL''^i_j \times \left\| F_j^i \right\| \right|, \quad 1 \le j \le f_i \ . \quad \textbf{(9)}$$

If $F_j^i \in E_i$ then we have $ref_j^i = 0$. Otherwise, $F_j^i \notin E_i$ and SEL''^i_j is calculated according to both the horizontal fragmentation strategy of C_i (primary or derived) and to the path expression evaluation direction. In a forward evaluation[1], $1 < i \le \ell$ and $1 \le j \le f_i$, we have:

- In P.H.F., $SEL''^1_j = 1$ and $SEL''^i_j = \dfrac{SEL'_{i-1} \times SEL_{i-1} \times D^i_{i-1,j}}{\left\| F_j^i \right\|}$; **(10)**
- In D.H.F., $SEL''^1_j = 1$ and $SEL''^i_j = \dfrac{part_j^i(SEL'_{i-1} \times SEL_{i-1}) \times D^i_{i-1,j}}{\left\| F_j^i \right\|}$. **(11)**

In equation (11), the function $part_j^i(factor)$ returns the participation of the fragment F_j^i in the objects selected by *factor* from C_i. Modeling this participation is important because if derived horizontal fragmentation is applied on C_i and some of its fragments are eliminated by their C_{i-1} primary fragments, then only non-eliminated C_i fragments contribute to REF_i objects. Indeed, the selectivity term (SEL'_{i-1} x SEL_{i-1}) is not proportionally distributed among all C_i fragments, but restricted to non-eliminated C_i fragments. Therefore:

$$part_j^i(factor) = \begin{cases} 1 & , \text{if } factor = 1, \\ factor + \dfrac{selElim'_i \times factor}{(1 - selElim'_i)} & , \text{otherwise.} \end{cases} \quad \textbf{(12)}$$

The selectivity factor $selElim'_i$ of objects from C_i fragments that were eliminated by the path expression selectivity is analogous to formula (7). Finally, the path

---

[1] Estimation in reverse evaluation is obtained analogously to (3), applying the function *part(factor)* if C_i has derived fragmentation.

expression selectivity and the nested predicate selectivity over a collection C_i that is horizontally fragmented are given respectively by:

- $SEL'_S = 1$ and $SEL'_i = \sum_{j=1}^{f_i} \left(sel_j^i \times SEL''^i_j \right);$ **(13)**
- $SEL_i = \sum_{j=1}^{f_i} \left(sel_j^i \times SEL_j^i \right).$ **(14)**

The term SEL'_S represents the selectivity factor of the path expression in the starting collection. Note that partial participation of collections in path relationships influences the estimation of the selectivity factors of each fragment involved in the path expression evaluation. In a distributed context, if total participation is assumed, then the difference from real values to estimates is even larger due to accumulation of many fragment deviations.

Path Expression Selectivity in Vertical Fragmentation. Let C_i, $1 \le i \le \ell$, be a vertically fragmented collection where only one C_i vertical fragment contains the reference attribute used in the path expression navigation. The remaining C_i fragments are accessed during the query evaluation only if their attributes are necessary to probe the predicate p_i. The selectivity factor of the path expression is the same in all C_i fragments and the total number of distinct C_i objects which are accessed during the path expression evaluation is obtained by:

$$REF_i = ref_*^i \ , \qquad \textbf{(15)}$$

$$\text{where} \quad ref_*^i = \lceil SEL'_i \times \|C_i\| \rceil . \qquad \textbf{(16)}$$

The term ref_*^i denotes the number of distinct C_i objects that are accessed in one C_i vertical fragment. Note that SEL'_i is obtained according to equations (2) and (3). However, each C_i object corresponds to f_i stored objects, according to C_i vertical fragments. Therefore, we estimate the total number of C_i objects which are accessed in the non-eliminated vertical fragments during the path expression evaluation as:

$$REF\_v_i = (f_i - \#E_i) \times ref_*^i \ . \qquad \textbf{(17)}$$

Finally, the nested predicate p_i has several selectivity factors according to C_i vertical fragments, thus its resultant selectivity factor is estimated as:

$$SEL_i = \min_{F_j^i \notin E_i} \left(SEL_j^i \right) . \qquad \textbf{(18)}$$

Both vertical and horizontal fragmentation estimates may be easily combined to calculate the selectivity factors of hybrid fragmentation techniques.

3 Experimental Analysis

In order to validate our cost model, we have compared its performance with results previously obtained [15] in practical experiments. These experimental results were obtained using the OO7 benchmark [4] on top of the GOA DBMS prototype [12].

Experimental and simulation results in terms of number of IO operations per query are shown in Figures 1 to 4. The results focus on the performance of the path expression evaluation in queries Q1-Q5 using strategy NP-F (forward naïve pointer chasing) and in queries Q1-Q2 using strategy VJ-R (reverse value-based join), disregarding the cost of displaying query results.

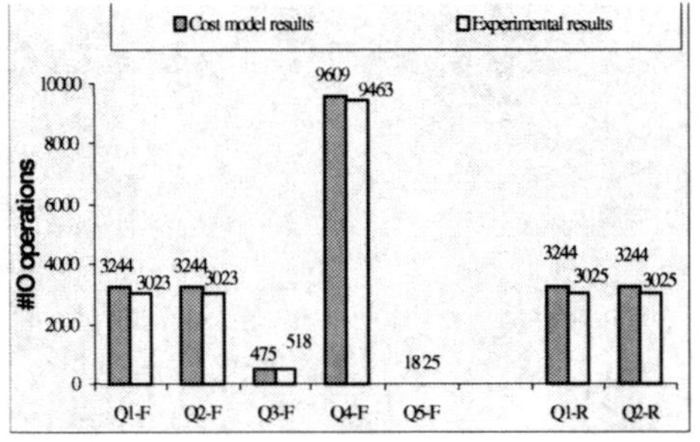

Fig. 1. NP-F and VJ-R execution IO cost (4Mbytes memory)

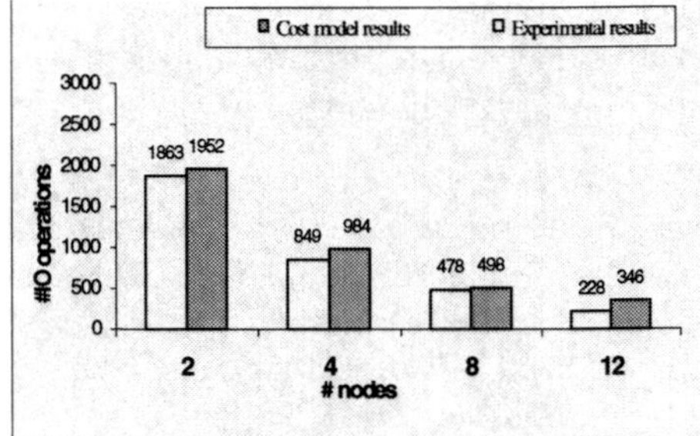

Fig. 2. IO cost per node of Q1-F execution in a distributed environment

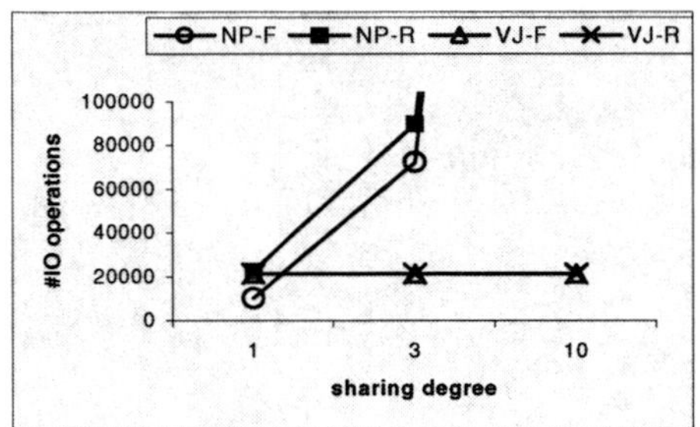

Fig. 3. IO cost varying the sharing degree (4Mbytes memory)

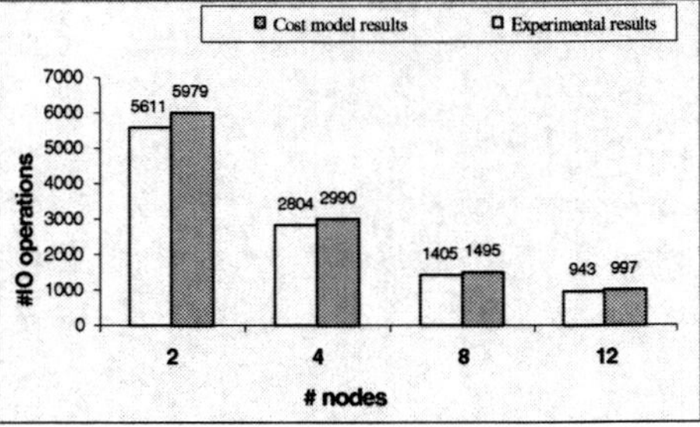

Fig. 4. IO cost per node of Q4- F execution in a distributed environment

Figure 1 shows the number of IO operations that occurred in the execution of each path expression evaluation strategy in the centralized environment, and compares them to the predictions of our cost model, showing that the estimates are very close to all the evaluated scenarios. As expected, most of the predicted results are slightly higher than the experimental ones, since some cost model formulas calculate the worst case for disk random access. Queries Q3 and Q5, however, presented the experimental result somewhat higher than the predicted by the cost model. This is due to the fact that they are very fast queries, thus the overhead of catalog access in the real experiment was more predominant.

Query Q4-F is defined over two large collections (AtomicParts and Connections). We assume that ||AtomicParts||=100000 and ||Connections||=300000. According to [1, 10], the number of accessed objects in the collection Connections is estimated as X_2=189637. Since the participation of the collections in the path expression is total, we observe that the real value of accessed objects from Connections should be 300000. According to our proposed formulas (1) and (2), the corresponding parameter is REF_2=300000. This example shows a difference, which is avoided in our estimation method, of approximately 37% between the result obtained by the traditional probabilistic estimation method and the real result.

In Figure 3, we analyzed the effect of varying the sharing degree (1, 3, and 10 in each collection) of the objects along a path expression with $\ell = 3$. The n-ary operator (NP-F and NP-R) has the worst behavior as share increases, since it ignores repeated object access and thus performs very poorly. The value-based join (VJ-F and VJ-R) presented a constant behavior because it avoids the bad effect of the object sharing and should be considered a good choice when object sharing is very high. This example shows that if the cost model does not consider the reverse direction or the value-based join algorithm, then the query execution strategy is limited to a very inefficient choice.

Queries Q1-F and Q4-F were executed in a distributed environment using 2, 4, 8, and 12 nodes. Figures 2 and 4 show the number of IO operations per node that occurred in the execution of each query. Our cost predictions are fairly close to values from experimental distributed execution, as in the centralized case.

4 Conclusions

Efficient processing of path expressions is fundamental for current query languages. The main contribution of this work is a new, realistic cost model to estimate the execution costs of evaluating path expressions in a distributed environment. The proposed cost model addresses binary and n-ary operators, as well as forward and reverse directions for path expression evaluation. It also considers issues such as the selectivity of the path expression, the sharing degree of the referenced objects which contributes to IO reload overhead estimate, physical clustering of the objects in disk, and the partial participation of the class collections in path relationships. These issues were combined and extended to encompass distributed processing, covering both horizontal (primary and derived) and vertical fragmentation of data.

We have shown the expressive deviation from real results in the traditional probabilistic method for estimation of the path expression selectivity when large collections with low selectivity factors are taken into account. Our selectivity estimation method avoids this deviation and presents low computational complexity, consequently diminishing processing costs in the optimization task. We also presented the limitations of always using the same algorithm and evaluation direction in path expression processing. The new cost model takes into account a large number of different factors, yet it remains fairly simple. The estimates generated by our cost model are very close to observed experimental results.

Currently we are working on extending this model for regular path expression processing. We are also experimenting the cost model to examine different strategies and new algorithms for evaluating path expressions.

Acknowledgement

This work was partially financed by CNPq and FAPERJ. The author G. Ruberg was supported by Central Bank of Brazil.

References

1. Bellatreche, L., Karlapalem, K., Basak, G.: Query-Driven Horizontal Class Partitioning for Object-Oriented Databases. DEXA 1998, 692-701
2. Bellatreche, L., Karlapalem, K., Li, Q.: Derived Horizontal Class Partitioning in OODBs: Design Strategies, Analytical Model and Evaluation. ER 1998, 465-479
3. Bertino, E., Foscoli, P.: On Modeling Cost Functions for Object-Oriented Databases. IEEE TKDE 9(3), 500-508 (1997)
4. Carey, M., DeWitt D., Naughton, J.: The OO7 Benchmark. ACM SIGMOD 22(2), 12-21 (1993)
5. Cho, W., Park, C., Whang, K., Son, S.: A New Method for Estimating the Number of Objects Satisfying an Object-Oriented Query Involving Partial Participation of Classes. Information Systems 21(3), 253-267 (1996)
6. Deutsch, A., Fernandez, M., et al.: Querying XML Data. IEEE Data Engineering Bulletin 22(3), 10-18 (1999)
7. Ezeife, C., Zheng, J.: Measuring the Performance of Database Object Horizontal Fragmentation Schemes. IDEAS 1999, 408-414
8. Fung, C. Karlapalem, K., Li, Q.: Cost-driven evaluation of vertical class partitioning in object oriented databases. DASFAA 1997, 11-20
9. Gardarin, G., Gruser, J., Tang, Z.: A Cost Model for Clustered Object-Oriented Databases. VLDB 1995, 323-334
10. Gardarin, G., Gruser, J., Tang, Z.: Cost-based Selection of Path Expression Processing Algorithms in Object-Oriented Databases. VLDB 1996, 390-401
11. Kossmann, D.: The State of the Art in Distributed Query Processing. ACM Computing Surveys 32(4), 422-469 (2000)
12. GOA++ Object Management System. URL: http://www.cos.ufrj.br/~goa
13. Ozkan, C., Dogac, A., Altinel, M.: A Cost Model for Path Expressions in Object Oriented Queries. Journal of Database Management 7(3), 25-33 (1996)
14. Ruberg, G.: A Cost Model for Query Processing in Distributed-Object Databases, M.Sc. Thesis in Portuguese, COPPE/UFRJ, Brazil (2001). Reduced version in English available in http://www.cos.ufrj.br/~gruberg/ruberg2001_english.pdf
15. Tavares, F.O., Victor, A.O., Mattoso, M.: Parallel Processing Evaluation of Path Expressions. SBBD 2000, 49-63

Profile Driven Data Management for Pervasive Environments*

Filip Perich, Sasikanth Avancha, Dipanjan Chakraborty, Anupam Joshi, and Yelena Yesha

Department of Computer Science and Electrical Engineering
University of Maryland Baltimore County
1000 Hilltop Circle, Baltimore, MD 21250, USA
{fperic1, savanc1, dchakr1, joshi, yeyesha}@csee.umbc.edu

Abstract. The past few years have seen significant work in mobile data management, typically based on the client/proxy/server model. Mobile/wireless devices are treated as clients that are data consumers only, while data sources are on servers that typically reside on the wired network. With the advent of "pervasive computing" environments an alternative scenario arises where mobile devices gather and exchange data from not just wired sources, but also from their ethereal environment and one another. This is accomplished using ad-hoc connectivity engendered by Bluetooth like systems. In this new scenario, mobile devices become both data consumers and producers. We describe the new data management challenges which this scenario introduces. We describe the design and present an implementation prototype of our framework, MoGATU, which addresses these challenges. An important component of our approach is to treat each device as an autonomous entity with its "goals" and "beliefs", expressed using a semantically rich language. We have implemented this framework over a combined Bluetooth and Ad-Hoc 802.11 network with clients running on a variety of mobile devices. We present experimental results validating our approach and measure system performance.

1 Introduction

The client/proxy/server model underlies much of the research in mobile data management. In this model, mobile devices are typically viewed as consumers of information, while data sources reside on the wired network. The main emphasis is on the development of protocols and techniques to deal with disconnection management and low bandwidth. The aim is often to allow applications built for the wired world (e.g., WWW, databases etc.) to run in wireless domains using proxy based approaches ([7]). In systems based on the 2.5/3G cellular infrastructure, the traditional client–proxy–server interaction is perhaps an appropriate model, where the "client" database can be extremely lightweight [1] or has a (partial) replicate of the main database on the wired side [13].

* This work was supported in part by NSF awards IIS 9875433 and CCR 0070802, DARPA DAML program, and IBM

R. Cicchetti et al. (Eds.): DEXA 2002, LNCS 2453, pp. 361–370, 2002.

With the spread of short-range ad-hoc networking systems (such as Bluetooth[1]) that enable devices to spontaneously interact with others in their vicinity, an alternative approach will be necessary. Mobile devices (hand-held, wearable or embedded in vehicles), computers embedded in the physical infrastructure, and (nano)sensors will all be able to discover and inter-operate with others in their vicinity. The mobile devices will be able to obtain more context-sensitive data by interacting with peers in their "vicinity" than by contacting a fixed data source on the wired network. In addition to the traditional challenges of mobile networks (i.e., low bandwidth and disconnection), this pervasive paradigm introduces new problems in terms of the environment's stability and accessibility. The connection time to a data source is often limited, as well as the likelihood of reconnecting to the same data source once disconnected. Accordingly, pervasive connectivity will require the mobile devices to be highly adaptive as well.

The objective of this paper is to articulate the requirements for, and present a preliminary implementation of, a robust infrastructure in which independent devices existing in a particular location will be able to collaborate with their mobile peers achieving higher data availability and currency. In this vision of pervasive computing environments, mobile devices are both sources and consumers of information and cooperate with others in their vicinity to pursue their individual and collective information needs.

The remainder of the paper is structured as follows. Section 2 discusses existing work in the area of distributed data management in mobile networks and in the area of user profiles. In section 3 we present new challenges and problems that this scenario introduced to pervasive environments that go beyond distributed database frameworks. In section 4 we describe the framework design and present system level details of its implementation. We conclude with section 5 and describe a future work.

2 Related Work

The problem of data management in a distributed environment has been well researched, both in terms of wired infrastructure and infrastructure-based wireless networks (e.g., MobileIP). The work on distributed and federated databases is well-known in the community [10]. Accordingly, we present work related to data management in wireless networks, and a short discussion of related work in the area of expressing user profiles.

Data Management in Wireless Networks: Chrysanthis *et al* [9] consider disconnected operations within mobile databases by presenting a mechanism, which they call a "view holder", that maintains versions of views required by a particular mobile unit. They also propose an extension to SQL that enables the profile- and capability-based programming of the view holders. Kottkamp and Zukunft [8] present optimization techniques for query processing in mobile database systems that include location information. They present a cost model and different strategies for query optimization incorporating mobility specific factors like energy and connectivity. Bukhres *et al* [3] propose an enhancement to the infrastructure-based mobile network model of Mobile Hosts (MHs) connected over a wireless virtual subnet and Mobile Support Stations (MSSs) connected to a wired static network. They recommend the addition of a mailbox, which serves as a central repository for the MHs that is maintained by the cellular provider and duplicated in all the MSSs.

[1] http://www.blutetooth.org/

Pitoura [11] presents a replication schema based on augmenting a mobile database interface with operations with weaker consistency guarantees. An implementation of the schema is presented by distinguishing copies into quasi and core; protocols for enforcing the schema are introduced. Finally, Demers *et al* [5] present the Bayou architecture, which is a platform of replicated, highly available, variable-consistency, mobile databases for building collaborative applications.

We note that in most of the previous work, the wireless networks are supported by the fixed, wireline infrastructure, where query optimization techniques require the support of wireline networks. Our work assumes no support from the fixed infrastructure. When the MH requires instantaneous information (e.g. traffic updates or bad weather warnings), it may be more easily accessible from other "local" MHs than a fixed node. In our work, a mobile device is always in nomadic mode, as defined by [3] and [8].

User Profiles: The data management community of late has been advocating the use of "profiles", especially when dealing with pervasive systems and stream data. For instance, Ren and Dunhamm [12] represent a profile as a collection of continuous location dependent data queries. The location dependent data is described in terms of tuples in a single-relational database (e.g., all hotels and restaurants in a city). A user then specifies her preferences by constructing several SQL queries based on the database schema. In a seminal paper, Cherniak *et al* [4] explore the use of profiles in the area of client/server based data recharging for mobile devices. They discuss the requirements for a successful profile as well as describe the need for a formal language that enables expressing such profiles. Their profile consists of two sections, namely the "domain", which is responsible for the data description, and the "utility", which is a numerical function denoting the data importance in respect to other information. While a step in the right direction, we argue in section 3 that this notion of profile is somewhat limited.

3 Challenges of Data Management in Pervasive Environments

If each entity in pervasive environments is capable of both posing and answering queries, we can describe this model as a type of mobile distributed database. However, it is far more complex than the conventional client-proxy-server based model. We illustrate this by classifying our environment along of four orthogonal axes, i.e., autonomy, distribution, heterogeneity, and mobility ([6]). This system is highly autonomous since there is no centralized control of the individual client databases. It is heterogeneous as we only assume that entities can "speak" to each other in some neutral format. The system is clearly distributed as parts of data reside on different computers, and there is some replication as entities cache data/metadata. Mobility is of course a given – in *ad-hoc* networking environments, devices can change their locations, and no fixed set of entities is "always" accessible to a given device. This is distinct from the issue of disconnection management that is traditionally addressed in the work on mobile databases. In those systems, disconnections of mobile devices from the network are viewed as temporary events and when reconnected, any ongoing transactions between the mobile and the server will either continue from the point of disconnection or be rolled back.

As devices move, their neighborhood changes dynamically. Hence, depending on the specific location and time a particular query is given, the originator may obtain different answers or none at all. Unlike traditional distributed database systems, the querying device cannot depend on a global catalog that would be able to route its query to the proper data source. Additionally, under high mobility conditions where current wireless networking technologies cannot support stable connections, there is no guarantee that the device will be able to access information that resides on neighboring devices. In other words, data is pervasive – it is not stored in a single repository but is distributed and/or replicated in an unknown manner among a large number of devices and only some of which are accessible at any given time. Querying is by similar reasoning *serendipitous*, if one asks a question to which the answer is stored in the vicinity then the query succeeds. Such a situation seems to leave too much to chance. To improve the chances of getting an answer to a question no matter when it is asked, each device should have the option to cache the metadata (e.g who has what data) and perhaps even the data obtained from neighbors in its current vicinity. To further complicate matters, each data source may have its own schema. Not all possible schema mappings can be done a-priori, and some devices will be unable to translate them due to their limited computational capabilities.

In addition, cooperation among information sources cannot be guaranteed. Clearly, the issues of privacy and trust will be very important for a pervasive environment, where transactions and involved entities are random [14]. Accordingly, there may be an entity that has reliable information but refuses to make it available to others, while another is willing to share information which is unreliable. Lastly, when an entity makes information available to another entity, questions regarding its provenance, as well as protection of future changes and sharing of that information arise.

In general, for pervasive systems to succeed, much of the interaction between the devices must happen in the background, without explicit human intervention. These interactions should be executed based on information in the profile. For instance, a diabetic user's profile can say "Always keep track of the nearest hospital", influencing what data the *InforMa* will seek to obtain and which information sources it will interact with. Of course, the question arises: "what exactly should a profile contain?" As we mentioned, perhaps the best work on profile driven data management is due to Franklin, Cherniak and Zdonik [4]. We argue that their profiles, which explicitly enumerate data and its utility, are not sufficient. A profile should not simply consist of information about utility values of fixed data domains, since in pervasive computing environments both the domains of data which a user may need, as well as its utility, will change with the changing context of the user. We believe that a profile should be described in terms of "beliefs", "desires", and "intentions" of the user, a model which has been explored in multi-agent interactions [2]. The "beliefs" represent information that should be treated as facts, and assigned "utility" and "reliability" values or functions to enable comparison with other information stored in a profile. For example, these may include information about user's schedule or cuisine preferences. The information in the profile of Cherniak *et al.* would in our system be treated as "beliefs". A "desire" represents a wish the user would like to accomplish. Each desire is also assigned "utility" value and function. Lastly, an "intention" represents a set of intended tasks – these can either be deduced from "desires", or be explicitly provided. For example, the profile may contain user's desire to listen to country music as performed by Shania Twain. The system should deduce from this the intention to download Shania Twain MP3s. This intention would then influence the information gathering behavior of the user's PDA. Alternately, a user may explicitly provide an intention to purchase Shania Twain CDs. Upon entering a mall, the device will try to obtain information about new releases from the local music stores. The "intentions" of user, modulated by the "beliefs" as well as contextual parameters, including location, time, battery power, and storage space, allow the *InforMa* of each entity to determine what data to obtain and its relative worth. We note here that the context information could also be regarded as "beliefs" that were dynamically asserted and retracted.

We believe that a semantically rich language, such as the one currently pursued by the W3C Consortium and DARPA (DAML+OIL[2]), provides a rich framework to represent our enhanced profiles. The advantages of this selection are two fold: By adhering to an already existing language, the syntax and rules do not have to be duplicated by creating a new formal language. Secondly, by utilizing a language used by the Semantic Web, the devices will be able to use the vast resources available on the Internet as well as the resources available in *ad-hoc* networks.

4 Framework Design and Implementation

Our framework is designed to handle serendipitous querying and data management efficiently and scalably in mobile *ad-hoc* environments. The framework consists of multiple instances of the following components: a meta-data representation, a profile, a communication interface, an information provider, and an Information Manager that we call *InforMa*.

4.1 Metadata Representation

The schema (ontology) for every information provider, information instances and even a profile must be understood by other entities in the environment. If this is not true, then the information is useless. At the same time, it is theoretically possible that all schemas are described in a different language. In this worst-case scenario, the existence of a schema translator becomes paramount. We can easily see that this is not a scalable solution and that the translator quickly becomes a bottleneck, preventing smooth exchange of information. We have, therefore, decided to use a common language to describe the schema for any information provider and chosen the semantic DARPA Agent Markup Language (DAML) for this purpose. In addition, instances of information, such as queries and answers, together with a user profile are also described in DAML.

We focused our efforts on developing ontologies that would be most useful for devices in moving vehicles. These include ontologies for describing user profiles, and for describing queries and answers [3]. Common well-known information providers, useful to such devices, are emergency related (e.g., police, medical, and fire department), traffic and road condition related, weather related, and maintenance related (e.g., gas station, towing service etc.). The ontologies are based on and very similar to the DAML-S ontology[4], which attempts to comprehensively describe services for the WWW. Using

[2] http://www.daml.org/

[3] http://mogatu.umbc.edu/ont/

[4] http://www.daml.org/services/

the DAML-S like description, we are able to match queries with information provider registration information as well as with particular answer instances. Accordingly, a device can describe itself by defining the appropriate service models it implements, the process models that provide the information, and the required inputs to be provided.

4.2 Profile

Since some entities in the *ad-hoc* environment are required to operate autonomously without an explicit human intervention, the entities must have access to individual rule-based profiles. These profiles are used to determine both the current and the future actions of the entities. We model a profile in MoGATU in terms of "beliefs", "desires", and "intentions", and encode it using DAML-based ontologies as we have previously discussed in Section 3. The "intentions" of user, modulated by the "beliefs" as well as contextual parameters, including location, time, battery power, and storage space, allow the *InforMa* of each entity to determine what data to obtain and its relative worth. We note here that the context information could also be regarded as "beliefs" that were dynamically asserted and retracted.

4.3 Information Providers

Every device manages a subset of the world knowledge repository that it can provide to itself and possibly to others. Of course, this subset may be inconsistent with the knowledge of other devices and may even be empty. An entity is an information provider when it possesses the capability to accept a query and generate an appropriate response based on the body of knowledge (mainly facts) under its control. These facts could be associated with practically anything in the world, for example the location of gasoline service stations in a certain area and price of gasoline at each station. Moreover, any device in our framework can provide information about more than one class of knowledge. At the same time, some devices may be too resource-limited or otherwise restricted to be able to store or share any information at all. These devices only use information advertised by peers in their environment.

Information providers register themselves with the local instance of *InforMa*. They may also register themselves or be registered with remote *InforMa*s. In the latter case, both information about information providers and the information under the control of those information providers is disseminated to all parts of the ad-hoc environment.

In our implementation, an information provider registers itself upon start-up with its *InforMa* by sending a registration request including a description of its schemas. *InforMa* adds it to its list of local and remote information providers. *InforMa* now knows how to route it any query that this provider is able to answer. On receiving a query, the provider attempts to answer it and sends back its response to the local *InforMa* which routes it back to the source. Renewal of registration information at a remote *InforMa* is the sole responsibility of the provider. *InforMa* simply removes the information related to the provider from its table, once the provider's lifetime has expired.

4.4 InforMa: Information Manager

Every entity implements *InforMa*, which is a local metadata repository that includes schema definitions for locally available information providers and particular facts such as queries and answers for local and non-local information providers. Accordingly, *InforMa* stores advertised schema for local information providers and also for those that it believes the device can reach by communicating with other devices in its vicinity. In addition, *InforMa* stores facts that were produced locally or that were obtained from others. For example, when a device has a local weather information provider and it furthermore knows that it is raining, *InforMa* includes metadata to reflect that knowledge.

Based on their model of interaction with their peers, we can define four basic types of *InforMa* instances. In the most simple form, the *InforMa* maintains required information about information providers locally present on the device. Each entity in the *ad-hoc* environment is required to implement this type of *InforMa*. We believe that this type would be most suitable for resource-limited devices. In addition, this particular form of *InforMa* is most suitable for entities whose environment changes rapidly. Any time a query is posed, *InforMa* is contacted to provide an answer. *InforMa* first attempts to determine whether any local information provider is capable of answering the query and contacts it. Otherwise, the *InforMa* tries to locate some remote information provider and requests its assistance. Finally, when all previous attempts fail, it attempts to contact all of its neighbors to ask them for their help. However, once the query is satisfied, the *InforMa* may choose to forget any information obtained from the other entities, in order to save memory. As an extension to the first type, the *InforMa* may decide to temporarily store the foreign information in the hope that a future query may be answered by reusing it. In this category, knowledge available to *InforMa* still remains restricted to the entity. For more resource-rich devices, the *InforMa* may decide to not only store information related to local information providers (and the ones obtained while answering local queries) but also accept information that was disseminated by other entities in its vicinity. Henceforth, *InforMa* is now more capable and efficient in satisfying queries that originate from its home entity. Finally, the most capable *InforMa* instance makes its knowledge available to all entities in its vicinity by accepting their query requests and by actively advertising its knowledge.

Query Answering: InforMa uses all the information encoded in the DAML metadata to find an appropriate answer or to locate an information provider that could potentially answer the query. In our framework, each *InforMa* first tries to find a valid non-expired answer. Next, it tries to match a local information provider, a remote information provider, or at least some other *InforMa* that could have a richer cache. The matching is done by finding the appropriate process model, and validating all inputs and outputs when necessary. We have implemented the current framework using graph and search techniques; however, it is possible that more capable *InforMa* entities may also utilize more powerful reasoning techniques using Prolog engines.

Caching: Every *InforMa* has a limited cache in which it stores registration information, queries and answers for a short period of time. Depending on its mode of operation, the cache size, the arrival rates of registration information and queries, and the lifetime of the registration information, *InforMa* may or may not be able to answer a certain query. In order to increase the chances of responding positively to a certain query and to decrease response time, *InforMa* can employ various cache-replacement algorithms to cache responses to previous queries together with information provider advertisements. We have implemented both hybrid Least Recently Used (LRU) and Most Recently Used (MRU) replacement algorithms utilizing a priority-based scheme allowing *InforMa* to determine what information to retain and what to discard. These algorithms work like the standard LRU and MRU algorithms; however, they assign the highest priority to local information providers first, followed by remote information providers, and the lowest priority to answers to previous queries. Additionally, we have implemented a preliminary semantic cache replacement algorithm that uses a profile. The user profile is used to generate standing queries as well as to determine the utility value of all cached information. The device uses these queries to contact other devices in its vicinity in the hope of obtaining information that the user may require in near future. The semantic replacement algorithm applies the utility values of all cached and incoming information to manage the limited cache size. Accordingly, along with time considerations of LRU and MRU algorithms, the semantic-based algorithm also covers other contextual dimensions.

Advertisement and Solicitation: In addition to supporting the registration of information providers, our framework also supports the concept of solicitation of information about information providers. Henceforth, every *InforMa* can periodically send solicitation requests to its peers. When a new information provider is discovered, *InforMa* caches the information if possible. Similarly, every *InforMa* can advertise its information providers to all its neighbors in the vicinity. One important point to emphasize here is that solicitation of information providers from remote *InforMa*s and broadcast-based advertisement is restricted to 1-hop neighbors only. This prevents unnecessary flooding of this information across the network.

Multi-Hop Networks and Routing: It is possible for a query to travel multiple hops within our framework. Every *InforMa* knows either the final destination of a particular message or a route to it. It obtains the information as follows: when a remote query or registration arrives on the Bluetooth or the Ad-Hoc 802.11 interface, *InforMa* stores the address of the remote device in its routing table. When, on the other hand, it receives a remote forwarded query or registration request, it notes in its routing table that the source of the message can be reached through the forwarder, unless it already knows how to reach the source. To facilitate this routing mechanism, we ensure that every message contains the Bluetooth or the 802.11 device address of the source.

4.5 Experimental Results

For evaluating our framework, we simulated the scenario of devices exchanging data while passing by one another. This was done with the use of several laptops and iPAQ 3870 devices. Connectivity was provided by Bluetooth (embedded in the iPAQs, Ericsson cards connected on serial ports on the laptops) and 802.11 cards in Ad-Hoc mode. Our first set of experiments simply validated the working of the system. A device was able to discover information from nearby devices, both directly connected and those more than a hop away. It was also able to cache data and respond to queries. The test consisted of four devices and was executed over a simulated period of 100 minutes. Device *A* was able to communicate with device *B*, which in turn was in range of devices *C* and *D*. Device *A* provided weather information and device *D* had information about locations and prices of nearby gas stations. We evaluated the system by randomly selecting a query and assigning it to one of the four devices while monitoring information present at each cache. For example, when device *A* asked for the closest gas station, it was able to deduce that device *D* contains the required information and that the query should be routed through device *B*. Moreover, when device *B* received the query, it was able to immediately return a cached answer instead of routing the request to device D.

We next studied the impact on the performance by varying the cache size of each *InforMa*. Since our present implementation must linearly scan the cache to see a matching DAML structure, increasing cache size increases the amount of time spent on this scan. However, even for a 30K cache, the processing time was on average 5ms per query after 100 runs. The network transmission time completely dominates this in Bluetooth environments (4.56s to transfer a 1.0KB "query" and to send the response). Even for the much faster 802.11 devices, the time needed to send the query and receive the answer over the network was five times longer (27ms combined round trip time)! We expect to incorporate ongoing research into creating indices for DAML statements in future versions of *InforMa* so as to increase the processing speed.

Next, we compared the performance of cache replacement policies, namely LRU, MRU and the semantics-based algorithm that we propose. Intuitively, the algorithm that can use the information in the profile to know that type of information the user needs should do a better job of caching. To validate this, we considered a scenario where the device is mobile and receiving two types of advertisements - one from local restaurants and the other from clothing stores over a simulated period of 100 minutes. The probability of the device receiving either advertisement type was 0.5. The profile indicated that the utility of the restaurant information was 9 times that of the clothing store information. As such, the simulated user queried about restaurants 9 times as often as about clothing stores. The goal of the device was to anticipate the user's future demand as dictated by the user's profile, consequently ensuring that the needed information was cached (if previously available). The worst performer in this scenario was MRU with success rate of 0.37. This was followed by LRU with success rate of 0.63. The best performance was the semantic replacement algorithm, with success rate of 0.87. The success of the semantic replacement algorithm is attributable to the high accuracy of the predictions based upon the profile.

Lastly, we studied the performance of our framework in one-hop and multi-hop networks. As we have described earlier, the transmission speeds for a single hop were 4.56s seconds in Bluetooth environment and 27ms seconds for 802.11 based devices. The measured results indicate that Bluetooth connectivity is fast enough to allow exchanges and interactions in relatively stable environments (e.g. a person in a mall, cars traveling in the same direction on a highway) which cover many of the pervasive computing scenarios. However, if the relative speed of objects in motion is high, then current networking technology clearly precludes the use of serendipitous querying.

5 Conclusions and Future Work

We have addressed the issues of mobile data management in pervasive environments by proposing a framework that is capable of handling a heterogeneous set of mobile devices.

We have presented the need for a robust framework enabling serendipitous querying in mobile *ad-hoc* environments. Each device is represented by one information manager, *InforMa*, and a number of information providers (data sources). Each device may also contain a profile reflecting the user's "beliefs", "desires", and "intentions". The profile and other information is encoded in a semantically rich language. Our implementation concurrently operates over both Bluetooth and 802.11 Ad-Hoc networks. The *InforMa* collects information about the current environment, and uses it in conjunction with the profile to predict its user's future requirements. We experimented and tested three alternative cache replacement policies as well as query routing over multi-node paths. Our results show that the semantic cache replacement algorithm outperforms both LRU and MRU replacement policies. Additionally, our results show that both Bluetooth and 802.11 support routing over multiple nodes.

In this paper, our focus was to address the issues concerned with querying and processing, which are similar to read-only mode operations in information access systems. We will extend our model by adding write-mode data access patterns allowing for full transaction capabilities.

References

1. C. Bobineau, L. Bouganim, P. Pucheral, and P. Valduriez. PicoDBMS: Scaling down Database Techniques for the Smartcard. In *VLDB*, 2000.
2. M. Bratmann. *Intentions, Plans, and Practical Reason*. Harvard University Press, 1987.
3. O. Bukhres, S. Morton, P. Zhang, E. Vanderdijs, C. Crawley, J. Platt, and M. Mossman. A Proposed Mobile Architecture for Distributed Database Environment. Technical report, Indiana University, Purdue University, 1997.
4. M. Cherniak, M. Franklin, and S. Zdonik. Expressing User Profiles for Data Recharging. *IEEE Personal Communications*, July 2001.
5. A. Demers, K. Petersen, M. Spreitzer, D. Terry, M. Theimer, and B. Welch. The Bayou Architecture: Support for Data Sharing among Mobile Users. In *Proc. IEEE Workshop on Mobile Computing Systems & Applications*, 1994.
6. M. Dunham and A. Helal. Mobile computing and databases: Anything new? *ACM SIGMOD Record*, 24(4), December 1995.
7. A. Joshi. On Proxy Agents, Mobility and Web Access. *ACM/Baltzer Journal of Mobile Networks and Applications*, 2000.
8. H. Kottkamp and O. Zukunft. Location-Aware Query Processing in Mobile Database Systems. In *Proc. of the ACM Symposium on Applied Computing*, Feb. 1998.
9. S. Lauzac and P. Chrysanthis. Utilizing Versions of Views within a Mobile Environment. In *DEXA*, pages 408–413, Aug. 1998.
10. M. Tamer Oezsu and Patrick Valduriez. *Principles of Distributed Database Systems*. Prentice Hall, Inc., New Jersey, 2nd edition, 1999.
11. E. Pitoura. A Replication Schema to Support Weak Connectivity in Mobile Information Systems. In *DEXA*, 1996.
12. Q. Ren and M. Dunham. Using Semantic Caching to Manage Location Dependent Data in Mobile Computing. In *ACM MobiCom'00*, 2000.
13. C. Tait, H. Lei, S. Acharya, and H. Chang. Intelligent File Hoarding for Mobile Computers. In *ACM MobiCom'95*, 1995.
14. J. Undercoffer, F. Perich, A. Cedilnik, L. Kagal, and A. Joshi. A Secure Infrastructure for Service Discovery and Access in Pervasive Computing. *ACM Monet: Security in Mobile Computing Environments*, Spring 2002.

INVISIP: Usage of Information Visualization Techniques to Access Geospatial Data Archives

Stefan Göbel[1], Jörg Haist[1], Harald Reiterer[2], and Frank Müller[2]

[1] Fraunhofer Institute for Computer Graphics, GIS department, Fraunhoferstr. 5, 64283 Darmstadt, Germany
{stefan.goebel, joerg.haist}@igd.fhg.de
http://www.igd.fhg.de/igd-a5/

[2] University of Konstanz, Department of Computer & Information Science, Universitätsstr. 10, 78457 Konstanz, Germany
{harald.reiterer, frank.mueller}@uni-konstanz.de
http://www.inf.uni-konstanz.de/iw_is

Abstract. Complex application examples or scenarios such as site planning need a lot of information, especially spatially referenced data[1] in order to find a best place for a new building or an industrial area and to solve individual planning tasks such as generating ecological, environmental or traffic reports. Recent initiatives to geospatial data archives offer access to a wealth of distributed data covered by the widespread information spectrum of different geodata disciplines (e.g. environmental data, geologic data, cadastral data, remote sensing data or socio-demographic data), but offer only basic levels of interactivity and user assistance. The EU-funded project INVISIP (Information Visualization in Site Planning, IST-2000-29640) addresses this lack of usability and aims to develop new concepts and methods to support all involved parties within the different phases of the multi-step site planning process. This paper describes INVISIP and introduces GeoCrystal and SuperTable as new information visualization techniques to support users in this process.

1 Introduction

Concerning this information demand in complex applications such as site planning, in the last decade a lot of scientific and organizational effort has been spent to structure the geodata market and to establish information systems and global infrastructures enabling data suppliers to describe (-> *e*Commerce, metadata) and users to find appropriate data (-> information retrieval, data mining). Most popular peculiarities of such information systems are metadata information systems (MIS) or catalogue systems (CS) on regional, national or international basis, online-shops or web-portals to geospatial data archives. Recent initiatives offer access to a wealth of distributed data covered by the widespread information spectrum of different geodata disciplines, but

[1] Studies have shown that the amount of spatial information (spatially referenced data, geodata) is 80-85 percent relating to all new data produced by the actual information society.

R. Cicchetti et al. (Eds.): DEXA 2002, LNCS 2453, pp. 371–380, 2002.

offer only basic levels of interactivity and user assistance within the different steps of the information retrieval process.

The EU-funded project INVISIP[2] addresses this lack of usability and aims to develop new concepts and methods to support all involved parties within the different phases of the multi-step site planning process. INVISIP has been initiated by the authors of this paper as technical driven project within action line III.4.2 (Information Visualization) of the actual IST-2000 call. The technical basis (background) for INVISIP builds the InGeo IC [8] as technical information and communication platform of the InGeoForum[3] and results of the INSYDER project referring to WWW search result visualization [13].

2 State-of-the-Art Analysis

The more information and data are produced in the actual information society, the more important become mechanisms and systems which organize data and provide information where to find which data. Most popular peculiarities of such information systems are web-based search engines (e.g. AltaVista, Lycos and Yahoo), digital archives, MIS or CS for geodata. Opposite to commonly used search engines, MIS/CS are mostly theme-specific taking into account the multidimensional characteristics of geodata (title, abstract, keywords, reference date, spatial and temporal extent, coordinate reference system, lineage and quality information such as resolution code, scale or accuracy, distribution formats, fees, etc.). Usually, these MIS for geodata provide both thematic and geographic access variants in addition to traditional keyword and full-text searches. Göbel and Jasnoch [4] give an overview of existing MIS and CS for geodata and point out technical strengths and weaknesses of existing approaches.

Most important results of a comprehensive state-of-the-art analysis concerning metadata-based search and visualization techniques within the different information retrieval phases [5] are:

1. All analyzed approaches offer some kind of keyword search and geographic search. Additionally, some systems offer temporal search mechanisms. Thematic access is realized by categories and domain values corresponding to metadata formats and well-defined terminology used in the special geodata application area.
2. GUI components consist of text fields, attribute/keyword lists and sometimes maps which are implemented as click-able image maps or web-based GIS (geographic information systems).
3. Search results are presented as textual result lists. There are first approaches which show the relevance score of results, but in general the comparison and interpretation of result sets is hardly possible, because there is no visual feedback referring to search parameters and its effects to search results. Besides, this also negatively influences query modification.

[2] INVISIP: Information Visualization in Site Planning, IST-2000-29640, http://www.invisip.de
[3] Information and Cooperation Forum for Geodata, see http://www.ingeoforum.de

With regard to search result presentation, results of the INSYDER approach have shown that users need a support when expressing their information need and reviewing and refining their search results [10]. The notoriously low precision of web search engines coupled with the ranked list presentation make it hard for users to find the information they are looking for. Surveys have shown that users have problems with the current paradigm of information retrieval systems for Web search simply presenting a long list of results. These long lists of results are not very intuitive for finding the most relevant documents in the result set. Here, empirical findings motivated us to develop a new type of user interface for Web retrieval that supports the user in the information seeking process by providing special visualisations (e.g. result table, scatterplot, bargraphs, segment view) in addition to the traditional result list. For this a dynamic search system with an on-the-fly ranking, a visualisation of the query and a relevance feedback option are used in the INSYDER system. The current redesign of INSYDER includes a new component – the SuperTable (see section 4.2). In this approach a new data model is used to maintain an independency from the field of application. The system is no longer restricted to the visualization of WWW search results, but provides the possibility to represent for example medical or geographic metadata.

Based on these facts the following lacks of usability respectively derived requirements to improve current approaches become obvious:

- Graphic-interactive components should offer easy thematic and geographic as well as application-driven access variants to interact with geospatial data archives. Concerning semantic aspects such as usage of promising keywords within the query formulation process, the latter access variant is very important.
- Visual feedback should facilitate locating appropriate data and should be integrated into all different steps of the information retrieval process. Especially search result visualization should enable users to understand and interpret results. This includes transparent ranking, comparison of hits and hints referring to query modification.

The necessity for these components underlines the current action line "III.4.2 Information Visualization" by the EU which aims to facilitate data handling and visual data mining in (often unfamiliar) information spaces. Here, special attention is paid to visual feedback and metaphor concepts in order to support all phases of the information retrieval process. The INVISIP approach exactly addresses these key issues and obstacles of existing systems and intends to establish a framework to access geospatial data archives.

3 INVISIP Framework

INVISIP provides a technical platform as an aid to facilitate information access and data handling for the site planning process (time-saving, intuitive analysis).

- The core of the system is a metadata browser, which facilitates user interaction and helps planners to search for appropriate topic-related geographic data and to visualize search results in an intuitive, transparent way. Here, new mechanisms for query formulation and query refinement as well as presentation respectively visualization of search results will be developed.

- Secondly, a knowledge base –in the form of a repository- will contain several visual data mining techniques to analyze received data and will provide context info, which helps users to understand data and to recognize semantic relationships between various geographic data domains.

A data integration component based on web-based GIS components will be the basis for the dissemination of the project results and transfer of technology to other countries and application domains.

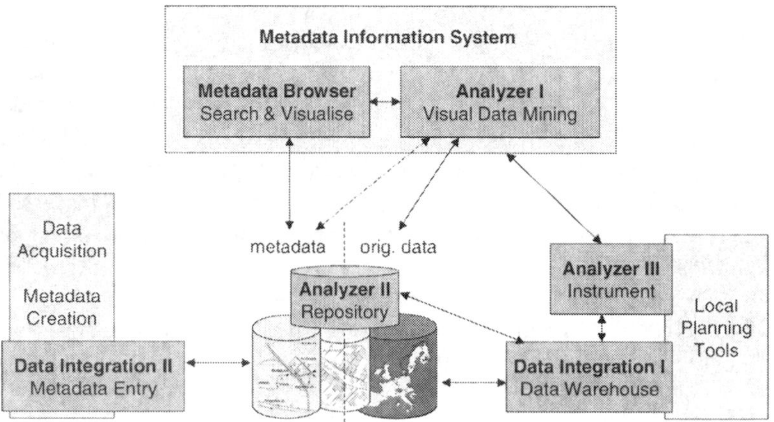

Fig. 1. INVISIP framework – proposed architecture: Components and Interfaces.

Figure 1 shows the proposed INVISIP framework (architecture/scenario) including components and interfaces. Simultaneously, these components represent the most important expected results:

1. A *Metadata Browser* contains mechanisms and information visualization techniques to support the search for appropriate geodata within the site planning process. From the technical point of view, the metadata browser is the most important and innovative component of the INVISIP framework as graphical user interface between users and the "geodata world". It is enhanced by information visualization techniques [1] and metaphors [12] to access geodata. Aside from metadata concepts (ISO standard [7], semantic network for geodata [3]) as information and navigation instrument to describe and locate appropriate geodata, information visualization techniques and metaphors are used to improve the usability of the metadata browser. Whereas information visualization techniques offer visual feedback in all steps of the data mining process, metaphors enable users to navigate in information spaces using intuitive spatial representations such as maps or well-known symbols settled in the library world like the book metaphor, information rooms or the complete library as 3D information and navigation space [14]. A visualization component facilitates browsing and comparing of geodata.
2. The interface to the (metadata-based) visual data mining component of the *Analyzer* enables users to navigate in unfamiliar information spaces and to determine

semantic relationships between necessary geodata. The main part of the analyzer builds the analysis instrument, which could be used as add-on for local planning tools. Thus, planners can use the instrument to contact a (regional, national or European wide) metadata information system and search for appropriate data. Further on, an analysis (context) repository will be established, which contains both metadata and original data, e.g. guidelines or laws, which have to be taken into account during the multi-step planning process.

3. The *Data Integration* component consists of two parts: Firstly, a data warehouse component that builds the interface between planning tools and original geodata. Similar to the analysis instrument it could be used as add-on for various planning tools already in use in different partner countries. Secondly, a Metadata Entry Tool will be established to enable geodata suppliers to describe their original data and to enter it into the infrastructure of INVISIP (MIS of INVISIP).

4 GeoLibrary

The GeoLibrary has been modeled in VRML and developed as 3D information and navigation space (using Java 3D) to improve orientation in the heterogeneous and multi-faceted geodata world. Different geodata disciplines and its terminology are used to structure the GeoLibrary. Analogue to a thematic classification of geodata application areas (environmental geodata, geo-basis and geo-scientific data and earth observation data) there are different floors: The first floor contains geo-basis and geo-scientific data, environmental data is located in the second floor and earth observation data is placed in the third floor below the roof. Users can poke around the GeoLibrary and graphic-interactively explore the geodata world and figure out semantic relationships between geodata of different application areas.

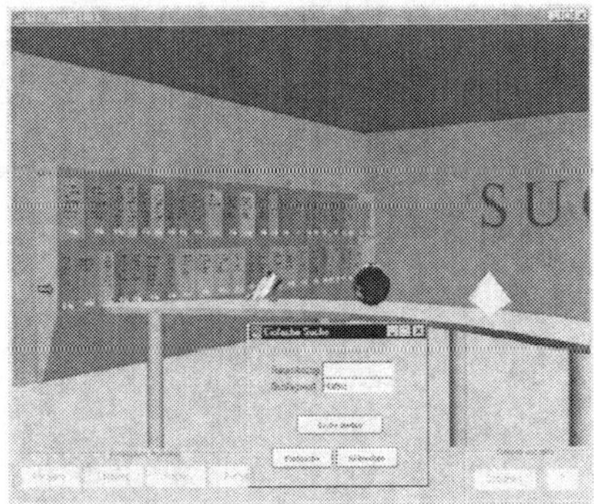

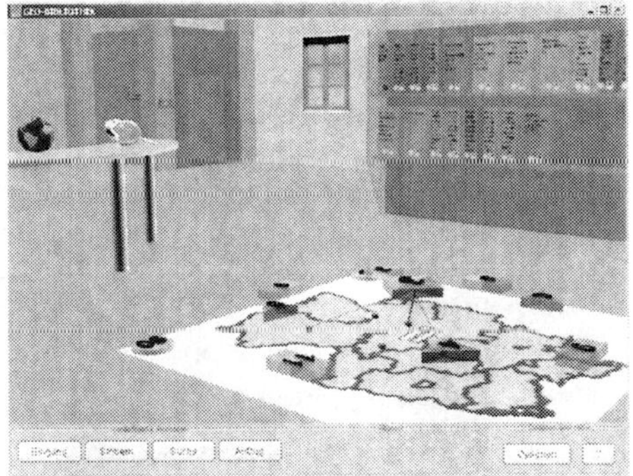

Fig. 2. GeoLibrary and GeoCrystal: Metadata based 3D information visualization technique to access geodata archives using metaphors – query formulation and search result presentation.

On the other hand the GeoLibrary offers an information desk which enables users to carry out "quick searches" similar to web-based search engines such as AltaVista or Yahoo. Thus it is not necessary for users to walk around in the library in order to find individual geodata sets (presented by books) or to compare different datasets (search results). With regard to both search result presentation and the comparison phase of results a graphic-interactive information room is used as information kiosk. This information kiosk represents the central place of the GeoLibrary. Entering the GeoLibrary users directly walk to the information desk (in front of the information kiosk), enter their tasks and goals and decide how to use the library. Different symbols on the information desk indicate various access variants:

1. A magnifying-glass initiates a search mode offering different easy (keyword search, spatial search by geographic names) and complex (based on metadata formats) search forms for casual and advanced users.
2. The globe symbolizes the "geodata world" and represents an entry point to dive into the wide range of application disciplines. Thus users can follow the different navigational hints and terms listed on blackboards in front of the elevator and bookshelves on the three floors of the library.
3. Triggering the rotating Crystal (symbolized as information pyramid) switches on GeoCrystal and fades in a map on the ground of the information room and the GeoCrystal elements in the 3D space above that map.
4. Additional thematic and application-driven access modes are symbolized by a tree-view diagram.

4.1 GeoCrystal

GeoCrystal [2] has been developed as new information visualization technique combining algebraic mechanisms (InfoCrystal [15]) with library (book, bookshelves, floors, etc.) and spatial metaphors (2D maps respectively 3D spatial information landscapes). The global aim of GeoCrystal is to improve understanding of search results by offering familiar metaphors settled in the field of set theory (algebra) combined with the provision of illustrated visual parameters such as spatial references of result sets. Hence the structure of GeoCrystal consists of two parts:

- On the ground of the information room there is a vector-based map realized as GIS component, which both enables users to specify spatial queries and supports spatial orientation and navigation.
- Above the map the result sets of a query are visually presented by block symbols indicating GeoCrystal elements, whereby the result sets are classified by the number of matching parameters corresponding to the query.

Result sets matching all query parameters are located in the center of the map at a high position (directly in the viewpoint of the user). Other result set classes (matching some, but not all query parameters) are positioned on spherical levels between the top of GeoCrystal and the base-map. Similar to InfoCrystal each query parameter is mapped to a color and represented by a circle at the corners of the GeoCrystal (on ground level closely placed to the interactive map). esult set classes are visually mapped to other symbols such as rectangular (matching two parameters), triangular (matching three parameters) or square blocks (matching four parameters) and are colored according to the colors of matching parameters. Additionally, each element of the GeoCrystal contains a number of matching result sets. Hence, users easily get an idea about the numerous distribution of results referring to special query parameters and how to modify the query in order to get better results.

With regard to the detailed analysis and comparison of result sets, users can interact with the elements of GeoCrystal and initiate several events. These events result in the provision of detailed textual and graphical presentations of the result sets, which are placed on two boards at the front side of the information room as well as on bookshelves placed at the over walls. Initial query search results are visualized as result lists indicating a check box, the global rank, title (with a hyperlink to the full metadata set) and iconic presentations of the metadata format used to describe the original dataset and the location of the geodata server respectively geospatial data archive of the matching dataset as well as links to contextual tooltips and to GeoCrystal. Activating the hyperlink below the title offers users the full meta dataset presented as HTML or XML-based file on the left board. Activating the GeoCrystal symbol initiates highlighting of the GeoCrystal element (class) containing the selected dataset. In order to compare several matching hits, user can select the checkboxes in first column of the result list and activate a "comparison button". Thus, another visualization is dynamically created offering detailed ranks such as a spatial rank, a thematic rank or a temporal rank to visualize the precision of individual search parameters (distance between a value of the geodata attribute/metadata element and the query condition of a search parameter). At this, GeoCrystal provides visualizations such as tile bars, scatter plots or proportional symbols.

Further on, picking of GeoCrystal elements in the 3D space causes the creation of an interactive list showing all datasets of that result class (e.g. datasets matching all query parameters at the top element of GeoCrystal). Then the selection of an individual dataset causes the creation of relations between a result, the map and the dataset itself represented as book on bookshelves:

- The spatial extent of a dataset is visualized as bounding box (west, north, south and east bounding coordinates) or highlighted area on the map.
- The locations of the geodata archive containing that dataset and other responsible parties involved in that dataset (place of the geodata originator, supplier, content provider, distributor, metadata provider, etc.) are visualized as point-features (filled circles) on different layers on the map.
- Optionally those points and highlighted areas are connected by pointers with the 3D elements of GeoCrystal.

4.2 SuperTable

The main goal of the SuperTable [9] is the Integration of Table Lens as seen in [11], ResultTable, HTML-List, BarGraph, and SegmentView into one component. There would be different predefined zoom-levels. Starting for example with a BarGraph view in a first zoom level, revealing document details in a one-line-per-document-mode for the whole table in a second level, a several-line-per-document-mode in a third level, and document information revealing segment details in a fourth level. In addition, tooltips or lens mechanisms can allow easy inspection of details for single documents. Power users can use multiple focus possibilities for comparisons. The SuperTable as an integrated component will be more complex than the former single components. With adequate design a subject who is starting to use the system may not be aware of this complexity, and therefore would not be distracted. The integration will minimize context-switching effort and is able to allow a smooth learning curve from beginner mode to power user mode.

The redesign of the INSYDER system combines the two approaches of SuperTable and ScatterPlot into a single window. *Level 1* represents an overview over all documents. All rows are as small as possible, so that in the best case all documents fit on the available space. Corresponding to the number of documents, the height of the rows can vary. Usually the rows will be too small to hold text, so only bars will be displayed. The length and the position of the bars encode various characteristics of the document, depending on the type of data they represent. The length of the bars (representing numeric data like size, relevance, ...) are equivalent to their numeric values. Nominal attributes can also be represented by a bar. For a few attributes we can code their values through position; for example the language, which can be english or french in our application (the left half of the cell means "english" and the right one means "french"). If there are too many different nominal values a visualization would be too confusing, which is for example the case with the title. Therefore this column will be empty. Different colors can additionally encode different search terms.

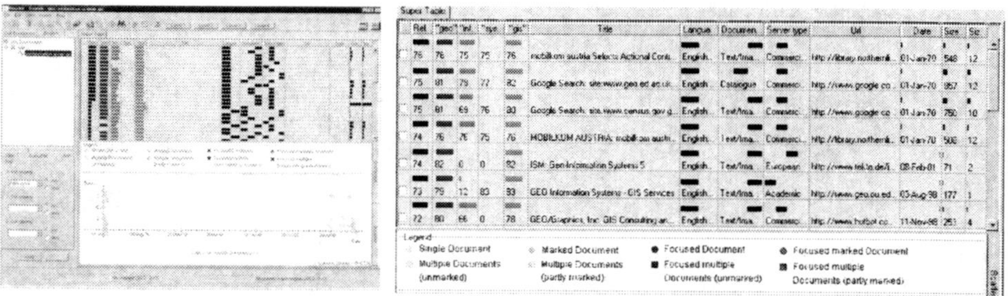

Fig.3. SuperTable (left: *Level 1*, right: *Level 2* zoomed in).

In *Level 2* more information will be visible in form of text, completing the visual representation of the multicolored bars. Now numeric values add detailed information about the bar displays from the initial, graphics-only display. Title and URL are now readable, but only upto the width of the respective column. All wider texts become truncated, clarified by three dots. *Level 3* provides the opportunity to read the whole text of those characteristics, which had to be abbreviated because of their size. Visualizations were cut off to gain space, so that title, url and abstract are now completely visible. In addition a new column is introduced, the so called "Relevance Curve". It represents a two-dimensional chart of the whole document, by dividing the document into a number of segments, e. g. sentences, subordinate clauses, etc. The height of single bars encodes the overall relevance for each individual segment. *Level 4* (Figure

4, right) displays only the (in our opinion) most important values of a document: Title, abstract and an extension of the relevance curve, the so called "Segment View", which uses tile bars as seen in [6]. In this case, every segment has the same length, not varying from one document to another. Consequentially the length of the Segment View differs from document to document, always corresponding to the real length of the document. The Tilebars are colored according to the colored search terms in the former levels. So it is easier to discover the segments, where all search terms can be found, not just a few of them. You can spot segments, that include only one or two search terms, and discern these from parts including all terms. Some terms may be seen more important than others, so a segment with a lower relevance can be important although not all terms are included.

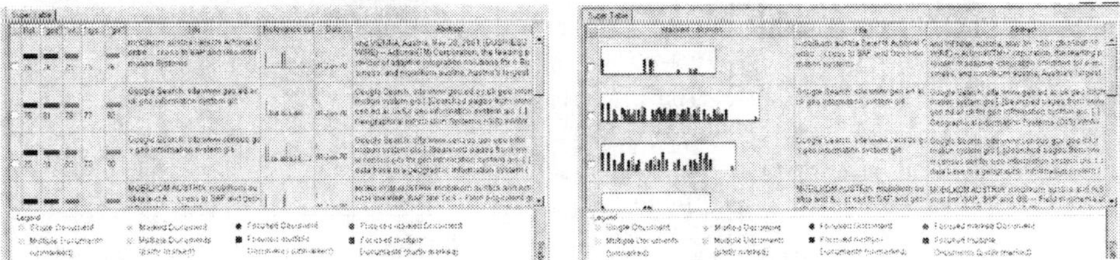

Fig. 4. SuperTable (left: *Level 3* zoomed in, right: *Level 4* zoomed in).

5 Conclusion

This paper describes the INVISIP approach which aims to support users in the data mining process of complex application areas such as site planning and to facilitate graphic-interactive access to geodata archives. Here, the idea is to provide metadata based information visualization techniques in the different information retrieval phases to locate appropriate geodata which is necessary to solve planning tasks, e.g. generation of ecological, environmental or socio-demographic reports.

GeoCrystal and SuperTable are introduced as new information visualization techniques to support users during the different information retrieval phases, especially search result presentation and comparison of search results (hints for query modification). Currently (May 2002) both techniques are integrated into a GeoLibrary as 3D information and navigation space using familiar metaphors such as books, bookshelves, an information desk or spatial landscapes (maps) within the first development phase of the INVISIP project.

From the application-oriented point of view, future work will be investigated to extend the GeoLibrary by applicaton-driven access variants. From the technical point of view further research work will consider different technologies in the field of artificial intelligence and knowledge management to improve the INVISIP MIS as basis for the GeoLibrary. Much effort is spent on the visual support within all information retrieval phases: query formulation, search result presentation and query refinement. Especially concerning the query formulation innovative concepts are developed taking into account not only information visualization techniques but also the ISO 19115 standard as structured format to describe geographic data. Besides, further information visualization techniques could be integrated within the different information retrieval phases to facilitate data mining (of original geodata) in general.

References

1. Card, S.K., Mackinlay, J.D., Shneiderman, B. Readings in Information Visualization. Using Vision to Think. Morgan Kaufmann Publishers, Inc, San Francisco, CA, 1999.
2. Göbel, S., Haist, J., Goebel, C. GeoCrystal : Graphic-Interactive Access to Geodata Archives. Proceedings SPIE 2002 – Visualization and Data Analysis, San Jose, CA, 2002.
3. Göbel, S., Jasnoch, U. Development of a semantic network for environmental geodata. Published in Sustainability in the Information Society, 15th International Symposium Informatics for Environmental Protection, Zurich, 2001, edited by Lorenz M. Hilty, Paul W. Gilgen. Metropolis Verlag, Marburg, 2001, pp. 679-684. ISBN 3-89518-370-9.
4. Göbel, S., Jasnoch, U. Metadata Information Systems for Geospatial Data, S.283-296 in Environmental Information Systems in Industry and Public Administration, edited by Claus Rautenstrauch, Susanne Patig. Idea Group Publishing, Hershey, USA, 2001. ISBN 1-930708-02-5.
5. Göbel, S., Jasnoch, U. Visualization Techniques in Metadata Information Systems for Geospatial Data. *Proc. ISESS'2000.* Zell a. See, Austria, 2000.
6. Hearst, M. TileBars: Visualization of Term Distribution Information in Full Text Information Access. *Proc. ACM SIGCHI'95*, pp. 59-66, Denver, CO, 1995.
7. ISO. Draft International Standard on Metadata for Geographic Information, ISO 19115-Metadata (status: DIS level), see http://www.statkart.no/isotc211/.
8. Jasnoch, U., Göbel, S., Balfanz, D. InGeo IC: The portal to Geodata. Proceedings *e*2000, Madrid, Spain. Published in Standford-Smith, Kidd: E-business. Key Issues, Applications, Technologies. IOS Press, Amsterdam, 2000.
9. Klein, P., Müller, F., Reiterer, H., Eibl, M.: Visual Information Retrieval with the SuperTable + Scatterplot, Accepted Paper at the 6th International Conference Information Visualization, London, England, 2002.
10. Mann, T.H.: Visualization of Search Results from the World Wide Web, PhD Thesis, University of Konstanz, 2002.
11. Rao, Ramana; Card, Stuart K.: The Table Lens. Merging graphical and symbolic representations in an interactive focus + context visualization for tabular information. In: Adelson, B.; Dumais, S.; Olson, J. S. (Eds.): CHI 1994: Conference Pro-ceedings Human Factors in Computing Systems. Conference: Boston, MA, April 24-28 1994. New York (ACM Press) 1994. p. 318-322. 1994
12. Rauber, A., Bina, H. A Metaphor Graphics based Representation of Digital Libraries on the World Wide Web: Using the libViewer to Make Metadata Visible. *Proc. DEXA ´99*, Florence, Italy, 1999.
13. Reiterer, H., Mußler, G., Mann, T., Handschuh, S.: *INSYDER – An Information Assistant for Business Intelligence*, Proceedings of the 23 Annual International ACM SIGIR 2000 Conference on Research and Development in Information Retrieval, ACM press, 2000, pp.112-119.
14. Robertson, B. biz viz gets real. Computer Graphics World, April 1999, S. 29-34.
15. Spoerri, A. InfoCrystal: A Visual Tool for Information Retrieval. *Proc. IEEE Visualization ´93*, San Jose, CA, 1993, pp. 150-157.

Eureka! : A Tool for Interactive Knowledge Discovery

Giuseppe Manco[1], Clara Pizzuti[1], and Domenico Talia[2]

[1] ISI-CNR
c/o DEIS, Università della Calabria
Via P. Bucci, 41C
87036 Rende (CS), Italy
{manco,pizzuti}@isi.cs.cnr.it
[2] DEIS, Università della Calabria
Via Bucci, 41C
87036 Rende (CS), Italy
talia@deis.unical.it

Abstract. In this paper we describe an interactive, visual knowledge discovery tool for analyzing numerical data sets. The tool combines a visual clustering method, to hypothesize meaningful structures in the data, and a classification machine learning algorithm, to validate the hypothesized structures. A two-dimensional representation of the available data allows a user to partition the search space by choosing shape or density according to criteria he deems optimal. A partition can be composed by regions populated according to some arbitrary form, not necessarily spherical. The accuracy of clustering results can be validated by using a decision tree classifier, included in the mining tool.

1 Introduction

The production of high-dimensional data sets in different application domains has grown the interest in identifying new patterns in data that might be of value for the holder of such data sets. Knowledge discovery is the process of analyzing data sets to identify interesting, useful and new patterns and trends in data [7]. The knowledge discovery process is a complex task that can involve the use of different data mining techniques. Data mining finds patterns or models that provide summarization of data while loosing the least amount of information. Examples of models comprise clusters, rules, tree structures, and others. The combination of different models in a Knowledge Discovery process may help users in finding what is interesting and significant in large data sets. The Knowledge Discovery is often referred as an interactive and iterative process that involves the following main phases: 1) data preparation and cleaning, 2) hypothesis generation, 3) interpretation and analysis. The hypothesis generation phase, generally, is completely automatic and realized using data mining algorithms based on machine learning and statistics techniques. A different approach aims at exploiting the perceptual and cognitive human abilities, when a visual representation of data is available, to detect the structure of data.

R. Cicchetti et al. (Eds.): DEXA 2002, LNCS 2453, pp. 381–391, 2002.

Visual data mining aims at integrating the human in the data exploration process, harnessing his interpretation abilities to large data sets. The basic idea of visual data mining is to present the data in some visual form, allowing the human to get insight into the data, draw conclusions, and directly interact with the data [13]. Visual data mining is especially useful when little is known about the data and the exploration goals are vague. Since the user is directly involved in the exploration process, shifting and adjusting the exploration goals is automatically done if necessary. Visual data mining exploits data visualization to guide the human user in the recognition of patterns and trends hidden in the data. Some interesting visual data mining experiences are described in [4,2,6,17,15,14]. When high dimensional data sets are to be mined, visual data mining tools may benefit of the use of dimension reduction techniques that maintain the main features of data.

In this paper we describe a human assisted knowledge discovery tool, named *Eureka*!, that combines a visual clustering method, to hypothesize meaningful structures in the data, and a classification machine learning algorithm, to validate the hypothesized structures. The tool applies the optimal dimensionality reduction method, known as *Singular Value Decomposition (SVD)* [21], to obtain a two-dimensional representation of the available data, and iteratively asks the user to specify a suitable partition of such a representation. The choice of a partition is demanded to the user, thus allowing the identification of clusters of any shape or any density. A partition can provide a separation of dense regions from regions containing sparse data, or it can be composed by regions populated according to some arbitrary polygonal or spherical regions. The accuracy of clustering results can be validated by using a decision tree classifier included in the mining tool. *Eureka*! has been implemented mainly as an extension of the Weka machine learning library [24]. Weka is a Java library defining standard interfaces for data sets loading and preprocessing (e.g., filter definition), mining algorithms and results representation.

The rest of the paper is organized as follows. Section 2 provides a brief introduction of the mathematical technique underlying the clustering tool. In section 3 we describe the interaction metaphor implemented into the system. In particular, section 3.1 covers the cluster generation technique, while section 3.2 is concerned with the cluster validation technique.

2 Background: Singular Value Decomposition

SVD is a powerful technique in matrix computation and analysis that has been introduced by Beltrami in 1873 [1]. More recently it has been used in several applications such as solving systems of linear equations, linear regression [21], pattern recognition [5], statistical analysis [12], data compression [16] and matrix approximation [19].

A *singular value decomposition* of an $n \times m$ matrix X is any factorization of the form

$$X = U \times \Lambda \times V^T$$

where U is an $n \times n$ orthogonal matrix, V is an $m \times m$ orthogonal matrix and Λ is an $n \times m$ diagonal matrix with $\lambda_{ij} = 0$ if $i \neq j$. It has been shown that there exist matrices U and V such that the diagonal elements of Λ are sorted: $\lambda_1 \geq \lambda_2 \geq \ldots \geq \lambda_m$. The diagonal elements λ_i are called *singular values* of X and it has been shown that they are the square root of the eigenvalues of the matrix $X^T X$.

The decomposition can equivalently be written as

$$X = \lambda_1 u_1 \times v_1^t + \lambda_2 u_2 \times v_2^t + \ldots + \lambda_m u_m \times v_m^t$$

where u_i and v_i are column vectors of the matrices U and V respectively, λ_i are the diagonal elements of Λ, and it is known as *spectral decomposition* [12]. SVD reveals an important information about the rank of the matrix X. In fact, if $\lambda_1 \geq \lambda_2 \geq \ldots \geq \lambda_r \geq \lambda_{r+1} = \ldots = \lambda_m = 0$ then r is the rank of X [8].

Geometrically this factorization defines a rotation of the axis of the vector space defined by X where V gives the directions, Λ the strengths of the dimensions and $U \times \Lambda$ the position of the points along the new axis. Intuitively, the U matrix can be viewed as a similarity matrix among the rows of X, i.e. the objects of the data set, the V matrix as a similarity matrix among the columns of X, i.e. the features that describe an object, the Λ matrix gives a measure of how much the data distribution is kept in the new space [11].

In the data mining area, SVD can be used to identify clusters by analyzing the U matrix. By visualizing the matrix $U \times \Lambda$ and considering only the first d dimensions, where $d \leq 3$, we obtain a compressed representation of the X matrix that approximates it at the best. The d kept terms are known as the *principal components* [12].

3 *Eureka!* : A Tool for Interactive Knowledge Discovery

Eureka! , is a semiautomatic tool for interactive knowledge discovery that integrates a visual clustering method, based on the Singular Value Decomposition technique, and a decision tree classifier to validate the clustering results. *Eureka!* has been implemented as an extension of the Weka machine learning library [24] by integrating additional functionalities such as a supervised discretization technique and visual clustering. *Eureka!* has been designed and implemented with the aim of making repeatable the knowledge discovery process on a data set and storing the steps done during the overall process into a repository in order to use it again at a later time. Thus *Eureka!* implements a fixed model of interaction with the user, in which the various steps of the data mining process are represented in a uniform way and executed according to a predefined schema. To this end *Eureka!* generates a hierarchical structure that describes the overall KDD process called *Repository.* The schema that models the KDD process is shown in fig. 1.

Intuitively, an analysis addressing some predefined objectives defines a *business-process.* A given business process is composed by one or more *kdd-process* items.

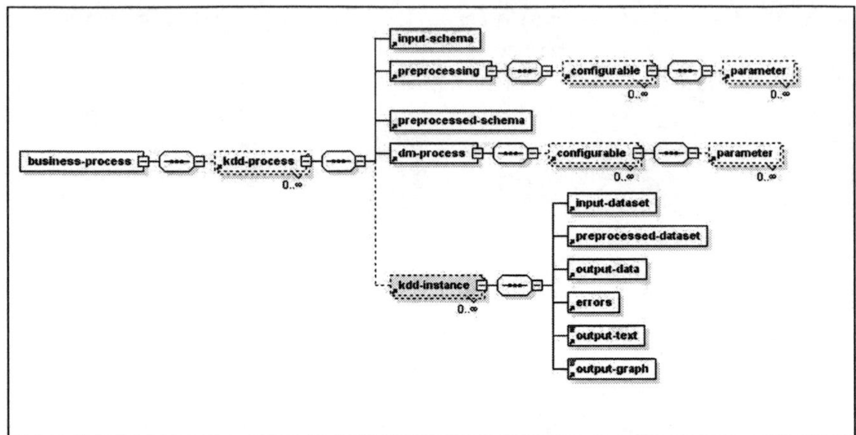

Fig. 1. The Interaction Model implemented in *Eureka!* .

Such items have the main objective of describing the meta-schema of each possible instantiation of the analysis: in particular, a *kdd-process* has a given data set (with a given structure described by the *input-schema* item), and it is subject to a given number of *preprocessing* steps, thus providing a *preprocessed-schema* item. The *dm-process* module describes the data mining techniques. Finally, a *kdd-instance* contains one or more possible instantiations of a KDD process. In particular, it contains an input data set conforming to the *input-schema*, the data set resulting from the preprocessing steps described in *preprocessing*, and the resulting patterns obtained from the application of the data mining algorithms.

The methodology employed in *Eureka!* is shown in figure 2. An input data set is transformed into a reduced data set by applying the SVD algorithm and visualized with respect to any two principal components. The user is then asked to choose a portion of the search space he deems interesting. The selected portion is identified as a cluster and the process is repeated on the remaining data until the user judges satisfactory the grouping obtained. At this point each tuple of the data set is labelled with the corresponding class decided by the user and a decision tree inducer can be run to verify the accuracy of the model found. Low misclassification errors should substantiate the detected groups. Thus, if the misclassification error is high, the user can backtrack on his choices and provide an alternative division of the search space, otherwise he can save the process done, and its results. In figure 3 the graphical interface of *Eureka!* is showed. It is composed of three main areas. On the left, the component referred as *Navigator* allows the generation and navigation of the *Repository*. The *Repository* is a hierarchical tree structure that maintains the step sequence done during the overall KDD process. It thus allows the creation and updating of a *business-process*. The bottom part of the interface provides messages about the *kdd-process* execution and the right part shows the current running task.

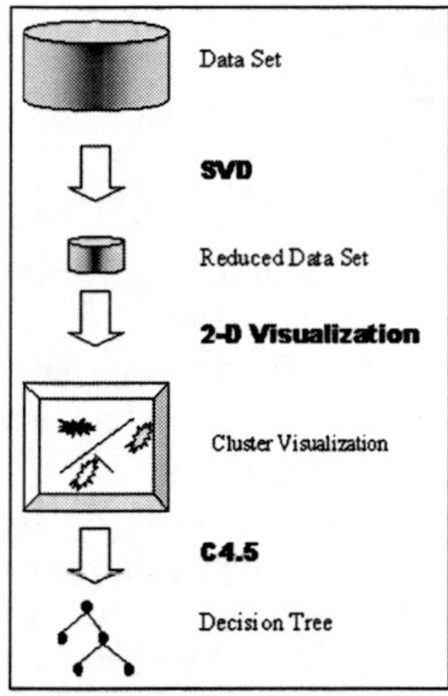

Fig. 2. Main steps of the data mining methodology.

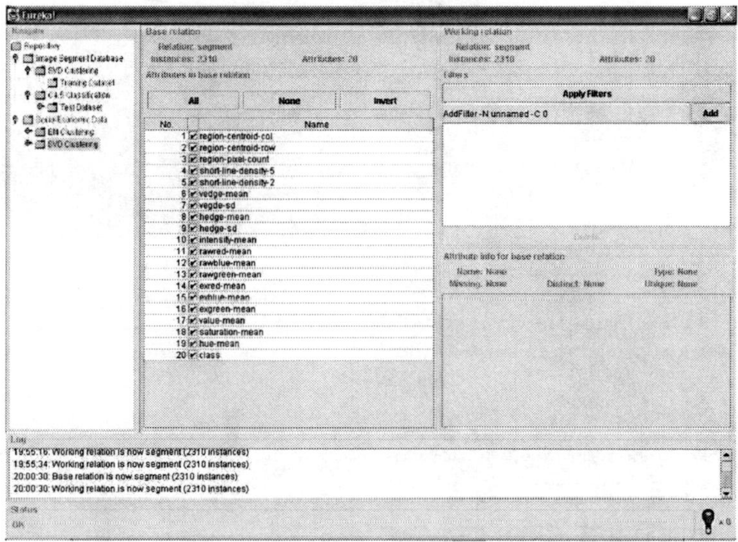

Fig. 3. *Eureka!* interface.

We now describe the main features of the system by means of a well-known example: the *image segmentation* database. The data set was taken from the UCI Machine Learning Repository [3] and describes a set of instances drawn randomly from a database of 7 outdoor images. The images where hand-segmented to create a classification for every pixel. The data set consists of 19 numeric attributes, describing the features of a 3×3 region that the instance represents. From the discussion above, we can detect two main steps in the clustering process: cluster generation and visualization, and cluster interpretation and validation. Let us analyze them in deeper details.

3.1 Cluster Generation and Visualization

As mentioned before, *Eureka!* implements an interactive divisive hierarchical clustering algorithm such that at each step clusters can be chosen visually in a two-dimensional space. Such an approach has the advantage of allowing to choose clusters that do not necessarily obey to predefined structural properties, such as density or shape [10,9]. At each step, a user can choose the cluster according to the criteria that are more likely to be applied. To this end, after the data set has been selected and preprocessed, the clustering task starts by choosing to apply the SVD transformation to the data set, as shown in figure 4 a). Initially, the visualization represents a single node in the cluster tree.

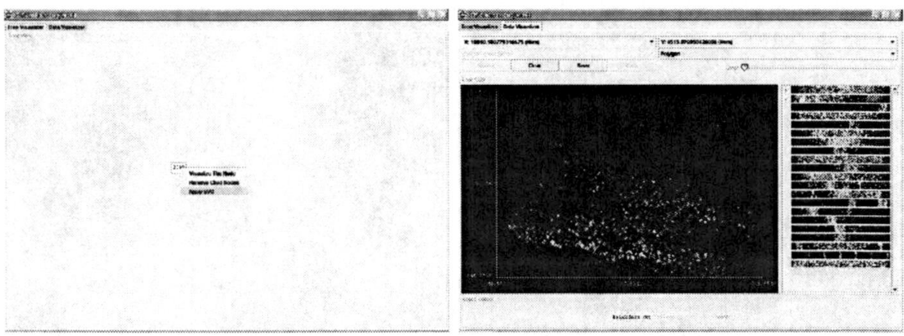

Fig. 4. a) *Eureka!* runs the SVD transformation to the overall data set. b) Visualization of the transformed data set with respect to the two principal components.

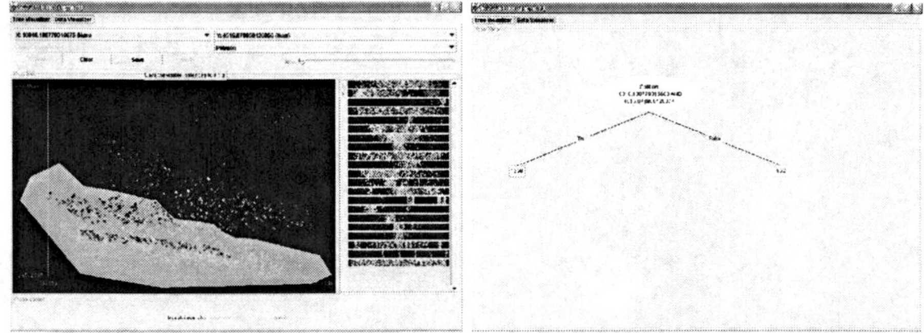

Fig. 5. a) Selection of a portion of the data set. b) Cluster tree after the first split.

By visualizing the transformed data set, figure 4 b), we can clearly distinguish at least three separate regions. In our visualization, separate regions represent clusters, i.e., elements that can be grouped together. In order to identify clusters, we need to draw the borders of a given region. More precisely, we can choose a region, and separate it from the rest of the space that is represented. *Eureka!* allows the user to separate a region by choosing an appropriate shape, as shown in figure 5 a). Once a region has been selected, we can store such a selection, thus obtaining a separation of the original space in a cluster tree representing two different groups, as shown in figure 5 b). The right node represents the selected region, and the remaining points are represented by the left node. We can choose any node in the Tree Visualizer Pane, thus allowing the corresponding visualization in the Data Visualizer Pane. In figure 6 the 1358 points of the left node and the 952 points of the right node are visualized.

New nodes can then be recursively split. In particular, the right node shows a clear separation among two different regions, and is worth a further splitting. This is shown in figure 7. An interesting aspect of the tool is the capability of

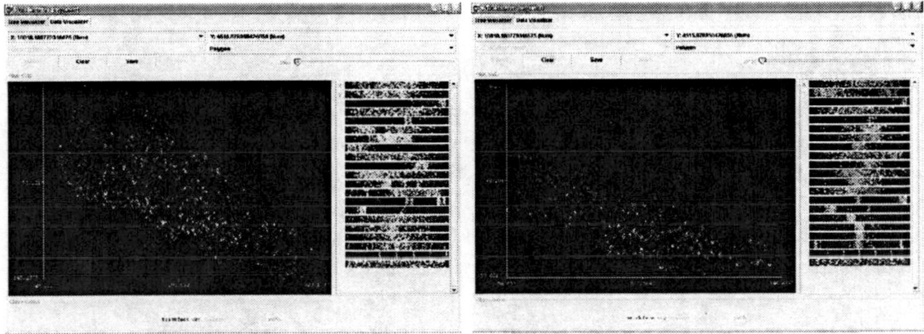

Fig. 6. Visualization of the first two selected portions.

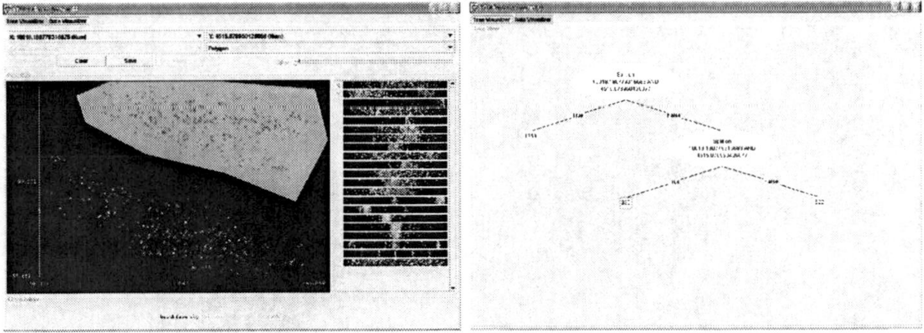

Fig. 7. Splitting of the right node.

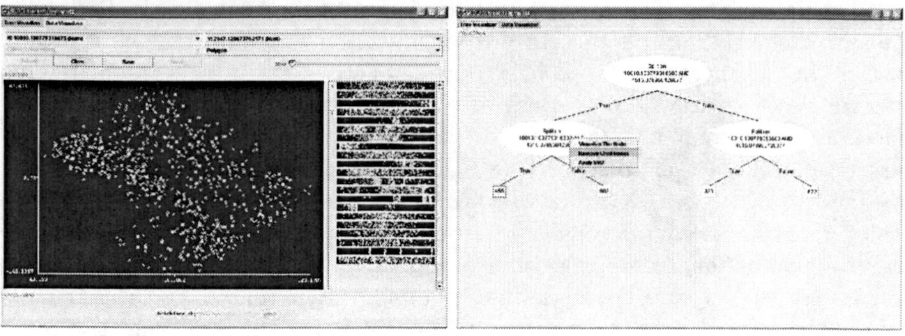

Fig. 8. a) Axe Modification. b) Deletion of unsatisfactory partitions.

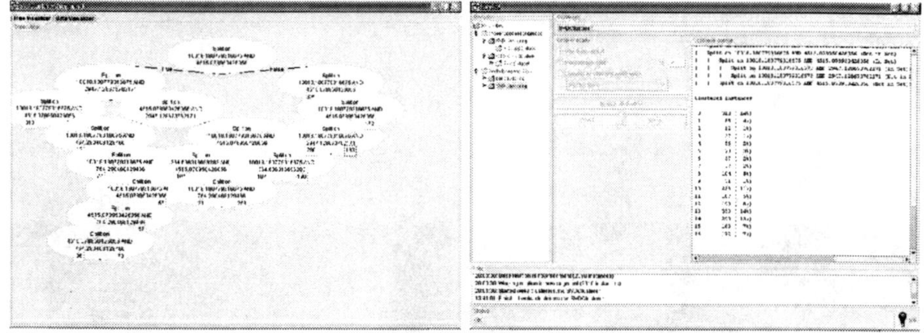

Fig. 9. Final Cluster Tree and data set distribution in *Eureka!* .

changing axes in the two dimensional representation. By default the mining tool provides a visualization of the first two dimensions (corresponding to the highest eigenvalues of the matrix Λ). However, by clicking over a given dimension among those shown in the left part of the Data Visualization pane, the user can change such a visualization as needed. A different visualization of the node shown in fig. 6 a), can be obtained by representing the Y axe using the fourth dimension in the SVD representation (fig. 8 a). Different visualizations can help a user in the cluster identification process. An unsatisfactory partition can be removed by directly acting on the cluster tree. For example, if the analysis of a node does not put in evidence a clear separation of the regions in the given data set partition, we can choose to delete it, as shown in figure 8 b).

Many further choices are available, in order to make separation as accurate as possible. In particular, we can choose non-convex regions, as shown in figure 5 a). The interaction of a given user within the cluster tree is stopped when no further significant splits can be detected. In the *segment* example, we obtained a tree containing 29 nodes and 17 leaves, as shown in fig. 9 a). The leaves of such a tree represent a partition of the data set in 17 groups.

3.2 Cluster Interpretation and Validation

A typical problem in clustering algorithm is the problem of assessing the quality of the results. The correctness of a clustering algorithm results has to be validated using appropriate criteria and techniques. Since clustering algorithms define clusters that are not known a priori, irrespective of the clustering methods, the final partition of data requires some kind of evaluation [9]. In [23,9], three main methods are described for assessing the validity of a clustering result:

- *external criteria*, when clustering results are evaluated according to a prespecified structure.
- *internal criteria*, when clustering results are evaluated in terms of the quantities that are computable from the available data (e.g., similarity matrix).
- *relative criteria*, when evaluation takes place in comparison with other clustering schemes.

In particular, when no predefined structure is available, a possibility is to evaluate clustering results using only quantities and features inherent to the data set. For example, one can evaluate the global quality of a clustering scheme by measuring both its *compactness* (i.e., how close the elements of each cluster are to each other) and *separation* (i.e., the difference between two distinct clusters). Clearly, various solutions are possible. For example, we can measure the compactness by looking at the maximal intra-cluster similarity:

$$\max_{\mathcal{C}_i} \sum_{\mathbf{x},\mathbf{y} \in \mathcal{C}_i} d(\mathbf{x}, \mathbf{y})$$

Many of these methods, however, cannot be used to compare different clustering algorithms. For example, it is not significant to compare algorithm that use different definitions of similarity (or distance). More importantly, often such quality measures are simple statistical indexes that do not describe sufficient properties useful to obtain an interpretation of each cluster.

In *Eureka!* , in order to evaluate the validity of a clustering scheme when no further information is available, we adopted a classification-based internal criterion. Such a criterion is mainly based on the observation that good clusters should be in easily separable regions, and hence a classifier could easily characterize them. Many classification schemes can be applied at this point. In particular, decision-tree classifiers [20] can be well-suited for identifying linearly separable regions. Practically, the criterion for assessing the validity of a cluster is that of building a predictor of the cluster label. A good clustering result should produce a low-error classifier. More importantly, a low-error decision-tree classifier provides a set of rules (directly obtained from the classification tree), that can reveal extremely useful to give an interpretation of each cluster resulting from the application of the clustering algorithm. In order to implement such a validation scheme, we exploited the functionalities available in Weka. Weka cluster interface, in fact, allows to automatically add a cluster label to the data set under consideration. Starting from this labelled data set, we can set up a new knowledge discovery process, in which we include a decision tree classifier with the aim of predicting the `cluster` attribute. The application of a decision-tree classification algorithm, (e.g., the C4.5 algorithm) ends up with a tree representing the interpretation of the cluster partition, and a set of measures (such as percentage of correctly classified instances, mean error rate, etc.), that assess the validity of the clustering scheme obtained so far.

We used the *Eureka!* tool in several data mining experiments. In particular, recently we used *Eureka!* on a data set of *social-economic data* representing a collection of measurements made in a given number of cities in an Italian district, and concerning social-economic factors such as unemployment rate, amount of companies, amount of agencies, etc.. The resulted knowledge discovery process produced very interesting results [22]. Due to space limit we discuss here the results obtained on the *segment* data set used in the previous sections as a running example. It is useful mainly to show the internal criteria approach. In the visual clustering process, we identified 17 clusters in the data set. Then a decision-tree classifier trained to predict the `cluster` attribute produced a tree with a degree of accuracy of 94% and produced 77 rules describing the features of the discovered clusters. It is interesting to compare such results with the results of a different clustering algorithm. For example, we compared such results with the clustering scheme resulting from the application of the EM algorithm [18] on the same data set. By imposing 7 classes (the optimal number of clusters, obtained via Cross-Validation), we obtain an error rate of 45%. Moreover, suggesting other clustering scheme to EM (e.g., different class numbers) produced a less accurate classification. This test case, as well as the social-economic data analysis, showed that a visual clustering methodology can produce more accurate results compared to that obtained using an oblivious clustering algorithm.

4 Conclusions and Future Works

In this paper we described the main features of an interactive knowledge discovery tool, named *Eureka*!, that combines a visual clustering method, to hypothesize meaningful structures in the data, and a classification machine learning algorithm, to validate the hypothesized structures. A two-dimensional representation of the available data allows a user to partition the search space by choosing shape or density according to criteria he estimates optimal. The accuracy of clustering results obtained through the user intervention can be validated by using a decision tree classifier which is a component of the mining tool. We used a simple data set to describe the tool features and how the discovery process is performed using it. Currently we are using *Eureka*! to mine different data sets in several application domains. At the same time, we are working on the tool improvements and extensions like in/out zooming features and automatic region separation suggestions provided to a user by the system at each splitting step.

References

1. E. Beltrami. Sulle funzioni bilineari [on bilinear functions]. *Giornale di Matematiche ad Uso degli Studenti delle Università*, 11:98–106, 1873.
2. S. Berchtold, H.V. Jagadish, and K.A. Ross. Independence Diagrams: A Technique for Visual Data Mining. In *Proceedings of Fourth Int. Conf. on Knowledge Discovery and Data Mining*, 1998.
3. C.L. Blake and C.J. Merz. UCI repository of machine learning databases, 1998.
4. K.C. Cox, S.G. Eick, G.J. Wills, and R. J. Brachman. Visual Data Mining: Recognizing Telephone Calling Fraud. *Data Mining and Knowledge Discovery*, 1(2):225–231, 1997.
5. R.O. Duda and P.E. Hart. *Pattern Classification and Scene Analysis.* Wiley, New York, 1973.
6. U. Fayyad, G.G. Grinstein, and A. Wierse. *Infomation Visualization in Data Mining and Knowledge Discovery.* Morgan Kaufmann, 2002.
7. U.M. Fayyad, G. Piatesky-Shapiro, and P. Smith. From Data Mining to Knowledge Discovery: an overview. In U. Fayyad et al., editors, *Advances in Knowledge Discovery and Data Mining*, pages 1–34. AAAI/MIT Press, 1996.
8. G.H. Golub and C.F. Van Loan. *Matrix Computation.* The Johns Hopkins University Press, 1989.
9. M. Halkidi, Y. Batistakis, and M. Vazirgiannis. On Clustering Validation Techniques. *Journal of Intelligent Information Systems.* To appear. Available at `http://www.db-net.aueb.gr/mhalk/papers/validity_survey.pdf`.
10. J. Han and M. Kamber. *Data Mining: Concepts and Techniques.* Morgan Kaufman, 2000.
11. A.K. Jain and R.C. Dubes. *Algorithms for Clustering Data.* Prentice Hall, 1988.
12. I.T. Jolliffe. *Principal Component Analysis.* Springer Verlag, 1986.
13. D.A. Keim and S. Eick. *Proceedings Workshop on Visual Data Mining.* ACM SIGKDD, 2001.
14. D.A. Keim and H.P. Kriegel. Visualization Techniques for Mining Large Databases: A Comparison. *IEEE Transaction on Knowledge and Data Engineering*, 8(6):923–938, 1996.
15. F. Korn et al. Quantifiable Data Mining Using Principal Component Analysis. *VLDB Journal*, 8(3–4):254–266, 2000.
16. F. Korn, H.V. Jagadish, and C. Faloutsos. Efficient Supporting Ad Hoc Queries in Large Datasets of Time Sequences. In *Proceedings of the ACM Sigmod Conf. on Magagment of Data*, 1997.
17. M. Macedo, D. Cook, and T.J. Brown. Visual Data Mining In Atmospheric Science Data. *Data Mining and Knowledge Discovery*, 4(1):68–80, 2000.
18. G.J. MacLahan and T. Krishnan. *The EM Algorithm and Extensions.* Wiley, 1997.
19. W. H. Press, S.A. Teukolsky, W.T. Vetterling, and B.P. Flannery. *Numerical Receips in C: The Art of Computing.* Cambridge University Press, 1992.
20. R. Quinlan. *C4.5: Programs for Machine Learning.* Morgan Kaufmann, 1993.
21. G. Strang. *Linear Algebra and its Applications.* Academic Press, 1980.
22. Telcal Team. Analisi della struttura produttiva ed occupazionale della regione calabria: Risultati. Technical report, Piano Telematico Calabria, 2001. in italian.
23. S. Theodoridis and K. Koutroubas. *Pattern Recognition.* Academic Press, 1999.
24. I. Witten and E. Frank. *Data Mining: Practical Machine Learning Tools with Java Implementation.* Morgan-Kaufman, 1999.

Electronic Tickets on Contactless Smartcard Database

Kimio Kuramitsu and Ken Sakamura

Interfaculty Initiative in Information Studies, University of Tokyo
{kuramitsu, sakamura}@iii.u-tokyo.ac.jp

Abstract. More recently, embedded databases and smartcard databases have emerged. To make such small databases practically useful, only a scale-down approach to a general-purpose relational database will be insufficient; some specializations for each application domain are also required. In this paper, we design a small database based on the experience of our electronic ticket project. The design includes a new data model that well represents a variety of small volume tickets, a role-based access control applied to each ticket, and a logging and rollback operations externalized in a way interacting with a preprocessor. We present that database functionality on a smartcard are helpful to build multi-party ticket applications.

1 Introduction

Does smartcard need database facilities? Since C. Bobineau et al presented PicoDBMS, database community has an increasing interest in a very small DBMS. In this paper we will address the usability of database facilities implemented on a smartcard throughout our experience of electronic ticket project [6,5].

In our project, a mission given to us first was how to well manage multiple kinds of tickets on a smartcard. The choice of the platform could be taken from a simple record-based card, like ISO-7816-4, to a program loadable one, like Multos and JavaCard. However several difficulties had appeared; a simple record file is less expressive for the properties of ticket applications, while an application program for implementing each ticket is too costly. These findings led to a simple data management system that supports a query language, access control, and transaction management.

The database we designed, on the other hand, differs from conventional databases in several ways. To represent a small volume of various tickets, a ticket is formed in a self-described object. To control accesses from different application contexts, a role-based authenticator is attached to each object. To reduce logging on the card, rollback operation in a transaction is externalized on a trusted host.

Another remark is that we presume for the first time a *contactless* card, whose power is considerably limited because it is transmitted through electro-magnetic wage or microwave. In comparisons to a contact card, the characteristic of such hardware limits not only processing power and storages, but also effectiveness

R. Cicchetti et al. (Eds.): DEXA 2002, LNCS 2453, pp. 392–402, 2002.

in wireless communication. We address several optimizations with preventing impractical implementation for such a platform.

The rest of the paper proceeds as follows. Section 2 describes the background of smartcard and electronic tickets. Section 3 defines a database model for ticket cards. Section 4 describes implementation model. Section 5 evaluates our design from electronic tickets. Section 6 concludes the paper.

2 Background

2.1 An Infrastructure for Electronic Tickets

An electronic ticket is a business application system, which make computerized all processes, including the issue of new tickets, buying and selling electronically, and automated examination at a check-in gate. We have designed the system as an infrastructure that allows multiple parties to conduct their business services. Figure 1 illustrates the overview of the infrastructure. The photo is a snapshot, where more than 100 users tested our electronic tickets at check-in gates at Yokohama International Stadium.

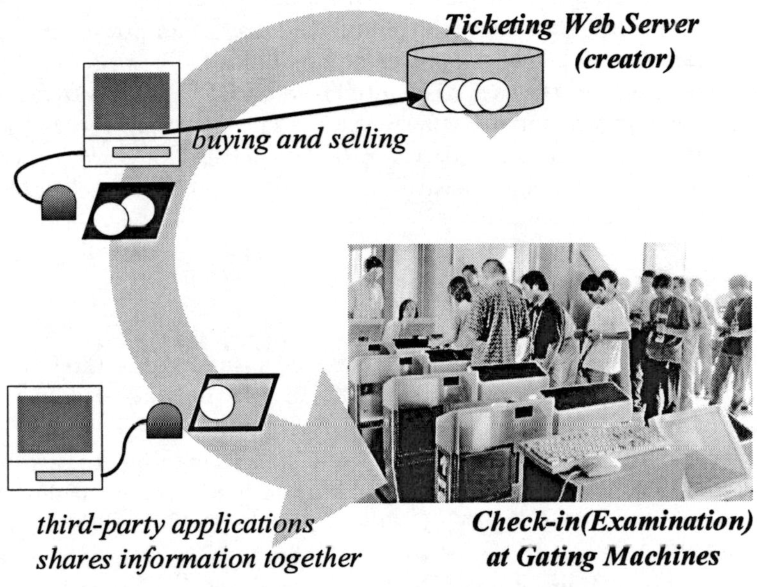

Fig. 1. The Overview of Electronic Ticket Infrastructure

In the infrastructure a smartcard is used as an *electronic wallet* on which several tickets are held, as well as a small amount of caches. More securely, we can also deposit our tickets in a security box over the Internet. The movement of tickets between a card and other holders is always available and ensured to be atomic. (The electronic transferability has been already reported in [6].) The strength of card-stored tickets is that it can encourage service compositions by sharing ticket information. For example, a vending machine at a station can suggest appropriate railway paths from ticket information on "today's game". The smartcard therefore requires the management of both expressive data structure for representing various kinds of tickets, and access control against various contexts of business services.

2.2 Contactless Smartcard

Smartcard [2] is one of the smallest computers, where all components (CPU, cryptographic coprocessors, RAM/ROM, nonvolatile storage such as E2PROM and FeRAM, and communication peripherals) are combined within a single chip. In addition to this, the smartcard is designed to be *tamper resistant*; all accesses from outside are fully controlled and, if needed, automatically encrypted. The tamper-resistant hardware enables us to secure database, as if a firewall system secures database servers in a guarded room.

From viewpoints of communications, we can categorize smartcard into two types: *contact card* and *contactless card*. In this paper, we chiefly focus on a contactless, whose power is transmitted with queries over electro-magnetic wave or microwave; a contactless smartcard limits the maximum power consumption of the processor and therefore the processor capabilities. The resources available in the state of the art of the card are limited to 8 bit CPU, 32 KB ROM and 512 bytes RAM for software and 4 KB for data storage. Although the development of higher performance cards is underway [10], the demand of powerless card will remain in the market for inexpensive devices for disposal or recyclable ticket wallets.

2.3 Related Work

We will turn to data management systems on a smartcard. First, there are several attempts based on a file system. IEC/ISO 7816 defines the hierarchical smartcard file system, like the directory in UNIX, and four kinds of file formats: transparent, records, variable records and cyclic file. To manipulate such files and their records, ISO 7816-4 specifies a set of standard commands, called APDUs (Application Protocol Data Units). On the other hand, SCFS (Smart Card File System) enable us to use the standard UNIX file APIs to access the smartcard files by being mounted on parts of the UNIX file system [3].

The research field of smartcard database was explored with PicoDBMS. In [8], several excellent techniques are discussed to optimize memory efficiency in a very small relational database. As well, the necessity for querying data on a smartcard has been recognized in a standardization process; ISO 7816-7 defines the specification of SCQL (Structured Card Query Language). Carraso's attempt is also known as the first development of an SCQL-based RDBMS on JavaCard [1].

However, these attempts are all based on the extension (or more preciously scale-down) of conventional data managements. The general-purpose functions restricted for scaling down do not always cover functions required in each application domain. In contrast, we emphasize on a specialization of ticket managements for making it practically available on a smartcard.

3 Database Model

Over a smartcard we can store electronic tickets, whose kinds might be different. Important is the management of variety, rather than that of volume. In this context, the relational database model seems to be fundamentally inadequate. This section defines a small database model specialized for managing small volumes of various tickets.

3.1 Data Representation

A ticket database consists of several objects. Let D be a database, and o be an object on D. We can define the structure of database.

Definition 1. A *ticket database* D is a finite set of objects, $\{o_1, o_2, .., o_n\}$, where each object corresponds to an *electronic ticket*. The relationship between D and o_i is interpreted as `has_a`, not `member_of`. That is, the user of the smartcard inherits the ownership of stored tickets on D.

We will turn to the internal structure of an object. An object consists of several elements. First, let $\mathbf{L}$ be a total set of labels, $\mathbf{T}$ be a total set of type, and $\mathbf{V}$ be a total set of values. We can define the structure of the element.

Definition 2. An *object element* is a triple of a label, a type, and its value, denoted as $\langle l, t, v\rangle$, where $l \in \mathbf{L}$, $t \in \mathbf{T}$, and $v \in \mathbf{V}$.

Now we can formulize the relationship between an object and its elements. Here, let L_i, T_i, V_i be sets over o_i, respectively containing labels, types, and values.

Definition 3. An object o_i is a *mapping* from a pair of label and type into a value. That is, we can denote the object as $o_i : L_i \times T_i \rightarrow V_i$, where $L_i \subset \mathbf{L}$, $T_i \subset \mathbf{T}$, $V_i \subset \mathbf{V}$.

Example 1. Following is an example of a ticket object (denoted o_a) used in our experimentation of electronic ticket.

o_a : (`type`, `string`) $\rightarrow$ `"ticket"`, o_a : (`id`, `serial`) $\rightarrow$ 100001
o_a : (`title`, `string`) $\rightarrow$ `"Concert of M. Imai"`, o_a : (`orgnizer`, `string`) $\rightarrow$ `"Kyodo"`
o_a : (`orgnizer`, `phone`) $\rightarrow$ `03-xxxx-xxxx`, o_a : (`place`, `string`) $\rightarrow$ `"Budokan"`
o_a : (`place`, `phone`) $\rightarrow$ `03-yyyy-yyyy`, o_a : (`date`, `date`) $\rightarrow$ `1999-10-07`
o_a : (`seat`, `code`) $\rightarrow$ `A00132`, o_a : (`enable`, `boolean`) $\rightarrow$ *true*
o_a : (`checkin`, `date`) $\rightarrow$ *null*
o_a : (`price`, `currency-yen`) $\rightarrow$ 1200, o_a : (`price`, `currency-usd`) $\rightarrow$ 10.00

Note that the data model shown here is based on the *ubiquitous data model* [4], which is designed to capture more real-world values; the type t is a *domain of values*, such as measurements of units, scale, and vocabularies. We believe that this model is expressive enough to represent ticket properties.

3.2 Access Control Model

The ticket database D is used in the context of multiple applications. On the other hand, the user will access each object by different permissions. For example, a creator of a ticket is not always a creator of another. The database therefore must control the access by each object, not by the whole database. Here we introduce a self-described authenticator to associate a user with different access controls in each object.

First, a *role* is introduced as the class of operation contexts, such as the creation and the examination of tickets. The access of a user can be controlled through a role by checking whether or not the user has the role. Here, using a basic password mechanism, we can formulize a role-based authenticator. Let r be a role name and $\mathbf{R}$ be a finite set of roles. Let p be a password and $\mathbf{P}$ be a finite set of passwords.

Definition 4. An authenticator α is a mapping $\alpha : \mathbf{R} \times \mathbf{P} \rightarrow \{\mathtt{t}, \mathtt{f}\}$, where $\mathtt{t}$ means authenticated, and $\mathtt{f}$ unauthenticated.

A user's requests can be controlled with a pair of (r, p). We attach the authenticator directly to an object. We denote that α_i is the authenticator of an object o_i. An object o_i accessible by role r_j is one that has $\alpha_i(r, p) \rightarrow \mathtt{t}$.

The access can be controlled in each object. Let us suppose that a user access with (r, p) to the database. The access to an object o_1 is allowed because $\alpha_1(r, p) \rightarrow \mathtt{t}$, while at the same time the access to o_2 is denied because $\alpha_2(r, p) \rightarrow \mathtt{f}$. Note that for the practical purpose we should apply the same authenticator to a class of objects, for example, tickets to the same game.

3.3 Query Language

As well as the object structure, the result of a query is formed in a self-described way, containing labels and types. Following is the syntax of select and update queries and their results.

select $\{(l_i, t_i)\}$ by $\{(r, p)\}$ where $\{(l_j, t_j)\ cmp\ v_j\}$ ..
$\rightarrow \{\langle l_i, t_i, o_a(l_i, t_i)\rangle\ \}$ ... $\{\langle l_i, t_i, o_b(l_i, t_i)\rangle\ \}$, ..
update $\{\rangle l_i, t_i, v_i\langle\}$ by $\{(r, p)\}$ where $\{(l_j, t_j)\ cmp\ v_j\}$
$\rightarrow \{\langle l_i, t_i, o_a(l_i, t_i)\rangle\ \}$, $\{\langle l_i, t_i, o_b(l_i, t_i)\rangle\ \}$, ..

Here the semantics of conventional SQL is preserved. The operator *cmp* in where clause is comparator and simplified to support only 6 operations $\{=, <>, <, >, <=, >=\}$. The uniqueness is the by clause that enables the user to switch roles in each query.

Note that the database answer queries without schematic systems, but it causes name conflict problems. To avoid this problem and increase data interoperability, we need to build ontologies for labels and types. However, building ontologies is beyond the scope of this paper. We assume shared ontologies hereafter.

4 Implementation Model

In this section, we set a virtual card $\mathcal{C}$ as a discussion stage for making our implementation independent of a particular smartcard product. We assume that the card $\mathcal{C}$ has 16 bit CPU, 32KB ROM for program, 4KB storage for data, and 106kbps for ISO-14443(B) communication. In the past experimentation of our electronic ticket [6][5], we developed prototyped database on the emulator of the card $\mathcal{C}$.

4.1 System Architecture

Clearly, computing resources over the $\mathcal{C}$ are too limited to provide full functions of the database model defined in Section 3. We have accordingly chosen a *wrapper* architecture, where some functions are externalized to the *preprocessor* on a host computer. The preprocessor is a transformer that decomposes from the query language to primitive *commands* executable over $\mathcal{C}$, and then recomposes the results of them. The symbols such as labels and types in the query language are also complied into bytecodes by using predefined mappings. In addition to this, cache management is incorporated for optimizing the transformation.

One of the points of the wrapper architecture is the sophistication of command sets on the card. Theoretically, we can wrap even a simple data card supporting only `read_record` and `write_record`. However, query decomposition increases interaction costs that lead to a critical bottleneck[1] in the ISO 14443(B) communication. We need expressive command sets that better specify operations in the application.

Another point is data privacy on the whole. The preprocessor can be practically regarded as *trusted* since it is authenticated through smartcard hardware mechanism and the interactions between them are also encrypted. However, the preprocessor is not tamper-resistant, where data privacy is not ensured. Therefore, the installing of access control in $\mathcal{C}$ should be prior to that of other functions. Figure 2 depicts the overview of the system architecture.

4.2 Storage Design

We will start by designing the structure of data storage. First we fix the size of a page to 64 bytes. This is derived from the physical size of one page on E2PROM. [2]

[1] In our experience of [5] the cost of one interaction exceeds about 100 ms, although it depends on vendors and their device drivers.

[2] Due to the compatibility, the FeRAM card sometimes inherits 64-byte page.

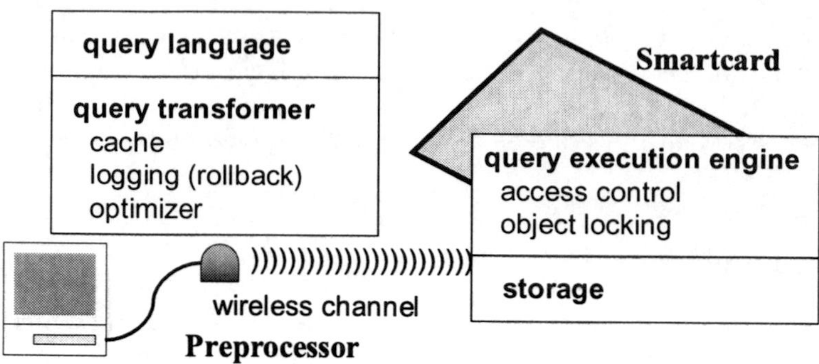

Fig. 2. System Architecture

Figure 3 illustrates the formatting layout of object storages. An object is partitioned by its element. To recombine them, we assign to each object an internal identifier `oid` (> 0). Following by `oid`, an element is formatted with length-fixed label and type in the `name` field, access control list in `acl`, encoding of value (such as int and char[]) in `enc`, and element value in `data`. In addition to the element partition, we introduce an *object header page* to control object managements; this page includes the fields `cpwd` and `spwd` for authenticating creator and service passwords, and the `lock` fields for concurrency control.

Note that we have chosen to use a flat structure since the card $\mathcal{C}$ has only 4KB for the storage. Comparing with results in [8], we need no indexing for such a small size. In addition, all commands are designed to be executable with *one-pass storage scanning* from the first element to the last one.

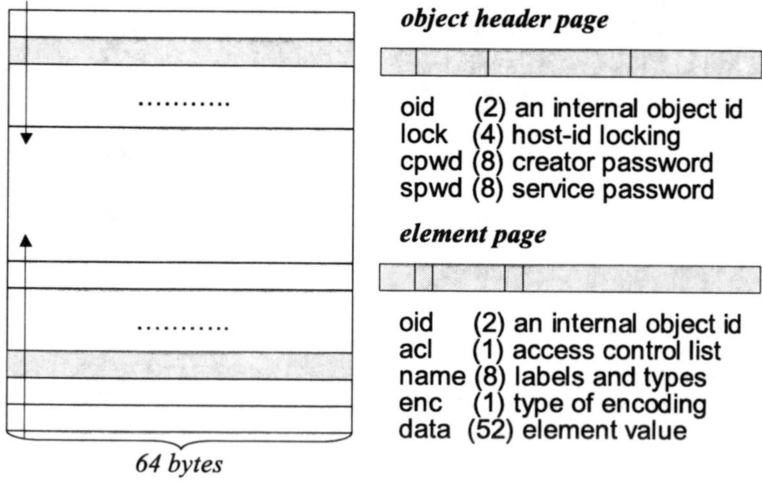

Fig. 3. The Formatting Layout of Object Storages

4.3 Primitive Query

The database supports all operations that need to implement the life cycle of a ticket: creation, transfer (trading), examination, and resignation. These operations are provided on the card $\mathcal{C}$ with primitive queries, or commands. To distinguish between the query language and commands, we use upper case letters to denote command names.

Here we focus on the following commands by which we can compose select and update queries. (Basically, the query select can be composed of SELECT and READ, and the update be of SELECT and UPDATE.)

SELECT [oid] n_1 CMP v_1 .. n_i CMP v_i END.
$\rightarrow \{\langle \texttt{oid}, n_1, o_{oid}(n_1)\rangle .. \langle \texttt{oid}, n_i, o_{oid}(n_i)\rangle\}$ END.
READ [oid] n_1 .. n_i END.
$\rightarrow \{\langle \texttt{oid}, n_1, v_1\rangle .. \langle \texttt{oid}, n_i, v_i\rangle\}$ END.
UPDATE [oid] n_1 v_1 .. n_i v_i END.
$\rightarrow \{\langle \texttt{oid}, n_1, o_{oid}(n_1)\rangle .. \langle \texttt{oid}, n_i, o_{oid}(n_i)\rangle\}$ END.

The results of these commands are returned in a form of $\langle \texttt{oid}, n, v\rangle$, where oid is an internal object id, n is the name corresponding to (l, t), v is the value of object $o_{oid}(n)$. (In UPDATE, the pre-updated value is returned for rollback logging.) The preprocessor shares oids on the host side for managing the cache of retrieved elements.

To make the commands more expressive, we add several enhancements. One is *object filtering*, which enables us to specify an executable object by using the first argument [oid] in a command. If oid $= 0$, then all objects are executed. Another is *command multiplexing*, which enables us to use multiple arguments in a command to avoid repeating the same type of command executions. To achieve one-pass storage scanning, the result is returned in an unordered *disjunction* of each result.

4.4 Access Control

To authenticate application contexts, we set four types of fixed roles: *creator*, *service*, *owner* and *others*. In the field acl on each element, we can specify read/write permission for each of these roles. The passwords of *creator* and *service* are recorded in the field cpwd and spwd in the object head. The owner *role* means the ownership of the database, whose password is consolidated in the database. If a password is not authenticated, we can use as the default role *others* for the access.

The authorization is done in each command. We can switch the specified role (and its password) in BY option. (For example, *COMMAND* BY (r, p) ..) If it is omitted, the role authorized in previous command is inherited.

4.5 Logging and Rollback Control

The hardware limitation of $\mathcal{C}$ does not allow harmonious coexistence of multiple users; only a single user can access to the database at a time. However contactless communication frequently causes the disconnection, where we must prevent inconsistency. For example, in a check-in process valid users should be gone through a gate without twice entrance and entire rejection.

To ensure data consistency, the execution of each command should be atomic. Let us recall the disconnection of communication simultaneously stops electric supply for the processor. Thus, both received command and formatting result should be stored and manipulated over nonvolatile memory. The atomic execution of multi-argument UPDATE command can ensure the consistency of a simple transaction, in which the user updates more than one element statically.

We will turn to a complex transaction. For that, we introduce *explicate locking* for each object. When we lock an object, a logical host identifier authenticated when opening a session is recorded in the field `lock` on the object header. This lock can exclude operations accessed by other host id. In addition to this, the UPDATE command is designed to be symmetric and return pre-updated values. The original values are recorded as logging on the host computer. Once the transaction is aborted, the preprocessor can recover modified values to these recorded values.

5 Evaluation

In this section we evaluate the database on the card $\mathcal{C}$ through our experience of electronic ticket project [6,5]. In the past experimentation, one ticket can be represented with about 20 elements on the database object. This corresponds to 1KB on the database storage. That is, the card $\mathcal{C}$ store at least 3 tickets. In this situation, we focus on query processing for ticket browsing and check-in transaction. The creation of tickets and the transfer of them have been already reported in [6].

5.1 Ticket Browsing

The owner of the smartcard can browse his or her tickets hold on the database. Using the browser on a host computer the owner can ask for a list of the tickets with a query:

$(Q1)$ select $(id, serial), (title, string), (date, date)$ by $(\texttt{owner}, p1)$ where $(type, string) =$ "*ticket*"

Consequently, the user can ask for furthermore information of a specific ticket with a query :

$(Q2)$ select $(*, *)$ by $(owner, p1)$ where $(id, serial) = 100001$

5.2 Check-in

In the check-in transaction, a gating machine searches a valid ticket from a card, and then updates the entrance records on it. First, a gating machine can ask for a valid ticket with a query:

Table 1. Results of Cost Estimations

commands	*Q1*	*Q2*	*Q3*	*Q4*
fully supported (matching and multiplexing)	2	2	1	1
partially supported (only matching)	4	7	3	2
not supported (only single read and update)	12	7	N/A	N/A

(Q3) select $(id, serial)$ by $(\texttt{service}, p2)$ where $(enable, bool) = true$

Let us note that each ticket has a different password for the gating service. That is, the access is filtered on the card to only tickets whose authentication is $\alpha(service, p2) \rightarrow$ authorized

The gating machine selects one of valid tickets, and continuously updates entrance records on the selected ticket with a query:

$(Q4)$ update $\langle enable, bool, no\rangle, \langle checkin, date, \text{2001-12-20}\rangle$ where $(id, serial) = 100001$

5.3 Cost Estimation

Using these access patterns specified in the queries *Q1* *Q4*, we analyze the performance of the implementation model. To start, we assume that we can ignore variants of each command execution costs; the execution of comparators underlying in each command will relatively lighter than the scanning of the object storage. In addition, we assume that the communication buffer is limited to 256 bytes per a transmission, which is derived from the length of one APDUs message. (Many of smartcards only supports this size of the buffer.) The execution costs therefore can be approximated with the number of interactions, although it depends on the number of stored tickets.

Here we estimate interaction costs in a case that there are three tickets that can be all accessed by the same role. Table 1 compares the effects of command variations. (The interacting messages are divided by 256 bytes.) The findings is that our optimization of command sets help reduce interaction costs in the context of ticket application.

6 Conclusion

Recently, embedded databases and smartcard databases have emerged. To make such small database practical, specialization for an application domain is to some extents required. In this paper we focused on a contactless smartcard that encourages database managements for multi-party ticket applications. The specialization includes a new data model for well representing a variety of small volume tickets, a role-based access control applied to each ticket, and a logging and rollback operations externalized in a way interacting with a preprocessor. These functions even if they are not general help us to build ticket applications such as customers' browsing and check-in process at an automated gate.

Currently, the ticket database has been only implemented on a Java-based emulator of the smartcard. This is simply because that we could obtain no smartcard with user friendly development environment. Fortunately, the development of the smartcard software begins to be opened to the academic. For the future, we intend to detail ticket managements implemented on a card.

Acknowledgement

This work was supported by a grant from the Ministry of Education of Japan. The authors would like to thank the members of Sakamura Laboratory (University of Tokyo) for their insightful suggestion.

References

1. L. C. Carrasco. RDBMS's for Java cards? What a senseless idea!, www.sqlmachine.com, (1999).
2. U. Hansmann (ed.) Smart Card Application Development Using Java. Springer Verlag, 1999.
3. N. Itoi, P. Honeyman, and J. Rees. SCFS: A UNIX Filesystem for Smartcards. In Proc. of USENIX Workshop on Smartcard Technology, (1999).
4. K. Kuramitsu and K. Sakamura. Semistructured Object: A Ubiquitous Data Model. IPSJ Transaction on Database, TOD12, 2002. (In Japanese)
5. K. Kuramitsu and K. Sakamura. Towards Ubiquitous Database in Mobile Commerce. In *Proc. of ACM International Workshop on Data Engineering for Wireless and Mobile Access*, pp. 84-89, 2001.
6. K. Kuramitsu and K. Sakamura. Tamper-Resistant Network: an infrastructure for moving electronic tokens. *TOWARDS THE E-SOCIETY E-Commerce, E-Business, and E-Government*, Kluwer Academic Publisher, pp. 113–129, (2001).
7. S. Ortiz. Industry Trends Embedded Databases Come out of Hiding. *IEEE COMPUTER*, pp. 16–19, Vol. 33, No. 3, (2000).
8. P. Pucheral, L. Bouganim, P. Valduriez, and C. Bobineau. PicoDBMS: Scaling down database techniques for the smartcard. *The VLDB Journal*, Vol. 10, No. 1, pp. 120-132, (2001).
9. International Standardization Organization (ISO), Integrated Circuit(s) Cards with Contacts – Part 7: Interindustry Commands for Structured Card Query Language (SCQL), ISO/IEC 7816-7, (1999).
10. K. Sakamura and N. Koshizuka. The eTRON Wide-Area Distributed-System Architecture for E-Commerce. *IEEE Micro*, Vol. 21, No. 6, (2001).

Mobile Agents for Distributed Transactions of a Distributed Heterogeneous Database System

D.Y. Ye, M.C. Lee, and T.I. Wang

Laboratory of Intelligent Network Applications
Department of Engineering Science
National Cheng Kung University
Taiwan
aska@linuxeagle.es.ncku.edu.tw
limigche@hotmail.com
wti535@mail.ncku.edu.tw

Abstract. A Distributed Heterogeneous Database System (DHDBS) is constituted of different kinds of autonomous databases connected to the network. A distributed transaction in such a system involves many sub-transactions and data movements among database sites. For the time being, most of the commercial database products implement their distributed transactions using the traditional client/server model that is suffering from enormous data movements. This paper proposes a new distributed transaction model which uses mobile agent technology to reduce data traffics in distributed transactions. The idea is backed by the well-known characteristics, such as mobility, autonomy, and concurrency, of mobile agents in supporting distributed computations. The aim is to boost the performance of distributed transactions of a heterogeneous database system in a loosely coupled environment (such as the Internet). An procedure is designed for distributed query decomposition. Some principles are observed for the path planning of a mobile agent roaming the network to carry out various sub-transactions.

1 Introduction

Mobile agents can roam among heterogeneous hosts in a network and communicate with each others to access distributed resources. The execution model of mobile agents is to ship the code (or the computation logic) to the data. They are proved, in many cases, quite friendly to the network traffic, and are particularly suitable for developing distributed applications [1][2][3][8]. Mobile agents may play important roles in many areas, including distributed information retrieval, network management, e-commerce, and etc. Among them, the distributed information retrieval, especially in a large scale distributed heterogeneous database, is obviously a big stage for mobile agents.

In general, a distributed heterogeneous database system is an integration of several different types of autonomous databases connected to a network [5][6][7]. At least two issues must be addressed in building a Distributed Heterogeneous

R. Cicchetti et al. (Eds.): DEXA 2002, LNCS 2453, pp. 403–412, 2002.

Database Management System (DHDBMS); one is the integration of different types of databases and the other is the distributed transaction management. The former is beyond the scope of this paper. The latter is about a mechanism to decompose a distributed transaction into mult iple sub-transactions that access databases on one or more computers across a network.

In dealing with distributed transactions, most of the current researches stick to the traditional client/server model [15] and come up with a centralized style management system. Although this style of transaction management has its advantages and the implementation is easy, it also yields a few drawbacks. As we know, distributed sub-transactions, if not well optimized, may trigger many unavoidable and unnecessary data movements among database sites. An obvious consequence is the significant performance dro pping owing to these unnecessary data movements. Enormous data movements also cause heavier network traffic that in turn increases the response time. Another is the inflexibility in the configuration of the entire DHDB. The system will be more tightly coupled under the client/server model. This will result in the less autonomy of each local DBMS as well as more reconfiguration work when local DBMS affiliating with or disappearing from the system. Using mobile agents to support DHDBMS preliminary provides th e following advantages:

- In contrast to the client/server model, interactions, i.e. control message exchanges, among distributed modules are rare, and thus the network traffic is reduced [9][10].
- With an optimized algorithm for decomposing distributed transactions, some unnecessary and even unavoidable data movements can be eliminated. The network traffic can be further reduced. This will greatly reduce the response time and make the transactions of large-scale and loosely coupled DHDB more acceptable [12].
- The management system can be more dynamic in both transaction processing and configuration of a distributed heterogeneous database. The integration and variance of the system can be more flexible; Even though sometimes there are local DBMS joining in or disappearing, reconfiguration of the whole DHDBMS is often unnecessary [13][14].
- Supports on transactions from and to mobile platforms can be easily integrated [4][15][16].

Other advantages resulted from using mobile agents will become clearer later in the paper. A framework is proposed in the following section to use mobile agents in accessing DHDB, which will fully utilize the characteristics of autonomy, mobility, and concurrency of mobile agents.

The rest of the paper is organized as follows. In section 2, the concept and the operation of a framework using mobile agents in accessing DHDB will be illustrated. Operations of each component are also described in detail in the section. Section 3 describes the policy and the algorithm of distributed database query, i.e. transaction decomposition. Section 4 presents some message formats that are involved in the framework. Some related works are discussed in section 5 and the last section draws the conclusi on.

2 The Concept and the Framework

Since the data involved in a distributed transaction spreads over the entire network, the transaction must be correctly decomposed into several sub-transactions for all the nodes accessed. The idea is to pack a sub-transaction into a mobile agent that will migrate to the node to which the sub-transaction access. This sub-transaction is processed locally at that node and the result is packed back into the mobile agent. If the result of the sub-transaction is involved with another sub-transaction by an operator, e.g. a join operator, the carrier agent will travel on to the new destination where its payload will be consulted in executing the operator. Otherwise it will move back to the transaction originator. All these decomposing analysis and navigating decisions will be done and made by the join forces of a Transaction Decomposer and a Transaction Coordinator.

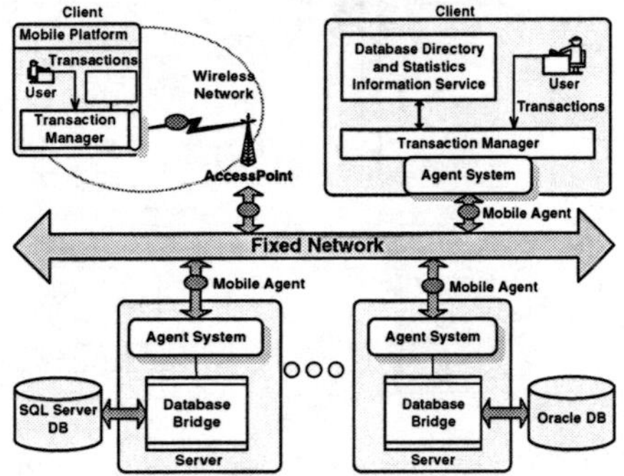

Fig. 1. The Mobile-Agent-Based Framework

Figure 1 shows the mobile-agent-based framework for supporting the processing of distributed transactions in a distributed heterogeneous database system. It has a simple but open architecture. The framework integrates different types of database systems by using mobile agent servers that contains two components, an Agent System and a Database Bridge. The former is to execute mobile agents that carry sub-transactions. The latter is the actual joint that connects a database system and the framework. The payload of a mobile agent, i.e. the sub-transaction, is extracted by the Agent System and handed to the Database Bridge. All the sub-transactions received by the Database Bridge will be converted into local queries to the local DBMS with right format. Different Database Bridges must be constructed for different types of DBMS; they are the only various components in the framework.

At the client side, there is a Transaction Manager and a Database Directory and Statistics Information Service. The Transaction Manager consists of a distributed transaction decomposer and a transaction coordinator not shown in the figure. A query form a user is analyzed by the Transaction Manager to produce necessary sub-transactions. During the decomposing process, the Transaction

Manager consults the Database Directory and Statistics Information Service component to make correct navigating decisions. All the sub-transactions are then handed to the Agent System to be packed into transactional mobile agents.

2.1 The Operation Model

The operation model and component details of the framework are shown in Figure 2; they are also summarized as follows. For the time being, the framework use a uniform SQL query and data format. Conversion between this uniform data format and a specific DBMS system is performed by the Database Bridge that connects the DBMS to the framework.

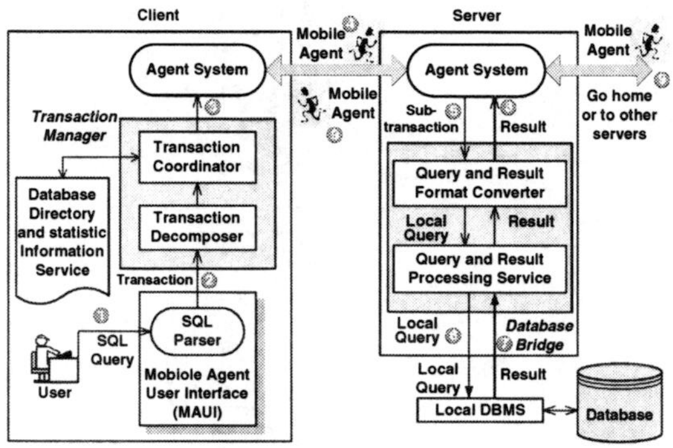

Fig. 2. The Operational Model of The Framework

1. When a SQL query (① in Fig.2) is entered by a user via a Mobile Agent User Interface, the SQL Parser will first scan and analyze the query. If no error is found, the generated transaction corresponding to the query is sent to the Transaction Manager (②).
2. The Transaction Decomposer of the Transaction Manager interprets the transaction and generates a distributed transaction context containing several sub-transactions and their associations. These associations are formed according to the operators, e.g. join, between two accessed distributed relations. When processing a context, for each sub-transaction the Transaction Coordinator first looks up the database node, at which the accessed relation of the sub-transaction resides, from the Database Directory and Statistics Information Service component. It then generates the navigation information for all sub-transactions according to the associations among them. Finally, the enriched context is dispatched to the Agent System (③) to generate transaction-carrier mobile agents. Concurrency among independent sub-transactions results in the production of multiple mobile agents. Ordered sub-transactions, on the other hand, will result in t he generation of multiple hops mobile agents. All the mobile agents then migrate to their own destinations (④).

3. After a mobile agent arrives at the Mobile Agent System of a database node, the sub-transaction, i.e. the payload of the mobile agent, is pulled out and handed to the Database Bridge (⑤). The Query and Result Format Converter within the bridge first converts the sub-transaction into a local query to the local DBMS with correct data format. This local query is then processed by the *Query* and Result Processing Service tha t will transmit the local to the local DBMS and trigger a real local transaction (⑥). The execution result of the local transaction is given back to the Database Bridge, and is collected by the same Query and Result Processing Service (⑦). Before going back to the Agent System, the data format of the execution result must be converted back to the uniform o ne of the framework by, again, the Query and *Result* Format Converter(⑧). Finally at the Agent System, the original mobile agent receives the result before it moves again. As mentioned above, which node is the next destination is determined by the navigation information packed into the mobile agent (⑨).

The flexibility also demonstrated here by the framework is that a mobile agent can be a single hop agent that visits a single database node for a single sub-transaction or a multiple hops agent that carries multiple sub-transactions for several database nodes. The optimal choice is yet to be evaluated.

3 A Distributed Transaction Decomposing Procedure

In this section, an example of decomposing a distributed transaction is given to demonstrate the spirit of the decomposing procedure. For the time being the procedure is specifically design for DBMSs of relation databases only. Also for simplicity, some optimization steps, such as redundancy elimination, are omitted from this paper.

3.1 The Decomposing Procedure

The steps of decomposing are described as follows with examples.

Step I : Scan the query clause, parse and decompose it into tokens. Then, classify the tokens into four categories and put them into a *Context*: *Command Type*, *referred Columns*, *referred Relations*, **and** *Conditions.*

Example 4-1: Suppose there is a query clause:

```
Select order.ord_id,customer.cust_id,employee.emp_name,
       prod.prod_id, prod.prod_name
From   order, customer,prod,employee
Where  not order.ord_id=13 and prod.prod_id=12  and
       (order.cust_id=customer.cust_id  or
        employee.emp_name='David')  or
       prod.prod_name in ('CD-ROM','CD-RW)
```

The result of step I would be:

```
Command Type     : Select
referred Columns: order.ord_id, customer.cust_id,
                  employee.emp_name, prod.prod_id,
                  prod.prod_name
referred Tables : order, customer,p roduct,employee
Conditions       : not order.ord_id=13                and
                  prod.prod_id=12                     and
                  (order.cust_id=customer.cust_id
                   or employee.emp_name='David')      or
                  prod.prod_name in ('CD-ROM','CD-RW')
```

Step II : Transform Conditions in the context into a relational algebra with internal symbols. Each internal symbol represents a simple predicate and is augmented with an operation tag; the operation tag eliminates the negation and specifies the operation that will perform on a predicate.

Example 4-2: The Conditions in Example 4-1 is transformed into:

```
Conditions       : not order.ord_id=13                and
                  prod.prod_id=12                     and
                  (order.cust_id=customer.cust_id
                   or employee.emp_name='David')      or
                  prod.prod_name in ('CD-ROM','CD-RW')

are transformed into:   A*B*(C+D)+(E)
    where:  ' ' is 'not'    '*' is 'and'    '+' is 'or'
with::
symbol      condition                          operation tag
'A'      order.ord_id=13                            reject
'B'      prod.prod_id=12                            select
'C'      order.cust_id=customer.cust_id             join
'D'      employee.emp_name='David'                  select
'E'      prod.prod_name in ('CD-ROM','CD-RW')       select
```

Step III : Transform the relational algebra by valid logic operations into a qualification in a quasi-disjunctive normal form:

$$(p_{11} * p_{21} * ... * p_{1n}) + ... + (p_{m1} * p_{m2} * ... * p_{mn})$$

The predicate in each conjunction (* predicates) is either a simple predicate (a single internal symbol) or a parenthesized disjunction of simple predicates. The reason for not using a 'exact' disjunctive normal form will become clear in the following example and steps.

Example 4-3: The relational algebra in example 4-2, the transformation is straight.

```
          A*B*( C +D)+ (E)                 (1)    A*B*C
=>        A*B*C +   A*B*D + E      => (2)    A*B*D
                                      (3)      E
```

where (1), (2), and (3) are independently, and can be executed independently. The final result is the union of the results of (1), (2), and (3).(**Note:** It seems that the resulting conjunctive sub-queries can be processed independent. While in practice, it may lead to **redundant work** if common expressions exist among these sub-queries. The following example will show this fact, and the next step will deal with it.)

Example 4-4: The relational algebra should be transformed into (forget about the coincidence):

```
          A*B*( C +D)+ (E)
=>        A*B*C +   A*B*D + E   => (1)    A*B*(C+D)
                                  (2)      E
```

where (1) and (2) are, same as in the above, independent, and can be executed independently. The final result is the union of th

Step IV : Refers to the database directory and statistics information and determines the execution site of each internal symbol. For selection predicate symbols, the execution site is determined by the location of the table involved. For join predicate symbols, the execution sites are determined by the following rules to minimize data movement:

- **Rule 1: if the involved two tables are at a same site, the site is selected.**
- **Rule 2: if the involved two tables are at different sites, the table with a smaller size is scheduled to be moved (replicated) to the other site.**

Example 4-5: For the resulting internal symbols in example 4-2, the result of step IV is:

```
symbol  condition                                  execution site
'A' is 'order.ord_id=13'                                        1
'B' is 'prod.prod_id=12'                                        2
'C' is 'order.cust_id=customer.cust_id' (1 => 2)                2
        assumes that  size(order) < size(customer)
'D' is 'employee.emp_name='David''                              3
'E' is 'prod.prod_name in ('CD-ROM','CD-RW)''                   2
```

Note: step III and step IV can be done concurrently.

Step V : Repeat for each internal symbol of each conjunctive sub-query generated in step III, assigning a mobile agent for its operation. Set the mobile agent as a multiple-hop agent if its execution result of the symbol will be used by the symbol to the right in the sub-query, and so on. Use the information obtained in step IV to help determine also the execution path of each mobile agent.

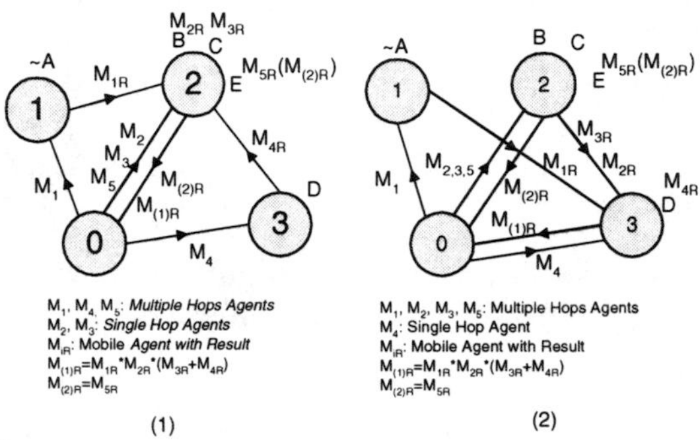

Fig. 3. Mobile Agents and Their Execution Path

Example 4-6: for the conjunctive sub-queries in example4-3, the assignment can be shown as follows and in figure3:

```
site          1   2    2   3          2
        (1)   A * B * (C + D)     (2) E
agents        M1  M2   M3  M4         M5
```

3.2 The Path Planning

Path planning for mobile agents in an application is not easy. As shown in the last example there can be multiple solutions for a single operation. To add more complexity, an optimal solution for an operation could be a worst solution for others. As mentioned above, exhaustive searches my yield an optimal solution only when the database directory and statistic information service is able to provide enough information for table size, attribute domain extremes, and etc.

4 Related Work

Although not many researches use mobile agents in distributed database systems, there are still some related works. Research in [12] proposed a "DBMS-aglet framework" for the applications of the popular World Wide Web, which has become the biggest universal information center, and has created the need for developing web-based DBMS client/server applications. Moreover, the widespread use of Java in network-centric computing, attributed mainly to its global portability and security control system, gives Java the lead in client/server programming and mobile computing. Through the well-established JDBC API and JDBC drivers, Java has become the main language in developing web-based DBMS. Thus, the main idea of this framework is to access web-based distributed DBMS based on Java-based mobile agents, using them to provide database connectivity, processing and communication, and consequently eliminate the overheads of the existing methodologies.

Mobile agents are used in distributed transactions in a similar way to distributed database systems. Many applications has been proposed, such as [14]. Another research is [13], which applied mobile agents to transactions of electronic commerce and proposed an architecture that offers fault tolerance and reliable agent transmission. This architecture additionally guarantees security for the host as well as security for the agent, and therefore an agent will be able to carry out financial transactions.

5 Conclusion

The most important reason of using mobile agents to support distributed transactions is two folds. Firstly, the resources of applications in distributed environment changes overtime; By using multiple, mobile, and autonomous agents to support global transactions makes it possible to monitor resources in distributed systems, and to react to changes in a very flexible manner. Secondly, because existing standardized middlewares for building distributed transactions, such as OTS based on CORBA, demand to know i n advance all resources used during the distributed transaction, they are not flexible enough for many of today's application scenarios. On the other hand, using mobile agents as a middleware of distributed transactions offers more flexibility and enhances these systems. This paper presents a new distributed database transaction management model based on mobile agent technology. With characteristics of high portability, autonomy and mobility, mobile agents can be a very competitive alternative to the traditional client/server techniques. A distributed transaction decomposition procedure and a couple of path-planning rules for the distributed transaction management are also presented in the paper. The rules are specially tailed for the concurrency characteristic of mobile ag ents. Compared to the traditional client/server model, mobile agent model can furnish a distributed transaction management system with higher local autonomy and concurrency; not to mention that they also reduce network traffic and, consequently, increase the performance of distributed transaction processing.

References

1. S. Covaci,; Zhang Tianning; I. Busse, "Java-based intelligent mobile agents for open system management", In Proceedings of Ninth IEEE International Conference on Tools with Artificial Intelligence, Page(s) 492 -501, 1997.
2. D. Kotz; R. Gray; S. Nog; D. Rus; S. Chawla; G. Cybenko, "AGENT TCL: targeting the needs of mobile computers", IEEE Internet Computing Volume 14 , Page(s) 58 -67, 1997.
3. Gunter Karjoth, Danny B. Lange, and Mitsutu Oshima, "A Security Model for Aglets,", IEEE Internet Computing, JULY,AUGUST 1997.
4. Bennett, Frazer, Richardson, Tristan , Harter, Andy, "Teleporting - Making Applications Mobile", Proc. of IEEE Workshop on Mobile Computing Systems and Applications, Santa Cruz, Dec.1994.
5. C.J. Date, "An Introduction To Database System", Addison Wesley Publishing Company, 1995.
6. D. Agrawal, A. El Abbadi, "Using Data Migration for Heterogeneous Databases", Interoperability in Multidatabase Systems, 1991. IMS'91 Proceedings., First International Workshop, Pages 226 - 229, 1991.
7. David Bell; Jane Grimson, "Distributed Database Systems", Addison Wesley Publishing Company, 1992.
8. Danny B. Lange and Mitsuru Oshima, "Programming And Deploying Java Mobile Agents With Aglets", Addison Wesley Publishing Company, Page(s)1-31,1998.
9. Jihoon Yang; V. Honavar ; L. Miller ; J. Wong, "Intelligent mobile agents for information retrieval and knowledge discovery from distributed data and knowledge sources", IEEE Information Technology Conference, Page(s) 99-102, 1998.
10. M. R. Genesereth ; S. P. Ketchpel,"Software Agents",Communications of the ACM,37(7) Page 48-53, July 1994.
11. S. Miyamoto, ; J. Fujimoto, "Development of environmental information systems with a distributed database", Environmentally Conscious Design and Inverse Manufacturing, 1999. Proceedings. EcoDesign '99, First International Symposium, Pages 148 - 153, 1999.
12. Stavros Papastavrou, George Samaras, Evaggelia Pitoura, "Mobile Agents for WWW Distributed Database Access", Data Engineering, 1999. Proceedings., 15th International Conference on , Page(s): 228 -237,1999.
13. H. Vogler; T. Kunkelmann; M. L. Moschgath, "Distributed transaction processing as a reliability concept for mobile agents", Proceedings of the Sixth IEEE Computer Society Workshop on Future Trends of Distributed Computing Systems, Page(s): 59 -64, 1997.
14. H. Vogler; A. Buchmann, "Using multiple mobile agents for distributed transactions", Proceedings. 3rd IFCIS International Conference on Cooperative Information Systems, Page(s) 114 -121, 1998.
15. T. I. Wang, "A Mobile Agent Carrier Environment with Mobile Computing Facilities", IIP: International Conference on Intelligent Information Processing, The 16th IFIP World Computer Congress, Beijin 21 25/08, 2000.
16. T. I. Wang, "A Mobile Agent Carrier Environment for Mobile Information Retrieval", 11-th International Conference on Database and Expert Systems Applications - DEXA 2000, Greenwich, London, 05 08/09, 2000.

An Adaptive Direction-Based Location Update Scheme for Next Generation PCS Networks[1]

Dong-Xiu Ou[1,2], Kam-Yiu Lam[1], and De-Cun Dong[2]

[1]Department of Computer Science City University of Hong Kong
83 Tat Chee Avenue, Kowloon Hong Kong
Email: cskylam@cityu.edu.hk
[2]Institute of Traffic Information Engineering and Control
Tong Ji University Shanghai, P.R. China

Abstract. This paper studies the location management problem in PCS network. An adaptive direction-based location update (ADBU) scheme is proposed in which a line-paging method is adopted to minimize the paging cost and an adaptive direction-based scheme is formulated for location update generation. Mobile terminals inspect their directions and a location update will be generated when the change in the direction of a mobile terminal is greater than the direction threshold. In the paper, we assume that the movement of a mobile terminal in a period of time can be divided into steps and each step has a destination. Then, we use a Gauss-Markov process to model the movement of a mobile terminal in each step. With the Gauss-Markov model and a feedback control mechanism, we estimate the optimal value for the direction threshold with the attempt to minimize the update cost and at the same time limit the paging cost using line-paging. Performance results have shown that the performance of ADBU is significantly better than another direction-based update scheme and the distance-based scheme a result of smaller paging cost and update processing cost.

1 Introduction

In recent years, the number of Personal Communications Service (PCS) subscribers increases rapidly. The main solution to support the growing population of mobile users is to reduce the cell size to increase the degree of limited bandwidth reuse. However, a serious problem resulted from using small cells is the high cost in location management. There are two basic operations in location management: *location update* and *paging*. The operation of recording the current location (cell) of a mobile terminal (MT) is called *location update* while the operation of searching the exact location (cell) of a MT is called *paging* [1]. In the PCS systems, location databases are used to record the location information of MTs. When a MT is being called, the location

[1] The work described in this paper was partially supported by a strategic grant from the City University of Hong Kong [Project No. CityU 7001259].

R. Cicchetti et al. (Eds.): DEXA 2002, LNCS 2453, pp. 413–422, 2002.

database will be searched. If the MT cannot be found in the cell recorded, a paging method will be used to search the called MT.

In the existing GSM network, a two-tier location database structure is used to manage the locations of MTs [13], and the mobile switching centers (MSCs) are responsible for maintaining user locations. One of the MSCs maintains a location database, called *Home Location Register (HLR),* which keeps the client profiles and the locations of MTs. Other MSC maintain a *Visitor Location Register (VLR)* for the location information of the MTs, which are currently located within the cells responsible by the MSC. When a MT moves out of its current cell (or location area LA[2]) and enters into another cell, a new entry of its location will be added into the VLR for the new cell, and then the HRL will be updated accordingly. This two-tier architecture is simple and easy to implement. However, it is obvious that it is not scalable and will make the location database to be the bottleneck of the system when the system is supporting a large population of MTs. Because a MT is permanently associated to an HLR, the overheads for locating a MT can be very heavy if the mobility of the terminal is high.

The central problem in the design of methods for location management in PCS network is how to minimize the total cost for location update and paging. Since MTs are free to move within the service area, when a call arrives, if the location information of the called MT maintained in the location database is out-dated, the system needs to search a large number of cells in order to identify the real location of the called MT for connection. To minimize the searching cost, it is important that the mobile terminals generate location updates to refresh the data items for its location in the location database whenever their locations are different from their last reported locations. However, if a MT generates an update to report its new location whenever it moves from one cell to another, the location update cost could be very heavy. This is especially expensive when the MT's call-to-mobility ratio (CMR) is low and the cell size is small.

In this paper, we propose an *adaptive direction-based location update (ADBU)* scheme with an attempt to minimize the total location management cost. It is assumed that the movement of a MT can be divided into steps and each step has a destination. We use a Gauss-Markov process to model the movement of a MT in each step. The MT inspects its direction periodically and a location update will be generated when its direction change is greater than the direction threshold defined for the step. There are two goods reasons for choosing the MT's direction as the key parameter for generating location updates. Firstly, based on the movement direction, we can use a line-paging scheme to minimize the paging cost. Secondly, since each MT has a pre-defined destination in mind in each step, the next direction of movement of a MT is correlated with its previous movement direction. We calculate the optimal direction threshold for generating location updates such that the total location management cost can be minimized. Since it is difficult to determine when a step starts and ends, a feedback mechanism is then formulated to dynamically adjust the optimal threshold value for each step based on the moving patterns of the mobile terminal.

This paper is organized as followings. Section 2 is the related work on location management in PCS systems. In section 3, we give an overview on our proposed

---

[2] To simplify the discussion, we assume that each LA consists of one cell.

scheme. Section 4 presents a practical model, Gauss-Markov model and give the formulations to calculate the total location management cost. In section 5, we introduce a control feedback mechanism for determining the optimal direction threshold for each movement step. The simulation results are presented in Section 6. Section 7 concludes the paper.

2 Related Work

For location management in the PCS network, the whole service area is partitioned into location areas (LAs). The major task of location management is to update the location of a MT when it moves from one LA into another. In order to reduce the total cost in location management, various location update generation schemes based on the mobile terminals' call and mobility patterns have been proposed. They include the *time-based* [1,2, 3], the *movement-based* [4,5] and the *distance-based* [6] schemes. Numerical results in [7] show that the distance-based update scheme may give a better performance in terms of a lower total cost for location update and paging as comparing with the timer-based and movement-based schemes.

In order to further reduce the location management cost, various schemes by exploring the mobility patterns of MTs have been proposed. In the *predictive distance-based update* scheme [8], a MT shares its location and velocity information with the system, and the system predicts the future location of a MT when a call on the MT arrives, and the MT performs location update whenever its distance exceeds a threshold distance, measured from the predicted location. In the *adaptive distance-based update algorithm* [9], an adaptive algorithm is proposed for supporting arbitrary cell topologies and general distribution of cell residence time.

Most all of the schemes use the ring-paging scheme, in which the system pages the MT from its last updated location to the predicted location or the threshold distance ring by ring. It is obvious that if the uncertainty in location is larger, a larger number of cells will be paged and the paging cost will increase rapidly with the uncertainty in location of the mobile terminal. For example, in a hexagonal cellular network, the cell number that may be paged is: $1+3d(d+1)$, $d=0,1, \ldots$ where d is the distance threshold.

To minimize the total cost in location management, a *direction-based location update (DBLU)* scheme was proposed [10]. Its line-paging method can significantly reduce the paging cost comparing with the ring-paging scheme. The paging cost is linearly proportional to the uncertainty in location of the MT. Its paging strategy is sequentially to page the cells along its movement line, i.e. the system pages the MT's last updated cell first, then pages the two adjacent cells along the line of movement and so on. It is obvious that if the distance is larger, the number of cells to be paged could be large, especially when the cell size is getting more and more smaller.

Although DBLU uses a line-paging method, it assumes that the next direction of a mobile terminal as a random process. This assumption may not be true. In real systems, a MT usually travels with a destination in mind, especially within a short period of time [8, 12]. Therefore MT's locations are usually correlated with their current locations and their mobility patterns [11]. In this paper we propose an adaptive mobility location update scheme in which the MT's direction is considered for update generation. It is assumed that every MT has its own mobility pattern within a period of time. According to the correlation in movement direction, we calculate the optimal direction threshold for generating location updates such that the location management total cost is minimized.

3 Overview of Adaptive Direction Update Scheme

Before the introduction of the proposed ADBU scheme, we would like to restate our model assumptions. It is assumed that the system consists of a large number of MTs, which move free within the system service area, and the service area is divided into a set of inter-connected cells. The cells may have different sizes. The cells are connected to a MSC. It is assumed that the mobile terminals may have different mobility patterns. The mobility pattern of a mobile terminal *MT* may be described as a function of time, i.e., $f_m(MT, t)$ returns the location of mobile terminal *MT*, its movement direction and speed at time *t*. It is further assumed that the mobility pattern of a mobile terminal may change with time and its mobility pattern over a long period of time can be divided into a sequence of steps. The length of each step can be different and each step has a destination such as shown in Fig. 1. Since each step has a destination, the mobility of the mobile terminal in each step is correlated with time and we model it using the Gauss-Markov process.

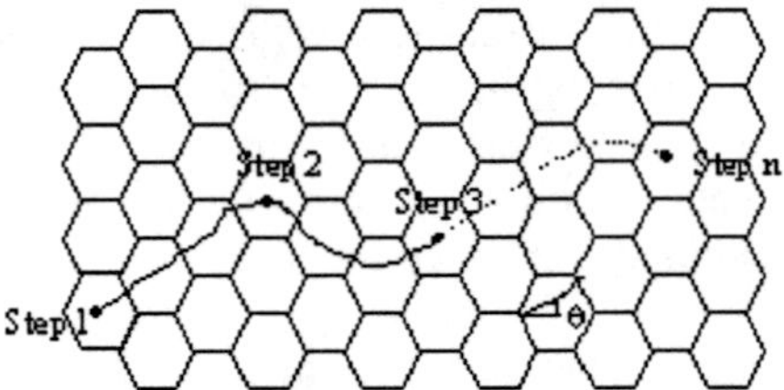

Fig. 1: MT moving in PCS network

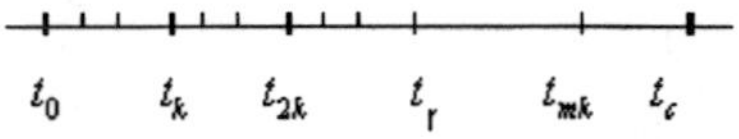

t_0 t_k t_{2k} t_r t_{mk} t_c

Fig. 2: A timing diagram

ADBU consists of three parts: location update generation, paging of mobile terminals and calculation of the optimal direction threshold for location updates.

Location Update Generation: While a MT is moving towards its destination, its movement direction may change with time. We define the direction by angle θ (Like the bottom of Fig. 1), which is calculated as the difference between the current movement direction and the movement direction at the time of last update. When θ is greater than the *direction threshold* (Φ) assigned to the mobile terminal, the system will update MT's location in the location database. After that this cell will be set as the initial location of the MT for detecting the MT's next direction.

Paging Strategy: In the existing PCS systems, when a call arrives, the system pages all the adjacent cells ring by ring to find the MT. Similar to DBLU, the paging used in ADBU is a line-paging scheme in which the cells along the movement direction of the called MT will be paged. If the speed is inspected at the same time [11], we can get an average speed (v_a) according to how the MT moves in the last previous of time. Assuming that the last location update is performed at time t_0, and the MT changes its direction at time *t*. Then, the displacement can be estimated as ($v_a(t-t_0)$). The system pages the MT in this cell first. If the MT is not found, then the system will page the two adjacent cells along the movement line and so on.

Calculation of Optimal Threshold: Different from DBLU, the definition of the direction threshold for location update generation is adaptively based on the movement directions of the MTs. In order to calculate the optimal direction threshold, we consider the total cost (C_{total}) in location management, $C_{total}=C_{LU}+C_{P,}$ where C_{LU} is the location update cost and C_P is the paging cost. C_{LU} depends on the number of location updates generated in a period time, and C_P depends on the number of cells being paged for searching the MT when it is being called. It is obvious that if the direction threshold is set to be small, the update cost will be high. On the other hand, if the direction threshold is set to be large, the paging cost will be heavy. Our objective is to choose the optimal direction threshold such that C_{total} is minimized.

Since the location of a MT is closely monitored if it is connecting with another MT, in the calculation of location management cost we only need to consider the time interval between the termination of the last call t_0 and the arrival of the next one t_c. In Fig. 2, we can see that each MT performs location inspection periodically, i.e. the MT examines its location and direction every k clock ticks (t_k). If the MT finds that its change in movement direction (θ) is greater than the direction threshold (Φ) at the mth examination, it will ask the system to update its location. However, the system will perform location update only if $t_{mk}<t_r$, where t_r is the time period that the MT resides in the cell. Therefore, if $\theta>\Phi$, but the MT is still in the same cell as its last update position, no location update will be performed. Thus the condition for location update is: $\theta>\Phi$, $t_{mk}>t_r$ and $t_{mk}<t_c$. Now we consider the paging cost. If we know the speed and the movement direction of a MT, we can calculate the displacement S_m for the time period, and the maximum number of cells to be paged is (S_m/S), where S is the cell size. Then, we can get the average location management cost for period t_c as:

$$C_{tc} = U \cdot P_r[\theta > \Phi] \cdot P_r[t_{mk} < t_c] \cdot P_r[t_{mk} > t_r] + P \cdot (S_m / S), \quad (1)$$

where U is the cost for processing a location update, P is the cost for paging one cell, and (S_m/S) takes the least integer which is larger than S_m/S.

We assume that call arrival to an MT is a Poisson process with mean λ_c, and the MT resides in the cell is a Poisson process with mean λ_r. Then the average total cos per unit time can be expressed as:

$$C_{total} = \lambda_r \cdot U \cdot P_r[\theta > \Phi] \cdot P_r[t_{mk} < t_c] \cdot P_r[t_{mk} > t_r] + \lambda_c \cdot P \cdot (S_m / S). \quad (2)$$

4 Model Formulation

4.1 Gauss-Markov Model

The future location of a MT before it reaches its destination in each step is correlated with its previous location, its speed and direction. Therefore, the random walk model is obviously not suitable to represent such kind of mobility pattern. If a mobile terminal is moving towards its destination, it is impossible that the mobile terminal has equal probability to move forward and backward [10]. A discrete Markov process is used in [10], and the direction of mobile has only three statements: backward, forward and changing direction. In this paper we assume that the mobile terminal's movement direction is a *Gauss-Markov model*, which is a more practice one for our system. It captures the essence of the correlation of the mobile terminal's direction in time. Gauss-Markov model is not just a Gauss process, which determines the distribution of direction amplitude. It is also a Markov process, which determines the transmission property of the process in time. In continuous-time, a stationary Gauss-Markov process [14] is described with a state differential equation:

$$\dot{\theta}(t) = -\beta\theta(t) + w(t), \tag{3}$$

where $\beta \geq 0$ determines the degree of memory in the mobility pattern and it is the correlation component. $w(t)$ is an independent, uncorrelated, and stationary Gauss process, with mean m_w=0 and the standard deviation σ_w=σ, presented as $N(0,\sigma^2)$. The statistics of a stationary Gauss-Markov process is completely described by the auto-correlation function $R(\tau)$ [14]:

$$R_\theta(\tau) = E[\theta(t), \theta(t+\tau)] = \sigma^2 e^{-\beta|\tau|}. \tag{4}$$

In this Gauss-Markov process, β determines the degree of correlation. For a given time interval τ, the correlation coefficient is large when β is small, and vice versa. The mean and deviation of direction $\theta(t)$ [15] are:

$$m_\theta(t) = 0, \qquad V_\theta(t) = \sigma^2 / (2\beta) \cdot (1 - e^{-2\beta t}). \tag{5}$$

Thus, the probability density function (PDF) of the direction is

$$p(\theta, t) = 1 \Big/ \sigma\sqrt{2\pi/\beta \cdot (1 - e^{-2\beta t})} \cdot \exp\left[\left(-\theta^2 \beta\right) / \left(2\sigma^2 (1 - e^{-2\beta t})\right)\right]. \tag{6}$$

In order to estimate how the direction of a mobile terminal changes, we define a discrete version of the movement direction [14] as:

$$\theta_{k+1} = e^{-\beta(t_{k+1} - t_k)}\theta_k + w_k. \tag{7}$$

We can see that if θ_{k+1} increases, β will become smaller for given values of θ_k and w_k. Assuming that $\Delta t = t_{k+1} - t_k$ is the clock-tick period. θ_0 is defined as the initial direction. As assumed in the above the MT examines its direction every k clock ticks, we can express θ_k explicitly in terms of the initial direction θ_0,

$$\theta_k = e^{-k\beta\Delta t}\theta_0 + \sum_{i=1}^{k-1} e^{-\beta(k-i-1)\Delta t} w_i, \tag{8}$$

where w_i, i=1,2,..., k-1, present a discrete Gauss noise $N(0,\sigma^2)$.

4.2 Location Tracking

Since the MT inspects its direction every $t_k = k \cdot \Delta t$, we can estimate its displacement in X and Y coordinates respectively in $k \cdot \Delta t$ as followings:

$$s_{xi} = v \cdot k \cdot \Delta t \cdot \cos\theta_k, \quad s_{yi} = v \cdot k \cdot \Delta t \cdot \sin\theta_k. \tag{9}$$

To simplify the equations, we transform the coordinate axes to make θ_0 zero at initial. We assume that the MT finds that the change in its movement direction is greater than the direction threshold at its mth inspection. Then the displacement from its last updated location is:

$$S_m = \sqrt{\left(\sum_{i=0}^{m} s_{xi}\right)^2 + \left(\sum_{i=0}^{m} s_{yi}\right)^2} . \tag{10}$$

4.3 Cost Evaluation of the Direction-Based Scheme

Since we assume that the call arrival and the residence time in a cell are Poisson processes with means λ_c and λ_r respectively, then the density functions of t_c and t_r are:

$$f_c(t) = \lambda_c e^{-\lambda_c t}, \quad f_r(t) = \lambda_r e^{-\lambda_r t} . \tag{11}$$

Then,

$$P_r[t_{mk} > t_r] = \int_0^{t_{mk}} \lambda_r e^{-\lambda_r t_r} dt_r = 1 - e^{-\lambda_r t_{mk}}, \quad P_r[t_{mk} < t_c] = e^{-\lambda_c t_{mk}} , \tag{12}$$

$$P_r[\theta > \Phi] = \int_{2l\pi+\Phi}^{2l\pi+2\pi-\Phi} p(\theta, t) d\theta. \tag{13}$$

Substituting (10), (12) and (13) into (2), we can calculate the total cost,

$$C_{total} = \lambda_r \cdot U \cdot \int_{2l\pi+\Phi}^{2l\pi+2\pi-\Phi} p(\theta, t) d\theta \cdot e^{-\lambda_c t_{mk}} \cdot \left(1 - e^{-\lambda_r t_{mk}}\right) + \lambda_c \cdot P \cdot \left(S_m / S\right) . \tag{14}$$

As shown in equation (14), C_{total} is determined by the cell residence rate λ_r, the call arrival rate λ_c, the cost of every location update U, the cost of paging one cell P, the probability of $\theta > \Phi$, $t_{mk} > t_r$, $t_{mk} < t_c$, and the number of cells to be paged.

5 An Adaptive Direction-Based Location Update Scheme

Since it is assumed that a mobile terminal has its own mobility pattern in each step, in each step there will be an optimal direction threshold Φ. However, it is difficult to predict when a step ends and when the next step starts. A new threshold may be needed after each location update if the mobility pattern of a mobile terminal has changed as it may enter into another step. Since it is difficult to predict when a MT changes it mobility pattern, we use a feedback control mechanism for the determining the optimal direction threshold for each step [16].

At the beginning, we assign an initial value to the direction threshold Φ say at $\pi/4$. The MT inspects its direction θ periodically. If $\theta \geq \Phi$, the system will update the location of the MT. The system then re-computes the new direction threshold Φ according to how the MT moves in the last previous of time. In the next inspection, this Φ will be set as the new direction threshold.

We continue to use the Gauss-Markov model to model the movement of a MT. From equation (3), we know that β determines the degree of memory in the mobility pattern. The direction threshold Φ depends on β. β changes with the movement model, and different movement models have different β values, and different optimal direction thresholds. Now we estimate β first. Based on β, we can get Φ.

As presented in Section 4, MT inspects it direction every $k \cdot \Delta t$ time period. Because at epoch $m \cdot k \cdot \Delta t$, MT finds its change in movement direction is greater than the direction threshold, so at epoch $k \cdot \Delta t$, $2k \cdot \Delta t$, $3k \cdot \Delta t$... $mk \cdot \Delta t$, the directions of the MT are known. They are θ_1, θ_2... θ_m. From equation (8), we can get:

$$\sum_{i=1}^{k-1} e^{-\beta(k-i-1)\Delta t} \cdot w_{i1} = \theta_2 - e^{-\beta k \Delta t} \cdot \theta_1, \quad \dots$$
$$\sum_{i=1}^{k-1} e^{-\beta(k-i-1)\Delta t} \cdot w_{i(m-1)} = \theta_m - e^{-\beta k \Delta t} \cdot \theta_{m-1}, \tag{15}$$

where w_i, i=1,2,..., k-1, are independent, discrete Gauss noise, $N(0,\sigma^2)$. Accumulating equation (15) and substituting the known values, we can solve the equation and get β.

6 Numerical Results and Comparisons

In this section, we report the analysis of the performance of the proposed update scheme, ADBU, and compare it with the distance-based (DB) method with a threshold distance d=1, and the direction-based update (DBLU) method proposed in [10]. In our simulation model, we assume that the call arrival time and the residence time in a cell follow Poisson distribution with mean λ_c and λ_r, respectively, and the change in movement direction is a Gauss-Markov process.

Table 1. Simulation Setting

Cell residence rate λ_r	0.05	Call arrival rate λ_c	0.2
Inspect time interval k	50	Clock tick Δt	0.01
Correlation coherent β	0.1	Standard deviation σ	0.2
Cost of one location update U	10	Cost of paging one cell P	5
Cell size S	5	Average speed v	1

If not mentioned, the parameters will take the values in Table 1. We have performed two sets of experiments. The first set of experiments investigates the total cost in ADBU when different values of direction threshold are used. Different values of β and CMR have been tested. In the second set of experiments, we compare ADBU with DBLU and DB under different parameter settings.

Fig. 3 shows the total location management cost of ADBU when the direction threshold is varied with β=(0.01, 0.1, 1.0). To calculate the total location management cost, we use equation (14), where $t_{mk}=m \cdot k \cdot \Delta t$. We can see that the total cost is large when the direction threshold value, Φ, is very small or very large. It is because when the direction threshold Φ is small, a large number of location updates are generated. On the other hand, when Φ is large, although the location update generation frequency is low, it will cause a high paging cost. As can be seen in Fig. 3, different values of β have different optimal Φ values. It is because when β is large, the directions of the mobile terminals change more smoothly. Thus the optimal Φ is smaller. Fig. 4 shows the results when CMR = (10^1, 10^0, 10^{-1}). It can be seen that when CMR is small, i.e., 10^{-1}, the optimal direction threshold will be large. It means that a frequent update is unnecessary when CMR is small.

Fig. 5 shows the total location management cost of the three schemes when λ_c is changed from $10^{-2.4}$ to 10^0. It can be seen that for the three schemes, C_{total} increases with λ_c. In DB, even when λ_c is small, the total cost is high and is much higher than DBLU and ADBU. It is because in DB the paging cost is heavy even when λ_c is small As shown in Fig. 5, the performance of ADBU is consistently better than DBLU for different λ_c values, and λ_c is larger ADBU is better. Fig. 6 shows the results when λ_r is varied from $10^{-2.4}$ to 10^0, with $\beta=0.04$. Both ADBU and DBLU are much better than DB with ADBU slightly better than DBLU. However when λ_r is large, the difference between ADBU and DBLU is small. It is because when λ_r is larger, the number of location update is smaller. Fig. 7 shows the results with CMR from $10^{-1.5}$ to $10^{1.5}$. Consistent with the results shown in Fig. 4, for the three schemes, when CMR is increased, the total cost increases also. The performance of ADBU is significantly better than both DBLU and DB. When CMR is larger, the performance of ADBU is better. Fig. 8 shows the results when the cost of paging one cell P is changed from 1 to 60, with $\lambda_r=\lambda_c=0.05$. It can be seen that the performance of ADBU is significantly better than DBLU and DB. As P increased, the total cost of DBLU is increased more rapidly than ADBU.

7 Conclusions

Location management plays an important role in the next generation PCS systems. It can ensure that the system can find the mobile terminals efficiently and minimize the total location management cost. In this paper, we study how to reduce the total location update cost and paging cost using an adaptive direction-based location update method, which uses a line-paging scheme to search the mobile terminals. Usually a mobile terminal moves to a destination in mind and its mobility pattern is correlated with its previous direction in a period time. To suit for this practical model we presented an ADBU scheme for location management based on Gauss-Markov to model the mobile terminal's movement direction. The simulation results show that the proposed ADBU method can give a better performance than both the distance-based method and the DBLU method under different system settings.

References

1. Leonardo P. Araujo and J. R. Boisson de Marca.: Paging and Location Update Algorithms for Cellular Systems. IEEE Trans. on Vehicular Technology, vol. 49, no. 5, Sep. 2000
2. Dong-Jun Lee and Dong-ho Cho.: On Optimum Timer Value of Area and Timer-based Location Registration Scheme. IEEE Communication Letters, vol. 5, no. 4, April 2001
3. C. Rose.: Minimizing the average cost of paging and registration: A timer-based method. ACM/Baltzer J. Wireless Networks (1996), vol.2, No.2, 109-116.
4. I.F. Akyildiz, J.S. Ho, and Y.B. Lin. Movement-based location update and selective paging for PCS Networks. IEEE/ACM Transactions on Networking, vol.4, 629-638, Aug. 1996.
5. Jie Li, Hisao Kameda, and Keqin Li. Optimal dynamic mobility management for PCS networks, IEEE/ACM Transactions on Networking, vol. 8, no. 3, June 2000.
6. Ian F. Akyildiz, Joseph S.M.Ho. A Mobile User Location update and Paging Mechanism Under Delay Constraints. ACM/Baltzer Wireless Networks, vol.1, no.4, 413-425, 1995.
7. A. Bar-Noy, I. Kessler, and M. Sidi. Mobile users: To update or not to update?. ACM/Baltzer J.Wireless Networks, vol.1, no.2, 175-195, July 1995.
8. Ben Liang, Zygmunt J. Haas. Predictive Distance-based Mobility Management for PCS Networks. in Proceedings of IEEE INFOCOM'99, New York, NY, March 21-25, 1999.
9. W.S. Wong, Victor C.M. Leung. An adaptive Distance-Based Location Update Algorithm for Next Generation PCS Networks. IEEE Journal on Selected Areas in Com., 2001.
10. H.W. Hwang, M.F. Chang, and C.C. Tseng. A Direction-Based Location Update Scheme with a Line-Paging Strategy for PCS Networks. IEEE Com. Letters, vol. 4, 149-151, 2000.
11. Yigal Bejerano, Israel Cidon. Efficient Location Management Based on Moving Location Areas, IEEE INFOCOM 2001.
12. Evaggelia Pitoura, George Samaras. Locating Objects in Mobile Computing. IEEE Transactions on Knowledge and Data Engineering, vol. 13, no. 4, July/August 2001

13. Il Han, Dong-ho Cho. Group Location Tracking Based on Representative Identity and Virtual VLR for Transportation Systems. IEEE Communication Letters, vol.5, no. 8, 2001
14. A.Gelb, Applied Optimal Estimation, The M.I.T Press, 1974.
15. J. Medhi, Stochastic processes, Wiley Eastern Limited, 1982.
16. M.J. Grimble, Adaptive Estimation and Control, Prentice Hall, 1991.

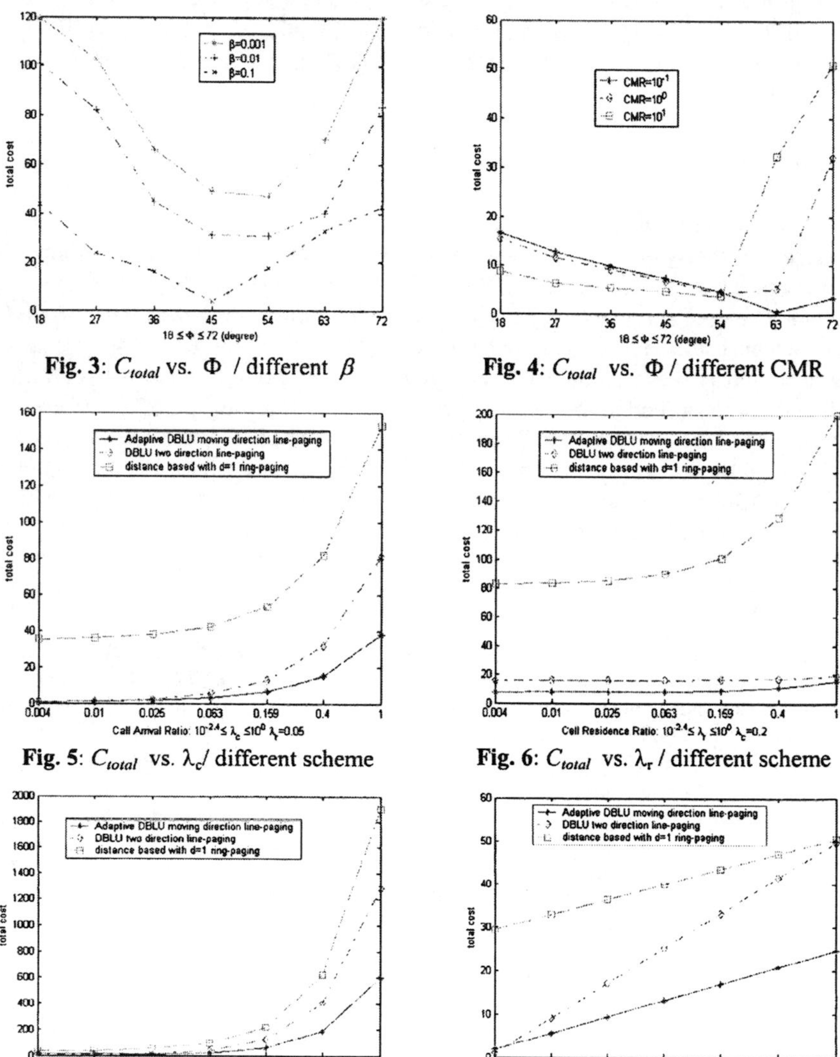

Fig. 3: C_{total} vs. Φ / different β

Fig. 4: C_{total} vs. Φ / different CMR

Fig. 5: C_{total} vs. λ_c/ different scheme

Fig. 6: C_{total} vs. λ_r / different scheme

Fig. 7: C_{total} vs. CMR /different scheme

Fig. 8: C_{total} vs. P / different scheme

ADEES: An Adaptable and Extensible Event Based Infrastructure

Genoveva Vargas-Solar and Christine Collet

IMAG-LSR, University of Grenoble, BP 72 38402 Saint-Martin d'Hères, France.
{Genoveva.Vargas, Christine.Collet}@imag.fr

Abstract. This paper describes ADEES, an open and evolutionary event-based architecture to develop complex distributed information systems. Different from most existing event supports that provide limited event description models and fixed management models, ADEES can be extended and customized on a per-application basis. It is not another "one-size-fits-all" event manager! It is used to generate event managers adopted by components to produce and consume events according to the event description and event management models they need (e.g. event as anonymous messages, specific composite event operators, synchronous/asynchronous detection, push/pull protocol).
The second aspect concerns the ability of a event service and event managers to reconfigure and adapt themselves with respect to application requirements and to their environment. Adaptability and extensibility is achieved, thanks to meta-programming and reflection techniques.

1 Introduction

Large-scale distributed information systems built out of heterogeneous components, using petabytes of structured, semi-structured or non-structured data and accessed by thousands of users are now a reality. Industrial and research activities are currently being carried out to develop suitable tools and related runtime infrastructures for supporting such systems. Middleware has emerged as an important architectural component and event-based architectures acquire a new impetus. Within such infrastructures, components cooperate by sending and receiving events, a particular form of message that has different semantics when considering communication protocols [5,10], distributed systems [8], middle-ware [8,3,7], or active databases [9].

The diversity of proposals show the potential and relevance of event-based infrastructures. However, existing technology suffers from several drawbacks. Event-based communication such as in Java must be hard coded; no separate event service module for managing events is provided. Middleware solutions encourage the specification of layer based architectures where the event service is embedded within the application architecture. In both approaches event management is reduced to event ordering and communication protocols. Other aspects of event management such as event persistence and composition must be implemented at the application level. In many cases, management policies are

R. Cicchetti et al. (Eds.): DEXA 2002, LNCS 2453, pp. 423–432, 2002.

implemented by different services. For example, CORBA [8] provides at least three services for managing event based asynchronous communication: a notification service, a message service and an event service.

Nevertheless, specific aspects of event management are to retain depending on the approaches: pull/push communication protocols, component oriented architectures and active database event management models. Yet there are several open issues that need to be addressed to integrate all these aspects in a single proposal and further to provide adaptable, extensible and plug and play event managers to develop complex information systems.

This paper introduces ADEES (ADaptable and Extensible Event Service), a meta event service suitable to develop a wide range of event managers supporting flexible cooperation and integration of distributed autonomous components at a middleware level. It describes how ADEES provides adaptability and extensibility to event management and how to build and exploit a service and its event managers. It also presents some experiences in using ADEES to develop Open and Distributed Active Systems (ODAS systems) [2].

Consistently the rest of the paper is organized as follows. Section 2 presents ADEES basic concepts and architecture considering an application example. Section 3 details how adaptable event managers are specified. Section 4 describes how an event service can be specialized and consequently the event managers it may support. Section 5 shows how event services and managers are specified and generated using ADEES. It also discusses some implementation and experience issues. Section 6 compares our proposal with other existing works. Finally, Section 7 concludes this paper and introduces some on-going and future research directions.

2 A Quick Tour of ADEES

Let us consider a financial system for buying and selling actions according to accounts credit availability and the financial market evolution. The system is composed of four components: A Bank Server that manages accounts and that can be accessed for executing banking operations. A Stock Exchange Server that can be accessed for buying and selling actions. It notifies stock exchange information. Financial Information Servers that manage histories about current economical indicators of companies and also indicators of specific areas. Such servers are refreshed periodically so that they can provide reliable information. An E-Trader application that provides information to investors such as stock exchange market evolution, capital state, financial transactions executed during the day. It also provides interfaces for accessing the bank and the stock exchange servers.

Situations are described by events such as *Telecom actions UpwardTrend* (e_1), *the Stock exchange session opens/closes* (e_2), *A bank account credit was updated* (e_3), *A purchase operation was executed* (e_4). Events are produced and consumed by the system components (bank and stock exchange servers, the E-Trader application). For instance, an E-Trader consumes events concerning actions (e.g., *Telecom actions UpwardTrend*) produced by the Stock Exchange Server.

Components have different characteristics and needs with respect to event production and consumption. For example, the Stock Exchange Server notifies its events explicitly, events representing banking operations, in contrast, are detected asynchronously. Similarly, the E-Trader consumes events representing the financial market as soon as they are produced, while Financial Information Servers wait until the end of the stock exchange session ([17:00]) to consume such events.

2.1 Event Based Communication with Managers

Figure 1 illustrates event based communication using an event service and its managers (built using ADEES). Two event managers EM_1 and EM_2 have been specialized for interacting with the financial application components. Both event managers are under the control of an Event Service Manager (ESM). The Bank Server produces events e_3 that are detected asynchronously by EM_1. The Stock Exchange Server signals events e_1, e_2 and e_4 explicitly to EM_2. Events consumed by the E-Trader and the Financial Information Servers are notified explicitly by the managers at different instants. For example, the E-Trader receives events concerning the stock exchange as soon as they are produced. Events representing banking operations arrive at the end of the day.

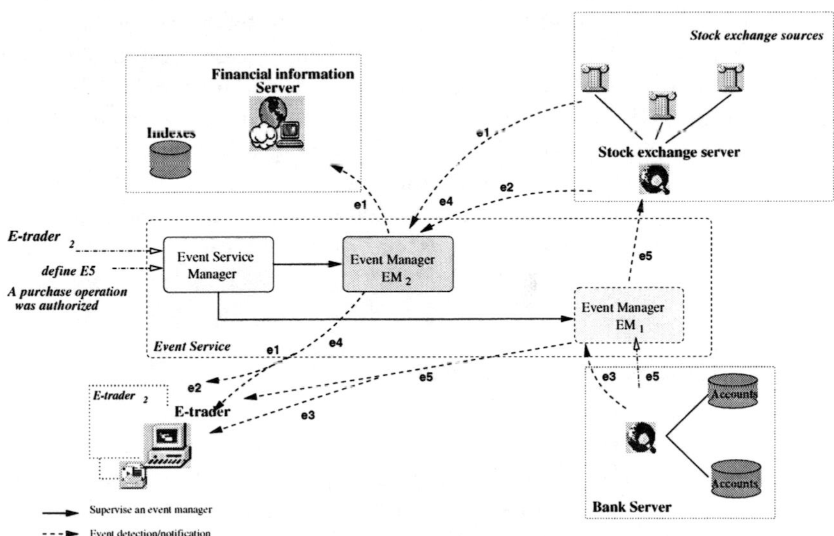

Fig. 1. Event based communication using an event service

Eventually a new E-Trader can connect to the system. According to the events he/she requires the Event Service puts him/her in contact with the corresponding event managers. Finally, traders may decide to add a new event type E_5 (*a purchase has been authorized by the bank*) to be notified as soon as produced.

This operation is done at the ESM level that handles the new definition and notifies it to the event manager EM_2. Under the control of the ESM, EM_2 has to be reconfigured for managing events of type E_5.

2.2 General Architecture of an Event Service

An event service built using ADEES is represented by an event service manager (ESM) and the event managers it monitors. Provided a schema, (i.e., an event type model and an event management model) the service (its ESM) generates an event manager. This manager can be used by a set of clients to specify instances of the underlying schema, i.e., types of events it is supposed to produce or consume and their associated management policies.

An ESM also supervises managers execution. First it provides means to specify, store and manage schemata and instances, together with deployment strategies for the specified event managers. Then, for each event manager specification, the ESM generates components for event detection, production and notification. It also defines listeners that will serve as proxies between the manager and subscribed producers (for event detection) and consumers (for event notification). According to a specific deployment strategy, the manager connects the client with a new listener or with an existing one.

A schema characterizes an event manager that can accept and manage different instances defined by producers and consumers that subscribe to it. Instances describe event types the manager is interested in and associated management policies used to manage events of those types (static adaptability). They can be then modified and added dynamically at execution time (dynamic adaptability).

Managers of a service share the same way of describing event type and management models: their schemata are described with respect to the same event type and event management meta-models. Schemata are instances of those meta-models and can be then modified to extend or reduce the functionalities of an event service and its managers (extensibility).

3 Adaptable Event Managers

Events produced and consumed by an event manager have to be characterized by event types and event management policies, respectively described using an event type model (i.e. concepts to describe event types) and a management model (i.e., concepts to describe event management policies). Both models are defined in a schema supported by the event manager. Components that want to share a schema subscribe themselves to the corresponding event manager as event producers and consumers. When subscribing to an event manager, a client (a producer or a consumer) specifies an *instance* (i.e., an event type and its associated management policies) using the concepts of the models given in the underlying schema. Each client subscribes several instances, one for each event type produced or consumed.

3.1 Event Manager Schema

A schema supported by an event manager associates an event type model with an event management model. It also includes a behavior control model that specifies policies for activating and deactivating event management (e.g., activate one or several types for one or several clients). The schema of our event manager EM_1 example can be defined as: $\mathcal{S} : \langle \varepsilon\tau_1, \varepsilon\mu_1 \rangle$ where $\varepsilon\tau_1$ is an event type model and $\varepsilon\mu_1$, an event management model.

Event Type Model Gives concepts and general structures used to describe event types that can be processed by a manager. For example, event types used in our financial application can be described using the event type model:

$$\varepsilon\tau_1 = \langle \text{ type name: string, } \{\langle \text{ variable name: } \{\text{real, integer, string}\}\rangle\}\rangle$$

As shown in the above description, the model characterizes event types as tuples of two elements: an event type name (i.e., a string); and a content (i.e., a set of tuples describing a variable name and its associated type). Using $\varepsilon\tau_1$, event types *Telecom Actions UpwardTrend* (e_1), *a bank account credit has been updated* (e_3) are expressed as follows :

ActionsUpwardTrend, {[price: real, domain: string, pays: string]}
where domain = 'Telecom' (e_1)

UpdateAccount, {[accid: string, owner: string, amount: real, date: string]} (e_3)

Note that where is a selection operator provided by $\varepsilon\tau_1$ to express constraints on the content of the set {[price: real, domain: string, pays: string]}.

Event Management Model An event management model describes the space of policies that can be used for managing events and the interfaces exported by a manager to control its execution. It is defined as dimensions chosen from a set of predefined ones that have been identified from an event management taxomony proposed in [11]. A dimension represents an aspect of the event management model (i.e., detection, production, notification, history management) and of management administration policies (i.e., management (de)activation, deployment strategies, operations associated to dimensions). Each dimension takes its value from a specific domain.

3.2 Instance

An instance comprises an event type and a management model. An Event Type is defined as an instance of an Event Type Model. The model describes the structure of event types: the way event type names are built and the type of information it can contain. A Management Model associates values to detection, production, notification dimensions (policies). Event management aspects appear as domain values. For a given producer or consumer and a given event type, the corresponding dimensions must have a unique value. Such a value is chosen from the domain associated to each dimension of the corresponding schema. In this way producers and consumers can specify different policies to be used to manage each of the event types they produce and/or consume.

Indeed, two consumers can receive events of the same type but managed using different policies. Furthermore, the same consumer or producer can receive/produce its event types using different policies.

3.3 Adaptability

Adaptability denotes the capability of an event manager to adapt its behavior with respect to a set of clients. Providing a schema and the possibility to define instances at subscription time ensures a first level of adaptability to the event manager. Another level of adaptability is provided as event managers are able to dynamically activate, deactivate and update instances (modify the event type and values associated to dimensions of the management model).

Instance activation is done with respect to a deployment strategy implemented by the manager. Clients interact with the event manager through listeners that implement schema instances. When a schema instance is activated, listeners are chosen or generated for managing it. Choosing or reusing a listener depends on the deployment strategy specified in an instance. Deployment strategies are out of the scope of this paper, more details can be found in [11]. Instances deactivation is executed by the event manager that contacts the listener, either to unsubscribe the client from its list or to disconnect it. The manager deactivates the processing of the corresponding instance.

According to the type of modification updates are immediate or differed. Management rules describing update execution policies are defined at the service level and they are configured when an Event Service Manager is created [11].

4 Extensible Event Managers

As they evolve, applications can modify and increase their requirements concerning event management. Thus, it must be possible to specialize models implemented by a manager and authorize the definition of new event types, the specification of new composition operators and new management policies. Also updates on models should be enabled. Consequently, models have been considered as data that must be described, materialized and managed by an event service. Meta-models are the core of ADEES. Due to the lack of space, we only describe these models informally. A formal specification can be found in [11].

4.1 Event Type and Management Meta-models

The event type meta-model is composed of two main meta-classes (abstract data types): EventType and Operator. An event type describes the structure of event names and it can be associated to information described by a set *Delta*. Each element of the set is represented by the meta-class Delta of the form $\langle varname : string, vartype : Type\rangle$, where *varname* is a string and *vartype* denotes basic data types (*Type*) such as integer, real, string, etc.

Operator is a data type that describes the type of operators that can be associated to an event type. It characterizes an operator as a function described by a symbol, a domain, a codomain and an Implementation. Domain and codomain are defined as Cartesian products of basic data types (integer, real, etc.) and EventType. The implementation can be defined in a formal language (e.g., lambda calculus) or in a specific programming language. In both cases, we suppose that it is correct so, from the meta-model point of view, it is a black box.

An event management meta-model characterizes event management phases (i.e., detection, production, notification, history management and administration) by *dimensions* associated to *values*. A value has an associated *implementation* that specifies its semantics. Dimensions are grouped into *components*. Each component represents an event management phase. Meta-classes are used to represent such elements (Metamodel, Component, Dimension). They characterize methods for adding and deleting components from a meta-model, dimensions from a component and values from a dimension (extensibility). The meta-model can be instantiated to define different event management models by specifying the components they consist of.

4.2 Extensibility

Extensibility denotes the capability of a service and its managers to extend and reduce their functionalities. It is controlled by the ESM, that can receive explicit requests from clients or detect situations that trigger schema updates. A first level of extensibility is provided by modifying statically existing schemata for defining new managers. Meta-models ensure consistent extensibility, that is to say, they ensure that updates on schemata are done with respect to meta-models dimensions.

A second level of extensibility is provided by the possibility to modify dynamically the schema of an existing manager. Updates can be done on type and management models that compose a schema. An event type model can be modified by adding, deleting and updating event type and operator implementations. At the manager level, updates in the schema imply the (de)activation of instances and the reconfiguration of their internal components (e.g., objects that implement new operators must be added and/or deleted). A management model is updated by adding, modifying and deleting values associated to dimensions. Such operations imply the modification of managers internal components and listeners, that must add, substitute or delete objects implementing those functionalities. According to the nature of the updates required, the execution of these operations can be immediate or differed to a specific check point. Updates execution policies are specified when the ESM is configured.

Extensibility at the event service level is materialized by meta-models updates. For example, it is possible to modify the structure of the EventType (e.g., change the types associated to the Delta attributes). Also, dimensions and components can be added and deleted to the management meta-model. For example, consider a meta-model that characterizes models that do not include event history management. New dimensions can be added to such a meta-model for describing the new functionality. This implies that new managers specified in the service will manage event histories but existing managers functionalities must be extended too. These operations cause the modification of the ESM and its associated managers.

5 Building a Service and Its Managers

ADEES mainly provides a kernel for programming an event service, i.e. its Event Service Manager (ESM). A programmer can configure specific parameters of an ESM: (1) The generic meta-model implemented by ADEES. (2) Policies to deploy generated managers. (3) Policies used for managing event managers.

5.1 Event Service General Architecture

The general architecture of an ESM consists of components that can be accessed by clients and managers through interfaces. Internally, an ESM is composed of three main components. (1) Instantiation: It receives a schema and its instances and instantiates an event manager given a schema, a set of instances an a deployment strategy. (2) Generation: Given a schema, its instances and a deployment strategy, this component generates an event manager component based on rules that specify the way schema and instances are integrated within the event manager component. (3) Subscription: Puts in contact clients with an event manager according to their associated schema instances and interacts with them for executing adaption requests.

5.2 Event Manager

An event manager is built as a set of components and two interfaces to communicate with its ESM and to execute adaption operations. Components implement manager functionalities. (1) Clients connection: Interaction between clients and managers is implemented by listeners. A connection component generates listeners that implement functionalities specified in schema instances. (2) Communication: Listeners implement communication policies for detecting and notifying events. Those concerning detection are managed by detectors, and those concerning notification by notifiers. According to a chosen deployment strategy, one or several clients can be connected to the same or different detectors or notifiers. (3) Management: Event composition, ordering, history management and notification is implemented by a management component. Each component provides an interface for modifying its structure when policies are activated or deactivated. (4) Execution: An execution engine monitors a manager execution and notifies adaptability and extensibility requests to management components. It interacts with the ESM through an interface that enables connection and disconnection of event managers.

6 Related Work

The event-based style and related technology has received a new impetus following the explosive development of Internet. The concept of event service has acquired different meanings and it is often difficult to identify the applicability of every single technology and the added value with respect to well known technologies.

TIB/Rendezvous [5] and USENET News system [10] are distributed infrastructures that offer an event notification service. The event services are similar to ours in the sense that they are independent components that support applications integration. However, our service compiles event processing strategies that are spread out in these products (subscription, filtering) to offer a general event management toolkit.

Distributed event-based infrastructures are frameworks of abstract classes (or interfaces) in an object oriented language [3,8]. The event service is not an independent component, rather it is embedded in objects code. Consequently, tuning components implies hard coding and weak re-usability possibilities. Our approach integrates communication protocols (pull/push) as defined by [8] but it provides an event processing layer to offer facilities (i.e., ordering, composing, storing) within a configurable environment.

Concerning interaction with clients, CORBA event service [8] and MOM [7] are channel based infrastructures similar to reliable multicast between channels and multicast addresses. TIBCO and USENET [5,10] are subject-based services that use an evolved form of channel based subscription (i.e., client addresses are determined by the subject). Clients can express interest in many subjects (channels) by specifying some form of expressions that are evaluated against the subject of an event. Our service adopts subject based interaction using event types that contain information about their conditions of production and filters associated to this information.

Similar to active services such as C^2offein [6], and FRAMBOISE [4] our work aims at specifying a service to extend classical DBMS functionalities without making the "huge black box" grow indefinitely. Unlike to our approach, they do not focus on an event service that interacts with "any" reactive component. Finally, as us they define adaptable services (statically) but they do not stress on strategies to provide extensibility.

7 Conclusion

The main contribution of our work is to provide ADEES an event service used to specify, generate and execute adaptable and extensible event managers that may process events in different contexts – i.e., (non) transactional, centralized, distributed, etc. Rather than providing "one-fits-all" managers and services, producers and consumers can tune the required functionalities by describing the models they need, the events they are interested in and the policies that must be used to detect, order, compose and notify events.

The first version of ADEES has been implemented using CORBA as underlying infrastructure for encapsulating distribution aspects but also for ensuring low level event communication between event managers and their clients (i.e., producers and consumers). We currently pursue the implementation of our event service and evaluate it with respect to performance requirements.

Concerning experiences in using ADEES, we already built Open Distributed Active Systems (ODAS) comprised of event managers and rule managers that can be easily deployed on the network [2]. ODAS systems have been used for our financial example. We are also currently using it to build a dynamic workflow management system used in Web-based electronic commerce applications and to ensure their dynamic evolution. More generally we plan to use it to develop services for supporting novel programming and execution environments that facilitate the structuring and cooperation of heterogeneous components [1].

References

1. C. Collet. The NODS Project: Networked Open Database Services. In *Proc. of the 14th European Conference on Object-Oriented Programming (ECOOP 2000)-Symposium on Objects and Databases*, Cannes, France, June 2000. http://www-lsr.imag.fr/Les.Groupes/storm/NODS/index.html.
2. C. Collet, G. Vargas-Solar, and H. Grazziotin-Ribeiro. Open active services for data-intensive distributed applications. In *Proceedings of the International Database Engineering and Applications Symposium, IDEAS'2000*, Yokahama-Japan, September 2000. IEEE.
3. Flanagan, editor. *JAVA in a nutshell.* O'Reilly, 1997. O'Reilly andssociates, Inc.
4. H. Frithschi, S. Gatziu, and K.R. Dittrich. Framboise – an approach to construct active database mechanisms. Technical Report 97.04, Department of Computer Science, University of Zurich, Zurich, April 1997.
5. TIBCO Inc. Rendezvous information bus, 1996. http://www.rv.tibco.com/rvwhitepaper.html.
6. A. Koschel, R. Kramer, G. Bültzingslöwen, T. Bleibel, P. Krumlinde, S. Schmuck, and C. Wein. Configuration Active Functionality for CORBA. In *Proceedings of the ECOOP97 Workshop*, Jyväskulä, Finnland, June 1997.
7. MOMA Educational Information: A Middleware Taxonomy. http://www.moma-inc.org/, 1998. White paper.
8. OMG, editor. *The Common Object Request Broker Architecture and Specification.* Object Management Group, 1997.
9. N. W. Paton. *Active Rules for Databases.* Springer Verlag, 1998.
10. Internet Requests For Comments (RFC)977, February 1986.
11. G. Vargas-Solar. *Service d'événements flexible pour l'intégration d'applications bases de données réparties.* PhD thesis, Université Joseph Fourier, Grenoble, France, december 2000.

Using J-Pruning to Reduce Overfitting of Classification Rules in Noisy Domains

Max Bramer

Faculty of Technology, University of Portsmouth, UK
Max.Bramer@bcs.org.uk
http://www.btinternet.com/~Max.Bramer

Abstract. The automatic induction of classification rules from examples is an important technique used in data mining. One of the problems encountered is the overfitting of rules to training data. This paper describes a means of reducing overfitting known as *J-pruning*, based on the *J-measure*, an information theoretic means of quantifying the information content of a rule, and examines its effectiveness in the presence of noisy data for two rule induction algorithms: one where the rules are generated via the intermediate representation of a decision tree and one where rules are generated directly from examples.

1 Introduction

The growing commercial importance of knowledge discovery and data mining techniques has stimulated new interest in the automatic induction of classification rules from examples, a field in which research can be traced back at least as far as the mid-1960s [1]. Most work in this field to date has concentrated on generating classification rules in the intermediate form of a decision tree using variants of the TDIDT (Top-Down Induction of Decision Trees) algorithm [2]. An alternative approach, which generates classification rules directly from examples, is Prism [3,4].

A problem that arises with all methods of generating classification rules is that of *overfitting* to the training data. In some cases this can result in excessively large rule sets and/or rules with very low predictive power for previously unseen data.

A method for reducing overfitting in classification rules known as *J*-pruning has previously been reported [5]. The method makes use of the value of the *J-measure*, an information theoretic means of quantifying the information content of a rule. The rules are *pre-pruned*, i.e. pruned as they are being generated.

In this paper the robustness of this technique in the presence of noise is examined. A comparison is made between the results obtained from the unpruned and J-pruned versions of both TDIDT and Prism for varying levels of noise added in a systematic fashion to three datasets from the UCI Repository of Machine Learning Datasets [6].

The use of J-pruning leads in all cases to a reduction in the number of rules generated and in many cases to an increase in predictive accuracy.

R. Cicchetti et al. (Eds.): DEXA 2002, LNCS 2453, pp. 433–442, 2002.

2 Automatic Induction of Classification Rules from Examples

2.1 Basic Terminology

It is assumed that there is a universe of *objects*, each of which belongs to one of a set of mutually exclusive *classes*. Objects are described by the values of a number of their *attributes*. There is a two-dimensional table of examples, known as a *training set*, each row of which (an *instance*) comprises the values of the attributes and the corresponding classification for a single object. The aim is to develop classification rules that enable the class to which any object in an unseen *test set* of further instances belongs to be determined from the values of its attributes. It will be assumed that the rules are to be in propositional form, each comprising a conjunction of *terms*, such as

IF x=a AND y=b AND z>34.5 AND w=k THEN Class=3

2.2 Top-Down Induction of Decision Trees

Many systems have been developed to derive classification rules of the above kind from a training set. Most (but not all) do so via the intermediate form of a decision tree constructed using a variant of the TDIDT (top-down induction of decision trees) algorithm given in Figure 1 below.

IF all cases in the training set belong to the same class
  THEN return the value of the class
ELSE

  (a) Select an attribute A to *split* on *
  (b) Sort the instances in the training set into non-empty subsets, one for each value of attribute A
  (c) Return a tree with one branch for each subset, each branch having a descendant subtree or a class value produced by applying the algorithm recursively for each subset in turn.

* When selecting attributes at step (a) the same attribute must not be selected more than once in any branch.

Fig. 1. The TDIDT Tree Generation Algorithm

The induced decision tree can be regarded as a set of classification rules, one corresponding to each branch.

The most widely used criterion for selecting attributes at step (a) is probably *Information Gain*. This uses the information-theoretic measure *entropy* to choose the attribute that maximises the expected gain of information from applying the additional test. This is the approach adopted in well-known systems such as C4.5 [2].

2.3 The Prism Algorithm

The Prism classification rule generation algorithm was developed by Cendrowska [3], primarily as a means of avoiding the generation of unnecessarily complex rules, which it was argued is an unavoidable but undesirable consequence of the use of a tree representation. The need to fit rules into such a representation requires them all to begin with a test on the value of the same attribute, even though that attribute may be irrelevant to many or most of the rules.

The Prism algorithm induces classification rules directly from a training set one rule at a time. Each rule is generated term-by-term, by selecting the attribute-value pair that maximises the probability of a chosen outcome class.

The version of Prism described in this paper is a modified form known as PrismTCS (standing for Prism with Target Class, Smallest first), which has been found to produce smaller sets of classification rules than the original form of the algorithm, with a similar level of predictive accuracy. With the original version of Prism, the training set is restored to its original state before the rules are generated for each class, thus requiring the training set to be processed once for each of the classes.

Instead PrismTCS makes use of a *target class,* which varies from one rule to the next as shown in Figure 2. With this form of the algorithm the full training set only needs to be processed once however many classes there are.

(1) Find the class with fewest instances in the training set (ignoring any with none). Call this the *target class* TC.

(2) Calculate the probability that class = TC for each possible attribute-value pair *

(3) Select the attribute-value pair with the maximum probability and create a subset of the training set comprising all instances with the selected combination (for all classes)

(4) Repeat 2 and 3 for this subset until it contains only instances of class TC. The induced rule is then the conjunction of all the attribute-value pairs selected in creating this subset

(5) Remove all instances covered by this rule from the training set

Repeat 1-5 until there are no instances remaining in the training set

* Any attribute that is part of an attribute-value pair already selected should not be used again for the same rule

Fig. 2. The PrismTCS Rule Generation Algorithm

3 Overfitting of Rules to Data

The principal problem with TDIDT, Prism and other algorithms for generating classification rules is that of *overfitting*. Beyond a certain point, specialising a rule by adding further terms can become counter-productive. The generated rules give a perfect fit for the instances from which they were generated but in some cases are too specific to have a high level of predictive accuracy for other instances. Another consequence of excessive specificity is that there is often an unnecessarily large number of rules. A smaller number of more general rules may have greater predictive accuracy on unseen data, at the expense of no longer correctly classifying some of the instances in the original training set. Alternatively, a similar level of accuracy may be achieved with a more compact set of rules.

3.1 Pruning Classification Rules to Reduce Overfitting

One approach to reducing overfitting, known as *post-pruning*, which is often used in association with decision tree generation, is to generate the whole set of classification rules and then remove a (possibly substantial) number of rules and terms, by the use of statistical tests or otherwise. An empirical comparison of a number of such methods is given in [7]. An important practical objection to post-pruning methods is that there is a large computational overhead involved in generating rules only then to delete a high proportion of them, especially if the training sets are large.

Pre-pruning a set of classification rules (or a decision tree) involves terminating some of the rules (branches) prematurely as they are being generated. Each incomplete rule such as

IF x = 1 AND z = yes AND q > 63.5 .... THEN ...

corresponds to a subset of instances currently 'under investigation'.

If not all the instances have the same classification the rule would normally be extended by adding a further term, as described previously. When following a pre-pruning strategy the subset is first tested to determine whether or not a termination condition applies. If it does not, a further term is generated as usual. If it does, the rule is *pruned*, i.e. it is treated as if no further attributes were available. Typically the rule will be treated as completed, with all the instances classified as belonging to the class to which the largest number belong.

Reference [5] reports on experiments with four possible termination conditions for pre-pruning rules as they are generated by TDIDT, e.g. truncate each rule as soon as it reaches 4 terms in length. The results obtained clearly show that pre-pruning can substantially reduce the number of terms generated and in some cases can also increase the predictive accuracy. Although they also show that the choice of pre-pruning method is important, it is not clear that (say) the same length limit should be applied to each rule, far less which of the termination conditions is the best one to use or why. There is a need to find a more principled choice of termination condition to use with pre-pruning, if possible one which can be applied completely automatically without the need for the user to select any 'threshold value' (such as the maximum number of terms for any rule). The *J-measure* described in the next section provides the basis for a more principled approach to pre-pruning.

4 Using the J-measure to Prune Classification Rules

4.1 Measuring the Information Content of a Rule

The *J-measure* was introduced into the rule induction literature by Smyth and Goodman [8] as an information theoretic means of quantifying the information content of a rule that is soundly based on theory.

Given a rule of the form **If Y=y, then X=x**, using the notation of [8], the (average) information content of the rule, measured in bits of information, is denoted by J(X;Y=y). The value of this quantity is the product of two terms:

- p(y) The probability that the hypothesis (antecedent of the rule) will occur - a measure of *hypothesis simplicity*
- j(X;Y=y) The *cross-entropy* - a measure of the *goodness-of-fit* of a given rule.

In what follows, it will be taken as a working hypothesis that a rule with a high J value (i.e. high information content) is also likely to have a high level of predictive accuracy for previously unseen instances.

4.2 Using J-Pruning with TDIDT and Prism

There are several ways in which J values can be used to aid classification tree generation using TDIDT. One method, which will be called *J-pruning*, is to prune a branch as soon as a node is generated at which the J value is less than that at its parent.

Thus for example consider an incomplete rule

IF attrib1 = a AND attrib2 = b .... (with J-value 0.4)

which is expanded by splitting on categorical attribute *attrib3* into the three rules

IF attrib1 = a AND attrib2 = b AND attrib3 = c1 .... (with J-value 0.38)
IF attrib1 = a AND attrib2 = b AND attrib3 = c2 .... (with J-value 0.45)
IF attrib1 = a AND attrib2 = b AND attrib3 = c3 .... (with J-value 0.03)

Assuming that none of the new rules is complete (i.e. corresponds to a subset of instances with only one classification) all three would be considered as candidates for J-pruning. As the J-values of the first and third are lower than that of the original (incomplete) rule each rule would be truncated, with all the corresponding instances classified as belonging to the class to which the largest number belong. For example, the first new rule might become

IF attrib1 = a AND attrib2 = b AND attrib3 = c1 THEN Class = 5

The second new rule has a larger J-value than the original rule and in this case the TDIDT algorithm would continue by splitting on an attribute as usual.

The difficulty in implementing this method is to know which classification to use when calculating the J-value of an incomplete rule. If there are only two classes the value of J is the same whichever is taken. When there are more than two classes an effective heuristic is to generate the J-value for each of the possible classes in turn and then to use the largest of the resulting values.

Reference [5] compares the results obtained using the TDIDT algorithm both with and without J-pruning for 12 datasets, mainly taken from the UCI Repository [6]. The results were calculated using 10-fold cross-validation in each case. TDIDT was used with the Information Gain attribute selection criterion throughout.

For many of the datasets a considerable reduction in the number of rules was obtained using J-Pruning (e.g. from 357.4 unpruned to 25.9 J-pruned for *genetics* and from 106.9 unpruned to 29.6 J-pruned for *soybean*). Averaged over the 12 datasets the number of rules was reduced from 68.5 to only 19.1. The effect on the predictive accuracy of the generated rulesets varied considerably from one dataset to another, with J-pruning giving a result that was better for 5 of the datasets, worse for 6 and unchanged for one, the average being slightly lower with J-Pruning than without.

In the case of PrismTCS classification rules J-pruning takes a simpler form. At each stage of rule generation the J-value of the incomplete rule is calculated and recorded. If at any stage adding an additional term would lead to a decrease in the J-value, the term is discarded. Provided the class to which the largest number of instances belongs is the current target class, the rule is completed with all the instances classified as belonging to the target class. Otherwise the incomplete rule and the corresponding instances are discarded.

Reference [9] compares the results obtained using PrismTCS both with and without J-pruning for 12 datasets, mainly taken from the UCI Repository [6]. The results were calculated using 10-fold cross-validation in each case.

The number of rules generated for the unpruned version of the PrismTCS algorithm was on average significantly smaller than for the unpruned version of TDIDT with the same datasets. Nevertheless the use of J-pruning with PrismTCS reduced the number of rules by more than one-third, with a substantial reduction from 87.7 rules to only 25.1 for *genetics* and a halving of the number of rules from 37.3 to 16.9 for *monk2*, in both cases accompanied by an increase in predictive accuracy. The predictive accuracy was larger for the J-pruned rule sets in seven cases and smaller for only three. On average there was a small increase in predictive accuracy despite the substantially reduced number of rules.

Although these results were very promising, as were those from the experiments with TDIDT, an important criterion for evaluating any classification rule generation algorithm is its *robustness*, particularly when noise is present in the data.

5 Experiments with Noisy Datasets

Many (perhaps most) real-world datasets suffer from the problem of *noise*, i.e. inaccurately recorded attribute or classification values. Although the user of a rule generation algorithm will generally be unaware that noise is present in a particular dataset, far less the proportion of values that are affected, the presence of noise is likely to lead to an excessively large number of rules and/or a reduction in classification accuracy compared with the same data in noise-free form.

The robustness of the unpruned and J-pruned versions of the TDIDT and PrismTCS algorithms to noise was investigated using the *vote* dataset from the UCI Repository [6]. The dataset comprises information about the votes of each of the members of the US House of Representatives on 16 key measures during 1984. The dataset has 300 instances, each relating the values of 16 categorical attributes to one of two possible classifications: *republican* or *democrat*. It seems reasonable to suppose that the members' votes will have been recorded with few (if any) errors, so the *vote* dataset in its original form will be considered noise-free.

From this dataset further datasets were created by contaminating the attribute values with progressively higher levels of noise. There were eight such datasets, named *vote_10*, *vote_20*, ..., *vote_80*, with the numerical suffix indicating the percentage of contaminated values.

The methodology adopted in the case of say *vote_30* was to consider the possibility of contaminating each attribute value in each instance in turn. For each value a random number from 0 to 1 was generated. If the value was less than or equal to 0.30 the attribute value was replaced by another of the valid possible values of the same attribute, selected with equal probability. The original classification was left unchanged in all cases. As the level of noise contamination increases from zero (the original dataset), through 10%, 20%, ... up to 80%, it is to be expected that (with any method) the predictive accuracy of any ruleset generated will decline.

5.1 Experimental Results: TDIDT

Figure 3 shows the number of rules generated using the TDIDT algorithm (with the 'Information Gain' attribute selection criterion) in its standard 'unpruned' form and with J-pruning for each of the datasets *vote_10*, *vote_20*, ... *vote_80*. Figure 4 shows the corresponding levels of predictive accuracy for the two forms of the algorithm for the nine versions of the *vote* dataset. All results were calculated using 10-fold cross-validation. The J-pruned algorithm clearly produces substantially fewer rules with at least as good predictive accuracy as the unpruned version.

This experiment was repeated for two further datasets taken from the UCI Repository: *genetics* and *agaricus_lepiota*. The *genetics* dataset comprises 3,190 instances, each with 60 categorical attributes and 3 possible classifications. The *agaricus_lepiota* dataset comprises 5,644 instances (after those containing any missing values were removed), each with 22 categorical attributes and 2 possible classifications. These datasets were chosen partly because all the attributes were categorical. It was considered that categorical values were less likely to be wrongly (or imprecisely) recorded than continuous ones. The results of the experiments for these datasets (again calculated using 10-fold cross-validation) are given in Table 1, with values rounded to the nearest integer.

The reduction in the number of rules obtained using J-pruning increases substantially as the percentage of noise in the data increases. In the most extreme case, for *agaricus_lepiota_80*, the unpruned version of TDIDT gives 2916 rules and the J-pruned version only 19. The predictive accuracy obtained using J-pruning was better than that for the unpruned version of TDIDT in all cases where the proportion of noise exceeded 10%.

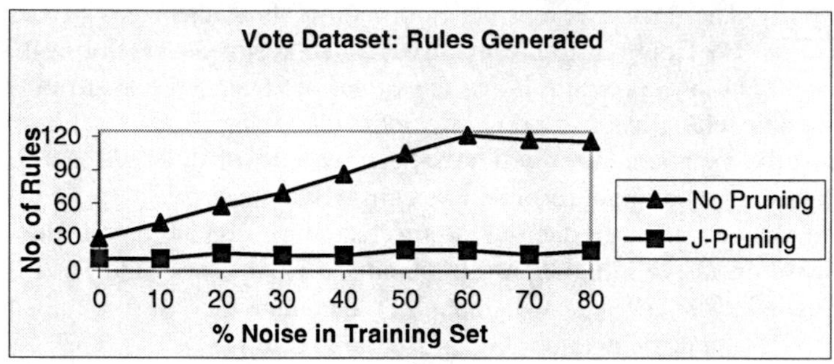

Fig. 3. Comparison of Number of Rules Generated: *vote* Dataset

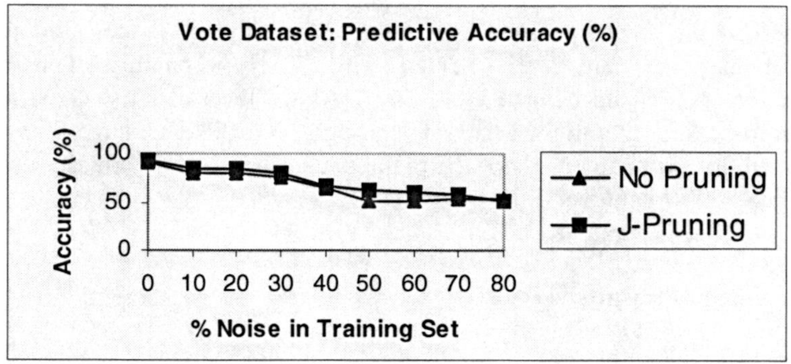

Fig. 4. Comparison of Predictive Accuracy: *vote* Dataset

Table 1. Rules Generated and Predictive Accuracy: *genetics* and *agaricus_lepiota*

	genetics				*agaricus_lepiota*			
Noise %	Rules		Accuracy (%)		Rules		Accuracy (%)	
	Un-pruned	Pruned	Un-pruned	Pruned	Un-pruned	Pruned	Un-pruned	Pruned
0	357	26	89	78	15	10	100	100
10	918	122	73	72	349	96	96	95
20	1238	158	60	67	794	128	89	91
30	1447	185	54	64	1304	149	81	86
40	1652	175	44	60	1827	159	72	80
50	1815	163	36	55	2246	167	64	76
60	1908	165	33	52	2682	167	55	71
70	1998	153	29	51	3003	184	48	67
80	2074	179	27	48	2916	19	52	74
Ave.	1490	147	49	61	1682	120	73	82

5.2 Experimental results: PrismTCS

The experiments described in Section 5.1 were repeated with the J-pruned and unpruned versions of the PrismTCS algorithm.

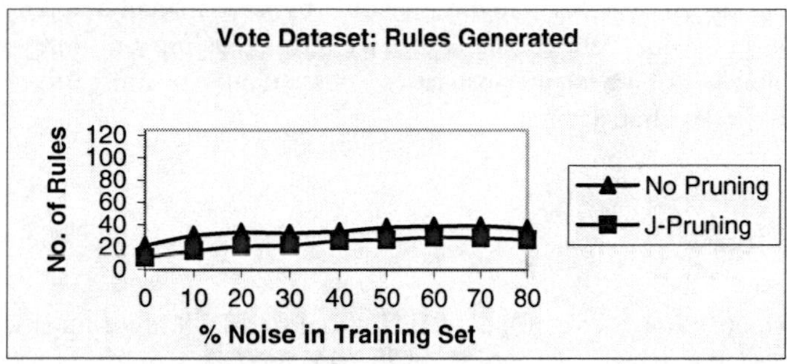

Fig. 5. Comparison of Number of Rules Generated: *vote* Dataset

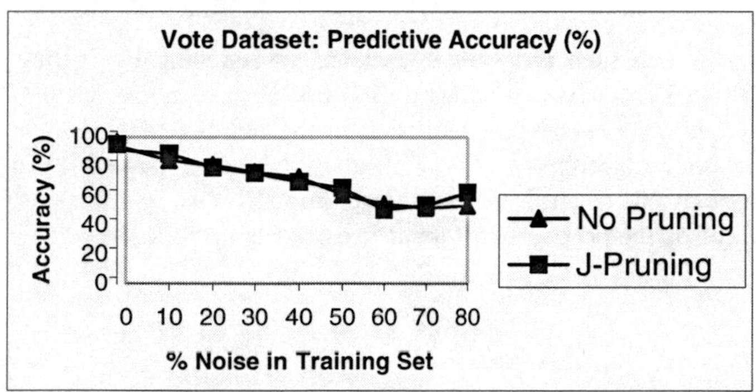

Fig. 6. Comparison of Predictive Accuracy: *vote* Dataset

Table 2. Rules Generated and Predictive Accuracy: *genetics* and *agaricus_lepiota*

Noise %	*genetics*				*agaricus_lepiota*			
	Rules		Accuracy (%)		Rules		Accuracy (%)	
	Un-pruned	Pruned	Un-pruned	Pruned	Un-pruned	Pruned	Un-pruned	Pruned
0	88	25	91	93	12	12	100	100
10	438	264	71	78	177	68	96	97
20	380	269	64	70	238	131	92	93
30	399	249	58	63	312	183	87	89
40	388	270	57	59	441	242	81	81
50	399	285	48	55	556	264	74	74
60	393	264	46	48	641	252	69	70
70	393	230	41	41	676	239	62	64
80	399	204	38	39	625	167	63	69
Ave	364	229	57	61	408	173	80	82

The results for the *vote* dataset are shown in Figures 5 and 6. Table 2 gives the results for *genetics* and *agaricus_lepiota*. In the case of the *vote* dataset, the increase in the number of rules as the percentage of noise increases is much less steep than for TDIDT. However, the use of J-pruning gives not only a smaller number of rules but in most cases slightly better predictive accuracy.

The *genetics* dataset is clearly highly sensitive to even a small amount of noise. However, for both this dataset and *agaricus_lepiota* using J-pruning not only reduces the number of rules, in most cases substantially, but also gives a small improvement in predictive accuracy.

6 Conclusions

Although a comparison between the TDIDT and PrismTCS algorithms is not the principal aim of this paper, it would seem that PrismTCS is more robust to noise than TDIDT. Although increasing the percentage of noise inevitably leads to an increase in the number of rules and a reduction in predictive accuracy with both algorithms, the effect is generally more extreme with TDIDT.

The J-pruning technique is a valuable means of reducing overfitting for both TDIDT and PrismTCS, which is robust in the presence of noise. Using J-pruning will generally lead to a substantial reduction in the number of classification rules generated for both algorithms. This will often be accompanied by a gain in predictive accuracy. In general, the advantage gained by using J-pruning becomes more pronounced as the proportion of noise in a dataset increases.

References

1. Hunt, E.B., Marin J. and Stone, P.J. (1966). Experiments in Induction. Academic Press
2. Quinlan, J.R. (1993). C4.5: Programs for Machine Learning. Morgan Kaufmann
3. Cendrowska, J. (1987). PRISM: an Algorithm for Inducing Modular Rules. International Journal of Man-Machine Studies, 27, pp. 349-370
4. Bramer, M.A. (2000). Automatic Induction of Classification Rules from Examples Using N-Prism. In: Research and Development in Intelligent Systems XVI. Springer-Verlag, pp. 99-121
5. Bramer, M.A. (2002). Using J-Pruning to Reduce Overfitting in Classification Trees. In: Research and Development in Intelligent Systems XVIII. Springer-Verlag, pp. 25-38.
6. Blake, C.L. and Merz, C.J. (1998). UCI Repository of Machine Learning Databases [http://www.ics.uci.edu/~mlearn/MLRepository.html]. Irvine, CA: University of California, Department of Information and Computer Science
7. Mingers, J. (1989). An Empirical Comparison of Pruning Methods for Decision Tree Induction. Machine Learning, 4, pp. 227-243
8. Smyth, P. and Goodman, R.M. (1991). Rule Induction Using Information Theory. In: Piatetsky-Shapiro, G. and Frawley, W.J. (eds.), Knowledge Discovery in Databases. AAAI Press, pp. 159-176
9. Bramer, M.A. (2002). An Information-Theoretic Approach to the Pre-pruning of Classification Rules. Proceedings of the IFIP World Computer Congress, Montreal 2002.

A Framework for Reasoning on Objects with Geometric Constraints

Hicham Hajji[1] and Evimaria Terzi[2]

[1] LISI-UFR Informatique, Université Claude Bernard Lyon 1
8, boulevard Niels Bohr, 69622 Villeurbanne - France
hhajji@bat710.univ-lyon1.fr
[2] Department of Computer Sciences
Purdue University, West Lafayette, IN 47907 - USA
edt@cs.purdue.edu

Abstract. This paper presents a framework for terminological reasoning by taking into account geometric representation of objects. We consider objects having shapes which are described by means of semi-algebraic sets[1]. We show how geometric representations can be used to define concepts. The formal semantics as well as the reasoning algorithms are given. We present a calculus for deciding satisfiability of a constraint knowledge base described in our language. The proposed language can be seen as an extensible core for applications such as multimedia databases or spatial and geographic databases.

1 Introduction

Spatial databases such as geographic databases in Geographic Information Systems (GIS), geometric databases in CAD, or image/video databases in Multimedia Information Systems and Medical Information Systems, are usually expected to store spatial information. Queries in these systems involve the derivation of different types of spatial relationships which are not explicitly stored. Hence, manipulation of geometric data is an important application area that requires reasoning techniques and arithmetic calculations. What could be sound criteria for achieving integration of reasoning on object structures and numerical computations for spatial reasoning? Some examples are (1) preserving the declarativity, (2) additional expressive power is desirable, but come without a serious loss of efficiency.

A collection of constraints can be geometrically viewed as an object in multi-dimensional space, containing all points in the space that satisfy the constraints. Spatio-temporal objects or, at least, their approximations, can be described using constraints, although their physical representation can differ for efficient manipulation. In order to adequately support decidable reasoning by taking into

[1] i.e., equalities and inequalities between integer polynomials in several indeterminates. That is, a relational approach as opposed to feature-vector approach and shape through transformation approach.

R. Cicchetti et al. (Eds.): DEXA 2002, LNCS 2453, pp. 443–453, 2002.

account spatial representation of objects, we extend the description logic $\mathcal{ALC}$ [5], on the basis of the general scheme given in [1]. The main idea of our approach is to deal with spatial objects using appropriate constructors whose arguments are semi-algebraic sets.

Combining spatial representations with the notion of objects with unique identifiers offers a powerful mechanism for spatial data specification and reasoning. Our technical contributions in this paper are as follows:

1. We describe how a formal object-based data model, namely a description logic, can be enhanced with constraints to naturally represent geometric shapes of objects.
2. We develop a calculus for deciding satisfiability of knowledge bases described by means of our language. As subsumption can be reduced to satisfiability problem, our algorithm is also a decision procedure for subsumption.

Although in the basic form that we give here, the formalism does not account for all aspects of spatial relations, it constitutes a kernel to be extended. Showing how we can formally specify and reason about spatial data at an abstract, logical level, is useful and significant.

Paper outline: Section 2 introduces some useful definitions. In Section 3, we develop our language, give its Tarski-style extensional semantics, and specify the components of a spatial knowledge base. Section 4 develops a calculus for deciding satisfiability of a knowledge base. Section 5 discusses related work. We conclude in Section 6.

2 Preliminaries

Before we give the syntax and semantics of our *abstract languages*, we introduce some useful definitions.

Definition 1. (Concrete Domains [1]) *A concrete domain* $\mathcal{D} = (\mathsf{dom}(\mathcal{D}), \mathsf{pred}(\mathcal{D}))$ *consists of:*

- *the domain* $\mathsf{dom}(\mathcal{D})$*,*
- *a set of predicate symbols* $\mathsf{pred}(\mathcal{D})$*, where each predicate symbol* $P \in \mathsf{pred}(\mathcal{D})$ *is associated with an arity* n *and an* n*-ary relation* $P^{\mathcal{D}} \subseteq \mathsf{dom}(\mathcal{D})^n$*,*

In many applications (in particular when modeling and querying databases), one would like to be able to refer to concrete domains and predicates on these domains when defining queries. An example of such a concrete domain could be the set of (nonnegative) integers with comparisons $(=, <, \leq, \geq, >)$.

Definition 2. (Real Formula) *A real formula is a well-formed first-order logic formula built from equalities and inequalities between integer polynomials in several indeterminates, i.e.,*

- *if* p *is a polynomial with real coefficients over the variables* $x_1, \ldots, x_m$ *over the real numbers, then* $p(x_1, \ldots, x_m)\ \theta\ 0$ *is a real formula with* $\theta \in \{=, <, \leq, >, \geq, \neq\}$*;*

– *if φ and ψ are real formulas, then so are $\varphi \wedge \psi$, $\varphi \vee \psi$, and $\neg\varphi$; and*
– *if x is a real variable and φ is a real formula in which x occurs free, then $\exists x \varphi(x)$ is a real formula.*

If φ is a real formula with m free variables $x_1, \ldots, x_m$, then it defines a subset $\varphi_{\mathbb{R}^m}$ of the m-dimensional Euclidean space $\mathbb{R}^m$, namely the set of points satisfying φ:

$$\varphi_{\mathbb{R}^m} := \{(u_1, \ldots, u_m) \in \mathbb{R}^m \mid \varphi(u_1, \ldots, u_m)\}.$$

Definition 3. (Semi-algebraic sets [2]) *Point-sets defined by real formulas are called semi-algebraic sets.*

For example, the set $V = \{(x, y) \in \mathbb{R}^2 \mid x^2 + y^2 = 1\}$ is semi-algebraic.

Note that semi-algebraic sets of $\mathbb{R}^m$ make the smallest family of subsets of $\mathbb{R}^m$ such that:

1. it contains all the sets of the form $\{(u_1, \ldots, u_m) \in \mathbb{R}^m \mid P(u_1, \ldots, u_m) \geq 0\}$, where $P(u_1, \ldots, u_m) \geq 0$ is a real formula;
2. it is closed with respect to the set-theoretic operations of finite union, finite intersection and complementation.

In this paper, we denote the domain of semi-algebraic sets, i.e., dom(semi-algebraic sets), by $\top_{\mathcal{SAS}}$.

Every real formula can effectively be transformed into a quantifier-free real formula [6]. As a consequence, it is *decidable* whether a real sentence is *valid* or *satisfiable* in the ordered field of the real numbers.

Figure 1 shows a part of geographic information about intercity highways and railroads. The names are fictitious. In this example, linear constraints (see table 1), which can be seen as linear restrictions of the polynomial constraints are used to specify spatial representations of different objects (here, for example, *cities*).

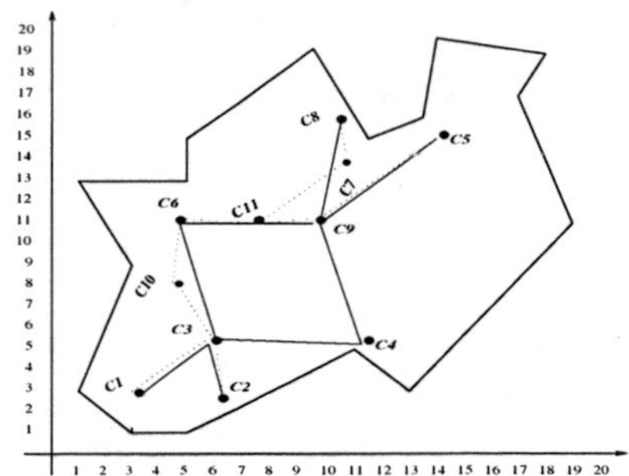

Fig. 1. Example of a geographical multimedia information about intercity highways and railroads

The linear data model is particularly suited to model spatial data in applications in which geometrical information is required and in which this information can be approximated by linear geometrical spatial objects. This model is opposed to the topological one which is suitable for applications in which rather than exact geometrical information, the relative position of spatial objects is of importance. For the expressive power and complexity of linear constraint query languages, see [3,7].

Table 1. City

Oid	Name	Population	Geometry
id_1	$C1$	250.000	$(x = 3.5) \wedge (y = 2.5)$
id_2	$C2$	290.800	$(x = 6.4) \wedge (y = 2.5)$
id_3	$C3$	1.004.928	$(x = 6) \wedge (y = 5.3)$
...	...	...	...

3 Language

3.1 Concept Language

Definition 4. (Syntax) *Let A be a concept name, R be a role name, and $\Phi_{\bar{V}}$ a m-ay real formula. For simplicity, we make use of the attribute* shape *whose semantics will be defined later. Concepts C and D can be formed by means of the following syntax:*

$$\begin{aligned} C, D \longrightarrow\ & A \mid \top \mid \bot \mid C \sqcap D \mid \\ & C \sqcup D \mid \neg C \mid \forall R.C \mid \exists R.C \mid \\ & in(\Phi_{\bar{V}}) \mid intersect(\Phi_{\bar{V}}) \end{aligned}$$

Definition 5. (Semantics) *The semantics is given by an interpretation $\mathcal{I} = (\Delta^{\mathcal{I}}, \cdot^{\mathcal{I}})$ which consists of an (abstract) interpretation domain $\Delta^{\mathcal{I}}$, and an interpretation function $\cdot^{\mathcal{I}}$. The interpretation function $\cdot^{\mathcal{I}}$ associates each concept C with a subset $C^{\mathcal{I}}$ of $\Delta^{\mathcal{I}}$, each role R with a subset $R^{\mathcal{I}}$ of $\Delta^{\mathcal{I}} \times \Delta^{\mathcal{I}}$, and the feature shape with a total function $shape^{\mathcal{I}} : \Delta^{\mathcal{I}} \rightarrow (\top_{\mathcal{SAS}} - \emptyset)$ ($\emptyset$ being the empty set denoted by unsatisfiable real formulas). Additionally, $\mathcal{I}$ has to satisfy the following equations:*

$$\begin{aligned} \top^{\mathcal{I}} &= \Delta^{\mathcal{I}} \\ \bot^{\mathcal{I}} &= \emptyset \\ (C \sqcap D)^{\mathcal{I}} &= C^{\mathcal{I}} \cap D^{\mathcal{I}} \\ (C \sqcup D)^{\mathcal{I}} &= C^{\mathcal{I}} \cup D^{\mathcal{I}} \\ (\neg C)^{\mathcal{I}} &= \Delta^{\mathcal{I}} \setminus C^{\mathcal{I}} \\ (\forall R.C)^{\mathcal{I}} &= \{d_1 \in \Delta^{\mathcal{I}} \mid \forall d_2, (d_1, d_2) \in R^{\mathcal{I}} \text{ then } d_2 \in C^{\mathcal{I}}\} \\ (\exists R.C)^{\mathcal{I}} &= \{d_1 \in \Delta^{\mathcal{I}} \mid \exists d_2, (d_1, d_2) \in R^{\mathcal{I}} \text{ and } d_2 \in C^{\mathcal{I}}\} \\ (in(\Phi_{\bar{V}}))^{\mathcal{I}} &= \{d \in \Delta^{\mathcal{I}} \mid shape^{\mathcal{I}}(d) \subseteq \Phi_{\bar{V}}\} \\ (intersect(\Phi_{\bar{V}}))^{\mathcal{I}} &= \{d \in \Delta^{\mathcal{I}} \mid shape^{\mathcal{I}}(d) \cap \Phi_{\bar{V}} \neq \emptyset\} \end{aligned}$$

The notation $shape^{\mathcal{I}}(d) \subseteq \Phi_{\bar{V}}$ means that all the points satisfying the formula describing the geometric shape of d satisfy the formula $\Phi_{\bar{V}}$. Similarly, $shape^{\mathcal{I}}(d) \cap \Phi_{\bar{V}} \neq \emptyset$ means that the set of points belonging to the geometric shape of d has a non-empty intersection with the set of points satisfying $\Phi_{\bar{V}}$.

Let A be a concept name and let D be a concept term. Then $A = D$ is a terminological axiom. A terminology (TBox) is a finite set $\mathcal{T}$ of terminological axioms with the additional restrictions that (i) no concept name appears more than once as a left hand side of a definition, and (ii) $\mathcal{T}$ contains no cyclic definitions.

An interpretation $\mathcal{I}$ is a model for a *TBox* $\mathcal{T}$ if and only if $\mathcal{I}$ satisfies all the assertions in $\mathcal{T}$.

3.2 Assertional Language

Individuals are specified by means of assertions. These assertions allow to link an individual to a concept, an individual to another individual through a role, or an individual to its real algebraic formula (i.e., its shape) through the feature *shape*.

The assertions on individuals are the following:

- $d : C$, the individual d is an instance of the concept C,
- $(d_1, d_2) : R$, the individual d_1 is linked to the individual d_2 through the role R,
- $(d, \Phi^d_{\bar{V}}) : shape$, the individual d has the geometric shape given by the real formula $\Phi^d_{\bar{V}}$.

where d, d_1, d_2 are abstract individuals, R is a role name, and *shape* is an attribute allowing to assign to the individual d the geometric shape defined by the real formula $\Phi^d_{\bar{V}}$.

An ABox $\mathcal{A}$ is a set of assertions. An interpretation $\mathcal{I}$ is a model for an ABox $\mathcal{A}$ if and only if $\mathcal{I}$ satisfies all the assertions in $\mathcal{A}$. The interpretation $\mathcal{I}$ satisfies:

- $d : C$ iff $d \in C^{\mathcal{I}}$
- $(d_1, d_2) : R$ iff $(d_1, d_2) \in R^{\mathcal{I}}$
- $(d, \Phi^d_{\bar{V}}) : shape$ iff $(d, \Phi^d_{\bar{V}}) \in shape^{\mathcal{I}}$ and $\Phi^d_{\bar{V}}$ is satisfiable

3.3 Spatial Knowledge Bases and Reasoning Services

A spatial knowledge base built by means of concept languages is generally formed by two components: The *intensional* one, called TBox, and the *extensional* one, called ABox.

An important service that must be provided is computing the subsumption hierarchy, i.e., computing the subconcept-superconcept relationships between the concepts of a TBox. This inferential service is usually called classification. The model-theoretic semantics introduced before allows the following formal definition of subsumption. Let $\mathcal{T}$ be a TBox and let A, B be concept names.

Then B *subsumes* A with respect to $\mathcal{T}$ (symbolically $A \sqsubseteq_{\mathcal{T}} B$) iff $A^{\mathcal{I}} \subseteq B^{\mathcal{I}}$ holds for all models $\mathcal{I}$ of $\mathcal{T}$.

For two concept terms C, D we say that D subsumes C (written $C \sqsubseteq D$) iff $C^{\mathcal{I}} \subseteq D^{\mathcal{I}}$ for all interpretations $\mathcal{I}$. Two concept terms C, D are said to be *equivalent* iff C subsumes D and vice versa. Equivalent terms denote the same set in every interpretation.

The subsumption problem for concept terms can now further be reduced to another interesting problem: the satisfiability problem for concept terms. Let C be a concept term. Then C is said to be *satisfiable* iff there exists an interpretation $\mathcal{I}$ such that $C^{\mathcal{I}} \neq \emptyset$. Thus an unsatisfiable concept term denotes the empty set in every interpretation, which means that it is worthless.

Obviously, we have $C \sqsubseteq D$ iff $C \sqcap \neg D$ is unsatisfiable. This means that an algorithm for deciding satisfiability of concept terms also yields a subsumption algorithm.

Finally, the *satisfiability* problem for concept terms (and thus also the subsumption problem) can also be reduced to the consistency problem for ABoxes. In fact, C is satisfiable iff the ABox $\{a : C\}$ is consistent.

In this paper, we follow the approach in which the satisfiability problem for concept terms is reduced to the consistency problem for ABoxes.

4 Testing Consistency for ABoxes

In this section we shall describe an algorithm which decides the consistency of an ABox for our language. Without loss of generality we assume that all the concept terms occurring in the ABox are in *negation normal form.* A concept term is in *negation normal form* iff negation signs occur only immediately in front of concept names. A concept in a negative normal form is called *simple.* Any concept can be rewritten into a simple concept by using the following rules, called *normalization rules*:

$$\begin{array}{l}
\neg\top \sim \bot \\
\neg\bot \sim \top \\
\neg(C \sqcap D) \sim \neg C \sqcup \neg D \\
\neg(C \sqcup D) \sim \neg C \sqcap \neg D \\
\neg\neg C \sim C \\
\neg(\forall R.C) \sim \exists R.\neg C \\
\neg(\exists R.C) \sim \forall R.\neg C \\
\neg in(\Phi_{\bar{V}}) \sim intersect(\neg\Phi_{\bar{V}}) \\
\neg intersect(\Phi_{\bar{V}}) \sim in(\neg\Phi_{\bar{V}})
\end{array}$$

Proposition 1. (**Equivalence**) *Any concept C can be transformed into an equivalent negative normal form. The normalization process is linear and it is only dependent of the size of the concept C.*

The algorithm for deciding consistency will start with the given ABox, and transform it with the help of certain rules until one of the following two situations occurs: (i) the obtained ABox is "obviously contradictory", or (ii) the obtained ABox is "complete", i.e., one can apply no more rules. In the second case, the complete ABox describes a model of the original ABox.

Propagation Rules. Let $\mathcal{A}$ be an ABox. The role of propagation rules applied to $\mathcal{A}$ is to make *explicit* (by adding assertions to the knowledge base) the part of the knowledge which is *implicitly* contained in the ABox. This knowledge is implied by the semantics of the constructors of the language. We call the obtained ABox for which no propagation rule applies a *complete* ABox, and denoted $\mathcal{A}^+$. Each rule takes an ABox $\mathcal{A}$ and adds assertions to this ABox. The algorithm terminates if none of the rules can be applied.

In the following, s, s_1, s_2 and t are abstract individual names or variables.

$\mathcal{A} \longrightarrow_\sqcap \{s : C_1, s : C_2\} \cup \mathcal{A}$
if 1. $s : C_1 \sqcap C_2 \in \mathcal{A}$ and
2. $s : C_1$ and $s : C_2$ are not both in $\mathcal{A}$

$\mathcal{A} \longrightarrow_\sqcup \{s : D\} \cup \mathcal{A}$
if 1. $s : C_1 \sqcup C_2 \in \mathcal{A}$ and
2. neither $s : C_1$ nor $s : C_2$ are in $\mathcal{A}$ and
3. $D = C_1$ or $D = C_2$

$\mathcal{A} \longrightarrow_\forall \{s_2 : C\} \cup \mathcal{A}$
if 1. $s_1 : \forall R.C \in \mathcal{A}$ and $(s_1, s_2) : R \in \mathcal{A}$ and
2. $s_2 : C \notin \mathcal{A}$

$\mathcal{A} \longrightarrow_\exists \{(s, y) : R, y : C\} \cup \mathcal{A}$
if 1. $s : \exists R.C \in \mathcal{A}$ and
2. y is a new variable and
3. there is no t such that $(s, t) : R \in \mathcal{A}$ and $t : C \in \mathcal{A}$

$\mathcal{A} \longrightarrow_{in} \{s : in(\Phi_{\bar{V}} \wedge \Phi'_{\bar{V}})\} \cup \mathcal{A} \setminus \{s : in(\Phi_{\bar{V}}), s : in(\Phi'_{\bar{V}})\}$
if 1. $s : in(\Phi_{\bar{V}}) \in \mathcal{A}$ and $s : in(\Phi'_{\bar{V}}) \in \mathcal{A}$ and
2. $s : in(\Phi_{\bar{V}} \wedge \Phi'_{\bar{V}}) \notin \mathcal{A}$

We have two groups of propagation rules. The first group are deterministic rules ($\longrightarrow_\sqcap$, $\longrightarrow_\forall$, $\longrightarrow_\exists$, $\longrightarrow_{in}$). The second group is constituted by the single rule $\longrightarrow_\sqcup$ which is non-deterministic. In addition, the rule $\longrightarrow_\exists$ is a generating rule because it allows to introduce new variables.

4.1 Clashes

Recall that the goal in applying propagation rules to an ABox $\mathcal{A}$ is to find a model for that ABox. As a result, we can obtain either a complete ABox $\mathcal{A}^+$ which represents a canonical model of $\mathcal{A}$, or an ABox containing a clash. Clashes that may occur in an ABox are the following:

- $s : \bot \in \mathcal{A}$
  s is in the denotation of the inconsistent concept $\bot$.
- $s : A \in \mathcal{A}$ and $s : \neg A \in \mathcal{A}$
  The individual s is instance of two contradictory concepts.

– $(s, \Phi^s_{\bar{V}}) : shape \in \mathcal{A}$, with $\Phi^s_{\bar{V}}$ unsatisfiable.
  The individual s has a geometric shape represented by $\Phi^s_{\bar{V}}$ which is unsatisfiable. That is, it denotes an empty set of points.
– $s : in(\Phi_{\bar{V}}) \in \mathcal{A}$, with $\Phi_{\bar{V}}$ unsatisfiable.
  The individual s is in the denotation of a concept whose formula $\Phi_{\bar{V}}$ specified by means of the constructor *in* is unsatisfiable.
– $s : intersect(\Phi_{\bar{V}}) \in \mathcal{A}$, with $\Phi_{\bar{V}}$ unsatisfiable.
  The individual s has a non-empty intersection with an empty set denoted by an unsatisfiable formula.
– $s : in(\Phi_{\bar{V}}) \in \mathcal{A}, (s, \Phi^s_{\bar{V}}) : shape \in \mathcal{A}$ and $(\neg\Phi^s_{\bar{V}} \vee \Phi_{\bar{V}})$ is unsatisfiable.
  The individual s is in the denotation of $in(\Phi_{\bar{V}})$. It has the geometric shape given by $\Phi^s_{\bar{V}}$, but some of the points denoted by this formula do not satisfy the formula $\Phi_{\bar{V}}$.
– $s : intersect(\Phi_{\bar{V}}) \in \mathcal{A}, (s, \Phi^s_{\bar{V}}) : shape \in \mathcal{A}$ and $(\Phi^s_{\bar{V}} \wedge \Phi_{\bar{V}})$ is unsatisfiable.
  The individual s is in the denotation of the concept $intersect(\Phi_{\bar{V}})$. It has the shape given by $\Phi^s_{\bar{V}}$, but there is no intersection between $\Phi_{\bar{V}}$ and $\Phi^s_{\bar{V}}$.

Let $\mathcal{A}$ be an *ABox*. We define the *canonical interpretation* $\mathcal{I}_\mathcal{A}$ and the *canonical* $\mathcal{I}_\mathcal{A}$*-assignment* $\alpha_\mathcal{A}$ as follows:

1. $\Delta^{\mathcal{I}_\mathcal{A}} := \{s \mid s \text{ is an object in } \mathcal{A}\}$
2. $\alpha_\mathcal{A}(s) := s$
3. $s \in A^{\mathcal{I}_\mathcal{A}}$ iff $s : A$ is in $\mathcal{A}$
4. $s \in (in(\Phi_{\bar{V}}))^{\mathcal{I}_\mathcal{A}}$ iff $s : in(\Phi_{\bar{V}}) \in \mathcal{A}$
5. $s \in (intersect(\Phi_{\bar{V}}))^{\mathcal{I}_\mathcal{A}}$ iff $s : intersect(\Phi_{\bar{V}}) \in \mathcal{A}$
6. $(s_1, s_2) \in R^{\mathcal{I}_\mathcal{A}}$ iff $(s_1, s_2) : R \in \mathcal{A}$

Theorem 1. **(Correctness)** *Let $\mathcal{A}^+$ be a complete ABox. $\mathcal{A}^+$ is satisfiable if and only if it does not contain a clash.*

4.2 Examples

Let us illustrate, by simple examples, the application of the propagation rules. We consider two reasoning services, namely, **Instantiation** and **Subsumption**.

Instantiation . Consider the following knowledge base $\Sigma =< \mathcal{T}, \mathcal{A} >$

$\mathcal{T} := \{\mathsf{CITY} = \exists \mathsf{name.STRING} \sqcap \exists \mathsf{state.STRING},$
$\quad \mathsf{CON}^2 = \mathsf{CITY} \sqcap \mathsf{in}((\mathsf{y} \geq 3) \wedge (\mathsf{x} \geq 0) \wedge (\mathsf{x} \leq 8))\}$
$\mathcal{A} := \{(\mathsf{chicago}, ((\mathsf{y} = 4) \wedge (\mathsf{x} = 5))) : \mathsf{shape}, \mathsf{chicago} : \mathsf{CON}\}$

Σ is a fragment of an hypothetical constraint knowledge base describing the map of the United States of America. It is easy to show that Σ is satisfiable and hence the instantiations in the ABox $\mathcal{A}$ are valid.

First, we replace in $\mathcal{A}$ the concept CON by its definition given in $\mathcal{T}$. This leads to the new ABox

[2] For CITY OF THE NORTH

$$\begin{array}{ll}
\mathcal{A}_3 := \mathcal{A}_2 \cup \{\mathsf{chicago} : \exists \mathsf{name.STRING}, & \\
\qquad \mathsf{chicago} : \exists \mathsf{state.STRING} \sqcap \mathsf{in}((y \geq 3) \wedge (x \geq 0) \wedge (x \leq 8))\} & \longrightarrow_{\sqcap} \\
\mathcal{A}_4 := \mathcal{A}_3 \cup \{\mathsf{chicago} : \exists \mathsf{state.STRING}, \mathsf{chicago} : \mathsf{in}((y \geq 3) \wedge (x \geq 0) \wedge (x \leq 8))\} & \longrightarrow_{\sqcap} \\
\mathcal{A}_5 := \mathcal{A}_4 \cup \{(\mathsf{chicago}, x_1) : \mathsf{name}, x_1 : \mathsf{STRING}\} & \longrightarrow_{\exists} \\
\mathcal{A}_6 := \mathcal{A}_5 \cup \{(\mathsf{chicago}, x_2) : \mathsf{state}, x_2 : \mathsf{STRING}\} & \longrightarrow_{\exists}
\end{array}$$

Fig. 2. A sequence of rule applications for instantiation

$\mathcal{A}_1 := \{(\mathsf{chicago}, ((y = 4) \wedge (x = 5))) : \mathsf{shape},$
$\mathsf{chicago} : \mathsf{CITY} \sqcap \mathsf{in}((y \geq 3) \wedge (x \geq 0) \wedge (x \leq 8))\}$
Then, we replace CITY in $\mathcal{A}$ with its definition in $\mathcal{T}$. We obtain the ABox
$\mathcal{A}_2 := \{(\mathsf{chicago}, ((y = 4) \wedge (x = 5))) : \mathsf{shape},$
$\mathsf{chicago} : \exists \mathsf{name.STRING} \sqcap \exists \mathsf{state.STRING} \sqcap \mathsf{in}((y \geq 3) \wedge (x \geq 0) \wedge (x \leq 8))\}$
In figure 2, we use the calculus to check the ABox $\mathcal{A}$ for satisfiability[3]. We start with $\mathcal{A}_2$. The figure shows a sequence of rule applications. In each step we give only the component of the ABox that changes. As completion, we obtain $\mathcal{A}_6$ which is clash-free, and hence the original ABox $\mathcal{A}$ is consistent.

Subsumption. Consider the following knowledge base $\Sigma = <\mathcal{T}, \mathcal{A}>$
$\mathcal{T} := \{\mathsf{CON} = \mathsf{CITY} \sqcap \mathsf{intersect}((y \geq 3) \wedge (x \geq 0) \wedge (x \leq 8)),$
$\mathsf{CAML}^4 = \mathsf{CITY} \sqcap \mathsf{in}((y \geq 3) \wedge (x \geq 3) \wedge (x \leq 4))\}$
$\mathcal{A} := \emptyset$

Let us see if CAML is subsumed by CON. That is, if $\mathsf{CAML} \sqsubseteq \mathsf{CON}$.

Recall that a concept C is subsumed by a concept D (written $C \sqsubseteq D$) iff the concept $C \sqcap \neg D$ is unsatisfiable. In our case, if $\mathsf{CAML} \sqcap \neg \mathsf{CON}$ is unsatisfiable. And the concept $\mathsf{CAML} \sqcap \neg \mathsf{CON}$ is unsatisfiable iff the ABox $\{a : \mathsf{CAML} \sqcap \neg \mathsf{CON}\}$, where a is an individual name, is unsatisfiable.

So, let $\mathcal{A} := \{a : \mathsf{CAML} \sqcap \neg \mathsf{CON}\}$

Before starting the application of propagation rules, we first replace concept names appearing in $\mathcal{A}$ by their definition in $\mathcal{T}$. We obtain the new ABox

$$\mathcal{A}_1 := \{a : \mathsf{CITY} \sqcap \mathsf{in}((y \geq 3) \wedge (x \geq 3) \wedge (x \leq 4))) \sqcap \\ \neg(\mathsf{CITY} \sqcap \mathsf{intersect}((y \geq 3) \wedge (x \geq 0) \wedge (x \leq 8)))$$

Then we normalize $\mathcal{A}_1$ by applying the normalization rules. We obtain the new ABox

[3] And hence the instantiations in $\mathcal{A}$ are valid
[4] For CITY AROUND MICHIGAN LAKE.

$$\mathcal{A}_2 := \{\mathsf{a} : \mathsf{CITY} \sqcap \mathsf{in}((\mathsf{y} \geq 3) \wedge (\mathsf{x} \geq 3) \wedge (\mathsf{x} \leq 4)) \sqcap (\neg\mathsf{CITY} \sqcup \mathsf{in}((\mathsf{y} < 3) \vee (\mathsf{x} < 0) \vee (\mathsf{x} > 8)))\}$$

Figure 3 shows a sequence of propagation rules application. At the end, we obtain two ABoxes, namely, $\mathcal{A}_5$ and $\mathcal{A}_6$ (because of the application of the nondeterministic rule $\longrightarrow_{\sqcup}$). $\mathcal{A}_5$ is unsatisfiable because it contains the clash $\{\mathsf{a} : \mathsf{CITY}, \mathsf{a} : \neg\mathsf{CITY}\}$. $\mathcal{A}_6$ is also unsatisfiable because the real formula $((\mathsf{y} \geq 3) \wedge (\mathsf{x} \geq 3) \wedge (\mathsf{x} \leq 4)) \wedge ((\mathsf{y} < 3) \vee (\mathsf{x} < 0) \vee (\mathsf{x} > 8))$ is unsatisfiable. Hence, CAML is subsumed by CON.

$$\begin{array}{ll}
\mathcal{A}_3 := \mathcal{A}_2 \cup \{\mathsf{a} : \mathsf{CITY} \sqcap \mathsf{in}((\mathsf{y} \geq 3)\wedge(\mathsf{x} \geq 3)\wedge(\mathsf{x} \leq 4)), & \\
\quad \mathsf{a} : (\neg\mathsf{CITY} \sqcup \mathsf{in}((\mathsf{y} < 3) \vee (\mathsf{x} < 0) \vee (\mathsf{x} > 8)))\} & \longrightarrow_{\sqcap} \\
\mathcal{A}_4 := \mathcal{A}_3 \cup \{\mathsf{a} : \mathsf{CITY}, \mathsf{a} : \mathsf{in}((\mathsf{y} \geq 3)\wedge(\mathsf{x} \geq 3)\wedge(\mathsf{x} \leq 4))\} & \longrightarrow_{\sqcap} \\
\mathcal{A}_5 := \mathcal{A}_4 \cup \{\mathsf{a} : \neg\mathsf{CITY}\} & \longrightarrow_{\sqcup} \\
\mathcal{A}_5' := \mathcal{A}_4 \cup \{\mathsf{a} : \mathsf{in}((\mathsf{y} < 3) \vee (\mathsf{x} < 0) \vee (\mathsf{x} > 8))\} & \longrightarrow_{\sqcup} \\
\mathcal{A}_6 := \mathcal{A}_5' \cup \{\mathsf{a} : \mathsf{in}((\mathsf{y} \geq 3)\wedge(\mathsf{x} \geq 3)\wedge(\mathsf{x} \leq 4))\wedge((\mathsf{y} < 3) \vee (\mathsf{x} < 0) \vee (\mathsf{x} > 8)))\} & \longrightarrow_{in}
\end{array}$$

Fig. 3. A sequence of rule applications for subsumption

5 Related Work

The idea of incorporating conceptual knowledge into spatial reasoning has been proposed in databases and Artificial Intelligence areas. We shortly discuss the relationship to modeling and reasoning with spatial data in Artificial Intelligence.

Spatial data representation and reasoning in Artificial Intelligence. Haarslev et *al.* [4] proposed an integration of quantitative spatial information with conceptual reasoning by the use of "generative" qualitative relations. Topological relation names (e.g., touching, covered-by) are used as role names. For example, a true-segment can be defined as a line_segment which satisfies some restrictions on the number of objects touching it. This is given by the following definition:

$$\mathsf{true\_segment} \doteq \mathsf{line\_segment} \sqcap (\geq 1\ \mathsf{touching}) \sqcap (\leq 4\ \mathsf{touching})$$

This proposal does not deal with spatial representation (i.e., shapes) of objects. The description logic framework can be seen as a language for encoding and reasoning with topological relations.

6 Conclusion

In this paper an approach for integrating terminological reasoning and spatial reasoning is presented. More precisely, we have proposed a formal spatial object data model in the style of KL-ONE based knowledge representation and reasoning system which is hybrid in two respects. On the one hand, it makes the usual distinction between two epistemological different kinds of knowledge, the terminological knowledge and the assertional knowledge. On the other hand, the terminological and assertional language, which usually describes the knowledge on an abstract logical level, is extended by allowing to refer to spatial data. The different parts of the system are integrated with the help of a unified model-theoretic semantics. Reasoning in the terminological and the assertional part can be done with the help of a single basic reasoning algorithm. This algorithm creates subtasks which have to be solved by the special purpose reasoner of the spatial domain. But there is no other interaction necessary between our basic algorithm and the reasoner on the spatial data.

The language we proposed can serve as a core for a knowledge base management system connected to a spatial database management system.

References

1. Franz Baader and Philipp Hanschke. A Scheme for Integrating Concrete Domains into Concept Languages. In *Proceedings of the 12th International Joint Conference on Artificial Intelligent (IJCAI'91). Sydney, Australia*, pages 452–457, 1991.
2. Riccardo Benedetti and Jean-Jacques Risler. *Real Algebraic and Semi-Algebraic Sets.* Hermann, editeurs des sciences et des arts, 293 rue Lecourbe, 75015 Paris, 1990. 340 pages.
3. Stéfane Grumbach, Jianwen Su, and Christophe Tollu. Linear Constraint Query Languages Expressive Power and Complexity. In Daniel Leivant, editor, *Proceedings of the International Workshop on Logic and Computational Complexity (LCC'94), Indianapolis, IN, USA*, pages 426–446, October 1994.
4. Volker Haarslev, Ralf Möller, and Carsten Schröder. Combining Spatial and Terminological Reasoning. In Bernhard Nebel and Leonie Dreschler-Fischer, editors, *Proceedings of the 18th German Annual Conference on Artificial Intelligence (KI'94), Saarbr"ucken, Germany*, pages 142–153, 1994.
5. Manfred Schmidt-Schauß and Gert Smolka. Attributive Concept Descriptions With Complements. *Artificial Intelligence*, 48(1):1–26, 1991.
6. Alfred Tarski. *A Decision Method for Elementary Algebra and Geometry.* University of California Press. Berkeley, 1951.
7. Luc Vandeurzen, Marc Gyssens, and Dirk Van Gucht. On Query Languages for Linear Queries Definable with Polynomial Constraints. In *Proceedings of the Second International Conference on Principles and Practice of Constraint Programming (CP'96), Cambridge, Massachusetts, USA*, pages 468–481. Springer Verlag, August 1996. LNCS 1118.

Deriving Abstract Views of Multi-granularity Temporal Constraint Networks

Claudio Bettini and Simone Ruffini

DSI - Università di Milano, Italy

Abstract. Temporal constraints are part of the specification of many complex application frameworks including activities to be scheduled, real-time components, temporal data management, e-commerce applications, and workflow management. This paper investigates the problem of creating an abstract view over a set of temporal constraints that may have been specified in terms of different granularities. The level of abstraction is determined by a specific time granularity chosen by the user among the ones in the system or created on purpose. An expressive formal model for time granularities is assumed including common granularities like hours and days as well as non-standard granularities like business days and academic semesters. The view derivation is based on a conversion technique exploiting the periodicity of time granularities.

1 Introduction

Integrated e-commerce applications are an example of frameworks where an advanced and efficient management of temporal aspects may be a significant advantage over the competition. In these complex systems the temporal relationships between events and activities involving different components are often described in terms of different time units. For example, the time between the receipt of an online order and the forwarding of item orders to the warehouses is described in minutes, while the time between the shipment of the order and the delivery is described in business-days.

This paper considers a formalization of the notion of temporal constraint with granularity and investigates the problem of creating an abstract view over a set of temporal constraints that may have been specified in terms of different granularities. The level of abstraction is determined by a specific time granularity chosen by the user among the ones in the system or created on purpose. In the above example we may want to have an abstract view of all the constraints in terms of business-days. In general, having an abstract view over a set of multi-granularity constraints may be desirable for at least two reasons: a) there are well-known algorithms to process temporal constraint networks where all the constraints are in terms of the same granularity [9], and b) it may be useful for the sake of application process monitoring to view all the constraints in terms of a particular granularity. In the e-commerce example, the abstract view in business days may be used to evaluate a guaranteed delivery time for the customer or for scheduling the internal processes.

R. Cicchetti et al. (Eds.): DEXA 2002, LNCS 2453, pp. 454–463, 2002.

Technically, the problem reduces to the conversion of each constraint into a corresponding one in terms of a different granularity. It will be immediately clear to the reader that the conversion problem is not a trivial one, even if we only consider common granularities like hours and days. For example, by saying that one event should occur the next day with respect to another one, we do not mean that the event should occur 24 hours after the other. Nor it is satisfactory to allow a range between 1 and 47 hours, as it may be suggested. Indeed 1 and 47 hours are actually the minimum and maximum distance between the occurrence of two events if they occur in consecutive days. However, a distance of 47 hours may also be the distance between two events whose occurrence is 2 days apart. This example actually says that an exact conversion does not exist, i.e., the constraint we obtain is not equivalent to the one we take as input.

Hence, our goal is, given a constraint in terms of a source granularity G, and given a target granularity H, to identify the constraint in terms of H which is the tightest among those implied by the input constraint or a good approximation of it. If $[m, n]G$ represents the constraint imposing a distance of at least m and at most n time units of G, then in the above example $[1, 47]$`hour` is the tightest among the constraints in terms of `hour` implied by $[1, 1]$`day`.

The concept of granularity as an abstraction tool has been deeply investigated in the AI and DB literature probably starting from [11]. The formalization of time granularity as adopted in this paper has been defined in [3] and used in several papers on the subject. Interesting recent work on this topic can also be found in [10], and [6]. Symbolic formalisms to represent time granularities have been proposed among others in [12],[5]. There are few approaches considering temporal constraints in terms of different granularities (e.g., [8],[10]), but in most cases they are restricted to common granularities. Our goal is to admit powerful constraints and very general user-defined granularities both to accurately model the new application domains and to select appropriate abstraction levels. A first comprehensive solution to this problem has been given in [3]. The main contribution of this paper with respect to [3] is the presentation of formal results which show how the algorithm can be implemented in practice for arbitrary periodical granularities, as well as a significant refinement of the conversion algorithm. A prototype system has been developed at the University of Milan and used for extensive testing.

Relevant applications of multi-granularity temporal constraints have been recently recognized in the area of data mining [4], workflow management [2], and clinical data management [7].

The rest of the paper is organized as follows. In the next section we introduce the formal notions of granularity and temporal constraints with granularities. In Section 3 we illustrate a general algorithm for granularity conversion, while in Section 4 we show how the algorithm can be implemented exploiting the periodicity of granularities. In Section 5 we give an example of abstract view derivation, and Section 6 concludes the paper. For lack of space, proofs are omitted, but can be found in [1].

2 Temporal Constraint Networks with Granularities

We first define a granularity system, called $\mathcal{GGR}$ (General Granularities on Reals) in [3], as the set of granularities satisfying the following definition.

Definition 1. *A* granularity *is a mapping G from the set of the integers to $2^{\mathcal{R}}$ (i.e., all subsets of reals) such that $G(i) = \emptyset$ for each non-positive integer i, and for all positive integers i and j with $i < j$, the following two conditions are satisfied:*

- *$G(i) \neq \emptyset$ and $G(j) \neq \emptyset$ imply that each real number in $G(i)$ is less than all real numbers in $G(j)$, and*
- *$G(i) = \emptyset$ implies $G(j) = \emptyset$.*

This is a very general notion of granularity modeling standard ones like `hour`, `day`, `week` and `month` as well as more specific ones like `academic semester`, `b-day` (business day), or `b-week` (business week), and arbitrarily user-defined granularities. For example, `b-week` may be defined by the mapping of its granules to the set of elements of the temporal domain denoting the period from a Monday through the next Friday every week. If we decide to model time starting from Monday 2001/1/1, then `b-week`(1), the first granule, is mapped to the instants denoting the period from 2001/1/1 through 2001/1/5, `b-week`(2) to the ones denoting 2001/1/8 through 2001/1/12, and so on.

In order to have finite representations of the granularities suitable to be automatically manipulated, we further restrict the granularities to those whose granules can be defined as a periodical pattern with respect to the granules of a fixed bottom granularity. For this purpose we first need to introduce a granularity relationship.

Definition 2. *A granularity G groups periodically into a granularity H if*

1. *for each non-empty granule $H(i)$, there exists a (possibly infinite) set S of positive integers such that $H(i) = \bigcup_{j \in S} G(j)$, and*
2. *there exist $R, P \in \mathbb{Z}^+$, where R is less than the number of granules of H, such that for all $i \in \mathbb{Z}^+$, if $H(i) = \bigcup_{r=0}^{k} G(j_r)$ and $H(i+R) \neq \emptyset$ then $H(i+R) = \bigcup_{r=0}^{k} G(j_r + P)$.*

Condition 1 says that any granule $H(i)$ is the union of some granules of G; for instance, assume it is the union of the granules $G(a_1), G(a_2), \ldots, G(a_k)$. The periodicity property (condition 2) ensures that if the Rth granule *after* $H(i)$ exists (i.e., $H(i+R) \neq \emptyset$), then it is the union of $G(a_1 + P), G(a_2 + P), \ldots, G(a_k + P)$. This results in a periodic "pattern" of the composition of R granules of H in terms of granules of G. The pattern repeats along the time domain by "shifting" each granule of H by P granules of G. The integer P is called the *period*. Many common granularities are in this kind of relationship, for example, both days and months group periodically into years. In general, this relationship guarantees that granularity H can be finitely described providing the specification of granules of H in terms of granules of G in an arbitrary period and the period value. For example, `b-week` can be described by the five business days in the first week of the time domain, and by the value 7 for the period. A granularity G_0 is called *bottom* granularity if G_0 groups periodically into each other granularity in the system.

We can now define a temporal constraint with granularity.

Definition 3. *Let $m, n \in \mathbb{Z} \cup \{-\infty, +\infty\}$ with $m \leq n$ and G a granularity. Then $[m, n]\, G$, called a* temporal constraint with granularity *(TCG), is the binary relation on positive integers defined as follows: For positive integers t_1 and t_2, (t_1, t_2)* satisfies *$[m, n]\, G$ if and only if (1) $\lceil t_1 \rceil^G$ and $\lceil t_2 \rceil^G$ are both defined, and (2) $m \leq (\lceil t_2 \rceil^G - \lceil t_1 \rceil^G) \leq n$.*

The $\lceil x \rceil^G$ function returns the index of the granule of G that includes $G_0(x)$. Intuitively, to check if a pair of instants (t_1, t_2) satisfies the TCG $[m, n]\, G$, we derive the indexes of the granules of G containing t_1 and t_2, respectively, and then we take the difference. If it is at least m and at most n, then the pair of instants is said to satisfy the constraint. For example, the pair (t_1, t_2) satisfies $[0, 0]$ `day` if t_1 and t_2 are within the same day. Similarly, (t_1, t_2) satisfies $[-1, 1]$ `hour` if t_1 and t_2 are at most one hour apart (and their order is immaterial). Finally, (t_1, t_2) satisfies $[1, 1]$ `month` if t_2 is in the next month with respect to t_1.

Definition 4. *A* constraint network (with granularities) *is a directed graph (W, A, Γ, Dom), where W is a finite set of variables, $A \subseteq W \times W$ a set of arcs, Γ is a mapping from A to the finite sets of temporal constraints with granularities, and Dom is a mapping from W to a possibly bounded periodical set of positive integers.*

A set of positive integers S is said to be periodical *if there exists a granularity G such that the bottom granularity periodically groups into G and $S = \{i \mid \lceil i \rceil^G$ is defined$\}$. The set is bounded if an integer U is given such that each value in the set must be less than or equal to U.*

Intuitively, a constraint network specifies a complex temporal relationship where each variable in W represents a specific instant (for example the occurrence time of an event) in terms of the bottom granularity. The domain of each variable is essentially a set of granules of the bottom granularity, represented through the positive integers corresponding to the granule indexes. The set of TCGs assigned to an edge is taken as conjunction. That is, for each TCG in the set assigned to the edge (X, Y), the instants assigned to X and Y must satisfy the TCG. Fig. 1 shows an example of a constraint network with granularities with no explicit constraint on domains ($Dom(X) = [1, \infty)$ for each variable X).

It is important to note that it is not always possible to replace a TCG $[m, n]\, G$ into a TCG in `seconds` Indeed, consider $[0, 0]$ `day`. Two instants satisfy the constraint if they fall within the same day. In terms of `second`, they could differ from 0 to $24 \times 60 \times 60 - 1 = 86399$ seconds. However, $[0, 86399]$ `second` has a different semantics from the original constraint. For example, if instant t_1 corresponds to 11pm in one day and instant t_2 to 4am the next day, then t_1 and t_2 do not satisfy $[0, 0]$ `day`; however, they do satisfy $[0, 86399]$ `second`.

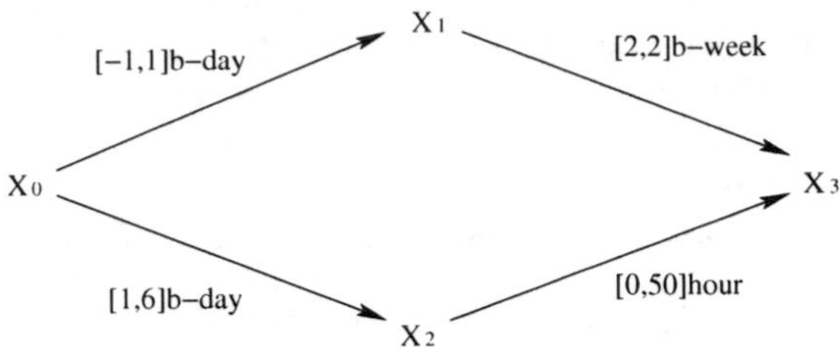

Fig. 1. A constraint network with granularities

3 Conversion of Constraints in Different Granularities

Consider the problem of converting a given TCG_1 in terms of G_1 into a logically implied TCG_2 in terms of G_2. (TCG_1 *logically implies* TCG_2 if any pair of time instants satisfying TCG_1 also satisfy TCG_2.) If we only have a total order of granularities with uniform granules, like e.g., `minute`, `hour`, and `day`, then the conversion algorithm is trivial since fixed conversion factors can be used. However, if incomparable granularities like `week` and `month`, or granularities with non-contiguous granules like `b-day` and `b-week` are considered, the conversion becomes more complex.

Moreover, given an arbitrary TCG_1, and a granularity G, it is not always possible to find a logically implied TCG_2 in terms of G. For example, $[0,0]$ `day` does not logically imply $[m,n]$ `b-day` no matter what m and n are. The reason is that $[0,0]$`day` is satisfied by any two events that happen during the same day, whether the day is a business day or a weekend day.

3.1 Allowed Conversions

In our framework, we allow the conversion of a TCG of a constraint network $\mathcal{N}$ into another TCG if the resulting constraint is implied by the set of all the TCGs in $\mathcal{N}$. More specifically, a TCG $[m,n]\,G$ on arc (X,Y) in a network $\mathcal{N}$ is *allowed* to be converted into $[m',n']\,H$ as long as $[m',n']\,H$ is *implied* by $\mathcal{N}$, i.e., for any pair of values t_X and t_Y assigned to X and Y respectively, if (t_X,t_Y) satisfies $[m,n]\,G$ and t_X and t_Y belong to a solution of $\mathcal{N}$, then (t_X,t_Y) also satisfies $[m',n']\,H$. To guarantee that only allowed conversions are performed, we assign to each variable X of a constraint network, a periodical set G_X which is the intersection of the domain of X and all the periodical sets defined by the granularities appearing in TCGs involving X. Then, a TCG on variables X and Y can be converted in terms of a target granularity H if each element in $G_X \cup G_Y$ is contained in a granule of H. It is easily seen that this condition guarantees the existence of an *allowed* conversion; indeed any pair of values t_X and t_Y assigned to X and Y respectively which is part of a solution must be in $G_X \cup G_Y$ (we only excluded values which could not satisfy TCGs), and if both values are contained in granules of H, their distance in terms of H can be evaluated.

Example 1. Consider the network in Fig. 1. The TCG in terms of `hour` cannot be converted in terms of `b-day` or `b-week` without considering the other constraints in the network. However, both G_{X_2} and G_{X_3} evaluate to the granularity obtained from `hour` by dropping all granules not included in a business day. Since both `b-day` and `b-week` cover the same span of time as this granularity, the constraint $[0, 50]$ `hour` can be converted in terms of `b-day` and `b-week`, obtaining $[0, 3]$ `b-day` and $[0, 1]$ `b-week`, respectively.

3.2 The Conversion Algorithm

We propose a general algorithm for constraint conversion based on the assumption that in most cases we know the relationship between each granularity and the bottom granularity.[1] Indeed, the algorithm, reported in Fig. 2, uses the distance functions *minsize*(), *maxsize*(), and *mindist-prim*() that take as one of their arguments the target granularity and return a value in terms of the bottom granularity. Intuitively, $minsize(G_2, k)$ and $maxsize(G_2, k)$ denote respectively the minimum and maximum length of k consequent granules of G_2, expressed in granules of the bottom granularity. For example, $minsize(\texttt{month}, 1) = 28$, and $maxsize(\texttt{month}, 1) = 31$ if `day` is the bottom granularity. The value of $mindist\text{-}prim(G_1, m)$ denotes the minimal distance in terms of granules of the bottom granularity between all pairs of instants in a granule of G_1 and in the mth granule after it, respectively. The conversion algorithm returns **undefined** when it is not possible to evaluate this distance for any pair of instants that are a candidate solution respectively for variables X and Y.

Steps 1 and 2 compute respectively the new minimum and maximum in terms of the target granularity. The algorithm imposes $n \in \mathbb{Z}^+$ if $n \neq +\infty$ for the input constraint. This is not a limitation since any constraint $[-n, -m]\, G$ on (X, Y) with $m, n > 0$ can be expressed as $[m, n]\, G$ on (Y, X). When both m and n are positive, the maximum and minimum distances identified by the constraint in terms of the bottom granularity are $maxsize(G_1, n{+}1)$ and $mindist\text{-}prim(G_1, m)$, respectively. We have to find these distances in terms of the target granularity. For the maximum we use the minimal length (*minsize*()) of a group of granules in the target granularity, since we want to maximize the number of granules needed to cover the given distance. Analogously, we use the maximal length (*maxsize*()) in the computation of the minimum value. If the lower bound is non-positive, we consider its absolute value and we treat it exactly as the upper bound except for reversing the sign of the result. When $m = -\infty$ and/or $n = +\infty$ the conversion algorithm simply keeps these constants also for the TCG in the target granularity. It is easily seen that this always leads to an implied TCG. However, when G_1 is bounded, the ∞ constants may be converted more precisely into finite values.

Theorem 1. *The conversion algorithm in Fig. 2 is correct: Any constraint obtained as output is implied by the original network.*

[1] This is very likely since the bottom granularity periodically groups into any other granularity.

INPUT: a network $\mathcal{N}$, a TCG $[m,n]\,G_1$, with $m \in \mathbb{Z} \cup \{-\infty\}$ and $n \in \mathbb{Z}^+ \cup \{+\infty\}$ associated with an arc (X,Y); a bottom granularity G; a target granularity G_2, s.t. $\forall i,t\ (t \in G_X(i) \cup G_Y(i) \Rightarrow \exists j\ t \in G_2(j))$.

OUTPUT: a logically implied TCG $[\overline{m},\overline{n}]G_2$ for (X,Y) or **undefined**.

METHOD:

if $\exists i,i',i'',m'$ s.t. $m \leq m' \leq n$, $G_1(i) \cap G_X(i') \neq \emptyset$, and $G_1(i+m') \cap G_Y(i'') \neq \emptyset$ **then**

Step 1 **if** $m = -\infty$ **then** $\overline{m} = -\infty$
  else if $m \leq 0$ **then** $\overline{m} = -min(R)$, **where**
  $R = \{r \mid minsize(G_2,r) \geq maxsize(G_1,|m|+1) - 1\}$
  else $\overline{m} = min(R) - 1$, **where**
  $R = \{r \mid maxsize(G_2,r) > mindist\text{-}prim(G_1,m)\}$
Step 2 **if** $n = +\infty$ **then** $\overline{n} = +\infty$
  else $\overline{n} = min(S)$, **where**
  $S = \{s \mid minsize(G_2,s) \geq maxsize(G_1,n+1) - 1\}$
Step 3 **return** $[\overline{m},\overline{n}]\,G_2$

else return undefined
where
$minsize(H,r) = min(Q)$ and $maxsize(H,r) = max(Q)$, with
  $Q = \{k \mid \exists j,i,\ k = min\{k' \mid (H(j) \cup \cdots \cup H(j+r-1)) \subseteq (G(i) \cup \cdots \cup G(i+k'-1))\}\}$

$mindist\text{-}prim(G_1,m) = min\{d \mid \exists i,j\ G(j) \cap G_1(i) \neq \emptyset$ and $G(j+d) \cap G_1(i+m) \neq \emptyset\}$

Fig. 2. Conversion of constraints through a bottom granularity

The conversion algorithm does not always return the tightest implied constraint, but, based on extensive experiments [1], it provides a very good approximation.

4 Implementation

In this section, we show how the conversion algorithm can be implemented. Essentially, this can be done by exploiting the periodicity of granularities and variable domains. First of all, we need to ensure that the conversion is allowed, as required by the condition specified on the INPUT in Fig. 2. From Section 3, we know that the conversion of a constraint on the distance from X to Y with target granularity G_2 is allowed if each element in $G_X \cup G_Y$ is in G_2. If we consider G_2' as the periodical set induced by G_2, it is easily seen that this condition holds if $G_X \cap G_2' \equiv G_X$ and $G_Y \cap G_2' \equiv G_Y$. Intersection of periodical sets can be easily implemented by considering their common period, and similarly can be implemented equivalence. (See [1] for details.) Secondly, we need to compute the values of the distance functions $minsize()$, $maxsize()$, and $mindist\text{-}prim()$ for arbitrary granularities and arbitrary parameters.

4.1 Computation of Distance Functions

Let us assume that `hour` is the bottom granularity (as we do in our system prototype), H is a generic granularity such that `hour` periodically groups into H, P is its period in terms of hours and R its number of granules in each period.

The method to compute the functions $minsize()$ and $maxsize()$ is based on two observations: a) Any group of consecutive R granules of H covers a span of time less than or equal to P hours; b) Any group of consecutive $R+1$ granules covers more than P hours.

Theorem 2. *Let P be the period of H and R the number of granules in P.*
If k MOD $R \neq 0$, then $minsize(H,k) = P*(k \text{ DIV } R)+minsize(H, k \text{ MOD } R)$ else $minsize(H,k) = P*((k-1) \text{ DIV } R) + minsize(H,R)$.
If k MOD $R \neq 0$, then $maxsize(H,k) = P*(k \text{ DIV } R)+maxsize(H, k \text{ MOD } R)$ else $maxsize(H,k) = P*((k-1) \text{ DIV } R) + maxsize(H,R)$.

Theorem 2 gives the value of $minsize(H,k)$ e $maxsize(H,k)$ for any k, given their value for $k = 0,\ldots,R$. To compute these values it is sufficient to consider each group of $1,\ldots,R$ consecutive granules of H in an arbitrary span of time of length $2*P$ (containing $2*R$ granules), taking the initial granule in the first period. For example, in order to evaluate $maxsize(b\text{-}day, 2)$ we consider each pair of consecutive business days from 2001/1/1 to 2001/1/14. The maximum size is obtained when we consider the pair (2001/1/5,2001/1/8), i.e., a Friday and the next Monday. The computation of these values can be easily implemented. We still have to determine how to compute $mindist\text{-}prim(H,k)$. A reasonable conjecture is that its value is given by $minsize(H,k-1)+1$. However, the real value may be greater than that if the granularity includes non contiguous granules, since the formula does not take into account the distance between the $(k-1)-th$ and the $k-th$ value. The following result gives the correct value for the function $mindist\text{-}prim()$.

Theorem 3. *Let P be the period of H and R the number of granules in P.*
If k MOD $R \neq 0$, then
$mindist\text{-}prim(H,k) = P*(k \text{ DIV } R) + mindist\text{-}prim(H, k \text{ MOD } R)$
else $mindist\text{-}prim(H,k) = P*((k-1) \text{ DIV } R) + mindist\text{-}prim(H,R)$

Analogously to $minsize()$ and $maxsize()$, $mindist\text{-}prim(H,k)$ can be efficiently computed for any k by the formulas in Theorem 3 if we precompute its value for $k = 0,\ldots,R$.

An implementation of the algorithm based on the above formulas has been developed in C and it is running on a Linux server at the University of Milan.

5 Deriving Abstract Views

Given a constraint network, we can derive an abstract view of it in terms of a target granularity H by applying the conversion algorithm to each constraint for which a conversion into H is allowed. Clearly, if some of the conversions are not allowed, an abstract view will have less constraints than the original network. Depending on the specific application it may be imposed that abstract views are generated only for granularities which admit a conversion of the complete network. The following example shows the derivation of an abstract view following the steps of the algorithm and the implementation techniques illustrated in the previous section.

Example 2. Consider the network in Fig. 1 and suppose we are asked to provide an abstract view of it in terms of business days. This means the constraints on arcs (X_1, X_3) and (X_2, X_3) must be converted. Considering $[2,2]$ `b-week`, since $m = 2$ (positive), we must calculate $\mathit{mindist\text{-}prim}(\texttt{b-week}, 2)$. For the granularity `b-week`, $R = 1$ and $P = 168$.

The value $\mathit{mindist\text{-}prim}(\texttt{b-week}, 1) = 49$ is the only we need to know, and $\mathit{mindist\text{-}prim}(\texttt{b-week}, 2) = P * 1 + \mathit{mindist\text{-}prim}(\texttt{b-week}, 1) = 168 + 49 = 217$. Now we must evaluate the minimum r such that $\mathit{maxsize}(\texttt{b-day}, r) > 217$. Granularity `b-day` has $R = 5$, $P = 168$. To calculate $\mathit{maxsize}(\texttt{b-day}, r)$ for every r, we need the value of $\mathit{maxsize}()$ for $r = 1$ to 5. These are respectively 24, 96, 120, 144, 168. The minimum r that satisfy the condition is $r = 7$, because $\mathit{maxsize}(\texttt{b-day}, 7) = P * (7 \text{ DIV } 5) + \mathit{maxsize}(\texttt{b-day}, 7 \text{ MOD } 5) = 168 + 96 = 264$, then $\overline{m} = 7 - 1 = 6$. With an analogous computation for n, we obtain $\overline{n} = 15$, and hence the new constraint $[6, 15]$ `b-day`.
The TCG in terms of `hour` cannot be converted in terms of `b-day` or `b-week` without considering the other constraints in the network, but G_{X_0}, G_{X_1}, G_{X_2} and G_{X_3} evaluate to the granularity obtained from `hour` by dropping all granules not included in a business day. Since both `b-day` and `b-week` cover the same span of time as this granularity, the constraint $[0, 50]$ `hour` can be converted in terms of `b-day` and `b-week`. Its conversion accordingly to the algorithm is $[0, 3]$ `b-day`, and the abstract view of the network in terms of `b-day` is shown in Fig. 3(a).

Similarly, we can obtain the abstract view in terms of `b-week` shown in Fig. 3(b). In this case, the constraints to be converted are those on arcs (X_0, X_1), (X_0, X_2) and (X_2, X_3). The algorithm derives $[-1, 1]$ `b-week`, $[0, 2]$ `b-week`, and $[0, 1]$ `b-week`, respectively.

The use of an intermediate granularity (the bottom granularity) in the conversion introduces an approximation that is reflected on the constraints of the de-

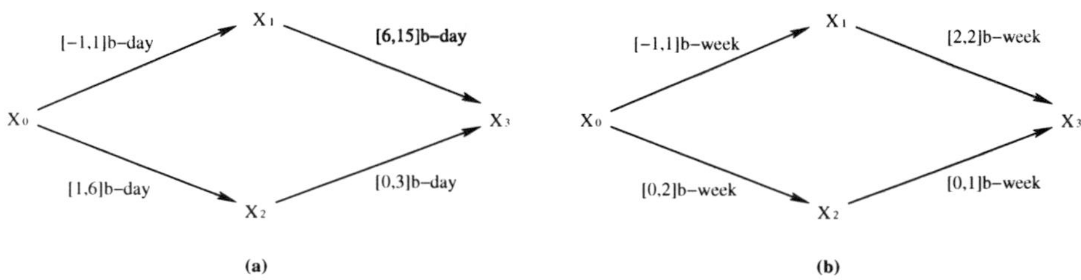

Fig. 3. An abstract view of the network (a) in `b-day`, and (b) in `b-week`

rived abstract view. In Example 2 the tightest implied constraint on arc (X_1, X_3) is $[6, 14]$ `b-day` and it is approximated by $[6, 15]$ `b-day`. Direct conversions avoid the approximation, but seem to be viable only for a very limited subset of granularities [1].

6 Conclusion

In this paper we proposed an algorithm and implementation techniques for the conversion of temporal constraints in terms of different granularities. By applying the algorithm, it is possible to derive abstract views of an original set of constraints. The conversion algorithm can also be integrated with arc and path consistency techniques for constraint propagation [9], leading to the derivation of implicit constraints in the abstract view and to the refinement of existing ones. As future work, we are investigating the application of the abstract view concept and algorithms to the problems of monitoring and scheduling in inter-organizational workflow management, an area where multi-granularity temporal constraints have been proven to be particularly useful [2].

References

1. C. Bettini, S. Ruffini. Granularity conversion of quantitative temporal constraints. DSI Technical Report N. 276-02, University of Milan, Italy, 2002.
2. C. Bettini, X. S. Wang, S. Jajodia. Temporal Reasoning for Supporting Workflow Systems. *Distributed and Parallel Databases*, 11(3):269-306, Kluwer, 2002.
3. C. Bettini, X. Wang, S. Jajodia. A general framework for time granularity and its application to temporal reasoning. *Annals of Mathematics and Artificial Intelligence*, 22(1,2):29–58, Kluwer, 1998.
4. C. Bettini, X. Wang, J. Lin, S. Jajodia, Discovering Frequent Event Patterns With Multiple Granularities in Time Sequences. *IEEE Transactions on Knowledge and Data Engineering*, 10(2):222–237, 1998.
5. R. Chandra, A. Segev, and M. Stonebraker, Implementing calendars and temporal rules in next generation databases, in *Proc. of ICDE*, 1994, pp. 264-273.
6. C. Combi, A. Montanari, Data Models with Multiple Temporal Dimensions: Completing the Picture, in Proc. of CAiSE, pp.187–202, 2001.
7. C. Combi, L. Chittaro, Abstraction on clinical data sequences: an object-oriented data model and a query language based on the event calculus *Artificial Intelligence in Medicine*, 17(3): 271-301, Elsevier, 1999.
8. T. Dean, Using temporal hierarchies to efficiently maintain large temporal databases *Journal of the ACM*, 36(4):687–718, 1989.
9. R. Dechter, I. Meiri, and J. Pearl, Temporal constraint networks, *Artificial Intelligence*, 49:61–95, Elsevier, 1991.
10. I.A. Goralwalla, Y. Leontiev, M.T. Ozsu, D. Szafron, C. Combi, Temporal Granularity: Completing the Puzzle. *Journal of Intelligent Information Systems*, 16(1): 41-63, Kluwer, 2001.
11. J.R. Hobbs, Granularity, in *Proc. of IJCAI*, Los Angeles, CA, 1985, pp. 432–435.
12. B. Leban, D. Mcdonald, and D. Foster, A representation for collections of temporal intervals, in *Proc. of AAAI*, 1986, pp. 367–371.

Representing Constraint Business Rules Extracted from Legacy Systems

G. Fu[1], J. Shao[1], S.M. Embury[2], and W.A. Gray[1]

[1] Department of Computer Science, Cardiff University, UK
{scmgf, J.Shao, W.A.Gray}@cs.cf.ac.uk
[2] Department of Computer Science, University of Manchester, UK
SEmbury@cs.man.ac.uk

Abstract. Constraints are a class of business rules that most information systems implement. However, due to staff turnover and lack of documentation, precise knowledge of what constraints are enforced by a system is often not available. This can seriously hinder an organisation's ability to understand the data stored in its systems, and to evolve the systems to implement new business policies. To help the situation, researchers have considered how to extract constraints out of legacy systems. While some powerful methods have been proposed for identifying constraints in application programs, little has been done so far to help users to comprehend the recovered constraints. To step up research in this direction, we study in this paper how the recovered constraints should be represented, so that they can be analysed, processed and then presented to the user in a comprehensible manner. We introduce a representation language that offers a balance between expressiveness, comprehensibility and reasoning power in handling the recovered constraints.

1 Introduction

Constraints are an important class of business rules that most information systems (ISs) implement. They describe the conditions under which an organisation operates. For example, a mobile phone service provider may have "new customers are eligible for free connections" as a constraint business rule.

Most ISs implement constraints. However, due to staff turnover and lack of documentation, what constraints are actually implemented in ISs may not be explicitly available or even lost. This can seriously limit organisations' ability to understand the data stored in their ISs, and to evolve the systems to implement new business policies.

To help the situation, researchers have considered how to recover constraints from ISs [9,5]. While these techniques are useful for identifying constraints from ISs, they do very little to help users to comprehend them. Typically, they recover constraints from ISs in the specific formats, such as program segments or logic statements, and then return them directly to the user. This is unsatisfactory for two reasons. First, the extracted constraints may have some hidden properties which, once established, can contribute to their comprehension. For

R. Cicchetti et al. (Eds.): DEXA 2002, LNCS 2453, pp. 464–473, 2002.

example, two or more constraints may be "related" according to certain criteria, or one constraint may conflict with another. Second, the recovered constraints may be used by different user groups, characterized by different interests, diverse background knowledge and specific responsibilities. For example, a system maintainer may like to understand a constraint in a form that will help him or her understand how it is implemented in ISs, whereas a business analyst may wish to understand the constraints in a business context. Clearly, direct returning the extracted constraints to the user will not meet this requirement.

What we need therefore is an intermediate representation of constraints that can support some form of reasoning (so as to recover implicit properties that may exist among the extracted constraints), and facilitate the interpretation of their semantics (in order to bridge the gap between implementation and conceptualisation). This is shown in Figure 1, i.e., where the extracted constraints are stored in a repository before being mapped to various presentation formats. A key issue here is the notation for representing the constraints: it must be expressive enough to represent a variety of extracted constraints, allow efficient analysis of their properties, and support their mapping to user preferred presentation formats.

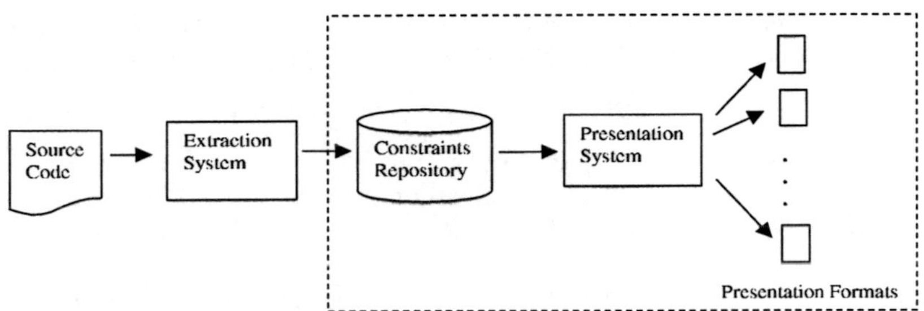

Fig. 1. A Framework for BR Presentation

In this paper, we introduce a language, $\mathcal{BRL}$, for representing a range of constraints that may be extracted from ISs. In contrast to other constraint representation languages [10,1,7], $\mathcal{BRL}$ offers a unique combination of and balance between expressiveness, comprehensibility and support for reasoning. Constraints are expressed in $\mathcal{BRL}$ in terms of business classes rather than the instances of these classes. This helps to bridge the gap between implementation and conceptualisation. Only a small set of representational constructs are included in $\mathcal{BRL}$ to capture the semantics that can realistically be expected from the reverse engineering of constraints. This makes our language compact and our reasoning efficient. Finally, $\mathcal{BRL}$ is designed within a logic framework, hence supports constraint analysis through logical inferences. We believe that these features of $\mathcal{BRL}$ provide essential support for the comprehension of extracted constraints.

The paper is organised as follows. Section 2 defines what we mean by constraints. Section 3 describes $\mathcal{BRL}$. We give its syntax and semantics first, and then discuss its main features by showing how the constraints are expressed in $\mathcal{BRL}$. Section 4 reviews the related work. Conclusions are given in Section 5.

2 Constraint Business Rules

Before introducing $\mathcal{BRL}$, it is necessary to explain what we mean by constraints and how constraints are classified.

Definition 1. *A structure is denoted by $S(S_1, S_2, \ldots, S_n)$, where S is the name of the structure and each S_i $(1 \leq i \leq n)$ is a component. If S does not have any component, S is a primitive structure. Otherwise, S is a composite structure.*

For example, `id` is a primitive structure and `customer(id, name, address)` is a composite one. Note that each component of a structure can also be a structure (primitive or composite), so a structure is recursively defined, e.g. `customer(id, name(first_name, last_name), address)` is a valid structure too.

Definition 2. *Each structure has an associated domain. Let S be a structure, the domain of S, denoted by $Dom(S)$, is recursively defined as follows:*

1. *If S is a primitive structure, then $Dom(S)$ is a set of values $\{v_1, v_2, \ldots\}$;*
2. *If S is a composite structure $S(S_1, S_2, \ldots, S_n)$, then $Dom(S) = Dom(S_1) \times Dom(S_2) \times \ldots \times Dom(S_n)$.*

A domain is essentially a set of elements from which a structure draws its instances. For example, `id` may draw its instances from $Dom(id) = \{c101, c102\}$, and `customer(id, name)` from $Dom(customer) = Dom(id) \times Dom(name)$.

Definition 3. *Let S be a structure and $Dom(S)$ be its domain. The state of S at time t, denoted by S^t, is a subset of $Dom(S)$. That is, $S^t \subseteq Dom(S)$.*

Not every subset of $Dom(S)$ is a valid state of S. To ensure that S^t is valid, constraints are introduced. We see constraints as "filtering functions" that eliminate the invalid states of S. This is explained in Figure 2.

Fig. 2. A Model of Constraints

That is, we see a valid state $\widehat{S^t}$ being derived by applying two sets of constraints ($\mathcal{C}_1$ and $\mathcal{C}_2$) as filters to the elements in $Dom(S)$. $\mathcal{C}_1$ are the constraints that eliminate the unwanted elements from $Dom(S)$. For example, `age > 17` is a typical $\mathcal{C}_1$-constraint which eliminates values below 18 from $Dom(age)$. $\mathcal{C}_2$ are the constraints that eliminate the unwanted states to be drawn from $\widehat{Dom(S)}$, i.e., the unwanted subsets from $\mathbb{P}(\widehat{Dom(S)})$, the power set of $\widehat{Dom(S)}$. Suppose that we have `custAcc(cust,ac)` and assume that $\widehat{Dom(custAcc)} = \{< c1, a1 >, < c1, a2 >, < c2, a1 >, < c2, a2 >\}$. That is, we have two customers (`c1` and `c2`) and each is allowed to open two types of account (`a1` and `a2`). Then "**`each customer can have no more than one account`**" is a $\mathcal{C}_2$-constraint which eliminates $\{< c1, a1 >, < c1, a2 >\}$ and $\{< c2, a1 >, < c2, a2 >\}$ from the set of states (subsets) that may be drawn from $\widehat{Dom(custAcc)}$.

Both $\mathcal{C}_1$ and $\mathcal{C}_2$ constraints may further be classified according to how they perform the elimination: they can be either conditional or unconditional. We therefore have four types of constraint. In the following, we will describe these types of constraint, and will use the following structure to describe the constraint business rules for a mobile phone service provider in our examples:

```
order(customer(id, name),
      service(network, freeTime)
      recommender(id, name))
```

Type-I (unconditional domain filtering constraints). This type of constraint determines which elements of $Dom(S)$ are allowed to be in $\widehat{Dom(S)}$. These constraints are usually associated with primitive structures. Suppose that $Dom(network)$ and $Dom(freeTime)$ are completely unconstrained, i.e. they are the Universe of Discourse (UoD). Then the following constraints

```
BR1. The company uses the following networks: Vodafone, Orange,
     one2one and BTcellnet.
BR2. The company offers 2 types of free talk: 300 and 600 minutes
```

will reduce $Dom(network)$ and $Dom(freeTime)$ to $\widehat{Dom(network)} = \{Vodafone, Orange, one2one, BTcellnet\}$ and $\widehat{Dom(freeTime)} = \{300, 600\}$, respectively.

Type-II (conditional domain filtering constraints). This type of constraint is to do with a composite structure $S(S_1, S_2, \ldots, S_n)$ and eliminates the unwanted elements from $Dom(S)$ by specifying a *dependency condition* that the values of some components of S must satisfy. Suppose that $Dom(service) = \widehat{Dom(network)} \times \widehat{Dom(freeTime)} = \{< Vodafone, 300 >, < Vodafone, 600 >, \ldots, < BTCellnet, 300 >, < BTCellnet, 600 >\}$. Then the constraint

```
BR3. Only Vodafone customers are entitled to 600 minutes free talk.
```

eliminates $< BTCellnet, 600 >$, $< Orange, 600 >$ and $< One2one, 600 >$ from $Dom(service)$, leaving $\widehat{Dom(service)} = \{< Vodafone, 300 >, < Vodafone, 600 >, < Orange, 300 >, < one2one, 300 >, < BTCellnet, 300 >\}$.

Type-III (unconditional state filtering constraints). This type of constraint eliminates one type of invalid state being drawn from $\widehat{Dom(S)}$. This is achieved by specifying a *size* requirement for a valid state. For example, the following is a Type-III constraint which ensures that no subset of $\widehat{Dom(customer)}$ whose size is greater than 100,000 may be returned as $\widehat{customer^t}$:

```
BR4. The company is allowed to provide services to up to
     100,000 customers by the regulator.
```

Type-IV (conditional state filtering constraints). This type of constraint is similar in function to Type-III, except that they eliminate invalid states by specifying a condition that the members of a subset drawn from $\widehat{Dom(S)}$ must collectively satisfy. This type of constraint can appear in various forms. They can specify *inclusion dependencies*, *association cardinalities* and other complex logical dependencies that must be obeyed by two or more states. For example, the following are all Type-IV constraints:

```
BR5. Recommenders must be existing customers.
BR6. A customer must use one, but no more than four services.
BR7. The total number of services, for which the free talk time
     is 600 minutes, must be less than 10,000.
```

BR5 ensures that an instance of $\widehat{recommender^t}$ must be an instance in $\widehat{customer^t}$ too. BR6 requires that each instance in $\widehat{customer^t}$ corresponds to between 1 and 4 instances in $\widehat{service^t}$. BR7 specifies that $\widehat{service^t}$ is valid if the number of instances in $\widehat{service^t}$ with respect to $freeTime = 600$ is less than 10,000.

The above classification of constraints is vital for us to design a language to represent the constraints. The four types of constraint we identified above are general enough to capture the constraints that may be extracted from ISs. By identifying the properties for each class of constraints, it is possible for us to introduce suitable constructs into $\mathcal{BRL}$ which we describe below.

3 The $\mathcal{BRL}$ Language

In this section, we first present the syntax and semantics of $\mathcal{BRL}$, and then discuss the features of $\mathcal{BRL}$ by showing how constraints are represented in it.

3.1 Syntax and Semantics of $\mathcal{BRL}$

$\mathcal{BRL}$ is a predicate logic based language. It has the usual predicate logic syntax. That is, a well formed formula (wff) is constructed according to the following:

$$\begin{aligned} < wff > ::= & \ Atomic\ Formula \mid \forall x < wff > \mid \exists x < wff > \mid \neg < wff > \mid \\ & < wff > \wedge < wff > \mid < wff > \vee < wff > \mid < wff > \rightarrow < wff > \end{aligned}$$

The wffs have their usual semantics and we assume that the reader is familiar with them. The construction of *atomic formula*, however, needs some explanation. First, we restrict our atomic formulas to be a set of *pre-defined* predicates:

$$\begin{aligned} < Atomic > \ ::= & \ TYPEOF(P, B) \mid ENUMERATE(P, \{O_1, ..., O_n\}) \mid \\ & EQUAL(P, A) \mid GREATERTHAN(P, A) \mid SUBSUME(P_1, P_2) \mid \end{aligned}$$

$DISJOINT(P_1, P_2) \mid ONEOF(P, \{P_1, ..., P_m\}) \mid ATMOST(P, n) \mid$
$ATLEAST(P, n) \mid ATLEAST(P_1, n, P_2) \mid ATMOST(P_1, n, P_2)$

Second, the terms used in these predicates are *meta-level* elements. More precisely, let $\mathcal{S}$ be a set of structure names, $\mathcal{P}$ be a set of path expressions (in the form $S_1.S_2 \ldots S_{m-1}.S_m$, $(m \geq 1)$, where each S_i is a structure name), $\mathcal{B}$ be a set of type names (e.g., String, Integer, etc) and $\mathcal{O}$ be a set of object names. A *term* in $\mathcal{BRL}$ is one of the following:

- a type $B \in \mathcal{B}$
- a path expression $P \in \mathcal{P}$
- an arithmetic expression A constructed from $O \in \mathcal{O}$, $P \in \mathcal{P}$ and usual arithmetic operators.

We give the semantics of $\mathcal{BRL}$ by mapping it into the corresponding instance level expressions in first order logic (FOL). First we have a translation function Φ that maps the terms of $\mathcal{BRL}$ to the corresponding instance level formulas as follows. The mappings for predicates are given in Table 1.

- For every $B \in \mathcal{B}$, $\Phi_x(B)$ produces a formula $B(x)$ with a free variable x. For example, $\Phi_x(Real)$ maps to $Real(x)$.
- For every path expression $P = S_1.S_2 \ldots S_m$, $\Phi_{x_1,x_2,...,x_m}(P)$ produces a formula $S_1(x_1) \wedge R_1(x_1, x_2) \wedge S_2(x_2) \wedge \ldots \wedge S_m(x_m)$ with free variables $x_1, x_2, ..., x_m$. $R_i(x_i, x_{i+1})$ is an auxiliary predicate used to specify the implicit relationship between x_i and x_j. For example, $\Phi_{x_1,x_2}(service.network)$ produces $service(x_1) \wedge R(x_1, x_2) \wedge network(x_2)$.
- For every arithmetic expression A, $\Phi_{x_1,...,x_m}(A)$ produces a formula $S_1(x_1) \wedge \ldots \wedge S_m(x_m)$ and a new arithmetic expression A' with free variables $x_1, ..., x_m$. $S_1, ..., S_m$ are the structure names appeared in A, $x_1, ..., x_m$ are free variables ranged over $S_1, ..., S_m$, respectively, and A' is the new arithmetic expression derived from A with $S_1, ..., S_m$ substituted by their corresponding variables $x_1, ..., x_m$. For example, $\Phi_x(freeTime + 100)$ produces a formula $freeTime(x)$ and a new expression $(x + 100)$.

For example, the following are valid formulas in $\mathcal{BRL}$:

(1) $ENUMERATE(service.network, \{Vodafone, Orange, one2one, BTcellnet\})$
(2) $EQUAL(service.talkTime, 600) \rightarrow EQUAL(service.network, Vodafone)$

and they have the following interpretation in FOL:

(1′) $\forall x, y(service(x) \wedge R(x, y) \wedge network(y) \rightarrow (y = Vodafone) \vee (y = Orange) \vee (y = one2one) \vee (y = BTcellnet))$
(2′) $\forall x, y_1, y_2(service(x) \wedge R_1(x, y_1) \wedge talkTime(y_1) \wedge R_2(x, y_2) \wedge network(y_2) \wedge (y_1 = 600) \rightarrow (y_2 = Vodafone))$

Table 1. Interpretation of Pre-defined Predicates in $\mathcal{BRL}$

$\mathcal{BRL}$ Predicates	Interpretation in FOL
$TYPEOF(P, B)$	$\forall x_1, ..., x_n(\Phi_{x_1,...,x_n}(P) \rightarrow \Phi_{x_n}(B))$
$ENUMERATE(P, \{O_1, ..., O_n\})$	$\forall x_1, ..., x_n(\Phi_{x_1,...,x_n}(P) \rightarrow (x_n = O_1) \vee ... \vee (x_n = O_n))$
$GREATERTHAN(P, A)$	$\forall x_1, ..., x_n(\Phi_{x_1,...,x_n}(P) \wedge \Phi_{y_1,...,y_m}(A) \rightarrow x_n > A')$
$EQUAL(P, A)$	$\forall x_1, ..., x_n(\Phi_{x_1,...,x_n}(P) \wedge \Phi_{y_1,...,y_m}(A) \rightarrow x_n = A')$
$SUBSUME(P_1, P_2)$	$\forall x_1, ..., x_n(\Phi_{x_1,...,x_n}(P_2) \rightarrow \exists y_1, ..., \exists y_{m-1}$ $(\Phi_{y_1,\cdots,y_{m-1},x_n}(P_1)))$
$DISJOINT(P_1, P_2)$	$\forall x_1, ..., x_{n-1} \neg \exists x_n(\Phi_{x_1,...,x_n}(P_1) \wedge \forall y_1, ..., y_{m-1}$ $(\Phi_{y_1,\cdots,y_{m-1},x_n}(P_2)))$
$ONEOF(P, \{P_1, ..., P_m\})$	$\forall x_1, ..., x_n(\Phi_{x_1,...,x_n}(P) \rightarrow \exists y_1, ..., y_{m-1}$ $\Phi_{y_1,\cdots,y_{m-1},x_n}(P_1) \vee ... \vee \exists z_1, ..., z_{k-1}\Phi_{z_1,\cdots,z_{k-1},x_n}(P_m))$
$ATLEAST(P, n)$	$\forall x_1, \ldots x_{m-1} \exists x_{m_1}, ..., \exists x_{m_n}(\Phi_{x_1,\cdots,x_{m_1}}(C) \wedge ... \wedge$ $\Phi_{x_1,\cdots,x_{m_n}}(P) \wedge (x_{m_1} \neq x_{m_2}) \wedge ... \wedge (x_{m_{n-1}} \neq x_{m_n}))$
$ATMOST(P, n)$	$\neg ATLEAST(P, n + 1)$
$ATLEAST(P_1, n, P_2)$	$\forall x_1, \ldots x_m(\Phi_{x_1,\cdots x_m}(P_1) \rightarrow \forall y_1, \ldots y_{k-1} \exists y_{k_1}, ..., \exists y_{k_n}$ $(\Phi_{y_1,\cdots,y_{k_1}}(P_2) \wedge ... \wedge \Phi_{y_1,\cdots,y_{k_n}}(C_2) \wedge$ $(y_{k_1} \neq y_{k_2}) \wedge ... \wedge (y_{k_{n-1}} \neq y_{k_n})))$
$ATMOST(P_1, n, P_2)$	$\neg ATLEAST(P_1, n + 1, P_2)$

3.2 Expressing Constraints

We now discuss how constraints are expressed in $\mathcal{BRL}$ and observe a number of its interesting properties. First, constraints are expressed in $\mathcal{BRL}$ using a set of pre-defined predicates. Though it is small, the set of predicates is actually quite powerful and adequate to represent four classes of constraints described in Section 2. This balance between expressiveness and simplicity is achieved by carefully considering the representation power needed for each class of constraints, and the possible constraints that may be recovered from ISs. This is explained in Table 2. As we see, we have introduced five groups of predicates into $\mathcal{BRL}$, each is necessary to represent certain kind of constraint. For example, `BR1` is a Type-I constraint and can be expressed using `ENUMERATE` predicate in Group 1:

$$ENUMERATE(network, \{Vodafone, Orange, one2one, BTcellnet\})$$

Table 2. Five Groups of Predicates

Group	Predicates	Characteristics	C-Type
1	$TYPEOF(P, B)$ $ENUMERATE(P, \{O_1, ..., O_n\})$	involving one structure, one type	I
2	$GREATERTHAN(P, A)$ $EQUAL(P, A)$	involving one structure, one expression	I, II, IV
3	$SUBSUME(P_1, P_2)$ $DISJOINT(P_1, P_2)$ $ONEOF(P, \{P_1, ..., P_m\})$	involving two or more structures	IV
4	$ATLEAST(P, n)$ $ATMOST(P, n)$	involving one structure, one cadinarlity spec	III
5	$ATLEAST(P_1, n, P_2)$ $ATMOST(P_1, n, P_2)$	involving two structures, one cardinality spec	IV

BR5 is of Type-IV and can be expressed using SUBSUME predicate in Group 3:

$SUBSUME(order.customer, order.recommender)$

Some constraints may not be expressible using these predefined predicates only, e.g. to expresss BR7, the implication operator "$\rightarrow$" will have to be used:

$EQUAL(service.freeTime, 600) \rightarrow ATMOST(service, 1000)$

The space limitation does not allow us to explain how various other constraints may be expressed in $\mathcal{BRL}$, but it is easy to verify how the predicates listed in Table 2 cover the four types of constraint we described in Section 2 adequately.

Second, constraints are expressed in $\mathcal{BRL}$ at the meta-level. Compared to the constraints represented at the instance level, it is much easier to derive constraint presentation from the $\mathcal{BRL}$ specifications. For example, given

$ATMOST(order.customer, 4, order.service)$

we can easily derive a high-level presentation from it (e.g. an ER model), than from an equivalent instance level expression in FOL:

$$\forall x, y(order(x) \wedge customer(y) \wedge R_1(x, y) \rightarrow \neg\exists z_1, z_2, z_3, z_4, z_5(service(z_1) \wedge \ldots \wedge service(z_5) \wedge R_2(x, z_1) \wedge \ldots \wedge R_2(x, z_5) \wedge (z_1 \neq z_2) \wedge (z_1 \neq z_3) \wedge \ldots \wedge (z_4 \neq z_5)))$$

Third, it is worth stressing that $\mathcal{BRL}$ is not designed for human users to specify constraints. Rather, it is designed to express constraints in such a way that it is easy for computers to analyse their properties and to interpret their semantics to the users. It is for this reason that the descriptive flexibility of $\mathcal{BRL}$ is rather limited. For example, we do not have a predicate in $\mathcal{BRL}$ to express $|\widehat{S^t}| = n$ (a Type-III constraint) directly. Instead, the following must be used:

$ATMOST(S, n) \wedge ATLEAST(S, n)$

This is obviously inconvenient to human users. But this is not a problem for the computer to capture the constraints internally and to analyse their properties.

Finally, $\mathcal{BRL}$, as a language based on predicate logic, supports the analysis of recovered constraints. For example, given the following constraint:

$ONEOF(customer, \{activeCustomer, inactiveCustomer\})$

we can deduce the following two constraints:

$SUBSUME(customer, activeCustomer)$
$SUBSUME(customer, inactiveCustomer)$

Since $\mathcal{BRL}$ allows only a limited set of predicates and represents constraints at the meta-level, constraint analysis is relatively simple. For example, if we have

$ATLEAST(service, 1000)$
$ATMOST(service, 900)$

then checking whether they conflict with each other can be done by a single integer comparison. See [6] for a detailed discussion of constraint analysis.

4 Related Work

Various languages have been proposed for representing constraints. Some express constraints at the instance level [1,10,8]. That is, they specify constraints by stating the properties that the instances of classes must satisfy. For example, BR7 may be represented in Alice [10] as follows:

```
SOME x in service (WHERE x.freeTime = 600) IMPLIES: COUNT(x) <= 1000
```

Such languages are typically based on First Order Logic, thus they are usually expressive enough to represent a wide range of constraints. However, constraints represented in these languages are not very comprehensible, due to the proliferation of variables and quantifiers – one has to interpret the relationships between various variables, quantifiers and logic connectives used in the formulas, and the semantics assumed by them, in order to present the constraints to the users in a meaningful way. Furthermore, representing constraints at the instance level can make it hard to perform constraint analysis efficiently.

$\mathcal{BRL}$ shares with these languages in that it is also a predicate logic based language, and supports property analysis through logical inference. However, $\mathcal{BRL}$ is different from these languages in that it allows only pre-defined predicates to be used and represent constraints at the meta-level. This allows the constraints represented in $\mathcal{BRL}$ to be efficiently analysed and naturally interpreted.

There also exists various languages in the literature which, like $\mathcal{BRL}$, represent constraints at the meta-level [7,4,2]. For example, BR5 can be expressed as a *constraint equation* [7] as follows:

$$order.recommender \sqsubseteq order.customer$$

Here, no variables representing instances are present; only the meta-level elements are involved. The general consensus is that constraints expressed at the meta-level is more natural to comprehend and easier to analyse. However, most of these meta-level languages are rather limited in what they can represent. For example, BR3 or BR6 given in Section 2 are not expressible as *constraint equations*, and BR3 and BR7 are hard to be expressed in *Classic* [3]. Furthermore, while most of these languages offer some efficient procedure for performing some constraint analysis, they are usually very limited and only applicable to the types of constraint they can represent. For example, description logic based languages have efficient procedures for deciding subsumption and satisfiability, but many constraint analysis problems can not simply be reduced to such problems.

$\mathcal{BRL}$ is a meta-level language, thus shares the many benefits that this group of languages have. Like them, $\mathcal{BRL}$ is also special propose language, limited to representing some classes of constraints and supporting some special forms of analysis. However, what distinguishes $\mathcal{BRL}$ from other meta-level languages is that $\mathcal{BRL}$ is designed with reverse engineering of constraints in mind. The constructs that we have introduced into $\mathcal{BRL}$ have been carefully chosen to represent only the constraints that may be recovered from legacy systems, and to facilitate their presentation to the users. Our initial experience with $\mathcal{BRL}$ shows that it is quite sufficient in meeting these requirements.

5 Conclusion

In this paper we have proposed a language for representing constraint business rules extracted from legacy ISs. The language has a number of useful features. Firstly, it is based on predicate logic. This makes it possible to analyse implicit links or properties among the constraints. Secondly, it is designed to work with the reverse engineering of constraints, i.e., we have included only a small number of pre-defined predicates to express the semantics that can be realistically expected from the reverse engineering of constraints. Finally, it supports expressing constraint at the meta level, which simplifies constraint analysis as well as constraint presentation. The work reported here is still on-going and a number of issues still remain. Based on the constraint represented in $\mathcal{BRL}$, we are investigating a range of suitable presentation formats to convey the semantics of constraints to users. We are also considering how to enrich the semantics of constraints by incorporating domain knowledge into constraint presentation.

Acknowledgement

This work is part of BRULEE project which is funded by Grant GR/M66219 from the U.K. Engineering and Physical Sciences Research Council.

References

1. N. Bassiliades and P. M. D. Gray. CoLan: A Functional Constraint Language and Its Implementation. *Data and Knowledge Engineering*, 14(3):203–249, 1994.
2. A. Borgida. Description Logics in Data Management. *IEEE Transactions on Knowledge and Data Engineering*, 7(5):671–682, 1995.
3. A. Borgida, R. J. Brachman, D. L. McGuinness, and L. A. Resnick. Classic: A Structural Data Model for Objects. In *SIGMOD Conference*, pages 58–67, 1989.
4. J. A. Chudziak, H. Rybinski, and J. Vorbach. Towards a Unifying Logic Formalism for Semantic Data Models. In *Proceedings of 12th International Conference on the Entity-Relationship Approach*, pages 492–507, 1993.
5. S. Embury, J. Shao, G. Fu, X. Liu, and W. Gray. A Framework for the Recovery of Data Semantics from Information Systems. Submitted for Publication, Department of Computer Science, Cardiff University, 2002.
6. G. Fu, J. Shao, S. M. Embury, and W. A. Gray. An Algorithm for Determining Related Constraints. In *Proceedings of 19th British National Conference on Databases (BNCOD2002) (to appear)*, 2002.
7. M. Morgenster. Constraint Equations: Declarative Expression of Constraints with Automatic Enforcement. In *Proceedings of 10th International Conference on Very Large Data Bases*, pages 291–300, 1984.
8. ORM. UML 2.0 OCL RFP. Available online http://www.omg.org/techprocess/meetings/schedule/uml_2.0_ocl_rfp.html, 2002.
9. P. Ruttan. Recovering Business Rules to Enable Legacy Transformation. Technical report, Netron Inc., 1999.
10. S. Urban. ALICE: An Assertion Language for Integrity Constraint Expression. In *Proceedings of the 13th Annual Conference on Computer Software and Application*, pages 292–299, 1989.

Agents for Industry Process Management

John Debenham
University of Technology, Sydney
debenham@it.uts.edu.au

Abstract. Industry processes are the trans-corporate business processes required to support the e-business environment. Industry process re-engineering is the re-engineering of trans-corporate business processes as electronically managed processes. Industry process re-engineering is business process re-engineering on a massively distributed scale. Industry processes will not be restricted to routine workflows that follow a more-or-less fixed path; they will include complex processes for which their future path may be unknown at each stage in their existence. So a management system for industry processes should be both highly scalable and should be able to deal with such complex processes. A multiagent process management system is described that can manage processes of high complexity. This system is built from interacting autonomous components so achieving system scalability.

1 Introduction

Business to Business (B2B) e-commerce is driving a new generation of Internet applications that can dramatically automate trans-corporate industry processes only if the business systems and the data that drive them are integrated across the component organisations [1]. Here *industry processes* includes both business transactions, and business processes and workflows. These Internet applications can only automate industry processes if there is a method to describe collaborative processes across organisations and to provide data interoperability. Improvements in process management can only be achieved through automation. Automation of processes leads to faster cycle times, reduced overhead and more competitive offerings. *Industry process re-engineering* is the re-engineering of trans-corporate processes as electronically managed processes. Companies that have implemented this e-business vision are saving tens of millions of dollars per year [2]. Industry process re-engineering must address the four issues of complexity, interoperability, communication and management:

- *complexity* of industry processes refers to their nature which includes *all* trans-corporate processes from routine workflows to high-level emergent processes [3];
- *interoperability* is an issue due to the heterogeneity of the diverse systems across a trading community. These systems vary in the applications that manage them and in the data formats that they employ;
- the *communication* and messaging infrastructure chosen will operate in a mission-critical environment, and
- process *management* which is responsible for tracking the automated trans-corporate processes that may include processes unique to individual trading

R. Cicchetti et al. (Eds.): DEXA 2002, LNCS 2453, pp. 474–483, 2002.

partners and will probably involve a wide range of process steps that must "make sense" to all involved.

That is, industry process re-engineering must deliver a secure, scalable and reliable solution for running a company's most critical core business processes. The complex nature of industry processes and their management is considered here.

Industry processes range in type from production workflows to high-level emergent processes. Processes all across this range are to be managed in the distributed and diverse e-business environment. High-level emergent processes are business processes that are not predefined and are ad hoc. These processes typically take place at the higher levels of organisations [1], and are distinct from production workflows [2]. Emergent processes are opportunistic in nature whereas production workflows are routine. How an emergent process will terminate may not be known until the process is well advanced. Further, the tasks involved in an emergent process are typically not predefined and *emerge* as the process develops. Those tasks may be carried out by collaborative groups as well as by individuals [4]. For example, in a manufacturing organisation an emergent process could be triggered by "lets consider introducing a new product line for the US market".

Multiagent technology is an attractive basis for industry process re-engineering [5]. A multiagent system consists of autonomous components that interact with messages. The scalability issue is "solved"—in theory—by establishing a common understanding for inter-agent communication and interaction. Specifying an inter-agent communication protocol may be tedious but is not technically complex. Standard XML-based ontologies will enable data to be communicated freely [1] but much work has yet to be done on standards for communicating expertise. Specifying the agent interaction protocol is a more complex as it in effect specifies the common understanding on the basis of which the whole system will operate.

2 Industry Processes

Following [6] a *business process* is "a set of one or more linked procedures or activities which collectively realise a business objective or policy goal, normally within the context of an organisational structure defining functional roles and relationships". Implicit in this definition is the idea that a process may be repeatedly decomposed into linked sub-processes until those sub-processes are "activities" which are atomic pieces of work. [viz (op.cit) "An *activity* is a description of a piece of work that forms one logical step within a process."]. A particular process is called a (process) *instance*. An instance may require that certain things should be done; such things are called *tasks*. A *trigger* is an event that leads to the creation of an instance. The *goal* of an instance is a state that the instance is trying to achieve. The *termination condition* of an instance is a condition which if satisfied during the life of an instance causes that instance to be destroyed whether its goal has been achieved or not. The *patron* of an instance is the individual who is responsible for managing the life of that instance [7]. At any time in a process instance's life, the *history* of that instance is the sequence of prior sub-goals and the prior sequence of knowledge inputs to the instance. The history is "knowledge of all that has happened already".

From a process management viewpoint, industry processes can be seen as consisting of sub-processes that are of one of the three following types:

- A *task-driven process* has a unique decomposition into a—possibly conditional—sequence of activities. Each of these activities has a goal and is associated with a task that "always" achieves this goal. Production workflows are typically task-driven processes.
- A *goal-driven process* has a process goal, and achievement of that goal is the termination condition for the process. The process goal may have various decompositions into sequences of sub-goals where these sub-goals are associated with (atomic) activities and so with tasks. Some of these sequences of tasks may work better than others, and there may be no way of knowing which is which [3]. A task for an activity may fail outright, or may be otherwise ineffective at achieving its goal. In other words, process failure is a feature of goal-driven processes. If a task fails then another way to achieve the process goal may be sought.
- A *knowledge-driven process* has a process goal, but the goal may be vague and may mutate [8]. Mutations are determined by the process patron, often in the light of knowledge generated during the process. After performing a task in a knowledge-driven process, the "next goal" is chosen by the process patron. So in so far as the process goal gives direction to goal-driven—and task-driven—processes, the growing body of process knowledge gives direction to knowledge-driven processes. The management of knowledge-driven processes is considerably more complex than the other two classes of process.

Fig. 1 shows a simplified view of the management of goal-driven process. The primitives shown in Fig. 1 are goals and plans. As the successful execution of a plan for a goal-driven process is not necessarily related to the achievement of the process goal each plan ends with a "success condition". A plan's *success condition* (SC) is a procedure that determines whether the plan's goal has been achieved. Some goals are associated with executable procedures. If a goal is not associated with an executable procedure then it should be the subject of at least one plan. The ideas shown in Fig. 1 are discussed in greater detail below.

Task-driven processes may be managed by a simple reactive agent architecture based on event-condition-action rules [7]. Goal-driven processes may be modelled as state and activity charts [9] and managed by plans that can accommodate failure [10].

3 Reasoning

The conceptual architecture of the process agents described here is a 3-layer, BDI hybrid architecture. As a hybrid architecture the process agent architecture exhibits both deliberative and reactive reasoning [11]. Deliberative reasoning is managed within a belief–goal–plan–intention framework [10]. Reactive reasoning is effected with triggers. Theses two forms of reasoning are balanced by giving reactive reasoning precedence over deliberative reasoning. That is, an attempt is made to fire all reactive triggers before each deliberative cycle commences.

3.1 Deliberative Reasoning

The process agent employs a form of "plan" that is rather more elaborate than many types of agent plan [10]. For goal-driven process management plans are prone to local failure. A form plan that can deal naturally with failure is described in [op. cit.].

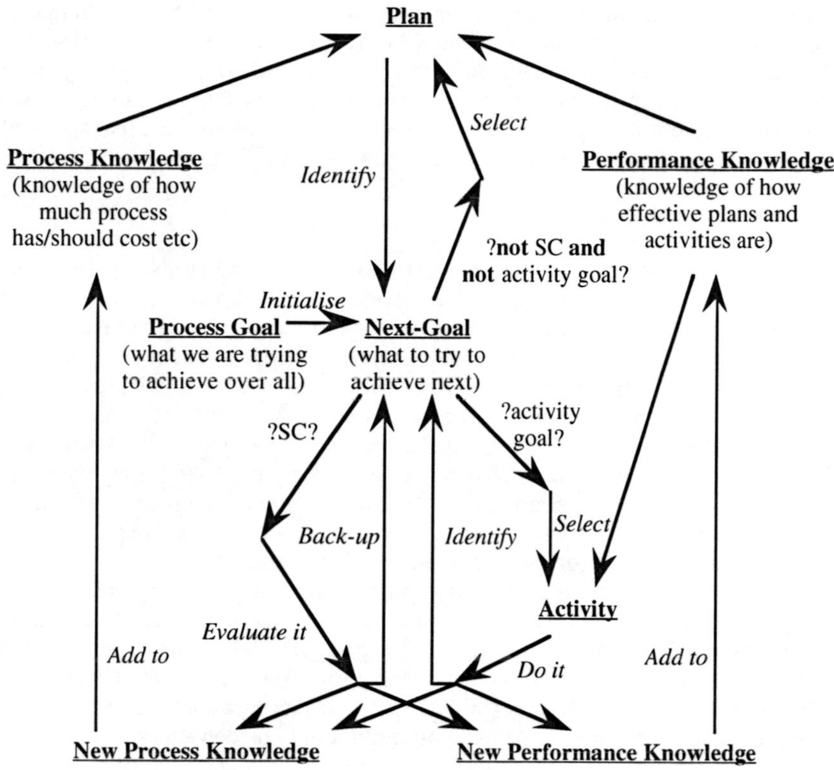

Fig. 1. Goal-driven process management (a simplified view)

Plans are built there from single-entry, triple-exit blocks; where the three exists represent success, failure and abort. Powerful though that approach is, it is insufficient for goal-driven processes because whether a plan has executed successfully is not necessarily related to whether that plan's goal has been achieved. In business process applications a necessary sub-goal in every plan body is a sub-goal called the "success condition". The *success condition* (SC) is a procedure whose goal is to determine whether the plan's goal has been achieved. The success condition is the final sub-goal on *every* path through a plan. The success condition is a procedure; the execution of that procedure may succeed (✓), fail (✗) or abort (**A**). If the execution of the success condition fails then the overall success of the plan is unknown (**?**). So the four possible plan exits resulting from a plan are success (✓), fail (✗), abort (**A**) and unknown (**?**).

Goal-directed business processes may be modelled as state and activity charts [9]. The primitives of that model are activities and states. For goal-driven sub-processes the *states* correspond to the goals associated with that sub-process. An *activity chart* specifies the data flow between activities. An activity chart is a directed graph in which the arcs are annotated with data items. A *state chart* is a representation of a finite state machine in which the transitions annotated with Event-Condition-Action rules. If the transition from state X to state Y is annotated with E[C]/A then this transition is followed if event E occurs and condition C holds in which case action A is performed.

The deliberative frequency is the frequency at which the deliberative process is activated. This process determines current options, selects current goals, and so on as described in the agent control architecture above. The deliberative frequency should be short enough to keep the system moving but not so fast that an individual's "In Tray" is seen to be constantly changing. For general business process management a deliberative frequency in the region of 5—20 minutes seems appropriate.

3.2 Reactive Reasoning

Reactive reasoning play three roles: first, it aborts a plan when its specified abort condition is satisfied, second, it passes data to partly executed plans for goals an agent is committed to achieve, and third, it deals with urgent messages. Of these three roles the third takes precedence over the first which takes precedence over the second.

Each plan contains an optional abort condition [ab] as described above. These abort conditions are realised as *abort triggers*. These triggers scan the agent's beliefs for the presence or absence of specific conditions. For example, "*if* I do not believe that X wants Y *then abort* the plan whose goal is to deliver Y to X" is an example of an abort trigger. Abort triggers are only active if the goal of the plan to which they are attached is a goal that the agent is presently committed to achieving. If a plan is aborted then any active sub-goals of that plan are also aborted.

Data is passed to partly executed plans using reactive triggers. A reactive trigger "watches" the agent's world beliefs. If and when this reactive trigger fires the next sub-goal is instantiated and is achieved. Reactive triggers of this form are associated with sub-goals. These triggers are activated when their associated sub-goal is committed to but has not been achieved. Triggers of this form provide a mechanism for passing data derived from inter-agent communication to such sub-goals.

4 Performance Knowledge

The performance knowledge is used to support task selection—ie who does what—through inter-agent negotiation. So its role is a comparative one; it is not intended to have absolute currency. The *performance knowledge* comprises performance statistics on the operation of the system down to a fine grain of detail. These performance statistics are proffered by an agent in bids for work. To evaluate a bid, the receiving agent defines payoff in terms of these statistics. In the case of a parameter, p, that can reasonably be assumed to be normally distributed, the estimate for the mean of p, μ_p, is revised on the basis of the i'th observation ob_i to $\mu_{p_{new}} = (1 - \alpha) \times ob_i + \alpha \times \mu_{p_{old}}$ which, given a starting value $\mu_{p_{initial}}$, and some constant α, $0 < \alpha < 1$, approximates the geometric mean $\frac{\sum_{i=1}^{n} \alpha^{i-1} \times ob_i}{\sum_{i=1}^{n} \alpha^{i-1}}$ where i = 1 is the most recent observation. In the same way, an estimate for $\sqrt{\frac{2}{\pi}}$ times the standard deviation of p, σ_p, is revised on the basis of the i'th observation ob_i to $\sigma_{p_{new}} = (1 - \alpha) \times | ob_i - \mu_{p_{old}} | + \alpha \times \sigma_{p_{old}}$ which, given a starting value $\sigma_{p_{initial}}$, and some constant α, $0 < \alpha < 1$, approximates the geometric mean $\frac{\sum_{i=1}^{n} \alpha^{i-1} \times | ob_i - \mu_p |}{\sum_{i=1}^{n} \alpha^{i-1}}$. The constant α is chosen on the basis of the stability of the observations. For example, if $\alpha = 0.85$ then "everything more than twenty trials ago" contributes less than 5% to the weighted mean, if $\alpha = 0.70$ then "everything more than ten trials ago" contributes less than 5% to the weighted mean, and if $\alpha = 0.50$ then "everything more than five trials ago" contributes less than 5% to the weighted mean.

Each individual agent/user pair maintains estimates for the three parameters: *time*, *cost* and *likelihood of success* for the execution of all of its plans, sub-plans and activities. "All things being equal" these parameters are assumed to be normally distributed—the case when "all things are *not* equal" is considered below. Time is the total time taken to termination. Cost is the actual cost of the of resources allocated. For example, if a person has a virtual document in their in-tray then the time observation will be the total time that that document spent with that person, and the cost may derived from the time that the person actually spent working on that document. The likelihood of success observations are binary—ie "success" or "fail"—and so the likelihood of success parameter is binomially distributed, which is approximately normally distributed under the standard conditions. These three parameters are useful, but the *value* parameter—that is the value added to a process by a plan or individual—is at least as important. Unfortunately, *value* is often very difficult to measure. It is dealt with by subjective estimates.

Finally, measurements of the *allocate* parameter for each individual are the amount of work w_i^j, allocated to individual j in discrete time period i. In a similar way to *time* and *cost*, the mean *allocate* estimate for individual j is made using $\text{allocate}_{new} = (1 - \alpha) \times w^j + \alpha \times \text{allocate}_{old}$, where w^j is the most recent observation for individual j. In this formula the weighting factor α is chosen on the basis of the number of individuals in the system, and the relationships between the length of the discrete time interval and the expected length of time to deal with the work. The *allocate* parameter is not normally distributed and the standard deviation is not estimated. The *allocate* and *value* estimates are associated with individuals. The *time*, *cost* and *likelihood of success* estimates are attached to plans.

The three parameters *time*, *cost* and *likelihood of success* are assumed to be normally distributed subject to "all things being equal". Inferred explanations of *why* an observation is outside expected limits may sometimes be extracted from observing the interactions with the users and other agents involved. For example, if Person X is unexpectedly slow in attending to a certain process instance then a simple interchange with X's agent may reveal that Person X will be working on the company's annual report for the next six days; this may be one reason for the unexpected observation. Inferred knowledge such as this gives *one possible cause* for the observed behaviour; so such knowledge enables us to *refine*, but *not* to *replace*, the historical estimates of parameters.

4.1 The Delegation Strategy

A *delegation strategy* is a strategy for deciding who to give responsibility to for doing what. For industry processes this delegation may involve delegation from an agent

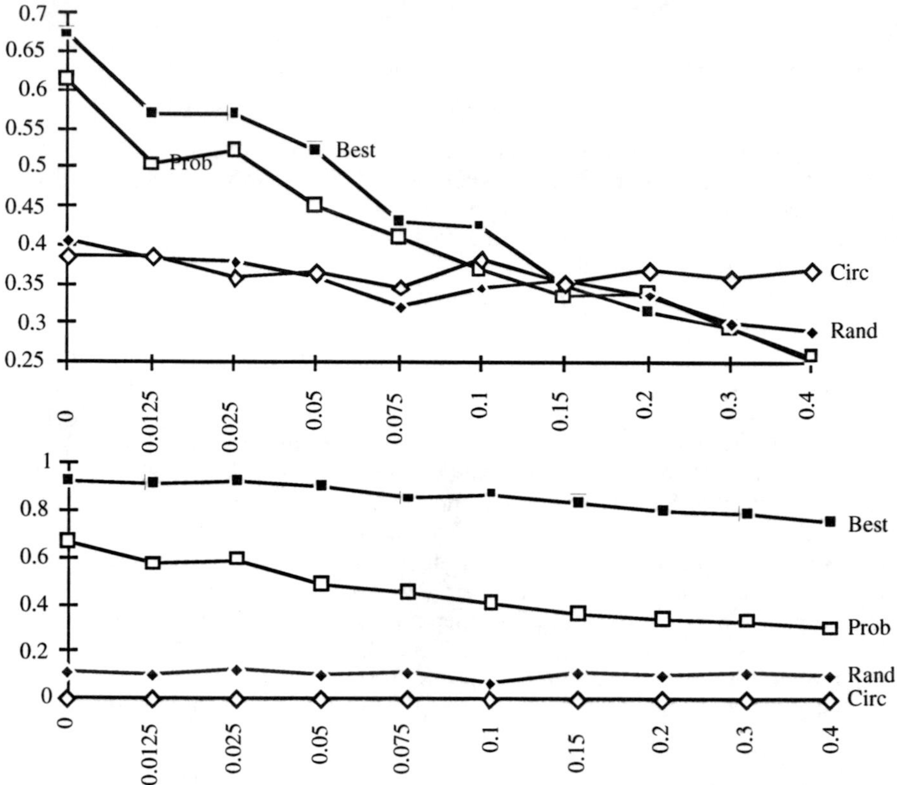

Fig 2 Payoff (top figure) and triple duplications (bottom figure) against the rebel factor for a learning rate = 0.1, death factor = 0.05, and α = 0.6.

within one organisation to an agent within another organisation. A user specifies the delegation strategy that is used by the user's agent to evaluate bids. In doing this the user has considerable flexibility first in defining payoff and second in specifying the strategy itself. Practical strategies in manual systems can be quite elementary; delegation is a job which some humans are not very good at. A delegation strategy may attempt to balance some of the three conflicting principles: maximising payoff, maximising opportunities for poor performers to improve and balancing workload. Payoff is defined by the user and could be some combination of the expected value added to the process, the expected time and/or cost to deal with the process, and the expected likelihood of the process leading to a satisfactory conclusion [12].

Given a sub-process, suppose that we have some expectation of the payoff D_i as a result of choosing the i'th individual (ie agent and user pair) from the set of candidates $\{X_1,...,X_i,...,X_n\}$ to take responsibility for it. A *delegation strategy* at time τ is specified as $S = \{P_1,...,P_i,...,P_n\}$ where P_i is the probability of delegating responsibility at time τ for a given task to individual X_i chosen from $\{X_1,...,X_i,...,X_n\}$. The system suggests an individual/task pair stochastically using the delegation strategy.

Corporate culture may determine the delegation strategy. Four delegation strategies are described. If corporate culture is to choose the individual whose expected payoff is maximal then the delegation strategy *best* is:

$$P_i = \begin{cases} \frac{1}{m} & \textit{if } X_i \text{ is such that } Pr(X_i \gg) \text{ is maximal} \\ 0 & \textit{otherwise} \end{cases}$$

where $Pr(X_i \gg)$ means "the probability that X_i will have the highest payoff" and *m* is such that there are *m* individuals for whom $Pr(X_i \gg)$ is maximal. In the absence of any other complications, the strategy *best* attempts to maximise expected payoff. Using this strategy, an individual who performs poorly may never get work. Another strategy *prob* also favours high payoff but gives all individuals a chance, sooner or later, and is defined by $P_i = Pr(X_i \gg)$. The strategies *best* and *prob* have the feature of 'rewarding' quality work (ie. high payoff) with more work. If corporate culture dictates that individuals should be treated equally but at random then the delegation strategy *random* is $P_i = \frac{1}{n}$. If the corporate culture dictates that each task should be allocated to *m* individuals in strict rotation then the delegation strategy *circulate* is:

$$P_i = \begin{cases} 1 & \textit{if } \text{this is the i'th trial and } i \equiv 0 \text{ (modulo n)} \\ 0 & \textit{otherwise} \end{cases}$$

The strategies *random* and *circulate* attempt to balance workload and ignore expected payoff. The strategy *circulate* only has meaning in a fixed population, and so has limited use.

A practical strategy that attempts to balance maximising "expected payoff for the next delegation" with "improving available skills in the long term" could be constructed if there was a model for the expected improvement in skills—ie a model for the rate at which individuals learn. This is not considered here.

An *admissible* delegation strategy has the properties:

- *if* $Pr(X_i \gg) > Pr(X_j \gg)$ *then* $P_i > P_j$
- *if* $Pr(X_i \gg) = Pr(X_j \gg)$ *then* $P_i = P_j$
- $P_i > 0 \ (\forall i)$

So the three strategies *best*, *random* and *circulate* are *not* admissible. An admissible strategy will delegate more responsibility to individuals with a high probability of having the highest payoff than to individuals with a low probability. Also with an admissible strategy each individual considered has some chance of being given responsibility. The strategy *prob* is admissible and is used in the system described in [4]. It provides a balance between favouring individuals who perform well with giving occasional opportunities to poor performers to improve their performance. The strategy *prob* is *not* based on any model of process improvement and so it can *not* be claimed to be optimal in that sense. The user selects a strategy from the infinite variety of admissible strategies:

$$S = \delta \times best + \varepsilon \times prob + \phi \times random + \gamma \times circulate$$

will be admissible if $\delta,\varepsilon,\phi,\gamma \in [0,1]$, $\delta + \varepsilon + \phi + \gamma = 1$ and if $\varepsilon > 0$. This leads to the question of how to select a strategy. As *circulate* is only meaningful in stable populations it is not considered here.

There are three ways that an 'optimal' strategy could be identified. First, theoretically given a specification of what strategy should achieve. Second, by trial and error in a real experiment. Third, by a laboratory simulation experiments. The value of a theoretical derivation depends on the validity of the model on which the derivation is based. In simple cases this can be done, for example to achieve uniform allocation of responsibility. Real experiments to evaluate delegation strategies are just not viable. Laboratory simulation experiments are cheap and indicate of how the strategies perform.

A world is designed in which the relative performance of the four strategies *best*, *prob*, *random* and *circulate* are simulated There are always three individuals in this world. If individuals die (ie they become unavailable) then they are replaced with new individuals. At each *cycle*—ie a discrete time unit—one delegation is made. There is a natural death rate of 5% for each individual for each cycle. The payoff of each individual commences at 0 and improves by 10% of "what there is still to learn" on each occasion that an individual is delegated responsibility. So an individual's recorded payoff is progressively: 0, 0.1, 0.19, 0.271, 0.3439, and so on, tending to 1.0 in the long term. The mean and standard deviation estimates of expected payoff are calculated as described above using a value of $\alpha = 0.6$. In addition the individuals have a strength of belief of the extent to which they are being given more work than the other two individuals in the experiment. This strength of belief is multiplied by a "rebel" factor and is added to the base death rate of 5%. So if work is repeatedly delegated to one individual then the probability of that individual dying increases up to a limit of the rebel factor plus 5%. A *triple duplication* occurs when work is delegated to the same individual three cycles running. The proportion of triple duplications is used as a measure of the lack of perceived recent equity in the allocation of responsibility. The payoff and proportion of triple duplications for the four strategies are shown against the rebel factor on the top and bottom graphs respectively in Fig. 2. The simulation run for each value is 2 000 cycles. The lack of smoothness of the graphs is partially due to the pseudo-random number generator used. When the rebel factor is 0.15—ie three times the natural death rate—all four strategies deliver approximately the same payoff. The two graphs indicate that the *prob* strategy does a reasonable job at maximising payoff while keeping triple duplications reasonably low for a rebel factor of < 0.15. However, *prob* may only be used when the chosen definition of payoff is normally distributed. The strategy *best* also assumes normality; its definition may be changed to "such that the expected payoff is greatest" [13] when payoff is not normal.

5 Conclusion

Managing trans-corporate industry processes involves managing processes across the full process spectrum in the distributed e-business environment. This spectrum is analysed as processes of three distinct types [14]. The management of knowledge-driven processes is not widely understood and has been described here. A multi-agent system manages goal-driven processes and supports the management of knowledge-driven processes [12]. The conceptual agent architecture is a three-layer BDI, hybrid architecture. During a process instance the responsibility for sub-processes may be delegated, and possibly out-sourced in the distributed, e-business environment. To achieve this, the system forms a view on who should be asked to do what at each step in a process, and tracks the resulting delegations of process responsibility [15]. This includes tracking delegations across component organisations.

References

[1] Skinstad, R. "Business process integration through XML". In proceedings XML Europe 2000, Paris, 12-16 June 2000.

[2] Feldman, S. "Technology Trends and Drivers and a Vision of the Future of e-business." In proceedings 4th International Enterprise Distributed Object Computing Conference, September 25-28, 2000, Makuhari, Japan.

[3] Dourish, P. "Using Metalevel Techniques in a Flexible Toolkit for CSCW Applications." ACM Transactions on Computer-Human Interaction, Vol. 5, No. 2, June, 1998, pp. 109—155.

[4] A. P. Sheth, D. Georgakopoulos, S. Joosten, M. Rusinkiewicz, W. Scacchi, J. C. Wileden, and A. L. Wolf. "Report from the NSF workshop on workflow and process automation in information systems." SIGMOD Record, 25(4):55—67, December 1996.

[5] Jain, A.K., Aparicio, M. and Singh, M.P. "Agents for Process Coherence in Virtual Enterprises" in Communications of the ACM, Volume 42, No 3, March 1999, pp62—69.

[6] Fischer, L. (Ed) "Workflow Handbook 2001." Future Strategies, 2000.

[7] Debenham, J.K. "Supporting Strategic Process", in proceedings Fifth International Conference on The Practical Application of Intelligent Agents and Multi-Agents PAAM2000, Manchester UK, April 2000.

[8] Debenham, J.K. "Knowledge Engineering: Unifying Knowledge Base and Database Design", Springer-Verlag, 1998

[9] Muth, P., Wodtke, D., Weissenfels, J., Kotz D.A. and Weikum, G. "From Centralized Workflow Specification to Distributed Workflow Execution." In Journal of Intelligent Information Systems (JIIS), Kluwer Academic Publishers, Vol. 10, No. 2, 1998.

[10] Rao, A.S. and Georgeff, M.P. "BDI Agents: From Theory to Practice", in proceedings First International Conference on Multi-Agent Systems (ICMAS-95), San Francisco, USA, pp 312—319.

[11] Weiss, G. (ed). Multi-Agent Systems. The MIT Press: Cambridge, MA (1999).

[12] Debenham, J.K. "Supporting knowledge-driven processes in a multiagent process management system." In proceedings Twentieth International Conference on Knowledge-Based Systems and Applied Artificial Intelligence, ES'2000: Research and Development in Intelligent Systems XV, Cambridge UK, December 2000.

[13] Sutton, R.S. and Barto, A.G. Reinforcement Learning. MIT Press, 1998.

[14] Riempp, G. Wide Area Workflow Management. Springer-Verlag, 1998.

[15] Wellman, M.P. and Derthick, M. Formulation of Tradeoffs in Planning Under Uncertainty. Morgan Kaufman Publishers, 1990.

A New Efficient Data Cleansing Method

Li Zhao, Sung Sam Yuan, Sun Peng, and Ling Tok Wang

Dept. of Computer Science, National Univ. of Singapore,
3 Science Drive 2, Singapore 117543
{lizhao,ssung,sunpeng1,lingtw}@comp.nus.edu.sg

Abstract. One of the most important tasks in data cleansing is to detect and remove duplicate records, which consists of two main components, detection and comparison. A detection method decides which records will be compared, and a comparison method determines whether two records compared are duplicate. Comparisons take a great deal of data cleansing time. We discover that if certain properties are satisfied by a comparison method then many unnecessary expensive comparisons can be avoided. In this paper, we first propose a new comparison method, LCSS, based on the longest common subsequence, and show that it possesses the desired properties. We then propose two new detection methods, SNM-IN and SNM-INOUT, which are variances of the popular detection method SNM. The performance study on real and synthetic databases shows that the integration of SNM-IN (SNM-INOUT) and LCSS saves about 39% (56%) of comparisons.

1 Introduction

Organizations today are confronted with the challenge of handling an ever-increasing amount of data. The data is very likely to be dirty because of misuse of abbreviations, data entry mistakes, missing fields, spelling errors, outdated codes etc [7]. Hence, we may have multiple records referring to the same real world entity. Since dirty data will distort information obtained due to the "garbage in, garbage out" principle, data cleansing is very important and necessary. In [11], data cleansing was identified as one of the database research opportunities for data warehousing into the 21st century.

Given a dirty database, the standard method to detect exact duplicates is to sort the database and then check if the neighboring records are identical. To detect inexact duplicates, [3] proposed *Sorted Neighborhood Method (SNM)*, which can be summarized in three phases:

- Create Key: Compute a key for each record. The key can be extracted from relevant fields or portions of fields;
- Sort Data: Sort the records using the key created;
- Merge: Move a fixed size window through the sorted records limiting the comparisons to those records in the window. If the window size is ω, then every new record entering the window is compared with the previous ω - 1 records to find duplicate records. The first record in the window slides out of the window.

R. Cicchetti et al. (Eds.): DEXA 2002, LNCS 2453, pp. 484–493, 2002.

Based on SNM, there are some variant algorithms. *Clustering SNM* [3] first partitions the database into independent clusters using a key extracted from the data, then applies SNM to each individual cluster independently. *Multi-pass SNM (MPN)* [3] is to execute several independent runs of SNM, each time using a different key and a relatively small window. *Duplicate Elimination SNM (DE-SNM)* [2] sorts the records on a chosen key and then divides the sorted records into two lists: a duplicate list and a non-duplicate list. A small window scan is first performed on the duplicate list to find the lists of matched and unmatched records. The list of unmatched records is merged with the original non-duplicate list and a second window scan is performed. As an alternative to SNM, *Priority Queue* is suggested in [9]. It uses a priority queue of sets of records belonging to the last few clusters detected. The algorithm scans the database sequentially and determines whether each record scanned is or is not a member of a cluster represented in a priority queue.

As the detection methods determine which records need to be compared, pare-wise comparison methods are used to decide whether two records compared are duplicate.

The comparison of records to determine their equivalence is a complex inferential process. One approach is using production rules based on domain-specific knowledge. *Equational Theory* was proposed in [3] to compare records. An equational theory is specified by a declarative rule language. Java Expert System Shell, which is a rule engine and scripting environment, is employed by IntelliClean [5]. The rule-based comparison methods are generally slow and do not clearly scale up for very large datasets.

Another approach is by computing the degree of similarity of records, which is a value between 0.0 and 1.0, where 0.0 means certain non-equivalence and 1.0 means certain equivalence [8]. This approach is based on the assumption that each field is a string. Naturally this assumption is true for a wide range of databases, including those with numerical fields such as social security numbers that are represented in decimal notation. In [9], this assumption is also identified as a major factor of domain-independent methods. Throughout this paper, we will adopt this assumption. *Longest Common Subsequence* and *Edit Distance* are useful measures for similarity of two strings. *Record Similarity (RS)* was introduced in [6] and record equivalence can be determined by viewing the similarity at three levels: token, field and record. In RS, field weightages are introduced to indicate the fields' importance.

All the methods we introduced are on the algorithms of matching, clustering and merging. Other work related to data cleansing includes proposing high level languages to express data transformation [1], and introducing data cleansing frameworks [10]. The algorithms are fundamental in the data cleansing, and the high level languages and data cleansing frameworks will benefit from the performance improvement of the algorithms.

The detection methods introduced above are independent from the comparison methods. That is, any detection method can use any comparison method to compare records. This independence gives freedom for applications but will result in a loss of useful information, which can be used to save expensive comparisons.

Let Y+X denote a method in which Y is a detection method and X is a comparison method used in Y. Consider SNM+RS, if the size of the window is ω, then every new record entering the window is compared with the previous ω - 1 records with RS to find duplicate records. We note that when a new record entering the window, all the records in the window have been compared with each other and should have achieved some knowledge on these comparisons. SNM+RS doesn't keep and make use of that comparison information and simply ignores it, which results in lots of unnecessary comparisons. For example, for records A, B and C, suppose that we have compared A with B, and B with C. SNM+RS will compare A with C in any case. However, intuitively, if A and B are very similar, and B and C are very similar/dissimilar, then A and C should be similar/dissimilar. If the comparison method can well describe this case such that $Sim(A, C)$, similarity of A and C, can be bounded by $Sim(A, B)$ and $Sim(B, C)$, and the previous two comparisons information ($Sim(A, B)$ and $Sim(B, C)$) can be saved and then efficiently used, there would be a chance to know whether A and C are duplicate or not without actually comparing them. Since the comparisons are very expensive, reducing the number of comparisons is therefore important in reducing the whole execution time. Thus the problem now is how to save the comparison information and use this information efficiently.

To solve this problem, in this paper, we first introduce a new comparison method, LCSS, based on the longest common subsequence. LCSS is efficient in detecting duplicate records and satisfies the following two useful properties:

- *Lower Bound Similarity Property (LP):*
  $Sim(A, C) \geq Sim(A, B) + Sim(B, C) - 1$
- *Upper Bound Similarity Property (UP):*
  $Sim(A, C) \leq 1 - |Sim(A, B) - Sim(B, C)|$

With the above properties, for any three records A, B and C, when $Sim(A, B)$ and $Sim(B, C)$ are known, we can evaluate the lower bound and upper bound for $Sim(A, C)$ without actually comparing A and C. Thus, these two properties provide a way to use previous comparison information (as similarity). To save that information, we set the *Anchor Record* in detection method, which is a particular record that keeps previous comparison information as a list of similarities. The anchor record serves as an anchor for future comparisons.

Based on the properties and anchor record, we then propose two new methods, SNM-IN and SNM-INOUT. They vary on the number of anchor records and their locations. SNM-IN has one anchor record and it is in the window. SNM-INOUT has two anchor records, one in the window and the other one outside the window.

A performance study has been conducted to compare the performance of SNM, SNM-IN and SNM-INOUT and the result shows that the integration of SNM-IN (SNM-INOUT) and LCSS can reduce the number of comparisons significantly.

The rest of the paper is organized as follows. In the next section, we introduce the comparison method LCSS, and show its properties. In Section 3, we describe the methods: SNM-IN and SNM-INOUT. We give the performance results in Section 4 and conclude in Section 5.

2 LCSS

2.1 Longest Common Subsequence

The *Longest Common Subsequence* has been studied extensively and has many applications, such as text pattern matching, speech recognition etc. In this paper, we follow the notation used in [4]. A subsequence of a string s is any string, which can be created from s by deleting some of the elements. More precisely, if s is the string $s_1 s_2 \cdots s_k$ then $s_{i_1} s_{i_2} \cdots s_{i_p}$ is a subsequence of s if $\forall j \in \{1, \ldots, p\}$: $i_j \in \{1, \ldots k\}$ and $\forall j \in \{1, \ldots, p-1\} : i_j < i_{j+1}$.

Consider two fixed strings $s = s_1 s_2 \cdots s_k$ and $t = t_1 t_2 \cdots t_m$. Among the strings which are subsequences of both s and t, there will be some of maximal length. Such subsequences are called longest common subsequences. Let $lcs(s,t)$ denote the (unique) length of the longest common subsequences of s and t.

Lemma 1. *For any three strings x, y and z, we have $lcs(x,y) + lcs(y,z) \leq |y| + lcs(x,z)$.*

To get a similarity value between 0.0 and 1.0, *post-normalization* by the maximal length of the compared strings is quite popular. Let $lcs_p(s,t)$ denote the post-normalization of s and t, i.e., $lcs_p(s,t) = lcs(s,t)/max\{|s|,|t|\}$. If $|s| \geq |t|$, we have $lcs_p(s,t) = lcs(s,t)/|s|$.

Let $d_p(s,t) = 1 - lcs_p(s,t)$. If $|s| \geq |t|$, we have $d_p(s,t) = 1 - lcs(s,t)/|s|$.

Theorem 1. *For any three strings x, y and z, we have*
$d_p(x,z) \leq d_p(x,y) + d_p(y,z)$.

Proof. For simplicity, we write d_p as d in the proof. Without loss of generality, we assume $|x| \geq |z|$.

(1) $|x| \geq |y| \geq |z|$

$$\begin{aligned}
&d(x,y) + d(y,z) = 1 - lcs(x,y)/|x| + 1 - lcs(y,z)/|y| \\
&= 1 - lcs(x,y)/|x| + (|y| - lcs(y,z))/|y| \\
&\geq 1 - lcs(x,y)/|x| + (|y| - lcs(y,z))/|x| \\
&= 1 - (lcs(x,y) + lcs(y,z) - |y|)/|x| \\
&\geq 1 - lcs(x,z)/|x| = d(x,z)
\end{aligned}$$

(2) $|x| \geq |z| \geq |y|$

$$\begin{aligned}
&d(x,y) + d(y,z) = 1 - lcs(x,y)/|x| + 1 - lcs(y,z)/|z| \\
&= 1 - lcs(x,y)/|x| + (|z| - lcs(y,z))/|z| \\
&\geq 1 - lcs(x,y)/|x| + (|y| - lcs(y,z))/|x| \\
&= 1 - (lcs(x,y) + lcs(y,z) - |y|)/|x| \\
&\geq 1 - lcs(x,z)/|x| = d(x,z)
\end{aligned}$$

(3) $|y| \geq |x| \geq |z|$
$d(x,y) + d(y,z) = 1 - lcs(x,y)/|y| + 1 - lcs(y,z)/|y|$
$= 1 - (lcs(x,y) + lcs(y,z) - |y|)/|y|$
$\geq min\{1, 1 - (lcs(x,y) + lcs(y,z) - |y|)/|x|\}$
$\geq min\{1, 1 - lcs(x,z)/|x|\}$
$\geq 1 - lcs(x,z)/|x| = d(x,z)$

Thus the theorem is proved. □

2.2 LCSS and Its Properties

Based on the normalized longest common subsequence, in the following, we propose the new comparison method, *LCSS*, and show its properties.

To indicate the relative importance of fields, field weightages are introduced on all fields. The sum of all field weightages equals to 1. Field weightages are also used in RS.

Suppose a database has fields F_1, F_2, $\cdots$, F_n, and the field weightages are W_1, W_2, $\cdots$, W_n respectively, $\sum_{i=1}^{n} W_i = 1$. To compute the similarity of records, we first compute the similarity of the corresponding field.

Given a field F, the field similarity for records A and B is given as:

$$Sim_F(A,B) = lcs_p(A_F, B_F),$$

where A_F and B_F are the strings in the filed F of A and B respectively.

Based on the field similarities, the similarity for records A and B is given as:

$$Sim(A,B) = \sum_{i=1}^{n} (Sim_{F_i}(A,B) \times W_i).$$

The similarity for any two records is between 0.0 and 1.0. Two records are treated as a duplicate pair if their similarity exceeds a certain threshold, denoted as σ (such as 0.8). Like all existed similarity methods, the computation of threshold is a knowledge intensive activity and demands experimental evaluation.

Let $d(A,B) = 1 - Sim(A,B)$, from the definitions of Sim_F and Sim and Theorem 1, we immediately have the following theorem.

Theorem 2. *For any three records A, B and C, we have* $d(A,C) \leq d(A,B) + d(B,C)$.

From the above theorem, we have

- $d(A,C) \leq d(A,B) + d(B,C)$
  $\Leftrightarrow 1 - Sim(A,C) \leq 1 - Sim(A,B) + 1 - Sim(B,C)$
  $\Leftrightarrow Sim(A,C) \geq Sim(A,B) + Sim(B,C) - 1;$
- $d(A,C) \geq d(A,B) - d(B,C)$
  $\Leftrightarrow 1 - Sim(A,C) \geq 1 - Sim(A,B) - (1 - Sim(B,C))$
  $\Leftrightarrow Sim(A,C) \leq 1 - (Sim(B,C) - Sim(A,B)).$
  Similarly, we can get $Sim(A,C) \leq 1 - (Sim(A,B) - Sim(B,C))$.
  Thus we have $Sim(A,C) \leq 1 - |Sim(B,C) - Sim(A,B)|$.

Let $L_B(A,C) = Sim(A,B) + Sim(B,C) - 1$ and $U_B(A,C) = 1 - |Sim(A,B) - Sim(B,C)|$, we then have

- *Lower Bound Similarity Property (LP)*: $Sim(A,C) \geq L_B(A,C)$
- *Upper Bound Similarity Property (UP)*: $Sim(A,C) \leq U_B(A,C)$

If B is understood, we write U_B and L_B as U and L respectively. The two properties show that when $Sim(A,B)$ and $Sim(B,C)$ are known, we can calculate the upper bound and lower bound for $Sim(A,C)$. Intuitively, if $L(A,C) \geq \sigma$ ($U(A,C) < \sigma$), we know that records A and C are duplicate (non-duplicate) and no actual comparison on them is required. Thus it reduces comparisons. For example, suppose $\sigma = 0.8$. If $Sim(A,B) = 0.9$, and $Sim(B,C) = 0.9$, then $Sim(A,C) \geq L(A,C) = 0.9 + 0.9 - 1 = 0.8 = \sigma$. Thus we know that records A and C are duplicate. If $Sim(A,B) = 0.9$, and $Sim(B,C) = 0.5$, then $Sim(A,C) \leq U(A,C) = 1 + 0.5 - 0.9 = 0.6 < \sigma$. Thus we know that records A and C are not duplicate.

3 New Detection Methods

In this section, we propose two new detection methods, SNM-IN and SNM-INOUT by efficiently using the properties that the comparison method satisfies.

We say that a record is an *anchor record* if the record has a list of similarities with all the other records in the current window. If the anchor record is in the current window, we call it an *inAnchor* record. Otherwise, we call it an *outAnchor* record.

Now, we propose the algorithm: Sorted neighborhood method with one anchor record. The anchor record is an inAnchor record. We call the algorithm *SNM-IN*.

Like SNM, SNM-IN can also be summarized in three phases: Create Key, Sort Data and Merge. The previous two phases are exactly the same with those in SNM. We show the Merge phase, which is divided into two stages, as follows.

1. *Initialization Stage:* Suppose the window size is ω. We firstly read the front ω records of the sorted dataset into the window. We do pair-wise comparisons on the ω records. We then set the last record as the inAnchor record and compute the similarity list for it.
2. *Scan Stage:* This stage can be divided into two parts:
   (a) *Comparison decision:* We denote the inAnchor record as R. When a new record, say L, moves into the window, we first compare L with R and get the similarity, $Sim(L,R)$. We also add $Sim(L,R)$ into the similarity list. After that, for each record in the current window, say A, with the $Sim(A,R)$ in the similarity list of R, if $L_R(A,L) = Sim(A,R) + Sim(L,R) - 1 \geq \sigma$, we treat L and A as duplicate and no comparison on them is required. Else if $U_R(A,L) = 1 - |Sim(A,R) - Sim(L,R)| < \sigma$, we treat L and A as non-duplicate and no comparison on them is require either. Otherwise, we compare them directly to determine whether they are duplicate or not.
   (b) *Anchor record choosing:* When the first record in the window slides out of the window and it is not the inAnchor record, we simply remove its

similarity from the similarity list, since it is out-of-date. If the first record is the inAnchor record, with sliding it out of the window we choose the last record in the window as the new inAnchor record. We also compare the last record with all the other records in the current window and compute the similarity list for the new inAnchor record.

The main difference between SNM and SNM-IN is as follows. While SNM compares the new record entering the current window with all previous records in the window, SNM-IN will first check whether the new record with previous records are duplicate or not with LP and UP. For those records having been determined as duplicate or non-duplicate with the new record, there is no need to compare them with the new record. Thus, with LP and UP, SNM-IN will reduce a lot of records comparisons. Notice that we only use LP and UP in SNM-IN, thus SNM-IN can employ any comparison method that satisfies LP and UP, such as LCSS. Further notice that the existing comparison methods, such as RS, do not satisfy them, therefore, they cannot be used by SNM-IN.

Let $<A, B>$ denote records A and B as a duplicate pair, DR(SNM) and DR(SNM-IN) be the duplicate results of SNM and SNM-IN respectively. We have the following theorem from that LCSS satisfies LP and UP.

Theorem 3. *If we run SNM and SNM-IN at the same window size, and with LCSS as the comparison method, we have DR(SNM-IN) = DR(SNM).*

Now we propose another algorithm: Sorted neighborhood method with two anchor records. One anchor record is an inAnchor record and the other is an outAnchor record. We call the algorithm *SNM-INOUT*. The Merge phase is shown in the following.

1. *Initialization Stage:* It is similar to the initialization stage of SNM-IN except that we set the outAnchor record as NULL.
2. *Scan Stage:* Similar to SNM-IN, this stage can also be divided into two parts:
   (a) *Comparison decision:* We denote the inAnchor record and outAnchor record as IR and OR respectively. Each anchor record keeps a list of similarity with all the other records in the current window. When a new record, say L, moves into the window, we first compare L with IR. We get the similarities, $Sim(L, IR)$, and add it into the similarity list of IR. If the record OR is not NULL, we also compare L with OR and add $Sim(L, OR)$ into the similarity list of OR. After that, for each record in the current window, say A, we first use the inAnchor record to determine whether L and A are duplicate or non-duplicate like SNM-IN does. If it cannot be determined with the inAnchor record and the outAnchor is not NULL, we then try to use the outAnchor record. If it still cannot be determined, we compare the records directly to determine whether they are duplicate or not.
   (b) *Anchor record choosing:* When the first record in the window slides out of the window and it is not the inAnchor record, we simply remove the first similarity from the similarity list of IR and OR. If the first record

is the inAnchor record, we set it as the outAnchor record and slide it out of the window. The original outAnchor record is discarded. We then choose the last record in the window as the new inAnchor record. We also compare the last record with all the records in the current window and compute the similarity list for the new inAnchor record.

We have shown the two methods, SNM-IN and SNM-INOUT. The main difference between them is on how many anchor records they have. SNM-INOUT has two anchor records while SNM-IN has only one anchor record. In SNM-INOUT, when a new record entering the current window, it is first compared with the two anchor records, which introduces one more comparison than SNM-IN does. However, in SNM-INOUT, for each record in the current window, the chance of determining the new record as a duplicate record or not is increased, which produce more chance to reduce comparisons than SNM-IN does. The performance result also proves this.

Since the outAnchor is outside the window and the last record in the window will compare with it, SNM-INOUT will obtain a few more duplicate pairs than SNM-IN does if both run at the same window size.

Let DR(SNM-INOUT) be the duplicate result of SNM-INOUT. We have the following theorem.

Theorem 4. *If we run SNM-IN and SNM-INOUT at the same window size, and with LCSS as the comparison method, we have DR(SNM-IN)* $\subseteq$ *DR(SNM-INOUT).*

As SNM is the core scheme of Clustering SNM, Multi-pass SNM and DE-SNM, similarly, we can propose Clustering SNM-IN, Multi-pass SNM-IN, and DE-SNM-IN by SNM-IN, and Clustering SNM-INOUT, Multi-pass SNM-INOUT, and DE-SNM-INOUT by SNM-INOUT.

4 Experimental Results

We test the performance on two databases, a small real database, company; and a large synthetic database, customer.

We get the company database from the authors of [5]. The company database has 856 records and each record has 7 fields: company code, company name, first address, second address, currency used, telephone number and fax number.

We generate the customer database as follows. We first generate a clean database with 5000000 records. Each record consists of 13 fields: social security number, first name, last name, gender, marital status, race, nation, education, home phone, business name, business address, occupation and business phone. Then we add additional 2390000 duplicate records into the clean database. Each record may be duplicated more than once. The error introduced in the duplicate records range from small typographical changes, to large changes of some fields.

Before testing, pre-processing on the records is conducted such as abbreviations and formats are standardized. Pre-processing the records is quite important

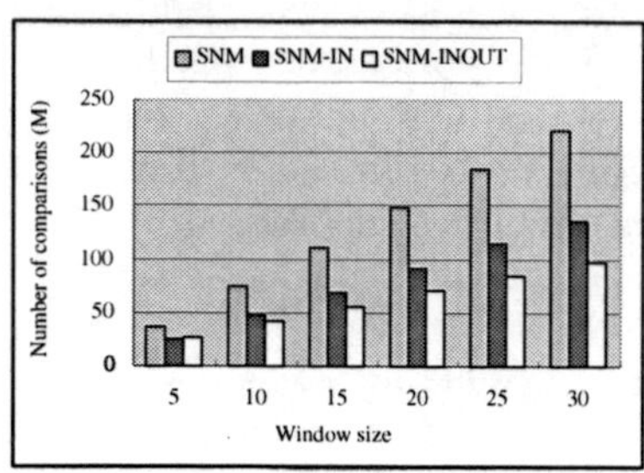

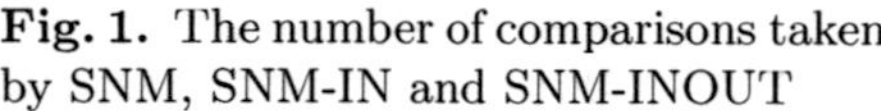

Fig. 1. The number of comparisons taken by SNM, SNM-IN and SNM-INOUT

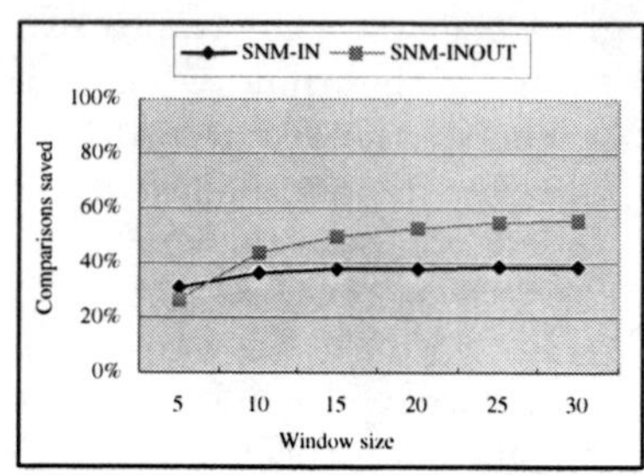

Fig. 2. The comparison saved by SNM-IN and SNM-INOUT as compared to SNM

and will increase the chance of finding duplicate records. More information on pre-processing can be found in [3] and [5].

We first compare SNM+LCSS with SNM+RS on the company and customer databases to understand the efficiency and accuracy of the comparison method LCSS . We run both methods at the window size of 10. The duplicate results obtained by both methods on the company database are exactly the same. Both obtain exactly the same 45 duplicate pairs, among which one pair is false positive (two records which do not represent the same real world entity are treated as duplicate). The duplicate results obtained by both methods on the customer database are almost the same. SNM+LCSS and SNM+RS obtain 2315225 and 2315242 duplicate pairs respectively, among which 2315163 duplicate pairs are the same in both methods. That is, more than 99.997% duplicate pairs obtained by both methods are the same. For the time, SNM+LCSS takes 8178 seconds and SNM+RS takes 8751 seconds. The time taken by SNM+LCSS is about 8% less than that taken by SNM+RS. Thus, the results show that the comparison method LCSS is as efficient as RS in capturing duplicate records and slightly faster than RS.

We then compare the methods SNM-IN and SNM-INOUT with SNM on the customer database to understand the comparisons saved with different window sizes. We run all methods from window size 5 to 30 with LCSS as the comparison method. From Theorem 3 and Theorem 4, we know that SNM and SNM-IN obtain exactly the same duplicate result, and SNM-INOUT obtains slightly more duplicate pairs than SNM-IN does. The results on comparisons are shown in Fig. 1 and Fig. 2, where Fig. 1 shows the number of comparisons taken by all methods and Fig. 2 shows the compassion saved (in percentage) by SNM-IN and SNM-INOUT compared with SNM.

From these two figures, we can see that the reduction in comparisons will increase when the window size increases. We see that SNM-IN saves comparisons from 32% to 39% and SNM-INOUT saves comparisons from 27% to 56% when the window size increases from 5 to 30. SNM-INOUT will take more comparisons than SNM-IN does when the window size is 5. It is reasonable since there are two anchor records in SNM-INOUT and each new record will compare with the two anchor records first, while in SNM-IN there is only one comparison with the inAnchor record. The two additional comparisons may not save more comparisons than one additional comparison since the window size is too small. However, when the window size increases, SNM-INOUT saves more comparisons than SNM-IN does, which is shown when the window size is increased to 30.

5 Conclusion

In this paper, we first propose a new comparison method, LCSS, based on the longest common subsequence, and discover its two useful properties, LP and UP. Take advantage of the two properties, we then propose two new detection methods, SNM-IN and SNM-INOUT. These two methods can efficiently use the properties satisfied by the comparison method to reduce unnecessary comparisons, while existing methods don't. The performance study on real and synthetic datasets shows that the integration of SNM-IN (SNM-INOUT) and LCSS saves comparisons significantly without impairing accuracy.

References

1. H. Galhardas, D. Florescu, D. Shasha, E. Simon, and C. A. Saita. Declarative data cleaning: Language, mode, and algorithms. In *Proc. 27th Int'l. Conf. on Very Large Databases*, pages 371–380, Roma, Italy, 2001.
2. M. Hernandez. A generalization of band joins and the merge/purge problem. Technical Report CUCS-005-1995, Columbia University, February 1996.
3. M. Hernandez and S. Stolfo. The merge/purge problem for large databases. In *Proceedings of the ACM SIGMOD International Conference on Management of Data*, pages 127–138, May 1995.
4. K. S. Larsen. Length of maximal common subsequences. Available from `http://www.daimi.au.dk/PB/426/PB-426.pdf`.
5. M. L. Lee, T. W. Ling, and W. L. Low. Intelliclean: A knowledge-based intelligent data cleaner. In *Proceedings of the sixth ACM SIGKDD international conference on Knowledge discovery and data mining*, pages 290–294, 2000.
6. M. L. Lee, H. J. Lu, T. W. Ling, and Y. T. Ko. Cleansing data for mining and warehousing. In *Proceedings of the 10th International Conference on Database and Expert Systems Applications (DEXA)*, pages 751–760, 1999.
7. Infoshare Limited. Best value guide to data standardizing. *InfoDB*, July 1998. Available from `http://www.infoshare.ltd.uk`.
8. A. E. Monge. Matching algorithm within a duplicate detection system. In *IEEE Data Engineering Bulletin*, volume 23(4), December 2000.
9. A. E. Monge and C. P. Elkan. An efficient domain-independent algorithm for detecting approximately duplicate database records. In *Proceeding of the ACM-SIGMOD Workshop on Research Issues on Knowledge Discovery and Data Mining*, Tucson, AZ, 1997.
10. V. Raman and J. M. Hellerstein. Potter's wheel: An interactive data cleaning system. In *Proc. 27th Int'l. Conf. on Very Large Databases*, Rome, 2001.
11. A. Silberschatz, M. StoneBraker, and J. Ullman. Database research: Achievements and opportunities into the 21st century. In *SIGMOD Record (ACM Special Interest Group on Management of Data)*, page 25(1):52, 1996.

Promoting Recommendations: An Attack on Collaborative Filtering

Michael P. O'Mahony, Neil J. Hurley, and Guenole C.M. Silvestre

Department of Computer Science, University College Dublin,
Belfield, Dublin 4, Ireland
{michael.p.omahony, neil.hurley, guenole.silvestre}@ucd.ie

Abstract. The growth and popularity of Internet applications has reinforced the need for effective information filtering techniques. The collaborative filtering approach is now a popular choice and has been implemented in many on-line systems. While many researchers have proposed and compared the performance of various collaborative filtering algorithms, one important performance measure has been omitted from the research to date - that is the *robustness* of the algorithm. In essence, robustness measures the power of the algorithm to make good predictions in the presence of noisy data. In this paper, we argue that robustness is an important system characteristic, and that it must be considered from the point-of-view of potential attacks that could be made on a system by malicious users. We propose a definition for system robustness, and identify system characteristics that influence robustness. Several attack strategies are described in detail, and experimental results are presented for the scenarios outlined.

1 Introduction

The information overload problem has prompted much research and various techniques have been proposed to improve matters. Content-based information retrieval algorithms filter information by matching user preference data against item descriptions and thereby eliminate irrelevant content. Collaborative filtering [4], [11] is an alternative class of retrieval algorithms and has gained in popularity in recent years. These so-called recommender systems attempt to filter in a personalised manner, and operate by recommending items to a user based upon the transactions of similar users in the system. Collaborative filtering algorithms have now been implemented in many application areas, ranging from on-line book stores, movie and music finders, job recruitment services, etc.

Many approaches to collaborative filtering have appeared in the literature. These include memory-based algorithms, which utilise the entire user database to make recommendations; and model-based approaches, where a model is first derived from the user database and is then used to make predictions [6], [12], [1], [3]. Many researchers have compared the performance of the various algorithms, with refinements and new ideas continuously emerging.

However one important performance measure has been omitted from the research to date - that is the *robustness* of the algorithm. In essence, robustness

R. Cicchetti et al. (Eds.): DEXA 2002, LNCS 2453, pp. 494–503, 2002.

measures the power of the algorithm to make good predictions in the presence of noisy data. Generally, collaborative filtering applications update their datasets whenever users input new ratings, without any quality assurance that the entered rating is a true reflection of a real user's preference. Indeed, since rating entry can be an onerous process, users may be careless in the values that they enter and inaccuracies (or noise) in the data must be expected. More sinisterly, it is possible to imagine scenarios in which malicious users may be motivated to deliberately attack the recommendation system and cause it to malfunction. (Imagine, for example, publishers wishing to promote their work by forcing a book recommendation system to output artificially high ratings for their publications). Depending upon the application, the cost of significantly modifying the recommendation system's output may be prohibitively high. Consider that the author may have to buy a book each time he wishes to modify the book's rating. Cost for other applications may simply be in terms of the amount of time required to input erroneous data.

Most recommendation applications operate in a web environment in which it is impossible to check the honesty of those who access the system. Hence, it is important to understand how much tolerance the recommendation algorithm has to noise in the dataset. In this paper, we propose a definition for system robustness, and identify system characteristics that influence robustness. Several attack strategies are described in detail, and experimental results are presented for the scenarios outlined.

2 Formal Framework

The performance of a system can only be measured with respect to some utility function which models the usefulness of a recommendation. Clearly, the utility of a recommendation depends upon the perspective of the players involved.

In our model of robustness, we take the end-user's perspective (to whom recommendations are delivered), and seek systems which are consistent in the recommendations that are made. Primarily, we examine how the system can be compromised by external third-parties (such as authors or publishers in the case of a book recommendation system). To such "attackers", the system is a black-box which can only be viewed through the recommendations that it outputs and can only be modified by the insertion of new data through the normal user interface.

We consider memory-based collaborative filtering (CF) in which the task is to predict the votes of a particular user (the *active* user) from a database of user votes, drawn from a population of other users. Let $\mathcal{U}$ be the universe of all users and fix some set of items I for which users vote. The votes of a user a on all items may be expressed as a vector, termed the *user profile* $\mathbf{v}_a \in V^m$ where V is a discrete set of vote values (including the special symbol $\perp$ interpreted as "not voted on") and m is the total number of items. A CF database D_U for $U \subset \mathcal{U}$ is a collection of votes $\{\mathbf{v}_a | a \in U\}$ for a particular set of users U.

Let $v_{i,j}$ be the jth element of $\mathbf{v}_i$ corresponding to the vote for user i on item j. Using the notation of [2], define I_i as the set of items on which user i has voted. The predicted vote of the active user a for item j, $p_{a,j}$ is given by

$$p_{a,j} = \bar{v}_a + \kappa \sum_{i=1}^{n} w(a,i)(v_{i,j} - \bar{v}_i) \ . \tag{1}$$

where $\bar{v}_i$ is the mean vote for user i, n is the number of users in the database with non-zero weights $w(a,i)$ and κ is a normalising factor.

The Pearson correlation coefficient weighting, proposed in [11] is adopted to explore and test our ideas on robustness in CF systems. Hence,

$$w(a,i) = \frac{\sum_j (v_{a,j} - \bar{v}_a)(v_{i,j} - \bar{v}_j)}{\sqrt{\sum_j (v_{a,j} - \bar{v}_a)^2 \sum_j (v_{i,j} - \bar{v}_i)^2}} \ . \tag{2}$$

where the sum is over those items which have been voted for by *both* user a and user i. From now on, we refer to this algorithm as *Resnick's algorithm* [11].

While various enhancements to this standard model have been proposed in the literature, such as default voting and case amplification [2], we restrict ourselves to the standard model as a solid and non-trivial basis upon which to develop our discussion. In our implementation of Resnick's algorithm, we have imposed a limit to the number of users involved in the calculation of the predicted rating, i.e. a nearest-neighbour approach is employed with the top-k nearest users chosen on the basis of highest (absolute) correlation with the active user.

3 Definitions of Robustness

One of the underlying claims of knowledge-based systems (KBS) is that they can deal with incomplete, inaccurate or uncertain data. In this regard, the previous work of Hsu and Knoblock [7], [8] and Groot et al [5], who propose methodologies for examining the robustness of knowledge discovery and knowledge-based systems, is of interest. However, much of the work done to date tends to focus on "normal" variations in the data. In this paper, we argue that robustness from the point-of-view of malicious attacks carried out on the system also needs to be considered.

We take the following approach to robustness of collaborative filtering. An *attack* is a transformation T which maps a database D_U to a new database $D'_{U'}$. Under the transformation, each vote in D_U $v_{i,j}$ is mapped to a new vote $v'_{i,j}$. If either $v_{i,j} = \perp$ or $v'_{i,j} = \perp$,this implies the addition of new votes or the deletion of existing votes, respectively. A transformation may also entail the addition of new users, so that $U \subseteq U'$.

Let $\mathcal{T}$ be the set of all possible attacks. Define a cost function $C : \mathcal{T} \rightarrow \mathcal{R}$. In general the cost of a transformation is application dependent. Various criteria can be used to construct a cost function. If the cost is related to the amount of effort it takes to perform the transformation, then this could be modelled by a monotonically increasing function of the number of user-item pairs which are modified by the transformation. There may also be a real cost, if ratings can only be entered into the system by purchasing the item in question.

Definition 1. *Fix a set, A, of unrated user-item pairs in the database, which remain unrated in the transformed database i.e.* $A \subseteq \{(a,j) | v_{a,j} = v'_{a,j} = \perp\}$. *We define robustness for the set A. Assuming that the set of vote values is bounded above by* R_{max} *and below by* R_{min}, *for each* $(a,j) \in A$, *the normalised absolute error, NAE, of prediction pre- and post-attack T is given by*

$$NAE(a,j,T) = \frac{|p_{a,j} - p'_{a,j}|}{\max\{|p_{a,j} - R_{max}|, |p_{a,j} - R_{min}|\}} . \tag{3}$$

Definition 2. *The* robustness *of prediction* $p_{a,j}$ *to attacks of cost c is given by*

$$Robust(a,j,c) = 1 - \max_{\{T \in \mathcal{T} : C(T) \leq c\}} NAE(a,j,T) . \tag{4}$$

Furthermore, the robustness of the CF recommendation system on the set A to attacks of cost c is given by

$$Robust(A,c) = \min_{(a,j) \in A} Robust(a,j,c) . \tag{5}$$

While the above definition gives a strong measure of robustness on the set A, it may also be useful to examine various other projections of the robustness (i.e. average or maximum robustness) over elements of A. Note that our definition of robustness does not contain any notion of "true" rating for the user-item pair. This reflects the distinction between the accuracy and robustness performance measures. A system which reports the same ratings regardless of the dataset is very robust, though it is unlikely to be very accurate.

The above definition is a useful measure when we are concerned with the general robustness of a system. However, additional metrics may be required depending on the nature of an attack. Consider, for example, a scenario whereby the objective is to force the predicted ratings of a particular item, or group of items, to a certain value. Given the set A of user-item pairs and an item j, let $A_j \subseteq A$ be those members of A who have rated j. Let $\mathcal{T}_c$ denote the set of all attacks of cost c from this class.

Definition 3. *We define* power of attack *(POA) for attack* $T \in \mathcal{T}_c$ *and item j by*

$$POA(A_j,j,T) = 1 - \frac{1}{|A_j|} \sum_{a \in A_j} \kappa_{a,j} . \tag{6}$$

where $\kappa_{a,j} = 1$ *iff* $p'_{a,j} = R_{target}$ *and* 0 *otherwise. We can now write the average POA for all such attacks of cost c over set* A_j *as*

$$POA(A_j,j,c) = \frac{1}{|\mathcal{T}_c|} \sum_{T \in \mathcal{T}_c} POA(A_j,j,T) . \tag{7}$$

Let I be the set of all items in A. Then the average POA of an attack of cost c on set A is:

$$POA(A, c) = \frac{1}{|I|} \sum_{j \in I} POA(A_j, j, c) . \quad (8)$$

In our experimental evaluation (Section 5), the cost is simply a function of the number of attack profiles that are added to the database.

Note that while an item-based attack may not force all of the post-attack predicted ratings to target, nevertheless the distribution of these ratings may be shifted significantly towards the target distribution. Therefore it is also worthwhile to compare the pre-and post-attack distributions of predicted ratings with the target distribution.

4 Attacks

Various forms of attack are possible on CF systems, and in this section we discuss some potential scenarios that may occur in practice. In all cases, the strategy used to mount an attack is the same. An attack consists of a set of malicious user profiles, which is inserted (via the normal user-interface) into the database.

Note that with Resnick's algorithm, the attack profiles added need to be sufficiently close or similar to the target users if they are to have an influence on the predicted ratings. For example, consider an attack designed to promote a particular product. The ideal scenario would be that the attack profiles would correlate perfectly with the target users and therefore maximise the predicted rating of the product. Attack parameters, such as size and number of profiles added, along with the items and ratings that comprise each profile, will need to be adjusted to implement the desired attack. In the following sections, we discuss these aspects in detail and identify some system characteristics that may be exploited to reduce system robustness.

4.1 Scenario 1: Random Attack

In a *random attack*, we consider that the goal of an attacker is to reduce the overall performance of a system as a whole. In these attacks, the focus is not on particular users or products, rather it is to target all users and items equally in an attempt to compromise the general integrity of the system. As a potential real-life scenario, consider a rival recommender system owner, who wishes to undermine the opposition and attract additional customers. The attack strategy in this case is relatively straightforward - the number of items in the attack profiles are randomly selected, along with the items and ratings that comprise them.

4.2 Scenario 2: Random Product Push/Nuke Attack

A *product push* or *nuke* attack attempts to force the predicted ratings of a particular item, or group of items, to some target rating. Imagine, for example, authors wishing to promote books by forcing a recommendation system to output high ratings for their work. In this scenario, an attacker implements the attack by building false profiles with the item to be pushed (or nuked) set to the maximum (or minimum) rating, and with the remainder of the items selected randomly as before.

4.3 Scenario 3: Focussed Product Push/Nuke Attack

Here again the attacker's goal is to target specific items, but in this case an important weakness in the Pearson correlation formula is exploited to implement the attack. The particular weakness in question is that the correlation between users is calculated only over the items that *both* users have rated. Hence, users can correlate strongly even though they have few items in common. While this weakness has been noted from the predictive accuracy point-of-view and some modifications to the standard model have accordingly been proposed, we highlight here its implications for robustness of recommendation.

With Pearson's formula, the correlation between users who have *exactly* two items in common is always $+1$ or -1. If the attacker adopts a strategy of building false user profiles consisting of the item to be pushed (or nuked) together with two other carefully selected items, then the probability of a successful attack is high. Ideally, two items about which there is strong consensus in the user population are selected to generate the attack profiles.

The remaining difficulty in this strategy is in ensuring that the attack profiles correlate in the same way (i.e. either positively or negatively) with all the target users. This implies that the attacker needs to know the ratings that the target users have given to the items contained in the attack profiles. However, some simple heuristics can suffice in practice. It is a fair assumption that items that have many ratings in the database (i.e. popular items) are generally rated higher than average. Such items are therefore appropriate choices when building attack profiles.

In addition, we discuss the scenario where multiple items are targeted in a single attack. In the next section, we demonstrate that by constructing a set of *independent* attack profiles it is possible to implement this type of attack successfully. Finally, we conclude by highlighting the vulnerability to attack that consistently and frequently rated items pose to a system, and the corresponding reduction in robustness that follows.

5 Results

We used two different datasets to evaluate the attack scenarios outlined in the previous section. The `Movielens` dataset [9] consists of 943 users, 1,682 movies and contains 100,000 transactions in total. Movies are rated on a scale of 1 to 5. The second dataset, `PTV` [10], is more sparse and consists of 1,542 users, 8,129 TV programs, and has 58,594 transactions. The rating scale for this dataset is from 1 to 4. From experiment we set the number of nearest neighbours to 50 for all attacks involving both datasets. An *all but one* protocol [2] is adopted in which the test set is obtained by removing a single user-item pair from the database. A prediction is then made for this pair using all the remaining data.

5.1 Scenario 1

A general random attack is performed on the `Movielens` and `PTV` databases. In the attack a number N of random attack profiles are generated. The number of items in each profile is a uniformly random number ranging between the minimum and maximum profile sizes that occur in the database. The results are presented in Fig. 1. Average robustness according to Eqn. 5 is plotted against $X\%$ (a percentage of the total number of users in the original dataset) of attack profiles added. For both databases, this attack is not very successful, with robustness falling to only 0.93 for `Movielens` and 0.85 for `PTV` at $X = 500\%$ (i.e. when 5 times the number of original users are added as attack profiles). This can be explained by the fact that randomly generated profiles are as likely to correlate positively as they are negatively with target users. This means that the attack profiles that contribute to predictions are likely to have no significant net effect.

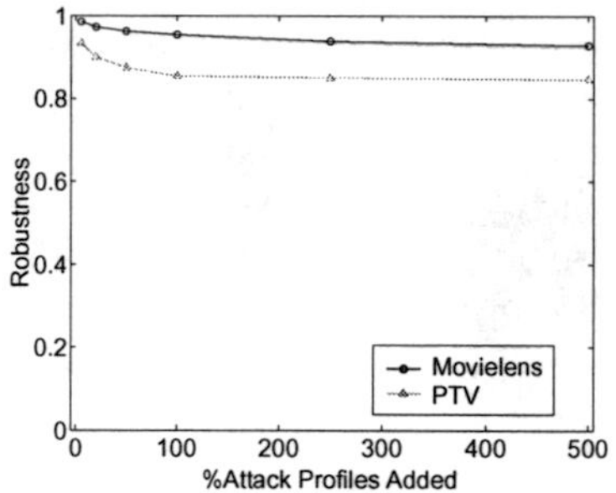

Fig. 1. Scenario 1: Robustness Degradation following Random Attack

5.2 Scenario 2

In this experiment, a random product nuke attack is performed. The attack profiles include the item to be nuked (set to the minimum rating), with the remainder of the items generated randomly as before. The number of attack profiles added is equal to the number of users in the original dataset. POA calculated according to Eqn. 8 are 0.98 for `Movielens` and 0.89 for `PTV`. In addition, the distribution means of the pre- and post-attack predictions are almost identical for both `Movielens` (3.18 and 3.33 respectively) and `PTV` (2.17 and 2.15 respectively), indicating that this type of random attack has little effect on predictions. As before, this is explained by the fact that randomly generated profiles are as likely to correlate positively as they are negatively with target users, thereby having no significant overall effect.

5.3 Scenario 3 - Experiment 1

In this experiment, a focussed product nuke attack is carried out. The attack proceeds by generating a 3 item attack profile consisting of the item to be nuked together with the two most popular items in the database. The identical attack profile is repeated a number N times. Note that this attack can only be successful for those users that have rated the two most popular items (35% of all users for `Movielens` and 18% for `PTV`). Therefore, we measure POA according to Eqn. 8 only over those users who have rated the items in question.

Fig. 2 presents POA against the size of the attack, N. For `Movielens`, POA falls to 0.5 when $N = 60$, showing that the attack was successful in forcing one half of all predictions to the minimum rating. Also the distribution means of pre- and post-attack predictions (3.24 and 2.34 respectively) further indicate a successful attack. For `PTV`, the attack is not successful, with POA falling only slightly below the baseline level (i.e. the POA at $N = 0$, corresponding to those user-item pairs for which predictions are already at the minimum rating). This is explained by the fact that the average number of attack profiles that contribute to predictions is significantly less for `PTV` than for `Movielens`. For example, consider the `Movielens` database, where, at $N = 60$, 73% of all profiles that contribute to predictions are attack profiles, as opposed to only 45% for `PTV`. Here we see the heuristic of assigning a higher rating to the most popular item in the attack profiles breaking down for `PTV`. This is due to the sparsity of the dataset, which is an order of magnitude more sparse than the `Movielens` dataset.

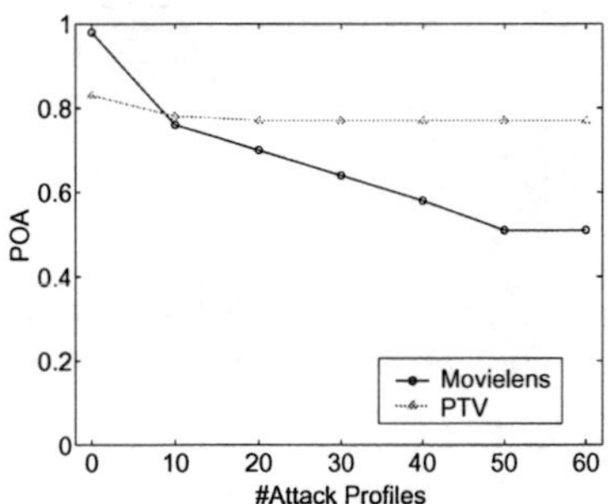

Fig. 2. Scenario 3 - Experiment 1: POA for Product Nuke Attack

5.4 Scenario 3 - Experiment 2

Again a product nuke attack is carried out on the `Movielens` and `PTV` databases, but this time the goal is to attack a *group* of items at once. In this case, N distinct attack profiles are generated, one for each of the items to be attacked. All attack profiles consist of 3 items, chosen in the same way as in Experiment 1 above. Thus each profile contains one of the items to be attacked, set to the minimum rating, together with two other items. If the attack profiles are independent of one another - and we can achieve this by ensuring that none of the items we wish to attack appear together in any of the attack profiles - then we can obtain similar results over the whole group as we achieved for the single-item attacks described in Experiment 1. This means, for example, that it would be possible for authors or publishers to demote or promote multiple titles in a single attack.

5.5 Scenario 3 - Experiment 3

It is clear that items which are rated identically over the entire database present a grave security risk from the point-of-view of robustness. This point is confirmed in this experiment, in which the database is initially modified so that two items have identical ratings over all users. These two items can now be used to generate very effective attack profiles to nuke (or push) any selected item in the database. We repeated the experiment outlined in Experiment 1 above on our modified database, using 60 attack profiles. The result was that POA over all items fell to 0.21 for `Movielens`, and 0.04 for `PTV`. The change in pre- and post- distribution means is also very significant - for `PTV` the means are 2.19 and 0.52 respectively; for `Movielens` the means are 3.17 and 1.03 respectively. Fig. 3 shows a histogram for `Movielens` of the recommendations made for all attacked user-item pairs, pre- and post-attack, which clearly illustrates the successful nature of the attack.

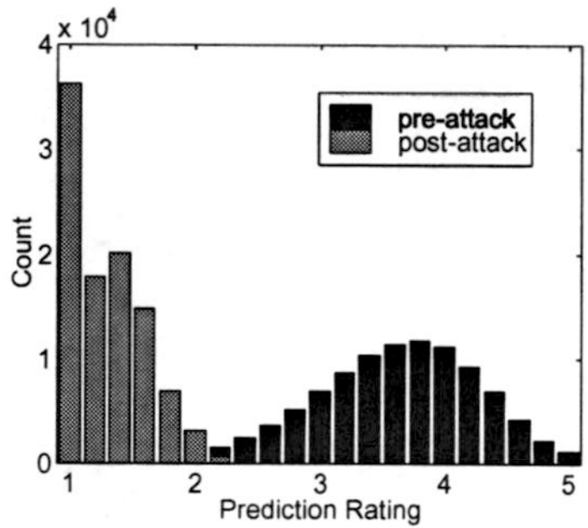

Fig. 3. Scenario 3 - Experiment 3: Histogram of Pre- and Post-Attack Predictions

Note that although it may seem unlikely that a real database will contain such agreement across all users for any item, it is reasonable to expect that there are groups of users who will agree on some common sets of items. This experiment shows that if the goal of an attack is simply to target a particular user group, then a simple and effective strategy is to seek those items on which the group agree and use them to build attack profiles.

6 Conclusion

In this paper we have introduced a new and important measure of performance, namely robustness, which has not previously been considered in the context of recommendation systems. We have demonstrated that a robustness analysis can highlight weaknesses in a system which do not become apparent by simply analysing recommendation accuracy. We have presented several attack scenarios and have shown that effective attack strategies can be devised to degrade the performance of the system. Future work will focus on robustness analysis of more sophisticated collaborative filtering systems and will investigate ways of securing systems against the types of deliberate attack that have been outlined in this paper.

References

1. C. C. Aggarwal, J. L. Wolf, K.-L. Wu, and P. S. Yu. Horting hatches an egg: A new graph-theoretic approach to collaborative filtering. In *Knowledge Discovery and Data Mining*, pages 201–212, 1999.
2. J. S. Breese, D. Heckerman, and C. Kadie. Empirical analysis of predictive algorithms for collaborative filtering. In *Proceedings of the Fourteenth Annual Conference on Uncertainty in Artificial Intelligence*, pages 43–52, July 1998.
3. M. Condliff, D. Lewis, D. Madigan, and C. Posse. Bayesian mixed-effects models for recommender systems. In *Proceedings of the ACM SIGIR Workshop on Recommender Systems: Algorithms and Evaluation, 22nd Intl. Conf. on Research and Development in Information Retrieval, 1999*, 1999.
4. D. Goldberg, D. Nichols, B. M. Oki, and D. Terry. Using collaborative filtering to weave an information tapestry. *Communications of the ACM*, 35(12):61–70, December 1992.
5. P. Groot, F. van Harmelen, and A. ten Teije. Torture tests: a quantitative analysis for the robustness of knowledge-based systems. In *European Workshop on Knowledge Acquisition, Modelling and Management (EKAW'00)*. LNAI Springer-Verlag, October 2000.
6. J. Herlocker, J. Konstan, A. Borchers, and J. Riedl. An algorithmic framework for performing collaborative filtering. In *Proceedings of the SIGIR*. ACM, August 1999.
7. C.-N. Hsu and C. A. Knoblock. Estimating the robustness of discovered knowledge. In *Proceedings of the First International Conference on Knwledge Discovery and Data Mining*, Montreal, Canada, 1995.
8. C.-N. Hsu and C. A. Knoblock. Discovering robust knowledge from dynamic closed-world data. In *Proceedings of AAAI'96*, 1996.
9. http://movielens.umn.edu/.
10. http://www.changingworlds.com/.
11. P. Resnick, N. Iacovou, M. Suchak, P. Bergstrom, and J.Riedl. An open architecture for collaborative filtering of netnews. In *Proceedings of the ACM Conference on Computer Supported Cooperative Work*. ACM, 1994.
12. B. M. Sarwar, G. Karypis, J. A. Konstan, and J. Riedl. Analysis of recommendation algorithms for e-commerce. In *ACM Conference on Electronic Commerce*, pages 158–167, 2000.

Bringing Together Description Logics and Database in an Object Oriented Model

Mathieu Roger, Ana Simonet, and Michel Simonet

Laboratory TIMC-IMAG- Osiris Team
La Tronche Cedex
Mathieu.Roger@imag.fr, Ana.Simonet@imag.fr,
Michel.Simonet@imag.fr

Abstract. Description logics have powerful deductive capabilities but rely on a weakly structured model. Databases provide storage optimization and offer better structuring capacities, especially within the object-oriented paradigm. We propose a model which offers the deductive capabilities of description logics and the structuring possibilities of the object approach. We distinguish between three types of classes : concrete classes, where objects are instantiated, virtual classes, which are subsets of concrete classes, corresponding to database object-preserving views, and abstract classes, which factor common properties of objects from different concrete classes. A schema in this model can be translated into a description logics schema and into a database schema. The former represents the deductive part and the latter deals with the storage aspect.

1 Introduction

Knowledge base systems are designed to express complex queries upon highly organised data whereas databases are meant to store and retrieve huge amounts of data in an efficient and secure way. Merging both approaches aims at combining their respective advantages and has been a hot topic for many years. Existing works differ both on database types (relational or object-oriented) and on knowledge base types (rule-based, constraint-based…).
Merging databases and DLs has already been investigated. [Borgida and Brachman 93] periodically insert all the objects from a database into a DL reasoner in order to detect incoherencies and perform deductions. [Bresciani 95] makes a connection between a DL system and a database, enabling the user to transparently execute DL queries with database objects. Although promising, these two approaches have their drawbacks. The first approach is well suited to already populated databases but it might be too late to abort the transaction when incoherent information is input. The second approach suffers from the lack of an automated translation between DL and database schemes. It is commonly thought that primitive concepts equate to classes and defined concepts equate to views, but translation from DL schemes to RDB schemes is not always possible: in DL systems one can describe an attribute within a defined concept, which is not common in relational views. Moreover a DL scheme contains no information about object storage, so persistence is under-optimised.

R. Cicchetti et al. (Eds.): DEXA 2002, LNCS 2453, pp. 504–513, 2002.

This work is part of the Osiris project [Simonet et al., 94] initiated by the P-Type data model proposed in [Simonet 84]. Its purpose was to design a DBMS centred on views, with an instance classification mechanism working with domain constraints and unknown values. After a study of Programming Languages and inheritance mechanisms, we extended this model to a set-oriented model with three kinds of classes: abstract, concrete and virtual, where abstract and virtual classes both allow for instance and class classification. This new proposition implements the classification process with a more general constraint language by using an existing DL demonstrator, namely Racer [Haarslev and Moller 01]. In this paper, which is the continuation of the work initiated in [Roger et al. 01], we consider DL systems as highly specialised reasoners that can perform inferences both on concepts and instances. We only use them as a deductive core implementation upon which we build a more complex system including database and programming language functionalities, as is also suggested in [Decker 98].

We describe the complete architecture of our system dealing with two translations, the first one is translation of classes into a language that gives our system the ability to check for schema coherence and instance classification. The second one is a translation to a relational database that gives us persistent data by using instance classification to perform object storage. We are conducting the implementation of that system, so it must be considered as work in progress.

This paper is organized as follows. The second part describes the syntax and semantics of our data modeling language. The third part describes the language in which we translate our data model. This translation is described in the fourth part with the storage translation, which relies on previous work [Roger et al., 01].

2 Data Model

2.1 Abstract Classes

Abstract classes are classes that do not carry any identity [Guarino and Welty 01], i.e., they do not provide any constructor. They describe only a small part of their objects' structure. The "canonical" example of an abstract class is the class THING that contains all objects: one cannot build a “thing” because one cannot decide if one already knows it or not!

```
abstract-class-definition ::
  abstract class name
    [(all|some) abstract-class-formula]
    [attribute-declarations]
    [constraints]
   end
```

This kind of class is now widely spread in OO languages. It is named *abstract class* in C++ and *deferred class* in Eiffel. In our model it is extended by the possibility of defining abstract classes by constraints, as shown by the class `YOUNG` in the following example.

```
abstract class AGED
  age : INTEGER ;
end
abstract class YOUNG all AGED
  age in [0..5] ;
end
```

Here we have a class of objects with an age and these objects will belong to various concrete classes (see 2.4). We also have the class YOUNG of all the objects that are in AGED with a particular range for age.

attribute-declarations is a sequence of *attribute-declaration* that define the "type" of the attribute, the cardinality range and the optional reverse attribute constraint.

constraints is a sequence of *constraint*. A *constraint* is a logical formula constructed with the logical operators **and**, **or** and **not**, and with atomic formulas that are *attribute-constraint*.

```
attribute-constraint ::
   attribute-name in set |
   Card ( attribute-name in set ) ≤ constant |
   Card ( attribute-name in set ) ≥ constant
set ::
   class |[constant..constant] |{constant (,constant)*}
```

abstract-class-formula are logical formulas constructed with the logical operators **and**, **or** and **and not**, and with atomic formulas that are class names. Distinguishing between equivalent and necessary condition is done through the **all | some** distinction. The **inheritance graph** is the directed graph with classes as edges and arrows representing the relationship USE such that C USE D iff D appears in the parent class formula of C.

2.2 Concrete Classes

Concrete classes are the most important kind of classes; they are the equivalent in this model to the "standard" notion of class in OO models. An object is created in a unique concrete class and remains in it during its lifetime. More precisely:

1. they are **primitive** classes, in the sense of Description Logics
2. they **supply an identity**, i.e., there exists a constructor for such a class
3. they are **rigid** [Guarino and Welty 01], i.e., an object belonging to a concrete class will remain in it forever
4. they are pairwise disjoint.

Because of these properties, an object belongs to a unique concrete class and never changes, and one can build an object from it. Concrete classes are primitive concepts, so the only authorised inheritance mean is **some**. In this version of our work we deal with two kinds of identity: **always new** that builds a completely new object at each constructor call, as in most OO languages, and **key** that allows to "build" several times the same object (such as each call to the constructor returns the same object).

```
identity ::
  always new |
  key attribute-name (, attribute-name)*
```

Note that the identity question relates database keys and OOPL constructor calls; we believe it is very promising for theoretical integration of database and OOPL issues. Concrete classes form a partition of the whole set of objects. They constitute the core of the model because they are the only classes that possess an identity.

```
concrete class CAR some AGED
  registration : STRING ;
  motor : STRING in {"gasoline", "diesel"} ;
  colour : STRING in {"red", "black", "white"} ;
  identity registration ;
end
concrete class PERSON some AGED
  name : STRING ;
  sex : STRING in {"male","female"} ;
  identity name, sex, age ;
end
```

Note that the attribute `age` is inherited from the abstract class AGED.

2.3 Virtual Classes

A **virtual class** is a <u>subset of a unique concrete class</u>. It is defined by a logical constraint that can comprise a set formula over other virtual classes.
From a Database viewpoint virtual classes are object-preserving views [Bertino 96], i.e., views that do not create new objects.

```
virtual class CAR-OWNER all PERSON
  cars : set(CAR) ;
end
virtual class DIESEL-CAR all CAR
  motor in {"diesel"} ;
end
virtual class DIESEL-OWNER all PERSON
  cars in DIESEL-CAR ;
end
```

2.4 Possible Classes

For a concrete class C we define **the set of possible classes for C** as the union of the set of all virtual classes of C and the set of all abstract classes that are connected to C through the <u>undirected</u> inheritance graph. This definition needs some explanation.
A **possible class for a virtual class V** is either its concrete class C or every possible class for C. The **set of possible classes for an abstract class A** is the union of all possible classes for the concrete classes C that are connected to A through the <u>undirected</u> inheritance graph. Intuitively, it means that an object of C will never be a member of a class that is not a possible class for C.

The **attributes of a concrete class C** are those defined in all the possible classes for C. In case of multiple definition their types must be the same one for predefined types and any class type for references to objects (the DL system will check for constraint compatibility). The **necessary attributes for a concrete class C** are those defined in the concrete class. An attribute that is not necessary is **optional**. As in [Chambers 93] all occurrences of attributes with the same name in a connected compound of the inheritance graph refer to the same attribute.

3 Description Logics

Description Logics provide a possible underlying data model for our work. DL languages are characterised by their concepts constructors; here we focus on the language ALCQI which is well adapted for object-oriented models [Calvanese et al. 95]. In the Osiris Prototype we use the RACER system to detect incoherent schemes, to check constraints and to classify instances.
A **TBox** (Term Box) is a triplet <C,R,A> where C is a set of concept names, R a set of role names and A a set of axioms. Informally, concepts are named sets of objects, roles are binary relationships between concepts, and axioms express constraints between concepts and roles. Given C and R, complex concepts can be constructed according to Table 1. An **interpretation** I is given by a set of entities (objects) Δ^I and an interpretation function $.^I$ which maps each concept from C to a subset of Δ^I, and each role from R to a subset of $\Delta^I \times \Delta^I$. Complex concepts are interpreted through $.^I$ accordingly to Table 1.

Table 1. Syntax and semantics for language ALCQI.

Constructor	Syntax	Semantics
Attribute typing	$\forall$ R.A	$\{ x \in \Delta^I \mid \forall y \in \Delta^I: (x,y) \in R^I \Rightarrow y \in A^I\}$
Intersection	$U \cap V$	$U^I \cap V^I$
Negation	$\neg U$	$\{x \in \Delta^I \mid x \notin U^I\}$
Union (U)	$U \cup V$	$U^I \cup V^I$
Cardinality constraints (Q)	$(\leq n\ R\ C)$	$\{x \in \Delta^I \mid \#\{y \in C^I, (x,y) \in R^I\} \leq n \}$
	$(\geq n\ R\ C)$	$\{x \in \Delta^I \mid \#\{y \in C^I, (x,y) \in R^I\} \geq n \}$
Inverse role (I)	R^{-1}	$\{(x,y) \mid (y,x) \in R^I\}$

Axioms are inclusion constraints between concepts (concepts from C or complex concepts), and then a **valid interpretation** is an interpretation that satisfies every axiom from A, i.e., if $C1 \subseteq C2$ is an axiom from A and I a valid interpretation then $C1^I \subseteq C2^I$. Intuitively, a Tbox may be safely considered as a Database scheme and an interpretation as a possible state for this scheme where there is only complete information.
An **ABox** (Assertion Box) is a finite set of assertions of one of the following forms :

1. $o \in C$ = object o belongs to concept C

2. (o1,o2) ∈ R = objects o1 and o2 are related through role R
3. closed(o,R) = all the objects linked to o through role R are given explicitly in the ABox

ABox reasoning consists in determining if a given ABox is **consistent** with a TBox. Description Logics systems provide an instance classification mechanism by allowing to ask if a given object belongs to a given concept; it is expressed in RACER with the *(instance-of? o C)* command that returns **true** if the object is proven to belong to C and **nil** otherwise. Given an ABox A, **instance classification** for an object **o** is done as follows: for each concept from C, ask both `(instance-of? o C)` and `(instance-of? o ¬C)`. If one of these questions answers true the classification is obvious; if none answers true, membership of **o** to C is unknown.

4 Translation

4.1 Translation into Description Logics

The translation of an Osiris scheme into a DL scheme is such that:

- each class corresponds to a concept with the same name
- each attribute corresponds to a role with the same name

Set formulas used for inheritance are translated into equivalent concept formulas by replacing **`and`** by ∩, **`or`** by ∪ and **`and not`** by ∩¬. For example, the formula `A` **`and`** `B` **`and not`** `C` is translated into the complex concept A ∩ B ∩ ¬C.

This translation might seem straightforward, but it is not the case. In fact, we need a special concept: **Undefined**. Its purpose is to allow an object not to be in a concept and to type-check values for optional attributes. If we do not impose constraints on optional attributes at the concrete class level, then, for let's say an optional attribute `student-number` declared in a virtual class `student` as an `integer`, then it is possible to build a person with a `string` as `student-number`: the object is not a `student`. We want to avoid this situation where an attribute value is not compatible with the declarations for this attribute, thus we have to say that possible values for optional attributes are in declared domains for this attribute, plus the case where it is not in any of these domains: in this case the value is in **Undefined**.

Translation into description logics allows us to check for satisfiability of classes through TBox reasoning and to deduce the classes an object belongs to (and the classes an object does not belong to) through ABox reasoning.

4.1.1 Concrete Classes

Attributes over predefined types need a special translation, because of elementary constraints such as `age in [0..5]`. We define a DL concept representing the domain of the attribute for each attribute over a predefined type that appears in a constraint; this domain is noted as `D_name`, where name is the name of the attribute. This domain is partitioned into smaller domains, called **stable sub-domains** [Simonet 84; Roger et al., 01] such that each elementary constraint on that attribute is translated into a DL constraint saying that all the values of the attributes are in a union of stable sub-domains.

Definition. Given an attribute A defined in a class C, let us call cons(A) the set of all elementary constraints involving A; a **stable sub-domain for A** is either a subset of cons(A) or the stable sub-domain sds-undefined$_A$. The interpretations of a stable sub-domain s are respectively $s^I = C^I \cap Cons_i^I - \cup Cons_j^I$, where $Cons_i \in s$ and $Cons_j \notin s$; and $\text{sds-undefined}_A{}^I = C^I \cap (\forall A.\textbf{Undefined})^I$.

The Calculation of stable sub-domains is done by the Osiris System. Stable sub-domains are translated into primitive disjoint concepts regardless of their meaning, i.e., the DL reasoner does not have to know what is the definition of the domain. The domain for the attribute is defined as the union of all its stable sub-domains. In fact, we consider a partitioned universe. Given a declaration of an attribute A with domain C, we define the following concept:

attribute-declaration-concept = ∀ A.C ∩ (≤ card-max A) ∩ (≥ card-min A)

For each necessary attribute of a class C we impose that:

C ⊆ attribute-declaration-concept

For each optional attribute of the class C we state the following constraint, where **DECLARATIONS(A,C)** is the set of all attribute declarations of A in any virtual class of C:

C ⊆ attribute-undefinition-concept(A) $\cup_{\textbf{X in DECLARATIONS(A,C)}}$ **X**
attribute-undefinition-concept(A) = ∀ A.UNDEFINED

Each constraint is translated into the corresponding constraint of ALCQI.

C ⊆ constraint, for all constraints of the class C.

The parent formula is also translated into a constraint:

C ⊆ Parent-Formula

For each distinct concrete class or predefined type attribute domain B and C and for the special concept **`Undefined`** we state that B and C are incompatible:

C ⊆ ¬B

Example 1. This example illustrates the translation for the concrete classes PERSON and CAR defined in the examples of section 2, and a special translation for predefined types.

```
PERSON ⊆ (∀cars.CAR ∪ ∀cars.UNDEFINED) ∩ AGED
CAR ⊆ ∀motor.D_motor ∩ (= 1 motor) ∩ AGED
```

The domain of the attribute motor is split into two parts, `D_motor1 = "diesel"` and `D_motor2 = "gasoline"`.

```
D_motor = D_motor1 ∪ D_motor2 ; D_motor1 ⊆ ¬D_motor2
```

The following constraints state that all concrete classes and domains for predefined types are pairwise disjoint.

```
CAR ⊆ ¬PERSON, CAR ⊆ ¬D_motor, PERSON ⊆ ¬D_motor, CAR
⊆ ¬Undefined, Person ⊆ ¬Undefined, D_motor ⊆
¬Undefined
```

4.1.2 Virtual and Abstract Classes

Consider an abstract or a virtual class V with `PARENTS` as the set formula, `Constraints` as constraints and `Attributes` as set of attribute declarations.
If the keyword is **`all`**, the extension of V is given by the following DL constraint:

$$\mathbf{V{=}PARENTS{\cap}(\cap_{C\in Constraints}C){\cap}(\cap_{Att\in Attributes}Att){\cap}(\cup_{C\in Possible(A)\wedge C\ concrete}\ C)}$$

If the keyword is **`some`**, the extension of V is given by the following DL constraint:

$$\mathbf{V{\subseteq}PARENTS{\cap}(\cap_{C\in Constraints}C)\cap(\cap_{Att\in Attributes}Att)\cap(\cup_{C\in Possible(A)\wedge C\ concrete}\ C)}$$

Example 2. This example shows the translation for virtual and abstract classes of our main example.

```
AGED = ∀age.D_age ∩ (= 1 age) ∩ (PERSON ∪ CAR)
YOUNG = AGED ∩ ∀age.D_age1 ∩ (PERSON ∪ CAR)
```

Because of constraints, the domain of the attribute age is split into two parts, `D_age1 = [0..5] D_age2 = INTEGER - [0..5]`. This domain is incompatible with other domains and concrete classes.

```
D_age = D_age1 ∪ D_age2, D_age1 ⊆ ¬D_age2, PERSON ⊆
¬D_age, D_motor ⊆ ¬D_age, CAR ⊆ ¬D_age, D_age ⊆
¬Undefined, CAR-OWNER = PERSON ∩ ∀cars.CAR, DIESEL-
OWNER = CAR-OWNER ∩ ∀cars.DIESEL, DIESEL = CAR ∩
∀motor.D_motor1
```

4.1.3 Translation of Objects

Object values need to be translated into ABox constraints. Each distinct object is assigned an oid by the main system; and this oid is also used as the unique name into the ABox reasoner. References to other objects are translated using the second form of ABox constraints (see 3.1), belonging to concepts by the first one, and the third one is used to "tell the end of a set". Values of predefined types are translated using the first form of constraints and the stable sub-domains, because values are not considered as ABox objects. Translation of the CAR object CAR(motor:"diesel", age:?, registration:"foo") whose oid is `oid27`.

```
oid27 ∈ CAR ; oid27 ∈ ∀motor.D_motor1
```

Translation of a PERSON object PERSON(cars:{oid27}, age:54) whose oid is `oid86`.

```
oid86 ∈ PERSON ; (oid86,oid27) ∈ cars ;
closed(oid86,cars) ; oid86 ∈ ∀age.D_age2
```

In the following we consider that all the objects are classified, i.e., for each class we know if an object belongs to it, does not belong to it or neither; this classification will be used as an indexing information for the object storage into a DBMS.

4.2 Translation into Relational DBMS

Each concrete class is translated into a table with an attribute for each mono-valued attribute from the concrete class and a external table for each multi-valued attribute. An additional attribute is built for each attribute to indicate if its value is Unknown, Undefined or Normal. Finally an extra attribute is added that references the **equivalence class** of the object as an external reference to an element of the EQ-CLASS table associated to the concrete class [Simonet et al., 94; Roger et al., 01].
Formally, an **EQ-CLASS** is an equivalence class for the relationship between objects having exactly the same membership status for each class. Practically, this table is used to indicate to which class an object belongs and to which it does not belong. Thus, the equivalence table of a concrete class is constituted from a key attribute and an numeric attribute for each possible class of the concrete class (1 means that the object belongs to the given class, 0 that the object does not belong to the class and any other value that we do not known whether or not the object belongs to the class).
Inserting an object into its table necessitates that its equivalence class (EQ-CLASS) is known. This ability is delegated to the deductive part of the Osiris system, and more specifically here to the Abox reasoner. Our architecture relies on a deep collaboration between a DL system and a RDBMS.
Example. This example shows the translation for the example used throughout the paper. It is constituted by the following relational tables.

```
Table CAR (oid:INT,age:INT, age_UndefUnknown:INT,
registration:STRING, registration_UndefUnknown:INT,
motor:STRING, motor_UndefUnknown:INT, colour:STRING,
colour_UndefUnknown:INT, EQ-CLASS:INT)
Table PERSON (oid:INT, age:INT, age_UndefUnknown:INT,
name:STRING, name_UndefUnknown:INT, sex:STRING,
sex_UndefUnknown:INT, cars_UndefUnknown:INT, EQ-
CLASS:INT)
Table PERSON_cars (oid_PERSON:INT,oid_CAR:INT)
Table EQ-CLASS-CAR (key:INT, CAR:INT, DIESEL-CAR:INT,
AGED:INT, YOUNG:INT)
Table EQ-CLASS-PERSON(key:INT, PERSON:INT, AGED:INT,
YOUNG:INT, CAR-OWNER:INT, DIESEL-OWNER:INT)
```

5 Conclusion

DLs and DBs are two kinds of systems bound to merge in order to respectively increase the reasoning power in DB (instance classification, query optimisation) and the amount of data efficiently processed in DL. But this convergence is hindered by the distance between database and DL representation models. Thus, works on

semantic query optimisation rely on persistent view maintenance (through defined concepts), but the lack of such a mechanism in most databases renders them unusable through this approach.
DB and DL coupling requires DB (a relational scheme in general) to DL scheme translation. Borgida and Brachman hide translation from a DB to a DL within programs. Bresciani handles translation from DL to DB as metadata (that must be stated by the user). Moreover, migration from DB to DL is a periodic process for Borgida, so the ABox must be able to handle a large amount of objects, which is still a critical issue in DL systems.
The solution advocated here is to generate both schemes (DL and storage) from a unique model that includes all the necessary meta-information and to strongly use instance classification for storage purposes.

References

[Abiteboul and Bonner 91] Serge Abiteboul and Anthony Bonner, Objects and Views, SIGMOD Conference 1991.

[Albano et al. 95] A. Albano, M. Diotallevi and G. Ghelli, Extensible Objects for Database Evolution: Language Features and Implementation Issues, DBPL'95

[Bassolet et al., 96]: C.-G. Bassolet, A. Simonet, M. Simonet, Probabilistic Classification in Osiris, a View-based OO DBMS and KBMS, In : DEXA'96, 7th International DEXA Workshop on Database and Expert Systems Applications, Sept. 1996, Zurich, pp 62-68.

[Borgida and Brachman 93] Alex Borgida and Ronald Brachman, Loading Data into Description Rreasoners, SIGMOD Record,vol 22, N° 2, 1993

[Bresciani 95] Paolo Bresciani, Querying Database from Description Logics, KRDB'95

[Bresciani 96] Paolo Bresciani, Some Research Trends in KR&DB (position paper), KRDB'96

[Calvanese et al. 95] Diego Calvanese, Giuseppe De Giacomo and Maurizio Lenzerini, Structured Objects: Modeling and Reasoning, DOOD'95

[Chambers 93] Craig Chambers, Predicate Classes, ECOOP'93

[Decker 98] Stefan Decker, On Domain Specific Declaration Knowledge Representation and DataBase Languages, KRDB'98

[Ducournau 01] Roland Ducournau, Spécialisation et sous-typage: Thème et variations, Rapport de Recherche 01-013, L.I.R.M.M., Montpellier, 2001.

[Guarino and Welty 01] Nicolas Guarino and Christopher Welty, Identity and subsumption, in R. Green, C. A. Bean, and S. Hyon Myaeng (eds.), *The Semantics of Relationships: An Interdisciplinary Perspective,* Kluwer 2001

[Guerini et al. 98] G. Guerrini, E. Bertino, R. Bal, "A Formal Definition of the Chimera Object-Oriented Data Model", *Journal of Intelligent Information Systems*, Vol.11, No.1, pp.5-40, July 1998.

[Haarslev and Moller 01] Volker Haarslev and Ralf Moller, RACER System Description, IJCAR'01

[Kuno and Rudensteiner 96] Harumi Kuno and Elke Rudensteiner, Using Object-Oriented Principles to Optimize Update Propagation to Materialized Views, ICDE'96

[Roger et al. 01] Mathieu Roger, Ana Simonet and Michel Simonet, Object Space Partitioning in a DL-like Database and Knowledge Base Management System, DEXA2001

[Simonet 84] Ana Simonet, Types Abstraits et Bases de Données: formalisation du concept de partage et analyse statique de contraintes d'intégrité, PhD, University of Grenoble, 1984

[Simonet et al. 94] Ana Simonet and Michel Simonet, Objects with Views and Constraints: From Databases to Knowledge bases, OOIS'94

Objects and Roles in the Stack-Based Approach*

Andrzej Jodłowski[1], Piotr Habela[3],
Jacek Płodzień[1,2], and Kazimierz Subieta[3,1]

[1] Institute of Computer Science PAS, Warsaw, Poland
[2] Warsaw School of Economics, Warsaw, Poland
[3] Polish-Japanese Institute of Information Technology, Warsaw, Poland
{andrzejj, jpl, subieta}@ipipan.waw.pl
phabela@pjwstk.waw.pl

Abstract. In the paper we propose a new approach to the concept of dynamic object roles. The approach assumes, among others, that: a role is a distinguished subobject for an object; a role dynamically inherits attributes' values and methods of its parent object; objects can be accessed by their names as well as by the names of their roles. The paper focuses on implications of this concept for an object data model and for an object data store. We also explain how it fits with other modern notions from the conceptual modeling field. Finally, we discuss some issues concerning a query language for the object data model with roles.

1 Introduction

Since its very beginning, conceptual modeling has been evolving to answer the needs of information systems analysts and designers. A great number of concepts and ideas has been proposed in the literature and introduced into practice. Some of them have been abandoned; some are still in use. Nevertheless, the need for more and more modern, useful, effective and easy-to-use modeling concepts is growing more and more. One of the most promising of them is dynamic object roles.

Roles, like classes, may be used to classify objects, but unlike class-based classification, role-based classification may be multiple and dynamic [7]. Some of the most popular features of roles are as follows [6]: a role comes with its own properties and behavior; an object may acquire and abandon roles dynamically; an object may play different roles simultaneously; an object may play the same role several times. For example, a certain person can simultaneously be a student, a worker, a patient, a club member etc. Moreover, a person can be a student two or more times. Therefore it is more precise to say that a person *becomes* a student for some time and later he/she terminates the student role, than to say that a student *is a* person. Similarly, a building can be an office, a house, a magazine etc.

* This work was partially supported by the European Commission project ICONS; project no. IST-2001-32429.

R. Cicchetti et al. (Eds.): DEXA 2002, LNCS 2453, pp. 514–523, 2002.

For several years dynamic object roles have had the reputation of a notion on the brink of acceptance/rejection. On the one hand, there are many papers advocating the concept, e.g. [1,2,5,11]. On the other hand, many researchers consider applications of the concept not sufficiently wide to justify the extra complexity of conceptual modeling facilities. Moreover, the concept is totally neglected on the implementation side – as far as we know, none of the popular object-oriented programming languages or database management systems (DBMSs) introduces it explicitly. Hence, there are several special techniques of representing roles indirectly [6], for instance, as named places of relationships and as specialization/generalization.

In our opinion, despite the significant number of ideas and papers, or rather due to it, the concept of dynamic roles should be revised. The paper describes our proposal for composite objects with roles, which possess a special structure and semantics. In our research we use the *stack-based approach* (SBA) and its query language SBQL; see e.g. [4,8]. A version of roles was implemented in the prototype system Loqis [9]. Currently we are working on a prototype of an object-oriented DBMS for intelligent content management for Web applications, where we intend to implement the ideas presented here.

The rest of the paper is organized as follows. Section 2 introduces the general idea of our proposal. Section 3 discusses the differences between the concept of dynamic roles (including our proposal) and the traditional object models in programming languages and DBMSs. Section 4 presents assumptions for an object store and Section 5 discusses some issues concerning a query language in our model with roles. Section 6 summarizes the paper.

2 General Idea of Our Proposal

The concept of dynamic object roles assumes that an object is associated with other objects (subobjects), which model its roles. In our terminology we distinguish between objects and roles: we assume that an object can contain many sub-objects called roles and a role belongs to a single object. These subobjects can be inserted and removed at run time. Object-roles cannot exist without their parent object. Deleting an object implies deleting all of its roles. Roles can exist simultaneously and independently.

A role can *dynamically inherit* from its object or from another role of this object (e.g. the specialization of a *Club_Member* role can be a *Club_President* role); inheritance between roles of different objects is forbidden. This kind of inheritance (known from prototype-based languages) is based on the same rule as the inheritance of class properties. A role, which inherits from a role, is sometimes called a *sub-role*; an inherited role is sometimes called a *super-role*.

A role can have its own additional properties (i.e. attributes, methods, associations etc). Two roles can contain properties with the same names, but this does not lead to any conflict, which is a fundamental difference in comparison to the concept of multiple inheritance. For example, a person can play simultaneously the role of a research institute employee with a *Salary* attribute and also the role of a service company employee with another *Salary* attribute. These two attributes exist at the same time, but except for the name no other feature is shared, including types, semantics and business ontologies.

Associations can connect not only objects with objects, but also objects with roles and roles with roles. This makes the referential semantics clean in comparison to the traditional object models.

Fig. 1 presents an example of objects with dynamic roles and their corresponding classes in our proposal's data model:

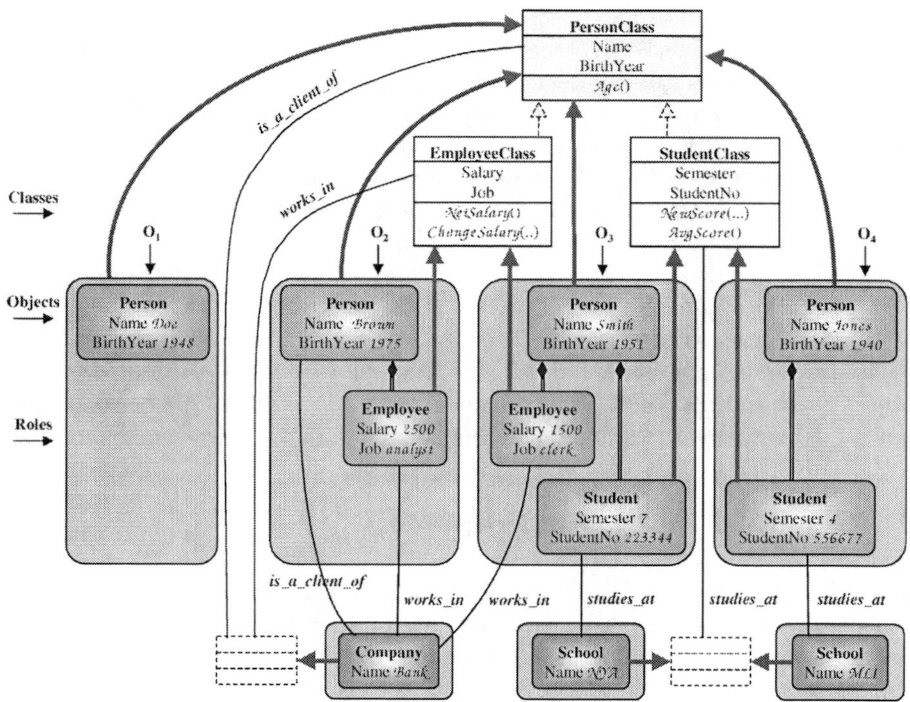

Fig. 1. Classes and objects with their roles

- Each object/role is connected to its own class. The connection is shown as a gray thick solid arrow. Classes contain invariant properties of the corresponding roles, in particular, their names (the first section), attributes and their types (the second section; the attributes' types are not shown), methods (the third section), associations etc.
- A special structure for an object (shown as a gray rectangle with round corners) contains this object (*Person*) and an arbitrary number of its roles (*Employee* and *Student*). We make no distinction between such a structure and its object.

- The *EmployeeClass* and *StudentClass* classes do not inherit statically from the *PersonClass* class. Instead, an *Employee* role and a *Student* role inherit dynamically all the properties of their *Person* super-roles, thus indirectly inherit the properties of *PersonClass*. We show this dynamic inheritance between *EmployeeClass*/*StudentClass* and *PersonClass* as a dashed arrow. However, if necessary, static inheritance between classes can still be applied in our model.
- Each object/role has its own name, which can be used to bind this object/role in a program or query. The presented objects can be bound through the name *Person* (each), through the name *Employee* (the objects O_2 and O_3) and through the name *Student* (the objects O_3 and O_4). The binding returns the identifier(s) of the appropriate object(s)/role(s).
- Each role is encapsulated, that is, its properties are not seen from other roles unless it is explicitly stated by a special link (shown as a double line with a black diamond end). In particular, an *Employee* role imports all the properties of its parent *Person* role. For example, if O_2 is bound by the name *Person*, then the properties {*Name* "Brown", *BirthYear* 1975} are available; however, if the same object is bound by the name *Employee*, then the properties {*Salary* 2500, *Job* "analyst", *Name* "Brown", *BirthYear* 1975} are available.

2.1 Links between Objects and Roles

As we have said, links can connect not only objects with objects, but also objects with roles and roles with roles. For example, in Fig. 1 a *works_in* link connects a *Company* object with an *Employee* role (a similar link *studies_at* connects *Student* roles with *School* objects). Fig. 1 shows also an *is_a_client_of* link between *Person* and *Company* objects. Accessing *Person* through this link implies that any role of that object remains invisible.

Creating links between roles is an important quality for analysis and design methodologies and notations (such as e.g. UML [10]), because in several cases links should be able to lead to parts of objects, not only to entire objects. To model this situation, the methodologies suggest using aggregation/composition. Such an approach implicitly assumes that e.g. an *Employee* is a part of a *Person* similarly as an *Engine* is a part of a *Car*. Although the approach achieves the goal (e.g. we can connect the *works_in* relationship directly to the *Employee* sub-object of *Person*), it obviously misuses the concept of aggregation, which normally is for modeling the "whole-part" situations. In our opinion, dynamic roles should be explicitly introduced into design methodologies and implementation environments.

3 Dynamic Object Roles vs. Classical Object-Oriented Models

Below we briefly discuss the most common features of roles advocated in the literature, which make the concept different in comparison to the classical object models:

- Multiple inheritance: Note that in Fig. 1 there is no *EmployeeStudentClass* class, which would inherit both from the *EmployeeClass* and *StudentClass* classes.
- Repeating inheritance: An object can have two or more roles with the same name; e.g. Brown can be an employee in two companies with a different *Salary* and *Job*. Such a feature cannot be expressed through the traditional inheritance or multi-inheritance concepts.
- Multiple-aspect inheritance: A class can be specialized for many aspects. Modeling tools, such as UML, cover this feature, but it is rather neglected in object-oriented programming and database models. One-aspect inheritance is not powerful enough and generally leads to multiple inheritance. Roles are a viable concept to avoid problems with this feature.
- Object migration: Roles may appear and disappear at run time without changing identifiers of other roles. In terms of the classical object models it means that an object can change its class(es) without changing its identity. This feature can hardly be available in the classical models, especially in models where the binding of objects is static.
- Referential consistency: In our model, relationships are connected to objects or roles, not to entire structures of objects and roles. Thus, for example, it is impossible to refer to Smith's *Salary* and *Job* when one navigates to its object from the *School* object. In the classical object models this consistency is enforced by strong typing, but it is problematic in untyped or weakly typed systems.
- Binding: An object can be bound by the name of any of its roles, but the binding returns the identifier of such a role rather than the identifier of the object. By definition, the binding is dynamic, because generally at compile time it is impossible to decide whether a particular object has a role with a given name.
- Typing: Because an object is seen through the names of its roles, it has as many types as it has different names for roles. Due to the dynamic nature of roles, typing must be (partly) dynamic.
- Subtyping: It can be defined in the standard manner; e.g. the *Employee* type is defined with the use of the *Person* type. However, it makes little sense to introduce a *StudentEmployee* type (cf. O_3 in Fig. 1). Encapsulated roles make it unnecessary (and impossible) to mix up the properties of a *Student* object and the properties of an *Employee* object within the same single data structure.
- Aspects of objects and heterogeneous collections: A big problem with classical database object models, for instance ODMG [3], is that an object belongs

to at most one collection. This is contradictory with both multiple inheritance and substitutability. For instance, we can include an *StudentEmployee* object into the extent *Students*, but we cannot include it into the extent *Employees* (and vice versa). This violates substitutability and leads to inconsistent processing. Dynamic roles have a natural ability to model heterogeneous collections: an object is automatically included into as many collections as the types of roles it contains.

4 Object Store

In the following we present the formal SBA models of an object-oriented data store without and with roles and compare them. For simplicity and for making the semantics clean, we assume object relativism (i.e. each property of an object is an object too) and consider all the properties of the store (including classes) first-class citizens. The store models a program/database *state* thus does not involve types, which we consider a checking utility rather than a "materialized" property of the state.

Formally, an object is a triple $<i, n, v>$, where i is a unique internal object identifier, n is an external object's name, and v is an object's value. The value can be atomic (e.g. "*Doe*"), can be a reference to another object, or can be a set of objects. Classes and methods are objects too. The classical SBA object store model (being some formal approximation of the object models of popular object-oriented systems) is a 5-tuple $<O, C, R, CC, OC>$, where:

- O is a collection of (nested) objects,
- C is a collection of classes,
- R is a collection of root identifiers (i.e. identifiers of objects being entries to the store),
- CC is a binary relation determining the inheritance relationship between classes,
- OC is a binary relation determining the membership of objects within classes.

In Fig. 2 (cf. Fig. 1) we present a simple example of an object store built in accordance with this definition (for simplicity we omit links).

Although the model seems to be natural and formally simple, there are several features which make it inconvenient, especially for defining a query language. The model results in anomalies with multiple, multiple-aspect and repeating inheritance. In the case of name conflicts it inevitably violates substitutability. Moreover, the model implies some problems with binding. For instance, suppose that a query contains the name *Person*, which has to be bound to the stored objects. According to the substitutability principle, it should be bound not only to i_1, but also to i_4 and i_9. However, these objects have the names *Employee* and *StudentEmployee*, hence the binding is not straightforward. The binding rules must "know" that *PersonClass* defines objects named *Person*, is specialized by *EmployeeClass*, *StudentClass* and *StudentEmployeeClass*, and objects of these classes, independently of their current name, should be bound to the name

Objects (*O*):
< i_1, *Person*, { < i_2, *Name*, *"Doe"* >, < i_3, *BirthYear*, *1948* > } >

< i_4, *Employee*, { < i_5, *Name*, *"Brown"* >, < i_6, *BirthYear*, *1975* >,
< i_7, *Salary*, *2500* >, < i_8, *works_in*, i_{127} > } >

< i_9, *StudentEmployee*, { < i_{10}, *Name*, *"Smith"* >, < i_{11}, *BirthYear*, 1951 >,
< i_{12}, *StudentNo*, *223344* >, < i_{13}, *Faculty*, *"Physics"* >,
< i_{14}, *Salary*, *1500* >, < i_{15}, *works_in*, i_{128} > } >

.....

Classes (*C*):
< i_{40}, *PersonClass*, { < i_{41}, *Age*, (*...code of the Age method...*) >,
...other properties of the PersonClass class... } >

< i_{50}, *EmployeeClass*, { < i_{51}, *ChangeSalary*, (*...code of the ChangeSalary method...*) >,
< i_{52}, *NetSalary*, (*...code of the NetSalary method...*) >,
...other properties of the EmployeeClass class... } >

< i_{60}, *StudentClass*, { < i_{61}, *AvgScore*, (*...code of the AvgScore method...*) >,
...other properties of the StudentClass class... } >

< i_{70}, *StudentEmployeeClass*, { } >

.....

Root identifiers (*R*): i_1, i_4, i_9, ...
Inheritance relationships between classes (*CC*): < i_{50}, i_{40} >, < i_{60}, i_{40} >, < i_{70}, i_{50} >, < i_{70}, i_{60} >, ...
Membership of objects in classes (*OC*): < i_1, i_{40} >, < i_4, i_{50} >, < i_9, i_{70} >, ...

Fig. 2. An example state of the object store in the classical SBA object model

Person. This information is not present in the given store model and must be introduced by some additional features.

The issue becomes even more problematic for weakly typed systems and/or dynamic binding. A similar problem concerns the semantics of references (in general, properties specific for a given subclass). For instance, if one accesses *Employee* objects through the name *Person*, then the *works_in* references should not be accessible.

To remove these disadvantages and include roles, we propose a modification to this store model. Its new version is defined as a 6-tuple <*O, C, R, CC, OC, OO*>, where:

- *C*, *CC* are defined as before,
- *O*, *R*, *OC* are defined both for objects and roles,
- *OO* is a binary relation determining dynamic inheritance between objects and roles.

The *OO* relation defines two functional aspects. On the one hand, the relation determines which objects/roles are inherited by roles. On the other hand, *OO* fixes the semantics of manipulating objects with roles. In particularly, copying an object implies "isomorphic" copying of all of its roles, and deleting an object implies deleting all of its roles. Deleting a role implies recursive deleting all of its sub-roles, but not its super-role. *OO* is a pure hierarchy (each role has at most one super-role; no cycles).

In Fig. 3 we present an object store built in accordance with the new definition. Note that the component *CC* is empty in this case (cf. Section 2).

The model does not imply problems with multiple inheritance. Because each role is an independent encapsulated entity, no name conflict is possible. The model also clearly shows the reason for multiple inheritance anomalies in the classical object models: they are caused by the fact that properties of different classes (perhaps incompatible) are not encapsulated, but mixed up in a single environment.

Objects and roles (*O*):
$< i_1$, *Person*, { $< i_2$, *Name*, "*Doe*" >, $< i_3$, *BirthYear*, *1948* > } >
$< i_4$, *Person*, { $< i_5$, *Name*, "*Brown*" >, $< i_6$, *BirthYear*, *1975* > } >
$< i_7$, *Person*, { $< i_8$, *Name*, "*Smith*" >, $< i_9$, *BirthYear*, *1951* > } >
$< i_{13}$, *Employee*, { $< i_{14}$, *Salary*, *2500* >, $< i_{15}$, *works_in*, i_{127} > } >
$< i_{16}$, *Employee*, { $< i_{17}$, *Salary*, *1500* >, $< i_{18}$, *works_in*, i_{128} > } >
$< i_{19}$, *Student*, { $< i_{20}$, *StudentNo*, *223344* >, $< i_{21}$, *Faculty*, "*Physics*" > } >
.....

Classes (*C*):
$< i_{40}$, *PersonClass*, { $< i_{41}$, *Age*, (*...code of the Age method...*) >,
...other properties of the PersonClass class...} >

$< i_{50}$, *EmployeeClass*, { $< i_{51}$, *ChangeSalary*, (*...code of the ChangeSalary method...*) >,
$< i_{52}$, *NetSalary*, (*...code of the NetSalary method...*) >,
...other properties of the EmployeeClass class... } >

$< i_{60}$, *StudentClass*, { $< i_{61}$, *AvgScore*, (*...code of the AvgScore method...*) >,
...other properties of the StudentClass class... } >
.....

Root identifiers (*R*): $i_1, i_4, i_7, i_{13}, i_{16}, i_{19}, ...$
Inheritance relationships between classes (*CC*): *Empty*.
Membership of objects/roles in classes (*OC*): $< i_1, i_{40} >, < i_4, i_{40} >, < i_7, i_{40} >, < i_{13}, i_{50} >, < i_{16}, i_{50} >, < i_{19}, i_{60} >, ...$
Inheritance between objects and roles (*OO*): $< i_{13}, i_4 >, < i_{16}, i_7 >, < i_{19}, i_7 >, ...$

Fig. 3. An example state of the object store in the SBA object model with roles

Moreover, the model does not imply the mentioned before problems with binding. Note that the identifier of each role belongs to the root identifiers *R*. Hence the name *Person* will be bound to i_1, i_4, i_7. The binding concerns only the *Person* objects; other objects and roles are invisible. Similarly, the name *Employee* will be bound to i_{13} and i_{16}, but after this binding the corresponding *Person* objects (i_4 for i_{13} and i_7 for i_{16}) become visible, according to the *OO* relation. Thus, for instance, *Employee.Name* and *Employee.Age()* are correct expressions. Similarly when the name *Student* is being bound.

The model is also consistent concerning references. For example, when the name *Person* is being bound, the *works_in* references are unavailable, because the *Employee* roles are invisible. This property holds independently of whether a system is strongly typed or untyped.

5 Query Language

The proposed model with roles requires modifying some elements of the "standard" SBA and the SBQL query language. Due to lack of space, the discussion concentrates only on some aspects of the issue.

Several mechanisms existing in the model without roles, for example binding and auxiliary names, remain the same for the new model. Among those that need modifying is an *environment stack*, which now can store binders for (root) roles. Moreover, new scopes pushed onto it by non-algebraic operators can contain sections opened for roles, sub-roles, sub-subroles etc.

After minor modifications, the well-known technique of casting has potential to be even more powerful than in the classical model. For instance, one may need to make an explicit conversion between a role and its object, between different roles of an object, or between an object and one of its roles. The syntax of such a cast operator is as follows:

(*name*) *query*

where *name* is the name of an object or a role, and *query* returns identifiers of objects or roles.

If *query* returns objects' identifiers, then the operator returns the identifiers of *name* roles within those objects. If *query* returns roles' identifiers, then the operator returns the identifiers of their objects (for *name* objects) or the identifiers of other roles within the same objects (for *name* roles). If an object has no role named *name*, then the result is empty.

The following examples illustrate it. Suppose that we want to receive *Employee* roles for Brown.

(*Employee*) (*Person* **where** *Name* = "Brown")

The evaluation of the subquery (*Person* **where** *Name* = "Brown") returns a collection of identifiers of *Person* objects for whom the value of the *Name* attribute is "Brown". Then the (*Employee*) operator converts each of these identifiers into the identifier(s) of Brown's *Employee* role(s); if an object has no *Employee* role, then the operator returns null. The result is a collection of the *Employee* roles' identifiers; nulls are ignored.

In another example we get those of students who work (i.e. who are employees):

(*Student*) *Employee*

The subquery *Employee* returns the identifiers of *Employee* roles in all objects in a store. Then the (*Student*) operator converts each of these identifiers into the identifiers of the appropriate *Student* roles.

Similarly we can introduce a Boolean operator testing the presence of a given role within an object. Another operator could return the names of the roles that are currently in an object. Such operators support the generic programming technique.

6 Summary

In the paper we have presented an object model with dynamic roles, which we consider an alternative to the classical database object models, such as the ODMG object model. Dynamic roles can support conceptual models of many applications and, in comparison to the classical models, do not lead to anomalies and disadvantages of multiple, repeating and multi-aspect inheritance. An advantage of the model with dynamic roles is conceptual clarity concerning the level of an object store and the level of a query language, including among others data naming, scope control, binding names and casting. The model leads to some new concepts for a schema definition language and metadata management; this issue requires further research.

References

1. Albano, A., Bergamini, R., Ghelli, G., Orsini, R.: An Object Data Model with Roles. Proc. of VLDB Conf. (1993) 39-51
2. Bertino, E., Guerrini, G.: Objects with Multiple Most Specific Classes. Proc. of ECOOP Conf. Springer LNCS 952 (1995) 102-126
3. Cattel, R.G.G., Barry, D.K. (Eds.): Object Data Management Group: The Object Database Standard ODMG, Release 3.0. Morgan Kaufmann Publishers (2000)
4. Płodzień, J., Kraken, A.: Object Query Optimization through Detecting Independent Subqueries. Information Systems. 25(8) (2000) 467-490
5. Richardson, J., Schwarz, P.: Aspects: Extending Objects to Support Multiple, Independent Roles. Proc. of SIGMOD Conf. (1991) 298-307
6. Steimann, F.: On the Representation of Roles in Object-Oriented and Conceptual Modeling. Data & Knowledge Engineering. 35(1) (2000) 83-106
7. Steimann, F.: Role = Interface: A Merger of Concepts. Journal of Object-Oriented Programming. 14(4) (2001) 23-32
8. Subieta, K., Kambayashi, Y., Leszczyłowski, J.: Procedures in Object-Oriented Query Languages. Proc. of VLDB Conf. (1995) 182-193
9. Subieta, K., Missala, M., Anacki, K.: The LOQIS System. Description and Programmer Manual. Institute of Computer Science, Polish Academy of Sciences. Report 695. Warsaw, Poland (1990)
10. OMG Unified Modeling Language Specification. Version 1.4. The Object Management Group (September 2001) http://www.omg.org
11. Wong, R.K.: Heterogeneous and Multifaceted Multimedia Objects in DOOR/MM: A Role-Based Approach with Views. Journal of Parallel and Distributed Computing. 56(3) (1999) 251-271

Dynamic Schema Evolution Management Using Version in Temporal Object-Oriented Databases*

Renata de Matos Galante, Adriana Bueno da Silva Roma, Anelise Jantsch, Nina Edelweiss, and Clesio Saraiva dos Santos

Federal University of Rio Grande do Sul, Cx Postal 15064,
91501-970 Porto Alegre - RS, Brazil
{galante, roma, anelise, nina, clesio}@inf.ufrgs.br

Abstract. In this paper, an analysis of the schema evolution process in object oriented databases is made using an object oriented data model that supports temporal features and versions definition - the Temporal Versions Model. A meta schema structure is defined to store information concerning to evolutionary schema states, as well as their classes, attributes and relationships. An implementation proposal is presented, combining specification and manipulation mechanisms including version and time concepts. Two alternatives are defined for the database extension management: multi-pool for schema versioning and single-pool for class versioning. Concerning the physical representation, both approaches can be used in the same application.

1 Introduction

Temporal aspects are present at any real life events. Several applications require the representation of these features to better serve their purposes. Some examples of these applications are flight reservation, financial systems, and geographical information systems (GIS). Temporal databases [11,14] allow capturing objects evolution with time.

This kind of evolution is called temporal versioning, in which each change in an object results in a new object version. However, only one version is valid, and all others are stored just to compose the database history. It may be desirable to store in the database not only the history of valid values, but also several object states, to allow alternative object versions. Advanced applications like CAD, CAM, CIM, engineering projects, and artificial intelligence, require project alternatives storage. To attend this purpose, the use of a versions model is fundamental.

Several recent works analyze versions support. One of these, the Versions Model [4], adds to object oriented models some concepts and mechanisms for the definition and manipulation of objects, versions and configurations. To allow the historical representation of changes, this model was extended with temporal features, resulting the Temporal Versions Model - TVM [10]. TVM allows storing object versions, and for each version, all the historical changes on dynamic attributes and relationships are also maintained. So, TVM brings together temporal features and versions management.

* This work has been partially supported by Capes and CNPq.

R. Cicchetti et al. (Eds.): DEXA 2002, LNCS 2453, pp. 524–533, 2002.

However, to represent reality in a strict way, not only the object evolution management is enough, because the conceptual schema may often change during the database life. Schema evolution and schema versioning are two techniques that allow schema modifications whereas consistency is maintained between schema and its data. The former stores only the current schema version and its data, but history is not retained. The later stores all schema versions and their associated data during schema changes.

Schema versioning with temporal features has been studied extensively in relational environments [1,9]. In a special way, bitemporal schema versioning [1] that enables retro and pro-active schema changes to produce past, present and future schema versions, was analyzed.

The main purpose of this work is to analyze the schema evolution process in object oriented databases under TVM. An implementation solution is defined that merges versions and temporal resources. This strategy is based on the form of data storage, which is divided in two different approaches: one for schema versions and the other for the class versions. The multiple repositories solution is adopted for the schema versions, and a single repository for class versions. Storage waste and data redundancy are avoided with this mechanism. A new schema version is created only when an important structure modification occurs.

This paper is organized as follows. In section 2 the Temporal Versions Model (TVM) is presented. Section 3 presents the TVM behavior in a schema evolution environment. In section 4, schema evolution with versions and time features management is defined. Implementation solutions are proposed in section 5. Section 6 presents a survey about related work in this area, and section 7 concludes the paper, introducing ongoing works concerning this subject.

2 Temporal Versions Model - TVM

Temporal Versions Model - TVM [10] is an Object Oriented data model supporting time and versions concepts. TVM allows storing object versions, objects lifetime, and keeps all the changes of dynamic values of data. Only the main features of TVM are presented here, which are necessary to understand the schema evolution process proposed in this paper.

Time is associated which objects, versions, attributes and relationships. An object has a time line for each of its versions. In this way, TVM supports two different temporal orders: branching time for a versioned object, and linear time within a version. Time variation is discrete, and is represented in the model through intervals as timestamps. These timestamps are bitemporal: valid time (when a fact becomes true in reality), transaction time (when a new value is posted to the database) and implicit [7].

Class attributes and relationships can be defined as static (past values are not stored in case of modification) or temporal (when all the defined value are stored in the database, composing the history). The user is responsible for classifying attributes and relationships as static or temporal, during the application specification. A class may present attributes and relationships of both kinds.

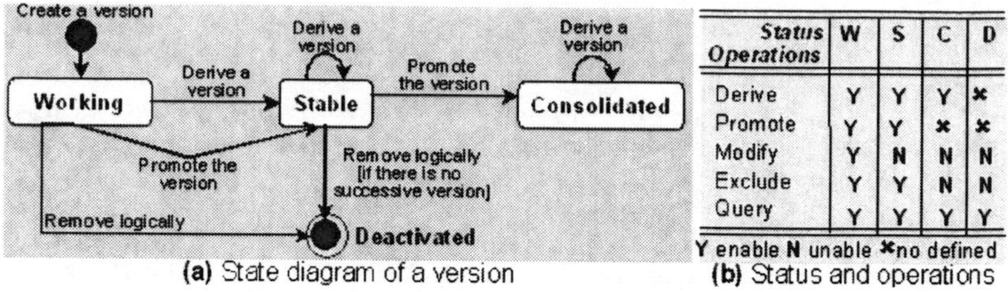

(a) State diagram of a version

Status / Operations	W	S	C	D
Derive	Y	Y	Y	×
Promote	Y	Y	×	×
Modify	Y	N	N	N
Exclude	Y	Y	N	N
Query	Y	Y	Y	Y

Y enable N unable ×no defined

(b) Status and operations

Fig. 1. State diagram of a version

Figure 1-a shows the state diagram of a version, showing the possible status, as well as the transitions among states, and the events that cause these transitions. Depending on status, operations can or cannot be applied to them (Figure 1-b).

3 Schema Versioning Using the Temporal Version Model

In order to complete the requirements to temporal management of applications, the occurrence of schema versions besides data evolution shall also be supported. TVM already presents versions and temporal features on the data level, as presented in the preceding section. This section adds to TVM the support to schema versioning.

Similarly to data versions, the schema versions also have states that represent the development phases. Figure 2 (a) illustrates the states that a schema version can go through, and the actions that can cause the transitions. A schema version is initially created in the working status. In this status the version represents a schema that is in a definition phase (all changes cause corrections). Differently from data versions, in this state the schema version does not have time associated to itself, cannot be instantiated nor referred, but can be physically removed.

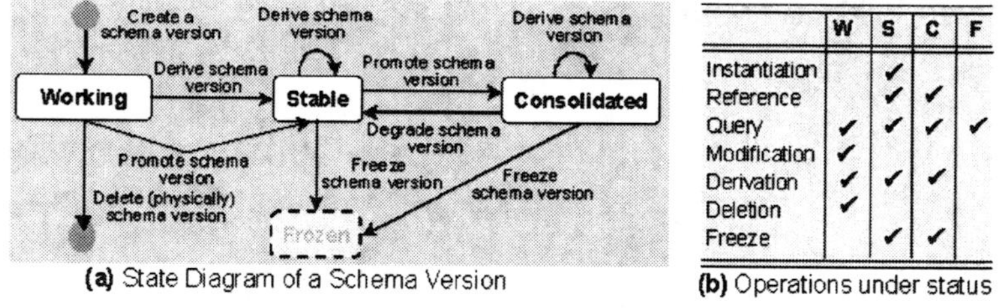

(a) State Diagram of a Schema Version

	W	S	C	F
Instantiation		✓		
Reference		✓	✓	
Query	✓	✓	✓	✓
Modification	✓			
Derivation	✓	✓	✓	
Deletion	✓			
Freeze		✓	✓	

(b) Operations under status

Fig. 2. Schema Version Status

A schema version in the stable status has the features of a data version in the same status. The consolidated status is also similar to consolidated status of data versions. However, a schema version in this stage can be returned to the stable state. The frozen status (which corresponds to the logic exclusion) is similar to the deactivated status of data versions, but schema versions in this status can be only used to solve queries. Figure

2 (b) presents a summary of the actions that can be performed in each of the schema version states.

4 Versions Temporal Management during Schema Evolution

In this section, schema evolution requirements are proposed, considering that *TVM* is used in the schema versioning. The goal is keeping the history of schema evolution as well as propagate the changes to the database instances. This can be developed in the following steps:

- *Update Primitives* - a group of operations which allows schema changes [3]. The primitives are classified according to the kind of change performed in the schema version, organized in three distinct categories: *Schema Structure Changes*, *Class Structure Changes* and *Class Behaviour Changes*.
- *Invariant Rules* - integrity rules [3] associated to the update primitives which assure correct schema changes. When an error is detected, the update primitive is cancelled and the user must be notified.
- *Evolution Manager* - controls the schema evolution management, separating the schema changes from the data propagation.
- *User Applications* - a database that stores the user applications and its associated data.

Data Intention Management. *Total versioning* [1] is adopted to control the schema version derivation. The update primitives can be applied to any schema version. Whenever a schema modification is performed, a new schema version is derived in order to maintain the modifications history.

Transaction and *valid time* are associated to each schema version (*Bitemporal Schema Versioning*), which allows retroactive and proactive changes in order to produce past, present and future schema versions states, keeping track of the defined schema versions. In this kind of versioning, a schema version can be handled through its transaction history, and through its validity history too.

Data Extension Management. When a schema version is modified, extensional data needs to be adapted to assure consistency between the new schema version and data. The approach adopted to accomplish instance change propagation, depends on the kind of implementation applied to the data repository, as extensional data may be stored using a *single repository*, or *multiple repositories* [1].

There are two important approaches for implementing instance migration mechanism [2]: *immediate* and *deferred*. Our proposal allows the user to choose between immediate or deferred approaches, depending on user application necessities.

In our approach *synchronous management* [1,9] is adopted. As each schema version has its associated data, query processing is always done according to the corresponding schema versions. This management is characterized for each temporal pertinence of a schema version that includes each corresponding temporal data pertinence along common temporal dimensions.

Instance propagation under a TVM schema evolution is very complex. For instance, if the delete primitive is applied to a class, which has subclasses, its instance propagation can be extremely complex because this change involves an inheritance hierarchy modification. In this case, all consequences must be analyzed to assure consistency during change propagations. But this study is out of paper's scope; instance propagation will be explored in future works.

5 Implementation Proposal

In this section, the implementation proposal to dynamic schema evolution management is presented. Two strategies are used, according to the kind of modification made in the schema structure. The multiple repositories solution is adopted for extensional database in case a schema update modifies the schema structure, for instance, if a class is added. Otherwise, when a schema change modifies the class structure, for instance, delete an attribute, the single repository solution is adopted for the storage of extensional database. However, both analyzed strategies can coexist in the same application domain, depending on the schema change which is performed.

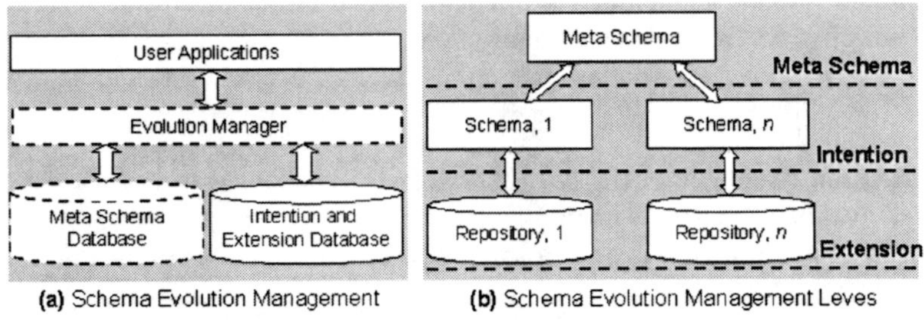

Fig. 3. Schema Evolution Management

Schema Evolution Management. The temporal schema evolution management is modelled through an intermediate layer (*Evolution Manager*), which controls the user applications and the database. This mechanism is illustrated in figure 3-a. The intentional and extensional database store the application schemas and the application data. In addition, another database stores the schema evolution. In this figure, the dotted lines show the processes that are controlled implicitly by the system.

The schema evolution management mechanism is split into three distinct parts: *meta schema*, *intention* and *extension* (see figure 3-b). The meta schema keeps temporal schema versions to provide a schema versioning mechanism. The intention stores the schema versions, whose associated instances are kept in the extension data. Extension data can be organized and managed through a join of single and multiple repositories.
Meta Schema The *meta schema level* is modelled through classes which maintain evolutionary information concerning the schemas, their corresponding classes, methods, attributes and relationships. Figure 4 illustrates the specification of a meta schema structure using an UML class diagram.

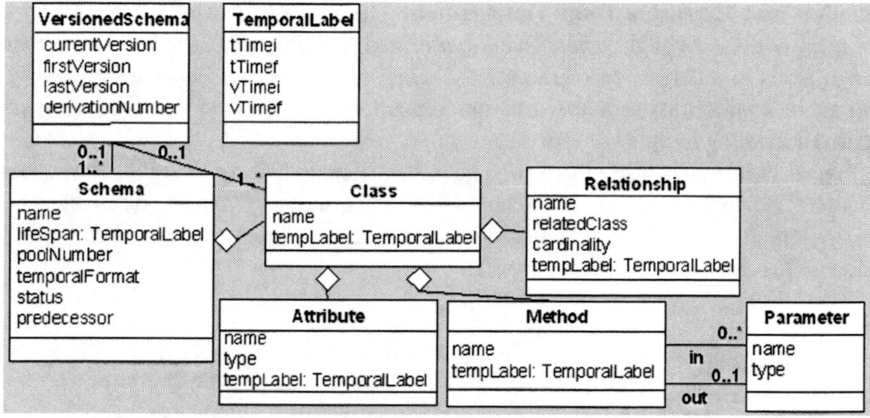

Fig. 4. Meta schema specification to a schema temporal versioning

The meta schema is modelled through the following main classes:

- `Versioned Schema` - keeps control of information about the schema versioning storage, including current version (`currentVersion`) [1], first version (`firstVersion`), last version (`lastVersion`) and version derivation number (`derivationNumber`).
- `Schema` - stores data concerning the schema versions. It includes the following attributes: schema name (`name`), data repository number (`poolNumber`), temporal format of extension data and lifespan (`lifespan`) of each schema version . In addition, the following attributes are defined to represent schema versioning: status version (`status`) and predecessor (`predecessor`) version number.
- `Class` - stores data about all classes associated with each schema version. It includes the following attributes: class name (`name`) and temporal label (`tempLabel`).
- `Attribute` - stores data concerning the attributes of the classes in each schema version, including the following attributes: attribute name (`name`), attribute length (`length`), attribute domain (`type`) and temporal label (tempLabel).
- `Method` - stores data concerning the methods of the classes, including the following attributes: method name (`name`), its parameters (name (`name`) and domain (`type`)), and temporal label (`tempLabel`).
- `Relationship` - stores data about the relationships between the classes, including relationship name (`name`), related class (`relatedClass`), relationship cardinality (`cardinality`) and temporal label (`tempLabel`).

Since bitemporal database is adopted to model the schema versioning mechanism, all temporal label must include the following attributes: initial transaction time (`tTimei`), final transaction time (`tTimef`), initial valid time (`vTimei`) and final valid time (`vTimef`).

[1] Current version can be defined by user. By default, it is the last created version

Intention and Extension Data Management The management of temporal schema evolution is done through *schema versioning* and *multiple repositories*. Any schema change leads to a derivation of the new schema version and a new data repository is created. In addition, data of the previous repository is copied to the new repository, updated according to the new schema.

Figure 5 illustrates the inclusion of a new class, named `Subject`, in the first schema version (`E1: Schema1`). A new schema version is derived (`E2: Schema2`), whose data are stored in the intention database. A new data repository containing the changes performed is created (`Repository,2`).

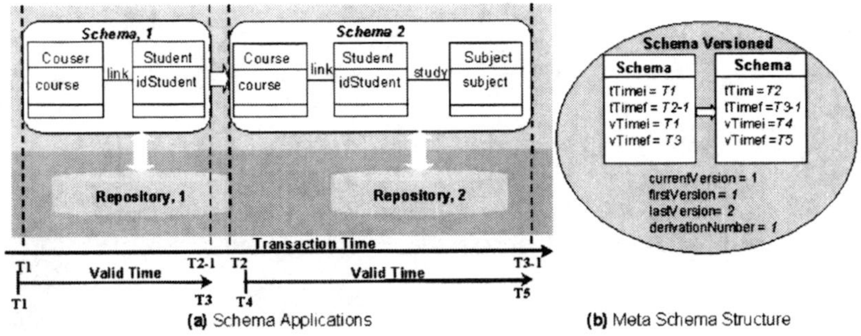

Fig. 5. Schema Versioning

The meta schema is implicitly updated in order to keep the preformed schema changes. The versioned schema class stores control data about schema versioning. In addition, each schema version stores temporal data in the Class, Attribute, Method, and Relationship.

Single Repository Storage. The schema versioning approach always handles versions of the complete schema, which can cause a high number of version derivations. In this case, the quantity of data repositories can be greatly increased. Another implementation proposal is defined here in order to improve the performance of the system, avoid frequency interruption during data propagation and assure the integrity of stored data.

In this context, a *class derivation mechanism* [3] is proposed. This approach has been applied to adapt the versioning concept in class level. Here, every class is seen as an independent versionable object. If the class description is changed, a new version of the class is stored. The propagation of changes is done in the same data repository in order to decrease data duplication, and all the history of the schema evolution is kept.

Figure 6 shows the class versioning mechanism. The `address` attribute is included in the Student class. In this case, the first class version (`Student,1`) is modified causing the derivation of a new class version (`Student,2`). The update changes are performed in the same schema version (`E1: Schema`). Also, the instance propagation is stored in the already existing data repository (`Repository,1`).

In order to represent the class evolution, the meta schema is implicitly updated to keep the performed class changes. Each versioned class must be associated with a versioned schema, which stores the versioning class data control. Figure 6 also shows the versioned

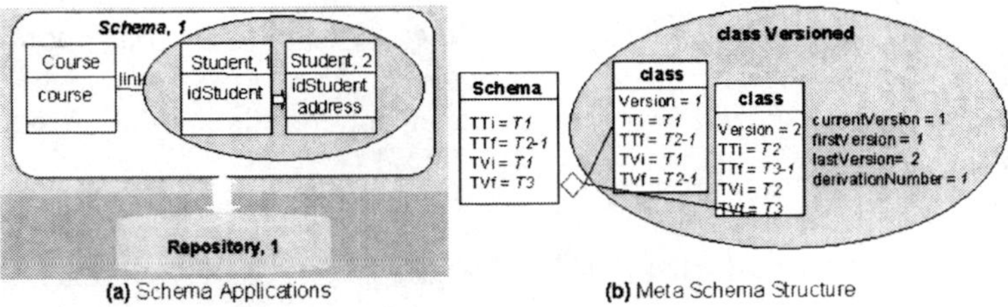

Fig. 6. Class Versioning

schema, with the associated class version. The meta schema must record data about class attributes, methods and relationships.

6 Related Work

The appropriate treatment of performed changes in a schema during its lifetime has been the objective of many researches. Consequently, a great number of proposals, which aim at dealing properly with this subject, have emerged. Concerning time and schema versioning, some researches have explored these concepts in the context of relational databases [1,9,12], and others have used the same concepts in object oriented databases [5,6,8,13].

The work presented in [13] defines formally a model that uses concepts of time and version in an object oriented environment. The model admits only transaction time. It defines axioms in order to ensure the schema consistency, but it does not define rules that guarantee the validity of the changed objects. According to this model, objects can be queried under the perspective of any schema version. The versioning granularity proposed is the class type. When a class is modified, the change is propagated to its respective class hierarchy.

Another formal model for schema version management is defined in [8]. In this work the author analyzes many features related to temporal schema versioning. This research defines an object oriented data model for schema versioning, which considers valid time and transaction time. The model supports defined collection of schema changes and for each schema change, a procedural semantics, based on the syntactic transformation of the schema version definition, is introduced.

In [6], a complete collection of schema modification operations is proposed. This proposal also uses the bitemporal versioning. The used versioning granularity is the temporal version, which is defined as a union of the schema version with the correspondent instances. The derivation follows the directed acyclic graph structure.

[5] proposes the use of a temporal object model for management of schema changes and adaptation of instances. For any process change the object adaptation is crucial, but only the affected object piece has to be changed.

The main differences among these proposals and the one presented in this paper are: the meta schema definition with the complete class specification necessary for bitemporal schema versioning management; the detailed analysis and definition of the states which a schema version goes through during its lifetime; the definition of operations in order to change the states of the schema versions; and, the presentation of an implementation proposal for dynamic schema evolution management considering the intentional and extensional levels.

7 Summary and Concluding Remarks

This paper proposes a dynamic schema evolution management approach, which is based on the Temporal Versions Model, thus adding time and version features to the class and schema levels.

The union of version and time concepts enables to keep different schema versions as well as to store the schema changes performed. It also allows both retroactive and proactive updates and queries in the schema and database. The use of the bitemporal schema versioning increases the flexibility of the proposal, allowing access to past, present and future schema versions.

To fulfill the requirements of the schema versioning, this work clearly defines the stages that the schema versions can go through as well as the different operations that can be used to change their states.

A meta schema structure is specified in order to maintain evolutionary information concerning schemas and their corresponding classes, attributes, methods and relationships. Additionally, one implementation proposal specifies two alternatives for the database extension management: multiple repositories for schema versioning and single repository for class versioning. Concerning physical representation, both approaches can be used in the same application. This characteristic is important due to the quantity of data repositories that can be greatly decreased.

This work is part of a project that aims at mapping the TVM and schema evolution mechanisms for the commercial database DB2. The schema evolution management is still in development. For further research, the instance propagation process will be analyzed, considering, considering the TVM as the basis for intentional and extensional database. Also, query language techniques will be analyzed in order to provide data retrieval through more than one schema version. Furthermore, the time order of the schema versioning is linear, which means that only one schema is valid in each instant of time. We have also researched the possibilities for adopting branched time, which would provide more than one active schema version at the same instant of time.

References

1. Castro, C. De; Grandi,F.;Scalas, M.R. Schema Versioning for Multitemporal Relational Databases. Information Systems, 22(5), 1997.
2. Ferrandina, F.; Meyer, T.; Zicari, R. Schema Evolution in Object Databases: Measuring the Performance of Immediate and Deferred Updates, 1997.
3. Galate,R.M.;Santos,C.S.;RUIZ,D.D.A. Um Modelo de Evolução de Esquemas Conceituais para Bancos de Dados Orientados a Objetos com o Emprego de Versões. In: SBBD, Brazil, 1998. In portuguese.
4. Golendziner, L.G. Santos, C. S. Version and configurations in object-oriented database systems: a uniform treatment. In: Int. Conf. on.Manag. of Data, 1995.

5. Goralwalla, I.A.; et. al. A Temporal Approach to Managing Schema Evolution in Object Database Systems. Data & Knowledge Engineering, v.28, n. 1, Nov 1998.
6. Grandi,F.; MAandreoli,F.; Scalas, M.R. A Generalized Modeling Framework for Schema Versioning Support. In: Australian Database Conference. IEEE Computer Society, v. 22, n.2, Jan. 2000.
7. Jensen, C. S. et al. The Consensus Glossary of Temporal Database Concepts - February 1998 Version. In: Temporal Databases Research and Practice. Berlin-Heidelberg: Springer-Verlag, 1998.
8. Mandreoli, Federica. Schema Versioning in Object-Oriented Databases. Università Degli Studi di Bologna: Dipartimento di Eletonica Informatica e Sistemistica, 2001.
9. Moreira, V.P.; Edelweiss, N. Schema versioning: queries to a Generalized Temporal Databases System. In: Workshop on Spatio-Temporal Data Models and Languages, in conjuntion with DEXA, 1999.
10. Moro, M. M., Saggiorato, S. M., Edelweiss, N., Santos, C. S. dos: Adding Time to an Object-Oriented Versions Model. In: DEXA, 2001. LNCS 2113.
11. Ozsoyoglu, G.; Snodgrass, R.T. Temporal and real-time databases: a survey. IEEE Transactions on Knowledge and Data Engineering, New York, v.7, n.4, Aug.1995.
12. Roddick, J. F.; et al. Beyond Schema Versioning: A Flexible Model for Spatio-Temporal Schema Selection. Geoinformatica, 2001.
13. Rodriguez, L.; Ogata, H.; Yano, Y. A Temporal Versioned Object-Oriented Data Schema Model. Computer & Mathematics with Applications, 2000.
14. Tansel, C.G.; et al. Temporal Databases theory, design and implementation. Redwood City: The Benjamin/Cummings Publishing Company, Inc., 1993.

Efficient Data Mining Based on Formal Concept Analysis

Gerd Stumme

Institut für Angewandte Informatik und Formale Beschreibungsverfahren AIFB, Universität Karlsruhe, D–76128 Karlsruhe, Germany
www.aifb.uni-karlsruhe.de/WBS/gst; stumme@aifb.uni-karlsruhe.de

Abstract. Formal Concept Analysis is an unsupervised learning technique for conceptual clustering. We introduce the notion of *iceberg concept lattices* and show their use in Knowledge Discovery in Databases (KDD). Iceberg lattices are designed for analyzing very large databases. In particular they serve as a condensed representation of frequent patterns as known from association rule mining.
In order to show the interplay between Formal Concept Analysis and association rule mining, we discuss the algorithm TITANIC. We show that iceberg concept lattices are a starting point for computing condensed sets of association rules without loss of information, and are a visualization method for the resulting rules.

1 Introduction

Knowledge discovery in databases (KDD) is defined as the non-trivial extraction of valid, implicit, potentially useful and ultimately understandable information in large databases [17]. For several years, a wide range of applications in various domains have benefited from KDD techniques and many work has been conducted on this topic. The problem of mining frequent patterns arose first as a sub-problem of mining association rules [1], but it then turned out to be present in a variety of problems [18]: mining sequential patterns [3], episodes [26], association rules [2], correlations [10,37], multi-dimensional patterns [21,22], maximal patterns [8,53,23], closed patterns [47,31,32,33]. Since the complexity of this problem is exponential in the size of the binary database input relation and since this relation has to be scanned several times during the process, efficient algorithms for mining frequent patterns are required.

The task of mining frequent patterns can be described as follows: Given a set G of objects, a set M of attributes (or items), a binary relation $I \subseteq G \times M$ (where $(g, m) \in I$ is read as "object g has attribute m"), and a threshold minsupp $\in [0, 1]$, determine all subsets X of M (also called *patterns* here) where the *support* $\operatorname{supp}(X) := \frac{\operatorname{card}(X')}{\operatorname{card}(G)}$ (with $X' := \{g \in G \mid \forall m \in X \colon (g, m) \in I\}$) is above the threshold minsupp.

The set of these *frequent patterns* itself is usually not considered as a final result of the mining process, but rather an intermediate step. Its most prominent

R. Cicchetti et al. (Eds.): DEXA 2002, LNCS 2453, pp. 534–546, 2002.

use are certainly association rules. The task of mining association rules is to determine all pairs $X \rightarrow Y$ of subsets of M such that $\text{supp}(X \rightarrow Y) := \text{supp}(X \cup Y)$ is above the threshold minsupp, and the *confidence* $\text{conf}(X \rightarrow Y) := \frac{\text{supp}(X \cup Y)}{\text{supp}(X)}$ is above a given threshold minconf $\in [0, 1]$. Association rules are for instance used in warehouse basket analysis, where the warehouse management is interested in learning about products frequently bought together.

Since determining the frequent patterns is the computationally most expensive part, most research has focused on this aspect. Most algorithms follow the way of the well-known Apriori algorithm [2]. It is traversing iteratively the set of all patterns in a levelwise manner. During each iteration one level is considered: a subset of candidate patterns is created by joining the frequent patterns discovered during the previous iteration, the supports of all candidate patterns are counted, and the infrequent ones are discarded. A variety of modifications of this algorithm arose [11,29,34,48] in order to improve different efficiency aspects. However, all of these algorithms have to determine the supports of *all* frequent patterns and of some infrequent ones in the database.

Other algorithms are based on the extraction of maximal frequent patterns, from which all supersets are infrequent and all subsets are frequent. They combine a levelwise bottom-up traversal with a top-down traversal in order to quickly find the maximal frequent patterns. Then, all frequent patterns are derived from these ones and one last database scan is carried on to count their support. The most prominent algorithm using this approach is Max-Miner [8]. Experimental results have shown that this approach is particularly efficient for extracting maximal frequent patterns, but when applied to extracting all frequent patterns, performances drastically decrease because of the cost of the last scan which requires roughly an inclusion test between each frequent pattern and each object of the database. As for the first approach, algorithms based on this approach have to extract the supports of *all* frequent patterns from the database.

While all techniques mentioned so far count the support of all frequent patterns, this is by no means necessary. In the next section, we will show that the knowledge of some supports is sufficient for deriving all other supports. This way, we are able to decrease computation time. An additional result is the visualization of representative frequent patterns in *iceberg concept lattices*, which is discussed in Section 3. In Section 4, we sketch the principle of one of the algorithms, called TITANIC. Last but not least, iceberg concept lattices allow to drastically reduce the number of rules that are to be presented to the user, without any information loss. This is the topic of Section 5. The paper summarizes joint work with Lotfi Lakhal, Yves Bastide, Nicolas Pasquier, and Rafik Taouil as presented in [5,6,42,43].

2 Mining Frequent Patterns with Formal Concept Analysis

Consider two patterns X and Y such that both describe exactly the same set of objects, i. e., $X' = Y'$. So if we know the support of one of them, we do not need to count the support of the other one in the database. In fact, we can introduce an equivalence relation θ on the powerset $\mathfrak{P}(M)$ of M by $X\theta Y \iff X' = Y'$. If we knew the relation from the beginning, it would be sufficient to count the support of one pattern of each class only — all other supports can then be derived.

Of course one does not know θ in advance, but one can determine it along the computation. It turns out that one usually has to count the support of more than one pattern of each class, but normally not of all of them. The percentage of patterns to be considered depends on how correlated the data are: The more correlated the data are, the fewer counts have to be performed.

This observation was independently made by three research groups around 1997/98, inspired by the theory of Formal Concept Analysis: L. Lakhal and his database group in Clermont–Ferrand, M. Zaki in Troy, NY, and the author in Darmstadt. The first algorithm based on this idea was Close [31], followed by A-Close [32], ChARM [55], PASCAL [6], Closet [33], and TITANIC [41,42], each having its own way to exploit the equivalence relation which is hidden in the data. In Section 4, we will sketch the TITANIC algorithm as an example.

All these algorithms make use of the theory of *Formal Concept Analysis (FCA).* Introduced in the early 1980ies as a formalization of the concept of 'concept' [51], FCA has over the years grown to a powerful theory for data analysis, information retrieval, and knowledge discovery [45]. In Artificial Intelligence (AI), FCA is used as a knowledge representation mechanism [46] and as conceptual clustering method [38,12,27]. In database theory, FCA has been extensively used for class hierarchy design and management [28,52,14,50,36,16]. Its usefulness for the analysis of data stored in relational databases has been demonstrated with the commercially used management system TOSCANA for Conceptual Information Systems [49].

FCA has been applied in a wide range of domains, including medicine, psychology, social sciences, linguistics, information sciences, machine and civil engineering etc. (cf. [45]). Over all, FCA has been used in more than 200 projects, both on the scientific and the commercial level. For instance, FCA has been applied for analyzing data of children with diabetes [35], for developing qualitative theories in music esthetics [25], for managing emails [13], for database marketing [19], and for an IT security management system [9].

FCA formalizes a concept of 'concept' as established in the international standard ISO 704: a concept is considered as a unit of thought constituted of two parts: its extension and its intension [51,15]. This understanding of 'concept' is first mentioned explicitly in the Logic of Port Royal [4]. To allow a formal description of extensions and intensions, FCA starts with the same type of data as association rule mining: a *(formal) context* $\mathbb{K} := (G, M, I)$ consists of a set G of objects [German: Gegenstände], a set M of attributes [Merkmale], and a binary relation $I \subseteq G \times M$. As above, we define, for $A \subseteq G$,

$$A' := \{m \in M \mid \forall g \in A\colon (g, m) \in I\} \ ;$$

and for $B \subseteq M$, we define dually

$$B' := \{g \in G \mid \forall m \in B\colon (g,m) \in I\} .$$

Now, a *formal concept* is a pair (A, B) with $A \subseteq G$, $B \subseteq M$, $A' = B$ and $B' = A$. A is called *extent* and B is called *intent* of the concept. The set $\mathfrak{B}(\mathbb{K})$ of all concepts of a formal context $\mathbb{K}$ together with the partial order $(A_1, B_1) \leq (A_2, B_2) :\Leftrightarrow A_1 \subseteq A_2$ (which is equivalent to $B_1 \supseteq B_2$) is called *concept lattice* of $\mathbb{K}$.

It turns out that each concept intent (here also called *closed pattern*) is exactly the largest pattern of the equivalence class of θ it belongs to. For any pattern $X \subseteq M$, the concept intent of its equivalence class is the set X''. The concept intents can hence be considered as 'normal forms' of the (frequent) patterns. In particular, the concept lattice contains all information to derive the support of all (frequent) patterns.

3 Iceberg Concept Lattices

While it is not really informative to study the set of all frequent patterns, the situation changes when we consider the closed patterns among them only. The concepts they belong to are called *frequent concepts*, and the set of all frequent concepts is called *iceberg concept lattice* of the context $\mathbb{K}$ for the threshold minsupp. We illustrate this by a small example. Figure 1 shows the iceberg concept lattice of the MUSHROOM database from the *UCI KDD Archive* [7] for a minimum support of 85 %.

The MUSHROOM database consists of 8,416 objects (mushrooms) and 22 (nominally valued) attributes. We obtain a formal context by creating one (Boolean) attribute for each of the 80 possible values of the 22 database attributes. The resulting formal context has thus 8,416 objects and 80 attributes. For a minimum support of 85 %, this dataset has 16 frequent patterns, namely all 2^4 possible combinations of the attributes 'veil type: partial', 'veil color: white', 'gill attachment: free', and 'ring number: one'. Only seven of them are closed. The seven frequent concepts are shown in Figure 1.

In the diagram, each node stands for formal concept. The intent of each concept (i. e., each frequent closed pattern) consists of the attributes labeled at or above the concept. The number shows its support. One can clearly see that all mushrooms in the database have the attribute 'veil type: partial'. Furthermore the diagram tells us that the three next-frequent attributes are: 'veil color: white' (with 97.62 % support), 'gill attachment: free' (97.43 %), and 'ring number: one' (92.30 %). There is no other attribute having a support higher than 85 %. But even the combination of all these four concepts is frequent (with respect to our threshold of 85 %): 89.92 % of all mushrooms in our database have one ring, a white partial veil, and free gills. This concept with a quite complex description contains more objects than the concept described by the fifth-most attribute, which has a support below our threshold of 85 %, since it is not displayed in the diagram.

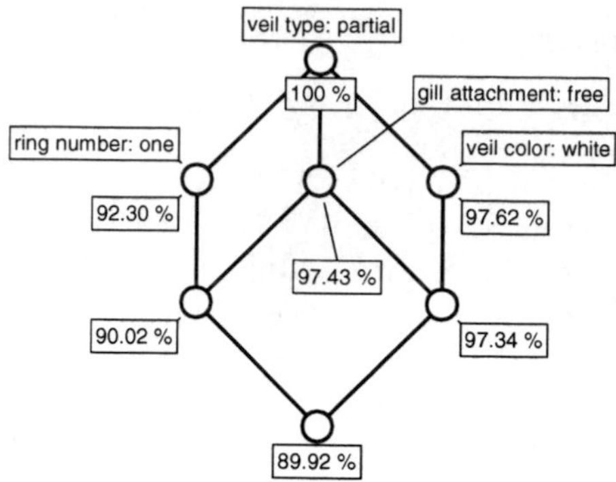

Fig. 1. Iceberg concept lattice of the mushroom database with minsupp = 85 %

In the diagram, we can detect the implication

$$\{\text{ring number: one, veil color: white}\} \Rightarrow \{\text{gill attachment: free}\} .$$

It is indicated by the fact that there is no concept having 'ring number: one' and 'veil color: white' (and 'veil type: partial') in its intent, but not 'gill attachment: free'. This implication has a support of 89.92 % and is globally valid in the database (i. e., it has a confidence of 100 %).

If we want to see more details, we have to decrease the minimum support. Figure 2 shows the MUSHROOM iceberg concept lattice for a minimum support of 70 %. Its 12 concepts represent all information about the 32 frequent patterns for this threshold. One observes that, of course, its top-most part is just the iceberg lattice for minsupp = 85 %. Additionally, we obtain five new concepts, having the possible combinations of the next-frequent attribute 'gill spacing: close' (having support 81.08 %) with the previous four attributes. The fact that the combination {veil type: partial, gill attachment: free, gill spacing: close} is not realized as a concept intent indicates another implication:

$$\{\text{gill attachment: free, gill spacing: close}\} \Rightarrow \{\text{veil color: white}\} \qquad (*)$$

This implication has 78.52 % support (the support of the most general concept having all three attributes in its intent) and — being an implication — 100 % confidence.

By further decreasing the minimum support, we discover more and more details. Figure 3 shows the MUSHROOMS iceberg concept lattice for a minimum support of 55 %. It shows four more partial copies of the 85 % iceberg lattice, and three new, single concepts.

The Mushrooms example shows that iceberg concept lattices are suitable especially for strongly correlated data. In Table 1, the size of the iceberg concept lattice (i. e., the number of all frequent closed patterns) is compared with the number of all frequent patterns. It shows for instance, that, for the minimum support of 55 %, only 32 frequent closed itemsets are needed to provide all infor-

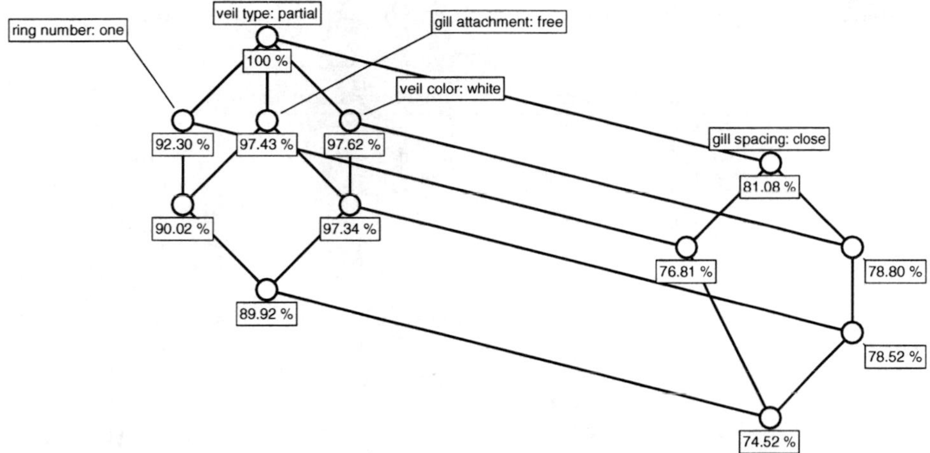

Fig. 2. Iceberg concept lattice of the mushroom database with minsupp = 70 %

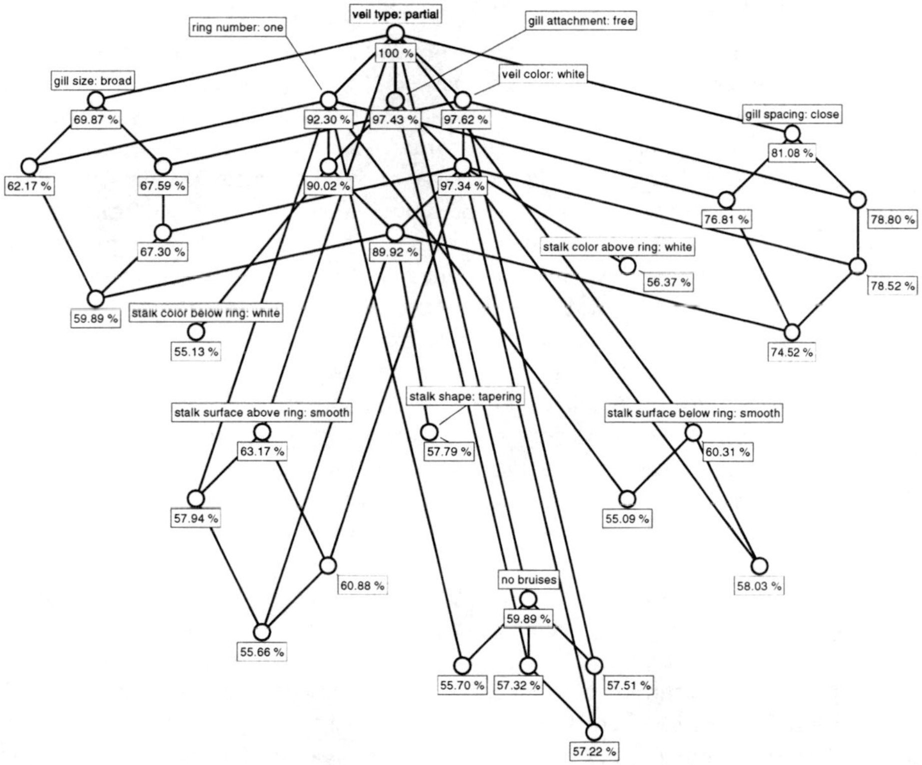

Fig. 3. Iceberg concept lattice of the mushroom database with minsupp = 55 %

Table 1. Number of frequent closed itemsets and frequent itemsets for the Mushrooms example

minsupp	# frequent closed itemsets	# frequent itemsets
85 %	7	16
70 %	12	32
55 %	32	116
0 %	32.086	2^{80}

mation about the support of all 116 frequent itemsets one obtains for the same threshold.

4 Computing the Iceberg Concept Lattice with Titanic

For illustrating the principles underlying the algorithms for mining frequent (closed) patterns using FCA, we sketch one representative called TITANIC. For a more detailed discussion of the algorithm, we refer to [42].

TITANIC is counting the support of so-called key patterns (and of some candidates for key patterns) only: A *key pattern* (or *minimal generator*) is every minimal pattern in an equivalence class of θ. TITANIC makes use of the fact that the set of all key patterns has the same property as the set of all frequent patterns: it is an order ideal in the powerset of M. This means that each subset of a key pattern is a key pattern, and no superset of a non-key pattern is a key pattern. Thus we can reuse the pruning approach of Apriori for computing the supports of all frequent key patterns. Once we have computed them, we have computed the support of at least one pattern in each equivalence class of θ, and we know the relation θ completely. Hence we can deduce the support of all frequent patterns without accessing the database any more.

Figure 4 shows the principle of TITANIC. Its basic idea is as the original Apriori algorithm: At the ith iteration, we consider only patterns with cardinality i (called *i–patterns* for short), starting with $i = 1$ (step 1). In step 2, the support of all candidates is counted. For $i = 1$, the candidates are all 1–patterns, later they are all i–patterns which are potential key patterns.

Once we know the support of all i–candidates, we have enough information to compute for all $(i-1)$–key patterns their closure, i. e., the concept intent of their equivalence class. This is done in step 3, using the equation $X'' = X \cup \{x \in M \setminus X \mid \text{supp}(X) = \text{supp}(X \cup \{x\})$.

In step 4, all patterns which are either not frequent or non-key are pruned. For the latter we use a characterization of key patterns saying that a pattern is a key pattern iff its support is different from the support of all its immediate subsets. In strongly correlated data, this additional condition helps pruning a significant number of patterns.

At the end of each iteration, the candidates for the next iteration are generated in step 5. The generation procedure is basically the same as for Apriori: An $(i+1)$–pattern is a candidate iff all its i–subpatterns are key patterns. As

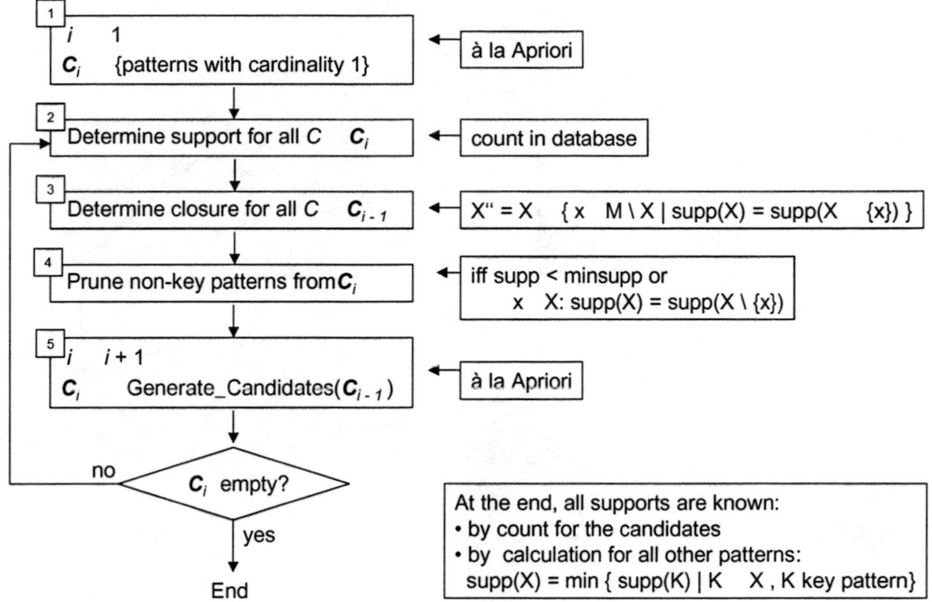

Fig. 4. The TITANIC algorithm

long as new candidates are generated, the next iteration starts. Otherwise the algorithm terminates.

It is important to note that — especially in strongly correlated data — the number of frequent key patterns is small compared to the number of all frequent patterns. Even more important, the cardinality of the largest frequent key pattern is normally smaller than the one of the largest frequent pattern. This means that the algorithm has to perform fewer iterations, and thus fewer scans of the database. This is especially important when the database is too large for main memory, as each disk access significantly increases computation time. A theoretical and experimental analysis of this behavior is given in [42], further experimental results are provided in [6].

5 Bases of Association Rules

One problem in mining association rules is the large number of rules which are usually returned. But in fact not all rules are necessary to present the information. Similar to the representation of all frequent patterns by the frequent closed patterns, one can represent all valid association rules by certain subsets, so-called *bases*. In [5], [56], and [43], different bases for association rules are introduced. The computation of the bases does not require all frequent patterns, but only the closed ones.

Here we will only show by an example (taken from [43]), how these bases look like. We have already discussed how implications (i. e., association rules

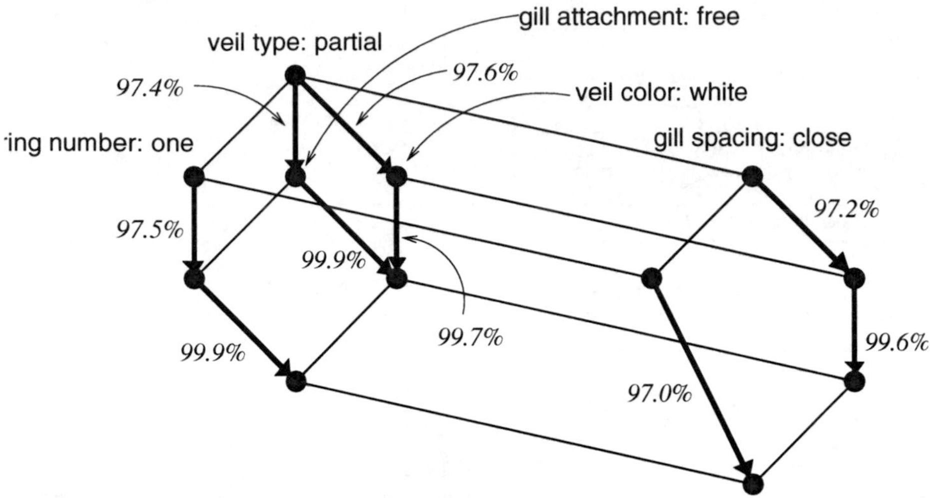

Fig. 5. Visualization of the Luxenburger basis for minsupp = 70 % and minconf= 95 %

with 100 % confidence) can be read from the line diagram. The Luxenburger basis for approximate association rules (i. e., association rules with less than 100 % confidence) can also be visualized directly in the line diagram of an iceberg concept lattice. It makes use of results of [24] and contains only those rules $B_1 \rightarrow B_2$ where B_1 and B_2 are frequent concept intents and where the concept (B_1', B_1) is an immediate subconcept of (B_2', B_2). Hence there corresponds to each approximate rule in the Luxenburger base exactly one edge in the line diagram. Figure 5 visualizes all rules in the Luxenburger basis for minsupp = 70 % and minconf = 95 %. For instance, the rightmost arrow stands for the association rule {veil color: white, gill spacing: close} $\rightarrow$ {gill attachment: free}, which holds with a confidence of 99.6 %. Its support is the support of the concept the arrow is pointing to: 78.52 %, as shown in Figure 2. Edges without label indicate that the confidence of the rule is below the minimum confidence threshold. The visualization technique is described in more detail in [43]. In comparison with other visualization techniques for association rules (as for instance implemented in the IBM Intelligent Miner), the visualization of the Luxenburger basis within the iceberg concept lattice benefits of the smaller number of rules to be represented (without loss of information!), and of the presence of a 'reading direction' provided by the concept hierarchy.

6 Conclusion

We have shown that results of Formal Concept Analysis increase on one hand the performance of data mining algorithms, and improve on the other hand the visualization of the results. There remains still a huge potential for further exploitation of FCA for data mining and knowledge discovery.

References

1. R. Agrawal, T. Imielinski, A. Swami. Mining association rules between sets of items in large databases. *Proc. SIGMOD Conf.*, 1993, 207–216
2. R. Agrawal and R. Srikant. Fast algorithms for mining association rules. *Proc. VLDB Conf.*, 1994, 478–499 (Expanded version in IBM Report RJ9839)
3. R. Agrawal and R. Srikant. Mining sequential patterns. In *Proc. of the 11th Int'l Conf. on Data Engineering (ICDE)*, pages 3–14, Mar. 1995.
4. A. Arnauld, P. Nicole: *La logique ou l'art de penser — contenant, outre les règles communes, plusieurs observations nouvelles, propres à former le jugement.* Ch. Saveux, Paris 1668
5. Y. Bastide, N. Pasquier, R. Taouil, G. Stumme, L. Lakhal: Mining Minimal Non-Redundant Association Rules Using Frequent Closed Itemsets. In: J. Lloyd, V. Dahl, U. Furbach, M. Kerber, K.–K. Lau, C. Palamidessi, L. M. Pereira, Y. Sagiv, P. J. Stuckey (eds.): *Computational Logic — CL.* Proc. 1st Intl. Conf. on CL (6th Intl. Conf. on Database Systems). LNAI **1861**, Springer, Heidelberg 2000, 972–986
6. Y. Bastide, R. Taouil, N. Pasquier, G. Stumme, L. Lakhal: Mining Frequent Patterns with Counting Inference. *SIGKDD Explorations* **2**(2), Special Issue on Scalable Algorithms, 2000, 71–80
7. S. D. Bay. The UCI KDD Archive [`http://kdd.ics.uci.edu`]. Irvine, CA: University of California, Department of Information and Computer Science.
8. R. J. Bayardo: Efficiently Mining Long Patterns from Databases. *Proc. SIGMOD '98*, 1998, 85–93
9. K. Becker, G. Stumme, R. Wille, U. Wille, M. Zickwolff: Conceptual Information Systems Discussed Through an IT-Security Tool. In: R. Dieng, O. Corby (eds.): *Knowledge Engineering and Knowledge Management. Methods, Models, and Tools.* Proc. EKAW '00. LNAI **1937**, Springer, Heidelberg 2000, 352–365
10. S. Brin, R. Motwani, and C. Silverstein. Beyond market baskets: Generalizing association rules to correlation. In *Proc. ACM SIGMOD Int'l Conf. on Management of Data*, pages 265–276, May 1997.
11. S. Brin, R. Motwani, J. D. Ullman, and S. Tsur. Dynamic itemset counting and implication rules for market basket data. In *Proc. ACM SIGMOD Int'l Conf. on Management of Data*, pages 255–264, May 1997.
12. C. Carpineto, G. Romano: GALOIS: An Order-Theoretic Approach to Conceptual Clustering. *Machine Learning.* Proc. ICML 1993, Morgan Kaufmann Prublishers 1993, 33–40
13. R. Cole, G. Stumme: CEM – A Conceptual Email Manager. In: B. Ganter, G. W. Mineau (eds.): *Conceptual Structures: Logical, Linguistic, and Computational Issues.* Proc. ICCS '00. LNAI **1867**, Springer, Heidelberg 2000, 438–452
14. H. Dicky, C. Dony, M. Huchard, T Libourel: On automatic class insertion with overloading. *OOPSLA 1996*, 251–267
15. B. Ganter, R. Wille: *Formal Concept Analysis: Mathematical Foundations.* Springer, Heidelberg 1999
16. R. Godin, H. Mili, G. Mineau, R. Missaoui, A. Arfi, T. Chau: Design of class hierarchies based on concept (Galois) lattices. *TAPOS* **4**(2), 1998, 117–134
17. J. Han and M. Kamber. *Data Mining: Concepts and Techniques.* Morgan Kaufmann, Sept. 2000.
18. J. Han, J. Pei, and Y. Yin. Mining frequent patterns without candidate generation. In *Proc. ACM SIGMOD Int'l Conf. on Management of Data*, pages 1–12, May 2000.

19. J. Hereth, G. Stumme, U. Wille, R. Wille: Conceptual Knowledge Discovery and Data Analysis. In: B. Ganter, G. Mineau (eds.): *Conceptual Structures: Logical, Linguistic, and Computational Structures.* Proc. ICCS 2000. LNAI **1867**, Springer, Heidelberg 2000, 421–437
20. Y. Huhtala, J. Kärkkäinen, P. Porkka, H. Toivonen: TANE: an efficient algorithm for discovering functional and approximate dependencies. *The Computer Journal* **42**(2), 1999, 100–111
21. M. Kamber, J. Han, and Y. Chiang. Metarule-guided mining of multi-dimensional association rules using data cubes. In *Proc. of the 3rd KDD Int'l Conf.*, Aug. 1997.
22. B. Lent, A. Swami, and J. Widom. Clustering association rules. In *Proc. of the 13th Int'l Conf. on Data Engineering (ICDE)*, pages 220–231, Mar. 1997.
23. D. Lin and Z. M. Kedem. Pincer-Search: A new algorithm for discovering the maximum frequent set. In *Proc. of the 6th Int'l Conf.on Extending Database Technology (EDBT)*, pages 105–119, Mar. 1998.
24. M. Luxenburger: Implications partielles dans un contexte. *Mathématiques, Informatique et Sciences Humaines* **29**(113), 1991, 35–55
25. K. Mackensen, U. Wille: Qualitative Text Analysis Supported by Conceptual Data Systems. *Quality and Quantity: Internatinal Journal of Methodology* **2**(33), 1999, 135–156
26. H. Mannila, H. Toivonen, and A. I. Verkamo. Discovery of frequent episodes in event sequences. *Data Mining and Knowledge Discovery*, 1(3):259–289, Sept. 1997.
27. G. Mineau, G., R. Godin: Automatic Structuring of Knowledge Bases by Conceptual Clustering. *IEEE Transactions on Knowledge and Data Engineering* **7**(5), 1995, 824–829
28. M. Missikoff, M. Scholl: An algorithm for insertion into a lattice: application to type classification. *Proc. 3rd Intl. Conf. FODO 1989.* LNCS **367**, Springer, Heidelberg 1989, 64–82
29. J. S. Park, M. S. Chen, and P. S. Yu. An efficient hash based algorithm for mining association rules. In *Proc. ACM SIGMOD Int'l Conf. on Management of Data*, pages 175–186, May 1995.
30. N. Pasquier, Y. Bastide, R. Taouil, L. Lakhal: Pruning Closed Itemset Lattices for Association Rules. *14ièmes Journées Bases de Données Avancées (BDA'98)*, Hammamet, Tunisia, 26–30 October 1998
31. N. Pasquier, Y. Bastide, R. Taouil, L. Lakhal: Efficient mining of association rules using closed itemset lattices. *Journal of Information Systems*, **24**(1), 1999, 25–46
32. N. Pasquier, Y. Bastide, R. Taouil, L. Lakhal: Discovering frequent closed itemsets for association rules. *Proc. ICDT '99.* LNCS **1540**. Springer, Heidelberg 1999, 398–416
33. J. Pei, J. Han, R. Mao: CLOSET: An Efficient Algorithm for Mining Frequent Closed Itemsets. *ACM SIGMOD Workshop on Research Issues in Data Mining and Knowledge Discovery 2000*, 21–30
34. A. Savasere, E. Omiecinski, and S. Navathe. An efficient algorithm for mining association rules in large databases. In *Proc. of the 21th Int'l Conf. on Very Large Data Bases (VLDB)*, pages 432–444, Sept. 1995.
35. P. Scheich, M. Skorsky, F. Vogt, C. Wachter, R. Wille: Conceptual Data Systems. In: O. Opitz, B. Lausen, R. Klar (eds.): *Information and Classification.* Springer, Berlin-Heidelberg 1993, 72–84
36. I. Schmitt, G. Saake: Merging inheritance hierarchies for database integration. *Proc. 3rd IFCIS Intl. Conf. on Cooperative Information Systems*, New York City, Nework, USA, August 20-22, 1998, 122–131

37. C. Silverstein, S. Brin, and R. Motwani. Beyond market baskets: Generalizing association rules to dependence rules. *Data Mining and Knowledge Discovery*, 2(1), Jan. 1998.
38. S. Strahringer, R. Wille: Conceptual clustering via convex-ordinal structures. In: O. Opitz, B. Lausen, R. Klar (eds.): *Information and Classification*. Springer, Berlin-Heidelberg 1993, 85–98
39. G. Stumme: *Conceptual Knowledge Discovery with Frequent Concept Lattices*. FB4-Preprint **2043**, TU Darmstadt 1999
40. G. Stumme, R. Taouil, Y. Bastide, L. Lakhal: Conceptual Clustering with Iceberg Concept Lattices. *Proc. GI–Fachgruppentreffen Maschinelles Lernen '01*. Universität Dortmund **763**, Oktober 2001
41. G. Stumme, R. Taouil, Y. Bastide, N. Pasquier, L. Lakhal: Fast computation of concept lattices using data mining techniques. *Proc. 7th Intl. Workshop on Knowledge Representation Meets Databases*, Berlin, 21–22. August 2000. CEUR-Workshop Proceeding. http://sunsite.informatik.rwth-aachen.de/Publications/CEUR-WS/
42. G. Stumme, R. Taouil, Y. Bastide, N. Pasqier, L. Lakhal: Computing Iceberg Concept Lattices with Titanic. *J. on Knowledge and Data Engineering* **42**(2), 2002, 189–222
43. G. Stumme, R. Taouil, Y. Bastide, N. Pasquier, L. Lakhal: Intelligent Structuring and Reducing of Association Rules with Formal Concept Analysis. In: F. Baader. G. Brewker, T. Eiter (eds.): *KI 2001: Advances in Artificial Intelligence*. Proc. KI 2001. LNAI **2174**, Springer, Heidelberg 2001, 335–350
44. G. Stumme, R. Wille, U. Wille: Conceptual Knowledge Discovery in Databases Using Formal Concept Analysis Methods. In: J. M. Żytkow, M. Quafofou (eds.): *Principles of Data Mining and Knowledge Discovery*. Proc. 2nd European Symposium on PKDD '98, LNAI **1510**, Springer, Heidelberg 1998, 450–458
45. G. Stumme, R. Wille (eds.): *Begriffliche Wissensverarbeitung – Methoden und Anwendungen*. Springer, Heidelberg 2000
46. G. Stumme: Formal Concept Analysis on its Way from Mathematics to Computer Science. *Proc. 10th Intl. Conf. on Conceptual Structures (ICCS 2002)*. LNCS, Springer, Heidelberg 2002
47. R. Taouil, N. Pasquier, Y. Bastide, L. Lakhal: Mining Bases for Association Rules Using Closed Sets. *Proc. 16th Intl. Conf. ICDE 2000*, San Diego, CA, US, February 2000, 307
48. H. Toivonen. Sampling large databases for association rules. In *Proc. of the 22nd Int'l Conf. on Very Large Data Bases (VLDB)*, pages 134–145, Sept. 1996.
49. F. Vogt, R. Wille: TOSCANA – A graphical tool for analyzing and exploring data. LNCS **894**, Springer, Heidelberg 1995, 226–233
50. K. Waiyamai, R. Taouil, L. Lakhal: Towards an object database approach for managing concept lattices. *Proc. 16th Intl. Conf. on Conceptual Modeling*, LNCS **1331**, Springer, Heidelberg 1997, 299–312
51. R. Wille: Restructuring lattice theory: an approach based on hierarchies of concepts. In: I. Rival (ed.). *Ordered sets*. Reidel, Dordrecht–Boston 1982, 445–470
52. A. Yahia, L. Lakhal, J. P. Bordat, R. Cicchetti: iO2: An algorithmic method for building inheritance graphs in object database design. *Proc. 15th Intl. Conf. on Conceptual Modeling*. LNCS **1157**, Springer, Heidelberg 1996, 422–437
53. M. J. Zaki, S. Parthasarathy, M. Ogihara, and W. Li. New algorithms for fast discovery of association rules. In *Proc. of the 3rd Int'l Conf. on Knowledge Discovery in Databases (KDD)*, pages 283–286, Aug. 1997.

54. M. J. Zaki, M. Ogihara: Theoretical Foundations of Association Rules, *3rd SIGMOD'98 Workshop on Research Issues in Data Mining and Knowledge Discovery (DMKD)*, Seattle, WA, June 1998, 7:1–7:8
55. M. J. Zaki, C.-J. Hsiao: ChARM: An efficient algorithm for closed association rule mining. Technical Report 99–10, Computer Science Dept., Rensselaer Polytechnic Institute, October 1999
56. M. J. Zaki: Generating non-redundant association rules. *Proc. KDD 2000.* 34–43

Two Approaches to Event Definition

Antony Galton[1] and Juan Carlos Augusto[2]

[1] School of Engineering and Computer Science, University of Exeter, UK
A.P.Galton@exeter.ac.uk
[2] Department of Electronics and Computer Science, University of Southampton, UK
jca@ecs.soton.ac.uk

Abstract. We compare two approaches to event definition, deriving from the Active Database and Knowledge Representation communities. We relate these approaches by taking a system of the former kind, displaying some of its shortcomings, and rectifying them by remodelling the system in the latter style. We further show the extent to which the original system can be recreated within the remodelled system. This bridge between the two approaches should provide a starting point for fruitful interaction between the two communities.

1 Events in Knowledge Representation and Databases

Events are ubiquitous in both life and computing. In both areas we frequently classify events, considering many individual events together as instances of some class, or event-type, to which we give a name (for example "plane crashes" or "user interrupts"). Each event-type gives rise to its own particular set of problems, but we may identify two as fundamental: 'How is the event-type defined?' and 'How can we detect when an event of that type has occurred?'. These two questions are clearly closely interrelated, but they are emphatically not the same question.

There are many areas of computing where event definition and detection are important. In this paper we focus on two areas representing two different approaches to events, which we have found it instructive to compare. These are knowledge representation and active databases. The former is generally more familiar to the AI community, the latter to the database community, but from our investigations it is clear that the concerns of both areas are relevant to both communities. Despite this, work in the two areas has for the most part proceeded separately, leading to divergence of notation and terminology. We believe it will benefit both areas to attempt to bridge this gap.

A database in the traditional, 'passive' sense is merely a repository (albeit perhaps highly structured) of information, which provides answers to queries posed by the user. The 'events' in the life of such a database are essentially the user-initiated updates and queries, and the responses to both types of events follow a rigid preprogrammed pattern. In particular, the database system itself is unable to produce behaviour except in direct response to individual external triggers. By contrast, an *active* database monitors the succession of events impinging on it from outside, and is endowed with the ability to detect not only events but also significant *patterns* of events, and to respond to these in accordance with some set of 'event-condition-action' (ECA) rules. Thus an active

R. Cicchetti et al. (Eds.): DEXA 2002, LNCS 2453, pp. 547–556, 2002.

database endowed with a set of ECA rules is in a certain sense capable of independent action, only indirectly triggered by inputs from its users.

A key feature of any active database system is its capacity to detect composite events of various descriptions. Systems may differ with respect to the available classes of primitive events, the variety of operators used for defining composite events from primitive ones, and the mechanisms by which composite events are detected. For example, the COMPOSE system of [1] provides four classes of primitive event (*object state events*, *method execution events*, *time events*, and *transaction events*), and a set of event-composition operators. The operators are selected so that their expressive power is exactly the same as that of regular grammars; this enables the event-detection mechanism to be implemented using finite automata, each event being associated with an automaton which reaches an accepting state exactly when that event occurs.

Another system, SAMOS [2, 3], combines active and object-oriented features in a single framework. Primitive events are *time events*, *method events*, *transaction events*, and *abstract events*, while composite events are built up from these using operators such as disjunction, conjunction, and sequential composition. Associated with each kind of primitive event is a method by which events of that kind are detected. These methods are used as the basis for a coloured Petri net which enables the detection of composite events. For each operator of the event algebra there is an associated structure in the net; these structures can be combined recursively as needed. When the primitive-event detector is activated the corresponding node in the net is activated and certain transitions fire. If as a result of these firings the node associated with some composite event acquires a token, then the composite event has been detected. The behaviour of the net is implemented by means of matrix-processing algorithms.

SNOOP [4] is another system emanating from the database community. We defer a description of this system to section 3, as it will provide the starting-point for the investigations reported in this paper.

Finally, we mention the work of [5], which provides a language for expressing event-based conditions in an OODB framework. As usual, basic and composite events are considered, the latter obtained by means of a predefined set of event constructors applied to other basic or composite events. Database events can be classified as *instantaneous* or *persistent*, while temporal events can be *absolute* (e.g., the first hour of a specific day), *periodic* (e.g., each working day), or *relative* (e.g., five hours after a modification to the database). The language resembles that of SNOOP, although the authors claim that it is strictly more expressive.

A feature that is common to all these systems is that all events, whether primitive or composite, are considered to be instantaneous, that is, the time associated with the event is an instant rather than an interval. In the case of a composite event built up from events occurring at different times, the associated instant is usually the time of the *last* of its contributory primitive events. This constraint is natural enough in a context where the prime focus of interest is on event detection, since typically a composite event will be detected at the time that its last contributory component is detected. However, this does lead to logical difficulties in the case of some composite event-types, as will be explained below. The only work on active databases we are aware of in which events are treated as having positive duration is [6]

Turning now to knowledge representation, one of the best-known proposals for the formalisation of temporal reasoning is the Interval Calculus [7, 8]. Here *all* events are regarded as durative, that is taking time, and accordingly intervals (rather than instants) are considered to be the basic temporal concept. A set of 13 basic relations between intervals is defined, and the rules governing the composition of such relations is regarded as a key factor in controlling temporal reasoning. Allen distinguishes between *properties*, *processes*, and *events*, the latter being related to intervals by means of a predicate $Occurs(E, i)$ which is used to assert that an event of type E occurs on the interval i. Events are assumed to be unitary in the sense of the formula $Occurs(E, i) \wedge In(i', i) \rightarrow \neg Occurs(E, i')$, where $In(i', i)$ means that i' is a *proper* subinterval of i. The main focus of this work is on the development of axioms to formalise the notions of action and causality. Event types are characterised in terms of necessary and sufficient conditions for their occurrence.

Event definition in terms of occurrence conditions also plays a prominent part in the Event Calculus of [9] (which is connected with temporal deductive databases rather than active databases), and in the work of Galton [10]. Rather than detection of events as they occur, the knowledge representation work on events has mainly concentrated on what inferences can be made from the fact that certain events are known to have occurred. These inferences may extend to the possibility of future events occurring, thus providing a link to another important theme of AI, planning. An exception is the work of [11], whose IxTeT system detects the occurrence of *chronicles* specified as conjunctions of instantaneous events together with constraints on their relative times of occurrence.

In the remainder of the paper, we first set up a simple discrete temporal framework (this is for convenience; the same issues arise in continuous time), then examine the SNOOP system in some detail as representative of the active database systems in which events are regarded as occurring at their time of detection and hence as instantaneous. In effect, events are defined in terms of their *detection conditions*. We next illustrate the problems that arise from the decision to treat events in this way, and go on to show that the problems do not arise if we adopt instead the assumption widespread in the knowledge representation community that events should be treated as durative and defined in terms of their *occurrence conditions*. We then investigate how far it is possible to reconcile the two accounts of events; we associate each event with a 'detection event' in such a way that detection of an event, in the database sense, can be exactly identified with the occurrence, in the knowledge representation sense, of its associated 'detection event'. The key question is whether the occurrence conditions of the latter can be precisely given; by determining precisely when they can and when they cannot, we provide a measure of the extent of the disagreement between the two approaches. Although this is only a beginning, we believe that this work can provide the foundation for a productive dialogue between the active database and knowledge representation communities.

2 A Temporal Framework

Whereas time is commonly conceptualized as a continuum, it is sufficient for many applications to treat it as a discrete system modelled by the integers under their usual ordering. In such a model, individual integers represent *atomic intervals*, chunks of time that are regarded as indivisible. It is assumed that no change can take place within an atomic interval. Longer intervals are specified by their initial and final atomic intervals; thus the interval [4,7] is composed of the atomic intervals 4, 5, 6, and 7. It is sometimes convenient to allow the notation [4,4] to refer to the atomic interval 4.

The main focus of interest in this paper will be on *events*. We distinguish the occurrence of an event from its detection. Typically an event is, or can be, detected at the end of the interval over which it occurs. We shall assume that event detection always occurs at an atomic interval, whereas the event itself may occur over an extended interval. We shall use the notation $\mathbf{D}(E, t)$ to mean that an event of type E is detected at time t, and $\mathbf{O}(E, [t, t'])$ to mean that such an event occurs over the interval $[t, t']$. An event-type which can only occur on an atomic interval will be called an *atomic event*. Events may be characterized either in terms of their detection conditions, or in terms of their occurrence conditions. These two approaches lead to rather different conceptions of events, which it will be one purpose of this paper to reconcile.

We assume that we are provided with a stock of *primitive event types*; we say nothing about how these are specified (although the primitive event types recognised by SNOOP are briefly described below), but shall assume that for each primitive event type E all facts of the form $\mathbf{O}(E, [t, t'])$ and $\mathbf{D}(E, t)$ are known. Our main interest in this paper will be in *composite event types*, which are constructed from the primitive event types by means of a set of operators. In the literature many such operators have been considered. In this paper we shall discuss those of the system SNOOP introduced by Chakravarty et al. [4].

3 Detectable Event-Types

An event-type defined in terms of its detection condition will be called a *detectable* event-type. To illustrate the use of detectable event types we describe the SNOOP system of [4]. In this system events are either primitive or composite, the latter being constructed from the former using the operators defined in the paper. Amongst primitive events are distinguished

1. database events, corresponding to database operations such as $retrieve$, $insert$, $update$, and $delete$;
2. temporal events, which pick elements of the passage of time itself, either absolutely (e.g., calendar dates, clock times) or relatively (in terms of some reference event, e.g., 3 seconds after a database update);
3. explicit events, which include any events detected by other application programs and input as primitive events into the DBMS.

The reader is referred to [4] for the original definitions of the operators used to form composite events. Here we attempt to provide equivalent definitions within the formalism laid out in the previous section; in cases where we found the original definitions ambiguous or unclear, we have resorted to informed guesswork in formulating the exact equivalents in our system. We consider the operators in the order they appear in the original paper.

or Disjunction of events: $\mathbf{D}(E_1 \nabla E_2, t) \stackrel{\text{def}}{=} \mathbf{D}(E_1, t) \vee \mathbf{D}(E_2, t)$.
and Conjunction of events. The events are not required to be simultaneous.

$$\mathbf{D}(E_1 \bigtriangleup E_2, t) \stackrel{\text{def}}{=} \exists t' \leq t((\mathbf{D}(E_1, t') \wedge \mathbf{D}(E_2, t)) \vee (\mathbf{D}(E_1, t) \wedge \mathbf{D}(E_2, t'))$$

any The original definition of this operator used a second-order condition, with a variable number of quantifiers depending on the number of events considered; in order to work within first-order logic, we define a series of "any" operators. For $m \leq n$, the event $\mathsf{ANY}^m_n(E_1, \ldots, E_n)$ occurs when m events out of n distinct specified events occur, in any order:

$$\begin{aligned}\mathbf{D}(\mathsf{ANY}^m_n(E_1, \ldots, E_n), t) \stackrel{\text{def}}{=} \; & \exists t_1 \leq \ldots \leq t_m = t \, \exists i_1, \ldots, i_m \in \{1, \ldots, n\} \\ & (\#\{i_1, \ldots, i_m\} = m \wedge \mathbf{D}(E_{i_1}, t_1) \wedge \cdots \wedge \mathbf{D}(E_{i_m}, t_m)).\end{aligned}$$

The first conjunct on the right-hand side ensures that the E_{i_j} are all distinct (here $\#X$ is the cardinality of X).
seq The sequential composition of two events:

$$\mathbf{D}(E_1; E_2, t) \stackrel{\text{def}}{=} \exists t' < t(\mathbf{D}(E_1, t') \wedge \mathbf{D}(E_2, t)).$$

A According to Chakravarthy et al., the 'aperiodic' operator A allows one to express the occurrence of an event E_2 within the interval defined by two other events E_1 and E_3. Their definition seems to express something different, however, namely that E_2 occurs within an interval beginning with E_1 at a time when E_3 has not yet occurred. There is no requirement for the event E_3 to occur at all. We thus have the definition:

$$\begin{aligned}&\mathbf{D}(\mathsf{A}(E_1, E_2, E_3), t) \stackrel{\text{def}}{=} \\ &\quad \mathbf{D}(E_2, t) \wedge \exists t' < t(\mathbf{D}(E_1, t') \wedge \forall t''(t' \leq t'' \leq t \rightarrow \neg \mathbf{D}(E_3, t'')))\end{aligned}$$

This can be expressed more simply by the introduction of a new predicate $\mathbf{D}_{in}$ which says that an event is detected at *some* point within a stated interval:

$$\mathbf{D}_{in}(E, [t_1, t_2]) \stackrel{\text{def}}{=} \exists t(t_1 \leq t \leq t_2 \wedge \mathbf{D}(E, t)).$$

We can then put

$$\mathbf{D}(\mathsf{A}(E_1, E_2, E_3), t) \stackrel{\text{def}}{=} \mathbf{D}(E_2, t) \wedge \exists t' < t(\mathbf{D}(E_1, t') \wedge \neg \mathbf{D}_{in}(E_3, [t', t]))$$

P The 'periodic' operator P caused us even more difficulty than A. However, we believe that $\mathsf{P}(E_1, n, E_3)$ is an event type which occurs every n time-steps after an occurrence of E_1 so long as E_3 does not occur. Note that, contrary to what one might think at first, the periodic operator does not express the periodic recurrence of some detectable event, but only that a certain period of time has elapsed a whole number of times since a given detectable event. It is thus a 'virtual' event rather than a 'real' one.

$$\begin{aligned}\mathbf{D}(\mathsf{P}(E_1, n, E_3), t) \stackrel{\text{def}}{=} \; & \exists t' < t \exists i \in \mathbb{Z}^+(t = t' + ni \wedge \mathbf{D}(E_1, t') \wedge \\ & \neg \mathbf{D}_{in}(E_3, [t' + 1, t]))\end{aligned}$$

not The non-occurrence of the event E_2 in an interval delimited by occurrences of E_1 and E_3:

$$\mathbf{D}(\neg(E_2)[E_1, E_3], t) \stackrel{\text{def}}{=} \exists t' < t(\mathbf{D}(E_1, t') \wedge \mathbf{D}(E_3, t) \wedge \neg \mathbf{D}_{in}(E_2, [t', t]))$$

4 Why Detection Conditions Are Inadequate

All the event-types defined in the previous section are detectable, assuming that all the event-types E_1, E_2, E_3 occurring in the definitions are detectable. This is because the events are defined in terms of detection conditions and not in terms of occurrence conditions. However, this leads to some problems; it means that the events that are defined are not always exactly the events that are, presumably, intended.

This is revealed when we consider a composite event such as $E_1; (E_2; E_3)$. Intuitively, since ';' expresses sequential composition, we should expect this event to occur whenever an occurrence of E_1 is followed by an occurrence of E_2 which is in turn followed by an occurrence of E_3. It should therefore be a different event from $E_2; (E_1; E_3)$. Now consider the detection conditions for the two events:

$$\begin{aligned}
\mathbf{D}(E_1;(E_2;E_3),t) &\iff \exists t' < t(\mathbf{D}(E_1,t') \wedge \mathbf{D}(E_2;E_3,t)) \\
&\iff \exists t' < t(\mathbf{D}(E_1,t') \wedge \exists t'' < t(\mathbf{D}(E_2,t'') \wedge \mathbf{D}(E_3,t))) \\
&\iff \exists t' < t, t'' < t(\mathbf{D}(E_1,t') \wedge \mathbf{D}(E_2,t'') \wedge \mathbf{D}(E_3,t))
\end{aligned}$$

$$\begin{aligned}
\mathbf{D}(E_2;(E_1;E_3),t) &\iff \exists t' < t(\mathbf{D}(E_2,t') \wedge \mathbf{D}(E_1;E_3,t)) \\
&\iff \exists t' < t(\mathbf{D}(E_2,t') \wedge \exists t'' < t(\mathbf{D}(E_1,t'') \wedge \mathbf{D}(E_3,t))) \\
&\iff \exists t' < t, t'' < t(\mathbf{D}(E_2,t') \wedge \mathbf{D}(E_1,t'') \wedge \mathbf{D}(E_3,t))
\end{aligned}$$

The two detection conditions are equivalent, which means that as detectable events defined according to SNOOP, $E_1; (E_2; E_3)$ and $E_2; (E_1; E_3)$ are equivalent. This in turn means that ';' so defined does not, after all, express sequential composition but something different.

For another example, consider the event $\neg(E_2 \bigtriangleup E_2')[E_1, E_3]$, the negation of a conjunction. Intuitively, one might expect this to occur so long as at least one of E_2 and E_2' fails to occur in the interval delimited by E_1 and E_3. Consider, however, the detection conditions:

$$\begin{aligned}
&\mathbf{D}(\neg(E_2 \bigtriangleup E_2')[E_1,E_3],t) \\
&\quad\iff \exists t' \le t(\mathbf{D}(E_1,t') \wedge \mathbf{D}(E_3,t) \wedge \forall t''(t' \le t'' \le t \to \neg\mathbf{D}(E_2 \bigtriangleup E_2',t''))) \\
&\quad\iff \exists t' \le t(\mathbf{D}(E_1,t') \wedge \mathbf{D}(E_3,t) \wedge \forall t''(t' \le t'' \le t \to \\
&\qquad\qquad \neg\exists t^* \le t''((\mathbf{D}(E_2,t^*) \wedge \mathbf{D}(E_2',t'')) \vee (\mathbf{D}(E_2,t'') \wedge \mathbf{D}(E_2',t^*))))) \\
&\quad\iff \exists t' \le t(\mathbf{D}(E_1,t') \wedge \mathbf{D}(E_3,t) \wedge \forall t''(t' \le t'' \le t \to \\
&\qquad\qquad \forall t^* \le t'' \neg((\mathbf{D}(E_2,t^*) \wedge \mathbf{D}(E_2',t'')) \vee (\mathbf{D}(E_2,t'') \wedge \mathbf{D}(E_2',t^*)))))
\end{aligned}$$

We need not spell this out any further to see that it imposes a very strong condition on the detection of events of types E_2 and E_2': a condition which refers to *all* times t^* earlier than some time t'' in the interval of interest. This takes us right outside the interval to a consideration of the entire past history, clearly not in keeping with the intuitive meaning.

5 Event-Types Defined in Terms of Occurrence

The problems encountered in the previous section all arise from the fact that the time associated with an event by the *Detect* predicate is an atomic interval; the event itself may occur over an extended interval, but in this case the *Detect* predicate carries no information about how far into the past that interval extends. To remedy this, we shall redefine the SNOOP operators in terms of occurrence conditions rather than detection conditions; this is more in keeping with the approaches to events in the Knowledge Representation tradition, as described above. We shall refer to the system of redefined operators as O-SNOOP ('Occurrence-based SNOOP') as distinct from the original system which we shall refer to as D-SNOOP ('Detection-based SNOOP').

or $\mathbf{O}(E_1 \nabla E_2, [t_1, t_2]) \stackrel{\text{def}}{=} \mathbf{O}(E_1, [t_1, t_2]) \vee \mathbf{O}(E_2, [t_1, t_2])$.

and $\mathbf{O}(E_1 \triangle E_2, [t_1, t_2]) \stackrel{\text{def}}{=} \exists t, t'(t_1 \le t \le t_2 \wedge t_1 \le t' \le t_2 \wedge ((\mathbf{O}(E_1, [t_1, t]) \wedge \mathbf{O}(E_2, [t', t_2])) \vee (\mathbf{O}(E_1, [t', t_2]) \wedge \mathbf{O}(E_2, [t_1, t])) \vee (\mathbf{O}(E_1, [t_1, t_2]) \wedge \mathbf{O}(E_2, [t, t'])) \vee (\mathbf{O}(E_1, [t, t']) \wedge \mathbf{O}(E_2, [t_1, t_2]))))$

any $\mathbf{O}(\mathsf{ANY}_n^m(E_1, \ldots, E_n), [t_1, t'_m]) \stackrel{\text{def}}{=} \exists t_2, \ldots, t_m, t'_1, \ldots, t'_{m-1} \in [t_1, t'_m] \exists i_1, \ldots, i_m \in \{1, \ldots, n\} (\#\{i_1, \ldots, i_m\} = m \wedge \mathbf{O}(E_{i_1}, [t_1, t'_{i_1}]) \wedge \cdots \wedge \mathbf{O}(E_{i_m}, [t_m, t'_{i_m}]))$.

seq We assume the events do not overlap:

$$\mathbf{O}(E_1; E_2, [t_1, t_2]) \stackrel{\text{def}}{=} \exists t, t'(t_1 \le t < t' \le t_2 \wedge \mathbf{O}(E_1, [t_1, t]) \wedge \mathbf{O}(E_2, [t', t_2]))$$

A The occurrence time for $\mathsf{A}(E_1, E_2, E_3)$ is the occurrence time for E_2—an occurrence of the event is an occurrence of E_2 in a certain context determined by E_1 and E_3. The rest of the occurrence condition specifies the context. There must be no occurrence of E_3 wholly within the interval between the occurrences of E_1 and E_2. To enable us to express this more concisely, we introduce a predicate $\mathbf{O}_{in}$ defined as follows:

$$\mathbf{O}_{in}(E, [t_1, t_2]) \stackrel{\text{def}}{=} \exists t'_1, t'_2(t_1 \le t'_1 \le t'_2 \le t_2 \wedge \mathbf{O}(E, [t'_1, t'_2])).$$

It will also be useful to define the end of an event by the rule:

$$\mathbf{O}(E\downarrow, t) \stackrel{\text{def}}{=} \exists t' \le t\, \mathbf{O}(E, [t', t]).$$

We now have

$$\mathbf{O}(\mathsf{A}(E_1, E_2, E_3), [t_1, t_2]) \stackrel{\text{def}}{=} \mathbf{O}(E_2, [t_1, t_2]) \wedge \exists t < t_1(\mathbf{O}(E_1\downarrow, t) \wedge \neg \mathbf{O}_{in}(E_3, [t, t_2])).$$

P As noted above, this operator expresses a virtual event which occurs at the moment of its detection; the occurrence time is therefore the same as the detection time. The non-occurrence of E_3 is handled as in the aperiodic case.

$$\mathbf{O}(\mathsf{P}(E_1, n, E_3), t) \stackrel{\text{def}}{=} \exists t' < t \exists i \in \mathbb{Z}^+(t = t' + ni \wedge \mathbf{O}(E_1\downarrow, t') \wedge \neg \mathbf{O}_{in}(E_3, [t' + 1, t]))$$

not What is the time of a non-occurrence? Since it is non-occurrence of E_2 in a predefined interval, the only credible time to assign to it is just that interval. The interval extends from immediately after E_1 finishes to immediately before E_2 starts. To help us express the occurrence condition, we define the start of an event by the rule

$$\mathbf{O}(\uparrow E, t) \stackrel{\text{def}}{=} \exists t'(t \le t' \wedge \mathbf{O}(E, [t, t'])).$$

We can now put

$$\mathbf{O}(\neg(E_2)[E_1, E_3], [t_1, t_2]) \stackrel{\mathsf{def}}{=} \mathbf{O}(E_1{\downarrow}, t_1) \wedge \mathbf{O}({\uparrow}E_3, t_2) \wedge \neg\mathbf{O}_{in}(E_2, [t_1, t_2]).$$

The problems we encountered with the D-SNOOP operators do not arise for O-SNOOP:

$$\begin{aligned}
&\mathbf{O}(E_1; (E_2; E_3), [t_1, t_2]) \\
&\iff \exists t, t'(t_1 \leq t < t' \leq t_2 \wedge \mathbf{O}(E_1, [t_1, t]) \wedge \mathbf{O}(E_2; E_3, [t', t_2]) \\
&\iff \exists t, t'(t_1 \leq t < t' \leq t_2 \wedge \mathbf{O}(E_1, [t_1, t]) \wedge \\
&\qquad \exists t^*, t^{**}(t' \leq t^* < t^{**} \leq t_2 \wedge \mathbf{O}(E_2, [t', t^*]) \wedge \mathbf{O}(E_3, [t^{**}, t_2]))) \\
&\iff \exists t, t', t^*, t^{**}(t_1 \leq t < t' \leq t^* < t^{**} \leq t_2 \wedge \\
&\qquad \mathbf{O}(E_1, [t_1, t]) \wedge \mathbf{O}(E_2, [t', t^*]) \wedge \mathbf{O}(E_3, [t^{**}, t_2]))
\end{aligned}$$

$$\begin{aligned}
&\mathbf{O}(E_2; (E_1; E_3), [t_1, t_2]) \\
&\iff \exists t, t'(t_1 \leq t < t' \leq t_2 \wedge \mathbf{O}(E_2, [t_1, t]) \wedge \mathbf{O}(E_1; E_3, [t', t_2]) \\
&\iff \exists t, t'(t_1 \leq t < t' \leq t_2 \wedge \mathbf{O}(E_2, [t_1, t]) \wedge \\
&\qquad \exists t^*, t^{**}(t' \leq t^* < t^{**} \leq t_2 \wedge \mathbf{O}(E_1, [t', t^*]) \wedge \mathbf{O}(E_3, [t^{**}, t_2]))) \\
&\iff \exists t, t', t^*, t^{**}(t_1 \leq t < t' \leq t^* < t^{**} \leq t_2 \wedge \\
&\qquad \mathbf{O}(E_2, [t_1, t]) \wedge \mathbf{O}(E_1, [t', t^*]) \wedge \mathbf{O}(E_3, [t^{**}, t_2]))
\end{aligned}$$

These two occurrence conditions are obviously inequivalent, and equally clearly in accordance with our intuitive understanding of triple sequential compositions.

In preparation for the next case, note that

$$\mathbf{O}_{in}(E_1 \triangle E_2, [t_1, t_2]) \iff \mathbf{O}_{in}(E_1, [t_1, t_2]) \wedge \mathbf{O}_{in}(E_2, [t_1, t_2]).$$

The proof is straightforward but rather tedious. We now have

$$\begin{aligned}
&\mathbf{O}(\neg(E_2 \triangle E_2')[E_1, E_3], [t_1, t_2]) \\
&\iff \mathbf{O}(E_1{\downarrow}, t_1) \wedge \mathbf{O}({\uparrow}E_3, t_2) \wedge \neg\mathbf{O}_{in}(E_2 \triangle E_2', [t_1, t_2]) \\
&\iff \mathbf{O}(E_1{\downarrow}, t_1) \wedge \mathbf{O}({\uparrow}E_3, t_2) \wedge \neg(\mathbf{O}_{in}(E_2, [t_1, t_2]) \wedge \mathbf{O}_{in}(E_2', [t_1, t_2])) \\
&\iff \mathbf{O}(E_1{\downarrow}, t_1) \wedge \mathbf{O}({\uparrow}E_3, t_2) \wedge (\neg\mathbf{O}_{in}(E_2, [t_1, t_2]) \vee \neg\mathbf{O}_{in}(E_2', [t_1, t_2]))
\end{aligned}$$

which unlike in D-SNOOP does not involve reference to times indefinitely far into the past, and is clearly in accord with our intuitive understanding of the logic of this case.

6 D-SNOOP and O-SNOOP Compared

The time associated with any event by D-SNOOP is the time at which the event is detected; in almost every case this is the time of its last constituent, so that event E is detected at the time of its termination $E{\downarrow}$. We could regard $E{\downarrow}$ as the *detection event* of E, making the detection of any event equivalent to the occurrence of its detection event. D-SNOOP rests on the premiss that reasoning about composite events can be satisfactorily accomplished using detection events only. In order for this to work, it would be necessary for every event-composition operator *Op* to obey a rule of the form

$$Op(E_1, \ldots, E_n){\downarrow} \leftrightarrow Op(E_1{\downarrow}, \ldots, E_n{\downarrow}){\downarrow}$$

(Note that the final $\downarrow$ operator can be omitted in those cases when the composite is already instantaneous.) The D-SNOOP operators automatically obey this rule, but as we have seen, their interpretation is problematic. An exact measure of the extent to which our remodelled O-SNOOP operators agree with those of D-SNOOP is furnished by what proportion of them obey the above rule.

For four of the operators it can be straightforwardly verified that the rule does indeed hold; the following are all theorems of O-SNOOP:

$$\begin{aligned}(E_1 \nabla E_2)\downarrow &= E_1\downarrow \nabla E_2\downarrow \\ (E_1 \bigtriangleup E_2)\downarrow &= (E_1\downarrow \bigtriangleup E_2\downarrow)\downarrow \\ \mathsf{ANY}^m_n(E_1,\ldots,E_n)\downarrow &= \mathsf{ANY}^m_n(E_1\downarrow,\ldots,E_n\downarrow)\downarrow \\ \mathsf{P}(E_1,n,E_3)\downarrow &= \mathsf{P}(E_1\downarrow,n,E_3\downarrow)\end{aligned}$$

That part of D-SNOOP which handles these operators can thus be exactly recreated within O-SNOOP.

This leaves three problematic cases, namely sequential composition, the aperiodic operator, and negation—two of these are, not surprisingly, the operators we had trouble with earlier. In all these cases, the fact that in O-SNOOP events are, in general, durative, whereas detection events are always instantaneous, vitiates any attempt to express detection of the composite event in terms of detection of its components. For example, it is not possible to define $(E_1;E_2)\downarrow$ in terms of $E_1\downarrow$ and $E_2\downarrow$. The reason for this is that in order for $E_1;E_2$ to occur, it is necessary for E_1 to finish—and thus to be detectable—before E_2 starts. But the start of E_2 cannot be expressed in terms of the detection of E_2, which only refers to its end. Thus the closest we can come to such expressions is

$$\begin{aligned}(E_1;E_2)\downarrow &= (E_1\downarrow;E_2)\downarrow \\ A(E_1,E_2,E_3)\downarrow &= A(E_1\downarrow,E_2,E_3)\downarrow \\ \neg(E_2)[E_1,E_3]\downarrow &= \neg(E_2)[E_1\downarrow,\uparrow E_3]\downarrow\end{aligned}$$

Crucially, it is E_2, and not $E_2\downarrow$, which is required on the right-hand side in each case.[3]

7 Conclusions and Further Work

We have drawn a contrast between two styles of event definition: the active database approach in which events are regarded as instantaneous and defined in terms of the conditions for their detection at an instant, and the knowledge representation approach in which events are for the most part regarded as durative and are defined in terms of the conditions for their occurrence over an interval. The contrast is starkly drawn in order to make a point; it is not suggested that there has been *no* dialogue and no commonality between the two approaches. We have explored this contrast in some detail by examining SNOOP, a system proposed within the active database community, displaying some of its shortcomings, and showing that these can be rectified by remodelling

[3] This gives the finishing time for $\neg(E_2)[E_1,E_3]$; but this event cannot be *detected* until the time of $E_3\downarrow$—the only mismatch between time of detection and time of finishing, a subtlety that doesn't arise for instantaneous events.

the system in the knowledge representation style. We further showed that SNOOP in its original form can be partially, but not totally, recreated within the remodelled system by mapping each event onto its associated detection event.

We regard this result as establishing a preliminary bridge between the approaches to events espoused by the two communities. To make further progress it will be necessary, from the active database side, to investigate the effect on their applicability of the remodelling of the event-forming operators, and, on the knowledge representation side, to investigate the relation of the SNOOP-style operators to the event-constructors already in common use in knowledge representation contexts. We believe that there is scope for fruitful dialogue between the two communities in these endeavours.

Acknowledgments

We should like to thank Brian Lings and Jonas Mellin for useful feedback on this paper, and Pernilla Rönn for pointing out an error in our original definition of $\triangle$.

References

1. N. Gehani, H. Jagadish, and O. Shmueli. Event specification in an active object-oriented database. In *Proc. ACM SIGMOD Int. Conf. on Management of Data*, pages 81–90, San Diego, Calif., 1992.
2. Stella Gatziu and Klaus R. Dittrich. Events in an active object-oriented database system. In *Proc. 1st Int. Conf. on Rules in Database Systems*, Edinburgh, 1993.
3. Stella Gatziu and Klaus R. Dittrich. Detecting composite events in active database sytems using Petri nets. In *Proc. 4th Int. Workshop on Research Issues in Data Engineering: Active Database Systems*, pages 2–9, Edinburgh, 1994.
4. S. Chakravarty, V. Krishnaprasad, E. Anwar, and S.-K. Kim. Composite events for active database: Semantics, contexts, and detection. In *20th International Conference on Very Large Databases*, pages 606–617, Santiago, Chile, September 1994.
5. Elisa Bertino, Elena Ferrari, and Giovanna Guerrini. An approach to model and query event-based temporal data. In *Proceeedings of the Fifth International Workshop on Temporal Representation and Reasoning (TIME'98)*, pages 122–131. IEEE Computer Science Press, 1998.
6. Claudia L. Roncancio. Towards duration-based, constrained and dynamic event types. In Sten F. Andler and Jörgen Hansson, editors, *Active, Real-Time, and Temporal Database Systems (Proc.2nd Int. Workshop ARTDB-97, Como, Italy, September 1997)*, pages 176–193. Springer-Verlag, 1997.
7. James Allen. Towards a general theory of action and time. *Artificial Intelligence*, 23:123–54, 1984.
8. James Allen and George Ferguson. Actions and events in interval temporal logic. *Journal of Logic and Computation*, 4:531–79, 1994.
9. R. A. Kowalski and M. J. Sergot. A logic-based calculus of events. *New Generation Computing*, 4:67–95, 1986.
10. Antony P. Galton. Space, time and movement. In Oliviero Stock, editor, *Spatial and Temporal Reasoning*, pages 321–352. Kluwer Academic Publishers, Dordrecht, 1997.
11. Malik Ghallab. On chronicles: Representation, on-line recognition, and learning. In Luigia Carlucci Aiello, Jon Doyle, and Stuart Shapiro, editors, *Principles of Knowledge Representation and Reasoning (Proceedings of KR'96)*, pages 597–606, San Francisco, CA, 1996. Morgan Kaufmann.

CoSMo: An Approach Towards Conceptual Security Modeling

Christine Artelsmair[1], Wolfgang Essmayr[2], Peter Lang[1], Roland Wagner[1], and Edgar Weippl[2]

[1]Institute for Applied Knowledge Processing (FAW)
Hauptstr. 99, A-4232 Hagenberg, Austria
{cartelsmair, plang, rwagner}@faw.uni-linz.ac.at
[2]Software Competence Center Hagenberg (SCCH)
Hauptstr. 99, A-4232 Hagenberg, Austria
{edgar.weippl, wolfgang.essmayr}@scch.at

Abstract: Security is generally believed to be a very important topic. However, during software development security requirements are hardly ever properly treated, least of all on the conceptual level. Security is considered as some kind of add-on which will be applied to the system after development. To fill this gap we work on the development of a conceptual security modeling method we refer to as CoSMo Conceptual Security Modeling). In this paper first a comprehensive summary of available security modeling methodologies is presented. Second, various security requirements and mechanisms which are necessary for building secure software systems are described systematically to give a clear distinction between requirements and mechanisms to enforce the security requirements. Finally, a modeling example is given to illustrate particular security requirements and mechanisms.
keywords: security, security modeling, conceptual modeling

1 Introduction

Today computer security is a large and crucial topic in computer science. A plethora of books and papers have been written about different aspects of security. Computer security encompasses a lot of different areas, for instance: access control, trusted systems, biometric devices, only to name a few topics. Historically, computer security was viewed as an unnecessary impediment getting work done. Recently, users increasingly start to take computer security more seriously. However, despite this increased interest, many users still do not really understand the fundamentals of computer security.

Because of booming electronic commerce and the Internet, nowadays, security is viewed as a necessary building block of a system; without it, a system cannot reach the desired customer acceptance; e.g. an online banking system will not be accepted by customers if the system lacks adequate security features. There are many low-level frameworks, APIs and technologies available which ease the development of new

R. Cicchetti et al. (Eds.): DEXA 2002, LNCS 2453, pp. 557–566, 2002.

systems. Nonetheless, security is often considered to be an add-on to a new system. This may be due to the lack of an appropriate conceptual modeling technique for security. Section 2 presents the state-of-the-art in security modeling techniques in literature. Section 3 and 4 introduce CoSMo (Conceptual Security Modeling) our approach towards conceptual security modeling. Finally, the paper is concluded with an outlook on future work.

2 Related Work

Although security is considered to be an important topic, not much work has been published on conceptual security modeling. Security requirements are described in different ways such as: semantic data modeling, modeling of business processes or risk analysis. This section gives a brief summary of each of these mentioned approaches.

Semantic Data Modeling

One of the first approach on conceptual security modeling was made in [1] and [2]. The author introduces the semantic data model for security (SDMS) which is based on a conceptual database model and a constraint language focusing on multilevel secure database systems. [3] introduces a security constraint language (SCL) and a graphical notation. The approach is restricted to multilevel secure database applications. The graphical notation is based on entity relationship diagrams ([4]). In [5] the approach of [3] is extended for object-oriented software development. The approach is based on OMT ([6]). Various OMT diagrams are extended by security aware elements which help to analyze different views of a real world situation.

Modeling of Business Processes

[7], [8] and [9] present an approach which primarily focuses on modeling secure business processes. The approach is called MOSS (Modeling Security Semantics of business transactions) where a business process is illustrated by some kind of activity diagram which is enriched with security aware elements. Furthermore, an infrastructure for secure and fair electronic commerce named COPS (Commercial Protocols and Services) is introduced. Last but not least, a three-layered framework is proposed. This framework helps security- and domain experts to build up a common view on a business process. The framework supports the development of secure software by offering a set of reusable components.

Risk Analysis

[10] and [11] deal with the analysis of the security risks in information systems. Based upon a formal model of an information system, a process model is presented which deals with the modeling of security risks. This process model contains six steps. After determining the security requests, possible threats for the system are identified and arising risks are collected. After rechecking the security requirements

will be refined based on the knowledge gained so far. Furthermore, the authors present a software tool to assist risk analysis according their approach.

Contribution of CoSMo

The modeling methods described and developed so far are not easily applicable for conceptual modeling and for developing secure software systems with UML. Either the developed method supports modeling of database applications with multilevel security or it focuses on the modeling of software systems for risk analysis. Methods developed for the analysis of secure business process are also not applicable for conceptual modeling of a single software system. Due to this lack of an appropriate method a method will be developed which is based on UML and deals with the conceptual modeling of secure information systems. The graphical representation of UML is easily understandable and helps to build up a common understanding of a new system. In the final version CoSMo will provide a method for conceptual modeling of secure software systems on the basis of UML.

3 CoSMo Security Modeling Basics: Security Requirements and Mechanisms

The security requirements of a system are specified by means of a security policy that is enforced by various security mechanisms. A security policy consists of a set of laws, rules and practices that regulate how an organization manages, protects and distributes sensitive information [3]. The following sections provide an overview of the most popular security requirements and security mechanisms which have been identified as the basics for security modeling in CoSMo.

Each security requirement can be enforced by one or more security mechanisms, resulting in a requirements/mechanisms matrix which is presented at the end of this chapter in Table 1. Security requirements and mechanisms are generically formu lated at a high level of abstraction.

Authenticity, Authentication, Identification

Authentication typically addresses the requirement of ensuring authenticity. Authenticity respectively authentication can take several forms:

- General identity authenticity/authentication
- Message content authenticity/authentication
- Message origin authenticity/authentication

General identity authentication is commonly handled by entering your username (identification) and password (authentication) on a login screen. *Message content authentication* is the process of verifying that the content of a received message is the same as when it was sent. Message content authentication itself includes the mechanism of *encryption* and is based on symmetric algorithms (refer to [12]). *Message origin authentication* is the process of verifying that the sender and origin of a received message are the same. It is enforced by the corresponding message origin authentication mechanism, including the concepts of *digital signatures*, *digital certificates* and *trusted third parties* (see below).

Integrity, Secrecy, Privacy

To ensure integrity (or consistency) requires to maintain only information that is correct and complete (*semantic integrity*) and to protect information from being modified by unauthorized actors (*protection integrity*) [13]. Semantic integrity is usually enforced by a schema, for example a database schema.

Secrecy (or confidentiality) denotes the protection of information from improper and unauthorized disclosure. Secrecy can be enforced by controlling who is granted access to the system (general identity authentication), and controlling the privileges of users (access control). Applying encryption is another way to keep information secret.

Privacy protection is a fundamental personal right of all individuals. Individuals have the right to expect that organizations will keep personal information confidential. Thus similar security mechanisms enforcing secrecy have to be applied.

Integrity Constraints, Secrecy Constraints

According to [1] there are two basic types of security constraints which correspond directly to integrity and secrecy. In general, *integrity constraints* are rules governing the update (i.e., create, modify, delete) and validation of data. *Secrecy constraints* are rules governing the classification of data and access to it. Both types of constraints are each further subdivided into two subtypes: semantic and access control constraints.

Semantic integrity constraints allow defining and maintaining the correct states of an information system during operation. Examples include: a student's birthday must be a valid date and every student must have an address. Semantic integrity constraints are used to enforce semantic integrity (see above).

Access control integrity constraints are the explicit statements of which users are authorized to modify which data items; for example, only the system administrator is allowed to add students or modify student data. Since access control integrity constraints can protect against malicious or accidental modification of information, they are a means to enforce protection integrity (see above).

Semantic secrecy constraints specify the level(s) at which data, and the associations between data, are classified. Examples include: the names of students are P (public), and the student's examination results are S (secret).

Access control secrecy constraints specify which users are authorized to access which data items. Example includes: students can only see data related to the examination which they have passed.

Both semantic secrecy constraints as well as access control secrecy constraints are applied to ensure secrecy and privacy.

Authorization, Access Control, Availability

Authorization is the specification of a set of rules about “who has which type of access to what information”. *Access control* is captured by procedures that control authorization by limiting access to stored data to authorized users only. Access control usually requires authentication as a prerequisite.

Authorization and access control mainly address the secrecy and privacy requirements for information systems.

Access control can take several forms [14]:

- Discretionary access control (DAC)
- Lattice-based access controls, also known as mandatory access controls (MAC)
- Role-based access control (RBAC)

Availability is the requirement of serving authorized actors with information whenever requested. To ensure availability requires to protect information from improper withholding from authorized actors. Keeping information available is a result of controlling access to data.

Accountability, Auditing, Non-repudiation

Accountability captures the requirement, that individuals can be made responsible for security relevant activities, which can be achieved by the mechanism of auditing.

Non-repudiation prevents an individual from denying having performed a particular action related to data. Non-repudiation is a particular case of accountability. Non-repudiation is a requirement achieved through *cryptographic methods* (see below). Additionally, the draft standard [15] promotes the use of *trusted third parties*: "Trusted third parties may be involved in the provision of non-repudiation services, depending on the mechanisms used and the non-repudiation policy in force."

The mechanism to keep records of all security-relevant actions issued by a user is called *auditing* [3]. Auditing consists of two components: the collection and organization of audit data and an analysis of the data to discover security violations.

Anonymity, Originality

Simply stated, *anonymity* is the absence of identity. [16] proposes a broader definition of the term anonymity: "Protecting certain activities from being traced back by unauthorized individuals or organizations".

Several situations require an electronic document's originality being proved. One must be sure of not holding a copy of the document. Electronic documents such as shares are only of value if they satisfy the criteria *originality*.

[17] have identified two different general approaches to provide anonymity in the Internet:

1. Anonymous services: Based on a non-anonymous transport system (layer 1-4 in the OSI reference model), try to implement anonymity in higher layers as far as it is desired.
2. Anonymous networks: Implement anonymity in the lower OSI layers and build different services upon it with anonymity to a certain extent (e.g. real anonymity, pseudo-anonymity, optional self-identification).

At this point we can introduce a new security mechanism, which is the concept of *infrastructure*. Consequently, by implementing some infrastructure (e.g., anonymous services or anonymous networks), one can achieve anonymity, when communicating over insecure channels such as the Internet.

Furthermore, in [18] the need for anonymity and originality in the context of electronic markets is discussed. In their work they specify a secure electronic market infrastructure for free tradable, anonymous and original emission permits by using *cryptographic methods* and organizational measures such as *trusted third parties* (see below).

Validity

Digital contracts and signatures do not only have a legal validity, since the rapid technical development may cause digital signatures to be invalid prior to the legal invalidity due to compromised keys or cracked algorithms. Proving validity of digital contracts or signatures requires additional *infrastructure* in the organization. For example, a new role in the organization is necessary which is responsible for re-signing documents when the corresponding certificate of the own enterprise is expired or is declared invalid and for the verification of signatures of contract partners.

Cryptography and Cryptographic Mechanisms

The cryptographic mechanisms most frequently applied according [12] are: i) encryption algorithms, ii) digital signatures and iii) integrity check functions (cryptographic hash function).

Encryption algorithms protect the confidentiality of data. An encryption algorithm, also called a *cipher*, enciphers plaintext under the control of a cryptographic key. Decryption with the appropriate decryption key retrieves the plaintext from the ciphertext. *Digital signatures* provide message integrity and authenticity. They are used for verifying that a message really is originated from a claimed sender. *Cryptographic hash functions* transform a variable-size input message into a fixed-size hash value, the message digest [16]. Hash functions are typically used in connection with digital signatures in order to reduce the message size for which a signature has to be given.

Digital Certificate, Trusted Third Party

Digital certificates are used for showing and proving the authenticity (message origin authenticity) of the involved communication participants. For instance, certifying a public key proves that it belongs to a particular individual or organization. A *certification authority* (CA) acts as a trusted third party and guarantees the link between user (organization) and cryptographic key by signing a document that contains username, key, name of the CA, expiry date, etc. More generally, *trusted third parties* are participants in electronic markets in which other participants are forced to trust, because they perform sensible tasks. In their use for public-key certification they offer an infrastructure to support legal binding of electronic documents. Another example is the usage of trusted third parties to realize fair electronic auction markets.

Summary

The sections above provide a comprehensive overview of traditional security requirements and security mechanisms as can be found in literature. The presented requirements and mechanisms are an extensible overview and do not have the demand to be complete.

As emphasized, there are several security mechanisms enforcing different security requirements. Table 1 gives a comprehensive overview and illustrates requirements to corresponding mechanisms.

Table 1. The requirements/mechanisms matrix: security requirements can be enforced by various security mechanisms

mechanisms \ requirements	general identity authenticity	message content authenticity	message origin authenticity	semantic integrity	protection integrity	secrecy	privacy	availability	accountability	anonymity	originality	validity	non-repudiation
identification	X												
general identity authentication	X					X	X						
message content authentication		X											
message origin authentication			X										
schema information				X									
semantic integrity constraints				X									
access control integrity constraints					X								
semantic secrecy constraints						X	X						
access control secrecy constraints						X	X						
access control						X	X	X					
auditing									X				
infrastructure										X		X	
encryption algorithms		X	X			X	X			X	X		X
digital signatures			X										X
digital certificates			X										
trusted third parties										X	X		X

4 Case Study

In this section an example to demonstrate the requirements for the CoSMo approach is presented. The above-mentioned separation between security requirements and mechanisms are taken into account. Furthermore, security requirements are named that already be dealt with at a conceptual level to give a basic idea of CoSMo. As example an application is described which supports the management of courses and examinations offered on a university. The use-case diagram shown in Fig. 1 represents a state-of-the-art UML diagram of some basic features of the system. For example, the claimed security requirement "a student must be identified before he executes use-case *register course* is not part of the use-case diagram but is part of the description of the use-case. In CoSMo it will be possible to model this security requirement on the conceptual level already in a use-case diagram. Important to note is that only the security requirements are demanded but there are no mechanism specified how to realize these requirements. The use-case diagram given may be enriched already at the conceptual level by the following security requirements:

- **authenticity:** Lectors and secretaries must authenticate themselves to execute use-cases *create course* and *edit course*. Students must authenticate themselves to register for a course. The use-case *view course* may be executed by any actor without authenticating himself.
- **non-repudiation:** Security relevant use-cases like *register course* may be audited, so that the user cannot deny having performed a particular action.
- **secrecy of data:** Lectors and secretaries have a different view on the data of a course than a student has.

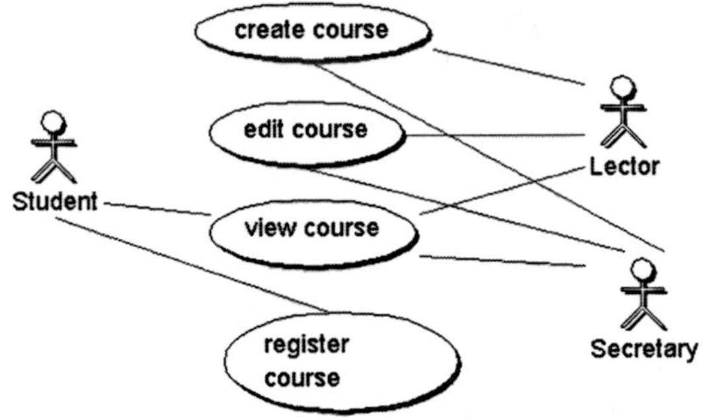

Fig. 1. use case "course administration"

The information system should not only support the administration of the teaching offers possible but also the handling of examinations. On the conceptual level the following sequence diagram (Fig. 2) may be used to express the following security requirements:

- **authenticity:** Students and lectors have to authenticate themselves if they want to execute the functions *fix date (of exam)*, *register for exam*, *correct examination papers* or *view grade*.
- **secrecy of data:** The Statistics user does not have the right to access individual grades but is allowed to read the grades for statistical purpose.

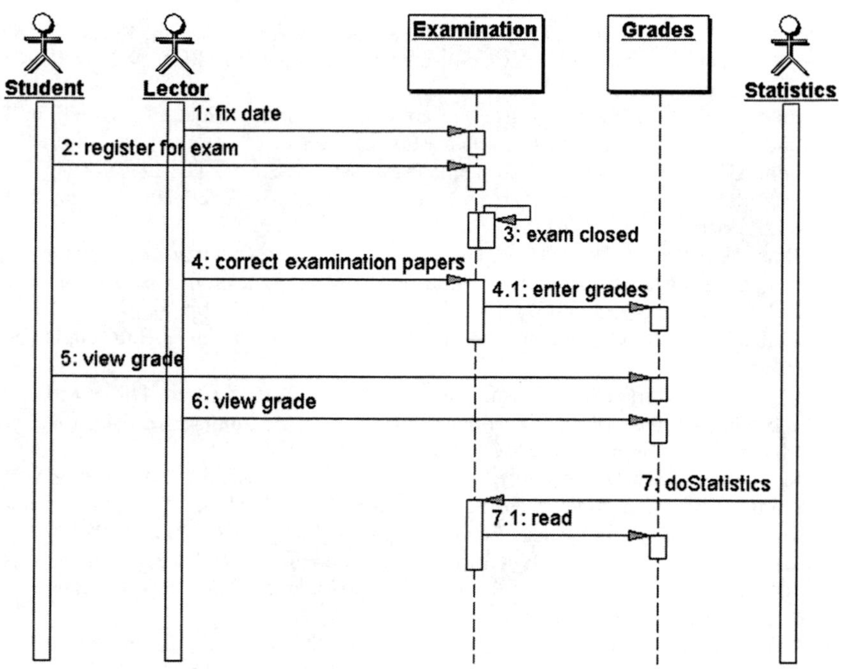

Fig. 2. sequence diagram "examination"

5 Conclusion

In this paper we first identified the need to integrate security considerations into the software modeling process. Conceptual modeling should have to encompass security requirements and high-level security mechanisms.

Prior to an overview of which security mechanisms can enforce which requirements, fundamental issues of security policies were elaborated. The aforementioned clear distinction between requirements and mechanisms is highlighted in an example application.

Our contribution is twofold: First and foremost we show how security considerations can be integrated into the process of conceptual modeling. Second, we systematically enumerate frequently encountered security requirements and clearly indicate which mechanisms are used to enforce them.

The next steps in the development of CoSMo will be the definition of a formal notation based on UML and the integration it into existing toolkits.

References

1. Smith, G. W., The Sematic Data Model for Security: Representing the Security Semantics of an Application, Proc. 6th Int'l Conf. on Data Engineering (ICDE'90), IEEE, Computer Society Press
2. Smith, G. W., Modeling Security Relevant Data Semantics, Proc. 1990 Symp. on Research in Security and Privacy, IEEE Computer Society Press
3. Pernul G., Database Security, Academic Press, 1994, ISBN# 0-12-012138-7
4. Chen, P. P., The Entity Relationship Model: Towards a Unified View of Data, ACM Trans. on Database Systems (TODS), Vol. 1(1)
5. Ellmer E., Pernul G., Kappel G., Object-Oriented Modeling of Security Semantics, Proceedings of the 11th Annual Computer Security Applications Conference (ACSAC'95), IEEE Computer Society Press, New Orleans (LA), Dec. 1995, pp. 52-61
6. Rumbauh, J. et al., Object-Oriented Modeling and Design, Prentice Hall, Englewood Cliffs, NJ, 1991
7. Herrmann G., Pernul G., Viewing Business Process Security from Different Perspectives, Proceedings of the 11th Int'l Bled Electronic Commerce Conference "Electronic commerce in the Information Society". Slovenia, 1998, pp. 89-103
8. Herrmann G., Security and Integrity Requirements of Business Processes – Analysis and Approach to Support their Realization, Proc. CAiSE*99 6th Doctoral Consortium on Advanced Information Systems Engineering, Heidelberg, 14-15. June, 1999, pp.36-47
9. Röhm A., Pernul G., COPS: A Model and Infrastructure for Secure and Fair Electronic Markets, IEEE Proceedings of the Hawai'i International Conference On System Sciences 32, January 5-8, 1999, Maui, Hawai'i.
10. Thoben W., Sicherheitsanforderungen im Rahmen der Bedrohungs- und Risikoanalyse von IT-Systemen, Datenbanksysteme in Büro, Technik und Wissenschaft (BTW '97), Springer-Verlag, S. 279-298, 1997
11. Schönberg A., Thoben W.., Ein unscharfes Bewertungskonzept für die Bedrohungs- und Risikoanalyse Workflow-basierter Anwendungen, Sicherheit und Electronic Commerce - Konzepte, Modelle und technische Möglichkeiten (WS SEC'98), A. Röhm, D. Fox, R. Grimm und D. Schoder (Hrsg.), S. 47-62, Vieweg-Verlag, Essen, Oktober 98
12. Gollmann D., Computer Security, John Wiley & Sohns, 1999, ISBN# 0-471-97844-2
13. Bichler P.: Conceptual Design of Secure Workflow Systems. An Object-Oriented Approach to the Uniform Modeling of Workflows, Organizations and Security. Dissertation,
14. Sandhu R., Samarati P., Authentication, Access Control and Audit, ACM Computing Surveys, Vol. 28, No.1, March 1996
15. International Organisation for Standardization (ISO): Information processing systems – Guidelines for the Use and Management of Trusted Third Parties – Part 2: Technical Aspects. International Standard ISO/IEC Draft 14516-2, Genf, 1995
16. Eßmayr W., Role-Based Access Controls in Interoperable Environments, Faculty of Natural Sciences and Engineering Johannes Kepler University Linz, PhD Thesis, January 1999
17. Berthold O., Federrath H., Köhntopp M. Project "Anonymity and Unobservability in the Internet", Workshop on Freedom and Privacy by Design CFP2000, Toronto, 2000
18. Gerhard M., Röhm A., A Secure Electronic Market for Anonymous Transferable Emission Permits, IEEE Proceedings of the Hawai'i International Conference On System Sciences 31, vol. 4, January 6-9, 1998, Kona, Hawai'i

Exploring the Concept of Group Interaction through Action in a Mobile Context

Rikard Harr

Department of Informatics, Umeå University, 901 87 Umeå, Sweden
rikard.harr@informatik.umu.se

Abstract. This paper explores the concept of interaction through action. The exploration is done empirically in the setting of bird hunting. Using qualitative research methods, we studied how a hunting group secure awareness in order to coordinate their actions and to collaborate. We analyzed the data using a modified CSCW-model and found that the methods for securing awareness and coordination are rather complex and that environmental constraints play important roles. Dealing with coordination and collaboration in a setting such as the one we study is not easy. Based on the empirical findings, we derive design implications to consider in the design of artifacts for supporting group activity grounded on the concept of interaction through action.

1 A Forgotten Field

Today the usage of information technology have increased and the IT support for group activities is highly developed. In organisations, groupware makes it possible to coordinate work and the communication infrastructure is very advanced. But it seems as if some human group activities are isolated from this evolution, the group activity of hunting for example. The activity takes place in a setting with a low frequency of artefacts and with lots of outer constraints such as variation in vegetation and weather. Group activities in the wild seem to have been left behind in the technological evolution. How do groups manage to coordinate their activities and secure collaboration between participants?

Reviewing the literature on the topic we found some research that had explored HCI issues in wild settings[1]. Authors are mostly concerned with technical demands on artefacts to support individual activities in such environments [4, 5, 6]. We also found literature about coordination, communication and collaboration in groups, but not in settings with a low frequency of artefacts and not through the aspects of interaction through action. Accordingly, no research so far has explored the aspects of interaction through action. How is the group activity of collaboration, coordination and communication structured in a context with a low level of artefacts and in an environment where ordinary methods to secure these issues are constrained?

In order to investigate the question empirically, we conducted an empirical study of a hunting group in northern Sweden. Using qualitative research methods, we studied how the group coordinate, communicate and collaborate in order to make the hunting session as fruitful and safe as possible. We analysed the data using the "CSCW framework" [7].

R. Cicchetti et al. (Eds.): DEXA 2002, LNCS 2453, pp. 567–576, 2002.

The rest of the paper is structured as follows: Section 2 contains a background describing how group activities are supported. Section 3 presents the theoretical framework. In section 4 we introduce the empirical study, i.e. bird hunting in Lövånger/Västerbotten, Sweden. Section 4 presents the main results from the study. We do so by applying the "CSCW framework" [7] on the empirical data. Finally in section 5 we conclude the paper and present implications to consider in the design of artifacts for supporting group activity grounded on the concept of interaction through action.

2 Background: Interaction through Action, Organization of Team Activities and Awareness

In this section we describe in more detail the concept of interaction through action, the organization of group activities and the importance of awareness.

2.1 Interaction through Action

One reason for people to collaborate is that they can achieve things together that is not possible to achieve for the individual [8]. A collaborative group can improve some aspects of their activities by doing it as a group and not as individuals. Co-watching a movie makes it more fun, co-diving makes diving safer and co-hunting is both more effective and safer.

The "CSCW framework" [7] shows aspects of group activities and describes the relation between participants, and participants and an object. The facilitation and study of this communication is very important to the field of CSCW, but it is not all there is to CSCW. The term implies that the participants often have some object that they are working upon. The nature of the object is what decides if one or more of the participants can control, modify or affect it. The participants will, under normal circumstances, be able to receive feedback of their own actions and receive feedthrough from the actions of others.

To be able to receive feedthrough from the actions of others is essential in many cooperative situations. Dix and Beale [7] claim that this feedthrough is many times more important than the direct communication. Their model is shown in figure 1:

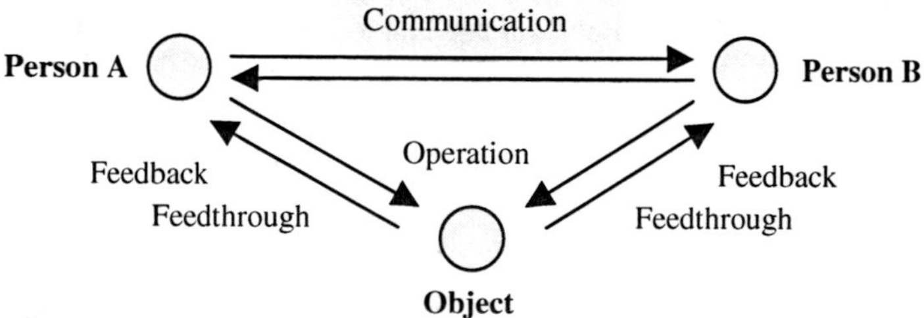

Fig. 1. The "CSCW framework" shows how collaboration is managed through action/reaction and a more or less shared view of situation.

2.2 Organization of Team Activities

There are two levels of activities and performance in a collaborating group. You have your own performance in relation to yourself and you have your performance in relation to the group. As Hutchins [8] claims, team performance make things possible to achieve for the group that would be impossible to achieve individually, at least in the same effective way. This is mainly why groups are formed, to achieve better results or in order to be more effective. There are other reasons for teams to be formed as well, for example social reasons.

The performances of teams can be classified as sequentially unconstrained or constrained. Hutchins [8] defines a procedure as sequentially unconstrained if "the execution of any enabled operation will never disable any other enabled but as yet unexecuted operation". If the task has no sequential constraints it can be accomplished by a "swarm of ants" strategy [8]. This means that there is no need for communication between the participants only feedthrough because of their effect on the shared environment. Hutchins defines a procedure as sequentially constrained "if the execution of any enabled operation will disable any other enabled but as yet unexecuted operation" [8]. This means that actions are dependent of the actions of others.

But the participants of a team also take action individually. This means that while performing, each and every participant of the group is involved in a "mixed-focus situation" [2]. Group members shift their attention continuously between group and individual activity. Therefore it is important that the environment allows quick gathering of information in order to maintain a feeling of awareness of what the other participants are doing and where they are.

Kirsh [9] discusses the coordination of a football team where the roles of the players are not specified completely, because of the dynamics of the situation in the field. They have to understand the point of their role in relation to the play as a whole. If things go well it leads to desirable results. A leader is required to add some constraints.

In order to form a platform for action, the use of "human interfaces" [8] is essential in a setting as the one we studied. The use of a human interface is when one person makes another person a human interface to a task. This means that a person acquire information about something through another person.

2.3 Awareness

The coordination of group activities highlights the need for awareness in group activities as it is impossible to know when to execute an operation for one participant if the operations of others are unknown. Sequentially unconstrained procedures on the other hand are more easy to distribute or can be solved by systems that are very loosely interconnected. Sequentially constrained procedures require coordination among the actions to be taken. However, there are ways to achieve this coordination. One way is to secure that each group member knows how to act when certain conditions in the environment are produced [8].

Awareness has been defined as "[...] an understanding of the activities of others, which provides a context for your own activity" [1].

In order to support awareness, one should see to it that information leaves the scene of work and that one's colleagues receive the information. The possibility to be aware of the actions of one's colleagues is better, the more information one receive. There is however is a flip side on that coin, the more information we receive from others, the greater the risk that the information will disturb our normal work [3]. One thing that is important to know is that it is never possible for anyone, at any point to have complete overview in a distributed and mobile setting [11].

In the coordination of group activities information about awareness is always needed [10]. Accordingly you have to be aware of the actions of others to be able to respond to them and in order to collaborate as a group and achieve coordination. Dourish and Belotti [10] claim that awareness provides a context for the action of any individual in the group through helping actors to understand the actions of others. Further, the context is used to guarantee that the contributions of every individual are relevant to the activity of the group, and to evaluate the actions of participants with respect to the goals of the group and the progress.

In an environment where you have full awareness of all participants of the group activity, it is easy to coordinate the action of each and every individual, and even if the procedures are sequentially constrained, it is not a problem. However in a situation where the possibility for securing awareness sometimes is bad, a need for buffers [8] arises. Hutchins claims: "buffering prevents the uncontrolled propagation of effects from one part of the system to another" [8].

3 Theoretical Framework

In order to explore interaction through action in a mobile setting, we found it necessary to develop a conceptual framework to guide the study, and in particular to analyse the empirical data. The fact that it, in the setting where we conducted our study, does not exist shared object, forced us to modify the model "CSCW framework" [7]. The one thing that to some extent is shared between participants is the view of situation. The modified model that we have used is shown in figure 2.

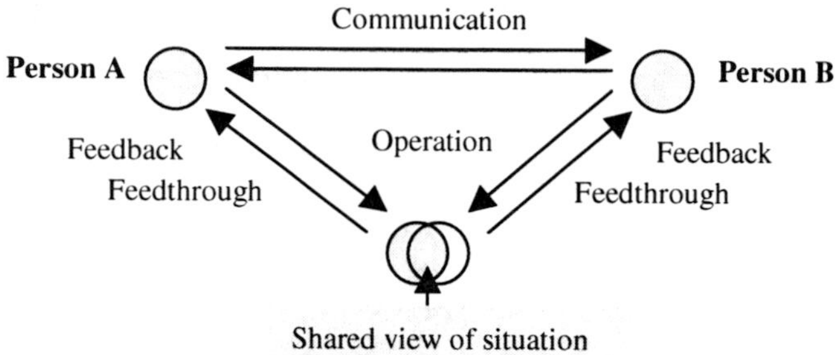

Fig. 2. The theoretical framework of the study

The framework above makes it possible to explore the procedure of interaction through action in a wild setting. The model suggests that communication is the exchange of some kind of information between people and that collaboration is when two or more people operate a shared view of situation. When one person changes his/her view of situation it changes the shared view. When doing that the person receive feedback and the other participant receives feedthrough. According to Ljungberg [12], we can in the context of the model conceive collaboration and communication as subsets of interaction. It is important to have some level of coincident view in order to secure some level of collaboration. If the coincident is complete, Person B also experiences everything about the situation that is experienced by Person A, and vice versa. And if the views of situation are totally different, then we have a breakdown.

4 Entering the Forgotten Field

We now wish to direct the attention to the results of the empirical study of this paper. The research issue we have explored is how group communication, coordination and collaboration is supported in mobile settings with a low level of artefacts.

4.1 Method

We used ethnographic techniques to collect data, i.e. qualitative interviewing and participating observation. Hammersly and Atkinson [13] describe ethnography as follows:

"In its most characteristic form it involves the ethnographer participating, overtly or covertly, in people's daily lives for an extended period of time, watching what happens, listening to what is said, asking questions – in fact, collecting whatever data are available to throw light on the issues that are the focus of the research. [13]"

Ethnography should last for an extended period of time, our study did not, but we used ethnographic techniques during our data collection phase. We made participant observations of a bird-hunting expedition. While studying the bird-hunting group we participated during two days, approximately 15 hours and afterwards we conducted tree qualitative interviews [14]. Only four hunters participated in the hunting session (one of them was the author of this paper) and that is why the number of interviews is relatively low. All interviews lasted between 30-45 minutes. The empirical data was analysed using the theoretical framework shown in figure 2 above.

4.2 Research Sites

The bird-hunting group is a group of three hunters (and me) who bird hunts together for a weekend every year. The host is a frequent hunter in the area, the rest of the participants have some knowledge of the terrain but for the author it was very limited. The hunting area is located in the north of Sweden, in a village named Lövånger, located approximately 90 km north of Umeå. The hunting session started an early Saturday morning in September.

A hunting session is normally divided into a couple of rounds. Every round starts with instructions from the guide. Normally he says something about the vegetation and he always say where the group shall reunite. Sometimes other information is of interest, for example rough passages or maybe an anecdote. Then the participants form a line with 30-50 meters in between and on a given signal they start moving. They try to move with a constant velocity in order to maintain the formation.

The shooting line is supposed to cover as much area as possible as the group move through the forest. The aim is to force birds to take off in front of the line so that a hunter can take a shot. The line is supposed to scare the birds and to force them to take off. The formation makes it easier to cover larger areas and if a bird takes off in front off the line it is more likely that some one or several of the hunters get the chance to shoot.

The guide normally walks on one of the ends of the shooting line in order to direct the movement. The one person next to him/her has to move according to the guide in order to keep the chain intact. The third person moves according to the second and so on. It is important to keep the line through keeping the same speed and direction as the person you orientate by. Being aware is crucial for the hunting session.

Besides the four hunters, there was also a dog participating in the hunting session. The dog is supposed to search for birds in front of the line and to force them to take off and land in a tree. The dog then distracts the birds with a constant barking. The birds then focus on the dog and one or more hunters can sneak within shooting distance and take a shot. Another area where the dog is useful is when a bird is wounded and a hunter need help to catch it.

The level of technological equipment to support collaboration used by the hunters is almost none, some hunters use a compass and some wear their cellulars (in case of emergency).

The activity of bird hunting, as this group pursue it can be viewed as follows:

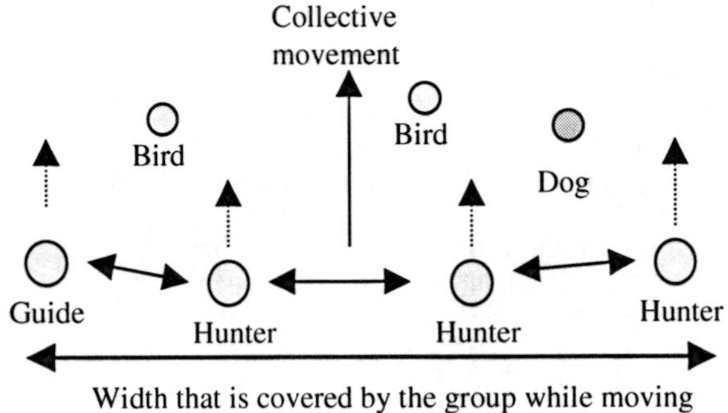

Fig.3. The activity of bird hunting, as this group pursue it

5 Results

We now apply the "CSCW framework" [7] on the model above, by going through the empirical data.

5.1 Feedback

The operations that a person does on his/her view of a situation give immediate feedback. There is however, a problem with feedback. If you drift off it and loose contact with the others it is very difficult to get feedback about the new situation you are in. This means that if you are not sharing view of situation with the others, it is almost impossible to take further actions. The support that you have for making your next move is the plan that the group made together in the beginning, and maybe a wild guess, and that is not enough.

5.2 Feedthrough

The level of feedthrough that other participants receive on the actions of a participant varies a lot. Because of the chain formation it is very rare that all participants receive the same feedthrough. Often the hunter next to the person that produces the feedthrough is the only one that receives it and can act accordingly. This means that the next person in line then have to receive feedthrough from the second person in order to act accordingly. If no feedthrough is provided the shared view of situation is impossible to achieve.

There is often a slack between an execution of an operation and for a participant to perceive the feedthrough of that operation, in that way feedthrough is communicated from one end of the firing line to the other. This means that it could take a while for it to reach all participants. For example if a person on the edge of the line avoids a certain area, maybe a ditch or trench, this may cause him to move towards the others. This starts a chain reaction where everybody moves further away. Only the second man in line does it because of the feedthrough from the action from the first person, the others they do it because the person next to them does it. Because of the slack it is therefore possible that the first person that avoided the obstacle may have returned to his position before the last person has responded to the first movement. This means that the firing line is almost always moving, not only forward, but also from side to side.

5.3 Communication

The ability to communicate with other participants varies a lot, depending on many factors. The density of the forest sometimes makes it difficult to signal to each other, and the level of communication through signalling is low. To speak or shout between participants is often out of the question since it scares the birds. This highlights the importance of buffers. Buffers are not something that is managed centrally but is managed inside the heads of every participant. For example if you do not know where the others are, then you have to remember the last time you saw someone and estimate the speed and direction that the person moved in on that occasion in order to act upon his/her movement. You also have to think about any obstacles that could have influenced the choice of path that the other person might have made, this is of course very difficult. This use of buffers is a part of communication through action and it means that lots of attention has to be directed towards other participants. But it also means that while a person is performing an egoistic operation, he is also communicating to the others. So by firing a shot, for example, you communicate something to everyone. But what you communicate is difficult to say, according to our study there are several reasons for firing: To shoot a bird, to signal where you are if you are lost or to notify the others that you've seen a bird.

During our interviews, we were told that the need for verbal communication is low during the sessions, but because of the social nature of hunting is the same need between the sessions high. One person gave an example were it is very frustrating not to be able to talk, and that is when the group walks in an open field and one participant spot something and want to direct the movement towards it. He complained that the possibilities to have some higher level of verbal interaction are low. However, the main opinion is that this is not a problem.

5.4 Operation

The operation is the actions that a hunter takes. Some operations provide a good feedthrough to the others, like a shot, and some operations do not, for example if a hunter drifts off or stops.

Because of the fact that you act upon the actions of the participants next to you and the feedthrough of their operations, it is possible that the actions of the participants on both sides of you provide feedthrough that collide. This means that the feedthrough is redundant and difficult to act upon. The opposite situation is also possible, when you do not receive feedthrough from anyone and you do not know how to act. This situation is often solved by going back to the plan, and through keeping the same direction as in the beginning, maybe with the help of a compass. This is what we call a breakdown, when you are not aware about the situations of the others and when you have low support for making decisions. In case of a breakdown, and if the hunter is not wearing a compass and the clouds make it impossible to orientate by the sun, things can get pretty ugly.

Normally the operations that a participant take is within the common sense of the group, for example you have to avoid a trench but you keep the contact with the shooting line, there are though, times when a participant break the pattern and then the awareness is threatened. There are in fact several events that could trigger a break of the shooting line: to get out of dense vegetation, to shoot at a bird, to sneak on a bird that one observes, if the dog starts barking and you sneak towards the bark or if someone shoots and you move into a better position.

5.5 View of Situation

The view of the situation that a person has is changing continuously. The use of buffers makes it possible to relate the movement and actions of oneself to the actions and movements of others. In that way you achieve a level of awareness. To be able to secure awareness the hunter uses eyes, ears, buffers, and memory of the direction, knowledge of the terrain and also knowledge of each other and the hunting plan. When something happens, for example when the dog starts barking, then the hunter has to decide how to act upon the event. If he feels that the dog is closest to him, then he moves toward it. With satisfying awareness and with a certain level of shared view of situation this makes the shooting line stop for a while and the hunter can operate without any risk. But if there is a low level of awareness and if the level of shared view is low, then there could be a risk. It is possible that more than one of the participants believe that he or she is the one that is closest to the dog. This means that hunters get within shooting range of each other and that they do not know where the others are.

The use of buffers is something that helps participants to maintain their view of the situation. If a hunter loose contact of the others he/she tries to remember the velocity and direction of the others in order to position himself in relation to them and create a view of his situation and also the shared situation.

5.6 Shared View of Situation

As we mentioned earlier it is a good thing if the shared view is indeed shared between the participants. In that way the coordination and collaboration is easy to achieve and the hunting session is safe and effective. The shared view is achieved through knowing each other, knowing the terrain, input through senses. To achieve a completely shared view within the group everyone would have to be standing at the same point and share the same values and knowledge. But then the hunting session would not be that effective.

It seems as if there are ways to achieve an acceptable level of shared view of situation under certain circumstances. These circumstances are good sensory input, terrain that is not too dense, good knowledge of each other's behaviour, the terrain and the plan. However this is seldom the case.

The fact that the goal and the starting point is briefed in the beginning and that the guide give some introduction to the hunting area makes it possible to keep a shared view. For example if the guide says that we should walk towards the sun for about 45 minutes, then we all know that it is a good thing to have the sun in the face, and as long as we do we are in some way coordinated with the others, and have somewhat a shared view with the others. If everyone used a compass it would be easier.

The shared view of situation is of course improved if the participants are familiar with the terrain in the area were the hunting session takes place. But even if the position of oneself is known, the possibility to know the positions of the others and the relative position is not secured.

7 Discussion

This paper has explored the concept of interaction through action in order to support collaboration for groups in mobile wild settings.

This paper has shown that the collaboration of a hunting group is structured in a very special way that leaves a lot to the judgement of every participant and there is a great variation in the way that participants operate, this variation is a problem. We have to remember that we are dealing with lethal weapons. Incidents do happen. Often, the only thing that happens is that the session is cancelled and the group has to look for a hunter that is lost, but every year people get shot in the forest. And during our interviews some examples of terrifying incidents were brought up. This group has hunted together before and they know each other in some way, but today it is quite common that a hunting group contains people that do not know each other, they may not even speak the same language.

So, if we were to think about implications for the design of some artefact based on the outcome of this study. First, while moving in the forest, there is a mixed-focus [2] situation indeed. The switch back and forth from the individual and the shared activity and vice versa is crucial. Because of this the time used to alternate from one to the other needs to be as short as possible.

A second implication is the fact that depending of the density of the vegetation, the distance between hunters varies from 15 to maybe 50 meters. The denser the vegetation is, the shorter distance. This is a method to secure awareness of each other and also to make the session as effective as possible. If you walk close the total width of the firing line gets small and this makes the area that is swept small and also the chance of finding birds, but the securing of awareness is easier to achieve in that way. The alternative is to keep a longer distance between the hunters in order to make the width of the firing line larger and in that way encounter more birds. This is a trade-off that is important to be aware off in future designs.

A third implication is that awareness is crucial in the activity of hunting. The way that this is secured today is through a rather complicated process with human interfaces and interaction through action. An artefact on which relative positioning could be presented would improve the hunt in many ways. Incidents where people get lost would occur less frequently, so would accidental shots.

A fourth implication is the fact that lots of the interaction during a hunt is interaction through action brings the conclusion that to be aware of the movements and positions of others is much more important than to be able to talk to each other. This means that the use of walkie-talkies never can solve all issues, but this does not mean that a walkie-talkie is not useful in this kind of setting, it is, but as a compass, it can only do so much.

The fifth implication that we would like to make is the fact that hunting has to be hunting. The unpredictability of hunting is very important and should never be threatened by any invention. But there are two reasons for using this kind of IT for bird hunters. First, during our interviews all respondents talked about some incident that could have led to a serious accident. The number of accidents that happens during hunting is not acceptable. The second reason is that the efficiency of the hunting session could be improved by IT. Today it is quite common to disorientate and get lost or left behind. This means that the hunter becomes inactive and the efficiency is damaged.

The final implication that we would like to make is that this study stresses another area for expert systems (ES) than the conventional one. Most work on ES has focused on applying ES technology on data processing areas [15]. The implications that this paper have for expert systems is that the setting is mobile and the support that is needed is on a local level in order to support local security and coordination of group activities.

References

1. Dourish, P.: Culture and Control in a Media Space. In proceedings of The Third European Conferens on Computer-Supported Cooperative Work, Milan, Italy, Kluwer Academic Publishers (1993) 125-138
2. Gutwin, C., & Greenberg, S.: Workspace Awareness for Groupware, CHI (1996)
3. Hollan, J., Hutchins, E., Kirsh, D.: Distributed Cognition: Toward a New Foundation for Human-Computer Interaction Research. ACM Transactions on Computer-Human Interaction, Vol 7, No. 2, (2000) 174-196
4. Pascoe, J., Ryan, N., Morse, D.: Using While Moving: HCI Issues in Fieldwork Environments. ACM Transactions on Computer-Human Interaction, Vol 7, No. 3, (2000) 417-437
5. Pascoe, J., Ryan, N., Morse, D.: Human-Computer-Giraffe Interaction: HCI in the field, proceedings of the 1999 ACM symposium on Applied Computing (February 1999)
6. Ranson, D.S., Patterson, E.S., Kidwell, D.L., Renner, G.A., Matthews, M.L., Corban, J.M., Seculov, E., Souhleris, C.S.: Rapid Scout: Bridging the Gulf Between Physical and Virtual Environments, Conference proceedings on Human factors in computing systems (1996)
7. Dix & Beale.: Remote Cooperation: CSCW Issues for Mobile and Teleworkers. Springer, New York (1996)
8. Hutchins, E.: Cognition in the wild, The MIT Press, Cambridge, Massachusetts, London, England (1995)
9. Kirsh, D.: Distributed Cognition, Coordination and Environment Design, proceedings of the European Cognitive Science Society (1999)
10. Dourish, P., Belotti, V.: Awareness and Coordination in Shared Workspaces, CSCW proceedings (1992)
11. Fagrell, H., Forsberg, K., Sanneblad, J.: Fieldwise: A Mobile Knowledge Management Architecture, The Viktoria Institute, Adera, ICTech, Newmad Technologies, Göteborg, Sweden (2000)
12. Ljungberg, F.: Exploring CSCW Mechanisms to Realize Constant Accessibility Without Inappropriate Interaction, Scandinavian Journal of Information Systems, (1999) 115-136
13. Hammersly & Atkinson.: Ethnography: Principles in Practice, Routledge, London (1995)
14. Holme, I.M., Solvang, B,K.: Forskningsmetodik, Om kvalitativa och kvantitativa metoder, Studentlitteratur 2nd edition, Lund, Sweden (1997)
15. Aiken, M.W., Liu Sheng, O.R., Vogel, D.R.: Integrating Expert Systems With Group Decision Support Systems. ACM transactions on Information Systems, Vol. 9, No. 1, (January 1991) 75-95

Inter-system Triggering for Heterogeneous Database Systems

Walter Guan and Raymond K. Wong

School of Computer Science & Engineering, University of New South Wales, Kensington, NSW, 2052, Australia, {wguan,wong}@cse.unsw.edu.au

Abstract. Most of the research in database triggers focused on the centralised active database systems. Because of the requirements from electronic commerce and Web applications, there are growing demands for inter-system level's triggers between different information sources. As a result, systems can interact with each other and react on the events happening on others. This paper proposes the concept of inter-system triggering, and discusses our implementation efforts. It also describes our proposed architecture, namely Advanced Triggering Database System (ATDS), for implementing inter-system triggers. Finally an application example of our preliminary prototype is presented.

1 Introduction

Since mid 1980s, the research in active database systems (ADS) had attracted many interests from the database community. A database system is said to be "active" if it has capacity to monitor events of interest, and to execute appropriate actions in a timely manner if monitoring events occur, without application intervention[3]. This capacity is provided by the use of triggers, which were also referred as active rules, demons, actors and assertions [11]. A trigger can be defined as a rule consisting of an event and an action, and optionally some conditions to be evaluated. When the specified event occurs, if there are no specified conditions, or if all the specified conditions are met, the action is executed [1].

Until early 1990s, triggers in various ADS proposed [4, 6, 8, 12, 10] but they only responded to events in a centralized database system. Furthermore, these centralised events were processed in a sequential manner. [2] proposed a mechanism for trigger rule processing in distributed and parallel environment and was provably equated to the rule processing in the corresponding centralised environment. The work was motivated by the fact of growing interests in distributed and parallel computing systems. Since then, a considerably number of research efforts have been devoted to ADS in distributed environment, e.g., [7, 9]. Database systems in these distributed/parallel environments were assumed to be within the same entities or federated frameworks.

However, as the electronic commerce and Web applications are becoming more dominant today, there are growing demands for interactions between database systems from different commercial entities. For instance, when the

R. Cicchetti et al. (Eds.): DEXA 2002, LNCS 2453, pp. 577–586, 2002.

stock of a product drops below its threshold level, the wholesaler's inventory database might have a user-defined trigger that notifies the wholesaler's staff to refill the inventory. Outside the wholesaler's company, a few suppliers may also be interested in monitoring this threshold level in real-time, so they can send the electronic quotations at the appropriate time. The wholesaler might be willing to give suppliers access to information regarding stock levels, but might not be willing to give them access to any other information. Furthermore, the wholesaler might want to give information of different sets of stock levels to different suppliers. It is not practical for a wholesaler to give database account to each supplier.

To address this issue, this paper proposes the concept of inter-system triggering for heterogeneous database systems. The implementing issues are investigated and discussed. We also propose a system called Advanced Triggering Database system (ATDS), with which we illustrate our approach to deal with the first implementing issues, and research issues within inter-system triggering, such as algorithm for finding applicable triggers etc. ATDS uses our invented execution model called RECRA (Registered Event-Condition-Registered Action), which is an extension of the HiPAC's ECA model [8]. Finally we demonstrate our concept by a marine data application.

This paper is organized as follows. Section 2 investigates the important implementation issues on inter-system triggering. The proposed ATDS system is then described in Section 3, and then in Section 4 we discuss our preliminary prototype in a marine data application at the Australian Navy. Finally, Section 5 concludes the paper.

2 Major Implementation Issues

The main implementing issues for heterogeneous systems triggering include: communication method, event/action messages format, event detection, and algorithm for executing remote functions, etc. Lingering research issues considered on traditional triggering such as scalability, development support, execution models, time-based events and uniformity [1] are also applied to inter-system triggering, discussion on our approach dealing with the first three lingering issues can be found in our longer version of this paper.[5]

The first issue is the communication method. Should these systems communicates with tcp/ip protocol, or more secured ssh protocol? Should the systems always keep an open network connection, or establishing a network connection on demand? We choose to use permanent connection to establish a communication channel in our system, for two main reasons. First, to reduce the time the system use to initialise a communication session when the event occurs. Two, if a foreign system is down, the breakdown of communication channel could trigger the system temporarily ignores all triggers related with this foreign system until the communication channel is re-established.

For ensuring the communication channel is secured and reliable, we plan to use ssh protocol when the system is more completed, we use tcp/ip during the developing stage. Furthermore, we use the following algorithm to ensure the channel is reliable. When two hosts first communicate, each of them generates a **host security string** which is a string of random data, and a binary index to identify other host (binary hostid). Then they store and exchange host security strings, and hostids. When a host wants to communicate with a foreign host, it will use the host security string and hostid generated by this foreign host to identify itself. Once a communication link is made, each system will also map the TCP/IP port number to the foreign host. Each message from a foreign host is identified by hostid, host security string, and TCP/IP port number, the correctness is therefore guaranteed. The hostid and host security string of the foreign host remain in the host database, until removal by database administrator. However, TCP/IP port number get updated when it changes, ie. the communication link breaks and then re-established.

The second issue is type of messages used to communicate between systems. The information need to be passing between database systems should at least include the monitoring events, and the name of functions/actions to be performed. For efficiency, we want the messages to be short and concise. We use binary indexing for hosts, objects on a host, events on the object, functions on host. An event notification contains a string consists of host id, host security string, object id, event id, and time stamp. An action message call contains hostid, host security string, function id, and time stamp.

Other interesting issue is that how a system detect events from other systems. For example, if system A interests in monitoring a particular event E on B, there are several different approaches for B notifying A about this event.**1.** On B, setup an complementary trigger, if event E occurs, signal A. **2.** On B, log all the registered exporting events, let A have access on this log. A periodically checks the log, and pulls the trigger if event E occurs. And **3.** (to authors' best knowledge, might be new to database research community) A setup an agent on B, which communicates with the host A. B doesn't need to be responsible for the message delivery, but just pass the registered interested events to this agent. The agent is responsible for the message delivery.

With our philosophy, we want to minimise CPU time on any systems. For minimising process time needed, a system should be passive on the event detections on the foreign systems. On the other hand, notifying other foreign systems about the interested events should not impose a high cost to the computation on event system, or should not decrease significantly the performance of the event system. Passing the events to an agent involves the least cost on the event system. Our approach is to run a daemon that seperated from the system that handle triggering, to monitor the event logs of the database. When it finds events that other system is interested, it constructs a message and send the message to the agent.

Our current implementation of an agent is a program that keep listening to a port, waiting for messages. When a message arrives, it conducts a basic parsing. if the message is of expected format, it translates the message into a query, and use the SPI libraries of Postgres to send the query back to the host. Our future plan is to compile the agent program as a loadable module for Postgresql, and create a new SQL command to load the agent module. A new research issue we found here is to find the efficient way to handle multiple agents, when there are many foreign system want to put their agents onto an event host.

Finally, how does a system execute the functions on other systems. There are also a few alternative options that system A could invoke a function on system B.**1.** through Remote Procedure Call.**2.** on B create a complementary trigger to fire the local functions, and allows A's trigger to pull this trigger. and **3.** A sends a message to B, saying the functions it wants B to invoke; B looks at its registry, and see if it should perform those functions for A, and acts accordingly.

We believe that for security reasons, a system should be active in monitoring the actions that all other foreign systems invoke. For example, if System B provides a trigger for System A to pull, in order to implement some actions on System B, System A has a process error, mistakenly pull the trigger 100 times, the result could be hazardous. Same level of risks applies if System B just allows System A to run the functions through Remote Procedure Call, where System B does not have direct controls on function execution. A safer strategy would be let System A informs System B about what functions it wants System B to execute, then System B decides whether or not to provide that service to System A. In our design, a system has a module to validate function call requests from all other foreign systems, and it also has a database containing information on the permissible functions for each authorised foreign system.

For execution model, immediate and deferred condition-action coupling might not be the best coupling model for inter-systems triggering. The reason is that since some triggers need to execute functions on other foreign systems, if triggers are processed in a sequential manner, the performance would be bad, if there are many triggers associated with a particular event. A better alternative would be the system could generate an optimized plan for evaluating conditions in applicable triggers to find executable functions, and an optimized plan for functions executing; condition evaluating module and function executing module are running concurrently and seperately. As a result, the execution model are both decoupled event-condition mode, and decoupled condition-action mode.

We propose a name for this execution model as "Registered Event-Condition-Registered Action (RECRA)". It is an extension to (Event-Condition-Action) ECA model, proposed in HiPAC. The main characteristics for this execution model is that a triggering process is broken up to three distinguish components: Event detection and notification according to registered interests, Condition evaluation, and Action Execution (according to registered authority if it is for foreign hosts). These three components are executed in a sequential order but independent to each other, optimization can be done seperately in each component.

3 System Architecture

We name our system as Advanced Triggering Database System (ATDS). It uses Registered Event-Condition-Registered Action (RECRA) model for inter-systems triggering. The overall system architecture for ATDS is shown in Figure 1. An ATDS consists of an event monitor(EM), a remote call validator (RCV), a triggering system(TS), a query optimizer (QO), and a database management system (DBMS).

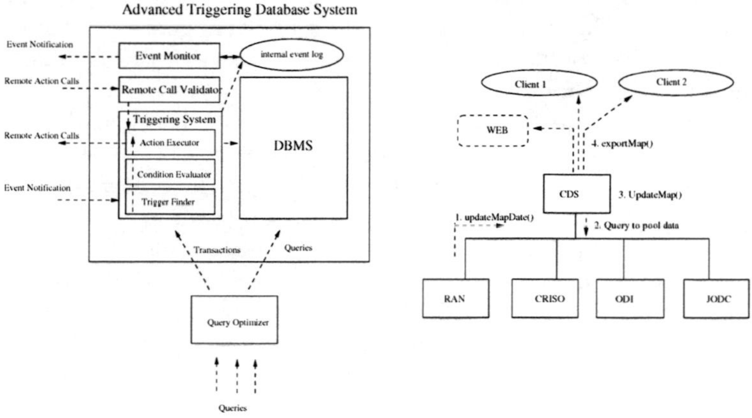

Fig. 1. L: ATDS Architecture, **R:**Automated Map Generation (See Sec:4)

EM monitors the event log generated by TS and notifies the events interested to the appropriate foreign ATDSs based on the registration. RCV receives remote action calls from foreign ATDSs, implementation for these requests taken place, via Action Executor in TS, if the requesting foreign ATDS is authorized to invoke the relevant functions. TS processes the internal transactions forwarded by QO, and the external events notified by EM in foreign ATDSs. TS consists of three modules: a Trigger Finder (TF), a Condition Evaluator(CE) and a Action Executor (AE). TF locates all the applicable triggers associated with the transaction/event, CE tests conditions specified in the condition part of the triggers, and if satisfies, AE implements the action part of the triggers. AE also executes functions for foreign ATDSs, supervised by RCV.

Query optimizer handles all the queries to database. If the queries are the transactions (such as insert, update, or delete etc), QO sends them to the TS; otherwise, to the DBMS. DBMS handles the traditional database management functions. Note that a traditional database management system might have its own triggering system, but in our ATDS, we uses our EM, RCV, TS to handle all triggering needs of the system for two reasons. First, execution model of our triggering system is somewhat different to the traditional one. Second, the way we define our triggers is also very different to that of traditional triggers. In our architecture, TS communicates with traditional DBMS through a query rewriting layer.

Detail discussion on how each of components works in ADTS can be found in [5]. we propose here an algorithm that used by TF to search applicable trigger quickly, we are investigating algorithms for optimizing condition evaluation, and optimizing action execution. Research on these algorithms and benchmark for ATDS as whole will be covered in our future work.

3.1 Registered Event-Condition-Registered Action (RECRA)

In our RECRA model, each trigger is only represented by a 16 bytes (128 bits) data structure. (see Figure 1). Such representation of triggers allow optimization of triggers searching, by using bitwise operation to search the database for all the applicable triggers for an event.

When a trigger is to be created on an ATDS(rule host), and it is set to be fired upon the occurrence of an event on a foreign ATDS(event host), this interested event is needed to be registered on the event host first, before the trigger can be validly defined on the rule host. Registration on the event host involves putting an entry in the Event Monitor's registry file.

Each entry contains objectid, eventid, the hostid of the rule host, and the method for message delivery. In ATDS, an event is represented by a combination of objectid, and eventid. The objectid is the binary index for the referring object in the database system objects table. The eventid is a 8 bit data string consists of two binary indexes. The first 4 bits represents the binary index for the type of the event (ie. insert, delete, update and etc) in the event types database. (ATDS could support up to 16 different event type) The last 4 bits represents the timing of an event (ie. before, after, during etc) in up to 16 different timing related to an event. (See Figure 2). The method for message delivery is either the name of rule host's agent, or function name for notifying the rule host.

Trigger Index Entry

| A | B | C | D | E | F | G | H | I |

A	3 bytes	Trigger Id	F	1 byte	Trigger Classification
B	1 byte	Host Id	G	3 bytes	Condition Id
C	2 bytes	Object Id	H	1 bypte	Action Priority
D	1 byte	Event	I	3 bytes	Action Id
E	1 byte	Priority			

Trigger types:		Trigger timings:	
0000	INSERT	0000	BEFORE
0001	UPDATE	0001	AFTER
0010	DELETE	......	

EVENT	Representation
BEFORE UPDATE	00010000
AFTER INSERT	00000001

Fig. 2. Left: Trigger Entry Elements, **Right:** Representation of Eventid

Once the event is registered on the event host, triggers invoked by this event can be defined on the rule system. In ATDS, a trigger is actually a string of index data, it contains indexes for referring event, condition and action in event database, condition database and action database respectively. These databases stores and indexes all the events, conditions and actions of all defined triggers seperately. In the triggering processing, Trigger Finder firstly finds the objectid and the eventid that represents the event, then it locates all the triggers containing the same objectid and eventid; Condition Evaluator uses the condition index to load the condition for evaluation, and Action Executor uses the action index to find the function needed to be executed. Such implementation of triggers matches our execution model of RECRA, the concept is that a trigger is somewhat defined by putting its three independent components together.

In most cases, the action host is the same as the rule host. But sometimes, an action is needed to be executed on a foreign host. In this case, on the destinated action host, a function to implement the task is to be written, and a registry entry for authorizing the rule host to execute this function is also needed to be added in Remote Call Validator. A registry entry consists of the hostid of the rule host and the functionid of the action host. One registry entry can only authorize one rule host for executing one local function. Then on the rule host, a function sending the remote action call message to the action host can be defined, and the binary index of this function in the action database becomes the action part of the trigger.

3.2 Triggers Searching Algorithm

For optimizing searching process, the trigger database is sorted by hostid, objectid and eventid with ascending orders in their binary values at runtime. Our search algorithm is to ensure the search engine locates all the triggers with the same hostid, objectid, the first four bits of the event string with the least possible comparisons. Within the search, TS first compares with hostid, if it finds the trigger with the same hostid, it starts comparing with hostid and objectid; when it finds the trigger with the same hostid, objectid, it starts comparing with hostid, objectid and first four bits of the event. When it finds a trigger with the same hostid, objectid, and first four bits, it start putting triggers into its memory, until it finds a trigger with any of the four bits, objectid, or hostid having greater binary value than the search one, then the search process stops.

The search process that comparing the hostid and objectid:

1. if hostid is less than search_hostid (in binary value), continue to go down.
2. if hostid equals to search_hostid, objectid less than hostid, continue to go down.
3. if hostid equals to search_hostid, objectid equal to hostid, continue to go down, and comparing the first four bits of event_string, until it stop.
4. if hostid equals to search_hostid, objectid greater than hostid, stop. or
5. if hostid is greater than search_hostid, stop.

The search process that comparing the first four bits of event_string.

1. if four_bits is less than search_four_bits, continue to go down.
2. if four_bits equals to search_four_bits, continue to go down, place this trigger database entry in memory.
3. if four_bits is greater than search_four_bits, stop. And this will cause a stop of the hostid and objectid search as well.

This algorithm for the trigger searching is capable for scaling up the number of triggers a system could have. Considering only 12 bytes (96 bits) of data is required for each trigger entry, assuming the system only allocates 16 Mb (16777216 bytes) of Memory to hold the whole trigger database, it is a capable of holding 1398101 triggers in its memory. This amount of triggers should be sufficient for the most, if not all, of database systems.

3.3 Triggering between ATDS

Once a communication link is established between two ATDSs, their Event Monitors notify the registered interested events to the Triggering Systems on the other side, when the monitoring events occur. Also, if the Action Executor on one ATDS fires a trigger that requires to invoke a function on the other ATDS, it sends the remote action call to the Remote Call Validator on the other ATDS. Figure 3 shows how the ATDSs communicate with each others.

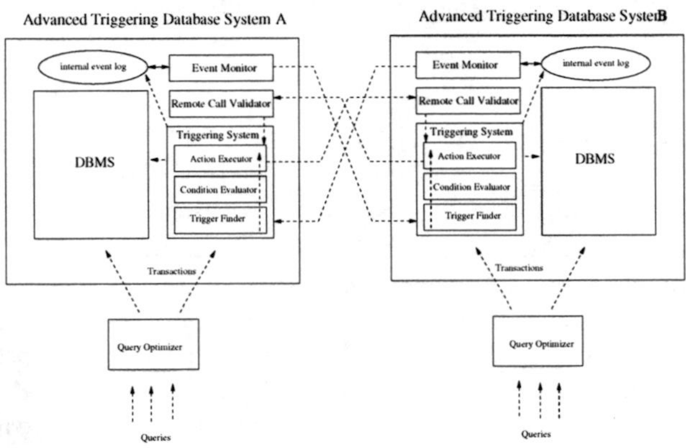

Fig. 3. Triggering between two ATDSs

Assuming we are using several ATDS to establish an e-commerce network, on each ATDS, all the events the foreign ATDSs interest in monitoring are registered, all the functions the foreign ATDSs want to invoke are authorized; Also, each ATDS has triggers that invoked by events in the foreign hosts, and/or execute functions on the foreign hosts. As these ATDSs are capable to react automatically to the events occur on others, a business model could be build in this network.

4 Example Application

We are apply our concept of inter-system triggering in providing automated map generation and exportation upon data change, as a solution for a marine data application problem experienced by Australian Ocean Datagraphic Centre. (Case details can be found in [5].) . We propose a prototype that could atuomatically generate a map, and exports the map to the client when there are some changes in the remote source databases.

We proposed here an electronic commerce network which consists 5 ATDS. 4 ATDS are to manage data source databases in RAN, CRSCO, ODI and JODC. 1 ATDS acts as the central database server (CDS) for AODC. (See Figure 1) This central database stores all the data needed to construct all graphs/reports. Update in the relevant tables in RAN, CRSCO, ODI and JODC will fire a trigger that sends CDS an Remote Action Call for invoking function updateMapData(). The function causes CDS queries the four ATDSs for pooling relevant data together, and updated its relevant tables. Such update triggers an instance of function updateMap() function, and then an instance of function exportMap(). The first converts the data into a grided temperature map, and save the map to a graph file, and second ftp the graph file to web server and the client site. A demo for the concept & its evaluation is available at `http://www.cse.unsw.edu.au/~wguan/demo` .

There maybe a case that more than two source database servers have their data updated at the time, thus have updateMapData() called twice. This is another research issue we found: when a large volume of transactions fire corresponding number of triggers that each invokes a same function once; but this function is only needed to be executed once for this volume of transactions, what is the efficient and optimized way to reduce the redundancy of functions invoked. We could propose three alternative approaches to the problem:

1. For triggers (Ts) with classification C, AE wait for a defined period of time to see if there are more Ts (with C) in the queue, before it fires action A.
2. For a large volume of triggers with C to be evaluated, CE only place one entry of Action A in its stack for passing to AE.
3. (**For comparison**) Adding an attribute called classification in struct Trigger (in trigger.h) of Postgresql, and adding relevant rules.

Evaluation & comparison of these approaches will be our future works.

Interestingly, through the application, we have also found three extra advantages in using the concept of inter-systems triggering. First, decomposition of traditional trigger to three components:(RE-C-RA)allows a function to be reused in all triggers with the same action. Second, introduction of Trigger priority allows users to specify the sequence of triggers fired. This feature, to authors' best knowledge, hasn't been implemented in any commercial database package yet. Third, defining external functions becomes more flexible. User only need to compile the codes for a function into a library, and place the library in the defined directory. An ATDS function then could be defined with the function name and the library name. Libraries are both portable (between the machines with the same machine architecture) and reusable.

5 Conclusion

We have proposed the concept of inter-systems triggering as the backbone for electronic commerce. Inter-system triggering allows a database system to react to the events occurred in other database systems. It also allows the database system to invoke the functions on other database systems if appropriate privileges are granted. We have discussed issues of inter-system triggering and presented our architecture called the Advanced Triggering Database System. The proposed architecture is based on the idea of Registered Event-Condition-Registered Action model for inter-systems triggering. Finally we presented an application example of our preliminary prototype in a marine data application.

References

1. S. Ceri, R. Cochrane, and J. Widom. Practical applications of triggers and constraints: Successes and lingering issues. In *Proceedings of the 26th International Conference on Very Large Data Bases*, Cairo,Egypt, 2000.
2. S. Ceri and J. Widom. Deriving Production Rules for Incremental View Maintenancehttp://www.vldb.org/conf/1991/P577.PDF . In *Proceedings of the 17th International Conference on Very Large Data Bases*, pages 577–589. Morgan Kaufmann, 1991.
3. U. Dayal, E. Hanson, and J. Widom. Active database systems. In *Modern Database System: The Object Model, Interoperability, and Beyond*, Reading. Addison-Wesley, Massachusetts, 1994.
4. N. H. Gehani and H. V. Jagadish. Ode as an Active Database: Constraints and Triggers. In *Proceedings of the 17th International Conference on Very Large Data Bases*, pages 327–336, 1991.
5. W Guan and R Wong. Advanced triggering database system. Technical report, University of New South Wales, Sydney, Australia, 2002.
6. E. N. Hanson. An Initial Report on the Design of Ariel: A DBMS With an Integrated Production Rule System. *SIGMOD Record*, 18(3):12–19, September 1989.
7. A. Koschel and Peter C. Lockemann. Distributed Events in Active Database Systems - Letting the Genie out of the Bottle. *Journal of Data and Knowledge Engineering (DKE)*, 25, 1998. Special Issue for the 25th Vol. of DKE.
8. D. R. McCarthy and U. Dayal. The Architecture of an Active Data Base Management System. In *Proceedings of the 1989 ACM SIGMOD International Conference on Management of Data*, pages 215–224, 1989.
9. S. Schwiderski. *Monitoring the behaviour of distributed systems.* PhD thesis, University of Cambridge, April 1996.
10. M. Stonebraker and G. Kemnitz. The Postgres next-generation database management system. *Communication of the ACM*, 34(10):78–92, 1991.
11. A. P. J. M. Siebes, M. H. Voort, and M. L. Kersten. Towards a design theory for Database triggers. In *Proceedings of the 3rd International Conference on Database and Expert Systems Applications*, pages 338–344. Springer, 1992.
12. J. Widom, R. J. Cochrane, and B. G. Lindsay. Implementing Set-Oriented Production Rules as an Extension of Starburst. In *Proceedings of the 17th International Conference on Very Large Data Bases*, pages 275–285, 1991.

Constructing Inter-relational Rules for Semantic Query Optimisation

Barry G.T. Lowden and Jerome Robinson

Department of Computer Science, The University of Essex
Wivenhoe Park, Colchester, Essex, CO4 3SQ, U.K.
lowdb@essex.ac.uk

Abstract. Semantic query optimisation is the process by which a user query is transformed into a set of alternative queries each of which returns the same answer as the original. The most efficient of these alternatives is then selected, for execution, using standard cost estimation techniques. The query transformation process is based on the use of semantic knowledge in the form of rules which are generated either during the query process itself or are constructed according to defined heuristics. Previous research has tended to focus on constructing rules applicable to single relations and does not take advantage of the additional semantic knowledge, inherent in most databases, associated with relational joins. Our paper seeks to address this weakness by showing how the rule derivation process may be extended to the generation of inter-relational rules using an approach based on inductive learning.

Keywords: Intelligent Information Systems, Semantic Query Optimisation, Rule Generation, Inductive Learning.

1. Introduction

Semantic query optimization is the process of transforming a query into an alternative query that is semantically equivalent but executes in a shorter time [4,5,6,7,8,12,19,26]. A semantically equivalent query returns the same result set as the original query and is generated from it by the application of rules. SQO differs, therefore, from conventional optimisation in that it uses semantic information rather than the statistical data held within the DBM system catalogue [1, 3, 16].

Rules can consist of 'integrity constraints' that hold for all states of the database or 'dynamic rules' that hold only for a given state. Generally, rules can be supplied by the database engineer or derived automatically. Automatic rule generation methods include heuristic based systems [20], logic based systems [9], graph based systems [24] and data driven systems [13, 23].

A weakness of these earlier approaches is that they do not take advantage of the semantic knowledge inherent in join relationships and, as such, are limited to the generation of rules associated with a single relation only. Siegel gives limited attention to the problem but does not address the general case.
As an example consider an employee relation:

E (name, department, salary, status, benefit)

R. Cicchetti et al. (Eds.): DEXA 2002, LNCS 2453, pp. 587–596, 2002.

for which the following rules apply:

(i) *department = 'computing'* $\rightarrow$ *benefit = 'car'*

(ii) *benefit = 'car'* $\wedge$ *salary > 30K* $\rightarrow$ *status = 'executive'*

and the relation is indexed on *status.*

A query of the form Q: *'retrieve names of all staff in computing who earn more than 35K'* may thus be transformed, using the above rules, into Q': *'retrieve names of all executives who work in computing and earn more than 35K'*. If executives represent only 5% of the workforce then it may be seen that this semantically equivalent query will execute in around 5% of the time taken by the original since, as *status* is indexed, only 'executive' tuples need be checked for the two original conditions.

Clearly this is a significant saving, however assume further that there also exists a department relation:

D (dept-name, budget, employee-count, executive-count) indexed on *dept-name*

and an inter-relational rule:

(iii) E.status = 'executive' $\wedge$ *E.department = D.dept-name* $\rightarrow$ *D.executive-count > 0*

Using this additional information, our original query may then be transformed into

Q'': *'retrieve names of all executives who work in computing and earn more than 35K' provided that the corresponding 'computing' tuple in relation D has a positive executive count'.*

A single access to D will determine whether this last condition is true or false and, if false, Q'' will return a NIL answer to the user without further processing thus reducing execution costs to a minimum. If the condition is true then the query will execute as Q'.

In general, given a query Q with conditions (C_1, ...C_k) and a rule set R, query transformation may be achieved by repeated use of the following reformulation operators:

(a) Addition – given a rule in R (x $\rightarrow$ y), if a subset of conditions in Q implies x, then we can add condition y to Q.
(b) Deletion – given a rule in R (x $\rightarrow$ y), if a subset of conditions in Q implies x, and y implies C_i, then we can delete C_i from Q.
(c) Refutation – given a rule in R (x $\rightarrow$ y), if a subset of conditions in Q implies x, and y implies $\neg C_i$, then we can assert that Q will return NIL.

In this paper we present a rule generation approach extended to include construction of inter-relational rules. The method runs as a background task, initially formulating a low cost alternative query using inductive learning [2, 11] and then deriving the rules needed to effect the transformation from the input query to the alternative. The rules may then be used to optimise subsequent queries formulated by the user.

The structure of the paper is as follows. In the next section we describe how the low cost alternative query is constructed and then show, in section 3, how this method may be extended to the inclusion of join conditions. Section 4 presents a rule derivation algorithm based on the equivalence of the input and optimum queries using a range of examples. Finally section 5 summarises our work and gives conclusions.

2. Constructing the Low Cost Alternative

To illustrate the underlying approach, we begin with a simple example based on a single relation. Consider the SALES database shown in Figure 1 together with an SQL-like user query of the form:

Q: *select * from salesemp where Ksalary > 30;*

The answer set of this query is referred to as the set of *positive* instances which is shown in italics. Instances, which are not in the answer set, are referred to as *negative* instances. An alternative query which is semantically equivalent to the input query must therefore return all the positive instances and no negative instances. With this basic requirement in place our method seeks to construct a cheaper alternative by evaluating conditions, on all attributes of the relation, which hold for the answer set.

Salesemp (emp#,	status,	Ksalary,	sales-code,	location (10 char))
E100	mgr	20	25	London
E105	mgr	22	35	Hull
E109	rep	15	24	Leeds
E115	***exe***	***40***	***33***	***Glasgow***
E120	***exe***	***35***	***34***	***London***
E122	***exe***	***37***	***23***	***Cardiff***
E125	***exe***	***42***	***25***	***Leicester***
E130	exe	28	36	Leeds
E150	sup	18	45	London
E155	sup	17	33	Leeds
E160	rep	16	22	Hull
E166	sup	19	36	Slough
E172	rep	14	27	Windsor
E180	mgr	24	31	Hull
E190	mgr	21	32	Leeds

Fig. 1. SALES Database.

In the example, these conditions are:

emp# in (E115, E120, E122, E125)

status = 'exe(cutive)'

sales-code >= 23 and <= 34

location in (Glasgow, London, Cardiff, Leicester)

together with the original query condition:

Ksalary > 30.

If *status* were an indexed attribute then intuitively we see that costs could be reduced by adding the condition *status = 'exe'* to the original query and evaluating only executive tuples for the Ksalary condition.

Specifically, we construct a condition cost table as shown in Figure 2. Entries are calculated by evaluating the product of (comparison cost of each condition C) with the (number of tuples to be compared T). For our example environment, the comparison cost is deemed to be 'string length' when applied to strings, 'member string length * number of members' when applied to sets, and '2' when applied to integers. The number of tuples to be compared will depend on whether the attribute is indexed and, for the purposes of our example, we assume that *status* and *sales-code* are indexed.

The *gain* of each condition is measured by the number of negative instances which it eliminates, as represented by the column G, and the *effectiveness* E of each condition is computed as G/C*T. Original conditions of the input query are included in the computation.

The values shown in the table serve only to illustrate the principles of the method, realistic figures will of course depend on the specific machine environment and take into account the associated access timings and mechanisms. For example it is likely that indexing would, in practice, require only one condition comparison thus increasing the value of E for that entry.

Candidate Conditions	**C**	**T**	**G**	**E**
emp# in (E115, E120, E122, E125)	*16*	*15*	*11*	*0.0458*
status = 'exe'	*3*	*5*	*10*	*0.6667*
sales-code >= 23 and <= 34	*4*	*10*	*5*	*0.1250*
location in (Glasgow, London, Cardiff, Leicester)	*40*	*15*	*9*	*0.0150*
Ksalary > 30	*2*	*15*	*11*	*0.3667*

Fig. 2. Condition Cost Table.

The algorithm for constructing the alternative query then proceeds as follows:

Algorithm A.

1. Let the alternative query condition list L := NULL;
2. Let the number of negative instances be N;
3. Evaluate conditions on all attributes which hold for the answer set (including original input query conditions);
4. Let x = the condition with highest E value;
5. Add x to L and subtract G(x) from N;
6. If N = 0 then return condition list L else re-compute table, with respect to L, and go back to step 3.

In our example the condition *status = 'exe'* has the highest E value, it is therefore added to the condition list L and the value of N is set to 1. The table is then recomputed with respect to the tuples identified by the conditions in L, as illustrated in Figure 3.

Candidate Conditions	**C**	**T**	**G**	**E**
emp# in (E115, E120, E122, E125)	*16*	*5*	*1*	*0.0125*
sales-code >= 23 and <= 34	*4*	*4*	*1*	*0.0625*
location in (Glasgow, London, Cardiff, Leicester)	*40*	*5*	*1*	*0.0050*
Ksalary > 30	*2*	*5*	*1*	*0.1000*

Fig. 3. Revised Condition Cost Table.

At this stage, the highest E value is associated with the input condition *Ksalary > 30* which is added to L. The value of N becomes zero. Hence L is returned as the condition list of the low cost alternative query:

Q' : *select * from salesemp where status = 'exe' and Ksalary > 30;*

which evaluates the Ksalary condition on the 5 'executive' tuples as opposed to the original input query which necessitated the retrieval of all tuples in the database.

Clearly it is not advantageous to use every user input query, for low cost query construction, and selection will normally be limited to those classed as the more expensive to execute. This will increase the probability of the derived rules being useful for optimisation of subsequent queries. Inclusion of the original input conditions in the evaluation process ensures that an alternative semantically equivalent query is always produced even though, trivially, it may be syntactically the same as the input query when a cheaper alternative cannot be found.

3. Inter-relational (Join) Constraints

We will first address the situation where an input query already includes a join condition and then examine the possibility of introducing further join conditions in order to generate a semantic equivalent.

Any well found user query, defined on more than one relation in a database, will reference, in the condition list, at least one attribute from each relation defined. Where there is more than one relation referred to in the output list then our system first decomposes the input query into a set of sub-queries comprising exactly one output relation and its associated condition list.

Let our SALES database schema now be extended to that of Figure 4 where join attributes are marked with an asterisk. It is possible to identify meaningful join attributes by their inclusion in user queries or, in some cases the system catalogue.

*salesemp (emp#, status, Ksalary, *sales-code, *location)*
*placement (main-town, *location, population)*
*contacts (name, company, credit-rating, *sales-code, address, position, commission)*

Fig. 4. Extended Relational Schema.

A possible query on this extended database is:

Q1: *select emp#, company from salesemp, contacts where Ksalary > 30 and salesemp.sales-code = contacts.sales-code and credit-rating > 5;*

which decomposes into two (single output relation) queries:

Q11*: select emp# from salesemp, contacts where Ksalary > 30 and salesemp.sales-code = contacts.sales-code ;*

and

Q12: *select company from salesemp, contacts where credit-rating > 5 and salesemp.sales-code = contacts.sales-code*

each of which is strongly related to Q1 but has wider applicability in terms of subsequent rule derivation.

Taking Q11 as our example and assuming the same answer set as our earlier query Q, we see that the set of candidate conditions shown in Figure 2 will be extended to include the inter-relational condition:

salesemp.sales-code = contacts.sales-code.

Condition costs may be evaluated as previously discussed and the number of tuples accessed will depend on whether either or both of the join attributes are indexed. If neither attribute is indexed then the value of T will depend on the cardinalities of the joining relations and associated selectivity factors. In this particular example we note that *salesemp.sales-code* is indexed hence the number of tuples accessed will be proportional to the cardinality of the relation *contacts.* If the cardinality of *salesemp* is 50K and that of *contacts* is 5K and the range of values of *contacts.sales-code* defined by the answer set of query Q11 may be associated with 10K tuples in *salesemp,* then the gain achieved by condition *salesemp.sales-code = contacts.sales-code* is 40K.

Inclusion of an inter-relational condition, in a partially constructed alternative query condition list L, permits the addition of candidate conditions on the set of attributes, associated with the joining relation, to the search space. These are then eligible for inclusion in L. In our example, if the join condition:

salesemp.sales-code = contacts.sales-code

were selected then conditions on each attribute in *contacts,* matching the answer set, would be evaluated and added to the candidate condition list. Where this leads to the inclusion, in the alternative condition list, of new join attributes linking additional relations then we may widen the search space for candidate conditions even further.

Note that, in the foregoing, the search space of candidate conditions is only extended to a further level if the related join condition is selected for inclusion in the partially completed alternative condition list ie. it is sufficiently cost effective. Where, however, a joined relation contains indexed attributes then candidate conditions are constructed on these attributes even if the join condition is not included in the alternative condition list. This simple heuristic ensures that potentially beneficial indexed conditions are not excluded from the evaluation process.

Expanding the search space of candidate conditions, in this way, is effected by ensuring that the above heuristic is included in step 3 of Algorithm A and also modifying the re-compute function in step 6 to include:

> If x is a join condition on a new relation S then construct conditions on the attributes of S and include them in the set of candidate conditions.

4. Rule Generation

The previous section has described the process for constructing an alternative query Q' which is semantically equivalent to the input query Q and cheaper to execute. We now use that equivalence as the basis for deriving the rules which would be needed to transform Q into Q'. The algorithm is shown in Figure 5.

Algorithm B:

Assume Q ≡ Q' (where Q = input query, Q' = cheaper alternative query);
Let the derived rule set R := NULL;
Let A be the output relation in the select clause of Q';
Let C_1 … C_n be the non-join conditions in the where clause of Q';
For each C
    Let consequent of new rule r = C;
    Construct P where P = shortest join path from C to A;
    Let antecedent of r = (condition list of Q) UNION (join conditions in P);
    If r not trivial then add r to R;
Return R;

Fig. 5. Rule Generation Algorithm.

In essence, for each non-join condition in the alternative query, Algorithm B determines the shortest join path to the output relation. New rules are constructed with the non-join condition becoming the consequent and the antecedent being formed from the UNION of the join path and the condition list of the input query. As before we will illustrate our approach by means of examples.
First we take the simple case of the query discussed in Section 2. There are no joins involved and the equivalence of conditions is straightforward:

$$(Ksalary > 30) \equiv (status = \text{'exe'}) \wedge (Ksalary > 30)$$

yielding the non-trivial rule:

$$(Ksalary > 30) \rightarrow (status = \text{'exe'})$$

As an example of a join query, we refer to the extended database schema of Figure 4.

Let the input query be:

Q: select emp# from salesemp, contacts, location
where salesemp.sales-code = contacts.sales-code and
salesemp.location = placement.location and
population > 40K and
commission > 0.5 and position = manager;

and our alternative cheaper equivalent:

Q': select emp# from salesemp, contacts
where salesemp.sales-code = contacts.sales-code and
credit-rating > 5;

The alternative query has a single non-join condition (*credit-rating > 5)* in the where clause and the shortest join path is (*salesemp.sales-code = contacts.sales-code).*

The derived rule (removing duplicate conditions) is therefore:

R1: (salesemp.sales-code = contacts.sales-code ∧ salesemp.location = placement.location ∧ population > 40K ∧ commission > 0.5 ∧ position = 'manager') → (credit-rating >5)

Clearly, however, rules which contain a large number of antecedent conditions tend to be very specific to the input query from which they were derived. The next stage of the process, therefore, attempts to decompose the rule into a set of shorter sub-rules more useful for optimising a wider range of user queries. This is achieved by identifying subsets of antecedent conditions which:

(a) maintain rule *cohesion*. A rule is cohesive if there is a connecting relational path through all antecedent and consequent conditions.

and where the condition subset

(b) still implies the consequent of the derived rule (by reference to the database).

The decomposition process considers each combination of the antecedent conditions and discards those which do not conform to the above criteria. Taking R1 as an example, the following resultant sub-rule is not cohesive:

(salesemp.sales-code = contacts.sales-code ∧ population > 40K)
→ (credit-rating >5)

since there is no path connecting either *salesemp* or *contacts* to *population.*

On the other hand the sub-rule:

(salesemp.sales-code = contacts.sales-code ∧ commission > 0.5)
→ (credit-rating > 5)

is cohesive and is checked against the database for validity.

All valid rules are eligible for inclusion in the rule base although some may be more effective than others in optimising subsequent queries. Also rule bases derived in this way can rapidly become very large and, as such, may degrade the efficiency of the optimisation process, a problem referred to as the *utility problem* [10, 17, 21, 27].

Our system addresses these issues by subjecting derived rules to statistical (Chi-square) analysis [10] which identifies and ranks rules according to their effectiveness. The rule set can be thus maintained at an optimum size and consists of only those rules which have wide applicability to the query space.

Rule validity may also be affected by changes to the database itself leading to potential inconsistent or weakened rules. For example if the range of values of a given attribute is extended, due to the addition of a new tuple in the database, then this may require modification of those rules which refer to that value range. Such rules are identified and modified in our system as part of the rule maintenance process [22, 18, 20], and then subjected to statistical re-evaluation and ranking.

5. Conclusions and Further Work

We have described a rule derivation approach, running as a background task, which includes the generation of inter-relational rules based on the semantic information inherent in relational joins. Such rules typically have long antecedents and a technique for rule decomposition has been presented to generate sub-rules which have more general applicability to the optimisation of subsequent queries. The method identifies both rules based on indexed attributes and also non-indexed rules which lead to a reduction in attribute comparison time

Simulation experiments on two 20K tuple model relations each consisting of nine non-indexed, three indexed and one join attribute show that the method performs well and identifies effective single relation and inter-relational rules which may be used in query transformation. We now intend to conduct more extensive field trials based on large publicly available datasets extracted from the University of Essex Data Archive incorporating the fast transformation algorithm described in [15].

References

[1] M.W. Blasgen and K.P. Eswaran. *'Storage and access in relational databases'*, IBM Systems Journal, 16(4), 363-377, 1977.

[2] Y. Cai, N. Cerone and J. Han, *'Learning in relational databases: an attribute-oriented approach'*, J. Computational Intelligence, 7(3), 119-132, 1991.

[3] A.F. Cardenas. *'Analysis and performance of inverted data base structures'*, Communications of the ACM, 18(5), 253-263, 1975.

[4] S. Chakravarthy, J. Grant and J. Minker, *'Logic-based approach to semantic query optimisation'*, ACM on Database Systems, 15(2), 162-207, 1990.

[5] S. Chaudhuri, *'An overview of query optimization in relational systems'*, PODS, 1998.

[6] Q. Cheng et al., *'Implementation of two semantic query optimisation techniques in DB2 universal database'*, Proc. 25th VLDB, Edinburgh, Scotland, September, 1999.

[7] P. Godfrey et al., *'Semantic query optimization for bottom-up evaluation'*, Proc. 9th International Symposium on Methodologies for Intelligent Systems, Poland, June, 1996.

[8] G. Graefe and D. Dewitt, *'The EXODUS optimiser generator'*, Proc. ACM-SIGMOD Conf. on Management of Data, 160-171, May 1987.

[9] J. Grant et al., *'Logic based query optimization for object databases'*, IEEE Transactions on Knowledge and Data Engineering, Vol. 12, No 4, August 2000.

[10] J. Han, Y. Cai and N. Cercone, *'Data-driven discovery of quantitative rules in relational databases'*, IEEE on Knowledge and Data Eng., 5(1), 29-40, 1993.

[11] D. Haussler, *'Quantifying inductive bias: AI learning algorithms and Valiant's learning framework'*, J. Artificial Intelligence, 36, 177-221, 1988.

[12] J. King, QUIST: *'A system for semantic query optimisation in relational databases'*, Proc. 7th VLDB Conf., 1981.

[13] B.G.T. Lowden, J. Robinson and K.Y. Lim, *'A semantic query optimiser using automatic rule derivation'*, Proc. Fifth Annual Workshop on Information Technologies and Systems, Netherlands, 68-76, December 1995.

[14] B.G.T. Lowden and J. Robinson, *'A statistical approach to rule selection in semantic query optimisation'*. Proc. 11th International Symposium on Methodologies for Intelligent Systems, LNCS, 330-339, Warsaw, June 1999.

[15] B.G.T. Lowden and J.Robinson, *'Improved information retrieval using semantic transformation'*, CSM 355, University of Essex, 2002.

[16] L. F. Mackert and G. M. Lohman, *'R* optimizer validation and performance evaluation for local queries'*, ACM-SIGMOD, 84-95, 1986.

[17] G.Piatetsky-Shapiro and C. Matheus, *'Measuring data dependencies in large databases'*, Knowledge Discovery in Databases Workshop, 162-173, 1993.

[18] J. Robinson and B.G.T. Lowden, *'Data analysis for query processing'*, Proc. 2nd International Symposium on Intelligent Data Analysis, London, 1997.

[19] J. Robinson and B.G.T. Lowden, *'Semantic optimisation and rule graphs'*, Proc. 5th KRDB Workshop, Seattle, WA, May 1998.

[20] J. Robinson and B.G.T. Lowden, *'Distributing the derivation and maintenance of subset descriptor rules'*, Proc. 7th International Conference on Information Systems and Synthesis, Orlando USA, July 2001.

[21] I. Savnik and P.A. Flach, *'Bottom-up induction of functional dependencies from relations'*, Proc. Knowledge Discovery in Databases Workshop, 174-185, 1993.

[22] A. Sayli and B.G.T. Lowden, *'Ensuring rule consistency in the presence of DB updates'*, Proc. XII International Symposium on Computer & Information Sciences, Turkey, October 1997.

[23] S. Shekhar, B. Hamidzadeh and A. Kohli. *'Learning transformation rules for semantic query optimisation: a data-driven approach'*, IEEE, 949-964, 1993.

[24] S.T. Shenoy and Z.M. Ozsoyoglu, *'Design and implementation of semantic query optimiser'*, IEEE Transactions on Knowledge and Data Eng., 1(3), 344-361, 1989.

[25] M. Siegel, E. Sciore and S. Salveter, *'A method for automatic rule derivation to support semantic query optimisation'*, ACM on Database Sys., 17(4), 563-600, 1992.

[26] Yu C. and Sun W., *'Automatic knowledge acquisition and maintenance for semantic query optimisation'*, IEEE Transactions on Knowledge and Data Engineering, Vol. 1, No. 3, 362-375, 1989.

[27] W. Ziarko, *'The discovery, analysis and representation of data dependencies in databases'*, Knowledge Discovery in Databases, AAAI Press, 195-209, 1991.

About Selections and Joins in Possibilistic Queries Addressed to Possibilistic Databases

Patrick Bosc[1], Laurence Duval[2], Olivier Pivert[1]

[1] IRISA/ENSSAT, Technopole ANTICIPA BP 447
22305 Lannion Cedex, France
{bosc|pivert}@enssat.fr
[2] IRISA/ENSAI, Campus de Ker Lann BP 37203
35170 Bruz Cedex, France
laurence.duval@ensai.fr

Abstract. This paper is situated in the area of the so-called fuzzy databases, i.e., databases containing imprecise information. It is now recognized that querying databases containing imperfect information raises several problems, including complexity. In this paper, we consider a specific kind of queries, called possibilistic queries, of the form "to what extent is it possible that a given tuple t belongs to the answer of Q (a regular relational query)." The major objective is to show that a reasonable complexity can be expected for a specific (although not too restricted) subset of possibilistic queries.

1. Introduction

In various application domains, there is a growing need for information systems capable of dealing with ill-known data. This is also the case in data warehouses where the gathering of information coming from various sources may induce imprecise data. Possibility theory [8] provides a purely ordinal model for uncertainty where imprecision is represented by means of a preference relation coded by a total order over the possible situations. This approach proposes a unified framework for representing precise values, as well as imprecise ones (regular sets), also called OR-sets [6], or vague ones (fuzzy sets) and various null value situations (see [4] for more details). Besides the representation issue, an important aspect is the manipulation of such data, and some pioneering works in the mid-80s have laid down some bases, especially for queries involving only "simple" operations, namely selections and projections [7]. For instance, a selection query returns a relation where each tuple is associated with a possibility and a necessity degree, which express the extent to which it is possible (respectively certain) that the considered tuple satisfies the selection condition imposed by the query.

R. Cicchetti et al. (Eds.): DEXA 2002, LNCS 2453, pp. 597–606, 2002.

Unfortunately, queries involving selections and projections only allow the handling of a single relation at a time and have a fairly restricted expression power. On the other hand, it has been proven [5] that "general" queries (i.e., those which make use of all relational operators) addressed to imprecise databases cannot be dealt with in practice. The reason is twofold: i) the possibilistic model (as well as the OR-set model) does not provide a representation system in the sense of [5] and ii) such queries require their evaluation over all the more or less possible worlds associated with an imperfect database. This last fact has two consequences: i) the difficulty for a user to interpret the result of a query made of a huge number of more or less possible (large) tables and ii) the prohibitive cost for such a processing (even when the database is not very big).

In [3], a relational query language supporting selections, projections and a specific join is suggested. Such an approach is compatible with a processing where worlds are not explicitly manipulated. Therefore, the method can be expected to be tractable. In the same spirit of feasibility/tractability, the idea developed in this paper (inspired from Abiteboul's proposal [1]) aims at moving to a specific kind of queries, called "possibilistic queries", for which, once again, worlds do not have to be explicited. A possibilistic query differs from a regular query in that it refers to a given tuple. More precisely, its general formulation is: to what extent is it possible that tuple t belongs to the answer of the regular relational query Q? We restrict the scope of this work to queries Q involving only selections, joins, and a final projection. We will also assume that a given relation is used only once in a query and that the possibility distributions involved are discrete (these limitations will be discussed in Section 3). The evaluation of possibilistic queries appears to constitute an original concern since (to our knowledge) no research works have dealt with this yet.

The remainder of the paper is structured as follows. In Section 2, the semantics of possibilistic queries is detailed. Their answer (a degree of possibility) is defined with respect to more or less possible worlds and the principle of an evaluation method where worlds are not explicited (called "compact calculus") is outlined. Section 3 describes the general principle of the approach we propose. The four main steps of the evaluation procedure are described in Section 4. They include the issue of making use of the knowledge of the target tuple, appropriate definitions of the operators appearing in Q in order to process it in a "compact way", and the computation of the final degree attached to the target tuple. In Section 5, some comments about the validity of the proposed procedure are made, some conclusions are drawn and directions for future works are identified.

2. Possibilistic Queries

In the remainder of this paper, the possibilistic relational framework introduced by Prade and Testemale [7] is considered. Let us recall that a possibilistic relation r over domains D_1, ..., D_n is a subset of the Cartesian product of the power set of the fuzzy sets over $D_1, \ldots, D_n$. In other words, the difference with a regular relation lies in the fact that any attribute value may be a possibility distribution rather than a singleton. A possibilistic database (made of possibilistic relations) is equivalent to a set of regular databases (where values of tuples are restricted to singletons), each of which is obtained by choosing one among the candidates for each imprecise value in a tuple. In such a representation, independence of imprecise values is assumed (i.e., any candidate can be taken regardless of the choices made for the other attribute values). Each world is associated with a degree corresponding to the minimum of the degrees tied to the candidates appearing in this world.

As mentioned before, a possibilistic query does not aim at the retrieval of a set of elements (as usual relational queries do). Its objective is to determine whether a given (regular) tuple may appear in the result of a query Q addressed to an imprecise relational database, where Q is a relational query restricted to selections, joins and a final projection in this work. A possibilistic query has the general form: "to what extent is it possible that tuple t belongs to the answer of Q". In the particular case of a database where imperfect values are represented as (nonweighted) disjunctive sets of candidates, the answer is just "yes" or "no". When possibility distributions are used, this result is a degree and more precisely, that of the most possible world where t belongs to the result of Q. In both cases, the key question concerns the way this degree can be computed. A naive approach is to build all more or less possible worlds and to process Q against each of them.

Example 1. Let us consider a database made of two relation schemas IMAGE(#i, t-a, date) and AIRCRAFT(t-a, lg, sp). Relation img(IMAGE) describes images by means of a number (#i), a possibly ill-known type of aircraft (t-a) and the date of the shot (date). Relation acf(AIRCRAFT) represents aircrafts with their type (t-a), length (lg) and maximal speed (sp). A possible extension is:

img

#i	t-a	date
i1	{1/a2+0.5/a1}	{1/d3+0.7/d1}
i2	{1/a3+0.8/a2+0.5/a4+0.2/a1}	{1/d2+0.2/d3}
i3	{1/a3+0.3/a4}	d1

acf

t-a	lg	sp
a1	20	1000
a2	25	1200
a3	18	800
a4	20	1200

A possibilistic query against this database would be: "to what extent is it possible that <d1, 20> belongs to the answer of the query Q looking for the pairs (date, length) such that there is (at least) an image taken on this date including an aircraft of this length". Among the 64 (more or less) possible worlds, some are leading to the desired tuple. <d1, 20> is a result of Q in the worlds (among others) involving acf and respectively:

img2

#i	t-a	date
i1	a1	d1
i2	a2	d2
i3	a3	d1

img3

#i	t-a	date
i1	a2	d3
i2	a3	d2
i3	a4	d1

which are respectively min(0.5, 0.7, 0.8, 1, 1) = 0.5 and min(1, 1, 1, 1, 0.3) = 0.3 possible ♦

Of course, the naive approach evoked previously is not realistic from a computational point of view. However, it constitutes the reference as to the validity/correctness of any other processing strategy which must be proven equivalent to it. Then, the objective is clearly to obviate this "extensive" calculus and (as far as possible) to replace it by a "compact" one where worlds are not made explicit. To do so, it is necessary to devise a processing technique in a "closed" framework where the inputs and outputs of operations involved in Q (i.e., intermediate results) are possibilistic relations, in order to ensure compositionality. The outline of the envisaged procedure consists of four steps which can be briefly described as follows:

1. removal of useless attributes, i.e., attributes that do not appear in query Q, from the initial possibilistic relations involved in Q (this step will not be detailed further);
2. propagation of the attribute values appearing in the target tuple t into the query Q (details are given in Section 4). This step will amount to introducing selections intended for retaining only those tuples likely to contribute to the production of the target tuple in the answer of Q. In the previous example, as we are interested in date d1, tuples of image whose set of possible date values does not contain d1 can be discarded;
3. evaluation of Q in a "compact" way, which requires the design of appropriate definitions for selection and join operations (these points, which constitute the heart of the contribution, are described in Section 4). It is worth mentioning that the goal is not to compute the exhaustive result of Q but only to fit the specificity of possibilistic queries, namely the determination of the final possibility degree associated with the target tuple;
4. computation of the final membership degree from the possibilistic relation issued from step 3 (see Section 4).

3. Context and Accepted Queries

Even if possibilistic queries are "simpler" to treat than regular queries, it turns out that their processing in a compact fashion is not exactly trivial. This leads us to restrict the family of possibilistic queries considered in this paper. Indeed, the constraints concern the components of the relational query which is part of the possibilistic query. As mentioned before, we have chosen to restrict ourselves to queries where only some operators are allowed (selections and joins which are the heart of many frequent queries). Hereafter, we point out a problem raised by certain queries and we describe the way we overcome these difficulties.

Let us first emphasize that the possibilistic relational model is unable to express constraints between candidates pertaining to different attributes. Indeed, independence is assumed in a relation in the sense that the choice of a candidate for an attribute in a given tuple is not conditioned by that of a previous choice for another attribute in that same tuple. Three main causes of dependencies are reviewed here.

The first two sources of dependencies originate in conditions which can appear in selections and joins. If we want to guarantee a safe use of an attribute in several operations (for instance a selection on attribute A of relation r, followed by a join of r and s where the joining condition refers to A again), it is mandatory to keep all the candidates which satisfy the selection. But, in some cases, it is not possible to keep satisfactory values for two (or more) attributes separately. A problem appears in two basic situations: i) a condition is made of a disjunction over more than one attribute (e.g., $A > 4$ or $B \leq 12$) which are used in further operations, or ii) an elementary condition involves two attributes (e.g., $A > B$) which are used in further operations. In both examples, a safe processing of further operations demands that all the combinations of attribute values are retained (i.e., pairs of values which satisfy the condition) along with their degrees. This requirement is not compatible with the hypothesis according to which the initial possibilistic model serves as a basis for the calculus.

Example 2. Let us consider the schema R(A, B, C) and a query involving the condition "$A > 100$ or $B < 20$" knowing that both A and B are used later. Moreover, let us assume that the A-value of a tuple u of r(R) is $\{1/90 + 0.7/80 + 0.2/120\}$ and its B-value is $\{1/30 + 0.5/10\}$. The correct result of this operation is made of the pairs (1/90, 0.5/10), (0.7/80, 0.5/10), (0.2/120, 1/30), (0.2/ 120, 0.5/10) and it is easy to see that this result cannot be represented in terms of "independent" A and B-values♦

If condition between two (reused) attributes raises the problem of value independence, it can be noticed that the situation where the comparison operator is the equality (which is very frequent in joining conditions) can be easily handled. In effect, in that case, it is sufficient to keep only one value (since the other is necessarily the same) along with the minimum of the two grades and the usual possibilistic model can be used. It is also the case when only one (or even none) of the attributes of an operation is used further.

The third situation likely to generate dependencies between candidate values arises when two (or more) copies of a same relation appear in the query Q and (at least) one of its attributes coming from distinct copies intervenes in a comparison. The approach we propose does not solve this problem, therefore we will consider in the following that no relation can be used twice in a query.

In our previous works [2], in order to avoid the problems induced by dependencies between attributes we had restricted the scope of the approach by imposing that an attribute could not be used twice in a query. Here we get rid of this constraint and we consider an alternative possibilistic model allowing to represent in a sound way the intermediate relations obtained during the processing of the possibilistic query. The key idea is to use several tuples to represent a (disjunctive) set of variants when necessary.

Example 3. Let us come back to example 2. All candidate solutions of the selection operation "A > 100 or B < 20" generated by tuple u = <{1/90 + 0.7/80 + 0.2/120}, {1/30 + 0.5/10}> can be represented by means of the two following tuples: <{1/90 + 0.7/80 + 0.2/120}, {0.5/10}>, and <{0.2/120}, {1/30 }>♦

In the context of possibilistic queries, it is legitimate to handle relations including disjunctive tuples since i) we are looking for the best alternative, i.e., the best representative of the target tuple in the result (the final degree is computed by means of a maximum), and ii) considering the type of queries considered, the operations of selection and join do not require the tuples to be independent (the queries do not involve any cardinality computation, in particular).

4. A "Compact" Way of Evaluation

The main objective of the third step is to define a "compact" computation procedure that avoids making explicit all possible worlds. The approach we propose uses the compact representation of a possibilistic database but, as mentionned in Section 3, we will consider that an intermediate relation resulting from a selection or a join may contain disjunctive tuples.

4.1 Restricting Initial Relations

This subsection covers the first two steps (out of 4) of the evaluation procedure we suggest (see Section 2). They aim at the production of possibilistic relations containing only useful columns and values. The first step performs the removal of unused attributes in each relation of Q. It does not raise any problem and is not worthy of details. The second step makes use of the target tuple t. When a relation r used in Q has a common attribute with t, the tuples of r likely to produce t must have a candidate value which is that of t. The objective is then to eliminate all tuples that are unable to produce t. Every relation whose schema does not overlap with that of t remains unchanged. Consider a relation r whose schema is R(A, X), A denoting a single attribute and X a set of attributes and let u be a tuple of r(R). If t.A does not appear as a candidate value in u.A, tuple u is not retained, otherwise u.A is reduced to t.A with its associated degree. This operation can also be seen as a specific selection defined as follows:

$$\text{sel}(r, A = t.A) = \{\langle \text{restr}(u.A, A = t.A), u.X\rangle \mid u \in r\} \quad (1).$$

where $\text{restr}(u.A, A\ \theta\ v) = \{\pi_i/a_i \mid a_i \in u.A \text{ and } \pi_i = \pi_{u.A}(a_i) \text{ and } a_i\ \theta\ v\}\}$, θ being a comparator and v a constant (this operation restricts the possibility distribution u.A to those candidate values that satisfy the filtering condition).

This operation will be applied for every attribute of the target tuple as illustrated in the following example.

Example 4. Let us come back to the relations img and acf of example 1 and let us consider the target tuple <a1, 20> relating to the attributes t-a and lg. According to the previous procedure, the two following restricted possibilistic relations img4 and acf1 are generated:

img4

#i	t-a	date
i1 i2	{0.5/a1} {0.2/a1}	{1/d3 + 0.7/d1} {1/d2 + 0.2/ d3}

acf1

t-a	lg	sp
a1	20	1000

In the first relation, the value of attribute t-a must be a1 (regardless of its degree) and in the second one, both t-a and lg are constrained (to a1 and 20 respectively)♦

4.2 Selections

We consider two types of atomic selection condition: those involving a comparison between an attribute and a constant (type 1), and those involving a comparison between two attributes (type 2). We first define the corresponding operations, then we deal with compound selection conditions.

The first type of condition aims at comparing an attribute value with a constant. If we consider a selection condition of type "A θ v" applying to relation r whose schema is R(A, X), a tuple u from r generates a tuple in the answer if at least one candidate value a_i in u.A satisfies the condition (a_i θ v). The resulting tuple u' has the same values as u for all attributes except for A: u'.A contains all of the candidates from u.A which satisfy the condition (a_i θ v). Such a selection operation can be defined the following way:

$$\text{sel}(r, A\ \theta\ v) = \{<\text{restr}(u.A, A\ \theta\ v), u.X> \mid u \in r\} \quad (2).$$

In case of a condition of the type "A θ B" applying to a relation r whose schema is R(A, B, X), a tuple u generates a tuple u' in the answer if at least one candidate value for u.A is in relation θ with at least one candidate value for u.B. As mentionned in Section 3, a tuple u may generate several disjunctive tuples that are stored in the resulting intermediate relation. To compute the answer we take all of the variants of u.A that match at least one variant of u.B. We generate a tuple u' for each of these u.A candidate values (a_i), the value of u'.A is a_i with its degree, the values of u'.B are all of the candidate values for u.B (b_j) which satisfy the condition a_i θ b_j. The number of tuples generated is then equal to the number of u.A candidates which are in relation θ with at least one candidate of u.B (let us notice that one might as well consider the symmetric solution that would consist in generating a tuple for each u.B candidate). More formally, such a selection operation can be defined the following way:

$$\text{sel}(r, A\ \theta\ B) = \{<\{\alpha_i/a_i\}, \text{restr}(u.B, a_i\ \theta\ B), u.X> \mid \exists\, u \in r \text{ such that } u.A = \{\alpha_1/a_1 + \ldots + \alpha_i/a_i + \ldots + \alpha_n/a_n\} \text{ and restr}(u.B, a_i\ \theta\ B) \neq \emptyset\} \quad (3).$$

Let us now deal with disjunctive selection conditions. As a typical example, let us consider the condition "($A\ \theta\ v_1$) **or** ($B\ \theta\ v_2$)" applying to a relation r whose schema is R(A, B, X). A tuple u of r (possibly) satisfies the selection condition if there is at least one candidate value a in u.A such that $a\ \theta\ v_1$ or one candidate value b in u.B such that $b\ \theta\ v_2$. The result of the selection applied to a given tuple is represented by means of two tuples in the answer. The first one includes all of the candidate values from u.A that satisfy the condition ($A\ \theta\ v_1$) along with all of the u.B candidate values. The second tuple is composed of all the candidate values which are not in the previous tuple namely all of the candidate values from u.B that satisfy the condition ($B\ \theta\ v_2$) along with all of the u.A candidate values that do not satisfy the condition ($A\ \theta\ v_1$). This operation can be formalized the following way:

$$\begin{aligned}\text{sel}(r, (A\ \theta\ v_1)\ \textbf{or}\ (B\ \theta\ v_2)) = \\ &\{<\text{restr}(u.A, A\ \theta\ v_1), u.B, u.X> \mid u \in r\} \cup \\ &\{<\text{restr}(u.A, \neg(A\ \theta\ v_1)), \text{restr}(u.B, B\ \theta\ v_2), u.X> \mid u \in r\} \quad (4).\end{aligned}$$

Other types of disjunctive selection conditions can be dealt with in a similar way (the formulas are omitted for space reason).

As far as conjunctive selection conditions are concerned, they can be in general processed using the usual possibilistic model (a given tuple generates at most one tuple) except in very special cases such as "$A_1\ \theta_1\ A_2$ and $A_1\ \theta_2\ A_3$", i.e., when a given attribute is involved in two comparisons with other attributes. In that case, disjunctive tuples must be considered too (this case is not detailed here).

Example 5. Let us consider the following relation r which describes satellite images of aircrafts. Each image is supposed to represent two aircrafts. The types of the aircrafts are supposed to be ill-known due to the imprecision inherent in the recognition process.

#image	aircraft1	aircraft2
1	{1/a1 + 1/a2 + 0.7/a3}	{0.8/a2 + 0.2/a3}
2	{0.2/a2 + 0.8/a3+ 0.2/a4}	{0.6/a1 + 0.1/a4}

Let us assume that the (sub)query considered is:

$$\text{sel}(r, \text{aircraft1} \neq \text{aircraft2})$$

The answer obtained is represented by the following relation containing disjunctive tuples:

#image	aircraft1	aircraft2
1	{1/a1}	{0.8/a2 + 0.2/a3}
1	{1/a2 }	{0.2/a3}
1	{0.7/a3}	{0.8/a2 }
2	{0.2/a2}	{0.6/a1 + 0.1/a4}
2	{0.8/a3}	{0.6/a1 + 0.1/a4}
2	{0.2/a4}	{0.6/a1}

♦

4.3 Joins

The definition of the join operation is similar to that of the selection involving a condition of type 2. When two tuples match, we keep all of the variants that match and we generate as many tuples as necessary. More formally, let us consider relations r and s whose respective schemas are R(A, X) and S(B, Y) and the joining condition A θ B. The join operation is defined as:

$$\text{Join}(r, s, A\ \theta\ B) = \{<\{\alpha_i/a_i\}, \text{restr}(v.B, a_i\ \theta\ B), u.X, v.Y> \mid \exists\, u \in r, \exists\, v \in s \text{ such that } u.A = \{\alpha_1/a_1 + \ldots + \alpha_i/a_i + \ldots + \alpha_n/a_n\} \text{ and } \text{restr}(v.B, a_i\ \theta\ B) \neq \varnothing\} \quad (5).$$

4.4 Computing the Final Degree

Let us notice that the final projection involved in Q has not yet been dealt with. The role of this fourth step is to perform this final treatment. By construction, the projection gives birth to a single tuple, i.e., the target tuple t. The only question resides in the determination of the degree attached to this tuple (which is indeed what the user is interested in). Let us denote by r' the relation obtained at the end of step 3. The possibility degree attached to a tuple of r' is the minimum over all the attributes of the maximal grades tied to each attribute value. According to the semantics of a projection (based on the existential quantifier), the final degree attached to the target tuple equals the maximum of those of the tuples in r'.

Example 6. Let us assume that the relation issued from step 3 is the following:

A	X	B	Y
{1/a1 + 1/a2 + 0.7/a3}	x	{0.8/b2 + 0.2/b3}	y
{0.8/a3}	x	{0.6/b1 + 0.1/b4}	y

in the context of a possibilistic query of the type: "to what extent is it possible that (x, y) belongs to ... ". During this final step, the pair (x, y) is assigned the degree:

$$\max(\min(\max(1, 1, 0.7), \max(0.8, 0.2)), \min(0.8, \max(0.6, 0.1))) = \max(\min(1, 0.8), \min(0.8, 0.6)) = \max(0.8, 0.6) = 0.8$$ ♦

5. Conclusion

The issue of querying possibilistic databases (where some attribute values may be imprecisely known and represented by means of possibility distributions) has been addressed in this paper. A new type of queries (called possibilistic queries) has been investigated in the perspective of avoiding the combinatorial growth tied to the explicitation of worlds. The general form of such queries is: "to what extent is it possible that a given tuple t belongs to the answer of the usual relational query Q". A four steps evaluation procedure has been devised, which covers only a subset of relational operations (selections and joins) but it is not too restrictive because in practice most of the queries use these operations. The present contribution constitutes a promising step insofar as it answers the complexity problem, even if for space reason, this issue has not been dealt with in detail here. For a similar reason, the formal proof of correctness of the procedure proposed is not given. Let us just say that, thanks to the constraints put into play, it would be quite easy to show that any tuple produced by a selection or join could be found by means of a world-based calculus and conversely (since no world is lost during the computations made here).

This work should be pursued in order to broaden the approach so as to be able to deal with a larger range of queries. In particular, the inclusion of set-oriented operators and the way self joins can be taken into account are two interesting lines of research.

References

1. Abiteboul, S., Hull, R, Vianu, V.: *Foundations of databases*, Addison-Wesley, 1995.
2. Bosc, P., Duval, L., Pivert, O.: About Possibilistic Queries Against Possibilistic Databases, to appear in the Proc. of the 17th ACM Symposium on Applied Computing *(SAC'2002)*, March 2002.
3. Bosc, P., Liétard, L., Pivert, O.: A function-based join for the manipulation of possibilistic relations, *16th ACM Conference on Applied Computing (SAC'2001)*, Las Vegas (USA), 472-476, 2001.
4. Bosc, P., Prade, H.: An introduction to fuzzy set and possibility theory-based approaches to the treatment of uncertainty and imprecision in data base management systems, *In: Uncertainty Management in Information Systems – From Needs to Solutions*, (Motro A. and Smets P. Eds.), Kluwer Academic Publishers, 285-324, 1997.
5. Imielinski, T., Lipski, W.: Incomplete information in relational databases, *Journal of the ACM*, 31,761-791, 1984.
6. Libkin, L., Wong, L.: Semantic representations and query languages for or-sets, *12th PODS Conference*, 37-48, 1993.
7. Prade, H., Testemale, C.: Generalizing database relational algebra for the treatment of incomplete/uncertain information and vague queries, *Information Sciences*, 34, 115-143, 1984.
8. Zadeh, L.A.: Fuzzy sets as a basis for a theory of possibility, *Fuzzy Sets and Systems*, 1, 3-28, 1978.

LeedsCQ: A Scalable Continual Queries System

Sharifullah Khan and Peter L. Mott

School of Computing, University of Leeds, Leeds, UK, LS2 9JT
{khan, pmott}@comp.leeds.ac.uk

Abstract

Continual Queries (CQs) are persistent queries that are issued once and then are run at regular intervals or when source data change until a termination condition is satisfied. Users receive new information automatically as it becomes available. CQs systems need to support a large number of CQs due to the scale of the Internet. This paper describes a novel architecture for a CQs system that scales to a large number of queries. In this system CQs are evaluated locally on the CQ server without accessing base relations after initial evaluation. Only group queries are run to retrieve auxiliary data. We optimize the retrieval of auxiliary data. A performance evaluation shows that the architecture reduces data transmission and I/O costs.

1 Introduction

Continual Queries (CQs) [5, 11] provide for personalized update monitoring on the Internet. They are persistent queries that are issued once and then are run at regular intervals or when source data change until a *termination condition* is satisfied. They relieve users from having to revisit Web sites and re-issue their queries. The users receive new information automatically as it becomes available.

A CQ is a typical SQL query Q having an additional *triggering condition*, and *termination condition*. CQs are of two types: *change-based* and *time-based*. Change-based CQs are fired when new data arrives at a source, while time-based CQs are fired at regular intervals. An example of a CQ is: *"notify me in the next one year whenever the BMW stock price drops by more than 5% in a day"*.

CQ systems need to support a large number of CQs due to the scale of the Internet. One approach to this problem is to use query grouping which optimizes the evaluation of queries by executing common operations in a group of queries just once [5, 13, 14]. However, traditional grouping techniques are not suitable in this situation [5, 9]. In addition, after initial evaluation, a CQ is only interested in those data that have been updated in the data source since its previous execution.

In this paper we present a novel architecture for a scalable CQ system called *LeedsCQ* which employs a scalable and dynamic grouping technique [9] and *differential evaluation* [8] for optimization of CQs. By differential evaluation, we mean that a CQ is evaluated on the whole base data only once. Subsequently

R. Cicchetti et al. (Eds.): DEXA 2002, LNCS 2453, pp. 607–617, 2002.

it is evaluated against the changes that have been made in the base data since its previous evaluation. These changes we call *differential updates* and store in a *differential relation.*

The rest of this paper is organized as follows. In section 2, we describe related work and identify their limitations. Section 3 proposes the architecture for a CQs system. Section 4 describes a technique for derivation of auxiliary queries. Section 5 presents a performance evaluation of our architecture in terms of data transferred and I/O's cost. Section 6 concludes this paper and presents future research.

2 Related Work

Considerable research on update monitoring has been done in databases. *Active databases*, *triggers*, *materialized views*, and CQ are tools of update monitoring. However, update monitoring over the Internet raises issues of scalability [4, 3, 11]. Active databases, triggers, and materialized views are not scalable and their performance quickly deteriorates when triggers are large in number or complex [4, 3, 11]. CQs can be scaled to a large number without performance deterioration [11, 5]. Early work on CQs was inspired by Terry et al. [16]. They developed continuous queries over append-only databases and their model for the update monitoring was purely time-based. This notion has been extended to a wide spectrum of environments in [2]. Recently a survey on continuous queries over data streams has been presented in [1].

Liu et al. [11, 10] proposed a new model for CQs that supports both content-based and time-based events and a termination condition. In their architecture the CQ server is responsible for evaluating each query individually over the data sources. Chen et al. [5] developed a scalable CQ system for Internet databases. In their architecture, queries are grouped over the CQ server and a representative group query (GQ) is chosen. GQ is evaluated over the data sources, while other queries of the group are evaluated from the result of their GQ.

The architectures mentioned in [11, 5] are not useful for grouped CQs because they do not comply with CQs characteristics and requirements: (1) A CQs system has to handle a large collection of CQs due to the scale of the Internet. (2) Users' requests are unpredictable and change rapidly. (3) When we group CQs, the group is dynamic, as old queries are deleted and new ones are added. In this case one or more groups may require dynamic re-grouping to maintain the effectiveness of groups [5]. (4) CQs in a group can have different evaluation times. For example, two users may request a similar CQ. One user may want to evaluate the CQ daily, while another may want to evaluate it when the profit increases 60%. This makes sharing computation difficult [5]. It proliferates the versions of query results in dynamic re-grouping of CQs in these architectures.

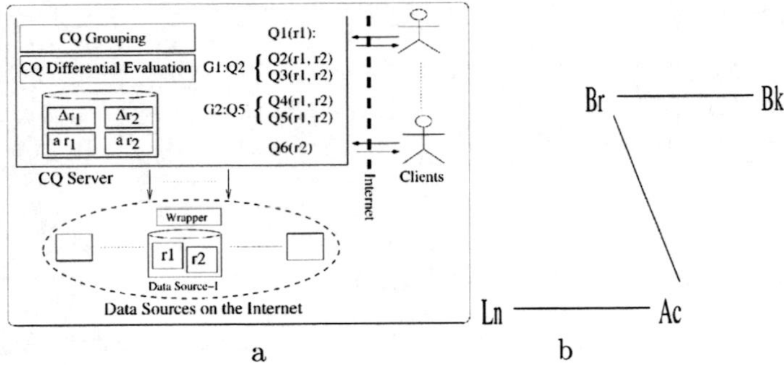

Figure 1: LeedsCQ Architecture and the Join Graph g_G of the group query G.

3 The Proposed Architecture for CQ System

In this section, we propose a scalable architecture (Figure 1(a)) designed to address the issues associated with current approaches. We maintain differential relations (Δr in the Figure 1(a)) on the CQ server. After the initial evaluation single relation CQs are evaluated against these differential relations and the differential relations are updated with changes at the data sources. However, multi-relation CQs can never be wholly evaluated against differential relations [12]. For example, the proposed expression to compute the changes of a 2-way join CQ over base relations, r_1, r_2, is (see [8] for details):

$$(\Delta r_1 \bowtie r_2) \cup (r_1 \bowtie \Delta r_2) \cup (\Delta r_1 \bowtie \Delta r_2)\,. \tag{1}$$

This expression specifies that CQ needs to access data drawn from base relations to compute changes, such data are called *auxiliary data* [12].

Auxiliary data can be obtained in two ways: (1) querying the data sources for each CQ (2) replicating base relations on the CQ server. However, both ways incur certain problems. The former may result in problems such as sending data repeatedly, which impacts on the base data's operations, and the periodic unavailability of data sources; while the latter may result in problems of storage consumption and maintenance costs.

We remarked above that each group of CQ is represented by a group query GQ. In the next section we shall show how GQs are used to derive the required auxiliary data. The fundamental features here are that GQs are pruned of projection operations and the results of GQs are collectively stored in differential and auxiliary relations. We believe our architecture: (1) avoids the replication of query results on the CQ server (2) avoids the proliferation of the version of GQ results in dynamic re-grouping (3) reduces storage consumption on the CQ server (4) makes our grouping technique more scalable.

Table 1: *Link()* and $Link^+$ () Function for the base relations.

(a)			(b)		
$Link\,(Bk,\,\mathcal{E})$	=	$\{Br\}$	$Link^+\,(Ln,\,\mathcal{E})$	=	$\{Ac,\,Br,\,Bk\}$
$Link\,(Br,\,\mathcal{E})$	=	$\{Bk,\,Ac\}$	$Link^+\,(Ac,\,\mathcal{E})$	=	$\{Ln,\,Br,\,Bk\}$
$Link\,(Ln,\,\mathcal{E})$	=	$\{Ac\}$	$Link^+\,(Br,\,\mathcal{E})$	=	$\{Ln,\,Ac,\,Bk\}$
$Link\,(Ac,\,\mathcal{E})$	=	$\{Br,\,Ln\}$	$Link^+\,(Bk,\,\mathcal{E})$	=	$\{Br,\,Ln,\,Ac\}$

4 Auxiliary Query and Its Derivation

In this section, we present a technique to derive auxiliary queries (AQs) from a GQ. AQs are used to extract the *auxiliary relations* needed in differential join queries. By *local conditions* we mean the selection conditions involving attributes from a single relation. First, we present few preliminary.

Definition 1 A *Join Graph* for a GQ $G\,(r_1, \cdots, r_n)$ is an undirected graph $g_G\,(\mathcal{R},\,\mathcal{E})$, where $\mathcal{R}$ is the set of vertices of the graph that represents the relations referenced in G, and $\mathcal{E}$ is the set of undirected edges, each connecting two vertices. An edge connecting r_i to r_j i.e. $e\,(r_i,\,r_j) \in \mathcal{E}$ represents a join condition $r_i.a = r_j.b$.

Definition 2 $Link\,(r_i,\,\mathcal{E}) = \{r_j \mid \exists\, e\,(r_i,\,r_j)\ \&\ e \in \mathcal{E}\}$ determines the set of relations in g_G to which a relation r_i joins on an attribute.

Definition 3 $Link^+\,(r_i,\,\mathcal{E})$ is the transitive closure of $Link\,(r_i,\,\mathcal{E})$.

When changes occur in r_i auxiliary data are needed from the set of relations r_j produced by $Link^+\,(r_i,\,\mathcal{E})$. The above definitions are illustrated through the following example.

Example 1 Consider a *Bank* database. The database comprises the following relations.

```
Bk(code, name, addr), Ac(ano, type, balance, cno, bno),
Br(bno, city, asset, code), Ln(lno, amount, date, bno, cno),
Cs(cno, name, phone, city).
```

Bk, Br, Ln, Ac, and *Cs* are abbreviation of bank, branch, loan, account, and customer respectively. Suppose we have a GQ:

$$G\,(Ln,\,Ac,\,Br,\,Bk) = \sigma_{amount \geq 10000 \wedge balance \leq 20000 \wedge city='Leeds' \wedge name='ABC'} (Ln \bowtie_{Ln.cno=Ac.cno} Ac \bowtie_{Ac.bno=Br.bno} Br \bowtie_{Br.code=Bk.code} Bk). \quad (2)$$

Figure 1(b) shows the Join Graph g_G of the GQ. Table 1 shows the *Link* and $Link^+$ relations derived from the Join Graph for this query.

Given a GQ $G\,(r_1, \cdots, r_n)$ defined over relations $r_1, \cdots, r_n$. A set of AQs is derived from G to retrieve auxiliary data when changes occur in a relation r_i. The set of relations supplying the needed auxiliary data are determined by $Link^+\,(r_i,\,\mathcal{E})$. An AQ for each of these relations may be derived from G. We formally define the AQ as follows.

Definition 4 An auxiliary query (AQ) $\partial G(r_i)$ for a relation $r_i \in G(r_1, \cdots, r_n)$ is a query that includes a selection on relation r_i followed by one or more semijoins with relations $r_j \in Link^+(r_i, \mathcal{E})$, provided that these relations satisfy their local conditions. The expression for AQ is:

$$\partial G(r_i) = \quad \sigma_{C_i}(r_i) \quad \ltimes \left\{ \sigma_{C_j}(r_j) \mid \exists r_j \in Link^+(r_i, \mathcal{E}) \right\}.$$

The AQs are dynamic and ad-hoc in nature. They retrieve all attributes of the respective base relation. Their result are stored on the CQ server in auxiliary relations (*ar* in the Figure 1(a)). In contrast to the conventional incremental view materialization method, this architecture employs one auxiliary relation for each base relation, which contains all the attributes of the base relation, and is used by all GQs. The procedure for the derivation of a set of AQs $\mathcal{S}$ from G is formally described in Algorithm 1. We call this algorithm the *Derivation of Auxiliary Queries* (DAQ) algorithm.

Algorithm 1 DAQ -Algorithm for Derivation of Auxiliary Queries.

Input: Group query $G(r_1, \cdots, r_n) = \sigma_C(r_1 \bowtie \cdots \bowtie r_n)$.
Output: Set of auxiliary queries $\mathcal{S}$.
Method:
Let $\mathcal{R}$ be the set of relations referenced in G.
Construct the graph g_G.
Push Selection down inside Join in G's description.
For every relation $r_i \in \mathcal{R}$,
  construct $Link(r_i, \mathcal{E})$ & $Link^+(r_i, \mathcal{E})$.
IF changes occurred in r_i,
  replace r_i with Δr_i for differential updates.
  For every relation $r_j \in Link^+(r_i, \mathcal{E})$,
    generate an auxiliary query $\partial G(r_j)$ as follows:
    $\partial G(r_j) = \sigma_{C_j}(r_j) \ltimes \left\{ \sigma_{C_k}(r_k) \mid \exists r_k \in Link^+(r_j, \mathcal{E}) \right\}$,
    C_j, C_k are the local selection condition over r_j, r_k and $C_j, C_k \in C$,
    where C is selection condition of group query G.

Consider the GQ defined in Example 1. Suppose changes occur in relation *Ln*. The AQs to retrieve the auxiliary data required by differential updates of ΔLn are generated as: (1) Construct the join graph of the GQ $G(Ln, Ac, Br, Bk)$, as shown in Figure 1(b). (2) Push selection down inside the joins in G. So the expression of G is:

$$\begin{aligned} G(Ln, Ac, Br, Bk) \quad = \quad & (\sigma_{amount \geq 10000} Ln) \bowtie_{Ln.cno=Ac.cno} (\sigma_{balance \leq 20000} Ac) \\ & \bowtie_{Ac.bno=Br.bno} (\sigma_{city='Leeds'} Br) \bowtie_{Br.code=Bk.code} \\ & (\sigma_{name='ABC'} Bk). \end{aligned}$$

This step restricts tuples to those that pass local conditions, thus reducing the size of the auxiliary relation. (3) Generate $Link()$ and $Link^+()$ for each relation of G to determine the set of relations to which *Ln* joins in G, shown in Tables 1-a and 1-b respectively. (4) Replace *Ln* with ΔLn as changes occur in *Ln*. This replacement does not affect the result (see [7] for details) but ΔLn restricts auxiliary data retrieval to differential updates and eliminates unnecessary data retrieval. (5) Take the set of relations of $Link^+$ $(Ln, \mathcal{E})$ and generate an AQ for each of these relations according to Definition 4. The AQ for Br is as follows.

$$\begin{aligned} \partial G\,(Br) \;\; = \;\; & (\sigma_{city='Leeds'} Br) \ltimes_{Br.bno=Ac.bno} (\sigma_{balance \leq 20000} Ac) \\ & \ltimes_{Ac.cno=Ln.cno} (\sigma_{amount \geq 10000} \Delta Ln) \\ & \ltimes_{Br.code=Bk.code} (\sigma_{name='ABC'} Bk)\,. \end{aligned}$$

The semijoin in the AQ reduces the number of Br's tuples by restricting it to contain only those tuples join-able with other relations. AQs for the other relations are generated similarly (see [7] for details). These AQs are sufficient to answer any continual queries in the group because the algorithm uses the $Link^+$ () function of an updated relation, which determines all the relations which can join with the updated relation in the join graph. As an additional optimization, *screen test*, or *change filtering* [12] could be used to determine which changes to the base relation are relevant to any of the GQs. (see [7] for details).

4.1 Handling Multiple Changes

Multiple changes (MCs) here means multiple tuples of a differential relation that have the same values for a join attribute. The modification operation of a tuple in the base relation is represented by deletion followed by an insertion of the tuple in the differential relation [8]. The *deferred* or *periodic* approach can be employed to refresh auxiliary relations. So, the differential relation actually maintains the changes made by several transactions to the base relation [8].

The DAQ algorithm treats the MCs and single changes uniformly because it uses semijoins to retrieve auxiliary data. A semijoin of two relations, r_1 and r_2, is $r_1 \ltimes r_2 = r_1 \bowtie (\pi_x (r_2))$, where x is a join attribute, i.e. $x = R_1 \cap R_2$. The semijoin projects the join attribute before joining and projection eliminates redundancy of distinct values of the join attribute. Therefore, the DAQ algorithm retrieves the auxiliary data for the MCs once instead of multiple times. Hence, the algorithm reduces data transmission over the network and I/O cost in cases of multiple changes.

4.2 Handling Changes to Multiple Relations

The DAQ algorithm handles the changes of one relation at a time if changes occur in multiple relations (MRs) since AQs generated by handling the changes of MRs simultaneously can produce incorrect results. Suppose changes occur in relations Ln and Ac simultaneously in Example 1. If the DAQ algorithm handles the changes of both relations at the same time, the algorithm will replace both relations Ln and Ac with their differential relations ΔLn and ΔAc in the AQ respectively. Then the AQ $\partial G\,(Br)$ in terms of the ΔLn changes is as follows:

$$\begin{aligned} \partial G\,(Br) \;\; = \;\; & (\sigma_{city='Leeds'} Br) \ltimes_{Br.bno=Ac.bno} (\sigma_{balance \leq 20000} \Delta Ac) \ltimes_{Ac.cno=Ln.} \\ & (\sigma_{amount \geq 10000} \Delta Ln) \ltimes_{Br.code=Bk.code} (\sigma_{name='ABC'} Bk)\,. \end{aligned}$$

Table 2: List of variables.

Variable	Meaning	Variable	Meaning
M	# of Memory blocks	v	# of distinct values of an att.
B	# of bytes transferred	R	Record length of a relation
IO	# of I/O's	BS	Block size, 1024 bytes
T	# of tuples in a relation	b	bytes

The result of $\partial G\,(Br)$ may not be correct because the tuples of auxiliary data required by ΔLn may not be available in ΔAc [8]. Similarly this can be the case in terms of the ΔAc changes. The DAQ algorithm derives AQs from a GQ by considering the changes of one relation at a time. However, in the case of insertions to MRs that can join with each other, the algorithm can handle changes to more than one relation at one time. This is becuase the new tuples of a relation do not need to access the existing tuples in other changed relations. This can be formally defined by a property as follows.

Property 1 (Insertion property) Consider a join operation $\{r_1 \bowtie_{a_1=a_2} r_2\}$ where tuples $\mu \in r_1$ and $\nu \in r_2$. If μ, ν are inserted in r_1, r_2 respectively at a time such that $\mu.a_1 = \nu.a_2$, then the expression to compute the change of the query in (1) will be as follows:

$$(\Delta r_1 \bowtie \Delta r_2)\,. \tag{3}$$

This property represents that the AQ of a changed relation in terms of other relations' changes is not required. Hence we define a rule on the basis of this property.

Rule 1 (Insertion rule) Let g_G be the join graph for a GQ G and $r_1 \in Link\,(r_2,\, \mathcal{E})$ and $r_2 \in Link\,(r_1,\, \mathcal{E})$. If insertions to r_1 and r_2 fulfill the Insertion property, then remove r_2 from $Link\,(r_1,\, \mathcal{E})$ and vice versa.

This rule eliminates an updated relation from the transitive closure of other updated relations. Suppose changes occur in relations Ln and Ac in Example 1 that are insertions that can join with each other. The tuples required by ΔLn are available in ΔAc and do not require the existing tuples of Ac. Similarly this is the case in terms of the ΔAc changes. When Rule 1 is applied to G in this case, then the arguments of $Link\,()$ and $Link^+\,()$ are changed, so that $Link\,(Ln,\, \mathcal{E}) = \{\}$, $Link^+\,(Ac,\, \mathcal{E}) = \{Bk, Br\}$ and $Link^+\,(Br,\, \mathcal{E}) = \{Ac, Bk\}$. So ΔLn needs no auxiliary data because its $link\,()$ function is empty whilst ΔAc needs auxiliary data from $\{Bk, Br\}$. The AQ for Br, when the DAQ algorithm handles the changes of both relations at the same time, is as follows:

$$\begin{aligned}\partial G\,(Br) \;\; = \;\; & (\sigma_{city='Leeds'}\, Br) \ltimes_{Br.bno=Ac.bno} (\sigma_{balance \le 20000} \Delta Ac) \\ & \ltimes_{Br.code=Bk.code} (\sigma_{name='ABC'}\, Bk)\,.\end{aligned}$$

5 Performance Evaluation

In this section we evaluate the performance of our architecture in terms of data transmission and I/O costs. We consider three architectures for CQs: (1) Each

Table 3: Relation statistics

Ac	size	Ln	size	Cs	size
R(Ac)	60b	R(Ln)	60b	R(Cs)	90b
T(Ac)	20,000	T(Ln)	20,000	T(Cs)	15,000
V(Ac,cno)	10,000	V(Ln,cno)	10,000	V(Cs,cno)	15,000
R(ΔAc)	60b	R(ΔLn)	60b	R(ΔCs)	90b
T(ΔAc)	100	T(ΔLn)	100	T(ΔCs)	100
V1(ΔAc,cno)	50	V1(ΔLn,cno)	50	V1(ΔCs,cno)	100
V2(ΔAc,cno)	100	V2(ΔLn,cno)	100	V2(ΔCs,cno)	100

CQ is evaluated individually at the data source. (2) CQs are grouped and the GQs are evaluated on the data source, while remaining CQs are deduced from the result of GQs on the CQ server. (3) Our architecture, where CQs are evaluated over differential and auxiliary relations on the CQ server after the initial evaluation. The AQs are evaluated on data sources to extract auxiliary data. We denote these architectures by m_1, m_2, m_3 respectively.

The evaluation is based on a "representative" scenario to illustrate the performance tradeoffs. It uses the variables listed in Table 2 and Table 3 presents parameters and their values which are assumed for the Bank database of Example 1. We define the following CQs over the Bank database for this evaluation:

$$\begin{aligned} Q_1 &= \sigma_{amout>10{,}000 \wedge balance<5000}\left(\Delta Ln \bowtie Ac \bowtie Cs\right), \\ Q_2 &= \sigma_{amout>15{,}000 \wedge balance<5000}\left(\Delta Ln \bowtie Ac \bowtie Cs\right), \\ Q_3 &= \sigma_{amout>12{,}000 \wedge balance<3000}\left(\Delta Ln \bowtie Ac \bowtie Cs\right). \end{aligned}$$

We further assume the length of a tuple in each CQ result set in m_1 & m_2 is *90 bytes*. CQs extract all the attributes of a relation in m_3. We employ methods described in [6], to compute the bytes of data transferred and the number of I/O's of queries.

5.1 Performance Based on Data Transferred

In order to determine B in a query, we compute the size of intermediate relations returned by the query. Let $r_1$and r_2 be two relations and x be the join attribute. We use *selectivity factor* $1/3$ for any inequality comparison. We estimate v of x in a relation after the effect of local conditions i.e., $v'(r_1, x)$, in the estimation of join result sizes by a common estimate [15]: $v'(r_1, x) = v(r_1, x) * (T'(r_1)/T(r_1))$, where, $T'(r_1)$ is the size of the relation after effect of local condition. We estimate the size of join result by a formula: $T(r_1 \bowtie r_2) = (T(r_1)T(r_2))/max(v(r_1, x), v(r_2, x))$. According to the formula, the size of the result of each of the above CQs is *66 tuples*. We formally define the saving of B as follows:

$$saving_B(G) = \sum_{i=1}^{k} B(Q_i) - B(G) \tag{4}$$

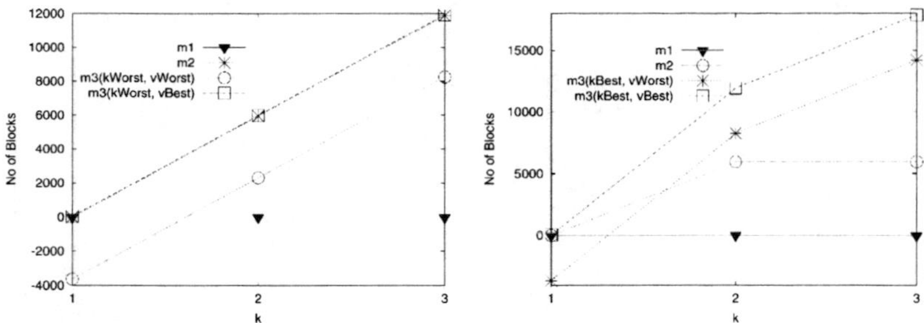

Figure 2: Saving in data transferred: S_1 (Left), S_2 (Right)

where k is the number of queries in G. It means that the saving of B increases as the number of queries increases in a group.

We believe that the *grouping ratio* k: number of queries in a group, in m_3 is greater than in m_2 because m_3 prunes queries of projection. We consider two cases for k: best and worst. The worst case, $kWorst$, is when the k of both architectures are equal and the best case, $kBest$, is when k in m_3 is greater by at least one query than in m_2. Moreover, the number of distinct values of join attributes, v, in case of MCs affects B in m_3. However, this does not apply to m_1 and m_2 because they do not use semijoin. We consider two cases: best and worst, for v in differential relations. The best case, $vBest$, is v is small e.g., V1(ΔA,cno) in Table 3; and the worst case, $vWorst$, is when v is large e.g., V2(ΔA,cno).

We consider two scenarios: S_1, S_2, based on k. In S_1 m_2 and m_3 group an equal number of queries i.e., we take $kWorst$ for m_3. The saving in B is shown by the graph in Figure 2(Left). In S_2 m_3 groups more queries than m_2, i.e., we take $kBest$ for m_3. The saving in B is shown by the graph in Figure 2(Right). It is shown that B depends on two factors in m_3: the number of queries in a group and v. The architecture m_3 becomes more efficient (i.e., achieves more saving) than the others as the number of queries in a group increases and v decreases.

5.2 Performance Based on I/O

We continue I/O's analysis with the same cases of k and v as we described in the previous section. We consider here only the $vWorst$ case of v because its effects on I/O's are minor. In addition, we assume here some more worst cases to facilitate the estimation of I/O's. That is, there are no indexes and relations are stored on identification key order and intermediate results are not materialized.

The saving in I/O's is different from the saving of B because queries in a group, except the GQ, do not transfer data between a data source and the CQ server, but they need I/O's on on the CQ server. So we make an amendment in (4) as follows.

$$saving_{IO}(G) = \sum_{i=1}^{k} IO(Q_i) - \left(IO(G) + \sum_{i=1}^{k} IO_{CQS}(Q_i) \right). \tag{5}$$

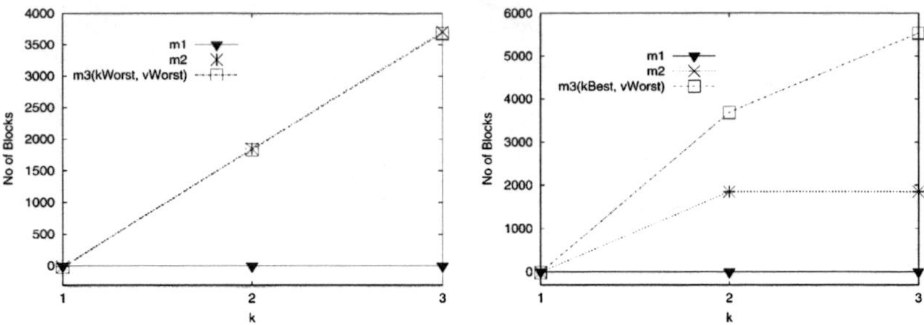

Figure 3: Saving in number I/O's: S_1 (Left), S_2 (Right)

$IO\,(G)$ is the number of I/O's of the GQ G, to read the data from a data source and to write them on CQ server, $IO_{CQS}\,(Q)$ is number of I/O 's of a query to read data at CQ server.

We consider the same scenarios: S_1, S_2, described in the previous section. Savings in the number of I/O of different architectures in S_1, S_2 are shown by the graphs in Figure 3. It is shown that the number of I/O's mostly depends on the number of queries in a group. Our architecture m_3 becomes more efficient than the others as queries in a group increases.

6 Conclusion

In this paper, we have presented a novel architecture for a scalable CQs system. This architecture employs grouping and differential evaluation of CQs for scalability and optimization. They are evaluated locally on the CQ server without accessing base relations after initial evaluation. Only GQs are run to access auxiliary data. The architecture reduces storage consumption on the CQ server and makes the grouping scalable. We have produced an algorithm to derive AQs from a GQ which reduces data transmission and I/O cost. It also reduces the size of an auxiliary relation. In other words, AQs optimize the retrieval of auxiliary data. Further, we have presented a performance evaluation of the architecture in terms of data transferred and I/O cost. The evaluation shows that the architecture needs fewer I/O's and reduces the data transmission for the large number of CQs in a group. In addition, it paves the way for dynamic re-grouping of CQs.

References

[1] S. Babu and J.Widom. Continuous queries over data streams. SIGMOD Record, 30(3):109-120, Sep. 2001.

[2] D. Barbara. The characterization of continuous queries. Int. J. of Cooperative Information Systems, 8(4):295-323, Dec. 1999.

[3] P. Bernstein et al. The asilomer report on database research. SIGMOD Record, 27(4), Dec. 1998.

[4] S. Ceri, R. Cochrane, and J. Widom. Practical applications of triggers and constraints: Successes and lingering issues. In Proc. of Int. Con. VLDB' 2000, pp 254-262, Cairo, Egypt, Sep. 2000.

[5] J. Chen, D. DeWitt, et al. NiagaraCQ: A scalable continuous query system for Internet Databases. In Proc. of Int. Con. ACM SIGMOD' 2000, pp 379-390, Dallas, USA, May 2000.

[6] H. Garcia-Molina, J.D. Ullman, and J. Widom. Database System Implementation. Prentice Hall Inc. 1st edn, 2000.

[7] S. Khan and P. Mott. LeedsCQ: A scalable continual queries system. Tech. report 2002.03, School of Computing, Uni. of Leeds, Leeds, LS2 9JT, UK, Feb. 2002.

[8] S. Khan and P. Mott. Differential evaluation of continual queries. Tech. report 2001.11, School of Computing, Uni. of Leeds, Leeds, LS2 9JT, UK, May 2001.

[9] S. Khan and P. Mott. Scalable and dynamic grouping of continual queries. Tech. report 2001.17, School of Computing, Uni. of Leeds, Leeds, LS2 9JT, UK, Sep. 2001.

[10] L. Liu, C. Pu, et al. Differential evaluation of continual queries. In Proc. of Int. Con. ICDCS' 96, pp 458-465, Hong Kong, May 1996.

[11] L. Liu, C. Pu, and W. Tang. Continual queries for Internet scale event-driven information delivery. IEEE Trans. on Knowledge and Data Engineering, 11(4):610-628, July/Aug. 1999.

[12] D. Quass, A. Gupta, I.S. Mumick, and J. Widom. Making views self-maintainable for data warehousing. In Proc. of Int. Con. on Parallel and Distributed Information Systems, pp158-169, Florida, USA, Dec. 1996.

[13] P. Roy, S. Seshadri, et al. Efficient and extensible algorithms for multi query optimization. In Proc. of Int. Con. ACM SIGMOD' 2000, pp 249-260, Dallas, USA, May 2000.

[14] T.K. Sellis. Multiple-Query Optimization. ACM Trans. on Database Systems, 13:(1)23-52, March 1988.

[15] A. Swami and K.B. Schiefer. On the estimation of join result size. In Proc. of Int. Con. EDBT' 94, LNCS, Vol.779, pp 287-300, Cambridge, UK, March 1994.

[16] D. Terry, D. Goldberg, et al. Continuous queries over append-only databases. In Proc. of Int. Con. ACM SIGMOD'92, pp 321-330, San Diego, USA, Jan. 1992.

TVQL - Temporal Versioned Query Language

Mirella Moura Moro[1], Nina Edelweiss[1],
Aglaê Pereira Zaupa[1, 2], and Clesio Saraiva dos Santos[1]

[1] Instituto de Informática - Universidade Federal do Rio Grande do Sul
Av. Bento Gonçalves, 9500 - Porto Alegre, RS, Brazil - CxP. 15064. CEP 91501-970
[2] Faculdade de Informática - Universidade do Oeste Paulista
R. José Bongiovani, 700 - Presidente Prudente, RS, Brazil. CEP 19050-260
[1]{mirella, nina, clesio}@inf.ufrgs.br, [2]aglae@apec.unoeste.br

Abstract. The Temporal Versions Model (TVM) is an Object Oriented Data Model developed to store the object versions and, for each version, the history of its dynamic attributes and relationships values. In this work, we propose a query language for this model. The language, called Temporal Versioned Query Language - TVQL, is based on SQL, adding new features to recover temporal information and versions. An alternative to its implementation on top of a commercial database is also presented.

1 Introduction

Information stored in a database evolves with time and, very often, it is necessary to keep track of such evolution. This fact led to researches concerning temporal database systems [2, 4, 5, 9, 10], which keep the evolution of data by associating timestamps to them. On the other hand, non-conventional applications, as CAD and CASE tools, often demand the support of many design alternatives. To fulfill such requirement, many works have focused on the question of versions support [1, 3, 6, 8, 11].

In [7], Moro et al. present a temporal object-oriented versions model (Temporal Versions Model - TVM), which brings together features of a version model and a temporal model. The Model allows the storage of all versions of an object and the history of dynamic attributes and relationships values. An approach to implement the TVM model on top of a commercial database is also presented in that work.

TVM is part of a project that aims implementing an integrated environment for class specification, object versioning, versions management, query, and visualization. There is an interface for temporal versioned class specification that allows the creation of tables in the database according to this specification. Now, this work presents a query language for TVM (Temporal Versioned Query Language – TVQL). The language adds new features to SQL for recovering temporal information and versions. An alternative to its implementation is also presented.

The paper is structured as follows. Section 2 illustrates the example to be used in the paper. Section 3 briefly exposes the Temporal Versions Model. Section 4 presents the query language TVQL. An alternative to its implementation on top of a commercial database is proposed in Section 5. Section 6 cites some related works. Section 7 summarizes the main ideas of this paper and presents future works.

R. Cicchetti et al. (Eds.): DEXA 2002, LNCS 2453, pp. 618–627, 2002.

2 Example

In order to illustrate different TVQL queries, TVM is used to model a simple application: a website design company, as presented in [7]. Beyond its clients' sites, the company keeps the professional pages of its employees. In order to simplify and make the concepts clearer, only the nucleus of the model is presented.

Each website is composed by one or more pages, one of them being the initial or main page. Each page is associated to a page pattern, which defines the background color and image, a banner, and the default font specification. The pattern is used as a standard for the employees' page layout. This pattern may vary according to the seasons of the year and commemorative dates, for instance. The class diagram corresponding to this example is presented in Fig. 1.

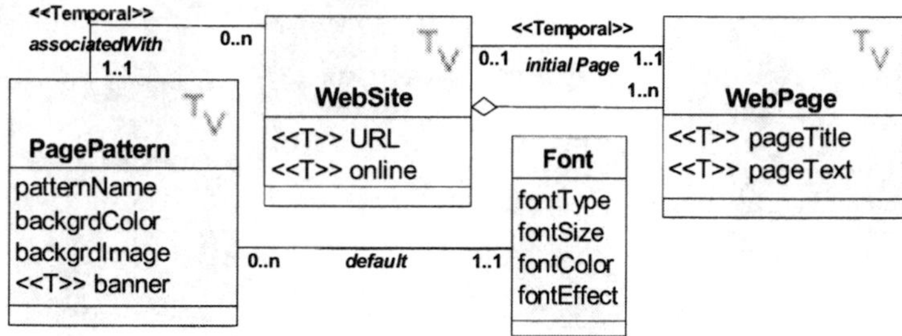

Fig. 1. Class Diagram of the example

3 Temporal Versions Model

The Temporal Versions Model (TVM) is proposed as an object-oriented (OO) data model that extends a version model by adding the temporal dimension to the instance versioning level [7]. Indeed, the user may model the database considering the design alternatives as well as the data evolution. It is important to notice that TVM does not require all classes to be temporal and versionable, allowing the integration with existing applications.

TVM allows the storage of different designed versions together with all updates in values of those attributes and relationships defined as temporal. Therefore, different versions coexist, representing branched time order that is not usual in other models, in which the time order is almost always linear. Within a version, the updates of temporal attributes and relationships vary in linear order.

Consider a Travel Agency as a client of the Website Company. The Agency has special tourism packages for international holydays with advertisements in the banner attribute. As illustrated in Fig. 2, a temporal versioned class may have instances with no versions and versioned objects. The instance *Fall* has no versions, while the instance *Summer* has three versions – the basic summer version *S*, a version to be used advertising the American July 4th, and a version for the French national date, July 14th. This figure also clarifies the evolving behavior of the temporal property *banner* whose value changes from *US-J4* to *FR-J14*. The temporal labels mean that a value is stored in the database and denotes the real world value on 06/28/2002; and another value is stored on 07/01/2002 but is valid only on 07/05/2002.

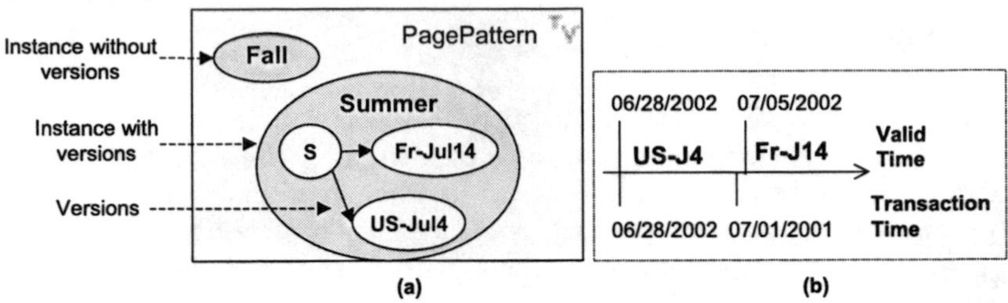

Fig. 2. a. An instance with no versions (*Fall*), and a versioned object (*Summer*) with three versions (*S*, *US-Jul4*, and *Fr-Jul14*). **b.** The evolving behavior of the temporal property *banner* with temporal labels.

4 Temporal Versioned Query Language

After this brief outline of TVM, this section shows its query language, Temporal Versioned Query Language (TVQL). The general form of a TVQL query is:

```
query ::=   SELECT [ EVER ] [ DISTINCT ] targetC { , targetC }
            FROM identificC { , identificC }     [ WHERE [ EVER ] searchC ]
            [ GROUP BY groupC { , groupC } [ HAVING logicalExpr ] ]
            [ ORDER BY orderC { , orderC } [ setOp query ] ;
targetC ::=          ( * | propertyName | aggregationFunctions | preDefInterval
                     | preDefInstant ) [ AS identifier ]
identificC ::=       className [ .VERSIONS ] [ aliasName ]
searchC ::=          logicalExpr | tempExpr
groupC ::=           propertyName | preDefInterval | preDefInstant
logicalExpr ::=      AnyLogicalExpression
tempExpr ::=         logicalExpr | PRESENT ( logicalExpr )
orderC ::=           groupC [ ASC | DESC ]
setOp ::=            UNION | INTERSECTION | DIFFERENCE
preDefInterval ::=   [ propertyName. ] ( tInterval | vInterval )
preDefInstant ::=    [ propertyName. ] ( tiInstant | tfInstant | viInstant | vfInstant )
                     | [ className. ] ( iLifeTime | fLifeTime )
```

Where brackets [ ] indicate optional segment, braces { } indicate optional repetitive segment (zero or more times), parentheses indicate set of options, | indicates "or", emphasized (bold) words are keywords.

TVQL is based on SQL and keeps its following features: base structure with *select-from-where*, alias for attributes (*select*) and classes (*from*), keyword *distinct* to eliminate duplicate values, operators for comparison, range and pattern matching (<, >, =, <=, >=, <>, *in*, *between..and*, *like*), arithmetic operators (+, -, *, /), logical operators (*or*, *and*, *not*), set operations (*union*, *intersection*, *difference*), aggregation functions (*count*, *sum*, *avg*, *min*, *max*), and other clauses (*group by*, *having*, *order by*).

By default, a TVQL statement retrieves current data stored in the current database state. Considering the temporal features of TVM, TVQL offers properties for pre-defined instants and intervals with a set of operators.

Several combinations of current and historic values may be declared in a query, depending on the use of the special keywords *ever* and *present*. *Ever* may be used after *select* and *where* to take into account not only the current values, but also the whole attributes and relationships histories. When *ever* is used in the *select* clause, the query retrieves the whole history of the chosen temporal properties. The use of *ever* in the *where* clause makes all values in a property history to be considered by the search condition. Another possibility is to retrieve historic values according to a current condition. This is done using *ever* in the *select* clause, and *present* in the *where* clause, which thus receives the current condition.

In order to retrieve and consider the temporal labels, TVQL specifies pre-defined temporal properties: *tInterval* (transaction time interval), *vInterval* (valid time interval), *tiInstant* (initial transaction time), *tfInstant* (final transaction time), *viInstant* (initial valid time), and *vfInstant* (final valid time). These properties are related to those attributes and relationships defined as temporal. Since there may be more than one temporal attribute in the same query, the user must specify to which attribute these properties are related. Otherwise, the query considers the temporal labels of all temporal attributes and relationships cited in the statement.

There are also two pre-defined properties related to the object lifetime: *iLifetime* (initial lifetime of the object), and *fLifeTime* (final lifetime of the object). All these pre-defined properties are defined to hide storage details from the user. Moreover, this feature allows greater implementation flexibility, as classes and attributes that store this information are not specified in TVQL.

TVQL proposes operators and behaviors for the existing operations to be included in the logical expressions of the *where* clause. There are operators for sequence of instants and intervals (*before*, *into*, *after*). The operators for temporal intervals are:

- *intersect* – returns true if the intervals have at least one common point.
- *overlap* – returns true if the second interval is within the first one.
- *equal* – returns true if both intervals start and finish in the same instants.

The user defines in the *from* clause which classes will be considered by a query. In TVQL, objects and versioned objects (current versions) are specified by the class name. The analysis of all versions is specified by adding the keyword *versions* to the class name. Consider the following queries:

1. Select banner from PagePattern; 2. Select banner from PagePattern.versions;

Query 1 takes into account *Fall* and the current version of *Summer*, while query 2 considers *Fall* together with all versions of *Summer* (*S*, *US-Jul4* and *Fr-Jul14*).

TVQL has three sets of functions to get specific information about versions and versioned objects. First, state functions evaluate the state of versions and return a boolean value – *isWorking*, *isWorkingAt* (if the version is in state "working" at a given time). Navigating functions evaluate the position of versions in the derivation sequence and return a boolean value – *isCurrent*, *isUserCurrent* (if the user defined it as the current one), *isFirst*, *isLast*, *isPredecessorOf*, *isSuccessorOf*. Finally, control functions retrieve information from the versioned object control – *firstVersion*, *lastVersion*, *versionCount*, *currentVersion*, *nextVersionNumber*, among others.

5 Implementing TVQL

The use of a powerful temporal data model does not require a specific database management system to support it. Existing commercial DBMSs may be used for this purpose as long as a proper mapping from the temporal data model to the data model underlying the adopted DBMS is provided. In order to show the feasibility of this approach, TVM was mapped to a commercial database in [7]. Now, this work presents the mapping from TVQL to SQL based on a mapping from TVM to a relational database. Instead of mapping TVM to an object-oriented database, this approach was chosen due to the widespread use and stability of relational databases. Basically, the mapping process joins the two parts of TVM mapping (representing the class model's hierarchy, and implementing the application classes) with a third one: the mapping of the TVQL functions and properties to SQL-92.

5.1 Mapping TVM to a Relational Database

In summary, the mapping from TVM classes to relational tables considers these steps:

1. If the class is standard, it is mapped to a table (*main table*) with the same name of the class, its attributes are mapped to columns, and the primary key is *tvoid.*
2. If the class is temporal versioned, it is also mapped to a main table with the same name of the class, with the following additional characteristics:
   3. The inherited attributes *alive*, *configuration*, *status* are mapped to columns in the main table.
   4. The inherited attributes *ascendant*, *descendant*, *predecessor* and *successor* are mapped to two special tables (*AscDesc* and *PredSucc*), which store the pairs and temporal labels (as these attributes are temporal).
   5. There is also a reference (*refVOC*, foreign key) to the *tvoid* of the respective versioned object control (which is mapped to the table *VOC* to store the information of all version controls, more details in reference [7]).
   6. Each temporal attribute and relationship is stored in a separated table (*auxiliary table*), which stores its history. These tables present the following columns: *tvoid* (foreign key related to the main table), *value* (with the same type of the attribute), and *itTime*, *ftTime*, *ivTime*, *fvTime* (temporal labels for initial and final transaction times, initial and final valid times). The primary key is composed by *tvoid*, *itTime* and *ivTime.*

Main tables store current data, and auxiliary tables store history values. The current values are also stored in the auxiliary tables in order to keep the temporal labels. This kind of implementation facilitates the query about current data, because only the main tables are considered. Similarly, queries about history consider only the auxiliary tables. Triggers and stored procedures are defined in order to manage current and historic data. For example, class *PagePattern* is mapped as shown in Fig. 3.

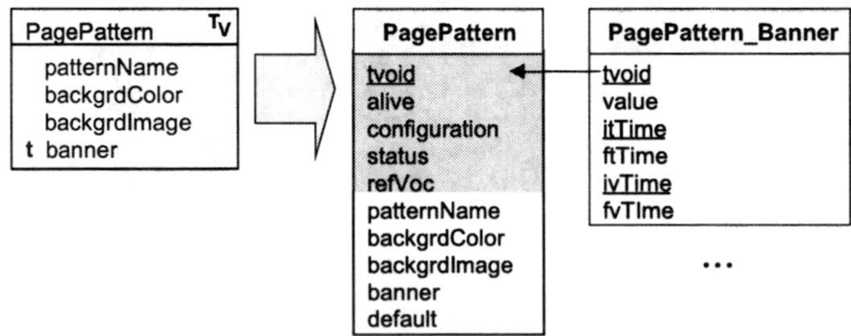

Fig. 3. A temporal versioned class (*PagePattern*) is mapped to a main table (*PagePattern*) and auxiliary tables in a relational database. The mapping is summarized with only one auxiliary table (*PagePattern_Banner*) graphically presented. Inherited attributes are presented in gray.

5.2 Mapping TVQL to SQL

The mapping from TVQL to SQL starts with the representation of the *from* clause, followed by the *select* and *where* clauses, and is divided in two parts: (i) mapping of classes, attributes and associations; and (ii) mapping of data restrictions. There is no special rule for mapping the general TVQL to SQL (keyword *distinct*; aggregation functions - *count*, *sum*, *avg*, *min*, *max*; and grouping clauses - *group by*, *having*, *order by*). Classes and properties involved in these cases are mapped to the respective tables implemented. In order to illustrate this procedure, some examples of TVQL queries with their mapping to SQL are presented in this section.

Mapping Classes, Attributes and Associations. The first step is to define in which tables of the database the classes and properties are stored. In *from* clause, classes are mapped to the main tables, and receive an alias (*t1*, *t2*, and so on). In *select* clause, attributes are mapped to the respective columns in the tables defined in *from*. In case of usual classes, the mapping is direct, as query 1.

Current data. Queries 1 and 2 consider only the current values stored in the main tables. The TVQL query is on the left side, and the respective SQL query is on the right.

Query 1) List all font types and sizes.

TVQL	**SQL**
SELECT fontType, fontSize FROM Font;	SELECT t1.fontType, t1.fontSize FROM Font t1;

In case of temporal versioned classes, if the keyword *versions* is not specified, the query must consider only the objects and current versions. Then, the table *VOC* is included in the *from* clause, and a special condition in the *where* clause, as the next query shows.

Query 2) List all current banners. The special condition means that either there is no reference to the versioned object control (the object has no versions) or there is a reference and the version is the current one. With keyword *versions*, this special condition is not used.

TVQL	**SQL**
SELECT banner FROM PagePattern;	SELECT t1.banner FROM PagePattern t1, VOC t2 WHERE (t1.refVOC = null) or (t1.refVOC = t2.tvoid and t1.tvoid = t2.currentVersion);

Data history. If the keyword *ever* is used after *select*, the auxiliary tables are also considered. As there is no temporal data restriction, queries 3 and 4 consider the current database state, which has final transaction time with value null or '12/31/9999'.

Query 3) List all banners in the history of all versions.

TVQL	**SQL**
SELECT EVER banner FROM PagePattern.versions;	SELECT t1.value FROM PagePattern_Banner t1 WHERE t1.ftTime = '12/31/9999';

Time and versions. Query 4) List the first version of all objects over history in class *PagePattern*, and the interval in which they are valid.

TVQL	**SQL**
SELECT EVER firstVersion, vInterval FROM PagePattern.versions;	SELECT t3.value, t3.ivTime || ".." || t3.fvTime FROM PagePattern t1, VOC t2, VOC_FirstVersion t1 WHERE t1.refVOC = t2.tvoid and t2.tvoid = t3.tvoid and t1.ftTime = '12/31/9999';

This query shows that getting the first version of a class is easy, while mapping to SQL is more complex. The possibility of querying the versioned object control directly by keywords, which are translated to its attributes, makes all query process involved in the implemented database transparent.

Mapping Data Restrictions. The second step is to map the data restrictions. In case of usual classes, the mapping is equal to SQL. In case of temporal versioned classes, a lot of possibilities must be considered, as presented in the next queries.

Temporal conditions. Query 5) Retrieve the current banner from versions of page patterns that have banner name beginning with letter A in its history.

TVQL	**SQL**
SELECT banner FROM PagePattern.versions WHERE EVER banner LIKE 'A%';	SELECT t1.banner FROM PagePattern t1, PagePattern_Banner t2 WHERE t1.tvoid = t2.tvoid and t2.ftTime = '12/31/9999' and t2.value like 'A%';

Query 6) Retrieve the current banner from versions of page patterns that have banner beginning with letter A as the database state on last December 31.

TVQL	**SQL**
SELECT banner FROM PagePattern.versions WHERE EVER banner LIKE 'A%' and '12/31/2001'into tInterval;	SELECT t1.banner FROM PagePattern t1, PagePattern_Banner t2 WHERE t1.tvoid = t2.tvoid and t2.value like 'A%' and t2.itTime <= '12/31/2001' and t2.ftTime >= '12/31/2001';

Queries 5 and 6 are very similar. The former considers the current database state, while the latter considers the database state as 12/31/2001. Another possibility for this query is to retrieve the history of banners based on current data, as query 7.

Query 7) Retrieve the history of banners that currently begin with letter A.

TVQL	**SQL**
SELECT EVER banner FROM PagePattern.versions WHERE PRESENT (banner LIKE 'A%');	SELECT t2.value FROM PagePattern t1, PagePattern_Banner t2 WHERE t1.tvoid = t2.tvoid and t2.ftTime = '12/31/9999' and t1.banner like 'A%';

Version features. Query 8) Retrieve pattern name and banner of stable versions in class PagePattern, with identification of their successors.

TVQL	**SQL**
SELECT p1.patternName, p1.banner, p2.tvoid FROM PagePattern.versions p1, PagePattern.versions p2 WHERE p1.isStable and p1.isPredecessorOf (p2);	SELECT t1.patternName, t1.banner, t2.tvoid FROM PagePattern t1, PagePattern t2, PredSucc t3 WHERE t1.status = 'S' and t3.predecessor = t1.tvoid and t3.successor = t2.tvoid and t3.ftTime = '12/31/9999';

Two or more Temporal Attributes. Query 9) Retrieve the *url* of online pages over the history. This query considers two temporal attributes in the same statement. The operation *intersect* appears in this query to assure that the result is not a Cartesian product between the histories of attributes *url* and *online*. Furthermore, it assures history consistency as the query retrieves only the *urls* that are valid when the pages are *online*.

TVQL	**SQL**
SELECT EVER url FROM WebPage.versions WHERE online = true and url.vInterval INTERSECT online.vInterval;	SELECT t1.value FROM WebSite_URL t1, WebSite_Online t2 WHERE t1.tvoid = t2.tvoid and t2.value = true and t1.ftTime = '12/31/9999' and t2.ftTime = '12/31/9999' and t1.ivTime<= t2.fvTime and t1.fvTime>= t2.ivTime;

6 Related Works

Temporal concepts and versions modeling are mostly treated individually in literature. Reference [7] cites at least eight works about temporal databases and seven about versions modeling, and just two models with time and versions, which are presented in this section. Other temporal query languages and version manipulation languages are also presented with their main particularities. Finally, we cite some similar and different features of these languages compared to TVQL.

The first model with time and versions is an extension for the OODAPLEX model, as a uniform model for temporal and versioned object-oriented databases, proposed by Wuu and Dayal [11]. The second one is a formal definition of a temporal versioned Object-Oriented data model (TVOO), proposed by Rodriguez, Ogata and Yano [8]. However, it has no query language specified.

In the OODAPLEX extension, queries are operations (functions) that map object (perhaps complex objects) to objects. Instead of *select*, the query structure uses *for each*, *for the*, *for all*, and *for some*. They uniformly combine retrieval on individual objects and aggregates of objects, associative retrieval and navigation retrieval. No special operators are necessary for temporal queries. However, while the retrieval of temporal and non-temporal information is uniformly expressed, the concept of version is not explicitly defined.

Some temporal query languages and version manipulation languages are presented as follows. VOHQL [3] is a visual query language for versions. The model represents the database as a graph of nodes and links. Expressing a VOHQL query consists of selecting links and performing operations from nodes of the graph. The language allows querying versions independent of others and versions organized into forests or trees. It has specific function for versions graph (*forest*, *unforest*, *tree*, *untree*), past and current links (*past*, *current*).

ATSQL [2] extends SQL using temporal modifiers or flags that may precede query statements (upward compatibility - UC, temporal upward compatibility - TUC, sequenced - SEQ, and non-sequenced queries - NONSEQ) in transaction and valid dimensions. It also allows coalescing and interval preservation.

TF-ORM [4] is a model with temporal functionality in objects with roles. Its language has special clauses *when* and *as on*, predicates (*is_valid_at*, *active_class* ...), operators (*always past*, *since*...) and temporal functions (*value*, *class_end_time* ...).

TSQL2 [9] supports time periods, multiple granularity, calendars, indeterminacy, selection operators (extractors, constructors and comparison).

SQL3 [10] adds object oriented features, the keywords *validtime*, *transactiontime* and *nonsequenced*, and temporal semantic to SQL.

TVQL is an SQL-based query language that allows usual SQL statements and retrieves data from the current and the past database states with time and versions information. Similarly to VOHQL, TVQL allows queries about independent versions as well as versions organized in the derivation graph.

Instead of new clauses and modifiers (as presented in TF-ORM, TSQL2, SQL3), TVQL retrieves historic data values using pre-defined temporal properties in the search clause, and the keyword *ever* to retrieve all history. It also allows to rollback the database to previous states using these same properties, ensuring an homogeneous behavior for valid and transaction times. Finally, TVQL can query current and historic values in the same statement by combining *ever* and *present* keywords.

Finally, as most temporal languages, TVQL has temporal operators for handling instants and intervals (*before*, *into*, *overlap*…). It also presents predicates for instance versions order, stored in the versioned object control (first, last, next, and current).

7 Summary and Concluding Remarks

This paper presented a query language (TVQL) for time-evolving systems with versions support that may be modeled using TVM. Although TVM is an object-oriented model, the query language is based on SQL, as part of an environment for temporal versions management under development on top of a relational database. The mapping from TVQL to SQL is also presented.

TVQL allows usual SQL statements. It also retrieves instances with time and versions associated to. Many examples of TVQL statements are presented with their mapping to SQL, covering the most important features of the language.

Instead of changing the base SQL structure (select-from-where), TVQL adds new properties to SQL clauses. These properties may retrieve past, current, and future data values, as well as current and past database states. Furthermore, the same query statement may consider current and historic values, by combining keywords *ever* and *present*. All these pre-defined properties are defined to hide storage details from the user. Therefore, this feature allows greater implementation flexibility, as the classes and attributes that store this information are not specified in TVQL.

A complete grammar was developed to formalize the structure and syntax of TVQL. Only a summary of the TVQL BNF is presented here, due to space limitation.

Among the language features are: retrieval of objects and versions independently and according to the derivation graph, querying over versions from one or more entities, homogeneous behavior for valid and transaction times, branched time information manipulation, querying over logically deleted instances, transparency of TVM specific features, and addition of few keywords to SQL.

Considering the intended integrated environment, the phase of TVM implementation is almost complete. There is an interface for temporal versioned class specification that allows creating tables in the database according to this specification. TVQL is mapped to SQL to run on top of the mapped tables.

Finally, the complete data manipulation language (with create, insert, update and delete statements) is also under development. Furthermore, the same project is extending TVM for supporting schema versioning and evolution, with a concrete plan already proposed. Other features must be added to TVQL when this part is complete.

References

1. Andonoff, E., Hubert, G., Le Part, A.: A Database Interface Integrating a Querying Language for Versions. In Procs. of Advances in Databases and Information Systems - ADBIS. Lecture Notes in Computer Science, Vol. 1475. Springer-Verlag, Berlin (1998) 200-211
2. Böhlen, M. H., Jensen, C. S., Snodgrass, R. T.: Temporal statement modifiers. ACM Transactions on Database Systems, ACM Press, Vol. 25, No. 4 (December 2000) 407-456
3. Conradi, R., Westfechtel, B.: Version Models for Software Configuration Management. ACM Computing Surveys, Vol. 30, No. 2 (June 1998) 232-282
4. Edelweiss, N., Hübler, P., Moro, M.M., Demartini, G.: A Temporal Database Management System Implemented on Top of a Conventional Database. In Procs. of Intl. Conf. of the Chilean Computer Science Society (2000) 58-67
5. Etzion, O., Jajodia, S., Sripada, E. (eds.): Temporal Databases: Research and Practice. Lecture Notes in Computer Science, Vol. 1300. Springer-Verlag, Berlin (1998)
6. Golendziner, L.G., dos Santos, C.S.: Versions and configurations in object-oriented database systems: a uniform treatment. In Procs. of Intl. Conf. Manag. of Data (1995) 18-37
7. Moro, M.M., Saggiorato, S.M., Edelweiss, N., Santos, C.S. dos.: Adding Time to an Object-Oriented Versions Model. In Procs. of Intl. Conf. on Database and Expert Systems Applications - DEXA. Lecture Notes in Computer Science, Vol. 2113. Springer-Verlag, Berlin (2001) 805-814
8. Rodríguez, L., Ogata, H., Yano, Y.: TVOO: A Temporal Versioned Object-Oriented data model. In Information Sciences, Elsevier Science, Vol. 114 (1999) 281-300
9. Snodgrass, R.: The TSQL2 Temporal Query Language. Kluwer Publishers (1995)
10. Snodgrass, R., Böhlen, M., Jensen, C., Steiner, A.: Transitioning Temporal Support in TSQL2 to SQL3. In: O. Etzion et al (eds.): Temporal Databases Research and Practice. Lecture Notes in Computer Science, Vol. 1300. Springer-Verlag, Berlin (1998) 150-194
11. Wuu, G. T. J., Dayal, U.A.: A Uniform Model for Temporal and Versioned Object-Oriented Databases. In: A. Tansel et al (eds.): Temporal Databases: Theory, Design, and Implementation. Benjamin/Cumming (1993) 230-247

Approach and Model for Business Components Specification

Philippe Ramadour and Corine Cauvet

Laboratoire SIS
Université d'Aix-Marseille III
Avenue de l'escadrille Normandie-Niemen
13397 Marseille Cedex 20
ramadour@netcourrier.com
corine.cauvet@univ.u-3mrs.fr

Abstract. The development of software through reusable parts that are thoroughly certified for their intended purposes is emerging as a new way of IS engineering. Thus, it seems necessary to propose design tools for components engineering. Research works on *"components"* focus rather on the implementation of components. We propose a model and guidelines for the specification of conceptual business components. Because, we notice it is possible to describe a business object in many ways, we believe that a business component should integrate variability. Such variability is necessary to make a component reusable in different contexts. The paper presents a business component model which allows identifying, abstracting and contextualizing this variability. *"Reuse graphs"* enable the expression of all the structures of one object while the *"context"* indicates, for each structure, the purpose intended by the structure and the constraints it solves. We also propose a software tool that manages business components as XML documents and that supports the reuse process.

1 Introduction

Considering information systems (IS) engineering, software industry increasingly needs to build more and more reliable software with more and more functionalities and to develop them faster and faster. The development of software through reusable parts that are thoroughly certified for their intended purposes is emerging as a new way for developing software. Component-based development ([1]) is recognised as an engineering activity that needs new and specific models, languages and processes.

At the technological level, propositions of component models provide mechanisms for the integration and management of components within software frameworks. Representative models of this trend are CCM (CORBA Components Model [2]) from the OMG, (D)COM/COM+ models ([3]) from Microsoft and EJB model (Enterprise Java Beans [4]) from Sun MicroSystem. Those models are models of implementation that propose mechanisms of communication between components and services to support object-based applications (object creation, object-persistence support, ...).

R. Cicchetti et al. (Eds.): DEXA 2002, LNCS 2453, pp. 628–637, 2002.

Those approaches aim at solving problems about integration of complex distributed applications.

At the conceptual level, there exist few propositions of components models. At this level, the objective is to define components to make domain knowledge reusable. Approaches based on business objects ([5, 6, 7]) try to reach this objective. At present, those approaches provide conceptual schema fragments (such as UML diagrams) expressing domain knowledge rather than proposing a model to structure this knowledge and make it reusable considering several contexts. Particularly, we think there is a lack of mechanisms to "capture" and represent the variability of domain knowledge ([8, 9, 10]).

This article contributes to the definition of component models for specifying structure and content of ***reusable business components***. It presents a model of specification of business components which provide domain knowledge reusable during IS engineering. A business component contains conceptual structures of objects and expresses common and discriminating properties of those structures. A business component also provides, for each structure, the context in which it can be reused.

The article is organised as follows. Section 2 presents the concept of "business components" and an approach for specifying business components. Section 3 introduces the model of business components. Sections 4 and 5 present the notions of *"reuse graph"* and *"context"* used for specifying the components. Section 6 proposes software tools to manage business components. Section 7 compares our approach with existing ones. Section 8 concludes and presents research perspectives.

2 Business Components: Definition and Approach of Specification

In this section, we define what business components are and we propose guidelines for specifying those components.

2.1 Business Components: Informal Presentation

Conceptual modelling is concerned with business goals identification, business activities definition and structuring business objects. Considering the activity of structuring objects, the IS engineer often has to choose a conceptual structure for an object regarding business requirements. For example, during the design of an IS for library management, we can consider an *"adherent"* in many ways: within the subscribing process it has a *"subscriber"* role, within the borrowing process it has a *"borrower"* role. In the same way, the object *"book"* could be described in many ways: its description can be different between a library and a bookshop but also between two libraries that have different requirements.

We think that a business component must express this kind of variability. Precisely, we think that variability is the gap between business components and information systems objects. We define a **business component** as **the abstraction of all structures of one business object**. This abstraction allows considering all structures of one object as a unique concept (the business component). It also allows expressing common and discriminating properties between those structures. Focusing on variability, those properties aim at guiding both engineering and reuse of business components. Regarding business objects design we can distinguish two levels of abstraction for knowledge:

- *"information system" level:* this is the level used in conceptual modelling of information systems. At this level object structures are defined within a conceptual schema for specific information system. Practically, object structures are expressed as UML class diagrams.
- *"business" level:* this level abstracts similar conceptual schemas of the information system level. This abstraction level allows describing similarities and differences between conceptual schemas. We place business components at this level.

2.2 Approach for Business Components Engineering

The proposed approach for specifying business components focuses on identification, expression of variability and contextualisation of domain knowledge:

- *business components identification* is based on a domain engineering approach ([11, 12]); the descriptions of objects are structures expressed as classes diagrams.
- *variability expression* is based on reuse graphs; those graphs expressed common and discriminating parts of different structures of one object.
- *contextualization* of an object structure allows indicating the constraints solved by the structure.

All the concepts used to specify business components are formalized in following sections. They constitute the business component model.

3 Model of Business Components

Business components are specified according to the business component model presented at figure 1[1].

The business components model is based on the knowledge levels we identified. A business component is described as an abstract representation of a set of structures of one business object. Indeed, as indicated below, a business object can be structured in many ways regarding domain, business processes and/or business rules. Thus, a **business component** defines a **set of structures describing one business object**.

---

[1] In this model, grey concepts proceed from the business level while white concepts proceed from information systems level and black concepts define methodological tools. We propose those tools (*"reuse graphs"* and *"context"*) for expressing and contextualizing the variability of business components. This model is the result of a research work presented in [13].

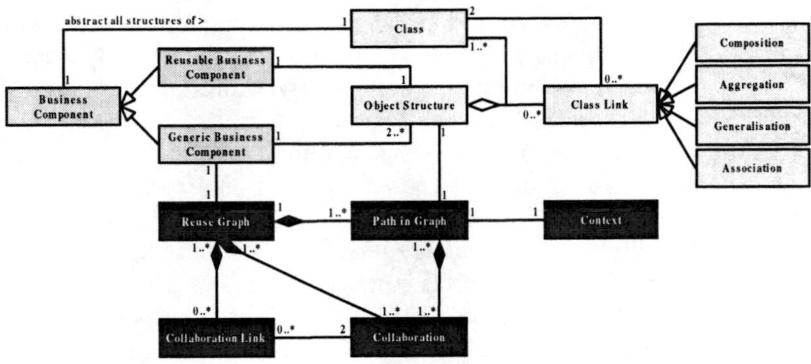

Fig. 1. Business component model

We define two types of business components:

- *reusable business components:* those components define a unique structure for a business object. This structure is reusable in any context. Those components are called "reusable" because they can be reused "simply" by integration of the proposed structure within a conceptual schema.
- *generic business components:* those components define several different structures for a same business object. They are called "generic" because the IS engineer must implement a process of selection to choose the most appropriate structure regarding the context in which the information system is developed. We associate a **reuse graph** with each generic business component to express common and discriminating properties between structures defined in the business component (each path of the graph expresses one structure). Finally, we associate a context with each path within the reuse graph. Those contexts indicate the situation in which the reuse of one structure seems to be relevant.

In a business component, object structures are expressed with classes (of information systems level) and usual links between classes (association, composition and generalization links). A class represents a business object which can be associated with another business component to abstract all of its structures.

4 Reuse Graphs

A **"reuse graph"** is the **representation of all structures of a business object**.

4.1 Nodes and Links in Reuse Graphs

A reuse graph exists for each generic business component. Paths in the graph define the set of all structures describing one business object. A reuse graph is composed of nodes, so-called *"collaborations"* of the graph, and oriented links, so-called *"collaborations links"*. A collaboration is an elementary fragment of one or many structures of a business object. Thus, a collaboration is a set of classes and links between classes figuring in one or many structures defined in a business component. A collaboration is an atomic artefact: all classes and classes links proceeded from a collaboration are considered as a whole at reuse time.

Depending on the considered business object, it may be possible to define a *"common collaboration"*. When this collaboration exists, it expresses the common fragment of structure contained in all structures of the business object. Other collaborations are called *"discriminating collaborations"*: they express fragments of structure discriminating some structures of the business object.

Links between collaborations support the assembly of collaborations. Each path within the graph defines a permitted structure for the business object. At reuse time the IS engineer elaborates a structure by choosing a path within the graph. We distinguish two kinds of links between collaboration A and collaboration B:

- *the optional link* from A to B indicates that the collaboration B **may** be reused when collaboration A is reused,
- *the compulsory link* from A to B indicates that the collaboration B **must** be reused when collaboration A is reused.

Moreover, we define an exclusion mechanism between links.

4.2 Reuse Graph Example

In the domain of library management, *"adherent"* business component can be used to define different structures of the business object *"adherent"*:

- in the context of the subscribing process, the structure of the *"adherent"* object defines a *"subscribing id"*, a *"subscription date"* and a *"subscribing state"* as properties and *"subscribe"*, *"suspend"* and *"strike out"* as methods.
- in the context of the borrowing process, the structure of *"adherent"* defines *"# of current borrowings"* and *"borrowing state"* as properties and *"borrow"* and *"return"* as methods; the class is also linked with *"book"* and *"borrowing"* classes.
- in the context of both processes, the structure of *"adherent"* defines all properties and methods listed below, except the *"subscribing state"* and *"borrowing state"* properties that are merged within the *"state"* property.

Thus, the *"adherent"* business component contains three structures (at least, but it is possible to define other structures). Those structures are represented within a reuse graph (see figure 2). This graph expresses a common collaboration, called *"CC"*, which presents class *"adherent"* with some properties and methods. The first discriminating collaboration, called *"CD1"*, contains class *"subscriber"* linked with class *"adherent"* by a generalisation link. The second discriminating collaboration, called *"CD2"*, contains class *"borrower"* linked with class *"adherent"* by a generalisation link. Finally, the third collaboration, called *"CD3"* contains class *"subscriber/borrower"* linked with class *"adherent"* by a generalisation link.

"CC" is a common collaboration; other collaborations of the reuse graph are discriminating ones linked with *"CC"* by a compulsory link. Moreover, collaboration *"CC"* must be reused (with a compulsory link) in conjunction with either *"CD1"* or

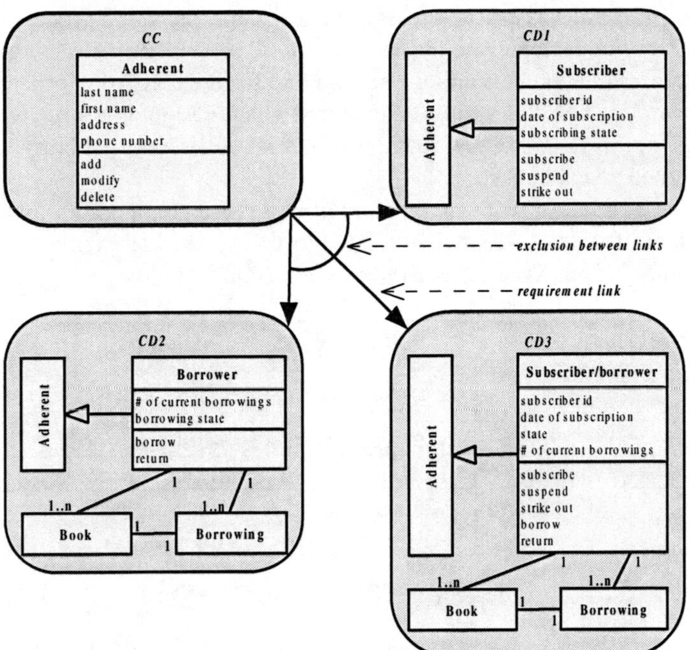

Fig. 2. Example of reuse graph

"CD2" or *"CD3"*; only one collaboration among *"CD1"*, *"CD2"* or *"CD3"* must be selected at the same time. Thus an exclusion mechanism is set up between compulsory links *"CC→CD1"*, *"CC→CD2"* and *"CC→CD3"*.

Reuse graphs express common and discriminating structure fragments of all structures of one business object. Each path of a graph is associated with one permitted structure, which is reusable within a specific conceptual schema.

5 Reuse Context

To guide the reuse of a business component, we have to characterize each structure provided by the component. The contextualization of those structures indicates the suitable situation(s) in which a structure can be reused: **context specifies specific requirements accomplished by a structure**. We propose to integrate both *"contextual knowledge"* and *"reusable knowledge"* (the structures of objects) within a business component. At reuse time, contextual knowledge will help the IS engineer to choose the most relevant structure according to the specific IS goals being developed.

We define the context as a set of constraints on object structures. We distinguish three levels of contextual constraints:

- *business goals:* a business component can provide structures for different domains. An object structure captures business goals. For example, description of a *"customer"* won't be the same in library management and in account management.

- *business processes:* The structure of an object depends on the process the object is involved in. For example, the object *"adherent"* presents two structures: a first one for the subscribing process and the second one for the borrowing process.
- *business rules:* those rules must be captured when designing a structure for a business object. For example, call to order or not an adherent of a library when he's in late for giving back books.

We associate a "context" with each path within a reuse graph and, so, with each specific structure of the business object related to the graph. For example, for the reuse graph of figure 2, contexts are those indicated in figure 3 below.

Path in the reuse graph of figure 2	**Reuse context constraints**		
	"Business goals" level	*"Business processes" level*	*"Business rules" level*
(CC, CD1)	Library management	Management of a subscribing process	-
(CC, CD2)		Management of a borrowing process	-
(CC, CD3)		Management of a subscribing process and of a borrowing process	-

Fig. 3. Examples of reuse contexts

Thus, context allows characterizing each path of a reuse graph and, so, each specific structure of a business object. At reuse time, contextual knowledge is used to support the selection process of a suitable structure.

6 Management of Business Components

The business component model supports business components design focusing on variability of objects structures. In this approach, a business component integrates both reusable knowledge (object structures) and contextual knowledge guiding the reuse of the component (reuse graphs and contexts). We present in this section an implementation of the model. This implementation manages the business components and supports their reuse[2].

6.1 Software Architecture

To provide guidance for design and reuse of business components, we propose to implement the components within XML formatted documents ([14]). The choice of XML presents two strong qualities: this is an open standard well-formed to deal with semi-structured data and it lets us use all free existing tools for management of XML data. The software prototype is structured according to ***three-tiered client-server architecture***. The three layers of the prototype are:

[2] Functional, software and hardware architectures of the prototype are detailed in [13].

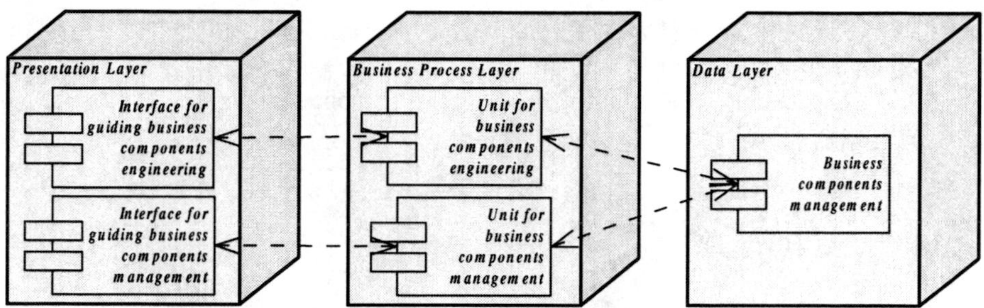

Fig. 4. Software prototype architecture

- *data layer:* this layer deals with storage and access of the XML documents that express the business components. We use *"XML-QL"* ([15]) as the query language to access to XML documents,
- *business process layer:* this application supports the reuse process of business components. It elaborates corresponding XML-QL queries and provides results to the interface layer. We use the PHP scripting language for implementing this layer,
- *presentation layer:* this layer deals with interactions with the IS engineer. For portability and facility reasons, we use a navigation tool for visualising HTML pages.

6.2 Business Components Reuse

The reuse process is supported by the application layer. The application layer uses a set of specific operations. Those operations exploit reuse graphs and contexts defined within business components. We distinguish reuse of reusable business components and reuse of generic business components:

- *reusable business components* provide only one object structure, unique, which can be reused in any situation and in any context. Thus, reuse of such components is immediate. The structure can be integrated within an IS conceptual schema.
- *generic business components* provide several structures for the same business object. Each structure is adapted to a specific context; thus, reuse of generic business components needs specific activities.

The proposed reuse process focused on the context associated with each structure provided by a component. This is a decision process and it is specified in four stages:

- the software prototype presents to the IS engineer a navigator on business components. It proposes to the engineer to indicate for which business component he would like to choose a specific structure.
- the IS engineer manipulates the selected business component through its reuse graph. Selecting an object structure consists in choosing a specific path in the graph. The selection of a path must be done regarding collaboration links and related context. The selected path must be associated with the context the most similar to the context in which the conceptual schema must be developed.

- the prototype helps the IS engineer to assembly contents of all collaborations of the selected path to design the corresponding structure.
- the IS engineer integrates this structure within the conceptual schema being developed.

7 Related Works

The notion of business component is used in several approaches ([6, 7, 16]) aiming at facilitating IS engineering. Those approaches often define business components as fragments of conceptual schemas. In these approaches, business components are used to define domain concepts (such as *"customer"*, *"subscriber"*, *"date"* ...) in a standard and normative way. In these approaches, a business component is a standard and unique structure (often called *"pattern"*) reusable within several domains ([17]).

Nevertheless, those propositions don't provide tools and guidelines for business components engineering. For example, the OMG approach ([2, 5]) defines structure of business objects but this structure doesn't take the variability of business objects into account. Thus, developed business objects only provide basic properties and methods available for all IS within one or several domains.

The *"San Francisco"* approach presented by IBM ([7]) takes into account variability through the notion of *"extension points"*. Nevertheless, the possible adaptations aren't characterised and contextualised. Common and discriminating properties aren't emphasized.

8 Conclusion

This article has presented a model and an approach for business components engineering. Business components provide both reusable structures of objects and knowledge to guide the reuse of those structures. The business component model allows abstracting all structures of a domain object within a business component. This model emphasizes the expression of the variability of all structures of an object. Reuse graphs and contexts provide specification tools for business components design. At reuse time those notions provide guidance in choosing an object structure adapted to specific requirements. Finally, a software prototype for business components management is presented. It implements the business components with XML formatted documents and also supports a business components reuse process.

Our actual research works aims at formalizing the contextual knowledge within business components. The notion of *"argument"* could be introduced to provide more guidance in choosing object structure in a specific situation. We also think that it would be possible to use the same approach for defining business components providing process structures and goal structures. Such business components already have been introduced in [13]. Finally, another research perspective concerns the integration problem of business components. We think that component integration should be dealt at the design stage of business component engineering. Integration is implemented with communication mechanisms available in software architectures.

References

1. Heineman G. T., Council W. T., *Component-Based Software Engineering – Putting the Pieces Together*, Addison-Wesley, 2001.
2. Wang N., Schmidt D. C., O'Ryan C., *Overview of the CORBA Component Model*, in *Component-Based Software Engineering – Putting the Pieces Together*, Heineman G.T. and Council W. T. coordinators, Addison-Wesley, 2001.
3. Ewald T., *Overview of COM+*, in *Component-Based Software Engineering – Putting the Pieces Together*, Heineman G.T. and Council W. T. coordinators, Addison-Wesley, 2001.
4. Blevins D., *Overview of the Enterprise JavaBeans Component Model*, in *Component-Based Software Engineering – Putting the Pieces Together*, Heineman G.T. et Council W. T. coordinators, Addison-Wesley, 2001.
5. Casanave C., Business-Objects Architectures and Standards, in *Proceedings of OOPSLA'97*, 1997.
6. Fowler M., *Analysis Patterns – Reusable Object Models*, Addison-Wesley Publishing Company, 1997.
7. Bohrer K. A., Architecture of the San Francisco frameworks, in *IBM Systems Journal*, vol. 37, n° 2, 1998, p. 156 (http://www.research.ibm.com/journals/sj37-2.html).
8. Motta E., Zdrahal Z., A Library of Problem-Solving Components Based on the Integration of the Search Paradigm with Task and Method Ontologies, in *International Journal of Human-Computer Studies*, vol. 49, n° 4, October 1998.
9. Weiss D., Lai C. T. R., Weiss D. M., *Software Product-Line Engineering, A Family-Based Software Development Process*, Addison-Wesley, 1999.
10. Jacob I., Krivine J.P., Monclar F.R., *De LISA à ELICO, des langages pour le développement de systèmes d'assistance à l'opérateur*, in Ingénierie *des connaissances, évolution récentes et nouveaux défis*, Charlet J., Zacklad M., Kassel G. and Bourigault D. coordinators, Eyrolles, 2000.
11. Wartik S., Priéto-Diaz R., Criteria for Comparing Domain Analysis Approaches, in *International Journal of Software Engineering and Knowledge Engineering*, vol. 2, n° 3, 1992.
12. Cauvet C., Rieu D., Front-Conte A., Ramadour P., *Réutilisation en ingénierie des systèmes d'information*, in *Ingénierie des systèmes d'information*, Cauvet C. and Rosenthal-Sabroux C. coordinators, éditions Hermès, 2001.
13. Ramadour P., Modèles et langage pour la conception et la manipulation de composants réutilisables de domaine, Pd. D. Thesis, University of Aix-Marseille, 17 December 2001.
14. eXtensible Markup Language (XML), World Wide Web Consortium (W3C) norm, available at http://www.w3.org/XML/.
15. eXtensible Markup Language Query Language (XML-QL), submission for the W3C, 19 august 1998, available at http://www.w3.org/TR/1998/NOTE-xml-ql-19980819/, HTTP project page available at http://www.research.att.com/sw/tools/xmlql/.
16. Carey J., Carlslon B., *Business Components*, in *Component-Based Software Engineering – Putting the Pieces Together*, Heineman G.T. and Council W. T. coordinators, Addison-Wesley, 2001.
17. Gamma E, Helm R., Johnson R., Vlissides J., *Design Patterns, Elements of Reusable Object-Oriented Software*, Addison-Wesley Publishing Company, 1995.

The TrailTRECer Framework – A Platform for Trail-Enabled Recommender Applications

Erich Gams, Tobias Berka, and Siegfried Reich

Salzburg Research - SunTREC
Jakob Haringer Strasse 5/III
5020 Salzburg, Austria
{egams, tberka, sreich}@salzburgresearch.at

Abstract. In their everyday work people are confronted with ever growing amounts of information and thus often feel overloaded with data. Trails, built from information about the users' browsing paths and activities, are an established approach to assist users in navigating vast information spaces and finding appropriate information. While existing systems focus on web browsers only, we argue that trails can be generated by any application. We describe *TrailTRECer*, a framework which supports trail-based information access, and which is open to any application. The usability of the framework and the concept of user trails were tested by building a trail-enabled browser client and a print manager client. Initial user evaluations indicate the usefulness of this approach.

1 Introduction

Looking for specific information or finding colleagues working on similar topics, has always been and still is an open issue. Growing numbers of documents within Intranets and - even more — on the World Wide Web make it increasingly difficult to find appropriate information. When navigating through information spaces people have to make choices without sufficient personal experiences of the alternatives available. In addition to the high number of choices available, these choices vary widely in quality. Therefore, following everyday life where people rely on recommendations from other people — either by directly getting in contact or indirectly through their trails — so-called recommender systems [17] propose to support the recommendation process by information technology and thus enable *social navigation* [5]. Recommendations can provide a manageable and useful view or filter of the whole information space. Such recommendations can be based on experiences and on opinions of other people who are more familiar with a particular domain.

In our work we take an approach based on user trails, much like, footprints users leave when handling information [14]. With trail-based recommender systems, which base access to and retrieval of information on user trails, users could manage their individual information spaces more efficiently. Most existing systems provide a kind of history mode of recently accessed web pages and thus focus on one application domain only. In this paper we present an open,

R. Cicchetti et al. (Eds.): DEXA 2002, LNCS 2453, pp. 638–647, 2002.

distributed and adaptable framework, named *TrailTRECer* which supports generation, manipulation and query by any application [15]. Due to this property we consider this to be an open system. For our project this means that implementation of new features can be added without modifying the basic structure. Its name indicates that, similar to the way "Trackers" follow trails in nature, "TrailTRECers" make their way through digital information spaces.

This paper is structured as follows: Section 2 is a survey of related work. After a brief discussion, we identify phases and the requirements for a framework supporting trail-enabled applications in Section 3. The framework will be based on a data model and an architecture defined in Section 4. For validation purposes of the framework and the data model that we constructed, we introduce two sample applications in Section 5, a BrowserManager and a PrintManager. Finally, Section 6 summarises the results of first user experiments and conclusions gained from them.

2 Related Work

Trail based systems recommend related items and provide assistance in navigation, and therefore share similarities with recommender systems and browsing advisors. Following the approach of recommending related items, two main groups have been derived: collaborative or social filtering systems and content based filtering systems [17]. Other research concerning assisting users in navigating the web can be loosely grouped together under the term browsing advisors. Trail based systems, providing recommendations based on user navigation, constitute an additional fourth category.

2.1 Content Based and Collaborative Filtering Systems

Content based filtering systems are based upon correlation between the content of a document and the user's preferences. Webwatcher [19] is a content based tour guide agent assisting users in browsing and navigating the Web. The agent accompanies the user by suggesting appropriate hyperlinks identified by keywords of interest. However, in order to expand the range of documents and in order to support serendipity, people rely on explorations. Letizia and Powerscout [10] are examples of so called reconnaissance agents — programs that look ahead in the user's browsing activities and recommend the best path to follow. Both learn a profile of user preferences by recording and analysing the user's browsing activities. Content based systems assume, that documents have to be machine parseable (hence most these systems focus on text documents) or attributes are assigned to them manually. By contrast trail based systems handle multimedia data by using navigation to implicitely determine the relevance of data.

Collaborative or social filtering systems generate personal recommendations by computing the similarity between a user's preferences and those of people with similar interests. PHOAKS [20] for instance collects URLs that have been positively mentioned in an electronic message or in a FAQ document. The URLs are filtered, e.g. through the number of distinct recommenders of a resource and provided to the people interested in a newsgroup. In Grouplens [9], a recommender system based on news messages, users assign numeric scores to each news article they read. The scores of different users are correlated with each other in order to find users who share a similar taste. Modified news clients allow rating by numbering. Summarizing collaborative filtering systems rely on user profiles, expressed by the users manually, or on algorithms automatically weighting people's interests with similar taste to produce recommendations. Users also need to use dedicated clients in addition to their favourite common applications.

2.2 Browsing Advisors

Broadway [7] is an example of a cooperative browsing advisor for the WWW, that uses case-based reasoning to advise pages by tracing past navigation sessions of users. The advise is mainly based on similarity of ordered sequences of past accessed documents. Footprints [21] consists of a set of tools that base access to interaction history between users and digital objects by navigation. The system doesn't use the history to make recommendations, but to contextualize Web pages the user is seeing.

2.3 Trail-Based Systems

Most browsing advisor systems reuse paths followed by a user or do analysis based on browsing behaviour. In the context of a trail based system, we assume the user not only to search for information on the Web to acquire additional knowledge, but also pass a workflow of creating or editing a document. Yet we differ from the approach of watching the interaction history of each document separately [6]. This qualifies trails for entirely different application domains than just browsing the Web [14]. In our understanding, trails constitute a specific path through a set of documents not limited to the WWW.

Thus, with respect to all the systems described above we conclude, that they do not fully support the notion of trails in terms of objects that can be created, copied and modified. Also, trails must not be dependent on the links an author of a hypertext created in the document e.g. links within a Web page. Trails can exists between documents of different type that have no explicit linkage between them. Memoir [18] has implemented the basic notion of trails within a Web environment and demonstrated the feasibility of trails for achieving the goals of matching users with similar interests. We argue that trail-based systems should be open with respect to the applications integrated and the activities traced. Consequently, we propose to develop an distributeable, adaptable component framework that provides an open set of services for recording, storing, processing and navigating trails through well-defined interfaces. By *Framework*, we refer to a software environment [2] that is designed to simplify the development and management of applications by providing a re-usable context for components; therefore, we see the framework and its components, as cooperating technologies [8]. In order to extract requirements for the construction of a trail based recommender system, we start with a brief overview of user scenarios. Basically these scenarios consist of: tracing and recording of trail data, finding related documents to the currently active one, finding related trails and related users (e.g. people with the same interest). The basic intention of getting recommendations is to find related documents and users with the same interests. By documents we refer to all kinds of nodes of a trail that can be identified by a URL.

3 Phases and Requirements

More precisely, three main phases can be extracted out of these scenarios: *Acquisition* of trail data from clients of everyday use, *Processing* of recorded trails to provide accurate recommendations to the user and *Management* of recorded trail data *over time* (forming a loop with processing)

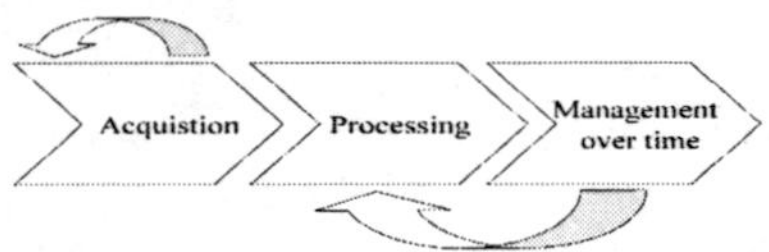

Fig. 1. Main phases of a trail-based system

Based on the phases of the trail processing workflow we have identified the following requirements, that will be implemented in the data model and the architecture of *TrailTRECer*:

R1 User Groups. When searching for information users are presumed to play different roles and thus can be assigned to one or more user group. Users can be divided into groups according to different tasks or projects or groups considering the departmental structure. Groups can have subgroups.

R2 Scalability. If the number of users increases, the recommendations should improve in terms of quality and trueness, but not in terms of quantity of the results. The performance should not slow down or make the system more a burden than a help for the user.

R3 Guaranteeing user's privacy. Recording a trail should be possible with guaranteeing the users' privacy, therefore it must be ensured that recording takes place only with the user's consent [13].

R4 Openness of the system to arbitrary applications. Users want to produce trails with common desktop applications. Trails can be generated by any application, i.e., mail clients, word processors, etc. not limited, as most systems do, to Web browsers [18,21,7]. Similar to the way open hypermedia link services offer themselves to a variety of adapted or purpose built applications the integration of trail-based client applications [4,22] with trail-services should be envisaged. A modified print manager, for instance, might be used to log those documents that have been printed (printing could indicate a document's importance). An interface between the components of the framework and the applications will provide access to basic functionalities, such as processing of trail data and management over time.

R5 Associate activity performed on a document with this document. As we argued in [15] the type of activity is important for the documents' relevance and therefore has to be associated with the document and traced. Activities can provide additional metadata and allow users to filter relevant documents from their trails. Moreover, the management of trails over time requires additional data for efficient filtering and retrieval of documents.

R6 Common and extensible data model. Besides activity the definition of trails also includes capturing contextual settings. For the basic entities see [15]. The data model should be open enough to support the addition of captured properties.

R7 Trails should be treated as first class objects. Trails are objects in their own right, which can be edited, deleted, or copied. Other services like exchanging trails between users would also be possible. A trail node can be anything (e.g. document, website) that can be clearly identified by a URL and has certain properties such as date, duration, activity.

R8 Trails defined as another hypertext domain. Following the Open Hypermedia Systems (OHS) community a trail-based system can be designed as another component of a Component-Based-OHS [16]. Trailbased functionality would be another hypertext application domain such as the navigational, taxonomic or spatial domain. Trails should be mapped into an Open Hypertext Model [11], offering new ways of navigation, representing trails in different views.

R9 The pertinence of trails can change over time. Knowledge and interests of people and also organisations change over time and so do trails. Some trails may attract more attention, than others. The frequency of trails' usage indicates that some trails are more important than others.

4 System Architecture

Based on the requirements above, we will describe the trail data model and the architecture of the *TrailTRECer* framework. Following the Open Hypermedia

Systems Working Group's reference architecture [16], trail functionality could simply be seen as another middleware service. However, an alternative option would be to follow the fundamental open hypermedia model (FOHM, [11]) and express trail data using that model. FOHM distinguishes between three basic hypertext domains. By adapting FOHM, interoperability between the different hypertext domains themselves will be possible (Adressing R4 and R8). FOHM is a common data model capable of representing structures and implementing operations from any of the three domains (See R8). The basic data model can briefly be summarized as follows: Associations hold vectors of bindings, a relationship type, and a structural type. Bindings glue data references and feature vectors together. Feature vectors can be defined arbitrarily.

Following that model, trails can be defined as associations. Trail marks resemble bindings, i.e., they relate nodes (which are references to the actual documents) and trails together. Activities are modeled as feature values. With respect to retrieving relevant trail marks (and subsequently nodes), we argue that FOHM should include a notion of relevance. This could be a standard feature that would in the simplest case accommodate a basic ranking mechanism; it could also include more elaborate definitions such as general contextual data (subject, place, and time). Additionally, sequential ordering of bindings is needed in order to allow for time dependent ordering and ranking. To summarize, FOHM could be adapted with some simple modifications to hold trail data.

The more accurate the system's recommendation to the users needs to be, the more complex the processing will be. Therefore, different paradigms such as software agents offer themselves for application in this domain [3]. SoFAR [12], the **So**uthampton **F**ramework for **A**gent **R**esearch, is a multi-agent framework that addresses the problem domain of distributed information management (addressing R2) and thus is well suited for our trail-based framework *TrailTRECer*. SoFAR provides information sharing between agents, promoted through the matchmaking mechanism of a registry agent. Every agent of the system subscribes to the registry agent in order to inform about the own functionality and to find certain capabilities supported by other agents running in the system.

In order to communicate and exchange information via an agent communication language, agent systems separate intention from content, by using a predefined set of performatives to carry the messages and an ontology as the topology of messages. We developed a trail ontology, which enables the exchange of related documents, trails or persons. The root of the ontology hierachy is an abstract term and a predicate, a term that can be queried about. *Related* is the parent predicate of the trail ontology. Any agent, that wants to receive related documents, can query for the *Related* predicate. *Related* only consists of a single field, namely *Trailmark*. Trailmark contains the properties of the current viewed document (See [15] for a definition) (also addressing R6 and R5). For exchange of related persons, documents or trails *Related* can be derived into different supported subtypes *RelatedPersons, RelatedDocuments, RelatedTrails*.

The *TrailTRECer* framework is built upon this trail ontology, enabling communication about any trail related information. All the tasks, such as collecting data, or visualization are distributed on different agents (addressing R1). Figure 2 depicts the architecture of the framework, containing two platforms, on which the agents reside.

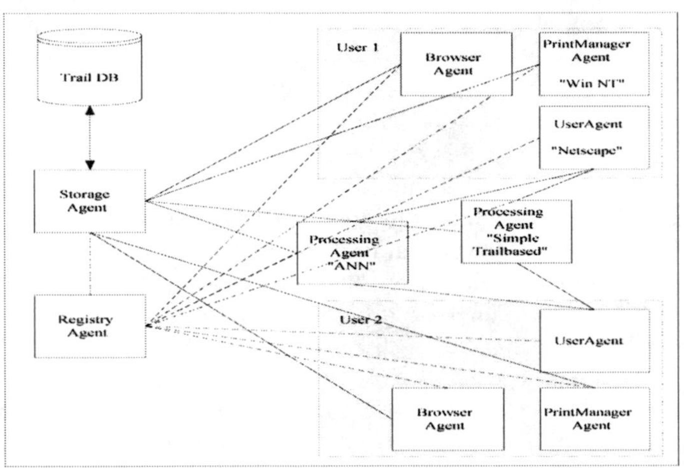

Fig. 2. Framework architecture

Each user holds an individual user platform, that contains all trail acquisition and trail visualization agents. Trail acquisition agent can be specialized in recording individual activities. Furthermore, each user can have an arbitrary number of individual trail acquisition and trail visualization agents (R4). The group platform acts as a wrapper for several users, preferably assigned according to the basic grouping of the recommender system. This platform hosts various agents, the processing agents, that can deliver "Related" documents or trails, and the storage agent, responsible for saving trails in a global database. In a further expansion, the framework can also hold agents managing the growth of trail data over longer usage of the system via aging algorithms (R9).

5 Sample Application Scenarios

In order to promote the feasability of trails for recommendation and to test the applicability of our framework, two trail recording agents a *Browser Agent* and a *PrintManager Agent* were implemented. The *Browser Agent* is wrapped around a HTTP proxy server watching and recording the browsing activity of the user. The *PrintManager Agent* has to be more dependent on the operating system used. For WinNT, we developed a component wrapped into a JNI interface, watching the print jobs of all running applications and recording the documents printed. Both agents pass their trails to the Storage Agent which connects to a relational database and stores them.

Furthermore two processing agents were integrated in the system. If the current document, identified by its URL, is found in a previous trail, the next neighbour documents will be recommended by the *Simple-Trail-Based Agent* ordered by the activity associated and the frequency of occurrence. A more advanced version will recommend a trail, that the user can follow, as a whole (R7). Additionally, an *Artificial Neural Network ANN Agent* recommends related domains based on ratings from an artificial neuronal network trained with trail data. (For details on the implementation see [1])

For a priming phase, trail data has been generated automatically from proxy access logs of several months browsing activity of the members of our department. In order to test the accurancy of recommendations, our *User Agent* connected to a sidebar integrated in Netscape 6.2. From there the user can access the delivered recommendations and also control the recording of trails (R3). The name of the processing agents together with the results fitting to the current viewed document are displayed. The documents viewed with the browser are indicated through the HTTP address and the documents printed through the file name. So far, no login component has been integrated into the framework, instead we identified the user by extracting the login name from the operating system (See R2). Figure 3 shows the recommendations of the two integrated processing agents in the left part of Netscape.

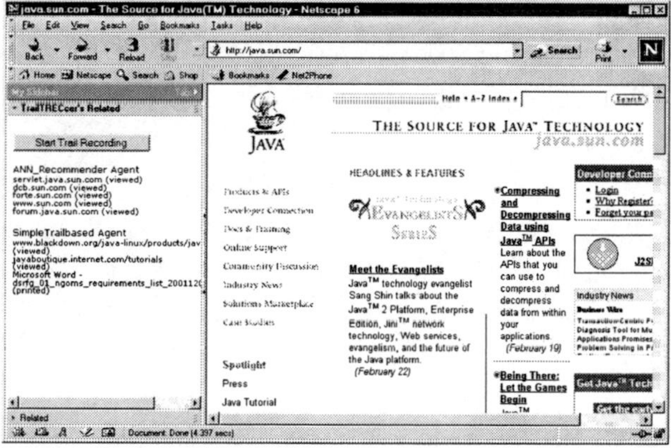

Fig. 3. Screenshot

The initial user evaluation of the *TrailTRECer* prototype included ten users with varying IT skills and educational backgrounds. The evaluation indicated that the processing agents' time consumption are acceptable, under the following conditions: The user can decide which agent to use, or other non-real-time methods of user notification are used, e.g. email [3]. The agent selection should be supported by a textual description of the agents.

Another important issue is the presentation of the agents' results. Since the algorithm parses a great number of documents, simply displaying the name or title of the document residing at that address may lack transparency, a problem which can be evaded by presenting the results in a manner similar to search engines (by displaying link target title, meta-data or excerpts). In the case of trails, it would be helpful to show the start and end trailmark, the trailmarks corresponding with the current trail, or extract a description out of the trail e.g. number of trailmarks (See R7).

6 Summary and Conclusion

In this paper, we introduced requirements, a software architecture and prototype components of a framework that enables the development of trail-enabled applications. Our framework focuses on reuseable, inter-operating components supporting services for processing, visualizing and for managing the relevance of trail data over time. The system can record and process trails with minimal effort from the user and at the same time provide recommendations appropriate to the currently active document. Furthermore, we proved the openness of our framework by implementing two sample applications, tracing print and browse activities of users. More clients can be easily integrated in the framework and involved in the recommendation process. Our next steps will focus on the integration of further applications, such as a newsgroup client and an email client, tracking email communication and newsgroup activities.

We believe that the usefulness of the approach chosen, i.e., using trails as basis for recommender systems, has been demonstrated by the positive feedback gained in the initial user study.

Acknowledgments

Trailist is supported by the Austrian Fonds zur Förderung der wissenschaftlichen Forschung (FWF) under grant No. P14006-INF.

References

1. Tobias Berka, Werner Behrendt, Erich Gams, and Siegfried Reich. A trail based internet-domain recommender system using artificial neural networks. *Accepted at the Int. Conf. on Adaptive Hypermedia and Adaptive Web Based Systems*, 2002.
2. Philip A. Bernstein. Middleware: A model for distributed system services. *Communications of the ACM*, 39(2):86–98, February 1996.
3. Leslie A. Carr, Wendy Hall, and Steve Hitchcock. Link services or link agents? In *Procs. of the '98 ACM Conference on Hypertext, 1998*, pages 113–122, 1998.
4. Hugh C. Davis, Wendy Hall, Ian Heath, Gary J. Hill, and Robert J. Wilkins. Towards an integrated information environment with open hypermedia systems. In *ECHT '92. Procs of the ACM conference on Hypertext, 1992*, pages 181–190, 1992.

5. Andreas Dieberger. Supporting social navigation on the world wide web. *Int. Journal of Human-Computer Studies*, 46(6):805–825, 1997.
6. W. Hill, J. Hollan, D. Wroblewski, and T. McCandless. Edit wear and read wear. In *Procs. of ACM Conf. on Human Factors in Computing Systems, CHI'92.*
7. Michel Jaczynski and Brigitte Trousse. Broadway: A case-based system for co-operative information browsing on the world-wide-web. In *Collaboration between Human and Artificial Societies*, pages 264–283, 1999.
8. Ralph E. Johnson. Frameworks = (components + patterns). *Communications of the ACM*, 40(10):39–42, October 1997.
9. Joseph A. Konstan, Bradley N. Miller, David Maltz, Jonathan L. Herlocker, Lee R. Gordon, and John Riedl. Grouplens: applying collaborative filtering to usenet news. *Communications of the ACM*, 40(3):77–87, 1997.
10. Henry Lieberman, Christopher Fry, and Louis Weitzman. Exploring the web with reconnaissance agents. *Communications of the ACM*, 44(8):69–75, 2001.
11. David E. Millard, Luc Moreau, Hugh C. Davis, and Siegfried Reich. FOHM: A fundamental open hypertext model for investigating interoperability between hypertext domains. In *Procs. of the '00 ACM Conference on Hypertext, 2000*, pages 93–102, 2000.
12. Luc Moreau, Nick Gibbins, David DeRoure, Samhaa El-Beltagy, Wendy Hall, Gareth Hughes, Dan Joyce, Sanghee Kim, Danius Michaelides, Dave Millard, Sigi Reich, Robert Tansley, and Mark Weal. SoFAR with DIM agents. An agent framework for distributed information management. In *Int. Conf. on The Practical Application of Intelligent Agents and Multi-Agents. PAAM 2000*, pages 369–388, 2000.
13. D. Nichols. Implicit rating and filtering. In *Procs. of the 5th DELOS Workshop on Filtering and Collaborative Filtering*, 1997.
14. Siegfried Reich, Leslie A. Carr, David C. DeRoure, and Wendy Hall. Where have you been from here? Trails in hypertext systems. *ACM Computing Surveys — Symposium on Hypertext*, 31(4es), December 1999.
15. Siegfried Reich and Erich Gams. Trailist - focusing on document activity for assisting navigation. In *Procs. of the Twelfth ACM Conference of Hypertext and Hypermedia*, pages 29–30, 2001.
16. Siegfried Reich, Uffe K. Wiil, Peter J. Nürnberg, Hugh C. Davis, Kaj Grønbæk, Kenneth M. Anderson, David E. Millard, and Jörg M. Haake. Addressing interoperability in open hypermedia: The design of the open hypermedia protocol. *New Review of Hypermedia and Multimedia*, 5:207–248, 1999.
17. Paul Resnick and Hal R. Varian. Recommender systems. *Communications of the ACM*, 40(3):56–58, March 1997.
18. D. De Roure, W. Hall, S. Reich, G. Hill, A. Pikrakis, and M. Stairmand. Memoir - an open distributed framework for enhanced navigation of distributed information. *Information Processing and Management*, 37:53–74, 2001.
19. D. Freitag T. Joachims and T. Mitchell. Webwatcher: A tour guide for the world wide web. In *Procs. of IJCAI97*, 1997.
20. Loren Terveen, Will Hill, Brian Amento, David McDonald, and Josh Creter. PHOAKS: A system for sharing recommendations. *Communications of the ACM*, 40(3):59–62, 1997.
21. Alan Wexelblat and Pattie Maes. Footprints: History-rich tools for information foraging. In *Conf. on Human Factors in Computing Systems*, pages 270–277, 1999.
22. Uffe Kock Wiil and Peter J. Nürnberg. Evolving hypermedia middleware services: Lessons and observations. In *Procs. of the ACM Symposium on Applied Computing (SAC '99)*, pages 427–436, 1999.

Adaptive Method for Range Top-k Queries in OLAP Data Cubes

Zheng Xuan Loh, Tok Wang Ling, Chuan Heng Ang, and Sin Yeung Lee

School of Computing
National University of Singapore
{lohzheng, lingtw, angch, jlee}@comp.nus.edu.sg

Abstract. In decision-support systems, the top k values are more informative than the max/min value. Unfortunately, the existing methods for range-max queries could not answer range top-k queries efficiently if applied directly. In this paper, we propose an efficient approach for range top-k processing, termed the Adaptive Pre-computed Partition Top method ($\mathcal{APPT}$). The $\mathcal{APPT}$ method pre-computes a set of maximum values for each partitioned sub-block. The number of stored maximum values can be adjusted dynamically during run-time to adopt to the distribution of the query and the data. We show with experiments that our dynamic adaptation method improves in query cost as compared to other alternative methods.

1 Introduction

With the rapid growth of enterprise data, the *On-Line Analytical Processing* (OLAP) [1] which uses a multi-dimensional view of aggregate data, has been increasingly recognized to provide quick access to strategic information for decision making. A popular data model for OLAP applications is the multi-dimensional database (MDDB), also known as data cube. A data cube [2, 3] is constructed from a subset of attributes in the database. Certain attributes are chosen as metrics of interest and are referred to as the *measure attributes*. The remaining attributes, are referred to as *dimensions* or the *functional attributes*. For instance, consider a database maintained by a supermarket. One may construct a data cube with SALES as a measure attribute, and DATE_OF_SALE and PRODUCT_NAME as dimensions; such a data cube provides aggregated total sales figures for all combinations of product and date.

Range Queries [4] apply a given aggregation operation over selected cells where the selection is specified by constraining a contiguous range of interest in the domains of some functional attributes. The most direct approach to answer range query is the naïve method. However, the naïve method is very expensive as all the involved cells in the data cube need to be scanned and compared before the final answer can be found. In order to speed up range queries processing in OLAP data cubes, comprehensive research has been done for aggregation functions sum [4, 5, 6, 7, 8] and max/min [4, 9, 10, 11]. Range-sum and range-max/min queries are very important in decision support system. However, another aggregation function, top k, has not received the deserved attention due to

R. Cicchetti et al. (Eds.): DEXA 2002, LNCS 2453, pp. 648–657, 2002.

its increased complexity. Aggregation function top k, which extends aggregation function max, is able to provide more precise information for decision-makers where the value of k is specified by the user. A *Range Top-k Query* finds the top k values in the given range. An example of range top-k query from the above supermarket data cube is to find the top 10 best selling products from 1st January 2002 to 7th January 2002. Queries of this form are commonly being asked by a supermarket manager to gain in-depth the overall performance of the sales before a precise decision can be taken. This query could not be answered directly by aggregation function max, but top k aggregation.

In the literature, in order to handle range-max queries which is a special case of range top-k queries when $k = 1$, the *Balanced Hierarchical Tree Structures* is proposed in [4] for storing pre-computed maximum values. However, if the cardinalities of domains are quite different in size, the height of the tree is up to the largest domain. The concept of *Maximal Cover* is proposed in [9] to represent the data distribution information with respect to range-max processing. In other words, the performance of this approach is highly dependent on the data distribution. For *Block-Based Relative Prefix Max* in [11], the auxiliary data structures keeps only the maximum values of each region. Using these structure, the second maximum value could not be deduced. Thus, frequent access to original data cube may be necessary. In another study, the *Hierarchical Compact Cube* [10] uses a multi-level hierarchical structure which stores the maximum value of all the children sub-cubes with the locations. However, by pre-storing only the maximum value for each disjoint region is insufficient for aggregation function top k (as explain in Section 2). This results in frequent access to the children sub-cubes and also the original data cube.

Optimizations of top-k queries in other domains were studied in [12, 13]. The probabilistic approach introduced in [12] optimizes the top-k queries by finding an optimal *cutoff parameter* to prune away the unwanted portions of the answer set in a relational database. On the other hand, [13] intends to find the top k tuples in a relational database which are nearest to a queried point by mapping a suitable range that encapsulates k best matches for the query. Thus, the concentration of both approaches is to find a suitable range in order to reduce the search space. In contrast, our focus on this paper is to explore the special property of aggregation top k that differs it from aggregation max and then find an efficient query method for range top-k queries.

For handling range top-k queries in OLAP data cubes, [14] proposed a physical storage structure for a partitioned data cube is proposed where dense and sparse partitions are stored in different data structures. The indices to the dense and sparse structures are stored in an auxiliary data structure together with the maximum value. Based on the maximum values, the query algorithm finds the top k values in the respective partition. This paper concentrates on the physical storage of a data cube, which is different from our studies.

In an interactive exploration of a data cube, it is imperative to have a system with low query cost. Therefore, our focus in this paper is to develop an algorithm to reduce the query cost of range top-k queries.

2 The $\mathcal{APPT}$ Method

Despite all the work on range-max queries, they cannot be applied directly to answer range top-k queries. In particular, most of the existing methods explore the idea that, given two disjoint regions A and B, if it is known that max(A) > max(B), region B can be ignored directly. However, for the case of top k where $k > 1$, even if it is known that max(A) > max(B), the effort of scanning the original data cube could not be waived for region A as the second maximum value may reside in region A. In this connection, pre-storing one value for each region may not be sufficient. The direct extension of these methods, therefore, is to store all the top k values for each region. This, however, poses the following problems:

1. the *storage* incurred by pre-storing all the top k values is very high
2. the *value of k is unknown* prior to queries and it may vary for queries

Nevertheless, the problem introduced by pre-storing one and k values can be minimized by keeping more than one value from each region (not necessary k values). For instance, for answering a top-3 query, if it is known that a_1, a_2, b_1 and b_2 are the top 2 values for region A and B, respectively, and the descending order of these values are a_1, b_1, a_2 and b_2, we may take the top 3 values that are known, a_1, b_1 and a_2, as the result without scanning region A and B. Thus, pruning is possible and the chance of scanning data cube can be reduced.

Making use of this essential idea, a data structure that stores at most r ($r > 1$) pre-computed maximum values for each partitioned region in a data cube is proposed. This structure is termed the *Location Pre-computed Cube* ($\mathcal{LPC}$) as the location of each pre-computed maximum value is stored as well. The location is needed to judge whether the maximum value is in the query range. In addition, the smallest pre-computed maximum value in each entry of $\mathcal{LPC}$ indicates the upper bound of the unprocessed values in the region. This also helps in pruning a search when the smallest pre-computed maximum value is smaller than all the k maximum values found.

The range top-k problem is also different from range-max problem in that the performance is influenced by the distribution of the maximum values over the data cube. For example, if the large values are mostly concentrated on a few region, then by pre-computing only r values for each region is insufficient unless $r \geq k$. A simple solution will be to increase the value of r to a large value. However, this forfeits storage efficiency as the increment of r applies to all the regions in the data cube. In contrast, this is not a restriction for range-max queries as $k = 1$. Thus, for handling non-uniformly distributed maximum values efficiently and cost effectively, the number of pre-stored values should be adjustable dynamically to adapt to the distribution of the query and data. To serve this purpose, a dynamic structure termed as the *Overflow Array* ($\mathcal{OA}$) is introduced in complement to the $\mathcal{LPC}$ to adaptively store additional maximum values for regions during run-time. Since $\mathcal{OA}$ is obtained from queries, it is more accurate than any analytical model that tries to predict the query pattern of the users.

2.1 The Data Structures

Definition 2.1 A *data cube* $\mathcal{DC}$ of d dimensions, is a d-dimensional array. For each dimension, the index can be ranged from 0 to $n_i - 1$ inclusively where n_i is the size of the ith dimension. Each entry in the data cube is called a *cell* and is denoted as $\mathcal{DC}[x_1, \ldots, x_d]$ where $0 \le x_i < n_i$.

	0	1	2	3	4	5	6	7	8
0	53	97	95	94	99	97	95	98	42
1	61	96	71	71	36	89	37	80	10
2	58	62	94	93	95	61	78	60	13
3	91	90	38	11	71	54	18	72	34
4	51	83	64	93	34	71	55	41	92
5	88	99	75	10	91	79	97	89	88
6	90	92	70	87	96	97	98	96	94

$n_1 = 7$

$n_2 = 9$

Fig. 1. A 2-dimensional data cube

Example 2.1 Figure 1 shows a 2-dimensional data cube. The size of the first dimension (n_1) is 7 and second dimension (n_2) is of size 9.

Definition 2.2 With respect to a data cube $\mathcal{DC}$ of d dimensions, a *range query* can be specified as $\{[l_1, \ldots, l_d], [h_1, \ldots, h_d]\}$ such that for each dimension i, $0 \le l_i \le h_i < n_i$ where n_i is the size of the ith dimension of $\mathcal{DC}$. A *range top-k query* finds the top-k values in the query range.

Example 2.2 The shaded area in Figure 1 represents range query $\{[2, 3], [5, 7]\}$.

Definition 2.3 A data cube of d dimensions, the size of each dimension is n_i $(1 \le i \le d)$, and d *partition factors* $b_1, \ldots, b_d$ can be partitioned into $\prod_{i=1}^{d}(\lceil n_i/b_i \rceil)$ disjoint sub-regions known as *sub-blocks*.

Example 2.3 Using partition factor 4 for n_1 and partition factor 3 for n_2, the data cube in Figure 1 is partitioned into $\lceil 7/4 \rceil \times \lceil 9/3 \rceil = 6$ sub-blocks.

Definition 2.4 Given a data cube $\mathcal{DC}$ of d dimensions and d partition factors $b_1, \ldots, b_d$, with the number of pre-computed values for each sub-block, r, a location pre-computed cube, $\mathcal{LPC}$ of $\mathcal{DC}$, is a cube such that

1. it has the same dimension d,
2. if the size of the ith dimension in $\mathcal{DC}$ is n_i, i.e., ranges from 0 to $n_i - 1$, then the dimension i in $\mathcal{LPC}$ will range from 0 to $\lceil n_i/b_i \rceil - 1$, and
3. each entry in $\mathcal{LPC}$, $\mathcal{LPC}[x_1, \ldots, x_d]$, corresponds to a partitioned sub-block in $\mathcal{DC}$ and stores two items:
   (a) the top r maximum values with the corresponding locations

(b) an index denoted as $\mathcal{LPC}[x_1, \ldots, x_d].Overflow$ that links an entry of $\mathcal{LPC}$, $\mathcal{LPC}[x_1, \ldots, x_d]$, to an record in the $\mathcal{OA}$. If there is no record in the $\mathcal{OA}$ for $\mathcal{LPC}[x_1, \ldots, x_d]$, it is set to NULL.

Definition 2.5 An overflow array, $\mathcal{OA}$, is a set of linked-list. Each element in the $\mathcal{OA}$ is termed as an *Overflow Record* which has the following structure:

1. f number of maximum values and the locations of these maximum values
2. an index specifying the next $\mathcal{OA}$ record if more values are needed, else NULL.

Initially, the $\mathcal{OA}$ contains no record and all the $\mathcal{LPC}[x_1, \ldots, x_d].Overflow$ are NULL. When processing queries, if access to the original data cube is needed for a sub-block, additional maximum values are added into the $\mathcal{OA}$ for this sub-block. In other words, an overflow record keeps the maximum values which are not pre-stored in the $\mathcal{LPC}$ or other overflow records of the sub-block. The construction of the $\mathcal{OA}$ is discussed in Section 2.2.

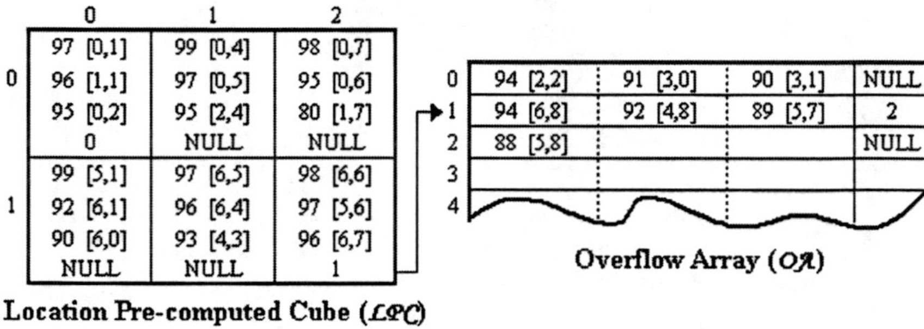

Fig. 2. Auxiliary Data Structures of $\mathcal{APPT}$ method

Example 2.4 Figure 2 presents the $\mathcal{LPC}$ and the $\mathcal{OA}$ of the data cube $\mathcal{DC}$ shown in Figure 1. The number of values kept for each sub-block (r) and overflow record (f), are set to 3. Note that $\mathcal{LPC}[1,2]$ holds the top 3 maximum values and the corresponding locations among the cells in $\mathcal{DC}[i,j]$ where $4 \leq i \leq 7$ and $6 \leq j \leq 8$. The value of $\mathcal{LPC}[1,2].Overflow$ is 1, shows that $\mathcal{OA}[1]$ is the first overflow record for $\mathcal{LPC}[1,2]$. The last field of $\mathcal{OA}[1]$ indicates that the next overflow record for $\mathcal{LPC}[1,2]$ is $\mathcal{OA}[2]$.

For simplicity and without loss of generality, in this paper, we assume the size of each dimension of a data cube is n and partition factor b for every dimension. In the subsequent sections, we can safely take $r = f$ as both factors represent the block size of each entry in the $\mathcal{LPC}$ and $\mathcal{OA}$, respectively.

2.2 Queries and $\mathcal{OA}$ Construction

Due to the possibility of pruning the search, it is highly beneficial to find a correct order for the evaluation of sub-blocks. As mentioned earlier, the values in the $\mathcal{LPC}$ represent the maximum values of every sub-block. Obviously, the $\mathcal{LPC}$ needs to be processed before the rest. On the other hand, the smallest pre-computed value indicates the upper bound of the unprocessed values in the sub-block; thus, higher priority of being processed is given to the sub-block with a higher upper bound value. Hence, our query algorithm first searches in all the entries of the $\mathcal{LPC}$ covered by the query range, and secondly, based on the smallest pre-computed values of all the entries in the $\mathcal{LPC}$, the $\mathcal{OA}$ and the $\mathcal{DC}$ are searched accordingly if necessary.

We now present an example to illustrate the idea mentioned. Using the data cube and range query $\{[2:3],[5:7]\}$ in Figure 1 and the $\mathcal{LPC}$ and $\mathcal{OA}$ in Figure 2, a range top-4 query, i.e. $k=4$, is performed.

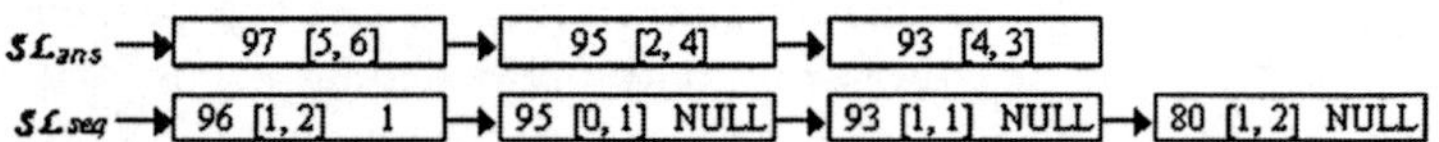

Fig. 3. Processing of $\mathcal{LPC}$

Firstly, all the maximum values in the $\mathcal{LPC}$ which are in the query range are inserted into sorted list $\mathcal{SL}_{ans}$ together with their locations. $\mathcal{SL}_{ans}$ stores the candidate answer to the range top-k query and the number of nodes is limited to k as only k answers are needed. As can be seen from Figure 3, $\mathcal{SL}_{ans}$ contains only three candidate answers, 95 from $\mathcal{LPC}[0,1]$, 93 from $\mathcal{LPC}[1,1]$ and 97 from $\mathcal{LPC}[1,2]$ whilst other pre-computed values in the $\mathcal{LPC}$ are out of the range.

For all the entries in the $\mathcal{LPC}$ covered by the query range, the smallest pre-computed values are inserted into another sorted list termed $\mathcal{SL}_{seq}$ together with their indices in the $\mathcal{LPC}$ and also the indices linked to the $\mathcal{OA}$. $\mathcal{SL}_{seq}$ is used to sort the priority of being processed in $\mathcal{OA}$ and $\mathcal{DC}$ based on the smallest pre-computed values. The constructed $\mathcal{SL}_{seq}$ is as shown in Figure 3.

The $\mathcal{SL}_{seq}$ is processed by dequeuing the first node and comparing the maximum value in the dequeued node with the candidate answers found. If the maximum value in the dequeued node is larger than any of the candidate answers found or the number of the candidate answers found is less than k, the $\mathcal{OA}$ is processed if the linked to the $\mathcal{OA}$ is not NULL, otherwise, the sub-block is scanned. As can be seen from Figure 4(a), the maximum value of the dequeued node is 96 from $\mathcal{LPC}[1,2]$. Since the candidate answers found so far is less than k, the overflow record linked by $\mathcal{LPC}[1,2]$, that is $\mathcal{OA}[1]$, is processed and 89 from $\mathcal{OA}[1]$ is inserted into $\mathcal{SL}_{ans}$ as shown in Figure 4(b). Since the number of candidate answers found is 4 and the smallest pre-computed value in $\mathcal{OA}[1]$ is not larger than the smallest candidate answer found, therefore, 89 from $\mathcal{OA}[1]$ is not inserted into $\mathcal{SL}_{seq}$.

As shown in Figure 4(b), the maximum value in the dequeued node is 95, which is larger than the smallest value in $\mathcal{SL}_{ans}$, i.e., 89. However, there is no overflow record for this entry and thus, the sub-block which corresponding to $\mathcal{LPC}[0,1]$ is scanned. The values which are not pre-stored in $\mathcal{LPC}$ but are larger

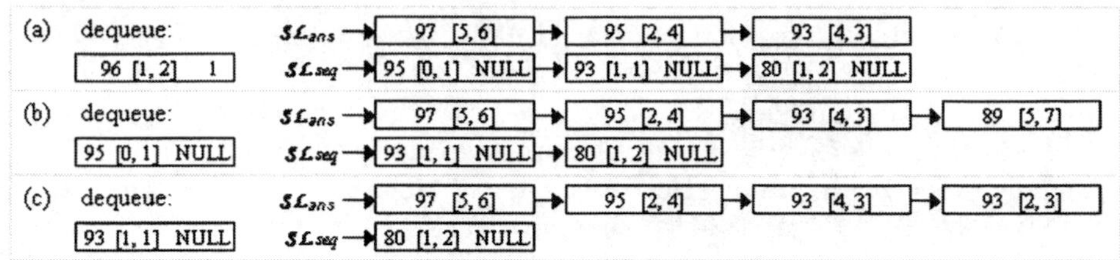

Fig. 4. Processing of $\mathcal{OA}$ and $\mathcal{DC}$

than 89 are 94 and 93. However, only 93 is inserted into $\mathcal{SL}_{ans}$ as 94 is out of range. In addition, 94 and 93 are inserted to $\mathcal{OA}[3]$ and $\mathcal{LPC}[0,1].Overflow$ is set to 3. As shown in Figure 4(c), the maximum value of the dequeued node is 93, which is equal to the smallest candidate answer found, thus, the algorithm stops and $\mathcal{SL}_{ans} = \{97, 95, 93, 93\}$ is returned as the answer.

Making use of the information given by the smallest pre-computed value in the $\mathcal{LPC}$ and/or $\mathcal{OA}$, the search to the $\mathcal{OA}$ and/or $\mathcal{DC}$ for sub-blocks corresponding to $\mathcal{LPC}[1,1]$ and $\mathcal{LPC}[1,2]$ are waived. This helps in reducing the search to the original data cube and thus, improving the response time of range top-k queries.

2.3 $\mathcal{OA}$ Maintenance

The $\mathcal{OA}$ is a global but fixed-size structure. If the $\mathcal{OA}$ is not full, any sub-block that requires more values during queries can request for a new allocation. In contrast, if the $\mathcal{OA}$ is full, the allocation must bear a higher "need" than the need of some existing blocks in order to replace it. To serve this purpose, we may have a "directory" structure which for each partitioned block the META-information of the access statistics of each block is stored. This gives a rough idea of how many data from each block will contribute to answer a query in average,

$$Mean\_Usage = \alpha \times Prev\_Mean\_Usage + (1 - \alpha) \times Cur\_Data$$

where Cur_Data is the number of values required besides $\mathcal{LPC}$ for answering the current query, Pre_Mean_Usage is the average number of values used from the previous query besides $\mathcal{LPC}$ and α is the "forgetting factor" for calculating the average. To find the most suitable overflow records for replacement, sub-block with the highest difference between the number of overflow records stored and the average number of overflow records used ($Mean\_Usage$) is chosen.

In preferable manner, all the additional values obtained from queries should be kept in the $\mathcal{OA}$. However, since a fixed size is allocated for the $\mathcal{OA}$, in certain cases, not all the desired values can be kept. Hence, a parameter β is introduced to represent the percentage of the desired values kept where $0 \leq \beta \leq 1$. For example, when $\beta = 0$, the $\mathcal{OA}$ is empty and when $\beta = 1$, all the additional values needed for queries are stored in the $\mathcal{OA}$.

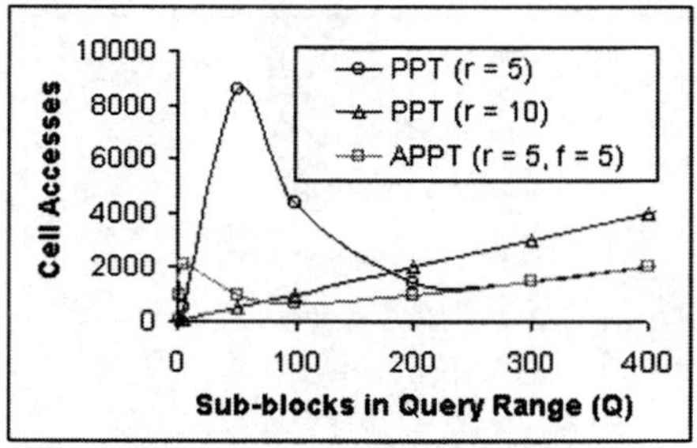

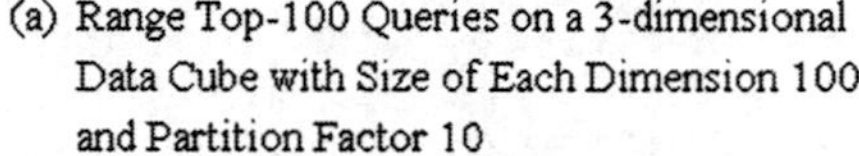
(a) Range Top-100 Queries on a 3-dimensional Data Cube with Size of Each Dimension 100 and Partition Factor 10

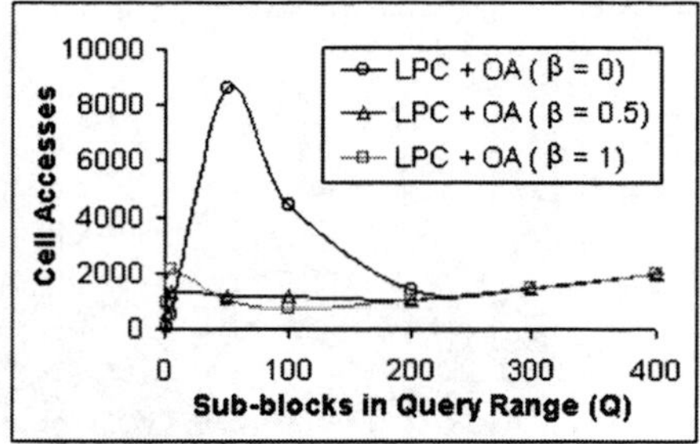

(b) Range Top-100 Queries on a 3-dimensional Data Cube with Size of Each Dimension 100 and Partition Factor 10

Fig. 5. Query Cost Improvement with the Existence of $\mathcal{OA}$

3 Experimental Results and Discussion

In order to have data cubes with non-uniformly distributed maximum values, Zipf distribution is used for determining the locations of cells holding the larger values. All the range queries are generated randomly and the query cost in terms of average cell accesses is measured.

Figure 5(a) depicts three separate experiments are executed on a set of range queries using i) $\mathcal{LPC}$ only with $r = 5$; ii) $r = 10$; and iii) both $\mathcal{LPC}$ and $\mathcal{OA}$ are used with size of the overflow record and the number of pre-computed values in the $\mathcal{LPC}$ equal to 5 ($r = 5, f = 5$). In general, the query cost when both $\mathcal{LPC}$ and $\mathcal{OA}$ are used is lower than the query cost of $\mathcal{LPC}$ only with $r = 5$, especially when the number of sub-blocks covered by the query (Q) is moderately small. Without $\mathcal{OA}$, a straightforward solution for improving the query cost for $\mathcal{LPC}$ only is to increase the r, e.g., $r = 10$. However, this solution only reduces the average cell accesses when Q is small as can be seen from Figure 5. Therefore, a better solution is to maintain an $\mathcal{OA}$ which gives a more stable query cost for different Q's.

As discussed in Section 2.3, due to storage limitation, not all the additional values needed for queries may be kept in the $\mathcal{OA}$ in the real-world cases. Therefore, the effect of β (the percentage of the additional values kept) is studied as shown in Figure 5(b). When $\beta = 0.5$, i.e., when 50% of the additional value required for queries can be kept in the $\mathcal{OA}$, the performance is slightly degraded for moderately small Q as compared to $\beta = 1$. When Q is very small, the performance of $\beta = 0.5$ is better than $\beta = 1$. This is because less number of overflow records is required when Q is small and the cost difference is the cost of accessing to the $\mathcal{OA}$. As a result, the requirement on $\mathcal{OA}$ maintenance can be relaxed (i.e., not storing all the desired values in the $\mathcal{OA}$) without sacrificing the performance significantly.

The same set of range queries are performed using the naïve method, general max method, the $\mathcal{APPT}$ method using $\mathcal{LPC}$ only and the $\mathcal{APPT}$ method using both $\mathcal{LPC}$ and $\mathcal{OA}$. Below are some observations made from Figure 6:

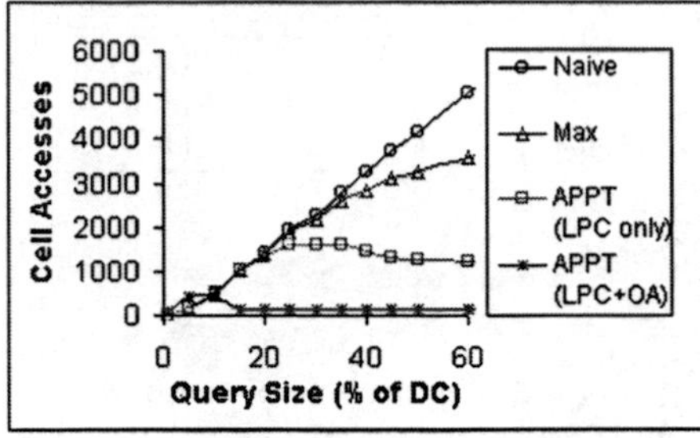

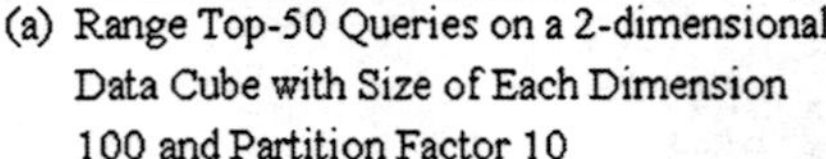
(a) Range Top-50 Queries on a 2-dimensional Data Cube with Size of Each Dimension 100 and Partition Factor 10

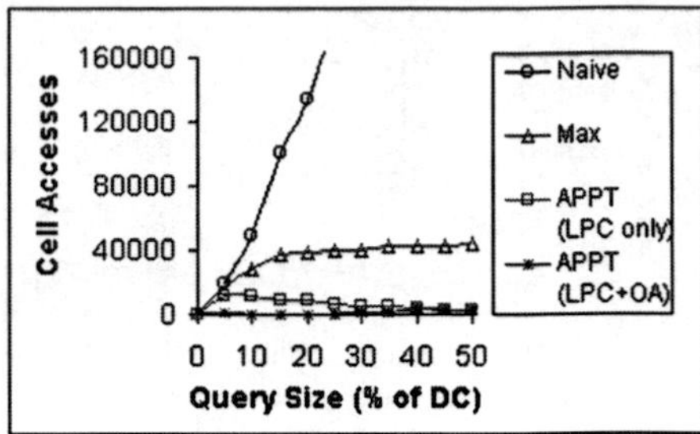

(b) Range Top-50 Queries on a 3-dimensional Data Cube with Size of Each Dimension 100 and Partition Factor 10

Fig. 6. Comparison with Alternative Methods

1. *naïve method*: the query cost increases linearly with the size of the query range as all the cells covered by the query range need to be accessed.
2. *general max method*: pre-compute only the maximum value for each sub-block. The query cost improvement over the naïve method increases with the increment of the query size as the pre-computed maximum value is able to waive some search to the data cube.
3. *$\mathcal{APPT}$ method ($\mathcal{LPC}$ only)*: with one additional pre-computed value than the max method, i.e., $r = 2$, the query cost is much lower than the general max method.
4. *$\mathcal{APPT}$ method ($\mathcal{LPC} + \mathcal{OA}$)*: with $\mathcal{OA}$, the query cost of the $\mathcal{APPT}$ method is further enhanced when the size of an overflow record and the number of pre-computed values for each sub-block equal to 2. For instance, for query size that covers 20% of the data cube, the query cost of the $\mathcal{APPT}$ method ($\mathcal{LPC} + \mathcal{OA}$) is only about 10% and 0.3% of the query cost of the naïve method for 2-dimensional and 3-dimensional data cubes, respectively. This shows that a higher query cost improvement can be gained when a higher dimensional data cube is used.

4 Conclusion

In decision-making environment, a number of top values are usually needed in order to make a precise decision. However, current approaches on range-max queries could not answer range top-k queries efficiently and cost effectively if applied directly. In this paper, we have presented an approach, the Adaptive Pre-computed Partition Top Method ($\mathcal{APPT}$), for range top-k queries processing. The main idea of the $\mathcal{APPT}$ method is to pre-store a number of top values for each sub-block in the Location Pre-computed Cube ($\mathcal{LPC}$). Based on the distribution of the maximum values, additional values required during queries are kept in a dynamic structure termed as the Overflow Array ($\mathcal{OA}$). In order to fully utilize the limited space of $\mathcal{OA}$, a technique is presented for $\mathcal{OA}$ maintenance. Through experiment, it is shown that the performance of the $\mathcal{APPT}$

method is further enhanced with the existence of $\mathcal{OA}$. Although the additional values needed for queries might not be fully stored in the $\mathcal{OA}$ due to storage constraints, the existence of $\mathcal{OA}$ still provides a high degree of performance improvement. Furthermore, the improvement in query cost gained from the $\mathcal{APPT}$ method compared to other alternative methods increases for higher dimensional data cube, e.g., for query size that covers 20% of the data cube, the $\mathcal{APPT}$ method requires about 10% and 0.3% of the query cost of the naïve method for 2-dimensional and 3-dimensional data cubes, respectively. This is very important as the data cube for OLAP applications are multi-dimensional.

References

1. The OLAP Council. *MD-API the OLAP Application Program Interface Version 5.0 Speci.cation*, 1996.
2. A. Agrawal, A. Gupta, S. Sarawagi. Modeling Multidimensional Databases. In *Proc. 13th Int'l Conf. on Data Engineering*, 1997.
3. J. Gray, A. Bosworth, A. Layman and H. Pirahesh. Data cube: A relational aggregation operator generalizing group-by, cross-tabs and sub-totals. In *Proc. 12th Int'l Conf. on Data Engineering*, pp. 152-159, 1996.
4. C. Ho, R. Agrawal, N. Me.ddo and R. Srikant. Range queries in OLAP data cubes. In *Proc. ACM SIGMOD Conf. on Management of Data*, 1997.
5. C. Y. Chan, Y. E. Ioannidis. Hierarchical Cubes for Range-Sum Queries. In *Proc. 25th Int'l Conf. on Very Large Databases*, pp. 675-686, 1999.
6. S. Ge.ner, D. Agrawal, A.E. Abbadi, T. Smith. Relative Pre.x Sum: An E.cient Approach for Querying Dynamic OLAP Data Cubes. In *Proc. 15th Int'l Conf. on Data Engineering*, pp. 328-335, 1999.
7. W. Liang, H. Wang, M. E. Orlowska. Range queries in dynamic OLAP data cube. *Data and Knowledge Engineering 34*, 2000.
8. H. G. Li, T. W. Ling, S. Y. Lee, Z. X. Loh. Range-sum queries in Dynamic OLAP data cube. In *Proc. 3rd Int'l Symposium on Cooperative Database Systems for Advanced Applications*, pp. 74-81, 2001.
9. D. W. Kim, E.J. Lee, M. H, Kim, Y, J. Lee. An e.cient processing of range-MIN/MAX queries over data cube. *Information Sciences*, pp. 223-237, 1998.
10. S. Y. Lee, T. W. Ling, H. G. Li. Hierarchical compact cube for range-max queries. In *Proc. 26th Int'l Conf. on Very Large Databases*, 2000.
11. H. G. Li, T. W. Ling, S. Y. Lee. Range-Max/Min queries in OLAP data cube. In *Proc. 11th Int'l Conf. on Database and Expert Systems Applications*, pp. 467-475, 2000.
12. D. Donjerkovic, R. Ramakrishnan. Probabilistic optimization of top N queries. In *Proc. 25th Int'l Conf. on Very Large Databases*, 1999.
13. S. Chaudhuri, L. Gravano. Evaluating Top-k Selection Queries. In *Proc. 25th Int'l Conf. on Very Large Databases*, 1999.
14. Z. W. Luo, T. W. Ling, C. H. Ang, S. Y. Lee, H. G. Li. Range Top/Bottom k Queries in OLAP Sparse Data Cubes. In *Proc. 12th Int'l Conf. on Database and Expert Systems Applications*, pp. 678-687, 2001.

dbRouter – A Scaleable and Distributed Query Optimization and Processing Framework

Wee Hyong Tok and Stéphane Bressan

School of Computing
National University of Singapore
{tokweehy, steph}@comp.nus.edu.sg

Abstract. In data integration systems, a central site often maintain a global catalog of all available data sources, and maintain statistics to allow the query optimizer to generate a good query plan. These statistics could be updated in a lazy manner during query execution time. A user query is often broken into several query fragments, and a centralized task scheduler schedules the execution of the respective query fragment, fetching data from the various data sources. This is then integrated at the central site and presented to the user. As data sources are introduced, there is a need to update the global catalog from time to time. However, due to the autonomous nature of the data sources, which are maintained by local administrators, it is difficult to ensure accurate statistics as well as the availability of the data sources. In addition, since the data are integrated at the central site, the central site could become a potential bottleneck. The unpredictable nature of the wide area environment further exacerbate the problem of query processing.

In this paper, we present our ongoing work on *dbRouter*, a distributed query optimization and processing framework for open environment. The dbRouter provides mechanisms to faciliate the discovery of new data sources, performs distributed query optimization, and manages the routing of data to its destination for processing.

1 Introduction

There has been a tremendous information boom, where information are made readily accessible either internally within a corporate intranet or externally on the internet. Various companies and organizations are putting up their data online. Examples of such data includes weather data, population census, stock trading/mutual funds statistics. At the same time, we see a wide availability of mobile electronic devices such PDAs and mobile phones with increasing processing capabilities. Mobile databases products have also increased. We see all these devices as potential data sources in which queries could be made. In additional, with the increasing processing capabilities of these devices, it is possible to delegate query processing tasks to these devices. [5,8,10] demonstrated the need to perform data integration over distributed collections of devices. The nature of

R. Cicchetti et. al. (Eds.): DEXA 2002, LNCS 2453, pp. 658–668, 2002.

the task would vary with the available processing and storage capabilities on the individual devices. With such a dynamic environment, traditional distributed and multidatabase query optimization techniques are ineffective to deal with such an open environment. Also, with the availability of large number of autonomous data sources, it is a challenge to maintain a know-all global catalog of metadata for all the data sources. Individual administrators maintain complete autonomy over the respective data sources, and hence changes are not readily propagated.

In the literature, there have been much work done on integrating data across diverse sources [6,7,9]. Three issues are prevalent and present challenges when designing a scaleable framework for an open environment. One of the issues is the automated discovery of new data sources. The second issue is how to perform distributed query optimization instead of relying on a centralized query optimizer. The last issue to be addressed is how to improve the initial response time of a query, and adapting to run-time fluctuations in the open wide-area environment. We will address each of this issue in the next few subsections.

1.1 Discovery of Available Data Sources

Data integration systems focus on integrating the data arriving from known heterogeneous data sources. New data sources are identified by the administrator and added to a global catalog. However, local administrators maintain autonomy over these data sources. New data sources might be introduced and existing data sources might be removed. In addition, there might be replicated data sources at different sites with different access costs (i.e. one source might incur less number of network hops than the other). As the number of sites providing data sources increases, maintaining a global catalog becomes a problem. This necessitates the need for an automated discovery mechanism that will discover the availability of data sources on a dynamic basis.

1.2 Distributed Query Optimization

Query optimization techniques in distributed database focused on exploiting data reducers such as semi-joins to minimize communication costs. In multi-databases, query optimization breaks the user query into query fragments, and send them to the respective database to be executed. As the indivudal databases are loaclly administerted, the multi-database query optimizer is unable to utilize the local information available on the individual databases. These information includes the use of various access methods, making use of specific join algorithms based on the query characteristics.

In addition, the unavailability of updated statistics is an impediment to query optimization. Similar to multi-databases, data integration systems usually decompose a user query into query fragments and rely on the use of wrapper modules to wrap each of the heterogeneous data sources, and exporting the results to a common data format to be integrated. A single query optimizer usually does query optimizations in all these systems.

Here, we wish to highlight that there is an important dischotomy between the notion of *distributed query optimization* and query optimization for distributed databases. In the literature, the notion of *distributed query optimization* oftens refers to query optimization in the context of distributed databases. However, our notion of *distributed query optimization* refers to decomposing a query optimization tasks into several subtasks, and delegating these smaller query optimization tasks to multiple sites for processing in a distributed manner.

1.3 Data Integration

Data integration systems often rely on a scheduler at the central site to adapt to changes in the characteristic of the arriving data. The scheduler might suspend query execution on one of the query fragments if it has been idling for a specific timeout period, and switching to perform other tasks. Many novel join techniques [14] and query scrambling techniques [1,2,15] have also been developed to adapt to the fluctuations in a wide-area environment. In addition, in most data integration systems, a centralized site integrates data coming from the various sources. However, as the number of data sources increases, the central site quickly becomes a bottleneck.

2 dbRouter

Our work focuses on defining a highly scaleable and open framework to provide efficient query optimization and processing in share-nothing wide-area environments. Data sources, ranging from relational databases, websites, personal digital assistants (PDAs) could be queried via a wrapper module. We will refer to the sites in which the data sources are located as nodes. All nodes are distributed in an open, share-nothing environment. The nodes in which the data source resides could also be delegated with local processing tasks, depending on available resources (storage, memory, processing capabilities).

2.1 Overview

A dbRouter encapsulates both query optimization and query processing mechanisms. However, it is not part of the data source, and resides externally and manages a set of data sources. Unlike traditional query optimization techniques that are performed by a single query optimizer, query optimization is performed amongst a group of dbRouters. During query optimization, the dbRouter first define coarse-grain plans, which are encapsulated within macro optimization blocks. The macro optimization blocks are then delegated to the respective dbRouters for further optimization.

Whenever a query is issued, the dbRouter would undergo the following phases:

- **Discovery Phase.** All relations and data sources that are referenced in the query would be resolved. Semantics and type checking of the query is also performed after all the relations are resolved. This is achieved by maintaining a lookup referal list. The lookup referal list provides the dbRouter with information about which dbRouters it should contact in order to resolve the relations referred to in a query.

- **Marco Query Blocks Optimization Phase.** Participating dbRouters would be delegated with macro optimization blocks for the data sources in which they manage, as well as the dependent data sources. For example, let us consider a join of relation A and B. dbRouter 1 might manage relation A, while dbRouter 2 manages relation B. From dbRouter 1's context, relation B would be a dependent relation, and vice versa.
- **Negotiation Phase.** In this phase, dbRouter would negotiate with other dbRouters the tuple flow. Each macro optimization block would have a well-defined input and outflow flow, and the dbRouters would then modify their respective input and output flow after negotiation.
- **Tuple routing Phase.** Instead of allowing the data to be integrated at a final assembly site, a tuple flow would be setup after the negotiation phase. Traditionally, query processing in data integration systems is characterized by single-site integration of arriving data. The bottleneck is commonly the data integration site. This design inhibits scalability as the number of data producing nodes increases. Our approach to query processing differs, in that the dbRouters operating at different nodes perform partial integration of the data. Each dbRouter then sends the processed tuple to the next dbRouter identified by its output stream. The tuples are then sent from dbRouter to dbRouter until it is directed back to the root node, where the user issued the query.

2.2 Automated Discovery of New Data Sources

The dbRouter at the node in which the query is issued would first try to find the data sources participating in the query. If it cannot find these data sources, it will contact the other dbRouters in its lookup referal list, and send a lookup message to ask the other dbRouters to resolve the unknown data sources specified. If any of these dbRouters is able to resolve the specified data sources, it would send a message back to the dbRouter in which the query is issued, indicating the location of the found relation. If a dbRouter could not resolve any of the specified relations, it would forward the lookup message to other dbRouters in its referal list. In order to prevent lookup messages from being forwarded in a cycle, a Time-To-Live (TTL) counter is maintained by all messages, and each time it is forwarded, the TTL is decreased by 1.

The algorithm for performing discovery of queried data sources is presented in Figure 1. The dbRouter at the node in which the user query forms the root node for the namespace. It is important to note that the namespace is established relative to the node in which the query is issued. The namespace is thus only valid in the lifetime of the query. We first start by discovering all relevant data sources at the root node. If we can find all the data sources, then the discovery algorithm terminates. If not, the dbRouter refers to its referal list for an alternative dbRouter. We then proceed to discover all the relevant data sources that the alternative dbRouter manages. We proceed from one dbRouter to another until all the data sources in the user's query are discovered. During the first part of the discovery algorithm, we might discover that there is more than one node for a particular data source. This could be due to a data source been replicated at multiple site. We proceed to prune away those data sources that have a greater access cost. At the end of the discovery algorithm, we are left with a list of nodes for the respective data sources which have the least access cost.

Let us consider a simple example as illustrated in Figure 2. dbRouter 1 to 3 are located at three different sites. A query is issued at the site in which dbRouter 1 located. Since the catalog for dbRouter 1 does not contain the information for the two relations A and B, it refers the query to other dbRouters in its referal list (i.e dbRouter 2). dbRouter 2 replies with a message that it manages relation A. Since the catalog for dbRouter 2 do not contain relation B, dbRouter 2 refers the query to dbRouter 3, which is in its referal list. dbRouter 3 then replies with a message to dbRouter 1 that it is managing relation B. This referal mechanism forms the basis for our automated discovery algorithm.

2.3 Distributed Query Optimization

In this section, we will discuss how distributed query optimization is performed. After the discovery phase, the nodes for the participating relations would be identified. We thus break the query plan into several query macro blocks. The query optimizer would then propagate each macro block to the dbRouters in which the participating relations are located. The number of macro blocks would be determined by the number of dbRouters participating in the execution of the query. Figure 3 presents the algorithm for populating the information in the macro blocks.

In addition, in order to ensure the processed tuples to flow from each dbRouter to the root node (i.e. node in which the query is issued), each macro optimization block has several well-defined input streams and an output stream. Prior to the propagation of the macro optimization blocks to the dbRouters, the input and output stream would have been defined. This could be changed during the negotiation phase of the dbRouters. For example, consider the query *Select * from A, B, C where A.rid = B.rid and B.sid = C.sid*. Let us suppose relation A, B and C are at dbRouter 2, 3 and 4 respectively. The query is issued at dbRouter 1. Based on the above query, 3 macro blocks would be created, and assigned to dbRouter 2, 3 and 4. Figure 4 shows the contents of the macro blocks and the assignment to the respective dbRouters.

2.4 dbRouter Negotiation

Once the macro blocks are assigned to the respective dbRouters, the respective dbRouters will negotiate with the dbRouters found in their dependent list. Negotiation between dbRouters are done in pairs. The basic motivation behind

```
Let R denote the set of relations in the query.
Let Q denote the set of relations found
Let G denote the optimization graph.
Nodes of the graph are either dbRouter or relation nodes

Let the rootNode be the node in which the query is issued Q = {}

// Discovery phase
routerNode = rootNode
currentdbRouter = dbRouter at rootNode

Initialize G

While ( Q != R ) {
 foundSet = currentdbRouter.RegisteredDataSource.getAllRelevantRelations();

 Perform type checking for the query which applies,
 If the attributes specified in of wrong type or semantically incorrect,
 then mark the predicates, projection list that are incorrect.

 Propagate these changes to the root node.

 Q = Q  ∪  foundSet;

 If  ( foundSet is not empty ) {
   For each relation r in foundSet {
     Create relationNode r, and add it to G
     Connect relationNode r to routerNode
   }
 }

 // Move on to the next router if not all relations specified in query
    has been found
 currentdbRouter = currentdbRouter.findBestRouter();

 Connect the node where currentdbRouter is to routerNode;
 routerNode = node(currentdbRouter);
}

// Pruning phase - Get rid of replicated data sources which have a greater
   accesscost
For all relationNodes node i in G {
  Remove node i from G if there exists node j
  s.t cost(node i) > cost(node j)

  Remove the routerNode in which node i is connected to if
  routerNode has no more connected relationNodes
}
```

Fig. 1. dbRouter discovery algorithm

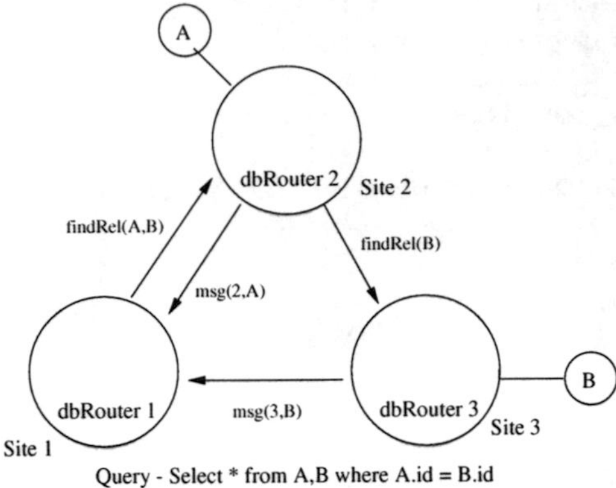

Fig. 2. Discovery of new data sources.

negotiation is to prevent shipping of a large base relation or intermediate results. During negotiation, statistics for the participating relations would be exchanged. The statistics include the join selectivity (if any), and the cardinality of the relations. Negotiation is always done between pairs of dbRouter. The dbRouter with smaller outgoing cost would send its output to the other. Once negotiation is completed. the input/output streams of each dbRouter are then modified accordingly. For example, consider 4. In plan 1, the tuples could flow from dbRouter 3 to dbRouter 2, where the join between B and C is performed, and the results flowing to dbRouter 1 where the final join is performed with A. Alternatively, in plan 2, the tuples could flow from dbRouter 2 to dbRouter 3, where the join between B and C is performed, and the results flowing to dbRouter 1 where the final join is performed. Hence, the choice of either plan 1 or 2 would depend on whether relation B or C has a smaller cardinalitiy,

Let *cost(X, Y)* denote the weighted sum of the normalized cost of connecting the output stream of dbRouter X to the input stream of dbRouter Y, and the normalized processing costs of processing the data first at dbRouter X, then dbRouter Y.

Let c_{xy} and c_{yx} denote the connectivity cost of connecting X to Y and Y to X respectively. The normalized cost of connecting X to Y, C , is defined as follows:

$$C = \frac{c_{xy}}{max(c_{xy}, c_{yx})}$$

Let p_x and p_y denote the processing cost at dbRouter X and Y respectively. The normalized processing cost of processing the data first at dbRouter X, P_x is defined as follows:

$$P_x = \frac{p_x}{max(p_x, p_y)}$$

Hence, the *cost(X, Y)* is defined as follows:

$$cost(X, Y) = \alpha C + \gamma P_x$$

where α and γ are tunable parameters.

```
Let MB denote the set of macro-blocks to be populated.
Let Q denote the query
Let P be the set of projection list in Q
Let S be the set of selection and join predicates in Q

Number of Macro Optimization Block = Number of dbRouters participating
in the query

For each macro block m in MB {
  // Assign projection attributes to the respective macro blocks
  For each attribute a in P {
    If a involves the relations in m, add a to m
  }

  For each predicate p in S {
    if p is a selection predicate {
      Check whether selection predicate is relevant to relations
      in macro block
      If it is relevant, add p to m
    }
    else if p is a join predicate {
      Check whether the left-hand side (LHS) attributes or the
      right-hand side (RHS) attributes are related to relations
      in macro block

      If it is relevant {
         Add p to m

         Check whether all relations in LHS and RHS are available in m
         Add those releations not available in m to the dependency list
         of m
      }
    }
  }
}
```

Fig. 3. Populating Macro Optimization Blocks

We would connect the output stream of dbRouter X to the input stream of dbRouter Y if

$$cost(X,Y) < cost(Y,X)$$

Negotiation is performed by all dbRouters in parallel. Suppose a dbRouter has more than one relation in its dependency list, and after the completion of the first negotiation, it realised it only have outgoing streams, but no incoming streams, it will then propagate its dependency list to the dbRouters where its outgoing streams is directed. The reason for the propagation is that since the dbRouter no longer has any incoming streams, it is likely that the original query graph have been modified as a result of the negotiation. Hence, there is

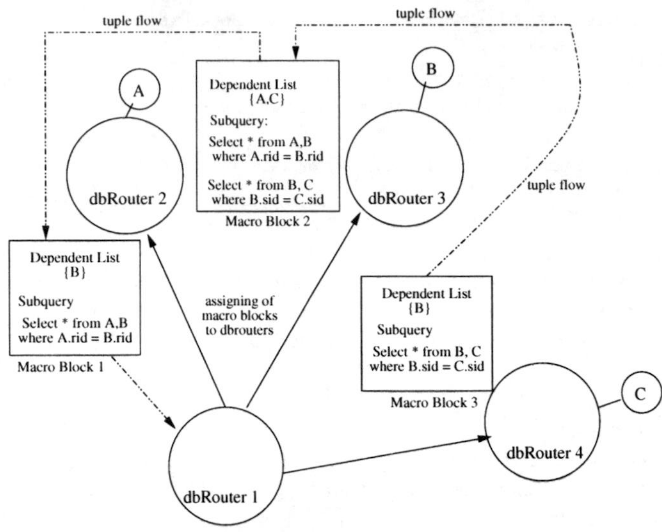

Fig. 4. Delegation of Macro-block to respective dbRouters

a need to perform a second negotiation after the propagation. dbRouters whose dependency list has changed after the propagation of dependency list would perform a second negotiation with dbRouters of the newly added relations. Once all dbRouters have finished negotiation, it will send a *negotiation_completed* message back to the dbRouter (i.e the root dbRouter) in which the query originated. Once the root dbRouter receives all the messages from the participating dbRouters, it will send a *go* message to these dbRouters, and query processing would proceed in a distributed manner.

2.5 Tuple Routing

Query execution proceeds immediately once negotiation between the dbRouters have completed. The role of the dbRouter now changes to that of a tuple routing mechanism. Since the input and output stream of each dbRouter has been setup, query processing executes in parallel at each respective dbRouter. A dbRouter might be delegated with collecting the results from a join being performed by a local relational database, or the dbRouter might be collecting results from a web wrapper module. These results are then routed by the dbRouter to the next dbRouter based on its output stream. At the same time, another dbRouter might be 'feeding' tuples to the current dbRouter. For specific data sources that have limited query processing capabilities, the dbRouter takes on a third role of performing local processing (e.g. filtering the data), before passing it on to the next dbRouter.

As the respective dbRouter performs various degree of processing, this helps to offload the root node's processing workload. This is in contrast to having a centralized site to perform the scheduling and integrating of the results, which quickly becomes a bottleneck.

3 Related Works

In [12], Mariposa, a distributed database management system for wide area networks was proposed. Mariposa allows autonomous DBMS's which are in a wide-area environment to work together to process queries. A query optimization technique based on a economic paradigm was used in which processing sites buy and sell data and query processing services. Using this model, a query broker at a central site selects the processing site for each plan chunk without contacting the sites prior. We note that our notion of macro blocks corresponds to the plan chunks used in Mariposa. However, our work differs from Mariposa in that instead of relying on a centralized query broker to determine the processing sites, the work is delegated to several dbRouters, working in parallel together to determine the optimal tuple flow.

In addition, the Telegraph project at the University of California, Berkeley aims to provide efficient and flexible mechanisms for distributed query processing across sites in wide area, and parallel query processing in a large shared-nothing cluster. It leverages on the success from the River project [3] and the eddies [4] work. We are currently studying the use of distributing the eddies at multiple sites, and connecting the output of the an eddy at one processing site to another eddy at another processing site for routing the tuples from site to site.

integration of data from heterogeneous information sources. Components were developed to extract properties from unstructured data objects, and translating them into a common object model to faciliate query processing and browsing of information across the data sources.

In [13], the Distributed Information Search COmponent (Disco) project studied the problems related to access to large number of heterogeneous data sources, such as unavailable data sources, and local autonomy of the individual data sources. A distributed mediator architecture was proposed to address the problems.

A general architecture of an agent-based approach for distributed query optimization and processing was proposed in [11]. *Database agents*, with task execution and learning capabilities was developed. The use of these agents in performing distributed query optimization was also explored.

Our main contribution lies in the proposal for a scaleable and distributed query optimization and processing framework for integrating data from diverse data sources. In addition, we presented an automated discovery algorithm for dynamiaclly identifying new data sources. We also present our preliminary study into performing distributed query optimization algorithm for an open environment. We introduced the notion of negotiation amongst the dbRouters in order set up a continuous flow of tuple from the various processing nodes to the root node where a query is issued. We are currently implementing the various dbRouter components for the proposed framework.

References

1. Laurent Amsaleg, Michael J. Franklin, and Anthony Tomasic. Dynamic query operator scheduling for wide-area remote access.
2. Laurent Amsaleg, Michael J. Franklin, Anthony Tomasic, and Tolga Urhan. Scrambling query plans to cope with unexpected delays, 1996.
3. Remzi H. Arpaci-Dusseau, Eric Anderson, Noah Treuhaft, David E. Culler, Joseph M. Hellerstein, David Patterson, and Kathy Yelic. Cluster i/o with river: Making the fast case common, 1999.
4. R. Avnur and J. Hellerstein. Eddies: Continuously adaptive query processing, 2000.
5. Philippe Bonnet, Johannes Gehrke, and Praveen Seshadri. Towards sensor database systems, Jan 2001.
6. Sudarshan Chawathe, Hector Garcia-Molina, Joachim Hammer, Kelly Ireland, Yannis Papakonstantinou, Jeffrey D. Ullman, and Jennifer Widom. The TSIMMIS project: Integration of heterogeneous information sources. In *16th Meeting of the Information Processing Society of Japan*, pages 7–18, Tokyo, Japan, 1994.
7. L. Haas, D. Kossman, E. Wimmers, and J. Yang. Optimizing queries across diverse data sources, 1997.
8. Tomasz Imielinski and Samir Goel. Dataspace - querying and monitoring deeply networked collections in physical space.
9. Z. Ives, D. Florescu, M. Friedman, A. Levy, and D. Weld. An adaptive query execution system for data integration. *Proceedings of ACM SIGMOD Conf., Philadelphia, PA, 1999.*, 1999.
10. Z.G. Ives, A. Y. Levy, J. Madhavan, R. Pottinger, S. Saroiu, I. Tatarinov, S. Betzler, Q. Chen, E. Jaslikowska, J. Su, W. Tak, and T. Yeung. Self-organising data sharing communities with sagres.
11. Michael Stillger, Johann K. Obermaier, and Johann Christoph Freytag. Aques: An agent-based query evaluation system, June 1997.
12. M. Stonebraker, P.M. Aoki, R. Devine, W. Litwin, and M. Olson. Mariposa: A new architecure for distributed data, Feb 1994.
13. A. Tomasic, L. Raschid, and P. Valduriez. Scaling access to heterogeneous data sources with disco, September/October 1998.
14. Tolga Urhan and Michael J. Franklin. Xjoin: A reactively-scheduled pipelined join operator, 2000.
15. Tolga Urhan, Michael J. Franklin, and Laurent Amsaleg. Cost-based query scrambling for initial delays, 1998.

Optimal Parallel I/O for Range Queries through Replication*

Keith Frikken[1], Mikhail Atallah[1], Sunil Prabhakar[1], and Rei Safavi-Naini[2]

[1] Purdue University, West Lafayette IN 47907, USA,
{kbf,mja,sunil}@cs.purdue.edu
[2] University of Wollongong Australia
rei@uow.edu.au

Abstract. In this paper we study the problem of declustering two-dimensional datasets with replication over parallel devices to improve range query performance. The related problem of declustering without replication has been well studied. It has been established that strictly optimal declustering schemes do not exist if data is not replicated. In addition to the usual problem of identifying a good allocation, the replicated version of the problem needs to address the issue of identifying a good retrieval schedule for a given query. We address both problems in this paper. An efficient algorithm for finding a lowest cost retrieval schedule is developed. This algorithm works for any query, not just range queries. Two replicated placement schemes are presented – one that results in a strictly optimal allocation, and another that guarantees a retrieval cost that is either optimal or 1 more than the optimal for any range query.

1 Introduction

Declustering data across multiple I/O disks is an effective technique for improving performance through parallel I/O. The problem of declustering multi-dimensional datasets has received a lot of attention due to the importance of multi-dimensional datasets. Examples of such datasets include relational databases (each ordered attribute of a relation can be viewed as a dimension), GIS and spatio-temporal databases, image and video data, pixels of a computer display, and scientific simulation datasets. The I/O devices can be magnetic disks, chips of main memory, or nodes in a shared-nothing environment.

By uniformly dividing the dataset along each dimension, the dataset is divided into tiles which are then distributed across multiple I/O devices. A range query over the dataset only needs to retrieve those tiles that intersect the query. Since the tiles are placed on multiple devices, they can be retrieved in parallel.

* Portions of this work were supported by Grant EIA-9903545 from the National Science Foundation, Contract N00014-02-1-0364 from the Office of Naval Research, by sponsors of the Center for Education and Research in Information Assurance and Security, the GAANN fellowship, NSF CAREER grant IIS-9985019 and NSF Grant 9972883.

R. Cicchetti et al. (Eds.): DEXA 2002, LNCS 2453, pp. 669–678, 2002.

The cost of retrieving a tile is assumed to be constant. The cost for executing a query from multiple devices is therefore proportional to the maximum number of tiles that need to be retrieved from a single device. For a query that retrieves m tiles, the optimal cost with k devices is given by $\lceil \frac{m}{k} \rceil$.

An ideal declustering scheme would achieve this optimal cost for all possible queries. Such a scheme is said to be *strictly optimal*. It has been established that for the case of two-dimensional data strictly optimal schemes exist only in very special cases [AE97]. Given the impossibility of finding strictly optimal schemes for the general case, researchers have focussed on developing schemes with average cost close to the optimal cost. This has resulted in the development of a large number of allocation schemes [DS82,FM89,LHY97,FB93,BBB$^+$97,PAAE98], [AP00,BSC00,SBC01]. The non-existence of strictly optimal allocations is based upon the assumption that each tile is allocated to a single device. This raises an interesting question: If tiles are allowed to be replicated and placed on multiple devices, then is it possible to obtain strictly optimal allocation? This is an important issue since the latency of access is (and will likely continue to be in the foreseeable future) more critical than storage capacity. To the best of our knowledge at the time of submission, the issue of replicated declustering for range queries had not been explored, however we have discovered that in [TF01] some work was done in this area (more on this at the end of the Section 2).

In this paper we investigate the use of replication for improving the declustering of two-dimensional data with an emphasis on range queries. While the techniques are applicable to multiple dimensions, we limit our discussion to the two-dimensional case. The allocation of tiles to disks can be viewed as a coloring problem – each device is considered to be a color. If a tile is allocated to device i, it is considered to be colored with color i. With replicated data placement, each tile can have multiple colors. Two questions naturally follow:

1. When given a grid that is colored in such a manner, choosing which disk to use for each block could dramatically increase the performance. How can an optimal selection be computed?
2. How should the tiles of the grid be colored to maximize performance?

We address both problems in this paper. The contribution of this paper are as follows:

- An efficient algorithm for determining a least cost retrieval schedule. This result applies to any arbitrary query – not just range queries.
- Two replicated data declustering schemes. The schemes differ in the degree of replication. One scheme achieves the strictly optimal cost by replicating each tile on each device. The second scheme requires $\sqrt{m}$ replicas of each tile where m is the number of devices and guarantees that the cost for any range query is either optimal or one more than the optimal.

The rest of the paper is organized as follows. Section 2 presents a brief discussion of the existing declustering (coloring) schemes, all of which assume non-replicated placement. In Section 3 we present an efficient algorithm to compute a least cost retrieval schedule for replicated placement. Section 4 addresses the issue of strictly optimal placement schemes with replication. Section 5 concludes the paper.

2 Related Work

Consider a two-dimensional data set that has been divided into tiles along each dimension. In the case of a screen display these tiles may correspond to single pixels, whereas in the case of a large image they may represent larger rectangular sections of the full image. For relational databases, they may correspond to subranges of two attributes. The I/O devices can be magnetic disks, chips of main memory, or nodes in a shared-nothing environment. In this paper we use the term *disk* to refer to any of these parallel I/O devices. We also use the terms *allocation*, *declustering* and *coloring* synonymously to refer to the assignment of tiles to I/O devices.

Given a two-dimensional array of $N_0 \times N_1$ tiles, and k colors (disks, or I/O devices), the coloring (declustering) function, ϕ, maps each tile (x_0, x_1), $0 \leq x_0 < N_0, 0 \leq x_1 < N_1$ to one of the colors, $0, \dots, k-1$. In [AE97], the necessary and sufficient conditions for the existence of strictly optimal coloring schemes are derived. In particular it is shown that strictly optimal colorings exist only in the following cases:

1. $k = 2, 3$, or 5; or
2. $k \geq N_0 N_1 - 2$; or
3. $N_0 \leq 2$, or $N_1 \leq 2$; or
4. $k = N_0 N_1 - 4$ and $\min\{N_0, N_1\} = 3$; or
5. $k = 8$ and $N_0 = N_1 = 4$

Of these cases, only the second case is of general interest. To demonstrate sufficiency of these conditions, a strictly optimal coloring is also developed in [AE97], which allocates tile (x_0, x_1) to color $(\lfloor \frac{k}{2} \rfloor) x_0 + x_1) \bmod k$. We will refer to this as the *HalfK* coloring. Figure 1(a) shows the coloring generated by the HalfK method for N_0=N_1=8 and $k = 5$.

Several coloring techniques have been proposed for improving range query performance in relational databases. These include the Disk Modulo or DM approach [DS82] also known as CMD [LSR92], the Fieldwise eXclusive or FX approach [KP88], the Gray code approach [GHW90] and the HCAM approach [FB93]. Two approaches based upon error correcting codes are [FM89] and [AE93]. Other techniques include [LHY97]. Coloring techniques for similarity query have also been developed in [BBB+97,PAE98b,PAE98a].

The Disk Modulo (DM) coloring proposed by Du and Sobolewski allocates tile (x_0, x_1) to color $\phi_{DM}(x_0, x_1) = (x_0 + x_1) \bmod k$. An example of the coloring generated by DM is shown in Figure 1(b) for the case $N_0 = N_1 = 8$, $k = 5$. A generalization of the DM method, the Generalized Disk Modulo or GMD, was also developed in [DS82], which allocates tile (x_0, x_1) to device $(ax_0 + bx_1) \bmod k$, where a and b are integers.

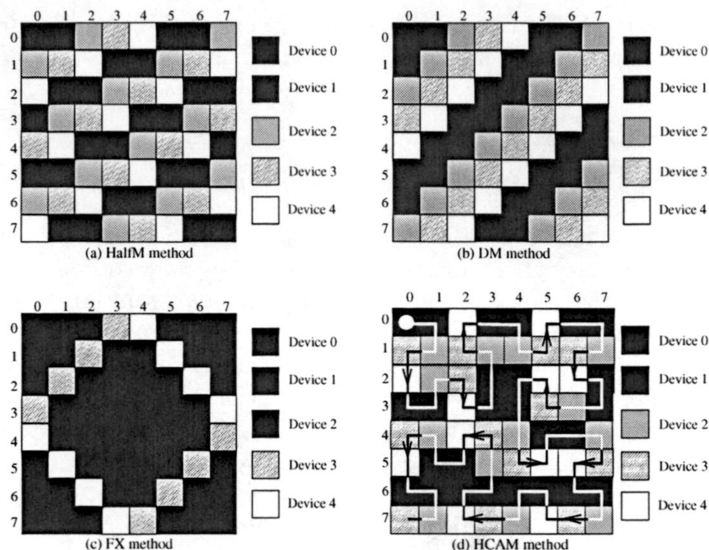

Fig. 1. Examples of colorings generated by non-replicating schemes.

The FX method proposed by Kim and Pramanik [KP88], requires that N_0, N_1 and k are all powers of 2. The FX coloring is defined as $\phi_{FX}(x_0, x_1) = (b_0 \oplus b_1) \bmod k$, where b_0 and b_1 are the binary representations of x_0 and x_1 respectively and $\oplus$ is the bit-wise exclusive-OR operation. Figure 1(c) shows an example of the coloring generated by the FX method for N_0=N_1=8, k=5.

The HCAM method is based upon the Hilbert space filling curves. Hilbert curves can be used to convert a discrete two-dimensional array into a linear sequence such that spatial proximity in the original array is preserved. Given an $N_0 \times N_1$ array of tiles, the HCAM method first converts the array into a linear sequence, and then allocates the tiles to devices in a round-robin fashion following the linear sequence. Figure 1(d) shows the coloring generated by HCAM for N_0=N_1=8, k=5. The linear path corresponding to the Hilbert curve is also shown.

A class of schemes called Cyclic Allocation schemes was developed in [PAAE98,PAE98c]. The cyclic schemes allocate tile (x_0, x_1) to color $(x_0 + Sx_1) \bmod k$, where $S \in \{0, \ldots, k-1\}$ is called the skip value. Each different value of S defines a unique scheme within the class of Cyclic schemes. The choice of S is shown to be critical for the performance of the scheme. Three methods for choosing good values for S are also presented in [PAAE98,PAE98c].

The Golden Ratio Sequences (GRS) scheme was developed by Bhatia et al. [BSC00]. The scheme is defined as: $\phi_{GRS}(x_0, x_1) = (x_0 - \Phi^{-1}((x_1) \bmod k)) \bmod k$, where Φ^{-1} is the inverse mapping of Φ. The mapping Φ is a permutation of the set $\{0, 1, \cdots, k-1\}$. The permutation is computed as follows: i) $\forall i \in \{0, \cdots, k-1\}$ compute the fractional part of $\frac{2i}{1+\sqrt{5}}$, and call it k_i. ii) Sort the k_i values and use this order to define the permutation Φ.

In [AP00], a coloring scheme with worst-case deviation from the optimal cost of $O(\log k)$ has been developed. The scheme was shown to be equivalent to one that maps tile (x_0, x_1) to device $(x_0 \oplus x_1^R) \bmod k$, where x_1^R is the reversal of x_1's binary representation in [SBC01]. The $O(\log k)$ is the tightest bound for any declustering scheme that does not replicate tiles [SBC01].

None of the existing schemes addresses the issue of replicated data placement. To the best of our knowledge, the issue of declustering schemes for replicated data as studied in this paper has not been addressed with the exception of two recent studies [SEK00,TF01]. The study in [SEK00], allows each data item to have at most one copy. An algorithm for finding a least cost retrieval schedule is developed. This study does not offer any particular algorithm for placing replicated data on disks. In [TF01] a retrieval computation algorithm is given for the case where an optimal scheduling exists, some suggested coloring schemes are given, and experimental data is provided for small numbers of disks. Our algorithm for scheduling is faster for large queries and is less restrictive (this difference is quantified in the first paragraph of the next section after some notation has been introduced).

3 Least Cost Retrieval with Replicated Placement

In this section we address the problem of finding a least cost schedule for retrieving the tiles required to answer a given query if the tiles are replicated on multiple disks. There are k disks, numbered $1, \ldots, k$. As a result of this particular query that we are processing, the tiles to be retrieved from the disks are numbered $1, \ldots, m$ (what we are describing works for any query, whether it is a range query or not). An identical copy of tile i resides on each of the q_i disks in the set $L_i = \{l_{i,1}, l_{i,2}, \ldots, l_{i,q_i}\}$, $q_i \leq k$, $1 \leq l_{i,j} \leq k$. Let $r = \max_{i=1 \ldots k} q_i$, be the level of replication, or equivalently the number of distinct disks that a record can be stored upon. The desired output is an assignment of each tile i to one of the disks in L_i so as to minimize the maximum number of tiles assigned to any disk (i.e., make the disk queues as evenly equal as possible). For the special case where records are placed on at most two disks, i.e. $r \leq 2$, an algorithm is given in [SEK00] which computes such an assignment. In [TF01], there is an algorithm that is given for an arbitrary level of replication, but only computes an assignment if the retrieval cost is optimal; this algorithm runs in time $O(\frac{rm^3}{k})$. Our algorithm executes in time $O(rm^2 + mk)$, and will compute the best retrieval schedule even if is not optimal.

It suffices to give an algorithm that, given any integer ℓ, tests whether there is a solution in which no disk is assigned more than ℓ tiles to retrieve (because such an algorithm can then be used in a binary search for the smallest such ℓ, at the cost of an extra logarithmic factor in the time complexity). Such an algorithm is given next.

Algorithm Test(ℓ)
Comment: Tests whether there is a solution in which no disk is assigned more than ℓ tiles to retrieve. If such a solution exists, it can also return (if needed) the corresponding assignment of each tile to a disk.

1. Create a directed graph G, whose edges have capacities, as follows:
   - There is one vertex for each disk, one vertex for each tile, and two additional special vertices called s and t; therefore there are $m + k + 2$ vertices.
   - There is a directed edge of capacity 1 from vertex s to the vertex for tile i, $1 \leq i \leq m$.
   - There is a directed edge of capacity 1 from the vertex of tile i to each of the q_i vertices corresponding to the disks in its L_i list, $1 \leq i \leq m$.
   - There is a directed edge of capacity ℓ from the vertex for disk j to vertex t, $1 \leq j \leq k$.
2. Run any polynomial-time maximum-flow algorithm on the above graph G (with s as source and t as destination). One known feature of such algorithms is that, if all edge capacities are integers, then the flow they produce is also integral (i.e., the flow through any edge is an integer).
3. If the value of the flow produced in the previous step is less than m, then answer "No". Otherwise answer "Yes" and, if the corresponding assignment is desired, assign each tile i to the disk j for which the edge (i, j) carries a flow of 1.

This algorithm ensures that no disk j is assigned more than ℓ tiles since no more than ℓ units of flow can go through j (because the capacity of the edge from j to t is ℓ). Also when the flow is m all of the records can be retrieved, since the flow from s to each record-node is 1.

Each probe of the binary search (for the smallest feasible ℓ) makes one usage of the above **Test** procedure (in "Yes/No" mode – there is no need to actually produce the assignment until the end of the binary search, when the best ℓ has been found). The most practical (and easiest to program) maximum-flow algorithm runs in time proportional to the cube of the number of vertices of the graph, therefore each probe in the binary search takes time $O((m + k)^3)$. There are $O(\log m)$ such probes, so that the overall running time of our method is $O((m + k)^3 \log m)$.

This previous algorithm can be optimized to remove the factor of $O(\log m)$ by taking advantage of the similarity between the residual networks created in each of the executions of AlgorithmTest.

First set up the max flow problem as before, use any Ford Fulkerson method to solve it, and have a global residual network so that information can be saved when a scheduling does not exist. Modify AlgorithmTest() so that it uses this global residual network. Another algorithm QuickAlgorithmTest() is created which takes the global residual network, adds one to the outflow from each disk to t, and then continues to execute Ford Fulkerson on the residual network to maximize the flow. QuickAlgorithmTest() returns true if the flow reaches M, otherwise it returns false. The following is an algorithm to find the minimum response time:

```
begin FindMinResponseTime
    L := ⌈m/k⌉ (note L is retrieval cost)
    D := AlgorithmTest(L)
    while D ≠ true do
        L := L + 1
        D := QuickAlgorithmTest()
    endwhile
end FindMinResponseTime
```

To analyze this algorithm we define f_0 = flow found in execution of AlgorithmTest(), and f_i = change in flow found in ith execution of QuickAlgorithmTest(). The total cost of FindMinResponseTime() will be $O(E(f_0 + f_1 + ... + f_{L-\lceil \frac{m}{k} \rceil}))$, where E is the number of edges in the flow graph, since Ford Fulkerson methods run in time $O(Ef)$ on integer flow graphs where f is the flow found. Now $E = O(mr + k)$, where r is the level of replication. Also, since the algorithm stops when a flow of m is reached, $(f_0 + f_1 + ... + f_{L-\lceil \frac{m}{k} \rceil}) = m$. Hence the running time is $O(rm^2 + mk)$.

4 Strictly Optimal Coloring with Replication

In the previous section we demonstrated that if tiles are placed on multiple disks that an optimal scheduling can be computed in polynomial time. The question now becomes, how do the tiles get placed on disk so that the query response time is minimized. In [SEK00] it was shown that if each tile was placed on two disks that are assigned randomly, then the probability of having a response time no more than one worse than optimal is very high. In [TF01] several replicated coloring were proposed that worked optimally when the number of disks was less than 15. We have two schemes for assigning disks to tiles. The first, Complete Coloring (CC), has optimal performance, and the second, Square Root Colors Disk Modulo (SRCDM) has performance that is no more than one from optimal.

Definition 1: The CC method places all tiles on all disks.

Theorem 1: The CC method has optimal query performance.

Proof: Sequentially, order the tiles in the query, call them $r_0, r_1, ...r_{n-1}$. Use disk i mod M for tile r_i. The response time is thus $\lceil \frac{n}{M} \rceil$, which is optimal. **QED**

Before we define SRCDM we need to specify some things about the query problem.

1. M is the number of disks in the system, and M is a perfect square such that $M = n^2$ for some $n \in \aleph$.
2. $Q(r, c)$ represents a query with r rows and c columns.
3. For any query $Q(r, c)$, r_1, r_2, c_1, and c_2 are defined such that $r = r_1 n + r_2$ where $0 \le r_2 < n$ and $c = c_1 n + c_2$ where $0 \le c_2 < n$. Furthermore,

let $d = r_2c_1 + r_1c_2$, and define d_1 and d_2 such that $d = d_1n + d_2$ where $0 \leq d_2 < n$

Definition 2: $\forall$i$\in \{0, .., n-1\}$, there is a corresponding set with n elements $< i >= \{in, in+1, ..., (i+1)n-1\}$.

Definition 3: The SRCDM (Square root colors disk modulo) coloring colors position (i,j) with the n colors in the set $< i + j(\bmod n) >$.

Lemma 1: Given n adjacent squares in a row(or a column), $\forall$i$\in \{0, .., n-1\}$ there exists a square colored with $< i >$ in SRCDM.

Proof: Wlog suppose that we are given n adjacent squares in a row, and that the leftmost square is colored with set $< j >$. $\forall$i$\in \{0, .., n-1\}$, the $((i-j) \bmod n)$th leftmost square is colored with the set $< i >$. **QED**

Theorem 2: SRCDM colors a grid with $M = n^2$ colors, in a way that the maximum response time of a query Q(r,c) is $\lceil \frac{rc}{M} \rceil + 1$ (i.e. no more than one from optimal).

Proof: Consider the optimal time for a query Q(r,c).
$rc = (r_1n + r_2)(c_1n + c_2) = r_1c_1n^2 + (r_1c_2 + r_2c_1)n + r_2c_2 = r_1c_1n^2 + dn + r_2c_2 = r_1c_1M + (d_1n + d_2)n + r_2c_2 = r_1c_1M + d_1n^2 + d_2n + r_2c_2 = (r_1c_1 + d_1)M + d_2n + r_2c_2$. Now $d_2n + r_2c_2 < 2M$, so $rc \leq (r_1c_1 + d_1 + 2)M$. Hence the optimal query response time $\lceil \frac{rc}{M} \rceil$ is subject to the following constraints: $(r_1c_1 + d_1) \leq \lceil \frac{rc}{M} \rceil \leq (r_1c_1 + d_1 + 2)$. Consider the query response time for SRCDM. We can partition Q into four regions (I, II, III, and IV) as shown in Figure 2. Consider region I, in

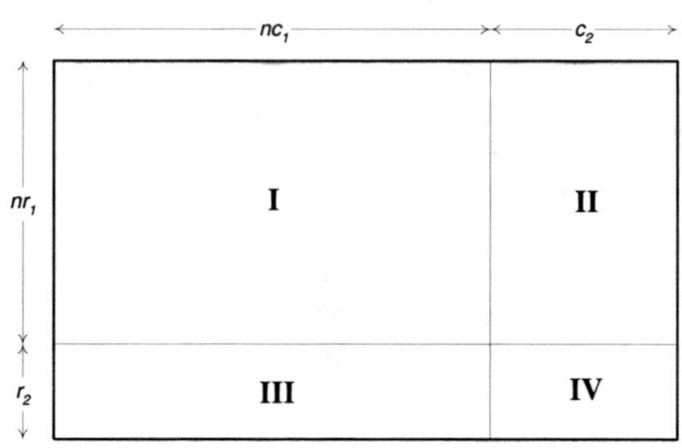

Fig. 2. Partitioning a Query

each row there are c_1 disjoint groups of n adjacent squares. Thus region I contains nr_1c_1 of these groups. By lemma 1 this implies that there are nr_1c_1 instances of each set $< i >$, hence region I requires a response time of r_1c_1. Consider regions II and III, in region II(III) each column(row) has $r_1(c_1)$ disjoint groups of n adjacent squares. Together these regions have $r_1c_2 + c_1r_2 = d_1n + d_2$ such groups, and thus require a response time $\leq d_1 + 1$. Consider region IV: It fits in an n by n square which implies its query response time will be ≤ 1. The maximum query response time in SRCDM will be $\leq r_1c_1 + d_1 + 2$. This is no more than one off optimal except for the case when the optimal response time is $r_1c_1 + d_1$, but in this case region IV would have area 0, which implies that region IV's response time will be 0, hence it will be no more than one from optimal. **QED**

For CC and SRCDM, a scheduling of disk accesses can be done in time proportional to the size of the query, and the algorithm in section 3 is unnecessary to compute it.

The colorings in this section have provable bounds for arbitrary large values of M, but they may be impractical to use in practice. However, our experimental results show that replication can help increase performance dramatically. A simple replication scheme would be to place would be to use any non-replicated coloring scheme for the first color and add $\frac{(i-1)M}{r}$ color modulo to get the ith coloring. We implemented this scheme and tested the performance of this scheme for values of $M \leq 32$ and $r = 2$. We found that this scheme increases performance for many colorings dramatically.

5 Conclusion

Tiling a multi-dimensional dataset and distributing it among multiple I/O devices is a well-known technique for improving retrieval performance for range queries. Since the non-existence of strictly optimal allocations has been established, researchers have focused on identifying schemes that approach this unachievable ideal. In this paper we addressed the impact of replicated placement of tiles. Two sub-problems arise with replicated placement: (a) Given a set of tiles to be retrieved, determining the lowest cost retrieval schedule and (b) Generating replicated allocations that result in good performance. We developed an efficient algorithm that generates a lowest cost retrieval schedule for any query (not just range queries). We show that it is possible (with full replication) to achieve a strictly optimal allocation. We also developed a scheme that requires $\sqrt{k}$ (where k is the number of parallel devices) replicas and guarantees that the retrieval cost is at most 1 more than the optimal for any range query. While the discussion in the paper focuses on two-dimensional data, all results with the exception of the performance guarantee for SRCDM are applicable to any number of dimensions.

References

AE93. K. A. S. Abdel-Ghaffar and A. El Abbadi. Optimal disk allocation for partial match queries. *Transactions of Database Systems*, 18(1):132–156, March 1993.

AE97. K. A. S. Abdel-Ghaffar and A. El Abbadi. Optimal allocation of two-dimensional data. In *Int. Conf. on Database Theory*, pages 409–418, Delphi, Greece, Jan. 1997.

AP00. M. J. Atallah and S. Prabhakar. (Almost) optimal parallel block access for range queries. In *Proc. of the 19th ACM Symposium on Principles of Database Systems (PODS)*, Dallas, Texas, May 2000.

BBB$^+$97. S. Berchtold, C. Bohm, B. Braunmuller, D. A. Keim, and H-P. Kriegel. Fast parallel similarity search in multimedia databases. In *Proc. ACM SIGMOD Int. Conf. on Management of Data*, pages 1–12, Arizona, U.S.A., 1997.

BSC00. R. Bhatia, R. K. Sinha, and C.-M. Chen. Declutering using golden ratio sequences. In *Proc. of Int'l. Conference on Data Engineering (ICDE)*, San Diego, California, March 2000.

DS82. H. C. Du and J. S. Sobolewski. Disk allocation for cartesian product files on multiple-disk systems. *ACM Trans of Database Systems*, 7(1):82–101, 1982.

FB93. C. Faloutsos and P. Bhagwat. Declustering using fractals. In *Proc. of the 2nd Int. Conf. on Parallel and Distributed Information Systems*, pages 18 – 25, San Diego, CA, Jan 1993.

FM89. C. Faloutsos and D. Metaxas. Declustering using error correcting codes. In *Proc. ACM Symp. on Principles of Database Systems*, pages 253–258, 1989.

GHW90. J. Gray, B. Horst, and M. Walker. Parity striping of disc arrays: Low-cost reliable storage with acceptable throughput. In *Proceedings of the Int. Conf. on Very Large Data Bases*, pages 148–161, Washington DC., August 1990.

KP88. M. H. Kim and S. Pramanik. Optimal file distribution for partial match retrieval. In *Proc. ACM SIGMOD Int. Conf. on Management of Data*, pages 173–182, Chicago, 1988.

LHY97. Y.-L. Lo, K. A. Hua, and H. C. Young. A general multidimensional data allocation method for multicomputer database systems. In *8th Int. Conf. on Database and Expert Systems Applications*, pages 357–66, Toulouse, France, September 1997.

LSR92. J. Li, J. Srivastava, and D. Rotem. CMD: a multidimensional declustering method for parallel database systems. In *Proceedings of the Int. Conf. on Very Large Data Bases*, pages 3–14, Vancouver, Canada, August 1992.

PAAE98. S. Prabhakar, K. Abdel-Ghaffar, D. Agrawal, and A. El Abbadi. Cyclic allocation of two-dimensional data. In *Proc. of the International Conference on Data Engineering (ICDE'98)*, pages 94–101, Orlando, Florida, Feb 1998.

PAE98a. S. Prabhakar, D. Agrawal, and A. El Abbadi. Data declustering for efficient range and similarity searching. In *Proc. Multimedia Storage and Archiving Systems III, (SPIE symposium on Voice, Video, and Data Communications)*, Boston, Massachusetts, November 1998.

PAE98b. S. Prabhakar, D. Agrawal, and A. El Abbadi. Efficient disk allocation for fast similarity searching. In *Proc. of the 10th Int. Sym. on Parallel Algorithms and Architectures (SPAA'98)*, pages 78–87, June 1998.

PAE98c. S. Prabhakar, D. Agrawal, and A. El Abbadi. Efficient retrieval of multidimensional datasets through parallel I/O. In *Proc. of the 5th International Conference on High Performance Computing, (HiPC'98)*, 1998.

SBC01. Rakesh K. Sinha, Randeep Bhatia, and Chung-Min Chen. Asymptotically optimal declustering schemes for range queries. In *Proc. of 8th International Conference on Database Theory (ICDT)*, pages 144–158, London, UK, January 2001.

SEK00. P. Sanders, S. Egner, and J. Korst. Fast concurrent access to parallel disks. In *11th ACM-SIAM Symposium on Discrete Algorithms*, 2000.

TF01. A. Tosun and H. Ferhatosmanoglu. Optimal Parallel I/O Using Replication. OSU Technical Report OSU-CISRC-11/01-TR26, 2001.

A Database for Repetitive, Unpredictable Moving Objects

Paul Werstein and J.R. McDonald

Department of Computer Science
University of Otago
Dunedin, New Zealand
{werstein, jrm}@cs.otago.ac.nz

Abstract. Recently much research has been done in applying database technology to tracking moving objects. Most techniques assume a predictable linear motion. We present a new application for moving object databases, characterized by repetitive, unpredictable motion with very high data rates. In particular, the domain of athletic and auto races is presented. We found existing moving object methods do not adequately address this application area. A data model is presented for efficiently storing the data. A spatiotemporal index is developed for fast retrieval of data. We give a set of queries likely to be of interest in this application domain. A study is presented showing our implementation has better performance than those based on relational DBMSs.

1 Introduction

In the last few years, much research has been done in applying database technology to tracking moving objects. The techniques developed to date assume a predictable, linear motion so an object can be represented as a position, time at that position, and some motion vector to give future locations.

This research looks at a class of applications which are characterised by repetitive, unpredictable motion and high data rates. Examples include sporting events such as athletic track and field races, bicycle races and car races. This class of applications cannot be represented using existing techniques.

The motion is repetitive since it involves many laps around a closed course. Each object (person, bicycle, car) covers approximately the same space which is the designated race course. This causes problems for indexing techniques using minimum bounding boxes since they expand to cover the entire data space. Problems also occur for techniques which divide the data space such as quadtrees since objects will appear in many of the rectangles.

The motion is unpredictable in the sense that an equation or set of equations cannot be used to describe the motion of the objects. It may be possible to describe mathematically an ideal path. However external, unpredictable factors cause the motion to vary frequently from the ideal path. In track and field races, factors include other athletes in the path, variation due to wind, and slips. In

R. Cicchetti et al. (Eds.): DEXA 2002, LNCS 2453, pp. 679–688, 2002.

auto races, factors include other cars in the path, debris or water on the track, unevenness of the track, drivers' skills, momentary loss of control and accidents.

This application class requires a high data rate to achieve the desired accuracy. We use Formula One car races as our example. The race cars are very close to each other and travelling at high speeds. At a top speed of approximately 360 kph, they travel 100 meters per second. We chose to have a resolution of 100 mm which means 1000 points per second are required. Fortunately, a race is relatively short and has a small number of objects (22 cars and about 90 minutes in our test set) which limits the amount of data to be stored. However it still amounts to over 7 GB of data.

The contribution of this research is a method of storing the locations of moving objects with a high data rate and indexing them for rapid retrieval. We found that conventional relational databases cannot handle adequately the data storage and retrieval needed to record a race and to allow display of the data in real time.

The next section positions this work in relation to other research. Section 3 describes how data is stored and indexed. Section 4 describes the performance of our database, and Section 5 has concluding remarks.

2 Related Work

Much of the current research on moving objects uses scenarios such as a car moving on a highway [9,2]. These types of applications are inherently different from our research scenario in the following ways:

- The requirements for positional accuracy are much higher in our application. For example, if a driver queries for hotels within 5 km, inaccuracy of even a few hundred meters is of little concern. However, for race cars traveling less than a meter apart, high accuracy is required.
- Speed changes are rather dramatic in our application. Most current research assumes fairly constant speed so the motion can be expressed as a linear equation [6]. Car races are characterised by continual speed changes. Formula One cars are capable of braking up to five G's and acceleration exceeding one G. They frequently slow for turns to about 50 kph and accelerate quickly to about 360 kph, so their speed changes very rapidly.
- It is difficult if not impossible to model a car's motion by an equation or set of equations. Many authors use a linear equation to define motion between observations [9,6,10]. For reasons mentioned previously, it is not possible to describe the actual path of a race car by a set of equations. Another application of our techniques is to track animals or hikers in a wilderness area. There are few if any constraints to their motion which makes mathematical description impossible.

Several data models have been proposed for representing moving objects in a database. The MOST data model, proposed in [9], incorporates dynamic attributes which are attributes whose values are a function of time. A dynamic attribute is represented by three sub-attributes, *A.value*, *A.updatetime*, and *A.function*. *A.function* is a function of time that has a value 0 at time = 0 and describes the manner in which the attribute value changes over time. The value of the attribute at *A.updatetime* is *A.value*. Thus at any future time, t > *A.updatetime*, the value of the attribute is *A.value* + *A.function(t)*.

Wolfson et al. use a data model which stores an object's start time, starting location, and a velocity vector [12]. Database updates are generated by the object when its location deviates more than a given threshold from the location that would be computed by the database.

In order to process queries in reasonable time, the data must be indexed. Some authors have discussed indexing present and future positions of moving objects [9,11,5,8,1]. Other authors discuss indexing the past positions of moving objects [7].

In [9], the authors propose indexing their dynamic attributes. Two alternate approaches are suggested in [11]. The first is the value-time representation space where an object is mapped to a trajectory that plots its location as a function of time. In the alternative intercept-slope representation space, the location is a function of time, $f(t) = a + vt$.

A dual transformation scheme is also used in [5] in which the trajectories of moving objects are transformed from the time-trajectory plane into a slope-intercept plane. They use an R*-tree and hB-tree to study the performance of the transform.

In [8], Saltenis et al. use a variant of the R*-tree called a TPR-tree (time parameterised tree) to index the current and future locations. While good for predicting locations in the near future, the minimum bounding boxes would grow to cover the entire track in our application.

An alternative indexing scheme for future locations is presented in [1], where constant speed motion in a straight line is assumed. Chon at al. present an index scheme for past, present, and future positions [2]. They use a space-time partitioning scheme where the data space is divided *a priori*. Their assumption is that moving objects have no more than hundreds of points. The grid is maintained in main memory.

In [7], the authors use variants of an R-tree, called STR-tree and TB-tree, to index past histories. These are variants in the sense that trajectories instead of locations are contained in the minimum bounding boxes. In our application, the trajectories are constantly changing which leads to a very large number of bounding boxes.

3 Data Storage and Indexing

Several authors have suggested building moving object databases on top of relational or object-relational databases [9,11,4,3,6,10]. However, our experiments show that relational DBMSs fall short in two ways.

First, a relational database returns a relation as the result of a query. In this paradigm, the database server usually creates a relation for the entire result and then delivers it to the requesting client. For some queries such as replaying an entire race, the result is far too large to deliver at once. Since the result cannot fit into main memory, it is temporarily written to disk, further adding to overhead. Instead we want to locate quickly the beginning of the data and then deliver it incrementally in a time frame that is no worse than actual race time. This allows for a reasonable visualisation of the data in a graphics display.

Secondly, we found that a sample of relational DBMSs simply cannot answer the queries we posed. These queries are given in Section 4. We tried our application on a popular commercial relational database, PostgreSQL and mySQL. The load times far exceeded the sample race time. In addition, some queries failed to complete in a reasonable time.

In our data model, data is stored as (t, x, y, l, s, h, Z) where t is the time of the sample; $(x\text{-}y)$ is the location at time t; l, s and h are the lap number, speed, and apparent heading at time t; and Z represents any other attributes that may be desired.

The data is stored on disk so that all data for each entrant is in time sequence. Thus once the start of the desired data is located, data may be read sequentially.

Considering the nature of the queries (described in Section 4), three indexes are constructed. The first index and the main contribution of this research is the spatiotemporal index. The approach we take is to partition the data space uniformly by the area covered. This is in contrast to the R-tree and its variants which use minimum bounding boxes to partition the data space. It is also in contrast to techniques such as a quadtree which recursively divides the area. Instead we divide the area into uniform subareas according to the expected data. This division is done before data is loaded although one could easily rebuild the index if another division were desired.

As an example, consider the case of an oval track. Figure 1 shows the track with a subdividing grid superimposed on it.

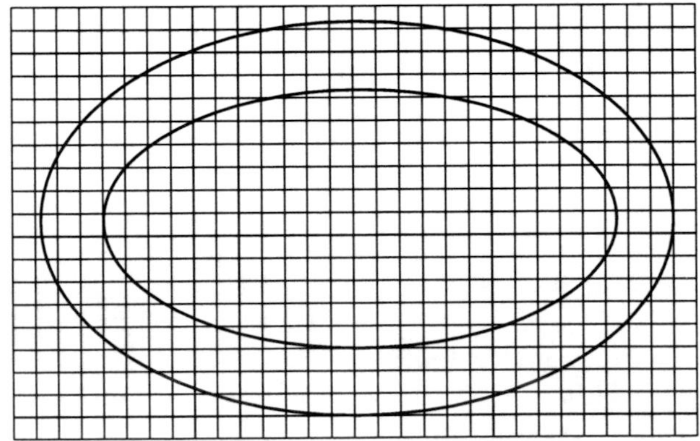

Fig. 1. An oval track with a grid superimposed

The spatiotemporal index employs two levels. At the first level is a logical X-Y matrix using sparse matrix techniques. That is, the only cells which are allocated memory or disk space are those that contain actual data (See Figure 2). We begin by allocating space for the entire distance expected to be covered in the X-axis. Cells are allocated for the Y-axis as needed. Thus the X-Y matrix only contains cells that cover area occupied at some point in time by the moving objects.

In Figure 2, the logical X-Y matrix is shown above the upper dashed line. The disk blocks containing the race data are shown below the lower dashed line. The internal part of the spatiotemporal index is shown between the dashed lines.

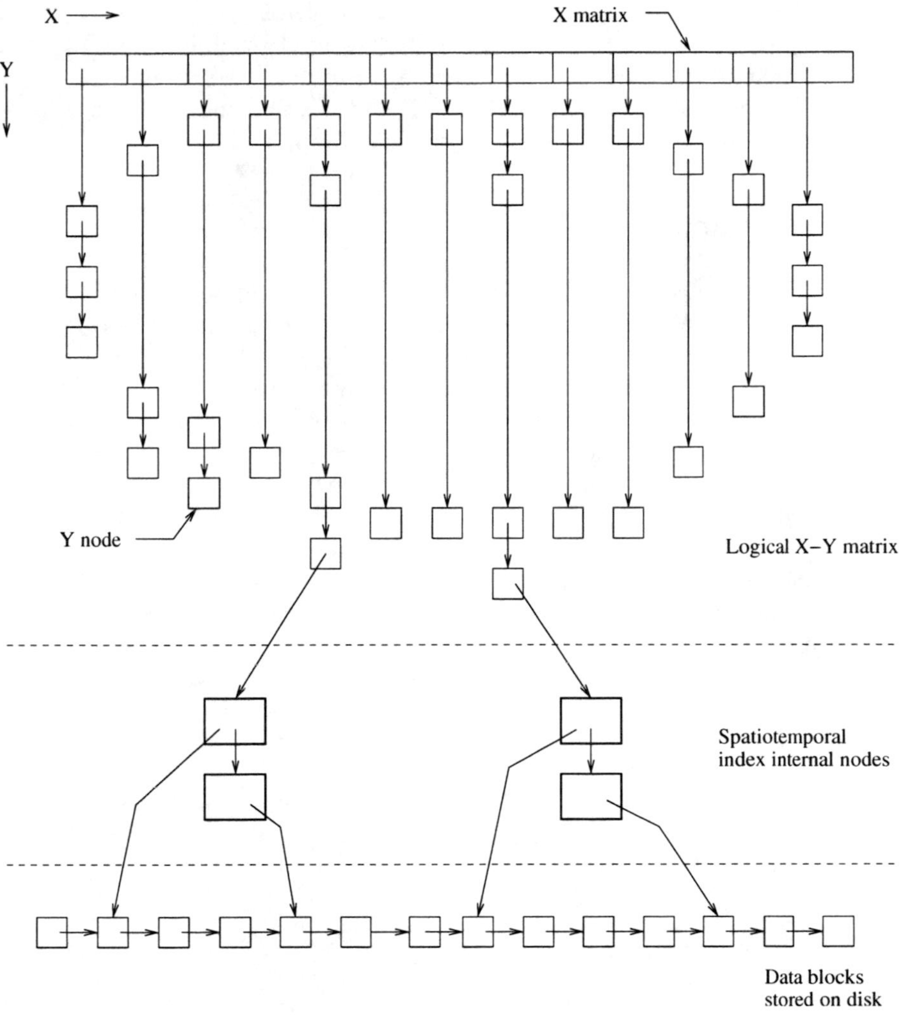

Fig. 2. Spatiotemporal index data structure

Each X-Y matrix cell is linked to one or more cells containing the internal spatiotemporal index entries. An index entry is of the form (t, l, d) where t is the time when the object entered that space, l is the lap number the object is on when it entered, and d is the data block on disk containing the actual data. The three entries, (t, l, d), are used to align query results properly (explained below).

The second index is a variation of a B^+-tree on time. This index is a variant in the sense that each node is full rather than one-half or two-thirds full since there is no need to leave room for future insertions. In addition there is only one entry for each data block. We call this a B^{++}-tree.

Splitting is done differently. When a node becomes full, a new node at the same level is created. Entries do not need to be moved between the original node and the new node. Instead the new entry is placed into the new node and pointer is sent up the tree where the process may be repeated. A node may be written to disk once it is full since it will not be subject to future splitting.

Finally, lap numbers are indexed by a B^{++}-tree. This index allows for very fast data location when playing back a particular lap.

4 Performance

We have implemented a database engine and the spatiotemporal indexing scheme in C++ on Linux. We call the implementation RSDB. The results described were obtained on a 500 Mhz Pentium III based PC with 128 MB of memory.

We use a data load and three queries to compare RSDB to relational databases. These queries represent the data required to replay certain parts of a race similar to the so-called ‘instant replays’ often seen on television broadcasts of such events. Comparisons are made against a commercial DBMS, PostgreSQL and MySQL. Our licensing agreement prevent us from publishing the results of the commercial DBMS. However it is fair to say that it also was lacking sufficient performance for this application.

To evaluate the performance of the indexing, a database was loaded with synthetic data which approximates a Formula One race. The files required to store the actual data use 330 MB of disk space per object. The time index uses 1 MB of disk space (0.3% of data space) and the spatiotemporal index uses 6.6 MB (2.0% of data space). Total disk space for the example race in our implementation was 7.6 GB.

For the relational DBMSs, each car has its own relation which makes it much more efficient when retrieving data for only a few cars. For RSDB, the data for each car is stored in a separate file.

4.1 Loading

A data generating program was developed for loading the test databases. This program generated data similar to the Formula One Grand Prix at Hockhenhiem, Germany. In 1999, the race lasted 4919 seconds (1 hour 22 minutes). The simulated race lasts 5064 seconds (1 hour 24.4 minutes). When the data generation program is not actually interfacing to a database, it takes 80 seconds to run. Thus the time to generate the data is small compared to the time of the simulated race.

The time to load the data and to build indexes is shown in Table 1.

Table 1. Time to load data and build indexes. Time in hrs:min:sec

System	Load data	Build indexes
PostgreSQL	59:01:05	5:55:40
MySQL	8:41:50	33:45:50
RSDB	1:00:56	0:16:35

Normal SQL commands were used to load the relational DBMSs. While there are more efficient means, none would have adequate performance given the time required to build the indexes. RSDB is able to load and rebuild the spatiotemporal index in 1:17:31 (less than simulated race time). For reasons of memory efficiency, RSDB writes its spatiotemporal index in a less than optimal manner during data load. It is then reorganized for more efficient retrieval after the load.

4.2 Playback Query

To provide a measure of performance, three queries were executed. The database client sends the data to /dev/null to alleviate any influence by the output device.

The first query retrieves all data for one car in time order. For the relational DBMSs, the following query was executed:

```
SELECT * FROM car1 ORDER BY racetime;
```

The actual race time is 5064 seconds. The results, given in Table 2, show that RSDB has more than adequate performance.

Table 2. Time to playback a race for one car. Time in seconds

System	Time
PostgreSQL	failed to complete
MySQL	gave error message
RSDB	406
RSDB (2 cars)	450
RSDB (3 cars)	528
RSDB (4 cars)	579
RSDB (5 cars)	612
RSDB (22 cars)	1451

4.3 Playback Lap Query

The second query retrieves data for a given lap for a car or a group of cars. For the relational DBMSs, a query of the following form was executed:

```
SELECT * FROM car1, car2, ...
   WHERE car1.lap=2 AND car2.lap=2 ...
      AND car1.racetime=car2.racetime ...
   ORDER BY car1.racetime;
```

The results are shown in Table 3. The actual race time for one lap is 113 seconds. PostgreSQL is marginal with 2 cars; MySQL can only handle up to 5 cars. RSDB can handle easily all 22 cars.

Table 3. Time to playback one lap. Time in seconds

System	Time
PostgreSQL	73
PostgreSQL (2 cars)	116
MySQL	12
MySQL (2 cars)	36
MySQL (3 cars)	58
MySQL (4 cars)	81
MySQL (5 cars)	105
MySQL (6 cars)	129
RSDB	9
RSDB (2 cars)	10
RSDB (3 cars)	12
RSDB (4 cars)	13
RSDB (5 cars)	13
RSDB (6 cars)	14
RSDB (22 cars)	34

4.4 Playback Lap and Section

This query further qualifies the playback to a given section of the track. While times are given for all the databases, it is difficult to compare the relational databases to RSDB. For the relational DBMSs, the track was arbitrarily divided into several sections and assigned a section number. Thus the section index in the relational case is simply an index on an integer. For RSDB, the spatiotemporal index described above is used.

For the relational databases, the SQL query was of the following form:

```
SELECT * FROM car1, car2, ...
   WHERE car1.section=1 AND car1.lap=2 ...
      AND car2.section=1 AND car2.lap=2 ...
      AND car1.racetime=car2.racetime
   ORDER BY car1.racetime;
```

Table 4. Time to playback a specified section. Time in seconds

System	Time
PostgreSQL	46
PostgreSQL (2 cars)	52
MySQL	2
MySQL (2 cars)	6
MySQL (4 cars)	11
MySQL (6 cars)	16
RSDB	2
RSDB (2 cars)	2
RSDB (6 cars)	3
RSDB (12 cars)	4
RSDB (22 cars)	see text (14)

The results are shown in Table 4. The actual race time for the selected section is 15 seconds.

For RSDB with 22 cars, it took 7 seconds to locate and coordinate the data. It then took 7 seconds to transmit the data to the client. The other RSDB results have a similar character, but the times are difficult to record because they are so short.

In our implementation, data is transmitted to the client in a buffer containing all data for a single time instance. The buffer contains logical slots for each entrant. If a given car is not in the section in a given time instance, its slot contains no data.

Due to the way the spatiotemporal index works and the way we want to display data, it is necessary to build internally portions of the index from disk and coordinate the times and locations. This time is the 7 seconds stated above. Once the data is ready, it can be sent in well under the time required in the actual race. The goal is to locate the data reasonably quickly which is shown to be possible and to transmit it in less than real time (which was done).

5 Conclusion

The storage and retrieval of high speed, repetitive, unpredictable moving objects is a new area of research with new challenges. We have described a method of storing the data and an index to answer expected queries quickly. These queries are significantly different from the queries normally presented in moving object research.

The use of Formula One races in the performance study presents a difficult challenge due to the large amount of data and demands for rapid retrieval. Our implementation was able to meet the goals, whereas implementations using relational databases were not able to meet the goals.

The research suggests several areas for future study. It may be possible to link the internal nodes of the spatiotemporal index according to the object's motion. This would allow a quick look (at a coarse level) at the path taken without retrieving actual data. It may be possible to use the internal linkage to retrieve more quickly the desired nodes instead of going through the upper level X-Y matrix.

References

1. Agarwal, P., Arge, L., Erickson, J.: Indexing moving points. In *Proceedings of the Nineteenth ACM SIGMOD-SIGACT-SIGART Symposium on Principles of Database Systems (PODS 2000)*, Dallas, Texas, USA (2000) 175-186
2. Chon, H., Agrawal, D., Abbadi, A.: Using space-time grid for efficient management of moving objects. In *Proceedings of the Second International Workshop on Data Engineering for Wireless and Mobile Access (MobiDE 2001)*, Santa Barbara, California, USA (2001) 59-65
3. Forlizzi, L., Güting, R., Nardelli, E., Schneider, M.: A data model and data structures for moving objects databases. In *Proceedings of the ACM SIGMOD 2000 International Conference on Management of Data*, Dallas, Texas, USA (2000) 319-330
4. Güting, R., Böhlen, M., Erwig, M., Jensen, C., Lorentzos, N., Schneider, M., Vazirgiannis, M.: A foundation for representing and querying moving objects. *ACM Transactions on Database Systems* **25** (2000) 1-42
5. Kollios, G., Gunopulos, D., Tsotras, V.: On indexing mobile objects. In *Proceedings of the Eighteenth ACM SIGMOD-SIGACT-SIGART Symposium on Principles of Database Systems (PODS 1999)*, Philadelphia, Pennsylvania, USA (1999) 261-272
6. Moreira, J., Riberiro, C., Saglio, J.-M.: Representation and manipulation of moving points: an extended data model for location estimation. *Cartography and Geographic Information Science* **26** (1999) 109-123
7. Pfoser, D., Jensen, C., Theodoridis, Y.: Novel approaches in query processing for moving object trajectories. In *Proceedings of the 26th International Conference on Very Large Databases*, Cairo, Egypt (2000) 395-406
8. Šaltenis, S., Jensen, C., Leutenegger, S., Lopez, M.: Indexing the positions of continuously moving objects. In *Proceedings of the ACM SIGMOD 2000 International Conference on Management of Data*, Dallas, Texas, USA (2000) 331-342
9. Sistla, A., Wolfson, O., Chamberlain, S., Dao, S.: Modeling and querying moving objects. In *Proceedings of the Thirteenth International Conference on Data Engineering*, Birmingham, UK (1997) 422-432
10. Vazirgiannis, M., Wolfson, O.: A spatiotemporal model and language for moving objects on road networks. In Jensen, C., Schneider, M., Seeger, B., Tsotras, V. (eds.): *Advances in Spatial and Temporal Databases, 7th International Symposium, SSTD 2001. Lecture Notes in Computer Science.* Vol. 2121. Springer-Verlag, Berlin (2001) 20-35
11. Wolfson, O. Xu, B., Chamberlain, S., Jiang, L.: Moving objects databases: issues and solutions. In *Proceedings of the 10th International Conference on Scientific and Statistical Database Management (SSDBM)*, Capri, Italy (1998) 111-122
12. Wolfson, O., Sistla, A., Chamberlain, S., Yesha, Y.: Updating and querying databases that track mobile units. *Distributed and Parallel Databases* (1999) **7** 257-287

Hierarchical Storage Support and Management for Large-Scale Multidimensional Array Database Management Systems[1]

Bernd Reiner[1], Karl Hahn[1], Gabriele Höfling[1], and Peter Baumann[2]

[1] FORWISS (Bavarian Research Center for Knowledge Based Systems)
Orleansstr. 34, 81667 Munich, Germany
{reiner, hahnk, hoefling}@forwiss.tu-muenchen.de
http://www.wibas.forwiss.tu-muenchen.de

[2] Active Knowledge GmbH, Kirchenstrasse 88,
81675 Munich, Germany
baumann@active-knowledge.com
http://www.active-knowledge.de

Abstract. Large-scale scientific experiments or simulation programs often generate large amounts of multidimensional data. Data volume may reach hundreds of terabytes (up to petabytes). In the present and the near future, the only practicable way for storing such large volumes of multidimensional data are tertiary storage systems. But commercial (multidimensional) database systems are optimized for performance with primary and secondary memory access. So tertiary storage memory is only in an insufficient way supported for storing or retrieval of multidimensional array data. To combine the advantages of both techniques, storing large amounts of data on tertiary storage media and optimizing data access for retrieval with multidimensional database management systems is the intention of this paper. We introduce concepts for efficient hierarchical storage support and management for large-scale multidimensional array database management systems and their integration into the commercial array database management system RasDaMan.

1 Introduction

In many large-scale scientific domains, experimental and scanning devices or simulation programs generate large volumes of data. Examples are atmospheric data transmitted by satellites, climate-modeling simulations, flow modelling of chemical reactors, computational fluid dynamics and simulation of the dynamics of gene expressions. In principle, many natural phenomena can be modeled as spatio-temporal array data of some specific dimensionality. Their common characteristic is that a huge

[1] This work was supported by the ESTEDI project (http://www.estedi.org). ESTEDI (European Spatio-Temporal Data Infrastructure for High-Performance Computing) is funded by the European Commission under FP5 grant no. IST-1999-11009.

R. Cicchetti et al. (Eds.): DEXA 2002, LNCS 2453, pp. 689–700, 2002.

amount (hundreds of terabytes) of multidimensional discrete data (MDD) has to be stored. Actually the common state of the art of storing such large volumes of data is tertiary storage systems (mass storage systems), where data are stored as file. Typically, such tertiary storage systems have robot controlled tape libraries or jukeboxes. They provide automated access to hundreds or thousands of media (e.g. magnetic tapes, magneto optical tapes, CD-ROMs, DVDs, etc.). Concerning data access the main disadvantages are high access latency compared to hard disk devices and to have no direct access to specific subsets of data.

If only a subset of such a large data set is required, the whole file must be transferred from tertiary storage media. Taking into account the time required to load, search, read, rewind and unload several cartridges, it can take many hours to retrieve a subset of interest from a large data set. Entire files (data sets) must be loaded manually from the magnetic tape, even if only a subset of the file is needed for a further processing.

On the other hand, multidimensional database management systems (DBMS) offer efficient retrieval or manipulation of MDDs. They have extended query languages with special multidimensional operations like geometric, induced and aggregation operations [1, 2]. Concerning data storage the possibility of tertiary storage access is lacking, so mass data can't be managed directly by multidimensional array DBMS. As a consequence, in high performance computing applications DMBS are typically used for meta-data management only, where meta-data contains the information about the location of the data sets (on which medium).

The ESTEDI[1] project addresses the delivery bottleneck of large high-performance computing (HPC) results to the users with a flexible data management for spatio-temporal data. ESTEDI, an initiative of European database developers, software vendors and supercomputing centers, will establish an European standard for the storage and retrieval of multidimensional HPC array data. To this end, the multidimensional array DBMS RasDaMan will be enhanced with intelligent mass storage handling and optimized towards HPC [3].

The intention of this paper is a concept of hierarchical storage support, by combining the advantages of both techniques, storing big amounts of data and realizing efficient data access for retrieval with the multidimensional array DBMS RasDaMan. Thus overcoming their shortcomings particularly for scientific applications. This paper is organized as follows: Section 0 gives an overview about the system architecture and describes the new-implemented tertiary storage support functionality. In section 0 we present a concept for efficient storage of multidimensional data. Section 0 will have a focus on the tertiary storage management and support for large MDDs. Performance aspects can be found in section 0. Section 0 summarizes the achievements and gives an outlook on future work.

---

[1] ESTEDI (European Spatio-Temporal Data Infrastructure for High-Performance Computing) project (http://www.estedi.org) is funded by the European Commission under FP5 grant no. IST-1999-11009. Project Partner are FORWISS (DE), Active Knowledge (DE), DLR (DE), MPIM (DE), University of Surrey (GB), CCLRC (GB), Numeca (BE), Cineca (IT), CSCS (CH) and IHPC&DB (RU).

2 System Architecture

We have implemented the hierarchical storage management concept and integrated it into the first commercial multidimensional array DBMS RasDaMan. RasDaMan is distributed by Active Knowledge GmbH (http://www.active-knowledge.com). The DBMS RasDaMan (Raster Data Management) is designed for multidimensional array data and provides an extended multidimensional query language RasQL [1, 2]. The original version of RasDaMan didn't have a connection to tertiary storage systems apart from conventional backup. Within the ESTEDI project we have extended the RasDaMan kernel with easy to use functionality to automatically store and retrieve data to/from tertiary storage systems. In Fig. 1 the architecture of the extended RasDaMan system can be seen.

The left side of the figure depicts the original RasDaMan architecture with the RasDaMan client, RasDaMan server and conventional DBMS (e.g. Oracle, which is used by RasDaMan as storage and transaction manager). The additional components for the tertiary storage interface are the Tertiary Storage Manager (TS-Manager), File Storage Manager and Hierarchical Storage Management System (HSM-System). The TS-Manager and File Storage Manager are included in the RasDaMan server. The HSM-System is a conventional product like SAM (Storage Archiving System) from LSC Incorporation or UniTree. Such an HSM-System (to the bottom right in Fig. 1) can be seen as a normal file system with unlimited storage capacity. In reality, the virtual file system of HSM-Systems is separated into a limited cache on which the user works (load or store his data) and a tertiary storage system with robot controlled tape libraries. The HSM-System automatically migrates or stages the data to or from the tertiary storage media, if necessary.

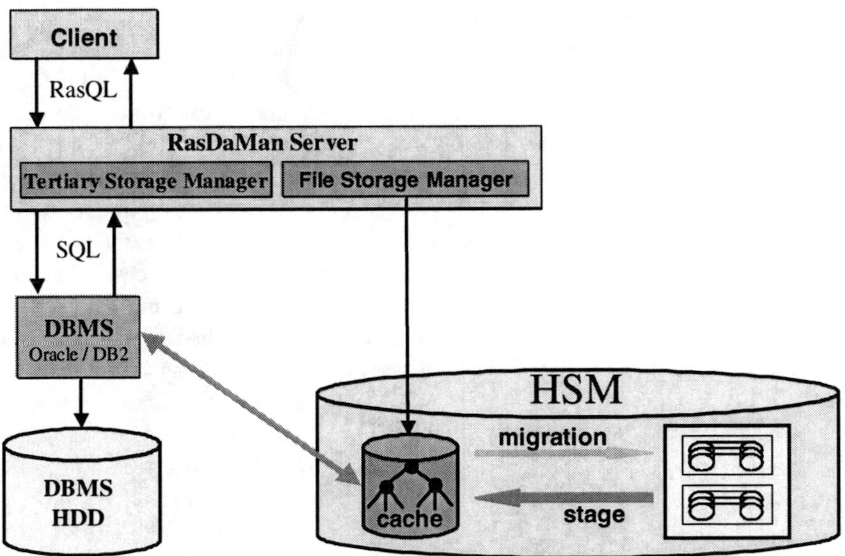

Fig. 1. Extended RasDaMan architecture with tertiary storage interface

All in all two possibilities are available for connecting tertiary storage systems to the database system RasDaMan. First, an existing system like an HSM-System can be used. The other possibility is to develop a proprietary and new connection to a tertiary storage system. We decided to use conventional HSM-Systems for the connection of tertiary storage devices to RasDaMan. Such HSM-Systems have been developed to manage tertiary storage archive systems and to handle thousands of tertiary storage media (e.g. magnetic tape). Leading HSM-Systems are sophisticated and support robotic libraries of many manufactures. Another important reason for this decision was that such HSM-Systems with big robotic libraries (more than 100 TByte storage capacity) are already in use by the ESTEDI partners, which are also using RasDaMan.

The new RasDaMan tertiary storage functionality is based on the TS-Manager module (shown in Fig. 1). This TS-Manager is implemented and integrated into the RasDaMan kernel. If a query (RasQL) is executed, the TS-Manager knows whether the needed data sets are stored on hard disk or on a tertiary storage media. This meta-data used by the TS-Manger are stored in RasDaMan respectively the underlying DBMS (e.g. Oracle). The performance is much higher if the meta-data are stored permanently in the DBMS and not exported to tertiary storage media. If the data sets are on hard disk (in the DBMS), the query will be processed without specific tertiary storage management. This is the normal procedure of the RasDaMan system without tertiary storage connection. If the data sets are stored on one or more tertiary storage media, the data sets must be imported into the database system (cache area for tertiary storage data sets) first. The import of data sets stored on tertiary storage media is done by the TS-Manager automatically whenever a query is executed and those data sets are requested. After the import process of the data sets is done, RasDaMan can handle the data sets (cached in the DBMS) in the normal way. The TS-Manager of RasDaMan has information and meta-data about all data sets, for example where the data sets are stored, how the data sets are organized on media, etc.

After an insert of new data sets they will not be exported to tertiary storage media automatically. Sometimes it is necessary to store the data sets only in the DBMS if the data access time is critical, e.g. some users have frequent access to the data sets. The user can decide, whether the data sets are to be stored on hard disk (which is already done by the insert tool) or whether the data sets should be exported on tertiary storage media. These two possibilities are flexible in several cases. For example, data sets are very often requested by users at the beginning (insert time of data sets) and after several months the data sets are less important for these users. In this case, the data sets first inserted into the DBMS can be exported to tertiary storage media after several months. If the data sets should only be stored in the DBMS, the user does not need to do anything else. When the data sets should be exported to tertiary storage media, one has to issue an export command. For exporting data sets a new statement was integrated into the RasDaMan query language (EXPORT FROM <data-set> WHERE <condition>). We can export complete data sets or only specific parts to the HSM-System (i.e. to tertiary storage media). Before we will describe details about tertiary storage support for multidimensional DBMS (section 0) we have to discuss basics about efficient storage of large multidimensional data in the following section.

3 Efficient Storage of Large Multidimensional Data

In this section we want introduce techniques of storing large multidimensional data efficiently. Later on this techniques will be extended for tertiary storage access. MDD, resulting from sampling and quantizing of phenomena like temperature or velocity in multidimensional space or represented statistical data, is a commonly used data type, in particular the 2D special case of raster images. A MDD object consists of an array of cells of some base type (e.g. integer, float or arbitrary complex types), which are located on a regular multidimensional grid. For example an MDD can be a 4 dimensional spatio-temporal object, resulting from scientific experiments or simulations and can become very large. Since linear storage of those MDDs as binary large objects (BLOB) makes it impossible to access only specific areas of interest from one MDD. Special multidimensional array DBMS (e.g. RasDaMan) are required for efficient MDD support.

The insufficient support for multidimensional arrays in commercial DBMS has inspired research on providing DBMS services (query language, transactions) for MDD, aiming at application areas different from traditional DBMS, for instance, scientific data management, geographic information systems, environmental data management, storage structures techniques. An often discussed approach is chunking or tiling of large data sets and is commonly used for multidimensional arrays in different application areas [5, 7, 13]. Chunking means subdividing of multidimensional arrays into disjoint sub-arrays with the same dimensionality as the original array. All chunks have the same shape and size and are therefore aligned. Tiling is more general than chunking, because sub-arrays don't have to be aligned or have the same size. MDDs can be subdivided in regular or arbitrary tiles. Regular or aligned tiling is identical with chunking and is the most common tiling concept in array systems. Further information about tiling strategies can be found in [8]. Fig. 2 depicts examples of arbitrary and regular tiling.

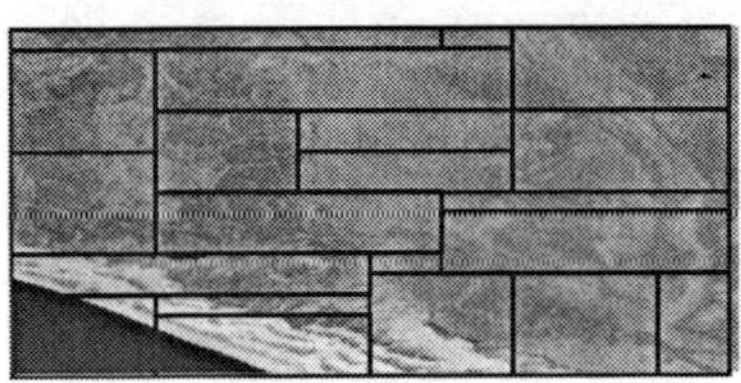

Arbitrary Tiling (2D)

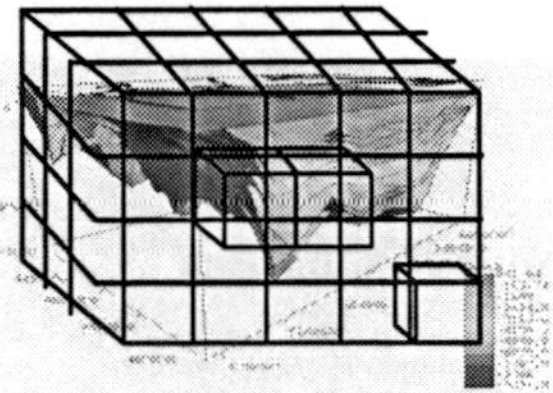

Regular Tiling (3D)

Fig. 2. Arbitrary and regular tiling strategy

If tiling is supported by DBMS (e.g. RasDaMan), it is possible to transfer only a subset of large MDDs from the database (or tertiary storage media) to client applications, because every tile is stored as one single BLOB in the relational database system. This will mainly reduce access time and network traffic. The query response time scales with size of query box, not with size of MDD. Now we can handle large data sets efficiently.

In the commercial DBMS RasDaMan, BLOBs (tiles) are the smallest units of data access. In order to manage these units in main memory, a limit on tile size is usually imposed. This limit should be set to multiples of one database page. Typical sizes of tiles stored in RasDaMan range from 32 KByte to 640 KByte and are optimized for hard disk access [8]. As we will see those tile sizes are much to small for data sets held on tertiary storage media. It is necessary to choose different granularities for hard disk and tape access, because they differ significantly in their access characteristics. Hard disks have fast random access, whereas tape systems have sequential access with much higher access latency. More details about performance of tertiary storage devices can be found in [10]. It is important to use data management techniques for efficiently retrieving arbitrary areas of interest from large data sets stored on tertiary storage devices. We have to find some partitioning techniques that partition data sets into clusters based on optimized data access patterns and storage device characteristics.

4 Tertiary Storage Support for Multidimensional DBMS

The average access time (e.g. load, switch, positioning time) for tape systems (20 – 180s) is by order of magnitude slower than for hard disk drives (5 - 12ms), whereas the difference between transfer rate of hard disk and tertiary storage systems isn't so important (factor 2 or 3). The main goal is to minimize the number of media load and search operations and to reduce the access time of clusters read from tertiary storage system when subsets are needed [6]. Generally there are several possibilities for optimization of the access costs. An important point is the granularity of the data stored on media and read from media. Particularly the size of the data blocks, which are moved from tape to the hard disk cache, is critical. On the one hand, preferably small data blocks should be transferred over the network to minimize the network traffic. On the other hand, the transfer rate of tertiary storage systems is not bad and the quantity of tape access should be minimized. On this reason the size of data blocks stored on tertiary storage media should be more than 100 MByte. It is unreasonable to increase the RasDaMan MDD tile size (32 – 640 KByte), because then we would loose the advantage of transferring only small subsets of the MDDs to the client application. A promising idea is to introduce an additional data granularity as provided by the so-called Super-Tile concept. In the following section we will present the newly developed Super-Tile concept.

4.1 The Super-tile Concept

The main goal of the new Super-Tile concept is a smart combination of several small MDD tiles to one Super-Tile for minimizing tertiary storage access costs. Smart means to exploit the good transfer rate of tertiary storage devices and to take advantage of other concepts like clustering of data. In ESTEDI, where RasDaMan is used as multidimensional DBMS the multidimensional index R+ tree for realizing fast random access of arbitrary tiles stored on disk is used [9, 12]. The conventional R+ tree index structure of the multidimensional DBMS was extended to handle such Super-Tiles stored on tertiary storage media. This means that information regarding which tiles are stored on hard disk and which are stored on tertiary storage media must be integrated into the index. Tiles of the same subindex of the R+ tree are combined into a Super-Tile and stored on tertiary storage medium. The specific tertiary storage manager knows on the basis of the structure of the multidimensional R+ tree that all tiles below this subindex (subtree of a R+ tree node) are combined to a Super-Tile and stored on the same tertiary storage media. A node of such a subindex is called a Super-Tile node.

Fig. 3 depicts an example of the R+ tree index of one MDD with the corresponding Super-Tile nodes. Only complete nodes of the R+ tree can become Super-Tile nodes (e.g. the ST1 node in Fig. 3). This means that all tiles of the included leaf nodes (in an R+ tree, data is only stored in leaf nodes) of one Super-Tile node are combined to one Super-Tile (light gray circle/oval). As a consequence, Super-Tiles can only be multiples of tiles.

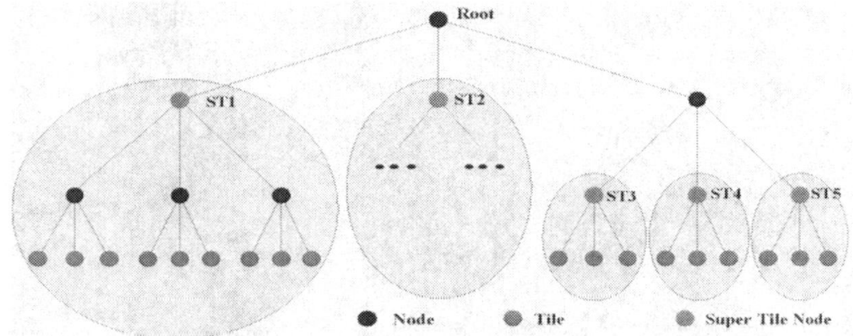

Fig. 3. Example R+ tree index of one MDD with Super-Tile nodes

Super-Tile nodes can be on arbitrary levels of the R+ tree. In the example of Fig. 3 we have 5 Super-Tile nodes (ST1 - ST5). The Super-Tile nodes ST1 and ST2 are on the second level of the tree and the corresponding Super-Tiles include 9 Tiles. The Super-Tile nodes ST3, ST4 and ST5 are on the third level of the tree and the corresponding Super-Tiles include only 3 Tiles.

We developed an algorithm for computing Super-Tile nodes inside the R+ tree. A general restriction of the Super-Tile algorithm is that only one Super-Tile node is contained in one path (from node to root) of the R+ tree. The algorithm traverse the R+ tree bottom-up and compute the size of the data (tiles), which is referenced in the subtree. For the detection of Super-Tile nodes the predefined size of the Super-Tiles is used. If the summarized size of the subtree of an index node is greater than the predefined Super-Tile size all child nodes get Super-Tile nodes. If the summarized size of tiles contained in the subtree of a node is smaller than the predefined Super-Tile size this node remains a candidate. The user can define suitable Super-Tile sizes, optimized for the data and tertiary storage access characteristics. If the user defines no Super-Tile size, a default maximum size of 200 MByte will be used. Extensive tests have shown that this Super-Tile size shows good performance characteristics in most cases and the Super-Tile algorithm produces Super-Tiles, which have about 60% to 80% of the size of the predefined Super-Tile size. More details about determining optimal file sizes on tertiary storage media can be found in [4].

Super-Tiles are the access (import/export) granularity of MDD on tertiary storage media. The retrieval of data stored on hard disk or on tertiary storage media is transparent for the user. Only the access time is higher if data stored on tertiary storage media. In order to improve performance, the whole index of all data (held on hard disk and tertiary storage media) is stored on hard disk. We will now discuss two further strategies for reducing tertiary storage access time, clustering and caching [11].

4.2 Strategies for Reducing Tertiary Storage Access Time

Clustering

Clustering is particularly important for tertiary storage systems where positioning time of the device is very high. The clustering of data sets reduces the positioning and exchange time of tertiary storage media. Clustering uses the spatial neighborhood of tiles within the data sets. Clustering of tiles according to spatial neighborhood on one disk or tertiary storage system proceed one step further in the preservation of spatial proximity, which is important for the typical access patterns of array data, because users often request data using range queries, which implies spatial neighbourhood. The used R+ tree index to address MDD's tiles already defines the clustering of the stored MDDs. With the developed Super-Tile concept we can distinguish intra Super-Tile clustering and inter Super-Tile clustering.

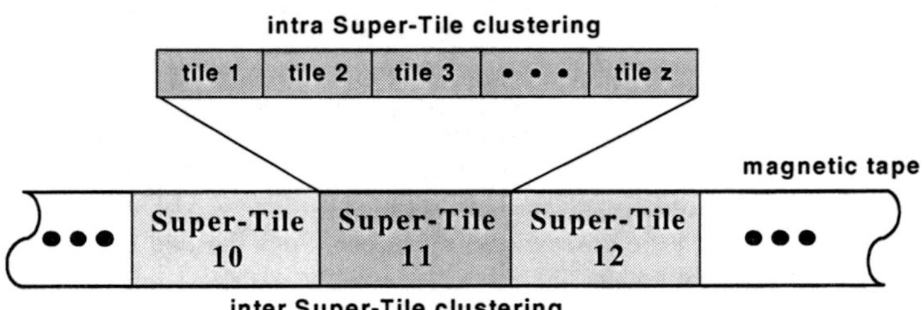

Fig. 4. Inter and intra Super-Tile clustering of tiles stored on magnetic tape

The implemented algorithm for computing the Super-Tiles (see chapter 0) maintains the predefined clustering of subtrees (of Super-Tile nodes) of the R+ tree index and realizes intra Super-Tile clustering. Inside one Super-Tile we have clustering, i.e. neighborhood of the spatial location of the included tiles. The export algorithm (export of Super-Tiles to tertiary storage) realizes the inter Super-Tile clustering within one MDD. The various Super-Tiles of one MDD are written to tertiary storage media in the clustered order (predefined R+ tree clustering). Inter and intra Super-Tile clustering of tiles stored on magnetic tape is shown in Fig. 4.

Caching

In order to reduce expensive tertiary storage media access the underlying DBMS of RasDaMan can be used as hard disk cache for data sets held on tertiary storage media. The general goal of caching tertiary storage data (Super-Tile granularity) is to minimize expensive loading, rewinding and reading operations from slower storage levels (e.g. magnetic tape). In the tertiary storage version, requested data sets held on tertiary storage media are migrated to the underlying DBMS of RasDaMan (see Fig. 1). The migrated Super-Tiles are now cached in the DBMS. After the migration the RasDaMan server transfers the requested tiles from the DBMS to the client application. For a better differentiation of data stored persistent in the DBMS (i.e. how data sets were held in the original version of the multidimensional DBMS) and data, which are only be, cached in the DBMS we call the storage location of the cached objects DBMS cache area.

The advantage of caching is that the data held on tertiary storage media doesn't have to be imported to the DBMS cache area for every request. The import of the requested data from the tertiary storage media is extremely expensive because the transfer from tertiary storage system to hard disk is slow (media loading time, media exchange time, media rewind time, seek time, read time, transfer rate, etc.). The second request to this data is very fast because the data is already held in the DBMS cache area. The tertiary storage Cache-Manager only evicts data (Super-Tiles granularity) from the DBMS cache area if necessary (the upper limit of the cache size is reached). At the moment the LRU (Least Recently Used) replacement strategy is supported and shows good performance. Other replacement strategies will be tested with tertiary storage devices. The general goal of these policies is to substitute only the data (Super-Tiles) that is least likely to be reused. In this research area, optimization algorithms especially for tertiary storage systems must be found.

5 Performance Aspects

First we show the main advantage of the developed hierarchical storage support for large-scale DBMS. The ESTEDI partners typically have to load whole MDDs (stored as single files) from tertiary storage devices, even if only a subset is required for further analysis. This means that the request response time scales with the size of the stored MDD. Using RasDaMan and the integrated tertiary storage access subsets of MDDs can be loaded and for this reason the query response time scales with the size of the query box and not with the size of the MDD (see Fig. 5).

In this example we assume a Super-Tile size of 200 MByte. On the left side of Fig. 5 we have a fixed query box size of 400 MByte and the MDD size is increasing, which means two Super-Tiles must be loaded at least and the access costs are stagnating. In the traditional case the access costs are scaling with the MDD size. If the MDD size is smaller than the predefined Super-Tile size the complete MDD has to be loaded and therefore the same access time is expected. Typically such small MDDs are not stored on tertiary storage medium. On the right side of Fig. 5 the MDD size is fixed (3 GByte) and the query box is increasing. If we have access with Super-Tile granularity the access costs are increasing step by step. Otherwise with traditional access we have constant access costs, as the complete MDD must be loaded.

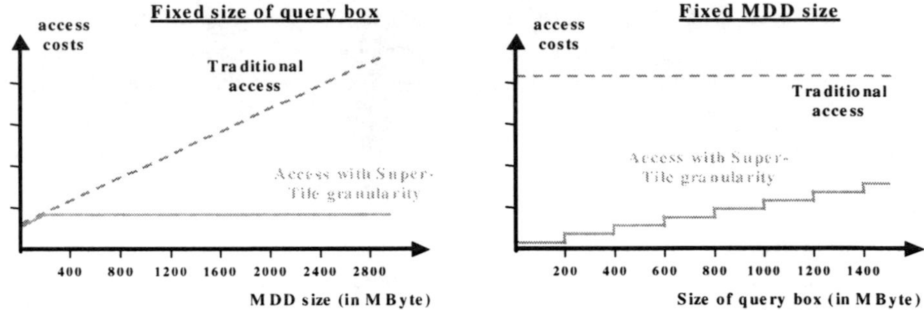

Fig. 5. Access comparison with fixed query box size and with fixed MDD size

Now we briefly discuss the performance of the export and retrieval functionality of the new tertiary storage version of RasDaMan. The export of data sets to tertiary storage media is very fast because the data sets just have to be written to the virtual file system of the HSM-System. This means storing data sets on the hard disk cache of the HSM-System. The migration of the data sets from the HSM cache to the tertiary storage media does not concern the RasDaMan system. For the retrieval functionality three cases must be distinguished. In the first case we assume that the data sets needed are already held in the DMBS cache area of RasDaMan. This request operation is very fast, because no import of data from the HSM-System has to be done. In the second case the data sets required are held in the hard disk cache of the HSM-System. This is quite likely because the size of the HSM cache is normally hundreds of GByte. In this case the import of the data sets is as fast as the export of the data sets because the data sets don't have to be staged from the tertiary storage media. This access is about factor 1.8 to 3 slower compared to normal DMBS access (dependent on network traffic, transfer rate, etc.). We assume for the third case that the data sets requested are not held in the HSM cache. This means the HSM-System must first stage the data sets needed from the tertiary storage media to the HSM cache and then the data sets are transferred to the RasDaMan system. Compared with DBMS access we measured a slowdown of factor 3 to 10 (dependent on tertiary storage device, transfer rate, etc.).

6 Conclusion and Future Work

The initial point of our development was that members of the ESTEDI project have large volumes of multidimensional array data, generated by scientific simulations, which are stored as files on tertiary storage media.

The main goal of our development was to realize a fast and efficient access to tertiary storage media and provide access functionality like retrieval of subsets as common for DBMS since a long time. This means the request response time scale now with the size of the query box, not with the size of MDD like the traditional case of the ESTEDI partner. In our approach we use a multidimensional array DBMS for optimal storage, retrieval and manipulation of large MDD. A major bottleneck of the commercial multidimensional array DBMS RasDaMan is that it was originally not designed to use tertiary storage media for storing hundreds of terabytes (up to petabytes). To handle the data amounts stored on tertiary storage an interface was presented to connect tertiary storage systems to the multidimensional array DBMS RasDaMan. Consequently, we created a hierarchical storage support and management system for large-scale multidimensional array DBMS, which is specifically designed and optimized (using clustering and caching of Super-Tiles) for storing multidimensional array data on tertiary storage media.

Future work will be the development of scheduling techniques for multidimensional array data streamlined for Super-Tiles. Scheduling for tertiary storage media means the optimization of the media read order. This optimization reduces expensive media seek and exchange operations. The focus is on scheduling policies that process all requests on a loaded medium before exchanging it in the loading station of the robotic library. We can differ intra and inter query scheduling. Intra query scheduling will optimize the request order within one query. Inter query scheduling can be done in RasDaMan by examining the query queue. If the actual query needs Super-Tiles from one MDD and a further query of the query queue also needs several Super-Tiles from the same MDD, all needed Super-Tiles will be imported at the same time into the RasDaMan cache area.

References

1. Active Knowledge GmbH: RasDaMan Query Language Guide version 5.0, Active Knowledge GmbH, Munich 2001
2. Baumann P.: A Database Array Algebra for Spatio-Temporal Data and Beyond, Proc. of the 4th Int. Workshop on Next Generation Information Technologies and Systems (NGITS), p. 76-93, 1999
3. Baumann P.: Array Databases Meet Supercomputing Data – the ESTEDI Project, Internal ESTEDI Report, 2000
4. Bernardo L. M., Nordberg H., Rotem D., Shoshani A.: Determining the Optimal File Size on Tertiary Storage Systems Based on the Distribution of Query Sizes, Proc. of the 10th Int. Conf. on Scientific and Statistical Database Management, p. 22-31, 1998
5. Chen L. T., Drach R., Keating M., Louis S., Rotem D., Shoshani A.: Efficient organization and access of multi-dimensional datasets on tertiary storage, Information Systems, vol. 20, no. 2, p. 155-183, 1995
6. Chen L. T., Rotem D., Shoshani A., Drach R.: Optimizing Tertiary Storage Organization and Access for Spatio-Temporal Datasets, NASA Goddard Conf. on Mass Storage Systems, 1995
7. Furtado P. A., Baumann P.: Storage of Multidimensional Arrays Based on Arbitrary Tiling, Proc. Of the ICDE'99, p. 480-489, 1999
8. Furtado P. A.: Storage Management of Multidimensional Arrays in Database Management Systems, PhD Thesis of Technical University Munich, 1999

9. Gaede V., Günther O.: Multidimensional Access Methods, ACM Computing Surveys, vol. 30, no. 2, 1998
10. Johnson T., Miller E. L.: Performance Measurements of Tertiary Storage Devices, Proc. of the 24th VLDB Conf., New York, USA, 1998
11. Reiner B.: Tertiary Storage Support for Multidimensional Data, VLDB Supercomputing Databases Workshop, Rome, September 2001
12. Rigaux P., Scholl M., Voisard A.: Spatial Databases – with application to GIS, Academic Press, 2002
13. Sarawagi S., Stonebraker M.: Efficient Organization of Large Multidimensional Arrays, Proc. of Int. Conf. On Data Engineering, volume 10, p. 328-336, 1994

Multiple Visual Representation of Temporal Data

Chaouki Daassi[1,2], Marie-Christine Fauvet[2,3], and Laurence Nigay[1]

[1] Laboratoire CLIPS-IMAG BP 53-38041, Grenoble cedex 9, France
[2] Laboratoire LSR-IMAG BP 53-38041, Grenoble cedex 9, Grenoble, France
[3] The University of New South Wales, Sydney NSW 2052, Australia
[Chaouki.Daassi, Marie-Christine.Fauvet, Laurence.Nigay]@imag.fr

Abstract. Temporal data are abundantly present in many applications such as banking, financial, clinical, geographical applications and so on. For a long time, tools for data analysis have been only based on statistics. A more recent and complementary research avenue involves visual data analysis, which is dedicated to the extraction of valuable knowledge by exploiting human visual perception capabilities. Examples of visual data analysis tasks, while manipulating temporal data, include correlating data evolution and identifying patterns. In this paper we present an interactive visualisation tool named INVEST, dedicated to visual analysis of temporal data. INVEST includes different visualisation techniques in order to address the variety of users' tasks.

Keywords: Visualisation Techniques, Temporal Data, Data Analysis.

1 Introduction

Data can be analyzed using statistical tools: many algorithms are developed to automatically extract valuable information from a set of data. A promising and complementary research avenue involves visual data analysis, which relies on interactive visualisation techniques. Adopting this approach, many studies focus on the design of visualisation techniques for data analysis [5, 15], but few of them are dedicated to temporal data [20, 8]. Our work focuses on visualisation techniques for temporal data analysis.

A temporal data denotes the evolution of an object characteristic over a period of time. The value of a temporal data is called a history. For the sake of simplicity, we define a history as a collection of instant time-stamped or interval time-stamped data items, although there are many other ways of representing a history [11, 9]. Fig. 1, shows a history of numeric values, where each time-stamp denotes a month. The set of timestamps is the temporal domain of the observed data.

In this paper we present the framework called INVEST (INteractive Visualisation and Explorative System of Temporal data) that several complementary visualisation techniques that have been designed with regard to user's tasks while manipulating temporal data. The paper is organized as follows: in section 2, we present two novel visualisation techniques among five available in the INVEST. Section 3 presents the

R. Cicchetti et al. (Eds.): DEXA 2002, LNCS 2453, pp. 701–709, 2002.

results of an experimental evaluation of the INVEST that confirm the offered. Finally, section 4 describes the INVEST architecture and implementation while section 5 concludes..

2 Visualisation Techniques

Visualisation techniques could be classified into two categories depending on whether they rely on item-based techniques or pixel-based ones. Within the first category (item-based technique), data values are mapped onto graphical objects such as polygons, circles, etc., drawn in 2D [12, 14] or 3D data spaces [1, 5]. Data values are easily distinguishable from each other, so that the users can easily compare two elements. However, this representation mode reaches its limits when displaying a huge amount of data. Consequently, these techniques must either be augmented with sliders, or the data space must be deformed [16, 18]. The second category is made up of the pixel-oriented techniques [14], in which each data value is mapped to a pixel colored with some intensity: a huge amount of data can therefore be represented in a limited screen area. The disadvantage of such techniques is that the users cannot compare two elements, but rather have a global representation of the data space.

Our research focuses on the design of item-based and pixel-based visualisation techniques in a 2D space. In the following two paragraphs, we present two INVEST visualisation techniques, namely the concentric circles and the superposed histograms.

On the other hand, we have considered the design of visualisation techniques with regard to users' tasks. As pointed out by [3, 19, 7], the utility of any visualisation technique is a function of the task that the technique is being used to support. In the context of task-based design, we therefore empirically established a list of user 's tasks that manipulate temporal data. These tasks concern data correlation, pattern identification, identification of concentration point of particular values, etc. To do so, we conducted interviews with geographers about the tasks they perform during a data analysis process and about the interpretation they make based on graphical representations.

2.1 Concentric Circles Technique (CCT)

The Concentric Circles Technique is dedicated to the visualisation of one or two quantitative histories. As shown in Fig. 2, its interface is made of a set of concentric circles, each one denoting the evolution of the visualised history(ies) during a fixed-length period of time. Values are denoted as rectangles adjacent to the circles. The height of each rectangle and its color's intensity are proportional to the value that it denotes. Circles are arranged so as to reflect the time order associated with the data.

We describe below the user's tasks addressed by the CCT. We compare our technique with the spiral representation of periodic data proposed in [4] (see Fig. 3).

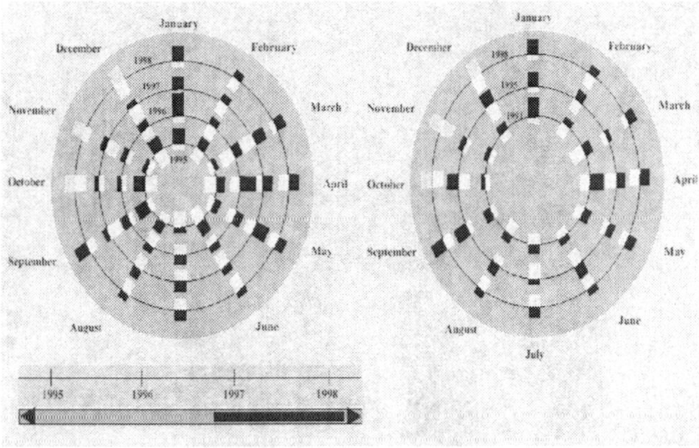

Fig. 2. The Concentric Circles Technique (CCT) .

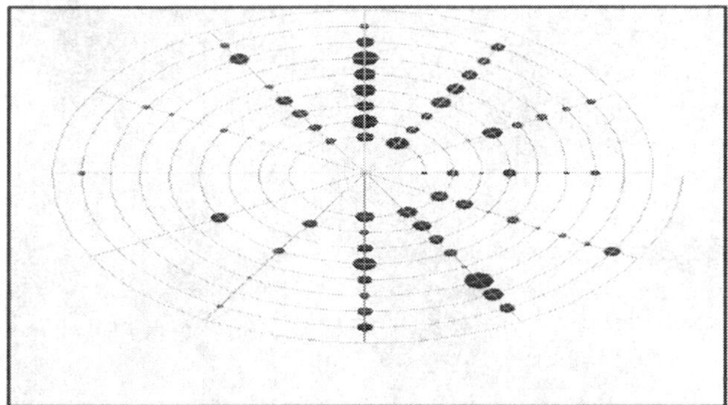

Fig. 3. Visualisation technique for serial periodic data [4].

The user's tasks addressed by the CCT are described below:

Navigate within a large data space. As shown in Fig. 3, in the spiral representation, the time axis is continuous and has a fixed origin. The size of the spiral is consequently proportional to the number of periods. It is clear that with a large number of periods (e.g. a hundred), the spiral representation cannot be applied, due to limitation of screen space. We face the same problem in the CCT, since the number of circles corresponds to the number of periods. To address this issue, the CCT's interface provides a time-slider, which allows the users to navigate through time. The displayed circles correspond to the periods falling within the time interval defined by the time-slider.

Correlate the evolution of two histories. The CCT supports the visualisation of two quantitative histories at a time. One of the histories is represented as explained above, while the other is represented with rectangles of a different color and oriented in an opposite direction. For instance, in Fig. 2, the rectangles denoting the values of one of the histories are blue-colored (dark gray in the gray scaled version) and oriented away from the center, and the values of the second history are red-colored (light gray) and oriented towards the center.

Compare periods. To facilitate the comparison of two elements positioned far from each other on the screen, the CCT interface provides two visualisation areas. The first one, located on the left in Fig. 2 and named the *reference area*, contains circles ordered in time. The second one located on the right and named the *working area*, enables the user to place selected circles in an arbitrary order. Putting circles close to each other facilitates the comparison of data values belonging to different periods. The width of a rectangle is proportional to the number of rectangles per period and to the radius of the circle. Only the height of a rectangle is proportional to the value that the rectangle denotes. By placing two circles next to each other (radii are similar), rectangles have nearly the same width, and comparison of their heights can be performed more easily.

Identify general trends. With the spiral representation users must scour the data space along the spiral to observe data evolution. As opposed to the spiral representation, with the CCT, the user can directly observe the evolution of the data during a given period (e.g. a year or a month) as well as compare the evolution of the data from one period to the next one. For instance, it can be seen in Fig. 3 that the values reached in January tend to be higher than the rest of the year, and that every year, the values tend to be low during June and December.

2.2 Superposed Histograms Technique (SHT)

Fig. 4 shows the superposed histograms technique (SHT) that offers a different approach for visual analysis of serial temporal data.

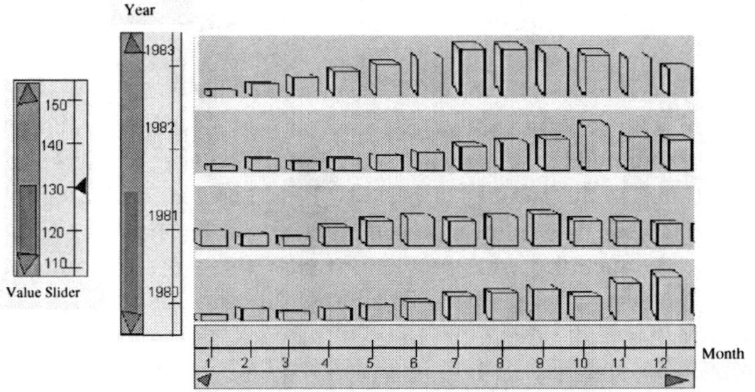

Fig. 4. Superposed Histograms Technique (SHT).

In SHT, data values have been mapped to 2.5 D objects (in the form of cubes). Time is represented along two dimensions. For this reason, the SHT includes two time-sliders, one vertical and one horizontal. Each data value is the result of a function *f* with two parameters that are two regular time-units. One time-unit *U1* is said to be regular with regard to another time-unit *U2*, only if each value of *U1* is composed of a fixed number of *U2*. A concrete example of regular units is *year* and *month*. Each year contains twelve months. In the example of Fig. 4, years and months are mapped onto two axes: years along the vertical axis and months along the horizontal axis. Each data value corresponds to ***f*** (year, month). The SHT addresses three user's tasks:

Navigate in time. The SHT provides two tools to navigate in time. Users can navigate using the vertical time-slider or the horizontal one.

Study data evolution according to one reference value. The value-slider, represented on the left of Fig. 4, is used to fix a threshold of data values: Only values greater than this threshold are visualised on the screen. The length of a given graphical object (cube) is the ratio of the corresponding data value minus the threshold, and the maximum value minus the threshold.

Compare periods. Periods are represented in the form of superposed histograms. Such a representation is well suited for the comparison of periods as explained in [2]: if the user's task is to compare periods, it is recommended to superpose them or represent them in a circular form.

3 Usability Assessment

In this section we describe the protocol of the evaluation we have carried out. The goal of the experiment was to evaluate the usability of the INVEST with regard to the user's tasks. The usability of a given visualisation technique V_i with regard to a given user's task T_j is defined as the value of the function $F(V_i, T_j)$, which is in the range of 0 and 1. The experimental evaluation lets us empirically identify these values $F(V_i, T_j)$. To do so we asked six participants (Ph.D. and master students in Geography) to use INVEST while manipulating their real data: a pollution measurement of NO and NO2. All participants were familiar with temporal data manipulation and graphic interpretation. Before starting an evaluation session, each participant had a document that describes how to use the techniques and for which tasks the technique has been designed. While manipulating the data, the participant could ask for help of the experimenter if s/he was facing a problem. At the end of the session, the participant has been asked to fill up one form per technique.

First, the participant specified the results s/he has obtained for each task. For example, for the task "trend observation", the participant has been asked to describe how the data evolve over time. Second, the participant has been asked to underline advantages and disadvantages of each technique with regard to a given task. In addition, s/he had to select a value between 0 and 20 to mark the usability of the technique according to a given task. The average of these values correspond to the values $F(V_i, T_j)$. Fig. 5 reports the results of the experiment according to five user's tasks and the two visualisation techniques CCT (light-grey) and SHT (dark-grey). Finally, the participant has been asked to propose other tasks it was easy to achieve using INVEST. By doing so, we could evaluate the completeness of our user's tasks list. For each participant, the session has lasted three hours and thirty minutes in average.

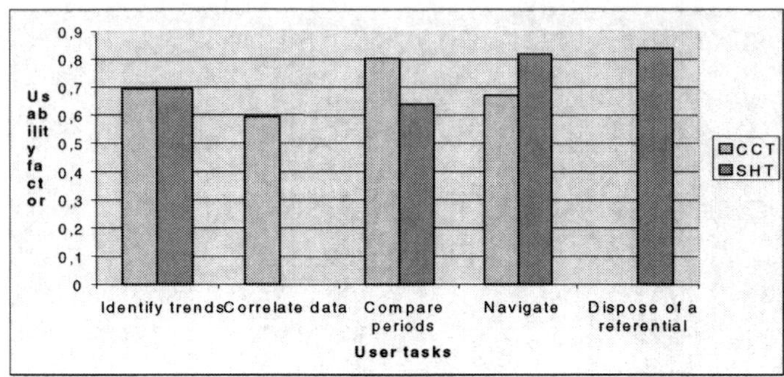

Fig. 5. Usability evaluation for both techniques (CCT and SHT).

The experimental evaluation leads to two conclusions:
First, we have empirically identified the $F(V_i, T_j)$ values. These values are embedded in the code of each technique. Indeed, in INVEST, each visualisation technique maintains knowledge about its usability factors according to each user's task. In the next section, we explain how we use these values at the implementation level.
Second, we experimentally prove that only one visualisation technique cannot fit all user's tasks. As shown in Fig. 5, for a given user's task Tj, each visualisation technique (V_i) does not have the same usability factor $F(V_i, T_j)$. For example, the SHT technique is not useful (usability factor equal to zero) when the user's task is to correlate two data evolutions, while it is very effective when the task is to observe data evolution according to a given referential. As a conclusion, visual data analysis systems should maintain a set of complementary visualisation techniques with regard to user's tasks. In the next section, we explain how we implement the multiple visualisation techniques within the software architecture model PAC-Amodeus.

4 Software Architecture of the INVEST System

Software designers of interactive systems usually distinguish two parts in a system: the interface and the functional core. The former defines the perceptual part of the system that is manipulated by the user. The latter implements the internal components that are dependent on the application domain. We clearly establish this distinction within the code of INVEST by applying the software architecture model PAC-Amodeus [17]. It is an hybrid multi-agent software architecture model that represents the organization of the components of interactive software. It is a blend of the five software components advocated by the Arch model [21] and the PAC refining process expressed in terms of agents [6]. Fig. 6 shows the five components of the PAC-Amodeus model and the Dialogue Controller refined in terms of PAC agents.

The Functional Core (FC) implements domain specific concepts in a presentation independent way. The FC hosts the temporal data. The Functional Core Adapter (FCA) serves as a mediator between the Dialogue Controller (DC) and the domain-specific concepts implemented in the FC. It is designed to absorb the effects of changes in its direct neighbors. The FCA operates as a translator between the representation of the temporal data in the FC and the data structure used in the DC. Data exchanged with the DC are conceptual objects independent of the representation used in the FC. This software design allows us to run INVEST using a temporal database or a set of temporal data files. Moreover, by only modifying the FCA, a relational database management system (new FC) can replace an object database management system (old FC).

At the other end of the spectrum, the Presentation Techniques Component (PTC) acts as a mediator between the DC and the Low Level Interaction Component (LLIC). The LLIC corresponds to the underlying platform, both hardware and software. In INVEST, this component corresponds to the AWT/Swing toolbox, INVEST being developed using JAVA. Because the PTC is platform independent, it is generally viewed as a logical LLIC. Presentation objects are translated in terms of interaction objects by the PTC. The distinction between presentation objects and interaction objects is subtle. A presentation object may correspond to an abstract interaction object or may correspond to a new interaction technique made of several interaction objects defined in the LLIC. Thus, the PTC defines a layer for portability, making the DC independent of the LLIC, as well as a layer for extending the LLIC services. For instance, each visualisation technique or part of it is defined by a JAVA bean, an extension of the toolbox. Such new interaction techniques belong to the PTC.

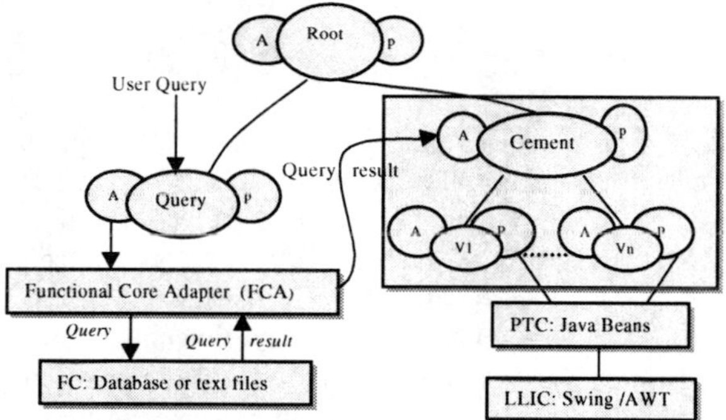

Fig. 6. INVEST architecture applying the PAC-Amodeus model.

The Dialogue Controller (DC) is the keystone of the model. It has the responsibility for task-level sequencing. The DC is decomposed into a set of cooperative PAC agents. The refinement of the DC in terms of PAC agents has multiple advantages including explicit support for concurrency (multithread dialogue, one dialogue per visualisation technique) and representation multiplicity (one representation per visualisation technique). A PAC agent is composed of three facets:
the Presentation implements the perceivable behavior of the agent. Within PAC-Amodeus, this facet is in direct contact with the Presentation Techniques Component (PTC); the Abstraction facet defines the competence of the agent. Within PAC-Amodeus, it is in direct contact with the Functional Core Adapter (FCA); the Control facet maintains the link between its two surrounding facets (i.e., Presentation and Abstraction) and the relationships with other agents.

Concretely, as shown in Fig. 6, the Dialogue Controller of INVEST is organized as a three-level hierarchy of PAC agents. One agent manages the query: its Abstraction facet communicates with the FCA to submit the query to the Temporal Database Management System. Once the query is executed, the FCA receives the data, translates them into a given data structure and submits them to the Abstraction of the Cement Agent. Each visualisation technique (V_i) is modeled as a PAC agent. The Presentation facet of a V_i agent relies on the corresponding JAVA bean in the PTC. Finally in order to establish communication between the Query agent and the Cement agent we add a Root agent. Within the hierarchy, the Cement Agent plays two roles:

First, it selects a subset of visualisation techniques that matches user's tasks. Let $N = \{N_1, N_2, .., N_k\}$ be the specified user's tasks. A given visualisation technique V_i is selected if $(\sum F(V_i, N_j) / card(N)) >=$ SelectivityFactor, where $N_j \in N$, $j \in \{1...k\}$ and SelectivityFactor $\in [0\text{-}1]$. Both user's tasks and the SelectivityFactor are specified by the user, along with the query or the set of data.

Second, it maintains the visual consistency between the current selected visualisation techniques. According to the software principle which stresses "mutual ignorance" to enhance reusability, agents which implement visualisation techniques should not know each other. Any action with a visual side effect on a view is reported to the cement agent which broadcasts the update to the other siblings [17].

5 Conclusion and Further Work

The goal of the work presented here has been to gain understanding of the design of visualisation techniques for temporal data. We have shown that different visualisation techniques are necessary in order to address the variety of users' tasks. Adopting this approach, we have presented INVEST, a multiple visualisation techniques platform to visually analyze temporal data. Two INVEST visualisation techniques among five supported by INVEST are presented and their experimental evaluation underlines the fact that the two techniques are complementary because they do not address the same user's tasks. We finally explained how the multiple visualisation techniques are implemented by applying our PAC-Amodeus architecture model. The software design guarantees the portability of INVEST with regard to the Functional Core component. We are planning to extend INVEST so that it can communicate with several Functional Cores including text files, XML files, and object database management system. Finally we also plan to carry out further usability experiments with more participants (colleagues of Geography Laboratory) in order to assess the usability of the visualisation techniques with regard to the user's tasks.

References

1. http://www.cs.auc.dk/3DVDM.
2. Bertin J., Graphics and Graphic Information Processing, Walter de Gruyter & Co, Berlin, 1981.

3. Casner S.. A task-Analytic Approach to the Automated Design of Graphic Presentations. ACM Transactions on Graphics, vol. 10, N° 2, April 1991, Pages 111-151.
4. Carlis J.V. and Konston J.A. Interactive Visualisation of Serial Periodic Data. In Proc. of the ACM Conference on User Interface Software and Technologie UIST'98, San Francisco, Ca, 1998.
5. Cook D., Virtual Reality: Real Ponderings, http://www.public.iastate.edu/~di5/Chance/paper.ps.gz.
6. Coutaz J., PAC-ing the Architecture of Your User Interface, DSV-IS'97, 4th Eurographics Workshop on Design, Specification and Verification of Interactive Systems, Springer Verlag Publ., P: 15-32.
7. Chuah Mei C., Roth Steven F., Mattis J. and Kolojejchick J. SDM: Selective Dynamic Manipulation of Visualisations. In proceedings of UIST'95 Conference, Pittsburgh PA USA, Pages 61-70.
8. Daassi C., Dumas M., Fauvet M-C, Nigay L. and Scholl P-C. Visual Exploration of Temporal Object Databases, In proc. of BDA00 Conference, 24-27 October 2000, Blois, France, P: 159-178.
9. Dumas M, Tempos: une plate-forme pour le développement d'application temporelles au dessus de SGBD à objets. Thèse de Doctorat de l'Université Joseph-Fourier, Grenoble, France, 2000.
10. Etzion E., Jajodia S. and Sripada S. M. (Ed.). Temporal Databases: Research and Practice. Springer Verlag Pub. LNCS 1399, 1998.
11. Fauvet M-C. Dumas M., and Scholl P-C. A representation independent temporal extension of ODMG's Object Query Language. In proc. of BDA99 Conference, Bordeaux, France, October1999.
12. Fredrikson A., North C., Plaisant C, and Shneiderman B.: Temporal, Geographical, and Categorial Aggregations Viewed through Coordinated Displays: A Case Study with Highway Incident Data. Workshop on New Paradigms in Information Visualisation and Manipulation 1999: 26-34.
13. Gram C. and Cockton G. Design Principles for Interactive Software. St Edmundsbury Press, 1996.
14. Keim D. Pixel-oriented Database Visualisation, SIGMOD Record, Special Issue on Information Visualisation, December. 1996.
15. Keim D. Visual Data Mining, Conf. On Very Large Databases (VLDB'97), Athens, Greece, 1997.
16. Mackinlay J.D., Robertson G., and Card S.K. The Perspective wall: Detail and Context smoothly integrated, Human factors in computing systems conference proceedings on Reaching through technology, 1991, Pages 173 – 176.
17. Nigay, L. and Coutaz, J. Software Architecture Modelling: Bridging Two Worlds Using Ergonomics and Software Properties, pp 49-73 in Formal Methods in Human-Computer Interaction, Palanque and Paterno (eds). Springer-Verlag, Berlin, 1997.
18. Nigay L. and Vernier F. Design Method of Interaction Techniques for Large Information Spaces, AVI'98, May 24-27, 1998, p: 37-46.
19. Roth Steven F., Kolojejchick J., Mattis J. and Goldstein J. Interactive Graphic Design Using Automatic Presentation Knowledge. In Proc. of CHI'94 conference, Boston USA, Pages 112-118.
20. Shahar Y. and Cheng C. Intelligent Visualisation and Exploration of Time Oriented Clinical Data. Technical Report TR SMI-98-0732, Stanford University, 1998.
21. The UIMS Workshop Tool Developers : A Metamodel for the Runtime Architecture of an Interactive System, SIGCHI Bulletin, 1992.

Query Optimization via Empty Joins

Jarek Gryz and Dongming Liang

York University
Toronto, Canada
{jarek,liang}@cs.yorku.ca

Abstract. A join of two relations in real databases is usually much smaller than their Cartesian product. This means that most of the combinations of tuples in the crossproduct of the respective relations do not appear together in the join result. We characterize these missing combinations as ranges of attributes that do not appear together and present experimental results on their discovery from real data sets. We then explore potential applications of this knowledge to query optimization. By modeling empty joins as materialized views, we show how knowledge of these regions can be used to improve query performance.

1 Introduction

A join of relations in real databases is usually much smaller than their Cartesian product. For example, the OLAP Benchmark from [8] with a star schema of six dimension tables with, respectively, 12, 15, 16, 86, 1000, and 10,000 tuples, has a fact table of the size of 2.4 millions tuples. The size of the fact table is thus 0.00009% of the size of the Cartesian product of the dimension tables.

This rather trivial observation about the relative size of the join and the respective Cartesian product, gives rise to the following questions: Can the non-joining portions of the tables (which we call *empty joins* in this paper) be characterized in an interesting way? If so, can this knowledge be useful in query processing? Consider the following example.

Example 1. Consider **Lineitem** and **Order** tables in TPC-H [24]. The **o_orderdate** attribute in the **Order** table stores information about the time an item was ordered, the **l_shipdate** attribute in the **Lineitem** table stores information about the time an item was shipped. The two attributes are correlated: an item cannot be shipped before it is ordered and it is likely to be shipped within a short period of time after it is ordered. Assume that an item is always shipped within a year from the time it is ordered. Thus, for a given range of **o_orderdate**, only the tuples from that range extended by one year of **l_shipdate** will be in the join of **Lineitem** and **Order**. None of the crossproduct between the remaining portions of the tables will appear together in the join result.

Call any query that involves a join and that evaluates to the empty table an *empty join*. Knowledge of empty joins may be valuable in and of itself as it

R. Cicchetti et al. (Eds.): DEXA 2002, LNCS 2453, pp. 710–720, 2002.

may reveal unknown correlations between data values which can be exploited in applications. For example, if a DBA determines that a certain empty join is a time invariant constraint, then it may be modeled as an integrity constraint. Indeed, the fact that an item cannot be shipped before it is ordered is defined in TPC-H as a check constraint [24].

But even if the discovered empty joins are not the result of a time invariant property or constraint, knowledge of these regions may be exploited in query optimization. Consider the following example.

Example 2. Consider the following query over TPC-H.

select sum(l_totalprice)
from lineitem l, order o
where l_orderkey = o_orderkey AND
    o_orderdate BETWEEN '1995.01.01' AND '1996.01.01'

Given the correlation of Example 1, a new condition *l_shipdate BETWEEN '1995.01.01' AND '1997.01.01'* can be added to the *where* clause of this query. By reducing the range of one or more of the attributes, or by adding new range predicates (which we have done in this example), we reduce the number of tuples that participate in the join execution thus providing optimization.[1] In the extreme case, when the predicates in the query fall *within* the ranges of an empty region, the query would not have to be evaluated at all, since the result is necessarily empty.

An empty join can be characterized in different ways. The most straightforward way is to describe it negatively by defining a correlation between data points that *do* join. Thus, for the two attributes from Example 1 we can specify their relationship as a linear correlation: *l_shipdate = o_orderdate + [0, 1] year*, where $[0,1]$ *year* is the correlation error. We explored this idea in [12] and showed how such correlations can be used in query optimization. We also learned, however, that such correlations are rare in the real data that we explored. Real data is likely to be distributed more randomly, yet not uniformly. In this paper, we are proposing an alternative, but complementary approach to characterizing empty joins as ranges of attributes that *do not* appear together in the join. For example, there are no tuples with *l_orderdate* > '1995.01.01' and *l_shipdate* < '1995.01.01' in the join of **Lineitem** and **Order**. In other words, the join of **Lineitem** and **Order** with thus specified ranges of *l_orderdate* and *l_shipdate* is empty. To maximize the use of empty joins knowledge, our goal in this work is to not only to find empty joins in the data, but to characterize fully that empty space. Specifically, we discover the set of all maximal empty joins in a two dimensional data set. Maximal empty joins represent the ranges of the two attributes for which the join is empty and such that they cannot be extended without making the join non-empty.

We suggest that empty joins can be thought of as another characteristic of data skew. By characterizing ranges of attributes that do not appear together,

[1] We are assuming that the selection is done *before* the join execution.

we provide another description of data distribution in a universal relation. Indeed, we show that data skew—a curse of query optimization— can have a straightforward, practical application for that very query optimization.

The optimization technique we present here is a straightforward generalization of the rewrite of Example 2. We show this technique to be useful in practice by experimental verification of the following two claims. First, real data sets contain a large number of empty joins, some of which are themselves very large. This is important as the likelihood of a query being eligible for a rewrite (that is, containing an empty join) increases with the size of an empty join. Second, the types of rewrites we propose indeed provide powerful optimization of query execution. We present experiments showing how the quality of optimization depends on the types and number of empty joins used in a rewrite. Last but not least, we develop this technique with a possible commercial implementation in mind. To that effect, we model the empty joins as materialized views, and so we can exploit existing work on using and maintaining materialized views in commercial systems. Our solution therefore has the highly desirable property that it provides new optimization method without requiring any change to the underlying query optimization and processing engine.

The paper is organized as follows. In Section 2, we present the results of experiments performed on real data, showing the nature and quantity of empty joins that can occur in large, real databases. In Section 3, we describe an optimization technique illustrating how knowledge of empty joins can be used in query processing and present experiments showing query performance improvements under various overlap scenarios. Related work is described in Section 4. Conclusions and future work are presented in Section 5.

2 Characteristics of Empty Joins

Consider a join of two relations $R \bowtie S$. Let A and B be attributes of R and S respectively over two totally ordered domains. (Note that A and B are **not** the join attributes.) We are interested in finding ranges $< x_0, x_1 >$ of A and $< y_0, y_1 >$ of B for which the join $R \bowtie S$ is empty, that is, $\sigma_{x_0 \leq A \leq x_1 \wedge y_0 \leq B \leq y_1}(R \bowtie S) = \emptyset$. We will say that the empty join is *maximal* if the ranges $< x_0, x_1 >$ and $y_0, y_1 >$ cannot be extended without making the join non-empty.

To characterize empty joins we used two real databases: the first, an insurance database; and the second, a department of motor vehicles database. We ran the empty joins mining algorithm[2] on 12 pairs of attributes. The pairs of attributes came from the workload queries provided with the databases. These were the attributes frequently referenced together in the queries (one from one table, and the other from a second table, and the tables are joined). For conciseness, we only present the results of five representative tests here.[3]

[2] The reader is referred to [10] for a full description of the mining algorithm.

[3] They are representative in the sense that they cover the spectrum of results in terms of the number and sizes of the discovered empty joins.

Table 1 contains the mining results: the number of discovered maximal empty joins E and the sizes of the 5 largest empty joins. The size of an empty join is defined formally in the following way. Let E be an empty join with the coordinates $(x_0, y_0), (x_1, y_1)$ over attributes A and B respectively in tables R and S respectively. The relative size of the join with respect to the covered area, $S(E)$, is defined as:

$$S(E) = \frac{(x_1 - x_0) * (y_1 - y_0)}{[max(A) - min(A)] * [max(B) - min(B)]} * 100\% \tag{1}$$

Table 1. Number and Sizes of Empty Joins

Test	E	Size of largest 5 empty joins				
1	269	74	73	69	7	7
2	29,323	68	58	40	37	28
3	13,850	91.6	91.6	91.3	91.3	83.1
4	7	8.8	2.1	1.2	0.6	0.3
5	25,307	39.9	39.8	24	20	20

We make the following observations:

1. The number of empty joins discovered in the tested data sets is very large. In some cases (see Test 3) it is on the order of magnitude of the theoretical limit of the possible number of empty joins [10].
2. In virtually all tests, extremely large empty joins were discovered. Usually, however, only a few are very large and the sizes drop dramatically to a fraction of a percentage point for the others.
3. The empty joins overlap substantially. The five largest empty joins from Test 1 overlap with, respectively, 7, 11, 16, 7, and 8 other empty joins discovered in that data set. These overlaps are a consequence of our decision to find *all* maximal empty joins.

Empty joins can have useful applications in data mining or estimating query result sizes (for example, in join histograms). Our focus in this paper is to use the information about empty joins in query optimization.

3 Using Empty Joins in Query Optimization

3.1 Query Rewriting

We now turn to the question of how to effectively use the knowledge about empty joins in query optimization. Our approach is to model the empty joins as materialized views. The only extra storage required is the storage required for the view definition since the actual materialized view will be empty.

Assume that the following query represents an empty join.

select $*$
from R, S
where $R.J = S.J$
and X between x_0 **and** x_1
and Y between y_0 **and** y_1

We can represent this query as a materialized view V and use it to rewrite future queries to improve their performance. Indeed, we can use existing results on determining whether a view can be used to answer a query and on rewriting queries using such views [23]. Rather than describing the algorithm, we present an example of how it would be applied here.

For example, if $x_0 \leq x_i, x_j \leq x_1$ and $y_0 \leq y_i \leq y_1 \leq y_j$, then the following rewrite of query Q is possible.

select $*$ *from* R, S *where* $R.J = S.J$ **and** X between x_i **and** x_j **and** Y between y_i **and** y_j	$\Rightarrow$	*select* $*$ *from* R, S *where* $R.J = S.J$ **and** X between x_i **and** x_j **and** Y between y_1 **and** y_j

This rewrite can be graphically represented, as shown in Figure 1, as a reduction of the area of the rectangle representing query Q with respect to the attributes X and Y, given the overlap with the empty join V.

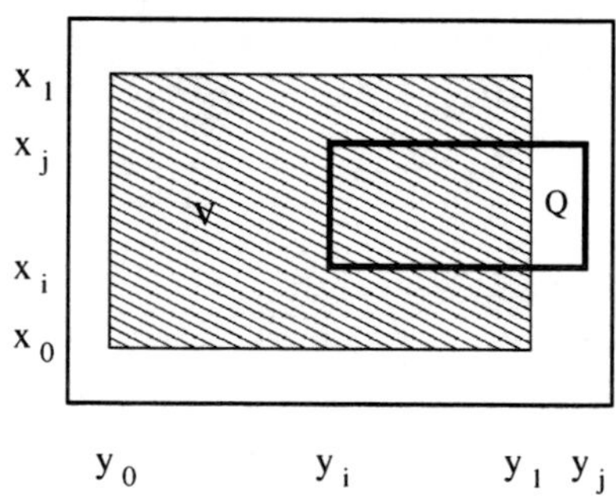

Fig. 1. Query Q (marked with thick lines) overlaps the empty View V.

Effectively, we are using the empty joins to reduce the ranges of the attributes in the query predicates. This, in turn, reduces the size(s) of the tables participating in the join, thus reducing the cost of computing the join.

3.2 Choosing Among Possible Rewrites

There are several ways such rewrites of the ranges can be done depending on the types of overlap between the ranges of the attributes in the query and the empty joins available. Previous work on rewriting queries using views can be used to decide when a view, in this case an empty view, can be used to rewrite the query [19,23]. However, this work does not give us a way of enumerating and prioritizing the possible alternative rewrites for the inequality predicates used in our queries and views.

As shown in Figure 1, a pair of range predicates in a query can be represented as a rectangle in a two dimensional matrix. Since the goal of the rewrite is to "remove" (that is, not to reference) the combination of ranges covered by an empty join, we need to represent the non-empty portion of the query, which we will call the *remainder query* [9]. Consider Figure 2, which illustrates five fundamentally different ways a query, represented as a rectangle with thick lines, can overlap with an empty join marked as a filled rectangle.

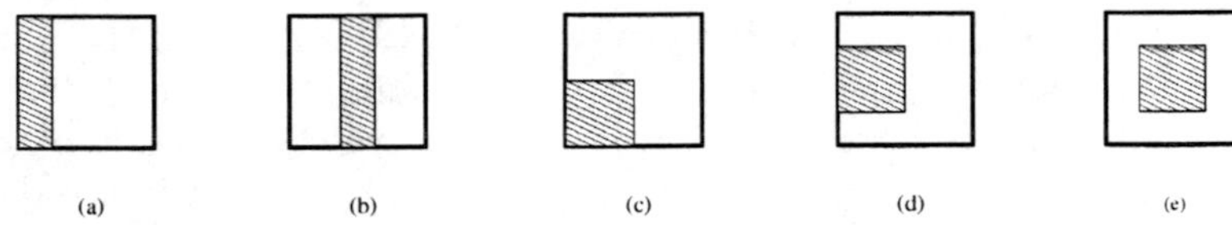

Fig. 2. Overlaps of increasing complexity between the query and empty joins.

In Case (a), the remainder query can be still represented as a single rectangle. Hence, the rewritten SQL query has a single non-empty query block. In Case (b), however, the remainder query has to be represented by at least two rectangles, which implies that the rewritten SQL query will be the UNION ALL of two non-empty query blocks (or an appropriate OR condition). Cases (c), (d), and (e) illustrate even more complex scenarios where three or four rectangles are needed to describe the remainder query. Indeed, it has been shown in [4] that blind application of materialized views may result in worse plans compared to alternative plans that do not use materialized views. This is also true about empty views. Our experiments reported below suggest that using rewrites containing multiple non-empty query blocks usually degrade rather than improve query performance. The decision about which empty joins to use in a rewrite must be made within the optimizer in a cost-based way. There are cases, however, when cost-based optimization can be avoided. For example, a rewrite of type (a) in Figure 3 is guaranteed not to produce worse performance than in the original query as the only change it makes in the query is to reduce the existing ranges of predicates. Our experiments also showed that a rewrite of type (b) consistently delivered optimization.

In the next subsection we investigate how the following factors affect the quality of optimization:

1. The size of the overlap between an empty join and a query.
2. The type of the overlap.
3. The number of empty joins overlapping the query used in the rewrite.

To demonstrate the utility of empty joins for query optimization under various overlap conditions, we performed several sets of experiments.

3.3 Quality of Optimization

The experiments described below were run on a PC with PII-700MHz, 320M Memory under Windows 2000, DB2 UDB V7.1 for NT.

We created two tables $R(id\ int, X\ int, J\ int)$ and $S(id\ int, Y\ int, J\ int)$, where J is a join column and X and Y are attributes with totally ordered domains. The range of values for both X and Y is $0-10,000$. R has 100k tuples, S has 10M tuples uniformly distributed over the domains of X and Y. The join method used in the queries below is sort-merge join.[4] No indexes have been created or used. In all experiments the query and the empty view had the form as Q and V in Section 3.1.

In the first experiment, we investigated the effect of the size of the overlap of the empty join and the query on the query performance. To this end, we created several empty joins with an increasing overlap with query. This was done by changing the values of one of the attributes so that the tuples in the designed range do not join with any tuples in the other table. The results of the experiment are presented in Table 2. As we expected, the reduction in query execution time

Table 2. Improvement in query execution time (in %) as the overlap with the empty join is increased.

Reduction of the size of the table (%)	5	10	20	25	33	50	66	83
Reduction of execution time (%)	2.4	6.6	16	39	41	48	56	67

grows monotonically with the increase of the overlap. On the other hand, the size of the overlap does not provide equivalent reduction in the query execution time. This is understandable, as the query evaluation involves not only the join execution, but also scanning of the two tables which is a constant factor for all tests. The only surprising result came from Test 4 (and in Test 5): the reduction of the query execution time jumps above the reduction of the table's size. As it turns out, the table became sufficiently small to be sorted in memory, whereas before it required an external sort.

In the second experiment we investigated the effect of the type of the overlap on query performance. Hence, we kept the size of the overlap constant at 25% of the size of the query, but changed the type of an overlap as shown in Figure 3.

[4] Similar results were obtained for nested-loops join. No optimization can be achieved for index nested-loops, since the join is executed before the selections.

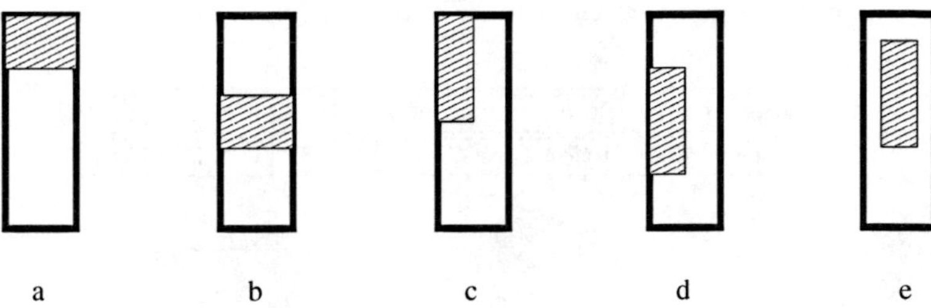

Fig. 3. Overlaps of increasing complexity between the query and empty joins.

Table 3. Impact of the type of the overlap used in rewrite on query performance.

Type of overlap	a	b	c	d	e
Reduction of execution time (%)	39	37	4.6	0	-13

As shown in Table 3, only the first two types of the overlap provide substantial performance improvement. As the number of OR conditions (or UNION's) necessary to express the remainder query increases, the performance deteriorates. For example, in Case (e), the query rewritten with ORs would have four separate blocks. Executing these blocks requires multiple scanning of relations R and S. Indeed, in all our experiments only the rewrites using overlaps of type (a) or (b) consistently led to performance improvement.

In the third experiment we kept the size of the overlap constant at 25% and used only type (a) and (b) of the overlap from the previous experiment. This time, however, we changed the number of overlapping empty joins with the query. We varied the number of empty joins used in a rewrite from 1 to 8 decreasing their sizes accordingly (to keep the total overlap at 25%) as shown in Figure 4.

The results are shown in Table 4. Interestingly, query performance degrades very slowly with the increasing number of empty joins used in a rewrite. The reason is, that despite an appearance of an increased complexity of the query after the rewrite a single scan of each table is still sufficient to evaluate the join.

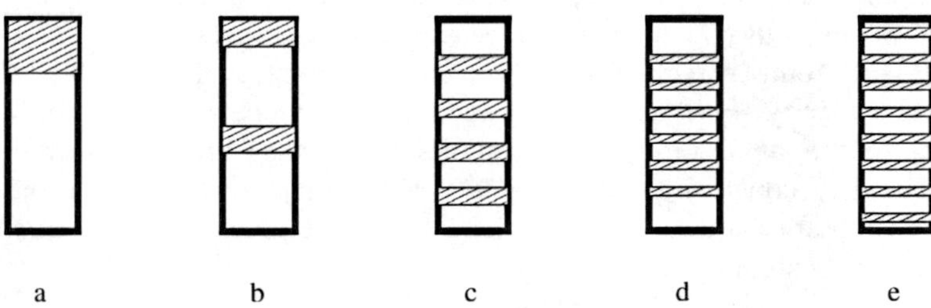

Fig. 4. Overlaps with increasing number of empty joins.

Table 4. Impact of the increasing number of overlaps used in rewrite on query performance.

Number of overlapping empty joins	1	2	4	6	8
Reduction of execution time (%)	39	38.4	38.3	35.9	34.3

We performed a number of experiments measuring the quality of optimization in the real workload of the insurance database using some of the empty joins described in Section 2. The results were consistent with those reported above. Ideally, we would have presented the optimization results performed with a publicly available workload, such as TPC-D, to allow for replication of the experiments. Unfortunately, the type of data distribution in TPC-D is not representative of a real data set. The data is synthetically generated, and the distribution of the attribute values tends to be uniform. We ran the mining algorithm on several pairs of attributes on TPC-D joins. In all cases the results were very different from what we discovered in real data sets. Although the number of empty joins was large, they all were very small thereby making them impractical for use by this technique. Indeed, we believe that the optimization technique presented in this paper would be most useful in datasets with large data skew where large empty joins might exist.

4 Related Work

We are not aware of any work on discovery or application of empty joins.

Extracting semantic information from database schemas and contents, often called *rule discovery*, has been studied over the last several years. Rules can be inferred from integrity constraints [1,2,25] or can be discovered from database content using machine learning or data mining approaches [5,7,15,20,22,25]. It has also been suggested that such rules be used for query optimization [16,20,22,25]. None of this work, however, addressed the specific problem we solve here.

Another area of research related to our work is answering queries using views. Since we model empty joins as a special case of materialized views (that are also empty), essentially all techniques developed for maintaining, and using materialized views for query answering apply here as well [13,19,4,23].

Also, since empty regions describe semantic regularities in data, they are similar to integrity constraints [11]. They describe what is true in a database in its current state, as do integrity constraints, but can be invalidated by updates, unlike integrity constraints. Using empty joins for query optimization is thus similar to semantic query optimization [3,14,17,18,21,6], which uses integrity constraints for that purpose.

5 Conclusions and Future Work

We presented a novel approach to characterizing data that is not based on detecting and measuring similarity of values within the data, but is instead based on the discovery of empty regions. We sketched an efficient and scalable algorithm that discovers all maximal empty joins with a single scan over sorted two dimensional data set. We presented results from experiments performed on real data, showing the nature and quantity of empty joins that can occur in large, real databases. Knowledge of empty joins may be valuable in and of itself as it may reveal unknown correlations between data values. In this paper, we considered using this knowledge for query optimization. We model the empty joins as materialized views, and so we exploit existing work on using and maintaining materialized views. We also presented experiments showing how the quality of optimization depends on the types and number of empty joins used in a rewrite.

We are currently working on adopting existing techniques for selecting and maintaining materialized views to empty joins. We believe that the most promising direction for future work in this area is to consider empty spaces within multi-way joins. Typical queries usually involve more than a two-way join. Although the technique described in this paper can still be used for such queries (by applying the rewrite to each pair of joining tables separately), a global approach may yield optimizations not available when performed piecemeal.

References

1. S. Ceri, P. Fraternali, S. Paraboschi, and L. Tanca. Automatic generation of production rules for integrity maintenance. *TODS*, 19(3):367–422, 1994.
2. S. Ceri and J. Widom. Deriving production rules for constraint maintanance. In *Proceedings of the* 16th *VLDB*, pages 577–589, Brisbane, Australia, 1990.
3. U. Chakravarthy, J. Grant, and J. Minker. Logic-based approach to semantic query optimization. *ACM TODS*, 15(2):162–207, June 1990.
4. S. Chaudhuri, R. Krishnamurthy, S. Potamianos, and K. Shim. Optimizing queries with materialized views. In *Proceedings of the 11th ICDE*, pages 190–200, Taipei, Taiwan, 1995. IEEE Computer Society.
5. I-Min. A. Chen and R. C. Lee. An approach to deriving object hierarchies from database schema and contents. In *Proceedings of the 6th ISMIS*, pages 112–121, Charlotte, NC, 1991.
6. Q. Cheng, J. Gryz, F. Koo, C. Leung, L. Liu, X. Qian, and B. Schiefer. Implementation of two semantic query optimization techniques in DB2 UDB. In *Proc. of the 25th VLDB*, pages 687–698, Edinburgh, Scotland, 1999.
7. W. Chu, R. C. Lee, and Q. Chen. Using type inference and induced rules to provide intensional answers. In *Proc. of the 7th ICDE*, pages 396–403, Kobe, Japan, 1991.
8. OLAP Council. APB-1 OLAP Benchmark Release II, November 1998. (www.olapcouncil.org).
9. S. Dar, M. Franklin, B. Jonsson, D. Srivastava, and M. Tan. Semantic data caching and replacement. In *Proc. of 22nd VLDB*, pages 330–341, Bombay, India, 1996.
10. J. Edmonds, J. Gryz, D. Liang, and R. J. Miller. Mining for empty rectangles in large data sets. In *Proceedings of the 8th ICDT*, pages 174–188, London, UK, 2001.

11. P. Godfrey, J. Gryz, and C. Zuzarte. Exploiting constraint-like data characterizations in query optimization. In *Proceedings of Sigmod*, pages 582–592, Santa Barbara, CA, 2001.
12. J. Gryz, B. Schiefer, J. Zheng, and C. Zuzarte. Discovery and application of check constraints in DB2. In *Proceedings of ICDE*, pages 551–556, Heidelberg, Germany, 2001.
13. A. Gupta and I. S. Mumick. Maintenance of materialized views: Problems, techniques, and applications. *Data Engineering Bulletin*, 18(2):3–18, 1995.
14. M.T. Hammer and S.B. Zdonik. Knowledge-based query processing. *Proc. 6th VLDB*, pages 137–147, October 1980.
15. J. Han, Y. Cai, and N. Cercone. Knowledge discovery in databases: An attribute-oriented approach. In *Proceedings of the 18th VLDB*, pages 547–559, Vancouver, Canada, 1992.
16. C. N. Hsu and C. A. Knoblock. Using inductive learning to generate rules for semantic query optimization. In *Advances in Knowledge Discovery and Data Mining*, pages 425–445. AAAI/MIT Press, 1996.
17. M. Jarke, J. Clifford, and Y. Vassiliou. An optimizing PROLOG front-end to a relational query system. In *SIGMOD*, pages 296–306, 1984.
18. J.J. King. Quist: A system for semantic query optimization in relational databases. In *Proc. 7th VLDB*, pages 510–517, Cannes, France, September 1981.
19. A. Y. Levy, A. O. Mendelzon, Y. Sagiv, and D. Srivastava. Answering queries using views. In *Proceedings of the 14th PODS*, pages 95–104, San Jose, California, 1995. ACM Press.
20. S. Shekar, B. Hamidzadeh, A. Kohli, and M. Coyle. Learning transformation rules for semantic query optimization. *TKDE*, 5(6):950–964, December 1993.
21. S.T. Shenoy and Z.M. Ozsoyoglu. Design and implementation of a semantic query optimizer. *IEEE Transactions on Knowledge and Data Engineering*, 1(3):344–361, September 1989.
22. M.D. Siegel. Automatic rule derivation for semantic query optimization. In *Proceedings of the 2nd International Conference on Expert Database Systems*, pages 371–386, Vienna, Virginia, 1988.
23. D. Srivastava, S. Dar, H.V. Jagadish, and A. Levy. Answering queries with aggregation using views. In *Proceedings of the 22nd VLDB*, pages 318–329, Bombay, India, 1996.
24. Transaction Processing Performance Council, 777 No. First Street, Suite 600, San Jose, CA 95112-6311, www.tpc.org. *TPC Benchmark*^{TM} *D*, 1.3.1 edition, February 1998.
25. Clement T. Yu and Wei Sun. Automatic knowledge acquisition and maintenance for semantic query optimization. *IEEE Transactions on Knowledge and Data Engineering*, 1(3):362–375, September 1989.

Efficient Processing of XPath Queries Using Indexes

Yan Chen[1], Sanjay Madria[1], Kalpdrum Passi[2], and Sourav Bhowmick[3]

[1] Department of Computer Science, University of Missouri-Rolla, Rolla, MO 65409, USA
madrias@umr.edu

[2] Dept. of Math. & Computer Science, Laurentian University, Sudbury ON P3E 2C6 Canada
kpassi@cs.laurentian.ca

[3] School of Computer Engineering, Nanyang Technological University, Singapore
assourav@ntu.edu.sg

Abstract. A number of query languages have been proposed in recent times for processing queries on XML and semistructured data. All these query languages make use of regular path expressions to query XML data. To optimize the processing of query paths a number of indexing schemes have also been proposed recently. XPath provides the basis for processing queries on XML data in the form of regular path expressions. In this paper, we propose two algorithms called Entry-point algorithm and Rest-tree algorithm that exploit different types of indexes, which we have defined to efficiently process XPath queries. We also discuss and compare two variations in implementing these algorithms; Root-first and Bottom-first.

1 Introduction

With the wide acceptance of XML as a common format to store and exchange data, it is imperative to query XML data. Several query languages have been proposed to query semistructured data, such as XQuery[4], XML-QL[7], XML-GL[3], Lorel[1], and Quilt[5].. XPath[6] is a language that describes the syntax for addressing path expressions over XML data. To improve the performance of the query on large XML files it is essential to employ indexes on XML data. Indexing techniques used in relational and object-oriented databases do not suffice for XML data due to the semistructured nature of the data.

In this paper, we introduce three types of indexes – name index, value index and path index to improve the performance of Xpath queries on XML data. We propose two algorithms called Entry-point algorithm and Rest-tree algorithm to efficiently process XPath queries using the proposed indexes and present performance evaluation of the algorithms. We present simulation results to show that XPath queries on large XML data execute faster using different types of indexes with the Entry-point algorithm proposed in the paper, when compared to traditional methods of querying with or without indexing. Without using indexes, the queries are implemented by traversing the complete XML DOM tree and also the methods that use indexes but do not exploit the index information of the ancestor nodes.

[1] Partially supported by UM Research Board Grant and Intelligent Systems Center.
[2] Partially supported by NSERC grant 228127-01 and an internal LURF grant.

R. Cicchetti et al. (Eds.): DEXA 2002, LNCS 2453, pp. 721–730, 2002.

1.1 Related Work

Semistructured data such as XML do not confirm to a rigid, predefined schema and have irregular structure. Indexing techniques in relational or object-oriented databases depend on a fixed schema based on a known, strongly typed class hierarchy. Therefore, such techniques are not directly applicable in XML data. Several indexing schemes have been proposed for semistructured data in [10,11], dataguides [8], 1-indexes, 2-indexes, and T-indexes [12], ToXin[13] and XISS[9].

Dataguides record information on the existing paths in a database, however they do not provide any information of parent-child relationships between nodes in the database as a result that cannot be used for navigation from any arbitrary node. **T-indexes** are specialized path indexes, which only summarize a limited class of paths. **1-index** and **2-index** are special cases of T-indexes. In our approach we add path information to every node that can trace the parent-child relationship for every node.

In **LORE** system four different types of index structures have been proposed [10], including: value, text, link, and path indexes. Value index and text index are used to search objects that have specific values; link index and path index provide fast access to parents of an object and all objects reachable via a given labeled path. Lore uses OEM (Object Exchange Model) to store data and OQL (Object Query Language) as its query language.

ToXin has two different types of index structure: the value index and the path index. The path index has two parts: index tree and instance functions, and these functions can be used to trace the parent-child relationship. Their path index contains only parent and children information but in our model, we store the complete path from root to each node. ToXin uses index for single level while we use multiple index for different levels. Also, in our proposal, we consider different types of indexes.

2 Indexing XML Data

Consider an XML file given in Figure 1 that has information about a bookstore containing say 100,000 books. The DOM tree for the XML fragment in Fig. 1 is shown in Fig. 2. If we need to retrieve all the books with author's name as "Chris" from the Benny-bookstore (a simple query which is often executed in information retrieval system), without using any optimization technique, we need to find all the nodes in the DOM tree with nodes labeled as BOOK. Then for each BOOK, we need to test the author's name. After about 100,000 comparisons we get a couple of books with author "Chris" as the output.

By using index on AUTHOR, we do not need to test author of each BOOK node. With the index of the key as "Chris", we can find all the author nodes faster (e.g. only two such nodes). The nodes obtained can be checked if they satisfy the query condition. The execution time can be reduced considerably by using the index. This is a "bottom-up" query plan. Such a plan is useful in the case when we have a relatively "small" result set at the bottom, which can be pre-selected. However, if the query is to find all the books with the name beginning with "glory" and the author as "Chris" and assume that "Chris" is such a famous author that she has more than 5,000 books in the store. The query plan could be to get all the books with the name "glory" disregarding their authors. If there is a small number of books satisfying the constraint, (e.g., four "glory" books), it might be useful to introduce another type of index, which is built on the values of some nodes. Here, we need index upon strings. On the basis of the nodes obtained in the first step, we can further test another condition on the query. Hence, we can build a set of nodes as the "entry set", which will depend on the specific query and on the type of XML data.

```
<BOOKSTORE name = "Benny-bookstore">
        <BOOK title = "Brave the new world">
                <ISBN>1-1-1</ISBN>
                <AUTHOR> David </AUTHOR>
        </BOOK>
        <BOOK title = "Glory days">
                <ISBN>1-1-2</ISBN>
                <AUTHOR> Chris </AUTHOR>
        </BOOK>
        <BOOK title = "I love the game">
                <ISBN>1-1-3</ISBN>
                <AUTHOR> Chris </AUTHOR>
        </BOOK>
        <BOOK title = "What lies beneath">
                <ISBN>1-1-4</ISBN>
                <AUTHOR> Michael </AUTHOR>
        </BOOK>
        <BOOK title = "Matrix II">
                <ISBN>1-1-5</ISBN>
                <AUTHOR> Jason </AUTHOR>
        </BOOK>
        <BOOK title = "The Root">
                <ISBN>1-1-6</ISBN>
                <AUTHOR> Tomas </AUTHOR>
        </BOOK>
</BOOKSTORE>
```

Fig. 1. An XML Fragment

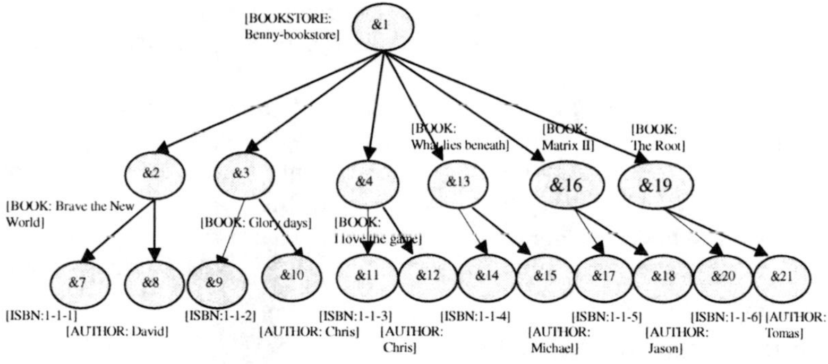

Fig. 2. Simple DOM Tree of Benny-bookstore

2.1 Types of Indexes

We now describe types of indexes that can be built over an XML file. We will then describe query plan operations that use the indexing structures. To speed up query processing in an XML file, we build three different types of index structures. The first type identifies objects that have specific values; the next two are used to efficiently retrieve the objects in an XML (DOM) tree. In XML Structures [2], each node has an ID. We exploit this attribute and establish a relationship between node ID and storage address to speed our search.

Name-index (Nindex)
A name index locates nodes with the tag names. Using this index, we group nodes that have the same tag name. We call this index as Name-index.

The Nindex for the incoming tag <BOOK> over the XML fragment in Fig. 2 will then be {&2, &3, &4, &13, &16, &19}.

Value-index (Vindex)
A value-index locates nodes with given value. XML has classified different data types, therefore, we do not need type coercion [10]. Vindex can be built selectively over basic types, such as numbers, strings or on other types.

The Value-index for the word "Chris" is {&10, &12}, for the word "the" is {&2, &4}. Apparently, not all values are worth building an index on each of them. The index on the word "the" seems to be redundant. The administrator or the user can decide which values would be useful as a value index.

The Nindex and Vindex can also be grouped together, as we need the name or type of nodes to restrict the value index. We can integrate these two indexes to facilitate and accelerate the query. In the simulation program, we extract the features of Nindex and Vindex to an abstract "type" index, which could be replaced by a specific index in actual environment.

Path-index (Pindex)
Pindex, a path index, locates nodes with the path from root node. To execute a query, after we get the first selected set of nodes, we need to test the nodes to see whether they satisfy the input expression. To make the testing efficient, it is helpful if we record the path from root to the current test node. This may be an extra attribute added to each node.

Path index is the information we attach to each node to record its ancestors' paths. This information is also very useful in our algorithm. As in some of the traditional algorithms [10, 8], if we do not execute the query from top to bottom, we need to get ancestors' of certain nodes at the middle level. Since we need to build this information on each node, an index will be useful.

In Fig. 2 the ancestral path information of &11 is {&1, &4}; node &7's ancestral path information is {&1, &2}.

Definition 1: Descent Number (DN)
Descent Number is the information we attach to every node to record the number of its descents. The descents of a node include all the arcs going out of that node and reaching the leaf nodes. This information is used to select one index node set among several index node sets. The usage of DN will be elaborated in our algorithms. In Fig. 2, the DN of node &11 is 0; the DN of node &3 is 2.

3 Entry-Point Algorithm

XPath is a language for addressing parts of an XML document. XPath also provides basic constructs for manipulation of strings, numbers and Boolean data. XPath operates on abstract, logical structure of an XML document, rather than on its surface syntax. XPath uses path notations for navigating through the hierarchical structure of an XML document. A query written in any of the query languages, such as XQuery[4], XML-QL[7], XML-GL[3], Lorel[1], and Quilt[5] is easily transformed in terms of an XPath expression. If we need to retrieve a relatively small part (data) from the large XML file under certain constraints expressed using XPath, it will be expensive to compare each node with given search conditions. Assuming that various types of indexes, such as Nindex, Vindex and Pindex defined in Section 2 have been created, we give two techniques to process and optimize the XPath expression generated from a given query. In the first technique we find an entry-point node among a set of middle level nodes in the XPath expression. Then we split the XPath expression at the entry-point and test for the path condition for the first part and eliminate nodes from DOM tree that do not satisfy the path condition. Then we test the remaining part of the XPath expression recursively eliminating nodes that do not satisfy the path condition. The algorithm can be implemented either using root-first approach or bottom-up approach. We explain the technique using the example in Fig. 1 before formally giving the algorithm.

Suppose we are given the following query:
Select BOOKSTORE/BOOK
Where BOOK.name="Glory days" and /AUTHOR.title = "Chris" and
BOOKSTORE.name = "Benny-bookstore"

The above query is transformed to the following XPath expression:
/BOOKSTORE [@name = "Benny-bookstore"]/child:: BOOK[@title = "Glory days"]/Child :: AUTHOR/child :: AUTHOR[@name = "Chris"]

Given several types of indexes can enable us to get some specific node sets. For example, we can use Nindex to get all BOOK nodes or AUTHOR nodes. There can be two ways we can approach the query to accelerate the execution. We can either get all books named "Glory Days" and then test the condition on each one of them if the author is "Chris", or first get all authors named "Chris", and then test the parent nodes if book name is "Glory Days". In the first strategy, we evaluate the former part of XPath expression first, that is,
/BOOKSTORE [@name= "Benny-bookstore"]/child:: BOOK[@title = "Glory Days"]

Then, we test each author child node, which is the latter part of XPath expression,
/Child :: AUTHOR/child :: AUTHOR[@name = "Chris"].

In terms of the XML DOM tree, we find an entry-point node among the "middle level" nodes using the index, and then test path information of these nodes to check if they match the first part of the XPath expression, and eliminate the entry-point nodes that do not satisfy the first part of XPath expression. Then, we start from the remaining entry-point nodes as the root nodes of a set of sub trees and eliminate nodes recursively from the sub trees to get the final nodes. The other bottom-up strategy is similar, except that the entry-point nodes will constitute the final result nodes set.

3.1 Entry-Point Algorithms

We now present two versions of Entry-point Algorithm; the Root-first Algorithm and the Bottom-first Algorithm.

```
INPUT: XPath expression
root/X1/X2/.../Xi/.../Xm
STEP 1: FOR each Xi
        BEGIN
         IF Xi is indexed THEN
           BEGIN
          get every node xi of
          type Xi. Get the DN
          ni of each xi
          Sumi = Σni
           END
        END
STEP 2: Get entry point Xn with minimum
Sum, add all xn to a node set S;
Consider the tree obtained after deleting all
branches that do not have the node xn in its
path.
split the XPath into root/X1/X2/.../Xn-1 and
/Xn+1/.../Xm by the entry point Xn;
STEP 3: FOR each node xn in S
        BEGIN
            IF the path starting
             from root to node xn
             is not included in
          the path
          root/X1/X2/.../Xn-1/Xn
         THEN
       delete the sub tree
       that does not satisfy
       the path condition
           END
STEP 4: FOR each node xn in S,
       consider all sub trees
       starting with xn
         BEGIN
         IF Xn+1/.../Xm is same as
           /Xm
         THEN  return nodes Xm
         ELSE INPUT = Xn/Xn+1/.../Xm
            GO TO STEP 1
             END
```

Algorithm 1.1 Entry-point Root-first

```
INPUT: XPath expression
root/X1/X2/.../Xi/.../Xm
STEP 1: FOR each Xi
        BEGIN
         IF Xi is indexed THEN
           BEGIN
          get every node xi of
          type Xi. Get the DN
          ni of each xi
          Sumi = Σni;
           END
         END
STEP 2: get entry point Xn with minimum
Sum, add all xn to a node set S;
Consider the tree obtained after deleting all
branches that do not have the node xn in its
path.
split the XPath into root/X1/X2/.../Xn-1 and
/Xn+1.../Xm  by Xn entry point;
STEP 3: FOR each node xn in S
        BEGIN
            IF the path starting
             from node Xn to a
             leaf  node is not
             included in the path
             Xn/Xn+1/.../Xm
         THEN
         delete the sub tree
         that does not satisfy
         the path condition
          END
STEP 4: FOR each node xn in S,
       consider all sub trees
       starting with xn as
       leaf nodes
       BEGIN
       IF root/.../Xn is same as
          /Xn
        THEN  return nodes Xm
       ELSE INPUT= root/X1/X2/.../Xn
          GO TO STEP 1
          END
```

Algorithm 1.2 Entry-point Bottom-first

Next, we illustrate the Entry-point Root-first Algorithm.

Example: Let the XPath expression to be evaluated be A/B/C/E//H. Thus, we need to retrieve the three nodes marked by circle in Fig. 3. Assume that the indexes have been built on nodes B and E.

In Step1, we find the entry point E by calculating descent numbers of the nodes that have indexes. In Fig. 3, the descents of nodes B and E are shown in brackets. The descent numbers for nodes B and E come out to be 31 and 18 respectively. Thus, node E becomes the entry point. After applying Step 2, we obtain the DOM tree shown in Fig. 4. It is important to note that it is possible that the DN of an entry-level node at a higher level might be smaller than the DN of an entry-level node at a lower level of the DOM tree. This is possible for the case when there might be a large number of entry-level nodes at the lower level as compared to the number of entry-level nodes at a higher level of the DOM tree.

In step 3, we test A/B/C/E on each E node and discard the right most sub tree with node E. The tree obtained is shown in Fig. 5.

In step 4, we evaluate E//H on each E and finally we get the three H nodes.

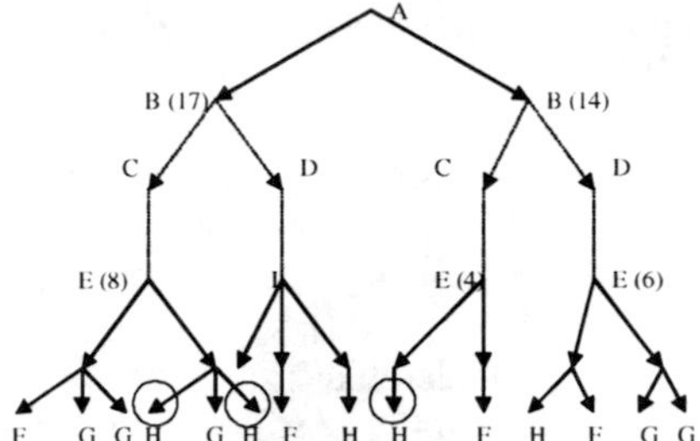

Fig. 3. Entry-point Algorithm

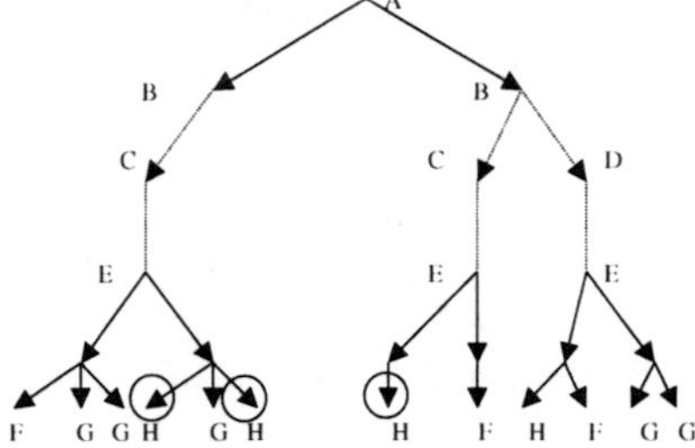

Fig. 4. Entry-point Algorithm (Cont.)

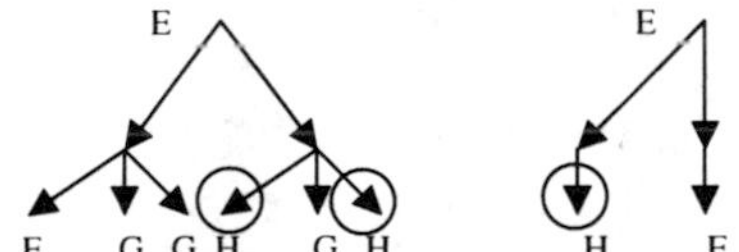

Fig. 5. Entry-point Algorithm (Cont.)

It is easy to see that the Entry-point algorithm will work with regular expressions too. We observe that if we are given an XPath expression of the form **root/X_1/X_2/.../X_i/.../X_m** where any expression X_i = *, we can check if the path of the entry point node x_n matches the given regular path **root/X_1/X_2/*/.../X_{n-1}/X_n** in Step 2 of the algorithm by using string matching and containment techniques. However, we need more study on "containment" relationship.

4 Rest-Tree Conception

In the Entry-point Algorithm we find an entry point among a number of middle level nodes and split the XPath expression to eliminate the nodes that do not satisfy the condition. Under certain conditions the Entry-point Algorithm may not perform well. For instance, in the BOOKSTORE database shown in Fig. 1, suppose we want to find out books written by "David" where the title of the book contains the word "book". The XML file might have hundreds of books having the word "book" in the title and further there might be a large number of books by author "David", but only one of them has the word "book" in its title. The Entry-point algorithm first eliminates all the nodes that do not have the word "book" in its title. Then it eliminates the nodes that do not have "David" as the author. Similarly in the Entry-point Bottom-first approach, the nodes that do not have "David" as the author name are eliminated first and then the parent nodes that do not have the word "book" in its title are eliminated. In this case, due to relatively large number of instances at the two levels, a large number of eliminations are required. We refine the Entry-point Algorithm to make it more efficient to handle such cases by selecting two or more entry-level points among the middle level nodes and eliminating the nodes based on those entry-level nodes.

Definition 2. Rest-Tree
The tree formed by the nodes that meet certain condition at its level, along with its descendant and ancestor nodes.

For example, in Figure 1, the Rest-tree of the node that satisfies the condition that the <BOOK> node has the word "glory" in its title, is formed by &1, &3, &9, and &10. In the first step we employ Entry-point Algorithm to find all nodes that meet the condition statements at each level. The final result will then be the intersection of the Rest-trees of these nodes.

In practice, we do not need to find the Rest-tree of every node satisfying the condition. Since we are left with only small set of nodes after applying the Entry-point Algorithm, we need to find the Rest-trees of a relatively small set of nodes within a small sub tree.

To get the intersection of rest-trees we note that the nodes that satisfy the query condition and that have the minimum number of descendants is available from the Entry-point Algorithm. The minimum level is the anchor level of the rest-tree algorithm. We just need to intersect the Rest-trees at this minimum level. For example, after the first step of Entry-point algorithm, we know there are 2000 nodes at Level A that meet say condition A, 1000 nodes at Level B that meet condition B, 200 nodes at Level C, 3000 at Level D, 400 at Level E. The minimum level is Level C and the ordering of the levels is C→E→B→A→D. As the ancestor node information is available as path-index, we can filter some nodes at Level C by checking the grandparent node information of the 400 nodes at Level E. Similarly, we can filter some other nodes at Level C by checking the parent node information of the nodes at Level B. The intersection at Level C will be complete by checking ancestor information at Level D nodes. The final step is to get all the nodes that satisfy the query requirement.

4.1 Rest-Tree Algorithm

The Entry-point algorithm finds the entry point and eliminates nodes at the entry level by checking ancestor level conditions, followed by checking descendant level conditions. However, as stated earlier, under certain conditions it might be better to check descendant level nodes and eliminate the nodes that do not satisfy the XPath expression. We can apply the elimination step either from the descendant level or ancestor level. It is better to begin with descendant level when the descent condition will eliminate more nodes than the ancestor level condition. Descendant level nodes have ancestor node information in the path-index. Using this information, we can eliminate entry-level nodes that do not satisfy the path condition of descendant nodes.

If the entry-level nodes are not in the set of ancestor nodes of valid descendant nodes, they are eliminated. Similarly, if the valid ancestor nodes are not in the path-information of entry-level nodes, those entry-level nodes are eliminated. Comparing the number of entry-level nodes that are eliminated in the Root-first and Bottom-first approach, it can be decided which level condition will be better to optimize the search. This can be implemented by testing if the number of valid descendant nodes is less than ancestor nodes; if so, select the descendant way, otherwise, vice versa. We now present the Rest-tree algorithm.

```
INPUT: XPath expression root/X_1/X_2/.../X_i/.../X_m
STEP 1:FOR each X_i
       BEGIN
              IF X_i is indexed THEN
            BEGIN
              get every node x_i of type X_i
          get the DN number n_i of each x_i
          Sum_i = Σn_i;
            END
       END
STEP 2: get entry point X_j with minimum Sum, add all x_j
     to a node set S_j;
          get comparison point X_k with second minimum Sum,
          add all x_k to a node set S_k;
STEP 3: IF level j > k THEN
       BEGIN
              FOR each node x_k in S_k
                     IF its ancestor is not in S_j THEN
                          delete x_k from S_k
            S_i = S_k
       END
       ELSE
            FOR each node x_j in S_j
                     IF its ancestor is not in S_k THEN
                          delete x_j from S_j
STEP 4: FOR each node x_j in S_j
        BEGIN
              IF the path starting from root to node x_j is
                 not included in the path root/X_1/X_2/.../X_j
              THEN
          delete the sub tree that does not satisfy the
          path condition
       END
STEP 5: FOR each node x_j in S_j, consider all sub trees
       starting with x_j
       BEGIN
           IF X_{j+1}/.../X_m is same as /X_m
                 THEN return nodes X_m
           ELSE INPUT = X_j/ X_{j+1}/.../X_m
                  GO TO STEP 1;
             END
```

Algorithm 2. Rest-tree Algorithm

5 Conclusions

In this paper, we have proposed three types of indexes on XML data to execute efficiently XPath queries. We proposed two algorithms to process XPath queries using these indexes to optimize the queries. We have simulated both Root-first and Bottom-first approaches and have observed that processing of XPath query using our Entry-point indexing technique performs much better than traditional algorithms with or without indexes (not reported here due to space constraint).

References

1. Abiteboul, S., Quass, D., McHugh, J., Widom, J., Wiener, J.L. The Lorel Query Language for Semistructured Data, International Journal on Digital Libraries. 1(1) (April 1997), pp. 68-88
2. Biron, P.V., Malhotra, A. (eds.). XML Schema Part 2: Datatypes W3C Recommendation, (May 2, 2001), http://www.w3.org/TR/xmlschema-2/ .
3. Ceri, S., Comai, S., Damiani, E., Fraternali, P., Paraboschi, S., Tanca, L. XML-GL: A Graphical Language for Querying and Restructuring XML Documents, In Proceedings of the 8th International World Wide Web Conference. Toronto, Canada (May 1999), pp. 93-109.
4. Chamberlin, D., Clark, J., Florescu, D., Robie, J., Siméon, J., Stefanescu, M.: Xquery 1.0: An XML Query Language. W3C Working Draft (20 December 2001).
5. Chamberlin, D., Robie, J., Florescu, J., Quilt: An XML Query Language for Heterogeneous Data Sources. In: International Workshop on the Web and Databases (WebDB) Dallas, TX (May 2000).
6. Berglund, A., Boag, S., Chamberlin, D., Fernandez, M.F., Kay, M., Robie, J., Siméon, J.: XML Path language (XPath) 2.0, W3C Working Draft, (20 December, 2001).
7. Deutsch, A., Fernandez, M., Florescu, D., Levy, A., Suciu, D., A Qquery Language for XML. In: Proceedings of the 8th International World Wide Web Conference, Toronto, Canada (May 1999), pp.77-91.
8. Goldman, R., Widom, J.: DataGuides: Enabling Query Formulation and Optimization in Semistructured Database. In: Proceedings of the Twenty-third International Conference on Very Large Data Bases. Athens, Greece (August 1997), pp. 436-445.
9. Li, Q., Moon, B. Indexing and Querying XML Data for Regular Path Expressions, In Proceedings of the 27th VLDB Conference, Roma, Italy (2001).
10. McHugh, J., Abiteboul, S., Goldman, R., Quass, D., Widom, J. Lore: A Database Management System for Semi-structured Data, SIGMQD Record, 26(3) (1997), pp. 54-66.
11. McHugh, J., Widom, J., Abiteboul, S., Luo, Q., Rajaraman, A. Indexing Semistructured Data. Technical Report, Stanford University, Stanford, CA (February 1998).
12. Milo, T., Suciu, D., Index Structures for Path Expressions, In Proceedings of the International Conference on Database Theory (1999), pp. 277-295.
13. Rizzolo, F., Mendelzon, A. Indexing XML Data with ToXin. Fourth International Workshop on the Web and Databases (in conjunction with ACM SIGMOD 2001), Santa Barbara, CA (May 2001).

Efficient Evaluation of Continuous Range Queries on Moving Objects *

D. Kalashnikov, S. Prabhakar, S. Hambrusch, and W. Aref

CS Dept., Purdue University, West Lafayette, IN 47907, USA
{dvk,sunil,seh,aref}@cs.purdue.edu

Abstract. In this paper we evaluate several in-memory algorithms for efficient and scalable processing of continuous range queries over collections of moving objects. Constant updates to the index are avoided by query indexing. No constraints are imposed on the speed or path of moving objects. We present a detailed analysis of a grid approach which shows the best results for both skewed and uniform data. A sorting based optimization is developed for significantly improving the cache hit ratio. Experimental evaluation establishes that indexing queries using the Grid index yields orders of magnitude better performance than other index structures such as R*-trees.

1 Introduction

The problem of handling different types of queries on moving objects has caught wide attention recently due to the development of location detection and wireless technologies [1][2][5][11]. Using these technologies, it is possible to develop systems where a local server tracks the locations of moving objects.

As an example, consider a system where aircraft are tracked by radar. Regions of space in which aircraft can be detected by enemy radar or anti-aircraft systems are identified by a server. The server continuously monitors the location of friendly aircraft with respect to these regions and issues alerts as soon as an aircraft is in a detection area. Alternatively, there might be areas where only specially designated aircraft are allowed to be. Such areas can be monitored continuously at the server to detect trespassers.

In this paper we address the problem of evaluating multiple concurrent continuous range queries on moving objects. In contrast to regular queries that are evaluated once, a continuous query remains active over a period of time and has to be continuously evaluated during this time. Each of these queries needs to be re-evaluated as the objects move. A solution for continuous *real-time* evaluation of queries that scales to large numbers of queries and objects is a major challenge.

Current efforts at evaluating queries over moving objects have focused on the development of disk-based indexes. The problem of scalable, real-time execution

* Work Supported by NSF grants 9988339-CCR, 9972883, 0010044-CCR, and Career award 9985019-IIS and a Gift from Microsoft Corporation.

R. Cicchetti et al. (Eds.): DEXA 2002, LNCS 2453, pp. 731–740, 2002.

of continuous queries may not be well suited for disk-based indexing for the following reasons: (i) the need to update the index as objects move; (ii) the need to re- evaluate all queries when any object moves; and (iii) achieving very short execution times for large numbers of moving objects and queries. These factors, combined with the drastically dropping main memory costs makes main memory evaluation highly attractive.

The location of a moving object can be represented in memory as a 2-dimensional point while its other attributes can be stored on disk. One local server is likely to be responsible for handling a limited number of moving objects (e.g. 1,000,000). For such settings, for even large problem sizes, all the necessary data and auxiliary structures, can be easily kept in the main memory of a high-end workstation.

In order for the solution to be effective it is necessary to efficiently compute the matching between large numbers of objects and queries. While multidimensional indexes tailored for main memory, as proposed in [5], would perform better than disk-oriented structures, the use of an index on the moving objects suffers from the need for constant updating as the objects move – resulting in degraded performance. To avoid this constant updating and to improve the processing of continuous queries, we propose a very different approach: *Query Indexing*. In contrast to the traditional approach of building an index on the moving objects, we propose to build an index on the queries. This approach is especially suited for evaluating continuous queries over moving objects, since the queries remain active for long periods of time, and objects are constantly moving.

In this paper we investigate several in-memory index structures for efficient and scalable processing of continuous queries. We evaluate not only indexes designed to be used in main memory but also disk-based indexes adapted and optimized for main memory. Our results show that using a simple grid-like structure gives the best performance for uniform and, surprisingly, also for highly skewed data. We also propose an effective technique for improving the caching performance and an analysis of the optimal grid size. The growing importance of moving object environments is reflected in the recent body of work addressing issues such as indexing, uncertainty management, broadcasting, and models for spatio-temporal data. Optimization of disk-based index structures has been explored recently for B^+-trees [10] and multidimensional indexes [5]. Both studies investigate the redesign of the nodes in order to improve cache performance. Neither study addresses the problem of executing continuous queries or the constant movement of objects (changes to data). The goal of our technique is to efficiently and continuously re-generate the mapping between moving objects and queries. Our technique makes no assumptions about the future positions of objects. It is also not necessary for objects to move according to well-behaved patterns as in [11]. The problem of scalable, efficient computation of continuous range queries over moving objects is ideally suited for main memory evaluation. Spatio-temporal database models and techniques for handling moving objects are also proposed in [3] [6] [7] [8] [12]. To the best of our knowledge no existing work addresses the main memory execution of multiple concurrent queries on moving objects as proposed in the following sections.

Due to space constraints several details have been omitted. A more detailed version of this paper is available [4]. The remainder of this paper is organized as follows. Section 2 describes continuous query processing, Query Indexing, and the index structures considered. We also present an effective technique for improving the cache hit rate. Section 3 presents the experimental results and Section 4 concludes the paper.

2 Continuous Query Evaluation

2.1 Query Indexing

The problem of continuous query evaluation is: *Given a set of queries and a set of moving objects, continuously determine the set of objects that are contained within each query*[1]. Clearly, with a large number of queries and moving objects, it is infeasible to re-evaluate each query whenever any object moves. A more practical approach is to re-evaluate all queries periodically taking into account the latest positions of all objects. In order for the results to be useful, a short re-evaluation period is desired. The goal of the query evaluation techniques is therefore to re-evaluate all queries in as short a time as possible.

A naïve solution is to compare each object against each query in every period. Another approach is building an index (e.g. R-tree) on the objects to speed up the queries. Although for regular queries this would result in improvements in performance over the naïve approach, it suffers a major drawback for the moving objects environment: the index needs to be continuously updated as object positions change. Maintaining such an index on mobile data is a challenging task [11].

This paper build on the idea of *Query Indexing* proposed in [9]. Instead of building an index on the moving objects (which would require frequent updating), create an index on the more stable queries . Any spatial index structure can be used to build the query index (e.g. R*-tree, Quad-tree, etc.).

The evaluation of continuous queries in each cycle proceeds as follows. For object P, let $P.qset$ denote the set of all queries in which P is contained. For query Q, let $Q.pset$ denote the set of objects contained in Q. The goal is to compute the set $Q.pset$ for each query Q based upon the current locations of the objects by the end of each cycle. Because of the lack of speed limitations $Q.pset$ and $P.qset$ are likely to be completely different from one cycle to the next. Consequently, incremental solutions are of little value. In each cycle, we first use the query index to compute $P.qset$ for each object P. Next, for each query Q in $P.qset$, we add P to $Q.pset$.

Some important consequences of indexing the queries instead of the data should be noted. Firstly, the index needs no modification unless there is a change

[1] This approach can be easily extended to compute point to query mapping, handle region queries, answer simple density queries (e.g. monitor how many people are in a building) etc.

to the set of queries a relatively less frequent event in comparison to changes to object locations since we are dealing with continuous queries. Secondly, the location of an object can change greatly from one cycle to the next without having any impact on the performance. In other words, there is no restriction on the nature of movement or speed of the objects. This is an advantage since many known object indexing techniques rely upon certain assumptions about the movement of objects. Next we discuss the feasibility of in-memory query indexing by evaluating different types of indexes for queries.

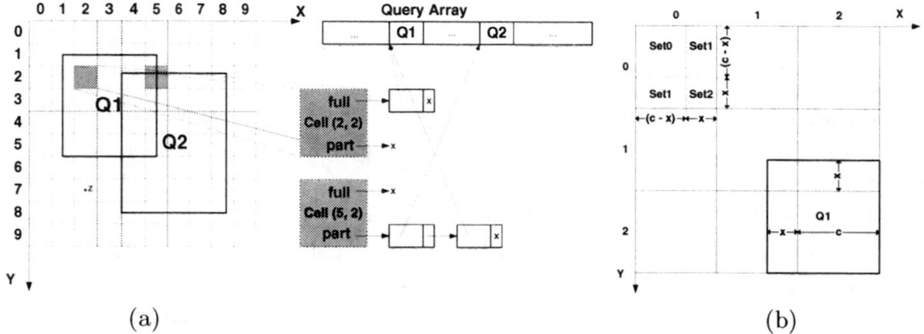

Fig. 1. (a) Example of Grid (b) Choosing grid size

2.2 Indexing Techniques

We consider the following five well-known index structures: R*-tree, R-tree, CR-tree, quad-tree, and Grid. The R-tree and R*-tree index structures are designed to be disk-based structures. The CR-tree [5], on the other hand, is a variant of R-trees optimized for main memory. All of these indexes were implemented for main memory use. In order to make a fair comparison, we did not choose large node sizes for these trees. Instead, we experimentally determined the best choice of node size for main-memory evaluation. All three indexes (R*-tree, R-tree, and CR-tree) showed best performance when the number of entries per node was chosen to be five. This value was used for all experiments.

Because many variations exist, we describe the Grid index as it is used here for query indexing. The Grid index is a 2-dimensional array of "cells". Each cell represents a region of space generated by partitioning the domain using a uniform grid. Figure 1a shows an example of a Grid. Throughout the paper, we assume that the domain is normalized to the unit square.

In this example, the domain is divided into a 10×10 grid of 100 cells, each of size 0.1×0.1. Since we have a uniform grid, given the coordinates of an object, it is easy to calculate the cell that it falls under in O(1) time. Each cell contains two lists that are identified as *full* and *part* (see Figure 1a). The *full* (*part*) list of a cell contains *pointers* to all the queries that fully (partially) cover the cell. The choice of data structures for the *full* and *part* lists is critical for performance. We implemented these lists as dynamic-arrays[2] rather than lists which improve performance by roughly 40%.

An analytical solution for the appropriate choice of grid size is presented in Section 2.3. As will be seen in the experimental section, this simple one-level Grid index outperforms all other structures for uniform as well as skewed data. However, for the case of highly skewed data (e.g. roughly half the queries fall within one cell), the *full* and *part* lists grow too large. Such situations are easily handled by switching to a two-tier Grid. If any of the lists grows beyond a threshold value, the grid index converts to a directory grid and a few secondary grids. The directory grid is used to determine which secondary grid to use. Each directory grid cell points to a secondary grid. The secondary grid is used in the same way as the one-level grid. While this idea of generating an extra layer can be applied as many times as is necessitated by the data distribution, three or more layers is unlikely to lead to a better performance in practice. Consider for example, that the domain of interest represents a 1000-kilometer by 1000-kilometer region. With a 1000×1000 grid, a cell of the two-tier grid corresponds a square of side 1 meter - it is very unlikely that there will be very many objects or queries in such a small region in practice.

Observe that the Grid index and the quad-tree are closely related. Both are space partitioning and split a region if it is overfull. There is, however, a subtle difference: the Grid index avoids many conditional ("if") branches in its search algorithm due to its shorter height. Furthermore, the Grid index is not a tree since siblings can point to a common "child" [4].

Another advantage of the Grid is that it typically has far more cells per level. A quad-tree therefore can be very deep, especially for skewed data. We expect that a quad-tree like structure that has more cells per level would perform better than a standard quad-tree. In order to test this hypothesis, we also consider what we call a 32-tree. The 32-tree is identical to a quad-tree, except that it divides a cell using a 32×32 grid, compared to the 2×2 grid used by the quad-tree. As with the Grid index, pointers to children are used instead of keeping an array of pointers to children. In order to further improve performance, we implemented the following optimization: In addition to leaf nodes, internal nodes can also have an associated *full* list. Only leaf nodes have a *part* list. A *full* list contains all queries that fully cover the bounding rectangle (BR) of the node, but do not fully cover the BR of its parent. Adding a rectangle (or region) to a node proceed as follows. If the rectangle fully covers the BR, it is added to the *full* list and the algorithm stops for that node. If this is a leaf node and there is space in the *part* list, the rectangle is added to *part* list. Otherwise the set of all relevant children is determined and the procedure is applied to each of them.

Storing *full* lists in non-leaf nodes has two advantages. One advantage is saving of space: without such lists, when a query fully covers a node's BR it would be duplicated in all the node's children. A second advantage is that it has

---

[2] A dynamic array is a standard data structure for arrays whose size adjusts dynamically.

the potential to speed up point queries. If a point query falls within the BR of a node then it is relevant to all queries in the *full* list of this node - no further checks are needed. A leaf node split is based on the *part* list size only. While many more optimizations are possible, we did not explore these further. The purpose of studying the 32-tree is to establish the generality and flexibility of the Grid-based approach.

2.3 Choice of Grid Size

We now present a sketch of an analysis of appropriate choice for the cell size for the Grid index in the context of main-memory query indexing. Consider the case where m square queries with side q - uniformly distributed on $[0, 1] \times [0, 1]$ - are added to index (see Figure 1a). Let c denote the side of each cell. Then q can be represented as $ic + x$, where $x \in [0, c)$ and i is an integer. By analyzing the average length of *part* list in each cell [4] proves that cell side size c should be chosen as: $c = \begin{cases} \frac{1}{4qm} & \text{if } q > \frac{1}{2\sqrt{m}}; \\ \frac{1}{\sqrt{m}} - q & \text{otherwise.} \end{cases}$ and smaller values of c give only minor performance improvement.

For our example in Figure 4a we have $m = 25,000$ and $q = 0.01$. Since $\frac{1}{2\sqrt{m}} = 0.001 < q$, the first formula should be used, i.e. $c = 1/4qm = 0.001$. This means that grid should be of size 1000×1000 and a finer grid will give only minor performance improvement while incurring a large memory penalty. We study the impact of tile size in the experimental section and show that the results match the analytical prediction.

2.4 Improving the Cache Hit Rate

The performance of main-memory algorithms is greatly affected by cache hit rates. In this section we describe an optimization that can drastically improve cache hit rates (and consequently the overall performance) for the query indexing approach. In each cycle the processing involves searching the index structure for each objects current location in order to determine the queries that cover it.

For each object, its cell is computed, and the *full* and *part* lists of this cell are accessed. The algorithm simply processes objects in sequential order in the array. If we expect that objects will maintain their locality, then we can improve cache-hit rates by altering the order of processing the objects. We re-order objects in the array such that objects that are close together in our 2D domain are also close together in the object array. In this situation everything relevant to a given cell is likely to remain in the CPU cache after the first processing and will be reused from the cache during the second processing. The speed up effect is also achieved because objects that are close together are more likely to be covered by the same queries than objects that are far apart, thus queries are more likely to be retrieved from the cache rather than from main memory.

Sorting the objects to ensure that objects that are close to each other are also close in the array order can easily be achieved by various methods. We choose to use a sorting based on the Z-order.

It is important to understand that *the use of this technique does not require that objects have to preserve their locality.* The only effect of sorting the objects according to their earlier positions is to alter the order in which objects are processed in each cycle. The objects are still free to move arbitrarily. Of course, the *effectiveness* of this technique relies upon objects maintaining their locality over a period of time. If it turns out that objects do not maintain their locality then we are, on the average, no worse than the situation in which we do not sort. It should also be noted that the exact position used for each object is not important. Thus the sorting can be carried out infrequently (say once a day).

3 Experimental Results

In this section we present the performance results for the index structures. Each index structure was implemented and tested, not simulated. The results report the actual times for the execution of the various algorithms. First we describe the parameters of the experiments, followed by the results and discussion.

In all our experiments we used a 1GHz Pentium III machine with 2GB of memory. The machine has 32K of level-1 cache (16K for instructions and 16K for data) and 256K level-2 cache. Moving objects were represented as points distributed on the unit square $[0,1] \times [0,1]$. The number of objects ranges from 100,000 to 1,000,000. Range-queries were represented as squares with sides 0.01. Experiments with other sizes of queries yielded similar results and are thus omitted. We considered the following distributions for objects and queries:

1. **Uniform**: Objects and queries are uniformly distributed.
2. **Skewed**: The objects and queries are distributed among five clusters. Within each cluster objects and data are distributed normally with a standard deviation of 0.05 for objects and 0.1 for queries.
3. **Hyper-skewed**: Half of the objects (queries) are distributed uniformly on $[0,1] \times [0,1]$, the other half on $[0,0.001] \times [0,0.001]$. Queries in $[0,0.001] \times [0,0.001]$ are squares with sides 0.00001 to avoid excessive selectivity.

We consider the skewed case to be most representative. The hyper-skewed case represents a pathological situation designed to study the performance of the schemes under extreme skew. In the majority of our experiments the Grid was chosen to consist of 1000×1000 cells. The testing proceeds as follows: First, queries and objects are generated and put into arrays. Then the index is initialized and the queries are added to it. Then in each cycle, we first update the locations followed by an evaluation of the query results.

Comparing efficiency of indexes: Figure 2a shows the results for various combinations of number of objects and queries with uniform distribution. The y-axis gives the processing time for one cycle in seconds for each experiment. Figure 2b shows similar results for the skewed case.

Each cycle consists of two steps: (i)*moving* objects (i.e., determining current object locations) and (ii)*processing*. From Figure 2b for the case of 100,000 objects and 100,000 queries we can see that the evaluation step for Grid takes 0.628

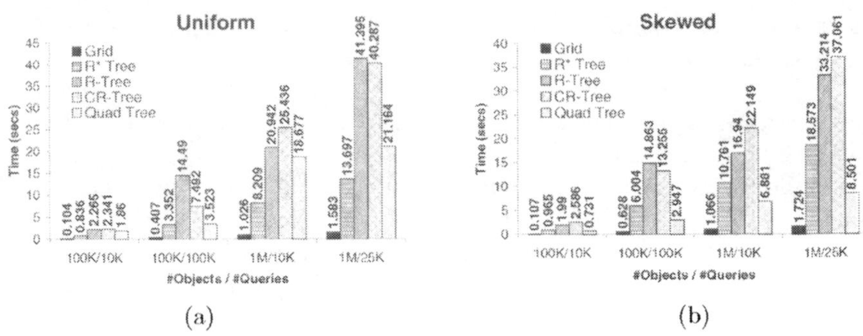

(a) (b)

Fig. 2. Index comparison for (a) uniform (b) skewed

seconds. Updating/determining object locations takes 0.15 seconds for 100K objects and 1.5 seconds for 1M objects on the average. Thus the length of each cycle is just 0.778 seconds on the average.

The Grid index gives the best performance in all these cases. While the superior performance of Grid for the uniform case is expected, the case for skewed data is surprising. For all experiments the Grid index consisted of only a single level. Figure 3a shows the results for the hyper-skewed case. For the hyper-skewed case, the grid switches from one-tier to two-tier due to an overfull cell. The processing time for a simple one-tier grid is too high, as expected, and is not shown on the figure. It is interesting to see that the Grid index once again outperforms the other schemes. There is a significant difference in performance of Grid and the other approaches for all three distributions. For example, with 1,000,000 objects and 25,000 queries, Grid evaluates all queries in 1.724 seconds as compared to 33.2 seconds for the R-tree, and 8.5 seconds for the quad-tree. This extremely fast evaluation implies that with the Grid index, the cycle time is very small - in other words, we can re-compute the set of objects contained in each query every 3.2 seconds or faster (1.7 seconds for the evaluation step plus

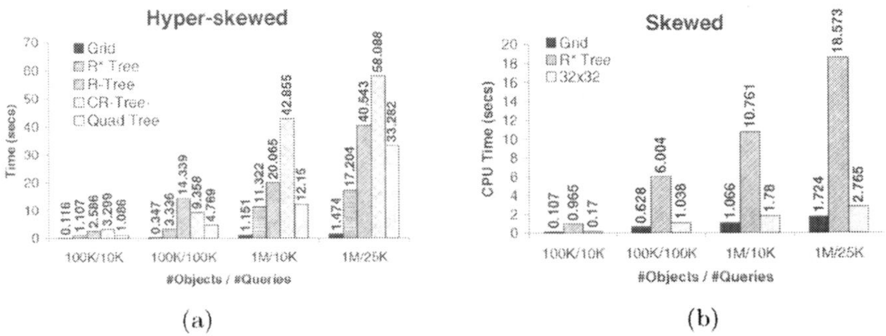

(a) (b)

Fig. 3. (a) Index comparison for hyper-skewed (b) Performance of 32-tree

1.5 seconds for updating the locations of objects). This establishes the feasibility of in-memory query indexing for managing continuous queries.

32-Tree index: The performance of the 32-tree (see Section 2.2) along with that for the Grid and R*-tree for skewed data is shown in Figure 3b. As can be seen from the graph our hypothesis is true: the performance of the 32-tree lies between that of the R*-tree and the Grid. Graphs for uniform and hyper-skewed data exhibit similar patterns and omitted due to the space limitations.

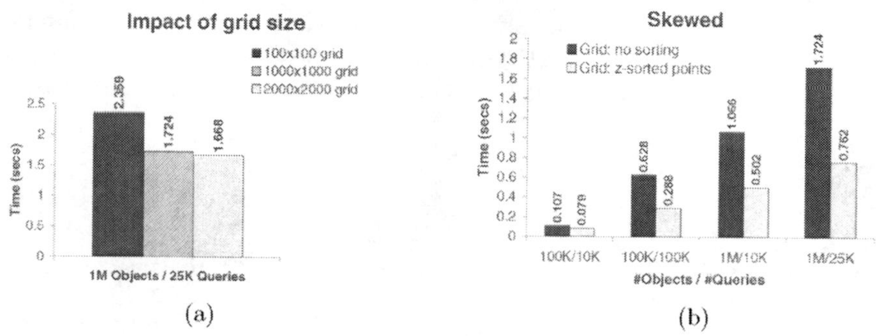

Fig. 4. a) Impact of grid size on processing time. b) Effectiveness of Z-Sorting.

Choice of Grid Size: In this experiment we study the impact of the number of cells in the grid. The analysis in Section 2.3 predicted that a 1000×1000 grid should be chosen for the settings of this example. Figure 4a presents the processing time needed with grid sizes 100×100, 1000×1000, and 2000×2000 cells. As can be seen, increasing the number of cells has the effect of reducing the average number of queries for a cell thereby reducing the processing time. There is a substantial increase in performance as we move from 100×100 cells to 1000×1000 cells. The increase is minor when we move from 1000×1000 to 2000×2000 cells for our case of 1M objects and 25K queries. This behavior validates the analytical results.

Z-Sort Optimization: Figure 4b illustrates the effect of the Z-Sort technique on evaluation time for ideally Z-sorted data. From the results, we see that sorting objects improves the performance by roughly 50%. The Z-sort technique was used only for this experiment.

Modifying the Grid: Although modifications to queries are expected to be rare, adding or removing queries is very efficient for the Grid. For example, 25K quereis were added or deleted (with equal probability) to/from an index which intially contained 25K queries in only 2.408 seconds. Therefore we see that even significant changes to the query set can be effectively handled by the Grid approach.

4 Summary

In this paper we studied in-memory evaluation of multiple concurrent continuous range queries on moving objects with the *Query-Indexing* approach. A significant characteristic of our approach is that no constraints are imposed on speed and path of movement of objects. We presented results for several different in-memory spatial indexes. The Grid approach showed the best result even for the skewed case. A technique of sorting the objects to improve the cache hit-ratio was presented. The performance of the Grid index was roughly doubled with this optimization. An analysis for selecting grid size and experimental validation was presented. Overall, indexing the queries using the Grid index gives orders of magnitude better performance than other index structures such as R*-trees.

References

1. P. K. Agarwal, L. Arge, and J. Erickson. Indexing moving points. In *Proc. of ACM SIGMOD-SIGACT-SIGART symposium on Principles of database systems*, Dallas, TX, May 2000.
2. L. Forlizzi, R. H. Guting, E. Nardelli, and M. Scheider. A data model and data structures for moving objects databases. In *Proc. of ACM SIGMOD Conf.*, 2000.
3. R. Guting, M.H.Bohlen, M. Erwig, C. Jensen, N. Lorentzos, M. Schneider, and M. Vazirgiannis. A foundation for representing and querying moving objects. *ACM Transactions on Database Systems*, 2000.
4. D. V. Kalashnikov, S. Prabhakar, S. Hambrusch, and W. Aref. Efficient evaluation of continuous range queries on moving objects. In *TR 02-015*, Purdue University, June 2002.
5. K. Kim, S. Cha, and K. Kwon. Optimizing mutidimensional index trees for main memory access. In *Proc. of ACM SIGMOD Conf.*, Santa Barbara, CA, May 2001.
6. G. Kollios, D. Gunopulos, and V. Tsotras. On indexing mobile objects. In *Proc. ACM PODS*, Philadelphia, June 1999.
7. A. Kumar, V. J. Tsotras, and C. Faloutsos. Designing access methods for bitemporal databases. 10(1), 1998.
8. D. Pfoser, C. Jensen, and Y. Theodoridis. Novel approaches in query processing for moving objects. In *Proc. of VLDB Conf.*, Cairo, Egypt, September 2000.
9. S. Prabhakar, Y. Xia, D. Kalashnikov, W. Aref, and S. Hambrusch. Query indexing and velocity constrained indexing: Scalable techniques for continuous queries on moving objects. In *IEEE Transactions on Computers, Special Issue on DBMS and Mobile Computing.* To appear.
10. J. Rao and K. A. Ross. Making B^+-trees cache conscious in main memory. In *Proc. of ACM SIGMOD Conf.*, Dallas, TX, May 2000.
11. S. Saltenis, C. Jensen, S. Leutenegger, and M. Lopez. Indexing the position of continuously moving objects. In *Proc. of ACM SIGMOD Conf.*, 2000.
12. O. Wolfson, P. A. Sistla, S. Chamberlain, and Y. Yesha. Updating and querying databases that track mobile units. *Distributed and Parallel Databases*, 7(3), 1999.

Partition-Based Similarity Join in High Dimensional Data Spaces

Hyoseop Shin[1], Bongki Moon[2], and Sukho Lee[3]

[1] Software Center
Samsung Electronics Co., LTD.
Seoul, Korea
hyoseop@samsung.com

[2] Department of Computer Science
University of Arizona
Tucson, AZ 85721
bkmoon@cs.arizona.edu

[3] School of Computer Science and Engineering
Seoul National University
Seoul, Korea
shlee@cse.snu.ac.kr

Abstract. It is not desirable in the performance perspective of search algorithms to partition a high dimensional data space by dividing all the dimensions. This is because the number of cells resulted from partitioning explodes as the number of partitioning dimensions increases, thus making any search method based on space partitioning impractical. To address this problem, we propose an algorithm to dynamically select partitioning dimensions based on a data sampling method for efficient similarity join processing. Futhermore, a disk-based plane sweeping method is proposed to minimize the cost of joins between the partitioned cells. The experimental results show that the proposed schemes substantially improve the performance of the partition-based similarity joins in high dimensional data spaces.

1 Introduction

Efficient processing of similarity joins in a high dimensional space is crucial in many application areas such as image and multimedia databases, time-series databases, and data warehouse and data mining.

For two data sets, R and S, of d-dimensional data points, a similarity join query is formulated as:

$$R \bowtie S = \{(r,s) | \left(\sum_{i=1}^{d} |r_i - s_i|^p \right)^{1/p} \leq \varepsilon, r \in R, s \in S\} \tag{1}$$

where r and s are represented as $[r_1, r_2, \ldots, r_d]$ and $s = [s_1, s_2, \ldots, s_d]$, respectively. The formula returns point pairs of R and S whose distances in the data

R. Cicchetti et al. (Eds.): DEXA 2002, LNCS 2453, pp. 741–750, 2002.

space are less than or equal to a cut-off similarity value, ε. The Euclidean distance, in which p is set to 2, is generally used to compute the distance between points.

Similarity join queries are similar to spatial join queries [4,7] or distance join queries [6,13] in the spatial databases in that both make use of the *overlap* or *distance* between objects in a data space to determine whether to pair them together or not. The difference mainly lies in the dimensionality. In a low dimensional space, many index structures including R-tree [5] and its variants [2,3] are available and these indexes can be useful in processing spatial joins efficiently. Even without indexes available, some partition-based spatial join algorithms [11,10] are known to be competitive to the algorithms using indexes. Basically, most of these spatial join methods are based on the assumption that a data space can be partitioned in an efficient way. Though space partitioning methods in the low dimensions may be applicable to similarity join queries in high dimensional spaces, its direct application may cause serious problems. First of all, it is not possible in practical point of view to partition a high dimensional space by employing all the dimension axes. This is because the number of cells resulted from partitioning explodes as the number of dimension axes participating in the partitioning increases, thus making any search method based on space partitioning impractical. For example, let each dimension axis be divided into 10 continuous sub-intervals, then the number of cells generated after being partitioned will be $10^8, 10^{16}, 10^{32}, 10^{64}$ for 8, 16, 32, 64 dimensions, respectively, and it is likely that these numbers are usually larger than the number of the points in the original data sets before being partitioned. Another problem of the partition-based methods for similarity join processing in high dimensional data spaces is that most of the cells after being partitioned are so sparse that the cost of disk I/O for join processing between cells is likely to be very high. Lastly, there are so many spatially-neighbored cells for each partitioned cell that the number of joins between cells becomes larger, too. For these reasons, it is not desirable to employ all the dimension axes in partitioning high dimensional data spaces.

To address this problem, in this paper we propose an algorithm to dynamically select partitioning dimensions based on a data sampling method for efficient partition-based similarity join processing. The algorithm not only determines the number of dimensions for use in partitioning but also yields dimension axes which partition the data spaces to most efficiently process similarity joins for given data sets and a cut-off similarity value, ε. Furthermore, a disk-based plane sweeping method is proposed to minimize the cost of joins between skewed cells.

This paper is organized as follows. In Section 2, related work is described. Section 3 explains the overview of the partition-based similarity join. Section 4 presents the dimension selection algorithm for efficient partition-based similarity join processing. Section 5 presents a disk-based plane-sweeping method for join processing between skewed cells. Experimental results for the proposed methods are reported in Section 6. In Section 7, the conclusion of this paper is presented.

2 Related Work

Several methods for similarity join processing in high dimensional data spaces have been reported in the literature. Shim et al. [12] proposed an indexing structure, ε-kdB-tree, to process similarity join queries. The data space is subdivided into a series of stripes of the width, ε, along one selected dimension axis. And then, each stripe is constructed as a main memory data structure, the ε-kdB-tree in which dimension axes are chosen in order to partition the space recursively so that the search space is reduced while processing joins between nodes of the ε-kdB-trees. The main drawback of this method is that severe performance decrease occurs due to possible random disk accesses if each tree does not fit in main memory. Koudas and Sevick [8] proposed to use space filling curves to partition the high dimensional spaces. Each data point is converted as a hypercube of the side-length, ε, and then each cube is assigned a level value corresponding to the size of the largest cell that contains the cube. In joining step, each cube is associated with the cubes in the other set of which level is higher than or same as its own level. This method also has been reported to suffer performance decrease with increasing dimensions, as most of the cubes are mapped to a very high level [1]. Böhm et al. [1] proposed the epsilon grid order algorithm for the similarity join problem. A regular grid of the side-length, ε, is laid over the data space, anchored in the origin. Then, the lexicographical order is defined on the grid cells. With this ordering of data points, it can be shown that all join mates of a point p lie within an interval of the file. The lower and upper limit of the interval is determined by subtracting and adding the vector $[\epsilon, \epsilon, \ldots, \epsilon]^T$ to p, respectively. This is illustrated in Fig. 1. In Fig. 1, the striped grid cells are considered to be computed for pairing with the specified grid cell, p. The number of grid cells in an interval, however, tends to get larger as the dimension increases.

The TV-tree [9] has been proposed as a structure to index the high dimensional data using only part of the entire dimensions. The TV-tree is mainly for efficient search on single data set, while the dimension selection method in this paper dynamically selects the dimensions for efficient similarity joins on two associated data sets.

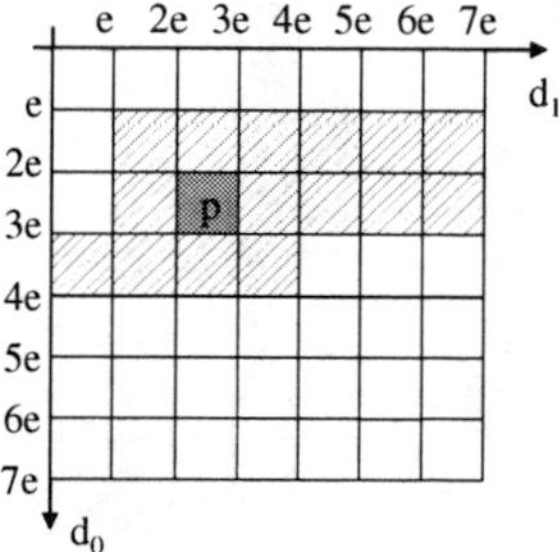

Fig. 1. Epsilon Grid Order-Based Similarity Join

3 Partition-Based Similarity Joins

In this section, the general approach of the partition-based similarity join is described and the difficulties in applying the approach for high dimensional data are explained. The partition-based similarity join consists of two steps, partition step and join step. In the partition step, the entire data space is partitioned into cube-shaped cells by dividing each dimension. We assume without loss of generality that all the data points are within an unit hypercube. As each dimension value ranges between [0,1], each dimension is partitioned into $\lceil 1/\varepsilon \rceil$ intervals of the width, ε. And then, each point in the data sets, R and S, which participate in the similarity join, is assigned to the cell to which it belongs. Note that two separate sets of cells exist for the two data sets. The Fig. 2 illustrates the partitioned data space after the partition step. The small rectangles in the figure represent the resulted cells.

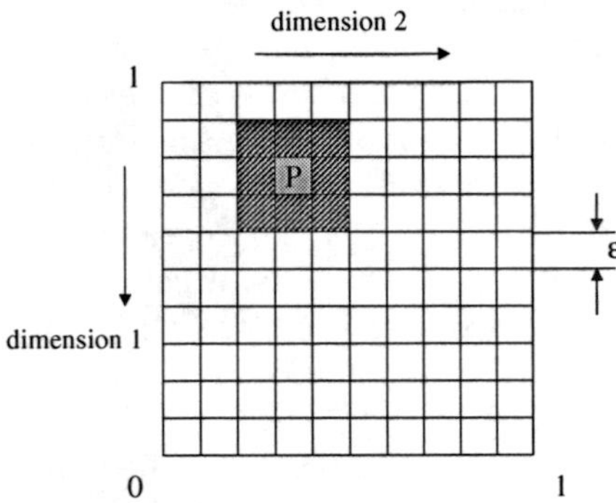

Fig. 2. Partition-Based Similarity Join : The Partition Step

In the join step of the partition-based similarity join, actual join computations are performed between cells from the two input data sets. Each cell from R does not need to be paired with every cell from S, but is paired only with the cells which it overlaps or neighbors in the data space. For example, in the Fig. 2, a cell, P shall be paired with one cell overlapping with it and eight cells surrounding it. Generally, in d dimensional data space, a cell in a data set that is not located at a border of the unit hypercube should be paired with 3^d cells in the other set.

4 Partitioning Dimensions

4.1 Motivation

In case of high dimensions, if a data space is divided by employing all the dimensions during the partition step, the number of cells resulted from the partitioning may explode so that the data skew problem can be serious. This consequently causes to lessen the effect of search space reduction by space partitioning, while increasing additional costs during the join step.

Theoretically, under an assumption that data points are uniformly distributed in the data space, given the two input data sets, R and S, and the number of partitioning dimensions, d_p, the CPU cost of the partition-based similarity join, which is computed by counting the number of distance computations between data points, is formulated as follows:

$$Cost(CPU) = |R| \times |S| \times (\frac{3}{\lceil 1/\varepsilon \rceil})^{d_p} \quad (2)$$

Meanwhile, the disk I/O cost, which is computed by counting the number of disk blocks visited, is formulated as follows:

$$Cost(IO) = |R|_{block} + 3^{d_p} \times |S|_{block} \quad (3)$$

for the total number of disk blocks, $|R|_{block}$ for R and $|S|_{block}$ for S.

According to the Equation 2 and 3, as the partitioning dimension, d_p, increases, the CPU cost of the partition-based similarity join decreases(if we assume that $\lceil 1/\varepsilon \rceil > 3$), while the I/O cost increases. This implies that there is a trade-off between the CPU cost and the I/O cost in regard to the performance of the partition-based similarity joins and it is desirable to determine the converging dimensionality. In this aspect, we propose methods for the partition-based similarity joins to determine the number of partitioning dimensions and to select partitioning dimensions.

4.2 The Number of Partitioning Dimensions

As mentioned in the previous section, all the dimensions cannot be used in dividing the data space. To determine the number of partitioning dimensions, we pre-estimated average cell size to be same as the size of a disk block. Then, the number of cells, N_p, to be generated after a partition step is computed as:

$$N_p = \frac{Min(|R|_{block}, |S|_{block})}{blockSize} \quad (4)$$

for the size of a disk block, $blockSize$. And also, the number of cells after the partition step can be computed in other way for given the number of partitioning dimension, d_p, and a partition sub-interval, ε:

$$N'_p = (\lceil 1/\varepsilon \rceil)^{d_p} \quad (5)$$

From the equation, $N_p = N'_p$, we can obtain the number of partitioning dimensions, d_p, as follows:

$$d_p = \frac{log \frac{Min(|R|_{block}, |S|_{block})}{blockSize}}{log \lceil 1/\varepsilon \rceil} \quad (6)$$

4.3 Selection of Partitioning Dimensions

With increasing dimensions, the domain cardinality of a data space grows exponentially ($O(c^d)$ for a dimension d), and accordingly data points in a high dimensional data space are likely to be distributed sparsely and skewedly in most regions of the data space. This data skewness can also happen when data points are projected into each dimension axis. So, it is desirable to select dimension axes that show more uniform data distributions for efficient partitioning of a data space. As the similarity join processing associate two input data sets, a dimension which yields rather uniform data distribution on one input data set may yield non-uniform data distribution on the other input data set. Futhermore, the degree of the uniformity even for one data set can change according to the cut-off similarity value. For these reasons, the partitioning dimensions for the similarity joins should be selected under the consideration of the associated two input data sets as well as the cut-off similarity value.

In this paper, to determine partitioning dimensions, we pre-computed the expected join cost for each dimension when data points of the input data sets are projected onto each dimension axis. After the join cost for each dimension compared, the d_p dimensions for which the join costs are smallest are selected as the partitioning dimensions. Note that the number of partitioning dimensions, d_p, is determined by the Equation 6. Algorithm 1 represents the algorithm, *DimSelect* which selects partitioning dimensions for the partition-based similarity joins.

The join cost for a dimension is computed as follows. First, as the space of a dimension axis is divided by a similarity cut-off value, ε, the space is divided into $\lceil 1/\varepsilon \rceil$ cells of length, ε. Second, the number of data points to be included in each cell from the input data sets are counted(line 4-6, 7-9). Third, each cell in one input data set is paired with three cells in the other input data set, a cell at the left side of it, one at the right side of it, and one overlapping with it. This is illustrated in Fig. 3 for the two input data sets, R and S.

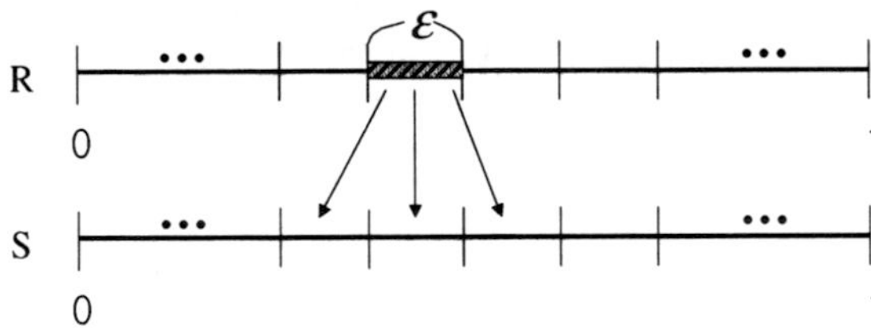

Fig. 3. The Computation of the Join Cost for a Partitioning Dimension

The cost of a join between two cells is computed by counting the number of distance computations between data points from the two cells. The number of distance computations between cells are computed by multiplying the number of data points of the cells(line 10-14). The total join cost for a dimension is obtained by the summation of the join costs between cells.

Note here that the data points of the two input data sets are not required to be actually partitioned into each cell to examine the number of data points belonging to each cell on a dimension. Moreover, to avoid a sequential scan of the entire data sets in estimating the join costs of the dimensions, we sampled small part of the data sets.

5 Disk-Based Plane Sweeping

The d_p partitioning dimensions chosen, the $(\lceil 1/\varepsilon \rceil)^{d_p}$ cells are generated for each input data set after the partition step. Each cell in one data set participates in cell-based join computations with 3^{d_p} cells in the other input data set which overlap or intersect with it in the data space. Cell-based joins are processed through a plane-sweeping method to reduce join costs. For a plane-sweeping processing, data points in each cell are sorted on a dimension axis during the partition step.

---

set the number of cells, $n_p \leftarrow \lceil 1/\varepsilon \rceil$;
initialize cell arrays, $P_R[1 \ldots d][1 \ldots d] \leftarrow 0, P_S[1 \ldots d][1 \ldots d] \leftarrow 0$;
initialize the number of distance computations for each dimension, $JoinCost[1 \ldots d] \leftarrow 0$;
// compute the number of entities for each partition
for *each entity* $(e_1, e_2, \ldots, e_d)$ *in* R_s **do**
    for *each dimension* i *in* $[1 \ldots d]$ **do**
        $P_R[i][\lceil n_p \times e_i \rceil] ++$;
    endfor
endfor
for *each entity* $(e_1, e_2, \ldots, e_d)$ *in* S_s **do**
    for *each dimension* i *in* $[1 \ldots d]$ **do**
        $P_S[i][\lceil n_p \times e_i \rceil] ++$;
    endfor
endfor
// compute the join cost for each dimension
for *each dimension* i *in* $[1 \ldots d]$ **do**
    for *each cell number* p *in* $[1 \ldots n_p]$ **do**
        if $i > 1$ **then** $JoinCost[i] \leftarrow JoinCost[i] + P_R[i][p] \times P_S[i][p-1]$;
        $JoinCost[i] \leftarrow JoinCost[i] + P_R[i][p] \times P_S[i][p]$;
        if $i < n_p$ **then** $JoinCost[i] \leftarrow JoinCost[i] + P_R[i][p] \times P_S[i][p+1]$;
    endfor
endfor
return the d_p dimensions for which $JoinCost[d]$ are the smallest;

Algorithm 1. *DimSelect*: Partitioning Dimension Selection Algorithm

---

As balanced data distributions among cells are not guaranteed, some cells may not fit in the memory buffer allowed in a system. In this case, a memory-based plane-sweeping method assuming that two sides participating in the plane-sweeping should be resident in the main memory may cause excessive disk I/O costs because data points remaining in the disk space should be read into the memory buffer every time a sweeping is processed. To prevent this overhead, we propose three different schemes of plane-sweeping under considering the relationships between the cell sizes and the memory buffer size.

First, if both the cells participating in a plane-sweeping fit in the buffer, a memory-based plane-sweeping method is applied without modification. This case is illustrated in Fig. 4-(a). Both cells are processed after being fetched into the buffer. Second, if only one of the cells fit in the buffer, the cell is fetched into the buffer and the other cell is split to fit in the buffer. plane-sweeping is processed over one to many relationships. This case is illustrated in Fig. 4-(b). Last, if neither of the cells fit in the buffer, both cells are splited before fetched into the buffer. This case is illustrated in Fig. 4-(c).

Note that for the last case, plane-sweeping is needless between splited sub-cells for which the axis distance is larger than ε. For example, in Fig.4-(c), $P_r - 1$ is not considered for pairing with $P_s - 2$ and $P_s - 3$.

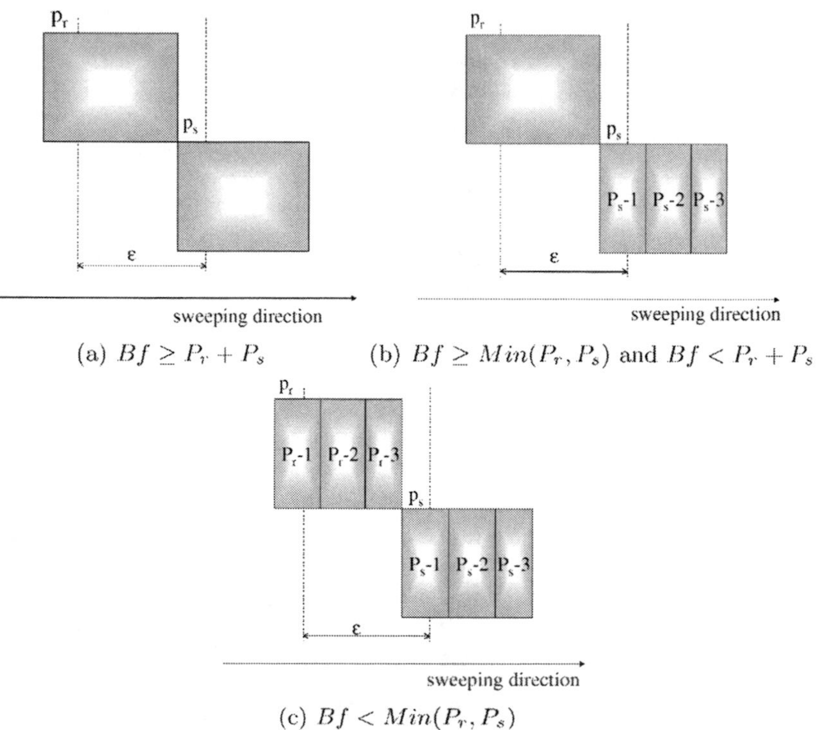

(a) $Bf \geq P_r + P_s$ (b) $Bf \geq Min(P_r, P_s)$ and $Bf < P_r + P_s$

(c) $Bf < Min(P_r, P_s)$

Fig. 4. Disk-based Plane-Sweeping

6 Experimental Results

In this section, we evaluate the proposed methods for the partition-based similarity join in high dimensional data spaces. We implemented three algorithms. The algorithm, $NaiveSJ$, computes the distances of all possible pairs of points from the given data sets to get results. The second algorithm, $PBSJ$ uses the method proposed in this paper for the selection of partitioning dimensions but the disk-based plane sweeping method is not included. The last algorithm, $S-PBSJ$ employs the disk-based plane sweeping method as well. In the experiments, we used two sets of 1,000,000 16-dimensional points, each of which is a color histogram value of an image.

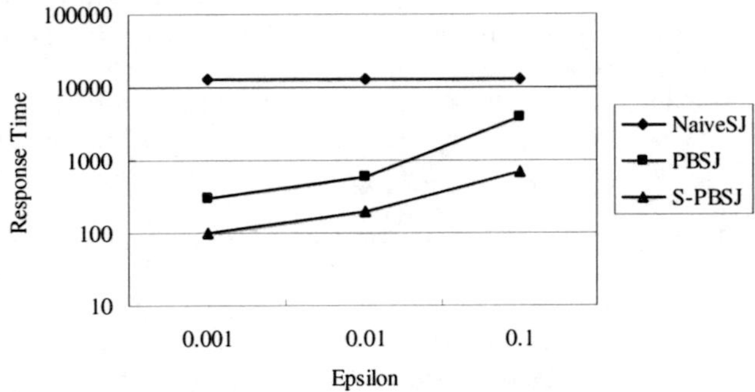

Fig. 5. Comparison of Response Times

The experiments were performed by varying cut-off similarity values, ε, into 0.001, 0.01, 0.1. As Fig. 5 shows the results, our algorithms, $PBSJ$ and $S-PBSJ$ were always better than $NaiveSJ$ by more than a magnitude. This result implies that the partition-based similarity join using the selective partion dimensions is quite effective compared with a naive method. Note that a partition-based similarity join of partitioning all the dimensions in high dimensional data spaces are worse than $NaiveSJ$, because the number of partitions explodes. For this reason, we did not consider the implementation of that method.

Between $PBSJ$ and $S-PBSJ$, $S-PBSJ$ performed better than $PBSJ$ by up to several times. This implies that the disk-based plane sweeping is quite effective in computing joins between partitioned cells. The disk-based plane sweeping caused to reduce the IO cost of joins as well as the CPU cost. Specifically, the reduction of the IO cost is caused by efficient accesses to the cells whose sizes are larger than main memory size during disk-based plane sweeping processing.

7 Conclusion

Partition-based approaches are not directly applicable to the similarity join processing in high dimensional data spaces. This is mainly because the number of cells resulted from partitioning is too large and thus unreasonable CPU and IO costs are spent. This paper proposed a dimension selection method which dynamically selects the most efficient dimensions to be partitioned for the similarity join. Furthermore, a disk-based plane sweeping method was proposed to minimize the cost of joins between partitioned cells. The experimental results showed that the proposed methods enhanced the partition-based similarity join in high dimensional data spaces by more than a magnitude. Future work includes an optimized soluiton to the disk-based plane sweeping as the data distributions among partitioned cells are very skewed.

References

1. C. Böhm, B. Braunmuller, F. Krebs, and H.-P. Kriegel. Epsilon grid order: An algorithm for the similarity join on massive high-dimensional data. In *Proceedings of the 2001 ACM-SIGMOD Conference*, 2001.
2. Norbert Beckmann, Hans-Peter Kriegel, Ralf Schneider, and Bernhard Seeger. The R^*-tree: An efficient and robust access method for points and rectangles. In *Proceedings of the 1990 ACM-SIGMOD Conference*, pages 322–331, Atlantic City, NJ, May 1990.
3. S. Berchtold, D. A. Keim, and H.-P. Kriegel. The X-tree: An index structure for high-dimensional data. In *Proceedings of the 22nd VLDB Conference*, Bombay, India, September 1996.
4. Thomas Brinkhoff, Hans-Peter Kriegel, and Bernhard Seeger. Efficient processing of spatial joins using R-Trees. In *Proceedings of the 1993 ACM-SIGMOD Conference*, pages 237–246, Washington, DC, May 1993.
5. Antonin Guttman. R-Trees: A dynamic index structure for spatial searching. In *Proceedings of the 1984 ACM-SIGMOD Conference*, pages 47–57, Boston, MA, June 1984.
6. Gisli R. Hjaltason and Hanan Samet. Incremental distance join algorithms for spatial databases. In *Proceedings of the 1998 ACM-SIGMOD Conference*, pages 237–248, Seattle, WA, June 1998.
7. Y.W. Huang, N. Jing, and E. Rundensteiner. Spatial joins using R-trees : Breadth-first traversal with global optimizations. In *Proceedings of the 23rd VLDB Conference*, 1997.
8. N. Koudas and C. Sevcik. High dimensional similarity joins: Algorithms and performance evaluation. In *Proceedings of the 1998 IEEE International Conference on Data Engineering*, 1998.
9. K. Lin, H. V. Jagadish, and C. Faloutsos. The TV-tree: An index structure for high-dimensional data. *VLDB Journal*, 3:517–542, 1995.
10. Ming-Ling Lo and Chinya V. Ravishankar. Spatial hash-join. In *Proceedings of the 1996 ACM-SIGMOD Conference*, pages 247–258, Montreal, Canada, June 1996.
11. Jignesh M. Patel and David J. DeWitt. Partition based spatial-merge join. In *Proceedings of the 1996 ACM-SIGMOD Conference*, pages 259–270, Montreal, Canada, June 1996.
12. K. Shim, R. Srikant, and R. Agrawal. High-dimensional similarity joins. In *Proceedings of the 1997 IEEE International Conference on Data Engineering*, 1997.
13. Hyoseop Shin, Bongki Moon, and Sukho Lee. Adaptive multi-stage distance join processing. In *Proceedings of the 2000 ACM-SIGMOD Conference*, pages 343–354, Dallas, TX, May 2000.

Heterogeneous Data Source Integration and Evolution

(Extended Abstract)

Mokrane Bouzeghoub[1], Bernadette Farias Lóscio[2],
Zoubida Kedad[1], and Assia Soukane[1]

[1] Laboratoire PRiSM, Université de Versailles
45, avenue des Etats-Unis 78035 Versailles, France
{Bouzeghoub, Kedad, Soukane}@prism.uvsq.fr
[2] Centro de Informática - Universidade Federal de Pernambuco
Av. Professor Luis Freire s/n, Cidade Universitária, 50740-540 Recife – PE, Brasil
(currently visiting PRiSM lab, University of Versailles)
bfl@cin.ufpe.br

1. Introduction

Data integration consists in providing a uniform view of a set of heterogeneous data sources. This allows users to define their queries without any knowledge on the heterogeneous sources. Data integration systems use the mediation architecture to provide integrated access to multiple data sources. A mediator is a software device that supports a mediation schema which captures user requirements, and a set of mappings between the mediation schema and the distributed sources. Mediation systems [20] can be classified according to the approach used to define the mappings between the data sources and the global schema [12,23]. The first approach is called global-as-view (GAV) and requires that each object of the global schema be expressed as a view (i.e. a query) on the data sources [6]. In the other approach, called local-as-view (LAV), mediation mappings are defined in an opposite way; each object in a given source is defined as a view on the global schema [11]. Both approaches allow to transform user queries, defined over the mediation schema, into subqueries defined over data sources. The transformation process is called a rewriting process and is done differently, depending on the approach used.

The main strengths and drawbacks pointed to each approach are the followings: the GAV approach is more natural and more simple to implement but not very flexible in evolving systems; each time a change occurs at a source definition, one has to scan all the mediation queries to check whether this change should be propagated or not. The LAV approach is very flexible as any change at the source level is reduced to the reformulation of one query or only the queries related to this source, but the rewriting process is very complex.

We focus on the GAV approach and address a set of problems such as: (i) how to generate the views defining the mediation schema, (ii) how to integrate data cleaning in the view expressions, (iii) how to maintain mediation schema and mediation queries when user requirement or data sources change. The following sections summa-

R. Cicchetti et al. (Eds.): DEXA 2002, LNCS 2453, pp. 751-757, 2002.

rizes the main research related to these problems and give an overview of our contributions to these problems.

2. Generation of Mediation Queries in the GAV Approach

The definition of mediation queries is a difficult manual task in the context of large scalable systems, regarding the amount of metadata necessary to explore before determining the queries. To help a designer during this process, we have proposed an approach for query discovery in a mediation system, following a global as view approach. In [10], we have proposed an approach which provides a support to discover view expressions over a set of heterogeneous sources. The proposed algorithm defines a solution space which provides the set of potential queries corresponding to an element of the mediation schema. Some heuristics and interaction with the mediation schema designer can be used to select the desired query. The approach assumes that all metadata describing the mediation schema and source schemas exist. Each schema is defined as a relational schema with its keys, foreign keys and functional dependencies. Equivalent concepts between data sources and the mediation schema are represented by integration assertions as usually done in schema integration methodologies [23].

The general approach is based on the definition of a set of mapping relations and transition relations. Given a relation V of the mediation schema, a mapping relation M_i is intuitively defined as a projection of a single source relation S_i on its keys and on the attributes appearing both in V and S_i. A transition relation T_j is intuitively defined as a projection of a source relation which allows a join between two mapping relations.

Given a set of mapping relations and transition relations, it becomes possible to explore all possible operations between these relations. For each pair of mapping/transition relations, the union operation is possible if the two relations have the same schema, the join operation is possible if the two relations have not the same schemas but have the same keys or are related by foreign keys. These operators form an operation graph from which potential queries can be enumerated.

The following steps sketch the process of discovering queries which define a view.

1. Selection of relevant sources which potentially allow to compute a given view: this step use the correspondence assertions between the mediation schema and the source schemas, particularly terminology assertions which define equivalent concepts. Each source which contains one or several attributes of the mediation view is considered as a relevant source.
2. Definition of the mapping relations and transition relations for a given mediation view. Mapping relations are derived as projections of relevant sources. Transition relations are defined if there is no direct way to join mapping relations. Transition relations are defined by following referential constraints paths within the same source or by matching keys between different sources.
3. Identification of possible relational operators to apply to a source or between different sources (more precisely to a mapping relation or between mapping or transi-

tion relations): Selection operators are derived from some integrity constraints defined over each view. Binary operators are derived using a set of rules which exploite meta data such as functional dependencies, keys and referential constraints.

4. Selection of relevant queries: Each path in the previous graph which includes all attributes of the view V is a potential query which defines V. But all potential queries are not necessarily relevant with respect to the semantics of the view. Some rules based on functional dependencies eliminate solutions which do not guarantee the satisfaction of these functional dependencies. Other heuristics such as quality factors defined on the sources can also be used to eliminate queries which do not correspond to the desired semantics.

Although the query generation process exploits metadata to deal with schemas heterogeneity, it does not consider the heterogeneity between source data. Consequently, the generated queries are considered just as abstract queries; they cannot be evaluated without including data transformations. This is the second issue which is addressed in the next section.

3. Cleaning Data through Mediation Queries

Data transformation and data cleaning is a process of reconciling heterogeneous data before integrating it or before delivering it to the final user. Data cleaning can be addressed in different ways depending on the access mode to the data sources. If the source data is accessed once for all or loaded periodically, the cleaning process is done by ad hoc procedures and is called *episodic cleaning*. If the source data is accessed for each user query in the context of mediation system, then the cleaning is called *intensive cleaning* and data transformations are integrated within mediation queries. We are interested in the second case and we aim to extend the previous query generation process with data transformations. Before summarizing our approach, let us have a brief look to the related work done in data cleaning. We can roughly distinguish three categories of contributions:

- The definition of specific data transformations devoted to numerical data conversion [7] or to the semantic equivalence of concepts or objects [9,15]. Depending on the type of transformation, some can be used in both approaches of episodic and intensive cleaning.
- The definition of cleaning patterns: patterns of queries or building blocks are defined as generic programs which can be instantiated for each specific domain and organized into a unique cleaning program which is executed on the data sources [8]. Interactive tools are proposed to help in the usage and execution of these building blocks [16,18]. These tools are very well suited to episodic cleaning but not applicable for intensive cleaning.
- The definition of a conceptual language which incorporates both querying facilities and data transformations. [5] have proposed the concept of *adorned queries* defined in description logic. Adornments allow to invoque external programs to convert or match heterogeneous data. The approach is defined within the local as view framework and applies to intensive data cleaning.

Our approach follows the third category but is defined within the GAV approach. Our aim is to extend the generation process of the mediation queries with data transformations. This extension is done in three stages:

- First, we extend the classical relational operators with mapping functions. These functions apply to tuples and transform their attribute values. This is already possible in Oracle with the usage of external functions within queries.
- Second, we replace the regular exact matching of select and join operators by an approximate matching. This can be done by using external approximate filtering functions as in Oracle or by redefining these operators as done in many query languages allowing approximate queries. This extension is particularly important when none of the values in source relations is a reference value, so that there exist a mapping function which transforms one value into another.
- Third, similarly to [8], we define new operators which realize 1-N or N-1 mappings: they allow respectively to explode a tuple into several tuples and to merge several tuples into one tuple. The operator allows to change the semantics of a table by changing one of its attributes, and the second operator to eliminate duplicates.

We see three advantages using this approach: (i) it allows a clear understanding of cleaning operations by giving a logical view which specifies explicitly and declaratively what kind of cleaning is done on source data, (ii) it is incremental as it extends in a natural way the relational algebra and can be extended again if new cleaning operators are necessary, (iii) given the queries at the logical level, it becomes easy to generate the corresponding SQL queries.

Given these extensions, the mediation query generation algorithm can be reformulated by incorporating mapping functions in the definition of mapping relations and by using the new operators concurrently with other relational operators depending on the heterogeneity of source data.

4. Evolution of Mediation Queries

One of the main challenges in data integration systems is to maintain the global schema consistent with the user requirements evolution and to maintain the mediation queries consistent both with the global schema evolution and with source evolution. The evolution of the mediation schema is in many aspects similar to the schema evolution problem in traditional databases; hence the novel and complex problem of evolution in mediation systems is the evolution of the mediation queries, especially in the GAV approach where mediated queries are very sensitive to changes in source description. The problem addressed in this paper can be stated as follows: given a change event occurring at the source level, how to propagate this change into the mediation queries.

Mainly two kinds of evolution have to be dealt with in a mediation-based system: the evolution of the user needs, and the evolution of the data sources:

- The evolution of the user needs may consist in adding, removing or modifying a user requirement. These changes impact the mediation schema by adding, modifying or deleting a mediated relation. Each change raised in the mediation schema may impact the mediation queries. If the change can be reflected in these queries (that is the current data sources still permit the computation of the new relation), the change on the mediation schema is committed, otherwise the change operation is rejected.

- If a change occurs in a source schema, it has to be propagated to the mediation level. The propagation may either modifies the mediation schema or the mediation queries. The mediation schema is modified if, for example, a relation in a global schema may no longer be computable when the source relations used in its mediation query are removed. The mediation queries are modified if the source relations on which they were defined are modified or when a new source relation is added or deleted.

We focus on the change which impacts the mediation queries and we propose to use the previous generation process of mediation queries to maintain their evolution. We assume that each mediation query is documented by the mapping relations and the transition relations which have been used to generate it during the design phase. Given a change operation at the source level (add a new source, delete an existing source, modify the definition of an existing source, etc.), a set of propagation rules are defined on the mapping relations and the transition relations to reflect the change occurred at the source level. This propagation may result in adding a new mapping/transition relation, deleting a mapping/transition relation, or updating their schemas. Then, the process of generating mediation queries is started again. Depending on the change reflected in the mapping and transition relations, the process may generate new mediation queries or ends by flagging the mediation relations which cannot be computed from the sources, i.e., the user requirements captured in the mediation schema cannot be satisfied.

As sketched before, change propagation occurred at the source level may result in changing mediation queries, changing mediation schema if some of its elements is not computable from the sources, and consequently disabling all existing user queries which cannot be evaluated over these elements. After another cycle of changing, some of these queries may become active as the corresponding mediation queries have been generated again. One interesting aspect to investigate in the future work is the impact of the propagation rules on the general quality of the system. Some quality factors could be defined and evaluated to determine if a given propagation rule increases or decreases the level of quality of the system.

5. Concluding Remarks

Mediation systems are powerful infrastructures which allow to interoperate with several autonomous, distributed and heterogeneous data sources. Most of the effort has been done in query processing through mediation schemas. Handling heterogeneity and evolution remain challenging problems whose complexity increases dramatically with XML and other semi-structured or non-structured data. However, without substantial effort done in this direction, important applications based on heterogeneous and evolving data sources, such as data warehousing, internet portals and other federated databases, cannot become a reality for their users.

References

1. Agarwal, S., Keller, A.M., Wiederhold, G., Krishna, S. «Flexible relation: an approach for integrating data from multiple, possibly inconsistent databases», Proceedings of the Eleventh International Conference on Data Engineering, (ICDE 95), march 1995, Philip S. Yu, Arbee L. P. Chen (Eds.)
2. Arens, Y., Knoblock, C.A., Shen, W.M., «Query Reformulation for dynamic information integration», International Journal on Intelligent and Cooperative Information Systems (6) 2/3, June 1996
3. Bergamaschi, S., Castano, S., De Capitani Di Vimercati, S., Montanari, S. and Vincini, M., "A semantic approach to information integration: the momis project," in *Proc. of Sesto Convegno della Associazione Italiana per l'Intelligenza Artificiale*, 1998.
4. Calvanese, D., De Giacomo, G., Lenzerini, M., Nardi, D., Rosati, R., « Source integration in data warehousing », DWQ technical report, October 1997
5. Calvanese, D., De Giacomo, G., Lenzerini, M., Nardi, D., Rosati, R., « A Principled Approach to Data Integration and Reconciliation in Data Warehousing », Proceedings of the CaiSE'99 Joint Workshop on Data Management and Data Warehouses, Heidelberg, June 1999.
6. Chawathe, S., Garcia-Molina, H., Hammer, J., Ireland, K., Papakonstantinou, Y., Ullman, J., Widom, J., «The TSIMMIS project: Integration of Heterogeneous Information Sources», Proceedings of the 10th Meeting of the Information Processing Society of Japan, (IPSJ'94), October 1994
7. Fan W., Lu H., Madnick S.E., Chueng D., Discovering and reconciling value conflicts for numerical data integration, Information Systems Journal, Vol 26, N°8, december 01.
8. Galhardas H., Florescu D., Shasha D., Simon E., Saita C, Declarative Data Cleaning: Language, Model and Algorithms, INRIA report n°4149, March 2001.
9. Hernandez,M.A., Stolfo, S.J., The Merge/Purge Problem for Large Databases, SIGMOD'95.
10. Kedad, Z. and Bouzeghoub, M., "Discovering View Expressions from a Multi-Source Information System", in Proc. of the Fourth IFCIS International Conference on Cooperative Information Systems (CoopIS), Edinburgh, Scotland, pp. 57-68, Sep. 1999.
11. Kirk, T., Levy, A.Y., Sagiv, Y., and Srivastava, D., "The Information Manifold", in *Proc. of the AAAI 1995 Spring Symp. on Information Gathering from Heterogeneous, Distributed Environments*, pp. 85-91, 1995.
12. Levy, A.Y., Rajaraman, A., Ordille, J.J., «Querying Heterogeneous Information Sources Using Source Description», Proceedings of 22th International Conference on Very Large Data Bases, (VLDB'96), September 1996, T. M. Vijayaraman, Alejandro P. Buchmann, C. Mohan, Nandlal L. Sarda (Eds.)
13. Low, W.L., Lee, M.L., T, Ling,.W., A knowledge based approach for duplicate elimination in data cleaning, Information Systems Journal, Vol 26, N°8, december 01.
14. Miller, R. J., Haas, L. M., Hernández, M.A.. "Schema Mapping as Query Discovery." VLDB 2000
15. Monge A.E., An adaptative and efficient algorithm for detecting approximately duplicate database records.

16. Raman, V., Hellerstein, J.M., Potter's Wheel: An Interactive Data Cleaning System, Proceedings of the 27th VLDB Conference, Roma, Italy, 2001.
17. Tejada, S., Knoblock, C.A. Minton, S., Learning object identification rules for information integration, Information Systems Journal, Vol 26, N°8, december 01.
18. Vassiliadis P., Vagena Z., Skiadopoulos S., Karayannidis N., Sellis T., ARKTOS: towards the modeling, design, control and execution of ETL processes, Information Systems, Vol 26, N°8, december 01.
19. Ullman, J. D., "Information integration using logical views", in Proc. of ICDT'97, vol.1186 of LNCS, pp.19-40, Springer-Verlag, 1997.
20. Wiederhold, G., «Mediators in the Architecture of Future Information Systems.», IEEE Computer 25(3), 1992
21. Wiederhold, G., Genesereth, M., «The basis for mediation», Proceedings of the Third International Conference on Cooperative Information Systems, (CoopIS-95), May 1995, Steve Laufmann, Stefano Spaccapietra, Toshio Yokoi (Eds.)
22. Zhou, G., Hull, R., King, R., «Generating Data Integration Mediators that Use Materialization.», Journal of Intelligent Information Systems (JIIS), 6(2/3), 1996
23. Halevy, A.Y., "Theory of answering queries using views", SIGMOD Record, vol. 29, no.4, pp.40-47, 2000.

Information Retrieval System for XML Documents*

Kenji Hatano, Hiroko Kinutani†,
Masatoshi Yoshikawa‡, and Shunsuke Uemura

Nara Institute of Science and Technology
8916–5 Takayama, Ikoma 630–0101, Japan
{hatano,hiroko-k,yosikawa,uemura}@is.aist-nara.ac.jp

Abstract. In the research field of document information retrieval, the unit of retrieval results returned by IR systems is a whole document or a document fragment, like a paragraph in passage retrieval. IR systems based on the vector space model compute feature vectors of the units and calculate the similarities between the units and the query. However, the unit of retrieval results are not suitable for document information retrieval since they are not congruent with the information which users are searching for. Therefore, the unit of retrieval results should be a portion of the XML document, such as a chapter, section, or subsection. That is, we think the most important concern of document information retrieval is to define the unit of retrieval results, that is meaningful for users. It is easy to construct the appropriate portion of XML documents as retrieval results because XML is a standard document format on the Internet and because XML documents consist of contents and document structures. In this paper, we propose an effective IR system for XML documents that automatically defines an appropriate unit of retrieval results by analyzing the XML document structure. We performed experimental evaluations and verified the effectiveness of our XML IR system. In addition, we also defined new recall and precision measures for XML information retrieval in order to evaluate our XML IR system.

1 Introduction

XML (Extensible Markup Language) [1] is becoming widely used as a standard document format in many application domains. In the near future, various kinds of documents will be expressed in XML. Accordingly, XML information retrieval (IR) systems will become very important as an end-user tool in many situations of document information retrieval. In spite of the big demand for XML information retrieval, XML IR systems are not yet available. This is because it is hard for users to enter the document structure as a query into an XML IR system to specify the logical structures of heterogeneous set of XML documents. Such the query is not clearly suitable for user interface of XML IR system. Therefore, we envision a much simpler form of queries for users. These queries would resemble those used in current Web search engines, in which typical queries consist of a few keywords. However, it is difficult to retrieve appropriate portions of XML documents without specifying the document structure in the query. We think the most important concern of XML information retrieval is to define beforehand the unit of retrieval results which is meaningful to users. It is easy to automatically

* This work was partly supported by the Ministry of Education, Culture, Sports, Science and Technology, Japan, under grants 12680417, 12780309 and 14780325, and by CREST Program "Advanced Media Technology for Everyday Living" of Japan Science and Technology Corporation.

† This author is currently with Japan Science and Technology Corporation, Japan.

‡ This author is currently with Nagoya University, Japan.

R. Cicchetti et al. (Eds.): DEXA 2002, LNCS 2453, pp. 758–767, 2002.

extract partial documents as retrieval results if the XML IR system utilizes XML parser programs. The problems include determining the granularity of the partial documents and the method of calculating the similarities between the partial documents and the query by using current IR techniques, because the similarities should accurately reflect the document structure.

In this paper, we develop an effective IR system for XML documents based on the vector space model (VSM) [11]. As stated earlier, we think the most important concern of our XML IR system is deciding the appropriate units of retrieval results. Hence, we define the units as partial documents, which are generated by analyzing the structure of the XML documents. Partial documents, which are intermediate in size between the whole document and a document fragment, like a paragraph in passage retrieval [9], are particularly appropriate for XML information retrieval. Therefore, if the unit of retrieval results is congruent with the information which users are searching for, and the similarities between the partial documents and the query are calculated exactly, then the retrieval accuracy of our XML IR system will be improved. We also propose a new method to calculate the similarities between partial documents and the query, based on the passage retrieval technique of our XML IR system. Moreover, to verify the effectiveness of our XML IR system, we define new recall and precision measures for XML information retrieval and we perform experiments using these ratios.

2 Background and Related Work

2.1 XPath Data Model

In this paper, we follow the notations and data model defined in XPath 1.0 [3]. In the XPath data model, an XML document is modeled as a hierarchical tree. Fig. 1 shows the logical structure of a sample XML document. Although there are seven types of nodes in the XPath data model, we limit our attention to the root node, element nodes, attribute nodes and text nodes for the sake of simplicity. In an XML tree, leaf nodes are text nodes or attribute nodes, and intermediate nodes are element nodes. The child element node of the root node is called the *document node*. In the XPath data model, a somewhat strange parent/child relationship between the element nodes and attribute nodes is used. An element node is a parent of an attribute node, but the attribute node is not a child of the element node. In our model, however, we regard the attribute node as a child of the element node[1]. This is the only difference between the XPath data model and our data model. The *expanded-name* of an element node (or attribute node) is the element type name (or attribute name) of the node. The *string-value* of a text node is the text itself[2], the *string-value* of an attribute node is the value of the attribute, and the *string-value* of an element node is the concatenation of the string-values of all text-node descendants of the element node.

Until now, two kinds of XML document retrieval model have been studied: one is based on non-overlapping lists and the other is based on proximal nodes. Our model of partial documents is similar to the model based on proximal nodes [8]. That is, our logical model of partial XML documents is a subtree whose root node is an element node. Therefore, we can identify a partial document by the reference number, n, of the root node of the partial document tree. We refer to such a partial document as "partial document #n." Our IR system is based on this model, and so it needs to define the units of retrieval results beforehand in order to analyize the XML document structures.

[1] If the element node has some attribute nodes which have brotherhood ties, they are owned by the element node.

[2] we do not consider hyperlinks in one document or between two or more documents.

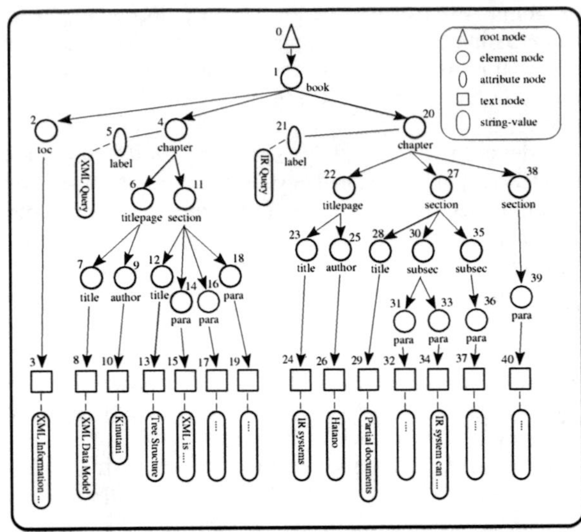

Fig. 1. A Tree Representation of an XML Document.

2.2 Passage Retrieval

In order to improve the degree of similarity between the documents and users' queries, many researchers have studied document retrieval. One area of research is passage retrieval [9], which is the identification and extraction of fragments from documents. To be more specific, passages are fragments of contiguous text belonging to a larger text: for example, fragments can be sentences, or sequences of sentences. In passage retrieval, the IR system manages documents based on these fragments and finds documents by using these fragments as retrieval results. We think the advantages of passage retrieval are the retrieval of the most relevant fragments of longer documents, the avoidance of document-length normalization problems, and the possibility of more user-friendly interfaces that return the most relevant fragments of a document. Moreover, passage retrieval can improve retrieval accuracy, particularly precision and recall, since it returns short fragments containing the highest density of the query keyword. On the other hand, the principal problems of passage retrieval are the segmentation algorithm used and the possibility of a dramatic increase in the number of document fragments collected. We think the recent research of passage retrieval [2, 5] could solve the algorithm problem; however, the problem of increasing numbers of fragments has not yet been solved.

In our research, we apply passage retrieval to an XML IR system. Our method divides documents into document fragments using XML document markup language. Since document fragments are text nodes and their string-values, partial documents are made from document fragments by analyzing the structure of the XML documents. In short, our proposed IR system conducts information retrieval on appropriate partial documents according to the XPath data model.

3 Development of an IR System for XML Documents

In order to improve the retrieval accuracy of document IR systems based on the VSM, we should divide documents into document fragments and calculate the similarities between the document fragments and the query, as in the passage retrieval described in Section 2.2, and then we should utilize the features of each fragment for information retrieval. We think this approach is also useful for information retrieval of XML documents; however, we have to solve the following problems:

- The number of document fragments is huge.
- The size of document fragments is small for XML information retrieval.

In this paper, we propose methods to solve the problems of passage retrieval and develop an XML IR system adopting these methods. Our IR system divides XML documents into document fragments, as is done in passage retrieval, and then our system constructs partial documents, which consist of document fragments based on the structures of the document. These partial documents are returned as retrieval results from our IR system. We believe these partial documents are the targets of information retrieval, and we believe the units of retrieval results are more meaningful for users than document fragments; that is, the size of the partial document is more appropriate than document fragments. Moreover, because there are fewer partial documents than document fragments, the problem of the retrieval of huge numbers of target information is solved. In order to develop our XML IR system, we implement the following procedures:

1. Our IR system divides stored XML documents into document fragments beforehand, according to their tags. When users enter keywords as a query into our IR system, it calculates the similarities of the document fragments and the query.
2. Our IR system defines partial documents as retrieval results of XML documents by analyzing their document structures. Since an XML document structure can be described as a tree, as in Section 2.1, the units of information retrieval in our XML IR system are defined as partial documents whose root node is every element node of the XML documents.
3. After our IR system decides the unit of information retrieval, it calculates the similarities between the partial documents and the query, calculated from the similarities between the document fragments and the query.

3.1 Division of XML Documents

The basic idea of passage retrieval suggests that larger the document, the greater the chance the document includes fragments irrelevant to a user's query. Therefore, document IR systems should divide documents into document fragments and utilize the features of each fragment for information retrieval. In traditional passage retrieval, the segmentation algorithm is a problem; however, this problem has already been solved, because XML is a markup language. In short, XML documents can be automatically divided into document fragments using their markup [5]; therefore, we can say passage retrieval is also useful for XML information retrieval.

In order to calculate the similarities of document fragments, our IR system conducts the following processes:

1. Our IR system divides the stored XML documents in the IR system into document fragments according to their markup. The document fragment is automatically and semantically divided as an element node, a text node whose parent node is the element node, and their string-values of XML documents.
2. Our IR system generates vectors of each document fragment. The generation of each vector is based on a term-weighting strategy, which is called the tf-idf scheme [10].

3. When a query is entered into our IR system, it generates a query vector and calculates the degree of similarity between each document fragment and the query. The similarity between the document fragments and the query is cosine of the angle between the vectors of the document fragments and the query.

3.2 Definition of the Unit of Retrieval Results

As we described in Section 2.2, targets of information retrieval in passage retrieval are whole documents or document fragments. However, whole documents and document fragments are not useful to users in the XML IR system. This is because the retrieval results of whole documents have a prolixity of expression and the document fragments may not be informative enough as retrieval results for users. That is, users may not understand what the retrieval results express. For example, let us consider the case when users enter the single keyword query "Hatano" to the XML document shown in Fig. 1. The minimum document fragment containing the character string "Hatano" is the partial document #25. However, this document fragment is not informative enough for users, because they could not know what "Hatano" has authored. Obviously, returning the whole document is not adequate either because the whole document has two chapters, and "Hatano" is the author of the second chapter.

We think retrieval results should offer a more meaningful portion of XML documents than document fragments. In order to extract the meaningful portions from XML documents, the XML IR system should utilize their document structures and use these structures to construct partial documents that consist of document fragments. As we consider the ideas described above, the partial document #20 in Fig. 1, for instance, will be the most relevant answer to the query. We define such a semantically consolidated granularity of documents as a *Coherent Subdocument (CS)*. CSs are portions of XML documents that are appropriate as retrieval results. However, it is difficult to extract CSs from XML documents; this is because XML documents have many kinds of document structures defined by DTD (Document Type Definition) or XML Schema language. Therefore, we define every partial document whose root node is an element node, which has at least one text node or one attribute node[3], as a CSs in our XML IR system. Thus, the CSs can be automatically extracted from XML documents by analyzing the document structures of the XML documents. As a result, the CSs include at least one document fragment; hence, there are fewer CSs than the document fragments. The problem, which is the huge number of retrieval results of the IR system, is solved. This point differs the most from the passage retrieval technique.

3.3 Similarity between CS and Query

After we decide the unit of retrieval results, our IR system calculates the similarity between the CSs and the query. In the VSM, the similarity is calculated as the cosine of the angle between the CS and the query vectors. Wilkinson has proposed similarity calculation methods for structured documents based on cosine measure [12]; however, we cannot adopt this method, because it can be adopted to only XML documents with same document structure. Therefore, we propose a new method to calculate the similarity between CSs and the query. Our proposed method utilizes the similarity between document fragments and the query to calculate the similarity between the CSs and the query.

In order to calculate the similarity between the CSs and the query, we should consider the following issues:

[3] The number of terms of text node or attribute node is limited to at least 30. If they do not have this number of terms, the tags of their nodes are eliminated from the XML documents.

- We have to integrate the similarities between document fragments and the query because a CS has at least one document fragment.
- We have to reflect the tree structure of the CSs in the similarity between the CSs and the query when our IR system integrates the similarities between the document fragments and the query.

We think that the first issue is the same as investigating the methods to integrate more than one value into a single value. We already know many kinds of functions that integrate some values into a single value, such as average function, minimum function, and so on. These functions are often used to model a human value judgment. In fuzzy set theory, which was founded by Zadeh [13] in the area of complex systems research, the human value judgment is the intersection or union of fuzzy sets. That is, all functions can be defined in fuzzy set theory. In fact, Lee [7] reported that the human value judgment can be expressed using fuzzy set theory because the functions were developed from fuzzy set theory. Therefore, we can adapt extended boolean models[4] to integrate the similarities between document fragments and the query into one value as the similarities between the CSs and the query. On the other hand, in order to reflect the tree structure of CSs in the similarity between the CSs and the query, we should reflect the parenthood relationship of the CSs' element nodes in the similarities between the CSs and the query. For example, let us consider the case when a user enters query Q into the XML IR system and the query returns the partial document #27, shown in Fig. 2, which is part of the XML document D shown in Fig. 1. The values of the text nodes in Fig. 2 indicate the similarities between document fragments #28, #31, #33, and #36, and query Q, respectively. In order to calculate the similarity between this CS, which is partial document #27, and the query, our IR system has to calculate the similarities between partial documents #28, #30, and #35 and the query. The similarity between partial document #28 and the query has already been calculated as 0.2, and the similarity of between partial document #35 and the query equals the similarity between partial document #36 and the query. The similarity between partial document #30 and the query can be calculated using a function of the extended boolean models. If we adopt a function $f()$ of the extended boolean models, the similarity between partial document #30 and the query is calculated as $sim(D^{30}, Q) = f(sim(D^{31}, Q), sim(D^{32}, Q))$. As a result, the similarity between this CS and the query is calculated as $sim(D^{27}, Q) = f(sim(D^{28}, Q), sim(D^{30}, Q), sim(D^{35}, Q))$. The formal definition of the similarity between CS and the query Q is as follows:

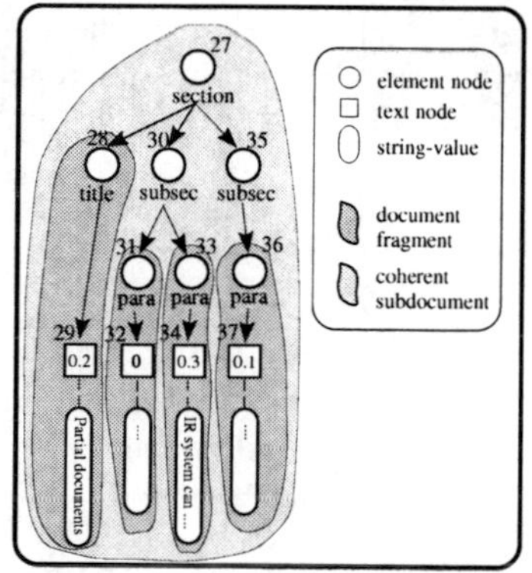

Fig. 2. Similarity of a CS and a Query.

Definition 1 (similarity between CS and query) *We assume that our IR system adopts a function $f()$ to integrate multiple similarities between document fragments and the query. For an element node whose reference number is n in an XML document,*

[4] Lee defined extended boolean models as fuzzy set, Waller-Kraft, Paice, p-norm, and Infinite-One in [6].

D, the similarity between the CS, which is the partial document #n, and the query Q is defined as follows:

$$\textbf{sim}(D^n, Q) = f(\textbf{sim}(c, Q), \textbf{sim}(c', Q), \ldots, \textbf{sim}(c^{(m)'}, Q)) \quad (1)$$

where $c, c', \ldots, c^{(m)'}$ *are child nodes of the element node #n,* $\textbf{sim}(c, Q)$ *indicates the similarity between partial documents whose root nodes are* $c, c', \ldots, c^{(m)'}$ *and query* Q. *If* $c^{(m)'}$ *is a text node,* $\textbf{sim}(c^{(m)'}, Q)$ *can be calculated as the similarity between the document fragment and the query.*

4 Experimental Evaluation

In order to verify the effectiveness of our IR system, we developed a prototype system which adopts our proposed methods described in Section 3, and compares them with other methods. Our methods apply the VSM to whole documents and CSs, and passage retrieval to document fragments. In the first approach, the IR system calculates the similarities between the XML documents and the query as the angles between the document vectors and the query vector. In the second approach, the IR system calculates the similarities between the partial documents and the query as the angles between the vectors of the partial documents and the query vector. In the last approach, the IR system calculates the similarities between the document fragments and the query as the angles between vectors of document fragments and the query vector. These three approaches differ in their definition of the unit of retrieval results and their method of calculating similarities between the CSs and the query.

4.1 Our IR System Setup

Our prototype system is separated into three modules: extracting the document fragments, constructing the CSs, and ranking the CSs.

1. First, our IR system analyzes XML documents using an XML parser called Xerces[5], and constructs DOM trees from the documents. Then, it extracts both the text nodes and their string-values as document fragments and constructs the CSs by analyzing the DOM trees described in Section 3.2[6].
2. Similarities between the CSs and the query are calculated based on the similarities of the document fragments and the query, as described in Section 3.3. A document fragment is a partial XML document whose root node is an element node with one text node, or one attribute node as a child node. Let e_j $(j = 1, 2, \ldots, N)$ be a document fragment. Our IR system calculates the frequency of the terms t_k $(k = 1, 2, \ldots, n)$ appearing in all XML documents, and generates the vectors $\boldsymbol{F}(e_j)$ of e_j. $\boldsymbol{F}(e_j)$ are calculated using a keyword-weighting strategy called the tf-idf scheme [10], as follows:
$$\boldsymbol{F}(e_j) = (w_{t_1}^{e_j}, w_{t_2}^{e_j}, \ldots, w_{t_n}^{e_j}) \quad (2)$$
where
$$w_{t_i}^{e_j} = \frac{tf(t_k, e_j)}{\sum_{j=1}^{N} \sum_{k=1}^{n} tf(t_k, e_j)} \cdot \log \frac{N_d}{df(t_i)},$$
$tf(t_k, e_j)$ is the term frequency appearing t_k in e_j, N_d is the number of XML documents, and $df(t_k)$ is the document frequency appearing t_k.

[5] http://xml.apache.org/xerces-j/index.html

[6] Using our reference collection described in Section 4.2, the number of CSs is 17, 4,344 and 3,171 in simple VSM plus passage retrieval and our method, respectively. The time taken to reconstruct CSs depends on the performance of the XML parser. In this case, our prototype system was able to construct CSs within one minute.

3. When a user enters keywords as a query into our IR system, our IR system generates a query vector $\boldsymbol{q}$. The base of the query vector is the same as that of $\boldsymbol{F}(e_j)$, and the element values of $\boldsymbol{q}$ do not depend on whether the keywords are included in the query keywords. Therefore, we can express the query feature vector $\boldsymbol{q}$ as follows:

$$\boldsymbol{q} = (q_{t_1}, q_{t_2}, \ldots, q_{t_n}). \tag{3}$$

If t_k is included in the query keywords, q_{t_k} is 1. If t_k is not included, q_{t_k} is 0. Then, our system calculates the similarities between the document fragments and the query. In the VSM, the similarity is calculated by the cosine of the angle between these two vectors, as follows:

$$\mathbf{sim}(\boldsymbol{F}(e_j), \boldsymbol{q}) = \frac{\boldsymbol{F}(e_j) \cdot \boldsymbol{q}}{|\boldsymbol{F}(e_j)||\boldsymbol{q}|} \tag{4}$$

4. Finally, our system calculates the similarities between the CSs and the query using the similarities between the document fragments and the query. As we described in Section 3.3, we adopt a function of the extended boolean models. In this paper, we adopt the p-norm function ($p = 2$) as follows:

$$f(s, s', \ldots, s^{(m)'}) = 1 - \left(\frac{(1-s)^p + (1-s')^p + \ldots + (1-s^{(m)'})^p}{m} \right)^{1/p} \tag{5}$$

We adopt the p-norm function because Lee also reported that it can provide better retrieval effectiveness when $p = 2$ [7].

4.2 Experiments and Evaluation of Our IR System

When we evaluate IR systems, we usually use reference collections. The reference collection quite often used is the TREC collection. Many kinds of reference collections have been created by NIST, although NIST has not yet presented a reference collection for XML documents. Therefore, we used XML documents obtained from the World Wide Web Consortium (W3C) Web site[7] and generated our own reference collection. Our reference collection consists of 17 translated XML documents, whose total size is about 7.2 MB, and 5 query/answer sets.

Using our reference collection, we evaluated four approaches: the retrieval method of whole documents on the VSM (*VSM-W*), the retrieval method of CSs using the VSM (*VSM-C*), that of document fragments on passage retrieval technique (*PR*), and that of CSs using our proposed method (*Proposed*). We drew their recall-precision curves. When we draw a recall-precision curve, we cannot use the recall and precision defined in standard IR textbooks. This is because we have to consider the contained relationship between the CSs and the answer set of partial documents of the reference collection. Hence, retrieval results of each approach are not always congruent with the answer set of partial documents. Therefore, we define new recall and precision measures of a CS whose rank is k in XML IR system as follows:

$$R_k = \frac{1}{a} \sum_{j=1}^{a} \frac{|(\bigcup_{i=1}^{k} RD_i) \cap SD_j|}{|SD_j|}, \quad P_k = \frac{1}{k} \sum_{i=1}^{k} \frac{|RD_i \cap (\bigcup_{j=1}^{a} SD_j)|}{|RD_i|} \tag{6}$$

where SD_j is the partial document that is the query answer of our reference collection, a is the number of the answer partial documents in our reference collection. Furthermore,

[7] http://www.w3.org/TR/

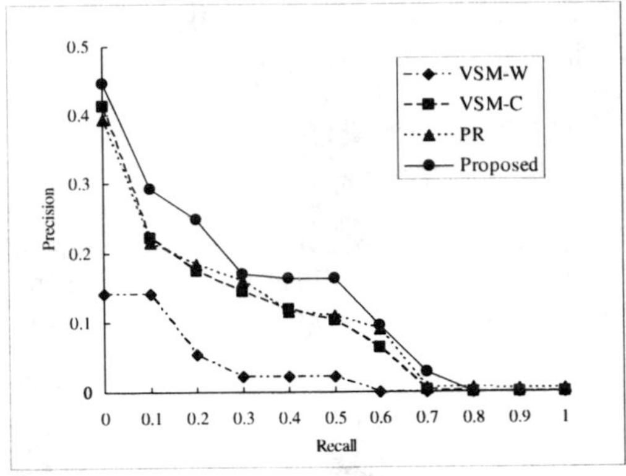

Fig. 3. Recall-Precision Curves of the Four Approaches.

RD_i is a retrieved CS whose subscript i indicates its rank, $|X|$ is the size of the partial document X. In this formula, R_k is expressed as the ratio of the intersection of the answer set of partial documents of our reference collection and retrieved CSs whose ranks are between the first and the k-th. P_k is the ratio including the answer set of partial documents of our reference collection in all retrieved CSs whose ranks are from the first to the k-th. Using these new recall and precision measures, we drew recall-precision curves to compare the four approaches in our experimental evaluation. In a comparison of these curves (see Fig. 3), we found that it is important to define the CSs as retrieval results for XML information retrieval because the *VSM-C* and the *Proposed* could retrieve more appropriate partial documents to the answer set of partial documents of our reference collection. We think whole documents and document fragments are not suitable for the unit of retrieval results; hence, these units are not congruent with the answer set of partial documents. We also found the effectiveness of our proposed method of calculating the similarity of the CSs. In fact, when we compared the *VSM-C* with the *Proposed*, the *Proposed* could achieve better retrieval accuracy than the *VSM-P*. However, the *Proposed* took more time to compute the similarities between the CSs and the query. In order to reduce the similarity calculation cost, we have to reduce the number of CSs. The root nodes of the CSs generated by our proposed method are all of the element nodes in the XML documents; however, we found that all CSs are not always suitable for XML information retrieval. In our previous research [4], we found that we could reduce the number of CSs if we utilized both the structures and the contents[8] of XML documents. If we adopt our previous research to construct an algorithm for reducing the number of the CSs, we think we will solve this problem, and the retrieval accuracy of our proposed method will improve. This is because the CSs which are constructed by this new algorithm could reflect both the structures and the contents of XML documents, so that the CSs will be more meaningful for users, that is, the CSs can be congruent with the answer partial documents.

[8] In [4], the contents are terms contained in XML documents and the expanded-name of XML document tags.

5 Conclusion and Future Works

In spite of a big demand for XML information retrieval, XML IR systems that can work like current Web search engines are not yet available. This is because a definitive unit of retrieval results has not been determined for XML information retrieval; hence, we cannot easily adopt the IR techniques to XML IR systems. In this paper, we developed an XML IR system whose unit of retrieval results is a partial document, which possesses the semantically consolidated granularity of an XML document. The CS was automatically used by our XML IR system to analyze the structures of XML documents. Moreover, we evaluated and discussed the validity of our developed XML IR system using the recall and precision measures which we specifically defined for XML information retrieval. We found that our XML IR system could provide better retrieval effectiveness than other systems.

However, we briefly discussed the efficiency of our XML IR system and our use of a small reference collection. Now, we are participating in INEX Project[9] which provides an opportunity to evaluate XML retrieval methods using large scale reference collection. Therefore, we will be able to carry out in-depth experiments until this December. Furthermore, we also consider the method to reduce the number of CSs. We think we might be able to utilize the class-partitioning techniques of object-oriented databases to construct CSs.

References

1. T. Bray, J. Paoli, C.M. Sperberg-McQueen, and E. Maler. Extensible Markup Language (XML) 1.0 (Second Edition). Oct. 2000.
2. J. Callan. Passage-level Evidence in Document Retrieval. In *Proc of ACM SIGIR'94*, pp.302–310, 1994.
3. J. Clark and S. DeRose. XML Path Language (XPath) Version 1.0. Nov. 1999.
4. K. Hatano, H. Kinutani, M. Yoshikawa, and S. Uemura. Extraction of Partial XML Documents Using IR-based Structure and Contents Analysis. In *Proc. of DASWIS-2001*, pp.189–202, Nov. 2001.
5. M. Kaszkiel and J. Zobel. Passage Retrieval Revisited. In *Proc. of ACM SIGIR'97*, pp.178–185. July 1997
6. J.H. Lee. Properties of Extended Boolean Models in Information Retrieval. In *Proc. of ACM SIGIR'94*, pp.182–190, 1994.
7. J.H. Lee. Analyzing the Effectiveness of Extended Boolean Models in Information Retrieval. Technical report, Cornell University, 1995.
8. G. Navarro and R. Baeza-Yates. Proximal Nodes: A Model to Query Document Databases by Content and Structure. *ACM TOIS*, 15(4):400–435, 1997.
9. G. Salton, J. Allan, and C. Buckley. Approaches to Passage Retrieval in Full Text Information Systems. In *Proc. of ACM SIGIR'93*, pp.49–58, June/July 1993.
10. G. Salton and C. Buckley. Term-Weighting Approaches in Automatic Retrieval. *Information Processing & Management*, 24(5):513–523, 1988.
11. G. Salton and M. Lesk. Computer Evaluation of Indexing and Text Processing. *Journal of the ACM*, 15(1):8–36, Jan. 1968.
12. R. Wilkinson. Effective Retrieval of Structured Documents. In *Proc. of ACM SIGIR'94*, pp.311–317, 1994.
13. L.A. Zadeh. Fuzzy Sets. *Information and Control*, 8:338–353, 1965.

[9] Initiative for the Evaluation of XML Retrieval (INEX): http://qmir.dcs.qmul.ac.uk/INEX/.

A System for Retrieval and Digest Creation of Video Data Based on Geographic Objects*

Takamasa Ueda**, Toshiyuki Amagasa, Masatoshi Yoshikawa***, and Shunsuke Uemura

Graduate School of Information Science, Nara Institute of Science and Technology
8916–5 Takayama, Ikoma, Nara 630-0101, Japan
{takama-u,amagasa,yosikawa,uemura}@is.aist-nara.ac.jp
http://db-www.aist-nara.ac.jp/

Abstract. With the advent of wearable cameras attached with wearable computers, we can record our daily lives as a large amount of video data. As a consequence, automatic creation of indexes on such video data is becoming important to support query retrieval or digest creation on them. This is because it is unrealistic to create indexes on long-sustained video data by hand. To cope with this problem, we propose a method to automatically create index on such video data on the basis of geographic objects. In this scheme, users wear a wearable computer, a GPS receiver, and a wearable video camera with gyroscope to record various kinds of context information as well as video data. The system then makes analysis of those data, and automatically creates indexes of the video data. To this end, we propose two kinds of weighting schemes for geographic objects, namely, distance- and direction-based weights. We introduce some variations of distance-based weighting functions, and a method to adaptively decide reasonable indexing area with respect to the position of the user and geographic objects.

1 Introduction

Wearable computers have been emerging as a new trend of computer technology for the past several years [1,2]. One wears a wearable computer as a part of his/her clothes at all time, and the wearable computer can support the owner's everyday life in many situations, by making analysis of various kinds of data captured by attached sensors.

Small-sized video cameras called "wearable cameras," that can be mounted on our body, are the most popular devices for wearable computers [3]. Wearable computers combined with wearable cameras make it possible to record video data of our viewpoint. Such video data can be used in many ways, for example, to support our memories, to create video diaries, and so on. Indeed, implementations of such applications were unrealistic in the past from some reasons, mainly because the limitations of storage

* This work is partially supported by the Ministry of Education, Culture, Sports, Science and Technology, Japan under grant 13780236, and by Core Research for Evolutional Science and Technology (CREST) Program "Advanced Media Technology for Everyday Living" of Japan Science and Technology Corporation (JST).

** Presently with KDDI Corporation, Japan
*** Presently with Information Technology Center, Nagoya University, Japan

R. Cicchetti et al. (Eds.): DEXA 2002, LNCS 2453, pp. 768–778, 2002.

capacities. However, remarkable progress on the technologies of storage devices and data compression is about to bring us microminiature-sized storages of tera-bytes (TB). As a consequence, recording our everyday life as video data is no longer unrealistic.

Another problem then arises; Our computer would be filled up with huge amount of video data. In spite of this, we should be able to retrieve video fragments we would like to see from those data quickly, say, "find video data of the travel when I was in Egypt in the last summer" or "find video data of the person who I met in front of the NARA station." In fact, comparing to conventional video data, such video data are different in some aspects: 1) the spans are very long and also the sizes are very large; 2) the pictures are quite unstable because the camera is mounted on human body; 3) most of those data are continuous, that is, once they start, there is no or little suspensions until they reach to the end; and 4) among all the video data, small parts of them are significant for us, in other words, most of them are out of our interest. For those reasons, we cannot apply conventional video retrieval techniques to wearable-camera videos as they are.

One promising approach for those problems is to use various information captured by sensors. In this paper, we propose a video retrieval system for wearable-camera videos, by which we can query those data based on geographic objects (geo-objects). A geo-object here means anything that appears on maps. To this end, we uses locational information of the user captured by a Global Positioning System (GPS) receiver, geographic information inferred from the locational information, and directional information of the camera captured by gyroscope. Specifically, we define the *importance* of geo-objects based on those information. The concept of *importance* is defined based on our behavior. If we are interested in a place or a building, we tend to stay there for a long time, and we tend to look at the place. We try to numerically express such behaviors in terms of *importance* of geo-objects. Finally, we can presume significant video fragments for a user using those values. Our approach is advantageous in the sense that we do not need any complicated data manipulation. We can therefore cope with the case that the data size is quite large.

The rest of this paper is organized as follows. Section 2 proposes the digest creation of video data recorded by wearable cameras based on geographic objects. In Section 3 we show the implementation of the proposed scheme. We evaluate the effectiveness of our scheme in Section 4. Section 5 discusses related work and Section 6 concludes this paper.

2 Digest Creation of Videos Based on Geo-objects

2.1 Preliminaries

In this paper, we assume that a user carries a wearable computer equipped with a wearable camera, a GPS receiver, and a gyroscope, at all the activity time, and records all his/her activities by the wearable computer. More precisely, video data, locational information, and directional information of the camera motion are recorded by the wearable camera, the GPS receiver, and the gyroscope, respectively. Incidentally, a GPS receiver is usable only in the open air, that is, we cannot obtain locational information when we are in the rooms. However, we do not care this shortcoming, because the topic is beyond of our discussion, and we believe that such information can be compensated by other means in the near future. We also assume that geographic databases are available, by which we can query names of places or landmarks by pairs of latitudes and longitudes.

2.2 Overview

In this study, we try to automatically index video data recorded by wearable cameras based on geo-objects. To this end, we make use of context data of the users, such as traces of the users' move, geographic information inferred from the trace data, and the directions of wearable cameras. Those context data enable us to search for video fragments based on the users' demand. Besides that, this approach has the clear advantages as follows. First, the computational cost is significantly lower than that is necessary for analyzing long-sustained video data themselves. This feature also brings new possibilities of the real-time video analysis running on wearable computers. In the next, queries users initiate can be expressed with more familiar ways for the users, like points on maps, or names of places or buildings, as long as such information is provided.

In our scheme, the key concept is *importance* of geo-objects. We defined the *importance* of a geo-object based on the following observations:

- For a user, a geo-object is more important if he/she stays close to the geo-object for a long time. In such a case, we make the *importance* of the place high.
- In spite of this, the place may not be important for the user if he/she does not look the place at all, that is, he/she looks another place staying near the place. In order to take such situations into consideration, we use directions of wearable cameras.

Those data concerning users' context can be used for various purposes: 1) we can retrieve video fragments based on names of places or buildings, and we can simply realize this function in terms of string matches; 2) if we have a large numbers of video fragments as the result of a query, we can give order among the results in the order of their *importance*; and 3) we can create a digest from a video data, by selecting significant video fragments for the user based on the *importance* and putting them together in a new video data.

2.3 Calculating Importance of Geo-objects

Distance-based weights. Let $P_t = (x_t, y_t)$ be the position of a user at time t and $O_k = (X_k, Y_k)$ be the position of a geo-object. The Euclidean distance $d(P_t, O_k)$ between the geo-object and the user is defined as follows:

$$d(P_t, O_k) = \sqrt{(X_k - x_t)^2 + (Y_k - y_t)^2}$$

If $d(P_t, O_k)$ is smaller than a given threshold r, we consider that the user has visited the geo-object. We put the name of geo-object as well as the time into the index. As readers can see, density of geo-objects changes depending on the places, and it is to be desired that we can tell the appropriate r with respect to the density. For this purpose, we can take another strategy in that k-nearest geo-objects from the user are recorded in the index. We will confirm the effectiveness of this approach in Section 4.

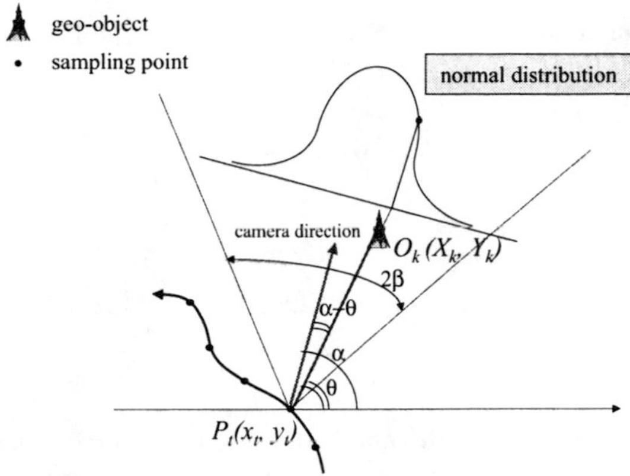

Fig. 1. Direction-based weighting of geo-objects.

At the same time, we compute the *weight* of the geo-object. Specifically, we calculate Euclidean distance between geo-objects and the user for every unit-time. The *weight* here should be calculated by a decreasing function from the above observations. Actually there are many functions that can be used for this purpose, for example, reciprocal of the distance, a linear decreasing function, and a normal distribution function. Due to the limitations of pages, we cannot describe the details, but we confirmed that the first one is the best through some experiments. We therefore employ the reciprocal of the Euclidean distance as the weighting function. The *weight* of the geo-object O_k ($w_{distance}(P_t, O_k)$) at time t is defined as follows:

$$w_{distance}(P_t, O_k) = \frac{1}{d(P_t, O_k)}$$

Direction-based weights. The *weights* of geo-objects solely based on distance are not adequate in many situations as mentioned in Section 2.2. In order to take the user's visual field into account, we introduce *weights* of geo-objects based on directions of wearable cameras.

Let us assume a user is placed in a map of north-side up, then a latitude line corresponds to an x-axis of the map. Let α_t be the angle between x-axis and the direction of the wearable camera at the time t, $\theta(P_t, O_k)$ be the angle between x-axis and the direction of a geo-object from the user. Figure 1 shows the relationship between the camera direction and the position of a geographic object. In that case, $\theta(P_t, O_k)$ can be calculated as:

$$\theta(P_t, O_k) = \tan^{-1} \frac{Y_k - y_t}{X_k - x_t}$$

In the next, we define the range of the user's vision. Let the range be β degree from the center of the user's view to right or to left. Consequently the range of the vision becomes $2 \times \beta$ degree. We are going to give higher *weight* as the geo-object comes close to the center of the user's view (α_t), that is, we give *weight* that follows the normal distribution

$N(0, \sigma^2)$ for the range of $-\beta < \alpha_t - \theta(P_t, O_k) < \beta$. Finally, $w_{direction}(P_t, O_k)$ is defined as:

$$w_{direction}(P_t, O_k) = \frac{1}{1-C} \exp\left(-\frac{(\alpha_t - \theta(P_t, O_k))^2}{2\sigma^2}\right) - \frac{C}{1-C}$$

where $C = \exp\left(-\frac{\beta^2}{2\sigma^2}\right)$. Note that the terms, $\frac{1}{1-C}$ and $\frac{C}{1-C}$, are for adjusting the *weight* in the range of $0 < w_{direction}(P_t, O_k) \leq 1$, and $w_{direction}(P_t, O_k) = 0$ if $|\alpha_t - \theta(P_t, O_k)| \geq \beta$.

Computing importance of geo-objects In order to make the best use of the two kinds of weights, we need to integrate those values into one. Taking (weighted) average of them is a simple way for that purpose. More precisely, we can do it by arithmetic and geometric averages. In this paper we use the geometrical average, and you can find the case of the arithmetic average in [4]. The integrated value then becomes:

$$w(P_t, O_k) = \sqrt{w_{distance}(P_t, O_k) \times w_{direction}(P_t, O_k)}$$

Intuitively, this formula tries to express the characteristics of our vision. That is, generally speaking, a geo-object is considered to be important for a user if he/she looks at the geo-object, but the *importance* degrades owing to the distance between the user and the place. Incidentally, the height of the geo-object plays an important role to decide the *importance*, but it is included in our future work.

Finally, we are ready to define the *importance* of geo-objects. Let $s \leq t \leq e$ be the times when $d(P_t, O_k) < r$ holds, the importance of O_k is defined as:

$$W(O_k) = \sum_{t=s}^{e} w(P_t, O_k)$$

In addition, in case of the user visits the geo-object for two or more times, the *importance* of O_k is defined as:

$$W(O_k) = \sum_{i=1}^{n} \sum_{t=s_i}^{e_i} w(P_t, O_k)$$

where s_i and e_i are the start and end times of the i-th visit.

2.4 Creating Digests

This section describes how we can create digests based on geo-objects and their *importance*. Figure 3 depicts overview of the process. The system receives three kinds of data, namely, video data, trace data of the user's move, and direction data of the wearable camera beforehand. Those data, except for video data, are recorded intermittently at a given interval, say, 1 second.

When computing *importance*, the system queries the names of geo-objects using the geographic database on the basis of the user's positions. Precisely, for each position, the system tries to find geo-objects where the user visited. The system then calculates the distance-based and direction-based *weight* values of each geo-object for each unit-time, using the formulae described above. After that, the system integrates those values as the *importance* of each geo-object.

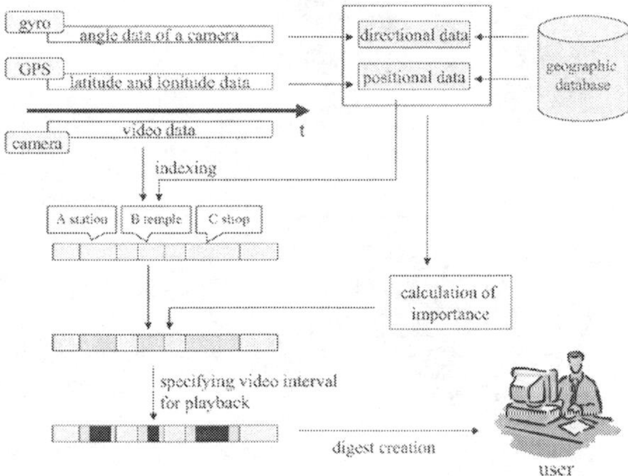

Fig. 2. Process overview.

When creating digests, the system first chooses geo-objects to be played with respect to the *importance* of geo-objects, and then retrieves video fragments corresponding to the selected geo-objects and put the results into a new video data. The detailed explanation follows:

1. The system requests the user to input the total playback time (t) and the number of scenes (n) to be included in the digest.
2. The system chooses n geo-objects in the order of *importance*, and shows the list of geo-objects to the user.
3. The user then refines the candidates in the list by selecting geo-objects not to be included in the final result.
4. The system recalculate the list of geo-objects by ordering the new candidates, and shows the result to the user again. (Repeat 3 and 4 until the list converges.)
5. The system searches for video fragments that include the geo-objects. For each fragment of the video, the actual playback time is decided by the algorithm below.
6. Finally, the system put the fragments into a new video, and returns it to the user.

Determining exact time-intervals for playback. Given the total time and the number of geo-objects to be played, we can take some strategies to allocate the playback time of each video fragment; One is to equally distribute the playback time for each fragment, and the other is to vary the playback time in proportion to the *importance*, that means we give longer times for the scenes in that the user is interested.

Another topic is how to decide the actual playback time-intervals for a given video data. Suppose we are going to include a geo-object in a digest, and 30 seconds are assigned for the scene. Practically, the recorded time in the original video data is much longer than that will be assigned in digests. The most simple approach is to divide the given time into equally sized two subintervals, and let the central time be the point where the *weight* of the geo-object indicates highest value. However, in general, we

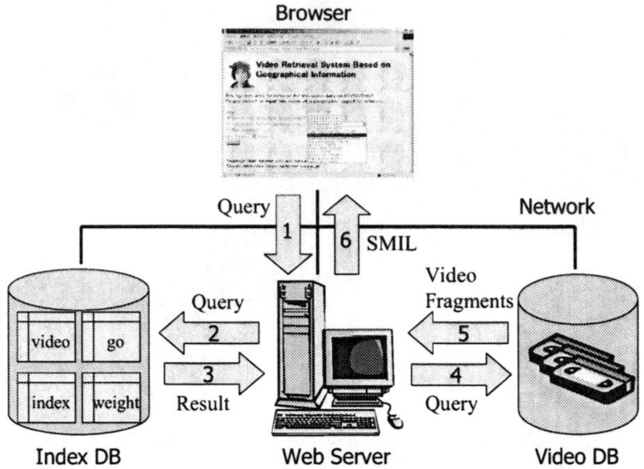

Fig. 3. System configuration.

have more interest in the scenes where we are coming close to geo-objects or we are doing something there than the scenes where we are going away from the place. Thus, we first decide the ratio of the playback times for the scenes before and after when the *weights* indicate the highest value. For example, let the ratio be $5:1$, the playback time be 1 minutes, and t be central time, the scene would be played for the time $[t-50, t+10]$.

3 Implementation

We have implemented a prototype system based on the above mentioned scheme. Figure 3 shows the configuration of the system. The system consists of a web server running CGI, an index database storing index information, and a video database. Users use web browsers to access to the system.

The database schema of the index database is as follows:

```
Video (id, name, date, starttime, endtime)
GO (id, name, latitude, longitude)
Index (video_id, go_id, starttime, endtime)
Weight (video_id, time, go_id, w_distance, w_direction)
```

where `Video` stores the metadata of each video data, `GO` stores the geo-objects and their positions that the user visited, `Index` stores the correspondence between the geo-objects and video intervals, and `Weight` stores *weights* of the geo-objects in every unit-time.

Given a request of query retrieval or digest creation from a user, the system queries the index database for appropriate video intervals. For example, video intervals containing "Nara National Museum" on "2001-05-18" can be retrieved by:

```
SELECT Video.name, Video.starttime, GO.starttime, GO.endtime
FROM   Video, Index, GO
WHERE  Index.video_id = Video.id
AND    Index.go_id = GO.id
AND    Video.date = '2001-05-18'
AND    GO.name like 'Nara National Museum';
```

Finally, the system retrieves the actual video fragments from the video database, and generates a SMIL (Synchronized Multimedia Integration Language) presentation [5] using the query results.

```
<smil>
  <head><layout>
      <region id="video-reg" left="0" top="0" height="210" width="340" />
      <region id="text-reg" left="0" top="210" height="20" width="340" />
  </layout></head>
  <body><par><seq>
        <video clip-begin="394.0s" clip-end="414.0s"
               src="file://d:/nara0518.mpg" region="video-reg" />
        <video clip-begin="833.0s" clip-end="853.0s"
               src="file://d:/nara0518.mpg" region="video-reg" />
  </seq>
  <textstream src="http://db-www.aist-nara.ac.jp/~takama-u/caption.rt"
              region="text-reg" fill="freeze" />
  </par></body>
</smil>
```

4 Evaluation

We have conducted experiments to confirm the effectiveness of our scheme, in particular, to see if the *importance* of geo-objects is meaningful or not. This section reports the experimental results, and gives some discussions.

4.1 Experimental Setup

We used Sony "CCD-MC100," a color video camera, as a wearable camera, and Sony "PCQ-GPS3SUG," a handy GPS receiver. Measurement error of PCQ-GPS3SUG is about 10 meters. We sampled user's locational data at every 1 second.

For geographic data, we used the numeric data including public facilities of Nara Prefecture in Japan, which is provided by Ministry of Land, Infrastructure, and Transport. In those data, 5,020 geo-objects are contained with their locations. However, it contains only public buildings, and does not contain geo-objects like temples, shrines, and shops. For this reason, we added some data concerning important geo-objects borrowed from "Atlas Z III" electronic map by hand.

In this experiment, we used the data of taking a walk in Nara Park, where there are many old temples and historical buildings. Figure 4 shows the route. As we can see from the figure, there are many geo-objects. Among the geo-objects, slanted-bold font represents the geo-objects we intended to visit, namely, "Todai Temple inner gate," "Todai Temple south big gate," "Nigatsu-do," and "Belfry."

4.2 Experimental Results

Tables 1 (a-1) – (a-3) show the experimental results. In (a-1), (a-2), and (a-3), we applied distance-based weights, direction-based weights, and both of them to compute the *importance* of each geo-object, respectively for 5-nearest geo-objects. We then created the rankings of the top twelve (12) geo-objects based on the *importance*. The underlined geo-objects represent the right answers. We can see from the tables, (a-3) was the best. In what follows, we can say that the combination of distance- and direction-based weights is effective. We can confirm this by another example. In this experiment, the tester looked at "Nigatsu-do" for a long time, and just behind of him was "Shigatsu-do."

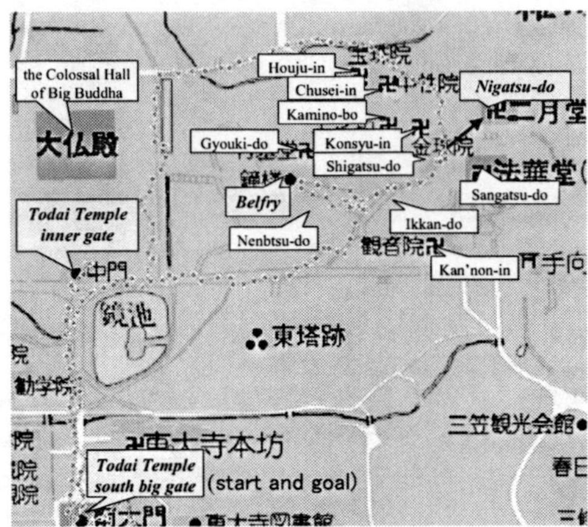

Fig. 4. The route used in the experiment.

For this reason, "Shigatsu-do" appears in the third in (a-1). By contrast, it degrades by taking the direction of camera into account in (a-3).

Additionally, we carried out another experiment to see the effectiveness of the k-nearest geo-objects strategy. Table 1 (b) shows the result in that we used fixed r ($r = 15$[1]). Recall that r represents the boundary between the user and a geo-object whether the object is indexed or not. By this strategy, we can adaptively change indexing areas owing to the density of geo-objects. In Figure 4 "Nigatsu-do" is isolated from the other geo-objects, and thus the ranking of "Nigatsu-do" was low in (b). However, it was improved in (a-3) by the approach.

5 Related Work

Until now, many researchers have devoted to the research of video data retrieval and digest creation, but few researches deal with video data recorded by wearable cameras. Nakamura et al.[6] proposed a method for analyzing video data recorded by wearable cameras. In this research, they defined two types of users' behaviors, "gaze at something in a short period" and "staying and continuously see something," by analyzing camera and object motion.

There are some researches dealing with bodily information, such as perspiration (Healey et al. [7]) and brain waves (Aizawa et al. [8]), in order to automatically organize video structures.

Our proposed method differs from the above mentioned researches in that we use user's positional information and camera's directional information at the same time. Combining those approaches and ours may be effective to achieve more satisfactory results.

[1] $r = 15$ is approximately 45 meters in the real-world.

Table 1. Ranking of geo-objects based on *importance*.

(a-1) 5-nearest / distance

Rank	Geo-object	Importance
1	Todai Temple inner gate	47.71
2	Todai Temple south big gate	39.20
3	Shigatsu-do	30.66
4	Ikkan-do	29.37
5	Belfry	27.98
6	Nenbutsu-do	26.60
7	Konshu-in	23.91
8	Gyouki-do	20.77
9	Shinkoku Shrine	16.79
10	Kamino-bo	15.84
11	Colossal Hall of Big Buddha	12.62
12	Nigatsu-do	12.02

(a-2) 5-nearest / direction

Rank	Geo-object	Importance
1	Todai Temple inner gate	378.05
2	Belfry	288.68
3	Nenbutsu-do	263.94
4	Todai Temple south big gate	229.37
5	Shinkoku Shrine	213.53
6	Gyouki-do	205.02
7	Ikkan-do	202.05
8	Colossal Hall of Big Buddha	183.98
9	Nigatsu-do	157.93
10	Konshu-in	112.68
11	Shigatsu-do	103.69
12	Sangatsu-do	92.90

(a-3) 5-nearest / distance and direction

Rank	Geo-object	Importance
1	Todai Temple south big gate	16.19
2	Todai Temple inner gate	15.18
3	Nenbutsu-do	11.14
4	Belfry	11.06
5	Nigatsu-do	9.66
6	Ikkan-do	8.62
7	Gyouki-do	6.79
8	Konshu-in	6.58
9	Shigatsu-do	5.53
10	Sangatsu-do	5.02
11	Shinkoku Shrine	4.76
12	Colossal Hall of Big Buddha	3.95

(b) $r = 15$ / distance and direction

Rank	Geo-object	Importance
1	Todai Temple south big gate	11.46
2	Todai Temple inner gate	7.14
3	Belfry	4.54
4	Nenbutsu-do	4.21
5	Shigatsu-do	2.81
6	Konshu-in	2.62
7	Ikkan-do	2.57
8	Nigatsu-do	1.53
9	Sangatsu-do	1.44
10	Chusei-in	1.39
11	Gyouki-do	1.35
12	Houju-in	0.83

6 Conclusions

In this paper, we proposed an approach to create a digest for video data recorded by a wearable camera based on geo-objects. Our method uses the notion of *importance* of geo-objects in order to infer important scenes in a given video data. We described a method for calculating importance of geo-objects from camera direction information obtained by gyroscope and distance between the user and geo-objects. We also showed the prototype implementation of the system, and conducted experiments to see the effectiveness of the proposed methods. As a result, we could confirm that the combination of distance- and direction-based *weights* of geo-objects was meaningful for us to automatically index video data recorded by wearable cameras.

In the future, we are going to take into account further information, such as height of buildings and extent of geo-objects. Besides that we are planning to use ontology of geo-objects in order to raise the accuracy of video retrieval.

References

1. Billinghurst, M., Bee, S., Bowskill, J., Kato, H.: Asymmetries in collaborative wearable interfaces. In: Proc. of Int'l Symposium on Wearable Computers (ISWC). (1999) 133–140
2. Rhodes, B.J., Minar, N., Weaver, J.: Wearable computing meets ubiquitous computing: Reaping the best of both worlds. In: Proc. of Int'l Symposium on Wearable Computers (ISWC). (1999) 141–149

3. Mayol, W., Tordoff, B., Murray, D.: Wearable visual robots. In: Proc. of Int'l Symposium on Wearable Computers (ISWC). (2000) 95–102
4. Ueda, T., Amagasa, T., Yoshikawa, M., Uemura, S.: Digest creation of video data recorded by wearable cameras using locational and geographical information. In: Proc of 1st Int'l Workshop on Wireless Information Systems (WIS–2002). (2002) 94–105
5. World Wide Web Consortium (W3C): Synchronized Multimedia Integration Language (SMIL 2.0) . (http://www.w3.org/TR/smil20/)
6. Nakamura, Y., Ohde, J., Ohta, Y.: Structuring personal experiences –analyzing views from a head-mounted camera. In: Proc. of Int'l Conference on Multimedea and Exposition (ICME). (2000) TP10–5
7. Healey, J., Picard, R.: Startlecam: A cybernetic wearable camera. In: Proc. of Int'l Symposium on Wearable Computers (ISWC). (1998)
8. Aizawa, K., Ishijima, K., Shiina, M.: Automatic summarization of wearable video – indexing subjective interest. In: Proc. of IEEE Pacific Rim Conference on Multimedia. (2001) 16–23

Similarity Image Retrieval System Using Hierarchical Classification

– Experimental System on Mobile Internet with Cellular Phone –

Masahiro Tada[1], Toshikazu Kato[1], and Isao Shinohara[2]

[1] Department of Industrial and Systems Engineering, Chuo University, 1-13-27, Kasuga, Bunkyo-ku, Tokyo 112-8551, Japan
{umehara, kato}@indsys.chuo-u.ac.jp
[2] Kyodo Printing CO.,LTD. 4-14-12 Koishikawa, Bunkyo-ku, Tokyo 112-8501, Japan
i_shinohara@kyodoprinting.co.jp

Abstract. We developed a similarity image retrieval system for database consists of various kinds and large amount of image data. Our system has the following features. (1) The similarity retrieval algorithm selects the most similar group to the visual key step by step as a search space so that the system could achieve less computation and better precision. (2) The system can easily adapt each user's subjective criterion for similarity. (3) The interface is so user friendly that just showing a key image is enough to invoke content-based image retrieval. Based on the features above, we developed and evaluated a similarity retrieval system using cellular phone with digital camera as a multimedia terminal.

1. Introduction

Most of the image retrieval systems at the major portal sites are designed on text based matching. Nevertheless text based matching has following problems. (1) Although text based matching is capable of retrieving candidate images having the same keywords, it is not capable of ordering them by the similarity of image contents. Thus, users are obliged to examine a large number of candidates by visual inspection. (2) Even to the same image, users may subjectively give their own interpretations based on their experience and knowledge. Therefore, keywords assigned to an image do not always suit every user. Furthermore, being once created, the keyword index cannot catch up with changes of users' interests. (3) There are many kinds of images which are hardly to describe their contents by simple keywords; such as texture images, graphic symbols, and design patterns. In order to retrieve such images by their contents, we have to show a similar instance or a hand-written sketch and to apply similarity retrieval with evaluating the graphical feature of the images.

Therefore, based on graphical features (GFs) of each image, we have developed a "Query by Visual Example (QVE)" system for database which consists of various kinds and large amount of image data. Here, GFs represent the pictorial content of the image in multi-dimensional vector form.

R. Cicchetti et al. (Eds.): DEXA 2002, LNCS 2453, pp. 779–788, 2002.

The objectives of our study are following;

(a) Computational modeling of visual perception process based on physiology and psychology: We employ statistical method to model the process in which each user subjectively judges similarity of images by his (or her) own experience and knowledge.

(b) Adapting the model to time-varying criterion of similarity: We develop a statistical supervised learning algorithm which is easy to rearrange the training examples and does not force users to cost much time and patience.

(c) Developing similarity retrieval algorithm: We develop an efficient algorithm in precision and computation for a large-scale database.

In this paper, we propose a modeling method using multivariate analysis for hierarchical classification of database. In this method, when a visual key is shown, the most similar set in hierarchically classified database is selected. Then, only the selected set is regarded as a retrieval domain. This method has achieved better precision and less computation in our experiments.

Since it is too tough to become accustomed to database languages for novice computer users, we also show our prototype system developed for mobile Internet environment. In this system, by using a cellular phone with digital camera (mobile camera) as a database terminal, a user has only to capture key image by mobile camera to retrieve similar images from the database. Thus, a user does not have to know much about database nor computer operations. We have evaluated its performance on our large amount of texture image database.

2. System Architecture

2.1 Content-Based Retrieval Mechanism

The QVE system uses an image itself as a visual key instead of keywords. Visual perception system of human being has nerve circuit which extracts local or global features of brightness and colors in its visual field. By integrating and evaluating these features, we perceive textures and shapes. Therefore, in our experiment, we extract the graphical features (GFs) to simulate the human visual perception in judging similarity. We have designed graphical features in multi-dimensional vector form to represent features perceived from each image (see Chap.3).

The system hierarchically traces the most similar set to the visual key on the bottom level of classification. The set is selected and regarded as a retrieval domain (see Chap.4).

2.2 User Friendly Interface

In Japan, more than 50% people have cellular phones, many of which are equipped with digital camera (mobile camera), and use them as the first aid to access to the Internet instead of personal computer. Cellular phones are very familiar to many people in capturing photos and exchanging them via email. Therefore, we adopt this type of cellular phone as a database terminal for content-based image retrieval.

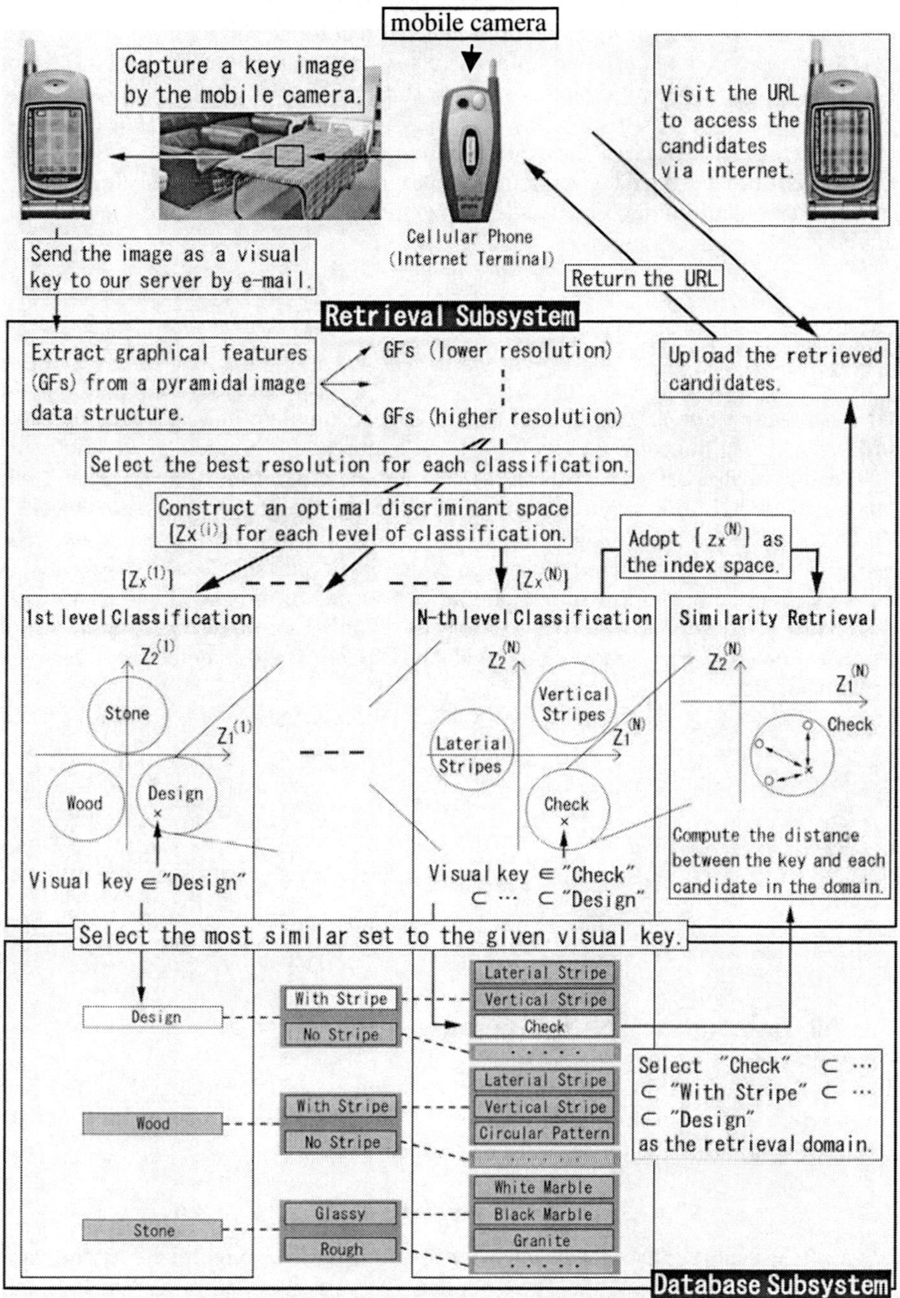

Fig. 1. Architecture of "Query by Visual Example" system using cellular phone

The user's operations for QVE are following;
(1) Capture a key image by the mobile camera on cellular phone.
(2) Send the image to our server as a visual key by e-mail (cellular phone's function)
(3) Receive the URL by e-mail where the summary report of the retrieved result is uploaded.
(4) Visit the URL to access the candidate images.
Our system can be operated without complex database languages. In this paper, we propose this kind of mobile database operation "Retrieve anytime, anywhere, by anybody ".

3. Graphical Features (GFs)

As discussed in Sec.2.1, we should design GFs to simulate human visual perception process which extracts local as well as global features of brightness and colors.

We should also design GFs as shift-invariant and noise-robust, because the camera angle and the lightning conditions are not same even if capturing the same object.

To measure the GFs of textures, local features in neighboring pixels as well as global features defined on whole image plane are important. In our experiment, we adopted 3×3 pixels window to compute local features of directions and curvatures of differentials. Therefore, we adopt relations of neighboring three pixels in the window as local features. Fig.2 shows the local mask patterns, the center of which is the reference point.

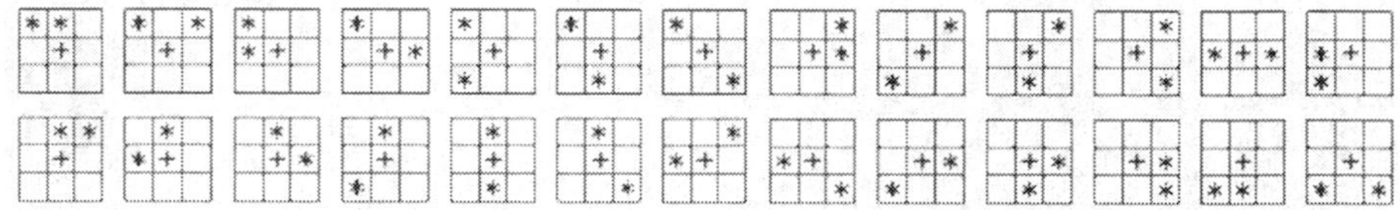

Fig. 2. Local mask patterns for GFs

3.1 Shift Invariance and Noise Robustness

It is well known that the autocorrelation function is shift-invariant. Otsu and Kurita proposed its extension to higher orders [3]. The Nth-order autocorrelation functions with N displacement vectors $\mathbf{a}_1, \quad, \mathbf{a}_N \in \mathrm{R}^2$ are defined by

$$y^{\mathrm{N}}(\mathbf{a}_1, \cdots, \mathbf{a}_N) = \int_P f(\mathbf{r}) f(\mathbf{r}+\mathbf{a}_1) \cdots f(\mathbf{r}+\mathbf{a}_N) d\mathbf{r},$$

where f(**r**) stands for the image intensity function on the image plane *P*, and $\mathbf{r} \in P$ is the image coordinate vector. They applied 0th, 1st and 2nd-order autocorrelation functions to face recognition [3] and texture classification [4].

Since the autocorrelation functions include multiplication of noisy intensity values, it is easily affected by noise. Therefore, based on Weber-Fechner's law, "equal increments of sensation are associated with equal increments of the logarithm of the stimulus," we defined tri-contrast as follows:

$$C^{(3)}(\mathbf{a}_1, \mathbf{a}_2, \mathbf{r}) = \frac{\{ g(\mathbf{r}+\mathbf{a}_1) - g(\mathbf{r}) \} + \{ g(\mathbf{r}+\mathbf{a}_2) - g(\mathbf{r}) \}}{| g(\mathbf{r}+\mathbf{a}_1) | + | g(\mathbf{r}+\mathbf{a}_2) | + 2 | g(\mathbf{r}) |} ,$$

where $\mathbf{a}_1$ and $\mathbf{a}_2 \in R^2$ are the displacement vectors (each "*" in Fig.2 denotes $\mathbf{a}_1$ and $\mathbf{a}_2$), function g(r) is defined on independent three-dimensional color space which is an extended version of f(r) which is defined on monochrome image, and $\mathbf{r} \in P$ is the image coordinate vector (each "+" in Fig.2 denotes $\mathbf{r}$).

Using tri-contrast defined above, we designed local GFs as follows:

$$x(\mathbf{a}_1, \mathbf{a}_2) = \int_P \frac{\{ g(\mathbf{r}+\mathbf{a}_1) - g(\mathbf{r}) \} + \{ g(\mathbf{r}+\mathbf{a}_2) - g(\mathbf{r}) \}}{| g(\mathbf{r}+\mathbf{a}_1) | + | g(\mathbf{r}+\mathbf{a}_2) | + 2 | g(\mathbf{r}) |} d\mathbf{r} .$$

The denominator and numerator of our tri-contrast denote a power of intensity and a difference of stimulus, respectively. Here, regarding S as intensity of stimulus, tri-contrast correspond to S / S. Hence, local GFs designed above correspond to

$$(1 / S)\, ds = \log S.$$

Therefore, our local GFs approximately follow Weber-Fechner's law:

$$I = K \log S + C,$$

where I, K, S, and C denote intensity of sensation, constant, intensity of stimulus and constant, respectively.

Since tri-contrast value is normalized by intensity of stimulus, local GFs are robust to noise. In addition, they are obviously shift-invariant.

Considering the independency of brightness and color, we adopted the L*a*b* color-space. L*, a* and b* denote luminosity, red-green chromaticity and yellow-blue chromaticity, respectively. Since L*a*b* color-space consists of three dimensional orthogonal coordinates, each tri-contrast value of L*, a*, b* is defined independently of the others. Therefore, without considering correlations with L*, a* and b*, we can compute local GFs regarding only each of the L*, a*, b* values of reference pixel r as g(r). In addition to these local GFs, we compute the average of each L*, a*, b* value as global GFs.

3.2 Optimal Resolution for GFs

GFs extracted from highest resolution may include only very detail information, while GFs from lower resolution do only very rough information. Since an optimal resolution for classification depends on target image sets, we can not fix the resolution of images beforehand.

A pyramidal image data structure gives a set of images of different resolutions from the highest to lower [5]. By extracting sets of GFs from each of the images in the pyramidal image data structure and selecting the most proper one for each target, an optimal set of GFs for each target are extracted.

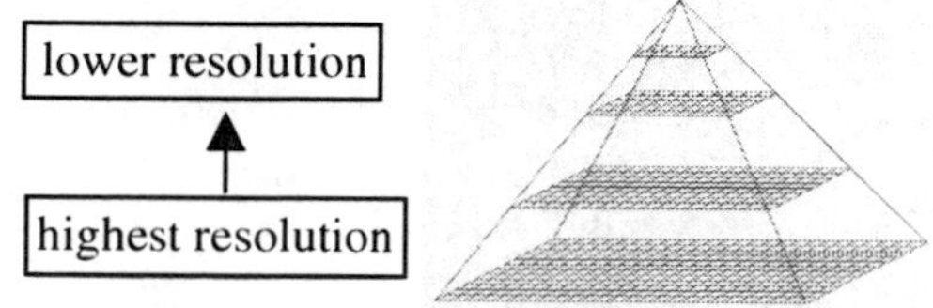

Fig. 3. An example of pyramidal image data structure

4. Hierarchical Classification

4.1 Advantages of Using Hierarchical Classification

To statistically model the process in which each user subjectively judges similarity of images by his (or her) own experience and knowledge, following requirements should be satisfied.

(1) The number of data: To apply reliable statistical supervised learning, we need a large number of training examples.
(2) Subjective criterion: We have to give the criterion on judging subjective similarity rule to the examples.
(3) Adaptation to time-varying criterion of subjective judgment: Experience changes user's subjective criterion for judging similarity. To adapt the model to this time-varying criterion, users have to repeatedly give a large number of training examples.

To give the criterion, one idea is to give it on judging subjective similarity rule in a similarity matrix form. In showing similarity matrix, each user has to assign the similarity score to each pair of samples. Another idea is to hierarchically classify the database according to subjective similarity. In hierarchical classification, each user subjectively classifies whole images into sets of similar images hierarchically by his (or her) own experience and knowledge. Such hierarchical classification has the following advantages;

(1) Compared with a similarity matrix form, non-hierarchical classification is only a rough approximation of subjective similarity, while a hierarchical classification gives rather detailed subjective similarity step by step.
(2) In giving criterion, a user may stop the hierarchical classification at any time. The system can apply supervised learning algorithm with the temporarily classified data. A user can continue the classification to give more detailed.
(3) Through hierarchical classification, comparison and similarity evaluation of data is rather localized. Therefore, to re-apply supervised learning, or to re-classify training examples, a user does not always have to rearrange the classification of whole training examples. In most cases, a user has only to re-classify the small portion of the database.

Therefore, hierarchical classification is more efficient than non-hierarchical classification.

4.2 Linear Discriminant Analysis (LDA)

An effective set of GF ($\subset$ GFs) for a classification as well as an optimal resolution for it depends on target image sets and classification levels. Therefore, we separately construct an optimal discriminant space $\mathbf{z} = (z_1, \ ,z_N)^T$ for a classification at each level by combinations of GFs $\mathbf{x} = (x_1, \ ,x_M)^T$.

Most simple way to combine GFs is to use weighted linear combination

$$\mathbf{z} = \mathbf{A}^T\mathbf{x},$$

where $\mathbf{A} = [a_{ij}]$ is a weighting matrix. To determine the weights, we apply linear discriminant analysis (LDA).

Given K sets C_i (i = 1, … , K) with a priori probabilities $_i$, the within-class and the between-class covariance matrices of GFs are computed as follows:

$$_W = \sum_{i=1}^{K} \ _i \ _i , \qquad _B = \sum_{i=1}^{K} \ _i (\overline{x}^{(i)} - \overline{x}) (\overline{x}^{(i)} - \overline{x})^T ,$$

where $\overline{\boldsymbol{x}}^{(i)}$, $\overline{\boldsymbol{x}}$, and $_i$ denote the mean vector of class C_i, the total mean vector, and the covariance matrix of class C_i, respectively.

Then the optimal weighting matrix **A** is given by the solution of the following eigen-equations,

$$_B \mathbf{A} = \ _W \mathbf{A} \quad , \quad \mathbf{A}^T \ _W \mathbf{A} = \mathbf{I},$$

where is a diagonal matrix of eigenvalues. The j-th column of **A** is the eigenvector corresponding to the j-th largest eigenvalue. The dimension of discriminant space **z** is bound by min(K−1, M).

4.3 Hierarchical Classification Algorithm

Our hierarchical classification algorithm is following.

(a) Regard whole database as a given set. Apply (b) to (d) while n >> k, where n and k denotes the number of images in a given set and the dimension number of GFs, respectively.

(b) Classify given set into a small number of subsets.

(c) Select the optimal resolution for the classification of subsets. Apply LDA to construct an optimal discriminant space by linear combinations of GFs.

(d) Regard each subset as a given set.

The number of discriminant spaces made on this algorithm is $\sum_{i=1}^{L-1} n_i$, where n_i and L denote the number of subsets in i-th level and the number of levels, respectively.

As discussed in Sec.4.2, the dimension of discriminant space **z** is bound by the number of target sets. Since the hierarchical classification algorithm of the image data reduces the number of target sets, it provides discriminant spaces of a small dimension.

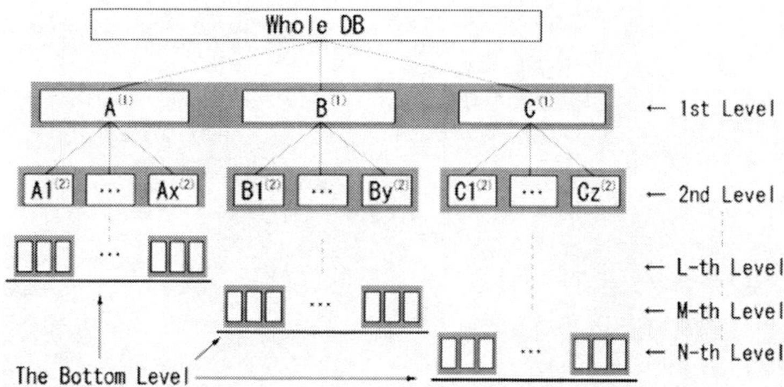

Fig. 4. An example of hierarchically classified database

4.4 Similarity Retrieval Algorithm

First, receiving the visual key, the most similar set in hierarchically classified database is selected step by step, from the top level of classification to the bottoms, using optimal discriminant spaces constructed in Sec.4.3. Secondly, regarding the selected set as a retrieval domain and the optimal discriminant space for the set as an index space, we compute the Euclidean distances between visual key and images in retrieval domain. Then the nearest image from the visual key is regarded as the candidate. By selecting the most similar set to the visual key, dissimilar images by the user's criterion are excluded from the retrieval domain.

Let us discuss the amount of computation in retrieval. By hierarchical classification, we have only to examine $O(\log N)$ to select the most similar subset, where N and $O(\log N)$ denote the number of whole data and proportional number to N, respectively. In the subset, we have to evaluate each distance for $O(M)$ times, where, M denotes the average number of data in each subset on the bottom levels. Even if the number of data grows to N' (N'>>N), the average number of data M remains in the same order, since users may give more detailed re-classification. Thus, the amount of computation does not increase in proportion to the growth of the database. Therefore, we achieve less computation and better precision in similarity retrieval.

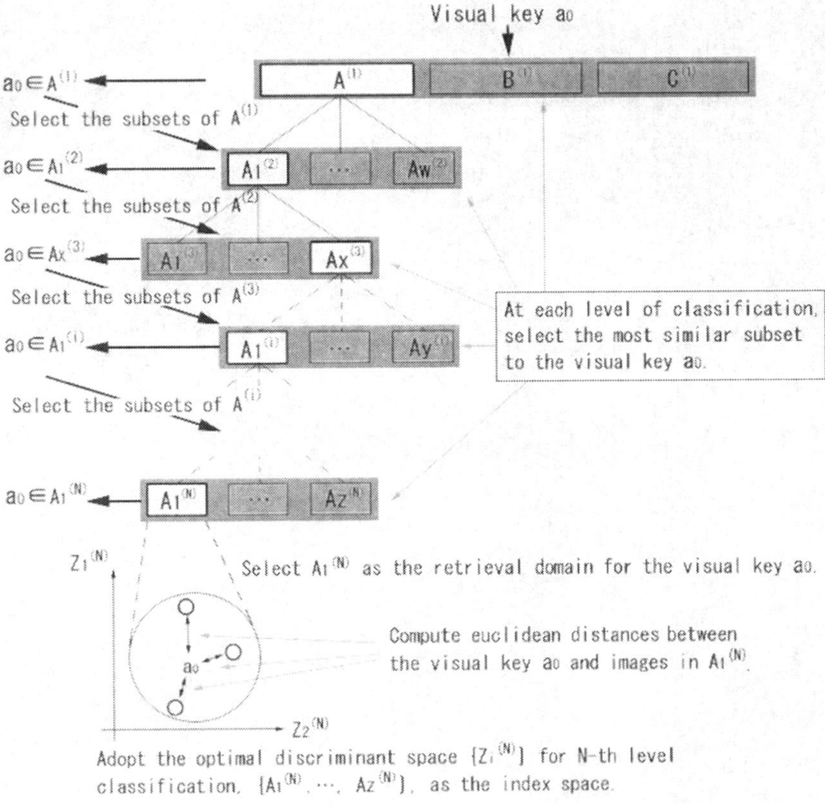

Fig. 5. Similarity retrieval algorithm

5. Experiments

5.1 Hierarchical Classification

As discussed in Chap.4, receiving a visual key, our system traces and selects the most similar set to the key step by step beforehand. Since mistracing may affect similarity retrieval, we need a good recognition ratio of each classification, usually required not less than 85%.

In our experiments, we prepared 5,700 images (240   320 pixels). Then, by using hierarchical classification algorithm introduced in Sec.4.3, we classified them into three levels (1st, 2nd, and 3rd level has three, six, and 18 sets, respectively) and constructed the optimal discriminant space for each classification (9 spaces in total). Here, we constructed pyramidal image data structure using reduced images in 1, 1/2, 1/4, and 1/8 resolution. Each set on 1st level has approx. 1,900 images, on 2nd level, each set has approx. 900 images, and on 3rd level, each set has approx. 300 images. When applying LDA to construct the optimal discriminant space, we used half of each set as training examples and the rest as test sets.

To evaluate the efficiency of our GFs and hierarchical classification (HC) method, we have compared recognition ratios on the test sets with each combination; our GFs and color histogram for parameters, HC and non-hierarchical classification (non-HC) methods. Table 1 shows the recognition ratios of each experiment. HC method on our GFs achieved much better recognition ratios than other methods.

Table 1. Recognition ratios of each classification on 3rd level (%)

Parameters	Methods	A	B	C	D	E	F	G	H	I
Our GFs	HC	98.0	92.4	85.2	91.3	88.5	87.5	100	89.9	93.0
	Non-HC	70.6	59.4	30.0	57.1	40.6	71.9	77.3	56.3	52.6
Color histogram	HC	50.6	42.8	44.3	47.0	41.0	40.6	72.2	67.8	67.5
	Non-HC	42.5	41.9	39.1	42.2	24.9	38.5	65.4	58.9	60.2

Parameters	Methods	J	K	L	M	N	O	P	Q	R	Average
Our GFs	HC	97.7	90.1	84.8	90.1	92.1	88.5	94.0	80.5	87.8	90.6
	Non-HC	74.1	65.1	66.7	40.8	65.9	60.1	74.5	54.8	62.8	60.0
Color histogram	HC	79.5	73.2	62.2	79.1	73.6	67.2	69.5	60.6	70.8	61.6
	Non-HC	68.3	60.8	54.0	50.8	54.9	47.1	60.5	52.0	59.1	51.2

5.2 Similarity Retrieval

As shown in Sec.5.1, recognition ratios using HC method on our GFs are good enough. Then, we evaluated the performance of our image retrieval system.

We prepared new 150 images and printed them out. Then, by the operations introduced in Sec. 2.2, we captured each of them by the mobile camera, showing it as a visual key, and invoked similarity retrieval. In our performance evaluation, we measured precision ratio. Precision ratio is defined as follows:

$$precision\ \ ratio = \frac{the\ number\ of\ relevant\ candidates\ retrieved}{the\ number\ of\ total\ candidates\ retrieved}.$$

In our experiments, the precision ratio by HC method on our GFs is 81.3%, while those by other methods are less than 40.0%.

From the viewpoint of computation, the index space is only two dimensions and retrieval domain contains approx. 300 images by HC method, while the index space is 17 dimensions and retrieval domain contains 5,700 images by non-HC method.

Therefore, by using HC method, we can achieve better precision and less computation at the same time.

6. Conclusion

We developed hierarchical classification method for similarity retrieval with better precision and less computation. In this mechanism, only a small number of subsets are traced to reduce the index space for similarity retrieval and exclude dissimilar patterns. Thus we achieved both better precision and less computation at the same time even for a large database.

This mechanism, QVE, also provides subjective criteria for content-based image retrieval, which means the system provides more user friendly service with his (or her) kansei model.

We developed our prototype systems for mobile Internet environment. Just capturing an image as a key, a user can retrieve pictorial information from the Internet in a user friendly manner.

References

[1] T. Kato, "Database architecture for content-based image retrieval," *The International Society for Optimal Engineering*, vol.1662, pp. 111-123, 1992

[2] K. Hirata and T. Kato, "Query by Visual Example," *Advances in Database Technology – EDBT '92*, pp. 56-71, 1992

[3] T.Kurita, N. Otsu, and T. Sato, "A Face Recognition Method Using Higher Order Local Autocorrelation And Multivariate Analysis," *Proc. of 11th International Conf. on Pattern Recognition*, vol. 2, pp. 213-216, 1992

[4] T. Kurita and N. Otsu, "Texture Classification by Higher Order Local Autocorrelation Features," *Proc. of Asian Conf. on Computer Vision*, pp. 175-178, 1993

[5] D.H.Ballrad and C.M.Brown, *Computer Vision*, Prentice-Hall, 1982

[6] L. Spillmann and J. S. Werner, *Visual Perception*, Academic Press, 1990

[7] M. Kreutz, B. Völpel, and H. Janßen, "Scale-Invariant Image Recognition Based on Higher Order," *Pattern Recognition*, vol.29, no.1, pp. 19-26, 1996

Information Extraction – Tree Alignment Approach to Pattern Discovery in Web Documents

Ajay Hemnani and Stephane Bressan

National University of Singapore,
3 Science Drive 2, Singapore 117543
{hemnania, steph}@comp.nus.edu.sg

Abstract. The World Wide Web has now entered its mature age. It not only hosts and serves large amounts of pages but also offers large amounts of information potentially useful for individuals and businesses. Modern decision support can no more be effective without timely and accurate access to this unprecedented source of data. However, unlike in a database, the structure of data available on the Web is not known apriori and its understanding seems to require human intervention. Yet the conjunction of layout rules and simple domain knowledge enables in many cases the automatic understanding of such unstructured data. In such cases we say that data is semi-structured. Wrapper generation for automatic extraction of information from the Web has therefore been a crucial challenge in the recent years. Various authors have suggested different approaches for extracting semi-structured data from the Web, ranging from analyzing the layout and syntax of Web documents to learning extraction rules from user's training examples. In this paper, we propose to exploit the HTML structure of Web documents that contain information in the form of multiple homogeneous records. We use a Tree Alignment algorithm with a novel combination of heuristics to detect repeated patterns and infer extraction rules. The performance study shows that our approach is effective in practice, yielding practical performance and accurate results.

1 Introduction

There are billions of terabytes of information on the World Wide Web. A significant amount of this information is semi-structured. By semi-structured, we mean data, for which no data model and schema are known apriori, but which can still be understood by a machine based on simple assumptions on the layout and syntax rules and possibly with some sufficient domain knowledge. Examples of such documents include online classifieds, product catalogs, staff directories, search engine listings, and so on. Manual parsing of these documents is tedious, time-consuming and unnecessary. This has motivated a lot of research efforts concerning the invention of information agents that automatically extract information from multiple websites. These agents rely on a set of extraction rules, and

R. Cicchetti et al. (Eds.): DEXA 2002, LNCS 2453, pp. 789–798, 2002.

are more commonly known as wrappers. For structured text, the rules specify a fixed order of relevant information. As for free text, an information extraction system needs several steps in addition to text extraction such as syntactic analysis, semantic tagging, recognizers for domain objects and so on. On the other hand, many Web documents such as search engine pages, online catalogs and classifieds contain data that is typically semi-structured. The data is usually organized in chunks called records, usually stored in the form of table rows, multiple paragraphs, lists, etc. These records are embedded within certain HTML tags. The fact that each web page usually displays a subset of these records implies the regular and repetitive nature of these embedding tags. Hence, the motivation behind building extraction rules based on these patterns has generated considerable interest in the research community. In this paper, we focus on syntactic analysis of such Web documents, taking advantage of the natural tree structure created by the nested HTML tags, with the help of an approximate tree-matching algorithm.

One of the existing approaches for Information Extraction that makes use of approximate tree matching algorithms relies on the use on template trees as proposed by Yih [13]. Although the approach is simple, the main drawback is the template generation process. It is time consuming, labor-intensive and proves to be tedious for novice users. Rahardjo B. [11] uses approximate string matching techniques to find textual similarities and differences between Web documents that form the basis for automatic extraction.

On the other hand, our main objective is to build a technique to extract information from Web documents such that the technique is robust, domain independent as well as requires no human intervention. The idea is based on the Tree Alignment algorithm [7] and our proposed heuristics. The purpose of the Tree Alignment algorithm is two-fold. This algorithm will facilitate the *detection* of "similar" subtrees (representing repeating patterns that could possibly be extraction rules) as well as *align* them to generate complete generalized extraction rules. Our heuristics are based on practical observations that we had made on several important and diverse websites over a significant period of time. In the interest of space, we will present the relevant performance studies of only a representative set of websites that we monitored.

The remainder of the paper is organized as follows. Section 2 discusses about related work. Section 3 describes the tag tree construction phase, demonstrates how the Tree Alignment algorithm works and its connection with the record boundary discovery problem. Section 4 presents the details of our proposed approach of using heuristics to facilitate the detection of repeated patterns based on the Tree Alignment algorithm. Section 5 reports our performance study that demonstrates the effectiveness of our proposed strategy. Finally, in Section 6, we conclude with directions for future work.

2 Related Work

Recent research efforts on structuring Web information have mainly focused on wrapper generation, natural language processing and Web data modelling. Automatic wrapper generation uses machine-learning techniques, and the wrapper research community has developed learning algorithms for a spectrum of wrappers from the simplest to the most sophisticated. Systems like ShopBot [3], WIEN [8], SoftMealy [6] and STALKER [10] use techniques that are tailored for relatively well-structured Web documents. These systems use delimiter-based extraction patterns and do not use syntactic or semantic constraints. Other systems like RAPIER [1], SRV [5] and WHISK [12] are examples of wrapper generators based on techniques intended for Web documents with a less rigorous structure. These systems must usually go through a training phase, where they are fed with training examples that have to be manually labeled. This poses a question of economy of scale.

On the other hand, Embley et al. [4] adopt a heuristic approach to discover record boundary in multiple-record Web documents In their approach, they capture the structure of the document as a tree of nested HTML tags, locate the subtree containing the records of interest, identify candidate separator tags using five independent heuristics, and select a consensus separator tag based on a combined heuristic. However, this one-tag separator approach fails when the separator tag is used elsewhere among a record other than the boundary. Continuing with the approach of analyzing structural content of Web documents, Lakshmi [9] proposes extracting information from the Web through exploiting the latent information given by HTML tags. For each specific extraction task, an object model is created consisting of the salient fields to be extracted and the corresponding extraction rules based on a library of HTML parsing functions. Chang et. al. [2] built a system that can automatically identify the record boundary by repeated pattern mining and multiple sequence alignment using a data structure called PAT trees to help in the discovery of repeated patterns. The main application of PAT trees is in the domain of exact matching. To allow approximate matching, the technique for multiple string alignment is adopted to extend the discovered exact repeats.

3 Extracting Information from Web Documents

This section describes the tag tree construction phase; demonstrates how the Tree Alignment algorithm works and its connection with record boundary discovery problem.

3.1 Tag Tree Construction

We adopt the algorithm used by Embley et al. [4]. This algorithm reads in a Web document D and builds a tag tree T after discarding "useless" tags and inserting all "missing" end tags. A "useless" tag is a tag that either starts with <! or is

an end tag that has no corresponding start tag. This Tag-Tree construction algorithm has time complexity O(n), where n is the length of the input Web document. After generating the tag tree T, the next task is to locate the subtree of T that contains the records. Embley et. al. use a conjecture that simply states that in a Web document with multiple records of interest, the subtree of T whose root has the highest fan-out should contain the records. The highest fan-out rule is very straightforward and works for most cases. However, in the case of certain Web documents, the subtrees with the highest fan-out do not contain the records of interest. For such documents, the subtree containing the records of interest will go undetected. The Web documents generated by Webcrawler are a good example. Therefore, to ensure that we process the correct subtree, we use a pre-defined list of tags that generally embed records of interest such as <P>, <TABLE>, <TR>, <TD>, <BLOCKQUOTE>, <HR>, <A> and so on. Once the subtree containing the records of interest in the tag tree has been identified, the next task would be to discover the record boundary and detect the repeating pattern of tags that embed these records, and align them to form generalized extraction rules that will cater to all the records in the relevant Web documents.

3.2 Alignment of Trees

The idea of alignment of trees was proposed by Jiang et. al. [7], and used for approximate tree matching to compute a measure of similarity between 2 ordered, labeled trees. An alignment A of trees T_1 and T_2 (see Figure 1) is obtained by first inserting nodes with no labels (empty spaces) into T_1 and T_2, to obtain T_1' and T_2', such that both of them have the same structure when the labels are ignored, and subsequently overlaying T_1' on T_2'. As a result of overlaying, each node will be a pair of labels. A score is defined for each pair. Each possible alignment has a value that is equal to the sum of the scores of all pairs of opposing labels. This value is called the **alignment distance**. An *optimal alignment* is one that minimizes the alignment distance over all possible alignments between T_1 and T_2. The time complexity of this Tree Alignment algorithm is O(|T1| . |T2| . $(\deg(T_1) + \deg(T_2))^2$), where $|T_i|$ is the number of nodes in T_i and $\deg(T_i)$ is the degree of T_i, i=1,2. The degree of a tree is the maximum number of children of any node in the tree. The idea of alignment of trees can be easily generalized to more than 2 trees. This provides a way to compare multiple trees simultaneously.

3.3 The Record Boundary Discovery Problem

Let S be the highest fan-out subtree containing the records of interest obtained from the tag tree T, as explained in section 3.1. Although it is very compelling to believe that each subtree under S is possibly a record by itself, it is not always the case with many of the Web documents. Hence, it is necessary to detect the boundary of these records, i.e. how many of the consecutive subtrees

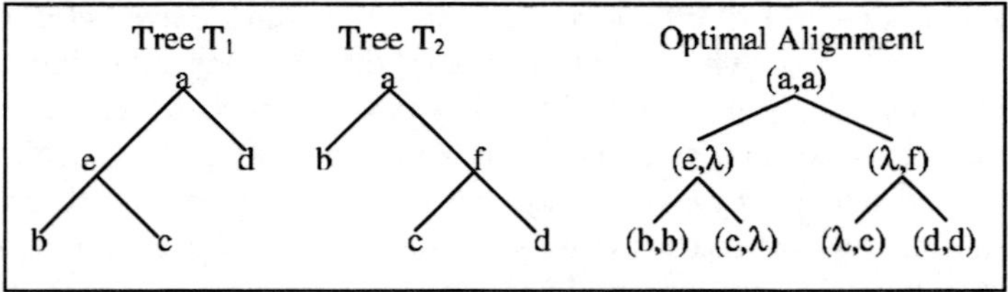

Fig. 1. Example of aligning tree T_1 with tree T_2

under S actually make up one record. A good example would be the MPH Online Bookstore website (see Figure 2). It presents its product listing as records in single-column table rows <TR><TD>Text</TD></TR>, and inserts an empty row <TR></TR> after every record row. Now it becomes very important to realize that each empty row after the record becomes part of the record itself. Hence, the generalized pattern should be:

<TR><TD>Text</TD></TR><TR></TR>

Failure to recognize this fact would result in the following generalized pattern:

<TR>[<TD>Text</TD> | -]</TR>

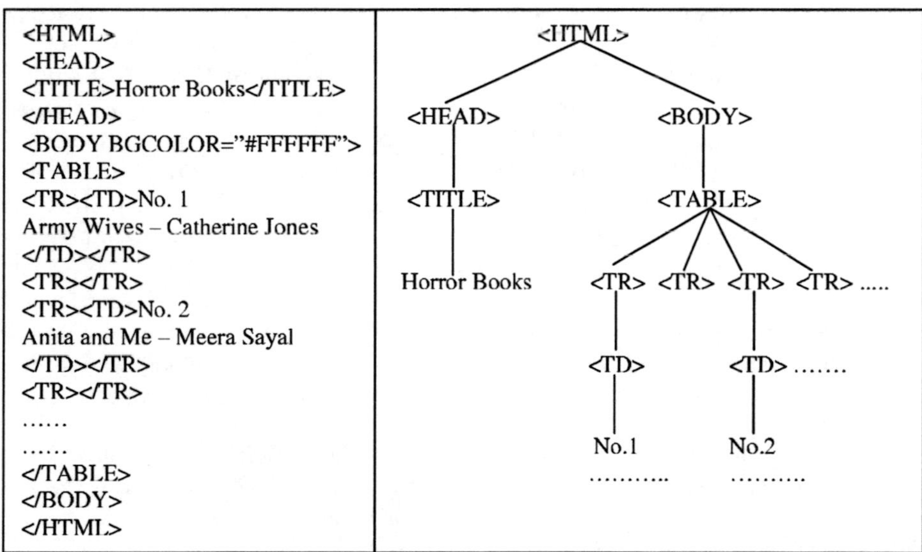

Fig. 2. A simplified Web document from MPH Online Bookstore and its corresponding tag tree

This would cause a lot of unwanted records data to be extracted and hence affect the accuracy rate. The record boundary discovery problem becomes even more difficult because of minor differences between records that result in different patterns. For example, we consider a Web document that displays second hand laptops for sale in a tabular fashion, with three columns showing the model, contact information and latest price. Now for some of the products, the latest price might not have been quoted. Thus, the generalized pattern would be:

<TR><TD>Text</TD><TD>Text</TD> [<TD>Text</TD> | -]</TR>

The square brackets indicate that some records do not have the third column and hence the dash (-). The Tree Alignment algorithm helps to integrate all the "similar" repeating patterns and align them in such a way so as to establish one generalized pattern that will be able to extract all the records of interest contained in the relevant Web documents.

4 The Proposed Strategy

We have reduced the problem of record boundary discovery to that of finding how many consecutive subtrees does a single record span. We define two heuristics, which we use in conjunction with the multiple tree alignment algorithm to cluster "similar" patterns together and align all the patterns in each of the clusters independently.

- **Alignment Distance Clustering (ADC) Heuristic:** As the name suggests, we compare all trees pairwise and compute the alignment distance of each pair of trees. For each tree, we cluster it together with trees based on smallest alignment distance measure. The key observation here is that similar trees will have smaller alignment distances; hence they have to be grouped as into the same pattern set. Each tree can belong to only one cluster.
- **Cluster Pattern Regularity (CPR) Heuristic:** Given t trees and c clusters, if the size of the smallest cluster C_s is less than $\lfloor 0.75t / c \rfloor$, then the aligned pattern from this cluster is merged with one of the remaining clusters with which it shares the smallest alignment distance. Sometimes, a few records may have very dissimilar patterns from majority of the records, and hence from an erroneous cluster. We need to make sure that there is enough evidence that the existence of a cluster is justified. Therefore, we use the regularity of the occurrence of these patterns as a certainty measure.

Having defined the heuristics, now we state the algorithm that detects the record boundary and recognizes the repeating patterns from portion of the tag tree containing the records of interest, validates and groups them and finally forms generalized extraction rules.

Algorithm RuleFinder

Input: A Web document D.
Output: Aligned Patterns representing Extraction Rules for D.

(1) Create the tag tree T.
(2) Identify the subtree S containing records of interest inside T using the enhanced highest fan-out rule.
(3) Compare all child trees of S pairwise.
(4) Use the ADC heuristic and cluster similar trees together.
(5) Align all the trees in each cluster.
(6) Apply the CPR heuristic to cluster C_s that has the lowest count of trees, and if the criterion is met, obtain the modified set of clusters.
(7) Repeat step 6 on the modified set of clusters until all existing clusters represent complete generalized patterns that are valid.

end

5 Performance Study

We tested the performance of our approach on two categories of Web documents: Search engines and Classifieds. We chose five different websites for each category. We analyzed ten Web documents from each website, 100 documents altogether. We use one Web document from each website as an input document for our system to generate the extraction rules, and then test the rules on all the ten documents for that website. We use performance metrics such as recall and precision rates to analyze the performance of our approach. *Recall rate* is defined as the ratio of number of records of interest extracted by the extraction rule to the number of records of interest contained in the input Web document. *Precision rate* is defined as number of records of interest extracted by the extraction rule to the total number of records extracted. It takes less than five minutes on average to detect and generate extraction rules from 100 Web documents. We conducted the experiments on 2 encoding levels:

- Encoding level 1: All tags are taken into consideration
- Encoding level 2: Text-enhancement tags (<B>, <I>, <U>) are ignored

Furthermore, to emphasize the contribution of the heuristics, we performed two rounds of experiments on the same dataset. The first round simply adopts the Multiple Tree Alignment algorithm and aligns all the trees under the highest fan-out subtree into one generalized pattern. The second round of experiments extracts records from the dataset using the heuristics-based approach. The results are presented in tables 1, 2 (search engine sites) and 3 (classifieds sites).

The experimental results confirm that the proposed heuristics-based approach improves the precision rate to a considerable extent. The recall rate, on

Table 1. Experimental results for Search Engines using the non-heuristic approach

Websites	Encoding (1)		Encoding (2)	
	Recall	Precision	Recall	Precision
www.yahoo.com	55%	93%	91%	93%
www.webcrawler.com	100%	96%	100%	96%
www.lycos.com	60%	90%	95%	90%
www.infoseek.com	100%	94%	100%	94%
www.savvysearch.com	100%	96%	100%	96%

Table 2. Experimental results for Search Engines using the heuristics-based approach

Websites	Encoding (1)		Encoding (2)	
	Recall	Precision	Recall	Precision
www.yahoo.com	55%	97%	91%	97%
www.webcrawler.com	100%	100%	100%	100%
www.lycos.com	60%	98%	95%	98%
www.infoseek.com	100%	97%	100%	97%
www.savvysearch.com	100%	96%	100%	96%

the other hand, improves when text-enhancement tags are ignored. For search engine sites, performance is better under encoding level 2. Table 2 shows that documents from Yahoo yield a recall rate of only 55% and those from Lycos only 60%. These sites usually encode the search terms in bold (<B>...</B>) wherever the terms appear in the records. For every record, these tags appear at random positions. Although the multiple Tree Alignment algorithm does formulate a generalized pattern for the sample input page, the pattern may not have accounted for some other possible placements of the tags in question, which might be prevalent in the other Web documents from the same website. Hence the recall rates for these 2 sites under encoding scheme 1 were less impressive. Since the other 3 search engines do not follow the same convention, they perform equally well under both encoding levels. The same case holds true for the documents from online classifieds websites. Hence the performance is impressive under both encoding schemes. Encoding level 2 is better between the 2 schemes, and therefore adopted for future.

Table 3. Experimental results for Online Classifieds

Websites	No Heuristics		With Heuristics	
	Encoding (1 & 2)		Encoding (1 & 2)	
	Recall	Precision	Recall	Precision
www.asiaone.com.sg	100%	91%	100%	97%
www.classifieds2000.com	100%	87%	100%	95%
www.catcha.com	100%	90%	100%	100%
www.asiaxpat.com.sg	98%	95%	98%	98%
www.herald.ns.ca/classifieds	100%	97%	100%	100%

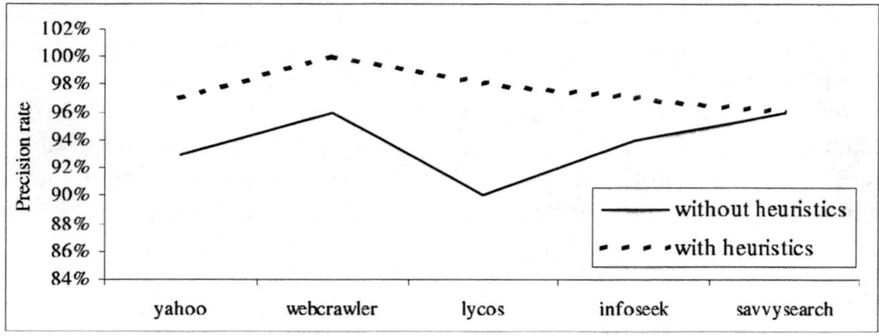

Fig. 3. Comparison of precision rates for search engine sites

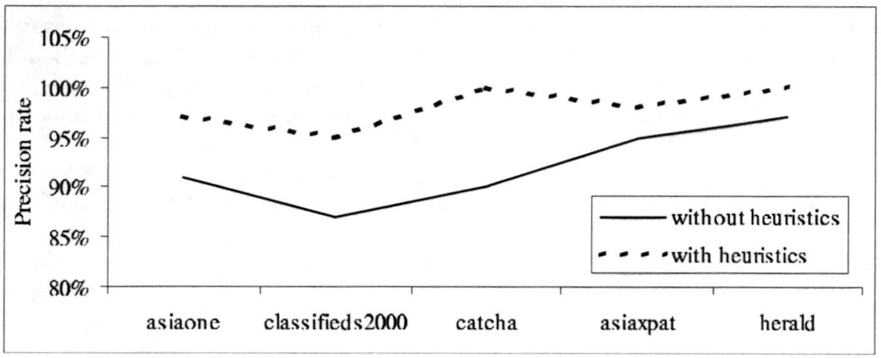

Fig. 4. Comparison of precision rates for online classifieds sites

The precision rates of the extracted results are plotted on the graph as shown in Figures 3 (search engine sites) and 4 (classifieds sites). It is evident that the heuristics-based approach form more accurate generalized patterns that extract correct and relevant records, thereby improving the precision rate. The experimental results also indicate that the encoding level does not have any effect on the precision rate. Under encoding level 2, our proposed heuristics-based approach has an average recall rate of 97.2% and an average precision rate of 97.6% for documents from search engines. As for online classifieds, recall rate averages to 99.6% and precision rate averages to 98%.

6 Conclusion and Future Work

This paper presents an automatic, domain-independent approach to generating extraction rules with the objective of extracting information from multiple-record Web documents. The technique utilizes the HTML structure of the pages to discover repeated patterns using a Tree Alignment algorithm. The adoption of the Tree Alignment algorithm to repeated pattern discovery is very suitable since multiple sequence alignment is handled implicitly. As exhibited by our extensive performance evaluation on several Web sources, the efficiency (time) is practical and the effectiveness (recall and precision) reasonable. Since no apriori knowledge of the different websites was used, our technique is expected to support most changes and therefore is robust. This work is the first step toward the design of a more complete solution in which syntactic and semantic knowledge can be combined and cross-leveraged for the automatic extraction of Web data.

References

1. Califf, M. E., Mooney, R. J.: Relational Learning of Pattern-Match Rules for Information Extraction. Working papers of the ACL-97 workshop in Natural Language Learning (1997)
2. Chang, C.H., Lui, S.C.: Information Extraction Based on Pattern Discovery. In Proc. 10th International World Wide Web conference on World Wide Web (2001)
3. Doorenbos, R.B., Etzioni, O., Weld, D. S.: A scalable comparison-shopping agent for the World Wide Web. In Proc. 1st international conference on Autonomous Agents. ACM Press., New York (1997) 39–48
4. Embley, D., Jiang, Y., and Ng, Y. -K.: Record-boundary discovery in Web documents. In Proc. ACM SIGMOD International Conference on Management of Data. Philadelphia, Pennsylvania, (1999) 467–478
5. Freitag, D. Information Extraction from HTML: Application of a general Machine Learning Approach. In Proc. 15th National Conference on Artificial Intelligence (1998)
6. Hsu, C.-N., Dung, M.-T.: Generating finite-state transducers for semi-structured data extraction from the Web. Journal of Information Systems, 23(8) (1998) 521–538.
7. Jiang, T., Wang L., Zhang, K.: Alignment of trees - an alternative to tree edit. Combinatorial Pattern Matching (1994) 75–86
8. Kushmerick, N., Weld, D., Doorenbos, R.: Wrapper induction for information extraction. In Proc. 15th International Joint Conference on Artificial Intelligence (1997).
9. Lakshmi, V.: Web structure Analysis for Information Mining. PhD Dissertation, National University of Singapore (2001)
10. Muslea, I., Minton, S., Knoblock, C.: A hierarchical approach to wrapper induction. In Proc. 3rd International Conference on Autonomous Agents (1999)
11. Rahardjo, B.: Information Extraction from Web using Matching techniques. PhD Dissertation, National University of Singapore (2001)
12. Soderland, S.: Learning Information Extraction Rules for Semi-structured and Free Text. Machine Learning, vol. 34 (1999) 233–272
13. Yih, W.T.: Template-based Information Extraction from Tree-structured HTML Documents. PhD Dissertation, National Taiwan University (1997)

Processing of Continuous Queries over Unlimited Data Streams

Ehsan Vossough[1] and Janusz R. Getta[2]

[1] Department of Computing and Information Technology,
University of Western Sydney,Macarthur
NSW, Australia,
e.vossough@uws.edu.au

[2] School of Information Technology and Computer Science,
University of Wollongong,
Wollongong, NSW, Australia,
jrg@cs.uow.edu.au

Abstract. This work addresses the problem of continuous query processing over infinite data streams. The paper defines new semantics for continuous queries and describes a continuous query processing system based on the concepts of continuous computations and online algorithms. A new programming control structure called as Continuous Iterator is proposed for implementation of continuous computations. The paper describes the semantics of three types of Continuous Iterators (composition, merge, and elimination), compares the iterators with the traditional relational algebra operations and proposes implementation of the iterators. The results of preliminary experiments are provided as well.

1 Introduction

Querying the streams of data propagated by the sources like financial stock markets, real-time sensing systems, network monitoring systems, etc, requires the invention of new query processing techniques. Processing of continuous queries over unlimited streams of data differs from the traditional processing of fixed size data sets with the single runtime queries. In theory, a continuous execution of a query over a fluctuating data streams can be implemented through re-computation of the same query over an almost identical database.

From the performance point of view, frequent repetition of the identical computations over entire data streams, each time one of the streams is extended or updated, is not feasible. Effective processing of continuous queries over infinite data streams has been already investigated in a number of research works [13,15,4,11,14,8,6]. The most recent review of the results achieved in the last decade is provided in [1].

The solutions invented so far are based on an idea of incremental computations such as INC, [10]. INC was originally developed to perform Incremental computations over nearly identical inputs where previous computations are taken into account for any new input. The INC paradigm however does not support

R. Cicchetti et al. (Eds.): DEXA 2002, LNCS 2453, pp. 799–809, 2002.

any general looping construct and does not explicitly address how to manage data arrivals at the EquiJoin inputs where the order of data is important. The Eddies system [5]and Telegraph project [9] which constructs and adapts query plans on the fly, come closest to what is proposed here. However, they are based on the traditional query processing languages such as SQL that operates on *all* the tuples from the incoming relations when they become available rather than continuously arriving tuples. Incremental processing of a query means that initially the query is computed over entire data streams and the incremental computations are then repeated over the modifications of the input streams. The results from the first iteration and the incremental results of second execution are combined together to get the results of the second iteration and so on. Incremental processing of query q over streams $R_1, \ldots, R_n$ is possible when the results of $q^i(R_1, \ldots, R_n)$ and the results of $q^{(i+1)}(\Delta R_1, \ldots, \Delta R_n)$ can be combined to find $q^{(i+1)}(R_1, \ldots, R_n)$. It is known that for non-monotonic queries [15] and time-varying queries [4] incremental processing cannot be applied.

This paper describes a new approach to processing of continuous queries over unlimited data streams. Our method is based on a simple observation that processing of continuous queries requires continuously running computations. The idea is to start processing of a query at time t_0 and run it all the time while the input data streams are modified. The partial results observed at times $t_0 + \Delta t$, $t_0+2*\Delta t$, $t_0+3*\Delta t$, ...etc may be considered as the results of continuous query processing. If no new data items are available then the processing is suspended and its state is saved. The computations are resumed when at least one of the input streams is extended or updated. The major difference between this approach and the methods based on incremental computations is that in our case the query is not restarted after each Δt to perform the incremental computations. Moreover, a continuously running process allows for recording of all variations on the output in response to the slightest modifications on the input. Our method needs a query processing algorithms that continuously produces outputs from the consumed input data streams. Such class of algorithms is well known in the computing literature as *on line algorithms*[7], [12]. Online algorithms can see only a part of their input and may therefore be less efficient than those that can see the complete input. One more problem is that query processing algorithms should be independent of the order in which the modifications of input streams arrive, i.e. for any increment ΔR_i of any stream R_i the query processor should be able to produce the latest partial result. To solve these problems we propose simultaneous processing of the query by more than one query processor. The idea is to run concurrently a number of query processing cycles, each one for an atomic modification of an input stream. To synchronize simultaneous processing of the same query we introduce a concept of *Continuous Iterator*, i.e. a loop that does more than what a query processor concurrently interprets. We show how to translate the queries expressed in relational algebra into programs with Continuous Iterators and we propose implementation of Continuous Iterators. The remaining sections of the paper are organized as follows. Section 2 presents some preliminary ideas and proposed approach by the introduction of continuous queries. Section 3 discusses a Continuous Iterator as the building block for a continuous query. Section 4 provides an overview of the Continuous Iterators versus relational algebra. In section 5 we discuss the implementation of the Continuous Iterator. Some experimental results are presented in section 6 and we conclude the paper with a general vision and plans for future development of the idea.

2 Continuous Queries

A simple intuition behind a concept of continuous query is that it is an ordinary query issued once and continuously processed over a database later on. To explain what *continuous processing* of a query means we may compare the properties of the results produced by the conventional and continuous queries. The results of one-time processing of a conventional query are static. They do not automatically change over time and they do not change when a database is updated. A conventional query must be issued one more time to get results that reflect the present state of the database. On the other hand, the results of a continuous query automatically follow the modifications of the database. Observation of these results is like observing the indicators that display in real-time the values of parameters of certain physical processes.

The semantics of continuous queries proposed in [15] states that the results produced by continuous query Q_M are a union of the results produced by the query Q issued at time t_{start} and recomputed at any moment of time $t > t_{start}$, i.e.

$$Q_m(t) = \bigcup_{t > t_{start}} Q(t)$$

Unfortunately, the accumulation of the results obtained from the continuous query processor may result in some problems. For example, when a database does not change in a period of time from t_1 to t_2 the it may still happen that a result of $Q(t_1)$ is not equal to $Q(t_2)$ due to the passing of time, e.g. comparison of date/time attribute with a call to $SYSDATE$ function. Then, the union of results obtained at t_1 and t_2 may lead to contradiction. This is why the semantics of continuous queries proposed by [15] does not assure consistency for all kinds of queries.

We propose a new semantics for continuous queries based on the observation of query results. Our semantics is applicable to all kinds of queries. We start from a concept of *database state*. A database state is a combination of all values of all properties of the objects described in a database at certain moment of time.

Let S by a set of all database states. Then, a *database history* is a function

$$h : Time \rightarrow S$$

such that at any moment of time t_0 a value of $h(t_0)$ is equal to a database state at time t_0. We define a *query* q as a function

$$q : S \times Time \rightarrow R$$

where R is a set of all results returned by query q. Evaluation of $q(h(t_1), t_2)$ returns the results of query q issued over a database state $h(t_1)$ and computed at t_2. Note, that for time-varying queries the results $q(h(t_1), t_1)$ and $q(h(t_1), t_2)$, $t_1 \neq t_2$ may be different.

If the results of $q(h(t), t)$ are computed by the system for all $t \geq t_{start}$) then query q is called as a *continuous query.* In practice none of the queries are really continuous due to the finite precision of timers in computer systems and time needed for re-computation of a query.

3 Continuous Iterators

This section describes a syntax and semantics of our system of Continuous Iterators and compares its expressive power with the classical relational algebra. To achieve a unified view of a database we consider fixed size data containers like data sets, relational tables, object classes, etc as streams of data elements. Data streams are sequences of data elements. Each data element is triple <*identifier, body, type*>. The first component uniquely identifies each element in a stream. Depending on the type of data container, an identifier can be a record number, primary key, object identifier, etc. Element body represents the contents of data element, e.g. it is either a record of data, a row from relational table, an instance of an object or something else. There are three types of data elements: positive, neutral and negative. Positive data elements represent the insertion of new data elements into a stream. Neutral elements are interpreted as updates. Theirs bodies replace the bodies of already appended elements which have exactly the same identifiers as neutral elements. Finally, the negative data elements represent deletions from a data stream. Whenever a new data element r_i arrives on input of data stream R_i then the first action is to modify the stream. Modification i.e. insertion, update, deletion, depends on a type of data element. If data element is neutral or negative and its identifier does not match identifier of any element already in the stream then the element is considered as irrelevant and no further action is taken. After each modification, all input streams consist of only positive data elements. After the stream is modified, the new data element is considered as an atomic modification of input and an iterator initiates a new processing cycle.

We distinguish three(*probably more than 3 in the future*) types of iterators: *composition, merge,* and *elimination* iterators. The syntax of *composition* iterator is the following;

forall $(r_1, \ldots, r_n)$ in $R_1 \times \ldots \times R_n$
  if $\phi(r_1, ...r_n)$ **then**
    $\varrho := e(r_1, \ldots, r_n)$
    insert(ϱ, *Result*)
  endif
endforall

Composition iterator scans through all combination of data elements from the input streams, picks the combinations that satisfy condition ϕ evaluates expression e and appends ϱ to *Result* data stream. The processing of composite iterator obeys the general rules for the processing of Continuous Iterators, i.e. the slightest modification in one of the input streams triggers a new processing cycle run by a separate query processor.

The syntax of *merge* iterator is as follows

```
forall (r) in R_1 + ... + R_n
    if φ(r) then
        ϱ := e(r)
        insert(ϱ, Result)
    endif
endforall
```

Processing of merge iterator starts when at least one of the input streams consists of at least one positive data element.

The syntax of *elimination* iterator is the following.

```
forall (r) in R_i ~ R_j
    if φ(r) then
        ϱ := e(r)
            insert(ϱ, Result)
    endif
endforall
```

Elimination iterator removes from the stream R_i all data elements that are in the stream R_j with an identical element body. When a new element r_i is appended to R_i then elimination process is governed by the following rules.

(i) If r_i is positive then the query processor checks if R_j contains no elements with the same body as r_i. If it is so, r_i is passed to the *Result* stream.
(ii) If r_i is neutral and it updates an element in R_i then the same procedure as above is applied.
(iii) If r_i is negative; it removes an element from R_i, then it is passed to *Result* stream.

When a new element r_j is appended to R_j then its processing follows the rules below.

(i) If r_j is positive then query processor scans through R_i and checks if there exists an element with the same body as r_j. If it is so, a negative r_j is passed to *Result* stream.
(ii) If r_j is neutral and it updates an element in r_j then the same procedure as above is repeated.
(iii) If r_j is negative and it deletes an element from R_j then query processor searches in R_i for an element with the same body as r_j. If such element exists, a positive r_j is passed to *Result*.

4 Continuous Iterators versus Relational Algebra

Implementation of continuous queries may to some extent follow a traditional path of query processing. In this approach, a query expressed in SQL and marked as a continuous query is translated to an extended relational algebra expression, the expression is syntax and cost optimized, a query processing plan is set up, and finally all relational algebra operations are replaced with Continuous Iterators. This method may work, for a moment, if we skip the performance problems; because the operations of relational algebra are easily expressible as special cases of Continuous Iterators.

Projection (π_x) and selection ($\sigma_p hi$) are the special cases of composition, merge or elimination iterators, consisting of one input stream and condition ϕ as the selection condition and expression e implementing row projection. Cross product ($\times$), Join ($\bowtie$), and intersection ($\cap$) are special cases of the composition iterator.

forall (r, s) in $R \times S$
  if $(r.x = s.x)$ **then**
    $\varrho := r \bullet s$
    insert(ϱ, *Result*)
  endif
endforall

Union ($\cup$) is a special case of merge and difference ($-$) is a special case of elimination iterator.

Replacement of relational algebra operations with Continuous Iterators makes the output streams of some iterators as the input streams for other iterators. Then, an atomic processing cycle is performed accordingly to a schema given in Fig. 1. Input to each Continuous Iterator C_i consists of

(i) the input streams R and S,
(ii) an atomic data element r, submitted to stream R either by external sources or by another iterator.

Output of iterator C_i consists of data elements $\Delta Result$ produced by an atomic processing cycle over element r and stream S and submitted to the *Result* stream. Processing of iterator C_i is performed in steps. First, data element r is applied (insert/update/delete) to R. If r has no impact on R then it is ignored otherwise an atomic cycle is performed by the processor. Processing of unary operations is performed in the same way as processing of the first argument of binary operations.

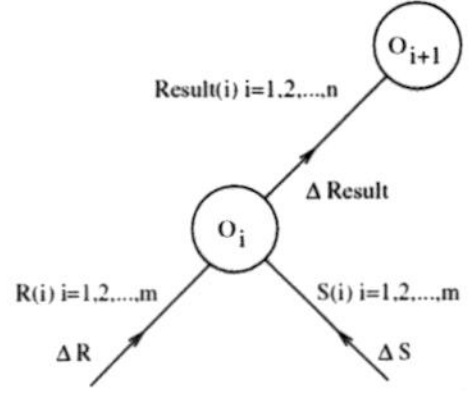

Fig. 1. Iterator processing schema

5 Implementation of Continuous Iterators

We consider the query operations that perform work on *single* tuples from infinite streams such that a newly arrived tuple in the stream is consumed by the query and the results are appended to the result stream. To facilitate the implementation of continuous iterators we introduced a Composite Boolean Table (CBT). Generally, CBT contains several columns as shown in Fig. 2. The first M

Merge Attributes			Streams		
a_1	..	a_m	S_1	..	S_n

Fig. 2. A general structure for CBT

columns store the attribute values $a_1..a_m$ from the composition expression that are used for merging streams $S_1..$ S_n. The next N columns store *pointers* to rows in streams $S_1..$ S_n that are the participants in the query (over one or more of the attribute values). At any moment in time, there are k streams to merge over l attributes, where $1 \leq k \leq N$ and $1 \leq l \leq M$. We do not compute the actual query results until the last moment when a window of tuples of size Z from all streams has been processed. At this stage, CBT would contain pointers to a combination of all tuples in the stored streams that are used by the query to produce the final results. Fig. 3 demonstrates a query block with several iterators that perform merge operations on the input streams S_1 .. S_n. In this paper we assume that all iterators within a query block perform the same type of merge. However, results of one block may be consumed by another block that may perform a different type of merge. Every block accommodates a local CBT.

An example of a CBT for a merge iterator between two streams is shown in Fig. 4. The first column stores the values of the attribute age. This column is indexed with a clustered Btree to improve the performance. The next two columns store pointers to tuples in streams A and B that can be merged over the attribute age. At first, CBT is empty and there will be no rows to perform

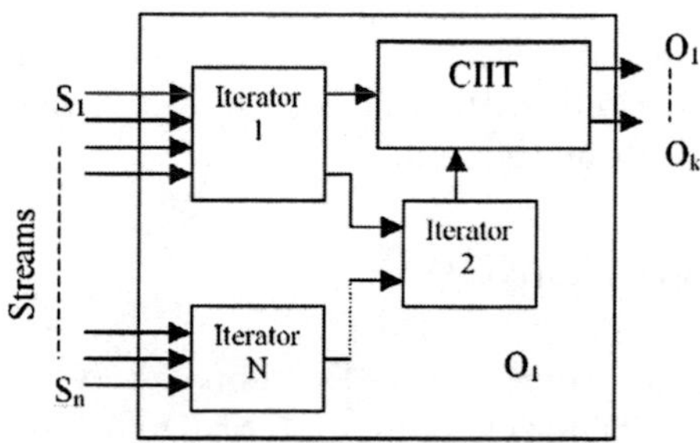

Fig. 3. Continuous iterators within a query block.

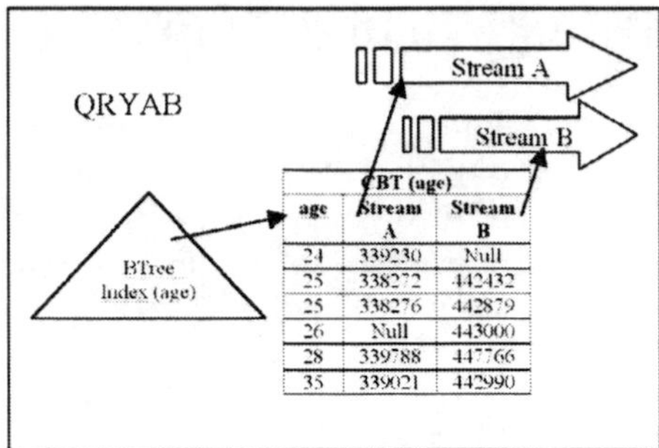

QRYAB
Stream A
Stream B
BTree
Index (age)
CBT (age)
age | Stream A | Stream B
24 | 339230 | Null
25 | 338272 | 442432
25 | 338276 | 442879
26 | Null | 443000
28 | 339788 | 447766
35 | 339021 | 442990

Fig. 4. CBT example

merge operations from one stream to another. A new tuple from stream A would result in a new row in CBT containing a value for the attribute age in the first column, a pointer to the tuple in stream A in the second column and a null value in the third column. This null value may be later updated with a pointer to a tuple in stream B that can merge with a corresponding tuple in stream A. Similarly, a new tuple from stream B will result in a new row in CBT with a null placed in the second column for a possible future merge with stream A. Arriving tuples from Streams A and B are then streamed into tables "store_A" and "store_B", respectively, for future merge operations.

A merge operation performs Cartesian crosschecks on all the tuples that are within a window of size Z in a stream. A new tuple from one stream may merge with the existing rows in another store and would update the CBT in three ways. Firstly, if CBT has no rows with the same attribute as the new tuple for a stream, then the new tuple is inserted in the table as was described previously. Secondly, if the CBT has null entries in a column that stores pointers to a stream and filled entries in other columns that store pointers to other streams, for particular attribute values, then a tuple from the same stream and with the same merge attributes updates these null entries with the pointer to the tuple in that same stream. Thirdly, if there are already pointers in a column with the same merge attributes as the new tuple, then new rows will be inserted in CBT that comprise of the pointer from the new tuple and pointers to all other rows in CBT with the same merge attributes. For a window of size Z, only rows that have no null entries are selected as having valid results that can be passed to other query blocks. Rows with Null entries are considered as having *partial results* and must wait to be updated.

6 Experimental Results

We used MSSQL Server 7 running on a Pentium 4 (1.7GHz) machine with 256M of memory. The Query Analyzer in the SQL SERVER provides a suitable client interface and several independent windows that can run different queries for different streams, simultaneously. Each customer having ages between 40 and

50, an ID, first Name, last name, address and phone number. The window size for customers can be adjusted depending on the restrictions on the duration of each experiment.

Customers arrive with no delay and they are processed immediately. This represents the worst scenario where there may be little or no processing time between the arrivals. If one stream is delayed then the remaining streams continue without waiting. The CPU time is shared in processing the streams. An average time to process a single tuple in a stream can be estimated from the results. The critical issue is to determine the required time to process the remaining data in each window and how this time compares with the conventional merging of the streams. If the remaining batch needs more time then our purpose in stream processing is defeated. A compromise must be reached where it may become necessary to abandon the stream processing in favor of the conventional merge process. This is a subject for future research. The results obtained so far are promising. For a streamed merge operation, the results were in close proximity of a normal merge operation.

6.1 Merge Operations between Streams Using a Single CBT

In this experiment $\text{CBT}_{AB(age)}$ is constructed from merge operations between customers in Streams A and B over the attribute age. In the beginning, Store_A and Store_B are empty. Incoming tuples populate the stores on a tuple by tuple basis. For every tuple, $\text{CBT}_{AB(age)}$ is populated with pointers to rows in any store that participated in the query for different values of customer age. Although SQL Server 7 provides *join hints* for loop, Hash or Merge operations, we allowed the Server to select an optimized plan for this experiment. Depending on the arrival delays between tuples in each stream, one stream may be setback in relation to other streams. This is observable when the results from one stream grow slower than results from other streams. In Fig. 5, Stream B result is delayed with respect to Stream A and is the determining factor for the conclusion of the merge operation. Stream B consumes 147 seconds to process 3000 tuples (or about 50 m Seconds per tuple). With an inter arrival time of 50 m Seconds per tuple, a normal stream would complete the merge operation after (3000 * 0.05 + 84) or 234 seconds. Stream B would complete in (3000 * 0.05 + 0.05) or 150.05 seconds. Next, we performed a tuple-by-tuple merge operation using three streams and a window size of 2000 requiring 8 billion comparisons. Results are shown in Fig. 6. In the conventional merge process, the server was unable to complete the merge after 4 hours. However, streamed process returned reasonable results in less than 2 hours.

7 Conclusions

The need to process continuous queries over infinite data streams is becoming a reality. Traditional DBMS systems are geared toward the processing of finite stored data sets rather than a constant flow of data. Building a complete DBMS

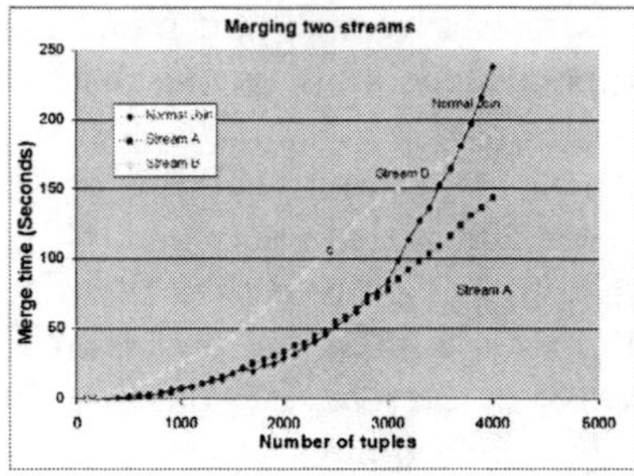

Fig. 5. Merging two streams A and B vs Normal merge operation

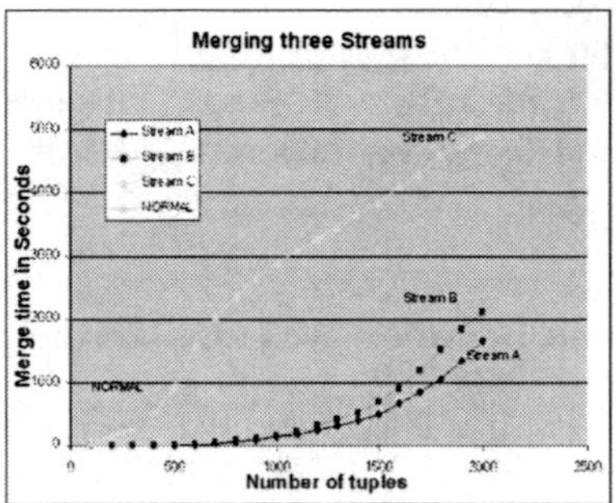

Fig. 6. Merging three streams A, B and C vs Normal merge operation

entails a significant amount of work. Our approach, however, is to modify or extend the existing DBMS to include the extra functionality needed to process queries with constantly arriving input data streams. This system is also adaptable to accommodate online data processing, approximate results, and adaptive query processing. We introduced the concept of a Continuous Iterator that is applied to normal expressions in the relational algebra and its implementation. Continuous Iterators are implemented within loops. Unlike the conventional loops, a partially iterated loop is capable of processing small increments of input data streams, disregarding the order of arrival of data streams i.e. a partially iterated nested join would fetch a new tuple from the current outer relation even if it did not finish rescanning the inner. We also presented the semantics for three types of iterators; composition, merge and elimination.

References

1. Shivnath Babu and Jennifer Widom, "Continuous queries over data streams," *SIGMOD Record*, vol. 30, no. 3, pp. 109–120, 2001.
2. Ehsan Vossough and Janusz Getta " Block level Query Scrambling Algorithm within Distributed Multi-database Environment," *4th IEEE Intl. workshop on Parallel and Distributed Databases: Innovative Applications and New Architectures, PADD2001, Munich*, pp. 123–127, 2001.

3. Ehsan Vossough, " Adaptable Processing of Large Data Sets in Distributed Environments," *EDBT 8th International Conference on Extending Databases Technology* , pp. 109–120, 2002.
4. Lars Baekgaard and Leo Mark, "Incremental computation of time-varying query expressions," *IEEE Transactions on Knowledge and Data Engineering*, vol. 7, no. 4, pp. 583–590, 1995.
5. Avnur R. Hellerstein, "Eddies: Continuously adaptive query processing," in *Proc. ACM-SIGMOD International Conference on Management of Data*, 1998, pp. 106–117.
6. Jianjun Chen, David J. DeWitt, Feng Tian, and Yuang Wang, "Niagaracq: A scalable continuous query systems for internet databases," in *Proceedings of the 2000 ACM SIGMOD International Conference on Management of Data*, 2000, pp. 379–390.
7. Amos Fiat and Gerhard J. Woeginger, *On Line Algorithms, The State of the Art*, Springer Verlag, 1998.
8. Joseph M. Hellerstein, Peter J. Haas, and Helen J. Wang, "Online aggregation," in *Proceedings of the 1997 ACM SIGMOD International Conference on Management of Data*, 1997, SIGMOD Record, pp. 171–182.
9. Joseph M. Hellerstein, J. Franklin, M. Chandrasekaran, S. Deshpande, A. Hildrum, K. Madden, S. Raman, and V. Shah, "Adaptive query processing: Technology in evolution," in *Bulletin of the IEEE Computer Society Technical committee on Data Engineering*, 2000, IEEE, pp. 7–18.
10. D. M. Yellin and R. E. Storm, "Inc: A language for incremental computations," *IBM T. J. Watson Research Center, ACM Transactions on Programming Languages and Systems*, , no. 2, pp. 211–236, 1991.
11. H. V. Jagadish, I.S. Mumick, and A. Silberschatz, "View maintenance issues for the chronicle data model," in *Proceedings of the 1995 ACM SIGMOD International Conference on Management of Data*, 1995, SIGMOD Record, pp. 113–124.
12. N. D. Jones, "Mix ten years later," in *ACM SIGPLAN Symposium on Partial Evaluation and Semantics-Based Program Manipulation*, 1995, pp. 24–38.
13. V. Srinivasan and Michael J. Carey, "Compensation-based on-line query processing," in *Proceedings of the 1992 ACM SIGMOD International Conference on Management of Data*, 1992, pp. 331–340.
14. Mark Sulliovan, "Tribeca: A stream database manager for network traffic analysis," in *Proceedings of the 22nd VLDB Conference*, 1996, p. 594.
15. Douglas Terry, David Goldberg, David Nichols, and Brian Oki, "Continuous queries over append-only databases," in *Proceedings of the 1992 ACM SIGMOD International Conference on Management of Data*, 1992, pp. 321–330.

ISA - An Incremental Hyper-sphere Approach for Efficiently Solving Complex Vague Queries

Tran Khanh Dang, Josef Küng, and Roland Wagner

FAW-Institute
Johannes Kepler University of Linz, Austria
{khanh, jkueng, rwagner}@faw.uni-linz.ac.at

Abstract. This paper presents an enhanced extension of the Vague Query System (VQS) [14, 15] to solve complex vague queries more efficiently and generally. The VQS is an extension to conventional database systems and can work on top of them to return records semantically close to user's query. It represents semantic information of arbitrary attributes by mapping them to the Euclidean space and this information is invisible to the users. Answering a complex vague query requires searching on multiple feature spaces of attributes and these spaces are usually multidimensional. The proposed approach in [15] is not general and has weaknesses lead to degenerate performance of the system. The new approach introduced in this paper overcomes all those defects and significantly improves the search performance in both concepts of CPU- and IO-cost. Our experiments on uniformly distributed data sets, which are managed by the SH-trees [6], have proven the advantages of this new approach.

1 Introduction

Conventional database management systems (DBMSs) may return an empty result set if the data do not match user's query precisely. An "elegant" database system should return results close to the query when no exact match is returned instead of the empty result set. However most existing DBMSs do not directly support this aspect, which is referred as vague retrieval capability [16], and thus the users must usually retry such queries with certain minor modifications until having a satisfactory result. There are some approaches proposed to enhance a conventional DBMS with vague retrieval capabilities, e.g. [13, 16, 14, 5, 1] etc.

First, Ichikawa et al [13] introduced the Associative Information Retrieval System (ARES), which is capable of performing a flexible interpretation of queries. The core of ARES is similarity relation that stores similarity between attribute values in a domain. Depending on similarity relations and a new operator "similar to", ARES can work on top of the conventional DBMSs to interpret users' queries flexibly when they expect. This approach, however, has some disadvantages. Each similarity relation needs n^2 entries with respect to n attribute values in the corresponding conventional relation [14] and this leads to high storage cost. Moreover, maintenance cost of similarity relations is also high because when a new attribute value is added, 2n+1 additional entries are necessary for the corresponding similarity relation. The extensions of the relational data model in ARES are unnecessarily complex [16].

R. Cicchetti et al. (Eds.): DEXA 2002, LNCS 2453, pp. 810–819, 2002.

In [16] Motro introduced a system called VAGUE that is an extension to the relational data model with data metrics and the standard query language with a comparator *similar-to*. There are four types of data metrics in VAGUE and each of them is a definition of distance between values in the same domain. In addition, VAGUE also allows multiple metrics over each domain with ability to select the appropriate metric for each query. Although VAGUE is a useful system, its design represents a compromise between the conflicting requirements for simplicity, flexibility and efficiency [16]. For examples, the users of VAGUE cannot provide their own similarity thresholds for each vague qualification but when a vague query does not match any data, VAGUE increases double all searching radii simultaneously and thus the search performance can be considerably deteriorated.

In [14] Kueng et al presented the Vague Query System (VQS), which bases on ARES and VAGUE as the background, to extend the conventional DBMSs so as to retrieve records semantically close to ad-hoc queries. VQS operates on top of the existing DBMSs and employs semantic background information, which is concealed behind mapped attribute values and invisible to the users. In fact, semantic background information in VQS is represented by mapping arbitrary types of attributes to the Euclidean space and stored in Numeric-Coordinate-Representation-Tables (NCR-Tables). In [15] Kueng et al introduced an Incremental hyper-Cube Approach (ICA) for finding the nearest record/tuple for complex vague queries (CVQs). Here we define a multi-feature vague query as a CVQ. This indicates that to answer a CVQ, the system must search on some feature spaces of attributes and then combine these search results to return the final ranked results to the user. In [14, 15] NCR-Tables take part as these feature spaces. Nevertheless, this proposed approach is not general and has weaknesses lead to degenerate the search performance of the system. In this paper we present an enhanced extension of the VQS to solve CVQs more efficiently and generally.

Solving CVQs efficiently has also been got special attention in the database research community because of its numerous application areas, e.g. multimedia databases [8, 4, 18, 17, 9, 3], digital libraries [11], text and fact databases [19] etc.

The rest of this paper is organized as follows. Section 2 summaries work related to addressing CVQs and specially elaborates on the ICA. Section 3 presents an incremental hyper-sphere approach and its advanced aspects to overcome weaknesses of the ICA. Section 4 gives a new algorithm to find k nearest neighbors for CVQs. Section 5 presents experimental results and section 6 gives conclusions as well as future work.

2 Related Work

This section briefly summaries some previous researches related to dealing with CVQs. First, in [8] Fagin proposed the algorithm A_0 for finding top-k matches for a user query involving several multimedia attributes. Each multimedia attribute is assumed to have a subsystem that can output results ranked in sorted order corresponding to this attribute. In the first phase of Fagin's algorithm, the system receives the ranked results from the subsystems until there are at least k matches in the intersection of all the subsystems. In the second phase, the system computes the score for each of the retrieved objects and returns the top-k objects. Fagin has shown that the algorithm A_0 is correct with monotone scoring functions[1].

Recently, there are some improvements of Fagin's algorithm as [17, 9]. However, as shown in [21], Fagin's algorithm makes some assumptions about multimedia systems, which do not hold in some cases, e.g. in distributed environment. In details, the algorithm assumes that random access is possible in the system. This assumption is correct only three following conditions hold: (1) there is at least a key for each subsystem, (2) there is a mapping between the keys, and (3) we must ensure that the mapping is one-to-one. Intuitively, the condition (1) is always satisfied in the VQS, however, the condition (3) does not hold. In the VQS, each *Fuzzy Field* is also the key for the corresponding NCR-Table but there is no the mapping one-to-one between *Fuzzy Fields* of the NCR-Tables. Consequently, Fagin's algorithm and also its improvements cannot be applied to the VQS.

Recent researches into multimedia systems also result in some new approaches to solving CVQ, e.g. [18, 3]. Ortega et al [18] presented an approach based on a variation of the Boolean model. This approach bases on probabilistic and fuzzy interpretations of distances between images and the query. Their query evaluation approach follows a *demand-driven data flow* approach [10], i.e. data items are only produced when needed. In [3] Boehm et al described a new evaluation technique called Generalized VA-File-based Search (GeVAS) to address multi-object multi-feature queries. However, GeVAS is mainly designed for multimedia systems and built on a peculiar index structure, the VA-File [22].

In [5] the authors introduced a solution to translate a top-k multi-feature query on continuous attributes to a range query that a conventional DBMS can process. In the other hand, this approach employs information in the histograms kept by a relational system and so the performance of the mapping techniques depends on accuracy of the available histograms. The accuracy of a histogram depends on the technique that it is generated and the amount of memory that has been allocated for it [5]. The performance may be decreased if the histograms are not up to date.

To enhance the VQS, in [15] Kueng et al presented the ICA for finding the best match for a given CVQ. This approach starts searching for each query criterion in the corresponding feature space, i.e. the NCR-Table, and retrieves all NCR-Values satisfying a hyper-cube range query with a predefined radius r_0 from the query criterion. The searching radius r_0 is incrementally extended until there is at least one tuple in the query relation that includes at least a returned NCR-Value from each NCR-Table related to the query (See [15] for more detailed explanations and illustrations). Depending on semantic information of attribute values according to the returned NCR-Values, the VQS compute total distance (TD) for tuple(s) found in the above phase. The tuples are later ranked by their TDs. To verify that whether a tuple having a minimum TD is the best match for the query, the VQS must enlarge the radius of each hypercube as formula 1 and do the search again. If there is a new tuple so that its TD is minimum among all new tuples found and smaller than the current minimum TD, it is the best match. Otherwise, the best match is the tuple having the minimum TD in the previous search phase.

[1] A function F is monotone if $a_i \leq b_i$ for i=1, 2, … n, then $F(a_1, a_2, \ldots a_n) \leq F(b_1, b_2, \ldots b_n)$

$$r_{inew} = D_i * TD_{curmin} * w_{sum} / w_i \quad (1)$$

where:

r_{inew}	new searching radius of query condition i
D_i	diameter of feature space i
TD_{curmin}	current minimum total distance
w_i	weight of query condition i
w_{sum}	sum of weights over all query conditions

Although the ICA is an innovative idea, it still has many defects. First, how to choose r_0 is not an easy problem because it affects the obtained object number and hence IO-cost and CPU-cost of the system. In other words, a "bad" r_0 may significantly decrease the search performance. Second, in case the algorithm needs to extend r_0, how to specify a new "good" radius is also difficult. In [15] the authors proposed the extension by a fixed proportion of the feature space diameter or it can be determined statistically. This solution is particularly domain-dependent. Moreover, the ICA is designed to retrieve only the best match record so it is not general because the users, in some cases, also need top-k records close to the query.

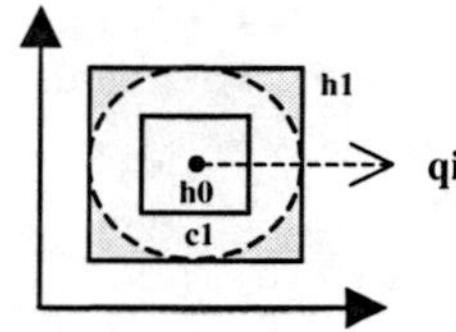

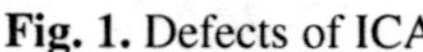

Fig. 1. Defects of ICA

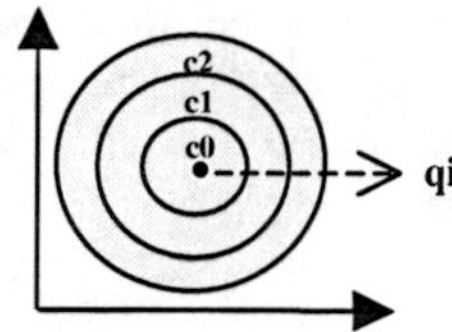

Fig. 2. An example feature space for ISA

Besides, figure 1 depicts an example feature space to show that the ICA accesses unnecessary disk pages and objects after the enlargement of the searching radii according to formula 1: Assume that the ICA found an appropriate tuple in the query relation according to the hyper-cube range query h_0 in the feature space i. To verify that if this tuple is the best match for the query, the ICA must extend the radius and found a new hyper-cube query h_1. Intuitively, objects located in gray area $s=h_1-c_1$ are unneeded to be verified but the ICA does it. Last, the ICA must do the hyper-cube range queries over all feature spaces repeatedly from scratch whenever there is an extension of the radii. This makes the IO-cost extremely high. For example, in figure 1, all disk pages accessed by query h_0 are also accessed again by query h_1. Section 5 shows that the ICA is inefficient even with only two feature spaces to be searched.

To overcome the ICA's weaknesses, we introduce a different advanced approach called Incremental hyper-Sphere Approach (ISA, for short). The next sections will detail this approach.

3 Incremental Hyper-sphere Approach

As mentioned above, we have to search on some multidimensional feature spaces to answer a CVQ. Although the VQS supports concept of multiple mappings, which means that an arbitrary attribute can be mapped to multiple NCR-Tables to express complex semantic definitions [15], without loss of generality we assume that each query condition of a CVQ will be evaluated by searching on a feature space. Furthermore, we also suppose that each feature space is maintained by a multidimensional index structure. Multidimensional access methods (MAM) facilitate similarity search efficiently and can rank the results based on their closeness to a particular value of an attribute [12]. This aspect is expected during searching on each feature space or NCR-Table in the VQS.

3.1 Basic ISA Version

Basis ISA version is intuitive: we replace all the hyper-cube range queries with hyper-sphere ones, which are created in a totally different and logical way. Concretely, in each feature space, the initial radius r_0 for the first hyper-sphere range query is set to distance of the nearest neighbor to the query condition corresponding to that feature space. After doing the first query in all the feature spaces, if there is no appropriate record found in the query relation, the algorithm will extend the searching radius for each query condition in the corresponding feature space and tackle the new hyper-sphere range queries. The radius of each new range query is the distance of the next nearest neighbor to the query condition. This extension process is repeated until at least an appropriate record is found in the query relation. Afterwards, the total distance is computed for each found record using formula 2 below.

$$TD = \left(\sum_{i} (d_i / D_i) * w_i \right) / w_{sum} \tag{2}$$

where:

TD	total distance of a record
D_i, w_i, w_{sum}	defined as formula 1
d_i	distance from query condition to NCR-Value returned in the corresponding feature space i

As the ICA, to verify that if the record having the minimum TD is the best match for the query, the new approach, ISA, must also extend the searching radii of the feature spaces as formula 1 and similarly continue processing. There is just only one difference that the new query after this enlargement is a hyper-sphere range query instead of a hyper-cube one. Therefore this basic version also omits redundant accesses to objects located in the gray area $s=h_1-c_1$ as depicted in figure 1.

There is one remaining problem in this basic approach: the algorithm still has to access unnecessary disk pages during the search. To make it clearer, we see an example feature space in figure 2 for the ISA: During the search, for example, the algorithm must tackle range queries c_0, c_1 and c_2. Intuitively, with the basic ISA version, the query c_1 again accesses all disk pages that the query c_0 accessed and disk pages intersect with area (c_1-c_0). Similarly, the query c_2 one more time accesses disk pages that the query c_1 accessed and disk pages intersect with area (c_2-c_1). This is an unexpected cost and it causes the search performance to be significantly degenerated.

To overcome the weakness of the basic ISA version, we have to address the nearest neighbor queries efficiently. The state-of-the-art algorithms with respect to the nearest neighbor problem-solving are presented in [12, 20]. Nevertheless, as shown in [2, 7], the algorithm introduced in [12] is optimal in terms of disk access number. In section

3.2, we present an adaptation of this algorithm to reject the weakness of this version. Section 3.3 will present an enhanced ISA version that employs this adaptation.

3.2 An Incremental Algorithm Adapted for Range Queries

The incremental nearest neighbor (NN) algorithm [12] returns objects one by one according to their distances to the query object. This algorithm is well suited for k-NN queries and k is possibly unknown in advance. Specially, when the k+1st neighbor is desired, this algorithm needs not to be recomputed (k+1)-NN query from scratch but it can continue the search from where it computed the kth neighbor. This algorithm employs a *priority queue* and traverses the index structure in a *best-first search manner*. That means when deciding which node in the index structure to traverse next, the algorithm picks the node with the least distance in the set of all nodes have been visited. Experiments in [7] with the adapted algorithm for the SH-tree [6] confirm that this incremental NN algorithm is optimal in terms of disk access number [2].

Adapting this algorithm for the ISA is easy because each feature space in this approach is also maintained by a multidimensional index structure[2]. Given a CVQ with n query conditions q_i (i=1, 2...n), we apply the algorithm to each of them in order to retrieve NCR-Values one by one. For each q_i there is only one priority queue is used during the search. Specially, due to the advantage of the applied algorithm, when a new hyper-sphere range query c_{i+1} is processed, the ISA does not have to again access disk pages accessed by the previous one c_i. Hence we can omit the last weakness of the basic ISA version. Note that the original algorithm in [12] is designed only for k-NN queries but here we must process the range queries. Fortunately, due to the way to create the hyper-sphere range queries, the original algorithm can easily be modified to meet the requirement. In details, for each range query with the radius r, the adapted algorithm will return all *data objects* at top of the priority queue until *the object (a data object or a node)* at top of the queue has the greater distance d_i to the query condition than r, i.e. d_i>r. In other words, when processing a k-NN query the adapted algorithm returns not only k nearest neighbors but also all data objects that the distance is equal to that of the kth nearest neighbor. See [12] for more details of the original algorithm. We name the adapted algorithm *incremental algorithm for range queries*. It is easily inferred from [2] that this new adapted algorithm is also optimal in terms of disk access number for each query condition q_i.

3.3 Enhanced ISA Version

This section presents an enhanced ISA version, which employs the incremental algorithm for the range queries, to find the best match for a complex vague query Q with n query conditions q_i (i=1, 2… n). Assume that F_i are the index structures that q_i will be searched on. The enhanced ISA is concisely described as follows.

1. Searching on each F_i for the corresponding q_i using the incremental algorithm adapted for hyper-sphere range queries.

---

[2] The index structures are required to use recursive and conservative partitioning [12, 2]

2. Combining the search results from all q_i to find at least an appropriate tuple in the query relation. The appropriate tuple must consist of the returned NCR-Values that corresponds to at least one tuple (record) of the query relation.
3. If there is no appropriate tuple that has been found then go back to step 1.
4. Computing the total distances for the found tuples using formula 2 and finding a tuple T_{min} with the minimum total distance TD_{cur}. Ties are arbitrarily broken.
5. Extending the searching radius for each q_i with respect to TD_{cur} using formula 1 and doing the new hyper-sphere range queries as step 1.
6. If there is any new appropriate tuple T_{new} with the smallest total distance $TD_{new}<TD_{cur}$ then return T_{new}. Otherwise, return T_{min}.

Obviously, after step 6 there is no any tuple (record) in the entire query relation having a smaller total distance to Q than that of the returned tuple. Therefore this enhanced ISA version correctly returns the best match for Q and totally overcomes the shortcomings of the ICA proposed in [15]. However, in step 5, we can process all the new hyper-sphere range queries more efficiently as follows.

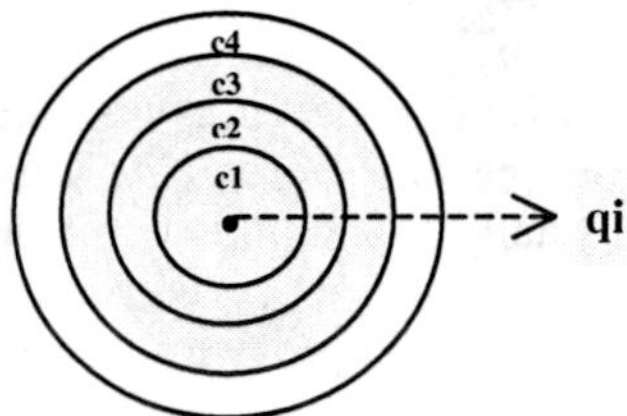

Fig. 3. Reducing the extended radius incrementally: the searched space is c_3 instead of c_4

Figure 3 illustrates an example: Assume that c_4 is one of the new queries in step 5 and c_1 is the old one in a searching feature space. Instead of processing c_4 directly we can continue the search as step 1 (the same for every F_i) and check whether any new appropriate tuple T_{new} found and its total distance $TD_{new}<TD_{cur}$. In case we found such a tuple, for example with c_2, we recompute the radii for every range query according to TD_{new} using formula 1. In figure 3, assume that the new radius creates a new range query c_3 then *c_4 contains c_3*. Now T_{new} takes role of T_{min} and this process is repeated until c_2's radius is greater than or equal to c_3's radius. Last, T_{new} is reported as the best match for the query. Processing the extended range queries in this manner will narrow the searched spaces and thus reduce the costs.

4 Finding k Nearest Neighbors for Complex Vague Queries

The enhanced ISA version just returns the best match for a CVQ. In practice, almost users need some top-k tuples (records) closest to the CVQ and k may be unknown in advance. This problem is easily solved by making some modifications to the enhanced ISA version as follows.

1. A priority queue PQ (or a sorted buffer) to keep all appropriate tuples found in step 4 of the enhanced ISA version is needed.

2. The next nearest neighbor of the query is verified similarly to the enhanced ISA version but here the tuple at the top of PQ takes part as T_{min} in the step 4.
3. When a tuple at the top of PQ is ensured to be the next nearest neighbor of the query, it will be added to the result set and be removed from PQ.
4. In the case PQ is empty and the user still needs more results then the search is continued normally on all the feature spaces. Due to the aspects of the incremental algorithm adapted for range queries, the search will continue from where it left when computing the previous nearest neighbor.

The correctness of this final ISA version is easily inferred from that of the enhanced ISA version. Besides, depending on this idea, the ICA can also be extended to answer k-nearest neighbor queries. In section 5 below we show experimental results to compare the ISA to the ICA.

5 Experimental Results

We did experiments for CVQs of only two query conditions and used uniformly distributed data sets of 4 and 8 dimensions. Each of them has 100K objects of form <id, values> and takes role as a feature space. Additionally, we used the SH-tree, a super hybrid index structure for multidimensional data [6], to manage the storage and retrieval of multidimensional objects in each feature space. We selected the SH-tree because it is one of the most flexible and efficient multidimensional index structures [7, 6]. The programs are implemented in C++. The page size is 8Kb for the data sets to meet the disk block size of the operating system.

For all experiments, we also simulated accesses to the query relation by comparing field *id* of the retrieved objects. For example, if a 4-d object <id_4, *values*> and an 8-d object <id_8, *values*> are retrieved during the search process and $id_4=id_8$, they are considered belonging to a tuple in the query relation. This tuple is called the appropriate one in this paper. Intuitively, for a particular query optimization processor in a database system, the retrieved object number in each feature space is directly proportional to the access cost to the database. Therefore we reported the disk access number and the retrieved object number for all the tests. Here the retrieved objects reported are ones located in the last hyper-sphere or hyper-cube range query.

Besides, for the ICA, each initial radius r_0 is set to maintain the selectivity at 0.001% in the corresponding feature space. For example, because the data sets are uniformly distributed, $r_0=\sqrt[4]{0.00001}$ in the 4-dimensional feature space. When the extension of each hyper-cube range query is necessary, the radius is increased by 1% of the corresponding feature space diameter to found the new hyper-cube range query.

For each feature space, 100 query points are randomly selected from the corresponding data set. The experimental results are shown in the below figures. Figure 4, 5 depict the results for 8-d data set and figure 6, 7 show the results for 4-d data set. For all the tests with k-nearest neighbor queries (k=1, 5, 10, 15, 20, 25 and 30), the ISA totally outperforms the ICA by an order of magnitude in both concepts of the disk access number and the retrieved object number. It means that the new approach, i.e. ISA, totally outperforms the previous proposed one, i.e. ICA, in both concepts of CPU-cost and IO-cost.

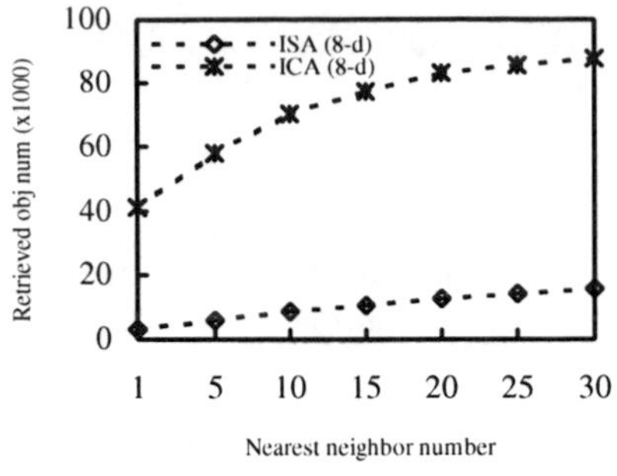

Fig. 4. Retrieved object number (8-d data set)

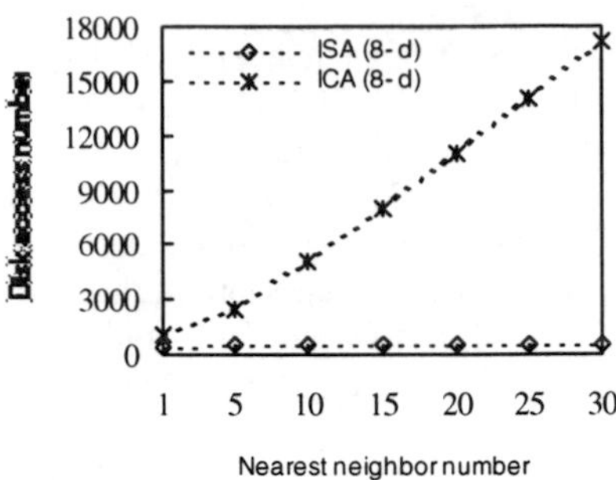

Fig. 5. Disk access number (8-d data set)

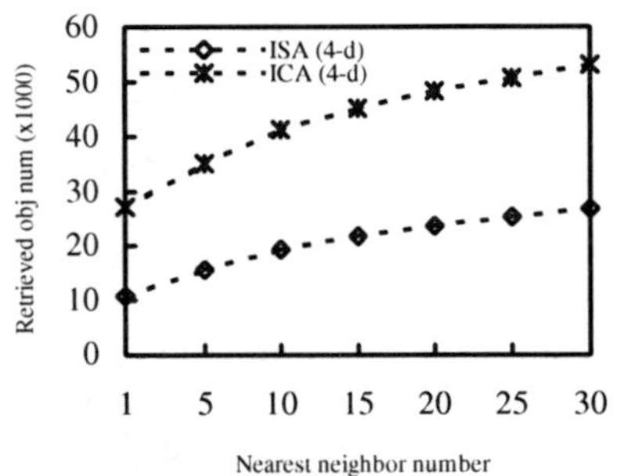

Fig. 6. Retrieved object number (4-d data set)

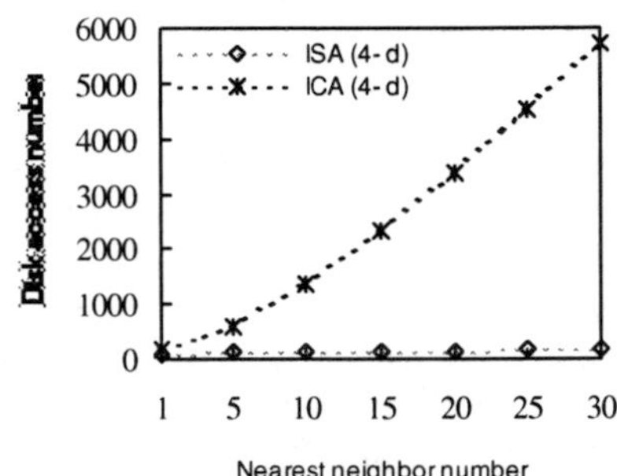

Fig. 7. Disk access number (4-d data set)

6 Conclusion and Future Work

In this article we presented a new approach called the ISA that can be applied to the VQS system [14] for efficiently solving CVQs. The ISA is superior to the ICA proposed in [15] in both concepts of CPU- and IO-cost. Besides, we also introduced an incremental algorithm adapted for range queries. It is proven to be an optimal algorithm in terms of the disk access number as the original one. This adapted algorithm considerably contributes towards accelerating the search for the nearest neighbors of CVQs using the ISA. Moreover, the ISA is more general and practical than the ICA in whatever sense and can be applied to every systems that the metadata have form as the NCR-Tables. Specially, the ISA is also usable in systems that the mapping one-to-one between keys in the NCR-Tables does not exist. This is a notable advantage of the ISA over Fagin's algorithm [8] and all its improvements.

Our future work will focus on applying the ISA, say the VQS, to real world application domains such as information retrieval, geographical and tourist information systems, medical databases, multimedia databases, etc. Furthermore, answering approximate CVQs in the VQS is also our future research.

References

1. R. Baeza-Yates, B. Ribeiro-Neto. Modern Information Retrieval. ACM Press Books, 1999
2. S. Berchtold, C. Böhm, D.A. Keim, H.P. Kriegel. A Cost Model for Nearest Neighbor Search in High-Dimensional Data Space. Proc. of 6th ACM SIGACT-SIGMOD-SIGART symposium on Principles of Database Systems, 1997
3. K. Böhm, M. Mlivoncic, H-J. Schek, R. Weber: Fast Evaluation Techniques for Complex Similarity Queries. VLDB 2001
4. S. Chaudhuri, L. Gravano. Optimizing Queries over Multimedia Repositories. Proc. of ACM SIGMOD International Conference on Management of Data, 1996
5. S. Chaudhuri, L. Gravano. Evaluating Top-k Selection Queries. VLDB 1999
6. T.K. Dang, J. Kueng, R. Wagner. The SH-tree: A Super Hybrid Index Structure for Multidimensional Data. Proc. of the 12th DEXA, Springer Verlag, LNCS 2113, ISBN 3-540-42527-6, pp. 340-349, Munich, Germany, Sep. 3-7, 2001
7. T.K. Dang, J. Küng, R. Wagner. Efficient Processing of k-Nearest Neighbor Queries in Spatial Databases with the SH-tree. Proc. of the 3rd iiWAS, ISBN 3-85403-150-5, pp. 425-435, Linz, Austria, Sep. 10-12, 2001
8. R. Fagin. Combining Fuzzy Information from Multiple Systems. Proc. of the 15th ACM SIGACT-SIGMOD-SIGART Symposium on Principles of Database Systems, June 1996
9. U. Guentzer, W.T. Balke, W. Kiessling. Optimizing Multi-Feature Queries for Image Databases. VLDB 2000
10. G. Graefe. Query Evaluation Techniques for Large Databases. ACM Computing Surveys (CSUR), Vol. 25, Issue 2, June 1993
11. A. Henrich, G. Robbert. Combining Multimedia Retrieval and Text Retrieval to Search Structured Documents in Digital Libraries. Pre-Proc. of the 1st DELOS Workshop on Information Seeking, Searching and Querying in Digital Libraries, Zürich, Switzerland, December, 2000
12. G.R. Hjaltason, H. Samet. Ranking in Spatial Databases. Advances in Spatial Databases - 4th Symposium, SSD'95, LNCS 951, Springer-Verlag, Berlin, 1995
13. T. Ichikawa, M. Hirakawa. ARES: A Relational Database with the Capability of Performing Flexible Interpretation of Queries. IEEE Trans. on Software Engineering, Vol. 12, No. 5, 1986
14. J. Kueng, J. Palkoska. VQS-A Vague Query System Prototype. DEXA 1997. IEEE Computer Society Press, Toulouse, France, September 1997
15. J. Kueng, J. Palkoska. An Incremental Hypercube Approach for Finding Best Matches for Vague Queries. DEXA 1999. LNCS, ISBN 3-540-66448-3, 1999
16. A. Motro. VAGUE: A User Interface to Relational Database that Permits Vague Queries. ACM Trans. on Office Information Systems, Vol 6, No. 3, July 1988
17. S. Nepal, M.V. Ramakrishna. Query Processing Issues in Image (Multimedia) Databases. Proc. of the 15th ICDE, Sydney, Australia, 1999
18. M. Ortega, Y. Rui, K. Chakrabarti, S. Mehrotra, T.S. Huang. Supporting Similarity Queries in MARS. Proc. of the 5th ACM International Conference on Multimedia, 1997
19. U. Pfeifer, N. Fuhr. Efficient Processing of Vague Queries Using a Data Stream Approach. Proc. of the 18th Annual International ACM SIGIR Conference on Research and Development in Information Retrieval, 1995
20. N. Roussopoulos, S. Kelley, F. Vincent. Nearest Neighbor Queries. Proc. of ACM SIGMOD International Conference on Management of Data, 1995
21. E.L. Wimmers, L.M. Haas, M.T. Roth, C. Braendli. Using Fagin's Algorithm for Merging Ranked Results in Multimedia Middleware. Proc. of the 4th COOPIS, Scotland, 1999
22. R. Weber, H.J. Schek, S. Blott. A Quantitative Analysis and Performance Study for Similarity-Search Methods in High-Dimensional Spaces. VLDB 1998

Parallel Query Support for Multidimensional Data: Inter-object Parallelism*

Karl Hahn[1], Bernd Reiner[1], Gabriele Höfling[1], and Peter Baumann[2]

[1] FORWISS, Bavarian Research Center for Knowledge Based Systems, Munich, Germany
{hahnk,reiner,hoefling}@forwiss.de
http://www.wibas.forwiss.tu-muenchen.de

[2] Active Knowledge GmbH, Munich, Germany
baumann@active-knowledge.com
http://www.active-knowledge.de

Abstract. Intra-query parallelism is a well-established mechanism for achieving high performance in (object-) relational database systems. However, the methods have yet not been applied to the upcoming field of multidimensional array databases. Specific properties of multidimensional array data require new parallel algorithms. This paper presents a number of new techniques for parallelizing queries in multidimensional array database management systems. It discusses their implementation in the RasDaMan DBMS, the first DBMS for generic multidimensional array data. The efficiency of the techniques presented is demonstrated using typical queries on large multidimensional data volumes.

1 Introduction

Arrays of arbitrary size and dimensionality appear in a large variety of database application fields, e.g., medical imaging, geographic information systems [7], scientific simulations, etc. Recently, integration of an application domain-independent and of a generic type constructor for such *Multidimensional Discrete Data (MDD)* into *Database Management Systems (DBMS)* has received growing attention. Current scientific contributions in this area mainly focus on MDD algebra and specialized storage architectures [1] [2] [3].

Since MDD objects may have a magnitude of several MB and much more and, compared to scalar values, operations on these values can be very complex, their efficient evaluation becomes a critical factor for the overall query response time. Beyond query optimization, parallel query processing is the most promising technique to speed up complex operations on large data volumes.

One of the outcomes of the predecessor project of *ESTEDI* (http://www.estedi.org), called *RasDaMan* (funded by the European Commission

* This work was supported by the ESTEDI project (http://www.estedi.org). ESTEDI (European Spatio-Temporal Data Infrastructure for High-Performance Computing) is funded by the European Commission under FP5 grant no. IST-1999-11009.

R. Cicchetti et al. (Eds.): DEXA 2002, LNCS 2453, pp. 820–830, 2002.

under grant no. 20073), in which the *Array DBMS RasDaMan* [2] has been developed, was the awareness that most queries on multidimensional array data are in fact CPU-bound [10]. Therefore, one major research issue of the succeeding project *ESTEDI* is the parallel processing of queries which is the topic of this paper. Furthermore, ESTEDI, an initiative of European software vendors and supercomputing centers, will establish an European standard for the storage and retrieval of multidimensional high-performance computing (HPC) data. It addresses a main technical obstacle, the delivery bottleneck of large HPC results to the users, by augmenting high-volume data generators with a flexible data management and extraction tool for multidimensional array data.

This paper discusses the suitability of concepts developed in parallel relational DBMS for intra-query parallelism in array DBMS. Special properties of array data, e.g. the size of one single data object combined with expensive cell operations require adapted algorithms for parallel processing. Suitable concepts found in relational DBMS were implemented and evaluated in the RasDaMan Array DBMS.

The remainder of this paper is organized as follows. Section 2 briefly describes the multidimensional data model, the multidimensional query language RasQL and the query execution in our example Array DBMS RasDaMan. In section 3, the architecture of the parallel RasDaMan server and the parallelizer module, which rewrites the query tree in order to distribute different sections of the tree to different processes, will be presented. The performance of the parallel implementation will be discussed, using a running example in section 4. We finally compare parallel algorithms of relational systems to our implemented techniques in order to evaluate their suitability regarding array data. Section 5 contains our conclusions and suggestions for future work.

2 Processing Multidimensional Data: The Array DBMS RasDaMan

In this section, we will describe a multidimensional data model, a multidimensional query language and the execution of multidimensional queries. As the parallel query processing was implemented in RasDaMan [2], we will first introduce the RasDaMan data model, the RasQL query language and its internal query tree and query execution. Nevertheless, the concepts for parallel query processing on array DBMS described in section 3 can be applied to other array DBMS as well.

2.1 Logical Data Model and Query Language

The fundamental concept of the RasDaMan data model is *Multidimensional Discrete Data (MDD)*. This can be defined as multidimensional array with (1) an arbitrary dimensionality, (2) a spatial domain, specified via lower bounds and upper bounds for each dimension, (3) a specific cell base type, consisting of a single scalar value or a complex type structure. An *MDD collection* holds an unordered set of MDD with the same dimensionality, spatial domain and cell base type.

In Fig. 2 (left top) we see a 3D MDD (data based on climate simulation model, provided by Max-Planck Institute for Meteorology, one of the application partners in the ESTEDI project). The dimensions specify longitude, latitude and time (months). The spatial domain is [0:63, 0:127, 0:119], i.e. the 3-dimensional array includes 64 x 128 x 120 cells. The cell values of scalar type double have a range of about 200 (dark regions near the poles) to 320 (bright regions near the equator), and define average temperatures on the earth surface in degrees Kelvin for 120 months. In Fig. 2 (left bottom), a collection of five MDD (each representing a decade of average temperature values) with the same dimensionality, spatial domain and cell type is illustrated. Internally each MDD is identified by a unique object identification number, here 28 to 32.

In order to invoke operations on array data and specify the multidimensional interval to be accessed, RasDaMan provides a query language RasQL which is derived from standard SQL. The simplified structure of such a RasQL query is

```
SELECT <array operation>
FROM collection 1, ..., collection n
WHERE <condition operation>
```

Array operations used in the select and where clause of the statement can be

1. geometric operations: the trimming operation specifies a sub-array with the same dimensionality, e.g. in our example [0:63,0:127,0:11] for the first 12 months. A section operation reduces the dimensionality by one, i.e. the data is projected to a hyperplane.
2. induced operations: operations which are defined on the base cell type are also defined on multidimensional arrays, e.g. the sum of two MDD with cell base type double.
3. aggregation operations: an MDD is reduced to one single scalar value. Operations of this class are quantifiers, maximum, minimum, average, etc.

The primary benefit of such a complex query language is the minimization of data transmission between database server and client. Areas of interest can be specified with geometric operators, and complex calculations can be executed on the server side, only transferring the result to the client instead of entire objects. A more detailed specification of the RasDaMan data model and the RasQL query language can be found in [2] and [3].

2.2 Query Execution: The RasDaMan Query Tree

Internally, the RasDaMan server builds up a query tree to process the query (Fig. 1). The query execution follows the open-next-close protocol (iterator concept) which is well known in database technology. First, the method `open()` is invoked on the root node α. In a post-order traversal, the method invocation is propagated through the query tree while initializing resources. Then, method `next()` is invoked repeatedly on the root node which again is propagated in a post-order traversal through the entire tree. Each time the method completes, this bottom-up process returns one element of the result collection. At the end, method `close()` is called to clean up resources allocated during execution.

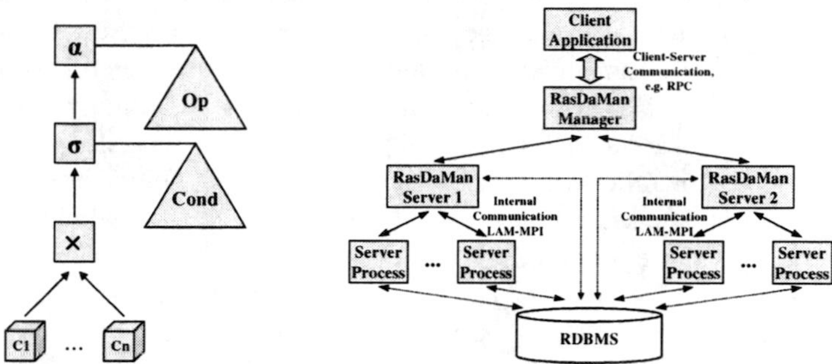

Fig. 1. Structure of a query tree for a RasQL statement (left). Architecture of the parallel RasDaMan server (right).

The iterator nodes of the query tree using the open-next-close protocol in Fig. 1 are

1. cross product _, representing the FROM clause of the RasQL statement. It delivers the cross product of all multidimensional objects of all referenced collections.
2. selection σ, representing the WHERE condition of the RasQL statement. The condition tree consists of multidimensional operations. A `next()` returns the next multidimensional data object for which the condition tree evaluates true.
3. application α, representing the SELECT operation of the RasQL statement. The operation tree executes array operations on the resulting multidimensional data.

It should be pointed out that the multidimensional data is not loaded at the bottom of the query tree (like the relational scan operator) but demand-driven during the evaluation of the condition tree, evaluated by the selection σ, and the operation tree, evaluated by the application α. Therefore, these operations of the query tree are the most expensive ones, because on the one hand the data loading is done there, and on the other hand the operation and condition itself are trees, which represent expensive array operations on the multidimensional data. Details on query optimization and execution in array DBMS can be found in [10].

3 Parallel Query Processing

Parallel query processing is a well established mechanism in relational DBMS [4] [6] [9] [11]. Different hardware architectures have been investigated regarding parallelism, i.e. multiprocessor computer (shared everything, symmetric multiprocessing, SMP) and shared disc / shared nothing systems (e.g. workstation cluster). Considering the facts that queries on array data are in most cases highly CPU-bound [10] and intermediate results can reach a size of several MB and more, we came to the conclusion that shared everything architectures are more appropriate for a parallel array DBMS, as performance will decrease with the transmission of large intermediate results over a network. Nevertheless, the architecture and the communication protocol used by the parallel RasDaMan server, which is LAM-MPI (http://www.lam-mpi.org), is not limited to any specific hardware architecture. LAM (Local Area Multicomputer) is an MPI (Message Passing Interface, http://www.mcs.anl.gov/mpi) programming environment and development system for heterogeneous computers within a network. With LAM, a dedicated cluster or an existing network computing infrastructure can act as one parallel computer solving one problem.

Furthermore, parallel processing of data can be classified into data parallelism, where different data sets are handled by different processes, and pipeline parallelism, where we can utilize a producer-consumer relationship within the query tree (a consumer executes operations on a data stream which is still being generated by the producer process). In this section we will describe the implemented data parallelism; a further discussion of the adaptation of parallel techniques in relational DBMS (e.g. pipeline parallelism) to Array DBMS will follow in section 4.

3.1 Parallel Architecture

The overall process structure of the parallel RasDaMan array DBMS is shown in Fig. 1. Several types of client applications currently exist. The most important is rView, a visualization application provided with RasDaMan [5]. Furthermore, several graphical front-ends for the visualization of data were implemented in the ESTEDI project, e.g., in the field of gene expression simulation, meteorological simulations, satellite image retrieval and information extraction, flow modeling of chemical reactors, etc. The clients are connected to the RasDaMan Manager using the RPC[1] or HTTP[2] protocol.

The RasDaMan manager distributes client request to different RasDaMan server processes which typically run on different computers. On this level, inter-query parallelism (multi-user functionality) is achieved: a query sent by the client application is transferred from the manager to a server process that is currently available.

Each RasDaMan server itself forks several internal processes at start-up time to realize intra-query parallelism. One designated process is responsible for the client-server communication and the distribution of the workload, all other processes are internal and therefore not visible from the client. The internal server processes have access to a relational DBMS which acts as a storage and transaction manager for the multidimensional array data (dotted lines in Fig. 1). At the time of writing, supported relational DBMS are Oracle, IBM DB2 and Informix.

As mentioned above, distributed processing of RasQL queries requires different processes and communication between them, e.g. to exchange requests or intermediate results. In order to avoid performance problems while evaluating a query, the processes do not fork during query execution but at start-up time of a RasDaMan server. So whenever a RasDaMan server is started, we create several internal server processes which reside in memory and are waiting for requests. We run 2 processes

[1] RPC: Remote Procedure Call

[2] HTTP: Hypertext Transfer Protocol

for administration tasks and an arbitrary number of processes for the computational work. In order to utilize CPU resources, but avoid unnecessary swapping of processes, we recommend n+2 processes with n being the number of processors of an SMP computer, resp. the number of nodes in a workstation cluster.

The parallel RasDaMan server distinguishes 3 classes of processes, where each process class reflects a part of the overall query tree (Fig. 1) that can be executed independently from other processes:

1. RasDaMan master server: this process is responsible for the server client communication via network, e.g., it connects the RasDaMan server to the rView client application using the RPC or HTTP protocol. It distributes controlling messages, the queries and therefore the workload to all other (internal) server processes. Query results are collected from the internal processes and transmitted to the client.
2. Internal tuple server: this process generates the cross-product of all MDD involved in the query. This is required to ensure a central administration of the multidimensional data objects for all processes. Upon receiving a request for the next data element, the server process accesses the underlying relational DBMS (only object identifiers are read not the whole objects), and sends the next tuple of object identifiers to the calling process.
3. Internal worker processes: a number of processes which do the actual query processing. Receiving a data identifier from the tuple server (invocation of `next()`) these processes evaluate the condition tree and the operation tree on this (tuple of) MDD.

3.2 Parallel Query Tree

The classification of the internal server processes presented above corresponds with the structure of the (parallel) query tree. In relational DBMS the optimization and parallelization phases, which both restructure the query tree, often show interferences. The optimization of a sequential execution plan contradicts an optimal parallel execution plan. Therefore, optimization and parallelization phases are often combined in one single module [8]. In RasDaMan, the optimization of the query tree does not conflict with parallel optimization, as optimization is primarily performed on the array operations of the operation and condition tree while the parallelizer works on the iterator nodes, so the parallelization module is invoked after the optimization phase.

The RasDaMan parallelization module works as follows: the algorithm identifies cross product iterator nodes in the query tree and inserts a pair of send/receive[3] nodes above it. The send/receive nodes encapsulate the transmission of requests (query execution protocol) and intermediate results between the internal server processes, using the MPI protocol. On the top of the query tree, the algorithm inserts another pair of send/receive nodes. This is necessary to designate one process as the master server process which also handles the server-client communication. It should be noted

[3] The semantics of the send and receive nodes refers to the direction of messages containing (intermediate) results.

that both 'expensive' nodes, the application and the selection nodes which evaluate the array operations, are executed within one process, instead of being split into two processes. We decided not to compute the application node and the selection node on different processes because this would avoid the usage of transient multidimensional data, i.e. memory-cached objects of the data read from the relational DBMS. It is very typical to execute selection and application operation on the same sub-arrays of data, therefore RasDaMan caches intermediate results within a query.

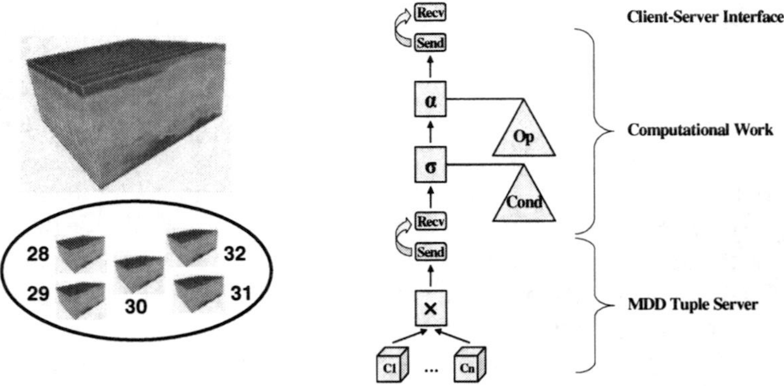

Fig. 2. 3-dimensional MDD (left top). Collection of five MDD (left bottom).Parallel query tree (right).

The algorithm splits the query tree into several sections which are interconnected by pairs of send/receive nodes. Fig. 2 illustrates an example of a query tree which was prepared for parallel query processing by the parallelizer module. The query tree is split into three parts which are processed by the different process classes presented above. The master process only holds one single receive node on the top of the query tree. It distributes the query execution, i.e. the open-next-close iterator concept, top-down in the query tree to the internal worker processes and collects the query results returned. The complete result is then encapsulated in a transfer structure and transmitted to the client.

Application and selection nodes of the query tree represent the expensive operations performed on the array data. This computational workload is distributed between several worker processes. Each internal worker process executes the query tree with the upper send node as its root node. Whenever it receives a `next()` request from the master process via MPI, it sends a next request down the query tree to the internal tuple server process and receives the MDD identifiers on which the operations are then evaluated. The resulting data is transmitted to the master which collects all results and transmits them to the client.

As mentioned above, the tuple server process executes the query tree beginning at the lower send node. It delivers the next valid identifier for a tuple of MDD, accessing the referenced collections. With this concept, a central allocation of MDD tuples to the worker processes is assured. Furthermore, this dynamic allocation of data identifiers to the worker processes using the iterator concept prevents data skew.

4 Performance and Evaluation

In order to evaluate the speed-up of the parallel RasDaMan server, we chose typical RasQL queries on 2-dimensional and 3-dimensional data. We will first give a detailed example of a test run, describing the test data, the RasQL query, the internal query execution and the intermediate results. Following the running example, parameters influencing the speed-up will be discussed in detail. Finally, the implemented techniques will be compared to techniques used for relational DBMS.

4.1 Running Example

Our example test scenario runs on a collection containing 60 3D MDD. The data was provided by the Max-Planck Institute for Meteorology (partner in the ESTEDI project). Each 3D cube represents temperature values in a specific height above sea level in degrees Kelvin for 10 years (120 months) and was calculated in meteorological simulations (see Fig. 2, left). The spatial domain of a MDD is [0:63,0:127,0:119], the base type is float; the size of one single MDD is 4 MB, the size of the entire collection is 240 MB.

The tests were performed on a SUN Ultra 250 with 2 UltraSPARC II CPUs running at 400MHz, approximately 1.1 GB of main memory and 100 GB of hard disc capacity. The relational DBMS used was Oracle 8.1.6, the parallel RasDaMan server version was 3.5. The query to be analyzed is

```
SELECT all_cells(a > 200.0)
FROM mpim3d as a
```

This simple RasQL statement analyzes each MDD of the `mpim3d` collection and returns a boolean value for each MDD, indicating if all cell values of the MDD are greater than 200.0 degrees Kelvin. This query is particularly well suited for parallel execution because

1. the application includes an induced operation '>' and an aggregation operation 'all_cells' in the operation tree, which are both CPU-bound,
2. the collection includes 60 MDD. The data volume is sufficient to let computational costs dominate over communication costs and to prevent data skew (as shown above, the load is distributed dynamically),
3. the results which have to be collected by the master server process and transmitted to the client are extremely small in this case, i.e. the intermediate result transferred from the worker processes to the master process is only one scalar value per MDD.

For these reasons, this query achieves a speed-up of about 1.91, measured on the RasDaMan server[4]. Typical speed-ups of CPU-bound queries lie within a range of 1.60 and 1.95 (if the response time of the query is not too short, see below). The time required by the different internal process classes is as follows:

- about 2% for the tuple server. This process does no computational work but central administration of the multidimensional objects.

[4] Response times on the client can differ because of slow network transfer rates.

- about 4% for the master process. In this case the result to be transmitted to the client is very small.
- 94% for the two worker processes. As the overall execution time is consumed by the processing of 60 data objects, the data skew in this example is minimal.

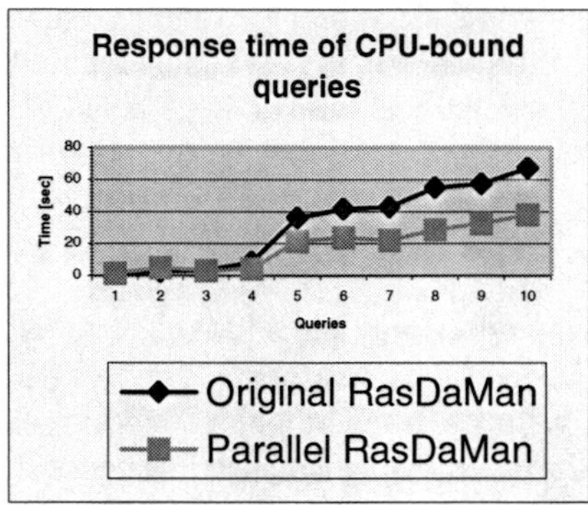

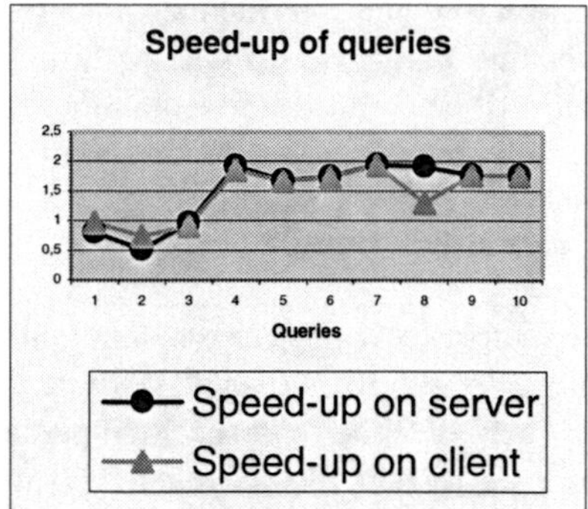

Fig. 3. Performance of the original server compared to the parallel implementation

Fig. 3 shows the performance for 10 CPU-bound queries with ascending response time. We can identify a threshold in the range of 3 seconds. This threshold distinguishes complex queries for which the parallel execution improves performance from simple queries where the overhead of parallelizing exceeds the performance improvement of a parallel execution. However, a response time less than 3 seconds is not typical for the processing array data, so we accept the performance loss for such simple queries. The more complex a query gets, the more speed-up is achieved. Finally, the speed-up of queries having a response time of 30 seconds or more (on the parallel RasDaMan server) is determined only by (1) the kind of array operations (I/O vs. CPU-bound, see section 2.1), (2) the kind of intermediate results which are transmitted by internal processes, (3) the number of MDD which have to be handled. A small number of MDD can lead to data skew.

The speed-up measured on the client application is typically less than the speed-up on the server (Fig. 3, right), especially if the result of the query which has to be transmitted over the network is very large (query 8).

4.2 Evaluation

Intra-query parallelism is a well established technique in relational DBMS, but to our knowledge it has not yet been examined for multidimensional array DBMS. The special properties of array data, such as the enormous size to be processed, the typical size of a single data element (MDD), typical queries being CPU-bound etc., require a detailed evaluation of the parallel algorithms used in relational database technology regarding their suitability for array DBMS:

1. data parallelism vs. pipeline parallelism

Data parallelism is an excellent way to speed up queries on MDD. Although multidimensional objects typically have a size of several MB (and more) and the operations are CPU-bound, the communication costs for the distribution of the objects are small compared to the costs for the array operations. Additionally, we tried to minimize communication costs by avoiding to transmit large intermediate results. Pipeline parallelism, on the other hand, destroys the utilization of transient multidimensional objects, i.e. cached MDD, and therefore compromises performance.

2. load balancing and data skew
   Expensive operations on large array data allow for dynamic load balancing. In contrast to relational DBMS which often access millions of very small data tuple array queries typically access up to several hundred data objects having a size of several MB or more. As a consequence, the next MDD to be evaluated can be allocated on demand instead of distributing the workload statically as done in relational systems. This procedure avoids data skew.
3. intermediate results
   Transferring intermediate results proves to be more complex in the case of array data than it is for relational data. Relational database pages filled with tuples have less complexity compared to multidimensional arrays, which consist of complex data of dynamic size, cell type etc. The parallelization module was adapted to this characteristic. Transmission of complex transient intermediate results was avoided where possible.

Summarizing, the implemented parallelism for array data requires methods different from relational techniques, but is well suited for the typical application scenarios involving processing of array data and achieves very good performance.

5 Conclusions

Parallel processing of multidimensional array data in an array DBMS has not attracted any attention in database research so far, although query execution time for processing this kind of data is mostly determined by CPU resources. Our goal was the utilization of parallel hardware in order to speed up CPU-bound queries, especially very expensive queries with execution times of several minutes or even hours. We designed a concept to dynamically split up the computational work on multidimensional objects between multiple processes. This required an adaptation and segmentation of the query tree to allow different parts of the query tree to be executed by different processes. In order to achieve good speed-up we minimized process initialization time and inter-process communication.

The concept described was fully implemented in the RasDaMan server kernel. Extensive test scenarios were performed regarding the structure of the resulting query tree and the intermediate results that have to be transmitted.

Performance measurements prove the validity of our concept. On a two processor machine we observed an increase in speed by a factor of up to 1.91 which is an extremely good result. Further performance measurements on computers with more processors and workstation clusters will follow. We expect similar performance improvements on these architectures as the concept implemented makes no assumptions regarding the number of processes or cluster nodes.

The implemented data parallelism partitions the data with a granularity of entire multidimensional objects. This has the benefit that the concept is straightforward and avoids excessive communication overhead which would lead to a loss of performance.

Summarizing, the parallel RasDaMan server shows extremely good performance, especially for computationally expensive queries.

Future work includes the investigation and the implementation of intra-object parallelism. In order to achieve performance improvements for a query which executes array operations on a single MDD, the concept described here is not suitable, as the granularity of our data parallelism is a complete multidimensional object. Speeding up such queries requires splitting up the MDD and processing the resulting fragments in parallel, which has to be investigated further in the future.

References

1. Agrawal, R., Gupta, A. Sarawagi, S.: Modeling Multi-dimensional Databases. Research Report, IBM Almaden Research Center, San Jose, USA, 1995
2. Baumann, P., Furtado, P., Ritsch, R., Widmann, N.: Geo/Environmental and Medical Data Management in the RasDaMan System. In Proc. of the Int. Conf. on Very Large Data Bases (VLDB), Athens, Greece, 1997
3. Baumann, P.: A Database Array Algebra for Spatio-Temporal Data and Beyond. In Proc. of the 4th International Workshop on Next Generation Information Technologies and Systems (NGITS), Zikhron Yaakov, Israel, 1999
4. Bouganim, L., Florescu, D., Valduriez, P.: Dynamic Load Balancing in Hierarchical Parallel Database Systems. In Proc. of the Int. Conf. on Very Large Data Bases (VLDB), Mumbai (Bombay), India, 1996
5. Dehmel, A., Baumann, P.: Visualizing Multidimensional Raster Data with rView. In Proc. of the Int. Workshop on Database and Expert System Application (DEXA), Greenwich, UK, 2000
6. DeWitt, D.J., Gray, J.: Parallel Database Systems: The Future of High Performance Database Systems, Communication of the ACM, Volume 35, 1992
7. DeWitt, D.J., Kabra, N., Luo, J., Patel, J., Yu, J.: Client Server Paradise. In Proc. of the Int. Conf. on Very Large Data Bases (VLDB), Santiago, Chile, 1994
8. Nippl, C., Mitschang, B.: TOPAZ: a Cost-Based, Rule-Driven, Multi-Phase Parallelizer. In Proc. of the Int. Conf. on Very Large Data Bases (VLDB), p. 251-262, 1998
9. Rahm, E.: Dynamic Load Balancing in Parallel Database Systems. In Proc. of EURO-PAR, Lyon, Springer-Verlag, Lecture Notes in Computer Science 1123, S.37-52, 1996
10. Ritsch, R.: Optimization and Evaluation of Array Queries in Database Management Systems, PhD Thesis, Technical University Munich, 1999
11. Tamer Özsu, M., Valduriez, P.: Principles of Distributed Database Systems, Second Edition. Prentice-Hall 1999

Pruning Training Corpus to Speedup Text Classification[1]

Jihong Guan[1] and Shuigeng Zhou[2]

[1] School of Computer Science, Wuhan University, Wuhan, 430079, China
jhguan@wtusm.edu.cn
[2] State Key Lab of Software Engineering, Wuhan University, Wuhan, 430072, China
Zhousg@whu.edu.cn

Abstract: With the rapid growth of online text information, efficient text classification has become one of the key techniques for organizing and processing text repositories. In this paper, an efficient text classification approach was proposed based on pruning training-corpus. By using the proposed approach, noisy and superfluous documents in training corpuses can be cut off drastically, which leads to substantial classification efficiency improvement. Effective algorithm for training corpus pruning is proposed. Experiments over the commonly used Reuters benchmark are carried out, which validates the effectiveness and efficiency of the proposed approach.

Keywords: text classification; fast classification; *k*-nearest neighbor (*k*NN); training-corpus pruning.

1 Introduction

As the amount of on-line textual information increases by leaps and bounds, effective retrieval is difficult without support of appropriate indexing and summarization of text content. Text classification is one solution to this problem. By placing documents into different classes according to their respective contents, retrieval can be done by first locating a specific class of documents relevant to the query and then searching the targeted documents within the selected class, which is significantly more efficient and reliable than searching in the whole documents repository.

Text classification has been a hot research topic in machine learning and information retrieval areas, and a number of methods for text classification were proposed [1, 2]. Among the existing methods, *k*NN is the simplest strategy that searches the *k*-nearest training documents to the test document and use the classes assigned to those training documents to decide the class of the test document [3, 4, 5, 6]. *k*NN classification method is easy to implement for it does not require the phase of classifier training that other classification methods must have. Furthermore, experimental researches show that *k*NN method offers promising performance in text

[1] This work was supported by the Natural Science Foundation of China (NSFC) (No. 60173027) and the Provincial Natural Science Foundation of Hubei of China (No. 2001ABB050).

R. Cicchetti et al. (Eds.): DEXA 2002, LNCS 2453, pp. 831–840, 2002.

classification [2, 6]. However, the kNN method is of low efficiency because it requires a large amount of computational power for evaluating a measure of the similarity between a test document and every training document and for sorting the similarities. Such a drawback makes it unsuitable for some applications where classification efficiency is pressing. For example, on-line text classification where the classifier has to respond to a lot of documents arriving simultaneously in stream format.

Some researchers in IR have addressed the problem of using representative training documents for text classification to improve classification efficiency. In [7] we proposed an algorithm for selecting representative boundary documents to replace the entire training sets so that classification efficiency can be improved. However, [7] didn't provide any criterion on how many boundary documents should be selected and it couldn't guarantee the classification performance. Linear classifiers [8] represent a category with a generalized vector to summarize all training documents in that category; the decision of the assignment of the category can be viewed as considering the similarity between the test document and the generalized vector. Analogously, [9] utilizes the centriod of each class as the only representative of the entire class. A test document is assigned to the class whose centroid is the nearest one to that test document. However, these approaches could not do well in the case that the sizes of different classes are quite different and distribution of training documents in each class is not regular in document space. Combining traditional kNN and linear classification methods, [5] uses a set of generalized instances to replace the entire training corpus, classification is based on the set of generalized instances. Experiments show this approach outperforms both traditional kNN and linear classification methods.

In this paper, our focus is also on the efficiency of kNN based text classification. We provide a robust and controlled way to prune noisy and superfluous documents so that the training corpuses can be significantly condensed while their classification competence is maintained as much as possibly, which leads to greatly improved classification efficiency. We design effective algorithm for text corpus pruning, and carry out experiments over the commonly used Reuters benchmark to validate the effectiveness and efficiency of our proposed approach. Our approach is especially suitable for on-line classification applications.

The rest of this paper is organized as follows. Section 2 introduces the vector space model (VSM), a clustering-based feature selection method and the kNN classification method. Section 3 first presents the concepts and algorithm for noisy and superfluous training documents pruning, and then gives a fast kNN classification approach based on the proposed training-corpus pruning algorithm. Section 4 describes some experiments for evaluating the proposed approach. Section 5 concludes the paper.

2 Preliminaries for kNN Based Text Classification

2.1 Documents Representation by Vector Space Model (VSM)

In kNN based text classification, the vector space model (VSM)[10] is used to represent documents. That is, a document corresponds to an n-dimensional document vector. Each dimension of the document vector corresponds to an important term appearing in the training corpus. These terms are also called document features. Given a document vector, its dimensional components indicate the corresponding terms' weights that are related to the importance of these terms in that document. Denote D a training corpus, V the set of document features, $V=\{t_1, t_2, \ldots, t_n\}$. For a document d in D, it can be represented by VSM as follows.

$$d = (w_1, w_2, \ldots, w_n). \tag{1}$$

Above, $\vec{d}$ indicates the vector of document d, $w_i (i=1\sim n)$ is the weight of term t_i. Usually, the weight is evaluated by *TFIDF* method. A commonly used formula is like this:

$$w_i = \frac{tf_i \times \log(N / n_i)}{\sqrt{\sum_{i=1}^{n} (tf_i)^2 [\log(N / n_i)]^2}}. \tag{2}$$

Here, N is the total number of documents in D, tf_i is the occurrence frequency of t_i in document d, and n_i is the number of documents where t_i appears. Obviously, document vectors calculated by (2) are unit vector. Given two documents d_i and d_j, the similarity coefficient between them is measured by the inner product of their corresponding document vectors, *i.e.*,

$$Sim(d_i, d_j) = \vec{d}_i \bullet \vec{d}_j. \tag{3}$$

2.2 Clustering Based Feature Selection

To calculate document vectors for training documents, the first step is to select a set of proper document features. A number of statistic methods have been used for document features selection in the literature [11]. However, in this paper we use a new method, which is referred to as *clustering-based feature selection*.

From the point of geometry view, every document is a unit vector in document space (n-dimensional space). Basically, documents belong to the same class are closer to each other in document space than those that are not in the same class, that is, they have smaller distance (or larger similarity). Documents in the same class form a dense hyper-cone area in document space, and a training corpus corresponds to a cluster of hyper-cones each of which corresponds to a class. Certainly, different hyper-cones may overlay with each other. Intuitively, the goal of feature selection task here is to select a subset of documents features such that the overlaying among different training classes in the document space is as little as possible.

The basic idea of our clustering-based feature selection method is like this: treating each training class as a distinctive cluster, then using a genetic algorithm to select a subset of document features such that the difference among all clusters is maximized. We define the difference among all clusters as follows.

$$Diff = \frac{1}{m} \sum_{k=1}^{m} \left(\frac{1}{|C_k| * (|C_k| - 1)} \sum_{\substack{d_i, d_j \in C_k \\ i \neq j}} sim(d_{ik}, d_{jk}) \right) - \frac{1}{(\sum_{k=1}^{m} C_k)^2 - \sum_{k=1}^{m} |C_k|^2} \sum_{k=1}^{m} \sum_{\substack{d_i \in C_k \\ d_j \notin C_k}} sim(d_i, d_j). \tag{4}$$

Above, m is the number of clusters, the first part indicates the average intra-cluster similarity, and the second part means the average inter-cluster similarity. Due to space limitation, we omit the details of the clustering based feature selection algorithm.

2.3 *k*NN Based Text Classification

The *k*NN based text classification approach is quite simple [2]: given a test document, the system finds the *k* nearest neighbors among training documents in the training corpus, and uses the classes of the *k* nearest neighbors to weight class candidates. The similarity score of each nearest neighbor document to the test document is used as the weight of the classes of the neighbor document. If several of *k* nearest neighbors share a class, then the per-neighbor weights of that class are added together, and the resulting weighted sum is used as the likelihood score of that class with respect to the test document. By sorting the scores of candidate classes, a ranked list is obtained for the test document. By thresholding on these scores, binary class assignments are obtained. Formally, the decision rule in *k*NN classification can be written as:

$$score(d,c_i) = \sum_{d_j \in kNN(d)} Sim(\vec{d},\vec{d}_j)\delta(d_j,c_i) - b_i. \quad (5)$$

Above, *k*NN(d) indicates the set of k nearest neighbors of document d; b_i is the class-specific threshold for the binary decisions, it can be automatically learned using cross validation; and $\delta(d_j,c_i)$ is the classification for document d_j with respect to class c_i, that is,

$$\delta(d_j,c_i) = \begin{cases} 1 & d_j \in c_i; \\ 0 & d_j \notin c_i. \end{cases}$$

Obviously, for a test document d, the similarity between d and each document in the training corpus must be evaluated before it can be classified. The time complexity of *k*NN classification is $O(n_t|D|\log(|D|))$ where $|D|$ and n_t are the size of training corpus and the number of test documents. To improve classification efficiency, a possible way is to reduce $|D|$, which the goal of this paper.

In this paper, we assume that 1) the class space has flat structure and all classes are semantically disjointed; 2) each document in the training corpus belongs to only one class; 3) each test document can be classified into only one class. With these assumptions, for test document d, it should belong to the class that has the highest resulting weighted sum in (5). That is, $d \in c$ only if

$$score(d,c) = \max\{score(d,c_i) \mid i = 1-n\}. \quad (6)$$

3 Training-Corpus Pruning for Fast Text Classification

Examining the process of *k*NN classification, we can see that outer documents or boundary documents (locating near the boundary) of each class (or document hyper-cone) play more decisively role in classification. On the contrary, inner documents or central documents (locating at the interior area) of each class (or document hyper-cone) are less important as far as *k*NN classification is concerned, because their contribution to classification decision can be obtained from the outer documents. In this sense, inner documents of each class can be seen as superfluous documents. Superfluous documents are just not tell us much about making classification decision, the job they do in informing classification decision can be done by other documents. Except for superfluous documents, there may be some noisy documents in training corpus, which are in-correctly labeled training documents. We seek to discard superfluous and noisy documents to reduce the size of training corpus so that classification efficiency can bee boosted. Meanwhile, we try to guarantee that the pruning of superfluous documents will not cause classification performance (*precision and recall*) degradation.

In the context of *k*NN text classification, for training document *d* in training corpus *D*, there are two sets of documents in *D* that are related to *d* in different way. Documents in one of the two sets are critical to the classification decision on *d* if *d* were a test document; for documents in the other set, *d* can contribute to the classification decisions on these documents if they were treated as test documents. Formal definitions for the two document-sets are as follows.

Definition 1. Given document *d* in training corpus *D*, the set of *k* nearest documents to *d* in *D* constitutes the *k-reachability* set of *d*, which is referred to as *k-reachability*(*d*). Formally, *k-reachability* (*d*)=$\{d_i \mid d_i \in D$ and $d_i \in k\text{NN}(d)\}$.

Definition 2. Given document *d* in training corpus *D*, there is a set of documents in the same class that *d* belongs to, in which each document's *k-reachability* set contains *d*. We define this set of documents the *k-coverage* set of *d*, or simply *k-coverage* (*d*). Formally, *k-coverage* (*d*)=$\{d_i \mid d_i \in D$ and $d_i \in$ *class*(*d*) and $d \in$ *k-reachability* $(d_i)\}$. Here, *class*(*d*) indicates the class to which *d* belongs.

Note that in definition 2, *k-coverage* (*d*) contains only documents from the same class that *d* belongs to. The reason lies in the fact: our aim is to prune training-corpus while maintaining its classification competence. Obviously, pruning *d* may impact negatively the classification decisions on the documents in the same class that *d* belongs to; however, it can benefit the classification decisions on the documents in the other classes. Hence, we need take care only the documents in the same class that *d* belongs to and whose *k-reachability* sets contain *d*.

Definition 3. Given document *d* in training corpus *D*, if it could be correctly classified with *k-reachability*(*d*) based on the *k*NN method, in other words, *d* can be implied by *k-reachability*(*d*), then it is a *superfluous document* in *D*.

Definition 4. Given document *d* in training corpus *D*, it is a *critical document* if one of the following conditions is fulfilled:

a) at least one document d_i in *k-coverage*(*d*) can not be implied by its *k-reachability*(d_i);
b) after *d* is pruned from *D*, at least one document d_i in *k-coverage*(*d*) cannot be implied by its *k-reachability*(d_i).

Definition 5. Given document *d* in training corpus *D*, if it is not a superfluous document and its *k-coverage* (*d*) is empty, then it is a *noisy document* in *D*.

In summary, a superfluous document is *superfluous* because its class assignment can be derived from other documents; a critical document is *critical* to other documents because it can contribute to making correct classification decisions about these documents; and a noisy documents is *noise* as far as classification is concerned because it is incorrectly labeled. In *k*NN classification, noise documents must be given up; superfluous documents can be discarded; however, critical documents must be kept in order to maintain training corpus' classification competence. Based on this consideration, we give a rule for training corpus pruning as follows.

Rule 1. The rule for training-document pruning.

For document *d* in training corpus *D*, it can be pruned from *D* if

1) it is a noisy document in *D*, or
2) it is a superfluous document, but not a critical document in *D*.

For the second case in Rule 1, the first constraint is the prerequisite for pruning a certain document from the training corpus, while the second constraint is put to guarantee that the pruning of a certain document will not cause degradation of classification competence of the training corpus.

While pruning superfluous documents, it is worthy of pointing out that the order of pruning is also critical because the pruning of one document may impact the decision on whether other documents can be pruned. Intuitively, inner documents of a class in the training corpus should be pruned before outer documents. This strategy can increase the chance of retaining outer documents as many as possible. Otherwise, if outer documents were pruned before inner documents, it would be possible to cause the Domino effect that a lot of documents are pruned from the training corpus, including outer documents, which would degrade greatly the classification competence of the training corpus. Therefore, some rule is necessary to control the order of documents pruning.

Generally speaking, inner documents of a certain class in the training corpus have some common features: 1) inner documents may have more documents of their own class around themselves than outer documents can have; 2) inner documents are closer to the center of their class than the outer documents are; 3) inner documents are further from the documents of other classes than the outer documents are. Based on these observations, we give a rule about superfluous document's pruning priority as follows. Here, we denote *H-k*NN(*d*) the number of documents in *k*NN(*d*) that belongs to the class of *d*; *similarity-c*(*d*) the similarity of document *d* to the center of its own class, and *similarity-ne*(*d*) the similarity of document *d* to the nearest document that does not belong to its own class.

Rule 2. The rule for setting priority of pruning superfluous documents.

Given two documents d_i, d_j in a class of the training corpus, both d_i and d_j are superfluous documents that can be pruned according to Rule 1.

1) if $H\text{-}k\mathrm{NN}(d_i) > H\text{-}k\mathrm{NN}(d_j)$, then prune d_i before d_j;
2) if $similarity\text{-}c(d_i) > similarity\text{-}c(d_j)$, then prune d_i before d_j;
3) if $similarity\text{-}ne(d_i) < similarity\text{-}ne(d_j)$, then prune d_i before d_j;

4) if they have similar *H-k*NN, *similarity-c* and *similarity-ne*, then any one can be pruned first;
5) the priority of using *H-k*NN, *similarity-c* and *similarity-ne*: *H-k*NN>*similarity-c*> *similarity-ne*.

Following is an algorithm for training corpus pruning. In algorithm 1, we assume that there is only one class in the training corpus. If there are multiple classes in the training corpus, just carrying out the pruning process in algorithm 1 over one class after another.

Algorithm 1. Pruning-training-corpus (*T*: training corpus, *P*: pruned corpus)

1) $P=T$; $S=\Phi$;
2) for each document d in T
3) compute *k-reachability*(d); compute *k-coverage*(d);
4) for each noisy document d in T
5) $S=S\cup\{d\}$; $T=T-\{d\}$; $P=P-\{d\}$;
6) for each document d_i in k-coverage(d)
7) remove d from k-reachability(d_i) and update k-reachability(d_i) in T;
8) for each document d_i in k-reachability(d)
9) remove d from k-coverage (d_i);
10) for each document d in T but not in S
11) if d can be pruned and have the highest priority to be pruned, then
12) $S=S\cup\{d\}$; $P=P-\{d\}$;
13) for each document d_i in k-coverage(d)
14) update k-reachability(d_i) in T.
15) return P.

Based on the technique of training corpus pruning, a fast algorithm for *k*NN text classification is outlined as follows.

Algorithm 2. Fast *k*NN classification based on training documents pruning (outline)

1) Selecting document feature with the proposed clustering based feature selection method; building training document vectors with the selected features;
2) Pruning the training corpus by using algorithm 1;
3) For each test document d, calculate its similarity to each training document in the pruned training corpus;
4) Sorting the computed similarities to get *k*NN(d);
5) Deciding d's class based on formula (5) and (6).

4 Experimental Results

We evaluate the proposed approach by using the Reuters benchmark compiled by Apte *et al.* for their evaluation of the SWAP-1 by removing all of the unlabeled documents from the original Reuters corpus and restricting the categories to have a training-set frequency of at least two [12]. Usually this corpus is simply referred to as

Apte[1]. We do not use the Apte corpus directly, instead we first remove training and test documents that belong to two or more categories, and then select the top 10 categories to form our own compiled Apte corpus. Statistic information of the compiled Apte corpus is listed in Table 1.

Table 1. Our complied Apte corpus (*TC-Apte*)

Category	Number of training docs	Number of test docs
Acq	1597	750
Coffee	93	25
Crude	255	124
Earn	2840	1170
Interest	191	90
money-fx	215	100
money-supply	123	30
Ship	111	38
Sugar	97	32
Trade	251	88
Total	5773	2447

We implemented a prototype with VC++ 6.0 under Windows 2000. Experiments were carried out on a PC with P4 1.4GHz CPU and 256MHz memory. The goal of experiments is to evaluate the performance (effectiveness and efficiency) of our approach. For simplicity, we denote the complied Apte corpus *TC-Apte*. In experiments, *TC-Apte* is pruned first by using our pruning algorithm; the pruned result corpus is denoted as *TC-Apte-pruned*. Classifiers are trained with *TC-Apte* and its corresponding pruned corpus *TC-Apte-pruned*, the trained classifiers' performances are then measured and compared.

Three performance parameters are measured: *precision* (*p*), *recall* (*r*), and *classification speedup* (or simply *speedup*), in which *p* and *r* are used for effectiveness measurements, and *speedup* is used for efficiency improvement measurement of our approach. Here we use the *micro-averaging* method for evaluating performance average across multiple classes. In the context of this paper (*i.e.* each document, either for training or for test, belongs to only one category), *micro-average p* (or simply *micro-p*) and *micro-average r* (or simply *micro-r*) have similar values. In this paper, we use *micro-p*, which can be evaluated as follows:

$$micro-p = \frac{the\ number\ of\ correctly\ assigned\ test\ documents}{the\ number\ of\ test\ ocuments}.$$

We define efficiency *speedup* in the following formula:

$$speedup = \frac{t_{TC-Apte}}{t_{TC-Apte-pruned}}.$$

Above, $t_{\text{TC-Apte}}$ and $t_{\text{TC-Apte-pruned}}$ are the time cost for classifying a test document (or a set of test documents) based on *TC-Apte* and *TC-Apte-pruned* respectively.

---

[1] Apte corpus is available at: http://moscow.mt.cs.cmu.edu:8081/reuters_21450/apte

Due to space limitation, here we give only partial experimental results. Fig. 1 illustrates the results of the impact of *k* value on pruning effectiveness and classification performance over *TC-Apte*. From Fig.1, we can see that by using our corpus-pruning technology, classification efficiency can get improved at a factor of larger than 4, with less than 3% degradation of micro-averaging performance. Obviously, this result is acceptable.

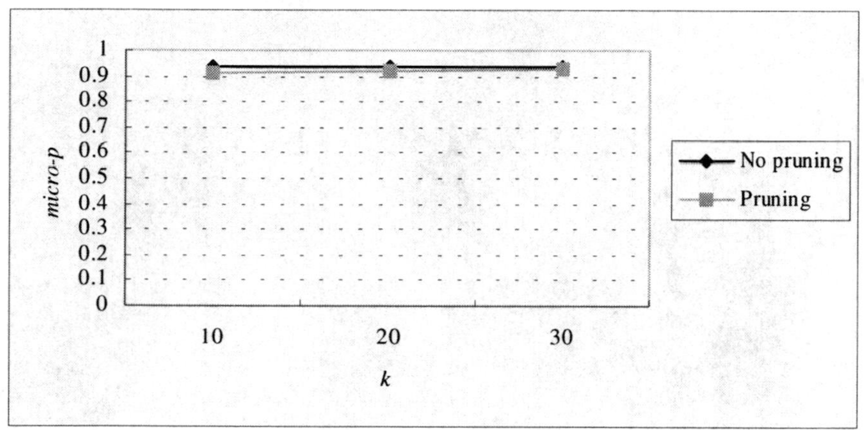

(a) *k* value vs. *micro-p*

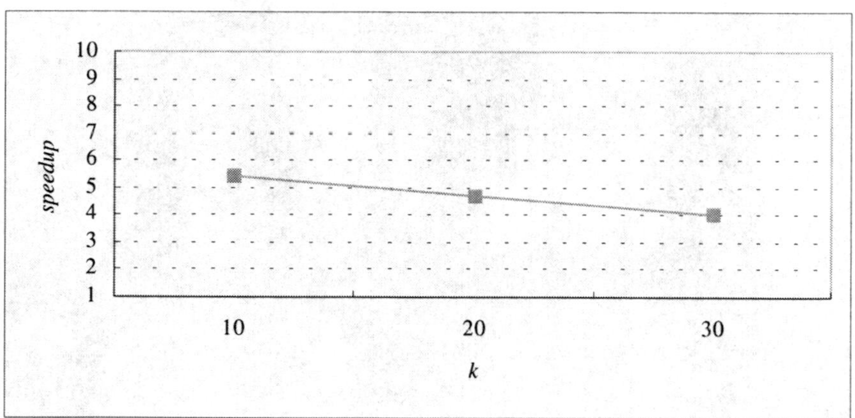

(b) *k* value vs. *speedup*

Fig. 1. Impact of *k* value on pruning effectiveness and classification performance

5 Conclusion

The rapid growth of text information available arises the requirement of efficient text classification method. Although *k*NN based text classification is a good method as far as performance is concerned, it is inefficient for it has to calculate the similarity of the test document to each training document in the training corpus. In this paper, we propose a training-corpus pruning based approach to speedup the *k*NN method. By using our approach, the size of training corpus can be reduced significantly while classification performance can be kept at a level close to that of without training documents pruning. Experimental results validate the efficiency and effective of the proposed approach.

References

1. Fabrizio Sebastiani. Machine learning in automated text categorization. *ACM Computing Surveys*, 34(1): 1-47, 2002
2. Y. Yang and X. Liu. A re-examination of text categorization. Proceedings of the 22nd Annual International ACM SIGIR Conference on Research and Development in Information Retrieval (SIGIR'99), 1999.
3. B. Masand, G. Linoff, and D. Waltz. Classifying news stories using memory-based reasoning. Proceedings of the 15th Annual International ACM SIGIR Conference on Research and Development in Information Retrieval (SIGIR'92), 1992, 59-65.
4. Y. Yang. Expert network: effective and efficient learning from human decisions in text categorization and retrieval. Proceedings of the 17th Annual International ACM SIGIR Conference on Research and Development in Information Retrieval (SIGIR'94), 1994, 13-22.
5. W. Lam and C. Y. Ho. Using a generalized instance set for automatic text categorization. Proceedings of the 21st Annual International ACM SIGIR Conference on Research and Development in Information Retrieval (SIGIR'98), 1998, 81-89.
6. S. Zhou, J. Guan. Chinese documents classification based on N-grams. A. Gelbukh (Ed.): Intelligent Text Processing and Computational Linguistics, LNCS, Vol. 2276, Spring-Verlag, 2002, 405-414.
7. S. Zhou. Key Techniques of Chinese Text Database. PhD thesis of Fudan University, China. 2000.
8. D. D. Lewis, R. E. Schapore, J. P. Callan, and R. Papka. Training algorithms for linear text classifiers. Proceedings of the 19th Annual International ACM SIGIR Conference on Research and Development in Information Retrieval (SIGIR'96), 1996, 298-306.
9. E. H. Han and G. Karypis. Centroid-based document classification algorithm: analysis & experimental results. Technical Report TR-00-017, Dept. of CS, Uni. of Minnesota, Minneapolis, 2000. http://www.cs.umn.edu/~karypis
10. G. Salton, A. Wong, and C. S. Yang. A vector space model got automatic indexing. K. S. Jones and P. Willett (Eds.), Readings in Information Retrieval. Morgan Kaufmann, 1997. 273-280.
11. Yang, Y., Pedersen J.P. A Comparative Study on Feature Selection in Text Categorization Proceedings of the Fourteenth International Conference on Machine Learning (ICML'97), 1997.
12. C. Apte, F. Damerau, and S. Weiss. Text mining with decision rules and decision trees. Proceedings of the Conference on Automated Learning and Discovery, Workshop 6: Learning from Text and the Web, 1998.

Towards Retrieval of Visual Information Based on the Semantic Models

Youngchoon Park, Pankoo Kim[1], Wonpil Kim, Jeongjun Song, and Sethuraman Panchanathan

Department of Computer Science and Engineering
Arizona State University,
Tempe, AZ 85287-5406, USA
{ycpark, sonjj, panch}@asu.edu

[1]Department of Computer Engineering
College of Electronics and Information
Chosun University, Kwangju Korea
{pkkim, kwpil}@mina.chosun.ac.kr

Abstract

Most users want to find visual information based on the semantics of visual contents such as a name of person and an action happening in a scene. However, techniques for content-based image or video retrieval are not mature enough to recognize visual semantic completely. This paper concerns the problem of automated visual content classification that allows semantic exploration of the visual information. To enable semantic based image or visual object retrieval, we propose a new image representation scheme called visual context descriptor (VCD) that is a multidimensional vector in which each element represents the frequency of a unique visual property of an image or a region. VCD utilizes the predetermined quality dimensions (i.e., types of features and quantization levels) and semantic model templates mined in priori. Techniques for creating symbolic representation (called visual term) of visual content and semantic model profile mining and matching have also been explored. The proposed model classification technique utilizes contextual relevance of a visual term to a target semantic class in visual object discrimination. Contextual relevance of a visual cue to a semantic class is determined by using correlation analysis of ground truth samples.

1. Introduction

Regardless of media type, users tend to find media objects based on their perceptual understanding of the media content [1][7]. Such perceptual understanding can be a semantic recognition of a localized visual object in an image, an emotional perception of a certain sound clip, an abstracted summary of a news video clip or a particular semantic event captured from a movie clip. These facts have been explored in our

[1] Corresponding author: This work was partially supported by the University Research Program grant from the Korean Ministry of Information and Communication.

R. Cicchetti et al. (Eds.): DEXA 2002, LNCS 2453, pp. 841–850, 2002.

human factors study in visual information retrieval. To enable conceptual level querying, the semantics of media content should be captured and represented in computable form. However, current content-based media retrieval techniques are not mature enough to answer semantic related queries [6][10]. This is due to the difficulties in extraction of semantic information from low-level media data.

Recently, few attempts have been made for classifying, and retrieving images on the basis of their semantic content. They mainly concern (i) visual feature transformation [5][8] and (ii) learning semantics from images [1][12]. Semantic object detection and recognition within a specific domain have long history in computer vision, however general purpose object detection for image retrieval (semantic classification/detection of the content into a number of classes) has not been fully explored. They mainly deal with a very limited number of classes (mainly two) and relatively simple domains [10][12]. Learning-based region labeling approach [1] highly depends on the meaningful image segmentation that is known to be an ill-posed problem [6]. Simple color filer based image categorization [13] shows marginal results. However, most current approaches mainly concern context-free visual data classification.

Based on the observations we have made on the many images (several thousands from various semantic categories), we may say there are certain occurrence relations among various feature primitives. For instance, certain colors are frequently observed from a single image/or a semantic object. A tiger can be detected by investigating the co-occurrence of orange, gray, white, and black. Similarly, appearance of a zebra or a penguin can be checked by the co-occurrence of white and black. Of course, these simple rules may results a number of false alarms in detection. However, they will reduce the size of search space significantly, and further refinements can be applied. In fact, contextual information can be added into an original image representation for improving the classification performance. Contextual information of a semantic visual model or a visual template can be obtained from many labeled image samples or bounded regions.

Underlying idea of classifying and retrieving the semantic visual content in this paper is based on the question, "Are there any hidden or observable co-occurrence relations of primitive visual cues among visual objects within a semantic class?". If so, how they can be captured, represented and used in indexing and retrieval. In the following sections, we will describe the proposed answers for the question.

2. Visual Term: Symbolic Representation of Atomic Element of the Visual Content

A visual term (or we will call visual cue) is a codeword of a quantized feature vector. In other words, a visual term is a symbolic representation of real valued multidimensional visual feature vector. It can be any types of visual features (e.g., a region color descriptor or a global geometric feature descriptor). Two homogeneous visual cues are considered as similar (called visual synonym) in feature vector space, when the similarity distance between them is less than a predefined threshold (e.g., $d(a, b) < threshold$ where d is a zero distance). Particular visual terms can take on an almost indefinite number of subtle meaning variations. In other word, a visual cue may be observed from many different visual contexts. This problem is also appeared in text domain. Scene disambiguation can be accomplished by employing contextual synonyms that two homogeneous or heterogeneous visual cues are considered as semantically related (or similar) terms, when they are highly correlated. (correlation(a, b) > threshold)

Target images are rendered with a subset of a universal visual term collection. The universal visual term collection can be seen as a dictionary of words in natural language and can be managed based on the visual term relations (e.g., visual synonyms, contextual synonyms, etc.,).

Visual term-based content representation requires a large collection of visual cues (i.e., universal codebook of heterogeneous visual cues) obtained from a number of regions, or whole images. From the image decoding point of view, a visual cue collection serves a universal codebook. Because of the size of codebook, highly efficient access method is desired. In fact, we use tree structured vector quantizer [3] that allows fast (i.e., O(logN)) access and reliable searching.

DCT based image feature (total of 18 coefficients, 6 coefficients per each color channel of an image block), edge-histogram, homogeneous texture descriptor, and a geometric property of an image (modeled by a line histogram)) are used in visual term generation (see [5] for more details). First three descriptors are used in region representation and a line histogram is used in global property description.

To select semantically relevant visual terms, we propose to use two techniques called "good-feature to track" [9], and "the rule of thirds". The first technique mimics the edge effect in human vision and the second captures the photocomposition heuristics. Iterative k means clustering algorithm with a large k (e.g., k = 4096 for DCT feature) has been employed to reduce the number of visual terms. A representative feature vector of a cluster is used as an input to tree structured vector quantizer (TSVQ) for translating a real valued feature vector into a symbolic (discrete) event model.

3. Learning Visual Concept: Semantic Model Learning

Visual concept is a profile of a visual object. A profile is a multidimensional vector, where each element represents a visual term to semantic object relevance measured by its normalized frequency within/across models. Profile creation is a model learning that is defined as a frequency (or probability) distribution function estimation of a visual object.

3.1 Model Representation with Visual Terms

Given a set of global features and local features, we can obtain a set of visual terms by using TSVQs. Then the content of an image is represented as a set of visual terms allowing multiple occurrences within an image or an image object. A training sample is provided as a form of $\boldsymbol{\tau} = \langle s_k, \mathbf{X}_i \rangle$, where s_k is the k-th semantic label, and

$\mathbf{X}_i = \langle x_{i1}, x_{i2}, \ldots, x_{iM} \rangle$ is a feature representation of a visual object. One of the simple forms of $\mathbf{X}_i$ is a binary representation (value of x_{ij} will be either 1 for observed or 0 for unobserved) in the i-th sample. Another representation is to use visual term frequencies. In this case $\mathbf{X}_i$ is a visual term histogram (x_{ij} is a frequency of visual term, x_j). For each semantic class, we use the following visual term-to-semantic class representation.

$$\mathbf{F}_{raw}^{S_k} = \begin{bmatrix} f_{raw}(x_0, o_0^{S_k}) & \cdots & f_{raw}(x_0, o_n^{S_k}) \\ \vdots & \ddots & \vdots \\ f_{raw}(x_M, o_0^{S_k}) & \cdots & f_{raw}(x_M, o_n^{S_k}) \end{bmatrix}$$

where, $o_j^{S_k}$ represents the j-th training sample of the k-th semantic class. The above representation is similar to term-to-document representation in latent semantic indexing. If we have a sufficiently large number of samples, then raw frequencies of visual terms can be easily translated into a relative frequency and can be used as model probability density function, and can be directly used in model matching. However, in practices, (i) incompleteness of samples, (ii) feature vector encoding errors, and (iii) non-uniformity of samples prevent the correct modeling of a visual concept of a semantic model. Therefore, reliable estimation of term frequencies is an important and necessary to produce quality semantic classification. For example, a blue region may have high frequency, while slightly dark blue sky may not be observed or have a single occurrence from landscape samples. In this situation, a semantic label prediction will not be considered the dark blue region as a sky in frequency based label prediction. In other word, rare events have to be estimated correctly. For this reason, we propose to use similarity-based visual term frequency estimation and contextual refinement.

3.2 Model Smoothing: Similarity-Based Unseen Term Frequency Estimation

The main idea is that, if two visual cues are similar enough in terms of visual similarity (one of them is not observed from samples), then unobserved visual term will receive credits based on the visual similarity. Given an unobserved visual term, x_i during the training phase of a semantic class, s_k its frequency is estimated by using the following equations.

$$f_{estimated}(x_i, s_k) = \alpha(n) \sum_j \kappa(d(x_i, x_j)) \times f_{raw}(x_j, s_k), \text{for all } x_j \in \Gamma(x_i)$$

$$\text{where, } f_{raw}(x_i, s_k) = \frac{1}{N} \sum_{l=0}^{N} f_{raw}(x_i, o_l^{S_k})$$

where, $f_{raw}(x_j, s_k)$ is a raw frequency of visual term *j* in a semantic class *k*, $\alpha(n)$ = 1/n, is a normalization function defined by the number of visual cues that are similar within a semantic class s_k, and κ is a weighting kernel function that determines the contribution factor of an observed visual cue in prediction based on the similarity distance. N is the total number of visual terms observed from training samples, $o_l^{s_k}$ in the k-th semantic class. A function, $\Gamma(x_i)$ returns a set of visual synonyms of x_i and it is called a synonym return function. A synonym set contains visual synonyms. Synonyms are computed in priori and maintained in an inverted list for fast searching.

The maximum value of the weighting function should be at zero distance, and the function should decay smoothly as the distance increases. A number of weighting kernels (e.g., $\kappa = 1 - d$, κ =exp(-*d***d*), κ =exp(|-*d*|), κ =1/(*d*+1) etc.) are available, however, there is no clear evidence that the choice of weighting kernel is critical in frequency estimation and model classification. $d(x_i,x_j)$ is a visual similarity distance between two visual terms, and it is in the interval [0,1].

The above frequency update model is based on the error-free encoding scenario. However, a codeword is lossy representation (i.e., representative vector of a cluster in TSVQ) of an observed visual vector because of encoding error. For this reason, additional error-based penalty model has to be included.

Let $\varepsilon = d(x_j^{src}, x_j^{TSVQ})$ be a distance function (or error) between a visual feature vector observed from the source object, x_j^{src} and, the best-matching visual feature to x_j^{src} in TSQV, x_j^{TSVQ}. Then the frequency with penalty model (ε is in the interval [0,1]) is computed with following equation.

$$f_{est\text{-}with\text{-}error}(x_j,s_k) = \varepsilon(x_j^{src}, x_j^{TSVQ}) \times f_{estimated}(x_j,s_k)$$

With the proposed approach, an unseen visual term frequency can be estimated by using observed visual synonyms. Rare events can be estimated with the proposed method, too. In fact, the proposed model is a weighted linear combination of estimations of visually similar cues by using non-parametric model.

3.3 Model Refinement

So far, we have described the method for creating model profiles. Further refinement is possible for improving the discrimination power by looking at the across model profiles. A visual term with high occurrences across training samples in a semantic object is a relevant cue to distinguish the semantic class from other classes. However, a visual term with high occurrences across semantic objects may not be a relevant in classification. However, if a certain visual term appears so frequently in a particular semantic class, then it will be a dominant cue to detect the semantic object across images. For this reason, we have defined the salient factor that measures the relevance of a visual term to a semantic class.

$$\gamma(x_j,s_k) = \frac{n_k^j}{N_k}$$

where, n_k^j is the number of semantically identical training samples that contains the visual term *j* at least once, and N_k is the total number of samples in the semantic class *k*. With the relevance factor and inverted visual content frequency, the frequency of a visual term i in a semantic class k is defined as follows:

$$f(x_i, s_k) = f_{estimated\text{-}with\text{-}error}(x_i, s_k) \times \frac{\alpha\left(\log_2\left(\frac{K}{n_i}\right)+1\right)+\beta\gamma(x_i, s_k)}{2}$$

where, α and β are weighting constants set to 1 and 1.2 respectively. Those values are obtained from experiments. A frequency of unseen visual term x_i is estimated based on the observed visual synonyms, x_j by considering (i) the encoding errors of visual synonyms, (ii) similarity distance between $\mathbf{x}_i$ and $\mathbf{x}_j$, and (iii) its relevance across semantic classes. In fact, the proposed weighting scheme is similar to TF*IDF [2] in document retrieval except for the last portion of the equation.

In summary, the proposed frequency estimation is a non-parametric probability density function estimation of unseen visual terms during the model learning by considering (i) similarity between an unobserved visual term and the observed similar visual terms, (ii) discrimination power of a visual term within a semantic class and (iii) discrimination power of a visual term across classes. One weak point of the proposed method is that it requires many samples and, however, it allows interactive and progressive approximation of probability density functions.

4. Visual Context Descriptor (VCD): Adding Contextual Information

Certain homogeneous or heterogeneous visual term pairs may be observed frequently within a semantic class. Example pairs are (hairy texture, skin color), (many horizontal/vertical lines and gray color), etc. Consider Fig.1. A visual term c (a hairy texture) is a contextual synonym with face colors in human face model. However, it is not correlated to dark brown horse skin color.

The main idea of visual context descriptor is to add unobserved visual terms that are highly correlated to the current observations. As shown in Fig. 1(b), the hairy texture can be added into the original visual term vector in matching with face template, however, it will not be added in matching with horse model. In the section, we will discuss the computation of contextual similarity and determination of appropriate frequency of a visual term that is not observed from the source, but is highly correlated to one of observed visual terms in a semantic model class.

A semantic similarity, $d^k_{sem}(x_i, x_j)$, between two visual terms in a semantic class *k* is calculated from a correlation matrix **C**, obtained from a visual term to a semantic object (or image) matrix, $\mathbf{A}_{s_k}$. Rows of $\mathbf{A}_{s_k}$ are corresponding to visual terms and columns of $\mathbf{A}_{s_k}$ are corresponding to a visual object samples annotated with the *k*-th semantic label. An element of visual term to semantic object matrix, $\mathbf{A}_{s_k}$ represents the raw frequency of visual term.

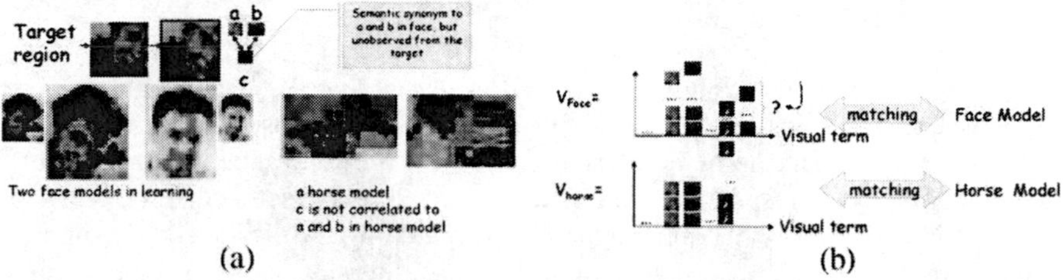

Fig. 1. Adding contextual information into the original visual term vector. (a) co-occurrence based contextual synonym detection within a semantic class, (b) adding unobserved contextual synonyms into the original visual term vector

A correlation matrix is a term-to-term similarity matrix defined in an image space by measuring correlation. All diagonal components of **C** are equal to 1. Two visual terms are considered as contextual synonym when they have a sufficiently large value in **C**. In other words, when two visual terms have high co-occurrences then they are considered as semantically related pair, (in fact, they have contextual association). Semantic similarity of two visual terms, x_i, and x_j in a semantic class k, $d^k_{sem}(x_i,x_j)$ has been developed for satisfying the following criteria:

$$d^k_{sem}(x_i,x_j)=0, \text{ iff } i=j, \text{ (i.e., } d^k_{sem}(x_i,x_j)=1-c_{ij}), \; d^k_{sem}(x_i,x_j)\neq 0, \text{ iff } (i\neq j)\wedge x_i\notin\Gamma(x_j)\wedge x_j\notin\Gamma(x_i)$$

A general form of distance dunction is as follows:

$$d^k_{sem}(x_i,x_j)=\delta(cor(x_i,x_j))$$

where, δ is a distance weighting kernel. We use $d^k_{sem}(x_i,x_j)=\exp(-(1-cor(x_i,x_j))*(1-cor(x_i,x_j)))$ as our semantic similarity distance function. A simple distance based semantic classification of an image object is based on the Euclidian distance.

Let $\mathbf{X}=\langle f(x_1),f(x_2),...,f(x_n)\rangle$ be an image object vector, a visual term frequency histogram. By considering the term to semantic class relevance and visual similarity-based frequency updating, we have *K* different versions of the image object vector, since each semantic model has its own term-to-relevance factor that is used for refining the original frequency vector. Let x_i be a visual term that is not observed from the source. If a visual term x_j is highly correlated to x_i in a semantic class k then a visual term frequency of x_i, $f(x_i,s_k)$ with correlation data, is defined as follows:

$$f_u(x_i,s_k)=\frac{total\_freq\_of(x_i,x_j,s_k)}{number\_of\_img\_obj(x_i,x_j,s_k)}\times d^k_{sem}(x_i,x_j)$$

The above equation estimates the frequency of an unseen visual term based on the contextual similarity and the average frequency of co-occurrences of contextual synonyms in training samples.

4.1. Model Matching and Classification

The proposed VCD will introduce unseen visual terms that are contextual synonyms of observed visual terms into the original image vector (at lease proportionally) and adaptively refines visual term frequencies based on the relevance factors. For each semantic class, a corresponding modified image object vector that conveys the contextual information is obtained and used in matching. A distance between a j-th modified vector, $\mathbf{x}_j = \langle f(x_1,s_j), f(x_2,s_j), \ldots, f(x_n,s_j) \rangle$ of the original image object vector, **X**, and a semantic model profile $\mathbf{y}_j = \langle f(y_1,s_j), f(y_2,s_j), \ldots, f(y_n,s_j) \rangle$ is defined as follows:

$$d_k(\mathbf{x}_k, \mathbf{y}_k) = \sqrt{(\mathbf{x}_k - \mathbf{y}_j)^T (\mathbf{x}_k - \mathbf{y}_k)}, k = 0, \ldots, K$$

A classification result will be obtained based on the following criterion:

$$\arg\min_k \{d_k(\mathbf{x}_k, \mathbf{y}_k)\}$$

The above classification takes best of the best as a classification result.

Then, model classification is a problem of finding the best semantic label. In this research, we are trying to achieve better classification results by modifying the original image vectors (or image object vectors). The result of visual term frequency or occurrence emphasis semantically relevant visual terms and introduces unobserved visual terms (semantically related) to the original image vector for overriding semantic context.

5. Experiments

We have built a retrieval prototype system that is accessible on the web (http://www.mpeg7tv.com). The current system contains more then 62,000 Corel image collection, and 25,000 images gathered from various sources (total of 87,221 images).

The size of codebook (the number of visual terms) created for this experiment is 5,440 (4096 DCT feature vectors, 1024 texture vectors, and 256 line histogram vectors and 64 local edge histogram vectors). Only image scaling is applied as a preprocessing. During the scaling, images are re-sized with pixel number constraints so that the total number of pixels is approximately equal to 102,400. More then 8,000 images (approximately 10% of the entire database content, also we use few artificially synthesized images) are considered in codebook design.

Four human subjects are involved in semantic object labeling, classification, outlining of bounding regions, and evaluations. The size of image patch is determined based on the patch size vs. region classification test on 100 image patches. Automated recognition test shows its best performance when the size of image region is 16x16 and ceases its classification performance when the size is larger then 16x16, while human performs more accurate classification. Based on this test, we set image patch size to 16x16. For the purpose of retrieval effectiveness evaluations, semantic-integrated image retrieval technique, denoted by M-1 [13] has been considered. For fair comparison, we use the same dataset that was used in M-1.

5.1 Corel Image Categorization Test

In this test, automated image categorization performance is evaluated. Similar test has also been conducted in [13] on 10 semantic classes on 1000 images (100 images per category). In fact, M-1 does not perform pre-classification of images. It actually performs the classification in query time based on region-to-region matching. As shown in Fig. 2., the proposed approach outperforms in semantic image classification (excluding card and dinosaurs class). Some classes show good classification results (such as building, flowers, and horses), while categories of Africa and buses show relatively poor classification result, because of visual content diversity in training data (lacking of coherences across images). For example, images containing people in the category of Africa are classified well since we are able to detect a coherence of visual terms across images, while many images containing animals are poorly classified because of the content diversity. In this situation, visual template does not have enough visual term frequency information to model rare occurrences of a certain semantic object. We have found that most terms representing part of animals in the category of Africa are filled with one or two frequencies. This indicates that training samples should be selected carefully, and we need a large enough number of semantic object samples that are visually coherent.

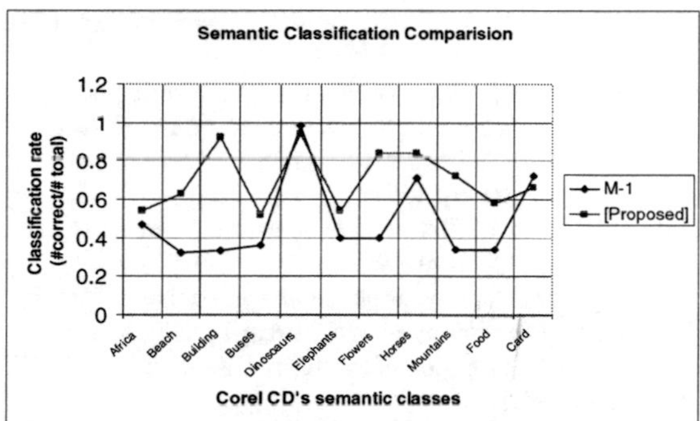

Fig. 2. Automated image categorization of Corel-data

There are certain semantic classes such as card and dinosaurs, where M-1 outperforms due to the fact that M-1's feature description has more accurate representation of spatial properties of images, while our current model does not take an account of spatial arrangement of image blocks. However, a distance based region co-occurrence model that is currently being developed may represent spatial constraints of the image contents. In summary, classification of 1,100 images into 11 semantic classes, we achieved average precision of 0.721 from the proposed method. Classification examples are available from http://www.mpeg7tv.com.

6. Conclusion

In this paper, we propose a novel visual content description scheme called visual context feature that is built from atomic visual content element called visual term. A visual term is a symbolic representation of multidimensional visual feature vector and its syntactic and semantic relations have been embedded into textual ontology. Visual term based image representation is similar to traditional document representation in information retrieval. Any visual features can be transformed into visual terms and can be easily integrated into a unified representation for future use. The proposed approach also supports various information retrieval techniques (e.g., logical imaging, latent semantic indexing, or vector space model) developed in text domain. Visual context descriptor mimics the human visual perception that faculties the contextual information in object recognition. A robust image classification without performing explicit segmentation is proposed and its effectiveness has been demonstrated. During the experiments, we do not consider spatial relation in representation. However, it can be easily integrated. Examples of such information are distance based visual term pair or angle based visual term pair.

Reference

1. K. Barnard and D.A. Forsyth, "Learning the semantics of words and pictures", Int. Conf. Computer Vision, 2001.
2. S. T. Dumais, "Improving the retrieval of information from external sources." Behavior Research Methods, Instruments and Computers, Vol. 23, No.2 , pp. 229-236, 1991.
3. Gersho, and R. M. Gray, *Vector Quantization and Signal Compression*, Kluwer International, 1992.
4. M. Gorkani and R. W. Picard, "Texture orientation for sorting photos at a glance", In Proc. Int. Conf. Pat. Rec., volume I, pages 459-464, Jerusalem, Israel, Oct. 1994.
5. ISO/IEC JTC1/SC29/WG11/M6808N3914, MPEG-7 Visual part of eXperimentation Model Version 8.19.0, Pisa, January 2001.
6. T. P. Minka and R. W. Picard, "Interactive learning using a society of models," MIT Media lab, Technical Report, No. 349, 1995.
7. Mojsilovic, and B. Rogowitz, "A Psychophysical approach to modeling image semantics", Proc. 2001 SPIE Human Vision and Electronic Imaging, San Jose, January 2001.
8. W. Picard and T. P. Minka, "Vision Texture for Annotation", MIT Media laboratory Technical Report No. 302, 1997
9. J. Shi, and C. Tomasi, "Good-feature to track", TR 93-1399, Cornell University, 1993.
10. Szummer and Rosalind Picard, "Indoor-Out door Image Classification", MIT Media Lab TR# 455, 199
11. Theodoridis, and K. Koutroumbas, *Pattern Recognition*, AP Professional, 1999.
12. Vailaya, M. Figueiredo, A. Jain, and H.J. Zhang, "Content-Based Hierarchical Classification of Vacation Images," in proceedings of IEEE Multimedia Computing and Systems, vol. 1:518-523, Florence, Italy, June 1999.
13. James Z. Wang, *Integrated Region-Based Image Retrieval,* Kluwer Academic Publishers, Dordrecht, 2001.

3D Object Retrieval by Shape Similarity

Jeong-Jun Song and Forouzan Golshani

Department of Computer Science and Engineering,
Arizona State University,
Tempe, AZ, 85287-5406
{jjsong, golshani}@asu.edu
http://media.eas.asu.edu

Abstract. We introduce a method for shape similarity based retrieval in 3D object model database. The proposed method leads us to achieve effectiveness and robustness in similar 3D object search supporting both query by 3D model and query by 2D image. Our feature extraction mechanism is based on observation of human behavior in recognizing objects. Our process of extracting spatial arrangement of a 3D object by surface point distribution can be considered as using human tactile sensation without visual information. On the other hand, the process of extracting 2D features from multiple views can be considered as examining an object by moving viewpoints(camera positions). We propose shape signatures for 3D object model by measuring features of surface point and the shape distance distribution from multiple views of 3D model. Our method can be directly applied to industrial part retrieval and inspection system where different geometric representations are used.

1 Introduction

One of the most important points in designing interactive 3D multimedia systems is how to handle 3D data in an efficient manner. A number of research groups in the field of computer graphics and computer vision have attempted to find efficient ways of representing 3D objects, specifically, to identify each object based on its geometric properties. There are two main three-dimensional object representation schemes. One is called "object-centered representation", and the other is "viewer-centered representation scheme". Object-centered representation often uses explicit three-dimensional descriptions of objects of interest in Euclidian space like solid geometry and surface-based representation. On the other hand, viewer-centered representation usually relies on a collection of range or intensity images of an object as the implicit description of its shape. Since features extracted from a 2D image do not immediately correspond to the object models, 3D to 2D or 2D to 3D transformations must be made before observed features can be matched with the 3D object model. The multi-view models can be quickly searched for matching features but require large amount of storage to keep numerous 2D images from multiple viewpoints. How to derive the appearance of an object from a novel viewpoint without keeping too many views is the main difficulty. Since we are interested in the design of a multimedia retrieval

R. Cicchetti et al. (Eds.): DEXA 2002, LNCS 2453, pp. 851–860, 2002.

system that provides various query methods for efficiency and robustness, the speed of retrieving object model in the database might be more important issue than storage issue. We follow the 3D object-centered representation scheme as a main object representation but also utilize 2D views from each sampled viewpoint to extract additional useful features that may enhance shape identification. Once features from projection images have been extracted, it is not necessary to keep them for later use. To obtain boundary information from 2D views of 3D object we adapt one of the 2D shape descriptors, Fourier Descriptor (FD), that have been used in many image-processing applications. Moment invariance and Curvature Scale Space are also well known shape descriptors currently available. Our object-centered feature extraction method, called histogram representation of distance distribution, is a kind of spherical depth map with a surface approximation.

This procedure involves sampling surface points from the object and measuring the depth between surface intersection points and their corresponding points on the unit sphere. For the object composed of many triangles with small variation of triangle size and shape, it may not be necessary to resample the surface points. We restrict our experiment of resampling to objects having small number of triangles and large variation in triangle size. Histogram representation of this spherical depth map can be a characteristic of spatial arrangement of the object of interest in 3D co-ordination system. Next, we explore shape distance distribution based on observation of Human Visual System (HVS) mechanism. HVS is well studied in cognition and psychophysical sciences. Examples include Ullman's High-level Vision [1] and Schiffman's Sensation and Perception [2]. From selected viewpoints, we extract shape features and compute Euclidian distance from them. These shape signatures are compared to one another during query processing to find similar object in the 3D object model database. The importance of this approach becomes obvious when we reflect on HVS. Consider how humans normally study three-dimensional object. We study the object by rotating the object and examining different views of the object. That is, we gather characteristic information while changing the viewpoints and infer the object appearance without explicitly constructing 3D alignment.

The organization of this paper is as follows. First, we will discuss background and related work on shape representation and matching in section 2. Next in section 3, we will introduce shape feature extraction methods based on object-centered methods and multiple views. Section 4 presents experimental result. In section 5 we discuss conclusions.

2 Related Work

There has been a great deal of study for shape descriptors in 2D images, ranging from simple geometric attributes to various transformation techniques. These techniques can be categorized as reconstructive and non-reconstructive techniques, depending on whether or not they allow the original shape of the object to be approximated. A good categorization of 2D shape description technique can be found in [3][4]. The choice of specific description techniques depends totally on the nature of applications. Shape similarity has also been studied for 3D geometric model of the objects in computer vision and other object recognition areas. In most cases, they utilize range data to compare 3D local surface information with existing 3D object model stored in the database. The most widely used 3D object model description in computer graphics is based on geometrical information such as vertex points, surface point cloud, edge lists, facets and normal vector information. 3D modelling software such as CAD applications utilizes a solid modelling concept along with surface description. To be useful in large databases especially content-based retrieval system, feature extraction techniques should be simple, inexpensive and robust. Surface points distribution has some simple and efficient characteristics. Since Gauss introduced a representation method that maps normal vectors of surface patch to the sphere [5], related representation method have been developed as extensions of this mapping scheme. Extended Gaussian Image (EGI) [6] maps mass to the corresponding point on the Gaussian sphere. This mass distribution depends on the shape of the object. Distributed EGI (DEGI) [7] has been derived to avoid the problem for non-convex object of EGI. This method tessellates viewing sphere and recalculates a partial EGI for each viewing direction to determine the attitude of a non-convex object.

The EGI uniquely defines a convex polyhedron. However, non-convex object that has more than two separated region with the same surface normal may have the same representation with any convex object. A direct way of expanding 2D descriptor to 3D is to consider the 3D shape as composition of infinite 2D slice stack along a given direction. This is a common technique in medical applications. The other straightforward approach is to describe 3D object with multiple projection images. Aircraft detection is one of the applications utilizing this approach. Other 2D and 3D shape descriptors that are currently used in different applications will be discussed in the next section. Distributed EGI, a partial EGI for each viewing direction is considered to avoid this drawback. The hidden area, which is occluded, does not contribute EGI mass on Gaussian sphere.

Complex EGI (CEGI) [8] is introduced which measures the distance from the arbitrary origin to each surface patch to discriminate non-convex object having the same EGI representation. The weight at each point is complex number, Ae^{jd} whose magnitude is the surface area and whose phase is the distance over the Gaussian sphere. The complex weight associate with a surface patch is, where A is the area of a patch with surface normal, the normal distance d to a fixed origin. Since Complex EGI has no surface location information more than two parts on an object may be mapped on the same point of the sphere with the same weight.

Spherical Attribute Image (SAI) [9] provides a method to make one to one mapping between a non-convex object surface and a spherical surface. Most of 3D models are represented by unstructured triangular patches called free-form surface. SAI method deforms tessellated sphere called geodesic dome to original object surface as close as possible before extracting Gaussian curvature from it. This is a process that provides structured mesh without surface segmentation. The distribution based on the simplex angle is referred to as the Spherical Attribute Image.

3 Shape Features

Our approach mimics the behavior of human object recognition by providing features from 2D visual information and 3D spatial arrangement of objects. Humans use tactile and visual sensations to recognize an object of interest. Using three-dimensional spatial arrangement from distribution of surface points can be considered as touching object by hands to recognize its global shape whereas using visual information such as 2D contour information from different viewpoints can be considered as exploring object by rotating object to recognize its appearance. The following figure in Fig. 1 shows overview of our proposed retrieval process based on spatial features. The concept of aligning a 3D model with its principal axes may play an important role in 3D object feature analysis. Since the bounding box of the 3D object may vary by its initial object pose, the object alignment by its principal axes eliminate rotation normalization process in 3D object feature analysis. The fundamental problem to obtain principal axes of the 3D object lies on its computational complexity. To improve this problem, some methods have been proposed such as 1) Principle Component Analysis(PCA) with vertex weight [10], 2) PCA with weight proportional to triangle area [11]. Another problem is that the different size of triangles consisting of the object surface may cause widely varying normalized coordinate frame for

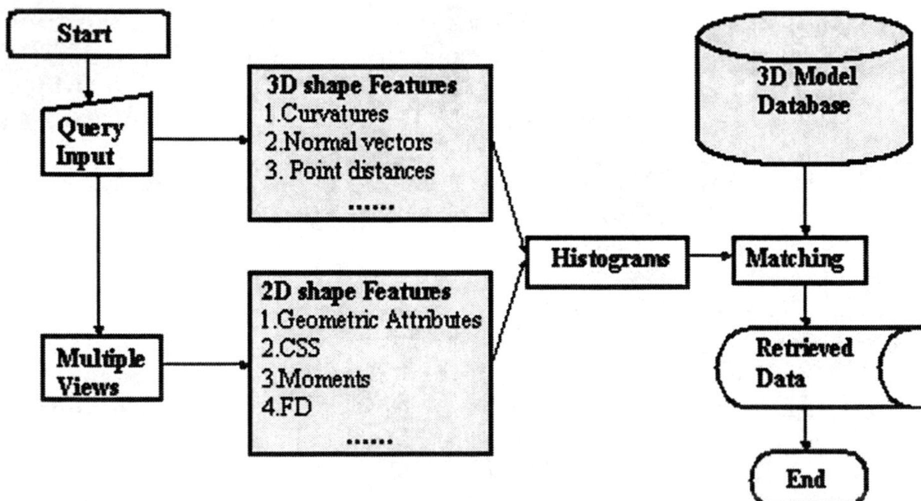

Fig. 1. Overview of proposed retrieval process. CSS: Curvature Scale Space, FD: Fourier Descriptor

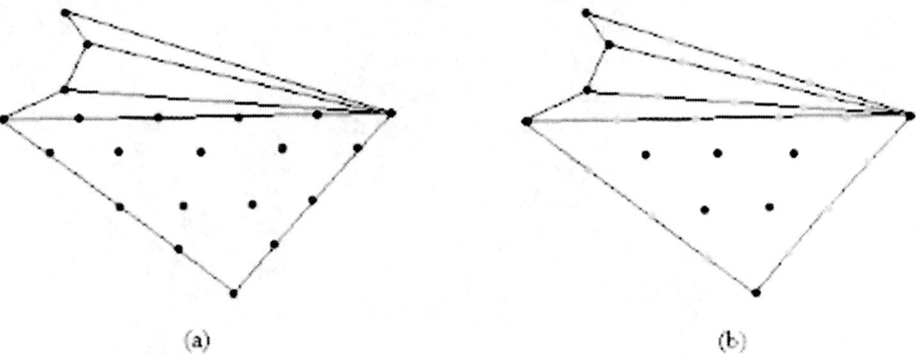

Fig. 2. (a) Problem of unbiased point distribution caused by various shape of triangle, (b) Biased point distribution after adding points

models that are identical. A typical method to generate unbiased random points with respect to the surface area of a polygon model is to subdivide triangles and obtain inner points. However, the various shape of triangle cause the biased point distribution. Our method improves it by adding points on triangle edges as well as faces as shown in Fig. 2. We first obtain inner points by applying recursive subdivision algorithm and add points on triangle edges recursively.

3.1 Depth Distribution

In order to make consistent environment for feature extraction we first generate unit sphere, where radius equals 1 (r = 1) and locate each object model in the center of the unit sphere. To make every object fit into unit sphere we need to find center of each object model and normalize it for size. The sampling points on a unit sphere can simply be obtain by subdividing polyhedron such as octagon, dodecahedron and icosahedrons. Once we determine the number of sampling points and find coordinates of each sampling point on the surface of the unit sphere, we shoot imaginary ray from each sampling point to the center of unit sphere. The length of each ray equals to 1, the radius of sphere. Since we locate 3D object model at the center of unit sphere, each ray is certain to intersect with the object. We compute intersection points and calculate distance between the starting point of the ray and the intersection point on the object surface. We use the heart of ray tracing technique to determine the intersection point of a ray with an object. To accomplish this task we use the parametric representation of a vector. Each point along the ray from A(x1, y1, z1) to B(x2, y2, z2) is defined by some value t such that

$$\left\{ \begin{array}{l} x = x_1 + (x_2 - x_1)t = x_1 + it \\ y = y_1 + (y_2 - y_1)t = y_1 + jt \\ z = z_1 + (z_2 - z_1)t = z_1 + kt \end{array} \right\} \tag{1}$$

Since we are using triangle mesh format for object models, we need to consider ray/plane intersection. A plane is a geometric entity that divides the space through which it passes in two. A plane, unlike a sphere, continues on infinitely; that is, it is unbounded. We begin with the equation of a plane, which is defined as:

$$A(x_1 + it) + B(y_1 + jt) + C(z_1 + kt) + D = 0 \tag{2}$$

Then the intersection is given by:

$$t = \frac{-(Ax_1 + By_1 + Cz_1 + D)}{(Ai + Bj + Ck)} \tag{3}$$

The point of intersection is calculated by substituting the value of t back into the ray equation. The next step is to determine if the intersection point is inside the polygon (triangle in our case). A number of different methods are available to solve this problem. One such algorithm works by shooting a ray in an arbitrary direction from the intersection point and counting the number of line segments crossed. If the number of crossings is odd, the point is inside the polygon; else it is outside. This is known as Jordan curve theorem. The detail explanation of ray tracing technique and Jordan curve theorem can be found in [12]. Now, we can calculate each distance between ray starting point and intersection point on the object surface and display each distance in a graph. This process corresponds to deformation of sphere to object surface as used in SAI. The advantage of our method is that we can get points from hidden surface. The fast ray-tracing algorithm can reduce computation time. To represent this distance distribution as a histogram we may set bin size to 0.1 for the distance (min 0.0, max 1.0) so that each distance belongs to one out of ten bins.

3.2 Spatial Arrangement Estimation

In this section, the histogram representations of 3D object features we devised for shape discrimination are described. The probability distributions of 3D object using distances of surface point pairs are discussed in [13]. In that paper, the authors utilized simple geometric attributes of surface points such as distance of two random points, angle between three random points, area of triangle between three random points and volume of tetrahedron between four random points and called them shape functions. We propose the way to estimate spatial arrangement of the object shape by utilizing Discrete Curvature and Normal Vectors as well as geometric attributes. The first step is to compute the Discrete Curvature of vertex points of triangle mesh. We use the Discrete Gaussian Curvature k which is defined as following Formula.

$$k = \frac{c}{A} \tag{4}$$

where c is the complete angle and A is barycentric area of triangles containing the corresponding vertex. The complete angle can be define as

$$c = 2\pi \sum_{i=1}^{m} \theta_i \tag{5}$$

and the barycentric area can be obtained from

$$A = \frac{1}{3} \sum_{i=1}^{m} t_i \tag{6}$$

Where m is number of neighborhood triangles containing the corresponding vertex, θ_i is adjacent angles between triangle edges containing the vertex and t_i is area of ith triangle. The curvature value paly an important role in sorting the surface points in an order. Simply, we can measure distances from random pairs of surface points, differences of Discrete Curvature values and angles of normal vectors. Then, we produce three histograms based on the measurements. These histograms are turned out to be three different signatures of the same 3D object. In order to reduce computation time to generate signatures we select some surface points which have high curvature values. Then, the computations for generating signatures can be performed only for those selected surface points. In later case every pairs of selected points can be involved to generate shape signatures.

3.3 Shape Signature from Multiple Views

According to the recent psychophysical finding human perceives three-dimensional object from multiple view of two-dimensional shapes not from construction of 3D alignment. Consider how we study three-dimensional object in our real life. We study an object by rotating it, or changing the viewing angles. Shimon Ullman argued for the theory that view-independent object recognition by human is not based on an internally stored model of the object, but upon the outputs of neurons that respond to various two dimensional views of that object. In this section we propose a shape signature of 3D object models from multiple views for shape discrimination. We compute circularity of each 2D shape from different viewpoints and measure the shape distance between them. The circularity can be obtained from the ratio of boundary and area. A simple geometric shape like circle, rectangle can be used as the basis of various shapes. Then, the distances of simple geometric attributes between the basis and each shape from different viewpoints can be measured. This distance histogram generated from the distance valuses is considered as shape signature of the 3D model. Alternatively we can also measure the 2D shape distances from a pair of randomly selected viewpoints and demonstrate the probability distribution of them for an object signature. Many 2D shape features can be used for our approach. Fourier Descriptor(FD) allows us to compactly describe 2D shape from arbitrary viewpoints. Curvature Scale Space and Moment invariants can be used as the other 2D shape descriptor as well.

4 The Experiments

In this experiment, we first generated 2D binary projection images of Boeing-747 aircraft from different viewing directions as shown in Fig. 3. We utilized basic

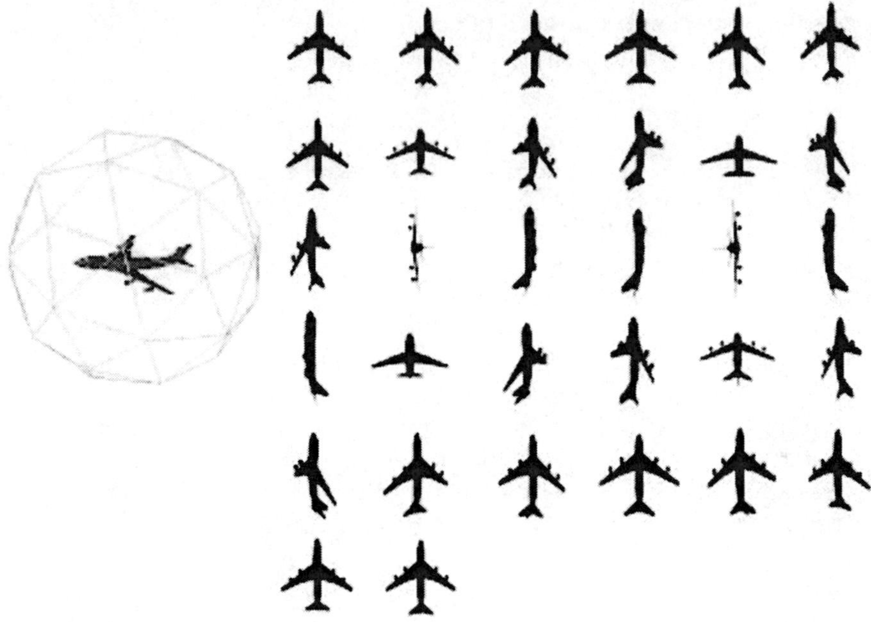

Fig. 3. Boeing 747 aircraft and its viewing sphere on the left and 2D projection binary images from different viewing directions on the left.

geometric attributes. For more reliable feature we will apply Curvature Scale Space and Moment Invariant features in future experiment. If we assume that 3D object have been initially located by principle axis we can directly consider the graph as a signature of the object model. However, since we have eliminated a procedure to find principle axis for the 3D model, the shape distance histogram can be used as the signature instead. Fig. 4(a) shows graph of geometric attribute (circularity) taken from 32 different viewpoints for Boeing 747 aircraft object. After computing circularity from each 2D images we can obtain distance from each pairs of circularity. This produces 1024 shape distances respectively. Then, histogram of shape distances for each geometric attribute will be obtained from them, which has 10 bins as shown in Fig. 4(b). Alternatively, shape distances can be obtained from random pairs of views.

5 Discussion and Conclusion

1D representation of the boundary of 2D shape has been developed in the context of image analysis for several decades. Our object-centered feature extraction approach can be conceptually extended from 2D shape feature extraction such as function of tangent angle and arc length, distance between shape centroid and boundary points, complex function using arc length parameter value. The dominant characteristic of our approach compared with others [14][15][16][17]

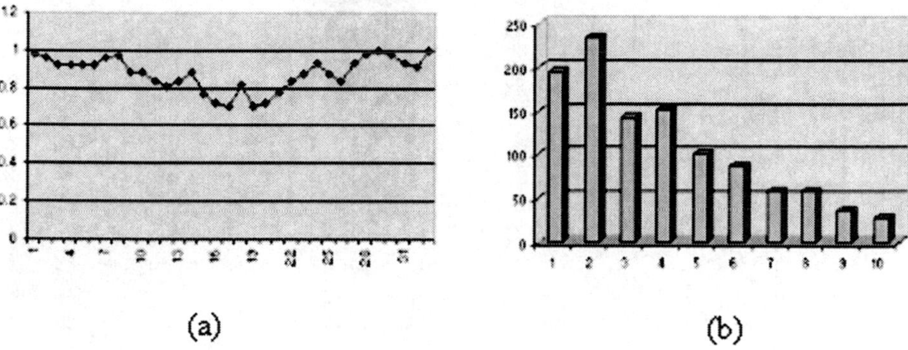

Fig. 4. (a)Graphs of circularity for Boeing 747 model x-axis: 32 different views y-axis: circularity. (b)Histogram of shape distance by circularity.

can be found in providing both object-centered and viewer-centered features by observation of human behavior for the object recognition. Especially, our view-centered approach mimics HVS to characterize 3D object by drawing several representative 2D view as appearance of a 3D object. Most view-based approach restrict its views to one viewing plane, namely, those generated be "walking around" the object without considering object pose which differ from the initial scanning. They usually assume that the object poses in stable condition, which is very ambiguous for object orientation. The main drawback is that it does not provide correspondences for arbitrary views of the object. In this paper we have proposed shape descriptors for general 3D object models based on object-centered and view-centered representation scheme respectively. We introduced 1D representation of the 3D shape using features of surface points. As another approach based on observation of HVS we explained a way to measure 2D shape distance from a pair of viewpoints and how to construct a histogram. These shape description method can be incorporated with the 3D shape distance measure that has geometrical differences in 3D model database. To be able to provide 2D image query interface our system need to develop efficient grouping algorithm based on 2D view similarity to reduce number of views of an object and clustering algorithm to hand large model database.

References

1. Shimon Ullman: High-level Vision, Object Recognition and Visual Cognition. The MIT Press(1996)
2. Harvey R. Schiffman: Sensation and Perception, An Integrated Approach. John wiley and sons, Inc.(1995)
3. Babu M. Mehtre, Mohan S. Kankanhalli, Wing F. Lee: Shape Measures for content based image retrieval: A comparision. Information processing and Management, Vol. 33, No.3 (1997) 319-337
4. Sven Loncaric: A survey of shape analysis Techniques. Pattern Recognition, Vol.31, No.8(1998) 983-1001

5. Gauss, K.F.: General Investigations of Curved Surfaces. Raven Press, New York(1965)
6. Horn, B.K.P.: Extended Gaussian Image. Proc. of IEEE, Vol. 72, No.12 December(1984)1671-1686
7. Ikeuchi, K. and Horn, B.K.P.: Picking up an Object from a Pile of Objects. in Robotics Research, The First International Symposium, J. M. Brady and R. Paul, The MIT Press, Cambridge, Massachusetts(1984) 139-162
8. Kang, S.B. and Ikeuchi, K.:The Complex EGI: New Representation for 3-D Pose Determination, IEEE Trans Pattern Analysis and Machine Intelligence, Vol. 15, No.7, July (1993) 707-721
9. Dellingette, H., Hebert, M., and Ikeuchi, K., " A Spherical Representation for the Recognition of Curved Objects," Proc. Intern. Conf on Computer Vision, May (1993) 103-112
10. D.V. Vranic and D. Saupe: Tools for 3D-object retrieval: Karhunen-Loeve Transform and spherical harmonics. submitted to IEEE Workshop on Multimedia Signal Processing, Cannes, France, Oct.(2001)
11. Paquet, E., Rioux, M.: A content-based search engine for VRML databases. Computer vision and Pattern Recognition Proceedings. IEEE Computer society conference(1998) 541-546
12. Andrew S. Glassner: An Introduction to Ray Tracing. ACADEMIC PRESS (1989)
13. R Osada, T Funkhouser, B Chazelle, and D Dobkin, "Matching 3D Models with Shape Distributions" ShapeModeling International , Genova, Italy, May, (2001)
14. C.C. Chang, S.M. Hwang and D.J. Buehrer: A shape recognition scheme based on relative distances of feature points from the centroid. Pattern Recognition 24(1991) 1053-1063
15. C. Zhang and T. Chen: Indexing and Retrieval of 3D models Aided by Active Learning. Demo on ACM Multimedia, Ottawa, Ontario, Canada, Oct.(2001) 1-5
16. C. M. Cyr, A. F. Kamal, T. B. Sebastian, and B. B. Kimia:2D-3D Registration based on Shape Matching. Proceedings of the IEEE Workshop on Mathematical Methods in Biomedical Image Analysis(2000) 198-203
17. C. M. Cyr and B. B. Kimia: 3d object recognition using shape similarity-based aspect graph. In ICCV, pages Accepted – To appear, (2001)

Binary-Tree Histograms with Tree Indices

Francesco Buccafurri[1], Filippo Furfaro[2], Gianluca Lax[1], and Domenico Saccà[3]

[1] DIMET, University of Reggio Calabria, 89100 Reggio Calabria, Italy,
bucca,lax@ing.unirc.it
[2] DEIS, University of Calabria, 87030 Rende, Italy,
furfaro@si.deis.unical.it
[3] ISI-CNR & DEIS, 87030 Rende, Italy,
sacca@unical.it

Abstract. In many application contexts, like statistical databases, transaction recording systems, scientific databases, query optimizers, OLAP, and so on, data are summarized as histograms of aggregate values. When the task of reconstructing range queries on original data from aggregate data is performed, a certain estimation error cannot be avoided, due to the loss of information in compressing data. Error size strongly depends both on how histograms partition data domains and on how estimation inside each bucket is done. We propose a new type of histogram, based on an unbalanced binary-tree partition, suitable for providing quick answers to hierarchical range queries, and we use adaptive tree-indexing for better approximating frequencies inside buckets. As the results from our experiments demonstrate, our histogram behaves considerably better than state-of-the-art histograms, showing smaller errors in all considered data sets at the same storage space.

1 Introduction

Often data is summarized over discrete ranges in order to create a database of manageable size allowing efficient storage, analysis, manipulation and display. For instance, query optimizations in relational databases is done by estimating selectivity of relational algebra operators from summarized data. Again, datawarehouses, transaction recording systems, OLAP applications, data mining activities, intrusion detection systems, scientific databases, and so on, operate on huge numbers of detailed records, but usually they do not care about detailed information, whereas extract useful knowledge only from condensed information consisting of summary data. Maintaining summary tables, with one histogram for each of a number of attributes, is used in statistical databases [7], where histograms represent a method for approximating probability distributions. Histograms are also used for improving the join processing in temporal databases [12]. Recently histograms have received a new deal of interest, mainly because they can be effectively used for approximating query answering in order to reduce the query response time in on-line decision support systems and OLAP [10], as well as the problem of reconstructing original data from aggregate information [1,4]. Histograms are created by partitioning the distribution of attribute

R. Cicchetti et al. (Eds.): DEXA 2002, LNCS 2453, pp. 861–870, 2002.

values into a number of buckets. Each bucket contains only aggregate summary information of the corresponding range of values, like the sum of occurrences in that range. For a given storage space reduction, the problem of determining the best histogram is crucial. Indeed, different partitions lead to dramatically different errors in reconstructing the original data distribution, especially for skewed data. This issue is being investigated since some decades, and a large number of techniques for arranging histograms have been proposed [5,6,9,3]. All these techniques adopt simple strategies (like Continuous Value Assumption [11] or Uniform Spread Assumption [9]) for estimating frequencies inside each bucket. Another common characteristic is that, besides the sum of frequencies, for each bucket, at least one boundary of the bucket must be kept in the histogram representation. In this paper we present a new type of histogram called *binary-tree histogram* which allows to save storage space thanks to a particular partition of the attribute domain, that frees us from the necessity of explicitly storing boundaries of buckets. The saved space is invested to improve the estimation of frequencies inside buckets, by adding, to each bucket, a suitable 32 bits tree-index. From this point of view our approach is related to that proposed in [2]. We use four types of tree-indices, suitable for different frequency distributions. During its construction, the histogram adapts to the actual distribution choosing the index capable of minimizing the error. Buckets of the histogram are hierarchically organized, in a binary-tree fashion in such a way that hierarchical queries can be quickly supported. The binary-tree histogram shows very high performance in terms of accuracy, as our experiments demonstrate. Experiments compare, at exactly the same storage space, our histogram with MaxDiff [9], V-Optimal [6] and Wavelet-based histograms [8], which represent the most meaningful and recent proposals in this context.

2 The Binary-Tree Histogram

Throughout this section consider given a *frequency vector* A of indices $1..n$ representing the number of occurrences of values of an attribute X of a relation R. W.l.o.g., the domain of X is assumed $1..n$. Thus, $A[i]$, for a given $1 \leq i \leq n$, is the *frequency of* i in R, i.e., the number of occurrences of the value i for the attribute X in R. Given any $1 \leq i \leq n$ such that $A[i] > 0$, the *spread* d_i of i is defined as 1 if i is the greatest attribute value with non-null frequency, or otherwise as the difference $j - i$, where j is the first index such that $j > i$ and $A[j] > 0$ (i.e., d_i is the distance from i to the next non-null value). A range r of indices of A is an interval $i..j$ such that $i \leq j \leq n$; for a range $r = i..j$, $lb(r)$ (i.e., lower bound of r) denotes i and $ub(r)$ (i.e., upper bound of r) denotes j. Given a range $r = i..j$ of A, we denote by $A[r]$ the portion of A identified by the indices $i..j$ and we call it *bucket* of A with lower bound i, denoted by $lb(A[r])$, and upper bound j, denoted by $ub(A[r])$. Given an aggregate function agg (among sum, $count$, avg, max, min) and a range r of indices of A, we denote as $agg(A[r])$ the result of the function agg applied to the elements of A contained in the range r. Thus, $sum(A[r])$ is the sum of such elements, $avg(A[r])$ returns the average value, $count(A[r])$ counts the number of non null elements occurring in $A[r]$, and $max(A[r])$ and $min(A[r])$ return the maximum and minimum value appearing in $A[r]$, respectively. Given a binary-tree T, we denote by $Nodes(T)$ the set of nodes of T, by $Root(T)$ the singleton containing the root of T, by $Left(T)$ the set $\{p \in Nodes(T) \mid \exists q \in Nodes(T) \wedge p \text{ is the left-hand child node of } q\}$, and by $Leaves(T)$ the set of leaf nodes of T. A *binary-tree partition* $BTP(A)$ of A is a binary tree whose nodes are ranges of A such that $Root(BTP(A)) = \{1..n\}$ and for each $q \in Nodes(BTP(A)) \setminus Leaves(BTP(A))$ the following holds: (1) q is full (i.e., it has two non-empty children), and (2) the left-hand child of q is $lb(q)..\lfloor(lb(q) + ub(q))/2\rfloor$, and (3) the right-hand child of q is $\lfloor(lb(q) + ub(q))/2\rfloor + 1..ub(q)$. Given a binary-tree partition P, we denote by $Store(P)$ the set $Root(P) \cup Left(P)$. A *binary-tree histogram* $BTH(A)$ on A is a pair $\langle P, S\rangle$ where P is a binary-tree partition of A and S is the set of pairs $\langle p, sum(A[p])\rangle$ where $p \in Store(P)$. For a node $p \in Store(P)$, we also denote by $S(p)$ the value $sum(A[p])$. Note that, for each node $q \in Nodes(P) \setminus Store(P)$, $sum(A[q])$ can be derived by using the set S. Indeed, $sum(A[q]) = sum(A[p]) - S(s)$, where s is the sibling node and p the parent node of q. Moreover, the value $sum(A[p])$ coincides with $S(p)$ in case $p \in Store(P)$. Given a binary-tree histogram $BTH = \langle P, S\rangle$ on A, P is said the *partition-tree* of BTH, and we denote it by $Part(BTH)$; S is said the *content set* of BTH and we denote it by $Cont(BTH)$. Given a node r of P, $A[r]$ is said a *terminal bucket* of BTH if $r \in Leaves(P)$, a *non-terminal bucket* otherwise.

2.1 Binary-Tree Histogram Representation

The storage space for a binary-tree histogram $BTH = \langle P, S\rangle$ is the space occupied by the representations of P and S. P can be represented by a string of bits: each bit is associated to a node of P and indicates whether the node is a leaf or not (i.e. whether the range corresponding to the node is split into two sub-ranges or not). Indeed, since the ranges associated to non leaf nodes of P are split into equal halves, it is not necessary to store any information about the lower bound and the upper bound of the ranges associated to the nodes. If the number of splits of P is t, then the string $Str(BTH)$ representing P contains $2 \cdot t + 1$ bits. The storage space for S is the space occupied by the set $\{s_i | \exists p_i \in Store(P) \wedge \langle p_i, s_i\rangle \in S\}$. Indeed, the information contained in S can be efficiently stored by means of an array $Agg(BTH)$ of size $t+1$ whose elements are the sums calculated inside each range in $Store(P)$. The order in which the sums are stored in such an array expresses their connection to the ranges in $Store(P)$. Fig.1 contains an example of a binary-tree histogram with the corresponding representation. Thus, the overall storage space for a binary-tree histogram on an array A with t splits is $size(BTH) = (2 \cdot t + 1) + (t + 1) \cdot W$, where W is the number of bits which are used for storing a sum. Note that a binary-tree histogram BTH uses less storage space than a classical histogram whose buckets are the terminal buckets of BTH (that is, the leaves of the partition tree). Moreover, in the average case, it is more efficient in estimating the answer to a range query since it uses the aggregate data of the non-terminal buckets (that is, the sums

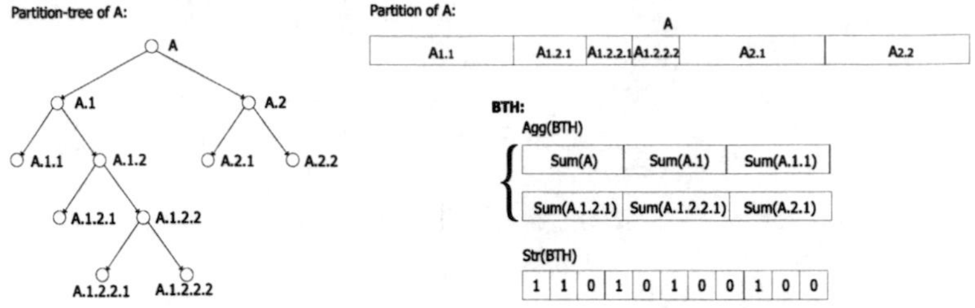

Fig. 1. A binary-tree partition with the representation of the corresponding histogram

of the ranges corresponding to the intermediate levels of the partition tree) and, thus, it is well-suitable for quickly answering to hierarchical queries.

3 Binary-Tree Histogram Construction

A classical problem on histograms is the estimation of the answer to a range query: that is, given a histogram H on A and a range $r = i..j$, with $1 \leq i \leq j \leq |A|$, estimate the overall frequency $\sum_{k=i}^{j} A[k]$. Clearly, while the contributions to the answer given by the sub-ranges coinciding with entire buckets can be computed exactly, the frequencies on the sub-ranges which partially overlap buckets can be only estimated, since the actual distribution of frequencies inside buckets is not available. The standard technique used for estimating the query inside buckets is the Continuous Value Assumption [11], (CVA, for short), basically consisting in a linear interpolation technique. For applying such a technique, no additional space is required. Another technique is the Uniform Spread Assumption [9]. Estimation is done by assuming that non null values inside buckets are distributed at equal distance each others. This technique requires 32 bit more for each bucket for storing the number of non null values occurring in it. However, in [2] it is shown that Uniform Spread Assumption does not give in general better accuracy than CVA. Anyway, also the way how the boundaries of buckets are defined, has strong impact on the estimation accuracy. We start by illustrating a new technique for defining the boundaries of buckets, leading to the construction of a *binary-tree histogram*. This is illustrated in the next subsection. Then we deal with the issue of increasing the accuracy of estimation inside the buckets.

3.1 Greedy Binary-Tree Histograms

Let A be the original frequency vector (containing also null values). Suppose that the storage space for the final binary-tree histogram is given, say it S. S limits the maximum number t of splits of the histogram, which can be easily derived as explained in the previous section. The value of t defines the set of all binary-tree histograms on A with the same number of splits. Among this set we could choose the best partitioned array w.r.t. some metrics. A reasonable metrics may be the total SSE of the histogram, defined as the sum of the SSEs of all of its terminal buckets. More formally, given a histogram H of k terminal buckets B_1, B_2, ..., B_k, $SSE(H) = \sum_{i=1}^{k} SSE(B_i)$, and given a terminal bucket $B = A[p..q]$, $SSE(B) = \sum_{i=p}^{q}(A[i] - avg(B))^2$. An *optimal binary-tree histogram* with t splits is any binary-tree histogram with $t+1$ terminal buckets with minimum SSE. In order to face the problem of determining an optimal binary-tree histogram, we propose the following greedy algorithm, building a binary-tree histogram with t splits from the array A:

1. $BTH := \langle\ P_0, \{\langle 1..n, sum(A[1..n])\rangle\}\ \rangle$
2. for each i from 1 to t
  2.1. Select $p \in Leaves(Part(BTH))$ such that: $SSE(A[p]) = max_{q \in Leaves(Part(BTH))}\{SSE(A[q])\}$ and set: $r = lb(p)..\lfloor(lb(p)+ub(p))/2\rfloor$
  2.2. $BTH := \langle\ Split(Part(BTH), p)\ ,\ Cont(BTH) \cup \{\langle r, sum(A[r])\rangle\}\ \rangle$.

where (i) P_0 is the partition tree containing only one node (corresponding to the range $1..n$), and (ii) the function *Split* takes as arguments a partition tree P_i and a leaf node l of P_i, and returns the partition tree obtained from P_i by splitting l into two halves. Informally, the algorithm builds a binary-tree histogram with t splits taking t steps. It starts from the binary-tree histogram whose partition tree has a unique node (corresponding to the range $1..n$) and, at each step, selects the (terminal) bucket having the maximum SSE and splits it.

3.2 Adding Tree Indices to Buckets

The technique presented in the previous section aims to build a histogram whose buckets contain frequencies with small differences, so that the CVA assumption in estimating a range query inside a bucket can be considered well-founded. Moreover, the binary-tree histogram uses a reduced storage space, due to the efficient representation of bucket boundaries: we do not need to explicitly store boundaries, but we can derive them from the binary-tree partition, whose representation is very compact. We may invest the saved space in order to improve the estimation technique *inside* buckets: Our idea consists in forcing the binary-tree approach inside buckets, limiting the total extra storage space required for each bucket to 32 bits. Clearly, having fixed this storage limit, the binary-tree technique inside each bucket could be applied *tout-court* only for one step (producing what we shall denote as *2 split* in the following). In case we want to construct an index-tree of splits we can use for each split less than 32 bits, progressively reducing the number of bits for lower splits in the tree. Like the binary-tree partition, intra-bucket indices may be unbalanced in order to spend more bits where it needs (that is, in the portion of the buckets with highest SSE). Actually, we define four different types of index, namely *2 split*, *3-Level Tree*, *4-Level Tree* and *5-Level Unbalanced Tree*, which occupy the same space used for storing a bucket (i.e. 32 bit), and we associate to each bucket the index which provides the most effective description of the frequencies contained in the bucket (the selection of the most suitable index is explained in detail further). In the description of the four types of index we will refer to Fig.2, which shows a partition of a bucket

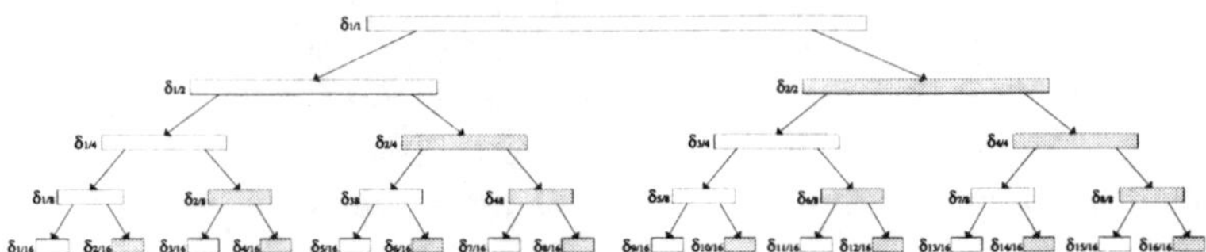

Fig. 2. 5-level tree

based on a tree with 5 levels. The symbol $\delta_{i/j}$ denotes the sum of the frequencies contained in the i-th of the contiguous j portions of the bucket whose size is one j-th of the size of the whole bucket (that is, $\delta_{1/1} = s$ is the total sum of all the frequencies in the bucket, $\delta_{1/2} = Sum(A[1..\frac{b}{2}])$ is the sum of the frequencies contained in the first half of the bucket, $\delta_{2/2} = \delta_{1/1} - \delta_{1/2}$ is the sum of the frequencies appearing in the second half of the bucket, and so on). The symbol $\widetilde{\delta}_{i/j}$ will denote the approximated value of $\delta_{i/j}$ which can be retrieved from the indices. Grey nodes in Fig.2 correspond to those portions of the bucket whose representation do not occupy any storage space: either the exact and the approximated values of the sum associated to such nodes can be calculated subtracting the value associated to their sibling from the value associated to their father.

3.3 Selection of the Most Suitable Index for a Bucket

The 5 indices we described in the previous paragraphs differ one from the other for the number and the size of the portions of the bucket they describe, and for the accuracy (i.e. number of bits) they associate to the portions. We point out that although 4LT and 5LUT indices split a bucket into a larger number of parts than 3LT and 2s do, we cannot state that they generate smaller errors in the estimation: indeed, the 4LT and 5LUT indices describe the portions with less accuracy (i.e. smaller number of bits). Thus, the selection of the most suitable index for a bucket depends on the actual distribution of the frequencies inside the bucket: for instance, the 2s index is the most suitable for those buckets whose halves contain uniformly distributed frequencies, the 5LUT is suitable for those buckets such that one of their halves contain uniform distributions of frequencies, but the other half contains a lot of frequencies with large differences, and so on. When associating a tree index to a bucket during the construction of a binary-tree histogram, we choose the most suitable index for a (terminal) bucket by comparing the average errors obtained using the different indices in estimating the queries over the ranges $[1..\frac{i}{16} \cdot b]$, with $1 \leq i \leq 15$, inside the bucket. That is, for each (terminal) bucket we build 5 indices (a 2s index, a 3LT index, a 4LT index, a *left*-5LUT index and a *right*-5LUT index) and evaluate 15 range queries using each of such indices. Next, we associate to the bucket the index which generates the minimum average error. We point out that the complexity of the choice of the most suitable indices using such a criterion is linear w.r.t. the number of splits t of the histogram: the number of terminal buckets that must be analyzed is $t + 1$, and for each bucket the number of operations which

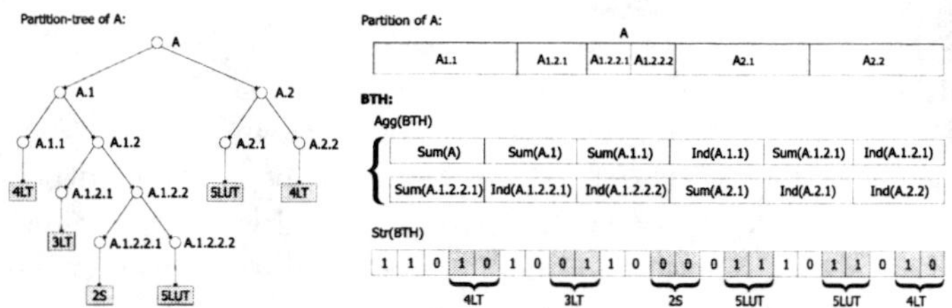

Fig. 3. A binary-tree histogram with tree indices

are necessary for building the 5 possible indices and evaluating the answers to the 15 range queries is constant (computing the exact answer to a range query can be done efficiently if we use the array of the cumulative frequencies).

3.4 Representation of a Binary-Tree Histogram with Tree Indices

The usage of tree indices for estimating a range query inside a terminal bucket makes it necessary to modify the representation of a binary-tree histogram: both the string of bits representing the structure of the partition tree and the array containing aggregate information must be changed. In particular, we add 2 bits for each terminal bucket to $Str(BTH)$, indicating which type of index the bucket is associated to. The values of the indices are added to $Agg(BTH)$. Thus, the storage space occupied by a binary-tree histogram with tree indices is given by: $S = (2 \cdot t + 1) + 2 \cdot (t + 1) + (t + 1) \cdot W + (t + 1) \cdot W = 4 \cdot t + 3 + 2 \cdot (t + 1) \cdot W$. Fig. 3 shows the partition tree and the representation of the binary-tree histogram obtained from that of Fig.1 by adding tree indices to its buckets.

4 Experiments: Comparison with Other Methods

In this section we compare our method with the main recently proposed types of histogram. In particular, we consider three well known approaches that are Max-Diff [3,9], V-Optimal [9,6] and Wavelet-based Histograms [8], which well represent the state of the art in this context. Experiments are conducted exactly at the same storage space using both synthetic and real-life data. First, we describe the query sets adopted for measuring the accuracy of different methods on synthetic and real-life data as well as the utilized error metrics.

Query set and error metrics: In our experiments, we use two different query sets for evaluating the effectiveness of the various methods: (1) $QS_1 = \{X \leq d : 1 \leq d \leq n\}$, and (2) $QS_2 = \{a \leq X \leq b : 1 \leq a \leq b \leq n\}$, where, we recall, X is the histogram attribute and $1..n$ is its domain. We measure the approximation error made by histograms on sets of queries extracted from the query sets above. For a set of queries Q we measure the *average relative error* $\frac{1}{|Q|} \sum_{i=1}^{|Q|} e_i^{rel}$, where e_i^{rel} is the *relative error* of the i-th query of the query set ($e_i^{rel} = \frac{|S_i - \widetilde{S}_i|}{S_i}$, where S_i and $\widetilde{S}_i$ are the actual answer and the estimated answer).

Synthetic Data

In this section we illustrate the synthetic data sets used for our experiments. **Distribution Classes:** For distribution class we mean a pair of statistic distributions, one characterizing the distribution for frequencies, the other characterizing the distribution for spreads. Frequency set and value set are generated independently, then frequencies are randomly assigned to the elements of the value set. We consider 3 distribution classes: **(1)** D_1: *Zipf-cusp_max(0.5,1.0)*. Frequencies are distributed according to a Zipf distribution with the z parameter equal to 0.5. Spreads are distributed according to a Zipf *cusp_max* [9] (i.e., increasing spreads following a Zipf for the first half elements and decreasing spreads following a Zipf distribution for the remainder elements) with z parameter equal to 1.0. **(2)** D_2 = *Zipf-zrand(0.5,1.0)*: Frequencies are distributed according to a Zipf distribution with the z parameter equal to 0.5. Spreads follow a $ZRand$ distribution [9] with z parameter equal to 1.0 (i.e., spreads following a Zipf distributions with z parameter equal to 1.0 are randomly assigned to attribute values). **(3)** D_3 = *Gauss-rand*: Frequencies are distributed according to a Gauss distribution with standard deviation 1.0. Spreads are randomly distributed.

$meth./dis.$	D_1	D_2	D_3	$mean$
WA	3.50	3.42	2.99	3.30
MD	4.30	5.78	8.37	6.15
VO	3.70	3.33	3.30	3.44
BT	0.26	0.27	0.27	0.27
BT^-	0.91	0.97	0.83	0.90

(a)

$meth./dist.$	D_1	D_2	D_3	$mean$
WA	13.09	13.06	6.08	10.71
MD	19.35	16.03	2.90	12.76
VO	8.51	8.98	5.67	7.72
BT	1.12	1.15	0.44	0.90
BT^-	4.06	4.88	1.42	3.45

(b)

$meth./dist.$	D_1	D_2	D_3	$mean$
WA	14.53	5.55	5.06	8.38
MD	11.64	6.65	3.30	7.20
VO	11.37	3.48	2.96	5.94
BT	1.51	3.50	0.91	1.97
BT^-	11.94	4.77	2.22	6.31

(c)

Fig. 4. (a): Errors for Population 1. (b): Errors for Population 2. (c): Errors for Population 3.

Populations: A population is characterized by the value of three parameters, that are T, D and u, and represents the set of frequency vectors with u non null elements which store the occurrence frequency of an attribute, namely X, defined on a domain with cardinality D belonging to a relation of cardinality T. *Population* P_1. This population is characterized by the following values for the parameters: $D = 4100$, $u = 500$ and $T = 100000$. *Population* P_2. This population is characterized by the following values for the parameters: $D = 4100$, $u = 500$ and $T = 500000$. *Population* P_3. This population is characterized by the following values for the parameters: $D = 4100$, $u = 1000$ and $T = 500000$. **Data Sets:** Each data set included in the experiments is obtained by generating 10 frequency vectors belonging to one of the populations specified above, according to one of the above described distribution classes. We consider the 9 data sets that are generated by combining all data distributions and all populations and evaluate errors by applying queries belonging to the query sets above.

Real-Life Data

We performed a number of experiments also on real-life data. We considered the attribute WSALVAL (Amount: Total Wage & salary) of the CENSUS database cpsm95p downloaded from the `URL: http://www.census.gov`. The attribute domain (representing yearly incomes), is the interval [1..200,000] and thus its cardinality is $D = 200,000$, the number of non null attribute values is $u = 4,298$, and the cardinality of the relation is $T = 32,263$.

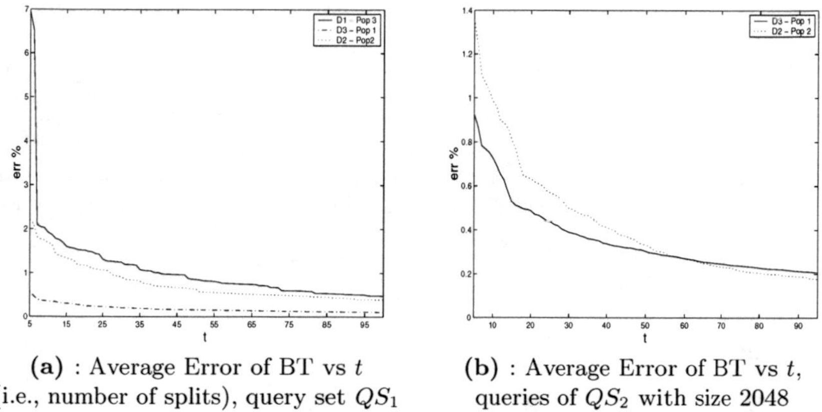

(a) : Average Error of BT vs t (i.e., number of splits), query set QS_1

(b) : Average Error of BT vs t, queries of QS_2 with size 2048

Fig. 5. Experimental Results

Experimental Results

Both experiments on synthetic data and real-life data show the superiority of our technique w.r.t. the other methods. For every methods, we used 32 bits for representing integers, and 32 bits for representing BTH indices. Tables in Figure 4 report the results obtained for the 9 synthetic data sets previously described. WA denotes the Wavelet-histogram, MD is MaxDiff, VO denotes V-Optimal and BT is the binary-tree technique with the usage of indices inside buckets. BT^- denotes the binary-tree method with no intra-bucket indices, where all the storage space is used for splitting buckets according to the binary-tree technique. As the results reported in the tables show, BT behaves considerably better than other methods. Results of BT^- demonstrate benefits given by the usage of indices inside buckets. The graph in Figure 5.(a) shows the dependency of the average error (of all queries of query set QS_1) of the binary-tree technique on the the number of splits (and, thus, on the total storage space) for 3 of the 9 synthetic data sets previously described. Graph of Figure 5.(b) is obtained by considering all the queries of the query set QS_2 with size 2048, and computing the average. Figure 6.(a) compares all methods for different query sizes (query set QS_2) on Population 3 and Distribution Class $D1$. Figure 6.(b) plots some results obtained on real-life data. Due to the large cardinality of the attribute domain (200,000), BT is compared only with MaxDiff, whose computational cost is linear as for our method. We report the dependency of the error on the storage space amount (expressed as number of 4-byte integers) showing that BT behaves considerably better than MaxDiff.

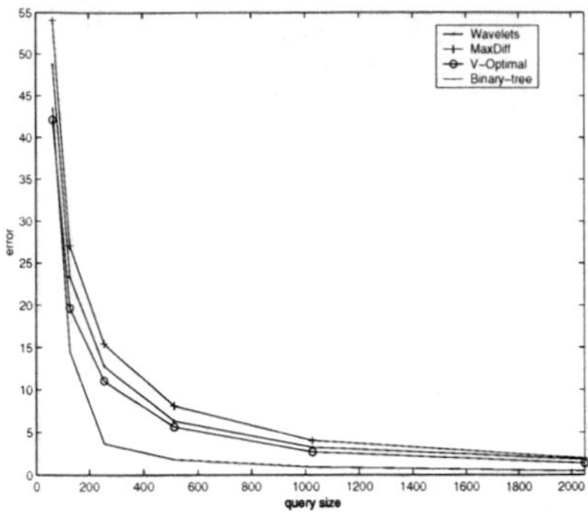

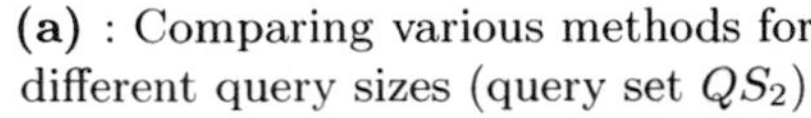
(a) : Comparing various methods for different query sizes (query set QS_2)

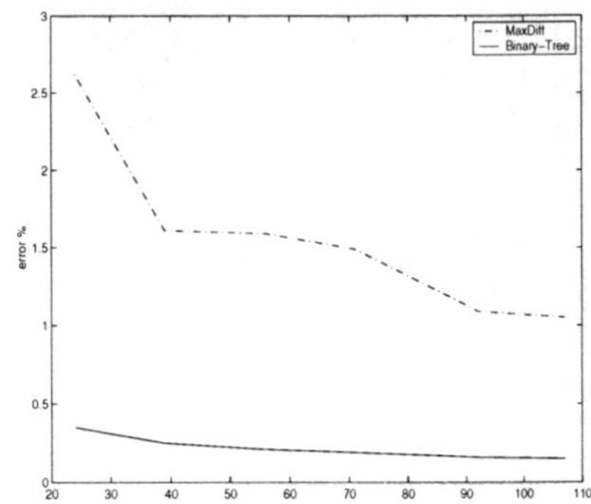

(b) : Average error for real data vs number of stored 4-byte integers (query set QS_1)

Fig. 6. Experimental Results

References

1. F. Buccafurri, F. Furfaro, F. Saccà, Estimating Range Queries using Aggregate Data with Integrity Constraints: a Probabilistic Approach, *Proc. of the 8th International Conference on Database Theory*, London(UK), 4-6 January 2001.
2. F. Buccafurri, L. Pontieri, D. Rosaci, D. Saccà, Improving Range Query Estimation on Histograms, *Proc. of the International Conference ICDE 2002*, San Josè, 2002.
3. S. Christodoulakis, Implications of Certain Assumptions in Data Base Perfomance Evaluations, *ACM TODS* 1984.
4. C. Faloutsos, H. V. Jagadish, N. D. Sidiripoulos. Recovering Information from Summary Data. In *Proceedings of the 1997 VLDB*, Athens, 1997
5. Y. Ioannidis, V. Poosala. Balancing histogram optimality and practicality for query result size estimation, In *Proceedings of the 1995 ACM SIGMOD International Conference on Management of Data*, San Josè (CA), May 1995
6. H. V. Jagadish, N. Koudas, S. Muthukrishnan, V. Poosala, K. Sevcik, T. Suel. Optimal histograms for quality guarantees, In *Proc. of the 1998 ACM SIGMOD Int. Conf. on Management of Data*, Seattle (Washington), June 1998
7. F. Malvestuto, A Universal-Scheme Approach to Statistical Databases Containing Homogeneous Summary Tables, *ACM TODS*, 18(4), 678–708, December 1993.
8. Y. Matias, J. S. Vitter, M. Wang. Wavelet-based histograms for selectivity estimation, In *Proceedings of the 1998 ACM SIGMOD International Conference on Management of Data*, Seattle, Washington, June 1998.
9. V. Poosala, Y. E. Ioannidis, P. J. Haas, E. J. Shekita, Improved histograms for selectivity estimation of range predicates, In *Proc. of the 1996 ACM SIGMOD Int. Conf. on Management of Data*, Montreal (Canada), June 1996.
10. V. Poosala, V. Ganti, Y.E. Ioannidis, Approximate Query Answering using Histograms, *IEEE Data Engineering Bulletin* Vol. 22, March 1999.
11. P. G. Selinger, M. M. Astrahan, D. D. Chamberlin, R. A. Lorie, and T. T. Price. Access path selection in a relational database management system, In *Proc. of ACM SIGMOD Internatinal Conference*, Boston (MA), May-June 1979.
12. I. Sitzmann, P.J. Stuckey, Improving Temporal Joins Using Histograms, *Proc. of 11th Int. Conf. on Database and Expert Systems Applications*, London(UK), 2000.

Indexing Genomic Databases for Fast Homology Searching

Twee-Hee Ong[1], Kian-Lee Tan[1,2], and Hao Wang[1]

[1] Department of Computer Science
National University of Singapore
3 Science Drive 2, Singapore 117543
{ongtweeh, tankl, wanghao}@comp.nus.edu.sg
[2] Genome Institute of Singapore
1 Science Park Road, The Capricorn #05-01
Singapore Science Park II, Singapore 117528
gistankl@nus.edu.sg

Abstract. Genomic sequence databases has been widely used by molecular biologists for homology searching. However, as amino acid and nucleotide databases are growing in size at an alarming rate, traditional brute force approach of comparing a query sequence against each of the database sequences is becoming prohibitively expensive. In this paper, we re-examine the problem of searching for homology in large protein databases. We proposed a novel filter-and-refine approach to speed up the search process. The scheme operates in two phases. In the filtering phase, a small set of candidate database sequences (as compared to all sequences in the database) is quickly identified. This is realized using a signature-based scheme. In the refinement phase, the query sequence is matched against the sequences in the candidate set using any local alignment strategies. Our preliminary experimental results show that the proposed method results in significant savings in computation without sacrificing on the accuracy of the answers as compared to FASTA.

1 Introduction

Molecular biologists frequently query genomic databases in their search for sequence homology. Traditionally, this process involves matching a query sequence against each of the database sequences where the similarity computations between two sequences typically have a complexity that is either linear or quadratic to the length of the sequences involved. However, several recent development have led to such brute force approach to be no longer practical. First, genomic databases are increasing in size in terms of both number of sequences and length of the sequence (doubling in size every 15 or 16 months [1]). Second, the number of queries directed at these databases are very large (over 40,000 queries per day [1]) and the user numbers and query rates are growing. Third, there is an increasing need to mine a sequence database for useful information. This typically requires all pairwise similarity between all the sequences to be computed.

R. Cicchetti et al. (Eds.): DEXA 2002, LNCS 2453, pp. 871–880, 2002.

Thus, the need to move away from exhaustive search techniques will keep getting stronger, and novel and efficient methods for searching genomic databases are necessary and called for.

One promising direction in the literature is to maintain an abstraction or index of the database sequences that can be used to identify a (small) subset of the database sequences that are broadly similar to the query. In this way, those database sequences that are not likely to be in the answer set can be pruned away without being accessed, thus saving both disk and computation cost. The candidate answer set is subsequently refined using a more effective alignment algorithm to pick out the final answer set.

Most of the existing works represent a sequence by its subsequences (also called *motifs*). Thus, sequences with the same set of motifs are likely to be homologues. However, these schemes typically restrict to fixed-length motifs. Moreover, they are storage inefficient, and their effectiveness (sensitivities) are limited because of the lack of inexact match when comparing motifs.

In this paper, we present a new indexing scheme to speedup homology search. The scheme is novel in the following ways. First, our approach can handle motifs of different length. Second, we account for inexact match when comparing motifs. Finally, a sequence's motifs are represented by a m-bit vector, called a *signature.* We note that m can be fine-tuned in order to trade off performance and storage. At one extreme, if m corresponds to the number of motifs, then, each motif can be mapped to a unique position in the vector. At the other extreme, if $m = 1$, then the vector is effectively useless as all motifs will be mapped to the same bit. The set of all signatures corresponding to the database sequences form the signature file.

The search process is a filter-and-refine strategy. In the filtering phase, motifs are extracted from the query sequence to generate a query signature. The query signature is matched against the signature file to return a candidate set of sequences. This step can be performed quickly as bitwise operations are very fast. In the refinement phase, the query sequence is matched against the candidate sequences using any exhaustive approach to pick out the answer set.

We implemented the proposed scheme, and conducted a preliminary experimental study on a real dataset. Our results show that a reasonable size m is sufficient for good performance. Moreover, the proposed scheme is significantly faster than FASTA [2] without sacrificing on the quality of the answers returned.

The rest of this paper is organized as follows. In the next section, we review some related work. Section 3 presents the proposed signature-based scheme. In Section 4, we report on the results of our experiments, and finally, we conclude in Section 5 with directions for further study.

2 Related Work

SSearch [3], FASTA [2] and BLAST [4] are all examples of exhaustive search tools. Each entry in the database is consulted before formulating an answer set to a query. Index-based systems have been studied. Here, we review three such schemes that we extract from [5].

RAMdb (Rapid Access Motif database) [6] is a system for finding short patterns (called *motifs*) in genomic databases. Each genomic sequence is indexed by its constituent overlapping intervals in a hash table structure. For each interval, an associated list of sequence numbers and offsets is stored. This allows a quick lookup of any sequences matching a query sequence. A long query sequence is split into shorter non-overlaping motifs that are used to query the database. RAMdb is best suited for the lookup of query motifs whose length is equal or slightly longer than the indexed interval length. RAMdb requires a large index twice the size of the original flat-file database (including the textual descriptions) and suffers from lack of special-purpose ranking schemes designed for identifying initial match regions. In addition, the non-overlapping interval of query motifs means false dismissals unless the frame happens to coincidentally align with the start of the interval frame.

The FLASH search tool redundantly indexes genomic data based on a probabilistic scheme [7]. For each interval of length n, the FLASH search structure stores, in a hash-table, all possible similarly-ordered contiguous and non-contiguous subsequences of length m that begin with the first base in the interval, where $m < n$. As an example, for a nucleotide sequence ACCTGATT the index terms for the first $n = 5$ bases, where $m = 3$, would be ACC, ACT, ACG, ACT, ACG and ATG; each of the permuted strings begins with the base A, the first base in the interval of length $n = 5$. The hash-table then stores each permuted m-length subsequence, the sequences that contain the permuted subsequences, and the offsets within each sequence of the permuted subsequence. The key idea of the flash scheme is that the permuted scheme gives an accurate model that approximates a reasonable number of insertions, deletions, and substitutions in genomic sequences. The authors found that FLASH was of the order of ten times faster for a small test collection than BLAST and was superior in accurately and sensitively determining homologies in database searching. FLASH utilizes a redundant index, which is stored in a hash-table and is uncompressed, and impractically large. For a nucleotide collection of around 100 Mb, the index requires 18 Gb on disk, around 180 times the collection size.

CAFE [1] is based on a partitioned search approach, where a coarse search using an inverted index is used to rank sequences by similarity to a query sequence and a subsequent fine search used to locally align only a subset of database sequences with the query. The CAFE index consists of three components: a search structure, which contains the index terms or distinct intervals, that is, fixed-length overlapping subsequences from the collection being indexed; inverted lists, which are a carefully compressed list of ordinal sequence numbers, where each list is an index of sequences containing a particular interval; and, a mapping table, which maps ordinal sequence numbers to the physical location of sequence data on disk. Queries are evaluated by representing the query as a set of intervals, retrieving the list for each interval, and using a ranking structure to store a similarity score of each database sequence to the query. Like FLASH, CAFE uses an overlapping interval. It uses a compression scheme to try to make the index size more manageable. The author notes that although it is more computationally efficient than the exhaustive methods, "exhaustive systems generally have better retrieval effectiveness".

3 Signature-Based Retrieval

In this section, we present the proposed signature-based retrieval scheme. The mechanism involves several components, and we shall discuss each of them. First, we need to extract a set of features that can be used to represent the sequences. Second, the extracted information is encoded as a signature, and a signature file is used to facilitate speedy retrievals. Third, we need to know how to compute the similarity between two sequences.

3.1 Representing the Semantics of a Sequence

In this paper, we represent each sequence by a set of *independent* subsequences extracted from the sequence. We refer to these subsequences as *motifs*. This concept resembles that of representing a document by its keywords in information retrieval research.

For the approach to be practical and useful, several issues have to be addressed. First, we need to determine a suitable set of motifs. Traditionally, one approach of finding motifs is to extract all subsequences whose length is between l_{min} and l_{max} that satisfy a given minimum support constraint [8]. Our algorithm, shown in Figure 1, is more robust and allows motifs of different length to be obtained. Essentially, given a subsequence, we count the number of database sequences that contain the subsequence. For those that are too small, i.e., below a minimum support constraint β, we do not treat them as motifs. For those that appear in too many sequences, i.e., above a maximum support constraint α, we also do not treat them as motifs. This is because such subsequences are not discriminating enough. Instead, we extend the subsequence length and use the extended subsequence as the motifs. We note that steps 1 to 10 of the algorithm allows the algorithm to pick a suitable starting length for motifs, if most of the subsequences of a certain length appear in many sequences, then it makes sense to start with a longer subsequence.

Second, given that we have identified a set of motifs, associate each database sequence with a subset of the motifs. To make the search effective, we want motifs of a sequence to be as unrelated or independent as possible. Two motifs are said to be dependent if and only if (a) either one is the prefix of the other or one is subsequence of the other, and (b) their intersection of their respective supporting sets is non-trivial [8]. Thus, for each sequence, we first find the set of motifs it supports and from this set we select a maximal set of independent ones.

To illustrate, Table 1 shows an example. On the left, we have 8 protein sequences. Suppose, we assume that we use a minimum support of 50%, i.e.,

Algorithm GenerateAllMotifs
Input: maximum support α, minimum support β, threshold γ

```
1. l_min ← 3
2. repeat
3.       tooShort ← False
4.       generate all subsequences of length l_min
5.       let k_i denote the number of sequences in the database that corresponds
         to motif m_i
6.       let M be the number of motifs whose k_i value is greater than α
7.       if M > γ
8.             tooShort ← True
9.             l_min ← l_min + 1
10. until not(tooShort)
11. for each subsequence s generated with length l_min
12. let c_s denote the number of sequences that contain s
13.       if α > c_s > β
14.             s is added into the list of motifs
15.       else if c_s > α
16.             extend s and include its extensions as motifs
17.             step 16 may be repeated for the extended motifs if their
                  count exceeds α
18. return the complete list of motifs
```

Fig. 1. Generation of motifs.

subsequences that appear in fewer than 4 sequences will be pruned away. Further, assume that we use a maximum support of 75%, i.e., subsequences that appear in 6 sequences or more will be extended. The middle table shows the motifs (those without '*') that will be generated. Consider a subsequence that has been marked with '*' in the table, say AQV. We note that AQV appears in 6 database sequences. As such, it is extended to AQVH (since it is the only one that appear in the database). Interestingly AQVH also appears in 6 database sequences, which resulted in it being further extended to AQVHK, AQVHM and AQVHP. Thus, the latter 3 subsequences are captured as motifs instead of AQV and AQVH. The table on the right shows the selected motifs for each database sequence. Here, we see that for sequence S_1, we have AQVH and AQVHK which are dependent, and AQVHK is selected as it is "maximal". Similarly, for sequence S_6, we have DAL and ALG which overlapped. In this case, we arbitrarily picked one of them.

The third issue concerns an efficient and compact strategy to represent the motifs of the database sequences. Our approach is to map each database sequence to a V-bit vector (called a *signature*) as follows. Consider a sequence with k motifs, $m_1, \ldots, m_k$. Initially, all the V bits of the signature is set to 0. We define a hash function $h(m)$ that maps a motif m to a value in the range 1 to V. Then, for motif m_i ($1 \leq i \leq k$), bit $h(m_i)$ is set to 1. Note that depending on the hash function used, *collision* can occur, i.e., it is possible for $m_i \neq m_j$ such that

Table 1. Motif generation example

Seq ID	Sequence
S_1	AQVHKHKKSVDAM
S_2	AQVHKKSGSDGLP
S_3	AQVHKHVAQIKDP
S_4	AQVHKALGPHKKS
S_5	DALGPAQVHMHKKS
S_6	AQIKDDALGPAQP
S_7	KKSPQIKDQVG
S_8	QIKDALGMAQVHP

Pattern	Support
ALG	4
*AQV	6
DAL	4
HKK	4
IKD	4
KKS	5
QIK	4
*QVH	6
QVHK	4
QVHM	1
QVHP	1
*AQVH	6
AQVHK	4
AQVHM	1
AQVHP	1

Seq ID	Selected Motifs
S_1	AQVHK, HKKS
S_2	KKS, AQVHK
S_3	AQVHK, IKD
S_4	AQVHK, ALG, HKKS
S_5	ALG, AQVHM, HKKS
S_6	DAL, IKD
S_7	KKS, IKD
S_8	ALG, AQVHP, IKD

$h(m_i) = h(m_j)$. In such a case, we expect *false drops* to occur, i.e., two dissimilar sequences may have the a significant number of bits set at the same locations and are treated as similar. The collection of all signatures produced by all the database sequences is the signature file.

3.2 The Similarity Measure

Two sequences are similar if they share some common motifs. Under the signature-based representation of sequences, the signatures representing both sequences are similar if they may only differ in some of the bits. This only requires a simple operation (logical AND) to compute the intersection between two signatures.

Let Q and D denote the signatures of a query sequence and a database sequence respectively. Then, the two sequences have the same motif if and only if the corresponding bits in both signatures are set (note that it is possible to be a false drop). Thus, the similarity measure, SIM, between Q and D can be determined as:

$$SIM(Q, D) = \frac{BitSet(Q \wedge D)}{BitSet(D)} \qquad (1)$$

where $BitSet(BS)$ denotes the number of bits in the vector BS that are set, and '$\wedge$' represents the bitwise logical-AND operation. Now, if both sequences share many common motifs, the similarity computed will be closed to 1.

3.3 The Retrieval Process

The retrieval process comprises two phases. In the first phase, we identify a small set of candidate sequences (from the database sequences) that are homologous to the query sequence quickly. This is done using the signature files as follows. Given a query sequence, we first determine its signature. This requires finding out the set of motifs that can be extracted from the sequence. This is done efficiently as follows. We use a window of length l_{min} and generate the subsequences of l_{min} as the window slides through the sequence. The subsequences are then sorted and compared against the motifs of the database sequences (this can be efficiently done using integer comparison, rather than string comparison). This process may be repeated for extended subsequences. Once the set of motifs is identified, the resultant signature is compared against those stored in the signature file. The database sequences that are similar can then be ranked and retrieved accordingly, and the top ranked sequences form the candidate set.

In the second phase, we compare the query sequence against each of the database sequences in the candidate set using a more comprehensive matching algorithm such as FASTA or BLAST. The best set of sequences can then be obtained.

3.4 Optimized Scheme for Improved Retrieval Effectiveness

In the above discussion, we have presented a very basic signature-based approach whose effectiveness may be limited. Here, we present extensions that can improve its effectiveness:

- In the similarity metric, when comparing two bit vectors, we have assumed that every motif is equally important. To account for frequently occurring low complexity motifs, we scale each of the motifs following the *inverse-document-frequency* methodology. This is also commonly used in information retrieval research. In this approach, if a particular motif appears in m out of n sequences, its weight is multiplied by $\log(n/m)$. The effect of this scaling is that infrequently occurring motifs are given higher weight than motifs that occur in almost every sequence.
- In our earlier discussion, we have pruned away those motifs whose counts fall below the minimum support. To avoid missing such motifs completely, we mapped such motifs to those that are similar to them. Referring to our example in Table 1, DAM in sequence S_1 may be treated as DAL.
- Another limitation in the above discussion is that the ordering of the motifs is not considered. To resolve this, we create an intermediate layer between the signature file and the database sequences. Each signature of a sequence also serves as an inverted list by pointing to the list of motifs associated with the sequence (note that the list of motifs is encoded, and not stored as strings). Instead of retrieving the database sequences, once the candidate sequences are identified, an alignment algorithm is applied on the list of motifs associated with them to further rank them. The refined ranking is then used to further prune the list of candidate set to a smaller set before the final matching of query and database sequences are performed.

4 Preliminary Results

To study the effectiveness (accuracy) and efficiency of the proposed signature retrieval method, we conducted some performance study. We implemented the basic signature scheme as described using the global approach [8] and present our results in this section. The dataset used for the experiment is essentially the entire protein sequence database, PIR1-PIR4, maintained by the National Biomedical Research Foundation (NBRF-PIR) at the Georgetown University Medical Center. This set has about 190,874 protein sequences.

4.1 On Retrieval Effectiveness

To study the retrieval effectiveness of the proposed method, we use FASTA as the basis for comparison. In other words, we consider our method accurate as long as it can return the same set of answers as that returned by FASTA.

Table 2 shows the results of the experiments. For the experiments, we set l_{min} to 3 and 4, and minimum support to 4.0% and 0.9% of the dataset respectively. For l_{min}=3, there are a total of 3322 motifs generated, while 3326 motifs were generated for l_{min}=4. In the figure, the first column represents the percentage of the database sequences that are retrieved as the candidate set after the filtering phase; the second and third column denotes the percentage of answers that are in FASTA but not contained among the database sequences retrieved in the signature scheme with l_{min} set to 3 and 4 respectively; the fourth column shows the percentage of answers that are in FASTA but not contained in the database sequences retrieved using an inverted file index (similar to that described in CAFE [1]), where length of q-gram was set to 4 [1].

From the results, we note that if we retrieve the top 10% of the sequences from phase 1 of the proposed scheme, the scheme missed about 12.5% of the answers produced by FASTA, with l_{min}=3. The results are slightly worse for l_{min}=4. This is expected as the probability of two sequences having longer exact motifs is lower. Also, by comparing the signature scheme to the inverted file implementation, we note that the accuracy of the inverted file is better than the scheme. This is expected, as the inverted file indexes all the q-grams that are present in the database, while for the signature scheme, the motifs that are below the minimum support are not present in the signature index. However, the space requirements of the inverted file is much more than that required by the signature scheme, and by a suitable length used for the motifs, we are able to obtain nearly the same accuracy as the inverted file implementation.

Also, it is encouraging to note that by scanning 20% of the database sequences, we can get reasonably good accuracy as the results obtained by FASTA. Our investigation also shows that the answers that are missed ranked fairly low under FASTA's answers. In other words, all the high ranking sequences are also ranked highly under the proposed scheme.

---

[1] At the time of the experiments, we were only able to obtain the implementation for q-gram of 4

Table 2. On retrieval effectiveness

% of sequences retrieved	% of answers missed (signature) l_{min}=3	% of answers missed (signature) l_{min}=4	% of answers missed (inverted file)
1%	40.0%	47.5%	13.3%
2%	35.0%	40.83%	9.17%
5%	16.0%	33.3%	5.83%
10%	12.5%	22.5%	5.83%
15%	11.67%	14.17%	5.0%
20%	7.5%	10.8%	4.16%

Table 3. On retrieval efficiency

length of query	signature-based method			FASTA	Inverted File
	Phase 1	Phase 2	Total		Phase 1
100 bp	58.8	0.18	58.98	78.41	13
200 bp	58.2	2.05	60.25	132.59	45
300 bp	58.4	15.11	73.51	177.55	71
400 bp	58.8	17.16	75.96	209.51	104
500 bp	58.9	20.76	79.66	240.74	127
600 bp	59.0	20.35	79.35	249.38	126

4.2 On Retrieval Efficiency

Table 3 shows the running time results of the experiments with l_{min} and length of q-gram for inverted file both set to 4. The results obtained are over multiple runs with multiple different queries. The timings for the proposed signature scheme are presented for all the stages; including phase 2 which is using FASTA on the top 10% of the database sequences retrieved in phase 1. The timings shown for the inverted file shows only the time to retrieve all records of all the q-grams present in the query sequence. First we observe that the query string length seems to have an effect on the cost of the algorithm: as the query length increases, the processing cost also increases. Second we note that all queries inccur approximately the same cost in phase 1. This is expected since each query sequence's bit vector has to be compared against all vectors in the signature file. Third, we find that the proposed scheme is generally more efficient for long query sequences. Its gain can be more than 50% that of FASTA. For short sequences, the gain is less significant.

5 Conclusion

In this paper, we have proposed a novel filter-and-refine approach to speed up homology search in large databases. In the filtering phase, a signature file is used to determine a small subset of candidate database sequences that are potentially homologous to the query sequence. In the refinement phase, the candidate set and the query sequences are aligned using any known alignment algorithm.

Our preliminary results on real data set showed that the proposed approach is promising. In particular, we can significantly reduce the processing cost without sacrificing much of the accuracy. We believe that the proposed scheme's efficiency can be further improved by partitioning the signature file according to the protein (super-)families. We would also like to exploit the sequence length to facilitate more efficient search. We are currently working in these directions.

References

1. H. Williams and J. Zobel. Indexing and retrieval for genomic databases. *IEEE Transactions on Knowledge and Data Engineering (to appear)*, 2001.
2. W.R. Pearson and D.J. Lipman. Improved tools for biological sequence comparison. In *Proceedings Natl. Acad. Sci. USA Vol. 85*, pages 2444–2448, 1988.
3. D. J. States, W. Gish, and S. F. Altschul. Improved sensivity of nucleic acid databas searches using application-specific scoring matrices. *Methods: A Companion to Methods in Enzymology*, 3(1):66–70, 1991.
4. S. F. Altschul, W. Gish, W. Miller, E. W. Myers, and D. J. Lipman. A basic local alignment search tool. *Journal of Moelcular Biology*, 215:403–410, 1990.
5. M. Dipperstein. Dna sequence databases. In *http://www.cs.ucsb.edu/ mdipper/dna/DNApaper.html*.
6. C. Fondrat and P. Dessen. A rapid access motif database (ramdb) with a search algorithm for the retrieval patterns in nucleic acids or protein databanks. *Computer Applications in the Biosciences*, 11(3):273–279, 1995.
7. A. Califano and I. Rigoutsos. Flash: A fast look-up algorithm for string homology. In *Proceedinsg of the International Conference on Intelligent Systems for Molecular Biology*, pages 56–64, Bethesda, MD, 1993.
8. V. Guralnik and G. Karypis. A scalable algorithm for clustering protein sequences. In *Proceedings of the BIOKDD 2001 Workshop (see http://www.cs.rpi.edu/ zaki/BIOKDD01)*, 2001.

Bitmap Indices for Speeding Up High-Dimensional Data Analysis

Kurt Stockinger

CERN, European Organization for Nuclear Research
CH-1211 Geneva, Switzerland
Institute for Computer Science and Business Informatics
University of Vienna, A-1010 Vienna, Austria
Kurt.Stockinger@cern.ch

Abstract. Bitmap indices have gained wide acceptance in data warehouse applications and are an efficient access method for querying large amounts of read-only data. The main trend in bitmap index research focuses on typical business applications based on discrete attribute values. However, scientific data that is mostly characterised by non-discrete attributes cannot be queried efficiently by currently supported access methods.
In our previous work [13] we introduced a novel bitmap algorithm called `GenericRangeEval` for efficiently querying scientific data. We evaluated our approach based primarily on uniformly distributed and independent data. In this paper we analyse the behaviour of our bitmap index algorithm against various queries based on different data distributions.
We have implemented an improved version of one of the most cited bitmap compression algorithms called `Byte Aligned Bitmap Compression` and adapted it to our bitmap indices. To prove the efficiency of our access method, we carried out high-dimensional queries against real data taken from two different scientific applications, namely High Energy Physics and Astronomy. The results clearly show that depending on the underlying data distribution and the query access patterns, our proposed bitmap indices can significantly improve the response time of high-dimensional queries when compared to conventional access methods.

1 Introduction

Over the last three decades many different index data structures were proposed to optimise the access to database management systems. Some of these are optimised for one-dimensional queries such as the B+tree whereas others are optimised for multi-dimensional queries such as the Pyramid-tree [3] or bitmap indices [8]. Recently, bitmap indices have gained wide acceptance in data warehouse applications and are an efficient access method for evaluating complex, multi-dimensional ad-hoc queries against read-only data.

The main trend in bitmap index research focuses on typical business applications based on discrete attribute values. However, scientific data that is

R. Cicchetti et al. (Eds.): DEXA 2002, LNCS 2453, pp. 881–890, 2002.

mostly characterised by non-discrete attributes cannot be queried efficiently by currently supported access methods.

In our previous work we introduced a novel bitmap algorithm called `GenericRangeEval` [13]. In addition, we proposed a cost model for predicting the performance of bitmap indices for scientific data and based our analysis primarily on uniformly distributed and independent data. In this paper we analyse the query performance of our bitmap indices based on different data distributions. We have implemented an improved version of one of the most cited bitmap compression algorithms called `Byte Aligned Bitmap Compression` and compare the performance to uncompressed bitmap indices. The main contribution of the paper is to demonstrate that bitmap indices can significantly improve the performance of high-dimensional queries against real data from different scientific disciplines.

The paper is organised as follows. In Section 2 we briefly review the related work on conventional bitmap indices and in Section 3 we discuss bitmap indices for scientific data. Section 4 is dedicated to an experimental evaluation of our bitmap compression algorithm. In Section 5 we present our results of applying bitmap indices to High Energy Physics and Astronomy. Conclusions and future work are given in Section 6.

2 Related Work

The simplest form of bitmap indices called *equality encoding* [8,4] encodes each distinct attribute value as one bitmap (or bit slice). This encoding technique is optimised for so-called *exact-match queries* [12] of the form $Q_e : v = a_i$. [4,5] proposed *range encoding* and *interval encoding* which are optimised for *one-sided range queries* $Q_{1r} : v_1 \; op \; a_i$ where $op \in \{<, \leq, >, \geq\}$ and *two-sided range queries* $Q_{2r} : v_1 \; op \; a_i \; op \; v_2$ respectively. *Interval encoding* is the most storage efficient encoding technique since it requires only half of the number of bitmaps when compared to *equality encoding* or *range encoding.*

[16] represented attribute values in binary form that yields indices with only $\lceil log_2 |A| \rceil$ bitmaps, where $|A|$ is the attribute cardinality. The advantage of this encoding scheme is that the storage overhead is even smaller than for *interval encoding*. However, query processing is in most cases more efficient with *interval encoding* since in the worst case only two bitmaps need to be read whereas binary encoding always forces all bitmaps to be read.

One of the main problems of bitmap indices is the large space overhead for high cardinality attributes. Thus, [19] proposed *range-based* indices. In this approach a bitmap is used to present an attribute range rather than a distinct attribute value. However, a detailed analysis and a possible solution to the problem of the additional overhead for retrieving data from disk ("sieving out" the matching attribute values), was still left an open issue.

Another possibility to overcome the storage overhead for high cardinality attributes is to compress the bitmaps. Various bitmap compression algorithms are discussed in [1,6,2,18].

3 Bitmap Indices for Scientific Data

3.1 Bitmap Evaluation Algorithm

Conventional bitmap indices encode each distinct attribute value with one bit slice. However, for non-discrete attribute values, attribute ranges rather than attribute values are encoded [9,12]. In our previous work we introduced a novel bitmap evaluation algorithm called `GenericRangeEval` [13]. An extended version can be found in [15]. Since we base all our analyses throughout this paper on this algorithm, we briefly review the main characteristics and outline the *candidate check problem.*

Assume a conventional range encoded bitmap index [4] with 6 physical bins which represents an attribute with cardinality 7. In our case, 7 attribute ranges are represented. Assuming that our encoded search space is in the range of [0;140), each bin represents a range that is a multiple of 20, as depicted in Figure 1.

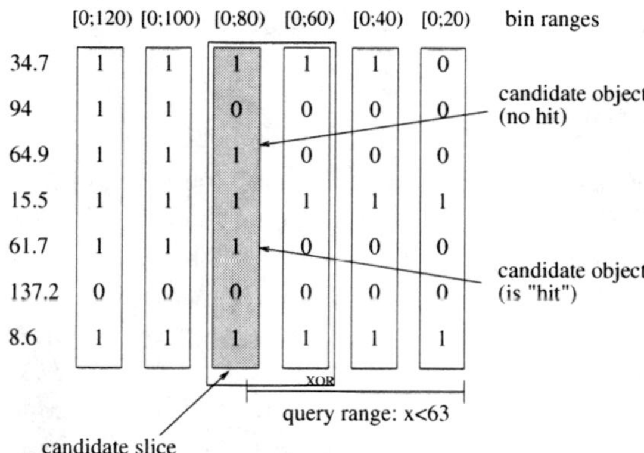

Fig. 1. One-sided range query on a range encoded bitmap index. The query $x < 63$ is evaluated via `GenericRangeEval`.

When we issue the following query $x < 63$, the preliminary foundset would be bin 3 (high-lighted in grey). Since this bin represents values in the range of [0;80), the foundset contains not only so-called *hits* (values 34.7, 15.5 and 8.6) but also *candidates* (values 64.9 and 61.7) that need to be checked against the query constraint. Candidates are all those attribute values in the current bin B_i that are not represented in bin B_{i-1}. We assume that the first bin is denoted by B_0. By XOR-ing B_i with B_{i-1} (see Figure 1) we yield two candidate objects with the values 64.9 and 61.7. These candidate objects need to be checked against the query constraint $x < 63$. Finally, the candidate object with the value 64.9 needs to be discarded since it does not fulfill the query constraint.

In this simple example we only outlined the behaviour of `GenericRangeEval` in a one-dimensional search space. For a detailed discussion about the behaviour in a multi-dimensional search space, we refer to [15].

3.2 Binning Strategies

An important tuning parameter of the bitmap indices for scientific data is the binning. In particular, we can distinguish between *equi-width* and *equi-depth* bins.

With *equi-width* bins, each bin has the same width and thus the distribution of the data values is also reflected in the number of entries for each bin. On the other hand, *equi-depth* binning guarantees that each bin has the same number of entries. Both binning strategies have advantages and disadvantages.

In short, the binning strategy depends on two factors, namely the *data distribution* and the *query access patterns* (or the query distribution). Equi-depth binning guarantees nearly constant access time for all kind of queries independent of the data distribution. One would chose this kind of binning when no query access patterns are available.

Since equi-width bins reflect the data distribution, this kind of binning is preferable if the query access patterns are such that those bins queried most have the least number of entries. Optimal binning strategies are discussed in [7].

4 Bitmap Compression

One of the disadvantages of bitmap indices for high cardinality attributes is the large space complexity, i.e. the high storage overhead for keeping a large number of bins persistently on disk. One way to reduce the space complexity is to compress the index. However, an important requirement for a bitmap compression algorithm is not only to have a good compression ratio but also to show good performance for the logical operations between the bit slices.

In the following section we discuss the impact of bitmap compression on range encoded bitmap indices based on `GenericRangeEval`. Together with Theodore Johnson from AT&T Labs-Research we implemented an improved version [6] of the original Byte-Aligned Bitmap Compression (BBC) algorithm by [1]. In addition, we also implemented the Boolean operations for two-sided BBC which was still left as an open issue in [6] due to the complexity of the algorithm.

We will now analyse the performance of compressed bitmap indices based on data following a typical exponential distribution of the form e^x (see Figure 2 a). We have chosen this kind of distribution since it is very common in High Energy Physics applications (see Section 5.1) which we mainly use for verifying our results. Our benchmark operates on 10^6 objects with 25 attributes (dimensions). Each range encoded bitmap index consists of 100 equi-width bins per indexed attribute. The benchmark was carried out on a Pentium II 400 under Linux Red Hat 6.1. The bitmap index is implemented with especially developed, persistent data structures on top of Objectivity/DB [14].

In Figure 2 b) we can see the compression ratio for each bin using two-sided Byte-Aligned Bitmap Compression (BBC2). We can observe that especially bins on the right side, i.e. bins with a high ordinal number, show good compressibility whereas bins with a low ordinal number show poor compressibility. The reason for the good compressibility is that due to the cumulative effect of range encoding [15], the bins with a high ordinal number have most of the bits set to 1. Similarily, bins with a low ordinal number have most of the bits set to 0 and can thus also be compressed. However, the compression ratio highly depends on the underlying data distribution.

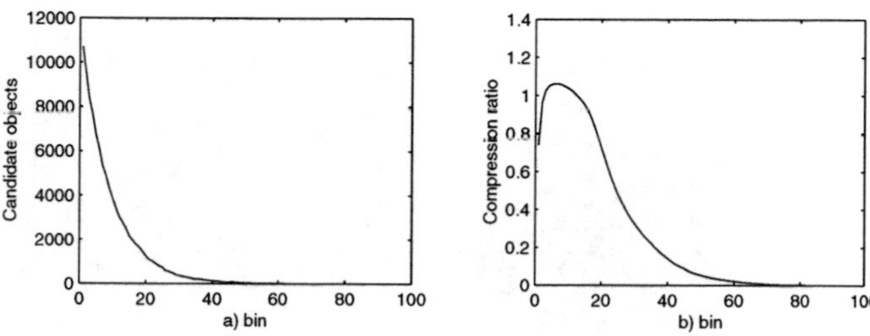

Fig. 2. Range encoded bitmap index based on data following an exponential distribution.

In the following we will compare the query response time of the compressed bitmap index (BBC2) with the response time of the uncompressed (verbatim) bitmap index. In Figure 3 a) and c) we plotted the query response time for the index I/O, i.e. not including the I/O operations for the candidate check. The graphs show the response times for one-sided 10-dimensional and 25-dimensional queries with various *query boundaries* ranging from bin 0 to bin 100. Let us explain this with an example.

Assume, for instance, an exponential distribution with values in the range of [0;10) and a bitmap index with 100 equi-width bins (as depicted in Figure 3). Thus, the boundary of the query $a_1 < 5$ is bin 50.

To sum up our results of Figures 3 a) and c), in the best case the compressed bitmap index is a factor of two faster than the verbatim bitmap index whereas in the worst case the compressed bitmap index is about a factor of two slower than the verbatim one. As we can see, the compressed bitmaps are faster for queries with high bin boundaries, i.e. for bins which show good compressibility. Thus, reading the compressed bit slice requires a smaller number of page I/Os. In addition, the logical operations can be performed faster when compared with verbatim bit slices. The total query response time, including the I/O operations for the candidate check, are given in Figures 3 b) and d).

Finally, we carried out the same benchmarks on a more powerful machine called "tier2" with higher CPU and disk I/O rates. The results are summarised in Figure 4. We can observe that the impact of bitmap compression yields only a slight performance improvement for queries with high bin boundaries when compared to the verbatim bitmap index. However, as we expect that in the

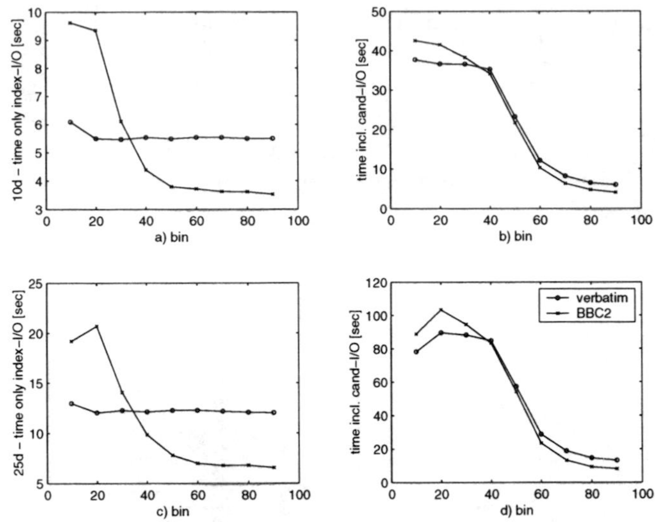

Fig. 3. Response time for verbatim vs. compressed bitmap indices.

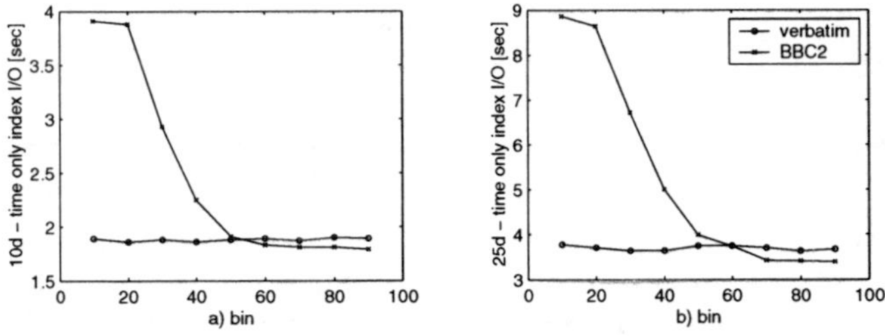

Fig. 4. Response time for verbatim vs. compressed bitmap indices on "tier2".

future the CPU speed will increase faster than the I/O rate, the performance improvement due to bitmap compression will be even more significant.

5 Applications

5.1 High Energy Physics

We will now evaluate the performance of the bitmap index with queries against real data taken from High Energy Physics. The data consists of 1,401,020 objects with 37 attributes each. The size of this data is 262 MB.

Similar to our previous benchmark, we created a bitmap index for each attribute consisting of 100 equi-width bins. The size of the whole bitmap index for all attributes is 790 MB. Out of these 37 attributes we have chosen 10 attributes which we study more carefully. The distributions of some of these attribute values are reflected by the distribution of the bins (see Figure 5).

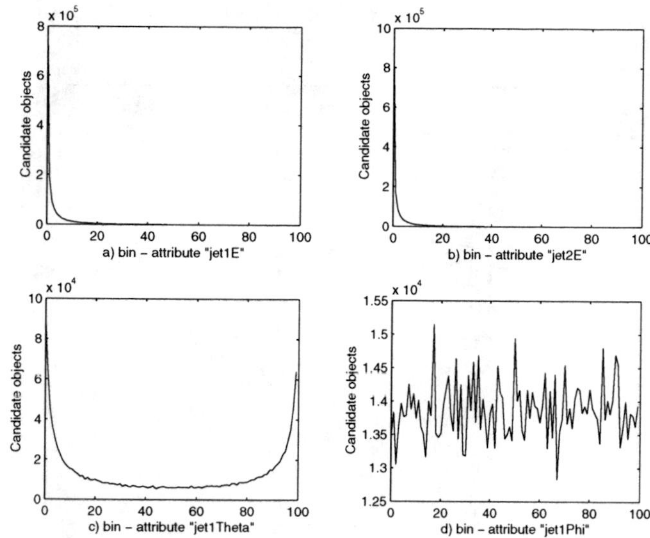

Fig. 5. Effect of equi-width binning for the attributes `jet1E`, `jet2E`, `jet1Theta` and `jet1Phi`.

All benchmarks are carried out on a machine with the following configuration: Dual 933 MHz Pentium III Linux server, 900 MB RAM, using a 600 GB 3ware RAID 0 array. Note, that currently all the data fits in main memory but in a few years the data of the physics experiments will be up to one Terabyte and thus will most likely not fit into main memory any more. However, for all our benchmarks we assured that the disk cache was trashed, i.e. the queries were run against a cold cache.

Based on some previous studies of access patterns in High Energy Physics [15], we have chosen a set of 13 example queries over one to ten dimensions. Due to space restrictions we only list one query and refer to [15] for more details:

```
Q8: Bitmaps ``jet1E > 1000 && jet2E > 1000 && part1E > 1000 &&
jet1Phi > 0 && part1Phi > 0''
```

Table 1 shows the response time for each of the 13 queries over various dimensions. Similar to [3], we also compare the query response time to the sequential scan. The results show that the bitmap index shows better performance than the sequential scan for high-dimensional queries. It is important to note that with a higher number of bit slices and with higher-dimensional queries, the performance improvement can be even more significant.

5.2 Astronomy

In this sub-section we will summarise the experience we gained when we evaluated the performance of bitmap indices for typical Astronomy queries of the

Table 1. Response time for 13 multi-dimensional sample queries - bitmap index vs. sequential scan.

Query	#dims	time [sec]	time seq. scan [sec]
Q1	1	6.9	3.6
Q2	1	5.8	3.6
Q3	2	6.3	5.5
Q4	3	6.6	8.0
Q5	4	6.8	10.1
Q6	4	6.8	10.1
Q7	4	6.8	10.1
Q8	5	7.0	12.3
Q9	5	15.1	12.3
Q10	5	7.0	12.3
Q11	8	20.6	20.6
Q12	10	20.8	23.2
Q13	10	13.9	23.2

Sloan Digital Sky Survey (SDSS) database [10]. All SDSS data is stored in Objectivity/DB and can be retrieved by a special SQL-like query interface developed by the astronomers. Our main challenge was to show that bitmap indices can even further improve the already optimised astronomy queries against the database [11].

The astronomy data consists of 6,182,527 objects with 65 attributes each. The total size is 1.9 GB. We created 65 bitmap indices with 100 equi-width bins each. The total size of all indices is 5.8 GB.

We evaluated the performance of the bitmap index against queries taken from the SDSS query server logs. In particular, the logs contained 357 queries of 41 different users; 49 out of these queries are against the data set called "sxGalaxy" which we studied in more detail. We took three representative range queries and compared the performance of the Sloan Sky Server against the performance of the bitmap index. One typical query looks as follows:

```
SELECT g,r,i FROM sxGalaxy
WHERE ((RA() between 180 and 185) && (DEC() between 1. and 1.2)
&& (r between 10 and 18) && (i between 10 and 18)
&& (g between 10 and 18))
```

Our results show a significant performance improvement of a factor of 10 to 20 when compared to the current implementation. The reason for the signifcant performance improvement is as follows. First, we clustered the data attribute-wise [14] rather than object-wise (as you would do for typical object oriented database management systems). Second, the queries against the highly specialised bitmap indices caused less page I/O than the current indices of SDSS. We have thus successfully demonstrated that with object oriented database management systems we can also get significant improvements with access methods and clustering techniques which are mainly used in relational database management systems. For further details of this study we again refer to [15].

6 Conclusions

In this paper we evaluated the performance of our bitmap index called `GenericRangeEval` against various queries based on different data distributions. We have implemented an extended version of one of the most cited bitmap compression algorithms called `Byte-Aligned Bitmap Compresion` and adopted it for our bitmap indices in order to cope with typical scientific data. We have demonstrated that the query response times of compressed bitmap indices can be significantly lower than for uncompressed bitmap indices. However, the speedup factor strongly depends on the ratio of CPU versus I/O speed. Since the CPU speed is expected to increase faster than the I/O rate, the performance improvements gained with bitmap compression will be even more significant in the future.

To prove the efficiency of our access method, we analysed the performance of bitmap indices for high-dimensional queries from two different scientific applications, namely High Energy Physics and Astronomy. In both cases the results clearly show that bitmap indices can lead to significant performance improvements when compared to conventional access methods. However, the performance improvement strongly depends on the underlying data distribution and the query access patterns. As part of our future work we will continue our investigation on a cost model for predicting the performance of bitmap indices based on various data distributions, in order to automate the choice between conventional access methods and bitmap indices for high-dimensional queries.

Acknowledgments

Our special thanks go to Erich Schikuta who always showed great enthusiasm during the write-up of this paper. We would also like to thank Jim Gray for the very fruitful discussions concerning the Astronomy data.

References

1. G. Antoshenkov, Byte-Aligned Bitmap Compression, *Technical Report, Oracle Corp.*, 1994.
2. S. Amer-Yahia, T. Johnson, Optimizing Queries On Compressed Bitmaps, *Proceedings of 26th International Conference on Very Large Data Bases*, Cairo, Egypt, Sept. 2000, Morgan Kaufmann.
3. S. Berchtold, C. Boehm, H.-P. Kriegel, The Pyramid-Tree: Breaking the Curse of D imensionality, SIGMOD 1998, *Proceedings ACM SIGMOD International Conference on Management of Data*, Seattle, Washington, USA, June 1998.
4. C. Chan, Y.E. Ioannidis, Bitmap Index Design and Evaluation, *In Proceedings ACM SIGMOD International Conference on Management of Data*, Seattle, Washington, USA, June 1998.

5. C. Chan, Y.E. Ioannidis, An Efficient Bitmap Encoding Scheme for Selection Queries, *Proceedings ACM SIGMOD International Conference on Management of Data*, Philadephia, Pennsylvania, USA, June 1999.
6. T. Johnson, Performance Measurements of Compressed Bitmap Indices, *Proceedings of 25th International Conference on Very Large Data Bases*, Edinburgh, Scotland, UK, September 1999, Morgan Kaufmann.
7. N. Koudas, Space Efficient Bitmap Indexing, *International Conference on Information and Knowledge Management*, McLean, VA, USA, November 2000.
8. P. O'Neil, D. Quass, Improved Query Performance with Variant Indexes, *Proceedings ACM SIGMOD International Conference on Management of Data*, Tucson, Arizona, USA, May 1997.
9. A. Shoshani, L.M. Bernardo, H. Nordberg, D. Rotem, A. Sim, Multidimensional Indexing and Query Coordination for Tertiary Storage Management, *11th International Conference on Scientific and Statistical Database Management*, Cleveland, Ohio, USA, July 1999.
10. Sloan Digital Sky Survey, *http://www.sdss.org*
11. A.Szalay, P. Kunszt, A. Thakar, J. Gray, D. Slutz, Designing and Mining Multi-Terabyte Astronomy Archives: The Sloan Digital Sky Survey, *Proceedings ACM SIGMOD International Conference on Management of Data*, Philadephia, Pennsylvania, USA, June 1999.
12. K. Stockinger, D. Duellmann, W. Hoschek, E. Schikuta. Improving the Performance of High Energy Physics Analysis through Bitmap Indices. *International Conference on Database and Expert Systems Applications*, London - Greenwich, UK, Sept. 2000. Springer-Verlag.
13. K. Stockinger, Design and Implementation of Bitmap Indices for Scientific Data, *International Database Engineering & Applications Symposium*, Grenoble, France, July 2001, IEEE Computer Society Press.
14. K. Stockinger, Performance Analysis of Generic vs. Sliced Tags in HepODBMS, *International Conference on Computing in High Energy and Nuclear Physics*, Beijing, China, September, 2001.
15. K. Stockinger, Multi-Dimensional Bitmap Indices for Optimising Data Access within Object Oriented Databases at CERN, *Ph.D. Thesis*, University of Vienna, Austria, November 2001.
16. M. Wu, A.P. Buchmann, Encoded Bitmap Indexing for Data Warehouses, *Proceedings of the Fourteenth International Conference on Data Engineering*, Orlando, Florida, USA, February 1998.
17. M. Wu, Query Optimization for Selections Using Bitmaps, *SIGMOD 1999, Proceedings ACM SIGMOD International Conference on Management of Data*, Philadephia, Pennsylvania, USA, June 1999.
18. K. Wu, E. J. Otoo, A. Shoshani, A Performance Comparison of Bitmap Indexes, *International Conference on Information and Knowledge Management*, Atlanta, Georgia, USA, November, 2001.
19. K. Wu, P.S. Yu, Range-Based Bitmap Indexing for High-Cardinality Attributes with Skew, *Technical Report, IBM Watson Research Center*, May 1996.

A Method of Improving Feature Vector for Web Pages Reflecting the Contents of Their Out-Linked Pages

Kazunari Sugiyama[1], Kenji Hatano[1],
Masatoshi Yoshikawa[1,2], and Shunsuke Uemura[1]

[1] Graduate School of Information Science, Nara Institute of Science and Technology,
8916-5 Takayama, Ikoma, Nara 630-0101, Japan
[2] Information Technology Center, Nagoya University,
Furo-cho, Chikusa-ku, Nagoya, Aichi 464-8601, Japan
{kazuna-s, hatano, yosikawa, uemura}@is.aist-nara.ac.jp

Abstract. TF-IDF schemes are popular for generating the feature vectors of documents. These schemes are proposed for characterizing one document. Therefore, in order to characterize Web pages using tf-idf schemes, the feature vectors of the Web pages should be reflected by the contents of Web pages linked with other pages via hyperlinks. In this paper, we propose three methods of generating feature vectors for linked documents such as Web pages. Moreover, in order to verify the effectiveness of our proposed methods, we compare our methods with current search engines and confirm their retrieval accuracy using recall precision curves.

1 Introduction

Many people use the World Wide Web (WWW) as a resource to obtain a variety of information. The amount of information on the Web has been increasing with the development of computer networks; therefore, it becomes more difficult to find valuable information amidst a large amount of information. Under these circumstances, search engines are essential tools to find information on the Web. These search engines are classified into three types: the directory type such as Yahoo![1], the robot-type such as Google[2], and meta-search engines which return the search results of some search engines. When users use the directory-type search engines, even if they can search information in a directory entering a keyword, they often cannot find information they really want. Moreover, even if the directories are meticulously constructed and Web pages are precisely classified, which directory the Web page belongs to is incomprehensible to users because not users but domain analysts determine the criterion of classification of Web pages. As a result, users encounter difficulty in finding information when using directory-type search engines. On the other hand, when users employ a robot-type search engine, the users cannot easily find valuable information because of the large amount of search results unless the users convey exact keywords to the search engines. Current robot-type search engines adopt a method for Web document retrieval such as PageRank [1] and HITS(Hypertext Induced Topic Search) [2] algorithm, which utilize the hyperlink structure of Web pages.

[1] http://www.yahoo.com/
[2] http://www.google.com/

R. Cicchetti et al. (Eds.): DEXA 2002, LNCS 2453, pp. 891–901, 2002.

In these algorithms, each hyperlink has a weight, and the terms included in a Web page is weighted based on the weight of the hyperlinks. In our opinion, however, the Web pages should be weighted by not only the weights of hyperlinks but also the contents of Web pages linked from the root Web page. Therefore, the robot-type search engines that apply these algorithms are inconvenient for users since they return the Web pages that is not relevant to queries users enter. In this paper, we propose three methods of generating a feature vector for Web pages. In our proposed methods, a feature vector of a Web page is reflected on the contents of Web pages which are linked from and are similar to the root Web page. In order to realize these processes, our prototype system analyzes the hyperlink structure of collected Web pages and classifies them using the K-means algorithm [3]. Moreover, we compare our methods with a current search engine that apply the PageRank algorithm and confirm our methods' retrieval accuracy using recall precision curves. In our experiments, we do not utilize an algorithm that reflects the weight of a hyperlink; but utilize only the algorithm that reflects the content of Web pages linked from the root Web page.

2 Related Work

A hyperlink structure is one of the features of Web pages because users can navigate the Web pages on the WWW using hyperlinks. In consideration of the way users employ the Web, similar Web pages are connected to each other by hyperlinks. Many studies in information retrieval have focused on the hyperlink structure of Web pages. In this section, we describe the searching methods using the hyperlink structure of Web pages.

We consider that the current techniques for retrieving Web documents using hyperlink structure can be classified into the following two categories:

- The retrieval technique based on the concept of "information unit."
- The retrieval technique based on the qualities of Web pages.

In regard to the first category, Tajima et al. [4] proposed the concept of "cut" to the documents on network environments such as E-mail, Netnews, and the WWW. The "cut" is composed of more than one document that has similar content and is used as the unit of document retrieval. Following this research, many researchers have proposed retrieval techniques based on the same concept, analyzing the hyperlink structure of the WWW and determining semantics of Web pages [5,6]. These information retrieval systems find the minimal sub-structures of the WWW hyperlink structure including all keywords users enter as unit of retrieval results and calculate their scores in order to rank them. However, the analysis of hyperlink structure and discovering the semantics of Web pages is time-consuming, and though they can find the minimal sub-structures exactly, the retrieval systems often find minimal sub-structures irrelevant to users' query.

Following these studies, a lot of studies have been performed based on the quality of the Web documents analyzing hyperlink structure. One of the most famous studies focuses on HITS algorithm [2]. The basic idea of HITS is that Web documents are classified into "authority" and "hub" pages, and if the degree of authority of a document has high value, the weight of terms in the document is high because the document is informative enough for query. Moreover, PageRank algorithm is applied to the search engine "Google." The PageRank algorithm depends on the vast hyperlink structure of WWW as an indicator of an individual Web document's value, and expresses the quality of a Web document in terms of the probability of following linked pages and that of navigating to irrelevant documents from a Web document of original interest [1]. These algorithms use only the hyperlink structure of the WWW to calculate the quality of Web documents. If the Web documents contain one specific topic as Amento et al. [7] have reported, we may use only the Web's hyperlink structure. However, we propose the use of not only hyperlink structure but also the general contents of each Web document in order to characterize it, since actual Web documents contain a variety of content. Chakrabarti et al. [8,9] have improved the HITS algorithm paying attention to this point. They have proposed a method considering the contents of Web documents extracted by both hyperlink structure and document structure. However, it is difficult to determine the extracted partial structure of Web documents, and the retrieval accuracy of their approach fluctuates in terms of the extraction method of the partial structure.

Considering these points, we propose a simple method of improving the feature vectors of Web pages. The feature vector of a Web page should reflect the contents of its out-linked pages because the contents of a Web page are similar to those of out-linked Web pages. When we reflect the contents of out-linked Web pages on the root Web page, we classify the out-linked pages using the K-means algorithm so that our proposed method performs as an adaptive retrieval algorithm for Web pages. In our method, it is expected we can extract keywords of a Web page more effective, and can obtain higher retrieval accuracy because of exploiting linked pages from a root Web page.

3 Proposed Method

In this section, we explain our methods of improving the feature vectors of a Web page. The basic idea is that we improve the feature vectors of Web pages generated by tf-idf schemes in advance by utilizing the feature vectors of its out-linked pages, which are generated likewise by tf-idf schemes. The pages out-linked from a certain Web page can be recognized because the contents that exist near the root Web page also exist near its linked Web pages. From now on, we refer to the Web page whose feature vectors we intend to improve as the "root page"; let this "root page" be p_r. Then, a Web page which exists in $i-$th hierarchy from p_r has N_i pages, $p_{i1}, p_{i2} \cdots, p_{iN_i}$. Though the hierarchy of numbers from p_r, can establish some paths; we define i as the number of links of the shortest path. Moreover, we denote the feature vector $\boldsymbol{w}^{p_r}$ of the root page p_r as follows:

$$\boldsymbol{w}^{p_r} = (w_{t_1}^{p_r}, w_{t_2}^{p_r}, \cdots, w_{t_m}^{p_r}), \tag{1}$$

where the element $w_{t_k}^{p_r}$ of $\boldsymbol{w}^{p_r}$ is defined as follows:

$$w_{t_k}^{p_r} = \frac{tf(t_k, p_r)}{\sum_{k=1}^{m} tf(t_k, p_r)} \cdot \log \frac{N_{web}}{df(t_k)}, \quad (k = 1, 2, \cdots, m) \tag{2}$$

where $tf(t_k, p_r)$ is the frequency of term t_k in root page p_r, N_{web} is total number of collected Web pages, and $df(t_k)$ is the number of Web pages in which term t_k appears.

From now on, we use $\boldsymbol{w}^{p_r}$ to indicate "initial feature vector". Then, we denote the improved feature vector $\boldsymbol{w}'^{p_r}$ as follows:

$$\boldsymbol{w}'^{p_r} = (w'^{p_r}_{t_1}, w'^{p_r}_{t_2}, \cdots, w'^{p_r}_{t_m}).$$

From now on, we use $\boldsymbol{w}'^{p_r}$ to indicate "improved feature vector". We propose the following three methods to improve the "initial feature vector" generated by tf-idf schmes:

1. The method of reflecting each linked page into a root page (**Method I**),
2. The method of reflecting centroid vectors of a group of out-linked Web pages from a root page (**Method II**),
3. The method of reflecting centroid vectors of a group of Web pages constructed by each i-th hierarchy from a root page (**Method III**).

3.1 Method I

This method reflects the contents of each page out-linked from root page. This method is based on the ideas that there are Web pages which are similar to the contents of pages out-linked from p_r and some pages which are similar to p_r exist closely linked pages, others may exist in distant out-linked pages. Using the ideas, we reflect the distance between p_r and its out-linked pages into each element of $\boldsymbol{w}^{p_r}$. For example, Figure 1 shows that $\boldsymbol{w}'^{p_r}$ is generated by reflecting the contents of all Web pages which exist in the second hierarchy from root page p_r. In this method, each element $w'^{p_r}_{t_k}$ of $\boldsymbol{w}'^{p_r}$ is defined as follows:

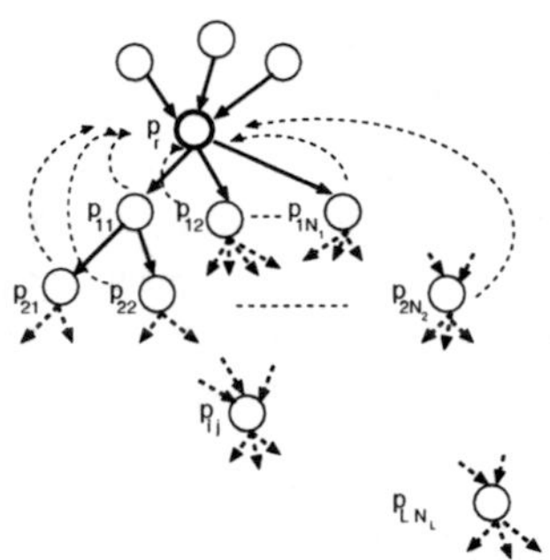

Fig. 1. The improvement of feature vectors as performed by method I.

$$w'^{p_r}_{t_k} = w^{p_r}_{t_k} + \sum_{i=1}^{L}\sum_{j=1}^{N_i} \frac{1}{dis(\boldsymbol{w}^{p_r}, \boldsymbol{w}^{p_{ij}})} w^{p_{ij}}_{t_k}. \tag{3}$$

Equation (3) shows that the product of weight $w^{p_{ij}}_{t_k}$ of term t_k in out-linked page p_{ij} and the reciprocal number of the distance between $\boldsymbol{w}^{p_r}$ and $\boldsymbol{w}^{p_{ij}}$, $dis(\boldsymbol{w}^{p_r}, \boldsymbol{w}^{p_{ij}})$ in vector space is added to weight $w^{p_r}_{t_k}$ of term t_k $\boldsymbol{w}^{p_r}$ calculated by equation (2), with regard to all out-linked pages which exist in the L-th hierarchy from p_r. We define $dis(\boldsymbol{w}^{p_r}, \boldsymbol{w}^{p_{ij}})$ as follows:

$$dis(\boldsymbol{w}^{p_r}, \boldsymbol{w}^{p_{ij}}) = \sqrt{\sum_{k=1}^{m}(w^{p_r}_{t_k} - w^{p_{ij}}_{t_k})^2}.$$

3.2 Method II

In this method, we cluster the set of all Web pages which exist up to i-th hierarchy from p_r, and generate $\boldsymbol{w}'^{p_r}$ by reflecting its centroid vectors on the $\boldsymbol{w}^{p_r}$ of root page

p_r. This method is based on the idea that when we observe the linked pages from p_r, the out-linked pages can be classified into certain topics. Using this idea, we reflect the distance between $\boldsymbol{w}^{p_r}$ and the centroid vector of the cluster on each element $w_{t_k}^{p_r}$ of $\boldsymbol{w}^{p_r}$. In other words, we make a group of Web pages, G_i as defined by equation (4),

$$\begin{aligned} G_i = \{ & p_{11}, p_{12}, \cdots, p_{1N_1}, \\ & p_{21}, p_{22}, \cdots, p_{1N_2}, \\ & p_{i1}, p_{i2}, \cdots, p_{iN_i}\}, \end{aligned} \tag{4}$$

and make K clusters in G_i by means of the K-means algorithm [3]. We make $\boldsymbol{w}'^{p_r}$ by reflecting the distance between each centroid vector, $\boldsymbol{w}^{g_c}(c = 1, 2, \cdots, K)$ and $\boldsymbol{w}^{p_r}$. For instance, Figure 2 shows that we make G_2, a group of Web pages which exist up to two links away from p_r, and make an improved feature vector by reflecting the K centroid vectors constructed by clustering G_2 on $\boldsymbol{w}^{p_r}$. In this method, each element $w_{t_k}'^{p_r}$ of $\boldsymbol{w}'^{p_r}$ is defined as follows:

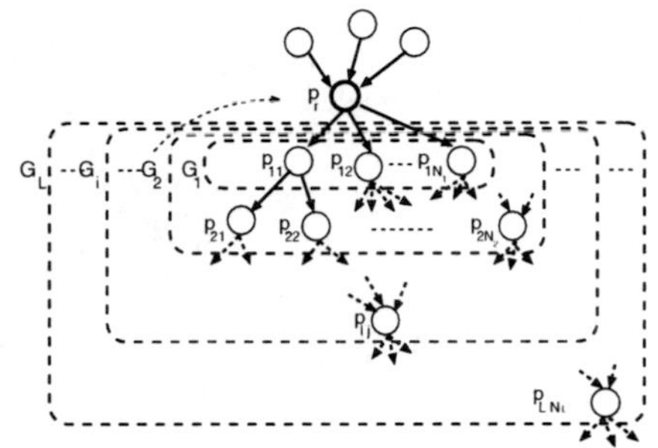

Fig. 2. The improvement of feature vectors as performed by method II.

$$w_{t_k}'^{p_r} = w_{t_k}^{p_r} + \sum_{c=1}^{K} \frac{1}{dis(\boldsymbol{w}^{p_r}, \boldsymbol{w}^{g_c})} w_{t_k}^{g_c}. \tag{5}$$

Equation(5) shows that the product of element $w_{t_k}^{g_c}$ of the centroid vector generated from the group of Web pages, and the reciprocal of the distance between $\boldsymbol{w}^{p_r}$, and $\boldsymbol{w}_c^{g}$, $dis(\boldsymbol{w}^{p_r}, \boldsymbol{w}^{g_c})$ is added to weight $w_{t_k}^{p_r}$ calculated by equation (2), with regard to the number of clusters, K. We define $dis(\boldsymbol{w}^{p_r}, \boldsymbol{w}^{g_c})$ as follows:

$$dis(\boldsymbol{w}^{p_r}, \boldsymbol{w}^{g_c}) = \sqrt{\sum_{k=1}^{m} (w_{t_k}^{p_r} - w_{t_k}^{p_{ij}})^2}.$$

3.3 Method III

In this method, we construct G_i, the group of Web pages which exist in each hierarchy linked from p_r, and generate $\boldsymbol{w}'^{p_r}$ by reflecting its centroid vector on $\boldsymbol{w}^{p_r}$. This method is based on the idea that the Web pages which exist in a certain hierarchy from p_r can be classified into certain topics. Using this idea, we reflect the distance between $\boldsymbol{w}^{p_r}$ and the centroid vector of a cluster on each element of the initial feature vector. In other words, we create a group of Web pages G_i as defined by equation (6),

$$G_i = \{p_{i1}, p_{i2}, \cdots, p_{iN_i}\}, \tag{6}$$

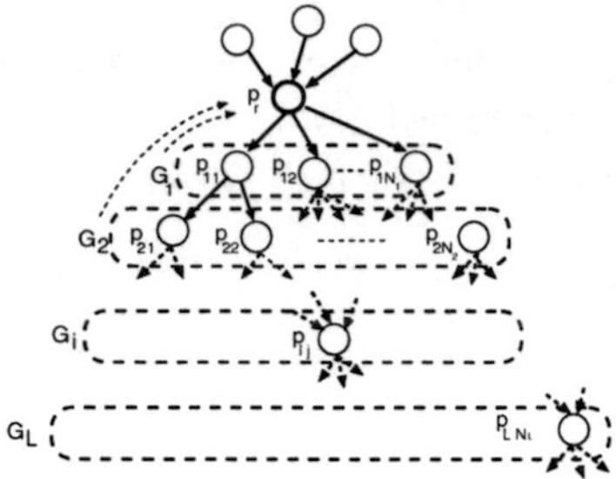

Fig. 3. The improvement of feature vectors as performed by method III.

and make K clusters in G_i by means of a K-means algorithm. We create an improved feature vector by reflecting the distance between each centroid vector $\boldsymbol{w}^{g_{ic}}(c = 1, 2, \cdots, K)$ and initial feature vector $\boldsymbol{w}^{p_r}$ of root page p_r. For instance, Figure.3 shows that we make a group of Web pages, G_1 and G_2, which exist in each hierarchy up to two links away from the root page p_r, and make an improved feature vector by reflecting the centroid vector constructed in each Web page group, G_1 and G_2, on $\boldsymbol{w}^{p_r}$. In this method, each element $w_{t_k}^{\prime p_r}$ of $\boldsymbol{w}^{\prime p_r}$ is defined as follows:

$$w_{t_k}^{\prime p_r} = w_{t_k}^{p_r} + \sum_{i=1}^{L} \sum_{c=1}^{K} \frac{1}{dis(\boldsymbol{w}^{p_r}, \boldsymbol{w}^{g_{ic}})} w_{t_k}^{g_{ic}}. \quad (7)$$

Equation (7) shows that the product of element $w_{t_k}^{g_{ic}}$ of the centroid vector, which is constructed from each group of Web pages constructed in each hierarchy up to i link away from p_r, and the reciprocal of the distance between $\boldsymbol{w}^{p_r}$ and $\boldsymbol{w}^{g_{ic}}$ in vector space, $dis(\boldsymbol{w}^{p_r}, \boldsymbol{w}^{g_{ic}})$ is added to weight $w_{t_k}^{p_r}$ of term t_k calculated by equation (2), with regard to all centroid vectors constructed in each hierarchy up to the L-th link away from p_r. We define $dis(\boldsymbol{w}^{p_r}, \boldsymbol{w}^{g_{ic}})$ as follows:

$$dis(\boldsymbol{w}^{p_r}, \boldsymbol{w}^{g_{ic}}) = \sqrt{\sum_{k=1}^{m} (w_{t_k}^{p_r} - w_{t_k}^{g_{ic}})^2}.$$

4 Experimental Results

We conducted the experiments in order to verify whether or not a term which has high value in the improved feature vector can be the keyword of a Web page (**Experiment I**), and to verify the precision of a search using an improved feature vector compared with the search results of an existing search engine (**Experiment II**). Our method described in section3is implemented using Perl on a desktop PC (CPU: AMD Athron 1.4GHz, Memory: 1GBytes, OS: Vine Linux2.1.5), and the experiments are conducted for 0.8GByte Web pages (about 250,000URLs).

4.1 Experiment I

We conduct the experiment to verify whether a keyword of the root Web page is extracted more precisely compared with tf-idf schemes. The procedure for this experiment is as follows:

1. We choose five terms beforehand as the correct keywords per Web page.
2. We calculate the cumulative rate of right answer which denote how many keywords are contained up to the top ten terms in the improved feature vector.

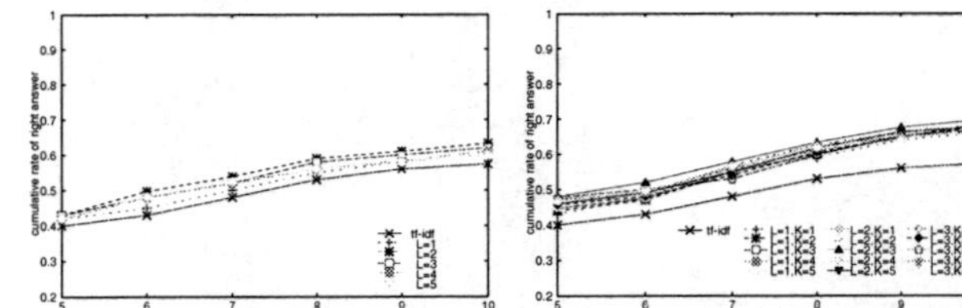

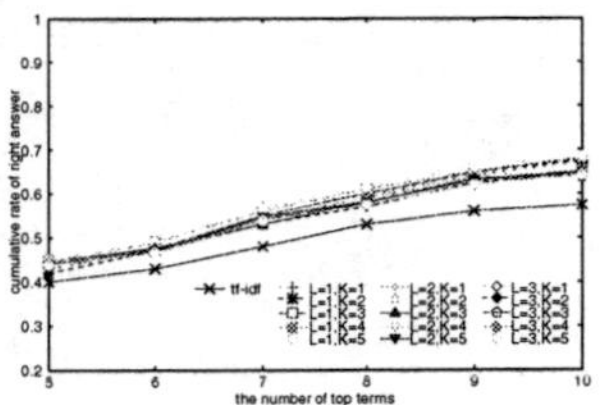

Fig. 4. Cumulative rate of right answer obtained by Method I.

Fig. 5. Cumulative rate of right answer obtained by Method II.

Fig. 6. Cumulative rate of right answer obtained by Method III.

Figures 4, 5, and 6 show the results obtained using proposed Methods I, II, III described in section3, respectively. Figure 4 shows the following characteristics of Method I:

- The keywords of a Web page are more exactly extracted by utilizing the contents of each Web page which exists up to $L = 2$, i.e., two links away from the p_r as compared with tf-idf schemes.
- The result of $L = 3$, i.e., in the case of reflecting the contents of a Web page three links away from p_r on its initial feature vector, is almost the same as the result of $L = 2$. Therefore, we found that, in Method I, an improved feature vector generated by urilizing Web pages at least two links away from p_r effectively extracted the keywords of the Web page.

Figure 5 shows the following characteristics of Method II:

- The result of $L = 2, K = 3$, i.e., in the case of generating an improved feature vector by exploiting the centroid vectors of three clusters constructed from a group of Web pages up to two links away from p_r, shows the most effective result in extracting the keywords of the Web page.

Finally, Figure 6 shows the following characteristic of Method III:

- The result of $L \geq 2$, i.e., in the case of generating improved feature vectors by exploiting the centroid vectors of clusters constructed from a group of Web pages which exists more than two links away from p_r, shows that it is less effective in extracting keywords of a Web page than $L = 1$, i.e., in the case of generating an improved feature vector by exploiting the centroid vector of clusters from a group of Web pages up to one link away from p_r, in extracting keywords of a Web page. In Method III, we cluster Web pages which exist in each hierarchy from p_r like Figure 3, so the continuity of contents between Web pages is lost. That is why we cannot obtain better results in the case of $L \geq 2$.

4.2 Experiment II

To compare our method with existing search engines, we conducted an experiment to verify whether an improved feature vector is effective as Web page index. Figure 7 shows an overview of our system. This system contains the following functions:

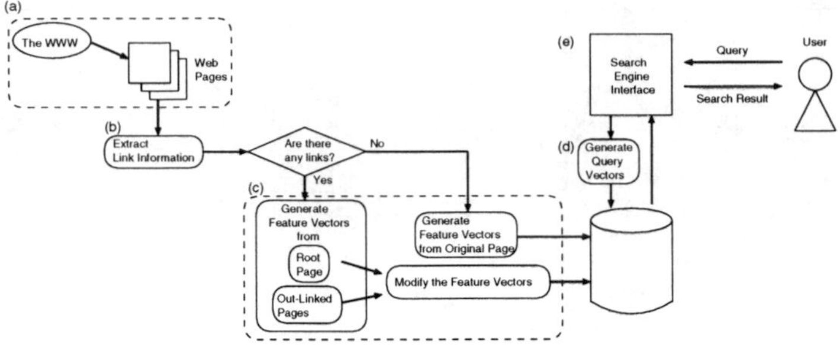

Fig. 7. Overview of our system.

(a) Collecting Web pages
This function collects Japanese Web pages by exploiting a Web crawler.

(b) Extracting link information
The link information of each collected Web pages are extracted. In this function, only forwarded links are extracted.

(c) Generating feature vectors of Web page
A feature vector of a Web page generated by tf-idf schemes is improved by exploiting our proposed method described in section 3.

(d) Generating query vector
We denote query vector $\boldsymbol{Q}$ as follows:

$$\boldsymbol{Q} = (q_{t_1}, q_{t_2}, \cdots, q_{t_m}), \tag{8}$$

where t_k is an index term, and the base of equation (8) is as same as that of equation (1). Each element q_{t_k} of equation (8) is defined as follows:

$$q_{t_k} = \left(0.5 + \frac{0.5 \cdot Qf(t_k)}{\sum_{k=1}^{m} Qf(t_k)}\right) \times \log \frac{N_{web}}{df(t_k)} \quad (k = 1, 2, \cdots, m), \tag{9}$$

where $Qf(t_k)$, N_{web}, and $df(t_k)$ is the number of index terms t_k, the total number of collected Web pages, and the number of Web pages in which the term t_k appears, respectively. As reported in [10], equation (9) is the element of a query vector which brings best search result.

(e) Search Engine interface
A user enters queries through this interface, and the system shows the search results to the user. This system calculates the similarity $sim(\boldsymbol{w}^p, \boldsymbol{Q})$ between feature vector $\boldsymbol{w}^p$ of Web page p and query vector $\boldsymbol{Q}$, and shows search results in descending order of $sim(\boldsymbol{w}_p, \boldsymbol{Q})$. The $sim(\boldsymbol{w}_p, \boldsymbol{Q})$ is defined as follows:

$$sim(\boldsymbol{w}^p, \boldsymbol{Q}) = \frac{\boldsymbol{w}^p \cdot \boldsymbol{Q}}{|\boldsymbol{w}^p| \cdot |\boldsymbol{Q}|}. \tag{10}$$

In our study, considering that Web pages have varied contents, we choose 14 Japanese terms as queries in order to cover a various contents of Web pages. We prepare ten relevance Web pages with regard to each query.

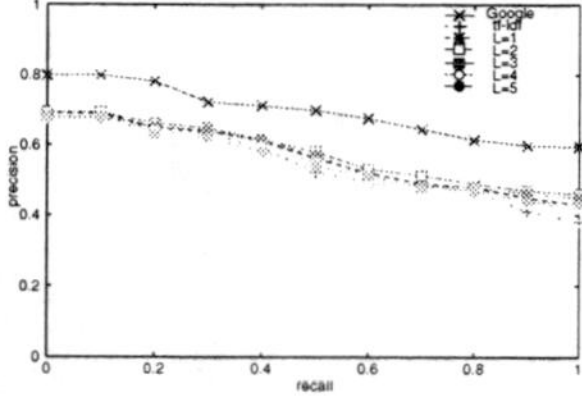

Fig. 8. Comparison of search accuracy obtained using Method I and that using an existing search engine.

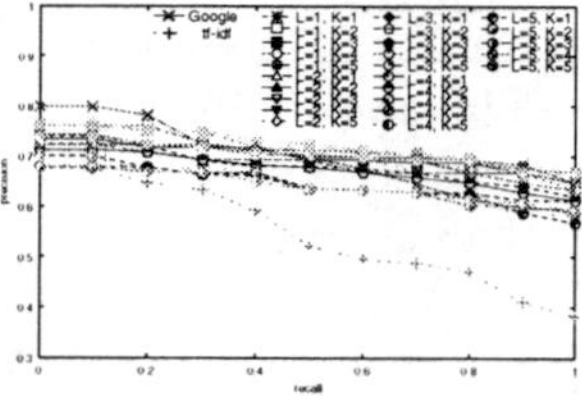

Fig. 9. Comparison of search accuracy obtained using Method II and that using an existing search engine.

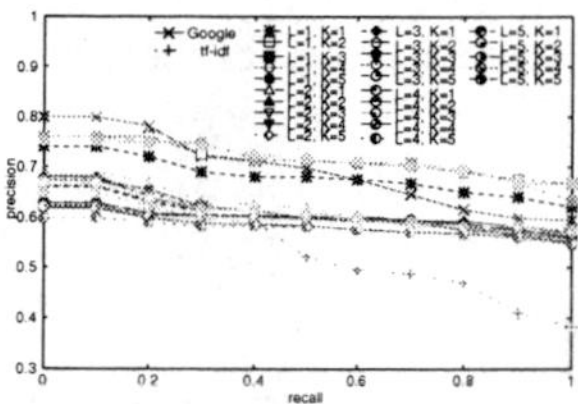

Fig. 10. Comparison of search accuracy obtained using Method III and that using an existing search engine.

We compare our method with the existing search engine Google[3], and evaluate retrieval accuracy using recall precision curves based on "precision at 11 standard recall levels" described in [11,12]. Figures 8, 9, and 10 show the results obtained by using the proposed Method I, II, and III described in section 3, respectively. Figure 8 shows the following fact with regard to Method I:

- The result of $L = 2, 3$, in the case of reflecting the contents of each Web page which exists two or three links away from root page p_r become better than $L = 1$, i.e., reflecting the content of each Web page which exists one link away from root page p_r.
- There is little difference between the result of $L = 2$ and that of $L = 3$.
- The result of $L \geq 4$ is worse than that of $L = 2, 3$.

In addition, we cannot obtain better retrieval accuracy than that of Google in exploiting the improved feature vector generated by Method I. Therefore, the Method I is not appropriate for creating an index for searching Web pages. Figure 9 shows the following characteristic of Method II:

- We can obtain higher retrieval accuracy at the point where recall is high than Google.
- The higher retrieval accuracy is obtained in the case of $L = 1, K = 3$, i.e. in the case of generating an improved feature vector by exploiting the centroid vector of three clusters constructed from a group of Web pages one link away from p_r, and $L = 2, K = 3$, i.e., in the case of generating an improved feature vector by exploiting the centroid vectors of three clusters constructed from a group of Web pages two links away from p_r. In particular, the result of $L = 2, K = 3$ shows that the contents of a Web page can be integrated up to two links away from p_r.

Moreover, we note that by using an improved feature vector, Web pages which correspond to the contents of a query can be ranked in an upper level of preference in comparison with Google which tends to rank many-linked Web pages with many links to other pages in an upper position. Finally, Figure 10 shows the following characteristic of Method III:

[3] http://www.google.com/intl/ja/

- The retrieval accuracy in the case of $L \geq 2$ is inferior to that of Method II. In Method III, Web pages are clustered in terms of their hierarchy from p_r as seen in Figure 3; thus, the continuity of the contents between Web pages is lost. This is why we cannot obtain better retrieval accuracy in the case of $L \geq 2$.

5 Concluding Remarks

We proposed three methods of generating feature vectors for Web pages. In our proposed methods, a feature vector of a Web page is reflected in the contents of out-linked Web pages that are similar to the root page. We also conducted experiments in order to verify the effectiveness of our proposed methods, obtaining the following results:

- We could extract appropriate index terms in the task of extracting the keywords of Web pages by using contents of their out-linked pages.
- We could obtain higher retrieval accuracy by improving feature vector of a root page exploiting feature vectors of Web pages two or three links away from the root page.

Our future work focuses on the following:

- In this paper, we use all the clusters generated from Web pages; however, we should select clusters which are more appropriate for generating feature vectors in order to obtain higher search accuracy.
- We have to verify the effectiveness of our method by conducting experiments using reference collections for Web pages.

References

1. S. Brin and L. Page. The anatomy of a large-scale hypertextual web search engine. In *In proc. of the 7th International World Wide Web Conference*, pages 107–117, 1998.
2. J. M. Kleinberg. Authoritative sources in a hyperlinked environment. In *In proc. of ACMSIAM Symposium on Discrete Algorithms*, 1998.
3. J. MacQueen. Some methods for classification and analysis of multivariate observations. In *Proc. of the 5th Berkeley Symposium on Mathmatical Statistics and Probability*, pages 281–297, 1967.
4. K. Tajima, Y. Mizuuchi, M. Kitagawa, and K. Tanaka. Cut as a querying unit for www, netnews, e-mail. In *Proc. of the 1998 ACM Hypertext Conference*, pages 235–244, 1998.
5. K. Tajima, K. Hatano, T. Matsukura, R. Sano, and K. Tanaka. Discovery and retrieval of logical information units in web. In *Proc. of the 1999 ACM Digital Libraries Workshop on Organizing Web Space*, 1999.
6. W. Li, K. Selc uk Candan, Q. Vu, and D. Agrawal. Retrieving and organizing web pages by 'information unit'. In *Proc. of the 10th International World Wide Web Conference*, pages 230–244, 2001.
7. B. Amento, L. Terveen, andW. Hill. Does 'authority' mean quality? predicting expert quality ratings of web documents. In *Proc. of the 22nd annual international ACM SIGIR Conference(SIGIR2000)*, pages 296–303, 2000.
8. S. Chakrabarti. Integrating the document object model with hyperlinks for enhanced topic distillation and information extraction. In *proc. of the 10th International World Wide Web Conference*, pages 211–220, 2001.

9. S. Chakrabarti, M. Joshi, and V. Tawde. Enhanced Topic Distillation using Text, Markup Tags, and Hyperlinks. In *Proc. of the 23nd annual international ACM SIGIR Conference(SIGIR2001)*, pages 208–216, 2001.
10. G. Salton and C. Buckley. *Term-weighting approaches in automatic retrieval.* Information Processing & Management, 24(5):513-523, 1988.
11. I. H. Witten and A. Moffatand T. C. Bell. *Managing Gigabytes.* Van Nostrand Reinhold, 149-150, 1994.
12. R. Baeza-Yates and B. Ribeiro-Neto. *Modern Information Retrieval.* ACM Press, 1999.

On Combining Link and Contents Information for Web Page Clustering

Yitong Wang and Masaru Kitsuregawa

Institute of Industrial Science, The University of Tokyo
{ytwang, kitusre@tkl.iis.u-tokyo.ac.jp}

Abstract Clustering is currently one of the most crucial techniques for dealing

(e.g. resources locating, information interpreting) with massive amount of heterogeneous information on the web, which is beyond human being's capacity to digest. In this paper, we discuss the shortcomings of pervious approaches and present a unifying clustering algorithm to cluster web search results for a specific query topic by combining link and contents information. Especially, we investigate how to combine link and contents analysis in clustering process to improve the quality and interpretation of web search results .The proposed approach automatically clusters the web search results into high quality, semantically meaningful groups in a concise, easy-to-interpret hierarchy with tagging terms. Preliminary experiments and evaluations are conducted and the experimental results show that the proposed approach is effective and promising. Keywords: co-citation, coupling, anchor window, snippet

1. Introduction

While web search engine could retrieve information on the Web for a specific topic, users have to step a long ordered list in order to locate the needed information, which is often tedious and less efficient due to various reasons like huge volume of information; users differ on requirements and expectations for search results; users may be just interested in "most qualified" information or one peculiar part of information etc. Especially, synonymity (different terms have similar meaning) and polysemy (same word has different meanings) make things more complicated. In general, the quality (recall and precision) and correspondent interpretation of search results for current search engines are far from satisfying and present big challenges for research in the fields of database, IR and data mining.

Many works [1,2,3,16,25] tried to explore link analysis to improve the quality of web search results or mine useful knowledge on the web. Kleinberg in [1] suggested that there are two kinds of pages on the web for a specific query topic: "hub" and "authority (the most authoritative page)" and they reinforce each other. A correspondent HITS algorithm was also proposed to locate the hubs and authorities from the search results given a query topic. However, sometimes one's "most authoritative" pages are not useful for others and further investigations on the above challenges are in high demand.

R. Cicchetti et al. (Eds.): DEXA 2002, LNCS 2453, pp. 902–913, 2002.

We think clustering web search results could help a lot. The goal of our work is to cluster high-quality pages in web search results into more detailed, semantically meaningful groups with tagging terms to facilitate user's searching and interpretation. When we talk about *web search results /search results*, we mean web pages returned from web search engine on a specific query topic. We use URLs or pages interchangeably when referring to search results.

Clustering approaches could be classified in two broad categories: term-based clustering [7,8,12,14,21,24] and link-based clustering [9,11,20,25]. Term-based clustering that is based on common terms shared among documents has been well studied in IR. However, it does not adapt well to web environment since it ignores the availability of hyperlinks between web pages and is susceptible to spam. Moreover, web search results are also different from a corpus of text documents in words distribution [25]. It is pointed out in [1] that many "authority" pages contain very little text. All these facts present difficulties in using term-based approach for web page clustering. In [20], we proposed a link-based clustering algorithm by co-citation and coupling analysis. According to preliminary experimental results, link-based clustering could cluster web search results into some medium size but high quality clusters. However, it suffers from the facts that pages without sufficient in-links (out-links) could not be clustered, which means the recall is low. So it is very natural to investigate how to combine link and contents information in clustering algorithm to overcome the above problems. Unlike clustering in other fields, web page clustering should separate irrelevant ones from relevant pages and only cluster relevant pages into meaningful groups.

The paper is organized as follows. Section 2 is an assessment of previous related work of clustering in web domain. In Section 3, we describe the proposed clustering algorithm combining link and contents analysis. Subsequently in Section 4, we report experimental results and evaluations. Conclusion and future work is in Section 5.

2. Related Work

Related work can be classified into two categories: clustering hypertext documents in a certain information space and clustering web search results. It is in [9] that a hierarchical network search engine is proposed to cluster hypertext documents to structure a given information space for supporting various services like browsing and querying based on the contents as well as the link structure of each hypertext document. In [21], a technique called LSH (Local-Sensitive-Hash) is proposed for web clustering. It plays more emphasis on the scalability of clustering. Snippet-based clustering is well studied in [7,8]. Shingle method, which is often used for duplicates removal is proposed in [14] to measure the similarity between pages for clustering. Applying the technique of association rule mining to term vectors is another clustering approach proposed in [24]. It can automatically produce groups of pages without defining the similarity between pages. These approaches differ with each other on clustering method and are all based on common terms shared among web pages. Clustering hypertext documents by *co-citation analysis* is explored in [11]. By applying HITS algorithm [1] to the vicinity graph around a seed URL, the approach proposed in [25] could find similar pages to the seed URL in a more narrow way, which is more focusing on finding similar pages than clustering web pages.

3. Combining Link and Contents Analysis in Clustering

Hyperlinks are helpful since they demonstrate objective opinions of the authors of other web pages to the pages they point to. **Co-citation** [19] and bibliographic **coupling** [18] are two more fundamental measures to be used to characterize the similarity between two documents. **Co-citation** measures the *number of citations (out-links) in common* between two documents and **coupling** measures the number of documents (*in-links*) that cite both of two documents under consideration. The anchor text or snippet of page *u* means anchor text or snippet attached with the hyperlink that points to *u in* search results. Anchor window of a hyperlink includes anchor text as well as text that surrounds the hyperlink, which might include concise and important terms to describe the main topic of the page that the link points to. We consider four parts of text in our contents analysis for each URL/page *u* in search results: snippet, anchor text, meta-content and anchor window of the in-link *v* of *u*. Meta-content is an optional tag for most web pages and gives the summary of the page by the author. We "glue" the four parts for each page *u* in search results and apply stemming processing to it to extract terms that summarizing the main topic of page *u*.

By combining contents and link analysis, the proposed approach clusters search results based on common terms, in-links and out-links shared among them. In the rest of our discussion in the paper, we have several notations: *n, m, M, N, L* are positive integers, *R* is the set of specified number of search results for a topic. We use *n* to denote specified number of search results used for clustering, *m* to denote specified number of in-links extracted for each URL/page in *R*. *M, N, L* denote total number of distinct in-links, out-links as well as terms after applying link and contents analysis mentioned above for all *n* pages in *R* respectively.

1) Representation of each page *P in R*

Each web page *P* in *R* is represented as three vectors: P_{Out} (*N*-dimension), P_{In} (*M*-dimension) and P_{KWord} (*L* – dimension). The *ith* item of vector P_{Out} indicates whether *P* has the correspondent out-link as the *ith* one in *N* out-links. If yes, the *ith* item is 1, else 0. P_{In} is identically defined. The *kth* item of vector P_{KWord} indicates the frequency of the corresponding *kth* term of *L* appeared in page *P*.

2) Centroid-based similarity measurement

We adopt traditional *Cosine* similarity measurement and the similarity of two pages *P, Q* includes three parts: out-link similarity *OLS (P, Q)*, in-link similarity *ILS (P, Q)* and contents similarity *CS (P,Q)*, which are defined as follows:

$$OLS(P,Q) = (P_{Out} \bullet Q_{Out}) / (\| P_{Out} \| \| Q_{Out} \|)$$

$$ILS(P,Q) = (P_{In} \bullet Q_{In}) / (\| P_{In} \| \| Q_{In} \|)$$

$$CS(P,Q) = (P_{KWord} \bullet Q_{KWord}) / (\| P_{KWord} \| \| Q_{KWord} \|)$$

$\| \ \|$ is length of vector.

Centroid or center point *C* is used to represent the cluster *S* when calculating the similarity of page *P* with cluster *S*, ***Sim(P, S)***. Centroid is usually just a logical point, which also includes three vectors. ***Sim(P, S)=Cosine(P, C) is defined as***

$$P1*OLS(P,C)+P2*ILS(P,C)+P3*CS(P,C),\ where P1+P2+P3=1 \quad (1)$$

Centroid C is defined as:

$$C_{Out} = \frac{1}{|S|}\sum_{P_i \in S} P_{iOut}\ C_{In} = \frac{1}{|S|}\sum_{P_i \in S} P_{iIn},\ C_{KWord} = \frac{1}{|S|}\sum_{P_i \in S} P_{iKWord} \quad (2)$$

|S| is number of pages in cluster *S*. By varying the value of *P1, P2 and P3*, we could get an in-depth understanding of the contributions of out-link, in-link as well as term to clustering process.

3) Clustering method

We extend standard K-means to overcome its disadvantages:

1. Define the similarity threshold
2. Filter irrelevant pages (associate with few links or terms)
3. Assign each relevant pages to the Top *C existing cluster(s)* based on the similarities (that above the similarity threshold) between the page and the correspondent centroids
4. The page will be one cluster itself if no *existing cluster* meet step 3
5. Recompute the centroids of the clusters if its cluster members are changed
6. Repeat Step 2 until 5 until all relevant pages are assigned and all centroids do not change any more
7. Merge two base clusters produced by step 6 if they share most members based on merge threshold.

Preliminary experimental results show that final clustering results are insensitive to the processing order; however, further investigation and proof of this point is needed, which is not discussed here. The convergence of the approach is guaranteed by K-means itself since our extension does not affect this aspect. The two parameters introduced here are *similarity threshold* and *merge threshold.*

4) Introducing some heuristic rules

- Differentiating among links

While link analysis usually suffers from the problem of orthogonality, we would like to alleviate it by weighting links to differentiate among them. It is very common for a page *u* that many of its in-link pages are from the same website. E.g. for page www.jaguar.com, more than 20 in-link pages are from website www.fort.com.

Rule For an URL/page *u*, if more than one in-link (out-link) page of it is from the same website, we replace these in-link (out-link) pages (e.g. the number is *K*) that from the same website with one website page with weight K1 (1<K1<K).

The value of K1 is determined according to the value of K. In our experimentation, we set K1 as 1, 2 or 3 when K with the value intervals as K=1, (1<K <20) or K>=20. For the above example, we replace all in-link pages that from the same website www.fort.com with one in-link as website page http://www.fort.com/ with weight 3.

- Hierarchical Clustering

We apply hierarchical clustering to clusters produced by previous steps to make the final clustering results more concise and easy to interpret. Another HR-merging threshold is used as the halt condition. Similarity between two clusters is identically calculated as in formula (1). The processing is as follows:

(a) Compute the similarity for every possible pair of clusters;

(b) For all pair of clusters that similarity is bigger than HR-merging threshold, we preserve them for further processing. We select one pair, say *(a, b)* and then merge them into a higher-level cluster *A*. Other cluster pairs that share one member with *A*, say *(a, c) or (b, c)* will be add into *A*, which result in *a, b, c* are in *A*. If there is no such cluster pair, select another cluster pair to process. The selection order is descendent based on the similarity values.

(iii) Repeat step (i), (ii) until the similarity of all possible pairs of cluster are smaller than HR-merging threshold.

5) Tagging each cluster

We attach tagging terms with each cluster since it is important for users to have a flavor of the main topic of each cluster by a glance of its tagging terms. Say for cluster *S*, *C* is its centroid, from C_{Kword} , it is easy to know the terms that have higher values and are most shared by the members of Cluster *S*, which might convey the main topic of the cluster.

4. Experiments and Evaluations

In this part, we mainly report our experimentations as well as evaluations on the proposed approach to investigate its effectiveness. We arbitrarily select eight topics, which include rather general ones like "food" and "chair"; relatively specific ones like "black bear attack" and "moon river"; as well as other topics like "jaguar", "big apple", "salsa", "jordan". Especially, we choose topic "jaguar" for detailed comparison. We test 200 URLs for each topic. For each page/URL in 200 search results, we get its 100 in-links. All results are obtained by using Google search engine. Just as mentioned, by varying the parameters in formula (1), it is possible to try different clustering approaches for a specific topic. Link-based clustering is denoted as "L" (with P1, P2, P3 as 0.5, 0.5, 0); term-based clustering is denoted as "C" (with P1, P2, P3 as 0, 0, 1); combining links and contents analysis is denoted as "M" (with P1, P2, P3 as 0.2, 0.3, 0.5). The choice of parameter values for clustering approach "M" is based on empirical evaluation. However, it needs further investigation, which is not the scope of discussion in this paper. Similarity threshold 0.1 and merge threshold 0.75 is used in our experimentation as recommended in [20] if we do not mentioned them particularly in the following discussion. In table 9, we have tried term-based clustering with different similarity thresholds. We use "C/0.1" or "C/0.15" to denote term-based clustering with similarity threshold 0.1 or 0.15. Another HR-merging threshold is introduced in the hierarchical clustering process. We deliberately choose a relatively strict one 0.4 for it since we would like to make sure that only clusters that are similar enough will be merged into one higher-level cluster. The anchor window we tried in our experimentation is 4, which include two word to the left and two words to the right of the anchor text.

4.1 Experimental Results

As final clustering results reveal, one page could belong to more than one cluster or belong to singleton cluster, which means that it cannot be grouped with other pages. In the rest of discussion, "pages/URLs clustered" means pages or URLs that appear in final clusters whose size are no less than 3. The size of a cluster is the number of pages in the cluster. We ignore singleton clusters or very small clusters. We present final clustering results (after hierarchical clustering process) for the eight topics in Table1 to Table8, which could give an impression of clustering results from the semantic point of view. Each entry in the tables is the main tagging terms we get according to part 5 of Section 3. The two numbers in the parenthesis of each entry in these tables are: a) the number of sub-clusters included in this cluster to indicate whether the cluster is a higher-level cluster; b) the number of distinct pages /URLs clustered in this cluster. E.g. for the first entry of term-based clustering "C" in Table1, the tagging words are company, furniture and the two numbers are 12 and 102. It means that the cluster is a higher-level cluster composed of 12 sub-clusters and there are totally 102 distinct URLs/pages are grouped in this cluster. Its main topic is about furniture companies that may manufacture or sell various kinds of chairs.

From Table1 to Table 8, we could know that for term-based clustering, it could only clearly identify the most popular ideas around the topic and fail to separate pages if they are differ slightly in topics. The fact holds for all topics no matter general or specific ones. Since it might be possible to "purify" the clusters by increasing the similarity threshold, we check the clustering results (before applying hierarchal clustering) for topic "jaguar" in more detail in Table 9. Each entry in Table 9 lists the top two terms with highest average weights bigger than 0.5 in parentheses for the correspondent cluster. We could see from Table 9 that clusters obtained by term-based clustering are rather "mixed". E.g. for C/0.1, different subtopics pages are mixed in Cluster No.1 as shown by both "car (1.7)" and "club (1.4)". Increasing the similarity threshold cannot solve the problem of "purity" of the cluster due to the fact that people use different words to express the same idea as shown in Table 9 for C/0.15 or C/0.2. Especially, text in snippets or anchor window usually brings noises, the final cluster quality depends heavily on how well the terms used to represent each vector. We use "**" in Table 1 to Table 8 to indicate that the correspondent cluster is not interpretable, which means that the most shared terms are meaningless, like "click". As for link-based clustering L/0.1, we could see that it could identify some medium size, tightly related meaningful clusters. The main disadvantages of link-based clustering are low recall and the quality of big clusters is not good. For M/0.1, it is clearly that it could "pull" some pages with the same topic but missing common links into the cluster by combining contents and links. In Fig.1, we give average clusters each URL belongs to for different topics based on three clustering approaches. The topics in the x axles of Fig.1 are in the same order with topics of Table 1 to Table 8.

Table 1. Final clustering results for topic "Chair"

	C	L	M
1	Company, furniture (12/102)	Company, furniture (1/56)	Company, furniture, (2/ 86)
2	University, department, engine (7/ 50)	University, department (2/ 19)	University, department (2/ 27)
3	Wheelchair, evacuate, stair (8/ 38)	Wheelchair, evacuate (1/ 11)	Wheelchair, evacuate, safety (2/ 15)
4	**	**	Shop, outdoor, service (3/19)
5		Rock, shop (1/ 10)	Electronic, history (1/7)
6		Ergonomic, seat (1/ 7)	Ergonomic, seat (1/ 8)
7		**	Toyota, armchair (1/6)

Table 2. Final clustering results for topic "Food"

	C	L	M
1	Safety, Association (3/ 107)	Safe, nation (2/ 53)	Safety, industry, science (3/ 72)
2	Recipe, cook, search (1/ 31)	Recipe, cook (1/ 14)	Recipe, cook, gourmet (3/20)
3	Nutrition, health (1/ 15)	Agriculture (2/ 16)	Wine, drink, export (3/ 14)
4	Genetic, organ (1/ 9)	Nutrition, online (2/ 16)	Canadian agriculture (2/1 9)
5	Restaurant, kitchen, (2/ 9)	Genetic, organ (1/ 9)	Nutrition, health (3/ 18)
6	Drug, guild (1 /10)	Restaurant, kitchen, chef (2/ 11)	New, product, standard (1/16)
7		Agriculture (1/10)	Genetic, organ (2/15)
8			Restaurant, kitchen, chef (2/ 8)
9			Drug, guild (1 /7)

Table3. Final clustering results for topic "Jaguar"

	C	L	M
1	Car , type (6/ 87))	Car, type, part (3/ 67)	Car, type, part, restore, race (4/ 68)
2	Club, Support (3/ 57)	Club (1/ 23)	Club (1/37)
3	Game, Atari (3/28)	Game, Atari (2/ 17)	Game, Atari (2/ 32)
4	Cat, onca (3/ 15)	Cat, onca (1/ 8)	Cat, wildlife, onca (2/ 13)
5	**	Book, magazine (1/ 6)	Book, jag, magazine (3/10)
6		Tour, reef (1/ 4)	Reef, tour, (1/ 5)

Table 4. Final clustering results for topic "Big Apple"

	C	L	M
1	New, York, City (4/ 98)	New, York, city (3/ 54)	New, York, City (2/ 76)
2	Theater, circus (6/ 41)	Circus (1/12)	Theater, Broadway, ticket (3/ 17)
3	Company, offer (1/ 18)	Game, user, group (1/ 9)	Circus, trapeze (2/14)
4		Sports (1/ 9)	Game, user, group (2/ 11)
5	Classic, Sybase, golf (1/ 11)		Sports, company, product (2/ /14)
6		Classic, Sybase, golf (1/ 3)	Classic, Sybase, golf (1/ 3)

Table 5. Final clustering results for topic "Jordan"

	C	L	M
1	Hashemite middle, east (3/ 90)	Hashemite Kingdom (2/ 54)	Hashemite Kingdom, east (3/ 74)
2	Michael Jordan, basketball (2/ 27)	Michael Jordan, basketball (1/ 13)	Michael Jordan, basketball (2/ 19)
3	Robot Jordan, author (1/ 21)	Robot Jordan, author (1/ 9)	Robot Jordan, author (2/ 17)
4	Tour (1/13)	Tourist, site (1/ 7)	Tourist, site (3/ 14)
5		Bank (1/ 5)	Bank (1/ 8)

Table 6. Final clustering results for topic "Salsa"

	C	L	M
1	Dance, Latin, music (5/ 97)	Dance, music (2/46)	Dance, Latin, music (3/ 95)
2	Pepper, sauce, hot (7/41)	Hot, sauce (1/ 14)	Recipe. Hot, sauce (4/ 39)
3	**	Club (1/ 9)	Artist, english, Palma (2/ 10)
4		Cook book, recipe (1/ 8)	Club (1/5)
5		Salsa in Germany (1/5)	

Table 7. Final clustering results for topic "Black Bear attack"

	C	L	M
1	Grizzly, fight (10 /105)	Country, fight (2/ 32)	Grizzly, country, fight (3/ 76)
2	Animal, wildlife (6/ 33)	Outdoor, camp (1/ 12)	Animal, kill, wildlife (4/ 38)
3	Alaska, hunt (2/ 6)	Grizzly, park (1/ 7)	Alaska, brown, hunt (3/ 20)
4	**	Report, info (1/4)	Outdoor, camp (3/14)

Table 8. Final clustering results for topic "Moon River"

	C	L	M
1	Music, mile, lyric, wide (5/ 103)	Music, seafood, visit (1/31)	Music, mile, lyric, wide (3/ 78)
2	Huston, river (5/ 43)	Theater, audio (1/13)	Huston, river (3/ 31)
3	Love, boat, message (1 /19)	William, author (1/ 8)	Gift, love, boat (2 /16)
4			Theater, audio (2/ 16)
5			William, author (3/ 10)

Table 9. Main tagging keywords for different clustering patterns for topic "jaguar" (before hierarchical clustering)

	C/ 0.1	C/0.15	C/0.2	L/0.1	M/0.1
1	Car (1.7), Club (1.4)	Car (1.8), Club (1.2)	Car (1.9), Club (1.2)	Car (1.6), Club (0.8)	Car (2.2), club (0.5)
2	Club, (1.7) Car (1.2)	Club (1.9), part (1.1), Car (0.7)	Club (1.6), car (1.0)	Club (1.5), frame (0.6)	Club (1.7), car (0.5)
3	Game (1.4), Atari (1.1)	Game (1.7)	Game (1.2)	Game (1.7)	Game (2)
4	Cat (1.1), type (0.8)	Cat (1.1), type (0.8)	Atari (0.8), Game (0.7)	Magazine (1.4), jag (1.2)	Atari Emulate (1.7)
5	Atari (0.8), Game (0.7)	Atari (0.8), Game (0.7)	Cat (1.1), type (0.6)	Cat (1.1), onca (0.9)	Cat (1.6), onca (0.9)
6	Java (0.9), video (0.6)	Java (0.9), video (0.6)	Classic (0.9), part (0.8)	Atari Emulate (1.5)	Magazine (1.3), jag (1.3)
7	Classic (0.7), type (0.6)	Classic (0.8), part (0.6)	**	Part (1.1), type (0.7)	Part (1.2), Type (0.9)
8	Club (1.5), part (0.9)	Classic (0.7), type (0.6)	Book (1.1), jag (0.9)	Race (0.9), formula (0.8)	Race (1.1) Formula (1.1), team (0.7)
9	Club (1.1.), support (0.7)	Club (1.0.), support (0.8)	Formula (0.9), team (0.7)	Reef (1.3), tour (0.9)	Tour, Reef (1.1)
10	Service (0.8), program (0.5)	Restore (0.7), jag (0.7)			Wildlife (1.2) Conservation (1.2)
11	Formula (0.9), dealer (0.6)	Formula (0.9), dealer (0.6)			Audio (0.6), saloon (0.5)
12	Restore (0.7), Jag (0.7)				Classic (1.0), restore (0.8)
13	Wildlife (0.8) leopard (0.5)				Amazon (0.9), book (0.9)
14	Frame (0.6), team (0.6)				
15	Panthera (0.5), rainforest (0.5)				

Term-based clustering usually has the highest overlap while link-based clustering gives the lowest. For rather general topics, more pages/URLs belong to more than one cluster; while for specific ones, most pages/URLs have only one unique topic. The interesting phenomenon is that for some topics like "jaguar", "salsa", which have different meanings under different contexts, the ratios of overlap for three clustering approaches are almost same.

4.2 Evaluation of Clustering Results

Validating clustering algorithm as well as evaluating its quality is complex because it is difficult to find an objective measure of quality of clusters. We would like to use three metrics *precisions, recall* and *average entropy* to evaluate the quality of final clusters. In our initiative evaluation, we manually check 200 web pages for each topic and give our judgment. Each page is given two estimates: relevant (to the query topic), its main topics and then create *classes* manually. Although this is time-consuming and it could lead to bias in our evaluation, it is possible to counteract potential bias by carrying out user experiment. Of all 200 pages, around 75% are marked "relevant" on the average.

4.2.1 Evaluation Metrics

We use A to denote the number of URLs clustered and B to denote the number of URLs that marked 'relevant', then we redefine *precision* and *recall* as follows:

Precision= $|A \cap B| / |A|$; *Recall*= $|A \cap B| / |B|$

Entropy provides a measure of "goodness" or "purity" for un-nested clusters by comparing the groups produced by the clustering technique to known classes. Low entropy means high quality of the cluster because of high intra-cohesiveness while high entropy means that the cluster members are not tightly related but covers more than one sub-topic under the general query topic. We adopt the computing of entropy introduced in [10]: Let CS is a cluster solution and *E(j)* is the entropy for cluster *j*. The average entropy for a set of clusters is calculated as the sum of entropy of each cluster weighted by its size. The definitions are as follows:

$E(j) = -\sum_i p_{ij} \log(p_{ij})$ · $E_{CS} = \sum_{j=1}^{m} \frac{n_j * E(j)}{n}$, p_{ij} is the "probability" that a member of cluster j belongs to the given class i. n_j is the size of cluster j, m is the number of clusters and n is the total number of page clustered. We also use "precision" and "recall" to indicate whether the proposed clustering approach separate irrelevant ones from high quality pages and clusters high quality pages as much as possible into meaningful groups. Since clustering is meant to group similar ones together, we think average entropy is more influential when evaluating the quality of a clustering algorithm.

4.2.2 Comparisons among Term-Based, Link-Based and Combining Link and Contents Clustering

Based on the evaluation metrics introduced in section 4.2.1, we compare the quality of clustering results produced by three different clustering approaches: term-based clustering, link-based clustering and combining link and contents clustering as demonstrated in Fig.2. The average entropy is calculated according to clustering results before applying hierarchical clustering.

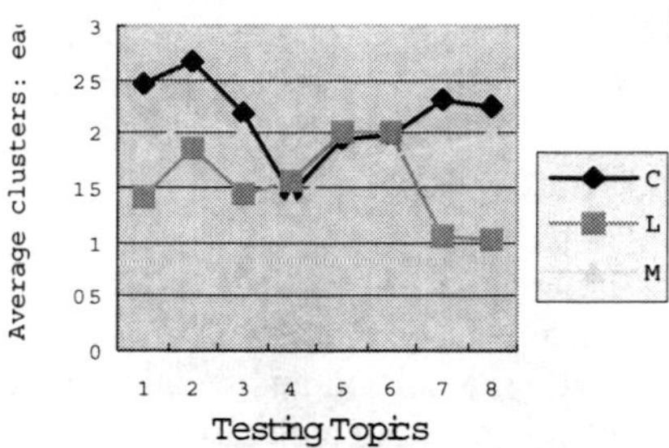

Fig.1 Average clusters each URL belongs for each topic based on three clustering approaches (see section4 for definitions of C, L, M)

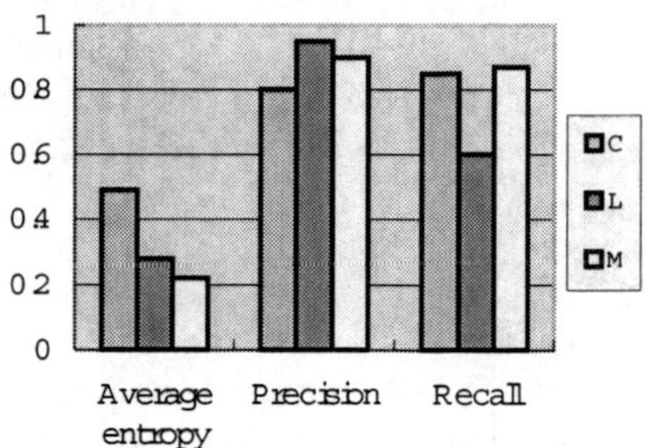

Fig 2. Evaluation of three clustering approaches based on three metrics (see section4 for definitions of C, L, M)

In general, the average entropy for term-based clustering (denoted as "C") is rather high, which means that the clusters obtained by this way are very coarse, noises are included in clusters and pages in one cluster actually cover different subtopics. Link-based clustering (denoted as "L") could improve a lot for this but with low recall since the clustering results for L are some medium but tightly related, meaningful clusters. Combining link and contents information (denoted as "M") could compensate this without sacrificing the "purity" but at a little cost of precision, which is clearly conveyed in Fig.2 since snippets and anchor windows usually bring noises. Since clustering web search results is meant to give clear classified information to facilitate user's locating and interpretation, combining link and contents information in clustering is effective and in general works much better than current term-based clustering and link-based clustering as well.

5. Conclusion

In this paper, we extend the previous work on link-based clustering by combining contents as well as links information appeared in anchor text, snippet, meta-content as well as anchor window of the in-links, which might give a brief summarization for the topic of the page under consideration. Our goal is to cluster high quality pages (by filtering some irrelevant pages) in search results returned from web search engine for a specific query topic into high quality, semantically meaningful groups with useful tagging terms to facilitate users' locating and information interpretation. Term-based clustering algorithms are less effective due to the facts that it ignores the availability of hyperlinks and extracting accurate, useful words from web pages directly is becoming more and more difficult because of sophisticated web-page generating techniques. Link-based clustering also suffers from the problems that pages with few/insufficient in-links or out-links will not be clustered and the "purity" of big-size clusters is also not so good (high entropy). Combining contents and links is a natural extension to link-based clustering and provide much help for the mentioned problems. We proposed a clustering algorithm by combining links and content analysis. We also extend the standard K-means algorithm to overcome its disadvantages and make it more suitable to clustering in web domain. By introducing some heuristic rules like differentiating among links as well as applying hierarchical clustering on clustering results, the final clustering results are presented in a concise, easy to interpret form of hierarchy. In order to investigate the effectiveness of the proposed approach, we have conducted experimentation and evaluation on eight topics, which include rather general ones like "chair", "food" and rather specific ones like "black bear attack", "moon river" as well as several other topics like "jaguar", "big apple" etc. Our evaluation is based on three metrics: average entropy, precision and recall, which we think that average entropy is more influential when evaluating a clustering algorithm. Experimental results suggest term-based clustering is too "coarse" to identify related pages in a more narrow way. Link-based clustering could identify tightly related, medium size but meaningful groups. However, low recall and high entropy for big-size cluster are its disadvantages. Experimental results and evaluations suggest that the proposed approach gives the significant improvements over term-based and link-based clustering approach in following several ways: 1) improve the recall without loss of quality (entropy) by "pulling" more pages into the cluster with same topic; 2) balance the clustering process to give reasonable clusters; 3) improve the average entropy as a whole. There are many works could be done to extend our current work. While our preliminary experimentation on the proposed approach gives positive results, more extensive investigations on other topics as well as the effect of parameters introduced in similarity measurement is among our next step work. We also plan to extend the current work to adapt it to clustering massive amount of web page that might cover more topics.

References

1. Kleinberg 98 Jon Kleinberg. *Authoritative sources in a hyperlinked environment.* In proceedings of the 9th ACM-SIAM Symposium on Discrete Algorithms (SODA), January 1998.
2. Ravi Kumar et. al. 99 Trawling the Web for emerging cyber-communities In Proceedings of 8th WWW conference, 1999, Toronto, Canada.
3. Brin and Page 98 Sergey Brin, and Larry Page. *The anatomy of a large scale hypertextual web search engine.* In Proceedings of WWW7, Brisbane, Australia, April 1998.
4. Oren Zamir and Oren Etzioni 99 *Grouper: A Dynamic Clustering Interface to Web Search Results* In Proceedings of 8th WWW Conference, Toronto Canada.
5. Richard C. Dubes and Anil K.Jain, *Algorithms for Clustering Data*, **Prentice Hall, 1988**
6. Oren Zamir and Oren Etzioni 97 *Fast and Intuitive clustering of Web documents,* KDD'97, pp287-290
7. Oren Zamir and Oren Etzioni 98 *Web document clustering: A feasibility demonstration* In Proceedings of SIGIR' 98 Melbourne, Australia.
8. Zhihua Jiang et. al. *Retriever: Improving Web Search Engine Results Using Clustering*
9. Ron Weiss et. al. 96 *Hypursuit: A Hierarchical Network Search Engine that Exploits Content-Link Hypertext Clustering* Hypertext'96 Washington USA
10. Michael Steinbach, George karypis and Vipin Kumar *A Comparison of Document Clustering techniques* KDD'2000. Technical report of University of Minnesota.
11. James Pitkow and Peter Pirolli 97 *Life, Death and lawfulness on the Electronic Frontier*. In proceedings of ACM SIGCHI Conference on Human Factors in computing, 1997

12. Cutting, D.R. et. al.92 *Scatter/gather: A Cluster-based approach to browsing large document collections*. In Proceedings of the 15th ACM SIGIR Conference on Research and Development in Information Retrieval. pp 318-329; 1992
13. A.V. Leouski and W.B. Croft. 96 *An evaluation of techniques for clustering search results.* Technical Report IR-76 Department of Computer Science, University of Massachusetts, Amherst, 1996
14. Broder et. al. 97 *Syntactic clustering of the Web.* In proceedings of the Sixth International World Wide Web Conference, April 1997, pages 391-404.
15. Lenoard Kaufman and Peter J. Rousseeuw. *Finding groups in Data: an introduction to cluster analysis* Wiley, 1990
16. Gibson, Kleinberg and Raghavan 98 David Gibson, Jon Kleinberg, Prabhakar Raghavan. *Inferring Web communities from link topology.* Proc. 9th ACM Conference on Hypertext and Hypermedia, 1998.
17. Agrawal and Srikant 94 Rakesh Agrawal and Ramakrishnan Srikanth. *Fast Algorithms for mining Association rules,* In Proceedings of VLDB, Sept 1994, Santiago, Chile.
18. M.M. Kessler, *Bibliographic coupling between scientific papers* , American Documentation, 14(1963), pp 10-25
19. H. Small, *Co-citation in the scientific literature: A new measure of the relationship between two documents*, J. American Soc. Info. Sci., 24(1973), pp 265-269
20. Yitong Wang and Masaru Kitsuregawa, *Use Link-based clustering to improve web search results*, WISE'01, pp. 119-128, 2001
21. Taher H.Haveliwa et. al. 99 *Scalable techniques for Clustering the Web.*
22. Taher H.Haveliwa et. al. *Similarity Search on the Web: Evaluation and Scalability Considerations* Extended Technical Report, 2000
23. Einat Amitay *Using common hypertext links to identify the best phrasal description of target web documents,* SIGIR'98 workshop for Hypertext IR for the web
24. Daniel Boley, Maria Gini *Partitioning-based Clustering for web document Categorization* The paper is also available at www.enterpriseware.net/EWRoot/Files/Boley1999a.pdf
25. J. Dean and M. Henzinger *Finding related page in the World Wide Web*. Proceedings of WWW8, 1999

MKL-Tree: A Hierarchical Data Structure for Indexing Multidimensional Data

Raffaele Cappelli, Alessandra Lumini, and Dario Maio

DEIS Università di Bologna, viale Risorgimento 2, 40136 Bologna - Italy.
{rcappelli, alumini, dmaio}@deis.unibo.it

Abstract. Recently, multidimensional point indexing has generated a great deal of interest in applications where objects are usually represented through feature vectors belonging to high-dimensional spaces and are searched by similarity according to a given example. Unfortunately, although traditional data structures and access methods work well for low-dimensional spaces, they perform poorly as dimensionality increases. The application of a dimensionality reduction approach, such as the Karhunen-Loève transform, is often not very effective to deal with the indexing problem, since the substantial loss of information does not allow patterns to be sufficiently discriminated in the reduced space. In this work we present a novel hierarchical data structure based on the Multi-space KL transform, a generalization of the KL transform, specifically designed to cope with locally correlated data. In the MKL-tree, dimensionality reduction is performed at each node, allowing more selective features to be extracted and thus increasing the discriminant power of the index. In this work the mathematical foundations and the algorithms on which the MKL-tree is based are presented and preliminary experimental results are reported.

1 Introduction

Multidimensional data management, which was initially limited to geographic information systems (GIS) and mechanical CAD, has become an important research area, with applications in many fields, such as robotics, computer vision, medical imaging, multimedia systems and data mining. In these applications, objects are usually represented through feature vectors belonging to high-dimensional spaces and are searched by similarity according to a given example. A variety of spatial data structures and access methods have been proposed in the literature in the past few years [5], but, for high-dimensional spaces (more than 20-30 dimensions), most of them are outperformed by a simple sequential scan. The low efficacy of traditional data structures to index high dimensions, is usually referred to as the "dimensionality curse": when the dimensions grow, the number of possible structural relations exhibits a more-than-exponential increase, data points are rather scattered and are usually clustered in proper subspaces of the whole high-dimensional space (multicollinearity). This problem is usually dealt with by reducing the dimensionality of the data to be indexed, by means of some dimensionality reduction techniques, such as the Karhunen-Loève

R. Cicchetti et al. (Eds.): DEXA 2002, LNCS 2453, pp. 914–924, 2002.

transform (KL transform) [4], or the Discriminant Analysis [11]. These transformations determine a subspace with a dimension much lower than the original space, by selecting only the components that are best suited to represent and discriminate the data points. Once projected in a reduced space, data can be indexed using a traditional structure. Unfortunately, representing data with a single global space reduction is often not very effective, since the substantial loss of information does not allow patterns to be sufficiently discriminated in the reduced space.

Recently a generalization of the KL transform, named Multi-space KL (MKL), has been introduced [2]: in MKL more subspaces are created to represent the different patterns belonging to a given dataset. Each subspace represents a subset of patterns which have similar characteristics, thus allowing more selective features to be extracted. It has been experimentally proved [1] that, in some application domains, such as pattern representation and classification, MKL markedly outperforms simple KL, since the creation of more subspaces allows the multicollinearity problem to be effectively dealt with; in fact, unlike the KL transform, which can handle only globally correlated data, MKL is also able to cope with locally correlated data. On the basis of the promising results obtained with the MKL transform, we decided to develop a hierarchical data structure that exploits MKL representation (MKL-Tree). In this work, the first formal studies and experimental results of the MKL-Tree are presented. The main contribution is the definition of the techniques adopted for representing the nodes of the structure and the introduction of algorithms for insertion, node splitting, point and range searches. In order to develop such algorithms, some novel concepts have been mathematically formalized and the KL and MKL transforms have been extended accordingly.

The rest of this paper is organized as follows: section 2 briefly summarizes the state of the art, in section 3, KL and MKL transforms are introduced and some useful results and properties extensively used throughout the paper are formalized. Section 4 describes the MKL-tree structure and presents the algorithms for implementing the main operations. Section 5 discusses experimental results and finally, in section 6, we draw our conclusions and include some proposals for future work.

2 Related Work

Recently, several new index structures adopting dimensionality-reduction have been developed to deal with high-dimensional data points: the TV-tree [8] is a hierarchical structure based on the idea of using a variable number of dimensions to represent data at different levels of the structure; SHOSLIF [11] is an image retrieval structure which uses principal component analysis for image representation and linear discriminant analysis for image retrieval, by means of the so-called Most Discriminant Features; Local Dimensionality Reduction (LDR) [3] is an indexing approach based on data partitioning in subsets that are locally correlated, each of which is projected into the KL subspace associated to its elements and indexed by a traditional structure, such as the R-tree. The idea behind LDR is quite similar to the MKL transform [2]; however, the resulting structure is substantially different from the MKL-tree introduced here, since in LDR the KL subspaces are only used at the first level of the tree instead of being used to represent each node as in MKL-tree. Moreover the LDR structure is essentially static and requires a large and representative training-set to be known a priori, while MKL-tree is totally dynamic and does not require a proper initialization.

3 KL and MKL Transforms

The Karhunen-Loève transform [4] is, among all the unitary transformations for dimensionality reduction, the one which guarantees the best Euclidean distance preservation, i.e. it minimizes the mean-square approximation error, defined as the mean distance between the points belonging to the training set and their back-projections from the reduced space.

Given $P = \{\mathbf{x}_i \in \Re^n \mid i = 1,...,m\}$, a set of *m n*-dimensional vectors belonging to the training set, the *k*-dimensional eigenspace associated to *P* is denoted as $S_P = [\overline{\mathbf{x}}_P, \Phi_P, \Lambda_P]$, where $\overline{\mathbf{x}}_P = \frac{1}{m}\sum_{\mathbf{x}\in P}\mathbf{x}$ is the mean vector, $\Phi_P \in \Re^{n\times k}$ (projection matrix) and $\Lambda_P \in \Re^{k\times k}$ are the matrices of the largest eigenvectors and eigenvalues of the covariance matrix $\mathbf{C}_P$ of *P*, respectively.

The *projection* of $\mathbf{x} \in \Re^n$ into the eigenspace S_P is $\mathbf{y} = \Phi_P{}^T(\mathbf{x} - \overline{\mathbf{x}}_P)$; the reconstruction from a projected vector is $\mathbf{x}' = \Phi_P\mathbf{y} + \overline{\mathbf{x}}_P$. The *distance from space* of a vector $\mathbf{x} \in \Re^n$ from a space S_P is defined as the distance between **x** and the back-projection of its projection onto S_P [2]: $d_{FS}(\mathbf{x}, S_P) = \sqrt{\left\|\mathbf{x} - \overline{\mathbf{x}}_P\right\|_2^2 - \left\|\Phi_P{}^T(\mathbf{x} - \overline{\mathbf{x}}_P)\right\|_2^2}$

The *reconstruction error* $\varepsilon(\mathbf{x}, S_P)$ of a vector **x**, is the approximation resulting from the projection/back-projection operations and it coincides with the distance of **x** from the space $S_P : \varepsilon(\mathbf{x}, S_P) = d_{FS}(\mathbf{x}, S_P)$; this error can be conceived as a measure of how far S_P is well-suited to represent **x**. It can be shown that the *mean-square error*, over all the patterns in *P*, corresponds to the sum of the $n-k$ discarded **C**'s eigenvalues.

Applying a single KL transform to a large set of points (global dimensionality reduction) may cause severe problems if their distribution cannot be approximated by a single Gaussian. In this case, a global dimensionality approach demonstrates its weakness in preserving distances between points and finally fails in data representation. The Multi-space KL (MKL) [2], where more subspaces are created to arrange the different patterns, have been introduced to deal with this problem. Each subspace represents a subset of patterns that have similar characteristics, thus allowing more selective features to be extracted.

For a given partition $\wp = \{P_1, P_2,..., P_s\}$ of the training set $P = \{\mathbf{x}_i \in \Re^n \mid i = 1,...,m\}$ and for a given set $K = \{k_1, k_2,..., k_s\}$ of scalars, the MKL transform is defined by the set of eigenspaces $S=\{S_1,S_2,...,S_s\}$, where S_i is the eigenspace of dimension k_i obtained from the training subset P_i. Please note that the KL transform represents a particular case of MKL, where s=1, $\wp=\{P\}$ and $K=\{k\}$. The partition $\wp$ is obtained by means of an ad hoc heuristic algorithm aimed to minimize the percentage mean-square reconstruction error, defined as the weighted sum of the percentage reconstruction errors related to each KL space S_i.

4 MKL-Tree Structure

MKL-tree is a disk-based hierarchical structure for n-dimensional points, where data are contained in the leaves, while internal nodes are used to route the search. Nodes correspond to disk blocks and represent the set of objects which are indexed by the corresponding subtree. The tree is height-balanced: all paths root-leaf have the same length h, named "height of the tree". Nodes are divided into two categories: *internal nodes,* containing a representation of their children and a pointer to the corresponding disk block, and *leaves,* containing representations and pointers to the indexed objects. The MKL-tree is an R-tree-like structure: it basically differs from R-tree in the node representation and in the insertion, search and split algorithms. The following subsections deal with all these topics.

4.1 Leaves and Internal Nodes Representation

A KL subspace of the original space is associated to each node, root excepted. The KL representation of the root is never calculated, since it is not useful to drive any search. Each element of a leaf node is the projection into the corresponding KL subspace of an indexed object and the pointer to the disk block in which the object is stored. Each element of an internal node corresponds to the KL subspace associated to a child node. The KL subspace associated to each (internal or leaf) node is the subspace that better represents the points in the corresponding subtree (that is, the subspace that guarantees the minimum reconstruction error for the points stored in the leaves of the subtree). As to the leaves, the related subspace is simply calculated starting from the corresponding data points, whereas, in the internal nodes, the subspace is determined by means of a "merging" procedure which creates a representative space starting from the KL subspaces associated to its children. In both cases however, the space associated to a node is characterized by a dimension k, markedly lower than the dimension n of the indexed data ($k << n$). The k value may be constant for the whole tree, or may vary among different nodes (for instance it could be low at leaf level and increase as it moves toward the root).

Nodes have a capacity (fanout), which denotes the maximum number of elements they can contain; this value is usually different for internal nodes (M_I) and leaf nodes (M_L). Some constraints are imposed to control the minimum loading factor of the nodes: each internal node, root excepted, must contain at least m_I elements; each leaf node must contain at least m_L elements. The ratio between the maximum and minimum node loading factor is a parameter that must be set at tree-creation time (e.g.

$m_I \geq \frac{1}{3} M_I$). These constraints help in balancing the element distribution among different nodes and enable a higher utilization of the structure to be achieved. The minimum and maximum capacity of the leaves are related to the dimension k of the corresponding KL subspace, to the size of disk blocks and the dimension n of the original data; in fact, in order to calculate the KL transform, at least $k+1$ elements must be present in the leaf, thus $m_L > k$. Moreover, the constraint $M_L \geq 2 \cdot m_L > 2 \cdot k$ is necessary to allow splitting of nodes. As far as internal nodes are concerned, the only constraint is $M_I \geq 2 \cdot m_I$. Figure 1 describes the general structure of an MKL-tree.

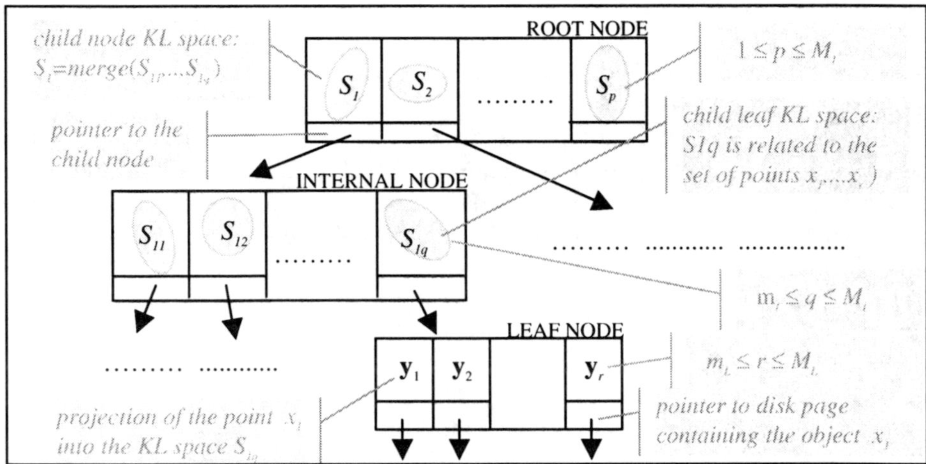

Fig. 1. An example of a three-levels MKL-Tree. Each node of the structure is represented by a KL subspace, denoted by S_i , which is maintained inside its parent node. Internal nodes contain the representation of their children, while leaves contain the projections of the indexed objects into the relative eigenspace. M_I and m_I are the maximum and minimum internal-node capacity, respectively. M_L and m_L are the maximum and minimum leaf capacity, respectively. The root is an internal node not having a minimum capacity.

4.2 Insertion of a New Point

In order to insert a new point the tree is visited to find the leaf most suited to contain it. If an overflow occurs, the leaf is split, otherwise the leaf is updated by recalculating the corresponding KL space contained in its parent node. Finally, each node on the path from the leaf to the root is updated, by using the incremental update technique for KL spaces reported in [9]. The KL space corresponding to the parent of the last node which has been split does not need to be updated, since the merging procedure already allows the new element to be taken into account. Updating the KL subspace associated to a leaf requires the projections of its points to be recalculated. On the contrary, modifying the KL subspace associated to internal nodes does not require updating its children, since they are always represented with respect to the original space. The insertion procedure is performed as indicated in the following pseudo-code. Searching for the leaf which is the best suited to contain the new point exploits the SELECTSUBTREE procedure, which routes the search among the different children of a node, by selecting the child which is associated to the nearest KL subspace. The distance from space (d_{FS}) is used to select the child node.

A KL subspace guarantees the minimum mean-square error for the training set *P* on which the KL transform has been calculated. In order to preserve this property, the KL transform should be recalculated each time a new element is added to or deleted from *P*; such an operation is quite complex and is too slow to be adopted in a hierarchical structure. For this reason, the MKL-tree adopts ad-hoc algorithms, which allow KL subspaces to be updated without recalculating them from scratch, when a new point is inserted, or two nodes have to be merged after a split. The proposed algorithms are reported in [9].

```
INSERT (element P)
Set N = root of the tree
while (N is not a leaf) do N = SELECTSUBTREE(N, P)
end while
Read the leaf N from disk and let E be the set of its elements
E = E ∪ {P}
if (#E ≤ M_L) then // Insert P in N
        Update the KL subspace associated to N
        Calculate the projection of P in the subspace associated to N
        Update the projections of the points in N
else // Overflow
        N = SPLIT(N, E)
end if
// Update the subspaces on the path G-root (G is the first node that must be updated, the
parent of the last node split, in case of overflow)
Set G to the parent node of N (NULL if N is the root)
Update the KL subspaces of the nodes in the path G-root

node SELECTSUBTREE (node N, element P)
Set F to the child F_N of N which minimizes the distance d_FS(P,F_N)
return F
```

4.3 Node Splitting

The splitting procedure is executed when the node capacity is exceeded. The procedure divides the node elements into two sets, each forming a new node. The two new nodes are inserted in the parent node in place of the split one; after this operation, the cardinality of the parent node grows by one element, thus the split can propagate all the way up to the root node. The split procedure returns a reference to the parent of the last split node; this reference is used by the insertion procedure as a starting point for updating the subspaces associated to the nodes.

```
node SPLIT (node N, element set E_N)
A=B=∅
PARTITION(E_N, A, B)
Create two new nodes N_A, N_B containing A and B sets of elements
Let G be the parent of N (a new node if N is the root) and E_G the set of its elements
Delete N from E_G and insert N_A, N_B in E_G
if (#E_G > M_I) then G = SPLIT(G, E_G) end if
return G
```

Due to the different characteristics of the leaf- and internal-node elements, the PARTITION procedure has two different implementations: as far as leaves are concerned, it coincides with the MKL clustering algorithm; as to internal nodes, a novel technique for partitioning subspaces has been specifically developed for solving the problem. The clustering algorithm of the MKL transform [2] has many degrees of freedom; in particular, it allows one to set: the maximum and minimum number of partitions to be created, the maximum dimensionality of the subspaces and the maximum reconstruction error. Furthermore, a balancing constraint on the partitions is imposed. When the algorithm is applied to the split of a leaf, just two partitions have to be created, the dimensionality of the subspaces is equal to the value k of the original node (a parameter which in our experiments has been fixed for the whole tree), and the points are partitioned so that the cardinality of a node is not lower than one third of that of the original node. The algorithm that performs the internal node splitting is conceptually similar to the MKL clustering, but, instead of clustering points, it has to partition subspaces. The search for an optimal division of the node elements is executed iteratively: first, two clusters containing the two farthest subspaces are created and the remaining subspaces are assigned to the clusters according to their distances from the first two subspaces. Next, at each step, first a reassignment procedure is performed to ensure that the two clusters are balanced, then the KL subspace corresponding to each cluster is determined by merging all subspaces [9] belonging to the cluster by means of the procedure MERGE. Finally, all the elements are reassigned again, according to their distance from the new merged spaces associated to the two clusters. Since both the elements to be partitioned and the partitions themselves are represented by KL subspaces, we define a distance between spaces d_s, (derived from [7]), as the minimum effective cluster radius such that the boundaries of the two hyper-ellipsoids intersect the segment between their mean vectors. The distance d_s between two KL subspaces $S_A = [\overline{\mathbf{x}}_A, \Phi_A, \Lambda_A]$ and $S_B = [\overline{\mathbf{x}}_B, \Phi_B, \Lambda_B]$ is defined as:

$$d_S(S_A, S_B) = c_1 c_2 \left(c_1 + c_2 - 2 \cdot \sqrt{c_1 \cdot c_2}\right) / (c_1 - c_2)^2$$

where $c_1 = \mathbf{a}^T \Lambda_A^{-1} \mathbf{a}$, $c_2 = \mathbf{b}^T \Lambda_B^{-1} \mathbf{b}$ and $\mathbf{a} = \Phi_B{}^T(\overline{\mathbf{x}}_A - \overline{\mathbf{x}}_B)$, $\mathbf{b} = \Phi_A{}^T(\overline{\mathbf{x}}_B - \overline{\mathbf{x}}_A)$ are the projections of each center on the other space.

```
PARTITION(element set E_N, element set A, element set B)
// Create the distance matrix among all elements in E_N
for each (S_i , S_j ∈ E_N )
        Md[i,j] = d_S(S_i , S_j)
end for
// Select the two farthest elements, to initialize the two clusters
(a,b) = arg max_{i,j} (Md[i, j])
A = A ∪ {S_a} ; B = B ∪ {S_b}
for i = 1 to #E_N  (i ≠ a, b) // Associates the remaining elements to the nearest cluster
        if (Md[i,a] ≤ Md[i,b]) then A = A ∪ {S_i}
        else B = B ∪ {S_i} end if
end for
repeat  // Reassignment
        BALANCE(A,B)
        // calculate the two subspaces corresponding to the clusters
        S_A= MERGE (A); S_B= MERGE (B);
        // reassign elements according to their distances from the new subspaces
        A = B = ∅
        for each S_i ∈ E_N
                if (d_S[S_i,S_a] ≤ d_S[S_i,S_b]) then A = A ∪ {S_i}
                else B = B ∪ {S_i} end if
        end for
until (the solution does not change or the max n° of iteration is reached)
```

The algorithm usually converges in a very small number of iterations (less than ten), in any case a maximum number of iterations is fixed, to avoid oscillatory phenomena which can rarely occur. The procedure BALANCE ensures that a sufficient number of elements are assigned to each cluster, by reassigning some elements if needed. Moving elements among clusters is performed according to a space similarity criterion: the KL subspace associated to the smaller cluster is calculated, then the nearest elements of the second space are moved until the balancing criterion is fulfilled. After the partitioning, two new nodes are generated from the elements of the two clusters A and B. If they are leaves, their KL subspaces are directly calculated from their points, which are finally projected into the new space. On the contrary, if the new nodes are internal, the related KL subspaces are the ones obtained by merging their elements.

4.4 Point and Range Searches

The point-search algorithm visits the tree starting from the root, by following the most promising path. To this aim, a heap queue of the nodes to be visited is maintained, ordered according to the distance (d_{FS}) from the searched point. At each step of the search, the first node in the queue is extracted: if it is an internal node, all its children, whose distance from the searched point is less than a threshold, are inserted into the queue; if it is a leaf, the presence of the searched point is checked. The search stops as soon as the searched element is found or the heap becomes empty.

The range-search algorithm is similar to the point-search one, except for the pruning criterion (that is the method used to determine whether a node has to be inserted into the heap queue or not). The pruning rule is based on probabilistic criteria: a node is visited only if the distance of the query center from its "bounding box" is less than the query radius; the approximate bounding box of a KL subspace is defined as the hyper-ellipsoid that is centered in the origin of the subspace and whose semi-axes lengths are three times the values of the corresponding standard deviation (which coincides with the square root of the related eigenvalue). If the points associated to a node have a Gaussian distribution, this approach guarantees that each point is within the bounding-box with a 99.73% probability; this statement is not true for other distributions but in any case, the loss of information is very low, as proved by the experimental results.

5 Experimental Results

In this section we present some experiments aimed at evaluating the effectiveness and efficiency of the MKL-tree in resolving similarity queries: the results are compared to the performance of a global-reduction indexing technique, based on a global KL transform coupled with an R-tree [6] indexing structure. The indicators used to measure the performance of the two approaches are:

- *I/O cost*: it is expressed as the number of disk blocks accessed
- *Precision*: it is defined as $\rho = |R_O| / |R_R|$, where R_0 is the number of n-dimensional objects which satisfy the search condition and R_R is the number of objects returned by the search procedure on the reduced dimensional space. Please note that a distance evaluated in the reduced space is a lower bound to the real distance in the original space, thus $R_0 \leq R_R$ and $\rho \in [0, 1]$.

Two databases of real data have been used as benchmarks:

- **FingDB**: it consists of 4000 vectors of dimension n=1680, representing the directional images of the fingerprints in the NIST DB4 [12].
- **COLHIST**: it consists of about 70000 vectors of dimension n=64 taken from the database of color histograms from Corel images [10].

In order to be indexed by an R-tree, the two datasets were previously projected, by means of a global KL transform, into lower dimensional spaces of dimensions $k = 10$ and $k = 8$, respectively. Note that, in order to perform a global dimensionality reduction, the whole dataset was considered available at index creation time. On the contrary, MKL-tree is a totally dynamic structure, since dimensionality reduction is performed at insertion time; the parameter k related to the reduced dimension of the subspaces associated to the nodes, has been fixed to the same value of the global approach, 10 and 8 for the two datasets, respectively.

On each dataset the following tests have been performed: point queries where each vector of the dataset has been searched and the average I/O cost has been evaluated, range queries, where 100 queries with a selectivity factor of about 2% have been executed to estimate both precision and I/O cost. The graphs in figure 2 show the average number nodes visited as a function of the number of points loaded in the index (i.e. the index size): MKL-tree is found to be more scalable than R-tree, since its performance decreases much more slowly as the index size grows.

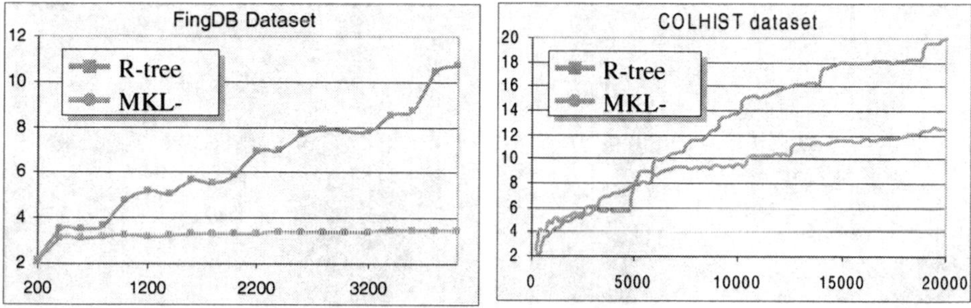

Fig. 2. Point search on the FingDB (left) and the COLHIST (right) dataset: average number of accesses to the leaves versus the number of points loaded in the index.

It has already been mentioned that a distance evaluated in the reduced space is always less or equal to a distance in the original space: this property guarantees that no points internal to the range sphere will be neglected by an "exact" search procedure, such as the one used by the R-tree. This is not true for MKL-tree, due to the probabilistic pruning criterion adopted in the range search algorithm. In the following experiments, the approximation error that is the percentage of missed points with respect to the exact result is also considered. Table 1 reports the results of range queries: MKL-tree outperforms R-tree both in precision and I/O costs, with a minimal amount of approximation. The better precision achieved by MKL-tree allows a large number of disk accesses to be avoided and a much lower number of matching calculations among elements in the original space to be performed in order to evaluate if the retrieved points are false positives.

Table 1. Average precision and I/O costs for 100 range queries on the FingDB and the COLHIST datasets. The approximation errors of the MKL-tree results are 2.67% and 1.28%.

	FingDB		COLHIST	
	Precision	I/O	Precision	I/O
R-tree	0.04	236	0.03	135
MKL-tree	0.07	165	0.21	46

6 Conclusions

In this work, a novel hierarchical structure for indexing high-dimensional data, based on the MKL transform, has been introduced. The mathematical foundations and the algorithms on which the tree structure is based have been presented and preliminary experimental results, aimed at comparing MKL-tree to R-tree, have been reported.

Several other tests, not reported here due to the lack of space, were performed to determine the best strategy for building the structure. Although the first results are very promising, a large margin for improvement exists and many comparative studies should be performed. In particular, the possibility of building an optimal tree structure when the whole dataset is known in advance should be investigated: at present, MKL-tree is a dynamic structure updated at each new insertion. If a large dataset is available at creation time, the tree may be "bulk loaded", thus obtaining a better organization of points among the nodes. In this way, the structure could become more stable, i.e less dependent on the data insertion order. As to node representation, a number of issues still remain open, such as developing a technique to determine the optimal value for the subspaces dimensionality (parameter k). Finally, algorithms for point deletion should be studied and methodologies to optimize range and nearest-neighbor queries may be investigated.

References

1. Cappelli R., Maio D., Maltoni D., "Fingerprint Classification based on Multi-space KL", in proc.Workshop on Automatic Identif. Adv. Tech. (AutoID'99), Summit (NJ), Oct. 1999.
2. Cappelli R., Maio D., Maltoni D., "Multi-space KL for Pattern Recognition and Classification", IEEE Transactions on PAMI, vol.23, no.9, pp.977-996, September 2001.
3. Chakrabarti K., Mehrotra S., "Local Dimensionality Reduction: A New Approach to Indexing High Dimensional Spaces", Proc. of the VLDB Conference, Cairo, Egypt. Sept. 2000.
4. Fukunaga K., Statistical Pattern Recognition, Academic Press, San Diego, 1990.
5. Gaede V, Günther O, "Multidimensional Access Methods", ACM Comp. Surv, 30(2), 1998.
6. Guttman A., "R-trees: A Dynamic Index Structure for Spatial Searching". Proc. ACM SIGMOD Int. Conf. On Management of Data, pp. 47-57, Boston, USA, 1984.
7. Kelly P.M., "An algorithm for Merging Hyperellipsoidal Clusters", Technical Report LA-UR-94-306, Los Alamos National Laboratory, Los Alamos, NM, 1994
8. Lin K., Jagadish H., Faloutsos C., "The TV-tree: An Index Structure for High-Dimensional Data", VLDB Journal, 3(4), pp.517-542, 1994.
9. Franco A., A. Lumini and D. Maio, "An efficient algorithm for eigenspace updating and merging", submitted to *IEEE Trans. on PAMI*
10. Ortega M., Rui Y., Chakrabarti K., Mehratra S., Huang T.S., "Supporting similarity queries in MARS", ACM Conf. on Multimedia, Seattle, USA, November, 1997.
11. Swets D.L., Weng J., "Hierarchical Discriminant Analysis for Image Retrieval", IEEE Transactions on Pattern Analysis and Machine Intelligence, 21(5), pp. 386-401, 1999.
12. Watson C.I., Wilson C.L., Nist Special Database 4, Fingerprint Database. U.S. National Institute of Standards and Technology, 1992.

Boolean Bounding Predicates for Spatial Access Methods
(Extended Abstract)

Megan Thomas and Joseph M. Hellerstein[1]

Computer Science Division, University of California, Berkeley
{mct, jmh}@cs.berkeley.edu

Abstract. Tree-based multidimensional indexes are integral to efficient querying in multimedia and GIS applications. These indexes frequently use shapes in internal tree nodes to describe the data stored in a subtree below. We show that the standard Minimum Bounding Rectangle descriptor can lead to significant inefficiency during tree traversal, due to false positives. We also observe that there is often space in internal nodes for richer, more accurate descriptors than rectangles. We propose exploiting this free space to form subtree predicates based on simple boolean combinations of standard descriptors such as rectangles. Since the problem of choosing these *boolean bounding predicates* is NP-complete, we implemented and tested several heuristics for tuning the bounding predicates on an index node, and several heuristics for deciding which nodes in the index to improve when available tuning time is limited. We present experiments over a variety of real and synthetic data sets, examining the performance benefit of the various tuning heuristics. Our experiments show that up to 50% of the unnecessary I/Os caused by imprecise subtree predicates can be eliminated using the boolean bounding predicates chosen by our algorithms.

1 Introduction

Spatial and multimedia databases often make heavy use of search-tree indexes like R*-trees [1] to provide efficient query processing. As an example, the Blobworld image search system [2] supports nearest neighbor queries over an index built on color vectors, to answer queries of the form "find me images like this one". A wide variety of multimedia and GIS applications can be accelerated by reducing the number of I/Os performed in index search.

The internal nodes of tree-based indexes typically contain a sequence of pairs (p, ptr), where ptr is a pointer to a subtree, and p is a descriptor – or "Bounding Predicate" (BP) – for the subtree below, such that each datum found in the leaves below satisfies p. The popular R*-trees, for example, use Minimum Bounding Rectangles (MBRs) as their BPs.

We observe that in many spatial and multimedia index scenarios, most of the I/O overhead is caused by imprecise BPs misdirecting the tree traversal algorithm. In this paper we present a simple but powerful BP representation

R. Cicchetti et al. (Eds.): DEXA 2002, LNCS 2453, pp. 925–934, 2002.

that improves the accuracy of bounding predicates without changing the tree structure – in particular, without expanding the height – of the index.

We achieve our performance benefits by exploiting unused space in the inner nodes of search-tree indexes. Indexes often leave some space on each node empty in order to accommodate future insertions [6]. We use this free space to store more accurate versions of the inaccurate bounding predicates on the node.

Multidimensional bounding predicates can in principle be arbitrarily complex geometric shapes; however, such complexity can consume much of the remaining free space on a node, and can complicate basic search primitives like spatial overlap. Inspired by Constructive Solid Geometry [3], we propose retaining the simplicity of basic shapes like rectangles, but combining them in boolean expressions. For instance, we can replace a simple MBR with the *union* of two smaller rectangles that, together, more tightly bound the same set of data items (points or rectangles). Alternately, we could describe a set of data items with the original MBR *minus* some smaller rectangle, where the smaller rectangle describes unpopulated space within the MBR. Generally, we refer to these combined descriptors as *boolean bounding predicates.*

For a given BP, a variety of possible ways to tune it exist, resulting in different boolean BPs. For a given node, a variety of choices exist for allocating the free space to the various BPs on the node for tuning. For a given index, there may be nodes that greatly benefit from tuning their BPs, and nodes that benefit less. These options lead to the set of design problems that we study here. First, we provide a simple language for refining BPs via boolean connectors. Second, we examine how to allocate free space to BPs on an individual node to minimize false positives during index tree traversal, a process we call *tuning* a node. Finally, we investigate how to prioritize nodes to tune, so that the tuning process need not visit the entire tree in cases where doing so is prohibitively expensive.

Our experimental results show that up to 50% of wasted index query I/Os can be eliminated using boolean bounding predicates chosen with our tuning algorithms.

Section 2 provides background and motivation for the work presented here, and Section 3 outlines our approach. Section 4 elaborates on our boolean bounding predicates. Sections 5 and 6 cover the tuning and prioritization algorithms we implemented and experimental results. We conclude in Section 7.

2 Background and Motivation

We implemented boolean BPs in the libgist Generalized Search Tree (GiST) package [4], which provides a convenient infrastructure for experimenting with new indexing schemes. We extended the GiST framework with a small set of interfaces for generalized boolean BPs, which we describe in the full paper [12].

To get a feel for typical performance problems in multimedia search, we used GiST and its companion profiling tool `amdb` [8] to analyze sample queries for the Blobworld [2] image retrieval application. We provide an intuitive overview of `amdb`'s profiling here. The only I/Os that are necessary in traversing a search-tree

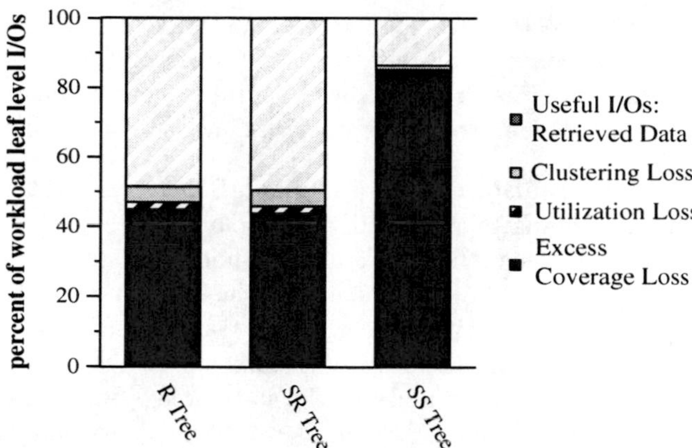

Fig. 1. I/Os performed during a query workload, broken down by underlying cause. Tests run on various spatial indexes built over sorted, bulk-loaded Blobworld data set.

index are those that lead the traversal algorithm to data that must be returned to the user; other I/Os are performance *losses* due to index inefficiency. The `amdb` analysis assigns each I/O to one of four causes: "retrieving useful data", "utilization loss" (under full index nodes), "clustering loss" (poor assignment of data items to leaves), or "excess coverage loss" (imprecise bounding predicates). As Figure 1 shows, most of the losses in our Blobworld experiments were attributed to imprecise BPs. Imprecise BPs lead to unnecessary I/Os because they result in "false positives", guiding the tree-traversal algorithm to leaf nodes that do not contain answers to the query. Such I/Os constituted from 10% to over 50% of the total I/Os performed by query workloads over R*-trees built on the various data sets we used for experiments.

We note that Blobworld – like many GIS and multimedia applications – has a read-mostly workload with very infrequent, batch updates. Because the data is largely static, it can be sorted and the index intelligently bulk-loaded [9]; this explains the low utilization and clustering losses in our experiments. In these scenarios, the key to good performance is to improve the precision of BPs to minimize excess coverage loss – the focus of this paper. However, we wish to stress here that an understanding of our static BP tuning problem is both of practical importance in many applications, and a prerequisite to addressing more dynamic environments.

3 Bounding Predicate Imprecision Problem

The crux of the boolean bounding predicate approach is to begin with a basic R*-tree[1], select a poorly performing inner node and use the free space on that

[1] The R*-tree was selected for general familiarity; our ideas are applicable to many tree-based indexes.

node to store extra rectangular components for some of the BPs on the node. We call this process *tuning*. Simple BPs are transformed into combinations of basic rectangles, united using the boolean operators *union* and *minus*.[2]

We have three problems to address in designing boolean bounding predicates:

1. **Boolean BP Creation:** Given a simple MBR, how should it be broken up into multiple rectangles combined with boolean operators? (Section 4.)
2. **Node Tuning:** Given a fixed-size internal node containing <BP, ptr> pairs and some free space, reallocate space to the BPs to generate boolean BPs that minimize false positives during index traversal. (Section 5.)
3. **Node Prioritization**: In some environments it may not be possible or worthwhile to tune every node in the index tree. So, given a search tree with k internal nodes and a budget $B < k$ of nodes to tune, select the best *B-subset* of the internal nodes for node tuning. (Section 6.)

Underlying the first two of these problems is the issue of judging the "badness" of a particular BP (BP_badness), in order to determine if we have available a "better" BP to replace it with. The third problem is based on judging the "badness" of the set of BPs on a node (node_badness), in order to determine how to prioritize nodes for tuning. Recall that our overall badness metric is excess coverage loss: the number of tree traversal I/Os that lead to irrelevant leaves. Given two different BPs and no other information, it is expensive to accurately determine which BP is going to contribute more excess coverage loss: the only way to be sure is to run the relevant query workload against both BPs. This measurement process is too expensive to perform in the inner loops of our tuning algorithms. Hence, for Node Tuning and Boolean BP creation we compare potential BPs using hyper-volume as our BP_badness metric. This mirrors the heuristics used in many other spatial data structure algorithms – e.g. the R-tree split algorithm. For Node Prioritization, the node_badness metric we use is amdb's excess coverage loss metric, as gathered by running a single characteristic workload over the untuned tree.

4 Creating Boolean Bounding Predicates

We begin by addressing how we transform simple MBRs into boolean BPs. Our basic operations are to replace a rectangle with either the union of two rectangles, or the difference of two rectangles.

TuneUnion (Figure 2) essentially splits one rectangle into two; this is a common operation in most multidimensional search trees during node splitting. However, in our case we are not splitting up the set of data items to separate them; we just want to more tightly circumscribe their extents. Hence our union split algorithm is a variant of the R*-tree node splitting algorithm [1], with a different

[2] A third boolean operator would be *intersection*. However, the intersection of two overlapping rectangles is simply one smaller rectangle so, for simplicity, we have not implemented *intersection*.

optimization goal. In particular, the R*-tree splitting algorithm works to minimize overlap between the resulting two bounding rectangles, which are intended to separate two subsets of data items. In our case overlap is perfectly acceptable because we are characterizing a single set of data items; we simply wish to minimize hyper-volume. So we take the R*-tree split algorithm and swap the calls to minimum "overlap-value" with minimum "area-value" (hyper-volume) in the subroutine ChooseSplitIndex. We also set the split imbalance parameter m to 5%, because it is perfectly acceptable in our scenario for the proportion of data items to rectangles to be skewed.

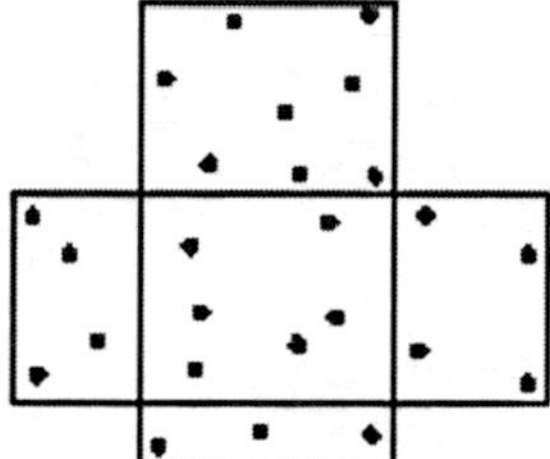

Fig. 2. Point Set Bounded by Two Unioned Rectangles

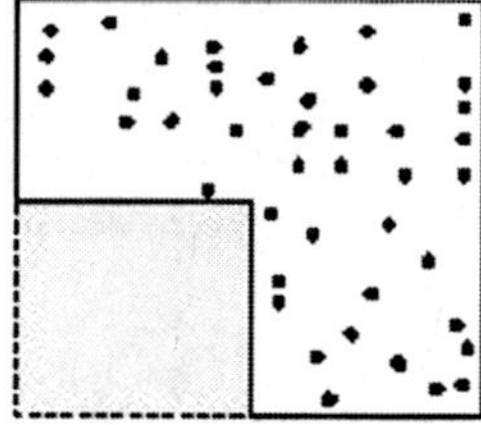

Fig. 3. Point Set Bounded by A Rectangle Minus A Second Rectangle

Our minus split algorithm, TuneMinus, does not have an obvious analogy in prior work. It is NP-complete to choose the best rectangle in d dimensions to subtract; indeed, it is NP-complete even under the constraint that the subtrahend is a corner of the original rectangle [5]. Intuitively, this corner constraint is attractive because MBR corners "stick out", and are likely parts of the MBR to unnecessarily overlap a large number of queries. Since even this constrained problem is NP-complete, we use a greedy heuristic that subtracts out the largest corner rectangle from the MBR (Figure 3). The full version of this paper details TuneMinus.

Both operations can be applied recursively using the logic laid out in Figure 4.

Note that boolean combinations of other shapes could be used analogously if they were more appropriate for a particular application. For example, boolean BPs are a generalization of the idea behind SR-trees [7]. From our perspective, every SR-tree BP is simply a rectangle and a sphere combined by an intersection operator.

5 Node Tuning

Given a particular index node to tune, we must decide which BPs in the node are most deserving of extra bytes, i.e., to which BPs we should allocate some

$$
\begin{array}{lll}
S & \Rightarrow & <\!fullrect\!> \mid (<\!union\!>) \mid (<\!minus\!>) \\
<\!union\!> & \Rightarrow & S \cup S \\
<\!minus\!> & \Rightarrow & (<\!fullrect\!> - <\!emptyrect\!>) \mid \\
 & & (<\!minus\!> - <\!emptyrect\!>) \mid (<\!union\!>) - <\!emptyrect\!> \\
<\!fullrect\!> & \Rightarrow & \texttt{MBR of some set of data items} \\
<\!emptyrect\!> & \Rightarrow & \texttt{rectangle bounding empty space}
\end{array}
$$

Fig. 4. Context-Free Grammar for Boolean Bounding Predicate Rectangle Combinations. Note that the < *emptyrect* > is always a simple rectangle, because there not likely to be benefit in refining rectangles that enclose empty space. The initial S is the minimum bounding rectangle.

```
A → (B ∪ C), where B, C are contained in A
A → (A − B), where B is an empty corner of A
A ∪ B → C, where C is the MBR bounding A and B
A − B → A
```

Fig. 5. State Transitions Used for A Single Step of Bounding Predicate Refinement In the Node Simulated Annealing (NSA) Algorithm: A can be either a single rectangle or a combination thereof.

free space to store an extra rectangle. We experimented with three different heuristics to handle node level tuning, which we call *NR* (Node Random), *NG* (Node Greedy) and *NSA* (Node Simulated Annealing).

NR selects a BP to tune by simply picking one BP at random from the set of BPs on the node and tuning it. If the BP has already been tuned into more than one rectangle, randomly select one of the two BP components to tune further, obeying the rules laid out in Figure 4. Once a BP (or BP component rectangle) to tune has been selected, randomly select the operation, TuneMinus or TuneUnion, to attempt. The return value from the TuneMinus or TuneUnion operation will be the change in BP_badness between the new BP and the old. If it is zero or negative, the new BP is discarded. In either case, the process of selecting and attempting to improve a BP is repeated until there is no longer sufficient free space to store another BP component.

NG tries both TuneMinus and TuneUnion on every existing BP (or component rectangle) on the node and selects the new BP which provides the greatest change in BP_badness over its corresponding old BP to replace. NG then repeats this procedure until it runs out of free space.

NSA uses a simulated annealing algorithm [11] to explore the space of BP possibilities. Figure 5 defines the state transitions each BP is allowed. Each step in the simulated annealing process consists of selecting a BP at random from those on the node and attempting a state transition. If the BP has already been tuned into multiple components, one of the subcomponent rectangles is randomly

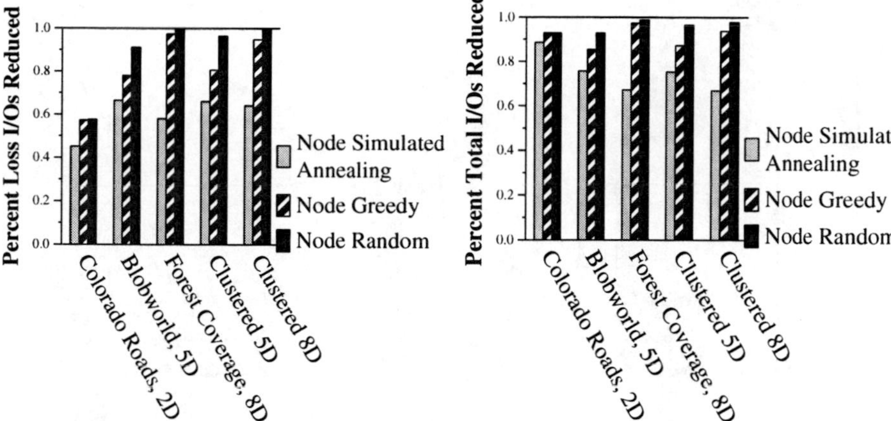

Fig. 6. Performance of Node Tuning: Percent change in *excess coverage loss* I/Os. Results after all nodes of indices over various data sets have been tuned. As you can see, NSA consistently outperforms the other algorithms at reducing the number of loss I/Os. The differences in percentage improvement between NG and NSA range from 12 to 39%; between NR and NSA the differences range from 12 to 41%.

Fig. 7. Performance of Node Tuning: Percent change in *total* I/Os. Results after all nodes of indices over various data sets have been tuned. As you can see, NSA consistently outperforms the other algorithms at reducing the number of query workload I/Os. The differences in percentage improvement between NG and NSA range from 4 to 30%; between NR and NSA the differences range from 4 to 31%.

selected, excluding the $<emptyrect>$ rectangles. Once a BP or combination of BP components has been selected, a state transition from Figure 5 is selected and applied. If the transition results in a reduction of BP hyper-volume, it is saved. If it does not, the simulated annealing oracle is consulted, and the new BP is saved with probability $e^{(-\Delta V/Temperature)}$.

The difficulty with NSA is tuning it. If the initial temperature is too high and the cooling rate too slow, it becomes, effectively, an inefficient exhaustive search. Because the number fed to the simulated annealing oracle is the change in hyper-volume between an existing and a proposed BP, the proper initial temperature is dependent upon the data set. We chose to set the initial temperatures to be $.00096 \times \prod_{i=1}^{d}(max(i) - min(i))$ where d is the dimensionality of the data set, $max(i)$ is the maximum value in that dimension and $min(i)$ is the minimum value. Examination of the return values from the simulated annealing oracle showed that these temperatures resulted in reasonable cooling; the oracle started by returning *true* frequently and ended by returning *false* frequently.

For each combination of tuning algorithm and node prioritization algorithm, we ran experiments over ten data sets; three real and seven synthetic, varying from 100K to 750K data points and from two to eight dimensions in the data points. Details are in the full version of this paper. Each data set was sorted

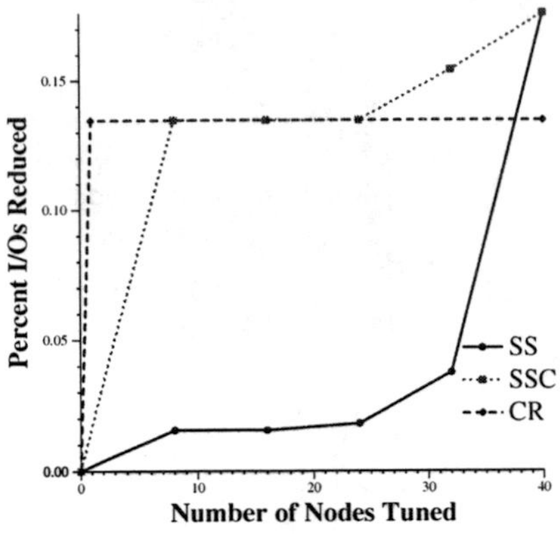

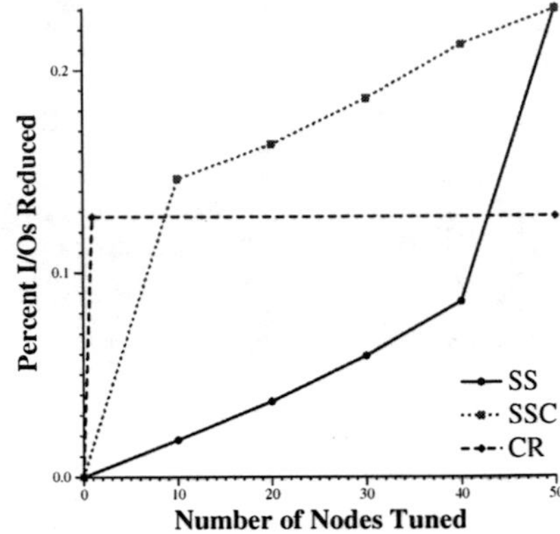

Fig. 8. Performance of Node Prioritization: Percent change in query I/Os over all nodes of Blobworld data set using NSA algorithm

Fig. 9. Performance of Node Prioritization: Percent change in query I/Os over all nodes of clustered 5D data set using NSA algorithm

using the Sort-Tile-Recursive algorithm from [9] and bulk-loaded into an R*-tree. For each data set we ran and analyzed nearest neighbor queries centered around ten percent of the total data points, selected at random from the data set, before we altered anything in the R*-trees, and analyzed the same query workload again after tuning nodes.

Figures 6 and 7 show the results of these experiments comparing the performance of the node level algorithms over a a variety of real and synthetic data sets. These graphs reflect the extent to which our techniques brought R*-tree performance toward ideal performance by eliminating wasted excess coverage loss I/Os. The absolute performance benefits of our techniques were also notable, with the best performers improving wall clock query set runtimes by about 25%.

NSA outperforms NG and NR for these data sets and others we tested, with the differences growing more pronounced as the dimensionality of the data grows. Node tuning runtimes for the various algorithms are similar, 5 – 30 wall clock seconds for most nodes in the index tree on a lightly loaded Sun Sparc Ultra 10 station with 256 MB memory.

6 Node Prioritization

To accomodate situations where there is not enough time to tune all the nodes in an index, we require a means of selecting the index nodes whose tuning will result in the greatest reduction in overall workload I/Os. When we do not know our tuning time budget in advance, we are interested in the *differential benefit* of tuning a single node – i.e., we want to maximize the slope of the graph where the x-axis represents the number of nodes tuned so far and the y-axis represents the number of I/Os saved.

Perfect node prioritization would require knowledge of the number of I/Os performed for a query workload before and after each possible set of nodes has been tuned. While it is possible to collect such knowledge by tuning each possible set of nodes and analyzing a test query workload, that would be prohibitively expensive. Therefore, we use heuristics to maximize the benefit of each node tuning step. We tested the performance of three heuristics that order nodes for tuning: Strict Sort (SS), Strict Sort and Climb (SSC) and Crop Root (CR).

For *SS* (Strict Sort), we tune the nodes in descending order of node_badness. SS does not require that the number of nodes to be tuned be known in advance; this is useful if, for example, a total tuning time is specified, but per-node tuning time is not well calibrated.

Our next heuristic, *SSC* (Strict Sort and Climb), requires a fixed budget to work correctly. Given a budget of B nodes to tune, SSC picks $b < B$ nodes with highest node_badness such that they have at most $B - b$ distinct ancestors and b is as large as possible. There may be a small (less than the height of the tree) number of unallocated tuning operations left if there is not enough room in the budget to make it from the node with the next highest node_badness all the way to the root. These remainder tunings are allocated to the nodes with the highest excess coverage losses not already in the set to be tuned. The B selected nodes are sorted by height in the index and tuned from the bottom of the index tree up in order to allow the increased precision of BPs lower in the tree to be reflected when the BPs higher up are tuned.

Because we noted that sharp drops in the number of I/Os performed over a workload frequently occurred just after the root node had been tuned, we added the Crop Root (CR) heuristic, which simply tunes the root node of the index tree. CR and SS have an advantage over SSC in that they do not require a budget B of nodes to be known in advance.

Figures 8 and 9 show the results of experiments comparing the performance of these heuristics. The algorithm which performs the least amount of work, CR, achieves almost as great I/O savings as SS and SSC achieve. The sharp rise in the SS line occurs after the root is tuned. In view of the fact that 13+% of the total I/Os (21% of the excess coverage loss I/Os) for the Blobworld data set index are eliminated through only tuning one node, the root, and that similar results were achieved for the other data sets, we believe the Crop Root algorithm is the best to use in the absence of time to tune all of the nodes.

7 Conclusions

We have presented new algorithms for spatial indexes, aimed at reducing the number of unnecessary I/Os an index performs during queries by making use of what free space may exist on index nodes to store more precise bounding predicates. We tested our algorithms using predicates that had simple rectangles as their building blocks, combined with the boolean operators union and minus. Tests show that 50% or more of the unnecessary I/Os performed by a query workload can be eliminated, with most of the benefit achieved through simply tuning the root node.

Space constraints preclude a discussion of related work, which appears in the full version of the paper.

Acknowledgments

This research was supported by fellowship stipend support from the National Physical Sciences Consortium and Lawrence Livermore National Laboratory. We thank Erik Demaine for the initial pointer to constructive solid geometry. Conversations with Kris Hildrum provided many useful insights.

References

1. N. Beckmann, Kriegel H.-P., R. Schneider, and B. Seeger. The R∗-tree: An efficient and robust access method for points and rectangles. In *Proc. of the ACM-SIGMOD Int'l Conference on Management of Data*, pages 322–331, 1990.
2. Blobworld image retrieval system. http://elib.cs.berkeley.edu/photos/blobworld/.
3. M. de Berg, M. van Kreveld, M. Overmars, and O. Schwarzkopf. *Computational Geometry: Algorithms and Applications, 2nd Ed.* Springer-Verlag, 2000.
4. J. M. Hellerstein, J. Naughton, and A. Pfeffer. Generalized search trees for database systems. In *Proc. of the 21st VLDB Conference*, Zurich, Switzerland, 1995.
5. K. Hildrum and M. Thomas. Jagged bite problem NP-complete construction. Technical Report UCB//CSD-99-1060, University of California at Berkeley, 1999.
6. T. Johnson and D. Shasha. B-trees with inserts and deletes: Why free-at-empty is better than merge-at-half. *Journal of Computer and System Sciences*, 47:45–76, August 1993.
7. N. Katayama and S. Satoh. The SR-tree: An index structure for high dimensional nearest neighbor queries. In *Proc. of the ACM-SIGMOD Int'l Conference on Management of Data*, pages 369–380, Tucson, AZ, May 1997.
8. M. Kornacker, M. Shah, and J. M. Hellerstein. An analysis framework for access methods. Technical Report UCB//CSD-99-1051, University of California at Berkeley, 1999.
9. S. T. Leutenegger, M. A. Lopez, and J. Edgington. STR: A simple and efficient algorithm for R-tree packing. In *Proc. of the 12th Int'l Conference on Data Engineering*, pages 497–506, New Orleans, LA, April 1997.
10. D. Lomet and B. Salzberg. The hB-tree: A multiattribute indexing method with good guaranteed performance. *ACM Transactions on Database Systems*, 15(4):625–658, December 1990.
11. W. Press, S. Teukolsky, W. Vettering, and B. Flannery. *Numerical Recipes in C: The Art of Scientific Computing, 2nd Ed.* Cambridge University Press, 1992.
12. M. Thomas and J. M. Hellerstein. Boolean bounding predicates for spatial access methods. Technical Report UCB//CSD-01-1174, University of California at Berkeley, 2002.
13. C. Zou and B. Salzberg. On-line reorganization of sparsely-populated B+-trees. In *Proc. of the ACM-SIGMOD Int'l Conference on Management of Data*, Montreal, Canada, June 1996.

Clustered Indexing Technique for Multidimensional Index Structures

Guang-Ho Cha and Yong-Ik Yoon

Department of Multimedia Science, Sookmyung Women's University
140-742 Seoul, South Korea
{ghcha, yiyoon}@sookmyung.ac.kr

Abstract. This paper presents an index clustering technique called the *segmented page indexing* (*SP-indexing*) for multidimensional index structures. The design objectives of the SP-indexing are twofold: (1) to improve the range query performance of the multidimensional indexing methods and (2) to provide a compromise between optimal index clustering and excessive full index reorganization overhead. The SP-indexing uses two kinds of I/O units: *pages* for random disk accesses and *segments* for sequential accesses. The SP-indexing improves the range query performance by offering high-performance sequential disk access within a *segment*. Experimental results demonstrate that the SP-indexing improves the range query performance up to several times compared with the traditional page-based indexing methods with respect to the total elapsed time.

1 Introduction

1.1 Motivation

In earlier generation databases, index structures were specially designed taking the page structure of disks into account. As database requirements grow to handle complex data types and as applications require frequent long range retrievals, the need is felt for specialized index structures other than traditional page-based one-dimensional index structures. For example, IBM's QBIC image retrieval system [5] has to process the query such as "find images that meet the condition of (20% ≤ red ≤ 30%) ∧ (50% ≤ green ≤ 70%) ∧ (40% ≤ blue ≤ 60%)." Applications which rely heavily on multidimensional complex data types include geographic information systems, multimedia databases, medical databases, CAD, and so on. However, the traditional page-based index structures do not satisfy the requirements for the multidimensional long range retrievals because they have to access many small index pages randomly. To overcome this problem, we develop a new multidimensional indexing technique for range queries that significantly improves the search performance compared with the traditional methods.

1.2 Background

More than ten years of database research have resulted in a great variety of multidimensional indexing methods to support range queries, for example, R*-tree [1], X-tree

R. Cicchetti et al. (Eds.): DEXA 2002, LNCS 2453, pp. 935–944, 2002.

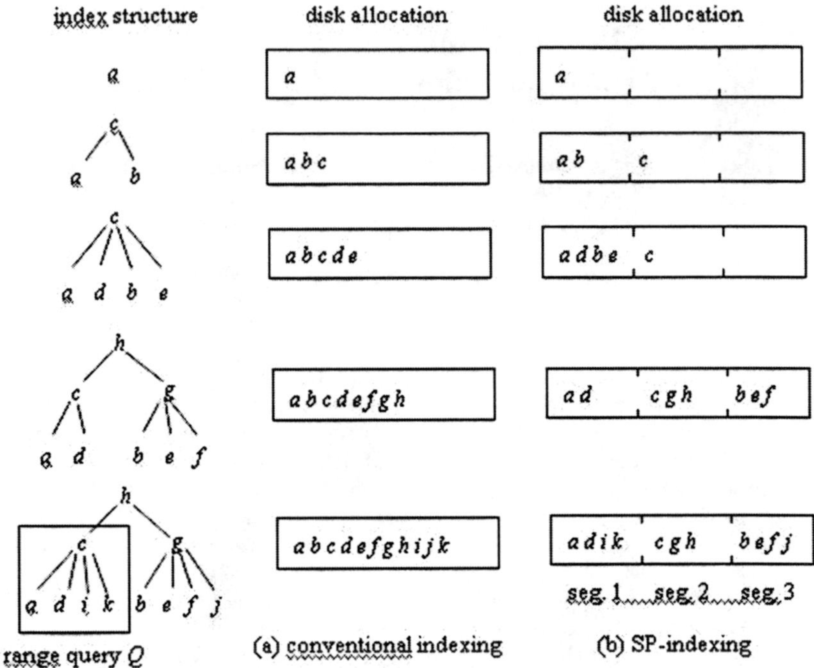

Fig. 1. Index tree growth and page allocation on disk

[2], M-tree [4], R-tree [7], LSD-tree [8], TV-tree [11], grid file [14], buddy-tree [16], and so on. Several characteristics are common to the existing multidimensional indexing methods:

- They have nodes whose size is a page,
- The size of a page is relatively small, e.g., 4 KB,
- They are *dynamic*,
- They do not exploit the clustering of index nodes,
- They use disk pages as the clustering unit and do not take into consideration the physical adjacency of individual pages.

The traditional page-based index structures do not satisfy the requirements for the multidimensional long range retrievals. The reasons are as follows: (1) Traditional 4 KB index pages are too small to handle the multidimensional long range retrievals efficiently. (2) However, simple larger index pages may consume much disk bandwidth. (3) They have to access many index pages randomly because the index pages are widely scattered on the disk due to dynamic page allocation. (4) To avoid this performance degradation, the related index nodes have to be clustered. However, existing indexing methods do not take into account the index clustering. They take into consideration only the clustering of data objects. Moreover, the dynamic index clustering requires the on-line index reorganizations, and the overhead of the global index reorganization is excessive. (5) They measure the search performance by the average number of disk page accesses, and do not take into consideration the physical adjacency of individual pages.

To overcome the drawbacks of the existing multidimensional indexing methods, we propose the *segmented page indexing* (*SP-indexing*) technique. The SP-indexing is based on the concept of *segments*. The SP-indexing considers the disk to be partitioned into a collection of segments. Each segment consists of a set of L contiguous pages on disk. A segment is the unit of clustering in the SP-indexing. Thus all disk pages in a segment can be read by a single disk sweep, and thus it saves much disk startup and seek time. In the SP-indexing, all disk pages are addressed by a pair of (segment no, page no). This addressing scheme means that we can access disk in page unit as well as in segment unit. When random accesses are required or when query ranges are very small, page-based disk accesses can be used instead of segment-based accesses.

The comparison between the traditional indexing methods and the SP-indexing method is best illustrated by an example. Fig. 1 shows an example process of index construction, i.e., creating index nodes and allocating associated disk pages, in conventional dynamic indexing methods and in the SP-indexing method. For the sake of simplicity and ease of explanation, we assumed that all nodes are of the same size, each disk page can hold up to four entries, each disk segment can hold up to four pages, and the data distribution is uniform. As shown in Fig. 1, the disk pages are allocated in sequence according to the order of node splits. In the SP-indexing, initially, a root node is stored in a single segment, i.e., (segment 1, page 1) in the example. We store the internal nodes and the leaf nodes in separate segments. In other words, we maintain two kinds of segments for internal nodes and leaf nodes. Let us suppose that the range query Q overlaps with the internal node c, as shown in the lower left portion of Fig. 1. Then we have to access the nodes h, c, a, d, i, and k in sequence during the range search. The conventional indexing methods require random disk accesses as many as the number of nodes that have to be accessed, i.e., six, in this example. However, if the nodes were clustered in the segments as shown in Fig. 1(b), it only needs two random disk accesses, i.e., segments 1 and 2. This smaller number of random disk accesses reduces I/O cost significantly during the search. The SP-indexing improves the range query performance considerably by clustering the index nodes close in the domain space into the same segment and by reading the pages in a segment sequentially. We note that the SP-indexing can be applied indistinguishably to most multidimensional indexing methods.

2 Related Work

The concept of the segment is similar to the idea of the *multi-page block* used in the SB-tree [15] and the bounded disorder (BD) access method [12, 13], which are variants of the B-trees, in the sense that they accommodate a set of contiguous pages and support multi-page disk accesses. However, this concept has not been applied to the multidimensional indexing methods because it might consume the disk bandwidth excessively with increasing dimensionality. As an instance, let us suppose that a query range overlaps only a half on each dimension of the data region occupied by a segment. Then the wasteness of the disk bandwidth caused by reading a segment instead of reading individual pages is ½ (= 1 – ½) in one-dimensional case, while it is $1 - (½)^d$ in d-dimensional case. In fact, however, the multi-page disk reads such as segment reads are more needed in high dimensions because the probability that the query range overlaps with the regions covered by the index nodes increases with the dimensionality due to the sparsity of the domain space, and thus more disk pages are required to be read in higher dimensions. In addition, unlike the multi-page blocks used in the B-trees in which all index nodes as well as all data objects have total ordering among themselves, the index nodes within segments for multidimensional indexing methods have no linear order among them. This makes the design and maintenance, such as partitioning and merging, of the segments in the multidimensional indexing method more difficult than those of the multi-page block in the B-trees.

The concept of segments has also some similarity to *supernodes* of the X-tree [2]. The supernodes are extended nodes over the usual page size, and thus the read of a large supernode at a time can be performed. In contrast to the segment which consists of smaller pages, the supernode is a larger node with variable size designed to avoid splits in the internal nodes. Thus, in the X-tree, larger supernodes are always read regardless of the exact match query or the range query, while, in the SP-indexing scheme, segments or pages can be read selectively depending on the query type. Additionally, the supernodes are applied only to the internal nodes of the index tree in order to maintain efficient internal index structures.

With respect to the index clustering, the SP-indexing also has some similarity to the bulk loading of multidimensional indexes [3]. However, in contrast to the SP-indexing which is a generic dynamic index structure creation method, the bulk loading is applied to the creation of initial index structure. In other words, the bulk loading assumes the initially empty index structure but the SP-indexing can be used dynamically in any time of the index creation.

3 The SP-indexing

In the following we introduce the SP-indexing which can be applied to any multidimensional indexing methods. To demonstrate the effectiveness of the SP-indexing, we apply the technique to the LSD-tree [8] and implement the LSD-tree designed by the SP-indexing technique, and we call it the *SP-tree*. The SP-tree is a multidimensional index structure to index d-dimensional point data. We chose the LSD-tree for our implementation because we are dealing with d-dimensional feature vectors for image databases, where d is the number of features we want to index.

3.1 The Structure of the SP-tree

The SP-tree considers the disk to be partitioned as a collection of segments. Segments are separated into *index segments* and *data segments*. The index segments accommodate internal nodes of the index tree and the data segments hold the leaf nodes. The reason why we separate the segments into two kinds is two folds: it simplifies the design of the index structure and it encourages the upper part of the index structure to reside in the main memory when we cache the index into the main memory. We call the index segment i-segment and the data segment d-segment.

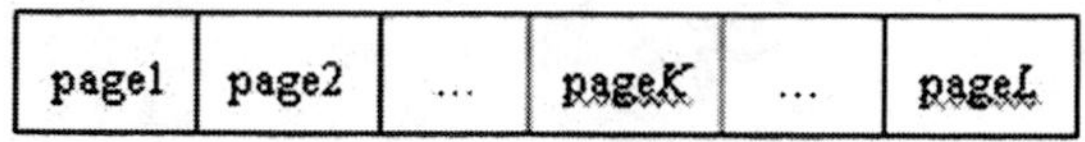

Fig. 2. A segment

Each segment consists of a set of L contiguous pages on disk (which can be read or written with a single sweep of the disk arm). In our implementation and experiments, we took $L = 16$. From the first page encountered by the disk head in reading and writing a segment to the last one in the segment, the pages are numbered 1, 2, ..., L. A segment has the following properties:

- A segment consists of a set of L nodes which reside on contiguous pages on disk as shown in Fig. 2. The number L is called the *fanout* of a segment.
- K, $1 \leq K \leq L$, nodes falling in a segment are filled contiguously from the beginning of the segment.
- The SP-tree reads K nodes from a segment at a time rather than all L nodes, and it saves the bandwidth.
- Every node of the SP-tree sits on segments.
- Leaf nodes reside in the *d*-segments and internal nodes are in the *i*-segments.

3.2 Building the SP-tree

The SP-tree has a hierarchical node structure. As usual for index structures which support spatial accesses for point data, the SP-tree divides the data space into pairwise disjoint data cells. With every data cell a data page is associated, which stores all objects contained in the cell. In this context, we call a data cell a *directory region*.

Successive parts of Fig. 3 show how the SP-tree grows and how its nodes are clustered in the segments. When the first entry of an SP-tree is inserted, a single page of the *d*-segment is allocated for the first node of the SP-tree. This node is a root node as well as a leaf node. The left side pictures in Fig. 3 show our example 2-dimensional data space. We assume that the range of each dimension is 0 to 100, and a pair of numbers on the directory regions indicates (*d*-segment number, page number).

Successive entries are added to this node until an insert forces a split in the root node. This node is then split into two leaf node pages which occupy page 1 and page 2 of the *d*-segment 1. An *i*-segment is allocated and the first page of the *i*-segment is assigned for new root node. The root node now contains a single separator and two pointers. A separator contains the information about the *split dimension* and the *split position* in the dimension. In our example of Fig. 3, the split is performed in dimension 1 at position 60. With subsequent insertions, overflows are occurred in the *d*-segment 1 and they cause the node split. Whenever a node split occurs, the SP-tree looks for an empty page on the segment containing the node receiving the insert. As we see from Fig. 2, this will be the page number K+1 in the containing segment, where K nodes already exist. We keep the information in the index header which tells us how many pages are occupied in each segment. If an empty page exists, we place the new node created by the split on that page. If there is no empty page in the segment, then a *segment split* is necessary. A new segment S is allocated, and the overfull segment R containing the splitting node is read into the memory. Then the L+1 nodes of the segment are distributed into two segments.

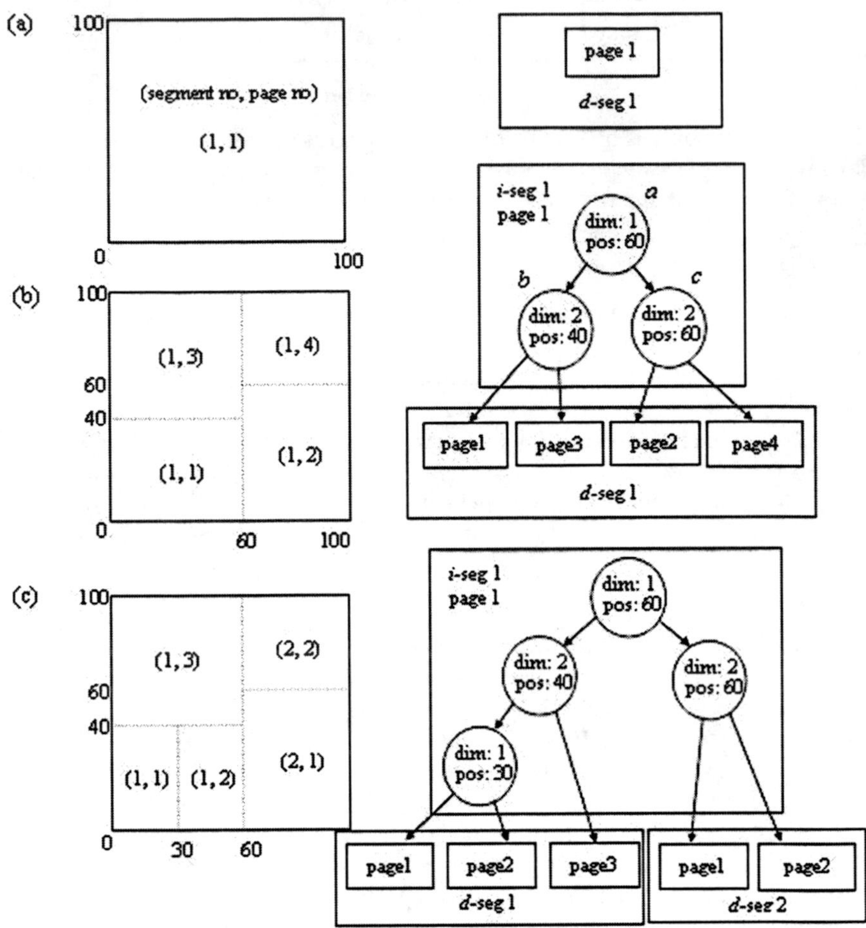

Fig. 3. The creation of the SP-tree using the SP-indexing

3.3 Segment Split Strategy

An important part of the insertion algorithm of the SP-tree is the segment split strategy which determines the split dimension and the split position. First, the SP-tree finds the internal node *u* which (directly or indirectly) plays a role of root for the overfull segment *R*. The separator of the internal node *u* has the dimension and the position to split the segment *R*. In Fig. 3(b), for example, if a new entry is inserted into the page (1, 1) and it causes the *d*-segment 1 to overflow, the SP-tree finds the internal node which plays a role of root of the *d*-segment 1, it is the internal node *a* in the case of Fig. 3(b). Since the SP-tree maintains an array to save the traversal path from the root of the SP-tree to the target page where a new entry to be inserted, it is not difficult to find the internal node that plays a role of root for the overfull segment. Starting from the root of the SP-tree, we check if the overfull segment can be split into two when we apply the separator (split dimension and split position) of the current internal node to split the segment. If the segment can be split using the separator, the corresponding internal node is selected as the root node of the overfull segment, and the segment is split. The data pages belonging to the right children of u are reallocated to the front positions of a new segment S, and the remaining pages are moved forward so that they fall on the front pages of the segment R. As a result of this segment split strategy, the data pages under the same internal node are collected in the same segment.

4 Performance Evaluation

To demonstrate the practical effectiveness of the SP-indexing, we implemented the SP-tree by using 64 KB segments. We performed an extensive experimental evaluation of the SP-tree and compared it to the pure LSD-tree. As before-mentioned, the SP-tree is the LSD-tree with the SP-indexing applied, but the specialized paging algorithm was not implemented and all index nodes were stored on the disk. Our experiments have been conducted under the Microsoft Windows NT 4.0 file system on Intel Pentium II 266 MHz processor with 192 MB of main memory. All experiments were performed on the local, uncached disk of our test machine. In other words, the memory buffer is flushed before each query.

4.1 Experimental Setup

For our tests we used two groups of synthetic data sets:

- Two-dimensional random data set which follows the random distribution.
- Two-dimensional skewed data set which follows the skewed distribution according to Zipf's law [9]. The Zipf distribution we used is as follows [10], and the value of z we used is 0.7:

$$f(i) = \frac{1/i^z}{\sum_{j=1}^{n} 1/j^z}, i = 1,2,\ldots,n$$

We also used real data set from the QBIC image database [5].

- 13,724 images of U.S. stamps and photos.

Stamps often come in series (e.g., states, birds, flowers) with common colors and related designs, and the U.S. Post Office has often used similar colors for many long-running stamps. As a result, this real image data set shows clustered distribution. Moreover, before storing images into the database, each image p is transformed to pTAp, where p represents 256-dimensional color histogram and A is a color similarity matrix. As a result of this transformation, most 256-dimensional images are gathered around the center of 256-dimensional hypercube. That is, the real image data set is strongly clustered around the center of the 256-dimensional hypercube. To reduce the influence of the dimensionality on the indexing method, we reduced the dimensionality of the image to 8 from 256 by selecting the most dominant 8 colors from 256 colors. As a result, we have an 8-dimensional real image data set. In addition, for a number of experiments we performed, a data set containing far more than 13,724 feature vectors was required. To obtain this larger database, the 13,724-vector data set was synthetically scaled up to one million, while retaining the original distribution of the

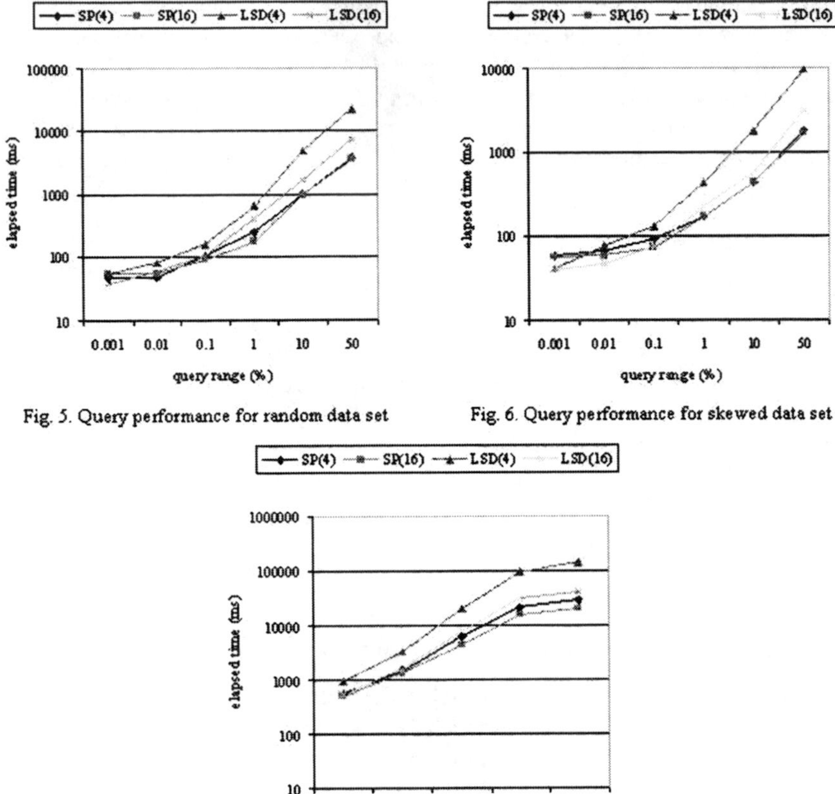

Fig. 5. Query performance for random data set

Fig. 6. Query performance for skewed data set

Fig. 7. Query performance for real data set

real image data set within each dimension. To generate a new image vector v, for each dimension i, 0 ≤ i ≤ 7, of v, we randomly select two out of 13,724 original vectors and average their values in dimension i of v. Since most original vectors are around the center of the hypercube, this method retains the original data distribution.

Each data set has 1,000,000 data points without duplicates. In all experiments, we used two kinds of page size, i.e., 4 KB and 16 KB. The segment size we used in all experiments was 64 KB. Thus, the fanout of a segment is 16 and 4 when 4 KB and 16 KB pages are used, respectively. To estimate the performance for range queries, we generated six groups of range queries. The regions of the six groups are squares varying in size which are 0.001%, 0.01%, 0.1%, 1%, 10%, and 50% of the whole data space and their centers are randomly distributed in the data space. For each experiment, 100 randomly generated range queries were posed and the results were averaged.

4.2 Total Elapsed Time

Figs. 5, 6, and 7 show the results of timing experiments for random, skewed, and real data sets. Notice that the scale of the *y*-axis is logarithmic in all Figures. SP(4) and SP(16) mean the SP-trees which use 4 KB and 16 KB pages, respectively. Similarly, LSD(4) and LSD(16) mean the LSD^h-trees which use 4 KB and 16 KB pages, respectively. In most experiments, the SP-trees which use 16 KB pages show the best performance except for some small size of range queries such as 0.001% range query in the random data set and 0.001% and 0.01% range queries in the skewed data set. The LSD^h-trees using 4 KB pages show the worst performance. As expected, the speed-up of the search time of the SP-tree increases with the growing query size and growing dimensionality. For the case of the small range of queries (e.g., 0.001% of the whole data space) in small dimensions (e.g., dimension 2), we can also perform the page-based disk access in the SP-tree because the SP-tree supports both of the segment-based access and page-based access.

Another point is that the absolute performance difference between the SP-indexing and traditional indexing methods is very large. In the case favorable to the SP-indexing, such as large query ranges in higher dimensions, the absolute performance superiority of the SP-tree is very high, that is, the difference of the total elapsed time between the SP-tree and the LSD-tree is more than 20 *sec* in the experiments. On the other hand, in the case unfavorable to the SP-indexing, the time difference is less than 20 *ms*.

We also conducted experiments for random access queries such as exact-match queries and the *k*-nearest neighbor queries to observe the performance of the SP-indexing in random accesses. The experimental results showed that there were almost no difference in the performance between the SP-trees and the LSD-trees when the page-based access was used.

5 Conclusion

We have introduced the SP-indexing technique and the cost model for range queries and insertions in multidimensional data spaces. Both the theoretical performance analysis and the experimental results demonstrate that in most cases the SP-indexing is superior to traditional multidimensional indexing methods for range queries. For random queries such as exact-match queries and *k*-nearest neighbor queries, there is almost no performance difference between the SP-tree and the LSD-tree when the page-based accessed is used. In addition, the performance degradation for updates in the SP-tree is negligible. The superiority of the SP-indexing increases greatly as the dimensionality of the domain space increases and the query range grows. High dimensionality and long range retrievals are quite common in today's environments such as multimedia databases. The performance advantage of the SP-indexing to traditional indexing methods was revealed up to several times in experiments depending on the data set and the size of range queries. In addition, it has been demonstrated that using larger pages (e.g., 16 KB) is more efficient for range queries than using traditional smaller pages (e.g., 4 KB). The performance advantage of the SP-indexing comes from saving much disk startup time. Moreover, storing a sequence of index pages contiguously within a segment provides a compromise between optimal index node clustering and the excessive full index reorganization overhead. Thus, the SP-indexing methods may be used as an alternative index clustering scheme. The SP-indexing is so generic that it can be applied to most multidimensional indexing methods.

References

1. N. Beckmann, H.-P. Kriegel, R. Schneider, and B. Seeger, "The R*-tree: An efficient and robust access method for points and rectangles," *Proc. of ACM SIGMOD International Conference on Management of Data*, pp. 322-331, 1990.
2. S. Berchtold, D.A. Keim, H.-P. Kriegel, "The X-tree: An Index Structure for High-Dimensional Data," *Proc. of the 22nd International Conference on Very Large Data Bases*, pp. 28-39, 1996.
3. J.v.d. Bercken, B. Seeger, and P. Widmayer, "A Generic Approach to Bulk Loading Multi-dimensional Index Structures," *Proc. of the International Conference on Very Large Data Bases*, pp. 406-415, 1997.
4. P. Ciaccia, M. Patella, and P. Zezula, "M-tree: An Efficient Access Method for Similarity Search in Metric Space," *Proc. of the International Conference on Very Large Data Bases*, pp. 426-435, 1997.
5. M. Flickner, H. Sawhney, W. Niblack, J. Ashley, Q. Huang, B. Dom, M. Gorkani, J. Hafner, D. Lee, D. Petkovic, D. Steele, and P. Yanker, "Query by image and video content: the QBIC system," *IEEE Computer*, Vol. 28, pp. 23-32, Sep. 1995.
6. Gray and G. Graefe, "The Five-Minute Rule Ten Years Later, and Other Computer Storage Rules of Thumb," *ACM SIGMOD Record*, Vol 26, No. 4, pp. 63-68, Dec. 1997.
7. Guttman, "R-Trees: A Dynamic Index Structure for Spatial Searching," *Proc. of the ACM SIGMOD International Conference on Management of Data*, pp. 47-57, 1984.
8. Henrich, "The LSD^h-tree: An Access Structure for Feature Vectors," *Proc. of the 14th International Conference on Data Engineering*, pp. 362-369, 1998.
9. D. Knuth, *The Art of Computer Programming, vol.* 3: *Sorting and Searching*, Addison Wesley, Reading, MA, 1973.
10. J.-H. Lee, D.-H. Kim, and C.-W. Chung, "Multidimensional Selectivity Estimation Using Compressed Histogram Information," *Proc. of the ACM SIGMOD International Conference on Management of Data*, pp. 205-214, 1999.
11. K.-I. Lin, H.V. Jagadish, and C. Faloutsos, "The TV-tree: An Index Structure for High-Dimensional Data," *VLDB Journal*, Vol. 3, No. 4, pp. 517-542, 1994.
12. W. Litwin and D.B. Lomet, "The Bounded Disorder Access Method," *Proc. of the IEEE International Conference on Data Engineering*, pp. 38-48, 1986.
13. D.B. Lomet, "A Simple Bounded Disorder File Organization with Good Performance," *ACM Transactions on Database Systems*, Vol. 13, No. 4, pp. 525-551, Dec. 1988.
14. J. Nievergelt, H. Hinterberger, and K.C. Sevcik, "The grid file: an adaptable, symmetric multikey file structure," *ACM Transactions on Database Systems*, Vol. 9, No.1, pp. 38-71, 1984.
15. P.E. O'Neil, "The SB-tree: An Index-Sequential Structure for High-Performance Sequential Access," *Acta Informatica*, Vol. 29, pp. 241-265, 1992.
16. Seeger and H.-P. Kriegel, "The Buddy-tree: An Efficient and Robust Access Method for Spatial Data Base Systems," *Proc. of the 16th International Conference on Very Large Data Bases*, pp. 590-601, 1990.

Database and Expert Systems 2002 "Quo vadis"?

A. Min Tjoa[1] and Roland R. Wagner[2]

[1] Institute of Information and Software Engineering,
Technical University of Vienna, Austria
tjoa@ifs.tuwien.ac.at

[2] Institute of Applied Knowledge Processing (FAW),
University of Linz, Austria
rwagner@faw.uni-linz.ac.at

Abstract. A summary of the development of the database and expert system applications research of this decade I given. The different trends and challenges are briefly analysed. The increasing shortening of the time-span between publication of an idea and the implementation and commercialisation of the idea is described.

1 Introduction

With the initiation of the first Database and Expert Systems Application Conference in 1990 a forum for dissemination and knowledge transfer for research results in the area of database and expert systems was established and well accepted in the scientific community (1,2,3,4,5,6,7,8,9,10,11,12). This paper should give an overview about the development of this area by means of the contributions given at the DEXA workshops (13,14,15,16,17,18,19) and other DEXA conferences (20,21,22,23,24).

2 The Development Since 1990

A number of important an still relevant trends in the area of database and expert systems applications were already presented at the first event in 1990. The coupling of relational databases with object management systems, the use of object oriented database management systems for non-standard applications, dynamic scheduling of transactions based on version consistency, advanced systems for management applications etc. are representative examples for this.

Beginning with 1991 the role of active database becomes more and more apparent for different applications. The building of adaptive applications using active mediators was presented in 1991. in this way applications instruct a mediator to actively monitor databases for change in information that the application depends on. Recent workflow approaches can be sought as direct continuations of these ideas.

The demonstration of the common sense business reasoner which was able to retrieve knowledge about certain business concepts and modify its knowledge base to include newly acquired information could also be seen as forerunner of efficient and advanced workflow systems.

R. Cicchetti et al. (Eds.): DEXA 2002, LNCS 2453, pp. 945–948, 2002.

The same holds for the interoperability between heterogeneous database systems with aspects as the implementation of multidatabase queries in federated databases with incremental growth. It was since this time that the role of data extraction and data mining has become more and more apparent. The reinvention and research on metadata and metavariables were important topics at DEXA 91 and DEXA 92.

In 1993 the role of user interfaces and the integration of hypertext/hypermedia was a main focus of the discussion at DEXA. New hypermedia data models which provide efficient and suitable data structure types for complex hypermedia objects containing textual, pictorial, sound and other hypermedia components are proposed to prevent the 'getting lost in hyperspace' phenomenon in the Web an to support the editing of links with its consistency side effects. The integration of hypermedia systems with object oriented database systems was also discussed in-depth in Prague at DEXA 93.

The 1994's DEXA was focused on the role of database and expert systems research as a catalyst for industrial innovation. The strategic role of information technology towards the information society was stressed at the conference in Athens.

In the information retrieval area the application of neural networks as an instrument for structuring of document sets was convincingly demonstrated by several authors. It is clear that this application will also become more and more relevant for ©data mining of huge amounts of formatted data in scientific and commercial databases.

The 1995's DEXA among others stressed the importance of support of Computer Supported Cooperative Work systems in the area of information security and workflow management. Also for our work as researchers and developers in a scientific environment the support by means of workflow management is essential. A workflow-based architecture to support scientific applications is therefore convincingly presented and discussed at last year's DEXA.

In 1996 many papers have discussed object-oriented and also active databases aspects. But also the emerging role of parallel architectures for database and expert systems applications can be observed by its increasing interest and its increase of valuable articles. Besides the applications a lot of theoretical database and expert systems aspects were discussed.

The 1997's DEXA in Toulouse has shown that again that object oriented, temporal, and active aspects in the area of database and expert systems application are very important. The invited speak has considered for the first time at a DEXA conference the connection of databases with the Web. Furthermore themes as multimedia databases, digital libraries, deductive databases, query languages, and federated databases were very actual.

In 1998 the content of the DEXA conference was very similar to the DEXA conference one year before. There is one observation that object oriented and active databases get more and more standard. On the other hand document management, information retrieval, transactions, and datawarehouses and knowledge discovery are the most important research areas.

It is very interested that at the DEXA 1999 conference in Florence the object oriented databases are again very important in the research are of database and expert systems applications. Further query aspects are increasing in this area, as well as heterogeneous, distributed and federated database and expert systems. In the area of data warehousing and data mining a lot of papers were accepted.

The 2000's DEXA continues with the very important area of query aspects and datawarehouses and knowledge discovery. Besides object oriented and multimedia database and expert systems the first papers in the direction of Web based systems were discussed at DEXA 2000.

In 2001 the content was very similar to 2000. A very important area is now the information retrieval, query aspects and also indexing. So the trends of the research areas from 1990 until 2002 were dramatically changing. Of course the Web is one the most important reason of the changing the areas in database and expert systems applications.

3 DEXA 1990 and DEXA 2002

1995 DEXA has started with DEXA workshops. The main idea was to discuss papers which were not really finished. Today the DEXA workshops are very important to have the possibility to discuss very specialised research areas. In 1998 it was clear to have an own conference about data mining and knowledge discovery (DaWaK) and one year later it was important to create an own conference in the area of Electronic Commerce and Web technologies. In the year 2001 a new workshop 'e-Government' was started. It was the most important workshop and therefore one year later the workshop was transferred in an own 'e-Government' conference.

So in summary the DEXA event consists of 4 conferences:

- DEXA
- DaWaK
- EC-Web
- eGOV
- and the DEXA workshops.

References

1. Tjoa A M., Wagner R.R.: First International Conference on Database and Expert Systems Applications DEXA 90 (Vienna), Springer Verlag 1990.
2. Karagiannis D.: Second International Conference on Database and Expert Systems Applications DEXA 91 (Berlin), Springer Verlag 1991.
3. Ramos I., Tjoa A M.: Third International Conference on Database and Expert Systems Applications DEXA 92 (Valencia), Springer Verlag 1992.
4. Marik V., Lanzansky J. Wagner R. R.: Fourth International Conference on Database and Expert Systems Applications DEXA 93 (Prague), Lectures Notes in Computer Science, Springer Verlag 1993.
5. Karagiannis D.: Fifth International Conference on Database and Expert Systems Applications DEXA 94(Athens), Lectures Notes in Computer Science, Springer Verlag 1994.
6. Revell N., Tjoa A M.: Sixth International Conference on Database and Expert Systems Applications DEXA 95 (London), Lectures Notes in Computer Science, Springer Verlag 1995.
7. Wagner R.R., Thoma H.: Seventh International Conference on Database and Expert Systems Applications DEXA 96 (Zurich), Lectures Notes in Computer Science, Springer Verlag 1996.

8. Hameurlain A., Tjoa A M.: Eighth International Conference on Database and Expert Systems Applications DEXA 97 (Toulouse), Lectures Notes in Computer Science, Springer Verlag 1997.
9. Quirchmay G., Schweighofer E., Bench-Capon T.J.M.: Ninth International Conference on Database and Expert Systems Applications DEXA 98 (Vienna), Lectures Notes in Computer Science, Springer Verlag 1998.
10. Bench-Capon T.J.M., Soda G., Tjoa A M.: Tenth International Conference on Database and Expert Systems Applications DEXA 99 (Florence), Lectures Notes in Computer Science, Springer Verlag 1999.
11. Ibrahim M., Küng J., Revell N.: Eleventh International Conference on Database and Expert Systems Applications DEXA 00 (London), Lectures Notes in Computer Science, Springer Verlag 2000.
12. Mayr H.C., Lazansky J., Quirchmayr G., Vogel P.: Twelfth International Conference on Database and Expert Systems Applications DEXA 01 (Munich), Lectures Notes in Computer Science, Springer Verlag 2002.
13. Revell N., Tjoa A M.: Sixth Workshop on Database and Expert Systems Applications (London), 1995.
14. Wagner R.R., Thoma H.: Seventh Workshop on Database and Expert Systems Applications 96 (Zurich), IEEE Computer Society, 1996.
15. Wagner R.R.: Eight Workshop on Database and Expert Systems Applications 97 (Toulouse), IEEE Computer Society, 1997.
16. Tjoa A M.,Wagner R.R.: Ninth Workshop on Database and Expert Systems Applications 98 (Vienna), IEEE Computer Society, 1998.
17. Tjoa A M.,Wagner R.R.: Tenth Workshop on Database and Expert Systems Applications 99 (Florence), IEEE Computer Society, 1999.
18. Tjoa A M.,Wagner R.R.: Eleventh Workshop on Database and Expert Systems Applications 00 (London), IEEE Computer Society, 2000.
19. Tjoa A M.,Wagner R.R.: Twelfth Workshop on Database and Expert Systems Applications 01 (Munich), IEEE Computer Society, 2001.
20. Mohania M. Tjoa A M.: Data Warehosing and Knowledge Discovery DaWaK 99 (Florence), Lecture Notes in Computer Science, Springer Verlag 1999.
21. Kambayashi Y., Mohania M. Tjoa A M.: Data Warehosing and Knowledge Discovery DaWaK 00 (London), Lecture Notes in Computer Science, Springer Verlag 2000.
22. Kambayashi Y., Mohania M. Tjoa A M.: Data Warehosing and Knowledge Discovery DaWaK 01 (Munich), Lecture Notes in Computer Science, Springer Verlag 2001.
23. Bauknecht K., Madria S.K., Pernul G.: Electronic Commerce and Web Technologies EC-Web 00 (London), Lecture Notes in Computer Science, Springer Verlag 2000.
24. Bauknecht K., Madria S.K., Pernul G.: Electronic Commerce and Web Technologies EC-Web 01 (Munich), Lecture Notes in Computer Science, Springer Verlag 2001.

Author Index

Lecture Notes in Computer Science

For information about Vols. 1–2358
please contact your bookseller or Springer-Verlag

Vol. 2359: M. Tistarelli, J. Bigun, A.K. Jain (Eds.), Biometric Authentication. Proceedings, 2002. X, 197 pages. 2002.

Vol. 2360: J. Esparza, C. Lakos (Eds.), Application and Theory of Petri Nets 2002. Proceedings, 2002. X, 445 pages. 2002.

Vol. 2361: J. Blieberger, A. Strohmeier (Eds.), Reliable Software Technologies – Ada-Europe 2002. Proceedings, 2002 XIII, 367 pages. 2002.

Vol. 2362: M. Tanabe, P. van den Besselaar, T. Ishida (Eds.), Digital Cities II. Proceedings, 2001. XI, 399 pages. 2002.

Vol. 2363: S.A. Cerri, G. Gouardères, F. Paraguaçu (Eds.), Intelligent Tutoring Systems. Proceedings, 2002. XXVIII, 1016 pages. 2002.

Vol. 2364: F. Roli, J. Kittler (Eds.), Multiple Classifier Systems. Proceedings, 2002. XI, 337 pages. 2002.

Vol. 2365: J. Daemen, V. Rijmen (Eds.), Fast Software Encryption. Proceedings, 2002. XI, 277 pages. 2002.

Vol. 2366: M.-S. Hacid, Z.W. Raś, D.A. Zighed, Y. Kodratoff (Eds.), Foundations of Intelligent Systems. Proceedings, 2002. XII, 614 pages. 2002. (Subseries LNAI).

Vol. 2367: J. Fagerholm, J. Haataja, J. Järvinen, M. Lyly, P. Råback, V. Savolainen (Eds.), Applied Parallel Computing. Proceedings, 2002. XIV, 612 pages. 2002.

Vol. 2368: M. Penttonen, E. Meineche Schmidt (Eds.), Algorithm Theory – SWAT 2002. Proceedings, 2002. XIV, 450 pages. 2002.

Vol. 2369: C. Fieker, D.R. Kohel (Eds.), Algorithmic Number Theory. Proceedings, 2002. IX, 517 pages. 2002.

Vol. 2370: J. Bishop (Ed.), Component Deployment. Proceedings, 2002. XII, 269 pages. 2002.

Vol. 2371: S. Koenig, R.C. Holte (Eds.), Abstraction, Reformulation, and Approximation. Proceedings, 2002. XI, 349 pages. 2002. (Subseries LNAI).

Vol. 2372: A. Pettorossi (Ed.), Logic Based Program Synthesis and Transformation. Proceedings, 2001. VIII, 267 pages. 2002.

Vol. 2373: A. Apostolico, M. Takeda (Eds.), Combinatorial Pattern Matching. Proceedings, 2002. VIII, 289 pages. 2002.

Vol. 2374: B. Magnusson (Ed.), ECOOP 2002 – Object-Oriented Programming. XI, 637 pages. 2002.

Vol. 2375: J. Kivinen, R.H. Sloan (Eds.), Computational Learning Theory. Proceedings, 2002. XI, 397 pages. 2002. (Subseries LNAI).

Vol. 2377: A. Birk, S. Coradeschi, T. Satoshi (Eds.), RoboCup 2001: Robot Soccer World Cup V. XIX, 763 pages. 2002. (Subseries LNAI).

Vol. 2378: S. Tison (Ed.), Rewriting Techniques and Applications. Proceedings, 2002. XI, 387 pages. 2002.

Vol. 2379: G.J. Chastek (Ed.), Software Product Lines. Proceedings, 2002. X, 399 pages. 2002.

Vol. 2380: P. Widmayer, F. Triguero, R. Morales, M. Hennessy, S. Eidenbenz, R. Conejo (Eds.), Automata, Languages and Programming. Proceedings, 2002. XXI, 1069 pages. 2002.

Vol. 2381: U. Egly, C.G. Fermüller (Eds.), Automated Reasoning with Analytic Tableaux and Related Methods. Proceedings, 2002. X, 341 pages. 2002.(Subseries LNAI).

Vol. 2382: A. Halevy, A. Gal (Eds.), Next Generation Information Technologies and Systems. Proceedings, 2002. VIII, 169 pages. 2002.

Vol. 2383: M.S. Lew, N. Sebe, J.P. Eakins (Eds.), Image and Video Retrieval. Proceedings, 2002. XII, 388 pages. 2002.

Vol. 2384: L. Batten, J. Seberry (Eds.), Information Security and Privacy. Proceedings, 2002. XII, 514 pages. 2002.

Vol. 2385: J. Calmet, B. Benhamou, O. Caprotti, L. Henocque, V. Sorge (Eds.), Artificial Intelligence, Automated Reasoning, and Symbolic Computation. Proceedings, 2002. XI, 343 pages. 2002. (Subseries LNAI).

Vol. 2386: E.A. Boiten, B. Möller (Eds.), Mathematics of Program Construction. Proceedings, 2002. X, 263 pages. 2002.

Vol. 2387: O.H. Ibarra, L. Zhang (Eds.), Computing and Combinatorics. Proceedings, 2002. XIII, 606 pages. 2002.

Vol. 2388: S.-W. Lee, A. Verri (Eds.), Pattern Recognition with Support Vector Machines. Proceedings, 2002. XI, 420 pages. 2002.

Vol. 2389: E. Ranchhod, N.J. Mamede (Eds.), Advances in Natural Language Processing. Proceedings, 2002. XII, 275 pages. 2002. (Subseries LNAI).

Vol. 2390: D. Blostein, Y.-B. Kwon (Eds.), Graphics Recognition. Proceedings, 2001. XI, 367 pages. 2002.

Vol. 2391: L.-H. Eriksson, P.A. Lindsay (Eds.), FME 2002: Formal Methods – Getting IT Right. Proceedings, 2002. XI, 625 pages. 2002.

Vol. 2392: A. Voronkov (Ed.), Automated Deduction – CADE-18. Proceedings, 2002. XII, 534 pages. 2002. (Subseries LNAI).

Vol. 2393: U. Priss, D. Corbett, G. Angelova (Eds.), Conceptual Structures: Integration and Interfaces. Proceedings, 2002. XI, 397 pages. 2002. (Subseries LNAI).

Vol. 2394: P. Perner (Ed.), Advances in Data Mining. VII, 109 pages. 2002. (Subseries LNAI).

Vol. 2395: G. Barthe, P. Dybjer, L. Pinto, J. Saraiva (Eds.), Applied Semantics. IX, 537 pages. 2002.

Vol. 2396: T. Caelli, A. Amin, R.P.W. Duin, M. Kamel, D. de Ridder (Eds.), Structural, Syntactic, and Statistical Pattern Recognition. Proceedings, 2002. XVI, 863 pages. 2002.

Vol. 2398: K. Miesenberger, J. Klaus, W. Zagler (Eds.), Computers Helping People with Special Needs. Proceedings, 2002. XXII, 794 pages. 2002.

Vol. 2399: H. Hermanns, R. Segala (Eds.), Process Algebra and Probabilistic Methods. Proceedings, 2002. X, 215 pages. 2002.

Vol. 2400: B. Monien, R. Feldmann (Eds.), Euro-Par 2002 – Parallel Processing. Proceedings, 2002. XXIX, 993 pages. 2002.

Vol. 2401: P.J. Stuckey (Ed.), Logic Programming. Proceedings, 2002. XI, 486 pages. 2002.

Vol. 2402: W. Chang (Ed.), Advanced Internet Services and Applications. Proceedings, 2002. XI, 307 pages. 2002.

Vol. 2403: Mark d'Inverno, M. Luck, M. Fisher, C. Preist (Eds.), Foundations and Applications of Multi-Agent Systems. Proceedings, 1996-2000. X, 261 pages. 2002. (Subseries LNAI).

Vol. 2404: E. Brinksma, K.G. Larsen (Eds.), Computer Aided Verification. Proceedings, 2002. XIII, 626 pages. 2002.

Vol. 2405: B. Eaglestone, S. North, A. Poulovassilis (Eds.), Advances in Databases. Proceedings, 2002. XII, 199 pages. 2002.

Vol. 2406: C. Peters, M. Braschler, J. Gonzalo, M. Kluck (Eds.), Evaluation of Cross-Language Information Retrieval Systems. Proceedings, 2001. X, 601 pages. 2002.

Vol. 2407: A.C. Kakas, F. Sadri (Eds.), Computational Logic: Logic Programming and Beyond. Part I. XII, 678 pages. 2002. (Subseries LNAI).

Vol. 2408: A.C. Kakas, F. Sadri (Eds.), Computational Logic: Logic Programming and Beyond. Part II. XII, 628 pages. 2002. (Subseries LNAI).

Vol. 2409: D.M. Mount, C. Stein (Eds.), Algorithm Engineering and Experiments. Proceedings, 2002. VIII, 207 pages. 2002.

Vol. 2410: V.A. Carreño, C.A. Muñoz, S. Tahar (Eds.), Theorem Proving in Higher Order Logics. Proceedings, 2002. X, 349 pages. 2002.

Vol. 2412: H. Yin, N. Allinson, R. Freeman, J. Keane, S. Hubbard (Eds.), Intelligent Data Engineering and Automated Learning – IDEAL 2002. Proceedings, 2002. XV, 597 pages. 2002.

Vol. 2413: K. Kuwabara, J. Lee (Eds.), Intelligent Agents and Multi-Agent Systems. Proceedings, 2002. X, 221 pages. 2002. (Subseries LNAI).

Vol. 2414: F. Mattern, M. Naghshineh (Eds.), Pervasive Computing. Proceedings, 2002. XI, 298 pages. 2002.

Vol. 2415: J.R. Dorronsoro (Ed.), Artificial Neural Networks – ICANN 2002. Proceedings, 2002. XXVIII, 1382 pages. 2002.

Vol. 2417: M. Ishizuka, A. Sattar (Eds.), PRICAI 2002: Trends in Artificial Intelligence. Proceedings, 2002. XX, 623 pages. 2002. (Subseries LNAI).

Vol. 2418: D. Wells, L. Williams (Eds.), Extreme Programming and Agile Methods – XP/Agile Universe 2002. Proceedings, 2002. XII, 292 pages. 2002.

Vol. 2419: X. Meng, J. Su, Y. Wang (Eds.), Advances in Web-Age Information Management. Proceedings, 2002. XV, 446 pages. 2002.

Vol. 2420: K. Diks, W. Rytter (Eds.), Mathematical Foundations of Computer Science 2002. Proceedings, 2002. XII, 652 pages. 2002.

Vol. 2421: L. Brim, P. Jančar, M. Křetínský, A. Kučera (Eds.), CONCUR 2002 – Concurrency Theory. Proceedings, 2002. XII, 611 pages. 2002.

Vol. 2423: D. Lopresti, J. Hu, R. Kashi (Eds.), Document Analysis Systems V. Proceedings, 2002. XIII, 570 pages. 2002.

Vol. 2425: Z. Bellahsene, D. Patel, C. Rolland (Eds.), Object-Oriented Information Systems. Proceedings, 2002. XIII, 550 pages. 2002.

Vol. 2426: J.-M. Bruel, Z. Bellahsene (Eds.), Advances in Object-Oriented Information Systems.Procedings, 2002. IX, 314 pages. 2002.

Vol. 2430: T. Elomaa, H. Mannila, H. Toivonen (Eds.), Machine Learning: ECML 2002. Proceedings, 2002. XIII, 532 pages. 2002. (Subseries LNAI).

Vol. 2431: T. Elomaa, H. Mannila, H. Toivonen (Eds.), Principles of Data Mining and Knowledge Discovery. Proceedings, 2002. XIV, 514 pages. 2002. (Subseries LNAI).

Vol. 2435: Y. Manolopoulos, P. Návrat (Eds.), Advances in Databases and Information Systems. Proceedings, 2002. XIII, 415 pages. 2002.

Vol. 2436: J. Fong, C.T. Cheung, H.V. Leong, Q. Li (Eds.), Advances in Web-Based Learning. Proceedings, 2002. XIII, 434 pages. 2002.

Vol. 2438: M. Glesner, P. Zipf, M. Renovell (Eds.), Field-Programmable Logic and Applications. Proceedings, 2002. XXII, 1187 pages. 2002.

Vol. 2440: J.M. Haake, J.A. Pino (Eds.), Groupware: Design, Implementation and Use. Proceedings, 2002. XII, 285 pages. 2002.

Vol. 2442: M. Yung (Ed.), Advances in Cryptology – CRYPTO 2002. Proceedings, 2002. XIV, 627 pages. 2002.

Vol. 2443: D. Scott (Ed.), Artificial Intelligence: Methodology, Systems, and Applications. Proceedings, 2002. X, 279 pages. 2002. (Subseries LNAI).

Vol. 2444: A. Buchmann, F. Casati, L. Fiege, M.-C. Hsu, M.-C. Shan (Eds.), Technologies for E-Services. Proceedings, 2002. X, 171 pages. 2002.

Vol. 2445: C. Anagnostopoulou, M. Ferrand, A. Smaill (Eds.), Music and Artificial Intelligence. Proceedings, 2002. VIII, 207 pages. 2002. (Subseries LNAI).

Vol. 2447: D.J. Hand, N.M. Adams, R.J. Bolton (Eds.), Pattern Detection and Discovery. Proceedings, 2002. XII, 227 pages. 2002. (Subseries LNAI).

Vol. 2451: B. Hochet, A.J. Acosta, M.J. Bellido (Eds.), Integrated Circuit Design. Proceedings, 2002. XVI, 496 pages. 2002.

Vol. 2453: A. Hameurlain, R. Cicchetti, R. Traunmüller (Eds.), Database and Expert Systems Applications. Proceedings, 2002. XVIII, 951 pages. 2002.

Vol. 2454: Y. Kambayashi, W. Winiwarter, M. Arikawa (Eds.), Data Warehousing and Knowledge Discovery. Proceedings, 2002. XIII, 339 pages. 2002.

Vol. 2455: K. Bauknecht, A M. Tjoa, G. Quirchmayr (Eds.), E-Commerce and Web Technologies. Proceedings, 2002. XIV, 414 pages. 2002.

CPSIA information can be obtained at www.ICGtesting.com
Printed in the USA
LVOW09s0746120616

492225LV00002B/8/P